McDougal Littell

CLASSZONE

Visit **classzone.com** and get connected.

ClassZone resources provide instruction, practice and learning support for students and parents.

Help with the Math

- @Home Tutor enables students to focus on the math and be more prepared for class, using animated examples and instruction.

- Extra examples similar to those in the book provide additional support.

- Hints and Homework Help offers assistance solving select homework exercises.

Practice, Practice, Practice

- eWorkbook includes interactive worksheets with additional practice problems.

- Problem of the Week features a new problem to solve every week.

Games and Activities

- Crossword puzzles, memory games, and other activities help students connect to essential math concepts.

- Math Vocabulary Flipcards are a fun way to learn math terminology.

Animated Math

- Engaging activities with animated problem-solving graphics support each lesson.

Access the online version of your textbook at classzone.com

Your complete text is available for immediate use!

McDougal Littell
Where Great Lessons Begin

NEW JERSEY

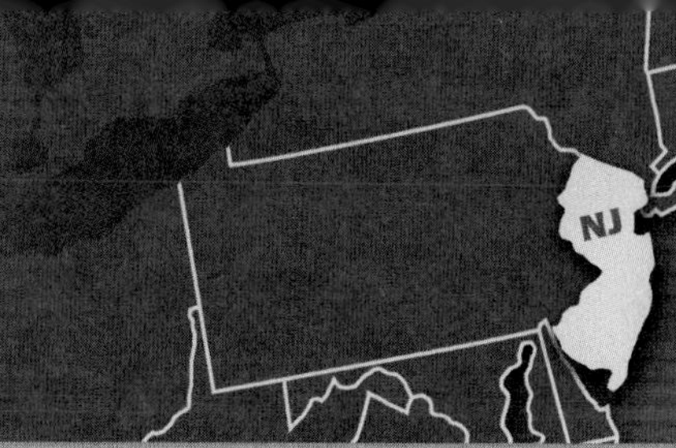

MATH
COURSE 2

Ron Larson
Laurie Boswell
Timothy D. Kanold
Lee Stiff

McDougal Littell
A DIVISION OF HOUGHTON MIFFLIN COMPANY
Evanston, Illinois • Boston • Dallas

McDougal Littell MATH

About Course 2

The focus of the early chapters in *McDougal Littell Math Course 2* is on rational numbers, their operations, and their algebraic representations. You will build your understanding of these concepts using models, such as rulers, number lines, and verbal models. You will also apply your skills to problem-solving situations and use estimation to check reasonableness. Topics from math strands, such as measurement conversions, area, averages, and data displays, are introduced early in the course and then integrated and expanded upon throughout.

Later chapters in *McDougal Littell Math Course 2* include topics such as equations and functions, geometry, square roots, and probability. The number and variety of problems, ranging from basic to challenging, give you the practice you need to develop your math skills.

Every lesson in *McDougal Littell Math Course 2* has both skill practice and problem solving, including multi-step problems. These types of problems often appear on standardized tests and cover a wide variety of math topics. To help you prepare for standardized tests, *McDougal Littell Math Course 2* provides instruction and practice on standardized test questions in many formats—multiple choice, short response, extended response, and so on. Technology support for course content and standardized test preparation is available at classzone.com.

ISBN-13: 978-0-618-88818-4
ISBN-10: 0-618-88818-7   3 4 5 6 7 8 9—0914—13 12 11
4500309842

Internet Web Site: http://www.mcdougallittell.com

About the Authors

Ron Larson is a professor of mathematics at Penn State University at Erie, where he has taught since receiving his Ph.D. in mathematics from the University of Colorado. Dr. Larson is well known as the author of a comprehensive program for mathematics that spans middle school, high school, and college courses. Dr. Larson's numerous professional activities keep him in constant touch with the needs of teachers and supervisors. He closely follows developments in mathematics standards and assessment.

Laurie Boswell is a mathematics teacher at The Riverside School in Lyndonville, Vermont, and has taught mathematics at all levels, elementary through college. A recipient of the Presidential Award for Excellence in Mathematics Teaching, she was also a Tandy Technology Scholar. She served on the NCTM Board of Directors (2002–2005), and she speaks frequently at regional and national conferences on topics related to instructional strategies and course content.

Timothy D. Kanold is the superintendent of Adlai E. Stevenson High School District 125 in Lincolnshire, Illinois. Dr. Kanold served as a teacher and director of mathematics for 17 years prior to becoming superintendent. He is the recipient of the Presidential Award for Excellence in Mathematics and Science Teaching, and a past president of the Council for Presidential Awardees in Mathematics. Dr. Kanold is a frequent speaker at national and international mathematics meetings.

Lee Stiff is a professor of mathematics education in the College of Education and Psychology of North Carolina State University at Raleigh and has taught mathematics at the high school and middle school levels. He served on the NCTM Board of Directors and was elected President of NCTM for the years 2000–2002. He is a recipient of the W. W. Rankin Award for Excellence in Mathematics Education presented by the North Carolina Council of Teachers of Mathematics.

Advisers and Reviewers

New Jersey Advisers and Reviewers

Linda Bohny
Mathematics and Business Supervisor
Mahwah High School
Mahwah, NJ

Jean Ferrara
Mathematics Supervisor
Glenn School
Old Bridge, NJ

Barbara Miller
Mathematics Teacher
Copeland Middle School
Rockaway, NJ

Curriculum Advisers and Reviewers

Susanne Artiñano
Bryn Mawr School
Baltimore, MD

Mary Atkinson
Mathematics Teacher
Lucio Middle School
Brownsville, TX

Lisa Barnes
Bishop Spaugh Academy
Charlotte, NC

Beth Bryan
Sequoyah Middle School
Oklahoma City, OK

Judy Carlin
Mathematics Teacher
Brown Middle School
McAllen, TX

Kathryn Chamberlain
McCarthy Middle School
Chelmsford, MA

Jennifer Clark
Mayfield Middle School
Oklahoma City, OK

Judith Cody
Mathematics Teacher
Deady Middle School
Houston, TX

Lois Cole
Pickering Middle School
Lynn, MA

Louis Corbosiero
Pollard Middle School
Needham, MA

Linda Cordes
Department Chair
Paul Robeson Middle School
Kansas City, MO

James Cussen
Candlewood Middle School
Dix Hills, NY

Kristen Dailey
Boardman Center Middle School
Boardman, OH

Sheree Daily
Canal Winchester Middle School
Canal Winchester, OH

Linda Dodd
Mathematics Department Chair
Argentine Middle School
Kansas City, KS

Curriculum Advisers and Reviewers

Melanie Dowell
Mathematics Teacher
Raytown South Middle School
Raytown, MO

Donna Foley
Curriculum Specialist for Math
Chelmsford Middle School
Chelmsford, MA

Rhonda Foote
Mathematics Department Chair
Maple Park Middle School
North Kansas City, MO

Shannon Galamore
Clay-Chalkville Middle School
Pinson, AL

Tricia Highland
Moon Area Middle School
Moon Township, PA

Lisa Hiracheta
Mathematics Teacher
Irons Junior High School
Lubbock, TX

Deborah Kebe
Canal Winchester Middle School
Canal Winchester, OH

Cas Kyle
District Math Curriculum Coordinator
Richard A. Warren Middle School
Leavenworth, KS

Rita Landez
Campus Instructional Coordinator
Sam Houston High School
San Antonio, TX

Jill Leone
Twin Groves Junior High School
Buffalo Grove, IL

Wendy Loeb
Mathematics Teacher
Twin Groves Junior High School
Buffalo Grove, IL

Melissa McCarty
Canal Winchester Middle School
Canal Winchester, OH

Myrna McNaboe
Immaculate Conception
East Aurora, NY

Deb Mueth
St. Aloysius School
Springfield, IL

Kay Neuse
Mathematics Teacher
Wilson Middle School
Plano, TX

Barbara Nunn
Secondary Mathematics Specialist
Broward County Schools
Fort Lauderdale, FL

Louise Nutzman
Mathematics Teacher
Sugar Land Middle School
Sugar Land, TX

Clarice Orise
Mathematics Teacher
Tafolla Middle School
San Antonio, TX

Jan Rase
Mathematics Teacher
Moreland Ridge Middle School
Blue Springs, MO

Angela Richardson
Sedgefield Middle School
Charlotte, NC

James Richardson
Booker T. Washington Middle School
Mobile, AL

Dan Schoenemann
Mathematics Teacher
Raytown Middle School
Kansas City, MO

Tom Scott
Resource Teacher
Duval County Public Schools
Jacksonville, FL

Gail Sigmund
Charles A. Mooney Middle School
Cleveland, OH

Dianne Walker
Traverse City Central High School
Traverse City, MI

Wonda Webb
Mathematics Teacher
William H. Atwell Middle School and
Law Academy
Dallas, TX

Stacey Wood
Cochrane Middle School
Charlotte, NC

Karen Young
Mathematics Teacher
Murchison Elementary School
Pflugerville, TX

NEW JERSEY

Overview
New Jersey Student Edition

New Jersey Table of Contents   *Page NJ 8 - NJ 22*

New Jersey Student Guide   *Page NJ 23 - NJ 63*

     New Jersey Mathematics Core Curriculum
Content Standards   *Page NJ 24 - NJ 30*

     New Jersey Assessment of Skills and
Knowledge (NJ ASK)   *Page NJ 31 - NJ 63*

New Jersey Chapter Support   *Throughout*

ᘒNJ **Daily practice in every lesson**

ᘒNJ **Weekly practice in the mid-chapter mixed review**

ᘒNJ **Summative practice in the end-of-chapter assessment**

Additional Standards-Based Lessons   *Page A1 - A34*

**New Jersey Mathematics Core Curriculum
Content Standards**   *Page S1*

Ocean City Beach, Ocean City, New Jersey © Corbis

Course 2 Overview

Number and Operations

Pre-Course Review
- ordering whole numbers, 736
- divisibility tests, 739
- whole number operations, 742–744
- whole number estimation, 745–748

Course 2 Content
- powers and exponents, 13
- order of operations, 17
- compare numbers, 56, 189, 269, 301
- decimal operations, 60–71
- estimation, 60, 66, 71, 219, 237
- scientific notation, 78, 274
- prime factorization, 165
- greatest common factor, 170

- least common multiple, 182
- write between fractions decimals, and percents, 199, 449, 460
- fraction operations, 219–237
- integer operations, 277–296
- rational and irrational numbers, 301, 582
- ratios, 399–409
- percent of change, 480–485

Algebra

Pre-Course Review
- commutative properties of addition and multiplication, 759
- associative properties of addition and multiplication, 760

Course 2 Content
- evaluate variable expressions, 8, 577
- use formulas, 25, 32, 296, 490, 588, 601
- identity and inverse properties, 301
- distributive property, 307
- write expressions and equations, 337

- solve equations, 347, 354, 361, 577
- solve inequalities, 366
- functions, 371–376
- slope of a line, 409
- solve proportions, 418, 423, 454, 542

Geometry and Measurement

Pre-Course Review
- units of time, 751
- using a ruler and compass, 753–754

Course 2 Content
- perimeter and area, 32, 594, 601, 612
- measure length, mass, and capacity, 84, 245
- convert measures, 90, 250
- scale drawings and models, 430
- classify angles, 511–516
- classify polygons, 521–529

- identify congruent and similar figures, 537
- transformations, 548–556
- Pythagorean theorem, 588
- circles, 607–612
- classify and sketch solids, 631–636
- surface area and volume, 642–662

Data Analysis and Probability

Pre-Course Review
- Venn diagrams and logical reasoning, 756
- reading data displays, 757–758

Course 2 Content
- mean, median, and mode, 109
- make and interpret data displays, 117, 126, 133, 138, 474

- appropriate data displays, 144
- find outcomes, 690–702
- find probability, 682, 709, 715

Problem Solving

Pre-Course Review
- make a model, 761
- draw a diagram, 762
- guess, check, and revise, 763
- work backward, 764
- make a list or table, 765
- look for a pattern, 766
- break into parts, 767
- solve a simpler problem, 768
- use a Venn diagram, 769
- act it out, 770

Course 2 Content

Problem solving is integrated throughout the course with a section of problem solving exercises in every lesson. The following problem solving features also occur throughout. For examples see:

- short response exercises, 6, 16, 24, 35, 48
- extended response exercises, 7, 21, 24, 41, 102
- choose a strategy exercises, 41, 65, 149
- Mixed Review of Problem Solving, 24, 42, 77, 96

Recognizing Patterns, p. 6
$64, 32, 16, 8, \ldots$
$\div 2 \div 2 \div 2$

Number Sense, Patterns, and Algebraic Thinking

Review Prerequisite Skills 1
    Get-Ready Game 1
    Vocabulary and Skill Check 2
    Notetaking Skills 2

Standards

4.3.A.1.a   **1.1** **xy ALGEBRA** Describing Patterns 3

4.3.D.3.b   **1.2** **xy ALGEBRA** Variables and Expressions 8

4.1.B.2   **1.3** **xy ALGEBRA** Powers and Exponents 13
    🔍 Investigation: Repeated Multiplication 12

4.1.B.3   **1.4** **xy ALGEBRA** Order of Operations 17
    Quiz for Lessons 1.1–1.4 22
    🖩 Technology Activity: Using Order of Operations ... 23
    New Jersey Mixed Review 24

4.3.D.2.b   **1.5** **xy ALGEBRA** Equations and Mental Math 25

4.2.E.1   **1.6** **xy ALGEBRA** Perimeter and Area 32
    🔍 Investigation: Investigating Area 31

4.5.A.1   **1.7** **A Problem Solving Plan** 37
    Quiz for Lessons 1.5–1.7 41
    New Jersey Mixed Review 42

   New Jersey **Assessment**

    Chapter Review 43
    Chapter Test 47
    New Jersey Test Preparation and Practice 48

    Animated Math classzone.com **Activities** 4, 14, 18, 26, 33, 38

New Jersey

ASSESSMENT

- New Jersey Practice Examples, 19, 34
- New Jersey Daily Practice, 7, 11, 16, 22, 30, 36, 41
- New Jersey Preparation and Practice, 5, 6, 7, 10, 11, 12, 15, 16, 19, 20, 21, 22, 24, 28, 29, 34, 35, 36, 40, 41, 42
- Writing, 6, 11, 12, 16, 20, 29, 31, 36, 40

PROBLEM SOLVING

- Real Life Examples, 3, 4, 9, 13, 17, 19, 27, 33, 34, 38
- Mixed Review of Problem Solving, 24, 42
- Multi-Step Problems, 7, 11, 16, 21, 24, 29, 34, 36, 40, 42
- Challenge, 7, 11, 16, 22, 29, 30, 36, 41

STUDENT HELP

- Homework Help, 5, 10, 15, 19, 27, 34, 39
  At classzone.com: @HomeTutor, Online Quiz, eWorkbook, Hints and Homework
- Reading and Vocabulary, 2, 3, 8, 13, 14, 17, 25, 32, 37, 43
- Notetaking, 9, 13, 17, 18, 26, 32, 38
- Avoid Errors, 9, 17

Multiplying Decimals, p. 67
Area = (2.5)(0.5)

Decimal Operations

Review Prerequisite Skills 52
    Get-Ready Game 52
    Vocabulary and Skill Check 54
    Notetaking Skills 54

Standards			
4.1.A.4	**2.1**	**Comparing, Ordering, and Rounding Decimals**	56
		🔍 Investigation: Modeling Decimals	55
4.1.B.1.a	**2.2**	**Adding and Subtracting Decimals**	60
4.1.B.1.a	**2.3**	**Multiplying Decimals**	66
4.1.B.1.a	**2.4**	**Dividing Decimals**	71
		Quiz for Lessons 2.1–2.4	76
		New Jersey Mixed Review	77
4.1.A.5	**2.5**	🔀 **ALGEBRA** **Scientific Notation**	78
		🖩 Technology Activity: Using Scientific Notation	82
4.2.D.2	**2.6**	**Measuring in Metric Units**	84
		🔍 Investigation: Measuring Length	83
4.2.D.1	**2.7**	**Converting Metric Units**	90
		Quiz for Lessons 2.5–2.7	95
		New Jersey Mixed Review	96

New Jersey **Assessment**

    Chapter Review 97
    Chapter Test 101
    New Jersey Test Preparation and Practice 102

 **Activities** 57, 60, 66, 71, 87

New Jersey

ASSESSMENT

- New Jersey Practice Examples, 68, 92
- New Jersey Daily Practice, 59, 65, 70, 76, 81, 89, 95
- New Jersey Preparation and Practice, 58, 59, 62, 63, 64, 65, 68, 69, 70, 74, 76, 77, 81, 88, 89, 92, 93, 94, 96
- Writing, 59, 64, 70, 75, 83, 89

PROBLEM SOLVING

- Real Life Examples, 56, 61, 67, 68, 71, 73, 78, 79, 85, 86, 92
- Mixed Review of Problem Solving, 77, 96
- Multi-Step Problems, 59, 61, 64, 68, 70, 73, 75, 77, 81, 84, 89, 92, 94, 96
- Challenge, 59, 65, 70, 76, 81, 89, 95

STUDENT HELP

- Homework Help, 58, 62, 68, 73, 80, 87, 92
  At classzone.com: @HomeTutor, Online Quiz, eWorkbook, Hints and Homework
- Reading and Vocabulary, 54, 56, 60, 66, 71, 78, 79, 84, 90, 97
- Notetaking, 56, 57, 66, 72, 78
- Avoid Errors, 61, 72, 84, 91

CHAPTER 3

Unit 1
Algebraic Thinking,
Decimals, and Data

New Jersey

Compare Data, p. 135
$44 - 3 > 48 - 15$

Data and Statistics

Review Prerequisite Skills 106
    Get-Ready Game 106
    Vocabulary and Skill Check 108
    Notetaking Skills 108

3.1 Mean, Median, and Mode 109
    Extension: Samples 115

Standards   4.5.E.1.d   **3.2 Bar Graphs and Line Graphs** 117
    Technology Activity: Making Data Displays 124

4.5.E.1.d   **3.3 Stem-and-Leaf Plots** 126
    Quiz for Lessons 3.1–3.3 130
    New Jersey Mixed Review 131

4.4.A.1.b   **3.4 Box-and-Whisker Plots** 133
    Investigation: Organizing Data using the Median 132

4.5.E.1.b   **3.5 Histograms** 138

4.4.A.1.a   **3.6 Appropriate Data Displays** 144
    Quiz for Lessons 3.4–3.6 149
    New Jersey Mixed Review 150

New Jersey Assessment

Chapter Review 151
Chapter Test 155
New Jersey Test Preparation and Practice 156
Cumulative Review 160

Animated Math classzone.com **Activities** 117, 126, 133

New Jersey

ASSESSMENT
- New Jersey Practice Examples, 111, 140
- New Jersey Daily Practice, 114, 123, 130, 137, 143, 149
- New Jersey Preparation and Practice, 111, 112, 113, 121, 122, 123, 128, 129, 130, 131, 136, 137, 140, 141, 142, 143, 146, 147, 148, 149, 150
- Writing, 112, 123, 129, 136, 137, 148, 150

PROBLEM SOLVING
- Real Life Examples, 109, 111, 115, 118, 126, 127, 133, 135, 139, 140, 145
- Mixed Review of Problem Solving, 131, 150
- Multi-Step Problems, 113, 117, 122, 126, 129, 131, 133, 137, 138, 143, 148, 150
- Challenge, 114, 123, 130, 137, 143, 148

STUDENT HELP
- Homework Help, 111, 120, 128, 136, 141, 146
  At classzone.com: @HomeTutor, Online Quiz, eWorkbook, Hints and Homework
- Reading and Vocabulary, 108, 109, 115, 117, 118, 126, 133, 138, 144, 151
- Notetaking, 109, 134, 144
- Avoid Errors, 110, 133, 139, 145

CHAPTER

4

Unit 2
Fractions
and Integers

Greatest Common Factor, p. 170
$48 = 4 \cdot 12, 24 = 2 \cdot 12, 36 = 3 \cdot 12$

Number Patterns and Fractions

Review Prerequisite Skills		162
Get-Ready Game		162
Vocabulary and Skill Check		164
Notetaking Skills		164

Standards	4.1.A.1.c	**4.1 Prime Factorization**	165
		4.2 Greatest Common Factor	170
	4.1.A.5	**4.3 Equivalent Fractions**	176
		🔍 Investigation: Modeling Equivalent Fractions	175
		Quiz for Lessons 4.1–4.3	180
		New Jersey Mixed Review	181
		4.4 Least Common Multiple	182
	4.1.A.4	**4.5 Comparing and Ordering Fractions**	189
		🔍 Investigation: Comparing Fractions	187
	4.1.A.5	**4.6 Mixed Numbers and Improper Fractions**	194
	4.1.A.5	**4.7 Fractions and Decimals**	199
		Quiz for Lessons 4.4–4.7	204
		🖩 Technology Activity: Fractions and Decimal Conversion	205
		New Jersey Mixed Review	206

New Jersey Assessment

Chapter Review	207
Chapter Test	211
New Jersey Test Preparation and Practice	212

Animated **Math** classzone.com **Activities** 171, 178, 185, 196, 201

🔧 New Jersey

ASSESSMENT

- New Jersey Practice Examples, 190, 201
- New Jersey Daily Practice, 169, 174, 180, 186, 193, 198, 204
- New Jersey Preparation and Practice, 167, 168, 169, 172, 173, 174, 178, 179, 180, 181, 184, 185, 190, 191, 192, 193, 197, 198, 201, 203, 204, 206
- Writing, 168, 169, 174, 175, 185, 188, 192, 198, 203

PROBLEM SOLVING

- Real Life Examples, 165, 170, 176, 177, 183, 189, 196, 201
- Mixed Review of Problem Solving, 181, 206
- Multi-Step Problems, 168, 174, 180, 181, 183, 186, 189, 190, 192, 195, 198, 204, 206
- Challenge, 169, 174, 180, 185, 193, 198, 204

STUDENT HELP

- Homework Help, 167, 172, 178, 184, 191, 196, 201
    At classzone.com: @HomeTutor, Online Quiz, eWorkbook, Hints and Homework
- Reading and Vocabulary, 164, 165, 166, 170, 176, 182, 189, 194, 199, 207
- Notetaking, 165, 189, 194, 195, 200
- Avoid Errors, 166, 171, 200

CHAPTER

5

Unit 2
Fractions
and Integers

New Jersey

Dividing Mixed Numbers, p. 241
$$600 \div 1\frac{1}{2} = 600 \times \frac{2}{3}$$

Fraction Operations

Review Prerequisite Skills 216
    Get-Ready Game 216
    Vocabulary and Skill Check 218
    Notetaking Skills... 218

Standards

4.1.B.1.a   **5.1 Adding and Subtracting Fractions**........................... 219

4.1.B.1.a   **5.2 Adding and Subtracting Mixed Numbers** 226
    🔍 Investigation: Modeling Addition of Mixed Numbers 225

4.1.B.1.a   **5.3 Multiplying Fractions and Mixed Numbers**................... 232
    🔍 Investigation: Multiplication of Fractions..................... 231

4.1.B.1.a   **5.4 Dividing Fractions and Mixed Numbers**...................... 237
    Quiz for Lessons 5.1–5.4.. 242
    🖩 Technology Activity: Fraction Operations 243
    New Jersey Mixed Review 244

4.2.D.2   **5.5 Measuring in Customary Units** 245

4.2.D.1   **5.6 Converting Customary Units**.................................. 250
    Quiz for Lessons 5.5–5.6... 255
    New Jersey Mixed Review 256

New Jersey   **Assessment**

    Chapter Review... 257
    Chapter Test... 261
    New Jersey Test Preparation and Practice 262

Animated **Math** **Activities** 221, 227, 233, 237, 239, 247, 251
classzone.com

New Jersey

ASSESSMENT	PROBLEM SOLVING	STUDENT HELP
• New Jersey Practice Examples, 221, 238, 247 • New Jersey Daily Practice, 224, 230, 236, 241, 249, 255 • New Jersey Preparation and Practice, 221, 222, 223, 224, 228, 229, 230, 234, 235, 236, 238, 240, 241, 244, 248, 249, 253, 254, 255, 256 • Writing, 223, 224, 229, 231, 235, 240, 249	• Real Life Examples, 221, 226, 232, 233, 238, 246, 250, 252 • Mixed Review of Problem Solving, 244, 256 • Multi-Step Problems, 223, 230, 236, 241, 244, 249, 254, 256 • Challenge, 224, 230, 236, 241, 242, 249, 255	• Homework Help, 221, 228, 234, 239, 248, 252 At classzone.com: @HomeTutor, Online Quiz, eWorkbook, Hints and Homework • Reading and Vocabulary, 218, 219, 226, 232, 237, 245, 246, 250, 257 • Notetaking, 219, 220, 226, 232, 233, 250 • Avoid Errors, 219, 227, 247, 251

Commutative Property, p. 305
$-15 + 21 = 21 + (-15)$

Integers

Review Prerequisite Skills 266
    Get-Ready Game 266
    Vocabulary and Skill Check 268
    Notetaking Skills 268

Standards			
4.1.A.4	**6.1**	**Comparing and Ordering Integers**	269
		Extension: Negative and Zero Exponents	274
4.1.B.1.a	**6.2**	**Adding Integers**	277
		🔍 Investigation: Modeling Integer Addition	276
4.1.B.1.a	**6.3**	**Subtracting Integers**	285
		🔍 Investigation: Modeling Integer Subtraction	283
		Quiz for Lessons 6.1–6.3	289
		New Jersey Mixed Review	290
4.1.B.1.a	**6.4**	**Multiplying Integers**	291
4.1.B.1.a	**6.5**	**Dividing Integers**	296
4.3.D.4.a	**6.6**	🅧🅨 ALGEBRA **Rational Numbers**	301
	6.7	🅧🅨 ALGEBRA **The Distributive Property**	307
4.2.C.1	**6.8**	🅧🅨 ALGEBRA **The Coordinate Plane**	313
		🔍 Investigation: Making a Scatter Plot	312
		Quiz for Lessons 6.4–6.8	319
		🖩 Technology Activity: Graphing in a Coordinate Plane	320
		New Jersey Mixed Review	321

New Jersey Assessment

Chapter Review 322
Chapter Test 327
New Jersey Test Preparation and Practice 328
Cumulative Review 332

Animated **Math** classzone.com **Activities** 272, 279, 292, 301, 308, 310, 317

New Jersey

ASSESSMENT
- New Jersey Practice Examples, 277, 297, 314
- New Jersey Daily Practice, 273, 282, 289, 295, 300, 306, 311, 318
- New Jersey Preparation and Practice, 271-273, 277, 280, 282, 287, 288, 289, 290, 293-295, 297, 299, 300, 304-306, 309-311, 314, 316, 317, 318, 321
- Writing, 271, 280, 284, 287, 294, 300, 306, 310

PROBLEM SOLVING
- Real Life Examples, 270, 279, 286, 292, 297, 298, 307, 308, 315
- Mixed Review of Problem Solving, 290, 321
- Multi-Step, 273, 282, 286, 288, 290, 295, 300, 306, 311, 315, 318, 321
- Challenge, 273, 282, 289, 295, 300, 306, 311, 318, 319

STUDENT HELP
- Homework Help, 271, 280, 287, 293, 298, 304, 310, 315
  At classzone.com: @HomeTutor, Online Quiz, eWorkbook, Hints and Homework
- Reading, Vocabulary, and Notetaking, 268, 269, 274, 277, 278, 285, 291, 296, 301, 302, 303, 307, 308, 313, 314, 322
- Avoid Errors, 270, 279, 296, 308

Addition Equations, p. 360
$$15 + 10 + 5 + p = 45$$

Equations, Inequalities, and Functions

Review Prerequisite Skills 334
    Get-Ready Game 334
    Vocabulary and Skill Check 336
    Notetaking Skills 336

Standards

4.3.C.2.a   **7.1**   ⓧⓨ **ALGEBRA** Writing Expressions and Equations 337

4.3.D.3.a   **7.2**   ⓧⓨ **ALGEBRA** Simplifying Expressions 342

4.3.D.2.b   **7.3**   ⓧⓨ **ALGEBRA** Solving Addition and Subtraction Equations 347
    🔍 Investigation: Modeling Addition Equations 346

4.3.D.2.b   **7.4**   ⓧⓨ **ALGEBRA** Solving Multiplication and Division Equations 354
    🔍 Investigation: Modeling Multiplication Equations 353
    Quiz for Lessons 7.1–7.4 359
    New Jersey Mixed Review 360

4.3.D.2.a   **7.5**   ⓧⓨ **ALGEBRA** Solving Two-Step Equations 361

4.3.D.4.a   **7.6**   ⓧⓨ **ALGEBRA** Solving Inequalities 366

4.3.A.1.a   **7.7**   ⓧⓨ **ALGEBRA** Functions and Equations 371

4.3.B.1.a   **7.8**   ⓧⓨ **ALGEBRA** Graphing Functions 376
    Quiz for Lessons 7.5–7.8 381
    📱 Technology Activity: Graphing Functions 382
    Extension: Direct Variation 383
    New Jersey Mixed Review 385

New Jersey Assessment

Chapter Review 386
Chapter Test 391
New Jersey Test Preparation and Practice 392

Animated **Math**
classzone.com   Activities 337, 348, 367, 372, 376

🔷 **New Jersey**

ASSESSMENT
- New Jersey Practice Examples, 356, 373
- New Jersey Daily Practice, 341, 345, 352, 359, 365, 370, 375, 381
- New Jersey Preparation and Practice, 339, 340, 344, 345, 350, 352, 356, 357, 358, 359, 360, 363-365, 368-370, 372, 373–375, 378, 380, 381, 383
- Writing, 340, 341, 345, 346, 352, 353, 358, 364, 369, 374, 380

PROBLEM SOLVING
- Real Life Examples, 338, 343, 349, 356, 362, 372, 377
- Mixed Review of Problem Solving, 360, 383
- Multi-Step Problems, 338, 341, 345, 352, 359, 360, 362, 365, 370, 372, 375, 376, 380, 383
- Challenge, 341, 345, 352, 359, 365, 370, 375, 381

STUDENT HELP
- Homework Help, 339, 344, 349, 356, 363, 368, 373, 378
  At classzone.com: @HomeTutor, Online Quiz, eWorkbook, Hints and Homework
- Reading, Vocabulary, and Notetaking, 336, 337, 338, 342, 347, 348, 354, 355, 361, 366, 371, 376, 377, 385, 386
- Avoid Errors, 337, 343, 348, 361, 367, 377

Slope, p. 410
$$\frac{\text{rise}}{\text{run}} = \frac{6 \text{ mi}}{4 \text{ h}}$$

Ratios and Proportions

Review Prerequisite Skills		396
Get-Ready Game		396
Vocabulary and Skill Check		398
Notetaking Skills		398

Standards

4.1.A.3	**8.1**	**Ratios**	399
4.1.A.3	**8.2**	**Rates**	404
4.1.A.3	**8.3**	XV **ALGEBRA** **Slope**	409
		Quiz for Lessons 8.1–8.3	414
		▦ Technology Activity: Finding Slope	415
		New Jersey Mixed Review	416
4.1.A.3	**8.4**	XV **ALGEBRA** **Writing and Solving Proportions**	418
		🔍 Investigation: Modeling Proportions	417
4.1.A.3	**8.5**	XV **ALGEBRA** **Solving Proportions Using Cross Products**	423
4.2.A.2.b	**8.6**	**Scale Drawings and Models**	430
		🔍 Investigation: Making a Scale Drawing	429
		Quiz for Lessons 8.4–8.6	435
		New Jersey Mixed Review	436

New Jersey Assessment

Chapter Review	437
Chapter Test	441
New Jersey Test Preparation and Practice	442

Animated Math
classzone.com **Activities** **400, 404, 410, 420, 431**

New Jersey

ASSESSMENT

- New Jersey Practice Examples, 405, 425
- New Jersey Daily Practice, 403, 408, 414, 422, 428, 435
- New Jersey Preparation and Practice, 401, 402, 403, 405, 406, 407, 408, 412, 413, 414, 416, 417, 421, 422, 424, 425, 426, 427, 428, 433, 434, 435, 436
- Writing, 402, 407, 413, 415, 417, 427, 429, 434

PROBLEM SOLVING

- Real Life Examples, 400, 404, 405, 411, 418, 420, 424, 425, 431
- Mixed Review of Problem Solving, 416, 436
- Multi-Step Problems, 400, 402, 405, 408, 410, 413, 416, 418, 420, 422, 424, 427, 434, 436
- Challenge, 403, 408, 414, 422, 428, 434, 435

STUDENT HELP

- Homework Help, 401, 406, 411, 420, 425, 432
  At classzone.com: @HomeTutor, Online Quiz, eWorkbook, Hints and Homework
- Reading and Vocabulary, 398, 399, 404, 409, 418, 423, 430, 431, 437
- Notetaking, 399, 418, 423, 424
- Avoid Errors, 400, 410, 420

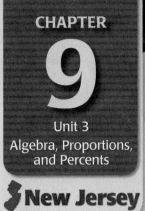

CHAPTER

9

Unit 3
Algebra, Proportions,
and Percents

New Jersey

Percents and Decimals, p. 460
$120\% = 1.2$

Percents

Review Prerequisite Skills 446
    Get-Ready Game 446
    Vocabulary and Skill Check 448
    Notetaking Skills 448

Standards			
4.1.A.3	**9.1**	**Percents and Fractions**	449
4.1.A.3	**9.2**	**Percents and Proportions**	454
		Investigation: Using Percent Bar Models	453
4.1.A.5	**9.3**	**Percents and Decimals**	460
4.1.A.3	**9.4**	**ALGEBRA** **The Percent Equation**	465
		Quiz for Lessons 9.1–9.4	470
		New Jersey Mixed Review	471
4.5.E.1.d	**9.5**	**Circle Graphs**	474
		Investigation: Measuring Angles	472
		Technology Activity: Making Circle Graphs	479
4.1.A.3	**9.6**	**Percent of Increase and Decrease**	480
4.1.A.3	**9.7**	**Discounts, Markups, Sales Tax, and Tips** ...	485
4.1.A.3	**9.8**	**ALGEBRA** **Simple Interest**	490
		Quiz for Lessons 9.5–9.8	494
		New Jersey Mixed Review	495

New Jersey **Assessment**

Chapter Review 496
Chapter Test 501
New Jersey Test Preparation and Practice 502
Cumulative Review 506

Animated Math classzone.com **Activities** 450, 457, 461, 472, 476, 481, 490

New Jersey

ASSESSMENT

• New Jersey Practice Examples, 460, 467, 487
• New Jersey Daily Practice, 452, 459, 464, 470, 478, 484, 489, 494
• New Jersey Preparation and Practice, 451, 452, 457, 458, 459, 460, 463, 464, 467, 468, 469, 470, 471, 477, 478, 482, 483, 484, 486, 487, 488, 489, 492, 493, 494, 495
• Writing, 452, 458, 469, 478, 484, 488, 493

PROBLEM SOLVING

• Real Life Examples, 450, 455, 461, 462, 466, 467, 476, 481, 486, 487, 491
• Mixed Review of Problem Solving, 471, 495
• Multi-Step Problems, 452, 459, 464, 469, 471, 475, 476, 478, 484, 485, 486, 489, 491, 493, 495
• Challenge, 452, 459, 464, 469, 470, 478, 484, 489, 494

STUDENT HELP

• Homework Help, 451, 456, 462, 467, 476, 482, 487, 492
   At classzone.com: @HomeTutor, Online Quiz, eWorkbook, Hints and Homework
• Reading, Vocabulary, and Notetaking, 448, 449, 450, 454, 456, 460, 465, 474, 480, 485, 490, 496
• Avoid Errors, 475, 476, 486, 491

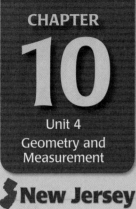
Multiplying Real Numbers, p. 90
Elevation $= 6416 + (-0.12)(50)$

Geometric Figures

Review Prerequisite Skills 508
    Get-Ready Game 508
    Vocabulary and Skill Check 510
    Notetaking Skills 510

10.1 Angles 511

10.2 Special Pairs of Angles 516

Standards   4.5.E.1.a   **10.3 XY ALGEBRA Triangles** 521
    Extension: Constructions 527

4.2.A.1.a   **10.4 Polygons** 529
    Quiz for Lessons 10.1–10.4 534
    New Jersey Mixed Review 535

4.2.A.3   **10.5 Similar and Congruent Polygons** 537
    🔍 Investigation: Investigating Similar Rectangles 536

4.2.A.2.a   **10.6 XY ALGEBRA Using Proportions with Similar Polygons** 542

4.2.B.1.c   **10.7 Transformations and Symmetry** 548
    🔍 Investigation: Investigating Symmetry 547
    Extension: Tessellations 554

4.2.C.2   **10.8 XY ALGEBRA Transformations in the Coordinate Plane** 556
    Quiz for Lessons 10.5–10.8 561
    🖩 Technology Activity: Translating Points 562
    New Jersey Mixed Review 563

   New Jersey   **Assessment**

    Chapter Review 564
    Chapter Test 569
    New Jersey Test Preparation and Practice 570

     Animated Math classzone.com **Activities** 511, 512, 530, 549, 550, 557

New Jersey

ASSESSMENT	PROBLEM SOLVING	STUDENT HELP
• New Jersey Practice Examples, 512, 523, 549	• Real Life Examples, 512, 518, 538, 543	• Homework Help, 513, 518, 524, 531, 539, 544, 550, 558
• New Jersey Daily Practice, 515, 520, 526, 534, 541, 546, 553, 561	• Mixed Review of Problem Solving, 535, 563	At classzone.com: @HomeTutor, Online Quiz, eWorkbook, Hints and Homework
• New Jersey Preparation and Practice, 512-515, 519, 520, 523-526, 532-535, 539-541, 544-546, 549, 551, 552, 553, 559-561, 563	• Multi-Step Problems, 515, 519, 526, 529, 531, 533, 535, 541, 545, 553, 560, 563	• Reading, Vocabulary, and Notetaking, 510, 511, 516, 521, 522, 523, 527, 529, 530, 537, 542, 548, 549, 554, 556, 557, 564
• Writing, 515, 520, 525, 526, 540, 545, 552, 560, 563	• Challenge, 515, 520, 526, 534, 541, 546, 553, 561	• Avoid Errors, 531, 537, 550

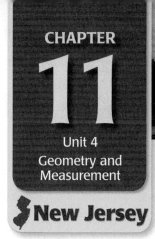

CHAPTER
11

Unit 4
Geometry and
Measurement

New Jersey

Circumference, p. 610
$C \approx (3.14)(135)$

Measurement and Area

Review Prerequisite Skills 574
    Get-Ready Game 574
    Vocabulary and Skill Check 576
    Notetaking Skills 576

11.1 **XY** **ALGEBRA** **Square Roots** 577

11.2 Approximating Square Roots 582

11.3 The Pythagorean Theorem 588
    🔍 Investigation: Modeling the Pythagorean Theorem 587
    Quiz for Lessons 11.1–11.3 592
    New Jersey Mixed Review 593

11.4 Area of a Parallelogram 594

Standards   4.2.E.1.a   **11.5 Areas of Triangles and Trapezoids** 601
    🔍 Investigation: Modeling Areas of Triangles and
    Trapezoids 599

4.2.E.1.a   **11.6 Circumference of a Circle** 607

4.2.E.1.b   **11.7 Area of a Circle** 612
    Quiz for Lessons 11.4–11.7 616
    📱 Technology Activity: Using Square Roots and Pi 617
    New Jersey Mixed Review 618

New Jersey Assessment

Chapter Review 619
Chapter Test 623
New Jersey Test Preparation and Practice 624

Animated **Math** Activities 589, 601, 613
classzone.com

New Jersey

ASSESSMENT

- New Jersey Practice Examples, 603, 613
- New Jersey Daily Practice, 581, 586, 592, 598, 606, 611, 616
- New Jersey Preparation and Practice, 580, 581, 585, 586, 590, 591, 593, 597, 598, 603–606, 610–615, 618
- Writing, 581, 586, 592, 597, 605, 610, 615

PROBLEM SOLVING

- Real Life Examples, 578, 583, 588, 589, 595, 602, 603, 609, 613
- Mixed Review of Problem Solving, 593, 618
- Multi-Step Problems, 581, 586, 591, 593, 597, 603, 606, 611, 613, 615
- Challenge, 581, 586, 592, 598, 606, 611, 616

STUDENT HELP

- Homework Help, 579, 584, 590, 596, 603, 609, 614
  At classzone.com: @HomeTutor, Online Quiz, eWorkbook, Hints and Homework
- Reading and Vocabulary, 576, 577, 579, 582, 588, 594, 601, 602, 607, 612, 619
- Notetaking, 588, 594, 595, 601, 602, 608, 612
- Avoid Errors, 584, 588, 595, 608

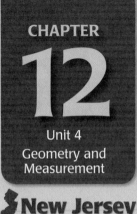

CHAPTER
12

Unit 4
Geometry and
Measurement

New Jersey

Surface Area, p. 660
$S = 64 + 4(20)$

Surface Area and Volume

Review Prerequisite Skills 628
    Get-Ready Game 628
    Vocabulary and Skill Check 630
    Notetaking Skills 630

Standards

4.2.A.2.c   **12.1 Classifying Solids** 631

4.2.A.2.c   **12.2 Sketching Solids** 636
    Extension: Viewing and Building Solids 640

4.2.A.2.c   **12.3 Surface Area of Rectangular Prisms** 642
    Quiz for Lessons 12.1–12.3 647
    New Jersey Mixed Review 648

4.2.A.2.c   **12.4 Surface Area of Cylinders** 649

4.2.A.2.c   **12.5 Volume of Rectangular Prisms** 655
    🔍 Investigation: Investigating Volume 654
    Extension: Surface Area and Volume of Pyramids 660

4.2.A.2.c   **12.6 Volume of Cylinders** 662
    Quiz for Lessons 12.4–12.6 666
    📓 Technology Activity: Surface Area and Volume 667
    New Jersey Mixed Review 668

New Jersey Assessment

    Chapter Review 669
    Chapter Test 673
    New Jersey Test Preparation and Practice 674

    Animated Math classzone.com **Activities** 632, 637, 667

New Jersey

ASSESSMENT
- New Jersey Practice Examples, 632, 662
- New Jersey Daily Practice, 636, 639, 647, 653, 659, 666
- New Jersey Preparation and Practice, 632, 633, 634, 635, 638, 639, 643, 644, 646, 647, 648, 651-653, 656, 657-659, 662, 664, 665, 666, 668
- Writing, 634, 639, 646, 653, 665

PROBLEM SOLVING
- Real Life Examples, 643, 650, 655, 656, 663
- Mixed Review of Problem Solving, 648, 668
- Multi-Step Problems, 635, 636, 637, 639, 640, 641, 642, 643, 646, 648, 653, 656, 658, 660, 661, 663, 666
- Challenge, 635, 639, 646, 647, 653, 659, 666

STUDENT HELP
- Homework Help, 633, 638, 644, 651, 657, 664
  At classzone.com: @HomeTutor, Online Quiz, eWorkbook, Hints and Homework
- Reading and Vocabulary, 630, 631, 636, 642, 643, 649, 655, 662, 669
- Notetaking, 642, 649, 655, 662
- Avoid Errors, 632, 656, 663

Permutations, p. 702
$3 \times 2 \times 1 = 6$

Probability

Review Prerequisite Skills 678
    Get-Ready Game 678
    Vocabulary and Skill Check 680
    Notetaking Skills 680

Standards

4.4.B.1   **13.1 Introduction to Probability** 682
       Investigation: Investigating Probability 681
    Extension: Number Sets and Probability 688

4.4.C.3   **13.2 Tree Diagrams** 690

4.4.C.3   **13.3 The Counting Principle** 696
       Investigation: Determining Outcomes 695
    Quiz for Lessons 13.1–13.3 700
    New Jersey Mixed Review 701

4.4.C.1.a   **13.4 Permutations and Combinations** 702
       Technology Activity: Finding Permutations and
       Combinations 708

4.4.B.3   **13.5 Disjoint Events** 709

4.4.B.3   **13.6 Independent and Dependent Events** 715
    Quiz for Lessons 13.4–13.6 721
    New Jersey Mixed Review 722

New Jersey   Assessment

    Chapter Review 723
    Chapter Test 727
    New Jersey Test Preparation and Practice 728
    Cumulative Review 732

Animated Math
classzone.com   **Activities** 683, 691, 709

New Jersey

ASSESSMENT
- New Jersey Practice Examples, 684, 691
- New Jersey Daily Practice, 687, 694, 700, 707, 714, 721
- New Jersey Preparation and Practice, 684, 685, 686, 687, 691, 692, 694, 697, 698, 699, 700, 701, 705, 706, 707, 712, 713, 714, 718, 719, 721, 722
- Writing, 687, 694, 695, 699, 706, 713, 719

PROBLEM SOLVING
- Real Life Examples, 684, 690, 697, 703, 704, 710, 711, 716, 717
- Mixed Review of Problem Solving, 701, 722
- Multi-Step Problems, 683, 687, 694, 697, 699, 701, 704, 707, 713, 716, 717, 720
- Challenge, 687, 694, 700, 707, 714, 720, 721

STUDENT HELP
- Homework Help, 684, 692, 698, 705, 712, 718
  At classzone.com: @HomeTutor, Online Quiz, eWorkbook, Hints and Homework
- Reading and Vocabulary, 680, 682, 683, 688, 690, 696, 702, 704, 709, 715, 716, 723
- Notetaking, 688, 696, 709, 710, 716, 717
- Avoid Errors, 697, 710, 717

Contents   **NJ 21**

Contents
of Student Resources

Additional Standards-Based Lessons
pp. A1–A34

Skills Review Handbook
pp. 735–760

Whole Number Place Value	735
Comparing and Ordering Whole Numbers	736
Rounding Whole Numbers	737
Number Fact Families	738
Divisibility Tests	739
Modeling Fractions	740
Using a Number Line to Add and Subtract	741
Addition and Subtraction of Whole Numbers	742
Multiplication of Whole Numbers	743
Division of Whole Numbers	744
Estimating Sums	745
Estimating Differences	746
Estimating Products	747
Estimating Quotients	748
Solving Problems Using Addition and Subtraction	749
Solving Problems Using Multiplication and Division	750
Units of Time	751
Solving Problems Involving Time	752
Using a Ruler	753
Using a Compass	754
Basic Geometric Figures	755
Venn Diagrams and Logical Reasoning	756
Reading Bar Graphs and Line Graphs	757
Reading and Making Line Plots	758
Commutative and Associative Properties of Addition	759
Commutative and Associative Properties of Multiplication	760

Problem Solving Handbook: Strategy Review
pp. 761–770

Make a Model	761
Draw a Diagram	762
Guess, Check, and Revise	763
Work Backward	764
Make a List or Table	765
Look for a Pattern	766
Break into Parts	767
Solve a Simpler Problem	768
Use a Venn Diagram	769
Act It Out	770

Problem Solving Handbook: Strategy Practice
pp. 771–775

Extra Practice for Chapters 1–13
pp. 776–788

Tables
pp. 789–794

Symbols	789
Measures	790
Formulas	791
Properties	792
Finding Squares and Square Roots	793
Squares and Square Roots	794

English-Spanish Glossary
pp. 795–830

Index

Credits
pp. 847–848

Selected Answers
pp. SA1–SA24

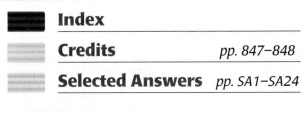

New Jersey Mathematics Core
Curriculum Content Standards
page S1

Student Guide to the Standards

The New Jersey Mathematics Core Curriculum Content Standards

- The New Jersey Mathematics Core Curriculum Content Standards are goals set by the state to ensure that you are being taught a thoughtful, complete curriculum.

- Teachers and other educators use the cumulative progress indicators when developing courses and tests.

- Lessons in your book connect to an indicator, which is listed next to the lesson in the table of contents beginning on NJ 8. These indicators are also shown on the first page of each lesson throughout the book.

 New Jersey Mathematics Core Curriculum Content Standards *page S1*

Ocean City Beach, Ocean City, New Jersey © Corbis

Guide to the New Jersey Mathematics Core Curriculum Content Standards

Learning the New Jersey Mathematics Core Curriculum Content Standards will help you hit a homerun!

Did you know...

...that baseball and math standards have some things in common?

...and, that your math standards have been written as a commitment to you, the New Jersey student?

So...

..."What are Math Standards and what do they have in common with baseball?"

Compare the standards to a set of rules that must be followed in a sport event. For example, in a baseball game, the batter must move from first base to second base and then third base before proceeding to the home plate to score a run. Learning this rule enables the team to win the game.

Without the knowledge of how a baseball game is played, the team will not have the fundamental concepts to compete.

Math standards, like the rules in baseball, help you focus on a common foundation of mathematical concepts that you will use in everyday life and later in the workplace.

And...

...How will learning the New Jersey Mathematics Core Curriculum Content Standards make a difference for you, the student?

It is important to learn material that is closely aligned to the math standards because they are what you will be tested on when it comes time to take your state test.

The New Jersey state standards have been written as a commitment to you, the student, to help you focus on the proper content to achieve both depth and understanding of mathematical knowledge.

New Jersey Mathematics Core Curriculum Content Standards Decoder

Part 1 The math standards for New Jersey are organized under the following standards:

1. Number and Numerical Operations
2. Geometry and Measurement
3. Patterns and Algebra
4. Data Analysis, Probability, and Discrete Mathematics

Part 2 Each standard is divided into strands.

Part 3 Each strand is broken down further into cumulative progress indicators. The information from the 3 parts will help you break the standard code!

Here is an example:

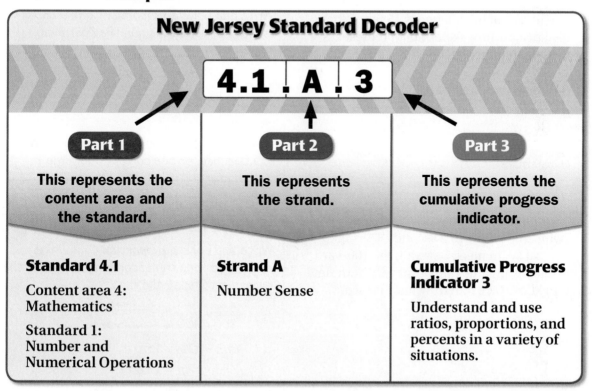

New Jersey Standard Decoder

4.1 . A . 3

Part 1

This represents the content area and the standard.

Standard 4.1

Content area 4: Mathematics

Standard 1: Number and Numerical Operations

Part 2

This represents the strand.

Strand A

Number Sense

Part 3

This represents the cumulative progress indicator.

Cumulative Progress Indicator 3

Understand and use ratios, proportions, and percents in a variety of situations.

STANDARDS

New Jersey Mathematics Core Curriculum Content Standards

Standard 4.1: Number and Numerical Operations

Strands

A: Number Sense

B: Numerical Operations

C: Estimation

What It Means To You

Understanding numbers is the basis for all math. Studying this standard will enable you to represent very large or very small numbers, know what number systems they belong to, and determine whether a problem needs a rough estimate or an exact answer.

Here is what questions might look like on the NJ ASK:

4.1.A.3 Understand and use ratios, proportions, and percents (including percents greater than 100 and less than 1) in a variety of situations.

Tonya drew a floor plan of her house. She used a scale of 1 inch equals 2 feet. The length of her kitchen is 15 feet. What distance on Tonya's floor plan represents the length of her kitchen?

A. 5.5 in.

B. 7.5 in.

C. 10 in.

D. 30 in.

Solution for Question 1

Write and solve a proportion to find the length l of her kitchen on the floor plan.

$$\frac{1}{2} = \frac{l}{15} \longleftarrow \text{inches} \atop \longleftarrow \text{feet}$$

$$1 \cdot 15 = 2 \cdot l$$

$$l = 7.5$$

The length of her kitchen on the floor plan is 7.5 inches, so the correct answer is B.

An athlete on the school swim team can swim 25 yards in 15.2 seconds. During the last swim meet, he swam the 100-yard event at the same rate of speed. About how long did it take him to swim this race?

A. 25 sec

B. 32 sec

C. 61 sec

D. 80 sec

Solution for Question 2

Write and solve a proportion to find the amount of time t in seconds that it took the swimmer to finish the race.

$$\frac{15.2}{25} = \frac{t}{100} \longleftarrow \text{time} \atop \longleftarrow \text{yards}$$

$$15.2 \cdot 100 = 25 \cdot t$$

$$t = 60.8$$

It takes the swimmer about 61 seconds to finish the race, so the correct answer is C.

Standard 4.2: Geometry and Measurement

Strands

A: Geometric Properties

B: Transforming Shapes

C: Coordinate Geometry

D: Units of Measurement

E: Measuring Geometric Objects

What It Means To You

Geometry is the study of points, lines, angles, surfaces, and solids. Studying spatial relationships gives us a visual way to understand the properties of geometric shapes. Measurement gives a numerical value to a characteristic of an object, such as length. Measurement is important because of all the ways we use it in everyday life.

Here is what questions might look like on the NJ ASK:

4.2.D.1 Solve problems requiring calculations that involve different units of measurement within a measurement system (e.g., 4'3" plus 7'10" equals 12'1").

Mia uses a square piece of construction paper as a base to make a photo collage of her summer vacation. The side length of the construction paper is 305 mm. What is the area of the construction paper in square centimeters?

A. 61 cm^2

B. 122 cm^2

C. 930.25 cm^2

D. 93,025 cm^2

Solution for Question 1

Convert 305 millimeters to centimeters

$$305 \text{ mm} \div 10 = 30.5 \text{ cm}$$

$A = s^2$ Formula for the area of a square

$\quad = (30.5)^2$ Substitute 30.5 for *s*.

$\quad = 930.25$ Multiply.

The area of the construction paper is 930.25 square centimeters. The correct answer is C.

A sports bottle holds 372 milliliters of water. If 7 soccer players each have their own bottle, how many liters of water will be needed to fill all the bottles?

A. 2.604 L

B. 26.04 L

C. 260.4 L

D. 2604 L

Solution for Question 2

Convert 372 milliliters to liters.

$$372 \text{ mL} \div 1000 = 0.372 \text{ L}$$

There are 7 bottles that each hold 0.372 liters of water.

$$0.372 \text{ L} \times 7 = 2.604 \text{ L}$$

The correct answer is A.

Standard 4.3: Patterns and Algebra

Strands	What It Means To You
A: Patterns **B:** Functions and Relationships **C:** Modeling **D:** Procedures	Algebra is the branch of mathematics in which symbols, usually letters, are used to represent numbers and quantities. Studying algebra will help you notice patterns, represent relationships, and analyze how things change.

Here is what questions might look like on the NJ ASK:

4.3.A.1.a Recognize, describe, extend, and create patterns involving whole numbers and rational numbers: Descriptions using tables, verbal rules, simple equations and graphs.

How can you find the next number in the sequence below?

$$4, 8, 16, 32, 64, \ldots$$

A. By adding 32 to the previous number

B. By adding 4 to the previous number

C. By dividing the previous number by 2

D. By multiplying the previous number by 2

Solution for Question 1

Look to see how each number is related to the preceding number.

Each number is two times the previous number, so the correct answer is D.

Two teachers rent movies to show students at the end of the school year. They rent 3 movies for $5 each and spend $9 on refreshments. They split these costs evenly. Which expression can be used to find the amount, in dollars, each teacher should pay?

A. $(5 + 9) \div 2$

B. $9 + 3 \times 5 \div 2$

C. $3 \times 5 + 9 \div 2$

D. $(3 \times 5 + 9) \div 2$

Solution for Question 2

The teachers spend $5 on each of 3 movies. So, they spend (3×5) dollars on movies. They also spend $9 on beverages. They are dividing the cost equally, so the sum of the money spent above divided by two is the amount each teacher should pay.

The expression is $(3 \times 5 + 9) \div 2$, so the correct answer is D.

Standard 4.4: Data Analysis, Probability, and Discrete Mathematics

Strands

A: Data Analysis

B: Probability

C: Discrete Mathematics—
Systematic Listing and Counting

D: Discrete Mathematics—
Vertex-Edge Graphs and Algorithms

What It Means To You

Data analysis involves processing information to solve problems that come up in work and in life. Probability is the study of the likelihood that a given event will occur. Studying data analysis and probability will give you the skills to analyze information, make predictions, and then draw conclusions based on the data. Discrete mathematics is the study of sets and systems that have a countable number of elements. You can use your discrete mathematics skills to solve logic games and break codes!

Here is what a question might look like on the NJ ASK:

4.4.A.2 Make inferences and formulate and evaluate arguments based on displays and analysis of data.

The circle graph shows how many people out of 100 prefer watching each sport.

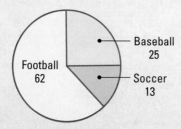

Which of the following statements is NOT supported by the circle graph?

A. Football is the most popular choice.

B. Thirty-eight people do NOT prefer football.

C. Soccer is NOT the least popular choice.

D. About twice as many people watch baseball as soccer.

Solution

The "Football" section is the largest section of the graph. So, football is the most popular choice.

To find out how many people *do not* prefer football, add the values in the "Baseball" and "Soccer" sections: $25 + 13 = 38$.

The number of people who prefer soccer is less than the number of people who prefer football and baseball. The statement "Soccer is *not* the least popular choice" is false.

So, the correct answer is C.

Countdown to the NJ ASK

Additional Test Practice
@ classzone.com

What is the NJ ASK?

- The New Jersey state test is called the New Jersey Assessment of Skills and Knowledge (NJ ASK). The NJ ASK is given in the spring to students in the 7th grade.

- The test is made up of multiple-choice and open-ended questions that evaluate your knowledge of the New Jersey Mathematics Core Curriculum Content Standards.

Getting Ready

You can use the questions on the following pages to practice for the NJ ASK. Each question addresses a cumulative progress indicator.

The questions are in the same format as those on the NJ ASK, and are organized by content standards. (For example, Standard 1 is Number and Numerical Operations.)

If you need practice with a particular cumulative progress indicator, use the chart on the next page to find which questions address that standard, strand, and cumulative progress indicator. If you need additional preparation, the chart lists lessons you can review.

You will have more opportunities to practice for the NJ ASK in every lesson and chapter throughout the book.

Ocean City Beach, Ocean City, New Jersey © Corbis

Countdown Reference Chart

This chart lists which questions address each cumulative progress indicator.
Lesson support is referenced and the full text of the standards is available on S1.

NJ Standards	Practice Questions for the NJ ASK	Lesson-by-Lesson NJ ASK Support
Standard 4.1: Number and Numerical Operations		
4.1.A.1	1, 2, 3	Lesson 6.6
4.1.A.1	4, 5, 6	Lesson 6.2, 9.3
4.1.A.2	7, 8, 9	Lesson 2.5
4.1.A.3	10, 11, 12	Lesson 1.7, 9.2
4.1.A.3	110, 111, 112	Lesson 9.1, 8.4, 8.5
4.1.A.4	13, 14, 15	Lesson 4.5, 6.1
4.1.A.4	113, 114, 115	Lesson 2.1, 6.1
4.1.A.5	16, 17, 18	Lesson 4.7, 9.1
4.1.A.5	116, 117	Lesson 4.7, 9.3
4.1.A.6	19, 20, 21	Lesson 4.7
4.1.B.1	22, 23, 24	Lesson 2.2, 2.3
4.1.B.1	25, 26, 27	Lesson 5.2, 5.3, 5.4
4.1.B.2	28, 29, 30	Lesson 1.3
4.1.B.3	31, 32, 33	Lesson 1.4
4.1.C.1	34, 35, 36	Lesson 2.4, 9.3
Standard 4.2: Geometry and Measurement		
4.2.A.1	37, 38, 39	Lesson 10.4
4.2.A.2	40, 41, 42	Lesson 8.6, 10.6
4.2.A.2	118, 119, 120	Lessons 8.6, 10.5
4.2.A.3	43, 44	Lesson 12.3, 12.4
4.2.A.3	45, 46	Lesson 12.4, 12.5
4.2.A.3	121	Lesson 12.5
4.2.B.1	47, 48	Lesson 10.7, 10.8
4.2.B.1	49, 50	Lesson 10.7
4.2.B.1	122	Lesson 10.8
4.2.C.1	51, 52, 53	Lesson 6.8
4.2.C.1	54, 55	Lesson 6.8
4.2.C.1	123	Lesson 6.8
4.2.C.2	56, 57, 58	Lesson 10.8
4.2.C.2	124, 125	Lesson 10.8
4.2.D.1	59, 60, 61	Lesson 2.7, 8.2

NJ Standards	Practice Questions for the NJ ASK	Lesson-by-Lesson NJ ASK Support
4.2.D.1	126, 127	Lesson 2.7, 5.6
4.2.D.2	62, 63	Lesson 2.6
4.2.D.2	64, 65, 66	Lesson 2.6
4.2.D.3	67, 68, 69	Lesson 2.6
4.2.E.1	70, 71, 72	Lesson 11.5, 12.4
4.2.E.1	128, 129	Lesson 11.5, 11.7
4.2.E.2	73, 74, 75	Lesson 12.6, Ext. 12.5
Standard 4.3: Patterns and Algebra		
4.3.A.1	76, 77, 78	Lesson 1.1
4.3.A.1	130, 131, 132	Lesson 1.1
4.3.B.1	79, 80	Lesson 7.8
4.3.C.1	81, 82, 83	Lesson 7.7, 8.3
4.3.C.2	84, 85, 86	Lesson 7.7
4.3.C.2	133	Lesson 1.7
4.3.D.1	87, 88	Lesson 6.2
4.3.D.1	89, 90	Lesson 6.3
4.3.D.2	134, 135, 136	Lesson 7.4, 7.5
4.3.D.3	137, 138, 139	Lesson 6.4, 7.1, 7.2
4.3.D.4	91, 92, 93	Lesson 6.6, 7.6
Standard 4.4: Data Analysis, Probability, and Discrete Mathematics		
4.4.A.1	94, 95	Lesson 3.3, 3.6
4.4.A.1	140	Lesson 3.1
4.4.A.2	96, 97	Lesson 3.3, 3.5
4.4.B.1	98, 99, 100	Lesson 13.1
4.4.B.2	141	Lesson 13.1 Investigation
4.4.B.3	101, 102, 103	Lesson 13.2
4.4.B.4	142	Lesson 13.1
4.4.C.1	104, 105	Lesson 13.3, 13.4
4.4.C.1	143, 144	Lesson 13.4
4.4.C.2	145	Lesson 13.5
4.4.C.3	106, 107, 108	Lesson 13.4
4.4.D.1	109	Lesson 6.8 Additional Lesson G

4.1.A.1 Extend understanding of the number system by constructing meanings for the following: a. Rational numbers; b. Percents; c. Whole numbers with exponents

1. Which temperature is less than $-6°F$?
   (p. 304, prob. 15–18)

   A. $-12°F$

   B. $-3°F$

   C. $2°F$

   D. $8°F$

2. Ed and Mary are underwater. Ed's depth is represented by -6 feet. Mary is above Ed. Which could be Mary's depth? *(p. 304, prob. 15–18)*

   A. -4 feet

   B. -8 feet

   C. -10 feet

   D. -12 feet

3. Tia had $43.50 in her bank account on Monday. On Tuesday she withdrew 10 dollars. On Wednesday she deposited 12 dollars. Which of the following numbers could represent Tia's withdrawal on Tuesday? *(p. 305, prob. 55)*

   A. $-\$33.50$

   B. $-\$10.00$

   C. $\$33.50$

   D. $\$53.50$

4. Which statement is true when $x = -5$ and $y = -4\frac{1}{2}$? *(p. 280, prob. 32)*

   A. $x > y$

   B. $y > x$

   C. $0 > y$

   D. $x > 0$

5. Which statement is *not* true when $a = |-6|$ and $b = -6$? *(p. 280, prob. 32)*

   A. $a = b$

   B. $a > 0$

   C. $y > 0$

   D. $0 > b$

6. Which is equal to 1.5%? *(p. 462, prob. 3)*

   A. 0.0015

   B. 0.015

   C. 0.15

   D. 1.5

Go On ➡

Standard 4.1 | Number and Numerical Operations

4.1.A.2 Demonstrate a sense of the relative magnitudes of numbers.

7. Which has a value between 50 and 100? *(p. 80, prob. 5–13)*

   A. 1.5×10^2

   B. 1.5×10^3

   C. 0.65×10^2

   D. 0.65×10^3

8. Which has a value that is closest to one million? *(p. 80, prob. 14)*

   A. 2×10^5

   B. 2×10^6

   C. 3×10^5

   D. 3×10^6

9. Which is equal to 175.01? *(p. 80, prob. 5–13)*

   A. 17.501×10^1

   B. 17.501×10^2

   C. 17.501×10^3

   D. 17.501×10^4

4.1.A.3 Understand and use ratios, proportions, and percents (including percents greater than 100 and less than 1) in a variety of situations.

10. You can bicycle at a constant speed of 20 miles per hour. How long will it take you to bike 35 miles at that speed? *(p. 41, prob. 7)*

   A. 35 minutes

   B. 70 minutes

   C. 105 minutes

   D. 350 minutes

11. The central angle measure of a sector in a circle graph is 108°. What percent of the circle graph does the sector represent? *(p. 452, prob. 61)*

   A. 252%

   B. 108%

   C. 30%

   D. 10.8%

12. The central angle measure of a sector in a circle graph is 126°. What percent of the circle graph does the sector represent? *(p. 452, prob. 61)*

   A. 12.6%

   B. 33.3%

   C. 35%

   D. 36%

Go On ➡

4.1.A.4 Compare and order numbers of all named types.

13. Which set of integers is in order from least to greatest? *(p. 271, prob. 16–21)*

    A. $-1, 4, 6, -8$

    B. $-2, -4, -6, -8$

    C. $-8, -6, -4, -2$

    D. $2, 3, 4, -5$

14. Which statement is false?
    (p. 191, prob. 9–14)

    A. $\dfrac{5}{7} > \dfrac{5}{8}$

    B. $\dfrac{5}{7} > \dfrac{4}{7}$

    C. $\dfrac{5}{7} > \dfrac{9}{14}$

    D. $\dfrac{5}{7} > \dfrac{4}{5}$

15. Which set of numbers is in order from least to greatest? *(p. 271, prob. 16–21)*

    A. $-7, -5, 0, 4, 8$

    B. $5, 7, 0, 4, 8$

    C. $0, 7, 5, 4, 8$

    D. $0, -4, 5, -7, 8$

4.1.A.5 Use whole numbers, fractions, decimals, and percents to represent equivalent forms of the same number.

16. Write the fraction as a decimal.
    (p. 201, prob. 3–12)

    $$\frac{11}{20}$$

    A. 0.21

    B. 0.55

    C. 1.81818

    D. 11.00

17. Which decimal is equal to $\dfrac{4}{11}$?
    (p. 201, prob. 3–12)

    A. 0.3

    B. 0.36

    C. $0.\overline{36}$

    D. $0.\overline{37}$

18. Which fraction or mixed number is equivalent to 37%? *(p. 451, prob. 2–11)*

    A. $\dfrac{3}{7}$

    B. $\dfrac{37}{100}$

    C. $3\dfrac{1}{7}$

    D. $3\dfrac{7}{10}$

Go On ➡

Standard 4.1 | Number and Numerical Operations

4.1.A.6 Understand that all fractions can be represented as repeating or terminating decimals.

19. Which decimal and fraction are *not* equal? *(p. 202, prob. 19–26)*

A. $0.15, \frac{1}{6}$

B. $0.6, \frac{6}{10}$

C. $0.5, \frac{6}{12}$

D. $2.0, \frac{6}{3}$

20. Which decimal and fraction are equal? *(p. 202, prob. 19–26)*

A. $0.8\overline{3}, \frac{5}{6}$

B. $0.67, \frac{2}{3}$

C. $0.\overline{4}, \frac{2}{5}$

D. $0.87, \frac{7}{8}$

21. Which decimal is equivalent to $\frac{3}{8}$? *(p. 202, prob. 19–26)*

A. 0.375

B. 0.38

C. 0.625

D. 0.75

4.1.B.1 Use and explain procedures for performing calculations with integers and all number types named above with: a. Pencil-and-paper; b. Mental math; c. Calculator

22. Which expression has the same value as 3×102? *(p. 68, prob. 5–20)*

A. $30 + 6$

B. $30 + 32$

C. $300 + 2$

D. $300 + 6$

23. What is the cost of 4 cans of tennis balls at $2.89 each? *(p. 69, prob. 26–33)*

A. $9.33

B. $11.26

C. $11.56

D. $12.46

24. Find the sum $48.8 + 304.05$. What is the tens digit of the sum? *(p. 62, prob. 3–14)*

A. 0

B. 4

C. 5

D. 9

Go On

COUNTDOWN *to* NJ ASK

4.1.B.1 Use and explain procedures for performing calculations with integers and all number types named above with: a. Pencil-and-paper; b. Mental math; c. Calculator

4.1.B.2 Use exponentiation to find whole number powers of numbers.

25. Which pair of expressions shows the best way to begin finding the sum $\frac{1}{4} + \frac{3}{10}$? *(p. 229, prob. 1–8)*

   A. $\frac{5}{5} \times \frac{1}{4}$ and $\frac{5}{5} \times \frac{3}{10}$

   B. $\frac{5}{5} \times \frac{1}{4}$ and $\frac{2}{2} \times \frac{3}{10}$

   C. $5 \times \frac{1}{4}$ and $2 \times \frac{3}{10}$

   D. $5 \times \frac{1}{4}$ and $5 \times \frac{3}{10}$

26. Which equation is true? *(p. 234, prob. 3–18)*

   A. $\frac{2}{5} \times \frac{4}{5} = \frac{2 \times 4}{5}$

   B. $\frac{2}{5} \times \frac{4}{5} = \frac{2 \times 4}{10}$

   C. $\frac{2}{5} \times \frac{4}{5} = \frac{2 \times 5}{5 \times 4}$

   D. $\frac{2}{5} \times \frac{4}{5} = \frac{2 \times 4}{5 \times 5}$

27. Which equation is true? *(p. 239, prob. 5–24)*

   A. $\frac{8}{15} \div \frac{2}{3} = \frac{8}{15} \times \frac{3}{2}$

   B. $\frac{8}{15} \div \frac{2}{3} = \frac{8}{15} \times \frac{2}{3}$

   C. $\frac{8}{15} \div \frac{2}{3} = \frac{15}{8} \times \frac{3}{2}$

   D. $\frac{8}{15} \div \frac{2}{3} = \frac{15}{8} \times \frac{2}{3}$

28. Which expression is *not* equivalent to the expression 6^2? *(p. 15, prob. 6–13)*

   A. 6×6

   B. 36

   C. 6 squared

   D. 12

29. What is the value of m^5 when $m = 2$? *(p. 15, prob. 6–13)*

   A. 10

   B. 16

   C. 32

   D. 64

30. What is the value of 8^4? *(p. 15, prob. 6–13)*

   A. 12

   B. 32

   C. 4096

   D. 65,536

Go On ➡

Standard 4.1 | Number and Numerical Operations

4.1.B.3 Understand and apply the standard algebraic order of operations, including appropriate use of parentheses.

31. Evaluate the expression. *(p. 19, prob. 3–14)*

$$6(5 + 2) + 7$$

- **A.** 39
- **B.** 49
- **C.** 84
- **D.** 294

32. Which could be the first step in evaluating $4 + 5^2(8 + 5) + 9 \div 3$? *(p. 19, prob. 3–14)*

- **A.** Multiply 5 by 2.
- **B.** Add 4 and 50.
- **C.** Add 4 and 5^2.
- **D.** Add 8 and 5.

33. Which statement is correct? *(p. 20, prob. 16)*

- **A.** $4 + 4 \cdot 7 - 2^3 = 6^2 + 4 \cdot 2^2$
- **B.** $6^2 - 5 \cdot 4 - 5 \cdot 2 = 2^2 + 2$
- **C.** $7 + 5 \cdot 2 = 7 \cdot 2 + 5$
- **D.** $2^3 + 3^2 = 5 + 3 \cdot 2^2 - 2$

4.1.C.1 Use equivalent representations of numbers such as fractions, decimals, and percents to facilitate estimation.

34. Which results in the greatest savings? *(p. 463, prob. 51–56)*

- **A.** a $59.95 item with a 10% discount
- **B.** a $44.95 item with a $\frac{1}{5}$ discount
- **C.** a $50.00 item with a $\frac{1}{10}$ discount
- **D.** a $40.00 item with a 20% discount

35. Which expression has the least value? *(p. 463, prob. 51–56)*

- **A.** $\frac{1}{3}$ of 120
- **B.** 33% of 90
- **C.** 0.3×105
- **D.** 0.4×48

36. Matt has 2.25 pounds of mixed nuts. He wants to share them equally with 3 friends. About how much should each person get, including Matt? Choose the best estimate. *(p. 74, prob. 43-46)*

- **A.** $\frac{1}{2}$ pound
- **B.** $\frac{3}{4}$ pound
- **C.** 1 pound
- **D.** $1\frac{1}{2}$ pounds

Go On

4.2.A.1 Understand and apply properties of polygons: a. Quadrilaterals, including squares, rectangles, parallelograms, trapezoids, rhombi; b. Regular polygons

37. Which is not a parallelogram?
(p. 529, prob. 5–7)

   A. square

   B. rectangle

   C. trapezoid

   D. rhombus

38. Which polygon always has congruent diagonals? *(p. 529, prob. 5–7)*

   A. parallelogram

   B. rectangle

   C. rhombus

   D. trapezoid

39. A regular polygon has 5 sides. Each side is 4 cm long. Which statement is true? *(p. 532, prob. 17)*

   A. Each angle has a measure of 90°.

   B. Each angle has a measure of 20°.

   C. The perimeter is 9 cm.

   D. The perimeter is 20 cm.

4.2.A.2 Understand and apply the concept of similarity: a. Using proportions to find missing measures; b. Scale drawings; c. Models of 3D objects

40. The scale on a map is 1 cm : 15 km. Find the actual distance in kilometers for a distance on the map that is 4.5 cm. *(p. 432, prob. 3–10)*

   A. 0.3 km   **C.** 18.5 km

   B. 3 km   **D.** 67.5 km

41. A scale model of an airplane is made using the scale 1 : 120. The length of a wing on the model is 16 centimeters. Which is the approximate length of the wing on the actual airplane?
(p. 432, prob. 3–10)

   A. 19 centimeters

   B. 192 centimeters

   C. 19 meters

   D. 192 meters

42. Given that $\triangle ABC : \triangle DEF$, what is the unknown length? *(p. 544, prob. 3–6)*

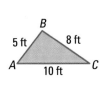 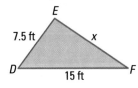

   A. 12 ft   **C.** 13 ft

   B. 12.5 ft   **D.** 16 ft

Go On

Standard 4.2 | Geometry and Measurement

4.2.A.3 Use logic and reasoning to make and support conjectures about geometric objects.

43. Which is a net of a rectangular prism?

(p. 644, prob. 3–6)

A.

B.

C.

D.

44. Which is the net of a cone?

(p. 653, prob. 29)

A.

B.

C.

D.

45. Which is the net of a cylinder?

(p. 651, prob. 6)

A.

B.

C.

D.

46. A rectangular prism has dimensions 3 inches, 5 inches, and 6 inches. Which statement below is true?

(p. 655, prob. 1–3)

A. At least one edge of the prism is 14 inches long.

B. The area of at least one face of the prism is greater than 25 square inches.

C. The volume of the prism is less than 18 cubic inches.

D. The volume of the prism is greater than 100 cubic inches.

Go On

4.2.B.1 Understand and apply transformations: a. Finding the image, given the pre-image, and vice-versa; b. Sequence of transformations needed to map one figure onto another; c. Reflections, rotations, and translations result in images congruent to the pre-image; d. Dilations (stretching/shrinking) result in images similar to the pre-image

47. In the diagram below, figure 1 is rotated to get figure 2. Which description of the rotation is most accurate?

(p. 550, prob. 4–6)

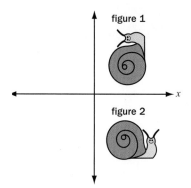

A. 90° clockwise

B. 180° counterclockwise

C. 270° clockwise

D. None of these

48. Identify the transformation. If it is a reflection, identify the line of reflection. If it is a rotation, give the angle and direction of rotation.

(p. 551, prob. 4–6)

A. Rotation, 90° clockwise

B. Translation

C. Reflection, x-axis

D. Rotation, 180° counterclockwise

49. What single transformation is shown?

(p. 551, prob. 3–6)

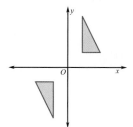

A. Translation

B. Reflection in x-axis

C. Rotation

D. Reflection in y-axis

50. What single transformation is shown?

(p. 551, prob. 3–6)

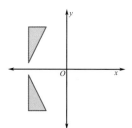

A. Translation

B. Reflection in x-axis

C. Rotation

D. Reflection in y-axis

Go On

Standard 4.2 | Geometry and Measurement

4.2.C.1 Use coordinates in four quadrants to represent geometric concepts.

51. Three vertices of a rectangle are (1,1), (6,1), and (6,3). What is the fourth vertex? *(p. 315, prob. 3–10)*

   A. (1, 3)

   B. (1, 6)

   C. (3, 3)

   D. (6, 6)

52. Two vertices of a right triangle are (1,4) and (5,4). Which could be the third vertex? *(p. 316, prob. 11–22)*

   A. (3, 4)

   B. (−1, 4)

   C. (1, −1)

   D. (−5, −4)

53. A polygon has vertices (−1,−1), (2, 2), (7, 2), and (4, −1). Which type of polygon is it? *(p. 316, prob. 11–22)*

   A. square

   B. trapezoid

   C. parallelogram

   D. pentagon

54. A circle passes through (0,−3), (3,0), and (0,−3). Which point below does the circle also pass through? *(p. 316, prob. 11-22)*

   A. (0, 3)

   B. (0, 0)

   C. (−3, −3)

   D. (3, −6)

55. A polygon has vertices (3, 3), (3, −3), (−2, −3), and (−2, 2). Which type of polygon is it? *(p. 314, prob. 11–22)*

   A. square

   B. trapezoid

   C. parallelogram

   D. rhombus

COUNTDOWN *to* NJ ASK

Go On

4.2.C.2 Use a coordinate grid to model and quantify transformations (e.g., translate right 4 units).

56. The line that contains the points $(-3, 1)$ and $(-5, -5)$ is reflected in the y-axis. What is the slope of the image line? *(p. 412, prob. 12, 13)*

   A. negative

   B. positive

   C. zero

   D. undefined

57. The point $(3, 5)$ is transformed to get the image point $(0, 5)$. Which of the following describes the transformation? *(p. 560, prob. 23)*

   A. reflection in the y-axis

   B. reflection in the x-axis

   C. translation 3 units left

   D. translation 5 units down

58. The point $(2, -6)$ is transformed to get the image point $(2, 6)$. Which of the following describes the transformation? *(p. 559, prob. 9-12)*

   A. reflection in the y-axis

   B. reflection in the x-axis

   C. translation 6 units up

   D. translation 6 units down

4.2.D.1 Solve problems requiring calculations that involve different units of measurement within a measurement system (e.g., 4′3″ plus 7′10″ equals 12′1″).

59. Sadie runs 8.6 miles in 1 hour 30 minutes. To the nearest tenth, what is Sadie's average speed in miles per hour? *(p. 407, prob. 33)*

   A. 4.3 miles per hour

   B. 5.7 miles per hour

   C. 6.5 miles per hour

   D. 12.9 miles per hour

60. A bird flies 65 miles in 150 minutes. What is its average speed in miles per hour? *(p. 407, prob. 33)*

   A. 32.5 miles per hour

   B. 26.5 miles per hour

   C. 26 miles per hour

   D. 22.5 miles per hour

61. Mason cut 42 centimeters off a board that was 2 meters long. How long was the remaining board? *(p. 95, prob. 55)*

   A. 40 centimeters

   B. 44 centimeters

   C. 1 meter 58 centimeters

   D. 2 meters 42 centimeters

Go On

Standard 4.2 | Geometry and Measurement

4.2.D.2 Select and use appropriate units and tools to measure quantities to the degree of precision needed in a particular problem-solving situation.

62. Use a ruler. What is the length of line segment *AB*, to the nearest eighth inch? *(p. 87, prob. 3–8)*

A •————————————————• B

- **A.** $2\frac{1}{8}$ inches
- **B.** $2\frac{1}{4}$ inches
- **C.** $2\frac{3}{8}$ inches
- **D.** $2\frac{1}{2}$ inches

63. Use a ruler. What is the length of line segment *CD*, to the nearest centimeter? *(p. 87, prob. 3–8)*

C •————————————————• D

- **A.** 2 cm
- **B.** 4 cm
- **C.** 5 cm
- **D.** 6 cm

64. Use a ruler. What is the value of *x*, to the nearest sixteenth inch? *(p. 87, prob. 3–8)*

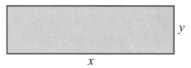

- **A.** $1\frac{5}{8}$ inches
- **B.** $1\frac{11}{16}$ inches
- **C.** $1\frac{3}{4}$ inches
- **D.** $1\frac{13}{16}$ inches

65. Which units are most appropriate for measuring the speed of a car on a highway? *(p. 89, prob. 45)*

- **A.** kilometers per hour
- **B.** miles per minute
- **C.** feet per second
- **D.** meters per hour

66. Christopher wants to determine how much water will fit in a baby's bottle. Which would be the most appropriate measuring tool? *(p. 89, prob. 48)*

- **A.** measuring cup
- **C.** scale
- **B.** ruler
- **D.** teaspoon

Go On

COUNTDOWN *to* NJ ASK

4.2.D.3 Recognize that all measurements of continuous quantities are approximations.

4.2.E.1 Develop and apply strategies for finding perimeter and area: a. Geometric figures made by combining triangles, rectangles and circles or parts of circles; b. Estimation of area using grids of various sizes

67. Which of the following is the most reasonable approximation for the mass of a pencil? *(p. 88, prob. 41-44)*

   A. 40 grams

   B. 400 grams

   C. 40 kilograms

   D. 400 kilograms

68. If Nate is measuring a length with a ruler divided into centimeters and millimeters, which is the most accurate measurement Nate could make?

(p. 89, prob. 50)

   A. 20 centimeters

   B. 19 centimeters

   C. 19.2 centimeters

   D. 19.27 centimeters

69. Four students measured the length of a stick. Each measured correctly. The results were: Ed (to the nearest yard) 1 yard; Milton (to the nearest foot) 2 feet; Abby (to the nearest inch) 26 inches; Carla (to the nearest half inch) $26\frac{1}{2}$ inches. Whose approximation will be most accurate? *(p. 89, prob. 50)*

   A. Ed   **C.** Abby

   B. Milton   **D.** Carla

70. What is the area of the composite figure formed by a semicircle and a trapezoid? Use 3.14 for π and round your answer to the nearest tenth.

(p. 651, prob. 3–5)

   A. 32.3 square centimeters

   B. 38.6 square centimeters

   C. 44.9 square centimeters

   D. 56.3 square centimeters

71. Which is the approximate surface area of the cylinder whose net is shown?

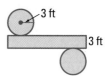

(p. 651, prob. 3–5)

   A. 28 ft^2 **C.** 56 ft^2

   B. 57 ft^2 **D.** 113 ft^2

72. What is the area of the figure shown below? *(p. 604, prob. 5–8)*

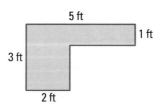

   A. 9 square feet   **C.** 11 square feet

   B. 10 square feet   **D.** 12 square feet

                              Go On ➡

Standard 4.2 | Geometry and Measurement

4.2.E.2 Recognize that the volume of a pyramid or cone is one-third of the volume of the prism or cylinder with the same base and height (e.g., use rice to compare volumes of figures with the same base and height).

73. JoEllen is using a cone to fill a cylinder with water. The cone and cylinder have the same base and height. How many full cones of water will it take JoEllen to fill the cylinder? *(p. 664, prob. 18)*

A. 1   **C.** 3

B. 2   **D.** 4

74. What is the relationship between the volumes of the two figures shown?
(p. 661, prob. 1-4)

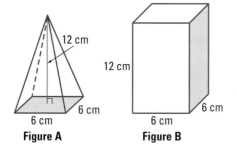

Figure A   Figure B

A. volume of (8✕) Figure A = $\frac{1}{4}$ volume of (8✕) Figure B

B. volume of (8✕) Figure A = $\frac{1}{3}$ volume of (8✕) Figure B

C. volume of (8✕) Figure A = $\frac{1}{2}$ volume of (8✕) Figure B

D. volume of (8✕) Figure A = volume of (8✕) Figure B

75. The volume of the cylinder below is 36π cubic units. What is the volume of a cone with the same base and height?
(p. 664, prob. 18)

A. 9π cubic units

B. 12π cubic units

C. 18π cubic units

D. 36π cubic units

Go On

COUNTDOWN *to* NJ ASK

4.3.A.1 Recognize, describe, extend, and create patterns involving whole numbers, rational numbers, and integers: a. Descriptions using tables, verbal and symbolic rules, graphs, simple equations or expressions; b. Finite and infinite sequences; c. Generating sequences by using calculators to repeatedly apply a formula

4.3.B.1 Graph functions, and understand and describe their general behavior: a. Equations involving two variables

76. Find the first five numbers of the described pattern. *(p. 5, prob. 5–16)*

Start with 4 and add 6 repeatedly.

A. 4, 16, 22, 28, 34

B. 4, 24, 48, 72, 96

C. 4, 10, 16, 22, 28

D. 6, 10, 14, 18, 22

77. Describe the pattern. *(p. 5, prob. 1–4)*

62,208; 10,368; 1,728; 288;…

A. Subtract 1,440 from the previous number.

B. Divide the previous number by 6.

C. Multiply the previous number by 6.

D. None of these

78. Write the next three numbers in the pattern. *(p. 5, prob. 1–4)*

121, 110, 99, 88, …

A. 88, 77, 66

B. 44, 22, 11

C. 66, 55, 44

D. 77, 66, 55

79. You are filling your bathtub with water. The graph on the right shows how many gallons are in the tub as a function of time. Which table represents the function in the graph? *(p. 381, prob. 45)*

Filling a Bathtub

A.

Input	0	1	2	3
Output	0	4	8	12

B.

Input	0	4	8	12
Output	0	1	2	3

C.

Input	0	1	2	3
Output	0	3	6	9

D.

Input	0	3	6	8
Output	0	1	2	3

80. The graph of which function is shown? *(p. 378, prob. 16)*

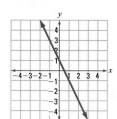

A. $y = x + 2$

B. $y = -\frac{1}{2}x + 1$

C. $y = \frac{1}{2}x + 1$

D. $y = -2x + 1$

Go On

Standard 4.3 | Patterns and Algebra

4.3.C.1 Analyze functional relationships to explain how a change in one quantity can result in a change in another, using pictures, graphs, charts, and equations.

81. Adam works at a bookstore. The graph shows his hourly wage for each year he has worked.

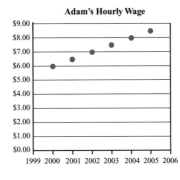

Adam's Hourly Wage

According to the graph, how much of an hourly pay increase has Adam received each year? *(p. 413, prob. 32, 37)*

A. $0.25   **C.** $1.00

B. $0.50   **D.** $1.50

82. You start with no money. Then you save $11 per week to buy a DVD player that costs $129. Which expression shows how many dollars you still need to save after *w* weeks? *(p. 379, prob. 29–36)*

A. $d = 129 - (11 + w)$

B. $d = 11w - 129$

C. $d = (129 - 11)w$

D. $d = 129 - 11\,w$

83. Which function gives the data in the table below? *(p. 374, prob. 16–23)*

Input x	1	2	3	4
Output y	1	3	5	7

A. $y = x + 1$ **C.** $y = 2x - 1$

B. $y = 2x + 1$ **D.** $y = 3x - 2$

4.3.C.2 Use patterns, relations, symbolic algebra, and linear functions to model situations: a. Using manipulatives, tables, graphs, verbal rules, algebraic expressions/ equations/ inequalities; b. Growth situations, such as population growth and compound interest using recursive formulas

84. Tennis balls are packaged in cans. The table below shows a relationship between the number of cans and the number of tennis balls of a certain brand.

Number of cans *x*	0	1	2	3
Number of tennis balls *y*	0	3	6	9

Which of the following is true about this situation? *(p. 374, prob. 16–23)*

A. $y = 3 + x$, and there are 18 tennis balls in 6 cans.

B. $y = 3x$, and there are 18 tennis balls in 6 cans.

C. $y = 3 + x$, and there are 21 tennis balls in 6 cans.

D. $y = 3x$, and there are 21 tennis balls in 6 cans.

85. Bill hikes 6 kilometers before lunch. After lunch he continues his hike, traveling at a speed of 4 kilometers per hour. If *x* represents the number of hours Bill hikes after lunch, which equation can be used to find *y*, the total number of kilometers Bill hikes for the day? *(p. 374–375, prob. 28–35)*

A. $y = 10 - x$ **C.** $y = 4 + 6x$

B. $y = 10 + x$ **D.** $y = 6 + 4x$

86. Carrie has read 15 pages of a 20-page chapter. Which equation can be solved to find the number of remaining pages in the chapter? *(p. 374–375, prob. 28–35)*

A. $x - 5 = 20$ **C.** $5 + x = 20$

B. $x - 15 = 20$ **D.** $15 + x = 20$

Go On

4.3.D.1 Use graphing techniques on a number line: a. Absolute value; b. Arithmetic operations represented by vectors (arrows) (e.g., "−3 + 6" is "left 3, right 6")

87. Use a number line to find the sum. *(p. 280, prob. 2–4)*

$$-7 + 3 + (-8)$$

- **A.** −12
- **B.** –2
- **C.** 12
- **D.** 18

88. Which expression has a value equal to (-5)? *(p. 280, prob. 13–24)*

- **A.** $-2 - 3$
- **B.** $-2 + 7$
- **C.** $-2 + 3$
- **D.** $-2 - 7$

89. Use a number line to find the difference. *(p. 287, prob. 6–17)*

$$19 - 22$$

- **A.** −41
- **B.** −3
- **C.** 3
- **D.** 41

90. Alex drew arrow A and then arrow B on the number line to represent an expression. Which expression did Alex represent? *(p. 287, prob. 2–17)*

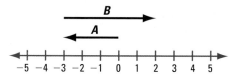

- **A.** $-3 + 5$
- **B.** $-3 + 2$
- **C.** $3 - 5$
- **D.** $3 - 2$

Go On ➡

Standard 4.3 | Patterns and Algebra

4.3.D.4 Understand and apply the properties of operations, numbers, equations, and inequalities: a. Additive inverse; b. Multiplicative inverse

91. What is the multiplicative inverse of $3\frac{1}{2}$? *(p. 304, prob. 3–6)*

    A. $-3\frac{1}{2}$

    B. $\frac{2}{7}$

    C. $\frac{5}{2}$

    D. $\frac{7}{2}$

92. What is the product of 6 and its multiplicative inverse? *(p. 304, prob. 1–6)*

    A. -6

    B. 0

    C. $\frac{1}{6}$

    D. 1

93. Which number line represents the solution set of the inequality $3x - 4 \geq 5$? *(p. 368, prob. 25–28)*

A.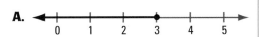

B.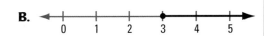

C.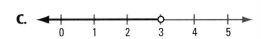

D.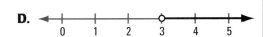

Go On

COUNTDOWN *to* NJ ASK

4.4.A.1 Select and use appropriate representations for sets of data, and measures of central tendency (mean, median, and mode): a. Type of display most appropriate for given data; b. Box-and-whisker plot, upper quartile, lower quartile; c. Scatter plot; d. Calculators and computer used to record and process information

94. The table shows data about the number of years of service of 32 police detectives who retired.

Years of Service	Detectives Retired
11–15	7
16–20	3
21–25	7
26–30	1
31–35	4

Which data display would be the most appropriate for the set of data?
(p. 146, prob. 3–9)

A. a line graph

B. a stem-and-leaf plot

C. a box-and-whiskers plot

D. a histogram

95. The stem-and-leaf plot below shows the number of calendars each of 11 students sold to raise money for the school band. How many students sold more than 12 calendars?
(p. 129, prob. 12–15)

Number of Calendars Sold

```
0 | 4  5  7  9
1 | 3  4  6  8  9
2 | 1  8
```
Key: 1 | 0 = 10

A. 5   **C.** 7

B. 6   **D.** 8

4.4.A.2 Make inferences and formulate and evaluate arguments based on displays and analysis of data.

96. Students at Montrose Middle School responded to a survey about how many minutes they spend on household chores each day. The histogram below shows the results of the survey. How many students reported spending more than 40 minutes each day on chores?
(p. 142, prob. 11)

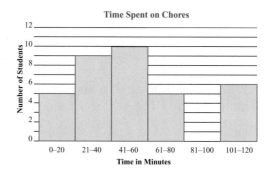

Time Spent on Chores

A. 2   **C.** 21

B. 3   **D.** 30

97. The stem-and-leaf plot shows the math quiz scores of 20 students.

```
 6 | 4  6
 7 | 0  0  2  8
 8 | 2  4  6  6  6  6
 9 | 0  2  2  2  4  8
10 | 0  0
```
Key: 9 | 2 = 92

How many students scored higher than the median? (p. 128, prob. 8)

A. 2   **C.** 10

B. 8   **D.** 11

Go On ➡

Standard 4.4 | Data Analysis, Probability, and Discrete Mathematics

4.4.B.1 Interpret probabilities as ratios, percents, and decimals.

98. A bag contains 12 marbles: 3 red, 4 black, and 5 white. You randomly choose a marble from the bag. Which is the probability that you will choose a red marble? *(p. 685, prob. 7–10)*

A. $\frac{1}{4}$ **C.** $\frac{1}{2}$

B. $\frac{1}{3}$ **D.** $\frac{3}{4}$

99. A bag contains 10 index cards. The cards are labeled with these numbers:

2 2 5 5 5 5 9 9 9 9

You randomly choose a card from the bag. Which is the probability that you will choose an odd number? *(p. 685, prob. 7–10)*

A. 33%   **C.** 80%

B. 67%   **D.** 90%

100. Lisa rolls a number cube labeled 1 through 6. Which is the probability that Lisa will roll an odd number? *(p. 685, prob. 7–10)*

A. 0.17   **C.** 0.50

B. 0.33   **D.** 0.83

4.4.B.3 Estimate probabilities and make predictions based on experimental and theoretical probabilities.

101. Carlita spun a color spinner 40 times. Her results were: 10 red, 8 blue, and 22 yellow. She plans to spin the spinner 10 more times. Based on her results so far, what is the most likely number of times she will spin blue in the next 10 spins? *(p. 693, prob. 8–10)*

A. 2 times   **C.** 6 times

B. 4 times   **D.** 8 times

102. A bag has 24 tiles. Each tile is labeled with a different number from 1 to 24. Jose chooses 8 tiles at random. He gets these numbers:

15 4 8 24 22 9 1 20

When Jose chooses the next tile at random from the remaining 16 tiles, which of the following intervals is that number *least likely* to be in? *(p. 693, prob. 15–18)*

A. 1 to 6   **C.** 13 to 18

B. 7 to 12   **D.** 19 to 24

103. Mark recorded the lunch choices of 100 students chosen at random. The choices are shown in the table below.

Cold Cut	Cheeseburger	Soup	Taco
20	20	25	35

Based on these results, what is the most likely number of students that will choose soup, out of the next 20 students? *(p. 693, prob. 19)*

A. 4   **C.** 6

B. 5   **D.** 8

Go On

4.4.C.1 Apply the multiplication principle of counting: a. Permutations-ordered situations with replacement vs. ordered situations without replacement

104. Prestige Builders has a development of new homes. There are five different floor plans, four exterior colors, and an option of either a two-car or a three-car garage. How many choices are there for one home? *(p. 705, prob. 7–10)*

 A. 20

 B. 34

 C. 40

 D. 60

105. A snack stand offers 6 choices of sandwiches and 3 choices of beverages. How many combinations of 1 sandwich and 1 beverage are possible?
(p. 705, prob. 13–16)

 A. 2

 B. 6

 C. 9

 D. 18

4.4.C.3 Apply techniques of systematic listing, counting, and reasoning in a variety of different contexts.

106. Beth, Joel, and Ingrid are lining up for auditions for the school play. How many different ways can they line up? *(p. 705, prob. 13–16)*

 A. 3 ways

 B. 6 ways

 C. 12 ways

 D. 24 ways

107. Ed is placing 4 books in a row on a shelf. How many ways can he arrange the 4 books? *(p. 705, prob. 13–16)*

 A. 4 ways

 B. 10 ways

 C. 16 ways

 D. 24 ways

108. Some of the different ways to arrange the letters X, Y, and Z in a row are shown below.

 XYZ   XZY   YXZ

How many more ways are there to arrange the letters? *(p. 705, prob. 13–16)*

 A. 1 more way

 B. 3 more ways

 C. 5 more ways

 D. 6 more ways

Go On

Standard 4.4 | Data Analysis, Probability, and Discrete Mathematics

Standard 4.1 | Number and Numerical Operations

**4.4.D.1 Use vertex-edge graphs to represent and find solutions to practical problems:
a. Finding the shortest network connecting specified sites; b. Finding the shortest route on a map from one site to another; c. Finding the shortest circuit on a map that makes a tour of specified sites**

109. On the grid below, the side of each small square is 1 unit long. Ray wants to start at point *A* and travel to point *B*. He wants to pass through the 3 other points shown on the grid. He can travel only on the grid lines. How long is the shortest possible path Ray can use? *(p. 316, prob. 24)*

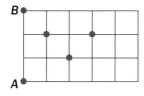

A. 6 units

B. 7 units

C. 8 units

D. 9 units

4.1.A.3 Understand and use ratios, proportions, and percents (including percents greater than 100 and less than 1) in a variety of situations.

110. (OE) The annual rainfall in one year was 40 inches, and in the next year it was 32 inches. What was the percent of decrease in rainfall? *(p. 452, prob. 56)*

111. (OE) What is the value of *n* in the proportion $\frac{7}{8} = \frac{n}{20}$? *(p. 425, prob. 2–17)*

112. (OE) There are 130 calories in a 40-gram serving of dried cranberries. How many calories are in a 100-gram serving of dried cranberries? *(p. 425, prob. 2–17)*

Go On ➡

4.1.A.4 Compare and order numbers of all named types.

113. (OE) Which point has a value between −2 and 1? *(p. 271, prob. 7–14)*

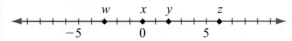

114. (OE) Order the integers 1, −6, 5, −14, 16 from least to greatest. *(p. 271, prob. 16–21)*

115. (OE) Below is a list of the finishing times of four cars in a race. Order the times from the least to greatest. Which car won the race? *(p. 58, prob. 16-21)*

Car	Time (in Minutes)
Red	25.42
Blue	25.5
Yellow	24.95
Green	25.327

4.1.A.5 Use whole numbers, fractions, decimals, and percents to represent equivalent forms of the same number.

116. (OE) Write the fraction $\frac{5}{8}$ as a decimal. *(p. 202, prob. 13)*

117. (OE) What decimal is equivalent to 0.4%? *(p. 462, prob. 3–14)*

Go On ➡

Standard 4.2 | Geometry and Measurement

4.2.A.2 Understand and apply the concept of similarity: a. Using proportions to find missing measures; b. Scale drawings; c. Models of 3D objects

118. (OE) A scale model of a house is made using the scale 1 : 16. The height of the front door in the model is 12.75 centimeters. What is the height of the actual front door of the house?

(p. 432, prob. 3–10)

119. (OE) The rectangles shown below are similar.

What is the value of *x*? *(p. 540, prob. 11–14)*

120. (OE) Griselda measures the distance on a map from town A to town B to be 9 centimeters. The scale on this map indicates that 1.5 centimeters represents 10 kilometers. *(p. 426, prob. 18–20)*

Part A Write and solve a proportion to find the actual number of kilometers from town A to town B.

Part B Griselda's car gets 8 kilometers per liter of gasoline. Write and solve a proportion to find the number of liters of gasoline needed to travel from town A to town B.

4.2.A.3 Use logic and reasoning to make and support conjectures about geometric objects.

121. (OE) The large box below is filled with sand. If all the sand is used to fill boxes that are identical to the small box, how many small boxes can be filled? Show your work and support your answer.

(p. 655, prob. 1–3)

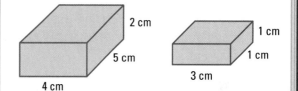

Go On

4.2.B.1 **Understand and apply transformations: a. Finding the image, given the pre-image, and vice-versa; b. Sequence of transformations needed to map one figure onto another; c. Reflections, rotations, and translations result in images congruent to pre-image; d. Dilations (stretching/shrinking) result in images similar to pre-image**

122. (OE) Graph $\triangle JKL$ with vertices $J(0, 1)$, $K(3, 1)$, and $L(1, 4)$. Then find the coordinates of the vertices of the image after applying the transformation $(x, y) \rightarrow (x + 4, y + 3)$ and graph the image on the same coordinate plane.

(p. 559, prob. 6–10)

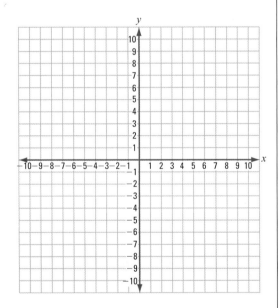

4.2.C.1 **Use coordinates in four quadrants to represent geometric concepts.**

123. (OE) The following points are the vertices of a section of a quilt stencil:

$A(3, 2)$, $B(2, 2)$, $C(2, 1)$, and $D(3, 1)$.

Part A Plot the points and draw figure *ABCD*.

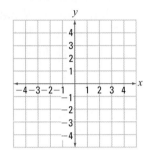

Part B Find the area of figure *ABCD*. Show your work.

Part C If each side of one grid square is 4 centimeters, what is the area of *ABCD* in square centimeters?

Show your work. **(p. 316, prob. 25–30)**

Go On ➡

Standard 4.2 | Geometry and Measurement

4.2.C.2 Use a coordinate grid to model and quantify transformations (e.g., translate right 4 units).

124. (OE) The point (2, 5) is reflected in the *y*-axis. What are the coordinates of the image? *(p. 560, prob. 24)*

125. (OE) The vertices of △*WRT* are $W(-1, -2)$, $R(1, 3)$, and $T(3, -3)$. Draw △*WRT* in a coordinate plane. Write a rule that will translate point *R* to the origin. What are the coordinates of the image of △*WRT* using this rule? *(p. 560, prob. 25)*

4.2.D.1 Solve problems requiring calculations that involve different units of measurement within a measurement system (e.g., 4′3″ plus 7′10″ equals 12′1″).

126. (OE) Find the difference. *(p. 253, prob. 17–29)*

   7 feet 6 inches
   − 3 feet 10 inches

127. (OE) A rectangle has length 3 feet 4 inches and width 2 feet 3 inches. What is the area of the rectangle in square inches? *(p. 93, prob. 36–38)*

4.2.E.1 Develop and apply strategies for finding perimeter and area: a. Geometric figures made by combining triangles, rectangles, and circles or parts of circles; b. Estimation of area using grids of various sizes

128. (OE) Find the area of the figure. *(p. 604, prob. 5–8)*

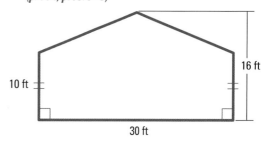

129. (OE) Find the area and the perimeter of the figure formed by the semicircle and triangle shown below. Use 3.14 for π. *(p. 615, prob. 25–27)*

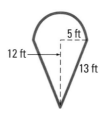

Go On

COUNTDOWN *to* NJ ASK

4.3.A.1 Recognize, describe, extend, and create patterns involving whole numbers, rational numbers, and integers: a. Descriptions using tables, verbal and symbolic rules, graphs, simple equations or expressions; b. Finite and infinite sequences; c. Generating sequences by using calculators to repeatedly apply a formula

130. (OE) Write a description of the pattern. *(p. 5, prob. 1-4)*

$$5, 20, 80, 320, \ldots$$

131. (OE) Ian planted crocuses in his garden. Crocuses have bulbs that divide and reproduce underground. The first year, Ian's garden produced 8 bulbs, the second year it produced 16 bulbs, and the third year it produced 32 bulbs. If this pattern were to continue, how many bulbs would the garden produce in the fourth year? *(p. 5, prob. 5–16)*

132. (OE) What three numbers would be next in the pattern below? Explain your thinking. *(p. 5, prob. 5–16)*

$$59, 55, 51, 47, 43, \ldots$$

4.3.C.2 Use patterns, relations, symbolic algebra, and linear functions to model situations: a. Using manipulatives, tables, graphs, verbal rules, algebraic expressions/ equations/ inequalities; b. Growth situations, such as population growth, and compound interest using recursive formulas

133. (OE) Admission prices at a theater are listed in the table below. Seven classes, each with 24 students, buy tickets as one large group. Write an expression that represents the total cost of all the tickets, in dollars. Find the value of the expression. *(p. 39, prob. 2–4))*

Tickets	Price for one ticket
1–35	$5.50
36–90	$5.10
Over 90	$4.90

4.3.D.2 Solve simple linear equations informally and graphically: a. Multi-step, integer coefficients only (although answers may not be integers); b. Using paper-and-pencil, calculators, graphing calculators, spreadsheets, and other technology

134. (OE) Solve the equation $2x - 3 = 7$. *(p. 357, prob. 37–42)*

135. (OE) Solve the equation $-2x + 1 = -5$. *(p. 357, prob. 37–42)*

136. (OE) What is the solution of the equation $2t + 6 = -12$? Show your work. *(p. 363, prob. 3–17)*

Go On

Standard 4.3 | Patterns and Algebra

4.3.D.3 Create, evaluate, and simplify algebraic expressions involving variables: a. Order of operations, including appropriate use of parentheses; b. Substitution of a number for a variable

137. (OE) Brandon owns 5 times as many state quarters as Lemont. Let x represent the number of state quarters Lemont owns. Write an expression that represents the number of state quarters Brandon owns. *(p. 340, prob. 45)*

138. (OE) Simplify $-3 - 4(a - 3)$. Show your work. *(p. 344, prob. 16–24)*

139. (OE) Evaluate the expression for the given values of the variables. *(p. 293, prob. 23–34)*

$7a + b$ when $a = -4$ and $b = 12$

Standard 4.4 | Data Analysis, Probability, and Discrete Mathematics

4.4.A.1 Select and use appropriate representations for sets of data, and measures of central tendency (mean, median, and mode): a. Type of display most appropriate for given data; b. Box-and-whisker plot, upper quartile, lower quartile; c. Scatter plot; d. Calculators and computer used to record and process information

140. (OE) Mike Piazza is a professional baseball player. The chart below shows the number of games he played each season for 11 seasons

Year	Number of Games Played
1992	21
1993	149
1994	107
1995	112
1996	148
1997	152
1998	151
1999	141
2000	136
2001	141
2002	135

Part A Find the mean, median, mode, and range for the data.

Part B Which of these measures best represents the data? Why?

(p. 112, prob. 27, 32, 34)

Go On ➡

4.4.B.2 Model situations involving probability with simulations (using spinners, dice, calculators and computers) and theoretical models: a. Frequency, relative frequency

4.4.B.4 Play and analyze probability-based games, and discuss the concepts of fairness and expected value.

141. (OE) Andy is on a 4-member committee. One member will be selected at random to be chairperson. Andy wants to use a simulation as a model to estimate the probability that he will be chosen as chairperson. Which of the following is the best simulation to use? Explain your reasoning. *(p. 681, investigation, prob. 1–2)*

a. Flip a coin 4 times. Let "heads" represent the event that Andy is chosen.

b. Use a spinner with 4 equal sections—red, blue, yellow, and black. Spin the spinner 10 times. Let "red" represent the event that Andy is chosen.

c. Roll a 1-to-6 number cube 10 times. Let "3" represent the event that Andy is chosen.

d. Write the numbers 1 through 10 on 10 index cards. Choose a card at random 4 times. Let "1" represent the event that Andy is chosen.

142. (OE) Kelly and Jim are playing a game with a pair of 1–6 number cubes. They take turns rolling the pair of number cubes. If Kelly rolls a sum of 6, she gets a point. If Jim rolls a sum of 12, he gets a point. The first player to have a total of 5 points wins the game. Is the game fair? Explain your answer. *(p. 681, investigation, prob. 1–2)*

Go On

Standard 4.4 | Data Analysis, Probability, and Discrete Mathematics

4.4.C.1 Apply the multiplication principle of counting: a. Permutations - ordered situations with replacement vs. ordered situations without replacement

143. (OE) Amy is on vacation. She packed 4 T-shirts, 2 hats, and 2 pairs of shoes. How many different outfits can she make, if each outfit has one T-shirt, one hat, and one pair of shoes?
(p. 705, prob. 7–10)

144. (OE) How many different ways are there to arrange the letters A, B, C, and D in a row? Explain your answer.
(p. 705, prob. 7–10, 13–16)

4.4.C.2 Explore counting problems involving Venn diagrams with three attributes (e.g., there are 15, 20, and 25 students respectively in the chess club, the debating team, and the engineering society; how many different students belong to the three clubs if there are 6 students in chess and debating, 8 students in debating and engineering, and 2 students in all 3?).

145. (OE) There are 18 students in the science club, 17 students in the math club, and 18 students in the drama club. There are 4 students who are in both the science club and math club, but not the drama club. There are 5 students who are in both the math club and drama club, but not the science club. There are 8 students who are in both the drama club and science club, but not the math club. There are 2 students who are in all three clubs. How many students are in exactly one of the three clubs? Draw a Venn diagram to show how you found your answer.
(p. 756, prob. 1–4)

1 Number Sense, Patterns, and Algebraic Thinking

Before

In previous courses you've . . .

- Completed number fact families
- Performed whole number operations

Now

New Jersey Standards

4.3.A.1.a	1.1	Extending patterns
4.3.D.3.b	1.2	Variable expressions
4.1.B.2	1.3	Powers and exponents
4.1.B.3	1.4	Order of operations
4.3.D.2.b	1.5	Solving equations
4.2.E.1	1.6	Perimeter and area
4.5.A.1	1.7	Problem solving

Why?

So you can solve real-world problems about . . .

- Hawaiian leis, p. 4
- ice hockey, p. 9
- video games, p. 19

Animated Math
at classzone.com

- Describing Patterns, p. 4
- Powers and Exponents, p. 14
- Perimeter and Area, p. 33

Get-Ready Games

Review Prerequisite Skills by playing *Going for Gold* and *Olympic Torch Run*.

Going for Gold

Skill Focus: Completing number fact families

- Each athlete above can only win gold medals whose sum, difference, product, or quotient is equal to the athlete's number.

- Find a way for each athlete to win two gold medals. Each medal can be won only one time.

Olympic Torch Run

START

4 — −3 — +5 —

+6   +5   +3

— +2 — ×4 —

÷2   ÷3   +8

— ×3 — +8 —

FINISH

Skill Focus: Using whole number operations

Carry the Olympic torch from START to FINISH. Begin at the circle marked START. Move along a path to an adjacent city. Perform the indicated operation on the number 4. Remember the result.

- Then move to a new city. Perform the indicated operation on your result from the previous move.

- You may carry the torch through each city only one time. You do not need to visit all the cities.

- Your goal is to get the greatest possible result at the FINISH.

Stop and Think

1. **WRITING** In *Going for Gold* is there more than one way that the athletes can each win two medals? Explain why or why not.

2. **CRITICAL THINKING** Suppose you want to visit all the cities in *Olympic Torch Run*. Describe two different paths from START to FINISH. Give the result for each path.

Review Prerequisite Skills

REVIEW WORDS
- **whole number,** *p. 735*
- **factor,** *p. 739*
- **sum,** *p. 742*
- **difference,** *p. 742*
- **product,** *p. 743*
- **quotient,** *p. 744*

VOCABULARY CHECK

Copy and complete using a review word from the list at the left.

1. In the multiplication sentence $3 \cdot 5 = 15$, 3 and 5 are called __?__ and 15 is called the __?__.

2. You subtract to find the __?__ of two numbers.

3. You divide to find the __?__ of two numbers.

4. You add to find the __?__ of two numbers.

SKILL CHECK

Copy and complete the statement. *(p. 738)*

5. $\underline{\;?\;} + 4 = 12$ **6.** $6 - \underline{\;?\;} = 3$ **7.** $7 \times \underline{\;?\;} = 35$ **8.** $\underline{\;?\;} \div 5 = 4$

Find the sum, difference, product, or quotient. *(pp. 742–744)*

9. $23 + 28$ **10.** $523 + 49$ **11.** $34 - 17$ **12.** $201 - 158$

13. 23×96 **14.** 392×105 **15.** $328 \div 8$ **16.** $190 \div 5$

@HomeTutor Prerequisite skills practice at classzone.com

Notetaking Skills   Keeping a Notebook

In each chapter you will learn a new notetaking skill. In Chapter 1 you will apply the strategy of keeping a notebook to Example 4 on p. 18 and Example 1 on p. 32.

Some useful items to put in your mathematics notebook are listed.

- vocabulary
- rules and properties
- worked-out examples
- symbols
- formulas
- assignments

When you write a rule in your notebook, also sketch any diagrams that help explain the rule. For example, a diagram can help you remember properties of rectangles and squares:

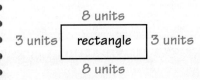

Opposite sides of a rectangle are equal in length.

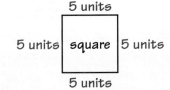

All four sides of a square are equal in length.

1.1 Describing Patterns

NJ 4.3.A.1.a Descriptions using tables, verbal and symbolic rules, graphs, simple equations or expressions

Before	You performed whole number operations.
Now	You'll describe patterns using whole number operations.
Why?	So you can schedule events, as in Example 1.

KEY VOCABULARY
- **add,** *p. 741*
- **subtract,** *p. 741*
- **multiply,** *p. 743*
- **divide,** *p. 744*

Scheduling Events You are a member of a summer movie club at your local movie theater. The club meets every Wednesday in July to watch a movie. The first meeting is on July 6. On what other dates in July will the club meet?

EXAMPLE 1 Recognizing and Extending a Pattern

To answer the question about the summer movie club above, start with July 6th and repeatedly add 7 days to the date.

Date of first meeting:	July 6	
		+ 7
Date of second meeting:	July 13	
		+ 7
Date of third meeting:	July 20	
		+ 7
Date of fourth meeting:	July 27	

▶ **Answer** The club will meet on July 13, July 20, and July 27.

Numerical Patterns To describe and extend a numerical pattern, find a relationship between the first and second numbers. Then see if the relationship is true for the second and third numbers, the third and fourth numbers, and so on.

EXAMPLE 2 Extending a Numerical Pattern

READING
The three dots at the end of a list of numbers mean that the numbers and the pattern continue without end.

Describe the pattern: 2, 7, 12, 17, ... Then write the next three numbers.

You add 5 to the previous number to get the next number in the pattern.

$$+5 \quad +5 \quad +5$$
$$2, \quad 7, \quad 12, \quad 17, \quad \textbf{22}, \quad \textbf{27}, \quad \textbf{32}, \ldots$$
$$+5 \quad +5 \quad +5$$

▶ **Answer** The pattern is *add 5*. The next three numbers are 22, 27, and 32.

EXAMPLE 3 Extending a Numerical Pattern

REVIEW
Need help with whole number operations? See pp. 742–744.

Describe the pattern: 2, 6, 18, 54, ... Then write the next three numbers.

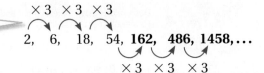

You multiply the previous number by 3 to get the next number in the pattern.

$$\times 3 \quad \times 3 \quad \times 3$$
$$2, \quad 6, \quad 18, \quad 54, \quad \textbf{162}, \quad \textbf{486}, \quad \textbf{1458}, . . .$$
$$\times 3 \quad \times 3 \quad \times 3$$

✓ **GUIDED PRACTICE** for Examples 1, 2, and 3

1. **Bus Schedule** A city bus drives by your house every 40 minutes during the afternoon. The first time you see the bus is at 2:20 P.M. At what other times will you see the bus before 5:00 P.M.?

Describe the pattern. Then write the next three numbers.

2. 28, 24, 20, 16, . . .   3. 256, 128, 64, 32, . . .

Visual Patterns To describe and extend a visual pattern, look for repeated colors and shapes, a change in the position of figures in the pattern, or a change in the number of figures in the pattern.

EXAMPLE 4 Extending a Visual Pattern

Hawaiian Leis A Hawaiian lei is a flower wreath given to symbolize friendship. What are the next three flowers in the pattern of the lei?

yellow carnation   red carnation

orchids

SOLUTION

Look for repeated flowers to find a pattern. The lei starts with a yellow carnation, two orchids, a red carnation, and then two orchids again. Notice that the carnations alternate between yellow and red.

▸ **Answer** The last flower is a red carnation, so the next three flowers are two orchids and then a yellow carnation.

Animated **Math**
at classzone.com

✓ **GUIDED PRACTICE** for Example 4

Describe the pattern. Then draw the next figure.

4.

5.

1.1 EXERCISES

★ = **STANDARDIZED TEST PRACTICE**
Exs. 18, 23, 34, 35, 36, 38, 41, and 59

○ = **HINTS AND HOMEWORK HELP**
for Exs. 13, 17, 19, 33 at classzone.com

SKILL PRACTICE

VOCABULARY **Match the pattern with its description.**

1. 0, 2, 4, 6, . . .

2. 30, 25, 20, 15, . . .

3. 1, 4, 16, 64, . . .

4. 10,000, 1000, 100, 10, . . .

A. Subtract 5 from the previous number.

B. Divide the previous number by 10.

C. Add 2 to the previous number.

D. Multiply the previous number by 4.

NUMBER PATTERNS **Describe the pattern. Then write the next three numbers.**

SEE EXAMPLES 1, 2, AND 3
on pp. 3 and 4
for Exs. 5–18

5. 1, 5, 25, 125, . . .

6. 100, 91, 82, 73, . . .

7. 640, 320, 160, 80, . . .

8. 2, 9, 16, 23, . . .

9. 0, 11, 22, 33, . . .

10. 4, 12, 36, 108, . . .

11. 80, 72, 64, 56, . . .

12. 729, 243, 81, 27, . . .

13. 1, 6, 36, 216, . . .

14. 1458, 486, 162, 54, . . .

15. 2, 3, 6, 11, 18, . . .

16. 1, 1, 2, 3, 5, 8, . . .

17. **ERROR ANALYSIS** A friend says that the next number in the pattern 1, 2, 4, 8, . . . is 13. Is your friend correct? *Explain.*

18. ★ **MULTIPLE CHOICE** Which operation describes the numerical pattern 1, 3, 9, 27, . . . ?

Ⓐ Add 3. **Ⓑ** Subtract 3. **Ⓒ** Multiply by 3. **Ⓓ** Divide by 3.

VISUAL PATTERNS **Describe the pattern. Then draw the next three figures.**

SEE EXAMPLE 4
on p. 4
for Exs. 19–22

19.

20.

21.

22.

23. ★ **MULTIPLE CHOICE** What is the next figure in the pattern?

Ⓐ **Ⓑ** **Ⓒ** **Ⓓ**

LETTER PATTERNS **Describe the pattern. Then write the next three letters.**

24. A, C, E, G, . . .

25. A, Z, B, Y, . . .

26. Z, W, T, Q, . . .

27. Z, M, Y, L, . . .

28. A, E, B, F, . . .

29. Z, P, F, V, . . .

30. PATTERNS Consider the pattern 12, 21, 30, 39, ... Will the 15th number have a value that is less than 100? less than 200? *Explain.*

31. CHALLENGE Each pattern below uses the same rule. Find the rule.

2, 11, 38, 119, . . .   3, 14, 47, 146, . . .   4, 17, 56, 173, . . .

PROBLEM SOLVING

SEE EXAMPLE 1
on p. 3
for Exs. 32–33

32. GUIDED PROBLEM SOLVING A radio station plays the day's top pop song during the afternoon at 2:10, 2:40, 3:10, 3:40, and so on. If you assume the pattern continues, when will the top pop song be played next?

   a. What is the relationship between the first time the song is played and the second time the song is played?

   b. Check that the relationship is true for all the other playing times.

   c. Use the relationship to find the next time the song will be played.

33. BASKETBALL There are 64 teams in the first round of a college basketball tournament. In each round after the first, there are half as many teams as in the previous round. How many teams are in the next three rounds?

34. ★ OPEN-ENDED MATH Give an example of a number pattern from your school day.

35. ★ WRITING You write a number pattern based on the rule "add the number to itself to find the next number." Your friend sees your list of numbers and says the pattern is "multiply by 2." Are you both describing the same pattern? *Explain.*

36. ★ MULTIPLE CHOICE There are 31 days in both July and August. Starting July 2, a swimming instructor offers lessons every 8 days throughout both months. On what date is the last lesson offered?

   (A) August 18   **(B)** August 26   **(C)** August 27   **(D)** August 31

37. CRAFTS Sketch the next three beads that will continue the pattern.

38. ★ SHORT RESPONSE Use the pattern 1, 5, 9, 13, 17, ... How many numbers will there be in the pattern when the value 85 appears? *Explain* how you found your answer.

39. ◆ MULTIPLE REPRESENTATIONS A pattern starts 1, 3, 5, 7, ...

   a. Describe in Words Describe the pattern in words.

   b. Draw a Pattern Draw a visual pattern that is related to the number pattern. *Explain* how the patterns are related.

40. PATTERNS Describe and complete the real-world pattern S, M, T, W, ... What real-life situation does the pattern represent?

41. ★ EXTENDED RESPONSE The diagram below shows the different phases of the moon over time. The number under each moon phase indicates the date on which the phase occurs.

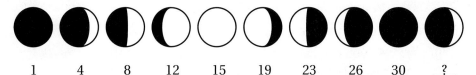

| 1 | 4 | 8 | 12 | 15 | 19 | 23 | 26 | 30 | ? |

a. **Patterns** Describe the visual pattern.

b. **Estimate** An equal amount of time passes from each phase to the next. Estimate the number of days that pass between phases.

c. **Predict** Suppose the first phase begins on May 1. Use the number pattern to predict the date of each phase during June.

42. REASONING Based on the rule "double the number and then add 3," you make the following list: 1, 5, 13, 29, 61. . . . Your friend says that this is the same as adding 4, then adding 4 × 2, then adding 4 × 2 × 2, and so on. Is your friend correct? Is your friend correct if you start with a whole number other than 1? *Explain.*

CHALLENGE Tell whether the result is *always, sometimes,* or *never* even. *Explain* your reasoning.

43. even × even × even × even . . .

44. even × odd × even × odd . . .

45. even + even + even + even . . .

46. even + odd + even + odd . . .

 NEW JERSEY MIXED REVIEW   **TEST PRACTICE** at classzone.com

47. Consider the heights of Taylor and her friends Zach, Elisa, and Cody. Zach is taller than Cody. Taylor is taller than both Cody and Elisa, but shorter than Zach. What information is needed to determine the order of the four friends from shortest to tallest?

   Ⓐ Is Zach shorter or taller than Taylor?

   Ⓑ Is Cody shorter or taller than Elisa?

   Ⓒ Is Elisa shorter or taller than Zach?

   Ⓓ Is Taylor shorter or taller than Cody?

1.2 Variables and Expressions

 4.3.D.3.b Substitution of a number for a variable

Before	You simplified numerical expressions.
Now	You'll evaluate variable expressions.
Why?	So you can calculate sports data, as in Example 3.

KEY VOCABULARY
- variable, *p. 8*
- variable expression, *p. 8*
- evaluate, *p. 8*

ACTIVITY

You can evaluate an expression by using a number strip.

STEP 1 Cut a long strip of paper. Write the numbers 1 through 9 on the strip.

> 1 2 3 4 5 6 7 8 9

STEP 2 Write "$n + 6$" on the remaining part of the paper. Cut two vertical slits (big enough for the number strip to fit through) on each side of the n.

> n + 6

STEP 3 Slide the strip through the slits so that one number shows. Record the resulting expression for each number. Then simplify.

> 5 + 6

Repeat the activity for the given expression. **1.** $n - 1$ **2.** $n \times 2$

Substituting In the activity, you substituted numbers for the variable n. A **variable** is a letter used to represent one or more numbers.

A **variable expression**, like $n + 6$, consists of numbers, variables, and operations. To **evaluate** a variable expression, you substitute values for the variables and then simplify the resulting numerical expression.

EXAMPLE 1 Evaluating Variable Expressions

a. Evaluate $x + 4$ when $x = 9$.

$x + 4 = 9 + 4$ **Substitute 9 for x.**

$\quad\quad = 13$ **Add.**

b. Evaluate $y - 3$ when $y = 7$.

$y - 3 = 7 - 3$ **Substitute 7 for y.**

$\quad\quad = 4$ **Subtract.**

 GUIDED PRACTICE   **for Example 1**

Evaluate the expression when $a = 3$ and $m = 9$.

1. $7 + m$ **2.** $a + 28$ **3.** $10 - a$ **4.** $m - 5$

KEY CONCEPT

For Your Notebook

Multiplication and Division Expressions

The expression 2×5 can also be written as $2 \cdot 5$. You can write multiplication and division expressions in several ways.

Multiplication $5n$ is another way of writing $5 \cdot n$.

ab is another way of writing $a \cdot b$.

$3(7)$ is another way of writing $3 \cdot 7$.

Division $\frac{x}{4}$ is another way of writing $x \div 4$.

AVOID ERRORS

Avoid using the multiplication symbol $\times$ in a variable expression. It could be confused with the variable x.

EXAMPLE 2 Evaluating Variable Expressions

a. Evaluate $4n$ when $n = 6$.

$4n = 4(6)$ **Substitute 6 for n.**

$= 24$ **Multiply.**

b. Evaluate $\frac{z}{2}$ when $z = 8$.

$\frac{z}{2} = \frac{8}{2}$ **Substitute 8 for z.**

$= 4$ **Divide.**

EXAMPLE 3 Evaluating Expressions with Two Variables

Ice Hockey Hockey players earn points for goals and assists. The expression $g + a$ can be used to find the points earned by a player who has g goals and a assists. Find the number of points earned by a hockey player with 12 goals and 29 assists.

SOLUTION

$g + a = 12 + 29$ **Substitute 12 for g and 29 for a.**

$= 41$ **Add.**

▶ **Answer** The hockey player earned 41 points.

✓ **GUIDED PRACTICE** for Examples 2 and 3

Evaluate the expression when $s = 5$ and $t = 10$.

5. $9s$

6. $18t$

7. $\frac{100}{t}$

8. $\frac{220}{s}$

9. $32t$

10. $14s$

11. $\frac{55}{s}$

12. $\frac{780}{t}$

13. What If? Suppose a hockey player had 18 goals and 41 assists in Example 3. Find the number of points the hockey player earned.

1.2 EXERCISES

HOMEWORK KEY

★ = **STANDARDIZED TEST PRACTICE**
Exs. 24, 25, 37, 38, 40, 41, and 51

◯ = **HINTS AND HOMEWORK HELP**
for Exs. 7, 11, 15, 17, 39 at classzone.com

SKILL PRACTICE

1. **VOCABULARY** Copy and complete: A __?__ is a letter used to represent one or more numbers.

2. **VOCABULARY** Give two examples of a variable expression.

EVALUATING Evaluate the expression for the given value.

SEE EXAMPLES 1 AND 2
on pp. 8 and 9
for Exs. 3–15

3. $x + 14$ when $x = 8$

4. $y - 5$ when $y = 13$

5. $7r$ when $r = 4$

6. $\frac{6}{s}$ when $s = 3$

7. $\frac{t}{3}$ when $t = 18$

8. $18 + a$ when $a = 17$

9. $y + 11$ when $y = 7$

10. $8b$ when $b = 9$

11. $24 - x$ when $x = 15$

12. $\frac{a}{4}$ when $a = 20$

13. $12y$ when $y = 2$

14. $b - 3$ when $b = 39$

15. **ERROR ANALYSIS** Describe and correct the error made in evaluating $2a$ when $a = 3$.

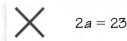

$2a = 23$

EVALUATING Evaluate the expression when $x = 3$, $y = 9$, $m = 13$, and $p = 25$.

SEE EXAMPLE 3
on p. 9
for Exs. 16–24

16. $p - m$

17. $y + p$

18. $m + p$

19. $m - y$

20. xy

21. mx

22. $\frac{y}{x}$

23. $\frac{39}{m}$

24. ★ **MULTIPLE CHOICE** What is the value of the expression $x + y$ when $x = 15$ and $y = 21$?

   (A) 6   (B) 30   (C) 36   (D) 42

25. ★ **MULTIPLE CHOICE** To play footbag, you kick a small beanbag to keep it in the air. The expression $3m$, where m is the number of minutes played, can be used to find the calories burned by a 100 pound person playing footbag. Which expression can *not* be used to find the calories burned by a 100 pound person playing footbag for 45 minutes?

   (A) 3(45)   (B) 3 · 45   (C) 3 × 45   (D) 345

COMPARING VALUES Copy and complete the statement using <, >, or = when $x = 7$ and $y = 15$.

26. $y + 9 \; \underline{?} \; 4x$

27. $x - 4 \; \underline{?} \; \frac{y}{5}$

28. $20 - y \; \underline{?} \; \frac{14}{x}$

29. $x + 12 \; \underline{?} \; 40 - y$

30. $3x \; \underline{?} \; y + 6$

31. $4y \; \underline{?} \; 52 + x$

CHALLENGE Tell whether the given expressions are *always*, *sometimes*, or *never* equal. *Explain* your reasoning and include examples.

32. $x + x; 2x$

33. $x + 4; x - 4$

34. $x + 4; x$

35. $\frac{x}{4}; 4x$

10   Chapter 1   Number Sense, Patterns, and Algebraic Thinking

SEE EXAMPLE 1
on p. 8
for Exs. 36–37

36. DANCE You pay $8 to see a modern dance show. The expression $s + 8$, where s is the cost of snacks you buy, can be used to find the total cost of going to the show. You buy snacks that cost $3. Find the total cost.

37. ★ MULTIPLE CHOICE To find the actual length in minutes of a TV show that airs in a one-hour time slot, evaluate $60 - c$, where c is minutes of commercials. How long is a show with 18 minutes of commercials?

Ⓐ 18 minutes   Ⓑ 32 minutes   Ⓒ 42 minutes   Ⓓ 52 minutes

SEE EXAMPLE 3
on p. 9
for Exs. 38–39

38. ★ SHORT RESPONSE If the variable expression $\frac{x}{y}$ has a value of 3, what are some possible values of x and y? Describe the relationship of x to y.

39. BAMBOO You can predict the growth for a stem of bamboo by evaluating the expression gn. In the expression, g is the average number of inches grown each day and n is the number of days. Predict the amount of growth in one week for bamboo that grows an average of 12 inches each day.

40. ★ WRITING Rewrite the phrase *two less than a number* as a variable expression. *Explain* how to evaluate it when $n = 5$.

Animated Math
at classzone.com

41. ★ OPEN-ENDED MATH Write a variable expression that has a decreasing value as the value of the variable increases.

42. PLUTO The expression $\frac{w}{17}$, where w is weight in pounds on Earth, can be used to approximate weight in pounds on Pluto. Tom weighs 153 pounds on Earth. Find his approximate weight on Pluto. Would a person who had twice Tom's weight on Earth also be twice Tom's weight on Pluto? *Explain.*

43. CHALLENGE Use $xy = 32$. Make a table of the possible whole number values of x and y, with the x-values in numerical order. Describe the pattern of the y-values. As the value of x increases, how does y change? *Explain.*

 NEW JERSEY MIXED REVIEW

 TEST PRACTICE at classzone.com

44. Jake just started a new bike-riding program. He bikes 1 mile every day during the first week, 2 miles every day during the second week, 4 miles every day during the third week, 8 miles every day during the fourth week, and so on. If this pattern continues, how far would you expect Jake to bike every day during the sixth week of the program?

Ⓐ 12 mi   Ⓑ 16 mi

Ⓒ 32 mi   Ⓓ 64 mi

GOAL
Introduce exponents by writing repeated multiplication expressions.

MATERIALS
• paper
• pencil

1.3 Repeated Multiplication

The number of times you fold a piece of paper is related to the number of sections formed by the folds.

EXPLORE Find the number of sections formed by folding a piece of paper 5 times.

STEP 1 **Fold** a piece of paper in half. Open the paper and count the number of sections formed.

Fold. → Open. →

1
2

STEP 2 **Copy** the table at the right. Record the number of sections you counted from Step 1.

Folds	1	2	3	4	5
Sections	2	?	?	?	?

STEP 3 **Close** the paper. Then fold the paper in half again. Count the number of sections formed and record this in your table. Keep folding, counting, and recording until you have completed 5 folds.

Fold. → Open. →

1	2
3	4

PRACTICE Complete the following exercises.

1. The number of sections you recorded in your table can be rewritten as a product of 2's. For example, 4 can be rewritten as 2 • 2. Add a *Rewritten form* row to your table and rewrite each number of sections as a product of 2's.

2. **WRITING** What can you conclude about the relationship between the number of folds and the number of times 2 is a factor in the rewritten form?

DRAW CONCLUSIONS

3. **REASONING** How many sections would be formed if you folded a piece of paper 6 times? Extend and complete your table for 6, 7, and 8 folds.

1.3 Powers and Exponents

4.1.B.2 Use exponentiation to find whole number powers of numbers.

Before	You multiplied pairs of numbers.
Now	You'll write repeated multiplication using exponents.
Why?	So you can count cells, as in Example 1.

KEY VOCABULARY
• **power,** *p. 13*
• **base,** *p. 13*
• **exponent,** *p. 13*

Biology A plant grows when its cells divide into pairs, as shown below. What is another way to write the number of cells after the fourth division?

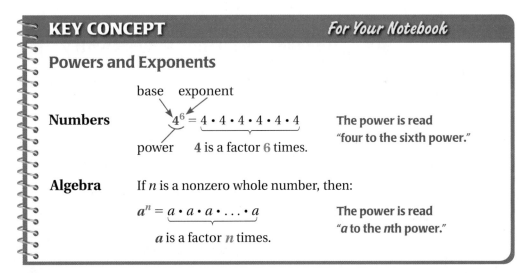

A **power** is a way of writing repeated multiplication. The **base** of a power is the factor, and the **exponent** of a power is the number of times the factor is used.

KEY CONCEPT   *For Your Notebook*

Powers and Exponents

Numbers

base   exponent

$$4^6 = \underbrace{4 \cdot 4 \cdot 4 \cdot 4 \cdot 4 \cdot 4}_{4 \text{ is a factor } 6 \text{ times.}}$$

power

The power is read "four to the sixth power."

Algebra   If n is a nonzero whole number, then:

$$a^n = \underbrace{a \cdot a \cdot a \cdot \ldots \cdot a}_{a \text{ is a factor } n \text{ times.}}$$

The power is read "a to the nth power."

EXAMPLE 1   Writing Powers

After the fourth cell division described above, there are $2 \cdot 2 \cdot 2 \cdot 2$ cells.

$$\underbrace{2 \cdot 2 \cdot 2 \cdot 2}_{2 \text{ is a factor 4 times.}} = 2^4$$

▶ **Answer** There are 2^4 cells after the fourth cell division.

EXAMPLE 2 Evaluating Powers

Evaluate the power.

a. 7^2 **b.** 4^3 **c.** 3^1

READING

You can read 7^2 as "7 to the second power" or as "7 squared."

You can read 4^3 as "4 to the third power" or as "4 cubed."

SOLUTION

a. $7^2 = 7 \cdot 7$ Write 7 as a factor 2 times.

$ = 49$ Multiply.

b. $4^3 = 4 \cdot 4 \cdot 4$ Write 4 as a factor 3 times.

$ = 64$ Multiply.

c. $3^1 = 3$ Write 3 as a factor 1 time.

Animated Math
at classzone.com

✓ **GUIDED PRACTICE** for Examples 1 and 2

Write the product as a power.

1. $8 \cdot 8 \cdot 8$ **2.** $5 \cdot 5 \cdot 5 \cdot 5 \cdot 5 \cdot 5$ **3.** $6 \cdot 6 \cdot 6 \cdot 6 \cdot 6$

Evaluate the power.

4. 2^6 **5.** 6^2 **6.** 5^4

EXAMPLE 3 Evaluating Powers with Variables

a. Evaluate x^2 when $x = 9$. **b.** Evaluate b^3 when $b = 7$.

SOLUTION

a. $x^2 = 9^2$ Substitute 9 for *x*.

$ = 9 \cdot 9$ Write 9 as a factor 2 times.

$ = 81$ Multiply.

READING

Numbers like 9^2 and 7^3 are written in *exponential form.* Numbers like 81 and 343 are written in *standard form.*

b. $b^3 = 7^3$ Substitute 7 for *b*.

$ = 7 \cdot 7 \cdot 7$ Write 7 as a factor 3 times.

$ = 343$ Multiply.

✓ **GUIDED PRACTICE** for Example 3

7. Evaluate m^8 when $m = 2$. **8.** Evaluate p^3 when $p = 10$.

9. Evaluate y^1 when $y = 3586$. **10.** Evaluate z^2 when $z = 17$.

11. What number greater than zero is equal to itself when raised to any power?

1.3 EXERCISES

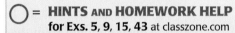

SKILL PRACTICE

1. VOCABULARY Name the base and the exponent in the power 9^4.

SEE EXAMPLE 1
on p. 13
for Exs. 2–5

WRITING PRODUCTS Write the product as a power.

2. $3 \cdot 3 \cdot 3 \cdot 3 \cdot 3$ **3.** $10 \cdot 10$ **4.** $a \cdot a \cdot a$ **5.** $k \cdot k \cdot k \cdot k$

SEE EXAMPLE 2
on p. 14 for
Exs. 6–13, 21

EVALUATING POWERS Write the power in words. Then evaluate the power.

6. 1^5 **7.** 5^2 **8.** 2^7 **9.** 0^8

10. 12^3 **11.** 6^2 **12.** 9^8 **13.** 5^1

XY ALGEBRA Evaluate the expression for the given value of the variable.

SEE EXAMPLE 3
on p. 14
for Exs. 14–20

14. y^2 when $y = 12$ **15.** b^1 when $b = 18$ **16.** m^3 when $m = 10$

17. x^4 when $x = 5$ **18.** w^6 when $w = 2$ **19.** c^5 when $c = 6$

20. ERROR ANALYSIS Describe and correct the error made in evaluating the expression b^4 when $b = 2$.

$$\times \quad \begin{aligned} b^4 &= 2^4 \\ &= 2 \times 4 \\ &= 8 \end{aligned}$$

21. ★ MULTIPLE CHOICE What is the value of 8^3?

(A) 24   **(B)** 64   **(C)** 72   **(D)** 512

WRITING POWERS Write the number as a power.

22. 49   **23.** 100   **24.** 81   **25.** 32

26. 27   **27.** 256   **28.** 625   **29.** 243

COMPARING POWERS Copy and complete the statement using <, >, or =.

30. 2^5 ? 5^2 **31.** 21 ? 3^7 **32.** 1^9 ? 1 **33.** 3^4 ? 4^3

34. 6^3 ? 9^2 **35.** 4^3 ? 2^6 **36.** 3^5 ? 5^3 **37.** 9^3 ? 7^4

XY CHALLENGE Tell whether the statement is *always, sometimes,* or *never* true for nonzero whole numbers. *Explain* your reasoning and include examples.

38. $2^x > x^2$ **39.** $2x > x^2$ **40.** $2^x < 2x^2$ **41.** $2^x < x^x$

PROBLEM SOLVING

42. DOG PEDIGREES A certificate of pedigree lists a dog's parents, grandparents, and so on. The power 2^6 describes the number of *great-great-great-great-* grandparents a dog has. How many is this?

43. **CHECKERS** A checkerboard has 8 rows of 8 squares. Write the number of squares on the checkerboard as a power. Use mental math to evaluate.

44. ★ **SHORT RESPONSE** Is a power with an exponent greater than one always greater than the base of the power? *Explain*, using examples.

SEE EXAMPLES
1 AND 2
on pp. 13–14
for Exs. 45–46

45. ★ **MULTIPLE CHOICE** Every hour a cell divides into 2 cells. Which expression represents the number of cells after 5 hours?

  (A) 2^5 **(B)** 5^2 **(C)** $2 \cdot 5$ **(D)** $2 \div 5$

46. ★ **WRITING** Given that $2^8 = 256$, describe how to find the value of 2^9 without multiplying nine 2's together.

47. **PATTERNS** Describe the pattern using powers.

48. **NUMBER SENSE** Without evaluating every power, write the following numbers in order from least to greatest: 6^2, 2^3, 9^2, 9, 2, 9^3, and 6. *Explain* your reasoning.

49. ◆ **MULTIPLE REPRESENTATIONS** You make a batch of green goo and split it into 3 portions. Then you split each of those portions into 3 portions. Again you split each of those portions into 3 portions.

  a. **Make a Model** *Describe* how to use a piece of paper to find the number of portions of goo you now have.

  b. **Write an Expression** Write and evaluate a power to find the number of portions of goo you now have.

50. **CHALLENGE** Evaluate the following powers: 3^4, 3^3, 3^2, and 3^1. What happens to the value of the power as the exponent decreases? Based on this pattern, what do you think is the value of 3^0?

 NEW JERSEY MIXED REVIEW **TEST PRACTICE** at classzone.com

51. You bought 3 dozen cans of soda priced at 6 cans for $2.48 and 15 bottles of water priced at 3 bottles for $1.86. What is the total amount of money you spent, not including tax, on the soda and bottled water?

  (A) $9.30 **(B)** $10.54 **(C)** $16.74 **(D)** $24.18

52. Kayla is making two banners for a basketball game. She wants the larger banner to be 9 feet long, and the smaller banner to be 4 feet shorter than the larger one. Which equation can be used to find the length n of the shorter banner in feet?

  (A) $n = 9 + 4$ **(B)** $n = 9 - 4$ **(C)** $n = 9 \cdot 4$ **(D)** $n = 9 \div 4$

1.4 Order of Operations

4.1.B.3 Understand and apply the standard algebraic order of operations, including appropriate use of parentheses.

Before You evaluated expressions involving one operation.

Now You'll evaluate expressions involving two or more operations.

Why? So you can find total cost, as in Example 1.

KEY VOCABULARY
• order of operations, *p. 17*

Music You buy a used guitar for $50. You then pay $10 for each of five guitar lessons. The total cost can be found by evaluating the expression $50 + 10 \times 5$. Is the total cost $100 or $300?

To make sure everyone gets the same result when evaluating an expression, mathematicians always use a set of rules called the **order of operations**.

KEY CONCEPT *For Your Notebook*

Order of Operations

1. Evaluate expressions inside grouping symbols.
2. Evaluate powers.
3. Multiply and divide from left to right.
4. Add and subtract from left to right.

EXAMPLE 1 Following Order of Operations

To find the guitar costs described above, evaluate $50 + 10 \times 5$.

$$50 + 10 \times 5 = 50 + 50 \qquad \text{First multiply 10 and 5.}$$

$$= 100 \qquad \text{Then add 50 and 50.}$$

▶ **Answer** The total cost is $100.

EXAMPLE 2 Evaluating a Variable Expression

Evaluate $x - 3y^3$ **when** $x = 25$ **and** $y = 2$.

AVOID ERRORS
Make sure you evaluate the power before you multiply.

$$x - 3y^3 = 25 - 3(2^3) \qquad \text{Substitute 25 for } x \text{ and 2 for } y.$$

$$= 25 - 3(8) \qquad \text{Evaluate the power.}$$

$$= 25 - 24 \qquad \text{Multiply 8 and 3.}$$

$$= 1 \qquad \text{Subtract 24 from 25.}$$

✔ **GUIDED PRACTICE**   for Examples 1 and 2

Evaluate the expression.

1. $5 + 6 \times 5$ **2.** $20 - 4^2 \div 2$ **3.** $10 \times 3 + 3^3$

4. Evaluate $a + 4b^2$ when $a = 6$ and $b = 5$.

Left-to-Right Rule When an expression has a string of additions and subtractions or a string of multiplications and divisions, you need to perform the operations in order from left to right.

EXAMPLE 3 **Using the Left-to-Right Rule**

a. $12 - 7 + 3 - 6 = 5 + 3 - 6$ Subtract 7 from 12.

$\qquad\qquad\qquad = 8 - 6$ Add 5 and 3.

$\qquad\qquad\qquad = 2$ Subtract 6 from 8.

b. $54 \div 9 \times 3 = 6 \times 3$ Divide 54 by 9.

$\qquad\qquad\quad = 18$ Multiply 6 and 3.

Grouping Symbols Grouping symbols indicate operations that should be performed first. The most common grouping symbols are parentheses ( ) and brackets [ ]. A fraction bar groups the numerator separate from the denominator.

EXAMPLE 4 **Using Grouping Symbols**

TAKING NOTES
In your notebook, you can write the letters PEMDAS to help you remember the order of operations:
Parentheses
Exponents
Multiplication
Division
Addition
Subtraction

a. $4(8 - 5) = 4(3)$ Subtract inside parentheses.

$\qquad\qquad = 12$ Multiply 4 and 3.

b. $\dfrac{13 + 7}{2 \cdot 5} = \dfrac{20}{10}$ Evaluate expressions grouped by fraction bar.

$\qquad\quad = 2$ Divide 20 by 10.

c. $(4 + 1)^2 \cdot 3 = 5^2 \cdot 3$ Add inside parentheses.

$\qquad\qquad\quad = 25 \cdot 3$ Evaluate the power.

$\qquad\qquad\quad = 75$ Multiply 25 and 3.

Animated **Math**
at classzone.com

✔ **GUIDED PRACTICE**   for Examples 3 and 4

Evaluate the expression.

5. $18 - 10 + 5 - 1$ **6.** $(3 + 7)(6 - 3)^2$ **7.** $\dfrac{8 \cdot 3}{4 + 2}$

8. $25 - 6 - 14 + 3$ **9.** $16 \div 2 \cdot 11$ **10.** $16(9 + 1) - 30$

EXAMPLE 5 Standardized Test Practice

Video Games The tricks and point values for a skateboarding video game are shown in the table. You complete one burntwist, three backflips, and four 360° flips. How many points do you score?

Trick	Points
Burntwist	500
Backflip	400
360° flip	150

ELIMINATE CHOICES
You can use mental math to determine that 3 backflips score 1200 points. So, you can eliminate choice A.

(A) 1050 points   **(B)** 1700 points

(C) 2100 points   **(D)** 2300 points

SOLUTION

You need to evaluate the expression $1 \cdot 500 + 3 \cdot 400 + 4 \cdot 150$.

$$\begin{aligned}
1 \cdot 500 + 3 \cdot 400 + 4 \cdot 150 &= 500 + 1200 + 600 && \textbf{Multiply first.} \\
&= 1700 + 600 && \textbf{Add 500 and 1200.} \\
&= 2300 && \textbf{Add 1700 and 600.}
\end{aligned}$$

▶ **Answer** You score 2300 points. The correct answer is D. Ⓐ Ⓑ Ⓒ ⬤

✓ **GUIDED PRACTICE** | for Example 5

11. What If? In Example 5, suppose you complete two burntwists, two backflips, and one 360° flip. How many points do you score?

1.4 EXERCISES

HOMEWORK KEY

★ = **STANDARDIZED TEST PRACTICE**
Exs. 16, 43, 44, 46, 48, 52, and 66

◯ = **HINTS AND HOMEWORK HELP**
for Exs. 9, 11, 15, 23, 45 at classzone.com

SKILL PRACTICE

VOCABULARY Copy and complete the statement using *before* or *after*.

1. To evaluate $7 + 8^2$, evaluate the power __?__ adding.

2. To evaluate $20 - 5 \div 5$, do the subtraction __?__ dividing.

EVALUATING EXPRESSIONS Evaluate the expression.

SEE EXAMPLES 1, 3, AND 4
on pp. 17–18
for Exs. 3–15

3. $6 + 7 \cdot 4$ **4.** $\dfrac{20 + 8}{4}$ **5.** $36 \div 3 \cdot 2^3$ **6.** $10 - 8 + 5 - 2$

7. $9(16 - 7)$ **8.** $40 - 12 \div 6$ **⑨.** $\dfrac{28}{7 - 3}$ **10.** $(1 + 6)(5 - 2)^2$

⑪. $\dfrac{12 + 6}{3 - 1}$ **12.** $9 \div 3 \times 3^4$ **13.** $16 \div (3^2 - 1)$ **14.** $(8 - 2)^2 + 12 \div 6$

⑮. ERROR ANALYSIS Describe and correct the error at the right.

$$\begin{aligned} 8 - 4 + 3 &= 8 - 7 \\ &= 1 \end{aligned}$$

SEE EXAMPLES 1 AND 3
on pp. 17–18
for Ex. 16

16. ★ **MULTIPLE CHOICE** What is the first step in evaluating the expression $4 + 3 \times 7^2 - 7$?

     (A) Add 4 and 3.   (B) Multiply 3 and 7.

     (C) Subtract 7 from 7.   (D) Evaluate 7^2.

XV ALGEBRA Evaluate the expression when $x = 8$ and $y = 2$.

SEE EXAMPLE 2
on p. 17
for Exs. 17–24

17. $4 + x \cdot y$ 18. $(x + 12) \div 5$ 19. $20 - y^4 + 6$ 20. $x - y^2 - 2$

21. $x - 2 \cdot y$ 22. $y - 16 \div x$ (23.) $11 \times 2(x \div 4)$ 24. $(x \div y)^2 + 5$

MENTAL MATH Copy and complete the statement, using $+, -, \times,$ or $\div$ to make the statement true.

25. $12 \div 4 \underline{\,?\,} 3 = 9$ 26. $16 \underline{\,?\,} 4 \times 2 = 24$ 27. $9 \underline{\,?\,} 18 \div 3 = 3$

28. $8 + 14 \underline{\,?\,} 2 = 36$ 29. $6 \underline{\,?\,} 2 + 8 \div 4 = 6$ 30. $9 + 8 \times 2 = 30 \div 6 \underline{\,?\,} 5$

31. $2^3 - 5 \times 6 \underline{\,?\,} 10 = 5$ 32. $10 \underline{\,?\,} 32 \div 8 = 6$ 33. $14 \underline{\,?\,} 7 \times 5 = 20 \div 4 \times 2$

REASONING Copy and complete the statement by placing parentheses to make the statement true.

34. $20 - 3^2 \times 2 + 8 \overset{?}{=} 110$ 35. $20 - 3^2 \times 2 + 8 \overset{?}{=} 30$

XV CHALLENGE Tell whether the value of the expression *increases*, *decreases*, or *stays the same* as the value of x increases.

36. $3^2 + 24 \div x$ 37. $40 - x \div 2^2 \div x$ 38. $x \times 4 \div 2^3$

39. $2x + 6^2 - x \times 3 + x$ 40. $12 + 20 \times 3 \div x^2$ 41. $(x + 2)^2 + 8 \div 4$

PROBLEM SOLVING

SEE EXAMPLE 5
on p. 19
for Exs. 42–43

42. **GUIDED PROBLEM SOLVING** A whale watching trip costs $32 for adults and $23 for students. How much will it cost for 4 adults and 20 students to take the trip?

     a. Write an expression for the cost of the adults. Write an expression for the cost of the students.

     b. Write an expression for the total cost of adults and students.

     c. Evaluate your expression using the order of operations.

43. ★ **MULTIPLE CHOICE** You buy 3 notebooks that cost $2 each, 5 pens that cost a total of $4, and 2 erasers that cost $1 each. You give the cashier $20. How much change do you receive?

     (A) $13   (B) $9   (C) $8   (D) $6

44. ★ **WRITING** Describe the steps you use to evaluate the expression $14 + 6^2 - 15 \div 3 + 1$.

SEE EXAMPLE 5
on p. 19
for Exs. 45, 47

45. **WEIGHTLIFTING** In an Olympic clean-and-jerk event, Cheryl Haworth lifted one 15 kilogram bar, four plates that each weighed 25 kilograms, and 2 plates that each weighed 20 kilograms. Write and evaluate an expression to find the total weight lifted.

46. ★ **SHORT RESPONSE** Write an expression with 4 terms and 3 different operations in which you work from left to right to evaluate. Write another expression that you cannot evaluate from left to right. *Explain* your process.

47. **PRINTING COSTS** A pack of paper costs $4. For every 10 packs of paper that you buy, you receive a discount of $11. Write and evaluate an expression to find the cost of buying 66 packs of paper.

48. ★ **EXTENDED RESPONSE** Use the pricing information for Joe's Joke Shop.

a. **Calculate** You want to buy a present for each of 6 friends. You have $20. Can you buy 6 chattering teeth? 6 hand buzzers?

b. **Make a List** You want to buy at least one of each item. Make a list of all the possible ways you can buy 6 presents regardless of the total cost.

c. **Reasoning** Write and evaluate an expression to find the total cost of each combination you listed in part (b). Which combinations of presents could you buy with $20?

Joe's Joke Shop	
Chattering teeth	$3
Hand buzzer	$4

READING IN MATH Read the advertisement below for Exercises 49–51.

Go Bowling!

If you are looking for an inexpensive, fun experience for your family, take them bowling. In addition to 30 lanes, **Strike** has a video arcade with games for all ages.

Are you planning a birthday party for your child? Consider **Strike** for the party.

3 games $**5**.00 per person

cake $**2**.00 per person

soft drink $**1**.00 per person

See our price list or consider the Deluxe Birthday package for 12–20 people. Only $125 for 3 games of bowling, cake, balloons, and unlimited soft drinks! **Strike** has friendly helpful staff who will provide your child with a memorable party.

49. **Calculate** You are planning a party at Strike for 10 people. Write and evaluate an expression for the total cost including 3 games of bowling, cake, and soft drinks.

50. **Calculate** You are considering the Deluxe Birthday package for 20 children. Write and evaluate an expression for the cost per person.

51. **Reasoning** What is the least number of people that would need to go for the Deluxe Birthday package to cost less than paying with the rates per person? *Explain* your reasoning.

52. ★ OPEN-ENDED MATH Pick a phone number without the area code. Replace the hyphen with an equal sign. Then insert symbols to try and make a true statement. (Not all phone numbers will work.)

CHALLENGE Evaluate the expression. Then rewrite the expression with parentheses so that its value is increased, and so that its value is decreased.

53. $8 \times 3 + 12 \div 3$

54. $36 \div 2 \times 6 + 7$

55. $4^2 + 5 \times 4 \div 2 + 8$

56. $28 + 2^5 - 36 \div 4 \times 2$

 NEW JERSEY MIXED REVIEW **TEST PRACTICE** at classzone.com

57. Which model represents 5^2?

Ⓐ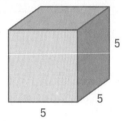

Ⓒ

Ⓑ

Ⓓ

QUIZ *for Lessons 1.1–1.4*

Describe the pattern. Then write the next three numbers. *(p. 3)*

1. 3, 6, 12, 24, . . .

2. 100, 95, 90, 85, . . .

3. 11, 15, 19, 23, . . .

4. Describe the pattern at the right. Then draw the next three figures. *(p. 3)*

5. SOCCER To find the number of points earned by a soccer player, you can evaluate the expression $2g + a$, where g is the number of goals scored and a is the number of assists. Find the number of points earned by a soccer player with 6 goals and 13 assists. *(p. 8)*

Evaluate the power. *(p. 13)*

6. 12^1

7. 13^2

8. 5^4

9. 3^5

Evaluate the expression. *(p. 17)*

10. $2 \cdot 6 \div 4 \cdot 10 \cdot 3$

11. $3 + 3^3 \div 3$

12. $5(12 - 6)^2 + 7$

1.4 Using Order of Operations

You can use the (,) , and ^ keys to evaluate expressions.

EXAMPLE 1 You buy 7 quarts of strawberries and 6 quarts of raspberries at a fruit stand. Each quart of fruit costs $3. What is the total cost?

SOLUTION

To find the total cost, evaluate the expression $3(7 + 6)$.

Keystrokes   **Display**

3 (7 + 6) =   **39**

▶ **Answer** The total cost is $39.

EXAMPLE 2 You can estimate the number of strawberries in one quart by evaluating 3^3. About how many strawberries are in 7 quarts?

SOLUTION

To estimate the number of strawberries in 7 quarts, evaluate the expression 7×3^3.

Keystrokes   **Display**

7 × 3 ^ 3 =   **189**

▶ **Answer** There are about 189 strawberries in 7 quarts.

PRACTICE Use a calculator to evaluate the expression.

1. $3 + 4 \cdot 5$
2. $9^2 - 3^2$
3. $\dfrac{14 + 6}{4 + 1}$
4. $(4 + 2)^2 + 5^2$

5. $\dfrac{26 + 9}{4^2 - 9}$
6. $314 - (3 + 3)^3$
7. $5 + \dfrac{8^3}{64}$
8. $6 \cdot 4^4 + 20$

9. BLUEBERRIES You can estimate the number of blueberries in one pint by evaluating 6^3. About how many blueberries are in 5 pints?

10. MEASUREMENT You can find the number of cubic inches in a cubic yard by evaluating 36^3. How many cubic inches are in 6 cubic yards?

Lessons 1.1–1.4

1. **PHOTO QUILT** You are making a photo quilt by transferring photos to 48 rectangular pieces of fabric. Each rectangle is 3 inches long and 2 inches wide. The fabric you buy is 24 inches wide. How long a piece of fabric do you need?

   A. 8 in.   **C.** 16 in.

   B. 12 in.   **D.** 18 in.

2. **STRAWBERRIES** You pay $7.50 for 3 quarts of strawberries. Later, you realize your recipe calls for 5 quarts of strawberries. How much will the additional strawberries cost?

   A. $2.50   **C.** $5.50

   B. $5   **D.** $12.50

3. **CALORIES** The number of calories in one serving of any food is the sum of the calories from fat, protein, and carbohydrate. The table shows the calories in 1 gram of each of the three food components.

Component	Calories in 1 gram
Fat	9
Protein	4
Carbohydrate	4

   A serving of cheddar cheese contains 14 grams of fat, 11 grams of protein, and 1 gram of carbohydrate. How many calories are in a serving of cheddar cheese?

   A. 70 calories   **C.** 174 calories

   B. 141 calories   **D.** 234 calories

4. **MINIATURE CARS** You collect miniature cars and display them on shelves that hold 20 cars each. Which expression describes the number of shelves needed for any number of miniature cars?

   A. $\dfrac{x}{20}$ **C.** $20x$

   B. $\dfrac{20}{x}$ **D.** None of the above

5. **GARDENING** A gardener has a rectangular garden with a length of 10 feet and a width of 5 feet. The gardener plans to increase the length of the garden by 3 feet. What will the area of the enlarged garden be?

   A. 25 ft^2 **C.** 65 ft^2

   B. 26 ft^2 **D.** 80 ft^2

6. **BIKE FRAME** The ideal height (in centimeters) of a mountain bike frame is about 10 centimeters less than two thirds of the bike rider's leg length (in centimeters). Two riders' leg lengths are 80 centimeters and 85 centimeters.
   To the nearest tenth of a centimeter, how much taller should the taller mountain bike frame be?

   A. 3.3 cm

   B. 5 cm

   C. 13.3 cm

   D. 23.3 cm

7. **OPEN-ENDED** An assistant at a veterinarian's office schedules appointments at 8:15, 9:00, 9:45, and 10:30. If you assume the pattern continues, when is the next scheduled appointment?

   • What is the relationship between the first appointment and the second appointment?

   • Check that the relationship is true for the other appointments.

   • Use the relationship to find the time of the next scheduled appointment.

1.5 Equations and Mental Math

NJ 4.3.D.2.b Solve simple linear equations informally and graphically. Using paper-and-pencil, calculators, graphing calculators, spreadsheets . . .

Before	You used mental math to add, subtract, multiply, and divide.
Now	You'll use mental math to solve an equation.
Why?	So you can find the duration of an activity, as in Ex. 43.

KEY VOCABULARY
- **equation,** *p. 25*
- **solution,** *p. 25*
- **solving an equation,** *p. 26*

ACTIVITY

You can use chips to find the value of a variable.

STEP 1 Use chips to model the statement $n + 4 = 7$. Let each chip represent 1.

$$n + \bullet\bullet\bullet\bullet = \bullet\bullet\bullet\bullet\bullet\bullet\bullet$$

STEP 2 Replace n with chips until you have the same number of chips on each side of the equal sign.

$$\bullet\bullet\bullet + \bullet\bullet\bullet\bullet = \bullet\bullet\bullet\bullet\bullet\bullet\bullet$$

STEP 3 Replacing n with 3 chips gives a total of 7 chips on each side, so $n = 3$.

$$\bullet\bullet\bullet\bullet\bullet\bullet\bullet = \bullet\bullet\bullet\bullet\bullet\bullet\bullet$$

Model with chips to help you find the value of the variable.

1. $6 + x = 10$ **2.** $y + 2 = 9$ **3.** $8 = m + 3$

In the activity, you solved *equations* by modeling with chips. An **equation** is a mathematical sentence formed by setting two expressions equal. A **solution** of an equation is a number that you can substitute for a variable to make the equation true.

EXAMPLE 1 Checking Possible Solutions

Tell whether the value of the variable is a solution of $n + 5 = 14$.

a. $n = 9$ **b.** $n = 7$

READING

Symbol	Meaning
$=$	is equal to
$\overset{?}{=}$	is equal to?
$\neq$	is not equal to

SOLUTION

a. $n + 5 = 14$ Write equation.

$9 + 5 \overset{?}{=} 14$ Substitute 9 for n.

$14 = 14$ **14 = 14, so 9 is a solution.**

b. $n + 5 = 14$ Write equation.

$7 + 5 \overset{?}{=} 14$ Substitute 7 for n.

$12 \neq 14$ **12 ≠ 14, so 7 is not a solution.**

Solving an Equation Finding all solutions of an equation is called **solving the equation.** You can use mental math to solve simple equations by thinking of the equation as a question.

EXAMPLE 2 **Using Mental Math to Solve Equations**

Equation	Question	Solution	Check
a. $9 + x = 12$	9 plus what number equals 12?	3	$9 + 3 = 12$
b. $n - 5 = 10$	What number minus 5 equals 10?	15	$15 - 5 = 10$
c. $4t = 20$	4 times what number equals 20?	5	$4(5) = 20$
d. $m \div 3 = 12$	What number divided by 3 equals 12?	36	$36 \div 3 = 12$

Animated Math at classzone.com

✓ **GUIDED PRACTICE** | **for Examples 1 and 2**

Tell whether the value of the variable is a solution of the equation.

1. $3x = 12$; $x = 4$ **2.** $7 = 13 - n$; $n = 5$ **3.** $6 \div y = 3$; $y = 2$

Solve the equation using mental math.

4. $7x = 35$ **5.** $15 = n - 6$ **6.** $12 + a = 32$ **7.** $24 \div n = 6$

Distance Problems Some distance problems can be solved using an equation that relates distance, speed, and time. For example, if you stand on a walkway moving at a speed of 2 feet per second for 30 seconds, you can use the formula below to find the distance you travel.

KEY CONCEPT *For Your Notebook*

Distance, Speed, and Time

Words Distance traveled is equal to the speed (rate of travel) times the travel time.

Algebra $d = rt$

Numbers distance = 2 feet per second • 30 seconds = 60 feet

Abbreviations are often used when referring to speeds. For example, miles per hour may be written as mi/h, feet per minute as ft/min, and meters per second as m/sec.

EXAMPLE 3 Using Mental Math to Solve an Equation

 Homing Pigeons A homing pigeon is a bird trained to fly back to its home. Homing pigeons can fly at a speed of about 50 miles per hour. About how long would it take a homing pigeon to fly 300 miles?

SOLUTION

$$d = rt$$ Write formula for distance.

$$300 = 50t$$ Substitute the values you know.

$$300 = 50 \cdot 6$$ Use mental math to solve equation.

▶ **Answer** It would take a homing pigeon about 6 hours to fly 300 miles.

✓ **GUIDED PRACTICE** for Example 3

8. **Traveling Speeds** A car travels on a highway at a constant speed. In 2 hours, the car travels 100 miles. At what speed is the car traveling?

1.5 EXERCISES

HOMEWORK KEY

★ = **STANDARDIZED TEST PRACTICE**
Exs. 28, 29, 45, 47, 50, 51, and 65

○ = **HINTS AND HOMEWORK HELP**
for Exs. 5, 13, 15, 43 at classzone.com

SKILL PRACTICE

1. **VOCABULARY** Copy and complete: A __?__ of an equation is a number that you can substitute for a variable to make the equation true.

2. **VOCABULARY** What is the difference between an expression and an equation? Give an example of each.

CHECKING SOLUTIONS Tell whether the given value of the variable is a solution of the equation.

SEE EXAMPLE 1
on p. 25
for Exs. 3–8

3. $5x = 35$; $x = 7$
4. $16 + y = 22$; $y = 8$
5. $9 = z - 12$; $z = 20$
6. $40 = 8z$; $z = 5$
7. $s + 5 = 11$; $s = 7$
8. $24 - a = 13$; $a = 9$

MENTAL MATH Solve the equation using mental math.

SEE EXAMPLE 2
on p. 26
for Exs. 9–20

9. $4a = 24$
10. $b - 6 = 7$
11. $18 = 9 + y$
12. $\frac{z}{3} = 7$
13. $8 = 25 - t$
14. $10x = 120$
15. $a \div 6 = 8$
16. $x + 8 = 15$
17. $\frac{36}{y} = 6$
18. $20 - b = 3$
19. $10 = x + 7$
20. $44 = 11p$

DISTANCE FORMULA Use the formula for distance to find the unknown value.

SEE EXAMPLE 3
on p. 27
for Exs. 21–26

21. $d = 100$ miles, $r = 25$ mi/h, $t = \underline{\ ?\ }$
22. $d = 16$ km, $r = \underline{\ ?\ }$, $t = 2$ h
23. $d = 9$ feet, $r = 3$ ft/sec, $t = \underline{\ ?\ }$
24. $d = \underline{\ ?\ }$, $r = 7$ in./min, $t = 9$ min
25. $d = 72$ miles, $r = \underline{\ ?\ }$, $t = 8$ hours
26. $d = 240$ yd, $r = 60$ yd/sec, $t = \underline{\ ?\ }$

27. ERROR ANALYSIS Describe and correct the error in writing the equation at the right.

What number divided by 7 is 28?
$7 \div x = 28$

28. ★ **MULTIPLE CHOICE** What is the solution of the equation $\frac{21}{a} = 3$?

(A) 3   (B) 7   (C) 18   (D) 63

29. ★ **MULTIPLE CHOICE** You are decorating a cake with 15 roses. You want an equal number of roses in each of the 3 rows on the cake. Which equation would you use to find the number of roses, r, in each row?

(A) $r + 3 = 15$ (B) $15 - r = 3$ (C) $3r = 15$ (D) $\frac{3}{r} = 15$

COMPARING SOLUTIONS Tell whether the equations have the same solution.

30. $x + 4 = 5$ and $x + 2 = 3$
31. $5y = 45$ and $6y = 48$
32. $12 - p = 11$ and $5 - p = 4$
33. $\frac{18}{b} = 6$ and $\frac{12}{b} = 3$

NUMBER SENSE Tell whether the equation has *no solution, one solution,* or *many solutions.*

34. $1 \cdot x = x$ **35.** $x + 3 = x + 4$ **36.** $0 \cdot x = 5$ **37.** $3x = 6x$

CHALLENGE Solve the equation using mental math.

38. $2p + 0 = 6$ **39.** $4 - 2a = 0$ **40.** $10 - 3y = 1$ **41.** $2x + 1 = 5$

PROBLEM SOLVING

SEE EXAMPLES 2 AND 3
on pp. 26–27
for Exs. 42–44

42. ST. LOUIS ARCH The elevator train inside the St. Louis Arch can carry a total of 40 people, with 5 people in each of the cars. Solve the equation $\frac{40}{c} = 5$ to find the number of cars in the elevator train.

43. AMUSEMENT PARKS You ride a log flume at an amusement park 6 times in a row. According to your watch, you spent a total of 18 minutes on the ride. Solve the equation $6n = 18$ to find the length (in minutes) of one ride.

44. BIKING You bike at approximately the same speed for 2 hours. You travel 24 miles. What is your speed?

SEE EXAMPLE 3
on p. 27
for Exs. 45–47

45. ★ **SHORT RESPONSE** An advertisement says that a ski lift can reach the top of a mountain in only 5 minutes. The distance the ski lift travels is 3000 feet. About how many feet per minute does the ski lift travel? *Explain* your reasoning.

46. **CHEETAHS** Find the approximate time it would take the cheetah in the diagram to run the distance shown.

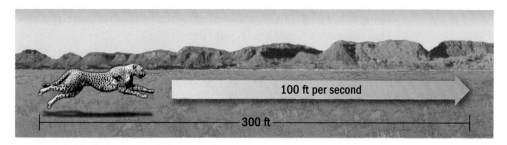

100 ft per second

300 ft

47. ★ **MULTIPLE CHOICE** Bats can fly at a speed of about 50 feet per second. At this speed, about how many seconds does it take a bat to fly 350 feet?

    A 6 seconds   **B** 7 seconds   **C** 70 seconds   **D** 300 seconds

48. **MULTI-STEP PROBLEM** The school treasurer has $40 to spend on a party for the students in band class. The party for the band class will cost $120.

  a. Solve the equation $x + \$40 = \$120$ to find how much more money the treasurer will need for the party.

  b. The class has 40 students. Use $\dfrac{\text{money needed}}{40} = \text{cost per student}$ to find how much each student will have to donate to pay for the party.

  c. If the number of students in the band class is greater than 40, what happens to the cost per student? *Explain.*

49. ◆ **MULTIPLE REPRESENTATIONS** Your friend is running a 1600 meter race. You can represent the situation using the equation $d + g = 1600$, where d represents the distance already run, and g represents distance still to go.

  a. Draw a Diagram Sketch a simple diagram of the situation, labeling d, g, and 1600.

  b. Make a Table Make a table to find possible values for g, using d-values of 0, 50, 100, 150, and 200.

  c. Use Words *Describe* the relationship between d and g using words.

50. ★ **OPEN-ENDED MATH** Describe a situation that could be modeled using the equation $x - 49 = 8$. Solve the equation. *Explain* what the solution represents in the situation.

51. ★ **WRITING** *Explain* why the equations $x + 3 = 5$ and $3 + x = 5$ have the same solution, but $x - 5 = 3$ and $5 - x = 3$ do not.

52. **CHALLENGE** You take 5 less than triple a number and add 7. The result is 14. Find the number. *Explain* how you found your answer.

53. CHALLENGE You spend half your money on a pair of shoes. You spend half of what you have left on a pair of pants. Then you spend half of what you have left on lunch. You have $10 left. How much money did you start with?

    a. Work Backward Use the strategy *work backward* to solve.

    b. Write an Equation Write and solve an equation to represent the situation.

    c. Compare Describe how the method in part (a) can help you write and solve the equation in part (b).

 NEW JERSEY MIXED REVIEW
 TEST PRACTICE at classzone.com

54. What is the value of the expression $36 \div 2 + (9 - 5)^2$?

    (A) 2   **(B)** 34   **(C)** 56   **(D)** 74

55. Which procedure can be used to determine how much longer the perimeter of rectangle A is than the perimeter of rectangle B?

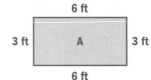 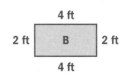

    (A) Add all the side lengths of rectangle A, and add all the side lengths of rectangle B. Then find the difference of the two values.

    (B) Add all the side lengths of rectangle A, and add all the side lengths of rectangle B. Then find the sum of the two values.

    (C) Multiply all the side lengths of rectangle A, and multiply all the side lengths of rectangle B. Then find the difference of the two values.

    (D) Multiply all the side lengths of rectangle A, and multiply all the side lengths of rectangle B. Then find the quotient of the two values.

Brain Game

Number Jumble

Copy the expression below. How can you fill in the boxes with the numbers 1, 2, 3, and 4 to make the expression have the greatest possible value? the least possible value?

 + **•** **−**

GOAL
Develop formulas for finding the areas of rectangles and the areas of squares.

MATERIALS
• graph paper

1.6 Investigating Area

The *area* of a figure is the number of square units needed to cover it. You can use graph paper to develop formulas for the areas of rectangles and squares.

EXPLORE **Find the area of a rectangle with a length of 10 units and a width of 4 units.**

STEP 1 On graph paper, draw a rectangle that has a length of 10 units and a width of 4 units.

STEP 2 Count the number of square units that cover the rectangle. The area is 40 square units.

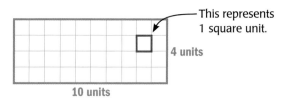

This represents 1 square unit.

4 units

10 units

PRACTICE **Find the area of the rectangle or square.**

1.

2.

3.

Using graph paper, draw a rectangle or square with the given dimensions. Then find the area.

4. Rectangle:
   length = 8 units
   width = 7 units
   area = __?__

5. Square:
   side length = 6 units
   area = __?__

6. Rectangle:
   length = 9 units
   width = 5 units
   area = __?__

7. The *perimeter* of a figure is the total length of its sides. For example, the perimeter of the rectangle above is 10 + 4 + 10 + 4, or 28 units. Find the perimeter of each rectangle or square in Exercises 1–6.

DRAW CONCLUSIONS

8. **WRITING** How can you use the length and the width of a rectangle to find its area? to find its perimeter? How can you use the side length of a square to find its area? to find its perimeter?

9. **REASONING** Write an equation that relates the area A, length l, and width w of a rectangle. Similarly, write an equation that relates the area A and side length s of a square.

10. **REASONING** Write equations for the perimeter of a rectangle and of a square.

1.6 Perimeter and Area

Before	You used properties of rectangles and squares.
Now	You'll use formulas to find perimeter and area.
Why?	So you can find the area of a wheelchair race course, as in Example 3.

KEY VOCABULARY
- perimeter, *p. 32*
- area, *p. 32*

The **perimeter** of a rectangle is the sum of the lengths of the sides. Perimeter is measured in linear units such as inches (in.), feet (ft), centimeters (cm), and meters (m).

The **area** of a rectangle is the number of square units needed to cover the rectangle. Area is measured in units such as square inches (in.^{2}), square feet (ft^2), square centimeters (cm^2), and square meters (m^2).

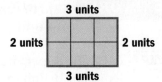

Perimeter = 3 + 3 + 2 + 2
= 10 units

Area = 6 square units

KEY CONCEPT

For Your Notebook

Perimeter and Area Formulas

	Rectangle	**Square**
	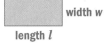 width w length l	side length s
Perimeter P	$P = 2l + 2w$	$P = 4s$
Area A	$A = lw$	$A = s^2$

EXAMPLE 1 Finding Perimeter

Find the perimeter of the rectangle or square with the given dimensions.

TAKE NOTES
You might want to write Example 1 in your notebook and include a diagram to help you remember the formulas for perimeter.

a. $l = 5$ feet, $w = 2$ feet

b. $s = 3$ centimeters

SOLUTION

a. $P = 2l + 2w$

$= 2(5) + 2(2)$

$= 10 + 4$

$= 14$

▶ **Answer** The perimeter is 14 ft.

b. $P = 4s$

$= 4(3)$

$= 12$

▶ **Answer** The perimeter is 12 cm.

EXAMPLE 2 Finding Area

 Find the area of the rectangle or square with the given dimensions.

REVIEW GEOMETRY
Need help with
rectangles and squares?
See p. 755.

a. $l = 5$ inches, $w = 3$ inches   **b.** $s = 10$ feet

SOLUTION

a. $A = lw$

$= 5(3)$

$= 15$

▸ **Answer** The area is 15 in.^{2}

b. $A = s^2$

$= 10^2$

$= 100$

▸ **Answer** The area is 100 ft^2.

✓ **GUIDED PRACTICE** | for Examples 1 and 2

Find the perimeter and area of the rectangle or square.

1.
2 m
6 m

2.
11 ft

3. Find the perimeter and the area of a rectangle that has a length of 6 inches and a width of 4 inches.

4. Find the perimeter and area of a square with sides that are 30 yards long.

EXAMPLE 3 Using Perimeter and Area

 Wheelchair Racing In a wheelchair slalom event, athletes weave around cones and race to the finish line. A diagram of the rectangular course is shown. Find the perimeter and the area of the course.

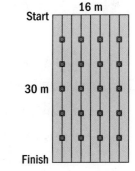
16 m
Start
30 m
Finish

SOLUTION

$P = 2l + 2w$

$= 2(30) + 2(16)$

$= 60 + 32 = 92$

$A = lw$

$= 30(16)$

$= 480$

▸ **Answer** The perimeter of the course is 92 m, and the area is 480 m^2.

Animated Math at classzone.com

✓ **GUIDED PRACTICE** | for Example 3

5. What If? In Example 3, suppose the wheelchair slalom course is 40 meters long and 24 meters wide. Find the perimeter and the area of the course.

EXAMPLE 4 Standardized Test Practice

Home Improvement You are planning to wallpaper one wall of your living room, as shown. You do not wallpaper over the window. One roll of wallpaper can cover 20 square feet. Which is the number of rolls of wallpaper you need to buy?

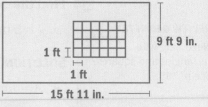

(A) 2 rolls   **(B)** 7 rolls   **(C)** 8 rolls   **(D)** 10 rolls

ELIMINATE CHOICES
The area of the entire wall is approximately 160 square feet. You will need a maximum of eight rolls of wallpaper. So, you can eliminate choice D.

SOLUTION

STEP 1 **Estimate** the wall's area using $l = 16$ feet and $w = 10$ feet.
$$A = \text{length} \times \text{width} = 16(10) = 160 \text{ ft}^2$$

STEP 2 **Calculate** the window's area: $A = \text{length} \times \text{width} = 6(4) = 24 \text{ ft}^2$.

STEP 3 **Subtract** to find the area you need to cover: $160 - 24 = 136 \text{ ft}^2$.

STEP 4 **Divide** the area by 20 to find the rolls needed: $136 \div 20 = 6 \text{ R } 16$.

▶ **Answer** You need more than 6 rolls of wallpaper. So, you will need to buy 7 rolls of wallpaper. The correct answer is B. **(A)** **(B)** **(C)** **(D)**

✓ **GUIDED PRACTICE** | for Example 4

6. **What If?** In Example 4, suppose the wall is 23 feet 11 inches long and 11 feet 10 inches high. How many rolls of wallpaper do you need?

1.6 EXERCISES

HOMEWORK KEY   ★ = **STANDARDIZED TEST PRACTICE**
Exs. 15, 29, 30, 31, and 44

○ = **HINTS AND HOMEWORK HELP**
for Exs. 3, 5, 7, 27 at classzone.com

SKILL PRACTICE

VOCABULARY Copy and complete the statement.

1. The sum of the lengths of the sides of a rectangle is the __?__ of the rectangle.

2. A 3 foot by 6 foot rectangle has a(n) __?__ of 18 __?__ feet.

SEE EXAMPLES 1 AND 2
on pp. 32–33
for Exs. 3–5

GEOMETRY Find the perimeter and the area of the rectangle or square.

3.  3 m
15 m

4. 20 in.

5. **ERROR ANALYSIS** Describe and correct the error at the right in finding the perimeter of the square shown.

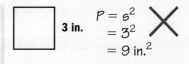

FINDING PERIMETER AND AREA Find the perimeter and the area of the rectangle or square with the given dimensions.

SEE EXAMPLES 1 AND 2
on pp. 32–33
for Exs. 6–13

6. $l = 12$ inches, $w = 4$ inches

7. $l = 9$ meters, $w = 7$ meters

8. $s = 2$ centimeters

9. $l = 20$ feet, $w = 2$ feet

10. $s = 17$ meters

11. $l = 11$ inches, $w = 6$ inches

12. $l = 15$ feet, $w = 4$ feet

13. $s = 12$ centimeters

14. MODELS The model at the right represents 8^2. Draw a model that represents 11^2.

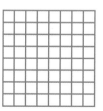

15. ★ **MULTIPLE CHOICE** Which of the following is *not* a perimeter?

Ⓐ 32 in. Ⓑ 60 ft Ⓒ 42 m Ⓓ 38 ft^2

ALGEBRA Find the unknown dimension of the rectangle or square.

16. $P = 24$ in., $s = $?

17. $A = 8$ ft^2, $l = 4$ ft, $w = $?

18. $A = 49$ cm^2, $s = $?

19. $P = 22$ m, $w = 3$ m, $l = $?

GEOMETRY The figures below can be divided into rectangles and squares. Find the perimeter and the area of each figure. *Explain* your method.

20.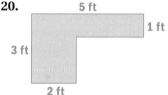

21.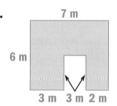

22.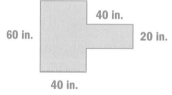

CHALLENGE Find the perimeter of the figure.

23. a square with an area of 144 ft^2

24. a square with an area of 196 ft^2

25. a rectangle with an area of 28 m^2 and a width of 4 m

PROBLEM SOLVING

SEE EXAMPLE 3
on p. 33
for Exs. 26–29

26. POOLS Your gym's pool has a length of 25 meters and a width of 12 meters. Find the perimeter and the area of the pool.

27. ART A rectangular painting has a width of 4 feet and a length of 7 feet. Find the perimeter and the area of the painting.

28. BASKETBALL A high school basketball court is a rectangle with length 84 feet and width 50 feet. Find the perimeter and the area of the court.

29. ★ **SHORT RESPONSE** A rectangular garden is 6 feet long and 4 feet wide. A square garden is 5 feet long. Which garden has the greater area? Which garden requires more fencing? *Explain*.

SEE EXAMPLE 4
on p. 34
for Ex. 30

30. ★ **MULTIPLE CHOICE** Your family is getting wall-to-wall carpeting installed in your living room and den, as shown. The carpeting costs $20 per square yard. What is the total cost for the carpeting?

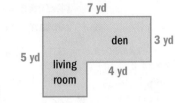

A $380   **B** $460   **C** $540   **D** $820

31. ★ **WRITING** Find the length of a side of a square whose perimeter and area are the same number, though not the same unit. *Explain* your reasoning.

THEATRE William Shakespeare's plays were originally performed in London's Globe Theatre.

SEE EXAMPLE 3
on p. 33
for Exs. 32–34

32. The original Globe Theatre was built in 1598 but no longer exists. Its rectangular stage had a length of 43 feet and a width of 28 feet. Find the stage's area and perimeter.

33. The new Globe Theatre, shown at the right, opened in 1997. Its rectangular stage has a length of 44 feet and a width of 25 feet. Find the stage's area and perimeter.

34. Compare your answers from Exercises 32 and 33.

35. **PAINTING** You are planning to spray paint the fronts and backs of two doors. Each door is 3 feet by 7 feet with a window of area 3 square feet. You will not paint the windows. One can of paint will cover between 22 and 30 square feet.

Estimate the least number of cans and the greatest number of cans you will need. How many cans of paint should you buy for this project? *Explain* your reasoning.

36. **CHALLENGE** If you fence a section of pasture in a square, then each side measures 20 feet. Find a way to fence the pasture in a rectangle with the same perimeter but less area. *Explain* whether it is possible to fence the land in a rectangle with greater area and less perimeter.

 NEW JERSEY MIXED REVIEW **TEST PRACTICE** at classzone.com

37. It takes Janet 30 minutes to walk home from school. She walks at a speed of 264 feet per minute. Which equation can be used to find the distance d, in feet, from school to her house?

A $d = 264 + 30$ **B** $d = (264)(30)$

C $d = 264 - 30$ **D** $d = 264 \div 30$

38. George can run 100 meters in 22 seconds. If he competes in a 500 meter race at that speed, about how many seconds will it take him to complete the race?

A 4 sec   **B** 110 sec   **C** 440 sec   **D** 11,000 sec

1.7 A Problem Solving Plan

 4.5.A.1 Learn mathematics through problem solving, inquiry, and discovery.

Before You used the problem solving strategy *look for a pattern*.

Now You'll use a 4-step plan to solve many kinds of problems.

Why? So you can choose the marching band's songs, as in Examples 1 and 2.

KEY VOCABULARY
- **sum,** *p. 742*
- **difference,** *p. 742*
- **product,** *p. 743*
- **quotient,** *p. 744*

Marching Band Your school's marching band can play for up to 14 minutes at the halftime show. The band must choose 3 songs from the table, and one of the songs must be the school song. What songs can the band play?

Marching Band Songs	Time (minutes)
School song	3
A	6
B	5
C	4
D	7

EXAMPLE 1 Understanding and Planning

To solve the marching band problem, you need to make sure you understand the problem. Then make a plan for solving the problem.

READ AND UNDERSTAND

What do you know?

The marching band can play for up to 14 minutes.

The table gives the playing times for songs.

The band must choose three songs, and one has to be the school song.

What do you want to find out?

What combinations of songs can the marching band play?

MAKE A PLAN

REVIEW PROBLEM SOLVING STRATEGIES To review problem solving strategies, see pp. 761–770.

How can you relate what you know to what you want to find out?

Find the time left available after playing the school song.

List all the possible combinations of two songs (excluding the school song) and the time it takes to play them.

Identify the combinations that fit within the available time.

✓ **GUIDED PRACTICE** for Example 1

1. In the table above, how many minutes long is the school song?

2. How many minutes does this leave for playing the other two songs?

EXAMPLE 2 Solving and Looking Back

USE A PATTERN

Notice the pattern of song pairings in the table:

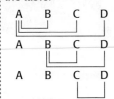

Using a pattern like this guarantees that you don't miss any song pairings.

To solve the marching band problem from the previous page, you need to carry out the plan from Example 1 and then check the answer.

SOLVE THE PROBLEM

Because of the school song requirement, there are $14 - 3 = 11$ minutes for playing the other two songs. Make a list of all the combinations of two songs, and the time it takes to play them.

Songs	Total Time
A: 6 min, B: 5 min	**11 min**
A: 6 min, C: 4 min	**10 min**
A: 6 min, D: 7 min	13 min
B: 5 min, C: 4 min	**9 min**
B: 5 min, D: 7 min	12 min
C: 4 min, D: 7 min	**11 min**

> Look for combinations that have a total playing time less than or equal to 11 minutes.

▸ **Answer** The marching band can play the school song and either songs A and B, songs A and C, songs B and C, or songs C and D.

LOOK BACK

Song C is the shortest song and song D is the longest song. So it makes sense that song C appears most often and song D appears least often. The answer seems reasonable.

Animated Math at classzone.com

✓ **GUIDED PRACTICE** for Example 2

3. **What If?** In Example 2, suppose song C is 6 minutes long. What songs can the marching band play with the school song?

KEY CONCEPT   *For Your Notebook*

The Problem Solving Plan

1. **Read and Understand** Read the problem carefully. Identify the question and any important information.

2. **Make a Plan** Decide on a problem solving strategy.

3. **Solve the Problem** Use the problem solving strategy to answer the question.

4. **Look Back** Check that your answer is reasonable.

1.7 EXERCISES

HOMEWORK KEY

★ = **STANDARDIZED TEST PRACTICE**
Exs. 7, 11, 12, 16, 20, and 28

◯ = **HINTS AND HOMEWORK HELP**
for Exs. 3, 5, 11, 13 at classzone.com

SKILL PRACTICE

1. VOCABULARY Describe all four steps of the problem solving plan.

UNDERSTANDING PROBLEM SOLVING In Exercises 2–4, identify what you know and what you need to find out. You do not need to solve the problem.

SEE EXAMPLE 1
on p. 37
for Exs. 2–4

2. You bought a package of 12 pens for $3. What is the cost per pen?

③. A customer bought a lunch that cost $4.99 and a drink that cost $.99. The customer paid with a $10 bill. How much change did the customer receive?

4. You take a ferry boat a distance of 50 miles to get to an island. The trip takes you 2 hours. At about what speed does the ferry boat travel?

SEE EXAMPLE 2
on p. 38
for Exs. 5–8

⑤. ERROR ANALYSIS Describe and correct the error made in solving the following problem.

You spent a total of $22 for yourself and a friend at the movies. You spent $6 on snacks. How much did each movie ticket cost?

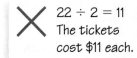

22 ÷ 2 = 11
The tickets cost $11 each.

6. BASEBALL A baseball game ticket costs $15. Tom goes to the game and has 3 hot dogs during the game. Hot dogs cost $2 each. Your friend says that Tom spent $21. *Explain* how to check your friend's answer.

7. ★ MULTIPLE CHOICE Which expression could you evaluate to find the answer to Exercise 3?

Ⓐ $4.99 + $.99

Ⓑ $10 − $4.99 + $.99

Ⓒ $4.99 − $.99

Ⓓ $10 − ($4.99 + $.99)

8. USING THE PROBLEM SOLVING PLAN You are ordering whole pans of lasagna for a party. One pan of lasagna serves 8 people. You expect 52 people at the party. How many pans of lasagna should you order?

  a. What are you trying to find?

  b. What operation should you use to find an answer?

  c. Write an expression to find the answer. Evaluate your expression.

  d. Is your answer reasonable? You cannot order part of a pan of lasagna.

9. CHALLENGE Mary and Donata have lunch, and each agrees to pay half of the $30 cost (which includes tax and tip). Mary has two $10 bills, and Donata has a $20 bill and two $5 bills. Is there a way for them to each pay half of the bill without getting change? *Explain.*

10. HOMEWORK Your favorite TV show starts at 9 P.M. Before it starts, you have to complete 20 minutes of social studies homework, 30 minutes of math homework, and 15 minutes of science homework. What is the latest time you can start your homework and be done by 9 P.M.?

11. ★ SHORT RESPONSE Why is it important to look back at your solution to a problem after you have solved the problem?

12. ★ MULTIPLE CHOICE A 6-pack of bottled water costs $2.19, and energy bars cost $1.39 each. Dan bought two 6-packs of water and 12 energy bars. Find the total amount he spent on water and energy bars.

(A) $21.06   **(B)** $29.82   **(C)** $34.20   **(D)** $42.96

13. ORIGAMI In origami, you can fold paper to make models of animals. The number of origami peacocks Jane makes on each of four days is given in the table. If she continues this folding pattern, on which day will Jane have a total of 70 peacocks?

Day	Peacocks
1	1
2	4
3	7
4	10

14. NUMBER SENSE The sum of the digits of a two digit number is 7. The tens' digit is 3 more than the ones' digit. What is the number?

15. LOOK FOR A PATTERN A drill team formation has 1 member in the first row, 3 in the second row, 5 in the third row, and so on. The formation has 8 rows. How many team members are in the formation?

16. ★ WRITING You buy a 5 pound bag of apples for $2.50. Do you have enough information to find the cost per apple? *Explain* your reasoning.

17. REASONING You want to place solar lanterns 3 yards apart on the perimeter of the backyard shown below.

Your friend says "you need 4 lanterns for each 9 yard side and 10 lanterns for each 27 yard side. So you need 2(4) + 2(10) = 28 lanterns." Do you agree with your friend? *Explain* why or why not. If not, how many lamps do you need?

18. USE A VENN DIAGRAM In your 32-student class, 14 students are wearing blue shirts and 17 are wearing gym shoes. If 7 students are wearing both blue shirts and gym shoes, how many students are wearing neither?

CHOOSE A STRATEGY Use a strategy from the list to solve the problem. Explain your choice of strategy.

Problem Solving Strategies
- Draw a Diagram *(p. 762)*
- Make a List *(p. 765)*
- Look for a Pattern *(p. 766)*

19. Karen, Ty, Mark, and Cindy are standing in line to buy movie tickets. Ty is directly behind Cindy. Mark is not last in line. Cindy is the first person in line. In what order are these four people standing?

20. ★ **EXTENDED RESPONSE** Manuel uses the small squares on a piece of graph paper to draw a 13-unit by 8-unit rectangle.

  a. What is the largest square Manuel can cut from the rectangle if the square is composed only of complete small squares? *Explain.*

  b. Manuel continues this with the remainder of the rectangle, cutting out the largest possible square each time, until he cannot make a square larger than a small square. Describe each square made.

  c. How many unused small squares are left from the original rectangle at the end of this process?

21. **CHALLENGE** You are camping and have only a 3 cup container and a 5 cup container. You need to measure 1 cup of water into a pot. How can you do this? Is there more than one way? *Explain.*

 NEW JERSEY MIXED REVIEW **TEST PRACTICE** at classzone.com

22. A farmer is planning to build a fence around a square field that has a side length of 145 feet. The fence is constructed using two strands of wire, as shown. One roll of wire covers 50 feet. How many rolls of wire are needed?

  A 11 rolls

  B 12 rolls

  C 23 rolls

  D 24 rolls

QUIZ *for Lessons 1.5–1.7*

Solve the equation using mental math. *(p. 25)*

1. $6 + m = 18$　　**2.** $83 = 90 - b$　　**3.** $16y = 32$　　**4.** $\dfrac{32}{z} = 4$

Find the perimeter and the area of the figure. *(p. 32)*

5. a 3 foot by 9 foot rectangle　　　**6.** a square with 15 inch sides

7. **TRAVEL** A train travels at a constant speed of 50 miles per hour for 150 miles. A bus travels at a constant speed of 60 miles per hour for 240 miles. Which trip takes less time? (*Hint:* Use the formula $d = rt$.) *(p. 37)*

Lessons 1.5–1.7

1. **SWIMMING POOL** The length and width of a swimming pool are shown.

10 feet

30 feet

A 4-foot wide walkway is put around the pool. What is the combined area of the pool and walkway?

A. 300 ft^2 C. 476 ft^2

B. 420 ft^2 D. 684 ft^2

2. **BUSINESS TRIP** Meredith drove from her company headquarters to visit 3 company offices, located in 3 cities. The distances in miles are shown. She drove at a constant speed of 30 miles per hour. She stopped for an equal amount of time at each office. She completed the entire trip in 3 hours. For how many minutes did she stop at each office?

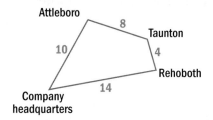

Attleboro

8

Taunton

10

4

Rehoboth

14

Company
headquarters

A. 25   B. 27   C. 30   D. 36

3. **AREA** Find the area of the shaded region.

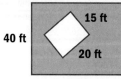

15 ft

40 ft

20 ft

50 ft

A. 180 ft^2 C. 1700 ft^2

B. 300 ft^2 D. 2000 ft^2

4. **SPEED** A car drives at a constant speed of 50 miles per hour. How long will it take the car to travel 200 miles?

A. 4 min

B. 2 h

C. 4 h

D. 10 h

5. **HIKING** On a 3-day hiking trip, you hiked the same distance on the first and second days, and 7 miles on the third day. You hiked a total of 23 miles. How many miles did you hike on the first day?

A. 7

B. 8

C. 16

D. 23

6. **OPEN-ENDED** You are trying to fit all of your family's home videos on two 2-hour videotapes. The table below lists the lengths in minutes of the video clips.

Clip	Minutes
A	40
B	60
C	10
D	80
E	20
F	30

• Which clips would you put on each videotape?

• Is there more than one way you could do this? *Explain.*

@HomeTutor
classzone.com
Vocabulary Practice

REVIEW KEY VOCABULARY

- variable, *p. 8*
- variable expression, *p. 8*
- evaluate, *p. 8*
- power, *p. 13*

- base, *p. 13*
- exponent, *p. 13*
- order of operations, *p. 17*
- equation, *p. 25*

- solution, *p. 25*
- solving an equation, *p. 26*
- perimeter, *p. 32*
- area, *p. 32*

VOCABULARY EXERCISES

1. Copy and complete: A(n) ___?___ of an equation is a number that you can substitute for the variable to make the equation true.

2. Copy and complete: The ___?___ of a rectangle is the number of square units needed to cover the rectangle.

3. What does an equation have that an expression does not?

4. What are the two parts of a power? Give an example of a power and label these two parts.

REVIEW EXAMPLES AND EXERCISES

1.1 Describing Patterns
pp. 3–7

EXAMPLE

Describe the pattern: 1, 7, 49, 343, ... Then write the next three numbers.

You multiply the previous number by 7 to get the next number in the pattern.

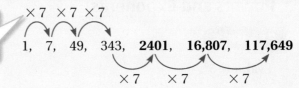

$\times 7 \quad \times 7 \quad \times 7$

1, 7, 49, 343, **2401, 16,807, 117,649**

$\times 7 \quad \times 7 \quad \times 7$

EXERCISES

Describe the pattern. Then write the next three numbers.

SEE EXAMPLES
2 AND 3
on pp. 3–4
for Exs. 5–10

5. 1, 11, 21, 31, . . .

6. 50, 44, 38, 32, . . .

7. 25, 50, 100, 200, . . .

8. 320, 160, 80, 40, . . .

9. 100, 97, 94, 91, . . .

10. 8, 20, 32, 44, . . .

Describe the pattern. Then draw the next three figures.

SEE EXAMPLE 4
on p. 4
for Exs. 11–12

11.

12.

Variables and Expressions   *pp. 8–11*

EXAMPLE

Evaluate the expression when $x = 5$.

a. $8x$

$8x = 8(5)$ **Substitute 5 for x.**

$\quad = 40$ **Multiply.**

b. $\dfrac{60}{x}$

$\dfrac{60}{x} = \dfrac{60}{5}$ **Substitute 5 for x.**

$\quad = 12$ **Divide.**

EXERCISES

Evaluate the expression for the given value of the variable.

SEE EXAMPLES 1, 2, AND 3
on pp. 8–9
for Exs. 13–22

13. $9x$ when $x = 7$

14. $14 + s$ when $s = 12$

15. $\dfrac{y}{8}$ when $y = 40$

16. $t - 3$ when $t = 11$

17. $a + 19$ when $a = 13$

18. $10p$ when $p = 16$

19. $\dfrac{k}{9}$ when $k = 63$

20. $5w$ when $w = 14$

21. $17 - c$ when $c = 8$

22. Games You are playing a game in which you try to hit a target with bean bags. Your total score can be found by evaluating the expression $10r + 5b$, where r is the number of times you hit the red zone and b is the number of times you hit the blue zone. Find your total score for hitting the red zone 6 times and hitting the blue zone 4 times.

1.3 **Powers and Exponents**   *pp. 13–16*

EXAMPLE

Evaluate 5^3.

$5^3 = 5 \cdot 5 \cdot 5$ **Write 5 as a factor 3 times.**

$\quad = 125$ **Multiply.**

EXERCISES

Evaluate the power.

SEE EXAMPLE 2
on p. 14
for Exs. 23–34

23. 10^2

24. 7^3

25. 2^5

26. 8^2

27. 3^5

28. 4^4

29. 9^3

30. 5^4

31. 15^1

32. 6^2

33. 1^4

34. 12^2

1.4 Order of Operations

pp. 17–22

EXAMPLE

Evaluate the expression $2 \times 3^3 + (20 - 6) \div 7$.

$$2 \times 3^3 + (20 - 6) \div 7 = 2 \times 3^3 + 14 \div 7 \qquad \text{Evaluate inside grouping symbols.}$$

$$= 2 \times 27 + 14 \div 7 \qquad \text{Evaluate powers.}$$

$$= \quad 54 \quad + \quad 2 \qquad \text{Multiply and divide from left to right.}$$

$$= 56 \qquad \text{Add and subtract from left to right.}$$

EXERCISES

Evaluate the expression.

SEE EXAMPLES 1, 3, AND 4
on pp. 17–18
for Exs. 35–46

35. $50 - 2 \cdot 10 + 4$ **36.** $\dfrac{5 \cdot 6}{6 + 9}$ **37.** $3(15 \div 3)^2$ **38.** $4 + 3(7 + 5)$

39. $6 - 15 \div 3 + 2$ **40.** $2(7^2 - 35) - 10$ **41.** $39 - (1 + 5)^2$ **42.** $\dfrac{(1 + 4)^3}{10 \div 2}$

43. $8(2 \times 3 \div 3)^3$ **44.** $12 + 1 - 3 \times 4$ **45.** $\dfrac{6^2 + 4}{9 - 1}$ **46.** $1 + 6(2 + 8)$

1.5 Equations and Mental Math

pp. 25–30

EXAMPLE

Solve the equation $n - 7 = 15$ using mental math.

Ask yourself "What number minus 7 equals 15?" Check 22 as a possible solution.

$$n - 7 = 15 \qquad \text{Write equation.}$$

$$22 - 7 \overset{?}{=} 15 \qquad \text{Substitute 22 for } n.$$

$$15 = 15 \qquad \text{The equation is true.}$$

EXERCISES

Solve the equation using mental math.

SEE EXAMPLE 2
on p. 26
for Exs. 47–62

47. $x + 9 = 13$ **48.** $36 = 14 + a$ **49.** $w - 10 = 11$ **50.** $8 - r = 2$

51. $25 = 5t$ **52.** $11p = 110$ **53.** $\dfrac{m}{4} = 7$ **54.** $\dfrac{32}{n} = 16$

55. $b - 5 = 25$ **56.** $18 = 2 + z$ **57.** $12 - c = 9$ **58.** $d + 11 = 33$

59. $16 = 4h$ **60.** $7q = 35$ **61.** $20 = \dfrac{y}{6}$ **62.** $\dfrac{70}{m} = 2$

1.6 Perimeter and Area

pp. 32–36

EXAMPLE

Floor Plans Your rectangular bedroom has a length of 11 feet and a width of 8 feet. Find the perimeter and the area of your bedroom.

$$P = 2l + 2w \qquad\qquad A = lw$$
$$= 2(11) + 2(8) \qquad\qquad = 11(8)$$
$$= 22 + 16 \qquad\qquad = 88 \text{ square feet}$$
$$= 38 \text{ feet}$$

SEE EXAMPLES 1 AND 2 on pp. 32–33 for Exs. 63–68

EXERCISES

Find the perimeter and the area of the rectangle or square with the given dimensions.

63. $l = 16$ ft, $w = 3$ ft   **64.** $l = 10$ m, $w = 7$ m   **65.** $s = 35$ in.

66. $l = 8$ cm, $w = 2$ cm   **67.** $s = 15$ yd   **68.** $l = 14$ mi, $w = 6$ mi

1.7 A Problem Solving Plan

pp. 37–41

EXAMPLE

Field Trip Your school is organizing a field trip for 81 students and 13 teachers. A bus can hold a maximum of 40 people. How many buses do you need for the field trip?

Read and Understand You want to find the number of buses needed to transport 81 students and 13 teachers.

Make a Plan You can divide the total number of people by the number of people one bus can hold to find the number of buses needed.

Solve the Problem Find the total number of people: $81 + 13 = 94$. Divide the total number of people by 40: $94 \div 40 = 2$ R14. So you need 3 buses.

Look Back Check your answer. Three buses can hold $40 \times 3 = 120$ people, which is more than the $81 + 13 = 94$ people in the group.

▸ **Answer** You need three buses for the field trip.

SEE EXAMPLES 1 AND 2 on pp. 37–38 for Ex. 69

EXERCISES

69. Vending Machines You put a dollar into a vending machine to get a $.65 bag of popcorn. List the different combinations of dimes, nickels, and quarters that you could receive as change.

CHAPTER TEST

Describe the pattern. Then write the next three numbers.

1. 10, 20, 40, 80, . . .

2. 99, 88, 77, 66, . . .

3. 16, 21, 26, 31, . . .

Evaluate the expression for the given value of the variable.

4. $28 - a$ when $a = 7$

5. $n + 14$ when $n = 19$

6. $8y$ when $y = 15$

Evaluate the power.

7. 4^3

8. 9^4

9. 5^5

Evaluate the expression.

10. $20 + 16 \div 4$

11. $15 - 3(5 - 3)^2$

12. $4 \cdot 8 + 8 \div 4$

13. $9 \cdot (2 + 14 \div 7)$

14. $(28 \div 2^2 - 6) + 10$

15. $3^3 + 7 - 5$

Solve the equation using mental math.

16. $13 + q = 27$

17. $7 = \dfrac{56}{w}$

18. $10r = 1000$

19. $x - 13 = 3$

20. $\dfrac{y}{7} = 8$

21. $t + 4 = 11$

Find the perimeter and the area of the rectangle or square with the given dimensions.

22. $l = 7$ in., $w = 5$ in.

23. $s = 14$ cm

24. $l = 9$ m, $w = 4$ m

25. **WALLPAPER** Describe the wallpaper pattern. Then draw the next three figures.

26. **SHOPPING** A clothing store is having a sale. If you buy one sweater, you can get another sweater of equal or lesser value for half price. You buy a $38 sweater and a $42 sweater. Evaluate the expression $42 + 38 \div 2$ to find the total cost of the sweaters.

27. **ARTS AND CRAFTS** You have several rectangular photographs that are each 7 inches long and 5 inches wide, and you have 80 inches of yarn. Around how many photographs can you put yarn borders?

28. **RUNNING** A runner is following the training schedule below. How many miles do you predict the runner will run on each of the next 3 days?

Days	Su	M	T	W	Th	F	S	Su	M	T	W	Th
Miles	0	3	5	3	0	3	6	3	0	3	7	3

REVIEWING THE PROBLEM SOLVING PLAN

To solve math problems, you need to approach the problem with an organized plan. You should read the problem carefully and identify all important information. Then make a plan and solve the problem.

EXAMPLE 1

Karate A community center is organizing karate classes. Each class can have a maximum of 22 people. There are 130 people interested in taking a karate class. How many classes should the center hold?

Solution

STEP 1 **Read and Understand** You need to find the number of classes that must be held to cover 130 people.

STEP 2 **Make a Plan** You can divide the total number of people by the maximum number of people one class can hold to find the number of classes needed.

STEP 3 **Solve the Problem** Divide: $130 \div 22 = 5$ R20. It does not make sense to hold part of a class. So, 6 classes are needed.

STEP 4 **Look Back** Check your answer. Six classes can hold $22 \times 6 = 132$ people, which is more than 130.

▶ **Answer** The recreation center should hold 6 classes.

EXAMPLE 2

Party Supplies Emma is planning a surprise birthday party for a friend. She has $25 to buy supplies. She buys 10 balloons for $1, 3 rolls of crepe paper for $2 per roll, 3 bottles of soda, and a cake for $10. What other information is necessary to find Emma's correct change?

Solution

Read and understand the problem. Then organize the given information in a table and identify what is missing.

Emma needs to know the cost of each soda bottle before she can determine her correct change.

Item	Cost
10 balloons	$1
3 rolls of crepe paper	$3 \times 2 = \$6$
a bottle of soda	$3 \times$ __?__ $=$ __?__
one cake	$10

PROBLEM SOLVING

Below are examples of problems in multiple choice format. Try solving the problems before looking at the solutions. (Cover the solutions with a piece of paper.) Then check your solutions against the ones given.

1. Mrs. Smith is buying supplies for her art room. She would like each of her students to have his or her own paintbrush. The table below shows the number of students in each of her art classes. Paintbrushes are sold in boxes of 15. How many boxes of paintbrushes should she buy?

Class	Number of students
1	22
2	28
3	18
4	32
5	16

A. 5 boxes

B. 6 boxes

C. 7 boxes

D. 8 boxes

Solution

Read and Understand You need to determine how many boxes of paintbrushes Mrs. Smith must buy so that each student has one.

Make a Plan Find the total number of students in all 5 classes. This is how many paintbrushes are needed. Divide this number by the number of paintbrushes in each box.

Solve the Problem

Find total: $22 + 28 + 18 + 32 + 16 = 116$.

Divide: $116 \div 15 = 7$ R11.

You cannot buy part of a box. So, Mrs. Smith must buy 8 boxes of paintbrushes.

Look Back Check your answer. Eight boxes contain $15 \times 8 = 120$ paintbrushes, which is more than the total number of students, 116.

The correct answer is D.

2. Your class is having a bake sale to raise money for a trip. You sell the cookies individually for $1 each or by the dozen for $8. You raised $78 on the first day of the bake sale. What necessary information do you need to find the total number of cookies you sold on the first day?

A. The number of cookies sold on day 2

B. The number of individual cookies that you sold the first day

C. The number of people selling the cookies

D. The number of cookies you made in preparation for the bake sale

Solution

You know the selling prices for the cookies.

one cookie = $1   dozen cookies = $8

You also know that $78 was raised on the first day of the bake sale.

You want to find the total number of cookies that you sold on the first day of the sale. To find this, you must know either the number of individual cookies sold or the number of dozens sold on the first day.

So the correct answer is B.

TEST PREPARATION

TEST PREPARATION

1. The director of a recreational center is organizing a girls' softball league. Each team can have a minimum of 9 girls. There are 96 girls are registered to play softball. How many teams should the league plan to have?

   A. 10 teams

   B. 11 teams

   C. 12 teams

   D. 13 teams

2. Alberta sells part of her stamp collection to make money. She sells the stamps for $2 each. She sold 25 stamps on Monday and 15 stamps on Tuesday. What information is necessary to find how many stamps she has remaining in her collection at the end of the day on Tuesday?

   A. Total number of stamps sold

   B. Number of stamps sold in the remaining portion of the week

   C. Total number of customers

   D. Number of stamps in her original collection

3. Mr. Collins wants to reseed his backyard but not his garden. Which expression gives the total area he must reseed?

   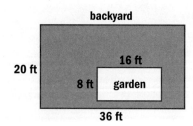
   backyard
   20 ft
   16 ft
   8 ft   garden
   36 ft

   A. $(20 \cdot 36)$

   B. $(20 \cdot 36) - (8 \cdot 16)$

   C. $(20 - 8)(36 - 16)$

   D. $(2 \cdot 20 + 2 \cdot 36) - (2 \cdot 8 + 2 \cdot 16)$

4. Nick, Katie, and Paul eat out at a restaurant. They decide to split the bill evenly. The total cost of the meals is $23, and they leave a $4 tip. Which strategy could you use to determine how much Katie should pay?

   A. Divide the total cost of the meals by 3 and then add $4.

   B. Divide the total cost of the meals by 3 and then subtract $4.

   C. Add $23 and $4. Divide the result by 3.

   D. Subtract $4 from $23. Divide the result by 3.

5. The bar graph shows the revenues of four different companies. Which statement is NOT supported by the graph?

   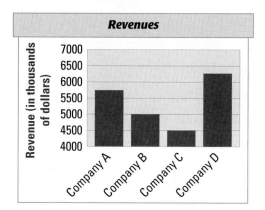
   Revenues

   A. Company A produced more revenue than Company D.

   B. Company B produced less revenue than Company A.

   C. Company C produced the least amount of revenue.

   D. Company D produced the greatest amount of revenue.

6. In what order should you perform operations to correctly evaluate the expression $64 - 8 \times 2^2$?

    A. Evaluate the power, subtract, and then multiply.

    B. Subtract, evaluate the power, and then multiply.

    C. Evaluate the power, multiply, and then subtract.

    D. Multiply, evaluate the power, and then subtract.

7. What is the approximate area of the rectangle shown below?

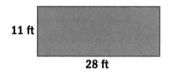

    11 ft

    28 ft

    A. 80 ft^2

    B. 200 ft^2

    C. 250 ft^2

    D. 300 ft^2

8. Josh bought 4 CDs for $18 each. About how much did he spend?

    A. Less than $59

    B. Between $60 and $79

    C. Between $80 and $99

    D. More than $100

9. Which expression is NOT equivalent to the expression $(5 - 3)^2 + 6 \div 2$?

    A. $2^2 + 6 \div 2$

    B. $(5 - 3)^2 + (6 \div 2)$

    C. $(2^2 + 6) \div 2$

    D. $(5 - 3)^2 + 3$

10. Evaluate the expression $13x + 2y$ when $x = 1$ and $y = 6$.

    A. 22

    B. 25

    C. 32

    D. 80

11. Which problem can be solved using the expression $2 \cdot 6 + 2 \cdot 12$?

    A. The width of a rectangle is 12 units long and the length is twice as long as its width. What is the perimeter of the rectangle?

    B. You can run 2 miles in 12 minutes and bike 2 miles in 6 minutes. How long would it take you to run 2 miles and bike 2 miles?

    C. A rectangle has a length of 12 units and a width of 6 units. What is the area of the rectangle?

    D. It costs $6 for a student and $12 for an adult to attend a baseball game. How much would it cost for 2 adults and 2 students to attend a game?

12. **OPEN-ENDED** Your family wants to carpet the rectangular floor at the right.

    16 ft

    11 ft

    Part A How many square feet of carpet are needed?

    Part B The carpet that your family picked out at a flooring store costs $2 per square foot. The store also charges $85 for installation. How much will the carpet and installation cost? *Justify* your answer.

TEST PREPARATION

2 Decimal Operations

Fish $58

Backpack $22

Ba

Before

In previous courses you've ...

- Added, subtracted, multiplied, and divided whole numbers
- Compared whole numberss

Now

New Jersey Standards

4.1.A.4	2.1	Comparing decimals
4.1.B.1.a	2.2	Adding and subtracting
4.1.B.1.a	2.3	Multiplying decimals
4.1.B.1.a	2.4	Dividing decimals
4.1.A.5	2.5	Scientific notation
4.2.D.2	2.6	Metric units
4.2.D.1	2.7	Metric conversions

Why?

So you can solve real-world problems about ...

- earthquakes, p. 59
- cornfield mazes, p. 63
- comets, p. 69
- gorillas, p. 94

 Animated Math

at classzone.com

- Adding Decimals, p. 60
- Multiplying Decimals, p. 66
- Decimal Eliminator, p. 71

Get-Ready Games

Review Prerequisite Skills by playing *Mall Math.*

Skill Focus:

- Comparing whole numbers
- Adding whole numbers

MALL MATH

MATERIALS

- *Mall Math* game board
- 1 number cube
- 2 place markers

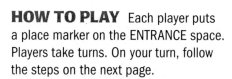

HOW TO PLAY Each player puts a place marker on the ENTRANCE space. Players take turns. On your turn, follow the steps on the next page.

1 **ROLL** the number cube and move that many spaces. You cannot move diagonally or pass through the empty spaces.

2 **BUY** the item in the space you have landed on. Cross out that space on the board. Players may land on that space on later turns, but they cannot purchase the item again.

3 **KEEP** a running tally of your spending by adding the price of the new item to your previous total.

$$\begin{array}{r} 42 \\ +\,17 \\ \hline 59 \end{array}$$

HOW TO WIN The first player to spend at least $500 wins.

Stop and Think

1. **WRITING** Suppose you are at the mall entrance. Describe how you could spend at least $500 in only 4 rolls. What would the rolls have to be, and what items would you buy?

2. **CRITICAL THINKING** Suppose you are on the goldfish space and you know that your next two rolls will be a 2 and then a 3. Where should you move on each roll in order to spend the greatest possible amount of money on the next two turns?

Review Prerequisite Skills

REVIEW WORDS
- **digit,** *p. 735*
- **number line,** *p. 736*
- **less than,** *p. 736*
- **greater than,** *p. 736*
- **round,** *p. 737*
- **dividend,** *p. 744*
- **divisor,** *p. 744*
- **quotient,** *p. 744*
- **estimate,** *p. 745*

VOCABULARY CHECK

Copy and complete using a review word from the list at the left.

1. In the division equation $42 \div 6 = 7$, 42 is called the __?__, 6 is called the __?__, and 7 is called the __?__.

2. If you __?__ 1723 to the nearest hundred, you get 1700.

3. The __?__ in the tens' place of the number 637 is 3.

SKILL CHECK

Round the number to the place value of the red digit. *(p. 737)*

4. 845   **5.** 12,047   **6.** 739,022   **7.** 2,993,438

Estimate the sum or difference. *(pp. 745, 746)*

8.
$$
\begin{array}{r}
905 \\
782 \\
+\ 179 \\
\hline
\end{array}
$$

9.
$$
\begin{array}{r}
54,036 \\
13,987 \\
+\ 32,053 \\
\hline
\end{array}
$$

10.
$$
\begin{array}{r}
2874 \\
-\ 1951 \\
\hline
\end{array}
$$

11.
$$
\begin{array}{r}
26,780 \\
-\ 17,702 \\
\hline
\end{array}
$$

Evaluate the expression. *(p. 17)*

12. $14 + 6 \times 7$ **13.** $12 \div 2 + 4$ **14.** $2 \times 4 + 5^2$ **15.** $5 - 2 \times 2$

@HomeTutor   Prerequisite skills practice at classzone.com

Notetaking Skills   Previewing the Chapter

In each chapter you will learn a new notetaking skill. In Chapter 2 you will apply the strategy of previewing the chapter to Example 1 on p. 66.

Before you begin a chapter, make a list of the chapter's lesson titles in your notebook. Write down at least one fact you predict you will need to know in order to understand each lesson.

Lesson 2.1 Comparing, Ordering, and Rounding Decimals

Prediction: I will need to know about place value.

Make similar predictions about the other lessons in Chapter 2.

This notetaking strategy will help you connect new topics with more familiar topics. It may make new concepts easier to understand.

INVESTIGATION
Use before Lesson 2.1

GOAL
Use models to write equivalent decimals.

MATERIALS
• base-ten pieces

2.1 Modeling Decimals

You can use base-ten pieces to model decimals. The three types of base-ten pieces and their values are shown below.

1 one

1 tenth

1 hundredth

EXPLORE Model 26 hundredths using the fewest number of base-ten pieces possible.

STEP 1 Model 26 hundredths.   **STEP 2** Use the fact that 10 hundredths are equal to 1 tenth.

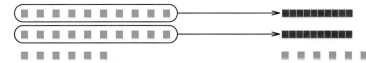

▶ **Answer** So, 26 hundredths = **2 tenths** and **6 hundredths**.

PRACTICE Copy and complete the statement. Use base-ten pieces as needed.

1. 4 tenths = __?__ hundredths

2. 4 ones = __?__ tenths

3. 30 hundredths = __?__ tenths

4. 11 tenths = __?__ hundredths

5. 25 tenths = __?__ ones and __?__ tenths

6. 17 hundredths = __?__ tenths and __?__ hundredths

DRAW CONCLUSIONS

7. **COMPARE** *Explain* how to use base-ten pieces to compare 74 hundredths to 8 tenths. Which is greater?

2.1 Comparing, Ordering, and Rounding Decimals

NJ 4.1.A.4 Compare and order numbers of all named types.

Before	You compared, ordered, and rounded whole numbers.
Now	You'll compare, order, and round decimals.
Why?	So you can compare race times, as in Example 1.

KEY VOCABULARY
• decimal, *p. 56*

Olympic Games In the 1968 Summer Olympics, Irena Szewinska of Poland won the women's 200 meter dash with a time of 22.5 seconds. In 2004, Veronica Campbell of Jamaica won the event with a time of 22.05 seconds. Whose time is faster?

The numbers 22.5 and 22.05 are *decimals*. A **decimal** is a number that is written using the base-ten place value system where a decimal point separates the ones' and tenths' digits. Each place value is 10 times the place value to its right.

KEY CONCEPT *For Your Notebook*

Decimals and Place Value

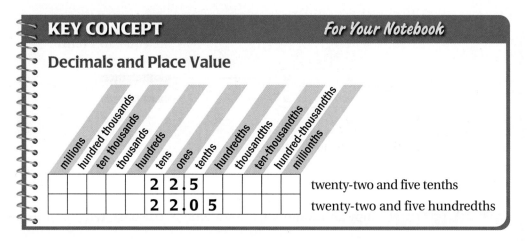

twenty-two and five tenths
twenty-two and five hundredths

Comparing Decimals To compare decimals, write the numbers in a column, lining up the decimal points. If needed, write zeros as placeholders so that all decimals have the same number of digits. Then compare digits from left to right.

EXAMPLE 1 Comparing Decimals

To determine which race time given above is faster, compare 22.5 and 22.05.

▼▼ ——— The tens' and ones' digits are the same.

22.50 ◄— Write a zero as a placeholder.
22.05

▲ ——— The tenths' digits are different. 5 > 0, so 22.50 > 22.05.

▶ **Answer** Because 22.5 > 22.05, Veronica Campbell's time is faster.

✓ **GUIDED PRACTICE**   **for Example 1**

Copy and complete the statement using <, >, or =.

1. 30.12 <u>?</u> 30.4   **2.** 7.7 <u>?</u> 7.70   **3.** 5.701 <u>?</u> 5.699

EXAMPLE 2   **Ordering Decimals**

Order 2.11, 2.21, 2, 2.06, and 2.24 from least to greatest.

On a number line, mark tenths between 2.0 and 2.3. Mark hundredths by dividing each tenth into ten equal parts. Then graph each number.

REVIEW NUMBER LINES
Remember that numbers on a number line increase from left to right.

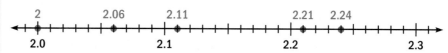

▶ **Answer** From least to greatest, the numbers are 2, 2.06, 2.11, 2.21, and 2.24.

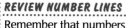 at classzone.com

---

KEY CONCEPT   *For Your Notebook*

Rounding Decimals

To round a decimal to a given place value, look at the digit in the place to the right.

- If the digit is less than 5, round down.
- If the digit is 5 or greater, round up.

EXAMPLE 3   **Rounding a Decimal**

ROUNDING
When rounding to a certain place value, include the digit of that place value even if it is zero.

2.301 → 2.30
8.96 → 9.0

Round 7.126 to the nearest tenth.

7.1**2**6

You want to round to the nearest tenth.

Because the hundredths′ **digit is less than 5, round down and drop the remaining digits.**

▶ **Answer** The decimal 7.126 rounded to the nearest tenth is 7.1.

✓ **GUIDED PRACTICE**   **for Examples 2 and 3**

Order the numbers from least to greatest.

4. 3.84, 4.4, 4.83, 3.48, 4.38   **5.** 5.71, 5.8, 5.68, 5.79, 5.6

Round the number to the nearest hundredth.

6. 34.0152   **7.** 1.5034   **8.** 22.6654   **9.** 125.7049

2.1 EXERCISES

HOMEWORK KEY

★ = **STANDARDIZED TEST PRACTICE**
Exs. 14, 30–33, 41–44, and 52

○ = **HINTS AND HOMEWORK HELP**
for Exs. 7, 17, 23, 27, 39 at classzone.com

SKILL PRACTICE

VOCABULARY Tell what place value the red digit is in.

1. 27.404

2. 3.579

3. 412.865

4. 15.26

COMPARING DECIMALS Copy and complete the statement using <, >, or =.

SEE EXAMPLE 1
on p. 56
for Exs. 5–15

5. 6.5 _?_ 6.45

6. 12.8 _?_ 12.801

7. 30.650 _?_ 30.65

8. 10.01 _?_ 10.10

9. 0.6 _?_ 0.61

10. 0.607 _?_ 0.66

11. 13.20 _?_ 13.2

12. 25.024 _?_ 26.023

13. 12.4312 _?_ 12.43112

14. ★ **MULTIPLE CHOICE** Which statement is true?

(A) 4.59 < 4.5   (B) 7.41 > 7.401   (C) 1.09 < 1.081   (D) 6.33 > 6.333

15. **ERROR ANALYSIS** A student compares the numbers 8.4 and 8.29 and determines that 8.29 > 8.4 because 29 > 4. Is the student correct? *Explain.*

ORDERING DECIMALS Order the numbers from least to greatest.

SEE EXAMPLE 2
on p. 57
for Exs. 16–21

16. 0.86, 0.03, 0.91, 0.2

17. 8.56, 7.65, 8.65, 7.635

18. 6.6, 6.6311, 6.8, 6.56

19. 7.34, 7.276, 7.3057, 7.266

20. 3.24, 3.907, 4.01, 3.8999

21. 9.6, 9.594, 9.701, 8.999

ROUNDING DECIMALS Round the decimal as specified.

SEE EXAMPLE 3
on p. 57
for Exs. 22–29

22. 17.6 (nearest one)

23. 32.09 (nearest tenth)

24. 0.25 (nearest tenth)

25. 0.73 (nearest one)

26. 12.5503 (nearest thousandth)

27. 9.104 (nearest hundredth)

28. 2.2949 (nearest hundredth)

29. 7.26073 (nearest ten-thousandth)

★ **OPEN-ENDED MATH Find a decimal number that is between the two numbers.**

30. 12.45, 12.47

31. 1.144, 1.145

32. 65.4, 65.49

33. 7.08, 7.0801

34. **NAMING DECIMALS** Write the numbers represented by the labeled points on the number line in decimal form and in words.

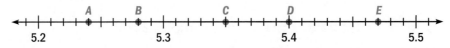

LOOK FOR A PATTERN Describe the pattern. Write the next two numbers.

35. 10, 1, 0.1, 0.01, . . .

36. 2.01, 2.002, 2.0003, 2.00004, . . .

37. **CHALLENGE** Find the decimal halfway between 0.1 and 0.8.

38. **CHALLENGE** Find the decimal three fourths of the way from 0.01 to 0.09.

SEE EXAMPLE 1
on p. 56
for Ex. 39

39. **SCULPTURE** The heights of two sculptures are 12.2 feet and 12.19 feet. Which is taller?

40. **SOAPBOX DERBY** The winning times in each division for a soapbox derby are 29.15 seconds, 29.78 seconds, and 29.74 seconds. Order the times from fastest to slowest.

41. ★ **WRITING** *Explain* in words how to round 19.96025 to the nearest tenth, to the nearest thousandth, and to the nearest ten-thousandth.

42. ★ **MULTIPLE CHOICE** During a camping trip, you and three friends carry lightweight tents. Your tent weighs 3.5 pounds, and your friends' tents weigh 3.25 pounds, 3.35 pounds, and 3.1 pounds. Which tent is the second lightest?

(A) 3.5 pounds **(B)** 3.25 pounds **(C)** 3.35 pounds **(D)** 3.1 pounds

43. ★ **SHORT RESPONSE** Moment magnitude is a measure used by scientists to describe an earthquake's power. Order the moment magnitudes from least to greatest. Does it make sense to round to the ones' place before comparing decimals? *Explain.*

Earthquake Location	Year	Moment Magnitude
Ecuador	1906	8.8
Chile	1960	9.5
Indonesia	2004	9.0

44. ★ **OPEN-ENDED MATH** Write two numbers that round *up* to 5.765 and two numbers that round *down* to 5.760. Do all four numbers round to the same hundredth? *Explain.*

45. **CHALLENGE** Write two numbers that are between 4.57 and 4.58. Write two numbers between the two numbers you chose. Now write two more numbers between these second two numbers. Is it always possible to find two numbers between any two given numbers? *Explain.*

NEW JERSEY MIXED REVIEW

 TEST PRACTICE at classzone.com

46. Jeff drives his car at a constant speed of 55 miles per hour to Neil's house. What additional information does he need to determine how long it will take him to get to Neil's house?

(A) The cost of fuel per gallon **(B)** The distance to Neil's house

(C) The maximum speed of his car **(D)** The number of miles per gallon his car gets

47. Alyssa scored between 14 and 24 points per game playing basketball. Which point total for all 6 games is most reasonable?

(A) 20 points **(B)** 80 points **(C)** 120 points **(D)** 150 points

 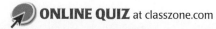

2.2 Adding and Subtracting Decimals

NJ 4.1.B.1.a Use and explain procedures for performing calculations with integers and all number types named above with: Pencil-and-paper

Before You added and subtracted whole numbers.

Now You'll add and subtract decimals.

Why? So you can calculate costs, as in Ex. 56.

KEY VOCABULARY

• front-end estimation, *p. 61*

ACTIVITY

You can use base-ten pieces to model decimal addition and subtraction.

STEP 1 **Model** the sum of 0.76 and 0.58 using base-ten pieces.

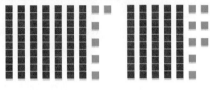

STEP 2 **Combine** and group the pieces.

STEP 3 **Trade** 10 tenths for 1 one and 10 hundredths for 1 tenth. The sum of 0.76 and 0.58 is 1.34.

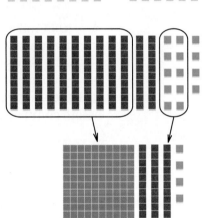

Use base-ten pieces to find the sum or difference.

1. $2.2 + 1.85$ **2.** $2.77 - 1.47$ **3.** $1.26 - 1.08$

Animated Math
at classzone.com

Decimal Operations Use a vertical format to add or subtract decimals. Begin by lining up the decimal points. Then add or subtract as you would with whole numbers. Be sure to write the decimal point in the answer.

EXAMPLE 1 Adding and Subtracting Decimals

a. $6.047 + 13.46$

$$
\begin{array}{r}
6.047 \\
+ \ 13.460 \\
\hline
19.507
\end{array}
$$
◄— Write a zero as a placeholder.

b. $9 - 5.28$

$$
\begin{array}{r}
9.00 \\
- \ 5.28 \\
\hline
3.72
\end{array}
$$
◄— Write zeros as placeholders.

EXAMPLE 2 Evaluating a Variable Expression

 Evaluate $6.7 + r - t$ when $r = 2.14$ and $t = 5.2$.

SOLUTION

$$6.7 + r - t = 6.7 + 2.14 - 5.2 \quad \text{Substitute 2.14 for } r \text{ and 5.2 for } t.$$
$$= 8.84 - 5.2 \qquad\qquad \text{Add.}$$
$$= 3.64 \qquad\qquad\qquad \text{Subtract.}$$

AVOID ERRORS
Don't forget to add and subtract from left to right when evaluating expressions horizontally.

Estimation One type of estimation is *front-end estimation*. To use **front-end estimation** to estimate a sum, add the front-end digits, estimate the sum of the remaining digits, and then add the results.

EXAMPLE 3 Estimating a Sum

Video Games For your birthday you receive a $25 gift certificate. You want to buy 3 used video games with prices as shown. Can you buy all 3 games using the gift certificate?

Game A	$8.79
Game B	$7.29
Game C	$7.89

SOLUTION

ANOTHER WAY
Round to the nearest dollar, then add.

$8.79		$9
$7.29	→	$7
+ $7.89		+ $8
		$24

STEP 1 Add the front-end digits: the dollars.

$$\begin{array}{r} \$8.79 \\ \$7.29 \\ + \$7.89 \\ \hline \$22 \end{array}$$

STEP 2 Estimate the sum of the remaining digits: the cents.

$$\begin{array}{r} \$8.79 \searrow \\ \$7.29 \longrightarrow \$1 \\ + \$7.89 \longrightarrow \$1 \\ \hline \$2 \end{array}$$

STEP 3 Add the results.

$$\begin{array}{r} \$22 \\ + \$2 \\ \hline \$24 \end{array}$$

▶ **Answer** The estimated sum is less than $25, so you can buy all three games using the gift certificate.

✓ GUIDED PRACTICE for Examples 1, 2, and 3

Find the sum or difference.

1. $8.41 + 2.6$ **2.** $1.937 + 2.28$ **3.** $6 - 3.74$ **4.** $4.59 - 3.17$

Evaluate the expression when $a = 4.2$ and $b = 6.27$.

5. $a + b$ **6.** $b - a$ **7.** $10.03 - a + b$ **8.** $a + 7.8 - b$

Estimate the sum or difference.

9. $3.85 + 5.21$ **10.** $5.78 - 2.63$

11. $6.41 + 3.27 + 1.96$ **12.** $8.26 - 3.82 - 1.92$

2.2 EXERCISES

HOMEWORK KEY

★ = **STANDARDIZED TEST PRACTICE**
Exs. 34, 38, 56, 59, 60, 61, and 71

◯ = **HINTS** AND **HOMEWORK HELP**
for Exs. 5, 9, 17, 27, 55 at classzone.com

SKILL PRACTICE

1. **VOCABULARY** *Explain* how to use front-end estimation to add decimals.

2. **VOCABULARY** What is the front-end digit of 9.653?

EVALUATING EXPRESSIONS **Evaluate the expression. Use estimation to check.**

SEE EXAMPLES 1 AND 3
on pp. 60–61
for Exs. 3–15

3. $15.8 + 7.6$

4. $124.6 + 47.01$

5. $53.24 + 14.023$

6. $4 - 3.456$

7. $90 - 7.5$

8. $24.98 - 3.3$

9. $467.2 + 5.63 + 11$

10. $27 - 3.204 - 10.8$

11. $8.55 + 20.4 - 15$

12. $0.032 + 0.29 + 1$

13. $26.17 - 9.002 + 1.9$

14. $3.876 + 2.2 - 4.10$

15. **ERROR ANALYSIS** Describe and correct the error made in finding the sum of 3.48 and 13.

$$\begin{array}{r} 3.48 \\ +\ \ 13 \\ \hline 3.61 \end{array}$$

✗ ALGEBRA **Evaluate the expression when $k = 5.874$, $m = 123.1$, $y = 26.3$, and $z = 12.28$.**

SEE EXAMPLE 2
on p. 61
for Exs. 16–24

16. $34 + z$

17. $y - z$

18. $30 - y + z$

19. $m - k + 6.401$

20. $140 - (k + m)$

21. $m - 6.78 - k + 28.3$

22. $k + y - z$

23. $m - y - 61.5$

24. $98.2 + (m - z)$

ESTIMATION **Estimate the sum or difference.**

SEE EXAMPLE 3
on p. 61
for Exs. 25–34

25. $5.24 + 9.79$

26. $3.44 + 8.38$

27. $4.11 + 5.90 + 8.02$

28. $5.78 + 9 + 2.2$

29. $8.75 - 5.67$

30. $6.6 - 4.45$

31. $9.7 - 5.45 - 2.12$

32. $4.89 - 3.91$

33. $5.72 + 6.15 + 1.05$

34. ★ **MULTIPLE CHOICE** Which of the numbers, when added to 8.43 using front-end estimation, results in an estimated sum of 15?

Ⓐ 6.59   Ⓑ 7.59   Ⓒ 8.04   Ⓓ 8.45

NUMBER SENSE **Write the decimal in expanded form. For example, 3.24 in expanded form is $3 + 0.2 + 0.04$.**

35. 6.912

36. 523.974

37. 43.07

38. ★ **MULTIPLE CHOICE** Assume the pattern on the number line starts with 0.14 and continues. What is the next number?

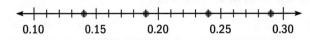

Ⓐ 0.39   Ⓑ 0.35   Ⓒ 0.34   Ⓓ 0.33

ESTIMATION Use estimation to copy and complete the statement using < or >.

39. $8.79 + 4.06 - 3.905$? 8

40. $6.91 + 2.08 + 3.83$? 12

41. $14.68 - 2.058 - 8.92$? 3

42. $11.81 - 9.45 + 2.61$? 4

43. $3.72 + 9.15 - 7.38$? 7

44. $10.19 - 4.24 - 1.853$? 6

CHOOSE AN OPERATION Would you *add* or *subtract* to find the answer? *Explain* your reasoning.

45. How much does it cost to buy a pair of jeans and a shirt?

46. How much warmer is today's high temperature than yesterday's high?

47. How much more does a cheeseburger cost than a hamburger?

xy **CHALLENGE** Solve the equation.

48. $6 - 2.4 + x = 8.8$

49. $4.28 + 0.72 - z = 0.7$

50. $9.73 + m - 4.22 = 12.6$

51. $7.93 + t - 6.17 = 13.03$

PROBLEM SOLVING

52. GUIDED PROBLEM SOLVING A tube of watercolor paints is $8.69, a paint brush is $3.78, and a canvas is $6.32. Is $20 enough money to buy the art supplies listed?

   a. Add the front-end digits.

   b. Estimate the sum of the remaining digits.

   c. Add the results. Is the sum *greater than* or *less than* $20?

For Exercises 53–55, use estimation to check that your answer is reasonable.

SEE EXAMPLE 3
on p. 61
for Exs. 53–55

53. CORNFIELD MAZES The first cornfield maze, grown in Annville, Pennsylvania, in 1993, covered 3.3 acres. The largest cornfield maze, grown in Lindon, Utah, in 1999, covered 12.6 acres. How many acres larger was the Lindon maze than the Annville maze?

54. MEASUREMENT Jared is 2.75 meters tall while on stilts and 1.6 meters tall without stilts. How far off the ground do the stilts raise Jared?

55. CAPACITY You mix a cleaning solution with 1.18 liters water, 0.15 liter vinegar, and 0.02 liter liquid soap. The container for this solution must have at least what capacity?

56. ★ SHORT RESPONSE You have $15. You want to buy a bouquet of tulips for $6.99 and a bouquet of assorted flowers for $7.50 at a flower shop. Do you have enough money to buy both bouquets? *Explain.*

57. SCAVENGER HUNT You are in a 3-part scavenger hunt. Your friend's team completed the game in 80.63 minutes. Your team's times for each part of the game are 22.34 minutes, 25.8 minutes, and 30.15 minutes. Is your team's total time faster than your friend's team's total time to complete the game? *Explain.*

58. DIRECTIONS Internet driving directions from Washington, D.C.'s National Zoo to the White House Visitor Center are shown below. How much shorter is the shortest route than the fastest route? The two directions start the same way. For how many miles are the directions the same?

Fastest Route	
Directions	**Distance**
Go SE on Connecticut Ave. NW	2.1 miles
Connecticut Ave. NW becomes 17th St. NW	0.2 mile
Turn left onto H St. NW	0.4 mile
Turn right onto 14th St. NW	0.3 mile
Turn right onto Pennsylvania Ave. NW	0.0 mile

Shortest Route	
Directions	**Distance**
Go SE on Connecticut Ave. NW	2.1 miles
Connecticut Ave. NW becomes 17th St. NW	0.5 mile
Turn left onto E St. NW	0.3 mile
E St. NW becomes Pennsylvania Ave. NW	0.0 mile

59. ★ WRITING When is the sum of two decimals a whole number? When is the difference of two decimals a whole number? *Explain* and give examples.

60. ★ MULTIPLE CHOICE A city had 3.57 inches of rain in April, 7.30 inches of rain in May, and 5.14 inches in June. Which is the *most reasonable* answer for an estimate of rainfall the city had during the three month period?

Ⓐ less than 15 inches   Ⓑ about 15 inches

Ⓒ about 16 inches   Ⓓ more than 17 inches

61. ★ EXTENDED RESPONSE The times, in seconds, below are for the first three legs of a 4-person relay race. Each leg of the race is 400 meters.

72.58   150.34   229.58   ?

   a. How long did runner 2 take?

   b. How long did runner 3 take?

   c. Your team wants to beat a previous team's record of 296.22 seconds. What is the maximum number of seconds the last runner can take? *Explain* your reasoning.

62. SALES As a salesperson, Tony makes $20.55 a day. He gets an additional $5.35 for each refrigerator he sells and an additional $4.24 for each dishwasher he sells. On Friday, he sold three dishwashers and four refrigerators. How much money did Tony make on Friday?

63. CHALLENGE The following snacks are available: water for $1.09, soda pop for $1.39, popcorn for $2.75, and candy for $1.99. List all of the possible combinations of snacks that you could buy with $5.

NEW JERSEY MIXED REVIEW

 TEST PRACTICE at classzone.com

64. The decimal 3.2 is found between which pair of decimals on a number line?

Ⓐ 2.1 and 2.9   Ⓑ 3.0 and 3.1   Ⓒ 3.1 and 3.3   Ⓓ 3.2 and 3.5

65. Two people each ordered a $13 meal at a restaurant. They paid for both meals with a $50 bill. Which expression can be used to find the amount of money they will get back?

Ⓐ $2 \times 13 - 50$

Ⓑ $50 + 2 \times 13$

Ⓒ $50 - 2 \times 13$

Ⓓ $50 \div 2 \times 13$

66. Which expression can be used to solve the problem below?

On a recent math test, Jill scored 3 points for each of the 18 multiple choice questions she answered correctly and 5 points for each of the 6 short response questions she answered correctly. What was her total score on the test?

Ⓐ $3 + 5 \cdot 18 + 6$

Ⓑ $3 + 18 \cdot 5 + 6$

Ⓒ $3 \cdot 5 + 18 \cdot 6$

Ⓓ $3 \cdot 18 + 5 \cdot 6$

Brain Game

Decode the Riddle

Find the values of **M, T, C, F, Y, R, E,** and **I** that make the sum and difference correct. Then replace the number in each box with its letter to find the answer to the riddle below.

$$
\begin{array}{r}
3.2T5 \\
+ \ M.TC2 \\
\hline
11.C1C
\end{array}
\qquad
\begin{array}{r}
0.3F1F \\
- \ 0.2C0F \\
\hline
0.091Y
\end{array}
\qquad
\begin{array}{r}
7.RE3 \\
+ \ 2.97R \\
\hline
10.E8I
\end{array}
$$

Why did the cookie go to the hospital?

| 5 | 4 | | 6 | 1 | L | 4 | | 7 | 2 | U | 8 | 8 | 0 |

2.3 Multiplying Decimals

NJ⑤ **4.1.B.1.a** Use and explain procedures for performing calculations with integers and all number types named above with: Pencil-and-paper

Before You multiplied whole numbers.

Now You'll multiply decimals.

Why? So you can calculate area, as in Example 3.

KEY VOCABULARY
• leading digit, *p. 66*

Modeling Products A 10×10 grid can be used to represent 1 whole. The width of each row or column is 0.1. The area of each small square is 0.01.

The shaded area at the right represents the product 0.7×1.3. There are 91 squares shaded, or 91 hundredths. So, $0.7 \times 1.3 = 0.91$.

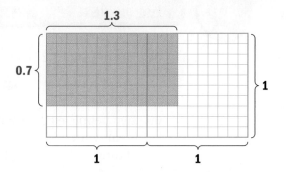

KEY CONCEPT *For Your Notebook*

Multiplying Decimals

Words Multiply decimals as you would whole numbers. Then place the decimal point in the product. The number of decimal places in the product is equal to the sum of the number of decimal places in the factors.

Numbers $0.7 \times 0.3 = 0.21$

TAKE NOTES
....
In previewing this lesson, notice that you need to know how to multiply whole numbers. List what you know about multiplying whole numbers to prepare for multiplying decimals.

EXAMPLE 1 **Multiplying Decimals**

$$
\begin{array}{r}
5.82 \\
\times\, 0.41 \\
\hline
582 \\
2328 \\
\hline
2.3862
\end{array}
$$

2 decimal places
+ 2 decimal places

4 decimal places

Animated Math at classzone.com

Check Reasonableness To check that the product in Example 1 is reasonable, round each factor to the place value of the *leading digit,* and then multiply. The **leading digit** of a number is the first nonzero digit.

5.82 ⟶ 6 **Round to the nearest whole number.**

0.41 ⟶ 0.4 **Round to the nearest tenth.**

Because $6 \times 0.4 = 2.4$, the product in Example 1 is reasonable.

EXAMPLE 2 Multiplying Decimals

a.
$$
\begin{array}{r}
6.45 \\
\times\ 18 \\
\hline
5160 \\
645 \\
\hline
116.10
\end{array}
$$

2 decimal places
+ 0 decimal places

2 decimal places

> After you place the decimal point, you can drop any zeros at the end of an answer.

b.
$$
\begin{array}{r}
1.273 \\
\times\ 0.06 \\
\hline
0.07638
\end{array}
$$

3 decimal places
+ 2 decimal places

5 decimal places

> Write a zero before the 7 as a placeholder so that the number has five decimal places.

▶ **Answer** $6.45 \times 18 = 116.1$

Check Because $6 \times 20 = 120$, the product is reasonable.

▶ **Answer** $1.273 \times 0.06 = 0.07638$

Check Because $1 \times 0.06 = 0.06$, the product is reasonable.

✔ **GUIDED PRACTICE** for Examples 1 and 2

Find the product. Then check that your answer is reasonable.

1. 1.4×7.2 **2.** 0.98×0.21 **3.** 2.351×1.6

Evaluate the expression when $m = 3.26$ and $n = 1.24$.

4. $2.6m$ **5.** $1.7n$ **6.** mn

EXAMPLE 3 Multiplying Decimals to Find Area

Central Park Central Park, in New York City, is a rectangular park about 2.5 miles long and about 0.5 mile wide. What is the area of Central Park?

SOLUTION

$A = lw$ **Write formula for area of a rectangle.**

$ = 2.5(0.5)$ **Substitute 2.5 for l and 0.5 for w.**

$ = 1.25$ **Multiply.**

▶ **Answer** The area of Central Park is about 1.25 square miles.

✔ **GUIDED PRACTICE** for Example 3

Find the area of the rectangle.

7.

2 in.

9.42 in.

8.

4.3 cm

8.4 cm

EXAMPLE 4 Standardized Test Practice

Farmer's Market You go to a farmer's market. You buy 14.4 pounds of fruits and vegetables. The prices range from $.25 to $2.10 per pound. What is the range of the amount of money that you could spend?

(A) $3.00 to $29.40   **(B)** $3.50 to $30.24

(C) $3.60 to $30.24   **(D)** $3.60 to $45.00

ELIMINATE CHOICES
An overestimate of your cost is 15 × 3 = 45. An underestimate is 12 × 0.25 = 3. So, you can eliminate choices A and D.

SOLUTION

STEP 1 **Calculate** the least total cost.

least total cost = 14.4 lb × least cost per lb

$C = 14.4 \times 0.25 = \$3.60$

STEP 2 **Calculate** the greatest total cost.

greatest total cost = 14.4 lb × greatest cost per lb

$C = 14.4 \times 2.10 = \$30.24$

▶ **Answer** The least cost for food is $3.60 and the greatest cost is $30.24. The correct answer is C. **(A) (B) (C) (D)**

✓ **GUIDED PRACTICE** | **for Example 4**

9. **What If?** In Example 4, suppose you buy 16.8 pounds of fruits and vegetables. What is the range of the amount you might spend?

2.3 EXERCISES

HOMEWORK KEY

★ = **STANDARDIZED TEST PRACTICE**
Exs. 22, 50, 51, 52, 53, and 65

○ = **HINTS AND HOMEWORK HELP**
for Exs. 7, 15, 23, 29, 49 at classzone.com

SKILL PRACTICE

VOCABULARY **Round to the leading digit.**

1. 3.5   **2.** 9.15   **3.** 18.06   **4.** 5.85

FINDING PRODUCTS **Find the product. Check your answer.**

SEE EXAMPLES 1 AND 2
on pp. 66–67
for Exs. 5–22

5. 0.4 × 0.03   **6.** 0.06 × 0.6   **7.** 0.8 × 3   **8.** 0.05 × 8

9. 3.4 × 6.5   **10.** 9.3 × 8.1   **11.** 3.9 × 0.91   **12.** 0.7 × 0.01

13. 78.1 × 4.4   **14.** 3.9 × 21.8   **15.** 0.14 × 0.09   **16.** 0.086 × 0.007

17. 94.2 × 0.14   **18.** 0.045 × 1.20 **19.** 25 × 0.052   **20.** 16.34 × 1.001

21. **ERROR ANALYSIS** Describe and correct the error made in finding the product of 6.21 and 0.04.

✗ 6.21 × 0.04 = 24.84

22. ★ **MULTIPLE CHOICE** Which description relates a term and its position n in a list?

Position	1	2	3	4	n
Value of term	1.5	3	4.5	6	?

(A) Add 0.5 to n.

(B) Divide n by 1.5.

(C) Subtract 1.5 from n.

(D) Multiply n by 1.5.

GEOMETRY Find the area of the rectangle.

SEE EXAMPLE 3
on p. 67
for Exs. 23–25

(23.)  3 mm

4.5 mm

24. 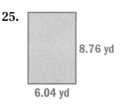 2.25 ft

8.23 ft

25. 8.76 yd

6.04 yd

ESTIMATION Estimate the product by rounding each factor to the place value of the leading digit.

SEE EXAMPLE 2
on p. 67
for Exs. 26–33

26. 3.45×90.2

27. 0.32×2.8

28. 4.57×199.4

(29.) 18.23×4.7

30. 6.92×0.08

31. 56.1×7.22

32. 15.75×1.39

33. 3.45×42.82

ALGEBRA Evaluate the expression when $p = 2.29$ and $q = 0.034$.

34. $7.654p$

35. $4.41q$

36. pq

37. $1.12pq$

EVALUATING EXPRESSIONS Evaluate the expression.

38. $12.54 \times 0.023 \times 11$

39. $35.054 \times 12.3 \times 2.01$

40. $0.34 \times (7.4 - 3.19)$

41. $(18.62 - 1.04) \times 12.7$

42. 9.9^3

43. 3.2^3

DESCRIBING PATTERNS Describe the pattern. Write the next three numbers.

44. $0.12, 0.6, 3, 15, \ldots$

45. $1, 0.5, 0.25, 0.125, \ldots$

46. $2, 3, 4.5, 6.75, \ldots$

47. CHALLENGE What decimal number(s) can you multiply by 2.3 to make the product less than 2.3? greater than 2.3? equal to 2.3? *Explain* your reasoning.

PROBLEM SOLVING

48. COMETS Halley's Comet takes about 23.06 times as long as Encke's Comet to orbit the Sun. Encke's Comet takes about 3.3 years. About how long does Halley's Comet take to orbit the Sun? Round to the nearest tenth.

(49.) AIR HOCKEY The surface of a rectangular air hockey table is 7.04 feet long and 3.7 feet wide. Find the area of the surface of the air hockey table.

50. ★ **SHORT RESPONSE** Laura has $10 to spend on nail polish. With tax, each bottle costs $2.89. Can Laura buy 3 bottles of nail polish? *Explain.*

51. ★ **WRITING** Find the value of $5.31x$ for the following values of x: 0.001, 0.01, 0.1, 1, 10, 100, and 1000. *Explain* the pattern in the products.

52. ★ **MULTIPLE CHOICE** A marathon is 26.2 miles. You average 8.5 minutes per mile. Which expression shows how many minutes it will take you?

    (A) $26.2 \div 8.5$ **(B)** 26.2×8.5 **(C)** $26.2 - 8.5$ **(D)** $26.2 + 8.5$

53. ★ **WRITING** *Describe* how to use dimes and pennies to find 2 tenths of $1.20. What number sentence does the model show?

SEE EXAMPLE 4
on p. 68
for Ex. 54

54. **GASOLINE** A car needs 8.7 gallons of gasoline to have a full tank. The prices range from $2.79 to $2.99 per gallon. What is the range of the amount of money that it costs to put 8.7 gallons of gasoline in the car?

55. **MEASUREMENT** The objects below have been magnified. Their actual width A is much smaller. Measure each object in millimeters.

Pollen	Algae	Blood cell

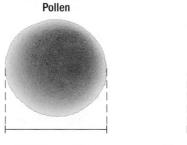  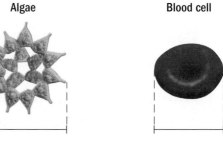

$A = 0.0013 \times$ width shown $A = 0.0037 \times$ width shown $A = 0.0006 \times$ width shown

   a. Use your measurements to find the actual width A of each object.

   b. Order the actual objects from least to greatest width.

56. **CHALLENGE** A store is selling crafts. The first week it prices 5 baskets at $20 each. After each week, if a basket is not sold, it will be priced to sell for 0.9 times the previous week's price. The store needs to sell the 5 baskets for a total of at least $53. If all 5 baskets sell in the same week, by the end of what week must they be sold?

 NEW JERSEY MIXED REVIEW   **TEST PRACTICE** at classzone.com

57. It took 1460 days to construct a building. Which expression can be used to find the number of years it took to construct the building?

   (A) 1460×365

   (B) 1460×52

   (C) $1460 \div 365$

   (D) $1460 \div 52$

2.4 Dividing Decimals

 4.1.B.1.a Use and explain procedures for performing calculations with integers and all number types named above with: Pencil-and-paper

Before	You divided whole numbers.
Now	You'll divide decimals.
Why?	So you can analyze the cost of the Louisiana Territory, as in Ex. 53.

KEY VOCABULARY
• **quotient,** *p. 744*
• **divisor,** *p. 744*
• **dividend,** *p. 744*
• **compatible numbers,** *p. 71*

Ticket Prices The cost of 11 tickets to see Blue Man Group was $574.75. How much did each ticket cost?

You can use long division to divide a decimal by a whole number. Divide as with whole numbers. Then line up the decimal points in the quotient and the dividend.

EXAMPLE 1   Dividing a Decimal by a Whole Number

To find the cost of each ticket as described above, divide 574.75 by 11.

```
          52.25
     11)574.75        Divide as you would with whole numbers.
        55            Line up decimal point in quotient with
        ──            decimal point in dividend.
        24
        22
        ──
        2 7
        2 2
        ───
          5 5
          5 5
          ───
            0         Stop dividing when you get a zero remainder.
```

▶**Answer** Each ticket cost $52.25.

ANOTHER WAY

You can also check your answer by multiplying the quotient and the divisor to see if it equals the dividend:
$52.25 \times 11 = 574.75$.

To check the reasonableness of a quotient, use *compatible numbers*. **Compatible numbers** are numbers that make a calculation easier.

11 ⟶ 10   **Round divisor to place of leading digit.**

574.75 ⟶ 570   **Round dividend to nearest multiple of 10.**

Because $570 \div 10 = 57$, the quotient in Example 1 is reasonable.

Animated Math at classzone.com

✓ GUIDED PRACTICE   for Example 1

Find the quotient. Then check your answer.

1. $20.1 \div 3$ **2.** $64.35 \div 5$ **3.** $380.32 \div 4$

Dividing by a Decimal Notice the pattern in the equations below.

$$6 \div 3 = 2 \qquad 60 \div 30 = 2 \qquad 600 \div 300 = 2 \qquad 6000 \div 3000 = 2$$

The quotient remains the same when the divisor and the dividend are both multiplied by the same power of 10. You can use this fact to divide by a decimal.

KEY CONCEPT   *For Your Notebook*

Dividing by a Decimal

Words   When you divide by a decimal, multiply both the divisor and the dividend by a power of ten that will make the divisor a whole number.

Numbers $12.5\overline{)8.75}$ ➡ $125\overline{)87.5}$ with quotient 0.7

EXAMPLE 2   Dividing Decimals

Divide: **a.** $3.804 \div 3.17$ **b.** $8 \div 1.6$ **c.** $0.114 \div 1.9$

SOLUTION

a. $3.17\overline{)3.804}$ ⟶

$$
\begin{array}{r}
1.2 \\
317\overline{)380.4} \\
\underline{317} \\
63\ 4 \\
\underline{63\ 4} \\
0
\end{array}
$$

Multiply the divisor and dividend by 100; move both decimal points two places to the right.

Line up decimal points.

b. $1.6\overline{)8.0}$ ⟶

$$
\begin{array}{r}
5 \\
16\overline{)80} \\
\underline{80} \\
0
\end{array}
$$

Multiply the divisor and dividend by 10; move both decimal points one place to the right. Write a zero as a placeholder in the dividend.

c. $1.9\overline{)0.114}$ ⟶

$$
\begin{array}{r}
0.06 \\
19\overline{)1.14} \\
\underline{1\ 14} \\
0
\end{array}
$$

Multiply the divisor and dividend by 10; move both decimal points one place to the right.

AVOID ERRORS
Don't forget to write zeros as placeholders in the quotient.

✓ **GUIDED PRACTICE**   for Example 2

Find the quotient.

4. $110.85 \div 1.5$ **5.** $0.234 \div 0.3$ **6.** $9 \div 0.3$ **7.** $0.208 \div 5.2$

8. *Explain* how the number line below can be used to check Example 2b.

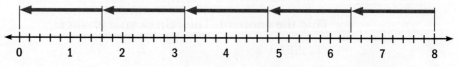

EXAMPLE 3 Rounding a Quotient

Collector's Cards You buy a pack of 8 Collector's cards for $2.15. Use a verbal model to find the price of each card. Round to the nearest cent.

STEP 1 Price of $=$ Price of $\div$ Number of cards
       1 card   package   in package

STEP 2 Divide $2.15 by 8.

$$
\begin{array}{r}
0.268 \\
8\overline{)2.150} \\
\underline{1\,6} \\
55 \\
\underline{48} \\
70 \\
\underline{64} \\
6
\end{array}
$$

> **ROUND YOUR ANSWER**
> To round to the nearest cent, or hundredth, divide only until the quotient reaches the thousandths' place. Then round.

STEP 3 **Round** to the nearest cent: $.268 $\longrightarrow$ $.27

▸ **Answer** The price of each card is about $.27.

✓ **GUIDED PRACTICE**   **for Example 3**

9. **What If?** In Example 3, suppose there were 12 cards in the pack. Find the price of each card. Round to the nearest cent.

2.4 EXERCISES

★ = **STANDARDIZED TEST PRACTICE**
   Exs. 40, 45, 47, 48, 65, and 66

○ = **HINTS AND HOMEWORK HELP**
   for Exs. 3, 11, 15, 43 at classzone.com

SKILL PRACTICE

1. **VOCABULARY** What two compatible numbers would you use to estimate the quotient 54.2 ÷ 6.7?

FINDING QUOTIENTS Find the quotient. Then check your answer.

> **SEE EXAMPLES 1 AND 2**
> on pp. 71–72
> for Exs. 2–13

2. 3.45 ÷ 15   **3.** 9 ÷ 7.2   4. 8.7822 ÷ 3.57

5. 0.3445 ÷ 6.5   6. 172.2 ÷ 82   7. 2199.24 ÷ 41

8. 1500.96 ÷ 16   9. 7 ÷ 1.4   10. 13 ÷ 6.5

11. 367.7 ÷ 3.677   12. 0.02997 ÷ 9.99   13. 1.387 ÷ 0.19

ROUNDING Find the quotient. Round your answer to the nearest hundredth.

> **SEE EXAMPLE 3**
> on p. 73
> for Exs. 14–22

14. 0.245 ÷ 6   **15.** 12 ÷ 6.4   16. 68 ÷ 3.1

17. 37.857 ÷ 7.5   18. 9.97 ÷ 2.9   19. 18.01 ÷ 3.28

20. 73.435 ÷ 3.8   21. 23.5 ÷ 0.66   22. 10.5 ÷ 0.37

2.4 Dividing Decimals   **73**

23. WHICH ONE DOESN'T BELONG? *Explain* your reasoning.

    A. $22.5 \div 18$ **B.** $22.5 \div 1.8$ **C.** $225 \div 18$ **D.** $2.25 \div 0.18$

24. ERROR ANALYSIS Describe and correct the error made in dividing 9.342 by 2.7.

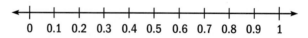

ESTIMATION Use compatible numbers to estimate the quotient.

25. $104.26 \div 4.98$ **26.** $1206.47 \div 29.2$ **27.** $1.90 \div 2.007$

28. $32.158 \div 14.974$ **29.** $143.865 \div 3.99$ **30.** $15.4 \div 2.461$

31. $202.099 \div 25.248$ **32.** $36.794 \div 9.018$ **33.** $358.1 \div 49.86$

XY **ALGEBRA Evaluate the expression when $x = 8.5$ and $z = 39.1$.**

34. $31.535 \div x + z$ **35.** $\frac{z}{x} - 0.23$ **36.** $50z \cdot 170.68 \div x$

37. $\frac{102}{3x} + 2z$ **38.** $x - 58.65 \div z$ **39.** $7(x + z) \div 9.8$

40. ★ MULTIPLE CHOICE What is the value of the expression $2.4 + 5.6 \div 0.02$?

    (A) 4.282   **(B)** 228.4   **(C)** 282.4   **(D)** 400

41. MODELING Copy the number line and show how to represent $0.8 \div 0.2$ to find the quotient.

```
  0   0.1  0.2  0.3  0.4  0.5  0.6  0.7  0.8  0.9   1
```

42. CHALLENGE Divide 3.24 by 0.1, 0.01, and 0.001. Multiply 3.24 by 10, 100, and 1000. *Explain* the relationship. *Write* a rule of this property.

PROBLEM SOLVING

43. CAR WASH Your class is holding a car wash to raise money for a field trip. You earn $4.75 for each car you wash. Estimate the number of cars you need to wash to reach your goal of $750.

44. WOOD How many pieces of wood measuring 3.75 inches long can be cut from a piece that is 30 inches long?

45. ★ MULTIPLE CHOICE You are knitting a scarf using 4 balls of yarn. The yarn costs a total of $24.88. How much does 1 ball of yarn cost?

    (A) $6.22   **(B)** $7.12   **(C)** $20.88   **(D)** $62.20

46. REASONING If you want to find out how many times heavier an alligator is than an iguana, would you *multiply* or *divide*? *Explain* your reasoning.

★ = STANDARDIZED TEST PRACTICE   ◯ = HINTS AND HOMEWORK HELP *at classzone.com*

47. ★ **SHORT RESPONSE** Copy the division problem at the right. Use estimation to place the decimal point in the quotient. *Explain* your reasoning.

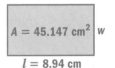

$$9.76\overline{)31.232}^{\;32}$$

48. ★ **WRITING** *Explain* how to use a number line model to find $1.5 \div 0.2$. Then explain how to use dimes and pennies to find $\$1.50 \div 0.2$.

49. **GEOMETRY** Use the formula $w = \dfrac{A}{l}$, where w is width, l is length, and A is area. Find the width of the rectangle.

$A = 45.147 \text{ cm}^2$ w

$l = 8.94 \text{ cm}$

READING IN MATH Read the passage below for Exercises 50–53.

Westward Expansion In 1803, the United States purchased the Louisiana Territory, 828,000 square miles of land west of the Mississippi River, from France for $15,000,000. The first of two payments to France for this land was $11,250,000; the second was for $3,750,000. In 1867, the United States purchased Alaska from Russia in one payment of $7,200,000.

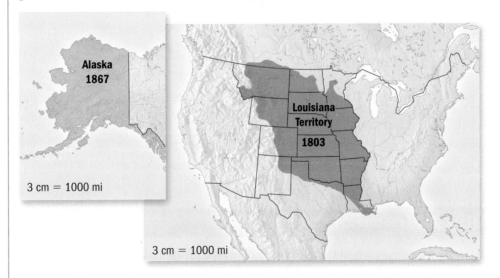

Alaska
1867

3 cm = 1000 mi

Louisiana
Territory
1803

3 cm = 1000 mi

50. **Compare** Use the maps to visually compare the sizes of the land areas purchased. Then compare the prices paid for those land areas.

51. **Estimate** The United States purchased Alaska for about $.02 per acre. About how many acres is Alaska?

52. **Measurement** Use the fact that $1 \text{ mi}^2 = 640$ acres. Find the number of square miles that were acquired in the purchase of Alaska.

53. **Reasoning** How much did the United States pay for each square mile of the Louisiana Territory? for each square mile of Alaska? Which was a better deal? *Explain* your reasoning.

54. **REASONING** The quotient of *a* and *b* is a whole number. Can *a* be a decimal number if *b* is a whole number? Can *b* be a decimal number if *a* is a whole number? Can both *a* and *b* be decimal numbers? Can the quotient be greater than *a*? *Justify* your answers using examples.

55. GEOMETRY A rectangle has a length of 12.3 feet and a width of 5.6 feet. A second rectangle has a length of 49.2 feet and a width of 22.4 feet.

    a. How many times as great as the perimeter of the smaller rectangle is the perimeter of the larger rectangle?

    b. *Compare* the areas of the two rectangles.

56. CHALLENGE *Describe* the possible values of the digits *a* and *b* in the quotient $a.b\overline{)3.6}$ such that the quotient is greater than the dividend.

 NEW JERSEY MIXED REVIEW **TEST PRACTICE** at classzone.com

57. Meredith buys 8 boxes of cereal at the grocery store. The prices per box range from $2.50 to $4.10. What is the range of the amount of money that she could spend?

    (A) $2.00 to $3.28

    (B) $20.00 to $32.00

    (C) $20.00 to $32.80

    (D) $25.00 to $41.00

58. Leslie drove the following distances, in miles, during the past five days: 62.4, 21.5, 8.3, 65.9, and 72.2. What was the total distance she drove during these days?

    (A) 228 mi   **(B)** 229.3 mi   **(C)** 230 mi   **(D)** 230.3 mi

---

QUIZ *for Lessons 2.1–2.4*

Copy and complete the statement using <, >, or =. *(p. 56)*

  1. 7.6 ? 7.63   **2.** 14.09 ? 14.1   **3.** 5.26 ? 5.260   **4.** 0.32 ? 0.0327

  5. Round 38.4985 to the nearest hundredth. *(p. 56)*

Find the sum or difference. *(p. 60)*

  6. $20.62 + 9.58$ **7.** $8.56 + 16.4$ **8.** $9.505 - 3.44$ **9.** $80.1 - 17.95$

10. SHOPPING You decide to buy a novel that costs $15.89, including tax. You give the cashier a $20 bill. How much change should you receive? *(p. 60)*

Find the product or quotient. Then check your answer.

  11. 9.58×6.19 *(p. 66)*   **12.** 3.45×1.66 *(p. 66)*

  13. $3.374 \div 0.35$ *(p. 71)*   **14.** $0.329 \div 28$ *(p. 71)*

15. CHOCOLATE In 1998, the average American consumed 12.2 pounds of chocolate. To the nearest hundredth pound, how much chocolate did the average American consume in one month? *(p. 71)*

Lessons 2.1–2.4

1. **ELECTRIC BILL** Lindsay's monthly electric bill is calculated on the following sliding scale using kilowatt-hours (kWh):

   • $15.25 for the first 100 kWh

   • $.07 for each additional kilowatt-hour up to and including 300 kWh

   • $.05 for each additional kilowatt-hour up to and including 450 kWh

   • $.04 for each kilowatt-hour over 450 kWh

   Her total bill for one month came to $38.55. How many kilowatt-hours did she use that month?

   A. 346 **B.** 358 **C.** 486 **D.** 495

2. **WOODWORKING** You cut squares with side lengths of 4.25 inches from a piece of wood that is 34 inches wide and 51 inches long.

   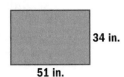

   51 in.
   34 in.

   How many squares with side length 4.25 inches can be cut from the wood?

   A. 40 **C.** 96

   B. 64 **D.** 144

3. **RACES** A race is 6.25 miles long. You average 9.2 minutes per mile. Your friend averages 9.6 minutes per mile. What was the difference in the number of minutes you and your friend took for the race?

   A. 1.5 **C.** 25

   B. 2.5 **D.** 57.5

4. **ART** Kelly is making a glass sculpture in the shape of a pyramid, as shown. The center of each of the four transparent triangular faces is connected to the center of every other face by wire. The wires cost $3.65 each. What is the total cost of the wires?

   A. $10.95 **C.** $21.90

   B. $14.60 **D.** $43.80

5. **SCHOOL FAIR** The table shows the amount of money raised by each of the 3 groups of seventh graders at a school fair. How much money did the 3 groups raise?

Group	7A	7B	7C
Money raised	$133.88	$148.59	$122.77

   A. $271.36 **C.** $405.24

   B. $282.47 **D.** $409.74

6. **OPEN-ENDED** An electric company calculates electric bills based on the following sliding scale:

   – First 100 kilowatt-hours (kWh): $15.25

   – Next 200 kWh: $.07 each

   – Next 150 kWh: $.05 each

   – Over 450 kWh: $.04 each

   • Lindsay's total bill for one month was $38.55. How many kilowatt-hours did she use that month? *Explain.*

   • Clyde's bill for one month was $27.40. Did he use more than 300 kilowatt-hours that month? *Explain.*

2.5 Scientific Notation

NJ 4.1.A.5 Use whole numbers, fractions, decimals, and percents to represent equivalent forms of the same number.

Before You multiplied whole numbers by powers of 10.

Now You'll read and write numbers using scientific notation.

Why? So you can express large numbers, as in Example 1.

KEY VOCABULARY
• scientific notation, p. 78

Models Joseph King constructed a 23-foot model of the Eiffel Tower using 110,000 toothpicks. How can you use powers of 10 to write 110,000?

One way to write large numbers is to use *scientific notation*, as shown below. Scientists write numbers in this form to make computations easier.

KEY CONCEPT   *For Your Notebook*

Using Scientific Notation

A number is written in **scientific notation** if it has the form $c \times 10^n$ where c is greater than or equal to 1 and less than 10, and n is a whole number.

Standard form	Product form	Scientific notation
2,860,000	$2.86 \times 1,000,000$	2.86×10^6

◆ EXAMPLE 1 Writing Numbers in Scientific Notation

 VOCABULARY

Powers of ten:
$10^1 = 10$
$10^2 = 100$
$10^3 = 1000$
$10^4 = 10,000$
$10^5 = 100,000$
$10^6 = 1,000,000$

As described above, Joseph King used 110,000 toothpicks to construct his Eiffel Tower model. To write 110,000 in scientific notation, use powers of 10.

Standard form	Product form	Scientific notation
110,000	$1.1 \times 100,000$	1.1×10^5
5 decimal places	5 zeros	Exponent is 5.

▶ **Answer** Joseph King used 1.1×10^5 toothpicks to make his model of the Eiffel Tower.

 GUIDED PRACTICE for Example 1

Write the number in scientific notation.

1. 450,000   **2.** 6,310,000   **3.** 10,000,000,000

4. 97,200   **5.** 348,400,000   **6.** 700

EXAMPLE 2 Writing Numbers in Standard Form

Write the number in standard form.

a. 7×10^3　　　　　**b.** 4.398×10^8　　　　　**c.** 5.2×10^{12}

SOLUTION

	Scientific notation	Product form	Standard form
a.	7×10^3	7×1000	7000
b.	4.398×10^8	$4.398 \times 100{,}000{,}000$	439,800,000
c.	5.2×10^{12}	$5.2 \times 1{,}000{,}000{,}000{,}000$	5,200,000,000,000

READING

You read 7×10^3 as "seven times ten raised to the third power," or "seven times ten cubed."

 GUIDED PRACTICE for Example 2

Write the number in standard form.

7. 3.71×10^4　　　　　**8.** 9×10^7　　　　　**9.** 4.652×10^{10}

10. 6.52×10^6　　　　　**11.** 1.22×10^3　　　　　**12.** 7.126×10^{10}

EXAMPLE 3 Comparing Numbers in Scientific Notation

Mars Mars has two moons, Phobos and Deimos. Phobos has a mass of 1.06×10^{16} kilograms. Deimos has a mass of 2.4×10^{15} kilograms. Which moon has the greater mass?

SOLUTION

To compare numbers written in scientific notation, first compare the exponents. If the exponents are equal, then compare the decimal parts.

Phobos: 1.06×10^{16}　　　　　**Deimos:** 2.4×10^{15}

Because $16 > 15$, $1.06 \times 10^{16} > 2.4 \times 10^{15}$.

▶ **Answer** Phobos has a greater mass than Deimos.

Check Write the numbers in standard form and compare.

$$1.06 \times 10^{16} = 10{,}600{,}000{,}000{,}000{,}000$$
$$2.4 \ \times 10^{15} = \ 2{,}400{,}000{,}000{,}000{,}000$$

So, $1.06 \times 10^{16} > 2.4 \times 10^{15}$. ✓

The Planet Mars

ANOTHER WAY

Think of 1.06×10^{16} as 10.6×10^{15}. Because $10.6 > 2.4$, 10.6×10^{15} is greater than 2.4×10^{15}. So, 1.06×10^{16} is greater than 2.4×10^{15}.

✓ **GUIDED PRACTICE** for Example 3

Copy and complete the statement using <, >, or =.

13. 9.74×10^{21} _?_ 2.1×10^{22}　　　　　**14.** 5.28×10^{12} _?_ 5.1×10^{12}

15. 1.06×10^{19} _?_ 7.5×10^{18}　　　　　**16.** 3.53×10^{37} _?_ 3.2×10^{37}

2.5 EXERCISES

 = **STANDARDIZED TEST PRACTICE**
Exs. 14, 40, 42, and 55

◯ = **HINTS** AND **HOMEWORK HELP**
for Exs. 9, 19, 21, 25, 39 at classzone.com

SKILL PRACTICE

VOCABULARY Tell whether the number is written in *scientific notation*, *standard form*, or *neither*. If neither, *explain* why.

1. 7.2×10^4 **2.** 34.2×10^5 **3.** 70,231   **4.** 1.764×10^{23}

WRITING IN SCIENTIFIC NOTATION Write the number in scientific notation.

SEE EXAMPLE 1
on p. 78
for Exs. 5–15

5. 41,200   **6.** 600   **7.** 29,200,000

8. 12,000,000   **9.** 154,000   **10.** 90,000,000,000

11. 102.4   **12.** 2000.1   **13.** 535

14. ★ **MULTIPLE CHOICE** What is 24,500,000 written in scientific notation?

(A) 2.45×10^5 **(B)** 24.5×10^6 **(C)** 2.45×10^7 **(D)** 24.5×10^7

15. **ERROR ANALYSIS** A friend says that the number 29,500,000 written in scientific notation is 29.5×10^6. Is your friend correct? *Explain.*

WRITING IN STANDARD FORM Write the number in standard form.

SEE EXAMPLE 2
on p. 79
for Exs. 16–24

16. 7.1×10^5 **17.** 2×10^3 **18.** 8.29×10^4

19. 1.5×10^2 **20.** 3.52×10^5 **21.** 5.884×10^9

22. 3.5802×10^7 **23.** 6.07×10^1 **24.** 4.40044×10^6

NUMBER SENSE Copy and complete the statement using <, >, or =.

SEE EXAMPLE 3
on p. 79
for Exs. 25–28

25. 8.12×10^{15} ? 1.5×10^{17} **26.** 2.33×10^{10} ? 7.6×10^{10}

27. 4.4×10^7 ? 44,000,000   **28.** 548,000,000 ? 5.48×10^7

29. **EXAMPLES AND NONEXAMPLES** Write three numbers in the form $c \times 10^n$ where the numbers are in scientific notation. Then write three other numbers in the same form, but not in scientific notation.

ORDERING Order the numbers from least to greatest.

30. 5.9×10^6 6.81×10^7 1.04×10^6 1.7×10^8

31. 3.25×10^5 3.5×10^5 7.98×10^4 2.61×10^6

32. 7.8×10^3 8.7×10^4 8.02×10^3 7.18×10^4

33. 1.101×10^8 1.1×10^8 1.11×10^8 1.10×10^7

ADDING NUMBERS IN SCIENTIFIC NOTATION Find the sum of the numbers.

34. $3.6 \times 10^{11} + 8.264 \times 10^{11}$ **35.** $9.37 \times 10^9 + 5.65 \times 10^9$

36. $1.25 \times 10^9 + 7.6 \times 10^8$ **37.** $2.4 \times 10^6 + 6.79 \times 10^9$

MONSTER TRUCKS **Use the following information.**

Bigfoot 5, the world's largest monster truck, is 15 feet 5 inches tall and weighs 38,000 pounds. Each tire is 10 feet tall and weighs 2.4×10^3 pounds.

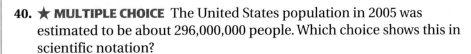

38. Write the weight of the truck in scientific notation.

39. Write the weight of one tire in standard form.

40. ★ **MULTIPLE CHOICE** The United States population in 2005 was estimated to be about 296,000,000 people. Which choice shows this in scientific notation?

Ⓐ 29.6×10^7 Ⓑ 2.96×10^8 Ⓒ 2.96×10^7 Ⓓ 296×10^6

41. **MATHEMATICIANS** Pythagoras, a Greek mathematician, was born about 2.6×10^3 years ago. Galileo, an Italian mathematician and astronomer, was born about 4.4×10^2 years ago. Who was born more recently?

42. ★ **SHORT RESPONSE** Which is greater: 6.7263×10^7 or 68.763×10^6? *Explain* your reasoning.

43. **LIGHT-YEARS** A *light-year,* the distance light travels in one year, is 5.88×10^{12} miles. The distance between Earth and the star Alpha Centauri A is 4.3 light-years. How many miles is this distance? Express your answer in standard form and in scientific notation.

44. **CABLE LENGTH** The distance around Earth's equator is about 1.32×10^8 feet. The total length of all of the wires on the Golden Gate Bridge is about 2.8 times this distance. What is the total length of the wires?

45. **CHALLENGE** Multiply the numbers 3.6×10^4 and 1.4×10^6. Express the product in scientific notation. What do you notice about the exponents of the factors and the product? Is your observation true when multiplying any two numbers in scientific notation? *Justify* your reasoning with examples.

 NEW JERSEY MIXED REVIEW   **TEST PRACTICE** at classzone.com

46. Greg is buying supplies for a company picnic. He can buy 3 loaves of white bread for $3.39 or 4 loaves of wheat bread for $4.56. He needs 12 loaves. Which bread should he buy to save as much money as possible and why?

Ⓐ Wheat bread because it is $1.14 for each loaf.

Ⓑ Wheat bread because there are more pieces in each loaf.

Ⓒ White bread because he can buy fewer than 12 loaves and still have enough bread for the picnic.

Ⓓ White bread because it is $1.13 for each loaf.

2.5 Using Scientific Notation

The **EE** key on a calculator is used to enter numbers written in scientific notation.

EXAMPLE 1 Earth has a mass of about 6×10^{21} metric tons. The mass of Neptune is about 17 times greater than the mass of Earth. What is the mass of Neptune?

SOLUTION

To find the mass of Neptune, multiply the mass of Earth by 17.

Keystrokes

6 **EE** 21 **×** 17 **=**

Display

$\boxed{1.02e+023}$

▶ **Answer** Neptune has a mass of about 1.02×10^{23} metric tons.

EXAMPLE 2 The distance between Earth and the Sun is about 9.3×10^{7} miles. The distance between Neptune and the Sun is about 2.7931×10^{9} miles. How many times farther is Neptune from the Sun than Earth?

SOLUTION

To find the number of times farther Neptune is from the Sun than Earth is, divide the distance between Neptune and the Sun by the distance between Earth and the Sun.

Keystrokes

2.7931 **EE** 9 **÷** 9.3 **EE** 7 **=**

Display

$\boxed{30.03333333}$

▶ **Answer** Neptune is about 30 times as far from the Sun as Earth is.

PRACTICE Use a calculator to evaluate the expression.

1. $(7.1 \times 10^{9}) + (2.0 \times 10^{8})$

2. $(5.67 \times 10^{5}) - (1.23 \times 10^{5})$

3. **ASTRONOMY** Earth's diameter is about 7.926×10^{3} miles. Neptune's diameter is about 3.0775×10^{4} miles. How many times greater is Neptune's diameter than Earth's diameter?

4. **STONE** The demand for crushed stone in the United States is 1.5×10^{9} tons per year. How much stone must be processed each day to meet this demand?

INVESTIGATION
Use before Lesson 2.6

GOAL
Measure objects using a metric ruler.

MATERIALS
• metric ruler

2.6 Measuring Length

The *metric system* is a decimal system of measurement. Two units of length in the metric system are *centimeters* and *millimeters*. To measure the length of an object using centimeters and millimeters, use a metric ruler.

EXPLORE Measure the length of the tube of paint.

STEP 1 **Line** up the ruler so that the top of the tube lines up with the 0 centimeter mark.

The distance between consecutive long tick marks is 1 centimeter

The distance between consecutive short tick marks is 1 millimeter

STEP 2 **Read** the measurement. A millimeter is equal to one tenth centimeter. Look for the tick mark closest to the end of the tube. It is closest to the fourth tick mark after 8 centimeters. So, the length of the tube of paint is 8.4 centimeters, or 84 millimeters.

PRACTICE Measure the length of the object in centimeters.

1. piece of chalk
2. pencil
3. staple
4. piece of paper
5. width of a belt
6. your shoe

DRAW CONCLUSIONS

7. **REASONING** Measure the objects in Exercises 1–6 in millimeters instead of centimeters. What do you notice about the measurements?

8. **ALGEBRA** Use your observations in Exercise 7. Write a rule for relating a length *c* of an object in centimeters to its length *m* in millimeters.

9. **WRITING** *Explain* why measuring to the nearest millimeter is more precise than measuring to the nearest centimeter.

2.6 Measuring in Metric Units

4.2.D.2 Select and use appropriate units and tools to measure quantities to the degree of precision needed in a particular problem-solving situation.

Before You used metric units.

Now You'll measure and estimate using metric units.

Why? So you can measure mass, as in Example 2.

KEY VOCABULARY
- **metric system,** *p. 84*
- **length: meter, millimeter, centimeter, kilometer,** *p. 84*
- **mass: gram, milligram, kilogram,** *p. 85*
- **capacity: liter, milliliter, kiloliter,** *p. 86*

The **metric system** is a decimal system of measurement. The metric system has units for length, mass, and capacity.

The **meter (m)** is the basic unit of length in the metric system. Three other metric units of length are the **millimeter (mm)**, **centimeter (cm)**, and **kilometer (km)**.

You can use the following benchmarks to estimate length.

1 millimeter thickness of a dime

1 centimeter width of a large paper clip

1 meter height of the back of a chair

1 kilometer combined length of 9 football fields

EXAMPLE 1 Using Metric Units of Length

Estimate the length of the bandage by imagining large paper clips laid next to it. Then measure the bandage with a metric ruler to check your estimate.

STEP 1 Estimate using large paper clips.

About 5 large paper clips fit next to the bandage, so it is about 5 centimeters long.

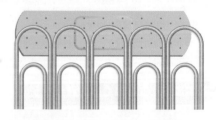

STEP 2 Measure using a ruler.

AVOID ERRORS
A typical metric ruler allows you to measure only to the nearest tenth of a centimeter.

Each centimeter is divided into tenths, so the bandage is 4.8 centimeters long.

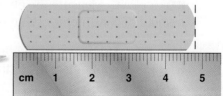

Mass Mass is the amount of matter that an object has. The **gram (g)** is the basic metric unit of mass. Two other metric units of mass are the **milligram (mg)** and **kilogram (kg)**.

EXAMPLE 2 **Measuring Mass**

Find the mass of the apples.

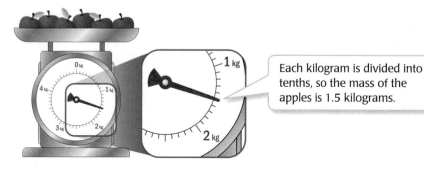

Each kilogram is divided into tenths, so the mass of the apples is 1.5 kilograms.

Mass Benchmarks You can use the following benchmarks to estimate mass.

1 milligram	**1 gram**	**1 kilogram**
grain of sugar	small paper clip	textbook

EXAMPLE 3 **Using Metric Units of Mass**

Copy and complete using the appropriate metric unit:
The mass of a CD is 16 __?__.

The mass of a CD is greater than the mass of 16 grains of sugar (16 mg), and it is less than the mass of 16 textbooks (16 kg). Because a good estimate for the mass of a CD is 16 paper clips, the appropriate metric unit is grams.

▶**Answer** The mass of a CD is 16 grams.

✓ **GUIDED PRACTICE** for Examples 1, 2, and 3

1. **What If?** Suppose you estimate with paper clips that a larger bandage is about 8 centimeters long. Is its actual length more likely to be 7.2 centimeters or 7.7 centimeters?

2. **What If?** Suppose there were only 3 apples on the scale in Example 2. Describe where the pointer would point relative to the 1 kg mark.

Copy and complete using the appropriate metric unit.

3. The mass of a baby is 4 __?__.   4. The mass of a tack is 200 __?__.

Capacity Capacity is a measure of the amount that a container can hold. The **liter (L)** is the basic metric unit of capacity. Two other metric units of capacity are the **milliliter (mL)** and **kiloliter (kL)**.

EXAMPLE 4 Measuring a Liquid Amount

Find the amount of liquid in the measuring cup.

Each 100 mL is divided into fourths, so the liquid is at the 225 mL level.

▶ **Answer** The measuring cup contains 225 milliliters of liquid.

Capacity Benchmarks You can use the following benchmarks to estimate capacity.

1 milliliter	**1 liter**	**1 kiloliter**
eyedropper	large water bottle	8 large trash cans

EXAMPLE 5 Using Metric Units of Capacity

What is the most reasonable capacity of a bathtub?

Ⓐ 750 mL   Ⓑ 14 L   Ⓒ 240 L   Ⓓ 5 kL

SOLUTION

Both 750 mL (750 eyedroppers) and 14 L (14 water bottles) are too little to fill a bathtub. Using 5 kL (40 large trash cans) would overfill a bathtub. That leaves 240 L (240 large water bottles), which seems reasonable.

▶ **Answer** The most reasonable capacity of a bathtub is 240 L. The correct answer is C. Ⓐ Ⓑ ● Ⓓ

 GUIDED PRACTICE for Examples 4 and 5

5. **What If?** Suppose there was twice as much liquid in the measuring cup in Example 4. Describe the liquid level relative to the mark for 400 mL.

Match the object with the appropriate capacity.

6. Tube of toothpaste   7. Large trash can   8. Bottle cap

A. 8 mL   B. 175 mL   C. 125 L

2.6 EXERCISES

SKILL PRACTICE

VOCABULARY **Copy and complete the statement.**

1. Milligrams, grams, and kilograms are metric units of __?__.

2. Milliliters, liters, and kiloliters are metric units of __?__.

ESTIMATION **Estimate the length of the object. Then measure the object using a metric ruler.**

SEE EXAMPLE 1
on p. 84
for Exs. 3–8

3. your foot
4. pencil eraser
5. this page
6. stapler
7. your thumb
8. calculator

FINDING MASS **Find the mass of the object.**

SEE EXAMPLE 2
on p. 85
for Exs. 9–12

9.

10.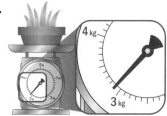

11.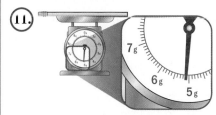

12.

CHOOSING UNITS **Copy and complete the statement using the appropriate metric unit.**

SEE EXAMPLES 1, 3, AND 5
on pp. 84–86
for Exs. 13–26

13. A tennis racket is 1.2 __?__ long.
14. A piece of paper is 0.1 __?__ thick.

15. The mass of a TV is 20 __?__.
16. The mass of a golf ball is 46 __?__.

17. A juice box contains 200 __?__.
18. A can of soup contains 0.4 __?__.

19. A building is 100 __?__ high.
20. The Hudson River is 507 __?__ long.

21. A width of a belt is 3 __?__.
22. The mass of a staple is 32 __?__.

23. The mass of a bike is 8 __?__.
24. The mass of a sock is 25 __?__.

25. A mug can hold 400 __?__.
26. A large bottle of soda holds 2 __?__.

Animated Math at classzone.com

SEE EXAMPLE 4
on p. 86
for Ex. 27

27. **WHICH ONE DOESN'T BELONG?** Which is *not* a measure of capacity?

    A. 40 mL
    B. 15 kg
    C. 2 L
    D. 75 kL

CAPACITY Find the amount of liquid in the measuring cup.

SEE EXAMPLE 4
on p. 86
for Exs. 28–31

28.

29.

30.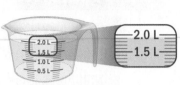

31.

★ **MULTIPLE CHOICE** In Exercises 32–34, choose the letter of the *most reasonable* measurement.

SEE EXAMPLE 5
on p. 86
for Exs. 32–34

32. What is the perimeter of a doormat?

Ⓐ 5 cm   Ⓑ 0.3 m   Ⓒ 2.5 m   Ⓓ 30 m

33. What is the mass of a toothpick?

Ⓐ 1 mg   Ⓑ 100 mg   Ⓒ 10 g   Ⓓ 1 kg

34. What is the capacity of a birdbath?

Ⓐ 90 mL   Ⓑ 2 L   Ⓒ 50 L   Ⓓ 2 kL

35. **ERROR ANALYSIS** A student claims that the mass of a desk is about 400 grams. Is this a reasonable estimate? *Explain* your reasoning.

MATCHING Match the object with the appropriate measurement.

36. cell phone   37. paper cup   38. snowboard   39. light bulb

A. 20 g   B. 80 g   C. 100 cm   D. 240 mL

40. **CHALLENGE** Name an object that has a large capacity and a small mass. Name an object that has a small capacity and a large mass.

PROBLEM SOLVING

NUMBER SENSE In Exercises 41–43, copy and complete using 3, 30, or 300.

㊶ **WHEELBARROWS** An empty wheelbarrow has a mass of about __?__ kg.

42. **BANANAS** Two bananas have a mass of __?__ g.

43. **STAMPS** A postage stamp has a mass of about __?__ mg.

44. **WOOD** Find the length of the piece of wood shown at the right.

45. ★ **MULTIPLE CHOICE** Which capacity could be used to describe the amount of syrup in two syrup bottles?

    (A) 500 L   (B) 50 mL   (C) 20 L   (D) 500 mL

46. ★ **WRITING** Julia thinks that the mass of a volleyball is about 300 grams. Her friend Bailey thinks that its mass is about 3 kilograms. Who is right? *Explain* your reasoning.

47. ★ **SHORT RESPONSE** Use benchmarks to order the measurements from least to greatest: 1 kg, 5 g, 10 kg, 50 mg. *Explain* your choice of benchmarks.

48. ★ **SHORT RESPONSE** You want to determine how much flour will fit into a container. Do you need to know the *mass* or the *capacity* of the container? Would an appropriate measuring tool be a *scale*, a *measuring cup*, or a *tablespoon*? *Explain* your reasoning.

49. ★ **OPEN-ENDED MATH** Find benchmarks other than those given on page 86 for 1 milliliter, 1 liter, and 1 kiloliter.

50. **CHALLENGE** You measure an object to the nearest gram. You find the measurement to be 8 grams. You then measure the same object to the nearest tenth of a gram. *Describe* the range of possible measurements. *Explain* your reasoning.

51. **CHALLENGE** A pool designed for swimming laps is 12 feet wide by 24 feet long by 4 feet deep. *Describe* the process you would use to estimate the capacity of the pool in liters.

 NEW JERSEY MIXED REVIEW   **TEST PRACTICE** at classzone.com

52. The sales of a new gadget from 2002 through 2004 are shown at the right. Assuming the trend continues, which is the best prediction of the number of gadgets sold in 2008?

    (A) 2×10^4 (B) 2×10^5

    (C) 2×10^6 (D) 2×10^7

Year	Number of gadgets sold
2002	20
2003	200
2004	2000

53. A jewelry store owner purchased several rings and sold them for $81.75 each. Four rings were sold in the first week, and 5 were sold in the second week. What piece of information is needed to find the profit made from the sales of rings in the first two weeks?

    (A) How much the owner paid for the rings

    (B) The number of rings sold in the third week

    (C) The total number of rings purchased

    (D) The total number of rings sold in the first two weeks

2.7 Converting Metric Units

 4.2.D.1 Solve problems requiring calculations that involve different units of measurement within a measurement system . . .

Before	You used metric units of length, mass, and capacity.
Now	You'll convert between metric units.
Why?	So you can calculate with metric units, as in Ex. 52.

KEY VOCABULARY
- meter, *p. 84*
- gram, *p. 85*
- liter, *p. 86*

Running In the 4 × 800 meter relay race, four teammates each run 800 meters. The total length of the race is 3200 meters. How many kilometers long is the race?

The metric system is a base-ten system. Metric prefixes are associated with decimal place values.

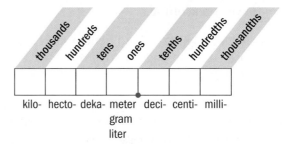

To convert between metric units *n* decimal places apart, multiply or divide as follows.

Multiply by 10^n.

larger unit ⟷ smaller unit

Divide by 10^n.

EXAMPLE 1 Converting Metric Units of Length

To find the length in kilometers of the relay race described above, convert 3200 meters to kilometers.

SOLUTION

You are converting from a smaller unit (meters) to a larger unit (kilometers), so *divide* by a power of 10.

From meters to kilometers, the decimal point is moved **3 places** to the left, so divide by 10^3, or 1000.

$$3200 \div 1000 = 3.2$$

$$3200 \text{ meters} = 3.2 \text{ kilometers}$$

▶ **Answer** The 4 × 800 meter relay race is 3.2 kilometers long.

EXAMPLE 2 Converting Units of Mass and Capacity

Copy and complete the statement.

a. 15 g = __?__ mg   **b.** 590 mL = __?__ L

SOLUTION

a. To convert from grams to milligrams, multiply by 1000.

$$15 \times 1000 = 15{,}000, \text{ so } 15 \text{ g} = 15{,}000 \text{ mg.}$$

b. To convert from milliliters to liters, divide by 1000.

$$590 \div 1000 = 0.59, \text{ so } 590 \text{ mL} = 0.59 \text{ L.}$$

✓ **GUIDED PRACTICE** for Examples 1 and 2

Copy and complete the statement.

1. 6800 m = __?__ km   **2.** 54 m = __?__ mm   **3.** 830 cm = __?__ m

4. 115 mm = __?__ cm   **5.** 9.25 kL = __?__ L   **6.** 100 g = __?__ kg

---

EXAMPLE 3 Comparing Metric Measurements

Copy and complete the statement using <, >, or =.

a. 320 cm __?__ 4 m   **b.** 0.2 kg __?__ 184 g

SOLUTION

a. 320 cm __?__ 4 m   **Strategy: Convert meters to centimeters.**

320 cm __?__ 400 cm   **4 × 100 = 400, so 4 m = 400 cm.**

320 cm < 400 cm   **Compare.**

▶ **Answer** 320 cm < 4 m

b. 0.2 kg __?__ 184 g   **Strategy: Convert kilograms to grams.**

200 g __?__ 184 g   **0.2 × 1000 = 200, so 0.2 kg = 200 g.**

200 g > 184 g   **Compare.**

▶ **Answer** 0.2 kg > 184 g

✓ **GUIDED PRACTICE** for Example 3

Copy and complete the statement using <, >, or =.

7. 1.4 kL __?__ 1400 L   **8.** 1.5 g __?__ 150 mg   **9.** 5.8 cm __?__ 580 mm

10. 4.9 m __?__ 490 cm   **11.** 7.2 L __?__ 7200 mL   **12.** 8.3 kg __?__ 83,000 mg

EXAMPLE 4 Standardized Test Practice

ELIMINATE CHOICES
Because 100 cm = 1 m, there are about 4 pieces per meter. The sandwich is 322.5 meters long, so 12.5 and 125 are too few sections. You can eliminate choices A and B.

Dividing with Decimals In 1979, Chef Franz Eichenauer made a submarine sandwich that was 322.5 meters long. Suppose the sandwich was cut into pieces that each measured 25.8 centimeters. How many pieces would there be?

A 12.5　　　**B** 125　　　**C** 1250　　　**D** 12,500

SOLUTION

AVOID ERRORS
Express both measures using the same unit before dividing.

STEP 1 **Convert** 322.5 meters to centimeters by multiplying by 100.

$$322.5 \times 100 = 32,250, \text{ so } 322.5 \text{ m} = 32,250 \text{ cm}$$

STEP 2 **Divide** the total length of the sandwich by the length of each piece to find the number of pieces.

$$32,250 \text{ cm} \div 25.8 \text{ cm} = 1250$$

▶ **Answer** The submarine sandwich would be divided into 1250 pieces. The correct answer is C. **A** **B** **C** **D**

✓ **GUIDED PRACTICE** | **for Example 4**

13. **What If?** In Example 4, suppose the sandwich was cut into pieces that each measured 37.5 centimeters. How many pieces would there be?

2.7 EXERCISES

HOMEWORK KEY

★ = **STANDARDIZED TEST PRACTICE**
Exs. 29, 49, 51, 55, and 69

○ = **HINTS AND HOMEWORK HELP**
for Exs. 5, 9, 21, 45 at classzone.com

SKILL PRACTICE

VOCABULARY Copy and complete the statement.

1. 1 liter = 1000 _?_

2. 1 meter = 100 _?_

3. 1 gram = 0.001 _?_

CONVERTING UNITS Copy and complete the statement.

SEE EXAMPLES 1 AND 2
on pp. 90–91
for Exs. 4–18

4. 72 mg = _?_ g

5. 49 m = _?_ cm

6. 890 mL = _?_ L

7. 470 mL = _?_ L

8. 1.25 km = _?_ m

9. 3.75 kg = _?_ g

10. 0.28 cm = _?_ mm

11. 0.75 L = _?_ mL

12. 1540 mm = _?_ cm

13. 3528 mm = _?_ cm

14. 45,250 g = _?_ kg

15. 840,000 mg = _?_ g

16. 2.42 kL = _?_ mL

17. 1.28 kg = _?_ mg

18. 1,250,000 mm = _?_ km

19. ERROR ANALYSIS Describe and correct the error made in converting 50 milligrams to grams.

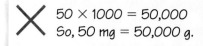

$50 \times 1000 = 50{,}000$
So, 50 mg = 50,000 g.

COMPARING MEASUREMENTS Copy and complete using <, >, or =.

SEE EXAMPLE 3
on p. 91
for Exs. 20–29

20. 160 mg ? 16 g   **21.** 740 L ? 0.74 kL   **22.** 2 km ? 2000 m

23. 4.1 g ? 410 mg   **24.** 6.5 m ? 65 cm   **25.** 8.9 mL ? 0.89 L

26. 2300 g ? 2 kg   **27.** 6.9 m ? 70 cm   **28.** 9.6 L ? 9600 mL

29. ★ **MULTIPLE CHOICE** Which amount is greater than 13 liters?

    A 1300 mL   **B** 130,000 mL   **C** 0.0013 L   **D** 0.013 L

EXPRESSIONS WITH UNITS Find the sum or difference. Write your answer using the smaller unit of measurement.

30. 3 cm + 11 mm   **31.** 4 L − 35 mL   **32.** 6000 g − 3.5 kg

33. 25 mg + 1 kg − 893 g   **34.** 95 m + 0.4 km − 225 mm   **35.** 3 kL + 2550 mL − 3001 L

PERIMETER AND AREA Find the perimeter of the rectangle in centimeters, then find the area of the rectangle in square centimeters.

36.
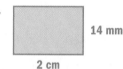
14 mm
2 cm

37.

8 mm
2.5 cm

38.

1.5 cm
5 mm

ORDERING MEASUREMENTS Order the measurements from least to greatest.

39. 60 g, 69 mg, 9.5 mg, 0.04 kg, 45 g   **40.** 15 L, 1.5 mL, 1500 mL, 1.5 kL, 0.15 kL

CHALLENGE Find the side length in millimeters of a square with the given area.

41. 9 cm^2 **42.** 36 cm^2 **43.** 100 cm^2

PROBLEM SOLVING

SEE EXAMPLE 4
on p. 92
for Exs. 44–46

44. GUIDED PROBLEM SOLVING You drink 1.44 liters of water per day. One fluid ounce is about 30 milliliters. How many 8 ounce glasses of water do you drink each day?

    a. How many milliliters are in 1.44 liters?

    b. How many ounces equals the number of milliliters from part (a)?

    c. How many 8 ounce glasses do you drink each day?

45. MEASUREMENT A chain of paper clips linked end to end is 2.7 meters long. Each paper clip is 4.5 centimeters long. About how many paper clips make up the chain?

46. WATER CONSERVATION A leaky faucet drips 23.64 liters per day. How many milliliters of water does the leaky faucet drip in one hour?

47. ORANGES An orange has a mass of 200 grams. You buy 20 oranges. What is the mass of the 20 oranges, in kilograms?

48. STAPLES A staple has a mass of 31 milligrams. What is the mass of 250 staples, in grams?

49. ★ OPEN-ENDED MATH *Describe* a situation where it would be helpful to use a change of unit.

50. MULTI-STEP PROBLEM A can of lemonade has a capacity of 355 mL.

   a. Convert the capacity of the can of lemonade to liters.

   b. How many liters are in seven two liter bottles?

   c. How many cans of lemonade does it take for their capacity to exceed the capacity of the seven two liter bottles? *Explain* the steps you used to find your answer.

51. ★ MULTIPLE CHOICE A rectangular deck is 16 meters long and 18 meters wide. What is the perimeter of the deck, in centimeters?

   Ⓐ 3400 cm   **Ⓑ** 6800 cm   **Ⓒ** 28,800 cm   **Ⓓ** 57,600 cm

52. GORILLA GROWTH A baby gorilla has a mass of about 2620 grams at birth. Baby gorillas grow at a fairly steady rate for the first month after birth.

   a. Determine the average number of grams the baby gorilla grows each day for the first 30 days.

   b. About how many kilograms is a 30-day-old gorilla?

Birth, 2620 g   10 Days, 2960 g   20 Days, 3300 g

53. MULTI-STEP PROBLEM The radius of Earth is approximately 6.38×10^6 meters.

   a. Mental Math Write the radius of Earth in standard form.

   b. Calculate Convert the radius from meters to kilometers.

   c. Explain What is the diameter of Earth, in kilometers? *Explain* how you found the answer. Then write the answer in scientific notation.

54. ◆ MULTIPLE REPRESENTATIONS Use the square to the right. Each side of the square is 0.25 decimeter.

   a. Draw a square that is 1 decimeter long on each side.

   b. Measure the sides of your square in millimeters.

   c. Find the area of your square in square millimeters. Represent this area as a power of 10.

0.25 decimeter

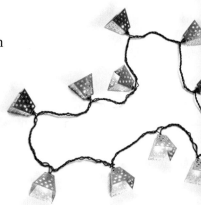

55. ★ **SHORT RESPONSE** Fifty mini-lights are equally spaced on a string of lights 7.5 meters long. There is a light at one end, and 15 centimeters between the last light and the plug at the other end. How many centimeters are between each light? *Explain.*

56. **CHALLENGE** Show two ways to find the area, in square centimeters, of a rectangle with a length of 4.5 meters and a width of 2.25 meters.

 NEW JERSEY MIXED REVIEW

TEST PRACTICE at classzone.com

57. Use a metric ruler to find the dimensions of the eraser at the right. Which best represents the perimeter of the eraser?

   Ⓐ 4.5 cm   **Ⓑ** 6 cm

   Ⓒ 7.5 cm   **Ⓓ** 9 cm

58. Which expression can be used to find the number of 2.3-inch wide coupons that can be placed across a piece of paper that is 11.5 inches wide?

   Ⓐ 11.5 + 2.3   **Ⓑ** 11.5 − 2.3   **Ⓒ** 11.5 × 2.3   **Ⓓ** 11.5 ÷ 2.3

QUIZ *for Lessons 2.5–2.7*

1. Write 987,000 in scientific notation. *(p. 78)*

2. **EARTH'S CORE** Beneath Earth's crust, there are 3 layers. The *mantle* is 1.8×10^3 miles thick, the *outer core* is 1.4×10^3 miles thick, and the *inner core* is 8×10^2 miles thick. Which layer is the thickest? *(p. 78)*

Copy and complete using the appropriate metric unit. *(p. 84)*

3. A skateboard is 85 __?__ long.   4. The mass of a pencil is 10 __?__ .

Copy and complete the statement. *(p. 90)*

5. 3200 mg = __?__ g   6. 16 L = __?__ mL   7. 57 cm = __?__ mm

8. **PUMPKIN CONTEST** A pumpkin contest is held at a county fair. The pumpkin with the greatest mass is declared the winner. Which pumpkins will be awarded first, second, and third place? *(p. 90)*

Name	Orange 1	Stumpy	Pie Guy	Pumped Up	Miss P.
Mass	18,000 g	45 kg	6300 g	37.5 kg	40,000 g

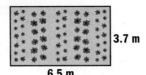
Lessons 2.5–2.7

1. **TOUR DE FRANCE** In 2004, the distance for the 20 stage Tour de France race was 3,395 kilometers. After 10 stages, the distance traveled is 1,581 kilometers. How many meters are left in the race?

   A. 1814

   B. 1.814×10^5

   C. 1.814×10^6

   D. 1.814×10^7

2. **AREA** What is the area of the garden below, in square centimeters?

   3.7 m

   6.5 m

   A. 24.05   **C.** 24,050

   B. 2405   **D.** 240,500

3. **SKIS** The length of a ski could be __?__.

   A. 10 m   **C.** 150 mm

   B. 80 cm   **D.** 175 m

4. **PERIMETER** A deck is 9 meters long and 14 meters wide. What is the perimeter of the deck, in centimeters?

   A. 46   **C.** 460

   B. 126   **D.** 4600

5. **SODA** You offer to bring soda to a party of 30 people. How many 2-liter bottles of soda do you need to bring so that every person can have two 300 mL glasses of soda?

   A. 2   **C.** 18

   B. 9   **D.** 180

6. **SPEED OF LIGHT** In 1676, with Earth at the point in its orbit farthest away from Jupiter, the Danish astronomer Ole Roemer found that light from Jupiter's moons took 16.55 minutes longer to get to Earth than it had when Earth was at its closest point. The difference in distance between these two points is now known to be 2.98×10^{11} meters. What is the approximate speed of light, in meters per minute, using these figures?

   A. 3.001×10^8

   B. 1.801×10^9

   C. 3.001×10^9

   D. 1.801×10^{10}

7. **FRIENDSHIP BRACELETS** You are making friendship bracelets out of colored string. For each bracelet, you need 75 centimeters of string. Each meter of string costs $.49. How much does it cost to buy the string needed for 12 bracelets?

   A. $4.41

   B. $8.46

   C. $36.75

   D. $44.10

8. **OPEN-ENDED** In 2004, the distance for the 20-stage Tour de France race was 3,385 kilometers.

   • Write the distance of the race in meters.

   • Write the distance in scientific notation.

   • After 10 stages, the distance traveled is 1840.5 kilometers. How many meters are left in the race? Write your answer in scientific notation.

REVIEW KEY VOCABULARY

- decimal, *p. 56*
- front-end estimation, *p. 61*
- leading digit, *p. 66*
- compatible numbers, *p. 71*
- scientific notation, *p. 78*
- metric system, *p. 84*

- meter, *p. 84*
- millimeter, *p. 84*
- centimeter, *p. 84*
- kilometer, *p. 84*
- gram, *p. 85*
- milligram, *p. 85*

- kilogram, *p. 85*
- liter, *p. 86*
- milliliter, *p. 86*
- kiloliter, *p. 86*

VOCABULARY EXERCISES

1. Give three examples of decimals.

2. What is the leading digit of 0.0398?

3. What is the difference between scientific notation and standard form?

In Exercises 4–6, copy and complete the statement.

4. Milliliters, liters, and kiloliters are metric units of __?__.

5. The __?__ is the basic unit of length in the metric system.

6. The __?__ is the basic metric unit of capacity.

REVIEW EXAMPLES AND EXERCISES

2.1 Comparing, Ordering, and Rounding Decimals   *pp. 56–59*

EXAMPLE

Compare 14.3 and 14.14.

$$14.30$$
$$14.14$$

— The tens' and ones' digits are the same.

— Write a zero as a placeholder.

— The tenths' digits are different. 3 > 1, so 14.30 > 14.14.

EXERCISES

In Exercises 7–9, copy and complete the statement using <, >, or =.

SEE EXAMPLES 1, 2, AND 3
on pp. 56–57
for Exs. 7–11

7. 8.54 _?_ 8.55

8. 6.11 _?_ 6.01

9. 0.051 _?_ 0.006

10. Order 1.11, 1.01, 0.01, 1.1, 0.11, and 0.1 from least to greatest.

11. *Explain* how to round a decimal to the nearest hundredth.

2.2 Adding and Subtracting Decimals

EXAMPLE

a. $9.325 + 17.38$

$$\begin{array}{r} 9.325 \\ + 17.380 \\ \hline 26.705 \end{array}$$ ← Write zero as a placeholder.

b. $8 - 3.74$

$$\begin{array}{r} 8.00 \\ - 3.74 \\ \hline 4.26 \end{array}$$ ← Write zeros as placeholders.

EXERCISES

Find the sum or difference.

SEE EXAMPLES
1, 2, AND 3
on pp. 60–61
for Exs. 12–24

12. $54.2 + 19.25$ **13.** $1.295 + 24.6$ **14.** $100 - 16.574$ **15.** $35.002 - 9.9$

Estimate the sum or difference using front-end estimation.

16. $28.07 + 10.89$ **17.** $6.4 + 6.573$ **18.** $34.77 - 14.19$ **19.** $8.32 - 3.84$

Evaluate the expression when $x = 2.75$ and $y = 16.2$.

20. $x + 10.32$ **21.** $5 + y + x$ **22.** $y - 3.909$ **23.** $22.02 - y + x$

24. Perimeter A rectangular floating dock is 9.2 feet long and 5.9 feet wide. Estimate the perimeter of the dock.

2.3 Multiplying Decimals

EXAMPLE

a.
$$\begin{array}{r} 7.32 \\ \times \quad 12 \\ \hline 1464 \\ 732 \quad\; \\ \hline 87.84 \end{array}$$
2 decimal places
+ 0 decimal places
2 decimal places

b.
$$\begin{array}{r} 2.354 \\ \times \quad 0.03 \\ \hline 0.07062 \end{array}$$
3 decimal places
+ 2 decimal places
5 decimal places

EXERCISES

Find the product. Then check that your answer is reasonable.

SEE EXAMPLES
1 AND 2
on pp. 66–67
for Exs. 25–33

25. 54×18.4 **26.** 2.5×34.6 **27.** 10.21×6.74 **28.** 0.002×9.009

29. 4.61×17.86 **30.** 9.156×21.007 **31.** 15×89.741 **32.** 195×1.984

33. Baseball Cal Ripken Jr. played major league baseball for 21 years. He played about 142.9 games each year. How many games did he play in his career? Round to the nearest whole number.

98   Chapter 2   Decimal Operations

2.4 Dividing Decimals

EXAMPLE

Find the quotient 6 ÷ 1.2.

$$1.2\overline{)6.0}$$

To multiply divisor and dividend by 10, move both decimal points 1 place to the right. Write a zero as a placeholder.

$$\begin{array}{r} 5 \\ 12\overline{)60} \\ 60 \\ \hline 0 \end{array}$$

EXERCISES

SEE EXAMPLES 1, 2, AND 3 on pp. 71–73 for Exs. 34–46

Find the quotient. Then check your answer.

34. 3.5 ÷ 14   **35.** 30.6 ÷ 9   **36.** 61.6 ÷ 7   **37.** 28.2 ÷ 3

38. 71 ÷ 0.5   **39.** 7434.44 ÷ 98.6   **40.** 1.4568 ÷ 6.07   **41.** 0.7866 ÷ 8.74

42. Silver Platter Mike gives his parents an engraved silver platter for their anniversary. The engraving says "Happy Anniversary" and costs a total of $13.60. How much does each letter cost to engrave?

Find the quotient. Round the quotient to the nearest cent.

43. $4.68 ÷ 5   **44.** $60.05 ÷ 2   **45.** $16.95 ÷ 6   **46.** $22.90 ÷ 50

2.5 Scientific Notation

EXAMPLE

Write the number 183,000 in scientific notation.

Standard form	Product form	Scientific notation
183,000	$1.83 \times 100{,}000$	1.83×10^5
5 decimal places	5 zeros	Exponent is 5.

EXERCISES

SEE EXAMPLES 1 AND 2 on pp. 78–79 for Exs. 47–54

Write the number in scientific notation.

47. 3,356,000   **48.** 5600   **49.** 780,000   **50.** 40,200

Write the number in standard form.

51. 4.06×10^8 **52.** 9.3×10^6 **53.** 1.25×10^2 **54.** 3.887×10^5

2.6 Measuring in Metric Units

pp. 84–89

EXAMPLE

**Copy and complete the statement using the appropriate metric unit:
The mass of a DVD is 22 _?_ .**

The mass of a DVD is greater than the mass of 22 grains of sugar (22 mg),
and it is less than the mass of 22 textbooks (22 kg). Because a good estimate
for the mass of a DVD is 22 paper clips, the appropriate metric unit is grams.

▶ **Answer** The mass of a DVD is 22 grams.

EXERCISES

SEE EXAMPLES
1, 2, 3, AND 4
on pp. 84–86
for Exs. 55–60

Copy and complete the statement using the appropriate metric unit.

55. The length of a parking space is 5.1 _?_ .   **56.** The mass of an insect is 15 _?_ .

Match the object with the appropriate measurement.

57. stapler   **58.** popsicle stick   **59.** computer keyboard   **60.** bottle

   A. 12 cm   **B.** 3 L   **C.** 42 cm   **D.** 75 g

2.7 Converting Metric Units

pp. 90–95

EXAMPLE

Copy and complete the statement.

   a. 32 g = _?_ mg

   To convert from grams to milligrams,
   multiply by 1000.

   $32 \times 1000 = 32{,}000$

   So, 32 g = 32,000 mg.

   b. 1300 mL = _?_ L

   To convert from milliliters to liters,
   divide by 1000.

   $1300 \div 1000 = 1.3$

   So, 1300 mL = 1.3 L.

EXERCISES

SEE EXAMPLES
1, 2, AND 3
on pp. 90–91
for Exs. 61–69

Copy and complete the statement.

61. 7 cm = _?_ m   **62.** 802 L = _?_ mL   **63.** 9.4 mg = _?_ kg

Copy and complete the statement using <, >, or =.

64. 240 cm _?_ 24 m   **65.** 9800 mg _?_ 9.798 g   **66.** 4.302 kL _?_ 4320 L

67. 57 g _?_ 0.57 kg   **68.** 762 mL _?_ 7.62 L   **69.** 1.450 m _?_ 1450 mm

@HomeTutor
classzone.com
Chapter Test Practice

Copy and complete the statement using <, >, or =.

1. 12.01 _?_ 12.101   **2.** 34.05 _?_ 34.04   **3.** 6.29 _?_ 6.3

Find the sum, difference, product, or quotient.

4. $4.88 + 219.405$ **5.** $6.67 + 2.36$ **6.** $6 - 2.65$ **7.** $30.105 - 9.9$

8. 0.94×0.63 **9.** 0.009×0.9 **10.** 0.16×8 **11.** 0.72×0.146

12. $60.25 \div 5$ **13.** $53.756 \div 8.9$ **14.** $0.291 \div 9.7$ **15.** $0.084 \div 0.2$

16. Evaluate $5.7 + 2.8 \div x$ when $x = 0.04$.

17. Write 786,000 in scientific notation.

18. Write 8.2×10^6 in standard form.

Copy and complete the statement.

19. 8.7 cm = _?_ mm   **20.** 28 kL = _?_ L   **21.** 1.7 g = _?_ kg

22. CURRENCY The exchange rates in U.S. dollars for several currencies are shown below. Write the values in order from least to greatest.

E.U. euro	U.S. dollar	Canadian dollar	Mexican peso	Japanese yen
0.8375	1	1.1648	10.767	114.18

23. SCHOOL SUPPLIES You are shopping for school supplies. You have $12. Can you buy everything on the list? Assume that there is no sales tax.

Notebook $1.99
Pen $1.15
Pencil $.65
Stapler $6.29

Copy and complete the statement using the appropriate metric unit.

24. The mass of a crayon is 25 _?_ .   **25.** The height of a giraffe is 5 _?_ .

26. Find the length of the eraser shown.

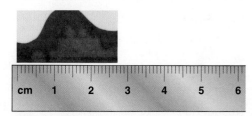

27. REFRESHMENTS You offer to bring soda to 30 people at a fundraiser. How many 2-liter bottles of soda do you need to bring so that every person but you can have two 300-mL glasses of soda? *Explain* your reasoning.

OPEN-ENDED QUESTIONS

TEST PREPARATION

PROBLEM

FUNDRAISER Your class is selling refreshments at a school dance to raise money for a class trip. You buy ten 2-liter bottles of soda. Each bottle costs $1.29. The soda is served in 250-milliliter plastic cups for $.75 a cup. How much money will you raise for your class trip by selling all of the soda? *Explain* your reasoning.

Below are sample solutions to the problem. Read each solution and the comments on the left to see why the sample represents full credit, partial credit, or no credit.

SAMPLE 1: Full Credit Solution

> This reasoning is the key to choosing the correct problem solving plan.

The amount of money raised by selling soda at a school dance is equal to the total soda sales minus the cost of buying the soda.

Find the total soda sales.

> The steps are clearly stated and reflect correct mathematical reasoning.

Total millimeters of soda in ten 2-liter bottles:

Total amount of soda: 10 bottles $\times$ 2 L = 20 L = 20,000 mL

Number of cups poured:

Number of cups: 20,000 mL $\div$ 250 mL = 80

Total soda sales:

Total soda sales = Number of cups $\cdot$ Price of each cup

Total soda sales = 80(0.75)

Total soda sales = $60

Find the total cost of buying the soda.

> All of the calculations are correct.

Total cost of soda = Number of bottles $\cdot$ Cost per bottle

Total cost of soda = 10(1.29)

Total cost of soda = $12.90

Find the amount of money raised.

Subtract the total cost from the total sales.

Money raised: $60 − $12.90 = $47.10

> The answer is correct.

A total of $47.10 will be raised for the class trip by selling all of the soda.

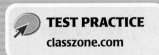

SAMPLE 2: Partial Credit Solution

Without explanation, the reasoning behind this calculation is unclear.

Soda sales

$20 \times 4 \times 0.75 = \$60$

Total cost for soda

$10 \times 1.29 = \$12.90$

A total of $47.10 will be raised for the class trip.

The answer is correct, but not justified.

SAMPLE 3: No Credit Solution

$10 \times 2 \div 250 \times 0.75 = 0.06$

A total of $.06 will be raised for the class trip.

No explanation is given and the answer is incorrect.

PRACTICE   Apply the Scoring Rubric

Score each of the following solutions to the problem on the previous page as *full credit, partial credit,* or *no credit*. *Explain* your reasoning. If you choose partial credit or no credit, explain how you would change the solution so that it earns a score of full credit.

1. Money earned from soda sales: $10 \times 2 \div 0.25 \times 0.75 - 60$

    Total cost: $10 \times 1.29 = 12.90$

    Money raised = Soda sales − Total cost

    Money raised = $60 - 12.90$

    Money raised = 47.10

    A total of $47.10 will be raised for the class trip.

2. You can find the total amount raised by finding the amount raised per bottle and multiplying the result by the total number of bottles.

    Amount of soda in milliliters in each bottle: $2 \text{ L} \times 1000 = 2000 \text{ mL}$

    Number of plastic cups needed per bottle: $2000 \div 250 = 8$

    Money earned per bottle minus buying cost:

    $8 \times 0.75 - 1.29 = 4.71$

    Money raised per bottle times total number of bottles:

    $4.71 \times 10 = 47.10$

    A total of $47.10 will be raised for the class trip.

TEST PREPARATION

1. A tuna can label indicates that there are 16 grams of protein in each serving. The can contains 2.5 servings. Which expression can be used to find the number of grams of protein in the can of tuna?

   A. 2.5 + 16

   B. 2.5 − 16

   C. 2.5 × 16

   D. 2.5 ÷ 16

2. Jana has $12.45 in her pocket. She spends $4.13 on food and $6.71 at the arcade. How much money does she have left?

   A. $1.61

   B. $5.74

   C. $9.87

   D. $23.29

3. Four tubes of toothpaste cost a total of $12.72. What method would you use to find the cost of one tube of toothpaste?

   A. Divide 12.72 by 4

   B. Multiply 12.72 by 4

   C. Add 4 to 12.72

   D. Subtract 4 from 12.72

4. Which list shows the order of 0.1, 1.0, 1.1, 1.01, and 1.11 from least to greatest?

   A. 0.1, 1.0, 1.01, 1.11, 1.1

   B. 1.11, 1.1, 1.01, 1.0, 0.1

   C. 0.1, 1.0, 1.01, 1.1, 1.11

   D. 0.1, 1.01, 1.0, 1.1, 1.11

5. The table shows the distance in miles from the interstate exit to the next exit. Exit 6 is after Exit 5. What is the distance from Exit 1 to Exit 6?

Interstate exit number	Distance to next exit
Exit 1	13.75
Exit 2	2.2
Exit 3	1.9
Exit 4	3.1
Exit 5	3.7

   A. 2.85 mi

   B. 3 mi

   C. 24.65 mi

   D. 25 mi

6. Simplify the expression below.

   $$72 \div 2 \times (3 - 1) \times 3^2$$

   A. 2

   B. 9

   C. 162

   D. 648

7. Heather rode her bike 23.4 miles in 2 hours. Which equation can she use to find her speed, r, in miles per hour?

   A. $23.4 = 2r$

   B. $2 = 23.4r$

   C. $23.4 - 2 = r$

   D. $2(23.4) = r$

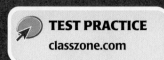

8. What is the perimeter of the driver's license shown below?

3.375 in.

2.125 in.

A. 5.5 in.

B. 7.2 in.

C. 8.875 in.

D. 11 in.

9. What is the length of the rectangle shown below?

$A = 6.6$ in.^{2} 1.1 in.

A. 0.6 in.

B. 5.5 in.

C. 6 in.

D. 60 in.

10. Wendy and Frank ordered food to be delivered and split the total cost. The food cost was $18.92, and they gave the driver $3.50 for a tip. The delivery took longer than 45 minutes, so $5 was taken off their bill. Which expression can be used to find how much money each paid?

A. $(18.92 + 3.5 - 5) \div 2$

B. $18.92 + 3.5 - 5 \div 2$

C. $18.92 + (3.5 - 5) \div 2$

D. $18.92 \div 2 + 3.5 - 5$

11. The weights in ounces of 5 apples are 3.2, 2.3, 3.1, 3, and 2. Which list orders the weights from greatest to least?

A. 3.2, 2.3, 3.1, 3, 2

B. 2, 2.3, 3, 3.1, 3.2

C. 3.2, 3.1, 3, 2.3, 2

D. 3, 3.2, 3.1, 2.3, 2

12. Dorothy's hair is 3 times as long as it was last year. Last year it was 5.7 inches long. What is the length of her hair now?

A. 8.7 in.

B. 11.4 in.

C. 17.1 in.

D. 18 in.

13. OPEN-ENDED Light travels about 300,000 kilometers per second. It takes about 500 seconds for light to travel from the sun to Earth.

Part A   Use the distance formula $d = rt$ to approximate the distance between the sun and Earth. Write your answer in standard form and in scientific notation.

Part B   The distance between Pluto and the sun is about 39.3 times greater than the distance between Earth and the sun. About how far is Pluto from the sun? Write your answer in scientific notation.

Part C   How many times longer does it take for sunlight to travel to Pluto than to Earth? *Explain* your reasoning.

TEST PREPARATION

3

Data and Statistics

Before

In previous chapters you've . . .

- Performed whole number operations
- Ordered decimals

Now

 New Jersey Standards

	3.1	Averages
4.5.E.1.d	3.2	Bar and line graphs
4.5.E.1.d	3.3	Stem-and-leaf plots
4.4.A.1.b	3.4	Box-and-whisker plots
4.5.E.1.b	3.5	Histograms
4.4.A.1.a	3.6	Appropriate displays

Why?

So you can solve real-world problems about . . .

- tornadoes, p. 122
- skiing, p. 129
- roller coasters, p. 133
- music, p. 139

 **Math**

at classzone.com

- Bar Graphs and Line Graphs, p. 117
- Stem-and-Leaf Plots, p. 126
- Box-and-Whisker Plot, p. 133

Get-Ready Games

Review Prerequisite Skills by playing
You're Out! and *Pitcher Shuffle.*

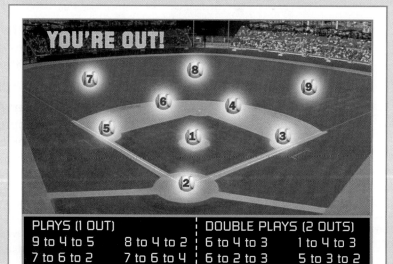

YOU'RE OUT!

PLAYS (1 OUT)		DOUBLE PLAYS (2 OUTS)	
9 to 4 to 5	8 to 4 to 2	6 to 4 to 3	1 to 4 to 3
7 to 6 to 2	7 to 6 to 4	6 to 2 to 3	5 to 3 to 2

Skill Focus: Using whole number operations

You and your partner each represent a baseball team that is on the field. You are in a race to get three outs.

- Each position on the field is associated with a number. A play or a double play is described using these numbers.

- Choose a play or a double play. Use the numbers to write a true statement using $=$ and one of the following: $+$, $-$, $\times$, or $\div$. If you can write a true statement, you get the out(s). Each play or double play can be used only once. The first player to get three outs wins.

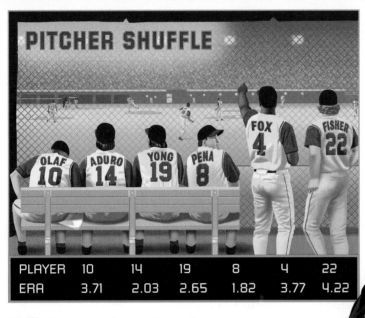

PITCHER SHUFFLE

PLAYER	10	14	19	8	4	22
ERA	3.71	2.03	2.65	1.82	3.77	4.22

Skill Focus: Ordering decimals

A pitcher's earned run average (ERA) indicates how successful the pitcher is at preventing players from scoring runs. In general, the lower the ERA, the better the pitcher.

• Order the ERAs of the pitchers from least to greatest. Then write the names of the pitchers in the same order.

• The first letters of the pitchers' names spell out the answer to the question below.

  What is the name of the pitch that follows a three-ball, two-strike count?

Stop and Think

1. **CRITICAL THINKING** In *You're Out!*, suppose the following numbers describe a triple play:
9 to 6 to 2 to 3. Use these numbers to write a true statement using = and one or more of the following: +, −, ×, or ÷.

2. **CRITICAL THINKING** In *Pitcher Shuffle*, make up a last name and an ERA for a seventh pitcher so that you can spell out the word PLAYOFF with the first letters of all seven pitchers' names.

Review Prerequisite Skills

VOCABULARY CHECK

REVIEW WORDS
- **number line,** *p. 736*
- **line plot,** *p. 758*

Copy and complete using a review word from the list at the left.

1. You can use a(n) __?__ to order and compare numbers.

2. A(n) __?__ uses a number line to show how often data values occur.

SKILL CHECK

The bar graph shows the average swimming speeds for some common fish. *(p. 757)*

3. What is the average swimming speed for carp?

4. What fish swims at an average speed of 8 kilometers per hour?

5. Which of the fish has the fastest average swimming speed?

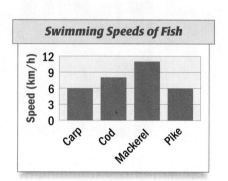

Swimming Speeds of Fish

Make a line plot of the data. *(p. 758)*

6. 10, 9, 8, 8, 9, 7, 11, 10, 8, 9, 8

7. 6, 7, 9, 5, 7, 9, 6, 5, 5, 7, 9, 7, 7

8. 1, 2, 2, 4, 1, 2, 3, 1, 4, 3, 3, 4

9. 16, 12, 14, 13, 13, 15, 12, 11, 15, 14

Order the numbers from least to greatest. *(p. 736)*

10. 11.6, 5.4, 22, 18.4, 13.8, 9.9

11. 12.1, 11.2, 13.8, 9.4, 13.4, 12

12. 4.2, 1.5, 5.31, 4.4, 6.2, 5.2

13. 6.28, 6.4, 6.2, 6.15, 6.6, 6, 6.5

@HomeTutor Prerequisite skills practice at classzone.com

Notetaking Skills — Including Vocabulary Notes

In each chapter you will learn a new notetaking skill. In Chapter 3 you will apply the strategy of including vocabulary notes on page 134 of Lesson 3.4.

You should include vocabulary words and their definitions in your notebook. Making a labeled diagram can help you understand and remember key terms.

base   exponent

$$3^5 = 3 \cdot 3 \cdot 3 \cdot 3 \cdot 3$$

power

3 is a factor **5** times.

3.1 Mean, Median, and Mode

Before You compared and ordered whole numbers and decimals.

Now You'll describe data using mean, median, and mode.

Why? So you can find average speeds, as in Ex. 29.

KEY VOCABULARY
- mean, *p. 109*
- median, *p. 109*
- mode, *p. 109*
- range, *p. 110*

Geysers Over a span of 12 hours, Old Faithful Geyser in Yellowstone National Park erupted 10 times. The lengths (in minutes) of the eruptions are shown.

2.8   4.5   4.1   3.7   3.5   4.5   2.2   4.9   2.6   4.2

What is the *average* length of the eruptions?

KEY CONCEPT *For Your Notebook*

Averages

The **mean** of a data set is the sum of the values divided by the number of values.

The **median** of a data set is the middle value when the values are written in numerical order. If a data set has an even number of values, the median is the mean of the two middle values.

The **mode** of a data set is the value that occurs most often. A data set can have no mode, one mode, or more than one mode.

EXAMPLE 1 Finding a Mean

To find the mean length in minutes of the eruptions of Old Faithful listed above, divide the sum of the 10 lengths of time by 10.

$$\text{Mean} = \frac{2.8 + 4.5 + 4.1 + 3.7 + 3.5 + 4.5 + 2.2 + 4.9 + 2.6 + 4.2}{10}$$

$$= \frac{37}{10}$$

$$= 3.7$$

▶ **Answer** The mean length of the eruptions is 3.7 minutes.

✓ **GUIDED PRACTICE** for Example 1

Find the mean of the data.

1. 6, 13, 12, 18, 14, 4, 7, 19, 15

2. 10, 1, 5, 14, 12, 5, 17, 13

Range To describe how spread out data are, you can find the *range*. The **range** of a data set is the difference between the greatest value and the least value.

EXAMPLE 2 Finding Median, Mode, and Range

Find the median, mode(s), and range of the numbers below.

$$64 \quad 60 \quad 64 \quad 38 \quad 52 \quad 65 \quad 61 \quad 48$$

SOLUTION

Write the data in order, least to greatest: 38 48 52 60 61 64 64 65

AVOID ERRORS
Make sure you first order a set of data when finding the median.

Median: Because there is an even number of data values, the median is the mean of the two middle values.

$$\text{Median} = \frac{60 + 61}{2} = \frac{121}{2} = 60.5$$

Mode: The number that occurs most often is 64.

Range: Find the difference between the greatest and the least values.

$$\text{Range} = 65 - 38 = 27$$

EXAMPLE 3 Choosing the Best Measure

Dance-a-Thon You receive the pledge amounts listed below for your participation in a dance-a-thon. Which measure best describes the data?

$1 $8 $12 $10 $45 $9 $1 $7 $6

SOLUTION

STEP 1 Find the mean: $\dfrac{1 + 8 + 12 + 10 + 45 + 9 + 1 + 7 + 6}{9} = \$11$

The mean suggests that most pledges are greater than they actually are.

STEP 2 Find the median: 1 1 6 7 **8** 9 10 12 45

The median is $8. It is the middle value of the nine values.

STEP 3 Find the mode: The pledge that occurs most often is $1.

The mode suggests that most pledges are less than they actually are.

STEP 4 Find the range: $45 - $1 = $44

The range suggests that the data are more spread out than they are.

▶ **Answer** The median best describes the pledge amounts.

EXAMPLE 4 Standardized Test Practice

City Parks A city council paid about $300 for 15 new trees for one of its parks. Two years later, 5 of the trees die and are replaced for $120. What is the mean cost of all the trees?

(A) $20   **(B)** $21   **(C)** $24   **(D)** $420

ELIMINATE CHOICES
Choice D can be eliminated because $420 is the *total* cost of all the trees.

SOLUTION

To find the mean cost of the trees, divide the sum of the costs by the total number of trees purchased.

$$\text{Mean} = \frac{300 + 120}{20} = \frac{420}{20} = 21$$

▶ **Answer** The mean cost of the trees is $21.
The correct answer is B. Ⓐ **Ⓑ** Ⓒ Ⓓ

 GUIDED PRACTICE   for Examples 2, 3, and 4

Find the median, mode(s), and range.

3. 9, 13, 19, 14, 16, 11, 7, 6, 13   **4.** 18, 52, 23, 79, 66, 17, 20, 10

5. What If? In Example 3, you receive three more pledges of $15, $20, and $22. Which measure best represents the pledge amounts?

6. What are the mode and median costs of the trees in Example 4?

3.1 **EXERCISES**

HOMEWORK
KEY

★ = **STANDARDIZED TEST PRACTICE**
Exs. 13, 25, 26, 30, 31, 34, 36, and 44

◯ = **HINTS** AND **HOMEWORK HELP**
for Exs. 3, 9, 13, 25 at classzone.com

SKILL PRACTICE

VOCABULARY **Tell whether the statement is *true* or *false*.**

1. The value that occurs the most often in a data set is the mode.

2. The range of a data set is the sum of the greatest and the least values.

FINDING AVERAGES AND RANGE **Find the mean, median, mode(s), and range of the data.**

SEE EXAMPLES 1 AND 2
on pp. 109–110 for Exs. 3–12

3. 17, 30, 38, 38, 42   **4.** 4, 4, 8, 11, 12, 16, 22

5. 108, 490, 502, 502, 502, 518   **6.** 20, 26, 31, 42, 44, 47, 51, 75

7. 46, 23, 63, 23, 81, 75, 46   **8.** 9, 63, 87, 45, 8, 87, 25, 12

9. 1.1, 0, 3, 2.8, 4.6   **10.** 7.6, 7.6, 6.1, 6, 14.3

11. 5.1, 5.3, 5.1, 5.2, 5.2, 5.3, 5.2   **12.** 68.4, 65.7, 63.9, 79.5, 52.5

SEE EXAMPLE 2
on p. 110
for Exs. 13–14

13. ★ **MULTIPLE CHOICE** The data below are the number of televisions that 11 students have in their homes. Find the mode of the data.

3, 2, 1, 1, 1, 5, 3, 1, 2, 1, 2

(A) 1   (B) 2   (C) 3   (D) 4

14. ERROR ANALYSIS Describe and correct the error made in finding the median of the data set.

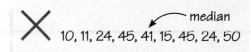

median

10, 11, 24, 45, 41, 15, 45, 24, 50

AVERAGES Find the three averages. Tell which average best represents the data.

SEE EXAMPLE 3
on p. 110
for Exs. 15–18

15. College class ages: 19, 17, 34, 22, 25, 54, 43, 23, 21, 28, 22, 31

16. Minutes waited in line at an amusement park: 11, 24, 16, 65, 5, 0, 35, 20, 45

17. Ages of players on a Little League team: 11, 11, 13, 13, 12, 13, 11, 12, 10, 13, 13.

18. Number of after-school activities for 10 students: 4, 1, 2, 7, 3, 2, 4, 4, 6, 9.

ALGEBRA Find the value of x that makes the mean the given number.

19. 5, 8, 9, 4, 1, x; mean = 5

20. 12, 7, 18, 15, 11, 9, x; mean = 12

21. 3.5, 1.5, 2.4, 4.6, 6.8, x; mean = 4.3

22. 3.0, 5.1, 9.8, 11.2, 12.5, 9.3, x; mean = 8.5

23. CHALLENGE Find five numbers with a mean of 16, a median of 15, a mode of 21, and a range of 11.

PROBLEM SOLVING

SEE EXAMPLE 4
on p. 111
for Exs. 24–26

24. DOLPHIN RESORT The following list shows how many dolphins at a resort for wild dolphins were present for the feeding session each day for a month. What is the most common number of dolphins that attended the feeding sessions?

7, 6, 6, 8, 8, 8, 8, 5, 6, 5, 5, 5, 5, 8, 6, 8,
4, 6, 10, 8, 8, 7, 5, 5, 5, 5, 9, 8, 8, 8, 8

25. ★ **MULTIPLE CHOICE** The amount of money you earned each week from baby-sitting is listed below. Find the mean of the data.

$15 $20 $10 $15 $20 $15 $15 $10

(A) $10   (B) $15   (C) $20   (D) $25

26. ★ **WRITING** A basketball team purchases 9 shirts, 9 pairs of basketball shoes, and 2 basketballs for the team. If the shirts cost $12 each, the shoes cost $65 each, and the balls cost $19 each, what is the mean total cost of the new gear? *Explain* why the median and mode are not acceptable to consider when figuring the average cost of one piece of new gear.

EARRINGS In Exercises 27 and 28, use the following information. Sixteen girls were asked how many pairs of earrings they own. The results are listed below.

23, 27, 12, 20, 11, 9, 5, 10, 16, 32, 14, 31, 13, 8, 37, 32

27. Find the mean, median, mode(s), and range.

28. Which measure best represents the data? *Explain* your reasoning.

29. **INDY 500** The table shows the speeds of the fastest qualifiers in the Indy 500 each year for 1999–2004. Find the median and mean rounded to the nearest thousandth. Which average better represents the speeds? Which 3 consecutive years had the least range? *Explain.*

Year	1999	2000	2001	2002	2003	2004
Speed (mi/h)	225.179	223.471	226.037	231.342	231.725	222.024

30. ★ **MULTIPLE CHOICE** You have 7 baseball cards worth a total $30. A few weeks later you add 5 cards to your collection with a combined value of $12. What is the average value of each card?

Ⓐ $2.40   Ⓑ $2.60   Ⓒ $3.50   Ⓓ $8.40

31. ★ **SHORT RESPONSE** Find the mode(s) of the following colors: red, yellow, red, blue, blue, yellow, red, blue, yellow, red. Why is the mode the only appropriate average?

MEMBERSHIP The line plot shows the ages of students in a comic book club.

on p. 110
for Exs. 32–35

32. Find the mean, median, mode(s), and range of the data.

33. Which measure best represents the data? *Explain* your reasoning.

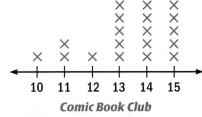

Comic Book Club

34. ★ **MULTIPLE CHOICE** In which data set are the mean, median, mode, and range all the same number?

Ⓐ 1, 2, 3, 3, 2, 1, 2   Ⓑ 1, 2, 3, 1, 2, 3, 1

Ⓒ 1, 3, 3, 3, 2, 3, 1   Ⓓ 2, 2, 1, 2, 3, 2, 3

35. **MULTI-STEP PROBLEM** Sally's scores on her science quizzes are listed below.

86 78 70 68 95 81 85 89 95

a. **Calculate** Find the mean, median, mode(s), and range of the data.

b. **Interpret** Which measure best represents Sally's scores? *Explain* your reasoning.

c. **Compare and contrast** Sally receives a score of 100 on the next quiz. How does this score affect the mean, median, and mode(s) of Sally's scores?

36. ★ **SHORT RESPONSE** Read the school news article below.

Survey Says!

The student council surveyed students about the number of hours they spend on homework each night. The responses spanned 3 hours, falling between 0 and 3 hours. The typical response was 1 hour and the most frequent response was 0.5 hour. ■

Which value in the paragraph represents the range? Which value represents the mode? Can you tell whether or not the other value given is the mean or the median? *Explain* your reasoning.

CHALLENGE **Create a set of at least seven data values that meet the conditions.**

37. The mean is not a good average to represent the data.

38. The data include at least four different values, and all three averages are equal.

NJ NEW JERSEY MIXED REVIEW   **TEST PRACTICE** at classzone.com

39. The table shows the results of a survey. Based on the information in the table, which of the following is a reasonable assumption?

Favorite Movie Type	
Movie Type	**Number of Students**
Comedy	12
Horror	5
Drama	6

Ⓐ Drama is the most popular type of movie.

Ⓑ Twice as many students like comedy as drama.

Ⓒ Comedy is not the most popular type of movie.

Ⓓ Three times as many students like comedy as horror.

Brain Game

What's My Age?

Use the following clues to find the age of each member of a family of five.

The median is 12.   The mean is 21.   The mode is 41.

The age of one of the family members is the median divided by 3.

Extension
Use after Lesson 3.1

Samples

GOAL Identify biased samples and surveys.

KEY VOCABULARY
• **population,** *p. 115*
• **sample,** *p. 115*
• **random sample,** *p. 115*
• **biased sample,** *p. 115*

A common way to gather data is through surveys. For example, television stations survey viewers, politicians survey voters, and retailers survey customers. Good surveying techniques lead to accurate predictions.

A **population** is the entire group of people or objects that you want information about. When it is difficult to survey an entire population, a **sample**, or a part of the group, is surveyed.

In a **random sample**, each person in the population has an equally likely chance of being selected. A non-random sample can result in a **biased sample** that is not representative of the population.

EXAMPLE 1 Identifying Potentially Biased Samples

School Spending The athletic department at a school has been given a donation. The coaches want students to help decide how to spend the money. The coaches will ask students to choose one of the options listed at the right.

Surveying all of the students will take too long, so a sample will be surveyed. Tell whether the survey method could result in a biased sample. *Explain.*

  a. Survey girls as they leave gym class.

  b. Survey students as they wait in line to buy school lunch.

  c. Survey the students on the baseball team.

SOLUTION

  a. This method could result in a biased sample because the girls are more likely to favor new lockers in the girls' locker room.

  b. This method is not likely to result in a biased sample because a wide range of students will be surveyed.

  c. This method could result in a biased sample because the baseball players are more likely to favor new baseball team uniforms.

Survey Questions The questions asked on a survey should be phrased in a way that reflects the opinions or actions of the people surveyed. If not, the results may be biased.

EXAMPLE 2 Identifying Potentially Biased Questions

Tell whether the question could produce biased results. Explain.

a.
> Do you, like most people your age, dislike listening to boring classical music?   ❑ yes   ❑ no

b.
> Do you agree with your town's policy for skateboarding on public property?   ❑ yes   ❑ no

SOLUTION

a. A response of "no" implies that this person disagrees with most people his or her age and likes listening to "boring" classical music. Therefore, the question encourages a response of "yes." So, the question could produce biased results.

b. This question assumes that the person responding knows the town's policy. Without information about the policy, the response may not be an accurate opinion. So, the question could produce biased results.

EXERCISES *for Examples 1 and 2*

LIBRARIES A town wants to know if residents will favor a tax raise for a library expansion. Tell if the method is likely to result in a biased sample. *Explain.*

1. Ask people as they leave the library.

2. Ask every fifth person who enters the bookstore in town.

3. Ask every tenth person listed in the phone book.

4. **Music** A radio station wants to know what type of music its audience would prefer to hear. *Describe* a sampling method that the radio station can use that is not likely to result in a biased sample.

Tell whether the question could produce biased results. *Explain.*

5. Would you rather spend a Friday night with your friends at an exciting movie or baby-sitting a crying baby?

6. How often do you read the school newspaper?

7. The fewer trash cans that a city has, the more litter the city has. Should our city include money in its budget for more trash cans?

8. Do you agree with this state's process for getting a driver's license?

3.2 Bar Graphs and Line Graphs

NJ 4.5.E.1.d Graphical representations (e.g., a line graph)

Before	You used a line plot to display data.
Now	You'll make and interpret bar graphs and line graphs.
Why?	So you can display tourism data, as in Example 1.

KEY VOCABULARY
• **bar graph,** *p. 117*
• **line graph,** *p. 118*
• **horizontal axis,** *p. 118*
• **vertical axis,** *p. 118*

Tourist Destinations The top five international tourist destinations and number of visitors are listed in the table. How can you represent the data visually?

You can represent data visually using a *bar graph*. In a **bar graph**, the lengths of the bars are used to represent and compare data.

Destination	Tourists (millions per year)
China	37
France	77
Italy	40
Spain	52
United States	42

EXAMPLE 1 Making a Bar Graph

You can use a bar graph to represent the tourist data above.

STEP 1 Choose a scale.

The largest data value is 77. So, start the scale at 0 and extend it to a value greater than 77, such as 90. Use increments of 15.

STEP 2 Draw and label the graph.

CHOOSE A DIRECTION
In a bar graph, the bars can be either vertical or horizontal.

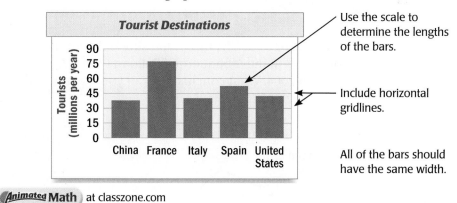

Use the scale to determine the lengths of the bars.

Include horizontal gridlines.

All of the bars should have the same width.

Animated Math at classzone.com

✓ **GUIDED PRACTICE** for Example 1

1. Make a bar graph of the data shown in the table.

Weekday Museum Visitors					
Day	M	T	W	T	F
Visitors	115	113	133	56	84

EXAMPLE 2 Making a Double Bar Graph

Sports The table shows the sports participation of students at a school.

Sport	Boys	Girls
Soccer	26	20
Basketball	17	21
Track and field	25	25
Volleyball	11	15

SOLUTION

To make a *double bar graph* of the data, start by drawing bars for the boys. Then draw bars for the girls. Be sure to choose a scale that works for all the data.

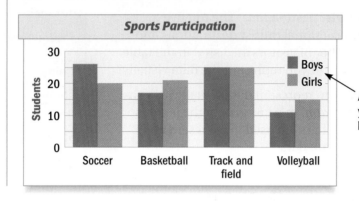

A *legend* tells you what each bar represents.

Line Graphs Another way to represent data visually is to use a *line graph*. In a **line graph**, points that represent data pairs are plotted using a horizontal number line, called a **horizontal axis**, and a vertical number line, called a **vertical axis**. The points are connected using line segments. Line graphs often show a change in data over time.

EXAMPLE 3 Interpreting a Line Graph

Hot Air Balloons The line graph shows the number of entries in the Albuquerque Balloon Fiesta from 1999 to 2004. What conclusions can you make about the line graph?

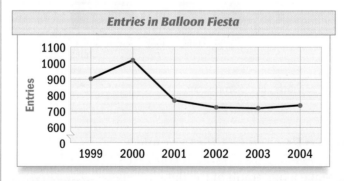

READING

In the line graph, the break in the vertical axis allows you to focus on the data values between 600 and 1100.

▶ **Answer** The line graph shows a sharp increase from 1999 to 2000, and a continued decrease from 2000 to 2003. Then the number of entries increased slightly from 2003 to 2004.

EXAMPLE 4 Making a Line Graph

Cell Phones Use the table to make a line graph of the number of cellular phone subscribers from 1998 through 2003. What can you conclude?

Year	1998	1999	2000	2001	2002	2003
Subscribers (millions)	69	86	109	128	141	159

SOLUTION

STEP 1 **Choose** horizontal and vertical axes.

Years from 1998 through 2003 will be shown on the horizontal axis. The greatest number of millions of subscribers is 159. So, start the vertical axis at 0 and end with 200, using increments of 40.

STEP 2 **Draw** and label the graph.

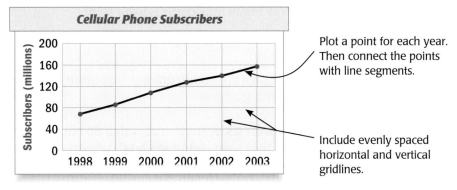

Plot a point for each year. Then connect the points with line segments.

Include evenly spaced horizontal and vertical gridlines.

▸ **Answer** The number of cell phone subscribers climbed steadily from 1998 to 2003.

✓ **GUIDED PRACTICE** for Examples 2, 3, and 4

2. **School Band** Make a double bar graph of the data about a school band.

Students in the School Band					
Instrument	**Flute**	**Clarinet**	**Saxophone**	**Trumpet**	**Drums**
7th graders	5	7	2	2	1
8th graders	8	4	2	1	2

3. What conclusions can you make about the double bar graph in Exercise 2?

4. Make a line graph of the number of people in line.

Number of People in Line at a Fast Food Restaurant					
Time	8 A.M.	10 A.M.	Noon	2 P.M.	4 P.M.	6 P.M.
People	11	4	18	6	9	12

3.2 EXERCISES

HOMEWORK KEY

★ = **STANDARDIZED TEST PRACTICE**
Exs. 15, 21, 22, 27, 28, and 42

◯ = **HINTS** AND **HOMEWORK HELP**
for Exs. 3, 5, 9, 19 at classzone.com

SKILL PRACTICE

1. **VOCABULARY** Copy and complete: In a line graph, points that represent data pairs are plotted using the scales on the __?__ and __?__ .

2. **VOCABULARY** How do bar graphs and line graphs differ?

INTERPRETING BAR GRAPHS The double bar graph shows the number of beverages purchased by students during one lunch.

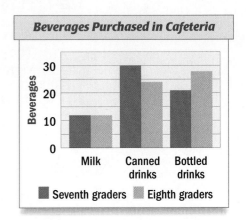

Beverages Purchased in Cafeteria

■ Seventh graders   ■ Eighth graders

**SEE EXAMPLES
1 AND 2**
on pp. 117–118
for Exs. 3–11

3. About how many bottled drinks were purchased by eighth graders?

4. About how many milk cartons were sold?

5. What type of beverage did seventh graders buy the most?

6. What beverage did eighth graders buy more than seventh graders?

7. **ERROR ANALYSIS** A student says that 30 more seventh graders bought canned drinks than eighth graders. Describe and correct the error made in drawing this conclusion from the graph.

MAKING BAR GRAPHS Make a bar graph of the data.

8.

Wingspans of Birds	
Bird	**Wingspan**
Seagull	1.7 m
Andean condor	3.2 m
Golden eagle	2.5 m
Grey heron	1.7 m
Gannet	1.7 m

9.

School Days per Year	
Country	**School Days**
Belgium	175
Japan	243
Nigeria	190
South Korea	220
United States	180

DOUBLE BAR GRAPHS Make a double bar graph of the data.

10.

Per Capita Personal Income by State (thousands of dollars)		
Year	**1990**	**2000**
Michigan	18.2	29.1
Texas	16.7	27.8
California	20.7	32.1
Maryland	22.1	33.5

11.

Household Pet Ownership (per 100 households)		
Year	**Dog**	**Cat**
1996	59	32
1998	61	32
2000	62	34
2002	62	34

SEE EXAMPLE 3
on p. 118
for Exs. 12–15

INTERPRETING LINE GRAPHS **The line graph shows the average price of gold for 1997–2003.**

12. About how many dollars per ounce was the average price of gold in 1998?

13. Between what years did the average price of gold decrease most sharply?

14. Estimate the total change in average gold price from 1997 to 2003.

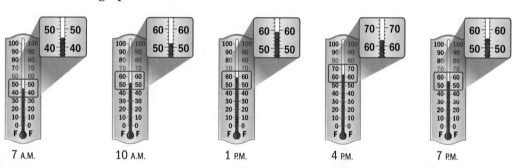

15. ★ **MULTIPLE CHOICE** Which conclusion is supported by the graph?

   Ⓐ The average price of gold was highest in 1997.

   Ⓑ The average price of gold increased from 1997 to 2001.

   Ⓒ The average price of gold was about the same in 1999 and 2000.

   Ⓓ The average price of gold decreased from 2001 to 2003.

SEE EXAMPLE 4
on p. 119
for Ex. 16

16. **MAKING LINE GRAPHS** Read the temperatures on the thermometers and make a line graph of the data.

   7 A.M.   10 A.M.   1 P.M.   4 P.M.   7 P.M.

17. **CHALLENGE** Use the line graph for average gold prices above. The plotted point in 2003 is about twice as far from the horizontal axis as the point for 2001. Does this mean that the average price of gold in 2003 was twice the average price of gold in 2001? *Explain* why or why not.

PROBLEM SOLVING

18. **GUIDED PROBLEM SOLVING** The table shows the average cost of a movie ticket since 1940.

Average Cost of a Movie Ticket						
Year	1940	1950	1960	1970	1980	1990	2000
Average Cost	$.24	$.53	$.69	$1.55	$2.69	$ 4.23	$5.39

   a. Draw a line graph to represent the data visually.

   b. Compare the steepness of each of the line segments. Write a statement that describes the change in cost over time.

WEATHER The line graph shows the number of tornadoes in the United States each year for 1991–1997.

SEE EXAMPLE 3
on p. 118
for Exs. 19–20

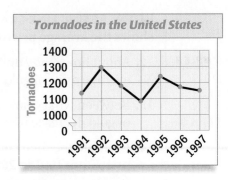

Tornadoes in the United States

19. Between which years was the decrease in the number of tornadoes greater: 1992–1993 or 1995–1996? *Explain* your answer.

20. Make a conclusion about the graph.

21. ★ **MULTIPLE CHOICE** The graph shows the average heights of boys and girls at specific ages. Which conclusion is supported by the graph?

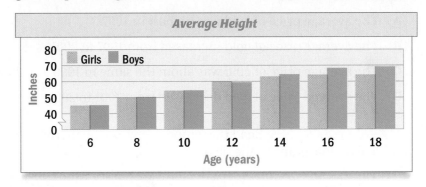

Average Height

Girls *Boys*

Inches

Age (years)

A Girls are taller than boys until the age of 14.

B Girls and boys grow the same amount each year.

C After the age of 14, boys grow faster than girls.

D Boys are always taller than girls.

22. ★ **OPEN-ENDED MATH** Ask the same number of seventh and eighth graders in your school what kind of pet(s) they have. Display the data in a double bar graph. Make a conclusion about your data.

23. **REASONING** Can the data collected in Exercise 22 be displayed in a double line graph? *Explain.*

NEWSPAPERS The table shows the circulation of daily newspapers each year for 1999–2003, grouped by morning and evening papers.

SEE EXAMPLES 3 AND 4
on pp. 118–119
for Exs. 24–26

24. Make a double line graph of the data. Use different colors for the morning and the evening papers.

25. Make a conclusion about how the circulation of morning and evening papers changed from 1999 to 2003.

26. *Predict* the circulation of morning and evening papers for 2004 and beyond.

Circulation (millions of papers)		
Year	**Morning**	**Evening**
1999	46.0	10.0
2000	46.8	9.0
2001	46.8	8.8
2002	46.6	8.6
2003	46.9	8.3

27. ★ **WRITING** Is it more appropriate to make a double bar graph or a double line graph to display the populations of two countries over time? *Explain* your reasoning.

28. ★ **EXTENDED RESPONSE** The horizontal bar graph shows the length of a day (in hours) for several planets.

    a. Name three pairs of planets whose day lengths are most similar.

    b. Make other conclusions about the data.

    c. As you go up the vertical axis, the planets become farther away from the sun. Does the length of a planet's day seem to be related to its distance from the sun? *Explain* why or why not.

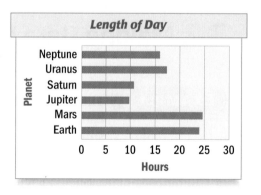

CHALLENGE The table shows the distance, to the nearest hundredth of a meter, of the gold medal winning discus throw for both men and women in the Olympics from 1976 to 2004.

Year	1976	1980	1984	1988	1992	1996	2000	2004
Women	69.00	69.96	65.36	72.30	70.06	69.66	68.40	67.02
Men	67.50	66.64	66.60	68.82	65.12	69.40	69.30	69.89

29. Make a double line graph of the data.

30. Notice the varying steepness of each of the line segments. In which years are the distances increasing the most? Decreasing the most? What could this imply? *Explain*.

 NEW JERSEY MIXED REVIEW   **TEST PRACTICE** at classzone.com

31. Audrey bought 5 compact discs for $60. Later she bought another compact disc for $9. What was the mean cost of all the compact discs?

    (A) $6.00   (B) $9.50   (C) $11.50   (D) $12.25

32. A woodworker records the measurements of 4 different parts of a dresser. The measurements are 5 mm, 3 cm, 20 cm, and 1.5 m. Which list shows the measurements written in meters in order from least to greatest?

    (A) 0.05 m, 0.3 m, 1.5 m, 2 m

    (B) 0.005 m, 0.03 m, 0.2 m, 1.5 m

    (C) 1.5 m, 3 m, 5 m, 20 m

    (D) 1.5 m, 0.2 m, 0.03 m, 0.005 m

3.2 Making Data Displays

EXAMPLE 1 The prices of the merchandise at a concert are shown at the right. Use spreadsheet software to make a vertical bar graph of the data.

	A	B
1	Merchandise	Price (dollars)
2	Hat	15
3	Long-sleeve shirt	35
4	Poster	10
5	Sweatshirt	40
6	T-shirt	25

SOLUTION

STEP 1 **Enter** the data in the first two columns of a spreadsheet, as shown above.

STEP 2 **Highlight** the data in cells A2:B6. The expression A2:B6 refers to the rectangular array of cells that has A2 and B6 at the corners.

STEP 3 **Use** the Insert menu to insert a graph. Select a vertical bar graph, or column chart, as the type of graph. Then choose the options for your graph, such as the titles and labels.

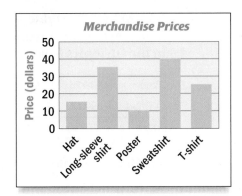

STEP 4 **Change** other features of your graph after it has been created by double clicking on the part of the graph that you wish to change and adjusting the formatting.

PRACTICE Use spreadsheet software and the table, which shows the number of shopping centers in Midwestern states.

1. Make a vertical double bar graph of the data. Follow the steps for a single bar graph, but highlight three columns of data. Adjust the scale on the vertical axis so that it starts at 600.

2. Make a horizontal double bar graph of the data. Follow the steps for a vertical bar graph but select horizontal bar graph from the Insert menu.

3. **REASONING** Make a conclusion about the number of shopping centers in the states listed.

Shopping Centers		
State	**1999**	**2000**
Illinois	2146	2175
Indiana	918	926
Michigan	1039	1056
Ohio	1716	1741
Wisconsin	629	637

EXAMPLE 2 Search the Internet to find the daily mean temperatures for each month in Chicago. Then make a line graph of the data.

SOLUTION

STEP 1 **Search** the Internet.

Search the Internet for:

| normal daily mean temperatures Chicago | Search |

STEP 2

Enter the data in the first two columns columns of a spreadsheet, as shown below.

	A	B
1	Month	Temperature (°F)
2	Jan.	22
3	Feb.	27
4	Mar.	37.3
5	Apr.	47.8
6	May	58.7
7	Jun.	68.2
8	Jul.	73.3
9	Aug.	71.7
10	Sep.	63.8
11	Oct.	52.1
12	Nov.	39.3
13	Dec.	27.4

STEP 3

Use the steps for making a bar graph, but select line graph instead.

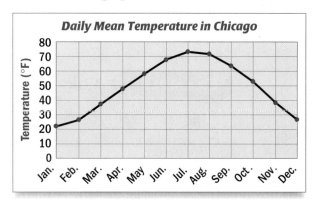

PRACTICE Use the Internet and spreadsheet software to complete the following exercises.

4. **OPEN-ENDED** Find the daily mean temperatures for each month of the year for a city in your state. Then make a line graph of the data.

5. **WRITING** *Compare* the daily mean temperatures for Chicago with those for the city you selected.

6. **SPORTS** Find the number of medals awarded to the country of your choice in the past five Winter Olympics. Use the phrase "International Olympics Committee Winter Olympics" to search for the data. Then make a line graph of the data.

3.3 Stem-and-Leaf Plots

Before	You displayed data using bar graphs and line graphs.
Now	You'll display data using stem-and-leaf plots.
Why?	So you can analyze ski race times, as in Ex. 15.

KEY VOCABULARY
- stem-and-leaf plot, *p. 126*

Speeds of Animals The table lists the maximum running speeds of various animals. How can the data be displayed to show the distribution of the speeds?

A **stem-and-leaf plot** is a data display that helps you to see the way data are distributed. You can use a stem-and-leaf plot to place data in increasing order.

Animal	Speed (mi/h)
Elk	45
Cheetah	70
Greyhound	39
Wildebeest	50
Quarter horse	47
Zebra	40
Giraffe	32
Coyote	43

EXAMPLE 1 Making a Stem-and-Leaf Plot

Display the speeds of the animals shown above in a stem-and-leaf plot.

SOLUTION

STEP 1 **Choose** the **stems** and **leaves**. The numbers range from 32 to 70, so let the stems be the tens' digits from 3 to 7. Let the leaves be the ones' digits.

STEP 2 **Write** the stems first. Draw a vertical line segment next to the stems. Then record each speed by writing its ones' digit on the same line as its corresponding tens' digit.

STEP 3 **Make** an ordered stem-and-leaf plot. Include a key to show what the stems and leaves represent.

> **ORDER A STEM-AND-LEAF PLOT**
> In the ordered plot, the leaves for each stem are listed in order from least to greatest.

Unordered Plot

```
3 | 9 2
4 | 5 7 0 3
5 | 0
6 |
7 | 0
```
Key: 4 |7 = 47

Ordered Plot

```
3 | 2 9
4 | 0 3 5 7
5 | 0
6 |
7 | 0
```
Key: 4 |7 = 47

> To order the data, order the leaves for each stem.

Animated **Math** at classzone.com

EXAMPLE 2 Interpreting a Stem-and-Leaf Plot

Bicycle Stunt Competition The point totals (rounded to the nearest tenth) for the 20 participants in a bicycle stunt competition are listed below. The rider with the greatest point total out of 100 points wins.

| **89.4** | 90 | 87.5 | 84.3 | 89.7 | 90.3 | 91.1 | 91 | 86 | 84.1 |
| 89.2 | 86 | 89.1 | 88.2 | 89.5 | 85.6 | 90.5 | 90.2 | 91.1 | 88.9 |

Use a stem-and-leaf plot to order the data. Make a conclusion about the data.

SOLUTION

Begin by making an unordered stem-and-leaf plot. Because the point totals range from 84.1 to 91.4, the stems are the digits in the tens' and ones' places. The leaves are the digits in the tenths' place.

Then make an ordered stem-and-leaf plot.

Unordered Plot	**Ordered Plot**
84 │ 3 1	84 │ 1 3
85 │ 6	85 │ 6
86 │ 0 0	86 │ 0 0
87 │ 5	87 │ 5
88 │ 2 9	88 │ 2 9
89 │ **4** 7 2 1 5	89 │ 1 2 4 5 7
90 │ 0 3 5 2	90 │ 0 2 3 5
91 │ 1 0 1	91 │ 0 1 1
Key: 87│5 = 87.5	Key: 87│5 = 87.5

▶**Answer** More than half of the participants finished near the top of the range, with 12 of the 20 participants having point totals greater than or equal to 89.

✓ **GUIDED PRACTICE** for Examples 1 and 2

1. **Test Scores** The test scores for the students in a social studies class are listed below. Make an ordered stem-and-leaf plot of the scores.

| 92 | 78 | 73 | 89 | 98 | 89 | 83 | 75 | 83 | 100 |
| 69 | 71 | 96 | 67 | 81 | 73 | 88 | 86 | 82 | 94 |

Use the stem-and-leaf plot from Exercise 1 to answer the questions.

2. How many test scores are greater than 84?

3. How many test scores are less than 80?

4. Identify the median of the data.

5. How many modes do the data have? What are they?

6. Make a conclusion about the test scores.

3.3 EXERCISES

HOMEWORK KEY

★ = **STANDARDIZED TEST PRACTICE**
Exs. 8, 9, 13, 15, 18, 20, 21, 22, and 30

◯ = **HINTS** AND **HOMEWORK HELP**
for Exs. 3, 5, 7, 13 at classzone.com

SKILL PRACTICE

1. **VOCABULARY** The key for a stem-and-leaf plot is 10|5 = 10.5. Which number in the key is the stem? the leaf?

2. **VOCABULARY** Copy and complete: In an ordered stem-and-leaf plot, the leaves are ordered from __?__ to __?__ .

MAKING STEM-AND-LEAF PLOTS **Make an ordered stem-and-leaf plot of the data.**

SEE EXAMPLE 1
on p. 126
for Exs. 3–7

3. Students in each class: 22, 29, 12, 27, 15, 19, 13, 27, 12, 9, 26, 10

4. Numbers of volunteers: 12, 11, 34, 11, 35, 29, 9, 30, 15, 10, 13, 11

5. Miles walked: 2.2, 4.1, 2.5, 0.5, 5.8, 6.6, 2, 3, 2.4, 1.1

6. Hours spent on the Internet: 4.3, 5.9, 4.1, 1.5, 0.8, 2.8, 1.1, 1.2, 2.4, 1.5

7. **ERROR ANALYSIS** Describe and correct the error in making the stem-and-leaf plot.

```
4 | 3 3 5 6
5 | 0 1 2
7 | 4 4 8 9 9   Key: 7|4 = 74
```
✕

SEE EXAMPLE 2
on p. 127
for Exs. 8–10

8. ★ **MULTIPLE CHOICE** What is the median of the data in the stem-and-leaf plot at the right?

Ⓐ 25.4   Ⓑ 25.8

Ⓒ 254   Ⓓ 258

```
23 | 4 5
24 | 4 7 9
25 | 0 4 8 8
26 | 3 8 9
27 | 1 2 5     Key: 24|7 = 24.7
```

9. ★ **MULTIPLE CHOICE** The prices of books in a bookstore are listed below. Which stem-and-leaf plot correctly displays the data?

8   20   26   30   45   6   18   20   28   32   14   15   25   20

Ⓐ
```
0 | 6 8
1 | 4 5 8
2 | 0 5 6 8
3 | 0 2
4 | 5       Key: 1|4 = 1.4
```

Ⓑ
```
0 | 6 8
1 | 4 5 8
2 | 0 5 6 8
3 | 0 2
4 | 5       Key: 1|4 = 14
```

Ⓒ
```
0 | 6 8
1 | 4 5 8
2 | 0 0 0 5 6 8
3 | 0 2
4 | 5       Key: 1|4 = 1.4
```

Ⓓ
```
0 | 6 8
1 | 4 5 8
2 | 0 0 0 5 6 8
3 | 0 2
4 | 5       Key: 1|4 = 14
```

10. **REASONING** When using a stem-and-leaf plot to find the median of a data set, why is it important to use an ordered stem-and-leaf plot?

128   Chapter 3   Data and Statistics

11. **CHALLENGE** Find the median of the
stem-and-leaf plot at the right. Make a
mark where the median occurs. Find the
median of the lower half of the data and the
median of the upper half of the data. What
do these values tell you about the data?

```
41 | 2
42 |
43 | 1 7
44 | 4 5 5 6 6 8
45 | 1 4 7 8 9
46 | 0 1 2 3    Key: 41|2 = 41.2
```

PROBLEM SOLVING

U.S. PRESIDENTS **The ages of recent U.S. Presidents at the time of their inaugurations are listed below.**

54   46   62   69   52   61   56   55   43   62   60   51   54   51

12. Make an ordered stem-and-leaf plot of the data.

SEE EXAMPLE 2
on p. 127 for
Exs. 13, 15–18

13. ★ **WRITING** Make a conclusion about the data.

SKIING **The data below show the times (in seconds) for the women's super giant slalom event at the 2002 Winter Olympics.**

73.86   74.08   73.95   74.44   74.28   73.99   73.59   74.99

74.73   74.89   75.13   73.64   74.84   74.83   75.17

14. Make an ordered stem-and-leaf plot of the data.

15. ★ **WRITING** Make a conclusion about the data.

FAMILY REUNION **The stem-and-leaf plot shows the ages of people at a reunion.**

```
0 | 2 5 5 7 9
1 | 1 1 3 4 7 9
2 | 2 5 7 8
3 | 2 3 4 4 9
4 | 0 2
5 | 3 7
6 | 0 1        Key: 5|3 = 53
```

16. How many people attended the reunion?

17. How old was the oldest person there?

18. ★ **WRITING** Make a conclusion about the data.

19. An *outlier* is a data value that is much less than or much greater than
most of the other values in the data set. Suppose that a 98 year old great-
grandfather attended the reunion. Why do you think his age is an *outlier*?

20. ★ **SHORT RESPONSE** The stem-and-leaf plot shows
the number of video games sold at a store each day
over two weeks. Find the mean, median, mode(s), and
range of the data. Make a conclusion about the data.

```
0 | 3
1 | 0 0 2
2 | 3 8 9
3 | 0 2 5 5 7 9
4 | 1          Key: 2|8 = 28
```

21. ★ **OPEN-ENDED MATH** Make a stem-and-leaf plot that has a mean of 25 and a median of 20.

22. ★ **EXTENDED RESPONSE** The heights, in inches, of plants grown using two fertilizers are listed below.

   Organic fertilizer: 23, 18, 38, 52, 46, 9, 36, 39, 40, 49, 50, 42, 47

   Chemical fertilizer: 42, 51, 36, 29, 12, 46, 30, 9, 18, 16, 23, 28, 24

   a. **Display** Make an ordered stem-and-leaf plot for each fertilizer.

   b. **Interpret** Make a conclusion about each stem-and-leaf plot.

   c. **Writing** Which of the two fertilizers is more effective? *Explain.*

23. **CHALLENGE** Use the bar graph at the right to make an ordered stem-and-leaf plot that shows the shoe sizes of a group of male students. Compare and contrast the two data displays.

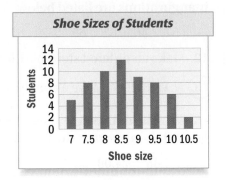

Shoe Sizes of Students

TEST PRACTICE at classzone.com

NEW JERSEY MIXED REVIEW

24. Martha ran the 50-yard dash 6 times. The table shows her time in seconds for each run. Which measure of data is represented by 35.3 seconds?

   (A) Mean   (B) Median

   (C) Mode   (D) Range

Race Times	
Race number	*Time (seconds)*
1	35.1
2	36.3
3	34.2
4	35.0
5	39.8
6	35.5

QUIZ *for Lessons 3.1–3.3*

Find the mean, median, mode(s), and range of the data. *(p. 109)*

1. 42, 16, 21, 34, 25, 28, 30, 20

2. 8.4, 8.9, 8.5, 8.5, 8, 7.9, 9.3

MUSIC The table shows the responses of students when asked to name their favorite type of music. *(pp. 117, 126)*

3. *Decide* whether to display the data in a bar graph or a line graph. Then make the data display.

4. Make a conclusion about the data.

5. Make an ordered stem-and-leaf plot of the data below.

   9.7, 10.6, 7.8, 7.2, 6.4, 8.3, 10.3, 7.7, 11.9, 10.1, 11.5, 6.4, 7.2

Music Type	Responses
Country	27
Hip-hop	36
Pop	58
Rock	34
Other	12

Lessons 3.1–3.3

1. **CAMPING** Which conclusion can you make from the line graph that shows the number of campsites being used at a campground each night?

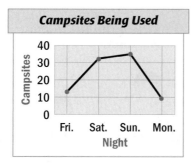

Campsites Being Used

   A. More campsites are used on weekends.

   B. The largest increase in the number of campsites used was from Saturday to Sunday.

   C. The least number of campsites used was on Friday.

   D. The number of campsites used increased each day.

2. **ELECTRONICS** The prices, in dollars, of DVD players in a store are listed. What is the median of the data?

   58, 70, 150, 95, 140, 68, 56, 130, 130, 66, 60, 95, 150, 142, 85, 125, 142, 76, 66, 120, 150, 110

   A. $95

   B. $102.50

   C. $110

   D. $150

3. **GEOMETRY** The mean of the perimeters of 3 square boxes is 36 inches. What is the mean side length of the boxes?

   A. 9 in.

   B. 12 in.

   C. 18 in.

   D. 36 in.

4. **SPORTS** The bar graph shows the home opener attendance for a school's baseball and hockey teams for 2000–2003. Compared to baseball, what prediction can be made about hockey home opener attendance in 2004?

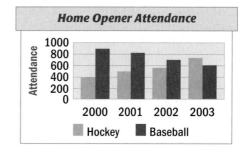

Home Opener Attendance

   A. Hockey attendance will be greater.

   B. Hockey attendance will be less.

   C. Hockey attendance will be the same.

   D. Hockey attendance will be 3 times greater.

5. **OPEN-ENDED** The stem-and-leaf plot below shows students' scores on a science quiz.

```
6 | 4 8            Key: 7 | 5 = 75
7 | 1 4 5 7
8 | 2 9
9 | 1 2 3 5 7 8 8
```

   • How many students are in the class?

   • What is the highest quiz score?

   • Make a conclusion about the data.

INVESTIGATION

Use before Lesson 3.4

3.4 Organizing Data Using the Median

EXPLORE Use the median to divide your class into groups according to the number of letters in students' first and last names.

STEP 1 **Count** the number of letters in your first and last name. Write the total on a piece of paper.

STEP 2 **Form** a line with your classmates. Hold up your papers, arranging yourselves from least to greatest.

STEP 3 **Determine** the median number of letters.

STEP 4 **Use** the median to divide the line into a lower half and an upper half. If there is an odd number of students, the median is not included in either the lower or upper half.

STEP 5 **Repeat** Steps 3 and 4 for each half. The original line should be divided into 4 parts.

PRACTICE Answer the following questions about the data for your class.

1. What is the median of your entire class?

2. What is the median of the lower half?

3. What is the median of the upper half?

4. What are the least and greatest numbers?

DRAW CONCLUSIONS

5. **REASONING** About what fraction of the class should have numbers of letters that are greater than or equal to the median of the lower half and less than or equal to the median of the upper half? Count the number of students that fall in this interval. Compare this number to the total number of students to check your answer.

3.4 Box-and-Whisker Plots

NJ 4.4.A.1.b   Box-and-whisker plot, upper quartile, lower quartile

Before   You displayed data using bar graphs and line graphs.

Now   You'll display data using box-and-whisker plots.

Why?   So you can compare sports data, as in Example 3.

KEY VOCABULARY
- **box-and-whisker plot,** *p. 133*
- **lower quartile, upper quartile,** *p. 133*
- **lower extreme, upper extreme,** *p. 133*
- **interquartile range,** *p. 134*

The **box-and-whisker plot** displays data beneath a number line that represents the range of the data. The display divides the ordered data into four parts using three points—the median, the *upper quartile*, and the *lower quartile*.

The median separates the upper half of the data from the lower half. The median of the lower half of the data is the **lower quartile**. The median of the upper half is the **upper quartile**.

The **lower extreme** is the least data value. The **upper extreme** is the greatest data value.

EXAMPLE 1   Making a Box-and-Whisker Plot

Roller Coasters   The heights, in feet, of 10 suspended roller coasters in the United States are 35, 42, 42.5, 60, 60, 70, 76, 78, 81, and 100. Make a box-and-whisker plot of the data.

SOLUTION

STEP 1   **Find** the median, the quartiles, and the extremes.

> **AVOID ERRORS**
> If a data set has an odd number of values, the median is not included in either the lower half or the upper half.

```
          Lower half                              Upper half
    ┌──────────────────┐                    ┌──────────────────┐
    35   42   42.5   60   60        ↑        70   76   78   81   100
    │         │                               │         │
  Lower     Lower                  Median    Upper     Upper
  extreme   quartile            60 + 70        quartile  extreme
                                ─────── = 65
                                   2
```

STEP 2   **Plot** the five values below a number line.

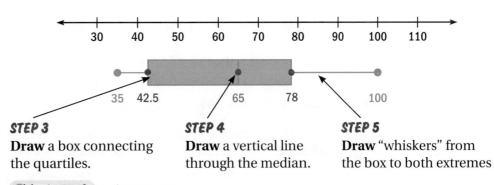

STEP 3
Draw a box connecting the quartiles.

STEP 4
Draw a vertical line through the median.

STEP 5
Draw "whiskers" from the box to both extremes

Animated Math at classzone.com

Interpreting a Box-and-Whisker Plot A box-and-whisker plot helps to show how varied, or spread out, the data are.

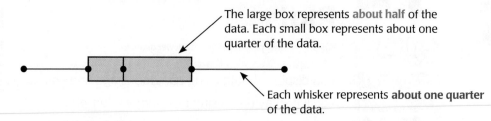

The large box represents **about half** of the data. Each small box represents about one quarter of the data.

Each whisker represents **about one quarter** of the data.

The **interquartile range** is the difference between the quartiles. The prefix "*inter*" means "*between*." So you can remember interquartile as being "between the quartiles." It is a measure of the spread of data.

EXAMPLE 2 Interpreting a Box-and-Whisker Plot

Watches The prices of the watches at a store are summarized in the box-and-whisker plot below.

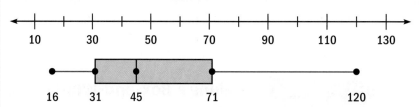

a. Suppose all of the watches under $31 are on clearance. About what fraction of the watches are on clearance?

b. Suppose all of the watches from $31 to $71 are on sale. About what fraction of the watches are on sale?

SOLUTION

a. The watches **less than $31** are about the same as the number in one of the whiskers, which represents **about one quarter** of the watches.

b. The watches between **$31 and $71** are about the same as the number in the large box of the plot, which represents **about half** of the watches.

 GUIDED PRACTICE for Examples 1 and 2

1. One weekend, a theater sold the following numbers of tickets to each screening of a new movie. Make a box-and-whisker plot of the data.

   497, 429, 746, 469, 504, 464, 326, 302, 509, 467, 401, 499

2. **What If?** In Example 2, suppose all of the watches under $45 were on clearance. About what fraction of the watches are on clearance?

3. In Example 2, is the number of watches between $71 and $120 greater than the number of watches between $16 and $31? *Explain.*

EXAMPLE 3 Comparing Box-and-Whisker Plots

Football The box-and-whisker plots represent the number of points scored in each game of the 2001–2002 season for the New England Patriots and the St. Louis Rams. What conclusions can you make about the data?

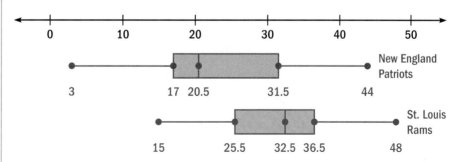

SOLUTION

In general, the Rams scored more points per game than the Patriots. The Patriots had more variability in their scoring than the Rams. The range for the Patriots was 44 − 3 = 41 and the range for the Rams was 48 − 15 = 33.

✓ **GUIDED PRACTICE** **for Example 3**

4. In Example 3, how do the lower extremes of the points scored compare?

3.4 EXERCISES

SKILL PRACTICE

VOCABULARY Tell whether the statement is *true*. Correct any false statements.

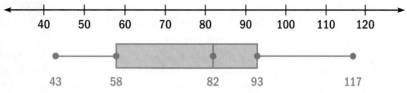

1. The upper extreme is 93.

2. The median is 82.

3. The lower quartile is 58.

4. The upper quartile is 117.

5. The range is 74.

6. The interquartile range is 24.

DISPLAYING DATA Make a box-and-whisker plot of the data.

SEE EXAMPLE 1
on p. 133
for Exs. 7–9

7. Hourly rates of pay: 8.75, 7.50, 9, 8, 6.50, 8, 6.50, 7, 6, 7, 6.25

8. Pages per chapter in a book: 21, 25, 20, 14, 15, 19, 14, 14, 10, 25

9. Ages of roller rink employees: 24, 22, 30, 18, 29, 38, 33, 17, 22, 25, 16, 41

10. ★ **MULTIPLE CHOICE** The box-and-whisker plot shows the heights, in feet, of waves at a beach during one day. What is the lower quartile?

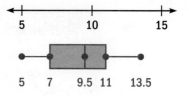

Ⓐ 5   Ⓑ 7

Ⓒ 9.5   Ⓓ 11

11. **WHICH ONE DOESN'T BELONG?** Which statement about the plot in Exercise 10 does not belong?

Ⓐ The smallest wave measured was 5 feet high.

Ⓑ About one quarter of the data lie between 9.5 feet and 11 feet.

Ⓒ About half of the data lie between 7 feet and 11 feet.

Ⓓ The range in heights is 4 feet.

12. **COMPARE GRAPHS** The weights, in ounces, of the snakes for sale at a reptile store are listed below. Make both a stem-and-leaf plot and a box-and-whisker plot of the data. *Compare* the two displays.

11, 14, 23, 18, 29, 33, 32, 17, 22, 25, 16, 28, 32, 24, 27, 20

CHALLENGE Tell whether the statement is *sometimes*, *always*, or *never* true.

13. When a data set has 13 items, the lower quartile is one of the items.

14. Exactly half of the items in a data set are greater than the median.

15. The upper extreme and the upper quartile are not the same number.

PROBLEM SOLVING

TREES The heights (to the nearest foot) of coastal redwood trees known to be over 340 feet tall are given below.

359, 361, 363, 358, 368, 361, 366, 360,
358, 359, 358, 366, 363, 364, 358, 363

16. ★ **WRITING** Make a box-and-whisker plot of the data. Write a conclusion about the data.

17. ★ **SHORT RESPONSE** Suppose the tallest tree is struck by lightning and its height is reduced to 352 feet. Make a box-and-whisker plot for the new data. Find as many differences as you can between this plot and the one that you made in Exercise 16.

DVD RENTALS The number of DVDs rented each day over two weeks is shown.

38   42   50   65   82   91   88   40   34   41   71   93   87   94

18. Make a box-and-whisker plot of the data.

19. ★ **WRITING** Make a conclusion about the data.

★ = STANDARDIZED TEST PRACTICE   ◯ = HINTS AND HOMEWORK HELP *at classzone.com*

FUEL ECONOMY In Exercises 20–22, use the box-and-whisker plots below. They show the average miles per gallon of gasoline used in city driving for 2002 models of small cars and sport utility vehicles (SUVs).

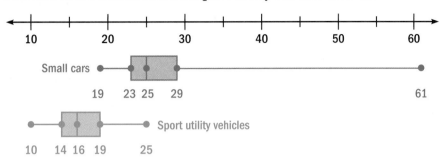

SEE EXAMPLE 3
on p. 135
for Exs. 20–25

20. Compare the number of small cars that get less than 25 miles per gallon with those that get more than 25 miles per gallon.

21. About what fraction of the SUVs get less than 14 miles per gallon?

22. ★ **WRITING** Make a conclusion about the gas mileage of the two groups of vehicles.

GOLF In Exercises 23–25, use the diagram below. It shows the distance, in yards, that Julia and Ty each hit 14 golf balls at a driving range.

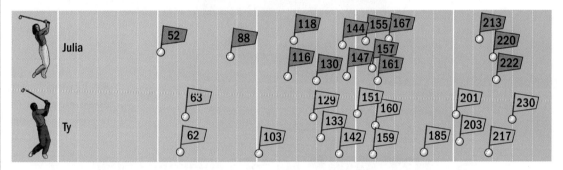

23. Using the same number line, make a box-and-whisker plot for each person.

24. ★ **WRITING** *Explain* the meaning of the interquartile range of each plot.

25. Make a conclusion about who can hit the ball farther.

26. **CHALLENGE** Suppose you make a box-and-whisker plot of the points scored in the games for each of two basketball players. Make conjectures about how the two plots would compare if one player is more consistent than the other.

NEW JERSEY MIXED REVIEW

TEST PRACTICE at classzone.com

27. You go to a craft store and buy several different types of ribbon. You buy a total of 6.8 yards of ribbon. The prices per yard range from $0.10 to $0.75. What is the range of the amount of money that you could spend?

Ⓐ $0.68 to $4.76   Ⓑ $0.68 to $5.10   Ⓒ $0.78 to $5.06   Ⓓ $5.10 to $6.80

3.5 Histograms

4.5.E.1.b Pictorial representations (e.g., diagrams, charts, or tables)

Before	You made bar graphs.
Now	You'll make and interpret histograms.
Why?	So you can interpret grouped data, such as butterfly data in Example 3.

KEY VOCABULARY
- frequency table, *p. 138*
- frequency, *p. 138*
- histogram, *p. 139*

You can use a *frequency table* to help organize and interpret data. A **frequency table** is used to group data values into intervals. The **frequency** of an interval is the number of values that lie in the interval.

Data Values

Calendars Sold in Mr. Moore's Homeroom

1, 7, 12, 2, 3, 22, 7, 5, 10, 1, 15, 9, 8, 2, 7, 17, 24, 14, 5, 4

Frequency Table

Interval	Tally	Frequency
1–5	ⅢⅡ III	8
6–10	ⅢⅡ I	6
11–15	III	3
16–20	I	1
21–25	II	2

A tally mark, I, represents one data value. The mark ⅢⅡ represents five data values.

EXAMPLE 1 Making a Frequency Table

Science The numbers of named stars in a group of 34 constellations are listed below. Make a frequency table of the data.

7, 5, 4, 10, 5, 7, 2, 6, 8, 1, 5, 1, 3, 1, 12, 11, 2, 11, 2, 5, 0, 6, 14, 8, 3, 1, 15, 10, 0, 2, 0, 15, 9, 1

SOLUTION

STEP 1 **Choose** intervals of equal size that cover all the data values, which range from 0 to 15. In the table, each interval covers 4 whole numbers. The first interval is 0–3 and the last interval is 12–15.

STEP 2 **Make** a tally mark next to the interval containing a given number of named stars.

STEP 3 **Write** the frequency for each interval by totaling the number of tally marks for the interval.

Interval	Tally	Frequency
0–3	ⅢⅡ ⅢⅡ IIII	14
4–7	ⅢⅡ IIII	9
8–11	ⅢⅡ II	7
12–15	IIII	4

Histograms A **histogram** is a graph that displays data from a frequency table. A histogram has one bar for each interval that contains data values. The length of the bar indicates the frequency for the interval.

EXAMPLE 2 Making a Histogram

Music Every Sunday morning, a radio station plays a countdown of the top 30 requested songs from the previous week. The table shows the number of weeks that each of the songs on this week's top 30 have been on the countdown.

Make a histogram of the data.

Weeks	Tally	Frequency
1–5	IIII	4
6–10	JHT JHT I	11
11–15	JHT IIII	9
16–20	IIII	4
21–25		0
26–30	II	2

SOLUTION

STEP 1 **Draw** and label the horizontal and vertical axes.

List each interval from the frequency table on the horizontal axis.

The greatest frequency is 11. So, start the vertical axis at 0 and end at 12, using increments of 2.

STEP 2 **Draw** a bar for each interval. The bars should have the same width.

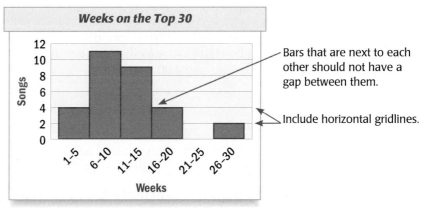

Bars that are next to each other should not have a gap between them.

Include horizontal gridlines.

AVOID ERRORS
Make sure that your histogram includes all of the intervals in the table, even the intervals that have a frequency of 0.

✓ **GUIDED PRACTICE** for Examples 1 and 2

1. **Typing Rates** The numbers of words that students in a typing class can type in a minute are listed. Make a frequency table and histogram of the data.

   25, 19, 23, 29, 34, 26, 30, 40, 33, 20, 35, 35, 25, 29, 36, 22, 31

2. **School Lunches** The number of students in your class who brought their lunch to school each day for the past two weeks is given below. Make a frequency table and histogram of the data.

   21, 12, 15, 21, 11, 8, 16, 18, 23, 27, 12, 14, 12, 12

★ **EXAMPLE 3** Standardized Test Practice

Butterflies The histogram shows the butterflies spotted in a butterfly garden between 8 A.M. and 8 P.M.

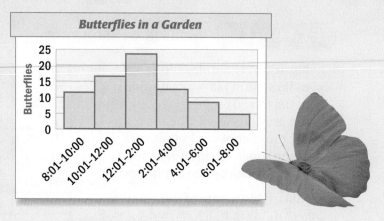

Butterflies in a Garden

Which statement is *not* supported by these data?

(A) The number of butterflies increased during the morning.

(B) More butterflies are spotted in the garden between 8:01 A.M. and noon than between 4:01 P.M. and 8:00 P.M.

(C) The number of butterflies spotted between 8:01 A.M. and 10:00 A.M. is about twice the number of butterflies spotted between 12:01 P.M. and 2:00 P.M.

(D) The number of butterflies spotted between 8:01 A.M. and 10:00 A.M. is about the same as the number of butterflies spotted between 2:01 P.M. and 4:00 P.M.

SOLUTION

The number of butterflies spotted between 8:01 A.M. and 10:00 A.M. is about 12. The number spotted between 12:01 P.M. and 2:00 P.M. is about 24.

▶ **Answer** The number of butterflies spotted between 8:01 A.M. and 10:00 A.M. is about *half* the number of butterflies spotted between 12:01 P.M. and 2:00 P.M. The correct answer is C. Ⓐ Ⓑ ⊙ Ⓓ

✓ **GUIDED PRACTICE** for Example 3

3. In Example 3, is the number of butterflies spotted between 8:01 A.M. and 2:00 P.M. greater than the number of butterflies spotted between 2:01 P.M. and 8:00 P.M.? *Explain.*

4. In Example 3, is the number of butterflies spotted between 12:01 P.M. and 4:00 P.M. greater than the number of butterflies spotted between 2:01 P.M. and 8:00 P.M.? *Explain.*

5. Make another comparison supported by the data in Example 3.

SKILL PRACTICE

1. **VOCABULARY** Copy and complete: The ? of an interval is the number of values that lie in the interval.

2. **VOCABULARY** *Describe* how a histogram differs from a bar graph.

MAKING FREQUENCY TABLES Copy and complete the frequency table.

SEE EXAMPLE 1
on p. 138
for Exs. 3–6

3. **Ages of camp counselors:**
19, 23, 26, 23, 16, 20, 26, 19, 21,
24, 21, 17, 27, 25, 22, 17, 16, 25

Interval	Tally	Frequency
16–18	?	?
19–21	?	?
22–24	?	?
?	?	?

4. **Minutes spent on phone daily:**
9, 19, 9, 13, 20, 8, 9, 19, 6, 12,
6, 18, 20, 10, 13, 17, 9, 5, 16, 5

Interval	Tally	Frequency
?	?	?
9–12	?	?
13–16	?	?
17–20	?	?

5. **ERROR ANALYSIS** The prices of televisions at a store are given below. Describe and correct the error(s) in the frequency table of the prices.

170, 135, 120, 175, 200, 260, 275, 160,
230, 165, 280, 150, 180, 280, 125, 100

Interval	Tally	Frequency
100–150	JHT	5
151–200	JHT I	6
200–250	II	2
251–300	IIII	4

6. ★ **MULTIPLE CHOICE** Which intervals can be used to make a frequency table of the lengths, in inches, of alligators at an alligator farm?

140, 127, 103, 140, 118, 100, 117, 101, 116, 129, 130, 105, 99, 143

Ⓐ 90–110, 111–130, 131–150   Ⓑ 91–110, 111–130, 131–150

Ⓒ 90–110, 110–130, 130–150   Ⓓ 81–100, 101–120, 121–140

◆ **MAKING HISTOGRAMS** **Make a frequency table of the data. Then make a histogram of the data.**

SEE EXAMPLES 1 AND 2
on pp. 138–139
for Exs. 7–9

7. **MATH TEST SCORES FOR A CLASS:** 70, 78, 68, 82, 91, 98, 76, 97, 89, 79, 88, 90, 85, 77, 84, 82, 90, 86, 93, 64, 94, 68, 86, 87

8. **HEIGHTS (IN FEET) OF TREES:** 5, 21, 18, 16, 8, 10, 16, 12, 21, 11, 7, 21, 19, 12, 13, 15, 8, 17, 11, 5, 9, 7, 20, 19

9. **PRICES (IN DOLLARS) OF WICKER FURNITURE:** 199, 329, 79, 149, 179, 149, 99, 69, 69, 99, 279, 129, 279, 79, 129, 189, 199, 79, 109, 89, 119, 119, 149, 99

10. CHALLENGE Write a survey question whose results can be displayed in a histogram. Make a prediction about your results. Then survey your class and display the results in a histogram. How does your prediction compare with your results?

PROBLEM SOLVING

SEE EXAMPLES
2 AND 3
on pp. 139–140
for Exs. 11–15

11. ★ **MULTIPLE CHOICE** The histogram shows the years that the 50 states were admitted to the Union. How many states were admitted during the years 1781–1810?

  Ⓐ 2   Ⓑ 8

  Ⓒ 17   Ⓓ 18

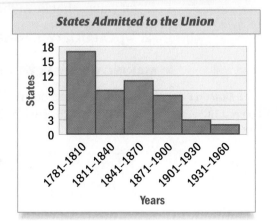

12. ★ **WRITING** Make a conclusion about the data displayed in the histogram at the right.

13. ★ **OPEN-ENDED MATH** Make a frequency table of the number of chapters in 10 different textbooks. What conclusions can you make?

WALKING TRAILS The frequency table below groups the lengths, in miles, of historical walking trails in the United States.

14. Make a histogram of the data.

15. ★ **WRITING** Make a conclusion about the data based on your histogram.

16. REASONING Can you determine the data values by looking at the frequency table or histogram? *Explain*.

17. ★ **SHORT RESPONSE** Use the frequency table in Exercises 14–16 to make a new frequency table with the following intervals: 3–6.9, 7–10.9, 11–14.9. How does changing the intervals affect the histogram?

Length	Frequency
3–4.9	4
5–6.9	5
7–8.9	17
9–10.9	2
11–12.9	6
13–14.9	1

18. ◆ **MULTIPLE REPRESENTATIONS** The number of minutes spent online by students during one day are listed below.

    15, 32, 8, 5, 0, 35, 19, 22, 60, 25, 38, 8, 7, 5, 2, 0, 30, 32, 45, 40, 25,
    20, 23, 32, 44, 18, 26, 35, 20, 10, 37, 18, 30, 8, 5, 36, 10, 21, 28, 15

  a. Make a Table Make a frequency table of the data.

  b. Make a Histogram Make a histogram of the data.

  c. Make a Box-and-Whisker Plot Make a box-and-whisker plot of the data.

  d. Compare Compare the box-and-whisker plot with the histogram. What information can you find in the box-and-whisker plot that you cannot find in the histogram? What information can you find in the histogram that you cannot find in the box-and-whisker plot?

19. ★ **EXTENDED RESPONSE** The point totals for each team in a Hawaiian canoe racing regatta are listed below. The team with the most points wins.

72, 69, 65, 54, 45, 44, 37, 36, 34, 33, 32, 32, 29, 27, 24, 21, 20, 18, 14, 14, 14, 13, 12, 11, 10, 10, 9, 8, 7, 7, 4, 4, 1, 0

a. Make a histogram of the data. *Explain* how you chose the intervals.

b. Make a stem-and-leaf plot of the data.

c. *Compare* the stem-and-leaf plot from part (b) with the histogram from part (a). How are they similar in describing the data? How are they different?

BUS DEPARTURES The histogram shows the number of departures from a bus station during a 24-hour period beginning at 12:01 A.M.

20. Find a range for the possible number of bus departures that took place between 8:01 A.M. and 2 P.M.

21. **CHALLENGE** From the histogram, can you determine the number of departures that took place between 4:01 P.M. and 4 A.M.? If so, find this number. If not, *explain* why not.

22. **CHALLENGE** Find a range for the possible number of bus departures that took place between 10:01 A.M. and 2 P.M.

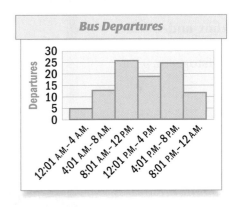

NJ

NEW JERSEY MIXED REVIEW

TEST PRACTICE at classzone.com

Isabella collected data on the number of pennies contributed for a fund drive by each homeroom in her grade. In Exercises 23 and 24, use the table that shows the results of the fund drive.

23. Which could be the number of pennies contributed by Mr. Hunter's class in order for the median and mode of the set to be equal?

Ⓐ 800　　　　Ⓑ 980

Ⓒ 1100　　　Ⓓ 1130

24. Mr. Hunter's class contributed 990 pennies. Which measure of data is represented by 270?

Ⓐ Mean　　　Ⓑ Median

Ⓒ Mode　　　Ⓓ Range

Fund Drive	
Homeroom Teacher	**Number of Pennies**
Mrs. Paulino	1000
Miss Steward	980
Mr. Williams	1200
Mr. Chang	1250
Mrs. Donahue	1130
Mr. Hunter	?

3.6 Appropriate Data Displays

Before	You displayed data using several types of graphs.
Now	You'll choose an appropriate display for a data set.
Why?	So you can display cycling data, as in Ex. 20.

KEY VOCABULARY
• **bar graph,** *p. 117*
• **line graph,** *p. 118*
• **stem-and-leaf plot,** *p. 126*
• **box-and-whisker plot,** *p. 133*
• **histogram,** *p. 139*

ACTIVITY

You can collect data and choose an appropriate display.

STEP 1 **Have** someone time you for 5 seconds as you write as much of the alphabet as you can. Record your result. Combine your result with those of your classmates.

STEP 2 **Work** with a group to decide how to display the data for the class. Then display the data and make a conclusion about the data. Compare your data display and conclusions with other groups.

Using appropriate data displays helps you make meaningful conclusions.

KEY CONCEPT *For Your Notebook*

Appropriate Data Displays

Use a *bar graph* to display data in distinct categories.

Use a *line graph* to display data over time.

Use a *stem-and-leaf plot* to group data into ordered lists.

Use a *box-and-whisker plot* to display how the data are spread out.

Use a *histogram* to compare the frequencies of data that fall in equal intervals.

EXAMPLE 1 Choosing an Appropriate Data Display

Bowling A professional bowler wants to display his scores for the year, without displaying individual data. What data display(s) should he use?

▶ **Answer** A line plot or a stem-and-leaf plot will show data values. A line graph or bar graph will not show distribution. Only a *box-and-whisker plot* or a *histogram* will show how the data are distributed without showing individual data.

USE A LINE PLOT?
Need help with line plots? See p. 758.

Misleading Data Displays You need to be able to identify potentially misleading data displays so that you interpret them correctly. Examples of potentially misleading data displays are shown below.

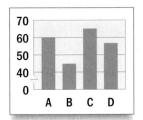

Broken Vertical Axis
The break in the axis exaggerates differences in bar lengths.

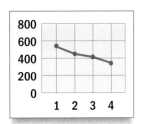

Large Increments
The large increments compress the graph vertically.

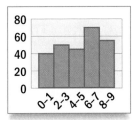

Small Intervals
The small intervals make it difficult to see the clustering of data.

EXAMPLE 2 Identifying Misleading Data Displays

Advertising Is the advertisement potentially misleading? *Explain.*

AVOID ERRORS
Make sure that you read the scale on the vertical axis of the data display in Example 2 carefully. Notice the break in the scale.

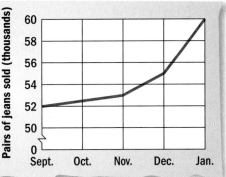

SOLUTION

The graph could be misleading because there is a break in the scale on the vertical axis, as it jumps from 0 to 50. The graph indicates a significant rise in sales. However, this rise would look less impressive if the vertical axis did not have a break in the scale.

✓ GUIDED PRACTICE for Examples 1 and 2

1. **Car Dealership** A car dealership sells seven makes of cars. Which data display(s) could be used to compare sales for each make of car last year?

2. **Profits** A store wants to display profits for this quarter. Which type of data display(s) could be used to compare this quarter's profits to last quarter's profits?

3. **What If?** Suppose you redraw the line graph in Example 2 with a scale from 0 to 60 using increments of 10. How does it compare with the graph in Example 2?

3.6 EXERCISES

HOMEWORK KEY

★ = **STANDARDIZED TEST PRACTICE**
Exs. 7, 11, 12, 13, 25, and 37

○ = **HINTS AND HOMEWORK HELP**
for Exs. 3, 5, 11, 13 at classzone.com

SKILL PRACTICE

1. **VOCABULARY** List five data displays that you have learned.

2. **VOCABULARY** Copy and complete: A __?__ is used to display data over time.

CHOOSING DISPLAYS In Exercises 3–5, choose an appropriate data display for the data. *Explain* your choice.

SEE EXAMPLE 1
on p. 144
for Exs. 3–7

3. You want to display the lengths of the long distance phone calls that you made last month so that the lengths are in four equal groups.

4. You want to display the change in heron population at a bird sanctuary over the last five years.

5. You want to display the results of a survey that asked people to name their favorite basketball team.

6. **ERROR ANALYSIS** A student wants to display the increasing value of a savings account over the past 10 months. The student chooses a stem-and-leaf plot to display the data. Describe and correct the error made in choosing that display for the data.

7. ★ **MULTIPLE CHOICE** Which data display would you use to compare frequencies of data falling in equal intervals?

   (A) Line plot
   (B) Stem-and-leaf plot
   (C) Box-and-whisker plot
   (D) Histogram

MAKING DISPLAYS Tell which of the two given types of data displays would *not* be appropriate for the set of data. Then make the appropriate data display.

8. A line graph or a stem-and-leaf plot

Price for a Gallon of Gasoline at Different Gas Stations						
$2.45	$2.25	$2.50	$2.31	$2.28	$2.46	$2.41
$2.29	$2.37	$2.19	$2.50	$2.27	$2.39	$2.44

9. A bar graph or a histogram

Ages of Students in a CPR Class						
Interval	10–19	20–29	30–39	40–49	50–59	60–69
Frequency	5	11	9	7	7	5

10. **CHALLENGE** Find a potentially misleading data display in a newspaper or a magazine. *Explain* why the display could be misleading.

SEE EXAMPLE 2
on p. 145
for Exs. 11–19

11. ★ **MULTIPLE CHOICE** The graph shows the donations collected during a fundraiser. What reason could cause the graph to be misleading?

Ⓐ Break in the vertical axis

Ⓑ Large increments on the vertical axis

Ⓒ Small intervals on the horizontal axis

Ⓓ Break in the horizontal axis

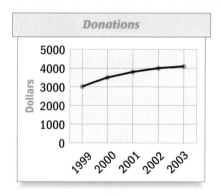

12. ★ **SHORT RESPONSE** The test grades for a science class are displayed in the histogram. *Explain* why the graph could be misleading.

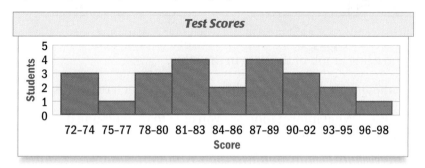

13. ★ **WRITING** Should a bar graph or a line graph be used to compare the number of restaurants of different types in a city? *Explain*.

FAVORITE MEALS The graph shows the results of a survey that asked students to choose their favorite meal. Tell whether the statement is *true* or *false*. *Explain* your reasoning.

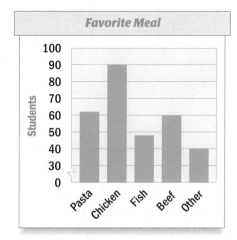

14. Chicken is twice as popular as beef.　　**15.** Pasta is twice as popular as fish.

16. Chicken is twice as popular as fish.　　**17.** Students chose beef twice as often as Other.

18. Pasta is twice as popular as Other.　　**19.** Beef is more popular than Pasta.

READING *IN* MATH Read the passage below for Exercises 20–22.

Tour de France The Tour de France is a long-distance cycling competition. For each of about 23 days, cyclists compete in stage races held mostly within the borders of France. Lance Armstrong has won the Tour more times than any other athlete.

The table shows the lengths in kilometers of each of the 20 racing stages of the 2004 Tour de France.

Stage	1	2	3	4	5	6	7	8	9	10
Km	202	197	210	64	200	196	204	168	160	237
Stage	11	12	13	14	15	16	17	18	19	20
Km	164	198	206	192	180	16	204	166	55	163

20. **Create a Display** Draw a box-and-whisker plot, stem-and-leaf plot, and a line graph of the data in the table.

21. **Compare** *Compare* the results you get from each of the displays.

22. **Writing** What information are you able to read off one display that you cannot read off another? *Explain.*

---

23. **MULTI-STEP PROBLEM** The graph shows the amounts of waste recycled in the United States.

   a. **Interpret** About how many times more waste was recycled in 2000 than in 1990?

   b. **Analyze** About how many times greater is the area of the recycle bin for 2000 than the area of the recycle bin for 1990? Does this agree with your answer to part (a)?

   c. **Make Conclusions** *Explain* why the graph could be misleading.

24. **COLLECT DATA** Ask at least 20 students how many CDs they own. Choose a data display for the data. *Explain* your choice. Then display the data and make conclusions about the data.

25. ★ **OPEN-ENDED MATH** Give an example of data that can be displayed in a line graph but not in a bar graph, and of data that can be displayed in a histogram but not in a line graph. *Explain* your answers.

DRAW VENN DIAGRAMS
For help with drawing Venn Diagrams, see page 769.

26. **CHALLENGE** In a high school 83 students take French, 110 students take Spanish, and 54 students take German. Eight students take both French and Spanish and 3 students take both German and Spanish. Create a Venn diagram and a bar graph of the data. *Compare* the displays.

27. Liz made different types of blankets. Six were red only, 4 were red and white, and 5 were red and blue. Which graph best represents these data?

(A)

Red and white | 5 | 6 | 4 | Red and blue

(B)

Blankets

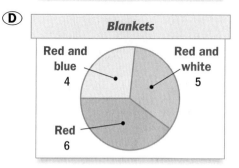

Number of blankets: 7 6 5 4 3 2 1 0

Red and white   Red   Red and blue

(C)

Blankets

Number of blankets: 7 6 5 4 3 2 1 0

Red and white   Red   Red and blue

(D)

Blankets

Red and blue 4

Red and white 5

Red 6

QUIZ *for Lessons 3.4–3.6*

1. Identify the upper and lower extremes, upper and lower quartiles, median, range, and interquartile range of the box-and-whisker plot shown. *(p. 133)*

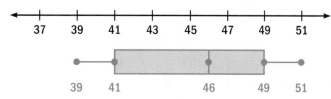

37   39   41   43   45   47   49   51

39   41   46   49   51

2. Make a box-and-whisker plot of the data below. *(p. 133)*

90, 102, 104, 120, 114, 95, 118, 105, 107, 106, 110, 109, 112

WORK WEEK **The hours worked during a week by each employee at a music store are listed below.** *(p. 138)*

29, 26, 23, 10, 17, 42, 38, 9, 29, 22, 16, 11, 39, 38, 26, 14

3. Make a histogram of the data. Use 0–9 as the first interval.

4. Make a conclusion about the data.

5. **BASKETBALL** You want to display the number of points scored during the season by each player on a basketball team. What display should you use to group the points into ordered lists? *(p. 144)*

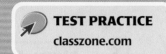
Lessons 3.4–3.6

1. **FOOTBALL** The histogram gives the numbers of points scored each game by a high school football team over the past several years. In what point range is the team most likely to score in the next game?

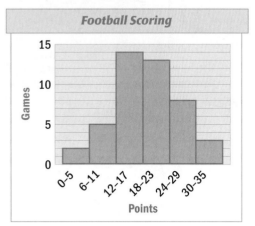

Football Scoring

A. 0 to 5   **C.** 12 to 17

B. 6 to 11   **D.** 18 to 23

2. **PIZZA** You want to display the results of a survey that asked students to name their favorite pizza topping. Which is an appropriate data display?

A. bar graph   **C.** line plot

B. line graph   **D.** stem-and-leaf plot

3. **AIRFARE** The prices, in dollars, of airplane tickets between two cities are listed. For what two additional values does a frequency table have equal frequencies for intervals 101–150, 151–200, 201–250, and 251–300?

　　135, 140, 145, 170, 175, 190, 195, 209, 240, 240, 250, 251, 275, 295

A. $150 and $250

B. $150 and $300

C. $151 and $250

D. $151 and $300

4. **LAND VALUE** The line graph shows the value of a plot of land over four years. What change would prevent the graph from being potentially misleading?

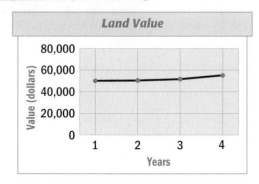

Land Value

A. Add more years to the horizontal axis.

B. Change the vertical axis to increments of 5000 from 0 to 60,000.

C. Change the vertical axis to start at 0 and end at 100,000.

D. Change the horizontal axis to show the value every 6 months.

5. **COPIES** The prices for making copies at a self-service copy center are listed in the table below. How much will it cost you to make 7 copies of a 30-page report?

A. $2.40

B. $10.50

C. $12.60

D. $16.80

Copies	Price per copy
1–100	$.08
101–200	$.06
over 200	$.05

6. **OPEN-ENDED** A teacher offers study sessions after school for upcoming tests. The data below show how many students attended each study session this year.

8, 2, 5, 6, 6, 1, 5, 9, 7, 11, 10, 4, 8, 7

- Find the extremes, the quartiles, and the median of the data.
- Make a box-and-whisker plot of the data.
- Make a conclusion about the data.

CHAPTER REVIEW

@HomeTutor
classzone.com
Vocabulary Practice

REVIEW KEY VOCABULARY

- mean, *p. 109*
- median, *p. 109*
- mode, *p. 109*
- range, *p. 110*
- bar graph, *p. 117*
- line graph, *p. 118*

- horizontal axis, *p. 118*
- vertical axis, *p. 118*
- stem-and-leaf plot, *p. 126*
- box-and-whisker plot, *p. 133*
- lower quartile, *p. 133*
- upper quartile, *p. 133*

- lower extreme, *p. 133*
- upper extreme, *p. 133*
- interquartile range, *p. 134*
- frequency table, *p. 138*
- frequency, *p. 138*
- histogram, *p. 139*

VOCABULARY EXERCISES

1. What data display is most appropriate for displaying data that are in distinct categories?

2. What data display is most appropriate for comparing data grouped into equal intervals?

3. What numbers do you plot to make a box-and-whisker plot?

4. What is the name of the difference between the upper quartile and the lower quartile of data?

Copy and complete the statement.

5. The __?__ of a data set is the sum of the values divided by the number of values.

6. The __?__ of a data set is the value that occurs most often.

7. An ordered __?__ is used to display data into an ordered list.

8. The number in the middle when the data is in an ordered list is the __?__ .

REVIEW EXAMPLES AND EXERCISES

3.1   Mean, Median, and Mode

pp. 109–114

EXAMPLE

Find the mean, median, mode(s), and range of the data.

$$5, 6, 11, 11, 16, 18, 19, 21, 21, 23, 24, 29$$

Mean: $\dfrac{5 + 6 + 11 + 11 + 16 + 18 + 19 + 21 + 21 + 23 + 24 + 29}{12} = 17$

Median: $\dfrac{18 + 19}{2} = 18.5$ **Modes:** 11 and 21   **Range:** $29 - 5 = 24$

EXERCISES

Find the mean, median, mode(s), and range of the data.

*SEE EXAMPLES
1, 2, AND 3*
on pp. 109–110
for Exs. 9–13

9. 0, 1, 2, 4, 4, 5, 7, 8, 10, 12, 13

10. 151, 183, 184, 163, 201, 162

11. 5.5, 6.3, 4.7, 4.6, 4.6, 7.1, 6.3, 7.4, 6, 7.5

12. 67.5, 70.7, 67.3, 71.2, 72.1, 71.2, 69.7

13. Reading The number of books read by 20 students in 3 months is listed below. Which average best represents the data? *Explain* your reasoning.

13, 19, 5, 9, 7, 8, 6, 2, 6, 5, 5, 7, 6, 2, 2, 8, 9, 7, 5, 9

3.2 Bar Graphs and Line Graphs

pp. 117–123

EXAMPLE

Snowboards The table shows the price of a snowboard at the same time each day during a five-day Internet auction. Make a line graph of the data.

Day	1	2	3	4	5
Price (dollars)	50	57	76	103	145

STEP 1 **Choose** horizontal and vertical axes.

Days from 1 through 5 are shown on the horizontal axis. The highest snowboard price is $145. So, start the vertical axis at 0 and end with 150, using increments of 30.

STEP 2 **Draw** and label the graph.

EXERCISES

*SEE EXAMPLES
1, 3, AND 4*
on pp. 117–119
for Exs. 14–15

14. Rivers Make a bar graph of the lengths of the rivers listed in the table.

Lengths of the Longest Rivers in the United States (miles)				
Mississippi	Missouri	Rio Grande	St. Lawrence	Yukon
2340	2540	1900	1900	1980

15. Allowance The table shows Holly's weekly allowance (in dollars) for each month during the first half of last year. Make a line graph of the data. Between which two months did Holly's allowance increase the most?

Month	January	February	March	April	May	June
Allowance	$15	$16	$16	$18	$19	$20

3.3 Stem-and-Leaf Plots

pp. 126–130

EXAMPLE

Make an ordered stem-and-leaf plot of the data.

38, 36, 10, 23, 19, 30, 6, 16, 39, 12, 12, 5, 27

0	5 6
1	0 2 2 6 9
2	3 7
3	0 6 8 9

STEP 1 **Choose** the stems and leaves. Let the stems be the tens' digits from 0 to 3. Let the leaves be the ones' digits.

STEP 2 **Write** the stems first. Record and order the leaves.

Key: 1 | 6 = 16

EXERCISES

Make an ordered stem-and-leaf plot of the data.

SEE EXAMPLE 1
on p. 126
for Exs. 16–17

16. Test scores: 98, 96, 83, 85, 89, 72, 84, 73, 88, 93, 89, 67, 83, 79, 83, 78, 75

17. Ages: 38, 38, 17, 23, 36, 35, 20, 12, 19, 39, 27, 36, 41, 30, 18, 22, 37, 25

3.4 Box-and-Whisker Plots

pp. 133–137

EXAMPLE

Make a box-and-whisker plot of the data.

11   4   28   16   6   13   21   15   5   21   4   20   17   26

STEP 1 **Order** the data. Identify the median, quartiles, and extremes.

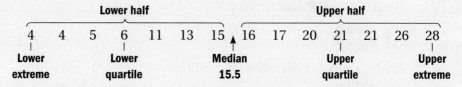

STEP 2 **Draw** a number line. Locate key points. Complete the graph.

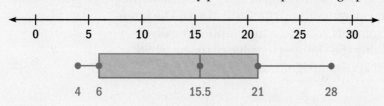

EXERCISE

SEE EXAMPLE 1
on p. 133
for Ex. 18

18. Car Speeds Make a box-and-whisker plot of the car speeds. 58, 62, 65, 65, 75, 72, 55, 56, 60, 61, 67, 70, 68, 69, 57, 64, 56

EXAMPLE

Prices The frequency table shows the prices of shoes in a store. Make a histogram of the data.

Price (dollars)	10–19	20–29	30–39	40–49
Frequency	10	22	16	11

STEP 1 **Draw** and label the axes. List the intervals. The greatest frequency is 22. So, start the vertical axis at 0 and end at 25, using increments of 5.

STEP 2 **Draw** bars of the same width for each interval.

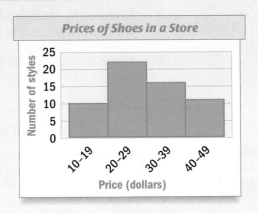

EXERCISE

SEE EXAMPLES 1 AND 2 on pp. 138–139 for Ex. 19

19. **Cleanup** The pounds of garbage collected by volunteers for a city cleanup project are listed below. Make a frequency table and a histogram of the data.

65, 29, 38, 50, 60, 43, 27, 48, 29, 79, 37, 45, 48, 32, 57, 35, 54, 53, 37, 47

EXAMPLE

Explain why the data display could be misleading.

The graph could be misleading because of the large increments on the vertical axis. The large increments compress the graph vertically, making the changes in value of the baseball card appear insignificant.

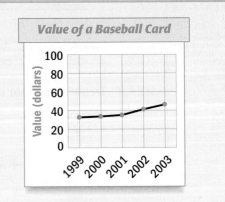

EXERCISE

SEE EXAMPLE 2 on p. 145 for Ex. 20

20. **Baseball Cards** Redraw the line graph above using a scale from 0 to 60 in increments of 5. *Compare* the two graphs. What do you notice?

3 CHAPTER TEST

@HomeTutor
classzone.com
Chapter Test Practice

In Exercises 1 and 2, find the mean, median, mode(s), and range.

1. 2, 7, 2, 7, 13, 7, 11, 9, 6, 5, 8

2. 48, 67, 88, 82, 41, 66, 72, 64, 49, 53

3. Find the missing values in the data below so that the mean is 28 and the mode is 15.

    20, 40, 36, __?__, 15, 38, __?__, 30, 41

FUNDRAISING In Exercises 4 and 5, use the data below, that show the numbers of tins of popcorn sold by members of a school band.

    40, 32, 16, 14, 11, 16, 11, 12, 26, 1, 15, 9, 6, 3, 27, 5, 12, 18, 23, 33, 17, 50

4. Make a stem-and leaf-plot of the data.

5. Use the stem-and-leaf plot to make a histogram of the data.

6. **PETS** The miles you walk your dog each day over two weeks are listed below. Make a box-and-whisker plot of the data.

    1.8, 2.6, 0.4, 2, 0.9, 2.5, 2, 1.9, 1.5, 1.5, 0.5, 0.8, 1.3, 1.6

BASEBALL Use the bar graph at the right. It shows the wins and losses for the Baltimore Orioles over three seasons.

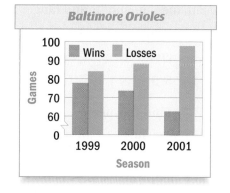

7. In which season did the Orioles lose 14 more games than they won?

8. About how many more games did the Orioles win in 1999 than in 2000?

9. Which of the three seasons would you consider the most successful? *Explain*.

10. **COMPUTERS** The table shows a computer's price over time. Make a line graph of the data. Then make a conclusion about the data.

Date	October 15	November 15	December 15	January 15	February 15	March 15
Price	$699	$699	$649	$629	$599	$499

11. **RESTAURANTS** What data display should a restaurant owner use to display the number of customers served on each Saturday night during the past year? *Explain* your choice.

MULTIPLE CHOICE QUESTIONS

If you have difficulty solving a multiple choice problem directly, you may be able to use another approach. Try to eliminate incorrect answer choices and obtain the correct answer.

PROBLEM 1

What are the mean, median, mode, and range of the ages?

10, 5, 23, 21, 28, 16, 5, 14, 22

A.	B.	C.	D.
mean = 16	mean = 32	mean = 16	mean = 24
median = 16	median = 16	median = 28	median = 28
mode = 5	mode = 5	mode = 10	mode = 5
range = 23	range = 23	range = 12	range = 12

METHOD 1

SOLVE DIRECTLY Use the definitions to find the mean, median, mode, and range.

STEP 1 **Write** the ages in order from least to greatest.

5, 5, 10, 14, 16, 21, 22, 23, 28

STEP 2 **Find** the mean.

$$\frac{5 + 5 + 10 + 14 + 16 + 21 + 22 + 23 + 28}{9} = 16$$

STEP 3 **Find** the median. Because there is an odd number of data values, the median is the middle age. The median is 16.

STEP 4 **Find** the mode. The age that occurs most often is 5.

STEP 5 **Find** the range. The difference between the greatest and the least values is $28 - 5 = 23$.

The correct answer is A.

METHOD 2

ELIMINATE CHOICES In some multiple choice questions, you can identify answer choices that can be eliminated.

The mode of the data is 5. You can eliminate choice C.

You can eliminate choice B because the mean cannot be larger than the largest value in the data set.

To find the range, you first have to write the ages in order from least to greatest. You can eliminate choice D because the range listed under choice D was found without placing the numbers in order.

The correct answer is A.

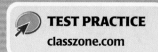

PROBLEM 2

The histogram shows the times, in minutes, that it took students at a school to run 1 mile. How many more students had times in the 7–8.9 minute interval than in the 9–10.9 minute interval?

A. 10   C. 20

B. 15   D. 41

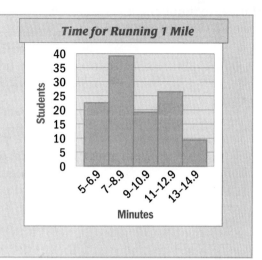

METHOD 1

SOLVE DIRECTLY Use the two bars that represent the number of students with times in the two specified intervals.

STEP 1 The scale on the vertical axis uses increments of 5.

STEP 2 Because there are about 4 increments of 5 separating the bars, the difference between the bars is about 20.

The correct answer is C.

METHOD 2

ELIMINATE CHOICES In some multiple choice questions, you can identify answer choices that can be eliminated.

For choice A, 10 units below the 7–8.9 bar would make the 9–10.9 bar end at about 30. ✗

For choice B, 15 units below the 7–8.9 bar would make the 9–10.9 bar end at about 25. ✗

For choice C, 20 units below the 7–8.9 bar would make the 9–10.9 bar end at about 20. ✓

The correct answer is C.

TEST PREPARATION

PRACTICE

Explain why you can eliminate the highlighted answer choice.

1. **SOCCER GOALS** The numbers of goals scored by a soccer team in each game over a season are listed below. What is the mean number of goals?

   6, 2, 1, 2, 5, 1, 3, 4, 4, 3, 7, 2, 1, 3, 0, 4

   A. 0   B. 2   C. 3   ✗ D. 8

2. **DAIRY CATTLE** A farmer wants to display the weights of the dairy cows. What data display should he use to see how the data are distributed, without displaying the individual data?

   ✗ A. stem-and-leaf plot   C. bar graph

   B. line graph   D. histogram

TEST PREPARATION

1. The histogram shows the numbers of minutes that 15 people used the phone.

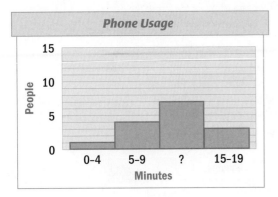

What is the missing interval?

A. 9–14

B. 9–15

C. 10–14

D. 10–15

2. The line plot shows the results of a questionnaire asking people how many days per week they exercise.

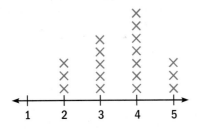

How many people exercise less than 4 days per week?

A. 3

B. 5

C. 7

D. 8

3. The graph shows the number of magazine subscriptions sold by a class during each month of a fundraiser.

Which statement is best supported by these data?

A. The class sold more magazine subscriptions in February than in January.

B. The class sold fewer magazine subscriptions in March than in January.

C. There were no sales in February.

D. The class sold the same number of magazine subscriptions in February as in January.

4. Mrs. Murphy bought 3 boxes of cereal at $2.98 each, 1 gallon of milk for $3.00, and 2 loaves of bread at $1.60 each. She paid 6% tax on everything. What other information is necessary to find Mrs. Murphy's correct change?

A. Total cost of all the items

B. Amount she paid in tax

C. Amount she gave the cashier

D. Cost of one dozen eggs

5. The table shows the distance David ran each day last week.

Running	
Day	**Distance (miles)**
Sunday	2.5
Monday	1.8
Tuesday	1.75
Wednesday	2
Thursday	1.5
Friday	2.2
Saturday	2

What was the total distance that David ran last week?

A. 11 mi

B. 13 mi

C. 13.75 mi

D. 15.75 mi

6. Which of the following CANNOT be used to find the perimeter of a rectangle with length l and width w?

A. $l + l + w + w$

B. $2l + w + w$

C. $l + w$

D. $2l + 2w$

7. Which description relates the position n of a term in the sequence and the value of the term?

Position n	1	2	3	4	5
Value of term	7	8	9	10	11

A. Subtract 6 from n

B. Add 6 to n

C. Divide n by 6

D. Multiply n by 7

8. Tony wants to paint a wall but not the door on the wall.

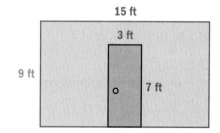

How many square feet of wall does Tony need to paint?

A. 21 ft^2

B. 34 ft^2

C. 114 ft^2

D. 135 ft^2

9. OPEN-ENDED Students' scores on a science quiz are listed below.

98, 100, 91, 64, 74, 98, 75, 68, 82, 97, 95, 77, 93, 71, 92

Part A Find the mean, median, and mode(s). Then decide which average best represents the data. *Explain* your reasoning.

Part B Two more scores, 59 and 60, are added to the list. *Describe* how the mean, median, and mode(s) will be affected.

3 CUMULATIVE REVIEW   Chapters *1–3*

Describe the pattern. Then write the next three numbers. *(p. 3)*

1. 5, 9, 13, 17, . . .
2. 19, 16, 13, 10, . . .
3. 3, 6, 12, 24, . . .
4. 128, 64, 32, 16, . . .
5. 89, 78, 67, 56, . . .
6. 210, 233, 256, 279, . . .

Evaluate the expression when $x = 3$ and $y = 6$.

7. $x + 15 - y$ *(p. 8)*
8. $3xy$ *(p. 8)*
9. $\dfrac{2y}{x}$ *(p. 8)*
10. x^2 *(p. 13)*
11. y^1 *(p. 13)*
12. x^3 *(p. 13)*
13. $2 + xy \div 10$ *(p. 17)*
14. $(y + 14) \div 2$ *(p. 17)*
15. $x^2 - y + 5$ *(p. 17)*

Round the decimal as specified. *(p. 56)*

16. 8.4 (nearest one)
17. 6.76 (nearest tenth)
18. 0.009 (nearest hundredth)

Copy and complete the statement using <, >, or =.

19. 5.4 _?_ 4.5 *(p. 56)*
20. 0.39 _?_ 0.40 *(p. 56)*
21. 0.580 _?_ 0.58 *(p. 56)*
22. 6×10^7 _?_ 2×10^8 *(p. 78)*
23. 2,400 _?_ 2.4×10^5 *(p. 78)*
24. 9,900,000 _?_ 9.9×10^4 *(p. 78)*
25. 3.8 cm _?_ 39 mm *(p. 90)*
26. 55 L _?_ 0.055 kL *(p. 90)*
27. 501 m _?_ 5010 cm *(p. 90)*

Evaluate the expression.

28. $42.6 + 81.9$ *(p. 60)*
29. $109.3 - 14.6$ *(p. 60)*
30. $5.37 - 4.1 + 23$ *(p. 60)*
31. 6.2×5.5 *(p. 66)*
32. 0.021×3.7 *(p. 66)*
33. $6.22 \times 1.5 \times 3.8$ *(p. 66)*
34. $4.8 \div 40$ *(p. 71)*
35. $4.45 \div 3.56$ *(p. 71)*
36. $23.4 \div 0.015$ *(p. 71)*

Choose an appropriate metric unit. *(p. 84)*

37. mass of a duck
38. length of a boat
39. capacity of a soup bowl
40. capacity of a bucket
41. length of a pencil
42. mass of a grain of sand

Find the mean, median, mode(s) and range of the data. *(p. 109)*

43. Hours of homework for one week: 10, 5, 25, 23, 28, 39, 16, 17, 5, 14, 9

44. Ages of people at an arcade: 22, 15, 5, 20, 17, 12, 9, 12, 27, 12

Make an ordered stem-and-leaf plot of the data. *(p. 126)*

45. 10, 13, 41, 55, 38, 22, 12, 55, 17, 27, 13, 19, 48, 25, 36

46. 78, 66, 45, 42, 86, 71, 60, 66, 78, 75, 64, 41, 86, 66

Make a frequency table and a histogram of the data. *(p. 138)*

47. Number of students in math classes: 22, 28, 17, 9, 15, 30, 26, 18, 19, 31, 29, 20, 24, 8, 18, 17

48. LAUNDROMAT The cost of doing 4 loads of laundry can be found by evaluating the expression $4(w + d)$, where w is the cost (in dollars) of doing one load in the washer and d is the cost (in dollars) of doing one load in the dryer. Find the cost for doing 4 loads of laundry when $w = 3$ and $d = 1$. *(pp. 8, 17)*

49. FERRY BOATS You take a ferry a distance of 80 miles to get to an island. The trip takes you 2 hours. At about what speed does the ferry travel? *(p. 25)*

50. RUGS The area of a rectangular rug is 24 square feet. The perimeter of the rug is 20 feet. Find the length and the width of the rug. *(pp. 32, 37)*

51. RACING EVENT You are in a 3-part racing event. Your friend's total time is 80.63 seconds. Your times for each part of the race are 22.34 seconds, 25.8 seconds, and 30.15 seconds. Is your total time faster than your friend's total time? *Explain. (pp. 56, 60)*

52. ASTRONOMY The table shows the approximate distances (in kilometers) from Earth to five of the stars nearest Earth. Write the stars in order from those closest to Earth to those farthest from Earth. *(p. 78)*

Altair	1.54×10^{14}
Barnard's Star	5.68×10^{13}
Proxima Centauri	3.97×10^{13}
Rigil Kentaurus	4.07×10^{13}
Wolf 359	7.28×10^{13}

53. OFFICE SUPPLIES Julie is purchasing office supplies and notes that bottles of correction fluid contain 20 milliliters of fluid. They come in packages of 12. How many packages does she need to purchase 1 liter of correction fluid. *(p. 90)*

54. MOVIES Students at a school were asked to name their favorite type of movie. Make a double bar graph of the results given below. *(p. 117)*

	Drama	Comedy	Action	Sci-Fi	Animated	Other
Boys	53	62	33	15	16	11
Girls	85	60	14	2	10	12

SPEED LIMITS In Exercises 55 and 56, use the stem-and-leaf plot. It shows the speeds (in miles per hour) of cars on a highway. *(pp. 126, 133)*

55. Make a box-and-whisker plot of the data.

56. A police officer decides to pull over anyone traveling 65 miles per hour or faster. About what fraction of the cars does the police officer pull over?

```
5 | 5 6 7 8
6 | 0 1 2 2 5 5 7 8 8
7 | 0 0 2 2 5 5
Key: 6|2 = 62
```

57. INTERNET You want to display the number of visits to a company's website each day over a week. Should you use a line graph or a histogram? *Explain. (p. 144)*

4 Number Patterns and Fractions

Before

In previous chapters you've . . .

- Worked with whole numbers
- Worked with decimals

Now

 New Jersey Standards

4.1.A.1.c	4.1	Prime factorization
	4.2	Common factors
4.1.A.5	4.3	Equivalent fractions
	4.4	Common multiples
4.1.A.4	4.5	Comparing fractions
4.1.A.5	4.6	Mixed numbers
4.1.A.5	4.7	Fractions and decimals

Why?

So you can solve real-world problems about . . .

- Chinese New Year, p. 168
- Rose Bowl floats, p. 173
- flying insects, p. 186

 **Math**
at classzone.com

- Greatest Common Factor, p. 171
- Mixed Numbers and Improper Fractions, p. 196
- Decimal and Fraction Converter, p. 201

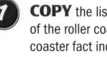 **Get-Ready Games**

Review Prerequisite Skills by playing *Coaster Commotion.*

> **Skill Focus:** Whole number division

COASTER COMMOTION

HOW TO PLAY Did you know that there are more roller coasters in the United States than in any other country? In this game, you'll use division to find out how many roller coasters there are in the United States.

 COPY the lists below. Each list corresponds to one of the roller coaster facts on page 163, and each roller coaster fact includes a trivia number. Determine whether each number in a list is a factor of its corresponding trivia number. If a number is a factor, cross it off the list.

A 2, 8, 10   **B** 4, 6, 8   **C** 3, 6, 9

2 MULTIPLY the remaining numbers to find the total number of roller coasters in the United States as of 2002.

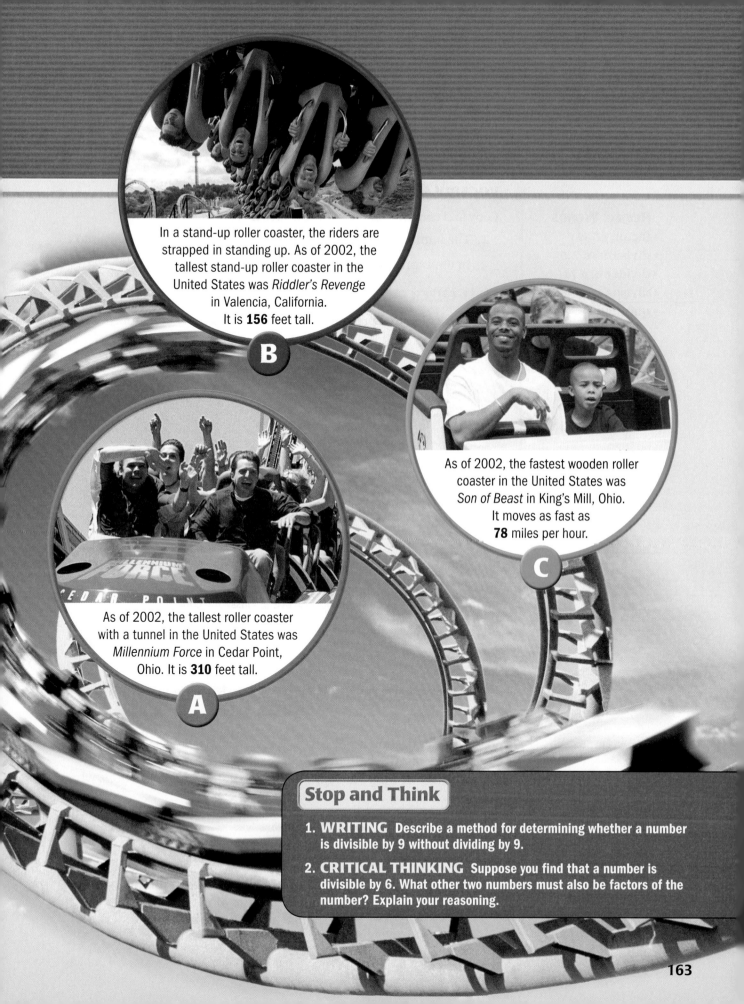

In a stand-up roller coaster, the riders are strapped in standing up. As of 2002, the tallest stand-up roller coaster in the United States was *Riddler's Revenge* in Valencia, California. It is **156** feet tall.

B

As of 2002, the fastest wooden roller coaster in the United States was *Son of Beast* in King's Mill, Ohio. It moves as fast as **78** miles per hour.

C

As of 2002, the tallest roller coaster with a tunnel in the United States was *Millennium Force* in Cedar Point, Ohio. It is **310** feet tall.

A

Stop and Think

1. **WRITING** Describe a method for determining whether a number is divisible by 9 without dividing by 9.

2. **CRITICAL THINKING** Suppose you find that a number is divisible by 6. What other two numbers must also be factors of the number? Explain your reasoning.

Review Prerequisite Skills

REVIEW WORDS
- **factor,** *p. 739*
- **divisible,** *p. 739*
- **dividend,** *p. 744*
- **divisor,** *p. 744*
- **quotient,** *p. 744*

VOCABULARY CHECK

Copy and complete using a review word from the list at the left.

1. The number 12 is said to be __?__ by 4 because 4 divides evenly into 12.

2. In the expression 144 ÷ 3, 144 is called the __?__.

SKILL CHECK

Write a fraction to represent the shaded part of the set or region. *(p. 740)*

3.   **4.**  **5.**

6.  **7.**   **8.**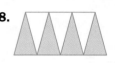

Find the product or quotient. *(pp. 743–744)*

9. 356×79	**10.** $592 \div 16$	**11.** $960 \div 12$
12. 827×654	**13.** $1590 \div 15$	**14.** 562×308
15. 1544×290	**16.** $3672 \div 9$	**17.** 1479×567

@HomeTutor Prerequisite skills practice at classzone.com

Notetaking Skills   Using Your Homework

In each chapter you will learn a new notetaking skill. In Chapter 4 you will apply the strategy of using your homework to Exercise 29 on p. 167.

Write a question mark next to a homework exercise you did incorrectly. Get help from your teacher or another student, and write down what you learned. Review homework corrections when you study for a test.

$$
\begin{array}{r}
1.07 \\
\times\ 0.03 \\
\hline
0.321
\end{array}\ ?
$$

$$
\begin{array}{r}
1.07 \\
\times\ 0.03 \\
\hline
0.0321
\end{array}
$$
← Number of decimal places in product is equal to the sum of the number of decimal places in the factors.

4.1 Prime Factorization

 4.1.A.1.c Extend understanding of the number system by constructing meanings for the following . . . : Whole numbers with exponents

Before You multiplied whole numbers to find their product.

Now You'll write a number as a product of prime numbers.

Why? So you can find possible group sizes, as in Example 1.

KEY VOCABULARY
- **prime number,** *p. 165*
- **composite number,** *p. 165*
- **prime factorization,** *p. 166*
- **factor tree,** *p. 166*

ACTIVITY

You can make a list of *prime numbers*.

STEP 1 **Write** the whole numbers from 2 through 48.

STEP 2 **Circle** 2 and cross out all multiples of 2 other than 2. (The first row in the list below has been done for you.) Then go to the next remaining number after 2, circle it, and cross out all its multiples other than itself. Repeat until every number is either circled or crossed out.

②	3	~~4~~	5	~~6~~	7	~~8~~	9	~~10~~	11	~~12~~
13	14	15	16	17	18	19	20	21	22	23	24
25	26	27	28	29	30	31	32	33	34	35	36
37	38	39	40	41	42	43	44	45	46	47	48

In the activity, the numbers that are circled are called *prime numbers*. A **prime number** is a whole number greater than 1 whose only whole number factors are 1 and itself. A **composite number** is a whole number greater than 1 that has whole number factors other than 1 and itself. The number 1 is neither prime nor composite.

EXAMPLE 1 Writing Factors of a Number

Field Trip A class of 36 students is on a field trip at the aquarium. The teacher wants to break the class into groups of the same size. Find all the possible group sizes by writing all the factors of 36.

SOLUTION

$36 = 1 \times 36$

$= 2 \times 18$

$= 3 \times 12$

$= 4 \times 9$ **36 isn't divisible by 5. Skip to 6.**

$= 6 \times 6$ **36 isn't divisible by 7 and 8. Skip to 9.**

$= 9 \times 4$ **Stop when the factors repeat.**

▶ **Answer** The possible group sizes are 1, 2, 3, 4, 6, 9, 12, 18, and 36.

TAKE NOTES
The divisibility tests on p. 739 will be useful in Chapter 4. You may want to copy them into your notebook.

EXAMPLE 2 Identifying Prime and Composite Numbers

Tell whether the number is *prime* or *composite*.

a. 56   **b.** 11

SOLUTION

a. The factors of 56 are 1, 2, 4, 7, 8, 14, 28, and 56. So, 56 is composite.

b. The only factors of 11 are 1 and 11. So, 11 is prime.

✓ **GUIDED PRACTICE**   for Examples 1 and 2

Write all the factors of the number.

1. 35   **2.** 32   **3.** 65   **4.** 23

Tell whether the number is *prime* or *composite*.

5. 47   **6.** 81   **7.** 34   **8.** 67

READING
To *factor* a number means to write the number as a product of its factors.

Prime Factorization To factor a whole number as a product of prime numbers is called **prime factorization**. You can use a diagram called a **factor tree** to write the prime factorization of a number. Use an exponent when a prime factor appears more than once in the prime factorization.

EXAMPLE 3 Using a Factor Tree

Use a factor tree to write the prime factorization of 54.

One possible factor tree: Another possible factor tree:

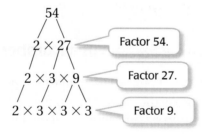

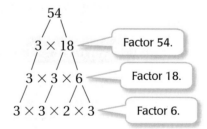

AVOID ERRORS
A number may be divisible by the same prime number many times. A factor tree is complete when the bottom row includes only prime numbers.

Both factor trees give the same result: $54 = 2 \times 3 \times 3 \times 3 = 2 \times 3^3$.

▶ **Answer** The prime factorization of 54 is 2×3^3.

✓ **GUIDED PRACTICE**   for Example 3

Use a factor tree to write the prime factorization of the number.

9. 30   **10.** 48   **11.** 44   **12.** 75

4.1 EXERCISES

HOMEWORK KEY

★ = **STANDARDIZED TEST PRACTICE**
Exs. 28, 48, 51, 52, 54, 55, and 62

◯ = **HINTS AND HOMEWORK HELP**
for Exs. 3, 7, 9, 21, 49 at classzone.com

SKILL PRACTICE

VOCABULARY Copy and complete the statement.

1. To factor a whole number as a product of prime numbers is called __?__ .

2. A whole number greater than 1 that has whole number factors other than 1 and itself, such as 22, is called a __?__ number.

SEE EXAMPLE 1
on p. 165
for Exs. 3–7

WRITING FACTORS Write all the factors of the number.

(3.) 20   **4.** 25   **5.** 13   **6.** 84   **(7.)** 100

CLASSIFYING NUMBERS Tell whether the number is *prime* or *composite*. *Explain* your reasoning.

SEE EXAMPLE 2
on p. 166
for Exs. 8–17

8. 88   **(9.)** 23   **10.** 39   **11.** 51   **12.** 61

13. 67   **14.** 41   **15.** 99   **16.** 201   **17.** 87

PRIME FACTORIZATION Use a factor tree to write the prime factorization.

SEE EXAMPLE 3
on p. 166
for Exs. 18–29

18. 49   **19.** 68   **20.** 50   **(21.)** 64   **22.** 26

23. 144   **24.** 225   **25.** 588   **26.** 612   **27.** 864

28. ★ **MULTIPLE CHOICE** What is the prime factorization of 72?

    A $2^2 \times 3 \times 6$ **B** $3^3 \times 2^2$ **C** $2^3 \times 3^2$ **D** $2^3 \times 9$

TAKE NOTES
Write a question mark next to Exercise 29 and seek help if you cannot answer the exercise.

29. **ERROR ANALYSIS** Describe and correct the error made in writing the prime factorization of 36.

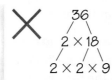

The prime factorization of 36 is $2^2 \times 9$.

REASONING Is the statement *true* or *false*? *Explain* your reasoning.

30. The prime factors of 15 are 1, 3, and 5.

31. All even numbers are composite.

32. The product of any two numbers is composite.

33. The product of any two prime numbers is always odd.

FINDING PRIMES Find all the prime numbers between the given numbers.

34. 15, 35   **35.** 50, 80   **36.** 108, 135

37. 180, 198   **38.** 230, 260   **39.** 270, 295

ALGEBRA Tell which values of *n*, from 1 to 10, make the expression *prime*.

40. $2n$ **41.** $2n + 1$ **42.** $4n + 1$ **43.** $4n + 3$

44. EXAMPLES AND NONEXAMPLES The prime factorizations of the numbers in Group A share a common property that is *not* true of the numbers in Group B. Find another number that belongs in Group A and another number that belongs in Group B.

Group A: 1764, 1089, 1225   **Group B:** 1232, 2310, 112

45. CHALLENGE Find the composite number between 50 and 60 whose prime factors have a sum of 11.

PROBLEM SOLVING

46. GUIDED PROBLEM SOLVING You are a tour guide and want to divide 90 people into the same size groups. The group size must be from 11 to 15 people. How many people should be in each group?

  a. Find all the factors of 90.

  b. Use the factors of 90 to find all the possible group sizes.

  c. Is more than one answer possible? *Explain* your reasoning.

47. SOUVENIR POUCHES As a volunteer at a museum, you fill souvenir pouches with semiprecious stones. Each pouch has the same number of stones, and there are no leftover stones. There is more than one stone per pouch. Is the total number of stones in all the souvenir pouches combined *prime* or *composite*? *Explain* your reasoning.

48. ★ WRITING *Explain* the difference between finding the factors of a number and finding the prime factorization of a number.

(49.) CLASS GROUPS A teacher wants to divide the 28 students in the class into groups for one assignment. Find all possible group sizes by writing all the factors of 28.

50. CHINESE NEW YEAR In the Chinese calendar, the year 2019 is the Year of the Pig. Is 2019 prime or composite? *Explain* your reasoning.

51. ★ SHORT RESPONSE A classroom in your school contains 32 desks, and another classroom contains 35 desks. Which classroom allows for more rectangular desk arrangements if you use all the desks? *Explain* your answer.

52. ★ OPEN-ENDED MATH Find two composite numbers whose prime factors each have a sum of 18.

★ = STANDARDIZED TEST PRACTICE   ◯ = HINTS AND HOMEWORK HELP *at classzone.com*

53. GOLDBACH'S CONJECTURE A *conjecture* is a statement believed to be true but not proved to be true. Christian Goldbach (1690–1764) made this conjecture about prime numbers: Every even number greater than 2 can be written as the sum of two prime numbers. Show that Goldbach's conjecture is true for every even number between 3 and 11.

54. ★ WRITING *Explain* how the divisibility tests help you find the prime factorization of a number like 180.

55. ★ EXTENDED RESPONSE List all the factors of 5 and 10, then of 27 and 54. Does the list of all the factors double when you double an odd number? *Explain.* List all the factors of 10, 20, 40, and 80. Does the list of all the factors double when you double an even number? *Explain.*

56. CHALLENGE The lengths of the sides of a triangle are consecutive whole numbers. Is it possible for the perimeter of this triangle to be a prime number? *Explain* your reasoning.

NEW JERSEY MIXED REVIEW

TEST PRACTICE at classzone.com

57. The histogram shows the number of cars that traveled through an intersection between 8 A.M. and 12 P.M. Which statement is NOT supported by the data?

(A) The busiest time was between 8:01 A.M. and 9:00 A.M.

(B) It was twice as busy between 11:01 A.M. and 12:00 P.M. as it was between 10:01 A.M. and 11:00 A.M.

(C) The intersection was busier between 10:01 A.M. and 12:00 P.M. than between 8:01 A.M. and 10:00 A.M.

(D) The busiest time was not between 9:01 A.M. and 10:00 A.M.

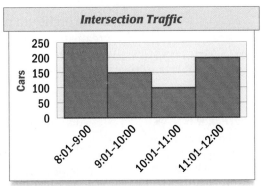

Brain Game

What am I?

If a number in the list below is a factor of 2,343,750, write its corresponding letter on a piece of paper. Unscramble the letters to answer the riddle.

2	3	4	5	6	7	8	9	10
C	A	E	H	M	L	N	R	T

Riddle: Take me out and scratch my head, I am now black, but once was red. What am I?

4.2 Greatest Common Factor

Before	You found all the factors of a whole number.
Now	You'll find the greatest common factor of two or more numbers.
Why?	So you can find ways to group items, as in Example 1.

KEY VOCABULARY
- **common factor,** p. 170
- **greatest common factor (GCF),** p. 170
- **relatively prime,** p. 171

Orchestra An orchestra conductor divides 48 violinists, 24 violists, and 36 cellists into ensembles. Each ensemble has the same number of each instrument. What is the greatest number of ensembles that can be formed? How many violinists, violists, and cellists will be in each ensemble?

A whole number that is a factor of two or more nonzero whole numbers is called a **common factor**. The greatest of the common factors is called the **greatest common factor (GCF)**. One way to find the greatest common factor of two or more numbers is to make a list of all the factors of each number and identify the greatest number that is on every list.

EXAMPLE 1 Making a List to Find the GCF

In the orchestra problem above, the greatest number of ensembles that can be formed is given by the greatest common factor of 48, 24, and 36.

ANOTHER WAY
List the factors of the least number. Find which of those numbers are factors of all the greater numbers, until you have checked your entire list.

Factors of 48: **1, 2, 3, 4, 6, 8,** (**12,**) 16, 24, 48

Factors of 24: **1, 2, 3, 4, 6, 8,** **12,** 24

Factors of 36: **1, 2, 3, 4, 6, 9,** (**12,**) 18, 36

The common factors are 1, 2, 3, 4, 6, and 12. The GCF is 12.

▶ **Answer** The greatest common factor of 48, 24, and 36 is 12. So, the greatest number of ensembles that can be formed is 12. Because there are 12 ensembles, divide each instrument group by 12. There will be 4 violinists, 2 violists, and 3 cellists in each ensemble.

 GUIDED PRACTICE for Example 1

Find the greatest common factor of the numbers by listing factors.

1. 16, 28   **2.** 60, 96   **3.** 14, 70, 91   **4.** 15, 75, 20

5. What If? What is the greatest number of ensembles that can be formed with 32 violinists, 40 violists, and 16 cellists? How many of each instrument will be in each ensemble?

Using Prime Factorization Another way to find the greatest common factor of two or more numbers is to use the prime factorization of each number. The product of the common prime factors is the greatest common factor.

EXAMPLE 2 Using Prime Factorization to Find the GCF

Find the greatest common factor of 180 and 126 using prime factorization.

Begin by writing the prime factorization of each number.

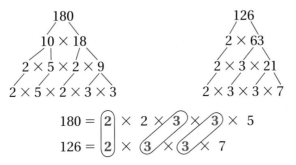

▶ **Answer** The common prime factors of 180 and 126 are 2, 3, and 3. So, the greatest common factor is $2 \times 3^2 = 18$.

Animated Math at classzone.com

Relatively Prime Two or more nonzero whole numbers are **relatively prime** if their greatest common factor is 1.

EXAMPLE 3 Identifying Relatively Prime Numbers

Tell whether the numbers are relatively prime.

AVOID ERRORS
To say that two numbers are relatively prime does *not* necessarily mean that one of the numbers is prime.

a. 28, 45   Factors of 28: 1, 2, 4, 7, 14, 28   The GCF is 1.
Factors of 45: 1, 3, 5, 9, 15, 45

▶ **Answer** Because the GCF is 1, 28 and 45 are relatively prime.

b. 15, 51   Factors of 15: 1, 3, 5, 15   The GCF is 3.
Factors of 51: 1, 3, 17, 51

▶ **Answer** Because the GCF is 3, 15 and 51 are not relatively prime.

✓ **GUIDED PRACTICE** for Examples 2 and 3

Find the greatest common factor of the numbers using prime factorization.

6. 90, 150   **7.** 84, 216   **8.** 120, 192   **9.** 49, 144

Tell whether the numbers are relatively prime.

10. 13, 24   **11.** 16, 25   **12.** 38, 48   **13.** 125, 175

4.2 EXERCISES

★ = **STANDARDIZED TEST PRACTICE**
Exs. 16, 32, 45, 47, 50, 51, 52, and 67

◯ = **HINTS AND HOMEWORK HELP**
for Exs. 5, 11, 17, 21, 43 at classzone.com

SKILL PRACTICE

VOCABULARY Copy and complete the statement.

1. A whole number that is a factor of two or more nonzero whole numbers is a ___?___.

2. The numbers 35 and 36 are ___?___ because their ___?___ is 1.

FINDING THE GCF Find the greatest common factor of the numbers by listing factors.

SEE EXAMPLE 1
on p. 170
for Exs. 3–15

3. 14, 21   **4.** 24, 32   **5.** 11, 33   **6.** 45, 76

7. 56, 81   **8.** 39, 52   **9.** 20, 55, 65   **10.** 42, 72, 84

11. 75, 90, 105   **12.** 48, 64, 96   **13.** 18, 30, 60   **14.** 36, 54, 135

15. ERROR ANALYSIS Describe and correct the error made in finding the GCF of 20 and 32.

Factors of 20: 1, 2, 4, 5, 10, 20
Factors of 32: 1, 2, 8, 16, 32
The GCF is 2.

SEE EXAMPLES 2 AND 3
on p. 171
for Exs. 16–28

16. ★ MULTIPLE CHOICE Find the greatest common factor of 180 and 225.

(A) 9   **(B)** 15   **(C)** 25   **(D)** 45

PRIME FACTORIZATION Find the greatest common factor of the numbers using prime factorization. Then tell whether the numbers are relatively prime.

17. 98, 140   **18.** 27, 117   **19.** 86, 154   **20.** 37, 93

21. 198, 216   **22.** 36, 168   **23.** 34, 85   **24.** 75, 285

25. 144, 264   **26.** 65, 112   **27.** 63, 84, 126   **28.** 39, 65, 182

REASONING Tell whether the statement is *always, sometimes,* or *never* true. *Explain* your reasoning.

29. The greatest common factor of two even numbers is 2.

30. Two composite numbers are relatively prime.

31. Two different prime numbers are relatively prime.

32. ★ MULTIPLE CHOICE Identify which number pairs are relatively prime.

I. 21, 32   II. 30, 36   III. 49, 72

(A) I and II   **(B)** I and III   **(C)** II and III   **(D)** I, II, and III

NUMBER SENSE Find a pair of numbers between 200 and 300 that have the given GCF. *Explain* how you found the pair of numbers.

33. 7   **34.** 18   **35.** 8   **36.** 13

GEOMETRY Find the area and perimeter of the rectangle. Are the two measures relatively prime? *Explain.*

37.
5
7

38.
8
10

39.
8
9

CHALLENGE Find the greatest common factor of the variable expressions.

40. $4xy$, $12xy$

41. $18r^3s^2$, $27r^2s^3$

42. $4y^2z^2$, $10y^2z$

PROBLEM SOLVING

SEE EXAMPLE 1
on p. 170
for Ex. 43

43. **SCIENCE CLASS** A science class with 15 girls and 12 boys is divided into groups. Each group has the same number of boys and the same number of girls. What is the greatest number of groups that can be formed? How many boys and girls are in each group?

44. **GUIDED PROBLEM SOLVING** You are making bags of school supplies for your friends. You have 12 markers, 18 pens, and 30 pencils. You want to put the same number of each kind of supply into each bag.

  a. Find the factors of 12, 18, and 30.

  b. What is the greatest common factor?

  c. What is the greatest number of bags you can make?

  d. How many of each kind of supply will be in each bag? *Explain* your reasoning.

45. ★ **MULTIPLE CHOICE** How many groups can be formed from 40 students and 24 teachers so that the same number of students and the same number of teachers are in each group?

  Ⓐ 3   **Ⓑ** 5   **Ⓒ** 8   **Ⓓ** 12

46. **ROSE BOWL FLOATS** You are decorating a Rose Bowl float. There are 108 red roses, 144 white roses, 48 yellow roses, and 72 purple roses. If bunches of roses are identical and no roses are left over, what is the greatest number of bunches that can be made? How many roses of each color are in each bunch?

47. ★ **SHORT RESPONSE** A school is preparing fruit baskets for a local nursing home using 162 apples, 108 oranges, and 180 bananas. The baskets are identical and no fruit should be left over. What is the greatest number of baskets that can be made? How many apples, oranges, and bananas are in each basket?

48. **FINDING COSTS** *Describe* the data you need in Ex. 47 in order to find the cost of one basket.

49. **REASONING** The lesser of two numbers is a factor of the greater number. What can you say about the GCF of the numbers? *Explain.*

50. ★ **WRITING** In your own words, describe how to find the greatest common factor of two numbers given their prime factorizations.

51. ★ **OPEN-ENDED MATH** Name 3 pairs of composite numbers between 50 and 100 that are relatively prime. *Explain* how you found the pairs.

52. ★ **SHORT RESPONSE** To find the GCF of 3, 15, 18, and 75, your friend says you need to check only the factors of 3 because the GCF cannot be greater than the least number. Is your friend correct? *Explain.*

53. **MULTI-STEP PROBLEM** A marching band has 81 trombonists, 36 flutists, 54 saxophonists, and 27 drummers. For a parade, the band is arranged into rows of equal length with one type of instrument in a row.

   a. What is the greatest number of musicians in each row?

   b. How many rows are there for each instrument?

   c. *Explain* why adding a row of 8 tuba players would not fit the arrangement, while adding 45 clarinetists would.

54. **CHALLENGE** The GCF of a number and 48 is 16. The sum of the number's digits is 13. Find two numbers that satisfy these conditions.

55. **CHALLENGE** You want to use sections of fence that are all of the same length to enclose the land shown at the right. How long can each section be? What is the least number of sections that are needed to enclose the land? *Explain* your reasoning.

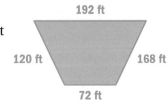

 NEW JERSEY MIXED REVIEW  **TEST PRACTICE** at classzone.com

56. Jimmy buys 12 baseballs for $30. He later buys 3 more baseballs for $12. What is the mean cost of all the baseballs?

   (A) $2.50   **(B)** $2.80   **(C)** $4   **(D)** $6.50

57. The rectangle below is divided into 3 equal sections. The area of the entire rectangle is *A*. Which expression gives the area of one section?

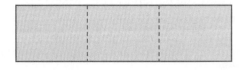

   (A) $A - 3$ **(B)** $A \times 3$ **(C)** $A \div 2$ **(D)** $A \div 3$

ONLINE QUIZ at classzone.com

GOAL
Use area models to find equivalent fractions.

MATERIALS
• paper
• colored pencils

4.3 Modeling Equivalent Fractions

You can use area models to find equivalent fractions.

EXPLORE Find two fractions equivalent to $\frac{4}{6}$.

STEP 1 **Draw** a rectangle on a piece of paper. Divide the rectangle into 6 equal parts, and shade 4 of the parts.

STEP 2 **Look** for other ways of dividing the rectangle into equal parts.

 There are 3 parts, and 2 are shaded.

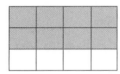 There are 12 parts, and 8 are shaded.

STEP 3 **Write** the equivalent fractions.
The fractions $\frac{2}{3}$ and $\frac{8}{12}$ are equivalent to $\frac{4}{6}$.

PRACTICE Draw a model of the given fraction. Then find two equivalent fractions.

1. $\frac{9}{18}$

2. $\frac{2}{14}$

3. $\frac{4}{5}$

4. $\frac{15}{20}$

DRAW CONCLUSIONS

5. **WRITING** How could you show that $\frac{3}{4}$ is equivalent to $\frac{18}{24}$?

6. **WRITING** How could you show that 1 is equivalent to $\frac{10}{10}$?

4.3 Equivalent Fractions

 4.1.A.5 Use whole numbers, fractions, decimals, and percents to represent equivalent forms of the same number.

Before	You factored whole numbers.
Now	You'll write equivalent fractions.
Why?	So you can simplify real-world fractions, as in Example 1.

KEY VOCABULARY
- fraction, *p. 176*
- numerator, *p. 176*
- denominator, *p. 176*
- equivalent fractions, *p. 176*
- simplest form, *p. 177*

A **fraction** is a number of the form $\frac{a}{b}$ ($b \neq 0$) where a is called the **numerator** and b is called the **denominator**. A fraction is used to describe equal parts of a whole. Fractions that represent the same part-to-whole relationship are called **equivalent fractions**.

❖ **EXAMPLE 1** Identifying Equivalent Fractions

There are 10 fish in an aquarium, and 2 of them are goldfish. The fish in the aquarium are arranged in the diagram below. What *fraction* of the fish in the aquarium are goldfish?

SOLUTION

Using the diagram, you can write two equivalent fractions:

$$\frac{\text{Number of goldfish}}{\text{Number of fish}} = \frac{2}{10}$$

$$\frac{\text{Number of groups of 2 goldfish}}{\text{Number of groups of 2 fish}} = \frac{1}{5}$$

The fractions $\frac{2}{10}$ and $\frac{1}{5}$ are equivalent fractions because they represent the same part-to-whole relationship.

❖ **EXAMPLE 2** Writing Equivalent Fractions

Write two fractions that are equivalent to $\frac{6}{8}$.

To find equivalent fractions, multiply or divide the numerator and denominator by the same nonzero number. Because you are multiplying or dividing by 1, the value of the fraction does not change.

MULTIPLY BY ANY NUMBER
You can multiply the numerator and denominator by *any* nonzero number to find an equivalent fraction.

$$\frac{6}{8} = \frac{6 \times 3}{8 \times 3} = \frac{18}{24}$$ **Multiply numerator and denominator by 3.**

$$\frac{6}{8} = \frac{6 \div 2}{8 \div 2} = \frac{3}{4}$$ **Divide numerator and denominator by 2, a common factor of 6 and 8.**

▶ **Answer** $\frac{18}{24}$ and $\frac{3}{4}$ are equivalent to $\frac{6}{8}$.

1. **Groceries** Two eggs in a carton of a dozen eggs are cracked. Write two equivalent fractions that represent the fraction of eggs that are cracked.

Write two fractions that are equivalent to the given fraction.

2. $\dfrac{1}{6}$ 3. $\dfrac{3}{10}$ 4. $\dfrac{8}{18}$ 5. $\dfrac{30}{45}$

Simplest Form A fraction is in **simplest form** if its numerator and denominator have 1 as their greatest common factor. To *simplify* a fraction, you divide its numerator and denominator by their GCF.

EXAMPLE 3 **Simplifying Fractions**

Write the fraction in simplest form.

a. $\dfrac{8}{28} = \dfrac{2 \cdot \cancel{4}^{1}}{7 \cdot \cancel{4}_{1}}$ **Divide out GCF of 8 and 28.**

$= \dfrac{2}{7}$

b. $\dfrac{8}{15}$ **The GCF is 1.**

The fraction is in simplest form.

EXAMPLE 4 **Using Fractions in Simplest Form**

Basketball At a basketball game, the home team made 14 out of 22 free throw attempts. The visiting team made 10 out of 25 free throw attempts. Write fractions for the number of free throws made by each team. Are the fractions equivalent?

Home Team $\dfrac{\text{Free throws made}}{\text{Free throws attempted}} = \dfrac{14}{22} = \dfrac{7 \cdot \cancel{2}^{1}}{11 \cdot \cancel{2}_{1}} = \dfrac{7}{11}$

Visiting Team $\dfrac{\text{Free throws made}}{\text{Free throws attempted}} = \dfrac{10}{25} = \dfrac{2 \cdot \cancel{5}^{1}}{5 \cdot \cancel{5}_{1}} = \dfrac{2}{5}$

▶ **Answer** No, $\dfrac{7}{11}$ and $\dfrac{2}{5}$ are not equivalent fractions.

COMPARE USING SIMPLEST FORM
Two fractions that do not have the same simplest form are not equivalent.

Write the fraction in simplest form.

6. $\dfrac{12}{16}$ 7. $\dfrac{15}{35}$ 8. $\dfrac{7}{28}$ 9. $\dfrac{14}{34}$

10. **What If?** In Example 4, suppose the home team made 6 out of 15 free throw attempts, and the visiting team made 8 out of 20 free throw attempts. Are the fractions equivalent? *Explain.*

4.3 EXERCISES

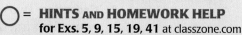

HOMEWORK KEY

★ = **STANDARDIZED TEST PRACTICE**
Exs. 6, 7, 8, 9, 10, 35, 41, 43, and 53

◯ = **HINTS AND HOMEWORK HELP**
for Exs. 5, 9, 15, 19, 41 at classzone.com

SKILL PRACTICE

1. **VOCABULARY** How can you tell if a fraction is in simplest form?

2. **VOCABULARY** Copy and complete: Fractions that represent the same part-to-whole relationship are called __?__ .

IDENTIFYING EQUIVALENT FRACTIONS Write two equivalent fractions that describe the model.

SEE EXAMPLE 1
on p. 176
for Exs. 3–5

3.

4.

5.

★ **OPEN-ENDED MATH** Write two fractions that are equivalent to the given fraction.

SEE EXAMPLE 2
on p. 176
for Exs. 6–10

6. $\dfrac{25}{120}$

7. $\dfrac{18}{21}$

8. $\dfrac{14}{34}$

9. $\dfrac{30}{52}$

10. $\dfrac{28}{32}$

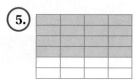 at classzone.com

WRITING IN SIMPLEST FORM Write the fraction in simplest form.

SEE EXAMPLE 3
on p. 177
for Exs. 11–21

11. $\dfrac{32}{72}$

12. $\dfrac{6}{21}$

13. $\dfrac{15}{21}$

14. $\dfrac{12}{35}$

15. $\dfrac{28}{48}$

16. $\dfrac{30}{45}$

17. $\dfrac{24}{32}$

18. $\dfrac{22}{27}$

19. $\dfrac{49}{105}$

20. $\dfrac{33}{81}$

21. **ERROR ANALYSIS** Describe and correct the error made in writing $\dfrac{24}{42}$ in simplest form.

$$\times \quad \frac{24}{42} = \frac{8 \cdot \overset{1}{\cancel{3}}}{14 \cdot \underset{1}{\cancel{3}}} = \frac{8}{14}$$

EQUIVALENT FRACTIONS Tell whether the fractions are equivalent.

SEE EXAMPLE 4
on p. 177
for Exs. 22–26

22. $\dfrac{14}{21}, \dfrac{24}{36}$

23. $\dfrac{15}{36}, \dfrac{40}{96}$

24. $\dfrac{56}{196}, \dfrac{132}{462}$

25. $\dfrac{34}{44}, \dfrac{136}{144}$

26. $\dfrac{45}{54}, \dfrac{8}{18}$

ALGEBRA Solve the equation by using equivalent fractions.

27. $\dfrac{18}{24} = \dfrac{n}{12}$

28. $\dfrac{12}{21} = \dfrac{x}{7}$

29. $\dfrac{3}{7} = \dfrac{18}{y}$

30. $\dfrac{12}{16} = \dfrac{6}{z}$

31. $\dfrac{10}{15} = \dfrac{x}{3}$

32. $\dfrac{4}{14} = \dfrac{20}{y}$

33. $\dfrac{2}{9} = \dfrac{n}{45}$

34. $\dfrac{16}{14} = \dfrac{8}{z}$

35. ★ **MULTIPLE CHOICE** Which fraction pairs are equivalent to three ninths?

(A) $\dfrac{9}{10}, \dfrac{1}{3}$

(B) $\dfrac{3}{19}, \dfrac{6}{38}$

(C) $\dfrac{1}{3}, \dfrac{5}{20}$

(D) $\dfrac{6}{18}, \dfrac{2}{6}$

CHALLENGE Find an equivalent fraction with the greatest denominator less than 100. Then find an equivalent fraction with the greatest denominator less than 1000.

36. $\frac{3}{8}$ **37.** $\frac{5}{9}$ **38.** $\frac{6}{7}$ **39.** $\frac{2}{3}$

PROBLEM SOLVING

SEE EXAMPLE 1
on p. 176
for Ex. 40

40. U.S. PRESIDENTS During the 1800s, there were 22 different presidents of the United States, and 6 of them were born in Virginia. Write a fraction, in simplest form, comparing the number of presidents born in Virginia with the total number of presidents in the 1800s.

41. ★ **MULTIPLE CHOICE** The highway speed limit in 20 states is 65 mi/h. In simplest form, what fraction of states have a speed limit of 65 mi/h?

Ⓐ $\frac{20}{65}$ Ⓑ $\frac{2}{5}$ Ⓒ $\frac{4}{10}$ Ⓓ $\frac{10}{25}$

42. FOOTBALL STATISTICS The diagram shows data for the quarterbacks (QB) of one game. It compares the numbers of passes completed to passes attempted for three lengths of passes. Write fractions for each data pair. For which length of pass do the two players have the same record?

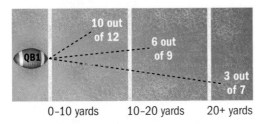

0–10 yards   10–20 yards   20+ yards

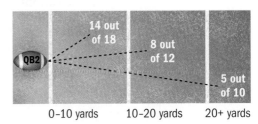

0–10 yards   10–20 yards   20+ yards

43. ★ **SHORT RESPONSE** You read 35 pages of a chapter in a book and have 15 pages left. What fraction of the chapter have you read? Write the fraction in simplest form. *Explain* how you found your answer.

44. ◆ **MULTIPLE REPRESENTATIONS** The table below shows the number of bones for different parts of the body.

Location	Number of Bones
Upper limbs	64
Wrists	16
Lower limbs	62
Ankles	14

a. Make a Model Draw a model for the fraction that represents the part of the upper limb bones that are found in the wrists.

b. Write a Verbal Model Write a verbal model that represents the part of the lower limb bones that are ankle bones.

c. Compare Rewrite your answers from parts (a) and (b) as fractions in simplest form. *Compare* your answers. Are the fractions equivalent?

4.3 Equivalent Fractions   **179**

45. PREDICTIONS You get 7 out of 11 answers correct on a quiz. About how many correct answers could you expect on a quiz that has 8 questions? 12 questions? 16 questions? *Explain.*

46. CHALLENGE The table shows the number of wins and losses of two baseball coaches.

   a. What part of the total games played were wins for each coach?

   b. Which coach has a better record?

   c. If you were going to hire one of these coaches, which would you choose? *Explain.*

Name	Number of Wins	Number of Losses
Coach Samuels	18	7
Coach Welsh	50	20

 NEW JERSEY MIXED REVIEW **TEST PRACTICE** at classzone.com

47. There are 16 girls in a classroom. The teacher is dividing the class into groups so that each group has the same number of boys and the same number of girls. What information is needed to find the greatest number of groups that can be formed?

  (A) The number of boys in the school

  (B) The number of students in the school

  (C) The number of boys in the classroom

  (D) The ages of the girls

48. Which number is most likely part of the following pattern: 0, 1, 3, 6, 10, 15, . . .?

  (A) 16   **(B)** 18   **(C)** 20   **(D)** 21

QUIZ for Lessons 4.1– 4.3

Tell whether the number is *prime* or *composite*. (p. 165)

  1. 75   **2.** 53   **3.** 61   **4.** 98

5. QUILT SQUARES You are making a quilt. You make 36 squares to be sewn together. *Describe* all the different rectangular arrangements you can make. *(p. 165)*

Find the greatest common factor of the numbers using prime factorization. Then tell whether the numbers are relatively prime. (pp. 165, 170)

  6. 12, 30   **7.** 10, 21   **8.** 28, 50   **9.** 117, 195

Write the fractions in simplest form. Tell whether they are equivalent. (p. 176)

  10. $\dfrac{15}{28}, \dfrac{45}{84}$ **11.** $\dfrac{7}{56}, \dfrac{12}{84}$ **12.** $\dfrac{27}{72}, \dfrac{36}{90}$ **13.** $\dfrac{45}{75}, \dfrac{81}{180}$

14. REASONING A number is a common factor of 96 and 144. The sum of the number's digits is 7. Find the number. *(p. 170)*

Lessons 4.1–4.3

1. **FIELD TRIP** There are 114 students going on a field trip. The teacher organizing the trip wants the students to be divided into groups of equal size. Which statement below is NOT correct?

   A. Each group can have 3 students.

   B. Each group can have 6 students.

   C. Each group must have an even number of students.

   D. Each group must have less than 58 students.

2. **FRUIT BARS** You divide a pan of fruit bars into 30 equal pieces, as shown below. You give away the bars that are shaded. Which fraction does NOT describe the amount of bars that you give away?

   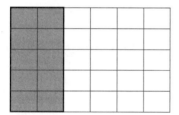

   A. $\frac{1}{3}$ **C.** $\frac{5}{6}$

   B. $\frac{2}{6}$ **D.** $\frac{10}{30}$

3. **MATH QUIZ** On a math quiz, Mario was asked to find a pair of composite numbers between 30 and 70 that are relatively prime. Mario chose 42 and 45. Why was Mario's answer incorrect?

   A. The numbers are not composite numbers.

   B. The numbers are not between 30 and 70.

   C. The numbers are not relatively prime.

   D. The numbers are prime.

4. **NATIONAL FLAG** Which fraction is equivalent to the number of horizontal stripes that are black in the flag of Zimbabwe below?

   A. $\frac{2}{8}$

   B. $\frac{5}{35}$

   C. $\frac{3}{9}$

   D. $\frac{9}{21}$

5. **SUMMER CAMP** A counselor wants to divide 48 boys and 30 girls into as many groups as possible. Each group must have the same number of boys, and each group must have the same number of girls. How many boys and girls are in each group?

   A. 6 boys, 6 girl

   B. 8 boys, 5 girls

   C. 16 boys, 10 girls

   D. 24 boys, 15 girls

6. **OPEN-ENDED** You buy 32 roses, 24 lilies, and 16 tulips. One rose costs $1.50. One lily costs $1. One tulip costs $.75.

   • You want to make as many identical bouquets as possible. What is the greatest number of bouquets you can make?

   • Use your answer to find how many flowers can be in each bouquet.

   • You want to make a profit of $40 after selling all of the bouquets. How much should you charge per bouquet? *Explain* how you found your answer.

4.4 Least Common Multiple

Before You found the GCF of two or more numbers.

Now You'll find the LCM of two or more numbers.

Why? So you can analyze sports performance, as in Ex. 31.

KEY VOCABULARY
- multiple, *p. 182*
- common multiple, *p. 182*
- least common multiple (LCM), *p. 182*

Model Trains Two model trains share a station, but they run on separate tracks. One of the trains returns to the station every 4 minutes. The other returns every 6 minutes. Both trains just left the station. When will the trains next return to the station at the same time? You will answer this question in Example 1.

A **multiple** of a number is the product of the number and any nonzero whole number. A multiple that is shared by two or more numbers is a **common multiple**. The least of the common multiples is the **least common multiple (LCM)**.

EXAMPLE 1 Using the Least Common Multiple

VOCABULARY
The similarity between the words "multiple" and "multiply" can help you to remember that a multiple is a product.

You can find when the model trains described above will return to the station at the same time by finding the least common multiple of 4 and 6. Begin by writing the multiples of 4 and 6. Then identify any common multiples.

Multiples of 4: 4, 8, 12, 16, 20, 24, 28, 32, 36, . . .

Multiples of 6: 6, 12, 18, 24, 30, 36, . . .

12, 24, and 36 are common multiples, so the LCM is 12.

▸**Answer** The trains will both return to the station in 12 minutes.

EXAMPLE 2 Finding the Least Common Multiple

Find the least common multiple of 7 and 8 by using a list.

Multiples of 7: 7, 14, 21, 28, 35, 42, 49, 56, . . .

Multiples of 8: 8, 16, 24, 32, 40, 48, 56, . . .

▸**Answer** The least common multiple of 7 and 8 is 56.

✓ **GUIDED PRACTICE** for Examples 1 and 2

Find the LCM of the numbers by listing multiples.

1. 3, 5
2. 12, 16
3. 9, 10
4. 2, 6, 14

5. 15, 20
6. 7, 11
7. 3, 12, 15
8. 21, 84

EXAMPLE 3 Using Prime Factorization to Find the LCM

Find the LCM of 84 and 360 using prime factorization.

STEP 1 **Begin** by writing the prime factorization of each number.

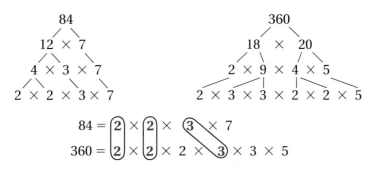

$$84 = \boxed{2} \times \boxed{2} \times \boxed{3} \times 7$$
$$360 = \boxed{2} \times \boxed{2} \times 2 \times \boxed{3} \times 3 \times 5$$

ANOTHER WAY
You could list all the multiples, but that usually would be impractical.

STEP 2 **Circle** the common factors. Then multiply the common factors (one for each pair) and all the uncircled factors.

$$2 \times 2 \times 2 \times 3 \times 3 \times 5 \times 7 = 2^3 \times 3^2 \times 5 \times 7 = 2520$$

▶ **Answer** The least common multiple of 84 and 360 is 2520.

EXAMPLE 4 Using the Least Common Multiple

Tour Bus Schedules Three tour buses leave the visitor's center at 9:00 A.M. Bus A returns to the visitor's center every 60 minutes, Bus B returns every 40 minutes, and Bus C returns every 75 minutes. What is the next time the buses will all return to the visitor's center at the same time?

SOLUTION

Find the least common multiple of 60, 40, and 75.

$$60 = 2^2 \times 3 \times 5 \qquad 40 = 2^3 \times 5 \qquad 75 = 3 \times 5^2$$

The least common multiple is $2^3 \times 3 \times 5^2 = 600$.

AVOID ERRORS
10 hours after 9:00 A.M. must be after noon rather than in the morning.

▶ **Answer** The buses all return at the same time in 600 minutes, or 10 hours, after 9:00 A.M., which is 7:00 P.M.

✓ **GUIDED PRACTICE** for Examples 3 and 4

Find the LCM of the numbers using prime factorization.

9. 36, 72   **10.** 24, 30   **11.** 54, 126   **12.** 20, 22, 55

13. What If? In Example 4, suppose Bus A returns every 30 minutes, Bus B returns every 20 minutes, and Bus C returns every 45 minutes. What is the next time the buses will all return at the same time to the visitor's center?

4.4 EXERCISES

SKILL PRACTICE

1. **VOCABULARY** What is the difference between finding the least common multiple and finding the greatest common factor of two numbers?

2. **VOCABULARY** Copy and complete: The product of a given number and any nonzero whole number is a ? of the given number.

FINDING MULTIPLES Find the first three common multiples of the numbers by listing multiples.

SEE EXAMPLES 1 AND 2
on p. 182
for Exs. 3–13

3. 9, 24   4. 12, 18   5. 16, 20   6. 30, 33

7. 5, 8, 12   8. 6, 11, 18   9. 9, 14, 21   10. 7, 20, 35

11. **WHICH ONE DOESN'T BELONG?** Which of the following is *not* a common multiple of 16, 30, and 36?

   A. 720   B. 2160   C. 3360   D. 17,280

12. **ERROR ANALYSIS** Describe and correct the error in finding the least common multiple of 6 and 16.

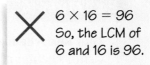

   6 × 16 = 96
   So, the LCM of
   6 and 16 is 96.

13. ★ **MULTIPLE CHOICE** What is the LCM of 8 and 36?

   Ⓐ 4   Ⓑ 8   Ⓒ 72   Ⓓ 288

SEE EXAMPLE 3
on p. 183
for Exs. 14–17

FINDING THE LCM Find the LCM of the numbers using prime factorization.

14. 42, 56, 140   15. 39, 52, 169   16. 28, 40, 144   17. 16, 25, 27

FINDING THE GCF AND LCM Find the GCF and the LCM of the numbers. Compare the product of the GCF and LCM to the product of the numbers.

18. 90, 165   19. 34, 66   20. 54, 132   21. 72, 168

xy ALGEBRA Copy and complete the factorizations to find the two numbers with the given LCM.

22. $2 \times$? ; $3 \times$? ; LCM 30   23. $17 \times$? ; $3 \times$? ; LCM 102

24. $5 \times$? ; $2 \times$? ; LCM 30   25. $2 \times$? ; $3 \times$? ; LCM 72

xy ALGEBRA Find the LCM of the variable expressions.

26. w^2, w^3 27. $3d, 9d$ 28. $4s^2, 2s^4$ 29. $12x^2, 16x$

30. **CHALLENGE** The greatest common factor of two numbers is 1. Is the least common multiple of these numbers always the product of the numbers? *Explain* your reasoning.

PROBLEM SOLVING

SEE EXAMPLE 1
on p. 182
for Exs. 31–33

31. **RUNNING LAPS** James and David are running laps on a quarter mile track. It takes James 3 minutes and David 4 minutes to run once around the track. They both start running from the starting line at the same time. After how many minutes will they next pass the starting line together?

32. **SUPPLIES** How many packs of each item do you need if you want to have the same number of napkins, paper plates, and plastic cups?

33. ★ **MULTIPLE CHOICE** You and a friend are building brick walls. Your bricks are 5 inches tall and your friend's bricks are 7 inches tall. Without cutting any bricks, what is the shortest brick wall that you can make so that you and your friend have brick walls of the same height?

    (A) 70 in.   **(B)** 48 in.   **(C)** 35 in.   **(D)** 12 in.

34. ★ **WRITING** Is the product of two whole numbers always a common multiple of the numbers? Is the product always the least common multiple of the numbers? *Explain* your reasoning.

35. **CHOOSE A STRATEGY** You want to find the LCM of 32 and 49. Would you list multiples or use prime factorization? *Explain* your choice.

    Animated Math at classzone.com

36. **REASONING** Is the number $2^5 \times 3^7 \times 7^{10} \times 13^{43}$ a multiple of 15? *Explain* your reasoning.

SEE EXAMPLE 4
on p. 183
for Ex. 37

37. **MAYAN CALENDARS** The Mayans used more than one calendar system, including using steps to represent days. One calendar had 365 days. Another calendar, considered sacred to the Mayans, had 260 days. If both calendars began on the same day, in how many days would they next begin on the same day?

38. ★ **OPEN-ENDED MATH** Find two numbers greater than 1 whose GCF is the lesser of the two numbers and whose LCM is the greater of the two numbers.

39. ★ **SHORT RESPONSE** Sarah and Jen are swimming laps. Sarah swims 7 laps in 5 minutes, and Jen swims 11 laps in 6 minutes. If they start and stop at the same time and swim a whole number of laps, what is the least amount of time they swim? In this amount of time, how many laps does each girl swim? *Explain* how you found your answer.

Temple of Kukulcan

40. GIVEAWAYS A store offers discounts, coupons, and prizes for its customers. How many customers will it take until a customer receives a discount, a coupon, and a prize? If 3600 people come to the store, how many will receive a discount, a coupon, and a prize?

20% discount for every 60th person!

$10 coupon for every 80th person!

Amazing prize for every 150th person!

41. MULTI-STEP PROBLEM Cicadas are flying insects that live underground until they are fully developed. It takes 13 years for one type of cicada and 17 years for another type of cicada to fully develop. In 1998, the two types emerged together in one area.

  a. Evaluate In how many years will the two types emerge together again?

  b. Analyze How is the answer found in part (a) related to 13 and 17?

  c. Predict Identify the years between 1998 and 2998 in which the two cicadas will emerge together. *Explain* your method.

42. CHALLENGE Mark has some trading cards. When he sorts them by 2s, 3s, 4s, and 5s, he has 1 left over each time. Mark has fewer than 100 cards. How many cards does he have?

43. CHALLENGE Two numbers less than 50 have a GCF of 5. If 5 is added to both numbers, the GCF is doubled but the LCM is reduced by 15. What are the two numbers?

NEW JERSEY MIXED REVIEW

TEST PRACTICE at classzone.com

44. The graph at the right shows the number and type of restaurants found in a city by a search engine. Which statement is best supported by these data?

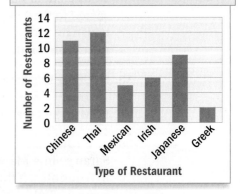

  Ⓐ There are more Thai restaurants than the others combined.

  Ⓑ There are half as many Irish restaurants as Thai restaurants.

  Ⓒ There are as many Irish restaurants as Mexican restaurants.

  Ⓓ There are 5 times more Chinese restaurants than Greek restaurants.

EXTRA PRACTICE for Lesson 4.4, p. 779   **ONLINE QUIZ** at classzone.com

4.5 Comparing Fractions

You can use area models to compare fractions with different denominators.

EXPLORE 1 Use models to compare $\frac{3}{4}$ and $\frac{5}{6}$.

STEP 1 **Draw** two rectangles of the same size. Divide one rectangle vertically into 4 equal parts and shade 3 of the parts. Divide the other rectangle horizontally into 6 equal parts and shade 5 of the parts.

STEP 2 **Divide** the two rectangles into the same number of equal parts by dividing the model for $\frac{3}{4}$ horizontally into 6 equal parts and dividing the model for $\frac{5}{6}$ vertically into 4 equal parts.

$$\frac{3}{4} = \frac{18}{24}$$

$$\frac{5}{6} = \frac{20}{24}$$

STEP 3 **Compare** the fractions. Because both rectangles are divided into the same number of equal parts, $\frac{18}{24} < \frac{20}{24}$, so $\frac{3}{4} < \frac{5}{6}$.

PRACTICE Model the two fractions. Then copy and complete the statement using <, >, or =.

1. $\frac{1}{3}$? $\frac{3}{8}$

2. $\frac{5}{6}$? $\frac{3}{5}$

3. $\frac{4}{7}$? $\frac{1}{2}$

4. $\frac{2}{9}$? $\frac{1}{4}$

5. $\frac{5}{6}$? $\frac{15}{18}$

6. $\frac{7}{11}$? $\frac{2}{3}$

7. $\frac{5}{12}$? $\frac{1}{3}$

8. $\frac{5}{15}$? $\frac{4}{12}$

Continued on next page

INVESTIGATION

On the previous page you compared $\frac{3}{4}$ and $\frac{5}{6}$ using models to write equivalent fractions with a common denominator of 24. You can represent what happens in Step 2 using multiplication.

$$\frac{3}{4} = \frac{3 \times 6}{4 \times 6} = \frac{18}{24} \qquad \frac{5}{6} = \frac{5 \times 4}{6 \times 4} = \frac{20}{24}$$

Notice that the 18 in $\frac{18}{24}$ is a result of multiplying the **3** in $\frac{3}{4}$ by the **6** in $\frac{5}{6}$.

Similarly, the 20 in $\frac{20}{24}$ is a result of multiplying the **5** in $\frac{5}{6}$ by the **4** in $\frac{3}{4}$.

These observations suggest a way to compare fractions using *cross products.*

EXPLORE 2 Compare $\frac{5}{8}$ and $\frac{7}{12}$ **using cross products.**

STEP 1 **Multiply** the denominator of the first fraction by the numerator of the second fraction.

$$8 \times 7 = \mathbf{56}$$
$$\frac{5}{8} \nearrow \frac{7}{12}$$

When you divide a model of $\frac{7}{12}$ into 8 equal parts, you get 56 shaded parts out of 96 total parts.

STEP 2 **Multiply** the denominator of the second fraction by the numerator of the first fraction.

When you divide a model of $\frac{5}{8}$ into 12 equal parts, you get 60 shaded parts out of 96 total parts.

$$12 \times 5 = \mathbf{60} \qquad 8 \times 7 = \mathbf{56}$$
$$\frac{5}{8} \swarrow \frac{7}{12}$$

STEP 3 **Compare** the two products. Because $60 > 56$, $\frac{5}{8} > \frac{7}{12}$.

PRACTICE **Compare the fractions using cross products. Then copy and complete the statement using <, >, or =.**

9. $\frac{1}{6} \underline{\ ?\ } \frac{2}{9}$ **10.** $\frac{1}{4} \underline{\ ?\ } \frac{3}{10}$ **11.** $\frac{3}{7} \underline{\ ?\ } \frac{2}{3}$ **12.** $\frac{4}{7} \underline{\ ?\ } \frac{6}{11}$

DRAW CONCLUSIONS

13. **WRITING** You are comparing $\frac{31}{36}$ and $\frac{24}{27}$. Which method is easier, drawing models or using cross products? *Explain.*

4.5 Comparing and Ordering Fractions

NJ 4.1.A.4 Compare and order numbers of all named types.

Before You compared and ordered decimals.

Now You'll compare and order fractions.

Why? So you can compare distances, as in Example 1.

KEY VOCABULARY
• least common denominator (LCD), *p. 189*

You can compare fractions by using the *least common denominator*. The **least common denominator (LCD)** of two or more fractions is the least common multiple of the denominators.

KEY CONCEPT *For Your Notebook*

Comparing Two or More Fractions

1. Find the LCD of the fractions.
2. Use the LCD to write equivalent fractions.
3. Compare the numerators.

EXAMPLE 1 Comparing Fractions Using the LCD

Kayaking Julie kayaks a distance of $\frac{7}{10}$ mile, and Seth kayaks $\frac{3}{4}$ mile. Who kayaks the greater distance?

SOLUTION

STEP 1 **Find** the LCD of the fractions, to compare $\frac{7}{10}$ and $\frac{3}{4}$. Because the LCM of 10 and 4 is 20, the LCD of the fractions is 20.

STEP 2 **Use** the LCD to write equivalent fractions.

Julie: $\frac{7}{10} = \frac{7 \times 2}{10 \times 2} = \frac{14}{20}$ **Seth:** $\frac{3}{4} = \frac{3 \times 5}{4 \times 5} = \frac{15}{20}$

STEP 3 **Compare** the numerators: $\frac{14}{20} < \frac{15}{20}$, so $\frac{7}{10} < \frac{3}{4}$.

▸ **Answer** Seth kayaks the greater distance.

Check Graph the numbers on a number line.

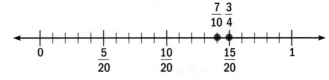

Because $\frac{14}{20}$ is to the left of $\frac{15}{20}$, $\frac{7}{10} < \frac{3}{4}$.

EXAMPLE 2 **Standardized Test Practice**

Which list shows $\frac{2}{3}, \frac{3}{8}, \frac{1}{6}$, and $\frac{3}{4}$ in order from least to greatest?

(A) $\frac{3}{8}, \frac{1}{6}, \frac{3}{4}, \frac{2}{3}$ **(B)** $\frac{1}{6}, \frac{3}{8}, \frac{2}{3}, \frac{3}{4}$ **(C)** $\frac{1}{6}, \frac{2}{3}, \frac{3}{4}, \frac{3}{8}$ **(D)** $\frac{1}{6}, \frac{3}{8}, \frac{3}{4}, \frac{2}{3}$

ELIMINATE CHOICES
You know that $\frac{3}{4}$ is greater than $\frac{3}{8}$, so you can eliminate choice C.

SOLUTION

STEP 1 **Find** the LCD. The LCD is the LCM of 3, 4, 8, and 6, which is 24.

STEP 2 **Use** the LCD to write equivalent fractions.

$$\frac{2}{3} = \frac{2 \times 8}{3 \times 8} = \frac{16}{24} \qquad\qquad \frac{3}{8} = \frac{3 \times 3}{8 \times 3} = \frac{9}{24}$$

$$\frac{1}{6} = \frac{1 \times 4}{6 \times 4} = \frac{4}{24} \qquad\qquad \frac{3}{4} = \frac{3 \times 6}{4 \times 6} = \frac{18}{24}$$

STEP 3 **Compare** the numerators: $\frac{4}{24} < \frac{9}{24} < \frac{16}{24} < \frac{18}{24}$, so $\frac{1}{6} < \frac{3}{8} < \frac{2}{3} < \frac{3}{4}$.

▶ **Answer** The order of the fractions from least to greatest is $\frac{1}{6}, \frac{3}{8}, \frac{2}{3}$, and $\frac{3}{4}$. The correct answer is B. **(A) (B) (C) (D)**

EXAMPLE 3 **Comparing Fractions Using Approximations**

Use approximation to tell which portion in each package is greater, $\frac{13}{24}$ or $\frac{17}{36}$.

Notice that the numerator of each fraction is about half the denominator.

You know that $\frac{1}{2} = \frac{12}{24}$, so $\frac{13}{24} > \frac{1}{2}$.

You know that $\frac{1}{2} = \frac{18}{36}$, so $\frac{17}{36} < \frac{1}{2}$.

24 Pencils

High Quality Wood Pencils

No. 2

36 Pencils

High Quality Wood Pencils

No. 2

▶ **Answer** You can conclude that $\frac{13}{24} > \frac{17}{36}$, so the package with $\frac{13}{24}$ of its pencils has a greater portion of pencils in it.

✓ **GUIDED PRACTICE** **for Examples 1, 2, and 3**

1. Copy and complete the statement using <, >, or =: $\frac{5}{8} \; \underline{?} \; \frac{7}{12}$.

2. Order the fractions from least to greatest: $\frac{9}{14}, \frac{5}{7}, \frac{3}{4}, \frac{5}{28}$.

Use approximation to tell which fraction is greater.

3. $\frac{8}{15}, \frac{11}{24}$ 4. $\frac{16}{33}, \frac{11}{18}$ 5. $\frac{23}{48}, \frac{31}{56}$ 6. $\frac{16}{30}, \frac{60}{130}$

4.5 EXERCISES

HOMEWORK KEY

★ = **STANDARDIZED TEST PRACTICE**
15, 21, 34, 35, 36, 37, 40, and 52

◯ = **HINTS** AND **HOMEWORK HELP**
for Exs. 5, 7, 11, 13, 31 at classzone.com

SKILL PRACTICE

1. **VOCABULARY** Copy and complete: The least common multiple of the denominators of two or more fractions is their ___?___.

2. **VOCABULARY** Use your own words to explain how to compare fractions with unlike denominators.

COMPARING FRACTIONS Copy and complete the statement using <, >, or =.

SEE EXAMPLE 1
on p. 189
for Exs. 3–8

3. $\frac{9}{16} \; ? \; \frac{3}{4}$

4. $\frac{5}{6} \; ? \; \frac{7}{8}$

5. $\frac{11}{15} \; ? \; \frac{2}{3}$

6. $\frac{17}{34} \; ? \; \frac{9}{18}$

7. $\frac{28}{81} \; ? \; \frac{7}{24}$

8. $\frac{13}{14} \; ? \; \frac{26}{28}$

ORDERING FRACTIONS Order the fractions from least to greatest.

SEE EXAMPLE 2
on p. 190
for Exs. 9–15

9. $\frac{1}{3}, \frac{2}{5}, \frac{3}{10}, \frac{11}{30}$

10. $\frac{3}{4}, \frac{2}{5}, \frac{5}{8}, \frac{7}{10}$

11. $\frac{3}{7}, \frac{1}{3}, \frac{1}{2}, \frac{9}{14}$

12. $\frac{3}{8}, \frac{9}{32}, \frac{1}{4}, \frac{5}{16}$

13. $\frac{7}{9}, \frac{32}{45}, \frac{20}{27}, \frac{2}{3}$

14. $\frac{17}{81}, \frac{5}{9}, \frac{13}{27}, \frac{2}{3}$

15. ★ **MULTIPLE CHOICE** Which fractions are in order from least to greatest?

  Ⓐ $\frac{8}{15}, \frac{5}{9}, \frac{3}{5}$
  Ⓑ $\frac{7}{18}, \frac{2}{9}, \frac{5}{12}$
  Ⓒ $\frac{5}{6}, \frac{13}{18}, \frac{16}{27}$
  Ⓓ $\frac{3}{8}, \frac{5}{16}, \frac{15}{32}$

SEE EXAMPLE 3
on p. 190
for Exs. 16–19

USING APPROXIMATION Use approximation to tell which fraction is greater.

16. $\frac{10}{21}, \frac{15}{28}$

17. $\frac{15}{31}, \frac{27}{50}$

18. $\frac{40}{79}, \frac{23}{48}$

19. $\frac{9}{17}, \frac{8}{16}$

20. **ERROR ANALYSIS** Describe and correct the error in comparing $\frac{15}{49}$ and $\frac{3}{4}$.

  ✗ 15 > 3 and 49 > 4, so $\frac{15}{49} > \frac{3}{4}$.

21. ★ **MULTIPLE CHOICE** The fraction $\frac{4}{7}$ lies between which pair of fractions on a number line?

  Ⓐ $\frac{7}{14}$ and $\frac{17}{28}$
  Ⓑ $\frac{8}{14}$ and $\frac{18}{28}$
  Ⓒ $\frac{9}{14}$ and $\frac{24}{28}$
  Ⓓ $\frac{10}{14}$ and $\frac{27}{28}$

22. **CHECKING REASONABLENESS** Use the LCD to tell which fraction is greater, $\frac{7}{15}$ or $\frac{15}{28}$. Approximate to check the reasonableness of your answer.

CHOOSE A METHOD Copy and complete the statement using <, >, or =. Tell whether you used *mental math* or *paper and pencil* to compare each pair of fractions. *Explain* your choice.

23. $\frac{15}{56}$? $\frac{1}{4}$

24. $\frac{7}{21}$? $\frac{1}{3}$

25. $\frac{13}{24}$? $\frac{19}{32}$

26. $\frac{13}{18}$? $\frac{5}{9}$

CHALLENGE Suppose x and y are nonzero whole numbers and $x < y$. *Describe* what happens to the value of each fraction as x gets closer to y. *Explain* your reasoning.

27. $\frac{x}{2y}$

28. $\frac{3x}{y}$

29. $\frac{x}{y}$

30. $\frac{y-x}{y}$

PROBLEM SOLVING

SEE EXAMPLE 1
on p. 189
for Ex. 31

31. **CAROUSELS** Carousel horses that move up and down are called *jumpers*. The Broadway Flying Horses carousel in San Diego has 28 jumpers out of 40 horses. The carousel at the San Francisco Zoo has 24 jumpers out of 36 horses. Which carousel has the greater fraction of jumpers?

32. **PIES** After Thanksgiving dinner, $\frac{1}{4}$ of an apple pie and $\frac{3}{10}$ of a pumpkin pie are left uneaten. Which pie has the greater portion left uneaten?

33. **WRENCHES** The sizes, in inches, of several wrenches are as follows: $\frac{11}{16}$, $\frac{3}{8}$, $\frac{3}{4}$, $\frac{1}{2}$, $\frac{5}{8}$, and $\frac{7}{16}$. Order the wrenches from smallest to largest.

34. ★ **WRITING** Jane says that $\frac{5}{6} < \frac{5}{12}$ because 6 is less than 12. Is she right? *Explain.*

35. ★ **MULTIPLE CHOICE** Choose the fraction that represents the best estimate of the portion of the granola bar covered with yogurt.

Ⓐ $\frac{1}{10}$
Ⓑ $\frac{3}{13}$
Ⓒ $\frac{4}{7}$
Ⓓ $\frac{5}{6}$

36. ★ **EXTENDED RESPONSE** Jon and Anne are raising money for a school project. Jon's fundraising goal is $225. Anne's fundraising goal is $275. So far, Jon has raised $150, and Anne has raised $190.

   a. Write fractions Write a fraction in simplest form for the portion of their fundraising goals that each student has raised.

   b. Analyze Who has raised the greater fraction of his or her goal?

   c. Compare *Compare* the students' progress in terms of fractions and in terms of absolute dollars they still need to raise. What do you observe?

37. ★ **SHORT RESPONSE** Alex says "You don't have to rewrite fractions using least common denominators to compare them. You can use any common denominator." Do you agree? *Explain* your answer using several examples.

38. **TENNIS** At a summer tennis camp, Veronica won 13 games and lost 15 games. Audrey won 19 games and lost 18 games. Write a fraction for the portion of games won by each girl. Who won the greater fraction of games? What was the fraction?

39. **XY ALGEBRA** How do the unit fractions $\frac{1}{a}$ and $\frac{1}{b}$ compare when $a > b > 0$? *Explain* your answer.

40. ★ **SHORT RESPONSE** Write a fraction that is exactly halfway between $\frac{3}{7}$ and $\frac{3}{5}$. *Explain* how you found the fraction.

41. **CHALLENGE** Write two fractions that are not equivalent. Add the numerators and add the denominators to get a new fraction. How does the new fraction compare to the two original fractions? Repeat, using two other fractions. How does each new fraction compare to your original fractions?

42. **CHALLENGE** Matt and Nina each weeded an equal sized garden. Monday, Matt weeded $\frac{2}{3}$ of his garden and Nina weeded $\frac{1}{2}$ of hers. Tuesday, Matt pulled $\frac{2}{5}$ of his remaining weeds and Nina pulled $\frac{3}{4}$ of hers. Who has the larger fraction of unweeded garden remaining? What is the fraction?

 NEW JERSEY MIXED REVIEW   **TEST PRACTICE** at classzone.com

43. Which of the following statements is supported by the data in the table?

x	2	3	4	5	6
y	4	6	8	10	12

   Ⓐ The least common multiple of *x* and *y* is *x*.

   Ⓑ The greatest common factor of *x* and *y* is *x*.

   Ⓒ When *x* is prime, *y* is prime.

   Ⓓ *x* and *y* have no factors in common.

44. The decimal 0.04 is found between which pair of decimals on a number line?
   Ⓐ 0.3 and 0.8   **Ⓑ** 0 and 0.009   **Ⓒ** 0.03 and 0.06   **Ⓓ** 0.003 and 0.03

4.6 Mixed Numbers and Improper Fractions

 4.1.A.5 Use whole numbers, fractions, decimals, and percents to represent equivalent forms of the same number.

Before You compared and ordered fractions.

Now You'll compare and order fractions and mixed numbers.

Why? So you can work with measurements, as in Ex. 40.

KEY VOCABULARY
- mixed number, p. 194
- proper fraction, p. 194
- improper fraction, p. 194

A **mixed number** has a whole number part and a fraction part. The number $2\frac{3}{4}$ is a mixed number. Model A represents $2\frac{3}{4}$.

A **proper fraction** is a fraction whose numerator is less than its denominator. A fraction is called an **improper fraction** if its numerator is greater than or equal to its denominator.

READING

The mixed number $2\frac{3}{4}$ is read "two and three fourths."

The mixed number $2\frac{3}{4}$ can be written as an improper fraction by dividing each of the 2 wholes into 4 equal sized parts, then counting the number of fourths. This is shown in Model B.

Model A

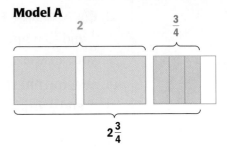

Model B

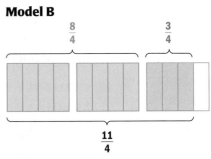

KEY CONCEPT *For Your Notebook*

Writing Mixed Numbers as Improper Fractions

Words To write a mixed number as an improper fraction, multiply the whole number part and the denominator, add the numerator, and write the sum over the denominator.

Numbers $2\frac{3}{4} = \frac{2 \cdot 4 + 3}{4} = \frac{11}{4}$

EXAMPLE 1 Writing Improper Fractions

Write the mixed number as an improper fraction.

a. $3\frac{5}{6} = \frac{3 \cdot 6 + 5}{6}$

$= \frac{23}{6}$

b. $4\frac{7}{8} = \frac{4 \cdot 8 + 7}{8}$

$= \frac{39}{8}$

KEY CONCEPT

For Your Notebook

Writing Improper Fractions as Mixed Numbers

Words   To write an improper fraction as a mixed number, divide the numerator by the denominator and write any remainder as a fraction.

Numbers $\dfrac{7}{3}$ ⟶ $7 \div 3 = 2 \text{ R1, or } 2\dfrac{1}{3}$

EXAMPLE 2   **Writing Mixed Numbers**

REVIEW DIVISION

Need help with dividing whole numbers? See p. 744.

Write $\dfrac{21}{6}$ as a mixed number in simplest form.

STEP 1   Write $\dfrac{21}{6}$ as a mixed number.

$$\begin{array}{r} 3 \text{ R3, or } 3\frac{3}{6} \\ 6\overline{)21} \\ \underline{18} \\ 3 \end{array}$$

You can write the remainder R3 as a fraction: $\dfrac{remainder}{divisor}$.

STEP 2   **Simplify.**

$$3\dfrac{3}{6} = 3\dfrac{1}{2}$$

▶ **Answer** $\dfrac{21}{6} = 3\dfrac{1}{2}$

EXAMPLE 3   **Comparing Mixed Numbers and Fractions**

Compare $\dfrac{17}{6}$ and $2\dfrac{1}{4}$.

STEP 1   Write $2\dfrac{1}{4}$ as an improper fraction: $2\dfrac{1}{4} = \dfrac{9}{4}$.

STEP 2   Rewrite $\dfrac{17}{6}$ and $\dfrac{9}{4}$ using the least common denominator, 12.

$$\dfrac{17}{6} = \dfrac{17 \times 2}{6 \times 2} = \dfrac{34}{12} \qquad\qquad \dfrac{9}{4} = \dfrac{9 \times 3}{4 \times 3} = \dfrac{27}{12}$$

STEP 3   Compare the fractions: $\dfrac{34}{12} > \dfrac{27}{12}$, so $\dfrac{17}{6} > 2\dfrac{1}{4}$.

✓ **GUIDED PRACTICE**   for Examples 1, 2, and 3

Copy and complete the improper fraction or mixed number.

1. $3\dfrac{3}{4} = \dfrac{?}{4}$ **2.** $1\dfrac{2}{5} = \dfrac{?}{5}$ **3.** $\dfrac{17}{3} = \underline{?}\dfrac{?}{3}$ **4.** $\dfrac{15}{7} = \underline{?}\dfrac{?}{7}$

Copy and complete the statement using <, >, or =.

5. $\dfrac{19}{6} \underline{?} 3\dfrac{5}{12}$ **6.** $\dfrac{14}{3} \underline{?} 4\dfrac{3}{5}$ **7.** $\dfrac{27}{4} \underline{?} 6\dfrac{3}{4}$ **8.** $\dfrac{49}{9} \underline{?} 5\dfrac{1}{2}$

EXAMPLE 4 Ordering Mixed Numbers and Fractions

Fitness The Presidential Physical Fitness Award involves a flexibility test called the V-sit reach. The distances, in inches, that four students were able to reach are listed below. Order the distances from least to greatest.

$$3\frac{5}{8} \qquad 3 \qquad \frac{17}{4} \qquad 3\frac{1}{2}$$

Another fitness test: Curl-ups

SOLUTION

The denominators are 8, 1, 4, and 2. Write the numbers as improper fractions using the least common denominator, 8.

WRITING WHOLE NUMBERS

3 can be written as $\frac{3}{1}$.

$$3\frac{5}{8} = \frac{29}{8} \qquad\qquad 3 = \frac{3}{1} = \frac{3 \times 8}{1 \times 8} = \frac{24}{8}$$

$$\frac{17}{4} = \frac{17 \times 2}{4 \times 2} = \frac{34}{8} \qquad 3\frac{1}{2} = \frac{7}{2} = \frac{7 \times 4}{2 \times 4} = \frac{28}{8}$$

▸ **Answer** From least to greatest, the distances are 3, $3\frac{1}{2}$, $3\frac{5}{8}$, and $\frac{17}{4}$.

 Math at classzone.com

✓ **GUIDED PRACTICE** for Example 4

9. Order the numbers 2, $2\frac{7}{8}$, $\frac{16}{5}$, and $2\frac{3}{4}$ from least to greatest.

4.6 EXERCISES

★ = **STANDARDIZED TEST PRACTICE**
Exs. 29, 43, 44, 45, 46, and 63

○ = **HINTS AND HOMEWORK HELP**
for Exs. 7, 11, 17, 23, 39 at classzone.com

SKILL PRACTICE

VOCABULARY Tell whether the number is a *mixed number,* a *proper fraction,* or an *improper fraction.*

1. $\frac{12}{12}$ **2.** $\frac{12}{17}$ **3.** $8\frac{3}{8}$ **4.** $\frac{21}{20}$

WRITING IMPROPER FRACTIONS Write the mixed number as an improper fraction.

SEE EXAMPLE 1
on p. 194
for Exs. 5–14

5. $5\frac{1}{3}$ **6.** $4\frac{2}{7}$ **7.** $2\frac{4}{9}$ **8.** $3\frac{3}{11}$ **9.** $4\frac{1}{8}$

10. $3\frac{4}{15}$ **11.** $11\frac{3}{8}$ **12.** $8\frac{6}{7}$ **13.** $4\frac{5}{16}$ **14.** $10\frac{2}{5}$

WRITING MIXED NUMBERS Write the improper fraction as a whole number or as a mixed number in simplest form.

SEE EXAMPLE 2
on p. 195
for Exs. 15–24

15. $\frac{27}{5}$ **16.** $\frac{42}{7}$ **17.** $\frac{67}{8}$ **18.** $\frac{95}{6}$ **19.** $\frac{24}{11}$

20. $\frac{99}{4}$ **21.** $\frac{126}{14}$ **22.** $\frac{107}{13}$ **23.** $\frac{159}{16}$ **24.** $\frac{58}{21}$

COMPARING MIXED NUMBERS AND FRACTIONS Copy and complete the statement using <, >, or =.

SEE EXAMPLE 3
on p. 195
for Exs. 25–29

25. $\frac{3}{2}$? $3\frac{1}{2}$ **26.** $\frac{8}{3}$? $2\frac{2}{3}$ **27.** $\frac{22}{3}$? $7\frac{1}{4}$ **28.** $\frac{29}{5}$? $6\frac{3}{5}$

29. ★ **MULTIPLE CHOICE** Which number is *not* equivalent to the number modeled below?

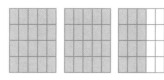

  A $\frac{52}{60}$ **B** $\frac{13}{5}$ **C** $2\frac{12}{20}$ **D** $2\frac{3}{5}$

SEE EXAMPLE 4
on p. 196
for Exs. 30–32

ORDERING NUMBERS Order the numbers from least to greatest.

30. $\frac{22}{2}, 2\frac{2}{3}, \frac{22}{11}, 2\frac{20}{33}$ **31.** $\frac{40}{40}, \frac{49}{42}, \frac{22}{20}, 1\frac{1}{9}$ **32.** $7\frac{1}{5}, 7, \frac{38}{5}, \frac{20}{7}$

(XY) ALGEBRA Plot the numbers on a number line, then solve the equation.

33. $x + 2\frac{1}{4} = \frac{21}{4}$ **34.** $3\frac{1}{2} - p = \frac{3}{2}$ **35.** $a + \frac{7}{5} = 8\frac{2}{5}$

36. ERROR ANALYSIS Describe and correct the error made in writing $5\frac{2}{3}$ as an improper fraction.

$$\times \quad 5\frac{2}{3} = \frac{(5 \cdot 3) + 3}{3} = \frac{18}{3}$$

CHALLENGE Order the given numbers from least to greatest. Then find values for *x* and *y* so that *x* is second in the list and *y* is fourth in the list.

37. $\frac{85}{9}, 9\frac{11}{20}, 9\frac{21}{40}, x, y$ **38.** $\frac{79}{7}, 11\frac{3}{11}, \frac{45}{4}, x, y$

PROBLEM SOLVING

SEE EXAMPLE 2
on p. 195
for Ex. 39

39. WALKING TO SCHOOL You walk to and from school five days a week. You live an eighth of a mile away from the school. Write the total distance you walk in a week as an improper fraction and as a mixed number in simplest form.

40. BUBBLE SOLUTION You are filling 5 bottles with bubble solution. To fill one bottle, you need $1\frac{1}{4}$ cups of water. You can find only a quarter-cup measure. How many quarter-cups of water do you need?

41. LONG JUMPS The four best long jumps at a track meet are $18\frac{7}{12}$ feet, $18\frac{2}{3}$ feet, $18\frac{3}{4}$ feet, and $18\frac{1}{3}$ feet. Order the numbers from least to greatest. What is the distance of the longest jump?

42. REASONING Which type of number is greater, an *improper fraction* or a *proper fraction*? *Explain* your reasoning.

43. ★ **WRITING** How could you order $3\frac{1}{4}$, $3\frac{3}{4}$, $3\frac{2}{7}$ and $3\frac{1}{8}$ from least to greatest without writing them as improper fractions? *Explain* your reasoning. Then order the mixed numbers from least to greatest.

44. ★ **OPEN-ENDED MATH** Choose two mixed numbers and two improper fractions between 4 and 5. Order the four numbers from least to greatest.

45. ★ **MULTIPLE CHOICE** At a restaurant, a serving of apple pie is one eighth of a pie. There are $2\frac{3}{4}$ apple pies. How many servings is this?

   (A) 2   **(B)** 11   **(C)** 19   **(D)** 22

46. ★ **SHORT RESPONSE** You cut two pizzas into eighths and two pizzas into sixths. You and your friends eat $1\frac{5}{8}$ of the first two pizzas and $1\frac{2}{3}$ of the other two. Draw models for the amounts of pizza eaten. Write the amounts eaten as improper fractions. Then compare the amounts eaten.

47. CHALLENGE Estimate the two whole numbers that the fractions $\frac{1284}{385}$ and $\frac{1520}{413}$ are between. *Explain* your reasoning.

 NEW JERSEY MIXED REVIEW   **TEST PRACTICE** at classzone.com

48. Which list shows $\frac{3}{4}$, $\frac{1}{2}$, $\frac{5}{8}$, and $\frac{2}{3}$ in order from least to greatest?

   (A) $\frac{1}{2}, \frac{2}{3}, \frac{3}{4}, \frac{5}{8}$ **(B)** $\frac{5}{8}, \frac{3}{4}, \frac{2}{3}, \frac{1}{2}$ **(C)** $\frac{1}{2}, \frac{5}{8}, \frac{2}{3}, \frac{3}{4}$ **(D)** $\frac{3}{4}, \frac{2}{3}, \frac{5}{8}, \frac{1}{2}$

49. Josie buys a dozen notebooks priced at 6 notebooks for $5.54. She also buys 30 blank CDs priced at $9.89 for 15 blank CDs. What is the total amount she spent, not including tax?

   (A) $15.43   **(B)** $20.97   **(C)** $25.32   **(D)** $30.86

50. The lengths of Kathy's last eight phone calls, in minutes, are 5, 12, 23, 12, 3, 16, 15, and 13. Which measure of data is represented by 12 minutes?

   (A) Mean   **(B)** Mode   **(C)** Median   **(D)** Range

4.7 Fractions and Decimals

4.1.A.5 Use whole numbers, fractions, decimals, and percents to represent equivalent forms of the same number.

Before	You wrote decimals and fractions.
Now	You'll write fractions as decimals and decimals as fractions.
Why?	So you can compare lengths, as in Exs. 43–45.

KEY VOCABULARY
- **terminating decimal,** *p. 199*
- **repeating decimal,** *p. 199*

You may recall that the fraction $\frac{a}{b}$ is equivalent to the expression $a \div b$. You can use this relationship to write any fraction as a decimal by dividing the numerator by the denominator.

EXAMPLE 1 Writing Fractions as Decimals

Write (a) $\frac{7}{20}$ and (b) $3\frac{5}{8}$ as decimals.

SOLUTION

REVIEW DIVISION
Need help with dividing decimals? See p. 71.

a.
```
      0.35
  20)7.00   ← Write zeros
     60        in dividend as
     ___       placeholders.
     100
     100
     ___
       0   ← Remainder is zero.
```

▶ **Answer** $\frac{7}{20} = 0.35$

b.
```
      0.625
   8)5.000   ← Write zeros
     48         in dividend as
     ___        placeholders.
     20
     16
     ___
     40
     40
     ___
      0   ← Remainder is zero.
```

▶ **Answer** $3\frac{5}{8} = 3 + 0.625 = 3.625$

✓ **GUIDED PRACTICE** for Example 1

Write the fraction or mixed number as a decimal.

1. $\frac{3}{10}$ **2.** $\frac{17}{200}$ **3.** $3\frac{4}{5}$ **4.** $2\frac{7}{8}$

VOCABULARY
In a terminating decimal, the digits *terminate*, or end. In a repeating decimal, the digits *repeat* with no end.

Terminating and Repeating Decimals When a long division problem results in a remainder of 0, the quotient is a **terminating decimal**. Sometimes, long division gives a **repeating decimal**, where one or more digits repeat without end. Repeating decimals can be written with a bar over the digit(s) that repeat.

$$0.4444\ldots = 0.\overline{4} \qquad \text{One digit repeats.}$$

$$3.0505\ldots = 3.\overline{05} \qquad \text{Two digits repeat.}$$

Writing Fractions as Repeating Decimals

Write (a) $\frac{5}{3}$ and (b) $\frac{13}{33}$ as decimals.

SOLUTION

a.
```
    1.666 ...  ←— The digit
  3)5.000        6 keeps
    3            repeating.
    ——
    20
    18
    ——
    20
    18
    ——
    20
    18        Remainder will
    ——    ←— never be zero.
     2
```
▶ **Answer** $\frac{5}{3} = 1.\overline{6}$

b.
```
      0.3939 ...  ←— The digits
  33)13.0000         3 and 9 keep
     99              repeating.
     ——
     310
     297
     ———
     130
      99
     ———
     310
     297       Remainder will
     ———   ←— never be zero.
      13
```
▶ **Answer** $\frac{13}{33} = 0.\overline{39}$

AVOID ERRORS
Only the digit(s) under the bar should be repeated. $1.\overline{6} = 1.666\ldots$, *not* $1.61616\ldots$.

REVIEW PLACE VALUE
Need help with place value? See p. 56.

Writing Decimals as Fractions To write a decimal as a fraction, use the place value of the last digit of the decimal to determine the denominator. For example, to write 0.45 as a fraction, 5 is in the hundredths' place, so write $\frac{45}{100}$.

Writing Decimals as Fractions

Write (a) 0.85 and (b) 4.375 as a fraction or mixed number.

SOLUTION

a. $0.85 = \frac{85}{100}$ 5 is in the hundredths' place.

$= \frac{17 \cdot \cancel{5}^{1}}{20 \cdot \cancel{5}_{1}}$

$= \frac{17}{20}$

b. $4.375 = 4\frac{375}{1000}$ 5 is in the thousandths' place.

$= 4\frac{3 \cdot \cancel{125}^{1}}{8 \cdot \cancel{125}_{1}}$

$= 4\frac{3}{8}$

TAKE NOTES
It is useful to know these common equivalents. Write them in your notebook.
$\frac{1}{2} = 0.5 \qquad \frac{1}{5} = 0.2$
$\frac{1}{3} = 0.\overline{3} \qquad \frac{2}{3} = 0.\overline{6}$
$\frac{1}{4} = 0.25 \qquad \frac{3}{4} = 0.75$

✓ **GUIDED PRACTICE**   for Examples 2 and 3

Write the fraction or mixed number as a decimal.

5. $\frac{7}{9}$ **6.** $\frac{13}{6}$ **7.** $2\frac{5}{11}$ **8.** $4\frac{3}{22}$

Write the decimal as a fraction or mixed number in simplest form.

9. 0.4   **10.** 2.65   **11.** 1.0025   **12.** 0.735

EXAMPLE 4 Standardized Test Practice

Geography The map below gives areas as fractions of the total area of the United States. Which of these states has the least area?

A California: $\frac{17}{400}$

ELIMINATE CHOICES
You can use mental math to determine that $\frac{1}{25} > \frac{1}{30}$. So, you can eliminate choice B.

B Montana: $\frac{1}{25}$

C New Mexico: $\frac{1}{30}$

D Texas: $\frac{9}{125}$

SOLUTION

Write the fractions as decimals and then compare the decimals.

California: $\frac{17}{400} = 0.0425$ **Montana:** $\frac{1}{25} = 0.04$

New Mexico: $\frac{1}{30} = 0.0\overline{3}$ **Texas:** $\frac{9}{125} = 0.072$

▶ **Answer** Because $0.072 > 0.0425 > 0.04 > 0.0\overline{3}$, the state with the least area is New Mexico. The correct answer is C. Ⓐ Ⓑ Ⓒ Ⓓ

Animated Math at classzone.com

✓ **GUIDED PRACTICE**   **for Example 4**

13. Order the fractions $\frac{1}{40}$, $\frac{21}{200}$, $\frac{1}{16}$, and $\frac{17}{125}$ from least to greatest.

4.7 EXERCISES

HOMEWORK KEY
★ = **STANDARDIZED TEST PRACTICE**
Exs. 13, 40, 41, 46, and 63

○ = **HINTS AND HOMEWORK HELP**
for Exs. 7, 11, 17, 21, 39 at classzone.com

SKILL PRACTICE

VOCABULARY Copy and complete the statement.

1. If the results of long division repeat without end, the quotient is a ___?___.

2. If a long division problem gives a remainder of 0, the quotient is a ___?___.

WRITING DECIMALS Write the fraction or mixed number as a decimal.

**SEE EXAMPLES
1 AND 2**
on pp. 199–200
for Exs. 3–12

3. $\frac{1}{2}$ **4.** $1\frac{1}{4}$ **5.** $1\frac{1}{3}$ **6.** $\frac{5}{6}$ **7.** $\frac{5}{18}$

8. $2\frac{2}{3}$ **9.** $2\frac{2}{5}$ **10.** $5\frac{4}{25}$ **11.** $3\frac{4}{9}$ **12.** $9\frac{7}{111}$

SEE EXAMPLE 1
on p. 199
for Ex. 13

13. ★ **MULTIPLE CHOICE** Which number is $4\frac{7}{8}$ written as a decimal?

(**A**) 4.78   (**B**) $4.7\overline{8}$ (**C**) 4.875   (**D**) 4.9

REPEATING DECIMALS Rewrite the repeating decimal using bar notation.

SEE EXAMPLE 2
on p. 200
for Exs. 14–18

14. 0.7777 . . .   **15.** 5.2121 . . .   **16.** 3.5888 . . .   (**17.**) 2.358358 . . .

18. ERROR ANALYSIS Describe and correct the error made in writing $\frac{5}{11}$ as a decimal.

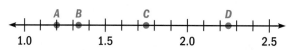

$$\frac{5}{11} = 0.4\overline{5} \quad ✗$$

WRITING FRACTIONS Write the decimal as a fraction or mixed number in simplest form.

SEE EXAMPLE 3
on p. 200
for Exs. 19–26

19. 0.8   **20.** 0.12   (**21.**) 0.475   **22.** 0.125

23. 6.24   **24.** 4.175   **25.** 2.245   **26.** 1.78

ORDERING NUMBERS Order the numbers from least to greatest.

SEE EXAMPLE 4
on p. 201
for Exs. 27–30

27. $\frac{2}{7}$, 0.25, $\frac{5}{2}$, 0.2, $0.\overline{2}$

28. 3.67, $3\frac{4}{5}$, $3\frac{2}{3}$, $\frac{16}{5}$, $3.6\overline{7}$

29. $\frac{8}{3}$, 1.9, 1.94, $\frac{9}{4}$, $1\frac{4}{9}$

30. $\frac{9}{10}$, 0.89, $\frac{6}{7}$, $0.\overline{90}$, $\frac{15}{20}$

MATCHING Match the number with its graph on the number line.

31. 1.75   **32.** $2\frac{1}{4}$ **33.** $\frac{6}{5}$ **34.** $1.\overline{3}$

CHALLENGE Write the decimal as a fraction or mixed number.

35. $1.\overline{3}$ **36.** $0.1\overline{3}$ **37.** $0.1\overline{6}$ **38.** $0.02\overline{6}$

PROBLEM SOLVING

SEE EXAMPLE 3
on p. 200
for Ex. 39

(**39.**) **RAINBOW BRIDGE** At 88.4 meters, Rainbow Bridge in Utah is the highest natural bridge in the world. Write the height as a mixed number in simplest form.

40. ★ **MULTIPLE CHOICE** The fraction of your stamp collection from the United States is $\frac{3}{5}$. What decimal represents the fraction of stamps from the United States?

(**A**) 0.25   (**B**) 0.35

(**C**) 0.4   (**D**) 0.6

41. ★ **WRITING** If you were comparing $5\frac{3}{5}$ and 5.75, would you change the mixed number to a decimal or the decimal to a mixed number? Why?

42. **REASONING** If you are using division to write a fraction as a decimal, how do you know when to stop dividing?

READING *IN* MATH Read the information below for Exercises 43–45.

Marsupials Marsupials are mammals with pouches. A tiny newborn marsupial can be as small as a lima bean. It spends the first few minutes of life in a difficult climb into its mother's pouch.

It spends its first few months of life in its mother's pouch. Some common types of marsupials are kangaroos, koalas, numbats, and wombats. They vary greatly in size, as the list at the right shows.

Marsupial	Length
Kangaroo	$72\frac{4}{5}$ in. to $84\frac{5}{16}$ in.
Koala	$23\frac{5}{8}$ in. to $29\frac{9}{16}$ in.
Numbat	$16\frac{5}{16}$ in. to $13\frac{4}{5}$ in.
Wombat	$31\frac{1}{2}$ in. to $51\frac{1}{5}$ in.

43. **Rewrite** Write each of the lengths as a decimal number of inches.

44. **Calculate** Multiply each length by 2.54 to find the number of centimeters long each marsupial can be. Round each length to the nearest 0.1 centimeter.

45. **Decide** An adult marsupial is 72 centimeters long. Which of these four marsupials is it most likely to be?

46. ★ **SHORT RESPONSE** There were 60 students who tried out for the school play. Only 0.7 of the students were selected to be in the play. What fraction of the students were *not* selected to be in the play? How many students were *not* selected to be in the play? *Explain* how you found your answers.

47. **INTERNET USE** A recent government report notes that the number of U.S. households using dial-up Internet service declined by about 1 in 8. Write the decline as a fraction and as a decimal. Is this more than 0.12? *Explain*.

48. **SPORT PARTICIPATION** The table shows the participation of 12–17 year-olds in selected sports activities in 2002.

  a. What fraction of the respondents exercise with equipment? Write your answer as a decimal rounded to hundredths.

  b. What fraction of the respondents skateboard? Write your answer as a decimal rounded to hundredths.

  c. How does the number of snowboarders compare to the sum of snowboarders and walkers? Write your answer as a decimal rounded to hundredths.

Type of Exercise	Number of 12–17 Year-olds
With equipment	5,069,000
Walking	4,482,000
Skateboarding	3,834,000
Snowboarding	1,659,000
Total respondents	24,265,000

49. MULTI-STEP PROBLEM Consider these fractions with whole number numerators: $\frac{1}{9}, \frac{2}{9}, \frac{3}{9}$, and $\frac{4}{9}$.

  a. Calculate Write each fraction as a decimal.

  b. Look for a Pattern What pattern do you notice?

  c. Make a Table Use the pattern you found in part (b) to make a table of equivalent fractions and decimals for proper fractions that are ninths.

50. CHALLENGE What is true about the denominator of any fraction in simplest form whose decimal form terminates rather than repeats?

 NEW JERSEY MIXED REVIEW **TEST PRACTICE** at classzone.com

In Exercises 51 and 52, use the following list of numbers.

$$\frac{5}{2}, 2\frac{1}{2}, 2\frac{1}{3}, \frac{8}{3}, \frac{32}{15}, 2\frac{7}{8}, 2\frac{1}{11}$$

51. Between which two numbers will the median of the numbers above most likely be located?

  (A) 1 and 2   **(B)** 2 and 3   **(C)** 3 and 4   **(D)** 3 and 5

52. Which method could you use to find the median of the numbers on the list?

  (A) Add all the numbers. Then divide by 7.

  (B) Find the number that occurs most frequently.

  (C) Order the numbers from least to greatest. Then find the middle value.

  (D) Subtract the smallest number from the largest number.

QUIZ for Lessons 4.4–4.7

Find the LCM of the numbers using prime factorization. *(p. 182)*

  1. 15, 27   **2.** 16, 18   **3.** 24, 50   **4.** 72, 147

Copy and complete the statement using <, >, or =. *(p. 189)*

  5. $\frac{7}{12} \underline{\ ?\ } \frac{2}{3}$ **6.** $\frac{3}{10} \underline{\ ?\ } \frac{3}{4}$ **7.** $\frac{5}{7} \underline{\ ?\ } \frac{1}{3}$ **8.** $\frac{22}{27} \underline{\ ?\ } \frac{55}{72}$

Write the mixed number as an improper fraction or the improper fraction as a mixed number in simplest form. *(p. 194)*

  9. $2\frac{3}{8}$ **10.** $5\frac{5}{7}$ **11.** $\frac{38}{4}$ **12.** $\frac{67}{6}$

13. SNOWFALL During the winter of 2002–2003, Anchorage, Alaska, accumulated a record 28.6 inches of snow during a single day for a United States city. Write the number as a mixed number and as an improper fraction in simplest form. *(p. 199)*

4.7 Fraction and Decimal Conversion

Some calculators allow you to work with fractions. You can use the ►F key to change decimals into fractions or mixed numbers. Use the ►D key to change fractions and mixed numbers into decimals.

EXAMPLE 1 **Write the decimal as a fraction or mixed number.**

a. 2.125 **b.** 0.85

SOLUTION

Keystrokes	Display
a. 2.125 ►F =	**2⊔1/8**
b. 0.85 ►F =	**17/20**

> The ⊔ in the display separates the whole number part from the fraction part of the mixed number.

EXAMPLE 2 **Write the fraction or mixed number as a decimal.**

a. $1\frac{3}{4}$ **b.** $\frac{23}{9}$

SOLUTION

> The UNIT key is used to write a mixed number. The display for the key is ⊔.

Keystrokes	Display
a. 1 UNIT **3** / **4** ►D =	**1.75**
b. 23 / **9** ►D =	**2.555555556**

PRACTICE **Write the decimal as a fraction or mixed number.**

1. 0.375 **2.** 1.825 **3.** 2.56 **4.** 0.9375

Write the fraction or mixed number as a decimal.

5. $15\frac{5}{6}$ **6.** $11\frac{7}{11}$ **7.** $\frac{20}{3}$ **8.** $\frac{123}{200}$

Lessons 4.4–4.7

1. PIZZA PARTY At a pizza party, all the pizzas are the same size, but they are cut into different numbers of equal slices, as shown.

Type of pizza	Number of slices
Pepperoni	8
Veggie	16
Pineapple	12
Cheese	4

Paul eats 5 slices of pepperoni pizza. Jared eats 9 slices of veggie pizza. Paige eats 8 slices of pineapple pizza. Trevor eats 3 slices of cheese pizza. Which list shows the people in increasing order according to the amount of a whole pizza each person ate?

A. Paul, Jared, Paige, Trevor

B. Jared, Paul, Paige, Trevor

C. Trevor, Paul, Paige, Jared

D. Paige, Jared, Paul, Trevor

2. FARM ANIMALS The table shows the number of animals on a family farm. What fraction of the farm animals are *not* pigs?

A. $\frac{3}{10}$

B. $\frac{7}{10}$

C. $\frac{3}{7}$

D. $\frac{7}{3}$

Animal	Number
Hens	4
Pigs	12
Sheep	10
Horses	8
Cows	6

3. CONFETTI You cut a strip of paper that is $5\frac{3}{8}$ inches long into $\frac{1}{8}$-inch pieces. How many pieces do you have?

A. 15

B. 39

C. 40

D. 43

4. BANK ACCOUNTS Every month Toni deposits one third of her salary into her checking account and one fourth of her salary into her savings account. Which statement is best supported by this information?

A. Toni deposits more of her salary into checking than savings.

B. Toni deposits more of her salary into savings than checking.

C. Toni deposits equal amounts of her salary into checking and savings.

D. There is not enough information to compare the amounts she deposits.

5. OPEN-ENDED A middle school was choosing a new mascot. Students voted for Wildcats, Cougars, or Lions. Each student voted once. The voting results are shown below.

Class	Wildcats	Cougars	Lions
A	5	10	10
B	8	12	4
C	10	12	6

- Which class had the greatest fraction of Wildcats votes? of Cougars votes? of Lions votes?
- A fourth class, Class D, voted and had a result of 0.32 of the class voting for Cougars. What is the order, from least to greatest, of the fraction of Cougars votes in the four classes?
- Suppose Class B had four students who did not vote. How would this affect the fraction of votes for each mascot? *Explain* your reasoning.

REVIEW KEY VOCABULARY

- prime number, *p. 165*
- composite number, *p. 165*
- prime factorization, *p. 166*
- factor tree, *p. 166*
- common factor, *p. 170*
- greatest common factor (GCF), *p. 170*
- relatively prime, *p. 171*
- fraction, *p. 176*

- numerator, *p. 176*
- denominator, *p. 176*
- equivalent fractions, *p. 176*
- simplest form, *p. 177*
- multiple, *p. 182*
- common multiple, *p. 182*
- least common multiple (LCM), *p. 182*

- least common denominator, *p. 189*
- mixed number, *p. 194*
- proper fraction, *p. 194*
- improper fraction, *p. 194*
- terminating decimal, *p. 199*
- repeating decimal, *p. 199*

VOCABULARY EXERCISES

1. The number 71 is a(n) __?__ because its only factors are 1 and itself.

2. The fraction $\frac{13}{8}$ is a(n) __?__ .

3. The __?__ of 2, 4, and 7 is 28.

4. The fractions $\frac{3}{10}$ and $\frac{4}{5}$ have a(n) __?__ of 10.

5. The __?__ of 2, 4, and 8 is 2.

REVIEW EXAMPLES AND EXERCISES

4.1 Prime Factorization
pp. 165–169

EXAMPLE

List the factors of the number. Tell whether it is *prime* or *composite*.

a. 36
The factors of 36 are 1, 2, 3, 4, 6, 9, 12, 18, and 36. It is composite.

b. 17
The only factors of 17 are 1 and 17. It is prime.

EXERCISES

Write all the factors of the number. Then tell whether the number is *prime* or *composite*.

SEE EXAMPLES 1, 2, AND 3 on pp. 165–166 for Exs. 6–14

6. 27	7. 68	8. 43	9. 72
10. 60	11. 91	12. 64	13. 31

14. Use a factor tree to write the prime factorization of 726.

4.2 Greatest Common Factor

EXAMPLE

Find the greatest common factor of 72 and 84.

Factors of 72: **1, 2, 3, 4, 6,** 8, 9, **12,** 18, 24, 36, 72

Factors of 84: **1, 2, 3, 4, 6,** 7, **12,** 14, 21, 28, 42, 84

▶ **Answer** The common factors are 1, 2, 3, 4, 6, and 12. The GCF is 12.

EXERCISES

Find the GCF using a list. Then tell whether the numbers are relatively prime.

SEE EXAMPLES 1, 2, AND 3
on pp. 170–171
for Exs. 15–22

15. 12, 18   **16.** 40, 51   **17.** 72, 136   **18.** 144, 192

Find the GCF using prime factorization.

19. 17, 85   **20.** 48, 60   **21.** 38, 45   **22.** 84, 360

4.3 Equivalent Fractions

EXAMPLE

Write two fractions that are equivalent to $\frac{12}{14}$.

Multiply or divide the numerator and denominator by the same nonzero number.

$$\frac{12}{14} = \frac{12 \times 4}{14 \times 4} = \frac{48}{56}$$ **Multiply numerator and denominator by 4.**

$$\frac{12}{14} = \frac{12 \div 2}{14 \div 2} = \frac{6}{7}$$ **Divide numerator and denominator by 2, a common factor of 12 and 14.**

EXERCISES

Write two fractions that are equivalent to the given fraction. If it is not in simplest form, write its simplest form as one of your fractions.

SEE EXAMPLES 2, 3, AND 4
on pp. 176–177
for Exs. 23–27

23. $\frac{3}{5}$ **24.** $\frac{6}{9}$ **25.** $\frac{4}{8}$ **26.** $\frac{2}{7}$

27. Test Scores On a test you earned 46 out of a possible 50 points. On another test, your friend earned 54 out of a possible 60 points. For each test, write the number of points earned as a fraction of possible points. Are the fractions equivalent? *Explain.*

4.4 Least Common Multiple

EXAMPLE

Use prime factorization to find the LCM of 10 and 18.

$10 = 2 \times 5$
$18 = 2 \times 3 \times 3$

▶ **Answer** The LCM of 10 and 18 is $2 \times 3 \times 3 \times 5$, or 90.

EXERCISES

Find the LCM using a list.

SEE EXAMPLES 2 AND 3
on pp. 182–183
for Exs. 28–35

28. 8, 20   **29.** 14, 21   **30.** 45, 81   **31.** 144, 156

Find the LCM using prime factorization.

32. 5, 35   **33.** 8, 9   **34.** 100, 250   **35.** 55, 70

4.5 Comparing and Ordering Fractions

pp. 189–193

EXAMPLE

Order the fractions $\frac{4}{7}, \frac{5}{8}, \frac{5}{14}, \frac{17}{28}$ from least to greatest.

The LCD is 56. Use the LCD to write equivalent fractions.

$$\frac{4}{7} = \frac{4 \times 8}{7 \times 8} = \frac{32}{56} \qquad \frac{5}{8} = \frac{5 \times 7}{8 \times 7} = \frac{35}{56}$$

$$\frac{5}{14} = \frac{5 \times 4}{14 \times 4} = \frac{20}{56} \qquad \frac{17}{28} = \frac{17 \times 2}{28 \times 2} = \frac{34}{56}$$

Compare the numerators: $\frac{20}{56} < \frac{32}{56} < \frac{34}{56} < \frac{35}{56}$, so $\frac{5}{14} < \frac{4}{7} < \frac{17}{28} < \frac{5}{8}$.

▶ **Answer** From least to greatest, the fractions are $\frac{5}{14}, \frac{4}{7}, \frac{17}{28}$, and $\frac{5}{8}$.

EXERCISES

Order the fractions from least to greatest.

SEE EXAMPLE 2
on p. 190
for Exs. 36–43

36. $\frac{3}{4}, \frac{49}{52}, \frac{25}{26}, \frac{11}{13}$ **37.** $\frac{8}{15}, \frac{1}{2}, \frac{7}{10}, \frac{2}{3}$ **38.** $\frac{5}{21}, \frac{1}{3}, \frac{3}{7}, \frac{2}{9}$ **39.** $\frac{6}{13}, \frac{25}{39}, \frac{5}{6}, \frac{17}{26}$

40. $\frac{2}{3}, \frac{3}{5}, \frac{5}{9}, \frac{7}{12}$ **41.** $\frac{5}{12}, \frac{11}{18}, \frac{4}{7}, \frac{9}{20}$ **42.** $\frac{5}{22}, \frac{1}{12}, \frac{3}{16}, \frac{2}{9}$ **43.** $\frac{9}{10}, \frac{11}{12}, \frac{6}{7}, \frac{7}{8}$

4.6 Mixed Numbers and Improper Fractions

EXAMPLE

Compare $\frac{37}{4}$ and $9\frac{7}{10}$.

STEP 1 Rewrite $9\frac{7}{10}$ as an improper fraction, $\frac{97}{10}$.

Then rewrite $\frac{37}{4}$ and $\frac{97}{10}$ using the LCD, 20.

$$\frac{37}{4} = \frac{37 \times 5}{4 \times 5} = \frac{185}{20} \qquad \frac{97}{10} = \frac{97 \times 2}{10 \times 2} = \frac{194}{20}$$

STEP 2 Compare the fractions: $\frac{185}{20} < \frac{194}{20}$, so $\frac{37}{4} < 9\frac{7}{10}$.

EXERCISES

SEE EXAMPLES
3 AND 4
on pp. 195–196
for Exs. 44–47

Copy and complete the statement using <, >, or =.

44. $\frac{9}{2} \underset{\text{?}}{} \frac{23}{5}$

45. $1\frac{4}{11} \underset{\text{?}}{} 1\frac{2}{9}$

46. $4\frac{3}{8} \underset{\text{?}}{} 4\frac{5}{14}$

47. $12\frac{3}{16} \underset{\text{?}}{} \frac{195}{16}$

4.7 Fractions and Decimals

EXAMPLE

a. Write $\frac{4}{5}$ as a decimal.

$$\begin{array}{r} 0.8 \\ 5\overline{)4.0} \\ \underline{4\,0} \\ 0 \end{array}$$

b. Write 0.825 as a fraction in simplest form.

$$0.825 = \frac{825}{1000} = \frac{33 \cdot \overset{1}{\cancel{25}}}{40 \cdot \underset{1}{\cancel{25}}} = \frac{33}{40}$$

EXERCISES

Write the fraction or mixed number as a decimal.

SEE EXAMPLES
1, 2, AND 3
on pp. 199–200
for Exs. 48–63

48. $\frac{11}{6}$

49. $5\frac{7}{8}$

50. $\frac{12}{25}$

51. $4\frac{7}{9}$

52. $\frac{3}{20}$

53. $\frac{17}{12}$

54. $2\frac{1}{6}$

55. $11\frac{3}{5}$

Write the decimal as a fraction or mixed number.

56. 0.75

57. 0.06

58. 5.125

59. 3.3125

60. 0.98

61. 2.25

62. 9.8

63. 0.45

210   Chapter 4   Number Patterns and Fractions

**Write all the factors of the number. Then tell whether the number is
prime or *composite*.**

1. 51   **2.** 63   **3.** 49   **4.** 67

Use a factor tree to write the prime factorization of the number.

5. 96   **6.** 128   **7.** 168   **8.** 260

**Find the GCF and the LCM of the numbers. Then tell whether the
numbers are relatively prime.**

9. 9, 16   **10.** 12, 15   **11.** 10, 25   **12.** 7, 13

13. 42, 66   **14.** 64, 120   **15.** 49, 84   **16.** 72, 144, 192

Write the fraction in simplest form.

17. $\frac{15}{80}$ **18.** $\frac{13}{78}$ **19.** $\frac{54}{81}$ **20.** $\frac{76}{135}$

Copy and complete the statement using <, >, or =.

21. $\frac{6}{7} \; ? \; \frac{9}{11}$ **22.** $\frac{5}{9} \; ? \; \frac{60}{108}$ **23.** $3\frac{2}{7} \; ? \; \frac{16}{5}$ **24.** $5\frac{5}{6} \; ? \; \frac{59}{10}$

Order the numbers from least to greatest.

25. $\frac{7}{4}, \frac{23}{12}, 1\frac{5}{6}, \frac{5}{3}$ **26.** $\frac{5}{6}, \frac{7}{9}, \frac{23}{27}, \frac{13}{18}$ **27.** $\frac{1}{2}, \frac{17}{42}, \frac{16}{21}, \frac{5}{7}$ **28.** $\frac{8}{5}, 1\frac{8}{15}, \frac{8}{3}, \frac{22}{15}$

Write the fraction or mixed number as a decimal.

29. $\frac{11}{5}$ **30.** $\frac{29}{11}$ **31.** $3\frac{14}{15}$ **32.** $5\frac{9}{16}$

Write the decimal as a fraction or mixed number.

33. 2.68   **34.** 0.56   **35.** 0.286   **36.** 3.048

37. DISTANCES Use the table at the
right to order the fractions from
least to greatest. Who rode the
farthest?

Rider	Suzie	Tom	Nikki	Lisa
Distance (miles)	$\frac{7}{9}$	$\frac{5}{6}$	$\frac{2}{3}$	$\frac{1}{2}$

38. FRIENDSHIP BRACELETS You have 280 green beads, 200 yellow beads,
and 240 blue beads to make friendship bracelets. If you use all the
beads, what is the greatest number of identical bracelets that you can
make? How many beads of each color would be on each bracelet?

REVIEWING FRACTION PROBLEMS

You may have to compare or rewrite fractions or mixed numbers when solving application problems. Read each application problem carefully. Then choose the appropriate strategy and solve.

EXAMPLE

Sports Terry is the coach of a cross country team. Each runner's mile time in minutes is recorded in the table. Which runners' times are slower than the median time?

Runner	Kyle	Penelope	Jennifer	Ted	Henry
Time (min)	$5\frac{3}{4}$	$6\frac{5}{6}$	$6\frac{1}{3}$	$5\frac{11}{12}$	$6\frac{1}{2}$

Solution

STEP 1 **Use** the LCD, 12, to write the mixed numbers as improper fractions.

Kyle: $5\frac{3}{4} = \frac{23}{4} = \frac{69}{12}$

Jennifer: $6\frac{1}{3} = \frac{19}{3} = \frac{76}{12}$

Henry: $6\frac{1}{2} = \frac{13}{2} = \frac{78}{12}$

Penelope: $6\frac{5}{6} = \frac{41}{6} = \frac{82}{12}$

Ted: $5\frac{11}{12} = \frac{71}{12}$

STEP 2 **Compare** the numerators: $\frac{69}{12} < \frac{71}{12} < \frac{76}{12} < \frac{78}{12} < \frac{82}{12}$. So, the numbers from least to greatest are $5\frac{3}{4}$, $5\frac{11}{12}$, $6\frac{1}{3}$, $6\frac{1}{2}$, and $6\frac{5}{6}$.

STEP 3 **Identify** the slower times. The times slower than the median time are the numbers *greater* than the median. The median is $6\frac{1}{3}$ minutes, so the slower times are $6\frac{1}{2}$ minutes and $6\frac{5}{6}$ minutes.

▶ **Answer** Henry's and Penelope's times are slower than the median time.

FRACTION PROBLEMS

Below are examples of fraction and mixed number problems in multiple choice format. Try solving the problems before looking at the solutions. (Cover the solutions with a piece of paper.) Then check your solutions against the ones given.

1. Lisa made 32 of 48 free throws last season and used the fraction $\frac{32}{48}$ to express her successes. Which method will write the fraction in simplest form?

   A. Divide the numerator and denominator by 4.

   B. Divide the numerator and denominator by 8.

   C. Divide the numerator and denominator by 16.

   D. Divide the numerator and denominator by 96.

Solution

To write a fraction in simplest form, divide its numerator and denominator by their GCF.

Find the GCF of 32 and 48.

$$32 = \boxed{2} \times \boxed{2} \times \boxed{2} \times \boxed{2} \times 2$$
$$48 = \boxed{2} \times \boxed{2} \times \boxed{2} \times \boxed{2} \times 3$$

The GCF of 32 and 48 is $2^4 = 16$.

So, divide the numerator and denominator by 16 to write the fraction in simplest form. The correct answer is C.

2. One basketball player can jump $\frac{23}{7}$ feet and another can jump $3\frac{1}{4}$ feet.

   Look at the problem solving steps below. Arrange the steps in the correct order to determine which basketball player can jump higher.

   Step P: Write the mixed number as an improper fraction.

   Step Q: Use the LCD to write equivalent fractions.

   Step R: Compare numerators.

   Step S: Find the LCD of the fractions.

   Which list shows the steps in the correct order?

   A. P, S, Q, R

   B. S, P, Q, R

   C. P, S, R, Q

   D. S, P, R, Q

Solution

In order to compare $\frac{23}{7}$ and $3\frac{1}{4}$, you need to write the numbers in the same form. So, the first step is P: write the mixed number as an improper fraction.

You need to be able to compare the fractions with a common denominator, so the next two steps are S then Q: find the LCD of the fractions and then use it to write equivalent fractions.

Finally, you can compare the numerators of the fractions to determine which is larger.

The correct order of steps is P, S, Q, and R, so the correct answer is A.

TEST PREPARATION

TEST PREPARATION

1. The table below shows the hat sizes of 4 people. Which list orders the names from those with the smallest size to those with the largest size?

Name	Hat Size
Pete	$7\frac{3}{8}$
André	7.25
Maria	$6\frac{7}{8}$
Anna	$7\frac{1}{8}$

   A. Maria, Anna, André, Pete
   B. Maria, André, Anna, Pete
   C. Maria, Pete, André, Anna
   D. Anna, Maria, André, Pete

2. A checkerboard is divided into 64 identical squares. Each of 2 players begins with 12 checkers. What portion of the checkerboard is covered with checkers at the start of the game?

   A. 0.1875
   B. 0.375
   C. 0.625
   D. 0.8125

3. Thirty-six coins out of a collection of 90 coins are state quarters. Which expression gives the simplest form of $\frac{36}{90}$?

   A. $\frac{36 \div 2}{90 \div 2}$
   B. $\frac{36 \div 3}{90 \div 3}$
   C. $\frac{36 \div 6}{90 \div 6}$
   D. $\frac{36 \div 18}{90 \div 18}$

4. Ty reached first base $\frac{3}{8}$ of the time while playing baseball. Which sentence explains the meaning of the fraction?

   A. Ty reached first base 3 times out of every 8 attempts.
   B. Ty reached first base 3 times for every 8 times he did not reach first base.
   C. Ty reached first base 8 times for every 3 attempts.
   D. Ty reached first base 8 times for every 3 times he did not reach first base.

5. Africa covers about $\frac{1}{5}$ of Earth's total land area, Asia covers about 0.3, North America covers about $\frac{4}{25}$, and South America covers about 0.12 of Earth's total land area. Which of these areas is the largest?

   A. Africa
   B. Asia
   C. North America
   D. South America

6. The lengths, in inches, of 4 plants are $\frac{31}{8}$, $3\frac{15}{16}$, $\frac{7}{2}$, and 4. Which list orders the lengths from least to greatest?

   A. $\frac{7}{2}, 3\frac{15}{16}, \frac{31}{8}, 4$
   B. $\frac{7}{2}, \frac{31}{8}, 3\frac{15}{16}, 4$
   C. $\frac{31}{8}, \frac{7}{2}, 3\frac{15}{16}, 4$
   D. $\frac{31}{8}, 3\frac{15}{16}, \frac{7}{2}, 4$

7. The table below shows the side length *s*, in feet, for several squares. Without calculating, which square has the largest perimeter?

Square	A	B	C	D
s	$12\frac{5}{12}$	12.4	$\frac{38}{3}$	$12\frac{1}{3}$

   A. Square A

   B. Square B

   C. Square C

   D. Square D

8. Sue's scores on two math quizzes were $\frac{7}{15}$ and $\frac{12}{20}$. Which method CANNOT be used to determine which score is greater, $\frac{7}{15}$ or $\frac{12}{20}$?

   A. Compare each fraction to $\frac{1}{2}$.

   B. Use the LCD to write equivalent fractions, and then compare.

   C. Write the fractions as decimals, and then compare.

   D. Write the fractions in simplest form and compare numerators.

9. What is the next number in the sequence below?

$$\frac{5}{4}, \frac{7}{4}, \frac{9}{4}, \frac{11}{4}, \ldots$$

   A. $\frac{13}{5}$

   B. 3

   C. $\frac{13}{4}$

   D. $\frac{15}{4}$

10. What number is NOT equivalent to $3\frac{3}{5}$?

    A. 3.6

    B. $\frac{18}{5}$

    C. $\frac{35}{10}$

    D. $3\frac{6}{10}$

11. The lengths, in inches, of six pointer fingers are 4.0, $3\frac{1}{2}$, 2.75, $3\frac{2}{3}$, $\frac{15}{4}$, and 3.8. What is the range of the lengths?

    A. $\frac{15}{4}$

    B. $3\frac{2}{3}$

    C. $\frac{5}{4}$

    D. 1.2

12. **OPEN-ENDED** Complete the table using the fractions to show the batting record of three players.

Player	Hits	At-bats	Hits / At-bats
Kendra	48	132	?
Charvone	62	186	?
Ashley	51	160	?

   Part A Compare the fractions.

   Part B Write each fraction as a decimal, and compare the decimals.

   Part C *Compare* the two methods.

5 Fraction Operations

Before

In previous chapters you've . . .

- Found the GCF and LCM of two or more numbers
- Written equivalent fractions

Now

New Jersey Standards

4.1.B.1.a	5.1	Adding fractions
4.1.B.1.a	5.2	Adding mixed numbers
4.1.B.1.a	5.3	Multiplying fractions
4.1.B.1.a	5.4	Dividing fractions
4.2.D.2	5.5	Customary units
4.2.D.1	5.6	Customary conversions

Why?

So you can solve real-world problems about . . .

- music, p. 224
- baseball, p. 226
- stained glass windows, p. 235
- pyramids, p. 254

 **Math**

at classzone.com

- Fractions with Different Denominators, p. 227
- Modeling Division, p. 237
- Penalty Shot, p. 239

Get-Ready Games

Review Prerequisite Skills by playing *Acrobat Triangle* and *Trapeze Math.*

Skill Focus: Finding the least common multiple

- The number on each acrobat above the bottom row is the least common multiple of the numbers on the two acrobats supporting the acrobat.

- Copy the number triangle and fill in the missing numbers.

Trapeze Math

Skill Focus: Writing equivalent fractions

• The numbers on the four trapeze artists shown above form a pair of equivalent fractions.

• Arrange the eight trapeze artists standing on the ground in two teams of four, so that each team forms two equivalent fractions.

Stop and Think

1. **WRITING** Is the number at the top of the *Acrobat Triangle* a multiple of all the numbers below it? Is it the least common multiple? Explain your reasoning.

2. **CRITICAL THINKING** Take one of your teams from *Trapeze Math* and see if you can rearrange the numbers to form other equivalent fractions. How many can you form?

5 *Getting Ready*

Review Prerequisite Skills

REVIEW WORDS

- **greatest common factor (GCF),** *p. 170*
- **equivalent fractions,** *p. 176*
- **simplest form,** *p. 177*
- **least common denominator (LCD),** *p. 189*
- **mixed number,** *p. 194*
- **improper fraction,** *p. 194*

VOCABULARY CHECK

Copy and complete using a review word from the list at the left.

1. Fractions that represent the same part-to-whole relationship are called ___?___ .

2. A(n) ___?___ is a number that has a whole number part and a fraction part.

3. The ___?___ of two or more nonzero whole numbers is the greatest whole number that is a factor of each number.

SKILL CHECK

Write the fractions in simplest form. Tell whether they are equivalent. *(p. 176)*

4. $\frac{14}{28}, \frac{12}{21}$

5. $\frac{8}{12}, \frac{10}{15}$

6. $\frac{15}{24}, \frac{25}{40}$

7. $\frac{24}{27}, \frac{36}{42}$

8. $\frac{9}{36}, \frac{6}{24}$

9. $\frac{15}{18}, \frac{18}{21}$

10. $\frac{10}{15}, \frac{30}{48}$

11. $\frac{16}{32}, \frac{10}{20}$

Write an improper fraction and a mixed number to describe the model. *(p. 194)*

12.

13.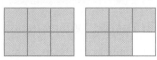

@HomeTutor Prerequisite skills practice at classzone.com

Notetaking Skills Using Your Notes

In each chapter you will learn a new notetaking skill. In Chapter 5 you will apply the strategy of using your notes to Example 3 on p. 233.

Take notes about examples that your teacher discusses. If you don't understand something, write a question in your notebook. Discuss questions with a friend or your teacher and write down what you learn.

Example: Write the mixed number $6\frac{2}{5}$ as an improper fraction.

$$6\frac{2}{5} = \frac{6 \cdot 5 + 2}{5}$$

Question: Why do you multiply 6 and 5, then add 2?

$$= \frac{32}{5}$$

Answer: To find the number of fifths in 6 wholes, multiply 6 by 5. Think of 6 as $\frac{30}{5}$ and combine that with $\frac{2}{5}$ to get $\frac{32}{5}$.

218

5.1 Adding and Subtracting Fractions

 4.1.B.1.a Use and explain procedures for performing calculations with integers and all number types named above with: Pencil-and-paper

Before You added and subtracted whole numbers and decimals.

Now You'll add and subtract fractions.

Why? So you can count musical beats, as in Exs. 62–65.

KEY VOCABULARY

- least common denominator, *p. 189*

ACTIVITY

You can use models to add and subtract fractions.

$$\frac{1}{3} \quad + \quad \frac{1}{3} \quad = \quad \frac{2}{3}$$

$$\frac{3}{5} \quad - \quad \frac{1}{5} \quad = \quad \frac{2}{5}$$

Use a model to find the sum or difference.

1. $\frac{2}{3} + \frac{1}{3}$ **2.** $\frac{1}{5} + \frac{1}{5}$ **3.** $\frac{7}{9} - \frac{3}{9}$ **4.** $\frac{3}{4} - \frac{1}{4}$

The activity suggests the following rules about adding and subtracting fractions with common denominators.

KEY CONCEPT   *For Your Notebook*

Fractions with Common Denominators

Words To add or subtract two fractions with a common denominator, write the sum or difference of the numerators over the denominator.

Numbers $\frac{1}{5} + \frac{2}{5} = \frac{3}{5}$ **Algebra** $\frac{a}{c} + \frac{b}{c} = \frac{a+b}{c}$ $(c \neq 0)$

$\frac{4}{7} - \frac{1}{7} = \frac{3}{7}$ $\frac{a}{c} - \frac{b}{c} = \frac{a-b}{c}$ $(c \neq 0)$

EXAMPLE 1   Adding Fractions

AVOID ERRORS
When adding fractions, you do not add the denominators.

$$\frac{2}{9} + \frac{5}{9} = \frac{2+5}{9}$$ **Add numerators.**

$$= \frac{7}{9}$$ **Simplify numerator.**

EXAMPLE 2 Subtracting Fractions

$$\frac{7}{8} - \frac{3}{8} = \frac{7-3}{8}$$ Subtract numerators.

$$= \frac{4}{8}$$ Simplify numerator.

$$= \frac{1}{2}$$ Simplify fraction.

SIMPLIFY FRACTIONS
Need help with simplifying fractions? See p. 176.

✓ **GUIDED PRACTICE** | **for Examples 1 and 2**

Add or subtract. Simplify if possible.

1. $\frac{3}{8} + \frac{1}{8}$ **2.** $\frac{3}{5} + \frac{4}{5}$ **3.** $\frac{4}{5} + \frac{2}{5}$ **4.** $\frac{11}{12} + \frac{5}{12}$

5. $\frac{5}{7} - \frac{2}{7}$ **6.** $\frac{7}{9} - \frac{1}{9}$ **7.** $\frac{11}{14} - \frac{4}{14}$ **8.** $\frac{23}{30} - \frac{13}{30}$

Different Denominators When adding or subtracting fractions with different denominators, rewrite the fractions so they have the same denominator. Then add or subtract the numerators as before.

KEY CONCEPT   *For Your Notebook*

Fractions with Different Denominators

1. Rewrite the fractions using the LCD.

2. Add or subtract the numerators.

3. Write the result over the LCD.

4. Simplify if possible.

EXAMPLE 3 Adding Fractions

$$\frac{3}{4} + \frac{2}{3} = \frac{9}{12} + \frac{8}{12}$$ Rewrite fractions using the LCD of $\frac{3}{4}$ and $\frac{2}{3}$.

$$= \frac{9+8}{12}$$ Add numerators.

$$= \frac{17}{12}$$ Simplify.

$$= 1\frac{5}{12}$$ Write as a mixed number.

MIXED NUMBERS
Need help with writing improper fractions as mixed numbers? See p. 194.

Check The addends $\frac{3}{4}$ and $\frac{2}{3}$ are both greater than $\frac{1}{2}$ and less than 1. The sum must be greater than 1 but less than 2. The answer is reasonable. ✓

 **EXAMPLE 4** **Standardized Test Practice**

Construction A piece of wood that is $\frac{5}{8}$ inch thick is sanded down to be $\frac{7}{16}$ inch thick. How much thinner is the wood now?

 A $\frac{1}{8}$ in. **B** $\frac{3}{16}$ in. **C** $\frac{1}{4}$ in. **D** $1\frac{1}{16}$ in.

ELIMINATE CHOICES
The piece of wood is $\frac{5}{8}$ inch thick. It is going to be made thinner, so the answer should be less than $\frac{5}{8}$. $1\frac{1}{16} > \frac{5}{8}$. Choice D can be eliminated.

SOLUTION

To find how much thinner the wood is, subtract $\frac{7}{16}$ from $\frac{5}{8}$.

$$\frac{5}{8} - \frac{7}{16} = \frac{10}{16} - \frac{7}{16}$$ Rewrite $\frac{5}{8}$ using the LCD of $\frac{5}{8}$ and $\frac{7}{16}$.

$$= \frac{3}{16}$$ Subtract numerators.

▶ **Answer** The wood is now $\frac{3}{16}$ inch thinner.

The correct answer is B. **A** **B** **C** **D**

at classzone.com

 GUIDED PRACTICE for Examples 3 and 4

Add or subtract. Simplify if possible.

9. $\frac{3}{4} + \frac{1}{12}$ **10.** $\frac{3}{5} + \frac{1}{2}$ **11.** $\frac{7}{8} - \frac{2}{3}$ **12.** $\frac{5}{6} - \frac{1}{10}$

13. What If? Suppose the $\frac{3}{4}$-inch thick wood in Example 4 is sanded down to be $\frac{19}{32}$ inch thick. How much thinner is the wood now?

5.1 **EXERCISES**

HOMEWORK KEY

★ = **STANDARDIZED TEST PRACTICE**
Exs. 31, 54, 56, 57, 60, and 80

○ = **HINTS AND HOMEWORK HELP**
for Exs. 3, 9, 15, 27, 53 at classzone.com

SKILL PRACTICE

1. VOCABULARY Copy and complete: To add fractions with different denominators, first rewrite the fractions using the __?__.

COMMON DENOMINATORS Evaluate the expression. Simplify if possible.

SEE EXAMPLES 1 AND 2
on pp. 219–220
for Exs. 2–13

2. $\frac{1}{10} + \frac{8}{10}$ **3.** $\frac{4}{7} + \frac{5}{7}$ **4.** $\frac{5}{7} + \frac{1}{7}$ **5.** $\frac{9}{20} + \frac{7}{20}$

6. $\frac{3}{5} - \frac{1}{5}$ **7.** $\frac{7}{12} - \frac{5}{12}$ **8.** $\frac{8}{9} - \frac{2}{9}$ **9.** $\frac{7}{9} - \frac{4}{9}$

10. $\frac{2}{20} + \frac{7}{20} + \frac{11}{20}$ **11.** $\frac{11}{12} - \frac{5}{12} + \frac{1}{12}$ **12.** $\frac{4}{9} + \frac{5}{9} - \frac{2}{9}$ **13.** $\frac{13}{15} - \frac{2}{15} - \frac{6}{15}$

SEE EXAMPLES 3 AND 4 on pp. 220–221 for Exs. 14–30

USING LEAST COMMON DENOMINATORS Evaluate the expression. Simplify if possible.

14. $\dfrac{3}{5} + \dfrac{7}{10}$

15. $\dfrac{5}{8} + \dfrac{3}{4}$

16. $\dfrac{2}{3} + \dfrac{1}{4}$

17. $\dfrac{1}{3} + \dfrac{5}{7}$

18. $\dfrac{1}{6} + \dfrac{3}{4}$

19. $\dfrac{1}{9} + \dfrac{5}{6}$

20. $\dfrac{11}{12} - \dfrac{3}{4}$

21. $\dfrac{4}{5} - \dfrac{3}{10}$

22. $\dfrac{3}{8} - \dfrac{1}{3}$

23. $\dfrac{4}{5} - \dfrac{3}{8}$

24. $\dfrac{3}{4} - \dfrac{1}{6}$

25. $\dfrac{7}{12} - \dfrac{5}{18}$

26. $\dfrac{3}{8} + \dfrac{5}{16} + \dfrac{7}{8}$

27. $\dfrac{5}{6} - \dfrac{7}{12} + \dfrac{2}{3}$

28. $\dfrac{2}{3} + \dfrac{3}{4} - \dfrac{2}{5}$

29. $\dfrac{5}{6} - \dfrac{7}{30} - \dfrac{2}{5}$

30. ERROR ANALYSIS Describe and correct the error made in finding the sum.

$$\dfrac{3}{4} + \dfrac{2}{3} = \dfrac{3 + 2}{4 + 3} = \dfrac{5}{7} \quad \times$$

31. ★ **MULTIPLE CHOICE** The sum of $\dfrac{1}{4}$ and which number is greater than $\dfrac{1}{2}$?

(A) $\dfrac{1}{8}$

(B) $\dfrac{1}{6}$

(C) $\dfrac{1}{4}$

(D) $\dfrac{1}{3}$

XY ALGEBRA Use mental math to solve the equation.

32. $\dfrac{5}{7} = \dfrac{3}{7} + x$

33. $x + \dfrac{4}{8} = \dfrac{5}{8}$

34. $\dfrac{3}{11} - x = \dfrac{1}{11}$

35. $\dfrac{6}{14} + x = \dfrac{11}{14}$

36. $x - \dfrac{7}{21} = \dfrac{9}{21}$

37. $\dfrac{13}{45} = \dfrac{25}{45} - x$

EVALUATING EXPRESSIONS Evaluate the expression. Write your answer as a fraction or mixed number.

38. $\dfrac{7}{10} - 0.6$

39. $\dfrac{5}{6} + 0.25$

40. $\dfrac{4}{15} + 0.9$

41. $0.9 - \dfrac{3}{10} - \dfrac{1}{5}$

42. $\dfrac{2}{9} + 0.7 + \dfrac{8}{27}$

43. $\dfrac{11}{12} + 0.35 - \dfrac{7}{8}$

CHOOSE A METHOD Copy and complete the statement using <, >, or =. Tell whether you used *mental math*, *estimation*, or *pencil and paper*.

44. $\dfrac{9}{10} - \dfrac{1}{10} \underset{?}{\quad} \dfrac{4}{5}$

45. $\dfrac{5}{12} + \dfrac{1}{6} \underset{?}{\quad} \dfrac{13}{24}$

46. $\dfrac{3}{4} + \dfrac{1}{20} \underset{?}{\quad} \dfrac{9}{10}$

47. $\dfrac{2}{3} - \dfrac{5}{9} \underset{?}{\quad} \dfrac{3}{18}$

48. $\dfrac{3}{8} + \dfrac{1}{2} \underset{?}{\quad} \dfrac{21}{24}$

49. $\dfrac{15}{21} - \dfrac{3}{7} \underset{?}{\quad} \dfrac{5}{14}$

50. LOOK FOR A PATTERN *Describe* the pattern: $\dfrac{1}{16}, \dfrac{1}{8}, \dfrac{3}{16}, \dfrac{1}{4}, \ldots$. Then write the next three fractions.

51. REASONING When you find $\dfrac{1}{6} + \dfrac{3}{8}$, what advantage does using the LCD of the two fractions have over using any other common denominator?

52. CHALLENGE Find the sum $\dfrac{1}{1 \times 2} + \dfrac{1}{2 \times 3} + \dfrac{1}{3 \times 4} + \ldots + \dfrac{1}{15 \times 16}$ by looking for a pattern in the sum of the first two fractions, the first three fractions, and so on. *Describe* the pattern.

★ = **STANDARDIZED TEST PRACTICE**   ◯ = **HINTS AND HOMEWORK HELP** *at classzone.com*

SEE EXAMPLE 3
on p. 220
for Ex. 53

53. **ALLIGATORS** A recently hatched alligator is $\frac{3}{4}$ foot long and grows $\frac{5}{12}$ foot over the next 5 months. How long is the alligator at 5 months old?

54. ★ **WRITING** *Describe* how $\frac{1}{4} + \frac{1}{3}$ is related to $\frac{3}{12} + \frac{4}{12}$.

SEE EXAMPLE 4
on p. 221
for Exs. 55–57

55. **RUNNING** Sara runs first in a $\frac{1}{2}$-mile relay running event. She runs $\frac{1}{8}$ mile. What is the total distance that her teammates have left to run?

56. ★ **SHORT RESPONSE** From the time you wake up, you need $\frac{3}{4}$ hour to get ready for school and $\frac{5}{12}$ hour to travel from home to school. Find the time, in fractions of an hour, it takes for you to get to school from the time you wake up. If you wake up at 6:30 A.M., can you get to school by 7:30 A.M.? *Explain* your reasoning.

57. ★ **MULTIPLE CHOICE** Which expression can you use to find how many pounds greater $\frac{9}{10}$ pound of bananas is than $\frac{4}{5}$ pound of bananas?

Ⓐ $\frac{9}{10} - \frac{4}{5}$ Ⓑ $\frac{4}{5} - \frac{9}{10}$ Ⓒ $\frac{4}{5} \times \frac{9}{10}$ Ⓓ $\frac{9}{10} + \frac{4}{5}$

58. **MULTI-STEP PROBLEM** Chris, Ted, and Leroy are practicing for a swimming event. They swim a total of $\frac{7}{8}$ mile. How far does Leroy swim? How much farther does Leroy swim than either Chris or Ted? *Explain* your reasoning.

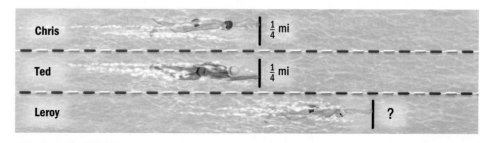

59. ◆ **MULTIPLE REPRESENTATIONS** A recipe for trail mix calls for $\frac{3}{4}$ cup of dried mixed fruit, $\frac{1}{2}$ cup of mixed nuts, and $\frac{1}{3}$ cup of granola. How many cups of trail mix does this recipe make?

  a. **Make a Model** Draw a model to answer the question.

  b. **Write an Expression** Write and evaluate a numerical expression to answer the question. Estimate to check your answer.

60. ★ **OPEN-ENDED MATH** Find three fractions greater than 0 and less than 1 whose sum is *greater than* 1. Find three fractions greater than 0 and less than 1 whose sum is *less than* 1.

61. **POSTCARD COLLECTION** In one postcard collection, $\frac{1}{2}$ are scenic, $\frac{1}{3}$ are comic, and the rest are advertising cards. What fraction of the cards have ads? If the collection contains 744 cards, how many of them have ads?

Music In music, a $\frac{4}{4}$ time signature means that there are 4 beats per measure and that a quarter note (♩) gets 1 beat. The beats for seven musical notes with this time signature are in the table.

Note	𝅝	𝅗𝅥	♩	♪.	♪	♪.	♪
Beats	4	2	1	$\frac{3}{4}$	$\frac{1}{2}$	$\frac{3}{8}$	$\frac{1}{4}$

62. Reading Music Does this measure contain 4 beats? *Explain.*

63. Reading Music Does this measure contain 4 beats? *Explain.*

64. Open-Ended Give three other measures with exactly 4 notes that have 4 beats.

65. Writing The note is called a sixteenth note. *Explain* why using the information given above.

66. CHALLENGE Consider the difference $\frac{1}{2} - \frac{1}{4} - \frac{1}{8} - \frac{1}{16} - \dots$. Find the difference of the first 4 terms shown. Find the difference of the first 6 terms. If the pattern continues, will the difference ever reach 0? *Explain* your reasoning.

67. CHALLENGE A *unit fraction* is of the form $\frac{1}{a}$ where $a \neq 0$. Rewrite $\frac{7}{10}$ and $\frac{4}{15}$ as a sum of unit fractions, where $a \leq 10$ and $a \leq 15$.

NJ NEW JERSEY MIXED REVIEW

TEST PRACTICE at classzone.com

68. Kayla shaded part of a grid as shown. What portion of the figure is shaded?

Ⓐ 0.36 Ⓑ 0.50

Ⓒ 0.64 Ⓓ 0.90

69. Which number belongs to the set?

$$\frac{9}{4}, \frac{36}{16}, \frac{27}{12}, \frac{54}{24}$$

Ⓐ $\frac{40}{25}$ Ⓑ $\frac{65}{32}$ Ⓒ $\frac{60}{28}$ Ⓓ $\frac{18}{8}$

INVESTIGATION
Use before Lesson 5.2

GOAL
Use area models to add mixed numbers.

MATERIALS
• paper
• pencil

5.2 Modeling Addition of Mixed Numbers

You can use area models to add mixed numbers.

EXPLORE Find the sum of $2\frac{3}{5}$ and $1\frac{4}{5}$.

STEP 1 **Draw** area models for $2\frac{3}{5}$ and $1\frac{4}{5}$.

   +

STEP 2 **Combine** the two models. Group the whole parts together, and group the fractional parts together.

$$2\frac{3}{5} + 1\frac{4}{5} = 3\frac{7}{5}$$

STEP 3 **Simplify.** Because $\frac{5}{5}$ is equivalent to 1,

$$3\frac{7}{5} = 3 + \frac{5}{5} + \frac{2}{5} = 4\frac{2}{5}.$$

PRACTICE Draw area models to find the sum. Simplify if possible.

1. $5\frac{1}{5} + 2\frac{3}{5}$

2. $3\frac{2}{3} + 1\frac{2}{3}$

3. $1\frac{2}{5} + 3\frac{4}{5}$

4. $4\frac{1}{4} + 2\frac{1}{4}$

DRAW CONCLUSIONS

5. **WRITING** *Explain* how to subtract $1\frac{1}{4}$ from $4\frac{3}{4}$ using an area model.

6. **REASONING** Is it possible for the sum of two mixed numbers to be a whole number? *Explain* your reasoning and give an example.

5.2 Adding and Subtracting Mixed Numbers

 4.1.B.1.a
Use and explain procedures for performing calculations with integers
and all number types named above with: Pencil-and-paper

Before	You added and subtracted fractions.
Now	You'll add and subtract mixed numbers.
Why?	So you can find totals, as with innings pitched in Example 1.

KEY VOCABULARY
- **least common denominator,** *p. 189*
- **mixed number, improper fraction,** *p. 194*

World Series In 2004, the Boston Red Sox won the World Series for the first time in 86 years. In the American League Championship Series leading up to the 2004 World Series, Tim Wakefield pitched $7\frac{1}{3}$ innings and his teammate Derek Lowe pitched $11\frac{1}{3}$ innings. What is the total number of innings they pitched?

To find the total number of innings, you need to add two mixed numbers using the rules below.

KEY CONCEPT
For Your Notebook

Adding and Subtracting Mixed Numbers

1. Find the LCD of the fractions, if necessary.
2. Rename the fractions, if necessary. Then add or subtract the fractions.
3. Add or subtract the whole numbers.
4. Simplify if possible.

EXAMPLE 1 Adding with a Common Denominator

ANOTHER WAY
Rewrite the mixed numbers as improper fractions, then add.
$$7\frac{1}{3} + 11\frac{1}{3} = \frac{22}{3} + \frac{34}{3}$$
$$= \frac{56}{3}$$
$$= 18\frac{2}{3}$$

To solve the real-world problem above, you need to find the sum of $7\frac{1}{3}$ and $11\frac{1}{3}$.

$$
\begin{array}{r}
7\frac{1}{3} \\
+\ 11\frac{1}{3} \\
\hline
18\frac{2}{3}
\end{array}
$$

Add the whole numbers.   **Add the fractions.**

▶ **Answer** Wakefield and Lowe pitched a total of $18\frac{2}{3}$ innings.

Check Estimate the sum by rounding each mixed number to the nearest whole number.
$$7\frac{1}{3} + 11\frac{1}{3} \approx 7 + 11 = 18 \checkmark$$

EXAMPLE 2 Subtracting with a Common Denominator

$$6\frac{7}{9} - 4\frac{1}{9} = 2\frac{6}{9}$$ Subtract fractions and then subtract whole numbers.

$$= 2\frac{2}{3}$$ Simplify.

EXAMPLE 3 Adding with Different Denominators

$$4\frac{5}{6} + 3\frac{3}{4} = 4\frac{10}{12} + 3\frac{9}{12}$$ Rewrite fractions using LCD of $\frac{5}{6}$ and $\frac{3}{4}$.

$$= 7\frac{19}{12}$$ Add fractions and then add whole numbers.

$$= 7 + 1\frac{7}{12}$$ Write improper fraction as a mixed number.

$$= 8\frac{7}{12}$$ Add whole numbers.

ESTIMATE ANSWERS
You can estimate the answer by rounding each mixed number to the nearest whole number. Because 5 + 4 = 9, the answer is reasonable.

Renaming When subtracting mixed numbers, sometimes the fractional part of the second mixed number is greater. If this is the case, then you have to *rename* the first mixed number so that you can subtract the fractional parts.

EXAMPLE 4 Renaming to Subtract Mixed Numbers

a. $6\frac{1}{6} - 3\frac{2}{3} = 6\frac{1}{6} - 3\frac{4}{6}$ Rewrite fractions using LCD of $\frac{1}{6}$ and $\frac{2}{3}$.

$$= 5\frac{7}{6} - 3\frac{4}{6}$$ Rename $6\frac{1}{6}$ as $5\frac{7}{6}$.

$$= 2\frac{3}{6}$$ Subtract fractions and whole numbers.

$$= 2\frac{1}{2}$$ Simplify.

b. $7 - 5\frac{5}{8} = 6\frac{8}{8} - 5\frac{5}{8}$ Rename 7 as $6\frac{8}{8}$.

$$= 1\frac{3}{8}$$ Subtract fractions and whole numbers.

AVOID ERRORS
To check that you renamed $6\frac{1}{6}$ properly, you can rewrite $6\frac{1}{6}$ and $5\frac{7}{6}$ as improper fractions and compare.

Animated Math
at classzone.com

✓ GUIDED PRACTICE   for Examples 1, 2, 3, and 4

Add or subtract. Simplify if possible.

1. $3\frac{1}{8} + 2\frac{5}{8}$ **2.** $7\frac{1}{5} + 1\frac{2}{5}$ **3.** $8\frac{5}{7} - 4\frac{1}{7}$ **4.** $12\frac{5}{6} - 9\frac{5}{6}$

5. $7\frac{1}{4} + 3\frac{1}{2}$ **6.** $1\frac{3}{4} + 4\frac{3}{8}$ **7.** $8 - 5\frac{1}{8}$ **8.** $8\frac{1}{6} - 6\frac{3}{4}$

5.2 EXERCISES

HOMEWORK KEY

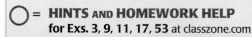

★ = **STANDARDIZED TEST PRACTICE**
Exs. 23, 54, 55, 57, 61, and 75

◯ = **HINTS** AND **HOMEWORK HELP**
for Exs. 3, 9, 11, 17, 53 at classzone.com

SKILL PRACTICE

1. **VOCABULARY** What is the difference between proper fractions and improper fractions?

2. **VOCABULARY** When is it necessary to rename a mixed number when subtracting?

USING COMMON DENOMINATORS Find the sum or difference. Then estimate to check the answer.

SEE EXAMPLES 1 AND 2
on pp. 226–227 for Exs. 3–10

3. $12\frac{3}{5} + 5\frac{1}{5}$ 4. $22\frac{2}{7} + 17\frac{4}{7}$ 5. $8\frac{7}{12} + 4\frac{5}{12}$ 6. $8\frac{3}{4} + 2\frac{3}{4}$

7. $3\frac{2}{3} - 2\frac{1}{3}$ 8. $7\frac{3}{5} - 3\frac{1}{5}$ 9. $8\frac{4}{9} - 5\frac{2}{9}$ 10. $13\frac{5}{6} - 9\frac{1}{6}$

EVALUATING EXPRESSIONS Find the sum or difference. Then estimate to check the answer.

SEE EXAMPLES 3 AND 4
on p. 227 for Exs. 11–24

11. $4\frac{1}{4} + 3\frac{3}{8}$ 12. $3\frac{2}{3} + 8\frac{1}{6}$ 13. $4\frac{3}{4} + 6\frac{2}{3}$ 14. $5\frac{1}{4} + 2\frac{5}{6}$

15. $6\frac{2}{5} + 11\frac{1}{6}$ 16. $8\frac{1}{6} - 5\frac{5}{6}$ 17. $8\frac{1}{8} - 1\frac{5}{8}$ 18. $12\frac{3}{4} - 9\frac{1}{6}$

19. $5\frac{5}{8} - 2\frac{1}{4}$ 20. $8\frac{2}{3} - 5\frac{4}{9}$ 21. $7 - 3\frac{3}{10}$ 22. $9 - 7\frac{4}{9}$

23. ★ **MULTIPLE CHOICE** Which of the following is the difference $8\frac{1}{4} - 3\frac{5}{6}$?

ⓐ $4\frac{1}{12}$ ⓑ $4\frac{1}{4}$ ⓒ $4\frac{5}{12}$ ⓓ $5\frac{7}{12}$

24. **ERROR ANALYSIS** Describe and correct the error made in finding the difference.

$$3\frac{1}{6} - 1\frac{5}{6} = 2\frac{4}{6} = 2\frac{2}{3} \quad ✗$$

ALGEBRA Evaluate the expression when $x = 7\frac{2}{5}, y = 5\frac{1}{3},$ and $z = 3\frac{3}{7}$.

25. $y + x$ 26. $y - z$ 27. $x - y + z$ 28. $z + y - x$

29. $8 - y + \frac{1}{2}$ 30. $2 + x - \frac{3}{8}$ 31. $y - 4 + z$ 32. $5 - z + x$

CHOOSE A METHOD Copy and complete the statement using <, >, or =. Tell whether you used *mental math, estimation,* or *pencil and paper.*

33. $3\frac{1}{4} + 4\frac{1}{4} \underline{?} 7\frac{1}{2}$ 34. $8\frac{1}{4} - 2\frac{1}{8} \underline{?} 6\frac{1}{2}$ 35. $10\frac{1}{10} + 16\frac{1}{2} \underline{?} 27\frac{1}{2}$

36. $12\frac{2}{3} - 2\frac{7}{9} \underline{?} 10\frac{2}{3}$ 37. $9\frac{4}{7} - 3\frac{11}{14} \underline{?} 5\frac{11}{14}$ 38. $7\frac{3}{4} + 4\frac{5}{12} \underline{?} 12\frac{1}{6}$

228   Chapter 5   Fraction Operations

COMBINING MIXED NUMBERS AND DECIMALS **Find the sum or difference.**

39. $2\frac{3}{8} + 3.25$

40. $12\frac{1}{10} - 6.8$

41. $4.625 - 2\frac{1}{6}$

42. $4.75 - 2\frac{1}{8} + 1.2$

43. $1\frac{1}{5} + 3.85 - 1\frac{1}{4}$

44. $9.48 - 6\frac{9}{10} + 11\frac{1}{2}$

(xy) SOLVING EQUATIONS **Solve the equation using mental math.**

45. $x + 2\frac{1}{2} + 1\frac{3}{4} = 5$

46. $x + 3\frac{2}{3} - 1\frac{4}{9} = 3\frac{1}{3}$

47. $x - 5\frac{3}{8} - 3\frac{1}{4} = 2$

48. $4\frac{5}{6} - x + 3\frac{7}{10} = 5\frac{7}{15}$

49. $3\frac{5}{6} + 4\frac{5}{8} + x = 10\frac{17}{24}$

50. $6\frac{1}{5} + x - 1\frac{1}{10} = 11\frac{1}{10}$

51. CHALLENGE Using each digit from 1 to 9 exactly once and only proper fractional parts, find an expression with the greatest value that has the form $a\frac{b}{c} + m\frac{n}{p} + x\frac{y}{z}$. What is the value of the expression?

PROBLEM SOLVING

SEE EXAMPLES 3 AND 4
on p. 227
for Exs. 52–54

52. RUNNING At track practice, you run $5\frac{1}{2}$ miles. You cool down by walking a distance of $1\frac{1}{3}$ miles. What is your total distance?

53. CHILD DEVELOPMENT Anastasia was $19\frac{1}{4}$ inches long at birth. At her 3 month checkup, she was $23\frac{1}{2}$ inches long. How much has she grown? If she grows the same amount before her next checkup, how long will she be?

54. ★ MULTIPLE CHOICE At the beginning of a trip, a boat's gasoline tank contained $14\frac{1}{5}$ gallons of gasoline. At the end of the trip, it contained $8\frac{2}{3}$ gallons. How many gallons of gasoline did the boat use?

(A) $5\frac{8}{15}$ gallons   **(B)** $6\frac{1}{4}$ gallons   **(C)** $6\frac{7}{15}$ gallons   **(D)** $22\frac{13}{15}$ gallons

55. ★ WRITING *Explain* how you can use mental math to find $7 - 3\frac{2}{5}$.

56. GEOMETRY A rectangle is $2\frac{1}{2}$ inches long. Its width is $1\frac{1}{8}$ inches less than its length. Find the perimeter of the rectangle.

57. ★ SHORT RESPONSE A car has a length of $14\frac{4}{5}$ feet. Another car is $1\frac{1}{10}$ feet longer. Can the two cars fit in a driveway that is $31\frac{1}{2}$ feet long? *Explain* how to estimate the answer.

58. REASONING Can you subtract two fractions with common denominators and get an answer with a different denominator? *Explain* your reasoning. If yes, provide two examples.

COINS In Exercises 59–63, use the table below.

Coin	dime	penny	nickel	quarter	half-dollar
Mass (grams)	$2\frac{1}{2}$	$3\frac{1}{8}$	5	$6\frac{1}{4}$	$12\frac{1}{2}$

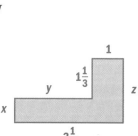

59. CALCULATE What is the difference in mass between a half-dollar and two dimes?

60. CALCULATE What is the sum of the masses of a penny, a dime, and a quarter?

61. ★ SHORT RESPONSE Is it correct to say that the mass of a penny is half the mass of a quarter, $9\frac{3}{8}$ grams less than a half-dollar, and 0.625 grams more than a dime? *Explain.*

62. REASONING You have 10 grams of coins. What is the greatest amount of money you can have? *Explain* your reasoning.

63. COMPARE Name a pair of coins in which the relationship between their value is comparable to the relationship between their masses. *Explain.*

64. CRAFTS You construct a wooden picture frame out of strips of wood that are $\frac{3}{4}$ inch wide. The dimensions of the outside of the frame are $6\frac{1}{2}$ inches wide by $8\frac{1}{4}$ inches long. Can you fit a picture that is 5 inches wide and 7 inches long in your frame? *Justify* your answer.

65. CHALLENGE Two ladybugs climb from the bottom of a window to the top. When the first ladybug finishes the $1\frac{1}{3}$ meter climb, the other ladybug is $4\frac{1}{2}$ centimeters behind. How far has the second ladybug climbed?

66. ⓧⓨ CHALLENGE The perimeter of this figure is $9\frac{3}{5}$. Find the values of *x*, *y*, and *z*.

(figure labeled with: 1, $1\frac{1}{3}$, y, z, x, $3\frac{1}{5}$)

 NEW JERSEY MIXED REVIEW  **TEST PRACTICE** at classzone.com

67. Mr. and Mrs. Carleton have $1000 to remodel their living room. The length of the room is $15\frac{1}{2}$ feet. Carpet is on sale for $2.60 per square foot. What piece of information is needed to find the amount of money that they have left after they carpet the entire floor?

   Ⓐ The dimensions of the windows in the room

   Ⓑ The width of the room

   Ⓒ The height of the walls in the room

   Ⓓ The original price of the carpet

INVESTIGATION
Use before Lesson 5.3

GOAL
Use models to multiply fractions.

MATERIALS
• paper
• colored pencils

5.3 Multiplication of Fractions

To model the product $\frac{3}{4} \times \frac{1}{3}$, you need to find $\frac{3}{4}$ *of* $\frac{1}{3}$.

EXPLORE Use a model to find $\frac{3}{4} \times \frac{1}{3}$.

STEP 1 **Draw** a unit square and divide it into 3 equal horizontal sections. Shade one of the sections to model $\frac{1}{3}$.

$\frac{1}{3}$

STEP 2 **Divide** the unit square into 4 equal vertical sections so you can select $\frac{3}{4}$ of the shaded part of the model.

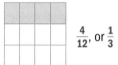
$\frac{4}{12}$, or $\frac{1}{3}$

STEP 3 **Select** $\frac{3}{4}$ of $\frac{1}{3}$. The product of $\frac{3}{4}$ and $\frac{1}{3}$ is $\frac{3}{12}$, or $\frac{1}{4}$.

$\frac{3}{12}$, or $\frac{1}{4}$

PRACTICE Use the given model to find the product.

1. $\frac{1}{2} \times \frac{3}{5}$

2. $\frac{1}{4} \times \frac{2}{3}$

Use a model to find the product.

3. $\frac{1}{2} \times \frac{3}{4}$

4. $\frac{1}{6} \times \frac{2}{3}$

5. $\frac{3}{5} \times \frac{1}{3}$

6. $\frac{2}{3} \times \frac{2}{3}$

DRAW CONCLUSIONS

7. **WRITING** You are using a model to find the product of two fractions. How is the number of sections in the model related to the product of the denominators of the fractions?

5.3 Multiplying Fractions and Mixed Numbers

 4.1.B.1.a Use and explain procedures for performing calculations with integers and all number types named above with: Pencil-and-paper

Before You added and subtracted fractions and mixed numbers.

Now You'll multiply fractions and mixed numbers.

Why? So you can find fractions of amounts, as of the votes in Example 2.

KEY VOCABULARY
- greatest common factor, *p. 170*
- mixed number, improper fraction, *p. 194*

Ice Cream Neapolitan ice cream is made up of one third chocolate, one third vanilla, and one third strawberry. How many gallons of strawberry ice cream are in a half gallon container?

To find a fraction *of* an amount, you *multiply*. For the problem above, you need to find $\frac{1}{3}$ of $\frac{1}{2}$, or $\frac{1}{3} \cdot \frac{1}{2}$.

KEY CONCEPT *For Your Notebook*

Multiplying Fractions

Words The product of two or more fractions is equal to the product of the numerators over the product of the denominators.

Numbers $\frac{1}{5} \cdot \frac{3}{8} = \frac{3}{40}$ **Algebra** $\frac{a}{b} \cdot \frac{c}{d} = \frac{a \cdot c}{b \cdot d}$ $(b, d \neq 0)$

READING

The rule for multiplying fractions states that *b* and *d* cannot equal zero because division by zero is undefined.

 EXAMPLE 1 Multiplying Fractions

To find the amount of strawberry ice cream in a half gallon of Neapolitan ice cream, multiply as shown.

$\frac{1}{3} \cdot \frac{1}{2} = \frac{1 \cdot 1}{3 \cdot 2}$ **Use rule for multiplying fractions.**

$= \frac{1}{6}$ **Multiply.**

▶ **Answer** A half gallon container has $\frac{1}{6}$ gallon of strawberry ice cream.

Check Use a model to find the product. ✓

 GUIDED PRACTICE **for Example 1**

Find the product. Simplify if possible.

1. $\frac{1}{3} \cdot \frac{5}{6}$ 2. $\frac{1}{4} \cdot \frac{7}{9}$ 3. $\frac{5}{7} \cdot \frac{2}{3}$ 4. $\frac{3}{5} \cdot \frac{1}{8}$

Dividing Out Common Factors When multiplying fractions, you can divide out common factors from the product's numerator and denominator so that the product will be in simplest form.

EXAMPLE 2 Multiplying Whole Numbers and Fractions

Election The winner for class president got $\frac{3}{5}$ of the votes. If 200 students voted, use a verbal model to find how many students voted for the winner.

SOLUTION

ANOTHER WAY
You can find the product using 200 chips. Divide the chips into fifths of 40 chips each. Then $\frac{3}{5}$ of 200 = 3 × 40, or 120 chips.

$$\text{Votes for winner} = \frac{3}{5} \text{ of 200 votes}$$

$$= \frac{3}{5} \times \frac{200}{1} \qquad \text{Write } \textit{of} \text{ as } \times \text{ and 200 as } \frac{200}{1}.$$

$$= \frac{3 \times \overset{40}{\cancel{200}}}{\underset{1}{\cancel{5}} \times 1} \qquad \text{Use rule for multiplying fractions. Divide out GCF of 200 and 5.}$$

$$= \frac{120}{1}, \text{ or } 120 \qquad \text{Multiply.}$$

▶ **Answer** There were 120 students who voted for the winner.

Multiplying Mixed Numbers When multiplying mixed numbers, first rewrite them as improper fractions. Then use the rule for multiplying fractions.

EXAMPLE 3 Multiplying Mixed Numbers

$$5\frac{1}{4} \times 4\frac{2}{3} = \frac{21}{4} \times \frac{14}{3} \qquad \text{Write } 5\frac{1}{4} \text{ and } 4\frac{2}{3} \text{ as improper fractions.}$$

TAKE NOTES
If you don't understand the process of dividing out common factors, write a question down in your notebook and discuss the question with a friend or teacher. Then write down what you learn.

$$= \frac{\overset{7}{\cancel{21}} \times \overset{7}{\cancel{14}}}{\underset{2}{\cancel{4}} \times \underset{1}{\cancel{3}}} \qquad \text{Use rule for multiplying fractions. Divide out GCF of 21 and 3 and GCF of 14 and 4.}$$

$$= \frac{49}{2}, \text{ or } 24\frac{1}{2} \qquad \text{Multiply; write as mixed number.}$$

Check Estimate by rounding each factor to the nearest whole number.

$$5\frac{1}{4} \times 4\frac{2}{3} \approx 5 \times 5 = 25 \checkmark$$

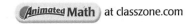 *Animated* **Math** at classzone.com

✓ **GUIDED PRACTICE** for Examples 2 and 3

Find the product. Simplify if possible.

5. $45 \cdot \frac{4}{5}$ **6.** $\frac{1}{6} \cdot 28$ **7.** $8 \cdot 6\frac{1}{2}$ **8.** $2\frac{3}{4} \cdot 20$

9. $12\frac{1}{9} \times \frac{3}{8}$ **10.** $\frac{2}{3} \times 6\frac{1}{2}$ **11.** $2\frac{3}{4} \times 3\frac{1}{6}$ **12.** $4\frac{4}{5} \times 1\frac{1}{9}$

5.3 EXERCISES

SKILL PRACTICE

1. **VOCABULARY** Copy and complete: When multiplying fractions, you can divide out common factors so that the product will be in __?__.

2. **VOCABULARY** Copy and complete: When multiplying two mixed numbers, you first write them as __?__.

MULTIPLYING NUMBERS Find the product. Simplify if possible.

SEE EXAMPLES 1, 2, AND 3
on pp. 232–233
for Exs. 3–19

3. $\frac{3}{7} \times \frac{5}{6}$ **4.** $\frac{1}{10} \times \frac{1}{12}$ **5.** $\frac{2}{5} \times \frac{1}{9}$ **6.** $\frac{1}{8} \times \frac{3}{4}$

7. $\frac{5}{6} \times 12$ **8.** $8 \times \frac{3}{4}$ **9.** $\frac{1}{3} \times 6$ **10.** $5 \times \frac{1}{5}$

11. $3\frac{1}{6} \times 2$ **12.** $1\frac{1}{4} \times 50$ **13.** $4\frac{1}{8} \times \frac{2}{11}$ **14.** $\frac{4}{9} \times 1\frac{1}{8}$

15. $1\frac{2}{5} \times 4\frac{2}{7}$ **16.** $3\frac{1}{3} \times 2\frac{7}{10}$ **17.** $8\frac{4}{5} \times 5\frac{5}{11}$ **18.** $7\frac{1}{2} \times 4\frac{2}{5}$

19. ERROR ANALYSIS Describe and correct the error made in finding the product.

$$2\frac{1}{3} \times 3\frac{1}{2} = 2 \times 3 + \frac{1}{3} \cdot \frac{1}{2}$$
$$= 6\frac{1}{6}$$

20. ★ MULTIPLE CHOICE Which of the following numbers, when multiplied by $4\frac{1}{3}$, results in a number greater than $4\frac{1}{3}$?

(A) 0   **(B)** $\frac{1}{4}$ **(C)** $\frac{7}{10}$ **(D)** $1\frac{1}{3}$

EVALUATING EXPRESSIONS Evaluate the expression.

21. $\frac{1}{2} + \frac{3}{8} \cdot \frac{2}{3}$ **22.** $\frac{3}{4} \cdot 10 + 2\frac{2}{3}$ **23.** $7\frac{3}{4} - 3\frac{5}{8} \cdot 1\frac{1}{3}$ **24.** $120 \cdot \frac{5}{48} - \frac{11}{13}$

25. $1\frac{3}{4}\left(\frac{1}{8} + \frac{3}{4}\right)$ **26.** $\left(\frac{5}{6} + \frac{5}{12}\right) \cdot \frac{7}{9}$ **27.** $\left(\frac{9}{16} - \frac{1}{4}\right) \cdot 2\frac{7}{10}$ **28.** $5\frac{1}{2}\left(\frac{2}{3} - \frac{1}{2}\right)$

ALGEBRA Evaluate the expression when $x = 3$ and $y = 6$.

29. $\frac{3}{4}x$ **30.** $\frac{1}{4} \cdot \frac{1}{x} + \frac{5}{6}$ **31.** $\frac{1}{5}y - \frac{1}{3}x$ **32.** $\frac{1}{y} + \frac{2}{5} \cdot \frac{x}{5}$

ESTIMATION Use estimation to copy and complete the statements with < or >. *Explain* your answer. Then find the exact product.

33. $\frac{9}{10} \times 1\frac{7}{9}$ _?_ 2   **34.** $\frac{1}{5} \times 5\frac{3}{5}$ _?_ 1   **35.** $1\frac{7}{8} \times 2\frac{2}{5}$ _?_ 2

36. $5\frac{1}{4} \times 1\frac{2}{7}$ _?_ $9\frac{3}{4}$ **37.** $4\frac{5}{6} \times 7\frac{1}{9}$ _?_ $35\frac{1}{5}$ **38.** $2\frac{2}{5} \times 5\frac{2}{9}$ _?_ 11

REASONING Copy and complete the statement using *always, sometimes,* or *never. Explain* your reasoning.

SEE EXAMPLES 2 AND 3
on p. 233
for Exs. 39–41

39. The product of a mixed number and a proper fraction is __?__ greater than 1.

40. The product of two proper fractions is __?__ equal to 1.

41. The product of two mixed numbers greater than 1 is __?__ greater than 1.

42. CHALLENGE Find $1\frac{1}{2} \cdot 4$. *Explain* how you can apply the process for multiplying a two-digit number by a one-digit number to multiply a mixed number by a whole number.

PROBLEM SOLVING

SEE EXAMPLES 2 AND 3
on p. 233
for Exs. 43–45

43. HORSE HEIGHT Trainers measure horses in *hands,* the distance across an adult's palm. The average height of a horse is $15\frac{1}{2}$ hands. A hand is about $\frac{1}{3}$ foot. About how tall is an average horse in feet?

44. ★ MULTIPLE CHOICE You have 50 bricks that are each $7\frac{5}{8}$ inches long. Which expression can you use to find how far, in inches, the 50 bricks would extend when laid out end to end?

(A) $50 + 7\frac{5}{8}$ **(B)** $50 - 7\frac{5}{8}$

(C) $50 \times 7\frac{5}{8}$ **(D)** $50 \div 7\frac{5}{8}$

45. ★ SHORT RESPONSE Each glass of lemonade requires $1\frac{1}{2}$ tablespoons of drink mix. Between 15 and 20 members usually attend your drama club meetings. Find a high and low estimate for how much drink mix is needed to serve each person a glass of lemonade. Is 20 tablespoons a reasonable guess? *Explain* your answers.

46. ★ WRITING Your water cooler contains 5 gallons of water. You drink $\frac{3}{5}$ gallon each day. Do you have enough water to last 6 days? *Explain* your reasoning.

47. STAINED GLASS The Darwin D. Martin house, built by Frank Lloyd Wright, has a rectangular stained glass window with a length of $41\frac{1}{2}$ inches and a width that is $15\frac{1}{4}$ inches less than the length. What is the area of the window?

48. ★ OPEN-ENDED MATH Give an example of a real-world situation you could model by multiplying each of the following: $20 \times 8\frac{1}{2}$ inches, $20 \times 8\frac{1}{2}$ feet, and $20 \times 8\frac{1}{2}$ miles.

49. ★ **EXTENDED RESPONSE** Jen wrote a 4-page book report. Each page took $\frac{3}{4}$ hour to write. She also spent 1 hour proofreading.

 a. Write and evaluate a numerical expression to describe the total amount of time Jen spent on the report.

 b. Including proofreading, Andre completed his 4-page report at a rate of one page per hour. Write and evaluate an expression to describe the time Andre spent on the report.

 c. *Compare* Jen's time with Andre's time.

50. **BAKING** A recipe that makes 24 apple muffins is shown. How should you change the recipe to make 32 muffins? Write the new recipe.

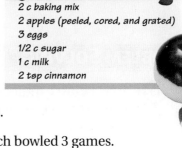

Recipe: **APPLE MUFFINS**
2 c baking mix
2 apples (peeled, cored, and grated)
3 eggs
1/2 c sugar
1 c milk
2 tsp cinnamon

51. **CHALLENGE** *Explain* how you could multiply $2\frac{1}{3} \times 6\frac{3}{8}$ without renaming the mixed numbers as improper fractions.

52. **CHALLENGE** Aubrey, Jasmine, and Neil each bowled 3 games. The mean of all 9 scores was $93\frac{1}{3}$. Aubrey's mean score was $81\frac{1}{3}$ and Neil's total for all the games was 291. Which bowler had the highest 3 game total? *Explain* your reasoning.

 NEW JERSEY MIXED REVIEW **TEST PRACTICE** at classzone.com

Amy is making four kinds of cookies for a party. The table shows the amount of flour needed for each recipe.

53. Amy plans on making one batch of each type. What is the total amount of flour needed?

 (A) $8\frac{7}{8}$ cups

 (B) $9\frac{3}{8}$ cups

 (C) $9\frac{5}{8}$ cups

 (D) 10 cups

54. Which recipe requires the most flour?

 (A) Chocolate chip

 (B) Sugar

 (C) Peanut butter

 (D) Pumpkin

Cookie Recipes	
Type	**Amount of flour (cups)**
Chocolate chip	$2\frac{3}{4}$
Sugar	2.5
Peanut butter	2.25
Pumpkin	$2\frac{1}{8}$

ONLINE QUIZ at classzone.com

5.4 Dividing Fractions and Mixed Numbers

 4.1.B.1.a Use and explain procedures for performing calculations with integers and all number types named above with: Pencil-and-paper

Before You multiplied fractions and mixed numbers.

Now You'll divide fractions and mixed numbers.

Why? So you can follow recipes, as in Ex. 42.

KEY VOCABULARY
• reciprocal, *p. 237*

You can use a model to find the quotient $2 \div \frac{1}{4}$.

First draw two unit squares. Then divide each square into fourths.

There are 8 fourths in the model. So, $2 \div \frac{1}{4} = 8$. You can also reason that there are 4 fourths in each square and there are 2 squares, so $2 \div \frac{1}{4} = 2 \times 4 = 8$. The numbers $\frac{1}{4}$ and 4 are *reciprocals*. Two nonzero numbers whose product is 1 are **reciprocals**.

VOCABULARY
Notice that two numbers are reciprocals if the numerator and denominator are swapped.

$\frac{2}{3}$ and $\frac{3}{2}$ are reciprocals, because $\frac{2}{3} \cdot \frac{3}{2} = 1$.

5 and $\frac{1}{5}$ are reciprocals, because $5 \cdot \frac{1}{5} = 1$.

$\frac{11}{8}$ and $\frac{8}{11}$ are reciprocals, because $\frac{11}{8} \cdot \frac{8}{11} = 1$.

at classzone.com

KEY CONCEPT *For Your Notebook*

Using Reciprocals to Divide

Words To divide by any nonzero number, multiply by its reciprocal.

Numbers $\frac{3}{4} \div \frac{2}{3} = \frac{3}{4} \cdot \frac{3}{2} = \frac{9}{8}$ **Algebra** $\frac{a}{b} \div \frac{c}{d} = \frac{a}{b} \cdot \frac{d}{c} = \frac{ad}{bc}$

$(b, c, d \neq 0)$

EXAMPLE 1 Dividing a Fraction by a Fraction

$\frac{5}{9} \div \frac{2}{3} = \frac{5}{9} \cdot \frac{3}{2}$ **Multiply by reciprocal.**

$= \frac{5 \cdot \overset{1}{\cancel{3}}}{\underset{3}{\cancel{9}} \cdot 2}$ **Use rule for multiplying fractions.**
Divide out common factor.

$= \frac{5}{6}$ **Multiply.**

EXAMPLE 2 Dividing a Fraction by a Whole Number

CHECK SOLUTION
You can check your answer by multiplying the quotient and divisor. The result should equal the dividend.
$$\frac{2}{5} \times 2 = \frac{2}{5} \times \frac{2}{1} = \frac{4}{5}$$

$$\frac{4}{5} \div 2 = \frac{4}{5} \cdot \frac{1}{2} \qquad \text{Multiply by reciprocal.}$$

$$= \frac{\overset{2}{\cancel{4}} \cdot 1}{5 \cdot \underset{1}{\cancel{2}}} \qquad \text{Use rule for multiplying fractions.} \\ \text{Divide out common factor.}$$

$$= \frac{2}{5} \qquad \text{Multiply.}$$

✔ **GUIDED PRACTICE**   **for Examples 1 and 2**

Find the quotient. Simplify if possible.

1. $\frac{5}{6} \div \frac{7}{9}$ **2.** $\frac{9}{2} \div \frac{3}{2}$ **3.** $\frac{1}{6} \div 3$ **4.** $\frac{2}{3} \div 4$

EXAMPLE 3 Standardized Test Practice

In-line Skating You set up an in-line skating course 21 feet long to practice weaving around cones. You want a cone every $3\frac{1}{2}$ feet, but not at the start or end of the course. How many cones will you need?

(A) 4 cones   **(B)** 5 cones   **(C)** 6 cones   **(D)** 7 cones

ELIMINATE CHOICES
You are placing the cones $3\frac{1}{2}$ feet apart, but $3\frac{1}{2} \cdot 7 > 21$. Choice D can be eliminated.

SOLUTION

METHOD 1 Draw a diagram on graph paper. Make the course 21 grid boxes long. Draw a point to mark the location of a cone every $3\frac{1}{2}$ grid boxes.

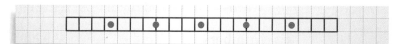

METHOD 2 Use division.

$$21 \div 3\frac{1}{2} = 21 \div \frac{7}{2} \qquad \text{Write } 3\frac{1}{2} \text{ as an improper fraction.}$$

$$= \frac{21}{1} \cdot \frac{2}{7} \qquad \text{Multiply by reciprocal.}$$

$$= \frac{\overset{3}{\cancel{21}} \cdot 2}{1 \cdot \underset{1}{\cancel{7}}} \qquad \text{Use rule for multiplying fractions.} \\ \text{Divide out common factors.}$$

$$= 6 \qquad \text{Multiply.}$$

▶ **Answer** 6 is the number of $3\frac{1}{2}$-foot spaces separated by cones. Subtract 1 to get the number of cones. You will need 5 cones. The correct answer is B. (A) **(B)** (C) (D)

EXAMPLE 4 **Dividing Two Mixed Numbers**

$$8\frac{3}{4} \div 2\frac{5}{8} = \frac{35}{4} \div \frac{21}{8}$$ Write $8\frac{3}{4}$ and $2\frac{5}{8}$ as improper fractions.

$$= \frac{35}{4} \cdot \frac{8}{21}$$ Multiply by reciprocal.

$$= \frac{\overset{5}{\cancel{35}} \cdot \overset{2}{\cancel{8}}}{\underset{1}{\cancel{4}} \cdot \underset{3}{\cancel{21}}}$$ Use rule for multiplying fractions.
Divide out common factors.

$$= \frac{10}{3}, \text{ or } 3\frac{1}{3}$$ Multiply.

Check Estimate the quotient by rounding each mixed number to the nearest whole number.

$$8\frac{3}{4} \div 2\frac{5}{8} \approx 9 \div 3 = 3 \checkmark$$

 Animated Math at classzone.com

✓ **GUIDED PRACTICE** for Examples 3 and 4

5. **What If?** In Example 3, you want the course to be 28 feet long with a cone at the beginning and end of the course. How many cones do you need? *Explain.*

Find the quotient. Then multiply or estimate to check the answer.

6. $3 \div \frac{6}{11}$ 7. $2\frac{2}{5} \div 12$ 8. $5\frac{2}{3} \div \frac{3}{5}$ 9. $4\frac{1}{2} \div 1\frac{1}{4}$

5.4 EXERCISES

HOMEWORK KEY

★ = **STANDARDIZED TEST PRACTICE**
Exs. 26, 27, 42, 43, 44, 46, and 59

◯ = **HINTS AND HOMEWORK HELP**
for Exs. 5, 11, 13, 19, 41 at classzone.com

SKILL PRACTICE

VOCABULARY Write the reciprocal of the number.

1. $\frac{5}{6}$ 2. 8   3. 1   4. $5\frac{2}{5}$

FINDING QUOTIENTS Find the quotient. Then check the answer.

SEE EXAMPLES 1, 2, 3, AND 4 on pp. 237–239 for Exs. 5–24

5. $\frac{3}{8} \div \frac{1}{4}$ 6. $\frac{6}{7} \div \frac{5}{14}$ 7. $\frac{9}{10} \div 6$ 8. $\frac{7}{12} \div 4$

9. $\frac{8}{9} \div 1\frac{2}{15}$ 10. $8 \div 2\frac{3}{4}$ 11. $10 \div 4\frac{1}{6}$ 12. $4\frac{1}{5} \div \frac{3}{10}$

13. $2\frac{5}{6} \div 7$ 14. $5 \div 3\frac{2}{3}$ 15. $9\frac{4}{5} \div 1\frac{1}{13}$ 16. $7\frac{1}{6} \div 2\frac{7}{12}$

17. $12 \div 3\frac{3}{5}$ 18. $6\frac{3}{16} \div 5\frac{1}{12}$ 19. $10\frac{2}{7} \div 4\frac{4}{11}$ 20. $8\frac{2}{9} \div 4\frac{3}{8}$

21. $8 \div 2\frac{2}{3}$ 22. $4\frac{3}{8} \div 3\frac{1}{3}$ 23. $6\frac{1}{5} \div 3\frac{4}{9}$ 24. $15\frac{3}{4} \div 7\frac{5}{7}$

SEE EXAMPLE 1
on p. 237
for Exs. 25–26

25. ERROR ANALYSIS Describe and correct the error made in finding the quotient.

$$\frac{7}{9} \div \frac{2}{3} = \frac{9}{7} \cdot \frac{2}{3} = \frac{18}{21} = \frac{6}{7} \quad \times$$

26. ★ MULTIPLE CHOICE Which multiplication expression is equivalent to the division expression $\frac{3}{20} \div \frac{4}{9}$?

(A) $\frac{3}{20} \times \frac{4}{9}$ (B) $\frac{3}{20} \times \frac{9}{4}$ (C) $\frac{20}{3} \times \frac{4}{9}$ (D) $\frac{20}{3} \times \frac{9}{4}$

27. ★ MULTIPLE CHOICE What is the value of $x \div 2\frac{2}{5}$ when $x = 1\frac{1}{2}$?

(A) $\frac{5}{8}$ (B) $1\frac{3}{5}$ (C) $2\frac{1}{5}$ (D) $3\frac{3}{5}$

XY ALGEBRA Evaluate the expression when $x = \frac{5}{8}$, $y = 3$, and $z = 2\frac{3}{16}$.

28. $x \div y$ **29.** $y \div x$ **30.** $4\frac{1}{6} \div y$ **31.** $x \div 10$

32. $(z \div x) \cdot y$ **33.** $(y \div z) \cdot x$ **34.** $(x + z) \div y$ **35.** $(y - z) \div x$

XY NUMBER SENSE *Describe* the whole number value(s) of x that make the statement true.

36. $x \div \frac{2}{3} = x$ **37.** $4\frac{1}{2} \div x = 9$ **38.** $1\frac{2}{5} \div x < 1\frac{2}{5}$ **39.** $x \div \frac{7}{8} > x$

40. CHALLENGE *Describe* what happens to the value of the expression $y \div 100$ as y gets closer to zero. *Describe* what happens to the value of the expression $100 \div x$ as x gets closer to zero. *Justify* your answers.

PROBLEM SOLVING

SEE EXAMPLES
2, 3, AND 4
on pp. 238–239
for Exs. 41–43

41. SANDWICHES To surprise the guests at a party, the host prepares a long submarine sandwich. The sandwich is cut into equal pieces as shown. Use a verbal model to help you find the length of each piece.

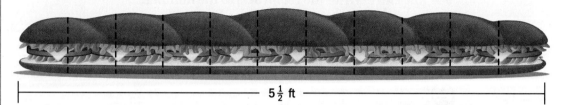

$5\frac{1}{2}$ ft

42. ★ MULTIPLE CHOICE Making pasta requires boiling 6 cups of water. Your measuring cup holds $1\frac{1}{2}$ cups. How many times do you need to fill the cup?

(A) 4 (B) $4\frac{1}{2}$ (C) 5 (D) 9

43. ★ WRITING *Explain* how to divide a mixed number by a mixed number.

44. ★ **SHORT RESPONSE** On a slalom skiing course, the distance from the start to the first gate is 15 meters, and the distance from the last gate to the finish is 20 meters. The slalom course is 637 meters long and the distance between gates is $10\frac{3}{4}$ meters. How many gates are needed for the course? *Explain* your answer.

45. ◆ **MULTIPLE REPRESENTATIONS** You are an editor for your school yearbook. Each row of student photos is $8\frac{5}{8}$ inches wide, including $\frac{1}{4}$ inch margins on each side of the page. The photos are $1\frac{1}{4}$ inches wide and $\frac{1}{8}$ inch apart.

　a. Make a Model On a sheet of paper make a model of one row of photos.

　b. Write an Expression Write an expression to represent the number of photos p that fit in each row. How many photos will be in each row? *Explain* your reasoning.

46. ★ **EXTENDED RESPONSE** A CD case is $\frac{3}{8}$ inch wide. A cassette case is $\frac{1}{4}$ inch wider than a CD case. You put 8 cassettes on a shelf that is 20 inches wide. How much space is left on the shelf? How many CDs will fit in the remaining space? *Explain* your reasoning.

UNIT RATES For each unit rate, *a* per *b*, write the unit rate *b* per *a*. *Explain* how the two unit rates are related.

47. $3\frac{1}{3}$ miles per hour　　**48.** $1\frac{1}{2}$ dozen eggs per carton　　**49.** $\frac{5}{8}$ ounce per box

50. CHALLENGE A customer paid more than \$12.50 but less than \$13 for $3\frac{1}{4}$ pounds of cheese. Find a range describing possible prices of a pound of cheese. Could the cheese have been \$3.84 per pound? \$4 per pound? *Explain* your reasoning.

 NEW JERSEY MIXED REVIEW **TEST PRACTICE** at classzone.com

51. Which model best represents the expression $\frac{1}{2} \times \frac{2}{5}$?

Ⓐ 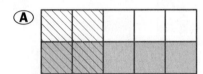　　Ⓑ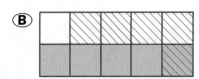

Ⓒ 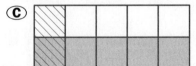　　Ⓓ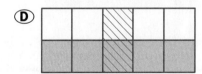

Find the sum or difference. *(pp. 219, 226)*

1. $\frac{2}{3} + \frac{1}{6}$

2. $\frac{3}{5} + \frac{1}{10}$

3. $\frac{5}{6} - \frac{5}{12}$

4. $\frac{7}{8} - \frac{3}{16}$

5. $11\frac{7}{8} + 24\frac{5}{12}$

6. $6\frac{3}{16} + 9\frac{7}{12}$

7. $21\frac{3}{4} - 5\frac{9}{14}$

8. $19\frac{2}{3} - 7\frac{2}{7}$

Find the product or quotient. *(pp. 232, 237)*

9. $13 \times \frac{17}{26}$

10. $2\frac{5}{8} \times 1\frac{5}{9}$

11. $17 \times \frac{15}{34}$

12. $1\frac{1}{3} \times 4\frac{2}{9}$

13. $3\frac{1}{3} \div \frac{1}{9}$

14. $5\frac{1}{2} \div 1\frac{3}{4}$

15. $5\frac{5}{11} \div \frac{1}{15}$

16. $3\frac{3}{4} \div 6$

17. **HIKING** At Mount Monadnock in New Hampshire, the distance from the parking lot to the top of the mountain along Red Spot Trail is $2\frac{3}{4}$ miles. You hike to the top and back down. How far have you traveled? *Explain.* *(p. 226)*

18. **BOOKS** Ryan gave away $\frac{1}{3}$ of his books and then sold $\frac{3}{4}$ of the remaining books. How many of his 180 books did he sell? *Explain* your answer. *(p. 232)*

Brain Game

Mix and Match

Play this game with a partner. Take turns doing the following:

1. Choose two fractions from those given. (Fractions cannot be used more than once.)

2. Let one fraction be the dividend and the other be the divisor.

3. Find the quotient. (Your partner should check your answer.)

4. Add the quotient to your score. (You both start with a score of zero.)

Once all the fractions have been used, the player with the greater score wins.

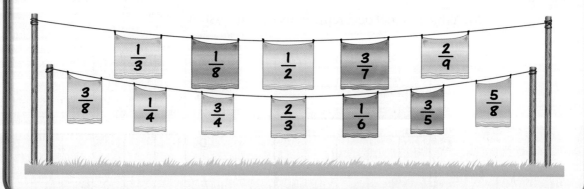

5.4 Fraction Operations

Some calculators allow you to perform operations with fractions and mixed numbers. If you have such a calculator, be sure it is set to display answers as mixed numbers in simplest form.

EXAMPLE How many $\frac{1}{2}$ minute commercials can a television station run during a $2\frac{1}{2}$ minute break?

SOLUTION

To find the number of commercials, you need to find the quotient $2\frac{1}{2} \div \frac{1}{2}$.

Keystrokes   **Display**

2 [UNIT] 1 [/] 2 [÷] 1 [/] 2 [=]   [5]

The [UNIT] key is used to write a mixed number. The display for the key is ⊔.

▶ **Answer** The television station can run 5 commercials during the break.

PRACTICE Use a calculator to evaluate the expression.

1. $\frac{5}{11} + \frac{7}{9}$

2. $\frac{2}{5} + \frac{5}{7}$

3. $\frac{19}{20} - \frac{3}{4}$

4. $\frac{2}{3} - \frac{2}{5}$

5. $5\frac{4}{7} \times \frac{1}{2}$

6. $\frac{3}{4} \times 10\frac{1}{15}$

7. $5\frac{11}{12} \div \frac{1}{4}$

8. $8\frac{1}{7} \div \frac{5}{9}$

9. $\frac{13}{20} \times \frac{7}{10} \div \frac{2}{5}$

10. $\frac{13}{25} \div \left(\frac{1}{3} + \frac{2}{7}\right)$

11. $\left(17\frac{9}{10} - 7\frac{5}{8}\right) \times 4\frac{1}{6}$

12. $\left(11\frac{2}{5} + 4\frac{3}{4}\right) \times \frac{3}{8}$

13. **POSTERS** A standard movie poster is $2\frac{1}{4}$ feet wide. The width of a wall is $13\frac{1}{2}$ feet. How many standard movie posters can you fit across the wall without overlapping? If each poster sells for $12.95, how much will it cost to put posters across the wall?

Lessons 5.1–5.4

1. **DELI MEAT** You have $\frac{3}{4}$ pound of roast beef and $\frac{1}{2}$ pound of turkey. You want to make 4 sandwiches, each with $\frac{1}{3}$ pound of meat. How could you determine whether you have enough meat?

   A. Compare the sum $\frac{3}{4} + \frac{1}{2}$ with $\frac{1}{3}$.

   B. Find the sum $\frac{3}{4} + \frac{1}{2}$ and divide by $\frac{1}{4}$.

   C. Divide the product $\frac{3}{4} \times \frac{1}{2}$ by $\frac{1}{3}$.

   D. Find $\left(\frac{3}{4} + \frac{1}{2}\right) \div 4$ and compare to $\frac{1}{3}$.

2. **RECIPE** In the recipe at the right, what fraction of the total amount of the ingredients is flour?

   Ingredients

   $\frac{1}{4}$ cup sugar

   $1\frac{1}{2}$ cups flour

   1 egg

   $\frac{1}{8}$ cup butter

   Note: 1 egg equals approximately $\frac{1}{4}$ cup.

   A. $\frac{17}{32}$

   B. $\frac{12}{17}$

   C. $2\frac{1}{8}$

   D. $3\frac{3}{16}$

3. **WATERMELON** A watermelon is cut into 16 equal sections. You divide one section into 4 equal slices. How much of the whole watermelon is one slice?

   A. $\frac{1}{64}$

   B. $\frac{1}{16}$

   C. $\frac{3}{16}$

   D. $\frac{1}{4}$

4. **RED PANDAS** The table gives the lengths, in feet, of 6 red pandas. What is the mean length of the pandas, in feet?

Panda	A	B	C	D	E	F
Length (feet)	$1\frac{2}{3}$	$1\frac{7}{8}$	$2\frac{1}{3}$	$1\frac{3}{4}$	$2\frac{1}{8}$	$2\frac{1}{2}$

   A. $\frac{13}{24}$

   B. $1\frac{7}{8}$

   C. $2\frac{1}{24}$

   D. $3\frac{1}{4}$

5. **BOUNCING BALL** A ball, dropped from a height of 6 feet, begins bouncing. The height of each bounce is $\frac{3}{4}$ of the height of the previous bounce. What is the height of the first bounce, in feet?

   A. $\frac{1}{8}$

   B. $\frac{3}{4}$

   C. $\frac{27}{8}$

   D. $\frac{9}{2}$

6. **OPEN-ENDED** You want to paint the outside of a storage building that has a square fountain. Each wall is $8\frac{3}{4}$ feet high and $12\frac{1}{2}$ feet long. You have two cans of paint that will cover 400 square feet each.

   • Find the total area of all four walls.

   • Do you have enough paint to cover all four walls? *Explain.*

   • Do you have enough paint to apply a second coat to all four walls? *Explain.*

5.5 Measuring in Customary Units

4.2.D.2 Select and use appropriate units and tools to measure quantities to the degree of precision needed in a particular problem-solving situation.

Before You measured and estimated using metric units.

Now You'll measure and estimate using customary units.

Why? So you can estimate weight with benchmarks, as in Ex. 28.

KEY VOCABULARY
- U.S. customary system, length: inch, foot, yard, mile, *p. 245*
- weight: ounce, pound, ton, *p. 246*
- capacity: fluid ounce, cup, pint, quart, gallon, *p. 247*

The units of measurement for length, weight, and capacity commonly used in the United States are part of the **U.S. customary system**.

Length The **inch (in.)** is a unit of length in the customary system. Three other customary units of length are the **foot (ft)**, **yard (yd)**, and **mile (mi)**. You can use the following benchmarks to estimate length.

1 inch
length of a
small paper clip

1 foot
distance from
shoulder to elbow

1 yard
width of
a door

1 mile combined length of 15 football fields

EXAMPLE 1 Using Customary Units of Length

To estimate the length of a barrette, think of small paper clips laid next to it. Then measure the barrette with a ruler to check your estimate.

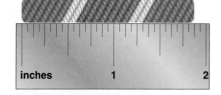

About $1\frac{1}{2}$ paper clips fit beside it, so it is about $1\frac{1}{2}$ inches long.

The ruler shows sixteenths of an inch, so it is $1\frac{14}{16}$, or $1\frac{7}{8}$, inches long.

✓ GUIDED PRACTICE for Example 1

1. **Length** Estimate the length of a pen in inches. Check with a ruler.

5.5 Measuring in Customary Units **245**

Weight The weight of an object tells you how heavy the object is. Three customary units of weight are the **ounce (oz)**, **pound (lb)**, and **ton (T)**. You can measure the weight of an object using a scale.

EXAMPLE 2 Measuring Weight

READING
Be careful to distinguish between mass and weight. Your mass is the same wherever you are, but your weight depends on gravity.

Find the weight of the bananas.

Each pound is divided into sixteenths, so the arrow is at the $1\frac{14}{16}$ lb or $1\frac{7}{8}$ lb mark.

▸**Answer** The bananas weigh $1\frac{7}{8}$ pounds.

You can use the following benchmarks to estimate weight.

| **1 ounce** | **1 pound** | **1 ton** |
| slice of bread | soccer ball | walrus |

EXAMPLE 3 Using Customary Units of Weight

Copy and complete the statement using the appropriate customary unit: The weight of a bowling ball is 14 _?_ .

The weight of a bowling ball is greater than the weight of 14 slices of bread (14 oz), and it is certainly less than the weight of 14 walruses (14 T). Because a good estimate for the weight of a bowling ball is the weight of 14 soccer balls, the appropriate customary unit is pounds.

▸**Answer** The weight of a bowling ball is 14 pounds.

✓ **GUIDED PRACTICE** for Examples 2 and 3

2. **Produce** Find the weight of the peppers.

Baseball Copy and complete the statement:

3. The weight of a baseball bat is 33 _?_ .

4. The weight of a leather catcher's mitt is 2 _?_ .

Capacity Capacity is a measure of the amount that a container can hold. Five customary units of capacity are the **fluid ounce (fl oz)**, **cup (c)**, **pint (pt)**, **quart (qt)**, and **gallon (gal)**. These units are also used to describe the amount of liquid in a container.

EXAMPLE 4 Measuring a Liquid Amount

Find the amount of liquid in the measuring cup.

Each cup is divided into fourths, so the liquid is at the $3\frac{3}{4}$ cup level.

▶ **Answer** There are about $3\frac{3}{4}$ cups of liquid in the measuring cup.

You can use the benchmarks shown to estimate capacity.

1 fluid ounce

EXAMPLE 5 Standardized Test Practice

What is the most reasonable capacity of a lemonade pitcher?

(**A**) 2 c   (**B**) 32 oz   (**C**) 2 qt   (**D**) 10 gal

ELIMINATE CHOICES
A fluid ounce is not the same as an ounce. Fluid ounces measure the capacity of a container holding liquid. Ounces measure the weight of the container. Choice B can be eliminated.

SOLUTION

The choices that are measures of capacity are 2 c, 2 qt, and 10 gal. Two cups of water is not enough to fill the pitcher and 10 gallons is too much. That leaves 2 quarts of water, which seems an appropriate capacity.

▶ **Answer** The most reasonable capacity of a lemonade pitcher is 2 qt. The correct answer is C. (**A**) (**B**) (**C**) (**D**)

Animated **Math**
at classzone.com

✓ **GUIDED PRACTICE**   for Examples 4 and 5

5. Find the amount of milk in the measuring cup.

Match the object with the appropriate capacity.

6. Juice glass   **7.** Paint can   **8.** Ice cube tray

A. 1 gal   **B.** 1 pt   **C.** 7 fl oz

5.5 EXERCISES

SKILL PRACTICE

SEE EXAMPLE 1
on p. 245
for Exs. 3–6

1. **VOCABULARY** Which unit measures capacity: *yard*, *cup*, or *pound*?

2. **VOCABULARY** Which unit measures weight: *foot*, *ton*, or *quart*?

ESTIMATION Estimate the length of the object in inches. Then measure the object using a ruler.

3. backpack   4. your shoe   **(5.)** calendar   6. picture frame

MEASURING WEIGHT Find the weight of the object.

SEE EXAMPLE 2
on p. 246
for Exs. 7–8

(7.)

8.

CHOOSING UNITS Copy and complete using the appropriate customary unit.

SEE EXAMPLES 3, 4, AND 5
on pp. 246–247
for Exs. 9–15

(9.) A newborn baby weighs $7\frac{1}{2}$ __?__ .

10. A tennis racket weighs $9\frac{1}{2}$ __?__ .

11. A shampoo bottle holds 12 __?__ .

12. A teakettle holds 10 __?__ .

13. **ERROR ANALYSIS** Describe and correct the error made in completing the statement: A mug weighs 16 __?__ .

A mug holds fluid, so a mug weighs 16 fluid ounces.

MEASURING LIQUID Find the amount of liquid in the measuring cup.

14.

(15.)

MEASURING Name a measurement tool that is appropriate for the given unit.

16. fluid ounce   17. inch   18. pound   19. yard

DETERMINING PRECISION Tell whether an *exact answer* or an *estimate* is more appropriate for the given situation.

20. Sawing wood to build a deck   21. Distance from home to the park

22. The amount of food you give your dog   23. Your finish time in a track race

24. ★ **MULTIPLE CHOICE** Which is the shortest distance?

　(A) 30 inches   (B) 3 feet   (C) $\frac{1}{2}$ mile   (D) 1 yard

25. CHALLENGE Can two filled containers have the same weight but different capacities? Can two filled containers have different weights but the same capacities? If so, give an example. If not, *explain*.

PROBLEM SOLVING

SEE EXAMPLE 1
on p. 245
for Exs. 26–27

26. ★ SHORT RESPONSE You want to measure the length of a wall. Would you use a *tape measure*, a *yardstick*, or a *12 inch ruler*? *Explain* your choice.

27. ★ MULTIPLE CHOICE What is the distance between Austin, Texas, and Tallahassee, Florida?

(A) 1760 yd (B) 7000 ft

(C) 600 in. (D) 800 mi

SEE EXAMPLE 3
on p. 246
for Exs. 28–29

28. ★ MULTIPLE CHOICE What is the weight of a typical Indian bull elephant?

(A) $3\frac{1}{2}$ T (B) 600 lb (C) 2000 oz (D) 100 lb

29. SUNGLASSES Dave thinks that a pair of sunglasses weighs about 2 ounces. Mary thinks that the weight is about 2 pounds. Who is right? *Explain*.

30. REASONING On one scale, each pound is divided into eighths. On another scale, each pound is divided into tenths. Which scale will give you a more precise measurement? *Explain* your reasoning.

31. ★ WRITING *Explain* how you can estimate how tall a person is in feet by using the width of a door.

32. EXAMPLES AND NONEXAMPLES A project requires you to use only units of length and units of capacity. List several customary units and tools that you may use. List several units and tools that you will not use.

33. ★ OPEN-ENDED MATH Give three examples of an object for which a reasonable weight would be 2 ounces.

CHALLENGE Which *customary* unit would you use to measure the item?

34. 10 cm leaf **35.** 3 meter wall **36.** 4 kilogram rock **37.** 1 liter fruit juice

 NEW JERSEY MIXED REVIEW

38. Which expression can be used to find the maximum number of $\frac{3}{10}$-meter lengths of string that can be cut from a piece of string that is $5\frac{3}{4}$ meters long?

(A) $\frac{3}{10} + 5\frac{3}{4}$ (B) $\frac{3}{10} \div 5\frac{3}{4}$ (C) $5\frac{3}{4} \div \frac{3}{10}$ (D) $5\frac{3}{4} \times \frac{3}{10}$

EXTRA PRACTICE for Lesson 5.5, p. 780   **ONLINE QUIZ** at classzone.com   **249**

5.6 Converting Customary Units

NJ 4.2.D.1 Solve problems requiring calculations that involve different units of measurement within a measurement system . . .

Before	You measured objects using customary units.
Now	You'll convert between customary units.
Why?	So you can convert lengths, as in Example 1.

KEY VOCABULARY
- **U.S. customary system, length: inch, foot, yard, mile,** *p. 245*
- **weight: ounce, pound, ton,** *p. 246*
- **capacity: fluid ounce, cup, pint, quart, gallon,** *p. 247*

Art In 1976, the artist Christo built a $24\frac{1}{2}$ mile long fabric fence in Marin and Sonoma Counties, California. He and his team joined together pieces of fabric, each 63 feet long, to form the fence. How many yards long was each piece?

KEY CONCEPT   *For Your Notebook*

Customary Units of Measure

Length	**Weight**	**Capacity**
1 ft = 12 in.	1 lb = 16 oz	1 c = 8 fl oz
1 yd = 3 ft = 36 in.	1 ton = 2000 lb	1 pt = 2 c
1 mi = 1760 yd = 5280 ft		1 qt = 2 pt
		1 gal = 4 qt

Converting Units To convert between customary units, the equations above can be used to multiply by a convenient form of 1. Some useful facts are:

- To convert inches to feet, multiply by $\dfrac{1 \text{ ft}}{12 \text{ in.}}$.

- To convert feet to inches, multiply by $\dfrac{12 \text{ in.}}{1 \text{ ft}}$.

EXAMPLE 1   Converting Customary Units of Length

To find the length, in yards, of each piece of fabric described above, convert 63 feet to yards.

$$63 \text{ ft} \times \frac{1 \text{ yd}}{3 \text{ ft}} = \frac{\overset{21}{\cancel{63 \text{ ft}}} \times 1 \text{ yd}}{\underset{1}{\cancel{3 \text{ ft}}}}$$

Use rule for multiplying fractions. Divide out common factor and unit.

$$= 21 \text{ yd}$$

Multiply.

MULTIPLY BY 1
Because 1 yd = 3 ft, the fraction $\frac{1 \text{ yd}}{3 \text{ ft}}$ is equivalent to 1.

▶ **Answer** Each piece of fabric was 21 yards long.

EXAMPLE 2   Converting Customary Units of Weight

Whales A humpback whale weighs 33 tons. How many pounds does the whale weigh?

SOLUTION

Use the fact that 1 T = 2000 lb.

$$33 \text{ T} \times \frac{2000 \text{ lb}}{1 \text{ T}} = \frac{33 \cancel{\text{T}} \times 2000 \text{ lb}}{1 \cancel{\text{T}}}$$
  Use rule for multiplying fractions. Divide out common unit.

$$= 66{,}000 \text{ lb}$$ Multiply.

▶ **Answer** The humpback whale weighs 66,000 pounds.

> **AVOID ERRORS**
> Make sure you use the correct form of the fraction so the common units divide out. In Example 2, use $\frac{2000 \text{ lb}}{1 \text{ T}}$, *not* $\frac{1 \text{ T}}{2000 \text{ lb}}$.

EXAMPLE 3   Converting Customary Units of Capacity

Convert 25 fluid ounces to pints. Use the fact that 1 c = 8 fl oz and 1 pt = 2 c.

$$25 \text{ fl oz} \times \frac{1 \text{ c}}{8 \text{ fl oz}} \times \frac{1 \text{ pt}}{2 \text{ c}} = \frac{25 \cancel{\text{fl oz}} \times 1 \cancel{\text{c}} \times 1 \text{ pt}}{8 \cancel{\text{fl oz}} \times 2 \cancel{\text{c}}}$$
  Use rule for multiplying fractions. Divide out common units.

$$= \frac{25}{16} \text{ pt, or } 1\frac{9}{16} \text{ pt}$$ Multiply.

> **CHECK UNITS**
> One way to check your answer is to make sure you end up with the correct units after simplifying.

EXAMPLE 4   Solve a Multi-Step Problem

Convert 26 fluid ounces to cups and fluid ounces.

STEP 1 **Convert** 26 fluid ounces to cups.

$$26 \text{ fl oz} \times \frac{1 \text{ c}}{8 \text{ fl oz}} = \frac{\overset{13}{\cancel{26}} \cancel{\text{fl oz}} \times 1 \text{ c}}{\underset{4}{\cancel{8} \cancel{\text{fl oz}}}}$$

$$= \frac{13}{4} \text{ c, or } 3\frac{1}{4} \text{ c}$$

STEP 2 **Convert** the fractional part from cups to fluid ounces.

$$\frac{1 \text{ c}}{4} \times \frac{8 \text{ fl oz}}{1 \text{ c}} = \frac{1 \cancel{\text{c}} \times \overset{2}{\cancel{8}} \text{ fl oz}}{\underset{1}{\cancel{4}} \times 1 \cancel{\text{c}}}$$

$$= 2 \text{ fl oz}$$

▶ **Answer** So, 26 fluid ounces = 3 cups 2 fluid ounces.

Animated **Math**
at classzone.com

   GUIDED PRACTICE   for Examples 1, 2, 3, and 4

Copy and complete the statement.

1. 10 yd = _?_ in.

2. 3000 lb = _?_ T

3. 6 c = _?_ fl oz

4. 9000 ft = _?_ mi _?_ ft

5. 35 oz = _?_ lb _?_ oz

6. 5 pt = _?_ qt _?_ pt

7. 450 in. = _?_ ft _?_ in.

8. 75 oz = _?_ lb _?_ oz

9. 4250 lb = _?_ T _?_ lb

Mixed Units When adding or subtracting measures given in mixed units, you may need to convert between units.

EXAMPLE 5 **Adding and Subtracting with Mixed Units**

Wakeboards One type of wakeboard weighs 7 pounds 6 ounces. Another type of wakeboard weighs 6 pounds 14 ounces.

a. Find the sum of the weights.

b. Find the difference of the weights.

SOLUTION

a. Add. Then rename the sum.

```
   7 lb   6 oz
 + 6 lb  14 oz
 ─────────────
  13 lb  20 oz
```

13 lb 20 oz = 13 lb + 1 lb 4 oz

▶ **Answer** The sum is 14 lb 4 oz.

b. Rename. Then subtract.

```
  7 lb  06 oz         6 lb  22 oz
 − 6 lb  14 oz   →   − 6 lb  14 oz
                     ────────────
                            8 oz
```

▶ **Answer** The difference is 8 oz.

RENAMING
16 oz = 1 lb,
so 20 oz is equal
to 1 lb + 4 oz.

✓ **GUIDED PRACTICE** **for Example 5**

10. What If? In Example 5, suppose the weights of the wakeboards are 6 pounds 15 ounces and 7 pounds 4 ounces. Find the sum and difference of the weights.

5.6 EXERCISES

HOMEWORK KEY

★ = **STANDARDIZED TEST PRACTICE**
Exs. 23, 42, 46, 53, 54, and 65

◯ = **HINTS AND HOMEWORK HELP**
for Exs. 7, 17, 21, 25, 43 at classzone.com

SKILL PRACTICE

VOCABULARY Copy and complete the statement.

1. 1 mi = 1760 __?__

2. 1 lb = 16 __?__

3. 1 mi = 5280 __?__

4. 1 pt = 2 __?__

5. 1 gal = 4 __?__

6. 1 ton = 2000 __?__

CONVERTING UNITS Copy and complete the statement.

*SEE EXAMPLES
1, 2, AND 3*
on pp. 250–251
for Exs. 7–16

(7.) 24 oz = __?__ lb

8. 15 pt = __?__ c

9. 35 in. = __?__ ft

10. 5 ft = __?__ in.

11. 16,320 ft = __?__ mi

12. $4\frac{5}{8}$ lb = __?__ oz

13. $1\frac{1}{4}$ T = __?__ lb

14. $3\frac{3}{4}$ c = __?__ fl oz

15. 25 c = __?__ pt

16. ERROR ANALYSIS Describe and correct the error made in converting 30 feet to inches.

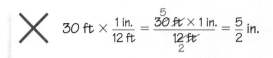

$$30 \text{ ft} \times \frac{1 \text{ in.}}{12 \text{ ft}} = \frac{\overset{5}{\cancel{30 \text{ ft}}} \times 1 \text{ in.}}{\underset{2}{\cancel{12 \text{ ft}}}} = \frac{5}{2} \text{ in.}$$

WRITING MIXED UNITS Copy and complete the statement.

SEE EXAMPLE 4
on p. 251
for Exs. 17–23

17. 40 in. = __?__ ft __?__ in.

18. 11 c = __?__ pt __?__ c

19. 2200 lb = __?__ ton __?__ lb

20. 96 in. = __?__ yd __?__ ft

21. 9 qt = __?__ gal __?__ qt

22. 70 oz = __?__ lb __?__ oz

23. ★ **MULTIPLE CHOICE** Which is equal to 130 ounces?

(**A**) 8 lb 2 oz   (**B**) 8 lb 2 fl oz   (**C**) 1 gal 2 oz   (**D**) 1 gal 2 fl oz

ADDING AND SUBTRACTING MEASUREMENTS Find the sum or difference.

SEE EXAMPLE 5
on p. 252
for Exs. 24–29

24.   3 c 5 fl oz
     + 8 c 6 fl oz

25.   6 lb 7 oz
     + 8 lb 9 oz

26.   45 lb   9 oz
     − 17 lb 13 oz

27.   6 ft   2 in.
     − 2 ft 11 in.

28.   10 ft 3 in.
     − 4 ft 9 in.

29.   12 mi   500 ft
     + 27 mi 5250 ft

COMPARING MEASUREMENTS Copy and complete the statement using <, >, or =.

30. 36 in. __?__ 3 ft

31. 10 pt __?__ 2 gal

32. 10 lb __?__ 64 oz

33. 3 yd __?__ 10 ft

34. 10 c __?__ 20 fl oz

35. 2 T __?__ 5000 lb

ORDERING MEASUREMENTS Order the measurements from least to greatest.

36. $\frac{1}{4}$ lb, 7 oz, $\frac{5}{8}$ lb, 0.5 lb, $\frac{32}{3}$ oz

37. 0.75 ft, 8.7 in., $\frac{37}{5}$ in., $\frac{5}{6}$ ft, $7\frac{3}{4}$ in.

⊗ **ALGEBRA** Copy and complete the statement.

38. There are __?__ mile(s) in x inches.

39. There are __?__ hour(s) in y seconds.

CHALLENGE Copy and complete the statement.

40. 60 miles per hour = __?__ feet per second

41. 15 oz per cup = __?__ pounds per gallon

PROBLEM SOLVING

**SEE EXAMPLES
1, 2, AND 3**
on pp. 250–251
for Exs. 42–44

42. ★ **MULTIPLE CHOICE** One lap of the Indy 500 is $2\frac{1}{2}$ miles long. How many feet are in three laps?

(**A**) 1250 feet   (**B**) 13,200 feet   (**C**) 39,600 feet   (**D**) 79,200 feet

43. CONTAINERS A container holds 20 fluid ounces of liquid. Convert this to cups and fluid ounces.

44. REASONING When converting from pounds to ounces, will the number of ounces be *greater than* or *less than* the number of pounds? *Explain.*

45. MULTI-STEP PROBLEM You have 10 jugs and 18 bottles of spring water. Each jug contains 1 gallon of spring water and each bottle contains 12 fluid ounces of spring water.

    a. How many cups of spring water do you have in the jugs?

    b. How many cups of spring water do you have in the bottles?

    c. How many cups of spring water do you have altogether?

46. ★ SHORT RESPONSE In some areas, fishing regulations set daily weight limits. When you catch a fish that makes the total weight of your caught fish greater than $7\frac{1}{2}$ pounds, you must stop fishing. If you catch a 4 lb 4 oz rainbow trout and a 3 lb 5 oz brook trout, can you continue to fish? *Explain.*

READING *IN* MATH Read the information below for Exercises 47–51.

Pyramids of Egypt The three great pyramids of Giza, Egypt, and their original heights and base widths are listed in the table. The tallest of these is The Great Pyramid, one of the Seven Wonders of the Ancient World. These three pyramids were built during the 4th Dynasty, between 2590 and 2540 B.C. It is believed that these massive structures took decades to complete.

Pyramid	Height	Width
Khafre	157 yd	8448 in.
Menkaure	2580 in.	344 ft
Khufu	481 ft	251 yd

47. Convert What are the heights of the pyramids in yards and in feet?

48. Reasoning Which pyramid is one of the Seven Wonders of the Ancient World?

49. Calculate How many yards taller is the tallest pyramid than the shortest pyramid? feet taller?

50. Compare Which pyramid has the least width?

51. Reasoning Are the heights of the pyramids all less than their base widths? *Justify* your answer.

52. BACKPACKS The total weight of a school backpack and the items it holds should not exceed 25 pounds. The following items are in your backpack, which weighs 1 lb 12 oz. Does the total weight exceed 25 pounds? If not, how much more weight can you add without exceeding 25 pounds? If so, by how much is it over 25 pounds?

Item	math book	notebook	calculator	history book	gym clothes and shoes
Weight	3 lb 14 oz	24 oz	9 oz	4 lb 10 oz	1 lb 9 oz

53. ★ WRITING You are subtracting two weights given in pounds and ounces. *Explain* how you can tell whether renaming is needed or not.

54. ★ **EXTENDED RESPONSE** You are building a CD rack with 3 shelves that are each 1 foot 3 inches long. Each end piece is 2 inches long.

   a. How many feet of wood will you need to buy for the shelves and six end pieces?

   b. Each CD has a width of $\frac{3}{8}$ inch. Estimate the number of CDs in one inch. Predict the number of CDs that will fit on a shelf. Calculate to find the exact number.

   c. Your friend asks you to build a CD rack for him. He has a collection of 100 CDs. How long should you make each of the 3 shelves?

55. **CHALLENGE** The length of a driveway is 12 yards and the width is $5\frac{1}{2}$ yards. Pavement sealer comes in containers that cover x square feet. Write an expression in terms of x that gives the number of containers of sealer that are needed. How many containers are needed if $x = 400$?

 NEW JERSEY MIXED REVIEW   **TEST PRACTICE** at classzone.com

56. In science class, four students measure the lengths of their index fingers. Which list shows the lengths in order from least to greatest?

   A $2\frac{1}{4}$ in., $2\frac{7}{8}$ in., $2\frac{7}{16}$ in., $2\frac{5}{8}$ in.   **B** $2\frac{1}{4}$ in., $2\frac{5}{8}$ in., $2\frac{7}{8}$ in., $2\frac{7}{16}$ in.

   C $2\frac{1}{4}$ in., $2\frac{7}{16}$ in., $2\frac{5}{8}$ in., $2\frac{7}{8}$ in.   **D** $2\frac{7}{8}$ in., $2\frac{5}{8}$ in., $2\frac{7}{16}$ in., $2\frac{1}{4}$ in.

57. What is the value of $(3 + 5)^2 \div 4 + 8$?

   A $5\frac{1}{3}$ **B** 15   **C** $17\frac{1}{4}$ **D** 24

QUIZ *for Lessons 5.5–5.6*

Tell what the measurement describes about a bottle of mouthwash. *(p. 245)*

   1. 17 ounces   **2.** 2 pints   **3.** 9 inches

Copy and complete the statement. *(p. 250)*

   4. $46\frac{2}{3}$ yd = __?__ ft   **5.** 11 qt = __?__ c   **6.** 22 qt = __?__ gal __?__ qt

Find the sum or difference. *(p. 250)*

   7.   6 gal 3 qt   **8.**   52 lb 8 oz   **9.**   12 yd 2 ft
       + 2 gal 2 qt   − 27 lb 13 oz   + 4 yd 1 ft

10. **COOKING** You are making soup that requires 4 cups of water. How many *fluid ounces* of water do you need? *(p. 250)*

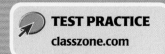
Lessons 5.5–5.6

1. **POTATOES** What is the difference in weight between the bag of potatoes shown and a single potato weighing 6 ounces?

A. $\frac{3}{8}$ pound

B. $\frac{7}{8}$ pound

C. $4\frac{3}{4}$ pounds

D. $5\frac{1}{4}$ pounds

2. **FILLING A TUB** The faucet in your 70-gallon bathtub is not working. You want to fill the bathtub halfway using a 2 quart pitcher. About how many times do you have to empty the pitcher into the bathtub?

   A. 35

   B. 70

   C. 140

   D. 280

3. **CITY BLOCK** The length of your stride when walking briskly is about $2\frac{1}{5}$ feet. You walk briskly from one end of a city block to the other and count 240 strides. About how long is the block?

   A. 0.1 mile

   B. 0.2 mile

   C. 1 mile

   D. 10 miles

4. **ELECTRONICS** A cell phone weighs about 3.5 ounces. A portable DVD player weighs about 2 pounds. About how many cell phones equal the weight of one DVD player?

   A. 0.2   **B.** 8   **C.** 9   **D.** 32

5. **DINOSAURS** The diagram below shows the heights and weights of an Ankylosaurus and a Stegosaurus. Which conclusion can be drawn from the information in the diagram?

Ankylosaurus
$3\frac{1}{2}$ tons   66 in.

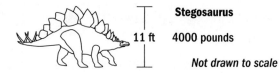

Stegosaurus
11 ft   4000 pounds

Not drawn to scale

   A. The Ankylosaurus was taller and weighed more than the Stegosaurus.

   B. The Stegosaurus was taller but the Ankylosaurus weighed more.

   C. The Stegosaurus was taller and weighed more than the Ankylosaurus.

   D. Taller dinosaurs weighed more than shorter dinosaurs.

6. **OPEN-ENDED** You are comparing the weight of a cell phone with the weight of a DVD player. Use customary units to answer the parts below.

   • A cell phone weighs about 3.5 _?_ .

   • A DVD player weighs about 2 _?_ .

   • About how many cell phones would it take to equal the weight of a DVD player?

CHAPTER REVIEW

5

@*HomeTutor*
classzone.com
Vocabulary Practice

REVIEW KEY VOCABULARY

- reciprocal, *p. 237*
- U.S. customary system, *p. 245*
- inch, *p. 245*
- foot, *p. 245*
- yard, *p. 245*

- mile, *p. 245*
- ounce, *p. 246*
- pound, *p. 246*
- ton, *p. 246*
- fluid ounce, *p. 247*

- cup, *p. 247*
- pint, *p. 247*
- quart, *p. 247*
- gallon, *p. 247*

VOCABULARY EXERCISES

1. Copy and complete: The __?__ of $\frac{3}{10}$ is $\frac{10}{3}$.

2. What is the product of a nonzero number and its reciprocal?

3. Which unit measures length: *pound, yard,* or *quart*?

4. Which unit measures capacity: *ounce, pound,* or *fluid ounce*?

5. How many inches are in a yard?

6. *Explain* the difference between an ounce and a fluid ounce.

7. Name three customary units of weight.

REVIEW EXAMPLES AND EXERCISES

5.1 Adding and Subtracting Fractions

pp. 219–224

EXAMPLE

$$\frac{1}{5} + \frac{3}{10} = \frac{2}{10} + \frac{3}{10}$$ **Rewrite fraction using 10 as the LCD of $\frac{1}{5}$ and $\frac{3}{10}$.**

$$= \frac{5}{10}$$ **Add numerators.**

$$= \frac{1}{2}$$ **Simplify.**

EXERCISES

Find the sum or difference.

SEE EXAMPLES 1, 2, 3, AND 4 on pp. 219–221 for Exs. 8–19

8. $\frac{3}{11} + \frac{5}{11}$

9. $\frac{7}{15} - \frac{4}{15}$

10. $\frac{6}{7} - \frac{4}{7}$

11. $\frac{11}{15} + \frac{1}{15}$

12. $\frac{9}{13} + \frac{2}{13}$

13. $\frac{8}{11} - \frac{5}{11}$

14. $\frac{1}{2} - \frac{1}{5}$

15. $\frac{3}{7} + \frac{1}{4}$

16. $\frac{5}{9} + \frac{1}{3}$

17. $\frac{7}{8} - \frac{3}{4}$

18. $\frac{13}{15} - \frac{3}{10}$

19. $\frac{5}{12} + \frac{3}{8}$

Chapter Review   **257**

5.2 Adding and Subtracting Mixed Numbers

pp. 226–230

EXAMPLE

$$10\frac{1}{4} - 4\frac{5}{6} = 10\frac{3}{12} - 4\frac{10}{12} \qquad \text{Rewrite fractions using LCD of } \frac{1}{4} \text{ and } \frac{5}{6}.$$

$$= 9\frac{15}{12} - 4\frac{10}{12} \qquad \text{Rename } 10\frac{3}{12} \text{ as } 9\frac{15}{12}.$$

$$= 5\frac{5}{12} \qquad \text{Subtract fractions and whole numbers.}$$

EXERCISES

Find the sum or difference.

SEE EXAMPLES
1, 2, 3, AND 4
on pp. 226–227
for Exs. 20–24

20. $2\frac{1}{5} + 3\frac{3}{5}$ **21.** $10\frac{5}{8} - 8\frac{7}{8}$ **22.** $9\frac{13}{14} - 8\frac{3}{7}$ **23.** $6\frac{4}{21} + 16\frac{1}{6}$

24. Knitting Carly is knitting a scarf for a friend. She wants the scarf to be $36\frac{5}{8}$ inches long. She has already knit $28\frac{3}{4}$ inches. How many more inches does Carly need to knit?

5.3 Multiplying Fractions and Mixed Numbers

pp. 232–236

EXAMPLE

$$3\frac{3}{4} \times 4\frac{2}{5} = \frac{15}{4} \times \frac{22}{5} \qquad \text{Write } 3\frac{3}{4} \text{ and } 4\frac{2}{5} \text{ as improper fractions.}$$

$$= \frac{\overset{3}{\cancel{15}} \times \overset{11}{\cancel{22}}}{\underset{2}{\cancel{4}} \times \underset{1}{\cancel{5}}} \qquad \begin{array}{l}\text{Use rule for multiplying fractions.}\\ \text{Divide out common factors.}\end{array}$$

$$= \frac{33}{2} \qquad \text{Multiply.}$$

$$= 16\frac{1}{2} \qquad \text{Rewrite improper fraction as a mixed number.}$$

EXERCISES

Find the product.

SEE EXAMPLES
1, 2, AND 3
on pp. 232–233
for Exs. 25–29

25. $\frac{3}{10} \times \frac{5}{8}$ **26.** $\frac{7}{12} \times 18$ **27.** $5\frac{5}{6} \times \frac{2}{7}$ **28.** $4\frac{7}{8} \times 2\frac{4}{9}$

29. Orchestra One half of an orchestra plays brass instruments. The horn section makes up $\frac{1}{7}$ of the brass instruments. What fraction of the whole orchestra is in the horn section?

5.4 Dividing Fractions and Mixed Numbers

EXAMPLE

$$\frac{5}{6} \div \frac{4}{9} = \frac{5}{6} \times \frac{9}{4}$$ **Multiply by reciprocal.**

$$= \frac{5 \times \cancel{9}^{3}}{\cancel{6}_{2} \times 4}$$ **Use rule for multiplying fractions.**
Divide out common factor.

$$= \frac{15}{8}$$ **Multiply.**

$$= 1\frac{7}{8}$$ **Rewrite improper fraction as a mixed number.**

EXERCISES

Find the quotient.

SEE EXAMPLES 1, 2, 3, AND 4 on pp. 237–239 for Exs. 30–34

30. $\frac{7}{8} \div \frac{1}{12}$ **31.** $\frac{3}{5} \div 6$ **32.** $36 \div 6\frac{3}{4}$ **33.** $10\frac{1}{8} \div 1\frac{7}{20}$

34. Storage A full shelf on a DVD rack is $21\frac{7}{8}$ inches wide. Each DVD is approximately $\frac{5}{8}$ inch wide. How many DVDs are on the shelf?

5.5 Measuring in Customary Units

EXAMPLE

Copy and complete the statement using the appropriate customary unit:
The weight of a fire extinguisher is about 8 ___?___ .

Use the benchmarks from Lesson 5.5. You know that the weight of a fire extinguisher is greater than the weight of 8 slices of bread (8 ounces) and is less than the weight of 8 walruses (8 tons). A good estimate for its weight is the weight of 8 soccer balls (8 pounds).

▶ **Answer** The weight of a fire extinguisher is about 8 pounds.

EXERCISES

Copy and complete using the appropriate customary unit.

SEE EXAMPLES 1, 3, AND 5 on pp. 245–247 for Exs. 35–39

35. An apple weighs 8 ___?___ .

36. The length of a chopstick is 9 ___?___ .

37. The capacity of a soup can is 19 ___?___ .

38. An airplane weighs 455 ___?___ .

39. Estimate the length of your math book in inches. Then use a ruler to check your estimate.

Chapter Review   **259**

EXAMPLE

Convert 5720 yards to miles.

Use the fact that 1 mi = 1760 yd.

$$\frac{5720 \text{ yd}}{1} \times \frac{1 \text{ mi}}{1760 \text{ yd}} = \frac{\overset{13}{\cancel{5720}} \text{ yd} \times 1 \text{ mi}}{1 \times \underset{4}{\cancel{1760}} \text{ yd}}$$ Use rule for multiplying fractions.
Divide out common factor and unit.

$$= \frac{13}{4} \text{ mi}$$ Simplify.

$$= 3\frac{1}{4} \text{ mi}$$ Rewrite improper fraction as a mixed number.

EXERCISES

Copy and complete the statement.

SEE EXAMPLES 1, 2, 3, AND 4
on pp. 250–251
for Exs. 40–46

40. 19 yd = __?__ in.

41. 8500 lb = __?__ T

42. 48 c = __?__ qt

43. 30 pt = __?__ gal __?__ pt

44. 200 ft = __?__ yd __?__ ft

45. 50 oz = __?__ lb __?__ oz

46. Fruit Punch You need to make 16 one-cup servings of punch for a party. How many quarts of punch do you need to make?

EXAMPLE

Find the sum or difference.

a.
```
    7 gal  3 qt
 +  7 gal  2 qt
 ─────────────
   14 gal  5 qt
```

14 gal 5 qt = 14 gal + 1 gal 1 qt

▶ **Answer** The sum is 15 gal 1 qt.

b.
```
   6 gal  1 qt  ──Rename──▶   5 gal  5 qt
 − 4 gal  3 qt              − 4 gal  3 qt
                           ─────────────
                             1 gal  2 qt
```

▶ **Answer** The difference is 1 gal 2 qt.

EXERCISES

Find the sum or difference.

SEE EXAMPLE 5
on p. 252
for Exs. 47–52

47.
```
   5 pt  1 c
 + 2 pt  1 c
```

48.
```
   9 ft  2 in.
 − 3 ft 11 in.
```

49.
```
   3 T   654 lb
 − 1 T  1541 lb
```

50.
```
   5 c  6 fl oz
 − 2 c  7 fl oz
```

51.
```
   20 mi  52 yd
 − 16 mi 763 yd
```

52.
```
   158 lb  9 oz
 + 22 lb 12 oz
```

Find the sum or difference.

1. $\dfrac{4}{5} + \dfrac{2}{15}$

2. $\dfrac{1}{2} + \dfrac{8}{9}$

3. $\dfrac{2}{3} - \dfrac{4}{7}$

4. $\dfrac{3}{4} - \dfrac{3}{10}$

5. $9\dfrac{3}{8} - 5\dfrac{1}{8}$

6. $14\dfrac{1}{6} + 12\dfrac{5}{6}$

7. $6\dfrac{2}{3} + 4\dfrac{3}{8}$

8. $7\dfrac{3}{4} - 5\dfrac{4}{5}$

Find the product or quotient.

9. $\dfrac{1}{5} \cdot \dfrac{1}{8}$

10. $\dfrac{4}{9} \cdot \dfrac{3}{16}$

11. $10 \cdot \dfrac{3}{4}$

12. $5\dfrac{1}{2} \cdot 2\dfrac{7}{9}$

13. $\dfrac{9}{17} \div \dfrac{3}{34}$

14. $\dfrac{7}{8} \div \dfrac{7}{12}$

15. $8\dfrac{2}{3} \div 5\dfrac{1}{6}$

16. $3\dfrac{6}{7} \div 1\dfrac{2}{7}$

Copy and complete the statement.

17. 20 lb = __?__ oz

18. 2 gal = __?__ pt

19. 5 yd = __?__ in.

20. 34 oz = __?__ lb __?__ oz

21. Find the length of the pencil to the nearest quarter inch.

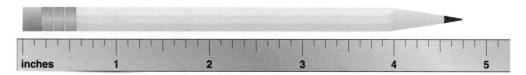

Copy and complete using the appropriate customary unit.

22. The weight of an empty wallet is 3 __?__.

23. The length of a toothbrush is 7 __?__.

24. The capacity of a kitchen sink is 20 __?__.

25. A lawn mower weighs 76 __?__.

26. **APPLE PIE** You have $2\dfrac{1}{3}$ pounds of apples, and your friend has $2\dfrac{1}{6}$ pounds. A pie recipe calls for $4\dfrac{1}{2}$ pounds of apples. Do you and your friend have enough apples to make this pie? *Explain.*

27. **RAIN** A rain gauge is used to collect rainfall data. During a rainstorm, a gauge reads $1\dfrac{3}{8}$ inches after the first three hours and $2\dfrac{1}{3}$ inches two hours later. How much rain fell in the last two hours?

28. **POPULATION** A middle school has 900 students. Seventh-grade students make up $\dfrac{2}{5}$ of all the students. How many of the students are in the seventh grade?

29. **NECKLACES** You want to make a necklace that has a bead placed every $1\dfrac{1}{4}$ inches. The necklace needs to be 20 inches long. There should be no beads at the ends of the necklace. How many beads do you need?

TEST PREPARATION

OPEN-ENDED QUESTIONS

Scoring Rubric

Full Credit
- solution is complete and correct

Partial Credit
- solution is complete but errors are made, or
- solution is without error, but incomplete

No Credit
- no solution is given, or
- solution makes no sense

PROBLEM

You are organizing a karaoke night at your school. You allow an average of $3\frac{1}{2}$ minutes for each singer to set up and $5\frac{1}{4}$ minutes for the song. How many singers can fit in a program that runs $1\frac{1}{2}$ hours? *Explain*.

Below are sample solutions to the problem. Read each solution and the comments on the left to see why the sample represents *full credit*, *partial credit*, or *no credit*.

SAMPLE 1: Full Credit Solution

Reasoning is key to choosing the correct operations.

The number of singers equals the total number of minutes for the program divided by the time for each singer.

Time for each singer = Set-up time + Song time

Time for each singer = $3\frac{1}{2} + 5\frac{1}{4} = 8\frac{3}{4}$

The steps of the solution are clearly written and the calculations are correct.

Singers = Total time ÷ Time for each singer

Singers = $90 \div 8\frac{3}{4}$

Singers = $90 \div \frac{35}{4}$

Singers = $90 \times \frac{4}{35} = \frac{72}{7} = 10\frac{2}{7}$

The question is answered correctly.

There is not enough time for 11 singers. The program can have 10 singers.

SAMPLE 2: Partial Credit Solution

The reasoning and the calculations are correct. The answer is incorrect. You cannot have a fractional number of singers.

Divide the total amount of time by the time needed for each singer.

Singers = $90 \div \frac{35}{4}$

Singers = $90 \times \frac{4}{35} = \frac{72}{7} = 10\frac{2}{7}$

The program can have $10\frac{2}{7}$ singers.

SAMPLE 3: Partial Credit Solution

The problem does not call for an estimated answer. ⤵

> The total amount of time for each singer is about 9 minutes.

The answer is correct, but it is not justified. ⤵

> You can have 10 singers.

SAMPLE 4: No Credit Solution

The units are not equivalent. Hours should be converted to minutes. ⤵

$$1\frac{1}{2} \div \left(3\frac{1}{2} + 5\frac{1}{4}\right) = 1\frac{1}{2} \div 8\frac{3}{4}$$

The calculations are incorrect. ⤵

$$1\frac{1}{2} \div \left(3\frac{1}{2} + 5\frac{1}{4}\right) = \frac{2}{3} \times \frac{35}{4}$$

$$1\frac{1}{2} \div \left(3\frac{1}{2} + 5\frac{1}{4}\right) = \frac{70}{12} = 5\frac{5}{6}$$

The answer does not make sense. ⤵

> You can have 6 singers.

PRACTICE Apply the Scoring Rubric

Score the solution to the problem below as *full credit*, *partial credit*, or *no credit*. *Explain* your reasoning.

> **PROBLEM** At a fish market, a pound of salmon costs $6 and a pound of shrimp cost $12. You buy $2\frac{1}{3}$ pounds of salmon and $3\frac{1}{2}$ pounds of shrimp. You pay using three $20 bills and are given $2 in change. Is your change correct? *Explain.*

1.
$$6\left(2\frac{1}{3}\right) + 12\left(3\frac{1}{2}\right) = 6\left(\frac{7}{3}\right) + 12\left(\frac{7}{2}\right)$$
$$6\left(2\frac{1}{3}\right) + 12\left(3\frac{1}{2}\right) = 14 + 42$$
$$6\left(2\frac{1}{3}\right) + 12\left(3\frac{1}{2}\right) = 56$$

The cost of purchasing the salmon and shrimp is $56. You paid with $60, so you should receive 60 − 56 = $4 change. You are owed $2.

2.
$$6\left(2\frac{1}{3}\right) + 12\left(3\frac{1}{2}\right) = \frac{6 \cdot 7 + 12 \cdot 7}{3} = \frac{126}{3} = 42$$

The cost of purchasing $2\frac{1}{3}$ pounds of salmon and $3\frac{1}{2}$ pounds of shrimp is $42. You paid with $60, so you should receive 60 − 42 = $18 change. You are owed $16.

TEST PREPARATION

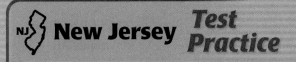
TEST PREPARATION

1. Christina and Timothy each own a kite. The string on Christina's kite is $75\frac{1}{2}$ feet long. The string on Timothy's kite is $1\frac{3}{4}$ feet shorter than Christina's. Which equation can be used to find l, the length of the string on Timothy's kite?

   A. $l = 75\frac{1}{2} + 1\frac{3}{4}$

   B. $l = 75\frac{1}{2} - 1\frac{3}{4}$

   C. $l = 75\frac{1}{2} \cdot 1\frac{3}{4}$

   D. $l = 75\frac{1}{2} \div 1\frac{3}{4}$

2. A recipe calls for $\frac{1}{2}$ cup of butter, $\frac{1}{4}$ cup of white sugar, $\frac{3}{4}$ cup of brown sugar, and $1\frac{1}{2}$ cups of flour. How much more flour is needed for the recipe than white sugar?

   A. $\frac{3}{4}$ cup

   B. $1\frac{1}{4}$ cups

   C. $1\frac{3}{4}$ cups

   D. $2\frac{1}{4}$ cups

3. A shelf is $20\frac{1}{2}$ inches wide. How many compact disc cases can it hold if each case is $\frac{7}{16}$ inch wide?

   A. 8

   B. 46

   C. 47

   D. 92

4. You cook 6 cups of pasta. One serving is $\frac{3}{4}$ of a cup. Which expression can you use to find the number of servings you cooked?

   A. $\frac{3}{4} \times \frac{1}{6}$

   B. $\frac{3}{4} \times 6$

   C. $\frac{3}{4} \div 6$

   D. $6 \div \frac{3}{4}$

5. Which figure is next in the pattern?

   A

   B

   C

   D

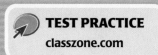

6. Which sequence follows the rule $3n + 5$?

   A. 3, 6, 9, 12, 15, . . .

   B. 6, 11, 16, 21, 26, . . .

   C. 8, 11, 14, 17, 20, . . .

   D. 8, 13, 18, 23, 28, . . .

7. Which of the following relationships is best represented by the data in the graph?

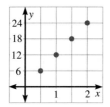

   A. Conversion of feet to inches

   B. Conversion of miles to feet

   C. Conversion of feet to yards

   D. Conversion of yards to inches

8. Bananas are on sale for $0.39 per pound. Greg bought 2.5 pounds of bananas. About how much did he pay for the bananas?

   A. Less than $0.50

   B. Between $0.50 and $1.00

   C. Between $1.00 and $1.50

   D. More than $1.50

9. Which is the greatest length?

   A. $\frac{1}{4}$ of a mile

   B. 1000 yards

   C. 1200 feet

   D. 9600 inches

10. Which model represents 5^2?

   A.

   B.
   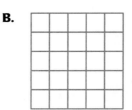

   C.

   D.

11. OPEN-ENDED The table shows the triple jump attempts made by 2 athletes in a track meet. Use the table to answer the questions below.

Athlete	1st Jump	2nd Jump	3rd Jump
Leslie	$41\frac{3}{5}$ ft	$39\frac{5}{6}$ ft	$40\frac{2}{3}$ ft
Jade	$40\frac{1}{12}$ ft	$38\frac{2}{3}$ ft	$42\frac{1}{4}$ ft

Part A Out of all the jumps, which athlete jumped the farthest?

Part B Find the difference between each athlete's longest jump distance and shortest jump distance.

Part C Which athlete has the greater mean jump distance?

TEST PREPARATION

6 Integers

Before

In previous chapters you've . . .

- Worked with whole numbers, decimals, and fractions
- Used order of operations

Now

 New Jersey Standards

4.1.A.4	6.1	Comparing integers
4.1.B.1.a	6.2	Adding integers
4.1.B.1.a	6.3	Subtracting integers
4.1.B.1.a	6.4	Multiplying integers
4.1.B.1.a	6.5	Dividing integers
4.3.D.4.a	6.6	Rational numbers
	6.7	The distributive property
4.2.C.1	6.8	The coordinate plane

Why?

So you can solve real-world problems about . . .

- miniature golf, p. 272
- planet temperatures, p. 288
- shipwrecks, p. 317

 **Math**
at classzone.com

- Adding Integers, p. 279
- Multiplying Integers, p. 292
- Rational Numbers, p. 301

Get-Ready Games

Review Prerequisite Skills by playing *Operation Scramble.*

Skill Focus:

- Using order of operations
- Writing expressions

OPERATION SCRAMBLE

MATERIALS

- 1 deck of *Operation Scramble* cards
- a pencil and paper for each player

HOW TO PLAY Deal four cards face up between you and your partner. The numbers on the cards are expression numbers. Deal a fifth card face up. The number on this card is the target number. For each round, both players should follow the directions on the next page.

Expression Cards   **Target Card**

1. **USE** all four expression numbers in any order and any of the operation symbols $+$, $-$, $\times$, or $\div$ to write an expression that equals the target number. You may also use parentheses.

2. **TELL** your partner when you are finished writing your expression. Both players must stop working if one person is finished. If both players agree that an expression cannot be written, turn over a new target number card.

3. **CHECK** the work of the player who finished writing an expression first. If the expression is correct, that player gets one point. If it is incorrect, deal new cards and try again.

$$3 + 4 - 2 \div 1 = 5$$

✓ **One point!**

HOW TO WIN Be the first player to get three points.

Stop and Think

1. **WRITING** In *Operation Scramble*, suppose you have only even numbers on the expression cards. The target number is odd. Give an example of a correct expression and a target number that fit this description. Explain which operations you had to use.

2. **CRITICAL THINKING** Use the numbers 5, 4, 3, and 2 as expression numbers. Show how you can write expressions equal to the whole numbers from 1 through 10.

Review Prerequisite Skills

REVIEW WORDS
- **power,** *p. 13*
- **base,** *p. 13*
- **exponent,** *p. 13*
- **order of operations,** *p. 17*
- **reciprocal,** *p. 237*

VOCABULARY CHECK

Copy and complete using a review word from the list at the left.

1. The __?__ of 5 is $\frac{1}{5}$.

2. When a power is expressed as a product, the __?__ is the repeated factor and the __?__ is the number of times the factor is used.

SKILL CHECK

Evaluate the expression. *(p. 17)*

3. $21 - 10 + 1$
4. $(2 + 5)(6 - 4)^2$
5. $13(2) - 4^2$
6. $\dfrac{3^2}{4 + 9 - 4}$

7. $28 - 21 \div 7$
8. $25 - (4^2 + 3)$
9. $\dfrac{7 - 3 \cdot 2 + 4}{6 \div 2 + 8 \div 4}$
10. $2^5 \div 8 \div 4$

Write the decimal as a fraction or mixed number. *(p. 199)*

11. 0.35
12. 4.5
13. 2.85
14. 0.745

Order the numbers from least to greatest. *(p. 199)*

15. $9, 7\frac{1}{3}, 8.9, 7.5, 0, 0.4$

16. $\frac{5}{6}, \frac{3}{4}, 0.25, 0.5, 1.23, 0$

17. $0.45, 4.5, \frac{4}{5}, \frac{5}{9}, \frac{9}{5}, 3.50$

18. $1, \frac{8}{9}, 1.123, \frac{9}{8}, 0.98, 1.12$

@HomeTutor Prerequisite skills practice at classzone.com

Notetaking Skills Recording the Process

In each chapter you will learn a new notetaking skill. In Chapter 6 you will apply the strategy of recording the process to Example 5 on p. 303.

You should record and summarize in your notebook the key steps that you take in performing a multi-step calculation. Referring to these steps can help you perform similar calculations.

Calculations	Key Steps
$6\frac{2}{3} \cdot 1\frac{4}{5} = \frac{20}{3} \cdot \frac{9}{5}$	Write mixed number as improper fractions.
$= \dfrac{\overset{4}{\cancel{20}} \cdot \overset{3}{\cancel{9}}}{\underset{1}{\cancel{3}} \cdot \underset{1}{\cancel{5}}}$	Use rule for multiplying fractions. Divide out common factors.
$= \dfrac{12}{1}$, or 12	Multiply.

6.1 Comparing and Ordering Integers

k7pe-0601-0001-h

 4.1.A.4   Compare and order numbers of all named types.

Before   You compared and ordered whole numbers and fractions.

Now   You'll compare and order integers.

Why?   So you can represent gains and losses, as in Example 1.

KEY VOCABULARY
- **integer,** *p. 269*
- **negative integer,** *p. 269*
- **positive integer,** *p. 269*
- **opposite,** *p. 269*

The following numbers are **integers**:

$$\ldots, -4, -3, -2, -1, 0, 1, 2, 3, 4, \ldots$$

Negative integers are integers that are less than zero. **Positive integers** are integers that are greater than 0. Zero is neither positive nor negative.

KEY CONCEPT   *For Your Notebook*

Integers and Their Opposites

k7pe-0601-0001-t

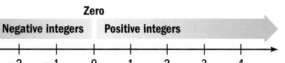

Two numbers are **opposites** if they are the same distance from 0 on a number line but are on opposite sides of 0. For example, 3 and −3 are opposites. The opposite of 0 is 0.

EXAMPLE 1   Writing Integers

READING

The integer −10 is read "negative ten." A number other than 0 that has no sign is considered to be positive, so the integer 9 is read "positive nine" or "nine."

a. In three plays of a football game, there is a gain of 7 yards, a loss of 10 yards, and a gain of 9 yards. Use integers to represent the gains and losses.

     7 yard gain: 7   10 yard loss: −10   9 yard gain: 9

b. A bank account has deposits of $100 and $150 and a withdrawal of $75. Use integers to represent the deposits and withdrawals.

     $100 deposit: $100 $150 deposit: $150 $75 withdrawal: −$75

✓ **GUIDED PRACTICE**   for Example 1

Write the opposite of the integer.

1. 15   **2.** −8   **3.** −35   **4.** 100

5. What If? The bank account from Example 1 has an additional deposit of $200 and withdrawals of $100 and $250. Use integers to represent the deposits and withdrawals.

Comparing Integers You can use a number line to compare and order integers. Remember that numbers decrease as you move to the left on a number line and increase as you move to the right.

EXAMPLE 2 **Comparing Integers Using a Number Line**

a. Compare -2 and -5.

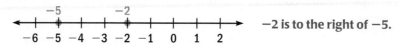

-2 is to the right of -5.

▸ **Answer** $-2 > -5$. You can also write $-5 < -2$.

b. Compare -6 and 1.

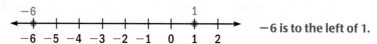

-6 is to the left of 1.

▸ **Answer** $-6 < 1$. You can also write $1 > -6$.

EXAMPLE 3 **Ordering Integers Using a Number Line**

Weather The table shows the average temperatures, in degrees Celsius, for six months in the Gobi Desert of Mongolia. Which of these months has the lowest average temperature?

Month	Nov.	Dec.	Jan.	Feb.	Mar.	Apr.
Average Temperature	$-6°$C	$-14°$C	$-15°$C	$-12°$C	$-3°$C	$6°$C

SOLUTION

You can graph each integer on a number line to order the temperatures.

The temperatures from least to greatest are: $-15, -14, -12, -6, -3, 6$.

▸ **Answer** At $-15°$C, January has the lowest average temperature.

Animated **Math** at classzone.com

✓ **GUIDED PRACTICE** for Examples 2 and 3

Copy and complete the statement using < or >.

6. $0 \ \underline{?} \ -7$ **7.** $-9 \ \underline{?} \ 4$ **8.** $-5 \ \underline{?} \ -4$ **9.** $-3 \ \underline{?} \ -13$

Order the integers from least to greatest.

10. $8, -4, -6, 4, -3, 1$ **11.** $-7, -12, -16, -10, -8$

6.1 EXERCISES

SKILL PRACTICE

1. VOCABULARY Which of the following numbers are integers?

$$2675, 0, -56, \frac{3}{4}, 75, 0.65$$

2. VOCABULARY What is the opposite of 12?

WRITING INTEGERS AND OPPOSITES Write the integer that represents the situation. Then write the opposite of the integer.

SEE EXAMPLE 1
on p. 269
for Exs. 3–6

3. 1333 feet above sea level

4. Sixteen degrees below zero

5. Nine million dollar loss

6. $15 account withdrawal

COMPARING INTEGERS Copy and complete the statement using < or >.

SEE EXAMPLE 2
on p. 270
for Exs. 7–15

7. 34 ? −43

8. −17 ? −13

9. 42 ? 37

10. 26 ? −267

11. −18 ? 3

12. −7 ? 4

13. −121 ? −125

14. 92 ? 96

15. ★ MULTIPLE CHOICE Which statement is true?

A −56 < −58

B 1 < −112

C −7 > −5

D −9 > −11

ORDERING INTEGERS Order the integers from least to greatest.

SEE EXAMPLE 3
on p. 270
for Exs. 16–22

16. −28, 18, 7, −17, 0, −12

17. 99, −42, 13, −2, 11, −49

18. −150, 235, −435, 345, −75

19. −66, 21, 9, −10, −22, 44

20. 320, −250, −19, 15, 2

21. −11, −93, −84, 0, 9, −3

22. ERROR ANALYSIS Describe the error in ordering the integers from least to greatest.

$$-1, -3, -7, -12 \quad \times$$

★ OPEN-ENDED MATH Draw a number line and graph the integer. Then give a real-world situation that the integer could represent.

23. −5

24. 0

25. 8

26. opposite of −7

27. −9

28. 4

29. −6

30. opposite of 3

ALGEBRA The statement $a < x < b$ means x is between a and b. Give two integer values of the variable that make the statement true.

31. $0 < d$

32. $c < 23$

33. $-10 > k$

34. $b > -9$

35. $-4 < m < 1$

36. $2 < p < 7$

37. $-3 > r > -11$

38. $9 > t > -2$

39. $-1 < k < 4$

40. $-22 < g < -12$

41. $7 > s > 4$

42. $52 < x < 60$

43. $-5 < y < 6$

44. $-1 < a < 2$

45. $6.3 > b > -9.7$

46. $3.6 > c > -8.2$

47. ⓧⓨ **ALGEBRA** Three times a given integer plus four is between −9 and 7. Give three possible values of this integer.

48. CHALLENGE The missing integer in the list of numbers below is the median of the numbers. What could the missing integer be?

$$-44, 23, -11, 12, -27, \underline{\ ?\ }, -4, 0, 1$$

PROBLEM SOLVING

SEE EXAMPLE 3
on p. 270
for Exs. 49–51

49. **MINIATURE GOLF** In miniature golf, the player with the least score wins. Order the scores given in the table from least to greatest. Who was the winner?

Player	Andrew	Mandy	Mitchell	Pedro
Score	−5	+3	0	−4

50. ★ **SHORT RESPONSE** The integers 17, −10, 32, −29, and 0 are temperatures in degrees Fahrenheit. Show how to find the median temperature. Would the median change if −29 was −28? if −29 was 29? *Explain.*

51. ROMAN BATTLES The location and date of five Roman battles are listed in the table. Use a number line to order the battles from earliest in time to most recent. Let positive integers represent the years A.D. and negative integers represent the years B.C. (for example, 89 B.C. = −89).

Location	Date
Alexandria	47 B.C.
Byzantium	196 A.D.
Carthage	147 B.C.
Jerusalem	70 A.D.
Syracuse	211 B.C.

52. FOOTBALL The diagram below shows 4 plays in a football game. Each tick mark represents 1 yard. How many total yards did the team gain or lose during these four plays if they were headed for the goal line shown? If they gained at least 9 yards, they made a touchdown. Did they make a touchdown?

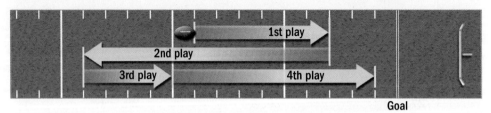

53. ★ **MULTIPLE CHOICE** The table below lists the freezing temperatures of five liquids. Which is the median of these temperatures?

Liquid	Benzene	Butane	Cesium	Mercury	Nitrogen
Freezing Temperature	5.5°C	−138°C	28.5°C	−38.87°C	−209.86°C

    Ⓐ 28.5°C   Ⓑ −38.87°C   Ⓒ −70.546°C   Ⓓ −352.73°C

54. ★ **EXTENDED RESPONSE** The table shows the high and low elevations on the seven continents.

Continent	High Elevation (ft)	Low Elevation (ft)
Africa	19,340	−512
Asia	29,035	−1349
Australia	7,310	−52
Europe	18,510	−92
North America	20,320	−282
South America	22,834	−131
Antarctica	16,066	−8383

   a. Order the continents by their high elevations from the greatest to the least.

   b. Order the continents by their low elevations from least to greatest.

   c. Find the median of each set of data.

   d. Copy and complete the graph below. Draw one horizontal bar for each continent. Include a title and labels on your graph. Which continent has the greatest range in elevation?

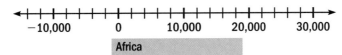

55. **CHALLENGE** The numbers *a*, *b*, and *c* are integers from −3 to 3. Two of the integers are negative and the other is positive. Use the clues to find the values of *a*, *b*, and *c*.

   Clues: $a < b$, $a > c$, $a < -1$, and $b < 2$

 NEW JERSEY MIXED REVIEW   **TEST PRACTICE** at classzone.com

56. Dallas spends a total of 52 hours per week at school and at football practice. He attends school from 8:50 A.M. until 3:50 P.M., Monday through Friday. Which equation can be used to find *t*, the number of hours Dallas spends at football practice each week?

   (A) $t = 52 - (5 \times 7)$

   (B) $t = 52 - (5 \times 8)$

   (C) $t = 52 - 7 + 7 + 7 + 7 + 7$

   (D) $t = 5 \times 7 - 52$

57. Austin is making a shelf for her bedroom. She needs to make wood lengths that are 2 feet 10 inches long. About how many wood lengths can she make from a board that is 9 feet 2 inches long?

   (A) Less than 2

   (B) Between 2 and 4

   (C) Between 4 and 6

   (D) More than 6

Negative and Zero Exponents

GOAL Evaluate powers with negative and zero exponents.

In Lesson 1.3, you wrote powers using positive exponents. You can also use negative integers and zero as exponents.

When you look down the table at the right, notice that as the exponents of 2 decrease by 1, the values of the powers are halved. This pattern suggests the following.

Power	Value
2^3	8
2^2	4
2^1	2
2^0	?
2^{-1}	?
2^{-2}	?
2^{-3}	?

$$2^0 = 2 \cdot \frac{1}{2} = 1 \qquad\qquad 2^{-1} = 1 \cdot \frac{1}{2} = \frac{1}{2^1}$$

$$2^{-2} = \frac{1}{2} \cdot \frac{1}{2} = \frac{1}{4} = \frac{1}{2^2} \qquad 2^{-3} = \frac{1}{4} \cdot \frac{1}{2} = \frac{1}{8} = \frac{1}{2^3}$$

These observations lead to the following definitions.

KEY CONCEPT *For Your Notebook*

Negative and Zero Exponents

Negative Exponent   For any integer n and any nonzero number a, a^{-n} is the reciprocal of a^n.

That is, $a^{-n} = \dfrac{1}{a^n}$.

Zero Exponent   For any nonzero number a, $a^0 = 1$.

EXAMPLE 1   **Evaluating Powers**

Evaluate the power.

a. 5^{-3} **b.** 10^{-5}

SOLUTION

a. $5^{-3} = \dfrac{1}{5^3}$ **Definition of negative exponent**

$\phantom{5^{-3}} = \dfrac{1}{125}$ **Evaluate the power.**

b. $10^{-5} = \dfrac{1}{10^5}$ **Definition of negative exponent**

$\phantom{10^{-5}} = \dfrac{1}{100{,}000}$ **Evaluate the power.**

$\phantom{10^{-5}} = 0.00001$ **Write fraction as a decimal.**

Scientific Notation In Lesson 2.5, you wrote large numbers in scientific notation using positive integers as exponents. You can also write small numbers in scientific notation using 0 and negative integers as exponents.

To change between scientific notation and standard form, first write the number as a product using the decimal form of a power of 10.

Power	Standard Form
10^0	1
10^{-1}	0.1
10^{-2}	0.01
10^{-3}	0.001
10^{-4}	0.0001
10^{-5}	0.00001
10^{-6}	0.000001
10^{-7}	0.0000001

EXAMPLE 2 Writing Numbers in Standard Form

Scientific notation	Product form	Standard form
a. 6×10^{-3}	6×0.001	0.006
b. 3.781×10^{-5}	3.781×0.00001	0.00003781

EXAMPLE 3 Writing Numbers in Scientific Notation

Standard form	Product form	Scientific notation
a. 0.00059	5.9×0.0001	5.9×10^{-4}
4 decimal places	Write product.	Exponent is -4.
b. 0.0000678	6.78×0.00001	6.78×10^{-5}
5 decimal places	Write product.	Exponent is -5.

EXERCISES

Evaluate the power.

1. 6^{-2} **2.** 4^{-4} **3.** 2^{-5} **4.** 10^{-6}

Write the number in standard form.

5. 2.1×10^{-2} **6.** 6.54×10^0 **7.** 8.92×10^{-3} **8.** 7.8×10^{-6}

9. Art A microscopic sculpture of a bull is about 0.0076 mm wide. A red blood cell has a diameter of about 8×10^{-3} mm. Which is greater, the width of the sculpture or the diameter of the cell?

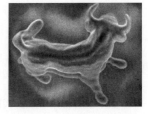

Write the number in scientific notation.

10. 0.004567   **11.** 0.0001   **12.** 0.00078   **13.** 0.0000932

GOAL
Model integer addition on a number line.

MATERIALS
• paper
• pencil

6.2 Modeling Integer Addition

You know from your earlier work that you can use a number line to model the addition of two positive numbers. You can use a similar approach when adding integers. Move right to add a positive number. Move left to add a negative number.

EXPLORE Find the sum $3 + (-2)$.

STEP 1 **Draw** a number line on a sheet of paper, or use a row of tiles on the classroom floor to represent a number line. Choose the edge of one tile to represent 0.

STEP 2 **Start** at 0. Move **3** units to the **right**.

STEP 3 **Move 2** units to the **left**.

STEP 4 **Find** your final position on the number line. You are at 1, 1 unit to the right of 0. So, $3 + (-2) = 1$.

PRACTICE Use a number line to find the sum.

1. $1 + 6$ **2.** $2 + 5$ **3.** $-3 + (-3)$ **4.** $-2 + (-3)$

5. $-7 + 3$ **6.** $-5 + 8$ **7.** $2 + (-5)$ **8.** $6 + (-2)$

DRAW CONCLUSIONS

9. REASONING Does order matter when adding integers? *Explain* your reasoning and give an example to support your answer.

10. WRITING Can the sum of a negative integer and a positive integer be positive? *Explain* your reasoning.

11. REASONING What is the sum of two integers that are opposites? *Justify* your answer.

6.2 Adding Integers

NJ 4.1.B.1.a Use and explain procedures for performing calculations with integers and all number types named above with: Pencil-and-paper

Before You compared and ordered integers.

Now You'll add integers.

Why? So you can find a diver's depth, as in Ex. 61.

KEY VOCABULARY
• absolute value, *p. 278*

Science Atoms, the building blocks of matter, are made up of protons that each have a charge of 1, neutrons that each have a charge of 0, and electrons that each have a charge of −1. One atom has 11 protons and 10 electrons. What is its total charge?

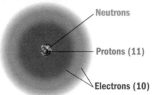

You can use a number line to add integers. Always start at 0. Move right to add a positive integer. Move left to add a negative integer.

EXAMPLE 1 Using a Number Line to Add Integers

Find the sum −5 + (−3) using a number line.

Start at 0. Move **5** units to the **left**.

Then move **3** more units to the **left**.

▸ **Answer** The final position is −8, so −5 + (−3) = −8.

EXAMPLE 2 Standardized Test Practice

The number line shows the charges of the atom described above. Which expression represents the total charge of the model?

(A) −11 + 10　　**(B)** 11 + (−10)　　**(C)** 11 + (−11)　　**(D)** 11 + 0

ELIMINATE CHOICES
Because the blue arrow points 11 units to the right, 11 is positive. So choice A can be eliminated.

SOLUTION

The model represents moving **11** units to the **right**, and then **10** units to the **left**, or 11 + (−10) = 1.

▸ **Answer** The correct answer is B.　Ⓐ **Ⓑ** Ⓒ Ⓓ

✔ GUIDED PRACTICE for Examples 1 and 2

Use a number line to find the sum.

1. −9 + (−5)　　　**2.** −7 + 4　　　**3.** 6 + (−13)　　　**4.** 12 + (−9)

Absolute Value The **absolute value** of a number is the distance between the number and 0 on a number line. The absolute value of a number *a* is written $|a|$.

EXAMPLE 3 Finding Absolute Value

Find the absolute value of the number.

a. 8   **b.** −7   **c.** 0

SOLUTION

a. The distance between 8 and 0 is 8. So, $|8| = 8$.

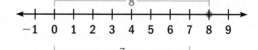

b. The distance between −7 and 0 is 7. So $|-7| = 7$.

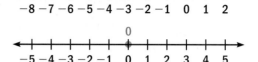

c. The distance between 0 and 0 is 0. So, $|0| = 0$.

✓ **GUIDED PRACTICE** for Example 3

Find the absolute value of the number.

5. 100   **6.** −9   **7.** −45   **8.** 22

Adding Integers In Examples 1 and 2 you added integers using a number line. You can add integers without using a number line by representing the length of each arrow using absolute value.

In Example 1, where the numbers being added have the same sign, you add the lengths of the arrows. In Example 2, where the numbers have opposite signs, you need to find the difference in their lengths. The longer arrow determines the sign of the sum. These observations are summarized below.

KEY CONCEPT   *For Your Notebook*

Adding Integers with Absolute Value

Words	Numbers
Same Signs Add the absolute values and use the common sign.	$10 + 14 = 24$ $-7 + (-5) = -12$
Different Signs Subtract the lesser absolute value from the greater absolute value and use the sign of the integer with the greater absolute value.	$13 + (-9) = 4$ $-11 + 6 = -5$
Opposites The sum of an integer and its opposite is 0.	$-4 + 4 = 0$

EXAMPLE 4 Adding Two Integers Using Absolute Value

a. Find the sum $-3 + (-12)$.

These integers have the same sign.

$$-3 + (-12) = -15$$

Add $|-3|$ and $|-12|$.

Both integers are negative, so the sum is negative.

b. Find the sum $-7 + 9$.

These integers have different signs.

AVOID ERRORS
Make sure your answer includes the sign of the integer with the greater absolute value.

$$-7 + 9 = 2$$

Subtract $|-7|$ from $|9|$.

Because $|9| > |-7|$, the sum has the same sign as 9.

✓ **GUIDED PRACTICE** for Example 4

Use absolute values to find the sum.

9. $-5 + (-11)$ **10.** $-9 + 6$ **11.** $0 + (-7)$

12. $-13 + 15$ **13.** $15 + (-8)$ **14.** $-12 + 12$

EXAMPLE 5 Adding Three or More Integers

Personal Finance Aaron has kept track of his earnings and expenses for one week. Find the sum of his earnings and expenses.

Allowance:	$12
School field trip:	−$3
Pay from mowing lawns:	$13
Repaid sister:	−$5

SOLUTION

You can find the sum by adding the integers two at a time.

ANOTHER WAY
You can add the integers in any order. You could add 12 and 13, then add −3 and −5, and then add the two sums together.

$$12 + (-3) + 13 + (-5) = 9 + 13 + (-5) \quad \text{Add 12 and } -3.$$
$$= 22 + (-5) \quad \text{Add 9 and 13.}$$
$$= 17 \quad \text{Add 22 and } -5.$$

Animated **Math**
at classzone.com

▶ **Answer** The sum of Aaron's earnings and expenses is $17.

✓ **GUIDED PRACTICE** for Example 5

15. What If? In Example 5, suppose Aaron records these earnings and expenses for a week:

$11, −$13, −$9, $3, $6

Find the sum of his earnings and expenses for the week.

6.2 EXERCISES

HOMEWORK KEY

★ = STANDARDIZED TEST PRACTICE
Exs. 32, 41, 60, 62, 63, 64, and 72

◯ = HINTS AND HOMEWORK HELP
for Exs. 3, 9, 15, 19, 59 at classzone.com

SKILL PRACTICE

1. **VOCABULARY** Tell whether the following statement is *true* or *false*, and explain your reasoning: The absolute value of an integer is its opposite.

MODELING ADDITION Write the addition expression modeled on the number line. Then find the sum.

SEE EXAMPLES 1 AND 2
on p. 277
for Exs. 2–4

2.

3.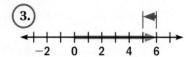

4.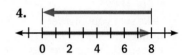

FINDING ABSOLUTE VALUE Find the absolute value of the number.

SEE EXAMPLE 3
on p. 278
for Exs. 5–12

5. -12 6. 0 7. 54 8. -3

9. -37 10. -567 11. 47 12. 19

ADDING INTEGERS Tell whether the sum will be *positive*, *negative*, or *zero*. Then find the sum.

SEE EXAMPLES 4 AND 5
on p. 279
for Exs. 13–25

13. $23 + 6$ 14. $9 + (-9)$ 15. $-13 + (-1)$

16. $-20 + 5$ 17. $0 + (-145)$ 18. $-4 + (-15)$

19. $-27 + 27$ 20. $-25 + (-5)$ 21. $-18 + (-7)$

22. $-37 + (-43)$ 23. $-4 + (-1) + (-5)$ 24. $-7 + 2 + (-1)$

25. **ERROR ANALYSIS** Describe and correct the error made in finding the sum $10 + (-15)$.

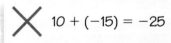

$10 + (-15) = -25$

COMPARING INTEGERS Copy and complete the statement using <, >, or =.

26. $\left|-5\right| \underline{?} 4$ 27. $0 \underline{?} \left|-1\right|$ 28. $\left|7\right| \underline{?} \left|-7\right|$

29. $-6 \underline{?} \left|2\right|$ 30. $\left|-9\right| \underline{?} \left|-2\right|$ 31. $\left|-12\right| \underline{?} 12$

32. ★ **MULTIPLE CHOICE** Which statement is true when $x = -3$ and $y = \left|-3\right|$?

(A) $y < x$ (B) $0 > y$ (C) $x < y$ (D) $x > 0$

ALGEBRA Evaluate the expression when $a = 6$ and $b = -3$.

33. $-2 + a$ 34. $b + (-6)$ 35. $b + a + (-1)$ 36. $7 + a + b$

37. $5 + b + (-4)$ 38. $3 + (-3) + b$ 39. $-8 + (-1) + a$ 40. $a + b + (-5)$

41. ★ **MULTIPLE CHOICE** Which expression has a value greater than -3?

(A) $4 + (-9)$ (B) $3 + (-8) + 1$ (C) $-10 + 8$ (D) $-1 + (-5) + 2$

COMPARING SUMS Copy and complete the statement using <, >, or =.

42. $-2 + 3 + (-10)$? $(-6) + 12$

43. $-9 + 13$? $11 + (-7) + (-10)$

44. $5 + (-8) + (-4)$? $2 + (-9)$

45. $-5 + (-10)$? $-4 + (-5) + (-6)$

MENTAL MATH Use mental math to solve the equation.

46. $-2 + d = 2$

47. $-7 = a + 10$

48. $c + (-5) = 0$

49. $8 = -8 + g$

50. $-17 = -9 + d$

51. $w + (-2) = -12$

XY ALGEBRA Solve for x.

52. $|x| = 15$

53. $|-x| = 7$

54. $|-x| = 2$

55. $|x| + 1 = 24$

56. $-9 + |x| = 11$

57. $|-x| + (-14) = 38$

58. CHALLENGE For the data set below, what are all the possible integer values of x so that $0 < x < |S|$, where S is the sum of the data? *Explain.*

$$-3, 2, 1, -6, -4, 2, -5, x$$

PROBLEM SOLVING

SEE EXAMPLE 5
on p. 279
for Exs. 59, 61

59. **BOARD GAMES** You are playing a board game with a friend. You draw one card each turn. If you draw a positive integer, you move forward. If you draw a negative integer, you move backward. You draw the five cards shown on your first five turns. How far and in what direction have you moved along the board after these five turns?

SEE EXAMPLE 3
on p. 278
for Ex. 60

60. ★ **WRITING** *Explain* why the absolute value of a number is never negative.

61. **SCUBA DIVING** A scuba diver dives to a depth of 60 feet, then rises 25 feet, sinks 10 feet, and then rises 25 feet. Write an addition expression using integers that gives the diver's final position relative to sea level. Then evaluate the expression.

62. ★ **WRITING** In his youth the English mathematician, Augustus DeMorgan (1806–1871), refused to use negative numbers, calling them "absurd." How would you convince him that addition involving negative numbers is perfectly legitimate?

63. ★ **MULTIPLE CHOICE** Which statement is correct?

Ⓐ The sum of a positive integer and a negative integer is always positive.

Ⓑ The sum of a positive integer and a negative integer is never positive.

Ⓒ The sum of three negative integers is always negative.

Ⓓ The sum of three positive integers is sometimes negative.

64. ★ **EXTENDED RESPONSE** Disc golf is a version of golf played with discs that are thrown at a target on each hole. *Par* is the expected number of throws needed to hit the target. Your score for each hole is the number of throws you make above or below par, and the player with the lowest total score wins. The table gives the scores of two players for the first 7 holes of a 9-hole disc golf course.

Hole	Par	Kyra	Mark
1	2	+3	+1
2	4	−1	0
3	4	+1	−1
4	3	−1	+2
5	2	0	+1
6	2	+1	+1
7	3	−1	−1
8	2	?	?
9	4	?	?

   a. **Calculate** What is each player's total score after Hole 7?

   b. **Apply** Mark scores −1 on Hole 8. For the score to be tied after Hole 8, what does Kyra need to score?

   c. **Predict** The game is tied after Hole 8. Both players usually need one more throw on Hole 9 than on Hole 8. *Predict* who will win the game. *Explain* your reasoning.

65. **CHALLENGE** You and three friends are playing a trivia game. A correct answer is worth 1 point, and an incorrect answer is worth −1 point. Ten questions are asked and answered by all. Beth's score is −2. Eduardo has six correct answers. What is your score if you are in second place? How many of your answers are correct?

66. **CHALLENGE** A local bike shop keeps track of each day's income and expenses by hand. The sum of all of the transactions for the day was $20. What amount should have been recorded for the new wrench set?

Transactions	
$95	bicycle sold
$5	flat tire repaired
?	new wrench set
$35	cycling jersey sold
−$40	newspaper ad

NEW JERSEY MIXED REVIEW

TEST PRACTICE at classzone.com

67. A wooden stake that is $8\frac{3}{4}$ inches tall is cut to a height of $6\frac{7}{12}$ inches. How much shorter is the stake now?

   (A) $1\frac{5}{6}$ in.   (B) 2 in.   (C) $2\frac{1}{6}$ in.   (D) $2\frac{1}{3}$ in.

68. The average yearly price for one share of a company's stock is shown in the table at the right. Which statement is supported by information in the table?

Year	Share price
2002	$1.50
2003	$2.21
2004	$4.42
2005	$3.75

   (A) The share price increased each year.

   (B) The share price decreased each year.

   (C) The share price increased the most from 2003 to 2004.

   (D) The share price is $1.25 more in 2005 than 2002.

ONLINE QUIZ at classzone.com

INVESTIGATION
Use before Lesson 6.3

GOAL
Model integer subtraction
on a number line.

MATERIALS
• paper
• pencil
• tiles (optional)

6.3 Modeling Integer Subtraction

You have used number lines to add integers. You can also use number lines to model the subtraction of integers.

To find $a - b$ using a number line, follow these steps.

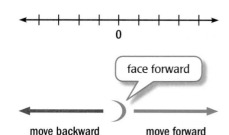

STEP 1 **Draw** a number line on a sheet of paper, or use a row of tiles on the classroom floor to represent a number line. Choose the edge of one tile to represent 0.

face forward

STEP 2 **Start** at 0. Move $|a|$ units forward if $a > 0$ or backward if $a < 0$.

move backward   move forward

STEP 3 **Interpret** the subtraction sign. It tells you to turn and face the opposite direction.

face the opposite direction

STEP 4 **Move** $|b|$ units forward if $b > 0$ or backward if $b < 0$.

move forward   move backward

EXPLORE 1 Find the difference $3 - 2$.

STEP 1 **Start** at 0. Because $3 > 0$, move $|3|$ units forward.

STEP 2 **Use** the subtraction sign. It tells you to turn and face the opposite direction.

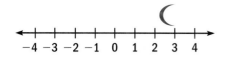

STEP 3 **Move** $|2|$ units forward because $2 > 0$. Now find your position on the number line. You are at 1, 1 unit to the right of 0. So, $3 - 2 = 1$.

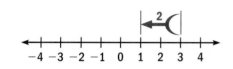

PRACTICE Use a model to find the difference.

1. $7 - 4$ 2. $3 - 6$ 3. $2 - 8$ 4. $0 - 5$

Continued on next page

EXPLORE 2 Find the difference $-2 - (-5)$.

STEP 1 **Start** at 0. Because $-2 < 0$, move $|-2|$ units backward.

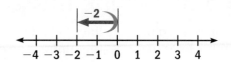

STEP 2 **Use** the subtraction sign. It tells you to turn and face the opposite direction.

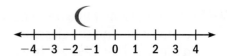

STEP 3 **Move** $|-5|$ units backward because $-5 < 0$. Now find your final position on the number line. You are 3 units to the right of 0, so $-2 - (-5) = 3$.

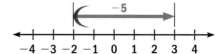

Animated Math at classzone.com

PRACTICE Use a model to find the difference.

5. $0 - (-4)$ **6.** $1 - (-3)$ **7.** $-1 - 6$ **8.** $-2 - (-8)$

Write the subtraction expression modeled by the figure. Then evaluate the expression.

9.
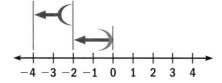

10.
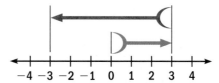

11.
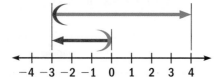

12.
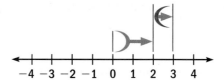

DRAW CONCLUSIONS

13. REASONING Write equivalent addition expressions for Exercises 9–12 and compare expressions and results. What do you notice?

14. WRITING Can the difference of two negative integers be positive? Can the difference of two negative integers be negative? *Explain* your reasoning and give examples to support your claims.

6.3 Subtracting Integers

 4.1.B.1.a Use and explain procedures for performing calculations with integers and all number types named above with: Pencil-and-paper

Before	You added integers.
Now	You'll subtract integers.
Why?	So you can calculate differences in dates, as in Ex. 49.

KEY VOCABULARY
• opposite, *p. 269*

Number line models of the subtraction expression $5 - 2$ and the addition expression $5 + (-2)$ are shown below.

Subtraction Model: $5 - 2$ **Addition Model: $5 + (-2)$**

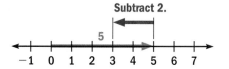   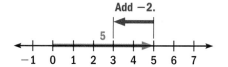

ANOTHER WAY
For another way to subtract integers see investigation on pp. 283–284.

Notice that the model for $5 - 2 = 3$ is identical to the model for $5 + (-2) = 3$. This suggests the following rule for subtracting integers.

KEY CONCEPT   *For Your Notebook*

Subtracting Integers

Words   To subtract an integer, add its opposite.

Numbers $5 - 7 = 5 + (-7)$ **Algebra** $a - b = a + (-b)$

EXAMPLE 1 Subtracting Integers

REVIEW OPPOSITES
Need help with adding integers? See p. 269.

a. $2 - 7 = 2 + (-7)$ To subtract 7, add its opposite, −7.

$\qquad\quad = -5$ Use rule for adding integers.

b. $12 - (-9) = 12 + 9$ To subtract −9, add its opposite, 9.

$\qquad\qquad\ = 21$ Use rule for adding integers.

c. $-3 - (-5) = -3 + 5$ To subtract −5, add its opposite, 5.

$\qquad\qquad\ \ = 2$ Use rule for adding integers.

✓ **GUIDED PRACTICE**   for Example 1

Find the difference.

1. $4 - 6$ **2.** $-7 - (-8)$ **3.** $-2 - 1$ **4.** $15 - (-3)$

EXAMPLE 2 Using Integer Subtraction

Geography The highest point in Asia is Mount Everest at 8850 meters. The shore of the Dead Sea, the lowest point in Asia, is about 410 meters below sea level. What is the difference between these elevations?

SOLUTION

SUBTRACTION ORDER
Order matters with subtraction. The difference of *a* and *b* means *a* − *b*, not *b* − *a*.

STEP 1 **Represent** the two elevations with integers.

Mount Everest: 8850 m   **Dead Sea:** −410 m

STEP 2 **Find** the difference of 8850 and −410 meters.

$$8850 - (-410) = 8850 + 410 \qquad \textbf{Rule for subtracting integers}$$
$$= 9260 \qquad \textbf{Add.}$$

▸ **Answer** The difference between the elevations is 9260 meters.

Amount of Change Subtraction can be used to find a change in a variable such as temperature or elevation. To find the change, subtract the old or start value of the variable from the new or end value of the variable.

EXAMPLE 3 Finding a Change in Temperature

Weather In Fairfield, Montana, on December 24, 1924, the air temperature dropped a record amount. At noon, the temperature was 63°F. Twelve hours later, the temperature was −21°F. What was the change in temperature?

SOLUTION

Change in temperature = **end temperature** − **start temperature**

$$= \mathbf{-21 - 63} \qquad \textbf{Substitute values.}$$
$$= -21 + (-63) \qquad \textbf{Rule for subtracting integers}$$
$$= -84 \qquad \textbf{Add.}$$

▸ **Answer** The change in temperature was −84°F, so the temperature dropped 84°F.

✓ **GUIDED PRACTICE** for Examples 2 and 3

5. **Elevation** Find the difference between an elevation of 535 feet above sea level and an elevation of 8 feet below sea level.

6. **Temperature** The temperature at 6 A.M. was −12°F. At 3 P.M. the temperature was 32°F. What was the change in temperature?

6.3 EXERCISES

HOMEWORK
KEY

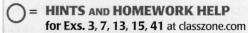

★ = STANDARDIZED TEST PRACTICE
Exs. 19, 44, 46, 47, and 58

◯ = HINTS AND HOMEWORK HELP
for Exs. 3, 7, 13, 15, 41 at classzone.com

SKILL PRACTICE

1. VOCABULARY Copy and complete: To simplify the expression $8 - (-9)$, you can add the _?_ of -9 to 8.

MATCHING EXPRESSIONS Match the subtraction expression with the equivalent addition expression. Justify using number line models.

SEE EXAMPLE 1
on p. 285
for Exs. 2–19

2. $-7 - 3$ **3.** $7 - (-3)$ **4.** $-7 - (-3)$ **5.** $7 - 3$

A. $-7 + 3$ **B.** $7 + (-3)$ **C.** $-7 + (-3)$ **D.** $7 + 3$

SUBTRACTING INTEGERS Find the difference.

6. $13 - (-4)$ **7.** $-9 - 3$ **8.** $10 - 12$ **9.** $-17 - 9$

10. $15 - (-18)$ **11.** $13 - 24$ **12.** $25 - 5$ **13.** $7 - (-7)$

14. $-5 - (-25)$ **15.** $-54 - (-7)$ **16.** $-56 - 28$ **17.** $33 - (-27)$

18. ERROR ANALYSIS Describe and correct the error made in finding $3 - (-6)$.

$$\times \quad 3 - (-6) = 3 - 6 = -3$$

19. ★ **MULTIPLE CHOICE** What is $-14 - (-7)$?

   A -21 **B** -7 **C** -2 **D** 7

ALGEBRA Evaluate the expression for the given value(s) of the variable(s).

20. $m - 5$ when $m = 4$ **21.** $x - y$ when $x = 9$ and $y = -11$

22. $10 + t - (-63)$ when $t = -17$ **23.** $-22 - x + 4$ when $x = -16$

COMPARING DIFFERENCES Copy and complete the statement using $<$, $>$, or $=$.

24. $4 - (-1) \underline{\,?\,} 7 - 4$ **25.** $-3 - (-9) \underline{\,?\,} 5 - (-2)$

26. $-6 - 8 - (-5) \underline{\,?\,} 2 - (-10)$ **27.** $2 - 9 \underline{\,?\,} -4 - (-3) - 6$

MENTAL MATH Copy and complete using $<$, $>$, or $=$.

28. $-4 - (-5) \underline{\,?\,} 0$ **29.** $5 - (-8) \underline{\,?\,} 0$ **30.** $-8 - 9 \underline{\,?\,} 0$

31. $6 - (-2) \underline{\,?\,} 4$ **32.** $3 - 5 \underline{\,?\,} 2$ **33.** $-4 - 5 \underline{\,?\,} -9$

CRITICAL THINKING For what types of numbers is the statement true?

34. $\left| a - b \right| = \left| a \right| - \left| b \right|$ **35.** $-\left| a - b \right| = \left| b - a \right|$ **36.** $\left| a - b \right| = \left| b - a \right|$

37. $\left| a + b \right| = \left| a \right| + \left| b \right|$ **38.** $\left| a + b \right| = \left| a \right| - \left| b \right|$ **39.** $\left| a + b \right| = -\left| a - b \right|$

40. CHALLENGE Find two integers whose sum is 2 and whose difference is 8.

PROBLEM SOLVING

SEE EXAMPLE 2
on p. 286
for Ex. 41

41. GEOGRAPHY The highest and lowest points in South America are Mount Aconcagua at 22,834 feet above sea level, and the Valdes Peninsula at 131 feet below sea level. Find the difference between these elevations.

SEE EXAMPLE 3
on p. 286
for Exs. 42–43

42. GUIDED PROBLEM SOLVING A professional cliff diver dives from a ledge 65 feet above the surface of the water. The diver reaches an underwater depth of 15 feet before returning to the surface. What was the diver's change in elevation from the highest point of the dive to the lowest?

a. What operation do you use to find a change in elevation?

b. Which integers represent the highest and lowest elevations of the dive?

c. Write and evaluate an expression to find the change in elevation.

43. DEATH VALLEY You are going to travel from the lowest point to the highest point in Death Valley, California. You will begin at 282 feet below sea level in Badwater and end up at 11,049 feet above sea level on Telescope Peak. What will your change in elevation be?

44. ★ WRITING A negative integer is subtracted from a positive integer. Is the result *positive* or *negative*? *Explain* your reasoning.

45. PLANET TEMPERATURES A temperature expressed using the Kelvin (K) unit can be converted to degrees Celsius (°C) by using the formula $C = K - 273$. Convert the temperatures given in the table to degrees Celsius.

Planet	Mean Surface Temperature
Mercury	452 K
Earth	281 K
Jupiter	120 K
Saturn	88 K
Pluto	37 K

46. ★ SHORT RESPONSE Describe the following pattern in two ways: 2, −1, −4, −7, . . . Then write the next three integers. *Explain* how this shows the relationship between integer addition and integer subtraction.

47. ★ OPEN-ENDED MATH Write and evaluate the addition expression that is equivalent to the subtraction expression −1 − (−4). Then give a real-world situation that the expression could represent.

48. CHEMISTRY Atoms have an electrical charge of 0. In the presence of chlorine, sodium atoms lose one electron, to become *ions*, or charged particles. Chlorine atoms each capture one electron to also become ions. Electrons have a charge of −1. Find the charge of each type of ion. Then write and evaluate an expression to find the difference between the charges of a sodium ion and a chlorine ion.

49. CHALLENGE The illustration shows the construction dates of significant landmarks. The positive integers represent the years A.D. and the negative integers represent the years B.C. Find the differences between each pair of events listed.

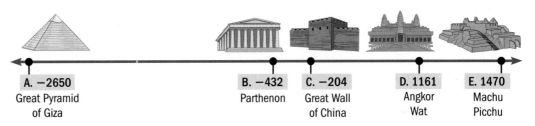

| A. −2650
Great Pyramid
of Giza | B. −432
Parthenon | C. −204
Great Wall
of China | D. 1161
Angkor
Wat | E. 1470
Machu
Picchu |

   a. D and A **b.** D and B **c.** E and B **d.** C and A

NEW JERSEY MIXED REVIEW

 TEST PRACTICE at classzone.com

50. The model shows the changes in the outside temperature. Which expression represents the total change in temperature?

   A $-3 + (-4)$ **B** $-3 + 4$ **C** $-7 + (-3)$ **D** $-3 + 7$

51. Simplify the expression below.

$$4(-2 + 5)^2 \div 6 - 2$$

   A -12 **B** -4 **C** 4 **D** 12

QUIZ for Lessons 6.1–6.3

1. Name two different integers that have an absolute value of 25. *(p. 277)*

Write the integer that represents the situation. *(p. 269)*

   2. profit of $85   **3.** loss of 7 yards   **4.** 12 degrees below 0

Order the integers from least to greatest. *(p. 269)*

   5. $-1, 3, -3, 0, -5$ **6.** $0, -7, 6, -3, 2$ **7.** $11, -11, 3, -3, -7$

Find the sum or difference.

   8. $-7 + (-4)$ *(p. 277)*   **9.** $21 + (-15)$ *(p. 277)*   **10.** $-11 + 5$ *(p. 277)*

   11. $30 - 63$ *(p. 285)*   **12.** $-9 - (-17)$ *(p. 285)*   **13.** $17 - (-17)$ *(p. 285)*

14. TEMPERATURE At dawn this morning, the temperature was $-3°$F. By noon, the temperature was $25°$F. What was the change in temperature? *(p. 285)*

15. PERSONAL FINANCE Find the sum of the following transactions recorded for a bank account over a one-week period: $25, −$35, $12, $14, −$43. *(p. 277)*

Lessons 6.1–6.3

1. NUMBER CLUES The clues below give information about the location of integers represented by the letters *a, b, c, d,* and *e* on a number line. How many of the integers are negative?

- *c* lies halfway between *e* and *a.*
- *a* is a positive integer.
- *b* lies 6 units to the right of *a.*
- *e* lies halfway between *d* and *c.*
- *c* is a negative integer.

A. 1

B. 2

C. 3

D. more than 3

2. GOLF SCORES The table gives the scores of two players for a 9-hole game of golf. The least total score wins. Noah won the game by 2 strokes. What did Collin score on the 9th hole?

Hole	Collin	Noah
1	−1	0
2	+1	−1
3	+1	+1
4	0	−1
5	+2	+1
6	+1	+2
7	−2	−1
8	−1	0
9	?	−1

A. −2

B. −1

C. +1

D. +2

3. ELEVATION On a mountain climbing expedition, a team descends from Camp B at 6250 meters to Camp A at 4595 meters. Which statement describes how to find the team's change in elevation?

A. Add 4595 and 6250.

B. Add −4595 and −6250.

C. Subtract 6250 from 4595.

D. Subtract 6250 from −4595.

4. SNOWFALL The table shows the average yearly snowfall totals for various cities in the United States. Which city's snowfall is closest to the mean?

City	Snowfall (in.)
Boston	43
Chicago	38
Cleveland	58
Milwaukee	47
Minneapolis	50
Pittsburgh	44

A. Boston

B. Pittsburgh

C. Milwaukee

D. Minneapolis

5. OPEN-ENDED A football team gained 2 yards on one play and lost 9 yards on the next play.

- Write an expression that represents the situation.

- Use a number line to evaluate the expression.

- *Explain* what the answer represents.

6.4 Multiplying Integers

 4.1.B.1.a Use and explain procedures for performing calculations with integers and all number types named above with: Pencil-and-paper

Before You multiplied whole numbers, decimals, and fractions.

Now You'll multiply integers.

Why? So you can apply rates to solve problems, as in Ex. 59.

KEY VOCABULARY
• **opposite,** *p. 269*

ACTIVITY

You can use patterns to find rules for multiplying numbers.

STEP 1 Copy and complete Table 1.

STEP 2 What pattern do you see as you read down the *Product* column in Table 1? Extend Table 1 using this pattern to find the next two products, $3 \cdot (-1)$ and $3 \cdot (-2)$.

STEP 3 What do you notice about the product of a positive integer and a negative integer?

STEP 4 Copy Table 2. Then use your answer from Step 3 to complete the table.

STEP 5 What pattern do you see as you read down the *Product* column in Table 2? Extend Table 2 using this pattern to find the next two products, $-3 \cdot (-1)$ and $-3 \cdot (-2)$.

STEP 6 What do you notice about the product of two negative integers?

Table 1

Expression	Product
$3 \cdot 3$	9
$3 \cdot 2$	?
$3 \cdot 1$	?
$3 \cdot 0$	?

Table 2

Expression	Product
$-3 \cdot 3$	?
$-3 \cdot 2$	?
$-3 \cdot 1$	?
$-3 \cdot 0$	?

REVIEW PATTERNS
Need help with describing and extending patterns? See p. 3.

In the activity, you may have found three rules for multiplying integers.

KEY CONCEPT

For Your Notebook

Multiplying Integers

Words	Numbers
Same Signs The product of two integers with the same sign is positive.	$4 \cdot 2 = 8$ $-4 \cdot (-2) = 8$
Different Signs The product of two integers with different signs is negative.	$4 \cdot (-2) = -8$ $-4 \cdot 2 = -8$
Zero The product of an integer and 0 is 0.	$4 \cdot 0 = 0$ $-4 \cdot 0 = 0$

EXAMPLE 1 Multiplying Integers

a. $-5(-7) = 35$ **The product of two integers with the same sign is positive.**

b. $-8(2) = -16$ **The product of two integers with different signs is negative.**

c. $-12(0) = 0$ **The product of an integer and 0 is 0.**

EXAMPLE 2 Evaluating Variable Expressions

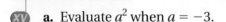

a. Evaluate a^2 when $a = -3$.

b. Evaluate xyz when $x = 2$, $y = -4$, and $z = 6$.

SOLUTION

a. $a^2 = (-3)^2$ **Substitute −3 for a.**

     $= -3(-3)$ **Write −3 as a factor two times.**

     $= 9$ **Multiply −3 and −3.**

b. $xyz = 2(-4)(6)$ **Substitute 2 for x, −4 for y, and 6 for z.**

     $= -8(6)$ **Multiply 2 and −4.**

     $= -48$ **Multiply −8 and 6.**

Animated Math
at classzone.com

EXAMPLE 3 Using Integer Multiplication

Greenland Most of Greenland is covered with ice that is almost two miles thick in some places. Scientists estimate that 3 feet of this ice melts each year. Find the change in the thickness of the ice after 10 years.

SOLUTION

You can find the total change in the ice thickness by multiplying the yearly change by the number of years. Use -3 for the yearly change because the thickness of the ice decreases by 3 feet each year.

     Change in ice thickness $= -3(10) = -30$

▶**Answer** The thickness of the ice will decrease 30 feet in 10 years.

ANOTHER WAY
You can use integer chips to find this product. Form 10 groups that represent −3. The total represents −3 (10), or −30.

✓ **GUIDED PRACTICE**   **for Examples 1, 2, and 3**

Find the product.

1. $-9(2)$ **2.** $-3(-4)$ **3.** $5(-5)$ **4.** $0(-14)$

5. Evaluate the expressions x^2y and $-3xy^2$ when $x = -2$ and $y = 3$.

6. **What If?** What is the change in the thickness of the ice in Example 3 after 18 years?

6.4 EXERCISES

HOMEWORK KEY

★ = STANDARDIZED TEST PRACTICE
Exs. 21, 22, 54, 56, 58, 60, and 71

◯ = HINTS AND HOMEWORK HELP
for Exs. 5, 9, 15, 33, 53 at classzone.com

SKILL PRACTICE

VOCABULARY Copy and complete using *positive* or *negative.*

1. The product of two negative integers is __?__ .

2. The product of a negative integer and its opposite is __?__ .

3. The product of three negative integers is __?__ .

SEE EXAMPLE 1
on p. 292
for Exs. 4–21

MULTIPLYING INTEGERS Find the product.

4. $4(8)$

5. $-3(11)$

6. $5(-6)$

7. $-2(-12)$

8. $11(10)$

9. $0(-15)$

10. $-9(-7)$

11. $-8(5)$

12. $6(-6)$

13. $15(-2)$

14. $-5(7)$

15. $-4(-7)$

16. $-13(0)$

17. $-4(-4)(-2)$

18. $10(0)(-7)$

19. $5(-1)(9)$

20. **ERROR ANALYSIS** Describe and correct the error made in finding the product of -3 and -6.

✗ $(-3)(-6) = -18$

21. ★ **MULTIPLE CHOICE** What is the product of -9 and -11?

(A) -99 (B) -20 (C) 2 (D) 99

SEE EXAMPLE 2
on p. 292
for Exs. 22–34

22. ★ **MULTIPLE CHOICE** What is the value of pt^2 when $p = 11$ and $t = -3$?

(A) -99 (B) -66 (C) 66 (D) 99

EVALUATING EXPRESSIONS Evaluate the expression when $a = -5$, $b = -2$, and $c = -7$.

23. $7c$

24. b^4

25. a^2

26. ab

27. $-12b$

28. $0 \cdot c^2$

29. $-ab$

30. $2bc$

31. $-3a^2c$

32. ab^4

33. $5 \cdot b^3$

34. $-c^3$

◆ **MULTIPLE REPRESENTATIONS** You can use repeated addition to model integer multiplication. For example, the number line below represents $3(-4)$ or $-4 + (-4) + (-4)$.

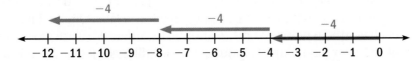

Use a number line to model the expression. Then find the product.

35. $3(-5)$

36. $2(-8)$

37. $4(-1)$

38. $5(-2)$

MENTAL MATH Solve the equation using mental math.

39. $-25s = -100$ **40.** $2n = -10$ **41.** $-6m = -60$

42. $-9p = 36$ **43.** $4a = -32$ **44.** $-5x = 65$

45. $-4m = -48$ **46.** $x^5 = -1$ **47.** $a^3 = -8$

NUMBER SENSE Find the missing numbers in the pattern.

48. __, -63, 189, __, 1701 **49.** 7, -28, __, __, 1792 **50.** -5, __, __, 625, -3125

51. CHALLENGE The first four numbers in a pattern are -1, 2, -3, and 4. What is the 25th number in the pattern? Write an expression for the nth number in the pattern.

PROBLEM SOLVING

SEE EXAMPLE 3
on p. 292
for Exs. 52–55

52. GUIDED PROBLEM SOLVING In degrees Fahrenheit, the lowest temperature recorded in May at McMurdo Station, Antarctica, is 3 times the average low temperature for May. The average low temperature for May is 16°F below 0°F. What is the lowest temperature recorded in May?

   a. What integer represents the average low temperature for May?

   b. What operation is needed to solve this problem?

   c. Write and evaluate an expression to find the lowest temperature recorded in May at McMurdo Station.

53. DIVING SEALS A seal dives at a speed of 2 meters every second. What integer represents the seal's change in position after 30 seconds?

54. ★ MULTIPLE CHOICE A whale dives down 3 feet each second. What integer represents the whale's change in position after 15 seconds?

   (A) -45 **(B)** -15

   (C) 18 **(D)** 45

55. AIRPLANE LANDING Suppose an airplane descends 4 feet every second prior to landing. Write and simplify an expression to represent the change in the altitude of the airplane after 10 seconds.

56. ★ WRITING *Explain* how to use an addition model to find $6(-8)$.

57. GAMES Peter is playing a card game in which you gain points for playing cards and lose points for cards not played. The Jack, Queen, and King are each worth 10 points. The Ace and the numbers 2–10 are worth 5 points each. Peter has gained 30 points, but he still has 2 Jacks, a 3, a 7, and an 8 in his hand. What is his score for the game?

58. ★ SHORT RESPONSE What is the least possible sum for two integers whose product is 36? *Justify* your answer.

294   ★ = STANDARDIZED TEST PRACTICE   ◯ = HINTS AND HOMEWORK HELP *at classzone.com*

59. PANAMA CANAL In the Panama Canal, a system of locks releases water from upper chambers into lower chambers so that ships can move through the canal. The water level in an upper chamber begins at 72 feet and falls about 3 feet every minute for 9 minutes. Write and evaluate an expression that represents the change in the water depth after 9 minutes. Then find the depth of the water after 9 minutes.

72 feet

60. ★ EXTENDED RESPONSE Your cousin is making a budget for herself. She has fixed expenses of $970 per month. She spends $350 per month on entertainment. Her job pays her $1295 per month after taxes. What is the monthly change in her money? How much does she need to reduce her entertainment expenses by to save $75 per month?

61. CHALLENGE Imagine creating a three-digit integer and a two-digit integer using each of the digits 1, 3, 5, 7, and 9 exactly once. The integers may be either positive or negative.

   a. What two integers give the greatest possible sum? the least possible sum? What are these sums?

   b. What two integers give the greatest possible difference? the least possible difference? What are these differences?

   c. What two integers give the greatest possible product? the least possible product? What are these products?

NEW JERSEY MIXED REVIEW

 TEST PRACTICE at classzone.com

62. The highest and lowest points in Australia are Mt. Kosciusko at 2228 meters above sea level, and Lake Eyre at 12 meters below sea level. Which expression can be used to find the difference between the elevations?

   A $2228 - 12$

   B $2228 - (-12)$

   C $-2228 - 12$

   D $-2228 - (-12)$

63. In which data set are the mean, median, and mode all the same number?

   A {6, 5, 6, 5, 6, 5, 6, 7}

   B {5, 6, 7, 5, 5, 6, 7, 7}

   C {7, 5, 5, 6, 6, 7, 6, 6}

   D {5, 7, 7, 6, 5, 7, 7, 5}

6.5 Dilviding Integers

NJ 4.1.B.1.a Use and explain procedures for performing calculations with integers and all number types named above with: Pencil-and-paper

Before You multiplied integers.

Now You'll divide integers.

Why? So you can convert temperatures, as in Ex. 52.

KEY VOCABULARY
• **mean,** *p. 109*

ACTIVITY

You can evaluate a division equation by using related multiplication.

STEP 1 **Copy** and complete the table.

Division Equation	Related Multiplication Equation	Quotient
18 ÷ 9 = __?__	? • 9 = 18	2
−15 ÷ 5 = __?__	?	?
−14 ÷ 7 = __?__	?	?
10 ÷ (−2) = __?__	?	?
−12 ÷ (−4) = __?__	?	?

STEP 2 **Copy** and complete the statement using *positive* or *negative*.

   a. A negative integer divided by a positive integer is __?__.

   b. A positive integer divided by a negative integer is __?__.

   c. A negative integer divided by a negative integer is __?__.

Rules for dividing integers are similar to rules for multiplying integers.

KEY CONCEPT *For Your Notebook*

Dividing Integers

Words **Numbers**

Same Signs The quotient of two integers with the same sign is positive. $10 \div 2 = 5, \dfrac{-24}{-3} = 8$

Different Signs The quotient of two integers with different signs is negative. $15 \div (-3) = -5, \dfrac{-18}{6} = -3$

Zero The quotient of 0 and any nonzero integer is 0. $0 \div 17 = 0, \dfrac{0}{-9} = 0$

AVOID ERRORS
Remember, you cannot divide by 0. To see why, rewrite 8 ÷ 0 = __?__ as __?__ • 0 = 8. Since this is never true, any number divided by 0 is *undefined*.

EXAMPLE 1 | Dividing Integers

a. $28 \div (-4) = -7$ The quotient of two integers with different signs is negative.

b. $\dfrac{-60}{-12} = 5$ The quotient of two integers with the same sign is positive.

c. $0 \div (-13) = 0$ The quotient of 0 and any nonzero integer is 0.

EXAMPLE 2 | Standardized Test Practice

Cold Temperatures The table shows the high temperatures for five days in January in Bangor, Maine. Which expression can be used to find the average daily high temperature?

Day	Temperature
Monday	3°C
Tuesday	−3°C
Wednesday	−5°C
Thursday	2°C
Friday	−7°C

(A) $3 + 3 + 5 + 2 + 7 \div 5$

(B) $(3 + 3 + 5 + 2 + 7) \div 5$

(C) $[3 + (-3) + (-5) + 2 + (-7)] \div 5$

(D) $3 + (-3) + (-5) + 2 + (-7) \div 5$

ELIMINATE CHOICES
Because some temperatures are negative, you can eliminate choices A and B.

SOLUTION

The mean is calculated by finding the sum of the high temperatures and then dividing by the number of days.

$$\text{Mean} = \frac{3 + (-3) + (-5) + 2 + (-7)}{5} = \frac{-10}{5} = -2.$$

The mean temperature for these five days was −2°C.

▶ **Answer** Only *C* divides the sum by 5. The correct answer is C. Ⓐ Ⓑ **©** Ⓓ

ANOTHER WAY
You can find the quotient $\dfrac{-10}{5}$ using integer chips. Divide chips representing −10 into 5 equal groups. Each group of −2 represents the quotient.

Temperature Conversions Operations with positive and negative numbers are needed to convert temperatures between degrees Celsius *C* and degrees Fahrenheit *F*.

KEY CONCEPT   *For Your Notebook*

Temperature Conversions

Words	Formulas	Numbers
Convert Celsius to Fahrenheit	$F = \dfrac{9}{5}C + 32$	$71.6 = \dfrac{9}{5}(22) + 32$
Convert Fahrenheit to Celsius	$C = \dfrac{5}{9}(F - 32)$	$22 = \dfrac{5}{9}(71.6 - 32)$

EXAMPLE 3 · Converting a Temperature

Biology During hibernation, an Arctic ground squirrel can decrease its body temperature to $-30°C$. Convert this temperature to degrees Fahrenheit.

SOLUTION

$F = \dfrac{9}{5}C + 32$ — Write formula for degrees Fahrenheit.

$ = \dfrac{9}{5}(-30) + 32$ — Substitute -30 for C.

$ = \dfrac{9 \cdot \overset{-6}{\cancel{(-30)}}}{\underset{1}{\cancel{5}} \cdot 1} + 32$ — Use rule for multiplying fractions. Divide out common factor.

$ = -54 + 32$ — Multiply.

$ = -22$ — Add.

▶ **Answer** The temperature $-30°C$ is equal to $-22°F$.

✓ **GUIDED PRACTICE** | **for Examples 1, 2, and 3**

Find the quotient.

1. $-24 \div 6$ **2.** $\dfrac{0}{-2}$ **3.** $\dfrac{-39}{-13}$ **4.** $19 \div (-1)$

5. Find the mean: -284 ft, -245 ft, -372 ft, -356 ft, and -343 ft.

Convert the temperature to degrees Celsius or to degrees Fahrenheit.

6. $0°C$ **7.** $-4°F$ **8.** $-45°C$ **9.** $77°F$

6.5 EXERCISES

HOMEWORK KEY

★ = **STANDARDIZED TEST PRACTICE**
Exs. 20, 55, 57, 58, and 70

◯ = **HINTS AND HOMEWORK HELP**
for Exs. 3, 7, 23, 27, 51 at classzone.com

SKILL PRACTICE

VOCABULARY Copy and complete the statement.

1. The quotient of a negative integer and a positive integer is __?__ .

2. The quotient of any number and __?__ is undefined.

DIVIDING INTEGERS Find the quotient.

SEE EXAMPLE 1 on p. 297 for Exs. 3–18

3. $-44 \div 11$ **4.** $-64 \div 32$ **5.** $70 \div (-10)$ **6.** $34 \div (-17)$

7. $-76 \div (-19)$ **8.** $-84 \div (-7)$ **9.** $63 \div (-9)$ **10.** $-52 \div 13$

11. $-24 \div 8$ **12.** $72 \div (-9)$ **13.** $0 \div (-121)$ **14.** $-96 \div (-12)$

15. $6 \div (-2)$ **16.** $36 \div (-12)$ **17.** $-26 \div 13$ **18.** $-42 \div (-7)$

SEE EXAMPLE 1
on p. 298
for Exs. 19–20

19. ERROR ANALYSIS Describe and correct the error made in finding the quotient of -20 and -5.

$$-20 \div (-5) = -4$$

20. ★ MULTIPLE CHOICE Which expression has a value of -6?

Ⓐ $-24 \div (-4)$ Ⓑ $42 \div 7$ Ⓒ $48 \div (-8)$ Ⓓ $-42 \div 6$

SEE EXAMPLE 2
on p. 297
for Exs. 21–26

FINDING MEANS Find the mean of the integers.

21. $-10, -6, 3, 9$ **22.** $7, -9, 9, -7, 0$ **23.** $-46, -33, 0, 11$

24. $10, -27, 4, -9$ **25.** $-17, -4, 5, 21, 30$ **26.** $8, -11, 18, -8, -3$

SEE EXAMPLE 3
on p. 298
for Exs. 27–30

CONVERTING TEMPERATURES Convert the temperature to degrees Celsius or to degrees Fahrenheit.

27. $-50°C$ **28.** $32°F$ **29.** $-13°F$ **30.** $-1°C$

ⅩⅤ ALGEBRA Evaluate the expression when $s = 16$ and $t = -5$.

31. $t \div (-1) - 1$ **32.** $s \div (-8) - 5$ **33.** $-64 \div s + 14$ **34.** $-64 \div 32 - t$

35. $t - 0 \div s$ **36.** $s \div (-4) + t$ **37.** $25 \div t - s$ **38.** $10 \div t + s$

COMPARING EXPRESSIONS Copy and complete the statement using <, >, or =.

39. $4 \div (-2) - 1 \underline{?} 4 \div 2 - 1$ **40.** $46 \div (-23) \underline{?} -46 \div 23$

41. $0 \div 4 + 9 \underline{?} 0 \div 7 + 9$ **42.** $-25 \div (-5) \div (-1) \underline{?} 5$

ⅩⅤ ALGEBRA Use the number line to complete the statement using <, >, or =.

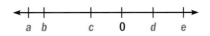

43. $a \div c \underline{?} 0$ **44.** $d \div c \underline{?} 0$ **45.** $e \div d \underline{?} a$

46. $0 \div a \underline{?} 0 \div e$ **47.** $e \div a \underline{?} e \div d$ **48.** $c \div d \underline{?} a \div b$

49. CHALLENGE The mean of a, $-a$, and b is 0. What is the value of b?

PROBLEM SOLVING

SEE EXAMPLE 2
on p. 297
for Exs. 50–51

50. BOWLING ALLEY A bowling alley's gains and losses over 5 months are $450, -$675, $1230, -$776, and -$95. Find the mean of the monthly gains and losses for the bowling alley.

51. GOLF Find the mean of the following golf scores for 9 holes of golf, expressed as strokes above or below par: $0, 5, -1, 1, 0, -3, 0, -2, 4$.

SEE EXAMPLE 3
on p. 298
for Exs. 52–54

52. MACAQUE MONKEYS During the winter in Japan, macaque monkeys find warmth in a hot spring that is fed by the Shirane Volcano. The water temperature is about $39°C$, while the air temperature can reach $-5°C$. Convert both to degrees Fahrenheit.

SEE EXAMPLE 3
on p. 298
for Exs. 53–54

53. BOILING POINT The boiling point of water is 100°C. What is this temperature in degrees Fahrenheit?

54. NITROGEN The melting point of nitrogen is about −346°F. What is this temperature in Celsius?

55. ★ WRITING What can you tell about two integers when their quotient is positive? negative? zero?

56. ESTIMATION *Explain* why the expression $2C + 30$ can be used to estimate the value of a Celsius temperature in degrees Fahrenheit. Then use the expression to estimate the value of −15°C in degrees Fahrenheit.

57. ★ SHORT RESPONSE *Explain* using an example why a negative integer divided by a negative integer is a positive integer.

58. ★ EXTENDED RESPONSE The temperature was −12°C at 6:00 A.M., 49°F at noon, and 4°C at 6:00 P.M.

  a. Model Make a line graph of the data in degrees Fahrenheit.

  b. Calculate What was the mean change in temperature in one hour, in degrees Fahrenheit, between 6:00 A.M. and noon? between noon and 6:00 P.M.?

  c. Reasoning The next day, the changes in temperature between 6:00 A.M. and noon and between noon and 6:00 P.M. were the same as the day before. If the temperature at 6:00 A.M. was −8°C, what was the temperature at noon and 6:00 P.M. in degrees Fahrenheit?

59. CHALLENGE The mean of five daily high temperatures is −3°C. Four of the temperatures are shown. Find the fifth temperature. *Explain* how to use integer chips or a number line to model the quotient.

    −2°C   −7°C   1°C   −4°C

 NEW JERSEY MIXED REVIEW   **TEST PRACTICE** at classzone.com

60. The table shows the change in altitude a in feet of a descending hot air balloon after t minutes. Which formula can be used to calculate the change in altitude a?

  Ⓐ $a = t - 25$

  Ⓑ $a = 25t$

  Ⓒ $a = -25t$

  Ⓓ $a = t - (-25)$

Time, t (minutes)	Change in altitude, a (feet)
1	−25
2	−50
3	−75
4	−100
5	−125

61. The fraction $\frac{5}{7}$ is found between which pair of fractions on a number line?

  Ⓐ $\frac{8}{14}$ and $\frac{15}{21}$ **Ⓑ** $\frac{9}{14}$ and $\frac{16}{21}$ **Ⓒ** $\frac{10}{14}$ and $\frac{17}{21}$ **Ⓓ** $\frac{11}{14}$ and $\frac{18}{21}$

6.6 Rational Numbers

 4.3.D.4.a Additive inverse

Before	You performed operations on positive fractions and decimals.
Now	You'll perform operations on rational numbers.
Why?	So you can calculate points multiple ways, as in Ex. 55.

KEY VOCABULARY
- rational number, p. 301
- additive identity, p. 302
- multiplicative identity, p. 302
- additive inverse, p. 302
- multiplicative inverse, p. 302

A **rational number** is a number that can be written as $\frac{a}{b}$ where a and b are integers and $b \neq 0$.

The Venn diagram shows the relationships among rational numbers, integers, and whole numbers. A few examples of each type are included. Notice that integers include whole numbers and rational numbers include integers.

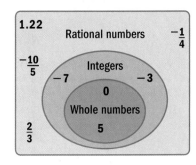

EXAMPLE 1 Identifying Rational Numbers

PLACING SIGNS
The negative sign in a negative fraction can appear in front of the fraction bar, in the numerator, or in the denominator.

Show that the number is rational by writing it in $\frac{a}{b}$ form.

a. $6 = \frac{6}{1}$ **b.** $-\frac{3}{5} = \frac{3}{5}$ **c.** $0.75 = \frac{3}{4}$ **d.** $-2\frac{1}{3} = \frac{-7}{3}$

Animated **Math** at classzone.com

EXAMPLE 2 Ordering Rational Numbers

Order $-1, -1.6, \frac{2}{5}, -1\frac{1}{4},$ and $-\frac{3}{8}$ from least to greatest.

Graph each number on a number line.

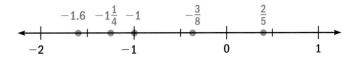

▶ **Answer** From least to greatest, the numbers are: $-1.6, -1\frac{1}{4}, -1, -\frac{3}{8}, \frac{2}{5}$.

✓ **GUIDED PRACTICE** for Examples 1 and 2

Show that each number is rational by writing it in $\frac{a}{b}$ form. Then order the numbers from least to greatest.

1. $2.5, -1, -\frac{5}{8}, -0.8$

2. $4\frac{1}{5}, -3.6, -3\frac{8}{9}, 0$

Familiar Properties You can perform operations with rational numbers as you did with decimals, fractions, and integers. You may recall the commutative and associative properties listed below. They can help you add and multiply rational numbers.

VOCABULARY

To help you remember the properties, recall that *commuters* are people who *move* or travel, and people you *associate* with are the friends in your *group*.

Commutative property of addition	$5 + 6 = 6 + 5$
Commutative property of multiplication	$5 \times 6 = 6 \times 5$
Associative property of addition	$(5 + 6) + 7 = 5 + (6 + 7)$
Associative property of multiplication	$(5 \times 6) \times 7 = 5 \times (6 \times 7)$

Four other number properties are shown below. You may have seen the identity properties called the properties of 0 and 1 in other courses.

KEY CONCEPT *For Your Notebook*

Inverse Property of Addition

Words The sum of a number and its **additive inverse**, or opposite, is 0.

Numbers $5 + (-5) = 0$ **Algebra** $a + (-a) = 0$

Identity Property of Addition

Words The sum of a number and the **additive identity**, 0, is the number.

Numbers $-7 + 0 = -7$ **Algebra** $a + 0 = a$

Inverse Property of Multiplication

Words The product of a nonzero number and its **multiplicative inverse**, or reciprocal, is 1.

Numbers $\frac{3}{4} \cdot \frac{4}{3} = 1$ **Algebra** For nonzero integers a and b, $\frac{a}{b} \cdot \frac{b}{a} = 1$

Identity Property of Multiplication

Words The product of a number and the **multiplicative identity**, 1, is the number.

Numbers $9 \cdot 1 = 9$ **Algebra** $a \cdot 1 = a$

EXAMPLE 3 **Identifying Properties**

Tell which property is being illustrated.

a. $-\frac{4}{5} \cdot \left(-\frac{5}{4}\right) = 1$ Inverse property of multiplication

b. $-3.5 + 3.5 = 0$ Inverse property of addition

c. $-4 + 8 = 8 + (-4)$ Commutative property of addition

d. $(-7.9)(1) = -7.9$ Identity property of multiplication

EXAMPLE 4 Using Familiar Properties

Evaluate the expression. Justify each step.

RECALL THE ORDER OF OPERATIONS
Using the order of operations, you would normally add $3 + (-10.6)$ first. Using the associative property to regroup can make the calculations easier.

a. $-10.6 + 3 + (-4.4)$

$= 3 + (-10.6) + (-4.4)$	**Commutative property of addition**
$= 3 + [(-10.6) + (-4.4)]$	**Associative property of addition**
$= 3 + (-15)$	Add -10.6 and -4.4.
$= -12$	Add 3 and -15.

b. $-25(7)(-4)$

$= 7(-25)(-4)$	**Commutative property of multiplication**
$= 7[(-25)(-4)]$	**Associative property of multiplication**
$= 7(100) = 700$	Multiply -25 and -4, multiply 7 and 100.

EXAMPLE 5 Using Properties

TAKE NOTES
In your notebook, record the key steps you take in evaluating an expression using properties. Referring to these notes can help you perform similar calculations.

a.

$\dfrac{2}{3} + \dfrac{7}{10} + \left(-\dfrac{2}{3}\right) = \dfrac{7}{10} + \dfrac{2}{3} + \left(-\dfrac{2}{3}\right)$	**Commutative property of addition**
$= \dfrac{7}{10} + \left[\dfrac{2}{3} + \left(-\dfrac{2}{3}\right)\right]$	**Associative property of addition**
$= \dfrac{7}{10} + 0$	**Inverse property of addition**
$= \dfrac{7}{10}$	**Identity property of addition**

b.

$-\dfrac{5}{3} \times \dfrac{7}{4} \times \dfrac{4}{7} = -\dfrac{5}{3} \times \left(\dfrac{7}{4} \times \dfrac{4}{7}\right)$	**Associative property of multiplication**
$= -\dfrac{5}{3} \times 1$	**Inverse property of multiplication**
$= -\dfrac{5}{3}$	**Identity property of multiplication**

✓ GUIDED PRACTICE for Examples 3, 4, and 5

Tell which property is being illustrated.

3. $-3 + 0 = -3$ **4.** $15 \times 8 = 8 \times 15$ **5.** $(5 + 4) + 6 = 5 + (4 + 6)$

Evaluate the expression. Justify each step.

6. $3.5 + [(-3) + 6.5]$ **7.** $5(-9)(-4)$ **8.** $-6(3)(-5)$

9. $2.8 + 7 + (-1.8)$ **10.** $0.5(7)(8)$ **11.** $0.9 + [9.1 + (-2)]$

12. $94 + 87 + (-94)$ **13.** $-53 + (-25) + 53$ **14.** $\dfrac{1}{3} \cdot \dfrac{5}{6} \cdot 3$

6.6 EXERCISES

HOMEWORK KEY

★ = **STANDARDIZED TEST PRACTICE**
Exs. 27, 55, 56, 57, and 76

○ = **HINTS AND HOMEWORK HELP**
for Exs. 11, 15, 19, 21, 53 at classzone.com

SKILL PRACTICE

VOCABULARY Copy and complete the statement.

1. The additive identity is the number __?__.

2. The multiplicative identity is the number __?__.

VOCABULARY Find the multiplicative and the additive inverses of the number.

3. $-\frac{2}{3}$ **4.** $5\frac{3}{7}$ **5.** 0.7 **6.** 21

WRITING RATIONALS Write the number in its rational form $\frac{a}{b}$.

SEE EXAMPLE 1
on p. 301
for Exs. 7–14

7. 0.4 **8.** $-3\frac{5}{8}$ **9.** 3 **10.** -12

11. $2\frac{1}{5}$ **12.** $-\frac{7}{9}$ **13.** -5.8 **14.** 0.98

ORDERING RATIONAL NUMBERS Order the numbers from least to greatest.

SEE EXAMPLE 2
on p. 301
for Exs. 15–18

15. $-3.1, -4, -\frac{10}{3}, -3\frac{3}{4}, -3.7$ **16.** $3, -2\frac{2}{3}, 0, -\frac{5}{4}, -0.85$

17. $\frac{3}{10}, -1\frac{1}{3}, 0.02, 1, -0.5$ **18.** $-4.25, 1, -\frac{22}{5}, -4\frac{7}{8}, -3$

IDENTIFYING PROPERTIES Tell which property is being illustrated.

SEE EXAMPLE 3
on p. 302
for Exs. 19–27

19. $-2.4 + 2.4 = 0$ **20.** $2 + 11 = 11 + 2$

21. $7 \times (12 \times 3) = (7 \times 12) \times 3$ **22.** $8 + 0 = 8$

23. $\frac{3}{5} \cdot \frac{5}{3} = 1$ **24.** $\frac{3}{5} \cdot \frac{5}{3} = \frac{5}{3} \cdot \frac{3}{5}$

25. $(-3 + 2) + 4 = -3 + (2 + 4)$ **26.** $5 \times (6 \times 19) = 5 \times (19 \times 6)$

27. ★ **MULTIPLE CHOICE** Which equation illustrates the associative property of addition?

(A) $5 + 22 = 22 + 5$ **(B)** $(15 + 3) + 67 = 15 + (3 + 67)$

(C) $5(-17) = -17(5)$ **(D)** $(6 \cdot 8) \cdot 10 = 6 \cdot (8 \cdot 10)$

MENTAL MATH Evaluate the expression. *Justify* each step.

SEE EXAMPLES
4 AND 5
on p. 303
for Exs. 28–36

28. $3 \cdot \frac{1}{2} \cdot \frac{1}{3}$ **29.** $4 + 17 + (-4)$ **30.** $-\frac{3}{4} + \frac{5}{6} + \frac{3}{4}$

31. $43 + 68 + 57$ **32.** $7(-8)(5)$ **33.** $-2.4 + [7 + (-0.6)]$

34. $\frac{1}{2} + \frac{4}{7} + \left(-\frac{1}{2}\right)$ **35.** $14 \cdot \frac{2}{3} \cdot \frac{1}{14}$ **36.** $2(3)(35)$

37. REASONING What numbers are their own multiplicative inverse? What number is its own additive inverse? *Explain* your reasoning.

WRITING EQUIVALENT FRACTIONS Tell which rational form of 1 is used to write the equivalent fraction.

38. $\frac{2}{3} \cdot \underline{\ ?\ } = \frac{24}{36}$

39. $\frac{3}{4} \cdot \underline{\ ?\ } = \frac{45}{60}$

40. $2\frac{7}{8} \cdot \underline{\ ?\ } = 2\frac{175}{200}$

COMPARING RATIONAL NUMBERS Copy and complete the statement using <, >, or =.

41. $-\frac{9}{11} + \frac{9}{11} \underline{\ ?\ } 1$

42. $-0.85 \underline{\ ?\ } -\frac{3}{4}$

43. $7 \cdot \frac{1}{7} \underline{\ ?\ } -1$

44. $\frac{6}{7} \cdot \frac{7}{6} \underline{\ ?\ } 1$

45. $1.25 \underline{\ ?\ } 1\frac{1}{5}$

46. $\frac{2}{3} + \frac{-2}{3} \underline{\ ?\ } 0$

XY ALGEBRA Evaluate the expression.

47. $(-x + x) \cdot y$

48. $\left(\frac{m}{n} \cdot \frac{n}{m}\right) + (-1)$

49. $\left(\frac{a}{b} \cdot \frac{b}{a}\right) \cdot [b + (-b)]$

CHALLENGE Tell whether or not the expressions are equal. Do exponents have associative and commutative properties? *Explain* your answer.

50. $2^3 \overset{?}{=} 3^2$

51. $(3^2)^3 \overset{?}{=} (3^3)^2$

52. $(2^2)^3 \overset{?}{=} 2^{(2^3)}$

PROBLEM SOLVING

SEE EXAMPLE 2
on p. 301
for Exs. 53, 54

53. **RAINFALL** The table shows the amount of rainfall, in inches, above or below the mean for four regions of Oklahoma during a recent drought. Order the numbers from least to greatest to determine which region's rainfall was the most above and the most below the mean.

Region	Panhandle	Northeast	Southwest	Southeast
Departure from Mean	-5.87	$-\frac{631}{100}$	$-8\frac{4}{25}$	1.97

54. **LOW TEMPERATURES** The record low temperatures by month in Minot, ND, are: $-44°C$, $-45°C$, $-1°C$, $-24°C$, $-13°C$, $-42°C$, $-3°C$, $-33°C$, $-16°C$, $-27°C$, and $-4°C$. Find the median of the data.

55. ★ **MULTIPLE CHOICE** Your team needs a total of 21 points to win a volleyball game. Your team's current score is 15. Which expression can *not* be used to find the number of points you need to reach 21?

(A) $21 - 15$ **(B)** $21 + (-15)$ **(C)** $-15 + 21$ **(D)** $15 - 21$

56. ★ **OPEN-ENDED MATH** Give an example of a rational number that is not an integer. Give an example of an integer that is not a whole number. Tell what each number could represent in the real world.

57. ★ **WRITING** You are given two rational numbers. Tell how to find a rational number that is between the two numbers. Does it make a difference how close together the given numbers are? *Explain.*

Stock Trading Shares of stock represent partial ownership in public companies, which are sold on the stock market. As the value of a company rises and falls, the value of each individual share in that company will vary.

You own shares of stock in seven companies. The changes in price (in dollars) of one share of each company for one day are shown below.

Stock A	Stock B	Stock C	Stock D	Stock E	Stock F	Stock G
0.13	−0.54	0.05	0.05	−0.1	−0.03	−0.56

58. Change Which stock had the greatest price change?

59. Predicting Gain If the price of stock A continues to change at the same rate, how many days will it take to gain over $1 per share?

60. Loss or Gain You own 100 shares of stock B. How much did you lose or gain on that day?

61. Total Gain or Loss You own 100 shares of each stock. What was your total gain or loss on that day?

62. REASONING Use the properties of addition to show that the expression $a + b + (-a) + (-b)$ is equal to 0. *Justify* each step you take.

63. CHALLENGE The average monthly temperatures for International Falls, Minnesota, in degrees Celsius are: −16.1, −11.7, −4.4, 3.9, 11.7, 16.7, 18.9, 17.8, 11.7, 5.6, −4.4, and −12.8. Find the mean of the data. *Describe* steps you could take to simplify the process.

NJ **NEW JERSEY MIXED REVIEW**   **TEST PRACTICE** at classzone.com

64. Use a ruler to measure the dimensions of the rectangle in inches. Which best represents its area?

   (A) 2 in.^{2} **(B)** 3 in.^{2}

   (C) 7.5 in.^{2} **(D)** 14 in.^{2}

65. The elevations of four different locations are −24 ft, 110 ft, −80 ft, and 5 ft. Which expression can be used to find the average elevation?

   (A) $24 + 110 + 80 + 5 \div 4$ **(B)** $(24 + 110 + 80 + 5) \div 4$

   (C) $(-24) + 110 + (-80) + 5 \div 4$ **(D)** $[(-24) + 110 + (-80) + 5] \div 4$

6.7 The Distributive Property

Before	You evaluated expressions using order of operations.
Now	You'll evaluate expressions using the distributive property.
Why?	So you can find combined areas, as in Example 1.

KEY VOCABULARY
- equivalent expressions, *p. 307*
- distributive property, *p. 307*

Theater A set designer is building a backdrop for a scene in the play *The Miracle Worker*. The plywood pieces used for the backdrop are made from a 4 foot by 6 foot rectangle joined to a 4 foot by 3 foot rectangle. What two expressions could you use to find the area of wallpaper needed to cover both pieces?

 EXAMPLE 1 Writing Equivalent Expressions

You can find the total area described above by finding the sum of the areas of the separate pieces or by finding the area of the pieces joined together.

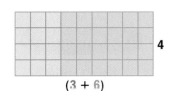

$$\textbf{Area} = 4(3) + 4(6) \qquad\qquad \textbf{Area} = 4(3 + 6)$$
$$= 12 + 24 = 36 \text{ ft}^2 \qquad\qquad = 4(9) = 36 \text{ ft}^2$$

 GUIDED PRACTICE for Example 1

1. **What If?** Suppose the set designer in Example 1 joins a rectangle of plywood with dimensions 2 feet by 7 feet to a rectangle with dimensions 2 feet by 4 feet. Model the area to be covered in wallpaper using equivalent expressions.

Expressions Both expressions in Example 1 are equal to 36. They are called **equivalent expressions** because they have the same value. These expressions are an example of the **distributive property**.

KEY CONCEPT *For Your Notebook*

The Distributive Property

Algebra For all numbers a, b, and c, $a(b + c) = ab + ac$ and $a(b - c) = ab - ac$.

Numbers $8(10 + 4) = 8(10) + 8(4)$ and $3(4 - 2) = 3(4) - 3(2)$

EXAMPLE 2 **Writing Equivalent Expressions**

Use the distributive property to write an equivalent expression. Check your answer.

 a. $-4(5 + 8)$ **b.** $4(50 - 3)$ **c.** $7(9) + 7(5)$

SOLUTION

READING

The *symmetric property of equality* lets you read an equation from left to right or from right to left. So, in Example 2 (c), if $a(b + c) = ab + ac$, then $ab + ac = a(b + c)$.

a. Expression: $-4(5 + 8) = -4(5) + (-4)(8)$ **Distributive property**

     Check: $-4(13) \stackrel{?}{=} -20 + (-32)$ **Simplify.**

         $-52 = -52$ ✓   **Answer checks.**

b. Expression: $4(50 - 3) = 4(50) - 4(3)$ **Distributive property**

     Check: $4(47) \stackrel{?}{=} 200 - 12$ **Simplify.**

         $188 = 188$ ✓   **Answer checks.**

c. Expression: $7(9) + 7(5) = 7(9 + 5)$ **Distributive property**

     Check: $63 + 35 \stackrel{?}{=} 7(14)$ **Simplify.**

         $98 = 98$ ✓   **Answer checks.**

EXAMPLE 3 **Using the Distributive Property**

Lava Lamps You are buying 8 small lava lamps as door prizes for a disco party that your school is having. Each lava lamp costs $15.95. Use the distributive property to find the total cost of the lamps.

SOLUTION

   $8(15.95) = 8(16.00 - 0.05)$ **Write 15.95 as a difference of a whole number and a decimal.**

AVOID ERRORS

Don't forget when using the distributive property to multiply the outside number by *both* numbers inside the parentheses.

       $= 8(16.00) - 8(0.05)$ **Distributive property**

       $= 128.00 - 0.40$ **Multiply.**

       $= 127.60$ **Subtract.**

▶ **Answer** The total cost of the lava lamps is $127.60.

Animated Math
at classzone.com

✓ **GUIDED PRACTICE**   for Examples 2 and 3

Use the distributive property to write an equivalent expression. Check your answer.

 2. $6\left(\dfrac{1}{7}\right) + 6\left(\dfrac{6}{7}\right)$ **3.** $-6(12 + 3)$ **4.** $8(12 - 5)$ **5.** $3(11) - 3(4)$

 6. What If? Suppose in Example 3 that each lava lamp costs $17.90. Find the total cost of buying 6 lamps.

6.7 EXERCISES

HOMEWORK KEY

★ = **STANDARDIZED TEST PRACTICE**
Exs. 8, 9, 45, 46, 48, 50, 53, and 64

◯ = **HINTS AND HOMEWORK HELP**
for Exs. 5, 11, 13, 43, 47 at classzone.com

SKILL PRACTICE

1. VOCABULARY Copy and complete: You can use the distributive property to write __?__ expressions.

WRITING EQUIVALENT EXPRESSIONS Use the distributive property to write an equivalent expression. Check your answer.

SEE EXAMPLES
1 AND 2
on pp. 307–308
for Exs. 2–8

2. $5(3 + 7)$

3. $4(4 + 5)$

4. $7(3) + 7(4)$

5. $8(100 - 4)$

6. $6\left(\frac{5}{12}\right) - 6\left(\frac{1}{12}\right)$

7. $4\left(\frac{3}{5}\right) + 4\left(\frac{2}{5}\right)$

8. ★ **MULTIPLE CHOICE** Match the expression $3(-4 + 3)$ with an equivalent expression.

Ⓐ $4(3) + 4(3)$ Ⓑ $3(-4) + 3(3)$ Ⓒ $4(3) - 4(3)$ Ⓓ $3(4) + 3(3)$

SEE EXAMPLE 3
on p. 308
for Exs. 9–19

9. ★ **MULTIPLE CHOICE** What is the value of the expression $9(8.5)$?

Ⓐ 36 Ⓑ 72.5 Ⓒ 76.5 Ⓓ 81

DISTRIBUTIVE PROPERTY Use the distributive property to evaluate.

10. $7(8.2)$

11. $6(16.85)$

12. $8(19.97)$

13. $3(7.3) + 3(2.7)$

14. $4(8.1) + 4(2.9)$

15. $9(13.2) + 9(6.8)$

16. $11\left(\frac{5}{8}\right) + 11\left(\frac{3}{8}\right)$

17. $13\left(\frac{3}{7}\right) - 13\left(-\frac{4}{7}\right)$

18. $3\left(\frac{2}{5}\right) - 3\left(\frac{-1}{5}\right)$

19. ERROR ANALYSIS Describe and correct the error made in using the distributive property to evaluate the expression $-8(5 + 4)$.

$$\times \quad \begin{aligned} -8(5 + 4) &= -40 + 32 \\ &= -8 \end{aligned}$$

EVALUATING EXPRESSIONS Evaluate the expression in two ways.

20. $14(3) - 27 + 14(7)$

21. $8(3) + 14 + 8(-4)$

22. $4(6) - 20 + 4(8 - 4)$

23. $17(2) + 16 + 17(8)$

24. $11(-5) + 12 + 11(6)$

25. $7(9 - 5) - 13 + 7(2 + 4)$

IDENTIFYING PROPERTIES Tell which property is being illustrated.

26. $-2 + 19 = 19 + (-2)$

27. $11 + (-11) = 0$

28. $\frac{3}{8} \cdot \frac{1}{8} = \frac{1}{8} \cdot \frac{3}{8}$

29. $3(11 \cdot 8) = (3 \cdot 11)8$

30. $\frac{2}{3} \times \frac{3}{2} = 1$

31. $3(11 + 8) = 3 \cdot 11 + 3 \cdot 8$

32. $5 \cdot 7 - 5 \cdot 15 = 5(7 - 15)$

33. $(-17)(1) = -17$

34. $23 + (9 + 3) = (23 + 9) + 3$

35. WHICH ONE DOESN'T BELONG? Which of the following does *not* use the distributive property correctly?

A. $6(2 + 5) = 6(2) + 6(5)$

B. $-3(8) + (-3)(2) = -3(8 - 2)$

C. $5(3) + 5(5) = 5(3 + 5)$

D. $4(12 - 7) = 4(12) - 4(7)$

XV ALGEBRA Write an equivalent expression using the distributive property. Simplify using the identity properties.

36. $p(r - s) + ps$ **37.** $mp + (-m)(n + p)$ **38.** $\frac{1}{a}(a - b)$

CHALLENGE Show how you can simplify the expressions using the distributive property twice to evaluate the expressions.

39. $(0.98)(7.03)$ **40.** $(1.1)(6.89)$ **41.** $(0.99)(9.98)$ **42.** $(3.01)(6.05)$

PROBLEM SOLVING

SEE EXAMPLE 1
on p. 307
for Ex. 43

43. PERIMETER The expression $2l + 2w$ is used to find the perimeter of a rectangle. Use the distributive property to write an equivalent expression for the perimeter. Show that both formulas give the same result for the perimeter of a rectangle that is 14 cm by 12 cm.

Animated Math at classzone.com

SEE EXAMPLE 2
on p. 308
for Exs. 44–45

44. PUMPKINS You buy 2 pumpkins to carve. The pumpkins weigh 10 pounds and 6 pounds, and cost $.70 per pound. Use the distributive property to write two equivalent expressions to represent the total amount that you pay for the pumpkins.

45. ★ MULTIPLE CHOICE You buy 5 CD's for $9.95 each. Which expression represents the total cost of the CD's?

   Ⓐ $5(10) - 5(0.05)$ **Ⓑ** $5(10 + 0.05)$ **Ⓒ** $5(10) - 0.05$ **Ⓓ** $10(5 - 0.05)$

46. ★ WRITING One meaning of the word *distribute* is to supply or deliver to each individual in a group. How can this meaning help you remember the distributive property?

47. TALENT SHOW At a talent show, each performer has 2 minutes to set up, 3 minutes for an introduction, and 5 minutes for the act. There are 20 people performing. Using the distributive property, find how long the talent show will be, in minutes.

48. ★ OPEN-ENDED MATH Describe an everyday situation that can be modeled by the equation $4(1 - 0.05)$. Then solve the problem and interpret the solution.

49. TRADING CARDS A friend is selling his collection of trading cards. He is selling each card for $.95, and you want to purchase 20 cards. Write an expression for the total cost of 20 cards. Then use the distributive property and mental math to evaluate the expression.

50. ★ SHORT RESPONSE You want to find the product 5×215, but the "2" button on your calculator is broken. How can you use the distributive property and your calculator to find the product? *Explain* your reasoning.

51. BANK A scale drawing of the layout of a bank is shown. Write two expressions for the actual perimeter of the bank, if the actual bank is x times as large as this drawing. Evaluate each expression when $x = 400$ and when $x = 282.8$.

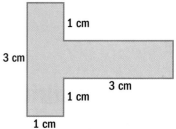

52. WALL AREA Two outer walls of a building have length 16 feet and height 12 feet. Each wall has one square window, with side length 3 feet. Write two equivalent expressions for the number of square feet of bricks needed to cover the walls. Then evaluate.

53. ★ **EXTENDED RESPONSE** A rectangular table is 3 feet wide and 6 feet long. Each of the shorter sides has a drop leaf, which can be raised to lengthen the table. The dimensions of each leaf are 3 feet by 1.5 feet.

  a. Use the distributive property to write two equivalent expressions for the area of the table with one leaf raised. *Illustrate* each expression with a diagram.

  b. If the dimensions of both the table and the leaves are doubled, does the area of the table with one leaf raised double? *Explain.*

54. CHALLENGE A club is selling sandwiches and pizzas to raise money. The club charges $4.75 for each sandwich and $5.75 for each pizza. It costs the club $2.25 for each sandwich and $2.50 for each pizza. The club sells 30 sandwiches and 20 pizzas. Write an expression to represent the total profit made. How much profit does the club make?

55. CHALLENGE You and two friends go to a baseball game. Together you have $50. Each ticket costs $10, and each of you buys a hot dog that costs $2 and a large drink. When you leave the stadium, all together you have $2 left. How much did each drink cost?

 NEW JERSEY MIXED REVIEW **TEST PRACTICE** at classzone.com

56. Mrs. Grace teaches dance lessons at a local studio. The line graph at the right shows the total number of students enrolled each year in her classes for the years 2000 to 2006. If the enrollment trend continues, which is the best prediction of the enrollment in 2008?

  Ⓐ Fewer than 50

  Ⓑ Between 60 and 80

  Ⓒ Between 90 and 110

  Ⓓ More than 120

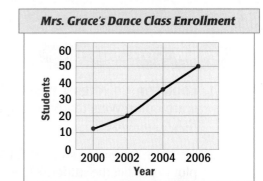

INVESTIGATION
Use before Lesson 6.8

GOAL
Make and interpret a scatter plot.

MATERIALS
• metric tape measure
• graph paper

6.8 Making a Scatter Plot

A *scatter plot* is a way to represent paired data visually. Each point on a scatter plot represents one data pair.

EXPLORE | Working in a group of six people, make a scatter plot that shows the relationship between height and lower-arm length.

STEP 1 **Make** a table like the one shown. Measure and record the height and lower-arm length of each person in your group to the nearest centimeter. Your lower-arm length is the distance between your elbow and your fingertips.

Name	Height (cm)	Lower-Arm Length (cm)
Damon	155	40
?	?	?

STEP 2 **Make** a scatter plot of your group's data by plotting each person's height and lower-arm length as a data pair. Label the axes and plot the points as shown.

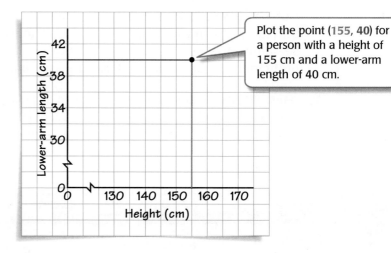

Plot the point (155, 40) for a person with a height of 155 cm and a lower-arm length of 40 cm.

DRAW CONCLUSIONS

1. **LOOK FOR A PATTERN** What do you notice about the points on the scatter plot? What tends to happen to a person's lower-arm length as height increases?

2. **PREDICT** Suppose a student is 170 centimeters tall. Use your scatter plot to predict the student's lower-arm length. *Explain* your reasoning.

6.8 The Coordinate Plane

NJ 4.2.C.1   Use coordinates in four quadrants to represent geometric concepts.

Before   You graphed and compared numbers on a number line.

Now   You'll identify and plot points in a coordinate plane.

Why?   So you can find broadcast distances, as in Exs. 49–50.

KEY VOCABULARY
- **coordinate plane,** *p. 313*
- **origin,** *p. 313*
- **quadrant,** *p. 313*
- **ordered pair,** *p. 313*
- **x-coordinate,** *p. 313*
- **y-coordinate,** *p. 313*
- **scatter plot,** *p. 315*

A **coordinate plane** is formed by the intersection of a horizontal number line, called the *x-axis*, and a vertical number line, called the *y-axis*. The x-axis and the y-axis meet at a point called the **origin** and divide the coordinate plane into four **quadrants**.

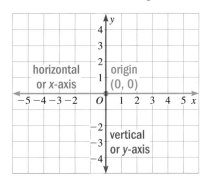

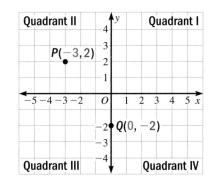

Points in a coordinate plane are represented by **ordered pairs** in which the first number is the **x-coordinate** and the second number is the **y-coordinate**. For example, point *P* is represented by the ordered pair (−3, 2) and lies in Quadrant II. A point on an axis, such as *Q*, does not lie in any quadrant.

EXAMPLE 1   Naming Ordered Pairs

Name the ordered pair that represents the point.

  a. *A*   **b.** *B*

SOLUTION

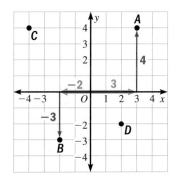

  a. Point *A* is 3 units right of the origin and 4 units up. So, the x-coordinate is 3 and the y-coordinate is 4. Point *A* is at (3, 4).

  b. Point *B* is 2 units to the left of the origin and 3 units down. So, the x-coordinate is −2 and the y-coordinate is −3. Point *B* is at (−2, −3).

 GUIDED PRACTICE   for Example 1

  1. Name the ordered pairs that represent points *C* and *D* in Example 1.

EXAMPLE 2 Standardized Test Practice

Which of the following points is located in Quadrant II?

(A) $P(3, -4)$ **(B)** $Q(-1, -3)$ **(C)** $R(0, 2)$ **(D)** $S(-2, 1)$

ELIMINATE CHOICES
Because point R lies on an axis, you know it does not lie in any quadrant. So, choice C can be eliminated.

SOLUTION

Plot points P, Q, R, and S on a coordinate plane. Point P is located in Quadrant IV. Point Q is located in Quadrant III. Point R lies on the y-axis. Point S is located in Quadrant II.

▶ **Answer** Point $S(-2, 1)$ is in Quadrant II.
The correct answer is D. **(A) (B) (C) (D)**

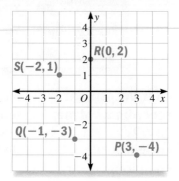

EXAMPLE 3 Finding Segment Lengths and Area

Find the length, width, and area of rectangle $ABCD$.

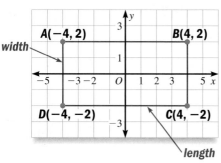

SOLUTION

The length of the rectangle is the *horizontal* distance between A and B. To find this distance, find the absolute value of the difference between their x-coordinates.

$$\textbf{Length} = \left| x\text{-coordinate of } A - x\text{-coordinate of } B \right|$$
$$= \left| -4 - 4 \right| = \left| -8 \right| = \textbf{8 units}$$

The width of the rectangle is the *vertical* distance between A and D. This distance is the absolute value of the difference between their y-coordinates.

$$\textbf{Width} = \left| y\text{-coordinate of } A - y\text{-coordinate of } D \right|$$
$$= \left| 2 - (-2) \right| = \left| 4 \right| = \textbf{4 units}$$

The area of the rectangle is found by multiplying the length and width.

$$\textbf{Area} = lw = 8(4) = \textbf{32 square units}$$

 GUIDED PRACTICE for Examples 2 and 3

Plot the points in the same coordinate plane. Describe the location of each point.

2. $A(2, 3)$ **3.** $B(0, 0)$ **4.** $C(-2, 0)$ **5.** $D(-1, -4)$

6. Geometry Find the length, width, and area of rectangle $ABCD$ formed by the points $A(-3, 4)$, $B(3, 4)$, $C(-3, -3)$, and $D(3, -3)$.

Scatter Plots You can use a coordinate plane to make a **scatter plot** of paired data. Each data pair is plotted as a point, and from the collection of plotted points you can recognize patterns and make predictions.

EXAMPLE 4 **Making a Scatter Plot**

Pine Trees The table gives the ages and heights of 10 pine trees. Make a scatter plot of the data. Then make a conclusion about the data.

WRITING ORDERED PAIRS
With a table, the first value is the *x*-value and the second value is the *y*-value. Use this information to write and plot ordered pairs.

Age (years)	0	1	6	10	13	18	21	32	36	39
Height (feet)	0	2	4	8	14	16	23	31	34	34

STEP 1 **Draw** the first quadrant of a coordinate plane and show ages on the *x*-axis and heights on the *y*-axis.

STEP 2 **Plot** the ordered pairs in the table.

STEP 3 **Look** for a pattern. The points tend to rise from left to right.

▶ **Answer** As the age of a pine tree increases, its height tends to increase as well.

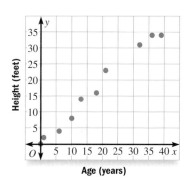

✓ **GUIDED PRACTICE** for Example 4

7. **What If?** Predict the height of a 27-year-old pine tree in Example 4.

6.8 EXERCISES

HOMEWORK KEY

★ = **STANDARDIZED TEST PRACTICE**
Exs. 23, 24, 42, 46, 47, and 62

○ = **HINTS AND HOMEWORK HELP**
for Exs. 7, 15, 21, 41, 43 at classzone.com

SKILL PRACTICE

VOCABULARY Copy and complete the statement.

1. In a coordinate plane, the horizontal number line is called the ___?___ .

2. The second number in an ordered pair is called the ___?___ .

NAMING ORDERED PAIRS Name the ordered pair that represents the point.

SEE EXAMPLE 1
on p. 313
for Exs. 3–10

3. *A*   4. *B*

5. *C*   6. *D*

7. *E*   8. *F*

9. *G*   10. *H*

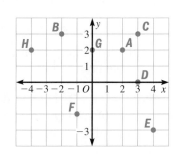

PLOTTING POINTS Plot and label the points in the same coordinate plane. Describe the location of each point.

SEE EXAMPLE 2
on p. 314
for Exs. 11–23

11. $L(-3, 3)$ **12.** $M(0, -3)$ **13.** $N(-2, -4)$ **14.** $P(4, 1)$

15. $R(-2, 5)$ **16.** $S(7, 0)$ **17.** $T(-1, -8)$ **18.** $U(6, 3)$

19. $V(4, -2)$ **20.** $W(-4, -5)$ **21.** $X(0, -4)$ **22.** $Y(5, -7)$

23. ★ **MULTIPLE CHOICE** In which quadrant is the point $K(4, -3)$?

(A) I   (B) II   (C) III   (D) IV

SEE EXAMPLE 3
on p. 314
for Exs. 24–31

24. ★ **MULTIPLE CHOICE** What is the length of a line segment with endpoints $G(3, 3)$ and $H(3, -4)$?

(A) -7 units   (B) 0 units   (C) 3 units   (D) 7 units

FINDING SEGMENT LENGTHS AND AREA Plot and connect the points to form a rectangle. Then find the length, width, and area of the rectangle.

25. $A(0, 0), B(6, 0), C(6, 2), D(0, 2)$ **26.** $M(7, 1), N(7, 5), U(8, 5), P(8, 1)$

27. $W(3, -4), X(-1, -4), Y(-1, 5), Z(3, 5)$ **28.** $I(-2, 2), J(8, 2), K(8, -1), L(-2, -1)$

29. $E(3, 4), F(-5, 4), G(-5, 2), H(3, 2)$ **30.** $Q(-4, 2), R(-4, 4), S(2, 4), T(2, 2)$

31. ERROR ANALYSIS Describe and correct the error made in finding the distance between A and B using the points $A(3, -14)$ and $B(3, -6)$.

$$
\begin{aligned}
\text{distance} &= -14 - (-6) \\
&= -14 + 6 \\
&= -8
\end{aligned}
$$

SEE EXAMPLE 4
on p. 315
for Ex. 32

32. REASONING Make a conclusion about the data shown in the scatter plot.

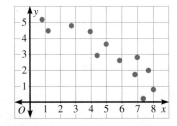

ALGEBRA Tell what you know about the numbers x and y, given the location of the point (x, y).

33. The point is in Quadrant I.   **34.** The point is in Quadrant IV.

35. The point is on the x-axis.   **36.** The point is on the y-axis.

37. The point is in Quadrant II.   **38.** The point is in Quadrant III.

39. GRAPHING EQUIVALENT FRACTIONS List 5 fractions equivalent to $\frac{2}{3}$. Use the list to graph 5 ordered pairs of the form (numerator, denominator). What conclusions can you make about this scatter plot?

40. CHALLENGE Let a and b be integers, both not zero. If you plot $O(0, 0)$, $P(a, b)$, and $Q(-b, a)$, you can connect these points to form $\angle POQ$. What type of angle is $\angle POQ$ regardless of the values of a and b? *Explain.*

PROBLEM SOLVING

SEE EXAMPLE 1
on p. 313
for Ex. 41

41. SHIPWRECKS Suppose a researcher uses a coordinate plane in which each unit is equal to 1 mile to record the location of a shipwreck. The research station is at the origin. The shipwreck is 15 miles west and 8 miles south of the station. What ordered pair can the researcher use to represent the location of the shipwreck?

 at classzone.com

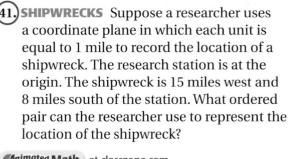

SEE EXAMPLE 3
on p. 314
for Ex. 42

42. ★ OPEN-ENDED MATH Draw a vertical line segment on a coordinate grid. Label the coordinates of the endpoints and show how to calculate the segment's length.

SEE EXAMPLE 4
on p. 315
for Exs. 43–47

FUEL ECONOMY In Exercises 43–45, use the table below showing the engine size, in liters, and highway mileage, in miles per gallon, for 12 cars.

Engine Size (L)	3	5	1	6	2	2	4	3	3	2	4	5
Highway Mileage (mi/gal)	28	23	47	19	33	31	25	24	25	37	24	22

43. Make a scatter plot of the data.

44. What can you conclude about the data?

45. Predict the highway mileage for a 5.5 liter engine.

46. ★ SHORT RESPONSE A group of scientists record information on a population of red foxes in a geographic region. The ordered pairs show the length, in feet, and the weight, in pounds, of 15 red foxes. Make a scatter plot of the data. Then make a conclusion about the data.

(3, 8), (3.4, 11), (3.1, 8.5), (3.5, 13), (3.5, 12.5), (3, 9), (3.7, 15), (3.7, 14.5), (3.4, 10), (3.3, 12), (3.2, 9), (3.2, 11.5), (3.6, 14.5), (3.6, 15), (3.5, 14)

47. ★ EXTENDED RESPONSE The table shows the freezing temperatures of water and of three bodies of water, and the salt content in each of these in parts per thousand (ppt).

	Water	Caspian Sea	Black Sea	Great Salt Lake
Approximate freezing temperature (°C)	0	−0.7	−1.0	−6.6
Salt content (ppt)	0	13	18	105

a. Graph Make a scatter plot of the data.

b. Analyze Describe the trend shown in the graph.

c. Calculate If ocean water averages a salt content of about 35 ppt, predict its freezing temperature. *Explain* your reasoning.

48. MULTI-STEP PROBLEM A computerized drill follows instructions given as ordered pairs in which the *x*-coordinate determines horizontal movement and the *y*-coordinate determines vertical movement. The drill begins at the origin and returns to the origin after each hole is drilled.

    a. Interpret You want the drill to make a stair step pattern beginning $(-4, -8), (-4, -6), (-3, -6), (-3, -4), \ldots$. What movement will the drill make to drill the first hole?

    b. Apply Write the next five instructions for the drill.

    c. Predict Will the twelfth hole be to the right or above the eleventh hole? What are the coordinates of the twelfth point?

BROADCAST RANGE The coordinate plane shows the broadcast area of a low-power radio station as a circle and its interior.

49. Which of the houses located at the following points are in the station's broadcast area?

    $A(9, 9), B(-6, -6), C(4, -5), D(-3, 9)$

50. CHALLENGE The scale on the coordinate plane is in miles. How far does the broadcast reach in a north east direction from the station? *Explain* your reasoning.

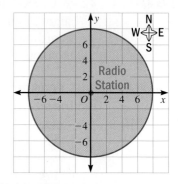

NJ **NEW JERSEY MIXED REVIEW**

TEST PRACTICE at classzone.com

51. What is the value of the expression below?

$$-2(-3 + 12) \div [-1 + (6 + 1)]$$

  A -13 **B** -3 **C** 3 **D** 23

52. Kara is driving from her house to the beach. She travels at a constant speed of 55 miles per hour. The total driving distance from Kara's house to the beach is 150 miles. Which equation can you use to approximate Kara's distance from the beach after driving *t* hours?

  A $d = 150 - \dfrac{t}{55}$ **B** $d = 150 - 55 - t$

  C $d = 150 + 55 + t$ **D** $d = 150 - 55t$

53. A $\dfrac{1}{2}$-inch pizza crust is flattened to a thickness of $\dfrac{3}{8}$ inch. By how much did the thickness of the crust decrease?

  A $\dfrac{1}{8}$ in.   **B** $\dfrac{1}{4}$ in.

  C $\dfrac{3}{8}$ in.   **D** $\dfrac{7}{8}$ in.

Find the product or quotient.

1. $-6(13)$ *(p. 291)*

2. $3(-25)$ *(p. 291)*

3. $-3(-12)$ *(p. 291)*

4. $-18 \div 9$ *(p. 296)*

5. $56 \div (-7)$ *(p. 296)*

6. $-15 \div (-3)$ *(p. 296)*

7. **STOCK MARKET** A newspaper reports these changes in the price of a stock over five days: $-0.1, -0.3, 0.5, -0.8, 2$. Find the mean daily change. *(p. 301)*

Evaluate the expression. *Justify* each step. *(p. 301)*

8. $(-5)(9)\left(-\dfrac{1}{5}\right)$

9. $\dfrac{1}{16}(-4)(16)$

10. $-3.4 + 7 + (-3.6)$

Use the distributive property to evaluate the expression. *(p. 307)*

11. $20(2) + 20(7)$

12. $12(9) - 12(3)$

13. $4(6.9)$

14. **CAR WASH** The members of a club hold a car wash and earn $4.25 for each car they wash and $3.75 for each car they wax. The club washes and waxes 16 cars. Use the distributive property to write and evaluate an expression for the total amount of money the club earned. *(p. 307)*

15. Plot the points $K(4, -5)$ and $L(-7, 0)$. *Describe* the location of each point. *(p. 313)*

16. Plot and connect the points $A(-5, 4)$, $B(2, 4)$, $C(2, -2)$, and $D(-5, -2)$ to form a rectangle. Then find the length, width, and area of the rectangle. *(p. 313)*

Brain Game

The More There Is, the Less You See!

To solve the riddle given in the title, fill in each blank with the letter located at the point represented by the ordered pair.

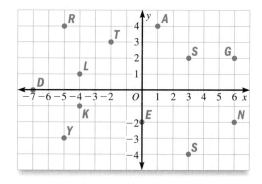

$\underline{\hspace{1cm}}$ $\underline{\hspace{1cm}}$ $\underline{\hspace{1cm}}$ $\underline{\hspace{1cm}}$ $\underline{\hspace{1cm}}$ $\underline{\hspace{1cm}}$ $\underline{\hspace{1cm}}$ $\underline{\hspace{1cm}}$

$(-7, 0)$ $\quad$ $(1, 4)$ $\quad$ $(-5, 4)$ $\quad$ $(-4, -1)$ $\quad$ $(6, -2)$ $\quad$ $(0, -2)$ $\quad$ $(3, 2)$ $\quad$ $(3, -4)$

6.8 Graphing in a Coordinate Plane

A graphing calculator allows you to graph ordered pairs in a coordinate plane.

EXAMPLE Graph the ordered pairs (4, −1) and (2, 3).

SOLUTION

STEP 1 **Clear** Lists 1 and 2 (L1 and L2) on your calculator. Then enter the *x*-coordinates of the ordered pairs in L1 and the *y*-coordinates of the ordered pairs in L2.

Keystrokes

2nd [STAT] ▶ 3 2nd [STAT] 1 , 2nd [STAT] 2 ENTER
[LIST] 4 ENTER 2 ENTER ▶ (−) 1 ENTER 3 ENTER

STEP 2 **Prepare** the calculator to graph the ordered pairs.

Keystrokes

2nd [PLOT] ENTER

Select the options as shown on the screen at the right. To select an item, put the cursor on the item and press ENTER .

STEP 3 **Graph** the ordered pairs by pressing ZOOM 6.

PRACTICE Graph the ordered pair and describe its location.

1. (6, 8)	**2.** (−4, 8)	**3.** (7, −8)	**4.** (−4, −4)
5. (−4, 0)	**6.** (3, 0)	**7.** (0, −2)	**8.** (0, 5)

Lessons 6.4–6.8

1. **CUTTING ROPE** You are going to cut a rope that is x feet long into sections that are $\frac{1}{x}$ as long as the entire rope. Then you will cut each section in half. Your friend says that no matter what the value of x is, the length of each final piece of rope will always be $\frac{1}{2}$ foot. Which property helps your friend to make this conclusion?

   A. Inverse Property of Addition

   B. Inverse Property of Multiplication

   C. Identity Property of Addition

   D. Distributive Property

2. **AREA** In the coordinate plane below, what is the area of rectangle $ABCD$?

   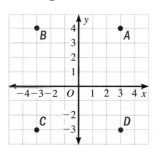

   A. 13 square units

   B. 21 square units

   C. 26 square units

   D. 42 square units

3. **NUMBER PATTERN** What are the next three numbers in the pattern below?

   $$2, -4, 8, -16, \ldots$$

   A. $18, -20, 22$

   B. $-18, 20, -22$

   C. $32, -64, 128$

   D. $-32, 64, -128$

STOCKS In Exercises 4 and 5, use the table below. You own shares of stocks in four companies. The table shows the changes in the prices, in dollars, of one share of each company's stock for one day. You own 100 shares of each stock.

Stock P	Stock Q	Stock R	Stock S
0.15	−0.25	$-\frac{1}{5}$	$\frac{1}{25}$

4. Which stock had the greatest price change?

   A. Stock P

   B Stock Q

   C. Stock R

   D. Stock S

5. What was the total change in the value of your stocks on that day?

   A. −$26

   B. −$0.26

   C. $0.26

   D. $26

6. **OPEN-ENDED** Use the coordinate plane to answer the questions below.

   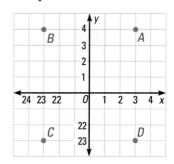

   • Name the point in Quadrant II.
   • What is the ordered pair represented by point D?
   • Find the distance between point C and point D.

REVIEW KEY VOCABULARY

- integer, *p. 269*
- negative integer, *p. 269*
- positive integer, *p. 269*
- opposite, *p. 269*
- absolute value, *p. 278*
- rational number, *p. 301*
- additive identity, *p. 302*

- multiplicative identity, *p. 302*
- additive inverse, *p. 302*
- multiplicative inverse, *p. 302*
- equivalent expressions, *p. 307*
- distributive property, *p. 307*
- coordinate plane, *p. 313*
- origin, *p. 313*

- quadrant, *p. 313*
- ordered pair, *p. 313*
- *x*-coordinate, *p. 313*
- *y*-coordinate, *p. 313*
- scatter plot, *p. 315*

VOCABULARY EXERCISES

1. Identify all integers and all pairs of opposites among the numbers 2.3, -4, 5, -2.3, -2, and 4.

2. *Explain* the difference between an additive inverse and an additive identity.

3. How is the multiplicative inverse of a number different from the additive inverse of a number?

4. How are the quadrants of a coordinate plane numbered?

REVIEW EXAMPLES AND EXERCISES

6.1 Comparing and Ordering Integers
pp. 269–273

EXAMPLE

Compare -2 and 3.

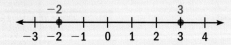

▶ **Answer** Because -2 is to the left of 3, $-2 < 3$ or $3 > -2$.

EXERCISES

Copy and complete the statement using < or >.

SEE EXAMPLES
1, 2, AND 3
on pp. 269–270
for Exs. 5–10

5. $12 \underline{\ ?\ } -23$

6. $-44 \underline{\ ?\ } 7$

7. $-21 \underline{\ ?\ } -19$

8. $-4 \underline{\ ?\ } -7$

9. Order the integers from least to greatest: 7, 9, 8, -8, -10, 11.

10. **Finance** Write the integer that corresponds to a bank withdrawal of $350.

6.2 Adding Integers

pp. 277–282

EXAMPLE

Find the sum $-2 + (-4)$ using a number line.

Start at 0. Move 2 units to the **left**.

Then move 4 more units to the **left**.

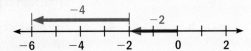

▶ **Answer** The final position is -6, so $-2 + (-4) = -6$.

EXERCISES

Find the sum.

SEE EXAMPLES 1 AND 4
on pp. 277, 279
for Exs. 11–23

11. $-14 + 29$ **12.** $31 + (-73)$ **13.** $-47 + (-13)$ **14.** $-16 + (-22)$

15. $52 + (-11)$ **16.** $-94 + 71$ **17.** $-36 + (-19)$ **18.** $-27 + (-68)$

Evaluate the expression when $x = -19$ and $s = 7$.

19. $x + (-6)$ **20.** $x + s$ **21.** $5 + (-s)$ **22.** $x + (-s)$

23. Lowest Points The lowest point in Europe is 28 meters below sea level. The lowest point in Australia is 16 meters higher than this. Write an addition expression involving integers that represents the elevation of the lowest point in Australia. Then evaluate the expression.

6.3 Subtracting Integers

pp. 285–289

EXAMPLE

Find the difference. Then check.

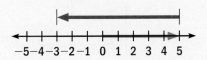

$5 - 8 = 5 + (-8)$	**Write as addition expression.**
$= -3$	**Use rule for adding integers.**

EXERCISES

Find the difference. Check using a number line.

SEE EXAMPLES 1 AND 2
on pp. 285–286
for Exs. 24–35

24. $1 - 8$ **25.** $11 - (-2)$ **26.** $-7 - 3$ **27.** $34 - (-41)$

28. $-15 - 7$ **29.** $19 - (-28)$ **30.** $12 - 35$ **31.** $-48 - (-39)$

Evaluate the expression when $a = -8$ and $b = 4$.

32. $b - 29$ **33.** $18 - a$ **34.** $a - b$ **35.** $a - (-b)$

6.4 Multiplying Integers

EXAMPLE

a. $-3(-8) = 24$ **The product of two integers with the same sign is positive.**

b. $-6(7) = -42$ **The product of two integers with different signs is negative.**

EXERCISES

Find the product.

SEE EXAMPLES
1, 2, AND 3
on p. 292
for Exs. 36–48

36. $-10(10)$ **37.** $-27(0)$ **38.** $-6(-3)$ **39.** $-9(-2)(-3)$

40. $-5(-7)$ **41.** $-19(6)$ **42.** $-8(-4)(-2)$ **43.** $-15(0)(-3)$

Evaluate the expression when $x = 5$, $y = -7$, and $z = -2$.

44. $z^2 x$ **45.** $-3xy$ **46.** yz **47.** $x^2 y$

48. Population Change Suppose the average population of a town has been decreasing by 115 people per year. How has the population changed over the last six years?

6.5 Dividing Integers

EXAMPLE

a. $36 \div (-9) = -4$ **The quotient of two integers with different signs is negative.**

b. $\dfrac{-56}{-8} = 7$ **The quotient of two integers with the same sign is positive.**

EXERCISES

Find the quotient.

SEE EXAMPLES
1 AND 3
on pp. 297–298
for Exs. 49–57

49. $-88 \div 22$ **50.** $96 \div (-32)$ **51.** $0 \div (-37)$ **52.** $-87 \div (-29)$

53. $-56 \div (-28)$ **54.** $19 \div (-1)$ **55.** $-84 \div 21$ **56.** $0 \div (-52)$

57. Freeze-Drying During the freeze-drying process, all of the water content is removed from the food item. To freeze-dry ice cream, regular ice cream is frozen at a temperature of $-40°$F and then dried in a vacuum. Convert this temperature to degrees Celsius.

6.6 Rational Numbers

EXAMPLE

Evaluate the expression. Justify each step.

a. $-10.6 + 3 + (-4.4)$

$= 3 + (-10.6) + (-4.4)$	**Commutative property of addition**
$= 3 + [(-10.6) + (-4.4)]$	**Associative property of addition**
$= 3 + (-15)$	**Add -10.6 and -4.4.**
$= -12$	**Add 3 and -15.**

b. $-25(7)(-4)$

$= 7(-25)(-4)$	**Commutative property of multiplication**
$= 7[(-25)(-4)]$	**Associative property of multiplication**
$= 7(100)$	**Multiply -25 and -4.**
$= 700$	**Multiply 7 and 100.**

EXERCISES

Show that the numbers are rational by writing each number in $\frac{a}{b}$ form.
Then order the numbers from least to greatest.

*SEE EXAMPLES
1, 2, 3, AND 4*
on pp. 301–303
for Exs. 58–63

58. $-3.7, 3\frac{5}{8}, -3.1, -\frac{16}{5}, 3$ **59.** $2.4, -2.1, -2\frac{4}{5}, 2, 2\frac{1}{9}$ **60.** $-6.2, 6\frac{1}{4}, 6.34, 6, \frac{-19}{3}$

Evaluate the expression. *Justify* each step.

61. $-\frac{2}{3} + \left(-\frac{2}{3}\right) + \frac{2}{3}$ **62.** $12 \cdot (-27) \cdot \frac{1}{12}$ **63.** $\frac{3}{7} \cdot (-1) \cdot \frac{7}{3}$

6.7 The Distributive Property

EXAMPLE

**Use the distributive property to write an equivalent expression for
$3(18 - 7)$. Check your answer.**

Expression: $3(18 - 7) = 3(18) - 3(7)$	**Distributive property**
Check $\qquad 3(11) \stackrel{?}{=} 54 - 21$	**Simplify.**
$\qquad\qquad 33 = 33 \checkmark$	**Answer checks.**

EXERCISES

Use the distributive property to write an equivalent expression. Then evaluate the expression.

SEE EXAMPLES 2 AND 3
on pp. 308–309 for Exs. 64–68

64. $9\left(\dfrac{5}{12}\right) + 9\left(\dfrac{7}{12}\right)$ **65.** $4(0.98)$ **66.** $6(1.03)$ **67.** $9(2.6) + 9(5.4)$

68. Lawn Mowing You mow lawns for 9 hours at $8.90 an hour. Use the distributive property to write an expression to find the amount you earn.

6.8 The Coordinate Plane

pp. 313–319

EXAMPLE

Name the ordered pair that represents the point.

   a. A **b.** B

SOLUTION

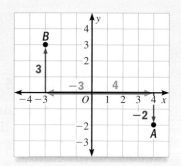

   a. Point A is 4 units to the right of the origin and 2 units down. So, the x-coordinate is 4 and the y-coordinate is -2. Point A is represented by the ordered pair $(4, -2)$.

   b. Point B is 3 units to the left of the origin and 3 units up. So, the x-coordinate is -3 and the y-coordinate is 3. Point B is represented by the ordered pair $(-3, 3)$.

EXERCISES

Name the ordered pair that represents the point.

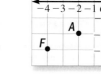

SEE EXAMPLES 1, 2, 3, AND 4
on pp. 313–315 for Exs. 69–80

69. A   **70.** B   **71.** C

72. D   **73.** E   **74.** F

Plot and label the points in the same coordinate plane. Describe the location of each point.

75. $A(0, -5)$ **76.** $V(5, -3)$ **77.** $X(-4, 3)$ **78.** $G(1, 4)$

79. Plot the points $P(-6, -7)$ and $Q(3, -7)$. Find the distance from P to Q.

80. Biology The ordered pairs show the widths and lengths, in centimeters, of nine butter clam shells. Make a scatter plot of the data. Then make a conclusion about the data.

      $(2.1, 2.7)$, $(3.1, 4.1)$, $(3.0, 4.0)$, $(2.8, 3.8)$, $(2.8, 3.5)$, $(2.6, 3.5)$, $(2.4, 3.2)$, $(2.9, 3.8)$, $(2.6, 3.4)$

Order the integers from least to greatest.

1. $16, -17, 32, 7, -15$
2. $38, -120, 201, -12, -422$
3. $-72, -54, 102, 33, 16$

Find the sum or difference.

4. $-12 + 10$
5. $11 + (-8)$
6. $-9 + (-9)$
7. $-4 - (-6)$
8. $7 - (-27)$
9. $36 - 56$

Find the product or quotient.

10. $-12(-3)$
11. $15(-3)$
12. $-46 \div (-23)$

Show that the numbers are rational by writing each number in $\frac{a}{b}$ form. Then order the numbers from least to greatest.

13. $9.6, -\frac{7}{9}, -5, -4\frac{5}{6}, 9\frac{1}{2}$
14. $2\frac{5}{6}, 0, -2.3, -3\frac{3}{4}, 2.4$

Evaluate the expression. Justify each step.

15. $\frac{2}{9} + \frac{8}{13} + \left(-\frac{2}{9}\right)$
16. $9 \cdot 16 \cdot \frac{1}{9}$
17. $5\left(\frac{5}{6}\right) - 5\left(-\frac{1}{6}\right)$
18. $4(8.5)$

Plot and label the points in the same coordinate plane. Describe the location of each point.

19. $Y(7, 25)$
20. $D(-12, 15)$
21. $F(26, -1)$
22. $Z(-11, -11)$

23. Plot and connect the points $C(-6, 0)$, $D(-6, -3)$, $E(-1, -3)$, and $F(-1, 0)$ to form a rectangle. Then find the length, width, and area of the rectangle.

24. **ELEVATION** Write the integer that represents an elevation of 36 feet below sea level.

25. **COLDEST TEMPERATURE** The coldest recorded temperature in South Carolina is $-28°C$, and the coldest recorded temperature in North Carolina is $-37°C$. Which state has the lower coldest recorded temperature?

26. **HOT AIR BALLOONS** A hot air balloon descends 210 feet each minute when landing. What is the change in the altitude of the balloon after 3 minutes?

27. **BABY-SITTING** You baby-sit for 5 hours at $7.75 an hour. Use the distributive property to write and evaluate an expression to find the amount you earn.

28. **GLITTER PENS** You buy three glitter pens. Each pen costs $.95. Use the distributive property to write and evaluate an expression to find the total cost of the pens.

REVIEWING DISTRIBUTIVE PROPERTY PROBLEMS

You can evaluate expressions by using area models or using the distributive property. The following examples illustrate both methods.

EXAMPLE 1

Evaluate the expressions $4(5 + 3)$ and $4(5) + 4(3)$ using area models. Then compare them.

Solution

Model the expression $4(5 + 3)$ by drawing a rectangle with a width of 4 units and a length of $(5 + 3)$ units. Then find the area of the rectangle.

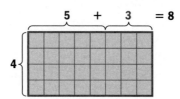

$$\begin{aligned} \text{Area} &= 4(\mathbf{5 + 3}) \\ &= 4(8) \\ &= 32 \end{aligned}$$

Model the expression $4(5) + 4(3)$ by drawing two rectangles: one with a width of 4 units and a length of 5 units and the other with a width of 4 units and a length of 3 units. Then find the sum of their areas.

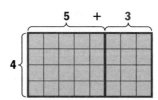

$$\begin{aligned} \text{Area} &= 4(\mathbf{5}) + 4(\mathbf{3}) \\ &= 20 + 12 \\ &= 32 \end{aligned}$$

Both expressions have the same value, 32. So, $4(5 + 3) = 4(5) + 4(3)$.

EXAMPLE 2

Evaluate the expressions (a) $4(80 + 6)$ and (b) $-8(47)$.

Solution

a. $\begin{aligned}[t] 4(80 + 6) &= 4(80) + 4(6) \\ &= 320 + 24 \\ &= 344 \end{aligned}$

b. $\begin{aligned}[t] -8(47) &= -8(50 - 3) \\ &= -8(50) - (-8)(3) \\ &= -400 + 24 \\ &= -376 \end{aligned}$

DISTRIBUTIVE PROPERTY PROBLEMS

Below are examples of distributive property problems in multiple choice format. Try solving the problems before looking at the solutions. (Cover the solutions with a piece of paper.) Then check your solutions against the ones given.

1. Which expression is equivalent to $7(7 - 13)$?

   A. $7(7) - 13$

   B. $7(7) - 7(13)$

   C. $7(7) - 13(13)$

   D. $7(13) - 7(13)$

Solution

By the distributive property, $a(b - c) = ab - ac$.

So, $7(7 - 13) = 7(7) - 7(13)$.

The correct answer is **B**.

2. Which area model represents the expression $3(8 - 3)$?

   A.

   B.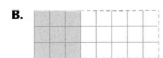

   C.

   D.

Solution

Identify the rectangle that has a width of 3 units and a length of $(8 - 3)$ units.

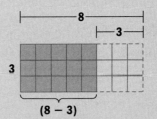

The correct answer is **C**.

3. Which expression is equivalent to $2(-6) + 2(11)$?

   A. $2(-6 + 11)$

   B. $2(-6) + 11$

   C. $2(2) + (-6)(11)$

   D. $(-6)(11) + 2(11)$

Solution

By the distributive property, $ab + ac = a(b + c)$.

So, $2(-6) + 2(11) = 2(-6 + 11)$.

The correct answer is **A**.

TEST PREPARATION

1. Which area model represents the expression $2(1 + 6)$?

A.

B.

C.

D.

2. Which of the following statements is NOT true?

   A. All whole numbers are integers.

   B. An integer is also a rational number.

   C. An integer must be either a positive or a negative whole number.

   D. The product of two integers always results in an integer.

3. Mr. Snyder wants to paint two adjacent walls, as shown. Which expression gives the total area he must paint?

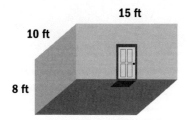

   15 ft

   10 ft

   8 ft

   A. $10 + 8(15)$

   B. $8(10) + 15$

   C. $8(10 + 15)$

   D. $10(8 + 15)$

4. Which expression is equivalent to $22(15 - 7)$?

   A. $22(15) - 7$

   B. $22(15) - 22(7)$

   C. $15 - 22(7)$

   D. $15(7) - 22(7)$

5. Which expression can be represented by the area models below?

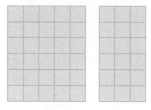

   A. $5(6) + 5(3)$

   B. $6(5) + 6(3)$

   C. $5(6) - 5(3)$

   D. $6(5) - 6(3)$

6. Evaluate the expression $-7x + 16y$ when $x = -1$ and $y = 5$.

   A. 9

   B. 23

   C. 73

   D. 87

7. The area of a rectangle is 1536 square inches, and the width of the rectangle is 24 inches. What is the length of the rectangle?

   A. 32 in.

   B. 64 in.

   C. 480 in.

   D. 744 in.

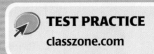
8. Which expression is represented by the model below?

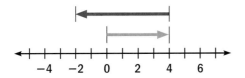

A. $4 + (-2)$

B. $4 + (-4)$

C. $4 + (-6)$

D. $4 + (-8)$

9. How many kiloliters are in 24.8 liters?

A. 0.0248 kL

B. 0.248 kL

C. 2480 kL

D. 24,800 kL

10. The line plot shows the results of a questionnaire asking tourists how many days they plan to spend on their vacation.

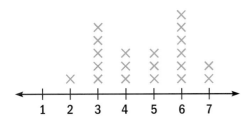

Which measure of data is represented by 6 days?

A. Mean

B. Median

C. Mode

D. Range

11. Which formula can be used to convert from d days to m minutes?

A. $m = 60d$

B. $m = 1440d$

C. $d = 60m$

D. $d = 1440m$

12. **OPEN-ENDED** Use the coordinate plane to answer the question below.

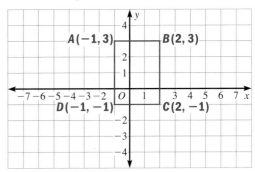

Part A Find the length, width, perimeter, and area of the rectangle.

Part B Draw a new rectangle that has twice the length and twice the width of the original rectangle. Find the perimeter and area of the new rectangle.

Part C Does the new rectangle have twice the perimeter of the original rectangle? Does the new rectangle have twice the area of the original rectangle? *Explain.*

TEST PREPARATION

Find the perimeter and the area of the rectangle or square with the given dimensions. *(p. 32)*

1. $s = 8$ inches

2. $l = 9$ feet, $w = 6$ feet

3. $l = 12$ meters, $w = 7$ meters

4. $s = 14$ centimeters

5. $l = 20$ feet, $w = 5$ feet

6. $s = 16$ meters

Copy and complete the statement. *(p. 90)*

7. 849 cm = _?_ m

8. 1280 mg = _?_ g

9. 3.625 L = _?_ mL

10. 2700 m = _?_ km

11. 63.75 kg = _?_ g

12. 410.6 kL = _?_ L

Make a box-and-whisker plot of the data *(p. 133)*

13. $59, 35, 28, 40, 48, 32, 47, 51, 42, 36$

14. $85, 76, 103, 94, 98, 82, 92, 86, 91, 72, 104$

Use a factor tree to write the prime factorization of the number. *(p. 165)*

15. 48

16. 90

17. 351

18. 495

Find the GCF and the LCM of the numbers. *(pp. 170, 182)*

19. $8, 14$

20. $15, 54$

21. $64, 144$

22. $42, 70, 105$

Find the sum or difference.

23. $\frac{1}{8} + \frac{1}{2}$ *(p. 219)*

24. $\frac{2}{3} + \frac{3}{4}$ *(p. 219)*

25. $\frac{8}{9} - \frac{5}{6}$ *(p. 219)*

26. $\frac{7}{12} - \frac{2}{5}$ *(p. 219)*

27. $3\frac{3}{8} + 1\frac{7}{8}$ *(p. 226)*

28. $8\frac{3}{16} - 4\frac{9}{16}$ *(p. 226)*

29. $7 + (-3)$ *(p. 277)*

30. $-16 - 12$ *(p. 285)*

31. $24 - (-15)$ *(p. 285)*

Find the product or quotient.

32. $\frac{1}{6} \times \frac{1}{9}$ *(p. 232)*

33. $\frac{4}{7} \times \frac{5}{12}$ *(p. 232)*

34. $\frac{7}{8} \div \frac{3}{4}$ *(p. 237)*

35. $\frac{7}{12} \div \frac{4}{5}$ *(p. 237)*

36. $3\frac{3}{4} \times 7\frac{7}{10}$ *(p. 232)*

37. $9\frac{3}{8} \times 6\frac{11}{15}$ *(p. 232)*

38. $5\frac{5}{9} \div 3\frac{1}{3}$ *(p. 237)*

39. $8\frac{2}{5} \div 2\frac{7}{10}$ *(p. 237)*

40. $8(-6)$ *(p. 291)*

41. $-16(-5)$ *(p. 291)*

42. $-36 \div (-6)$ *(p. 296)*

43. $-56 \div 14$ *(p. 296)*

Order the rational numbers from least to greatest. *(p. 301)*

44. $-\frac{7}{4}, -1\frac{5}{8}, -2.3, -1\frac{7}{16}, -2$

45. $-0.8, 1\frac{1}{4}, \frac{5}{12}, 1.4, -\frac{3}{4}$

Plot and connect the points to form a rectangle. Then find the length, width, and area of the rectangle. *(p. 313)*

46. $A(-1, 2), B(3, 2), C(3, -3), D(-1, -3)$

47. $E(-4, 4), F(2, 4), G(2, 1), H(-4, 1)$

48. HEIGHT Four friends stand in order from shortest to tallest for a photograph. Mary is taller than Jack. Harry is standing between Jack and Alicia. Jack is not the shortest. What is the order in which the friends are standing? *(p. 37)*

49. MARBLES You are filling bags with marbles to give out as gifts to children. There are 80 blue marbles, 112 green marbles, 144 yellow marbles, and 192 red marbles. The bags of marbles will be identical and there will be no leftover marbles. What is the greatest number of bags that can be made? How many marbles of each color are in each bag? *(p. 170)*

50. PRECIPITATION The table shows the annual average days of precipitation in four U.S. cities. Write the number of days in Grand Junction as a fraction of the number of days in Madison, and write the number of days in Dodge City as a fraction of the number of days in Lexington. Are the fractions equivalent? *(p. 176)*

City	Days
Grand Junction, CO	72
Dodge City, KN	78
Madison, WI	120
Lexington, KY	130

51. ELECTRONIC MESSAGES Three computers check for electronic messages at 8:00 A.M. The first computer is set up to check for messages every 7 minutes, the second computer checks every 15 minutes, and the third computer checks every 20 minutes. What is the next time that all three computers check for messages? *(p. 182)*

52. DIAMONDS A diamond's weight is measured in carats. If a ring has one $\frac{1}{4}$-carat diamond and two $\frac{1}{8}$-carat diamonds, what is the total weight of the diamonds on the ring? *(p. 219)*

53. CONTAINERS You have a bottle of water with 36 fluid ounces that you would like to pour into a container that has a capacity of $2\frac{3}{4}$ pints. Will all of the water fit into the container? If so, how much more water could you add to the container? If not, how much of the water will not fit into the container? *(p. 250)*

54. WIND CHILL FACTOR The wind chill factor tells how cold it feels outside based on the temperature and wind speed. The wind chill factor was 18°F at 8:00 A.M. but dropped to −14°F by 1:00 P.M. What was the change in wind chill factor? *(p. 285)*

55. BASEBALL The table below shows the home runs hit each season by a baseball player from the time he was 27 years old until he was 36 years old. Make a scatter plot of the data. Then make a conclusion about the data. *(p. 313)*

Age (years)	27	28	29	30	31	32	33	34	35	36
Home runs	20	24	29	31	48	33	44	25	22	20

7 Equations, Inequalities, and Functions

Before

In previous chapters you've ...

• Evaluated variable expressions
• Solved equations with mental math

Now

NJ **New Jersey Standards**

4.3.C.2.a	7.1	Writing equations
4.3.D.3.a	7.2	Simplifying expressions
4.3.D.2.b	7.3	Solving equations
4.3.D.2.b	7.4	Properties of equality
4.3.D.2.a	7.5	Two-step equations
4.3.D.4.a	7.6	Solving inequalities
4.3.A.1.a	7.7	Functions and equations
4.3.B.1.a	7.8	Graphing functions

Why?

So you can solve real-world problems about ...

• space exploration, p. 349
• marathons, p. 358
• scuba diving, p. 375

 **Math**
at classzone.com

• Solving Inequalities, p. 367
• Functions and Equations, p. 372
• Graphing, p. 376

Get-Ready Games

Review Prerequisite Skills by playing *Deciphering Ancient Numbers* and *Stone Tablet*.

Deciphering Ancient Numbers

Skill Focus:

• Evaluating variable expressions

• Solving equations using mental math

Suppose the equations above are written using an ancient number system. Each symbol represents a number from 1 through 10. Copy and complete the table by matching each symbol with its value.

Value	1	2	3	4	5	6	7	8	9	10
Symbol	?	?	?	?	?	?	?	?	?	?

Stone Tablet

? 1	? 1	2	? 1
? 1	10	? 1	8
9	? 1	7	? 1
4	15	? 1	1

Skill Focus:

- Evaluating variable expressions

- Solving equations using mental math

Suppose an ancient stone tablet contains numbers that an archeologist suspects are arranged in a magic square. The archeologist has translated most of the numbers on the tablet. Unfortunately, some have been worn away. Copy and complete the magic square using the information below.

- Each integer from 1 through 16 is used exactly once.

- The sum of each row, column, and diagonal is 34.

Stop and Think

1. **CRITICAL THINKING** Write expressions that equal 20, 24, 36, and 150 using the symbols in *Deciphering Ancient Numbers.*

2. **WRITING** Suppose you multiply each number on the *Stone Tablet* by 2. Show that the resulting square is a magic square. Are there other ways you could use the *Stone Tablet* magic square to generate new magic squares? Explain your reasoning.

Review Prerequisite Skills

REVIEW WORDS
- **variable,** *p. 8*
- **variable expression,** *p. 8*
- **evaluate,** *p. 8*
- **equation,** *p. 25*
- **solution,** *p. 25*

VOCABULARY CHECK

Copy and complete using a review word from the list at the left.

1. A mathematical sentence formed by setting two expressions equal is called a(n) __?__ .

2. A letter used to represent one or more numbers is called a(n) __?__ .

3. To __?__ a variable expression, substitute values for the variables and then simplify the resulting numerical expression.

SKILL CHECK

Use mental math to solve the equation. *(p. 25)*

4. $15r = 30$ **5.** $w + 4 = 9$ **6.** $p - 3 = 12$ **7.** $63 = 21t$

8. $\dfrac{q}{2} = 10$ **9.** $5 + h = 11$ **10.** $4r = 28$ **11.** $w - 7 = 13$

Evaluate the expression when $x = 4$, $y = 2$, and $z = -3$. *(pp. 17, 291)*

12. $5x^2y$ **13.** $zx - 3y$ **14.** $7 - yz + x$ **15.** $3 - xyz$

16. $y^2 + z^2$ **17.** $5y - 2x$ **18.** $yz^2 - 3x$ **19.** $xy - yz$

Plot the point in a coordinate plane. *(p. 313)*

20. $Q(-3, 4)$ **21.** $R(0, 2)$ **22.** $S(-2, -1)$ **23.** $T(3, -5)$

@HomeTutor   Prerequisite skills practice at classzone.com

Notetaking Skills   Comparing and Contrasting

In each chapter you will learn a new notetaking skill. In Chapter 7 you will apply the strategy of comparing and contrasting on pages 354 and 355 of Lesson 7.4, and on page 366 of Lesson 7.6.

You can compare and contrast related concepts in your notebook. For example, noting similarities and differences between integers and their opposites can help you remember them.

Integers and Their Opposites

Similarity: The integers n and $-n$ are both $|n|$ units from 0 on a number line.

Difference: If $n > 0$, then n is to the right of 0 on a number line, and $-n$ is to the left of 0 on a number line.

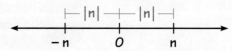

7.1 Writing Expressions and Equations

 4.3.C.2.a Using manipulatives, tables, graphs, verbal rules, algebraic expressions/ equations/inequalities

Before	You evaluated variable expressions.
Now	You'll write variable expressions and equations.
Why?	So you can find heights of objects, as in Example 3.

KEY VOCABULARY
• **verbal model,** *p. 338*

Caves You are exploring a cave in which rock formations called *stalagmites* grow up from the cave floor. The tour guide tells you that the tallest stalagmite in the cave is underwater in a pool 55 feet deep, and the distance between the tip of the stalagmite and the surface of the water is 41 feet. How tall is the stalagmite? You'll find the answer in Example 3.

Translating Phrases and Sentences To solve real-world problems, you need to translate verbal phrases and sentences into variable expressions and equations. Look for key words that indicate addition, subtraction, multiplication, and division.

Addition	*Subtraction*	*Multiplication*	*Division*
plus	minus	times	divided by
the sum of	the difference of	the product of	the quotient of
increased by	decreased by	multiplied by	separate into equal parts
total	fewer than	of	
more than	less than	twice	
added to	subtracted from		

Order is important in subtraction and division expressions. For example, "2 less than a number" is written as $x - 2$, not $2 - x$. Similarly, "a number divided by 5" is written as $x \div 5$, not $5 \div x$.

EXAMPLE 1 Translating Verbal Phrases

Verbal phrase	Expression
a. A number increased by 5	$x + 5$
b. 7 less than a number	$x - 7$
c. 3 more than twice a number	$2x + 3$
d. 4 decreased by the quotient of a number and 7	$4 - \dfrac{x}{7}$

Animated **Math** at classzone.com

EXAMPLE 2 Translating Verbal Sentences

Verbal phrase	Equation
a. 16 increased by a number is 27.	$16 + y = 27$
b. The difference of twice a number and 3 equals -4.	$2y - 3 = -4$
c. The product of $\frac{1}{2}$ and a number is 36.	$\frac{1}{2}y = 36$
d. -3 is equal to twice the sum of a number and 2.	$-3 = 2(y + 2)$

✓ **GUIDED PRACTICE** for Examples 1 and 2

Write the verbal phrase or sentence as a variable expression or equation. Let *n* represent the number.

1. 14 added to a number

2. 22 less than $\frac{1}{2}$ of a number

3. 42 divided by a number equals 7.

4. 5 minus twice a number is 17.

Verbal Models You can use verbal models to solve real-world problems. A **verbal model** uses words to describe ideas and math symbols to relate the words.

❖ EXAMPLE 3 Writing and Solving an Equation

Caves To find the height of the stalagmite described at the top of page 337, you can write and solve an equation.

STEP 1 **Use** a diagram like the one at the right to write a verbal model. Let *h* represent the height of the stalagmite.

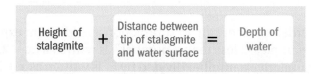

41 ft

55 ft

h

STEP 2 **Write** an equation using the verbal model.

$$h \quad + \quad 41 \quad = \quad 55$$

STEP 3 **Solve** using mental math: $14 + 41 = 55$, so $h = 14$.

▶ **Answer** The height of the stalagmite is 14 feet.

✓ **GUIDED PRACTICE** for Example 3

5. Hiking While hiking, you descend 2000 feet from the start of a trail to an elevation of 5200 feet. Write and solve an equation to find the elevation at the start of the trail.

7.1 EXERCISES

HOMEWORK
KEY

★ = **STANDARDIZED TEST PRACTICE**
Exs. 21, 45, 46, 47, 51, and 60

○ = **HINTS AND HOMEWORK HELP**
for Exs. 5, 13, 15, 19, 45 at classzone.com

SKILL PRACTICE

VOCABULARY Copy and complete the statement.

1. A(n) _?_ uses words to describe ideas and math symbols to relate the words.

2. Phrases such as *decreased by* and *fewer than* indicate _?_.

MATCHING Match the verbal phrase with its variable expression.

SEE EXAMPLE 1
on p. 337
for Exs. 3–14

3. 4 more than a number

4. The quotient of a number and 4

5. The difference of 4 and a number

6. 4 less than a number

A. $4 - x$

B. $x + 4$

C. $x \div 4$

D. $x - 4$

WRITING EXPRESSIONS Write the verbal phrase as a variable expression. Let *n* represent the number.

7. A number added to -7

8. The product of a number and 2

9. $\frac{1}{3}$ of a number

10. A number divided by 16

11. -50 decreased by a number

12. Twice a number

13. The quotient of a number plus 6 and 3

14. 4 added to the square of a number

WRITING EQUATIONS Write the verbal sentence as an equation. Let *n* represent the number.

SEE EXAMPLE 2
on p. 338
for Exs. 15–20

15. The sum of a number and -9 equals 24.

16. A number times -5 is 10.

17. The product of 3 and a number is twice 23.

18. The sum of -4 times a number and 3 is 27.

19. 2 plus $\frac{1}{3}$ of a number is equal to -8.

20. 13 is equal to 5 minus a number.

21. ★ MULTIPLE CHOICE A vehicle rental company charges $25 to rent a moving van plus $.50 for each mile traveled. Which expression represents the total cost of renting a van and driving *d* miles?

(A) $25 + d$

(B) $25 + 0.50d$

(C) $25 - 0.50d$

(D) $25d + 0.50$

WRITING PHRASES AND SENTENCES Write a verbal phrase or sentence for the variable expression or equation.

22. $3 + a$

23. $13b$

24. $c - 2$

25. $10 \div d$

26. $4p = 16$

27. $q + 8 = 34$

28. $15n = 60$

29. $90 \div s = 1$

30. $x \div 6 = 9$

31. $a - 11 = 2$

32. $2r - 9 = 15$

33. $k + 9 = 52$

7.1 Writing Expressions and Equations **339**

34. ERROR ANALYSIS A student says that "7 more than a number is 15" is written as "$7 + 15 = x$." Describe and correct the error.

WRITING PHRASES Write a verbal phrase for the variable expression.

35. $\dfrac{x^3}{y - 8}$ **36.** $(3q)(9 - r)$ **37.** $\dfrac{a + 12}{b^2}$

38. MENTAL MATH The quotient of 2 times a number a and 4 is 1. The difference of 10 and the product of 3 and a number b is 1. Which is greater, a or b? *Explain.*

39. CHALLENGE John and Jane are asked to write the sentence "4 times this number plus 8 equals 64" as an equation and then find the value of the number. John writes $4n + 8 = 64$, so $n = 14$. Jane writes $4(n + 8) = 64$, so $n = 8$. Are they both right? *Explain.*

PROBLEM SOLVING

Write the real-world phrase as a variable expression. Identify what the variable represents.

40. 3 years older than Theo

41. Twice a team's score

42. Half of your class

43. 5 inches shorter than Ann

SEE EXAMPLE 3
on p. 338 for
Exs. 44, 45, 47

44. GUIDED PROBLEM SOLVING The Colorado River, which is 1450 miles long, is 450 miles shorter than the Rio Grande. How long is the Rio Grande?

　　a. Draw a diagram of the situation.

　　b. Use the diagram to make a verbal model that represents the situation.

　　c. Use the model to write an equation. Then solve it using mental math.

45. ★ **MULTIPLE CHOICE** You buy a digital video recorder for $99 and the cost per month for the recorder's data service is d dollars. What is your total cost for 1 year?

　　(A) $12d$　　　**(B)** $(99 + 12)d$　　　**(C)** $99 + 12d$　　　**(D)** $99d$

46. ★ **WRITING** *Describe* real-world situations that can be represented by the expressions $n + 3$, $n - 3$, $3n$, and $n \div 3$.

47. ★ **EXTENDED RESPONSE** A hot air balloon travels downward as shown at right.

　　a. Write an equation to represent the situation. Then use mental math to find the balloon's original altitude.

　　b. The balloon takes 5 minutes to reach the ground from its original altitude. To find how many feet per minute the balloon travels, write an equation and use mental math to solve it.

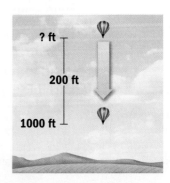

? ft

200 ft

1000 ft

　　★ = **STANDARDIZED TEST PRACTICE**　　◯ = **HINTS AND HOMEWORK HELP** *at classzone.com*

In Exercises 48 and 49, write an equation to represent the situation. Then use mental math to solve the equation.

48. **SWIMMING** In 1994, Tammy and John Van Wisse became the first brother and sister to swim across the English Channel. Tammy's crossing time of 512 minutes was 15 minutes longer than her brother's crossing time. How long, in hours and minutes, did it take John to swim across the English Channel?

49. **TEMPERATURE** The water temperature dropped by 24°F from 75°F. Water freezes at 32°F. By how many more degrees does the temperature need to drop to reach the freezing point?

50. **DENTAL COSTS** Amy has an orthodontist's appointment to get her braces checked every 6 weeks. A check-up costs $40. About how much money does she spend getting her braces checked for 1 year? *Justify* your estimate.

51. ★ **SHORT RESPONSE** Is "three less than a number" equivalent to "the difference of three and a number"? *Explain* your reasoning.

52. **GEOMETRY** Write an expression for the area of a rectangle whose length is 5 inches longer than its width. Evaluate this expression to find the area of this rectangle if the width is 3 inches.

53. **CHALLENGE** Your age is x. Your older brother's age y is 3 years more than your age. Your younger brother's age z is 4 years less than your older brother's age. Write an equation using y and z that represents your younger brother's age.

54. **CHALLENGE** You walk at 4 miles per hour for $\frac{1}{2}$ hour, and then jog at 6 miles per hour for h hours. The total distance that you cover both walking and jogging is 6 miles. Write an equation that represents this situation. For how long do you jog?

 NEW JERSEY MIXED REVIEW  **TEST PRACTICE** at classzone.com

55. The points $(-4, -2)$ and $(0, -2)$ are plotted on the coordinate plane. Which other two points could you plot to form a square?

   Ⓐ $(-4, 3), (0, 3)$ Ⓑ $(-4, 2), (0, 2)$

   Ⓒ $(-4, 4), (0, 4)$ Ⓓ $(-4, -6), (0, -6)$

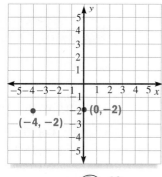

56. Simplify the expression below.

$$2(-3) - 2(4 - 8) \div 2^2$$

   Ⓐ -4 Ⓑ $\frac{1}{2}$ Ⓒ 1 Ⓓ 10

7.2 Simplifying Expressions

NJ 4.3.D.3.a Create, evaluate, and simplify algebraic expressions involving variables: Order of operations . . .

Before You wrote variable expressions.

Now You'll simplify variable expressions.

Why? So you can simplify perimeter expressions, as in Ex. 36.

KEY VOCABULARY
- **terms,** *p. 342*
- **like terms,** *p. 342*
- **equivalent variable expressions,** *p. 342*
- **coefficient,** *p. 342*
- **constant term,** *p. 342*

The distributive property can be used to simplify a variable expression:

$$2x + 3x = (2 + 3)x$$
$$= 5x$$

The parts of an expression that are being added together, such as $2x$ and $3x$ in the expression $2x + 3x$, are called **terms**. Terms that have identical variable parts are **like terms**. In the expression $2x + 3x$, $2x$ and $3x$ are like terms. The distributive property allows you to *combine like terms*.

EXAMPLE 1 Combining Like Terms

Simplify the expression $7c + 9 - 3c$.

$7c + 9 - 3c = 7c + 9 + (-3c)$	**Write expression as a sum.**
$= 7c + (-3c) + 9$	**Commutative property of addition**
$= [7 + (-3)]c + 9$	**Distributive property**
$= 4c + 9$	**Simplify.**

READING
After Example 1, the step of using the distributive property to combine like terms will not be shown.

In Example 1, $7c + 9 - 3c$ is *equivalent* to $4c + 9$. **Equivalent variable expressions** are expressions that are equal for every value of each variable.

In a term that is the product of a number and a variable, the number is called the **coefficient** of the variable. A term that has a number, but no variable, is a **constant term**. In the expression $4a + 1$, 4 is the coefficient of a, and 1 is a constant term.

EXAMPLE 2 Coefficients, Constant Terms, and Like Terms

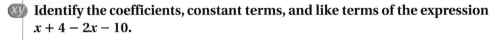

Identify the coefficients, constant terms, and like terms of the expression $x + 4 - 2x - 10$.

First, write the expression as a sum: $x + 4 + (-2x) + (-10)$.

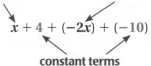

Coefficient is 1.   Coefficient is −2.

$$x + 4 + (-2x) + (-10)$$

constant terms

x and −2*x* are like terms.
4 and −10 are like terms.

EXAMPLE 3 Simplifying an Expression

 Simplify the expression $5(w - 4) + w + 8$.

$$5(w - 4) + w + 8 = 5w - 20 + w + 8 \qquad \text{Distributive property}$$
$$= 5w + (-20) + w + 8 \qquad \text{Write as a sum.}$$
$$= 5w + w + (-20) + 8 \qquad \text{Commutative property}$$
$$= 6w + (-12) \qquad \text{Combine like terms.}$$
$$= 6w - 12 \qquad \text{Rewrite without parentheses.}$$

 GUIDED PRACTICE for Examples 1, 2, and 3

Identify the coefficients, constant term(s), and like terms of the expression. Then simplify the expression.

1. $-3z + 1 + 4z$ **2.** $15 - 9r + 7r - 6$ **3.** $2y + 8 - 2y - 4$

4. $16 - 8k + 9k - 8$ **5.** $6a - 18 - 1 - 6a$ **6.** $-7m + 5 + 2m$

EXAMPLE 4 Writing and Simplifying an Expression

Exercise Mats A rectangular exercise mat is twice as long as it is wide. Write and simplify an expression for the perimeter of the mat in terms of the width w.

SOLUTION

Because the mat is twice as long as it is wide, its length is $2w$.

$$\text{Perimeter} = 2l + 2w \qquad \text{Formula for perimeter of a rectangle}$$
$$= 2(2w) + 2w \qquad \text{Substitute } 2w \text{ for } l.$$
$$= 4w + 2w \qquad \text{Multiply.}$$
$$= 6w \qquad \text{Combine like terms.}$$

▶ **Answer** An expression for the perimeter of the mat is $6w$.

 GUIDED PRACTICE for Example 4

7. A rectangle is 6 inches longer than it is wide. Write and simplify an expression for the perimeter of the rectangle in terms of the width w.

8. A rectangle is three meters longer than it is wide. Write and simplify an expression for the perimeter of the rectangle in terms of the width w.

7.2 EXERCISES

HOMEWORK KEY

★ = **STANDARDIZED TEST PRACTICE**
Exs. 25, 36, 37, 38, 39, and 46

◯ = **HINTS** AND **HOMEWORK HELP**
for Exs. 7, 13, 21, 25, 37 at classzone.com

SKILL PRACTICE

1. **VOCABULARY** In the expression $5z - 7 + 2z + 1$, identify the coefficients, constant terms, and like terms.

2. **VOCABULARY** Terms that have identical variable parts are called __?__.

COMBINING LIKE TERMS Combine like terms to simplify the expression.

SEE EXAMPLE 1
on p. 342
for Exs. 3–11

3. $3a + 9 - a$

4. $18 + 4b + 6$

5. $-8c + 4 - 5$

6. $14t + 15 - 2t$

7. $4k - 10 + 7 - 7k$

8. $6 - 2l - 7 + 3l$

9. $10x + 4.5 + x - 9$

10. $14.9 - y + y + 5.78$

11. $-p + 3 + 2.4p - 2p$

IDENTIFYING COEFFICIENTS AND TERMS Identify the coefficients, constant term(s), and like terms of the expression.

SEE EXAMPLE 2
on p. 342
for Exs. 12–15

12. $3x + 4 - x$

13. $10 - 4y + 5y - 8$

14. $7z - 9z + 2 + z$

15. **ERROR ANALYSIS** Your friend says that the coefficients of y in the expression $6y + 5 - 3y$ are 6 and 3. Is your friend right? *Explain.*

SIMPLIFYING EXPRESSIONS Simplify the expression.

SEE EXAMPLE 3
on p. 343
for Exs. 16–25

16. $6(1 - j) + 2j$

17. $5(z + 2) - 8$

18. $4b - 2 + 2(b + 1)$

19. $7(m - 2) - 2m + 1$

20. $12v - 3(2 + 4v) + \frac{1}{3}$

21. $2\left(2t + \frac{2}{7} - 2t\right) + 8t$

22. $5 - s(4 - 7) + 3s$

23. $5 + 2(n - p) + 2n - 4$

24. $5a - 2(2 + b) + 3b$

25. ★ **MULTIPLE CHOICE** Which expression shows $-4(n - 3) + 2n$ in simplified form?

Ⓐ $-2n - 12$ Ⓑ $-6n - 12$ Ⓒ $-2n + 12$ Ⓓ $-4n + 12 + 2n$

GEOMETRY Write and simplify an expression for the figure's perimeter.

SEE EXAMPLE 4
on p. 343
for Exs. 26–28

26.

$2c$

$3c$

27.

x

$x + 10$

28.

$z + 1$

$3z$

COMPARING EXPRESSIONS Tell whether the expressions are equivalent.

29. $7x + 2x^2$;
$9x^2$

30. $6x \cdot x + 3x$;
$2x^2 + 3x + 4x^2$

31. $3x^3 - 2x^3$;
$-4x^3 + 5x^3$

CHALLENGE Assume $x \geq 1$. Copy and complete the statement using <, >, or =.

32. $4(x^2 + 1)$ __?__ $2x^2 + 4$

33. $5 + 2(x - 3)$ __?__ $2x + 2$

34. $3x^2 + 6x$ __?__ $3(x^2 + 2x)$

PROBLEM SOLVING

SEE EXAMPLE 4
on p. 343
for Exs. 35–37

35. GEOMETRY A rectangle is three times as long as it is wide. Write and simplify an expression for the perimeter of the rectangle in terms of the width, *w*.

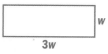

w

3w

36. ★ SHORT RESPONSE A rectangular soccer field is 30 yards longer than it is wide. Write expressions for the field's perimeter and area in terms of the width, *w*. Can these expressions be simplified? *Explain* why or why not.

37. ★ MULTIPLE CHOICE A rectangular garden has a length of $3x + 1$ and a width of *x*. Which expression does *not* represent the garden's area?

(A) $(3x + 1)x$ **(B)** $3x^2 + 1$ **(C)** $3x^2 + x$ **(D)** $(3x)(x) + 1(x)$

38. ★ WRITING *Explain* how you can use the distributive property to combine like terms. Include two examples.

39. ★ EXTENDED RESPONSE You have just returned from a 3-day trip. On day 1 of your trip, you took 10 photographs. On day 3 of the trip, you took twice as many photographs as you did on day 2.

  a. Write and simplify an expression for the total number of photographs you took on the trip.

  b. If you took 12 photographs on day 2, how many photographs did you take in all? *Explain* your reasoning.

  c. Your sister took 9 pictures on the trip. She took 4 of the same pictures as you. If you took 20 pictures on day 2, how many different pictures have you and your sister taken? *Explain*.

40. CHALLENGE A rectangular piece of cardboard is 4 times as long as it is wide. You make a box by cutting squares with side length *x* from the corners of the cardboard and turning up the resulting flaps. Write an expression involving *x* and the original width of the cardboard *w* that represents the perimeter of the base of the box. Then simplify the expression. *Explain* what the possible values of *x* can be.

NEW JERSEY MIXED REVIEW

TEST PRACTICE at classzone.com

41. The table shows the change in the value (in cents) of a stock over 5 days. Which expression can be used to find the average daily change in the value of the stock?

Day	Change in value
1	15
2	−65
3	35
4	12
5	−7

  (A) $15 + 65 + 35 + 12 + 7 \div 5$

  (B) $(15 + 65 + 35 + 12 + 7) \div 5$

  (C) $15 + (-65) + 35 + 12 + (-7) \div 5$

  (D) $[15 + (-65) + 35 + 12 + (-7)] \div 5$

INVESTIGATION
Use before Lesson 7.3

GOAL
Model and solve addition equations.

MATERIALS
• algebra tiles

7.3 Modeling Addition Equations

You can use algebra tiles to model and solve simple addition equations.

x-tile

An *x*-tile represents the variable *x*.

1-tile

A 1-tile represents positive 1.

EXPLORE Solve $x + 2 = 5$.

STEP 1 **Model** $x + 2 = 5$ using algebra tiles.

STEP 2 **Take** away two 1-tiles from each side.

STEP 3 **Identify** the solution. The *x*-tile is equal to three 1-tiles. So, the solution of the equation $x + 2 = 5$ is 3.

Check $3 + 2 = 5$ ✓

PRACTICE Use algebra tiles to model and solve the equation.

1. $x + 3 = 8$

2. $x + 4 = 5$

3. $x + 1 = 7$

4. $6 + x = 11$

5. $9 + x = 13$

6. $2 + x = 10$

DRAW CONCLUSIONS

7. **WRITING** *Explain* why, in the example shown above, it is important to take away two 1-tiles from each side and not just the left side of the equation.

8. **REASONING** *Describe* how you would use algebra tiles to solve the equation $4 + x + 2 = 10$. Then solve the equation.

7.3 Solving Addition and Subtraction Equations

 4.3.D.2.b Using paper-and-pencil, calculators, graphing calculators, spreadsheets, and other technology

Before You wrote equations.

Now You'll solve addition and subtraction equations.

Why? So you can find the duration of a moon landing, as in Example 4.

KEY VOCABULARY
• inverse operations, *p. 347*
• equivalent equations, *p. 347*

You can use equations to help you solve real-world problems. One way to solve an equation is to use *inverse operations*. An **inverse operation** is an operation that "undoes" another operation. Addition and subtraction are inverse operations.

Performing the same operation on each side of an equation results in a new equation that has the same solution as the original equation. Two equations that have the same solution(s) are **equivalent equations**.

KEY CONCEPT *For Your Notebook*

Subtraction Property of Equality

Words Subtracting the same number from each side of an equation produces an equivalent equation.

Algebra $x + a = b \longrightarrow x + a - a = b - a$

EXAMPLE 1 Solving an Addition Equation

 Solve the equation $x + 7 = -10$.

$$x + 7 = -10 \qquad \text{Write original equation.}$$
$$\underline{-7 \qquad -7} \qquad \text{Subtract 7 from each side.}$$
$$x \qquad = -17 \qquad \text{Simplify.}$$

ANOTHER WAY
You can use mental math to solve simple equations by thinking of the equation as a question. In Example 1, think of $x + 7 = -10$ as "what number plus 7 equals -10?"

Check $x + 7 = -10 \qquad \text{Write original equation.}$
$$-17 + 7 \overset{?}{=} -10 \qquad \text{Substitute } -17 \text{ for } x.$$
$$-10 = -10 \checkmark \qquad \text{Solution checks.}$$

 GUIDED PRACTICE for Example 1

Solve the equation. Check your solution.

1. $t + 8 = 15$ **2.** $n + 10 = 4$ **3.** $8 + x = -4$

Addition Property of Equality

Words   Adding the same number to each side of an equation produces an equivalent equation.

Algebra $x - a = b$ ⟶ $x - a + a = b + a$

EXAMPLE 2   **Solving a Subtraction Equation**

Solve the equation $-9 = y - 12$.

AVOID ERRORS

Whether you add or subtract vertically or horizontally to solve equations, remember to perform the same operation on each side of the equation.

$-9 = y - 12$	Write original equation.
$-9 + 12 = y - 12 + 12$	Add 12 to each side.
$3 = y$	Simplify.

Check

$-9 = y - 12$	Write original equation.
$-9 \stackrel{?}{=} 3 - 12$	Substitute 3 for *y*.
$-9 = -9$ ✓	Solution checks.

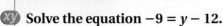 at classzone.com

---

EXAMPLE 3   **Combining Like Terms**

Solve the equation $2 = 1.3 + a + 4$.

$2 = 1.3 + a + 4$	Write original equation.
$2 = 1.3 + 4 + a$	Commutative property of addition
$2 = 5.3 + a$	Combine like terms.
$2 - 5.3 = 5.3 - 5.3 + a$	Subtract 5.3 from each side.
$-3.3 = a$	Simplify.

Check

$2 = 1.3 + a + 4$	Write original equation.
$2 \stackrel{?}{=} 1.3 + (-3.3) + 4$	Substitute -3.3 for *a*.
$2 = 2$ ✓	Solution checks.

✓ **GUIDED PRACTICE**   **for Examples 2 and 3**

Solve the equation. Check your solution.

4. $8 = m - 6$ **5.** $r - 10 = 14$ **6.** $p - (-2.2) = 5.6$

7. $5 = 4 + c - 2$ **8.** $2y - 1 - y = -3$ **9.** $3.4 + s - 1.3 = 6.8$

EXAMPLE 4 Writing and Solving an Equation

Space Exploration The *Apollo 11* mission lasted about 195.5 hours. The flight from Earth to the moon lasted about 103 hours, and the flight from the moon back to Earth lasted about 71 hours. About how many hours did the *Apollo 11* astronauts spend on the moon?

SOLUTION

Write a verbal model. Let t represent the number of hours the astronauts spent on the moon.

Length of Mission	=	Length of flight to moon	+	Time spent on moon	+	Length of flight to Earth

$195.5 = 103 + t + 71$	Write equation.
$195.5 = 174 + t$	Combine like terms.
$195.5 - 174 = 174 - 174 + t$	Subtract 174 from each side.
$21.5 = t$	Simplify.

▶ **Answer** The *Apollo 11* astronauts spent about 21.5 hours on the moon.

✓ **GUIDED PRACTICE** for Example 4

10. **Decorations** You spent a total of $50 for streamers, balloons, and flowers. You spent $12.50 on streamers and $15 on balloons. Write and solve an equation to find how much you spent on flowers.

7.3 EXERCISES

HOMEWORK KEY

★ = **STANDARDIZED TEST PRACTICE**
Exs. 19, 20, 43, 48, 52, 54, and 69

○ = **HINTS** AND **HOMEWORK HELP**
for Exs. 7, 17, 19, 25, 51 at classzone.com

SKILL PRACTICE

1. **VOCABULARY** Name a pair of inverse operations.

2. **VOCABULARY** Copy and complete: Two equations that have the same solution(s) are called __?__.

SOLVING EQUATIONS Solve the equation. Check your solution.

SEE EXAMPLES 1 AND 2
on pp. 347–348
for Exs. 3–17

3. $c + 5 = 8$

4. $n + 7 = 10$

5. $6 + p = -11$

6. $t - 3 = 2$

7. $2 + s - \dfrac{3}{7} = \dfrac{6}{7}$

8. $\dfrac{3}{8} = \dfrac{5}{16} + x - 1$

9. $n + 9 = 18$

10. $y + 13 = -17$

11. $14 = c + 10$

12. $13 + w = -7$

13. $r + 10 = -10.2$

14. $-5.1 = x - 14.2$

15. $h - 9.3 = 28$

16. $t - 6.8 = 13.9$

17. $-7 = b - (-7)$

SEE EXAMPLES
1 AND 2
....
on pp. 347–348
for Exs. 18–20

18. ERROR ANALYSIS Describe and correct the error made in solving the equation $x - 5 = 22$.

$$\times \quad \begin{array}{r} x - 5 = 22 \\ \underline{-5 \quad -5} \\ x = 17 \end{array}$$

19. ★ **MULTIPLE CHOICE** Which equation has a solution of 5?

    A $x - 5 = 10$ **B** $5 + x = 10$ **C** $10 + x = 5$ **D** $10 = 5 - x$

20. ★ **MULTIPLE CHOICE** The difference of a number x and 3 equals 2. What is the value of x?

    A -5 **B** -1 **C** 1 **D** 5

SEE EXAMPLE 3
....
on p. 348
for Exs. 21–29

COMBINING LIKE TERMS Solve the equation.

21. $2 + n - 3 = 6$ **22.** $3 = 5 + x - 1$ **23.** $2k + 6 - k = 17$

24. $5.7 = 9 + p - 1$ **25.** $2.3 + h - 3.1 = 27$ **26.** $8.6 = 5p - 4p + 2.4$

27. $3y - 2y + 8 = 4$ **28.** $7.2 = 4z + 3 - 3z$ **29.** $17.9 - 3h + 9 + 4h = 12.3$

SENTENCES Write the verbal sentence as an equation. Then solve.

30. 5 less than a number p is -17.

31. The sum of 6 and a number x is 3.

32. 6 more than a number n is 13.

33. A number t decreased by 1 is -3.

34. A number y minus 11 is -16.

35. A number r added to -4 is 8.

36. $2\frac{1}{3}$ more than a number n is $4\frac{1}{2}$.

37. A number z decreased by 7.2 is -12.9.

REASONING Give the reason for each step in solving the equation.

38.
$$\begin{array}{ll} 24 + x - 14 = 2 & \\ 24 + x + (-14) = 2 & \underline{\quad?\quad} \\ 24 + (-14) + x = 2 & \underline{\quad?\quad} \\ 10 + x = 2 & \underline{\quad?\quad} \\ 10 - 10 + x = 2 - 10 & \underline{\quad?\quad} \\ x = -8 & \underline{\quad?\quad} \end{array}$$

39.
$$\begin{array}{ll} 1 = -6 + x + 9 & \\ 1 = -6 + 9 + x & \underline{\quad?\quad} \\ 1 = 3 + x & \underline{\quad?\quad} \\ 1 - 3 = 3 - 3 + x & \underline{\quad?\quad} \\ -2 = x & \underline{\quad?\quad} \end{array}$$

GEOMETRY Write and solve an equation to find the unknown side length.

40. Perimeter: 13 ft   **41.** Perimeter: 21.5 in.   **42.** Perimeter: 42.5 m

43. ★ **OPEN-ENDED MATH** Write 3 different addition equations that each have a solution of -5.

CHALLENGE Describe the values of x that make each statement true.

44. $5x + 5 = 5(x + 1)$ **45.** $x - 7 - x = 0$ **46.** $3x - x + 16 = 2(x + 8)$

PROBLEM SOLVING

SEE EXAMPLE 4
on p. 349
for Exs. 47–51

47. GUIDED PROBLEM SOLVING You and your friend are going on a jet ski tour as shown at right. The tour takes you from the dock to a coral reef, then to an island, and back to the dock. The tour is 5 miles long. How far is it from the reef to the island?

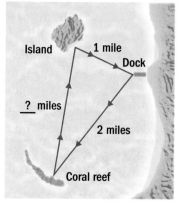

   a. Write a verbal model that represents the situation.

   b. Use the verbal model to write an equation. Let x represent the distance between the reef and the island.

   c. Solve the equation.

48. ★ **MULTIPLE CHOICE** Judy is 7 years younger than Lily. Which equation can be used to find Lily's age L, if Judy is 14 years old?

   A $14 = L + 7$ **B** $14 = L - 7$ **C** $14 = 7L$ **D** $14 = 7 - L$

49. SCHOOL SUPPLIES Locker mirrors are on sale for $5.75. This is $1.50 less than the regular price. Write and solve an equation to find the regular price of the mirrors.

50. ATOMIC MASS For any element, the atomic mass of a single atom is approximated by the sum of the numbers of protons and neutrons it contains. Write and solve equations to find the number of neutrons in an atom of each element in the table.

Element	Gold	Silver	Mercury
Atomic mass	197	108	201
Protons	79	47	80

51. INDIRECT MEASUREMENT While holding his cat, Bill steps on a scale. The scale reads 127 pounds. Alone, Bill weighs 112 pounds. Write and solve an equation to find the weight of Bill's cat.

52. ★ **WRITING** Jared solves the equation $-5 + x = 2$ by subtracting -5 from each side. Carlos solves the same equation by adding 5 to each side. Are they both correct? *Explain.*

53. COSTUME PARTY You need to make a costume to wear to your friend's costume party. You have $25 to spend. Write and solve an equation to find how much money you have left after buying 2.5 yards of fabric, a wig, 2 sheets of poster board, and face paints.

Item	Fabric	Wig	Poster board	Face paints
Cost	$3.50 per yard	$5.39	$1.99 per sheet	$4.25

54. ★ **SHORT RESPONSE** *Describe* a real-world situation that can be represented by the equation $d + 12 = 20$. *Explain* what d represents.

55. MULTI-STEP PROBLEM At a store, you can buy used CDs for $3.49, used DVDs for $8.99, or used video games for $12.50. You have $25, but you have to buy a package of CD holders which cost $4.75.

    a. Write and solve an equation to find out how much you can spend on other items.

    b. Use your answer to (a) to write and solve an equation to find how much money you will have left if you buy a video game.

    c. After buying the CD holders and a used video game, what else can you buy? *Explain.*

56. CHALLENGE Bronson is x years old. Natalie's age is 4 more than triple Bronson's age. Iris is 2 years older than Natalie. Find each person's age if 7 times Bronson's age equals the sum of Natalie's and Iris's ages.

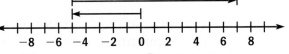

NEW JERSEY MIXED REVIEW

TEST PRACTICE at classzone.com

57. Which expression is represented by the model at the right?

  Ⓐ $-5 + 0$ **Ⓑ** $-5 + 7$ **Ⓒ** $-5 + 10$ **Ⓓ** $-5 + 12$

58. The price p of a taxable item and its tax t are given. Which formula can be used to calculate the tax?

  Ⓐ $t = p + 0.07$ **Ⓑ** $t = p \div 0.07$

  Ⓒ $t = p \times 0.07$ **Ⓓ** $t = p \times 1.07$

p	t
$3	$.21
$4	$.28
$5	$.35
$6	$.42

Brain Game

Orderly Words

The solution of each equation corresponds to a letter of the alphabet ($1 = A$, $2 = B$, $3 = C$, $4 = D$, and so on). Solve the equations to answer the following question.

Question: What is the longest word in the English language that has all of its letters in alphabetical order?

Answer:

$x + 9 = 10$ $x - 7 = 5$ $26 - x = 13$ $x - 18 = -3$ $x + 2.4 = 21.4$ $x + 14 = 34$

 ONLINE QUIZ at classzone.com

GOAL
Model and solve multiplication equations.

MATERIALS
• algebra tiles

7.4 Modeling Multiplication Equations

You can use algebra tiles to model and solve simple multiplication equations.

EXPLORE Solve $3x = 12$.

STEP 1 **Model** $3x = 12$ using algebra tiles.

STEP 2 **Divide** the x-tiles and 1-tiles into 3 equal groups.

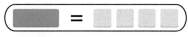

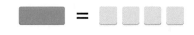

STEP 3 **Identify** the solution. One x-tile is equal to four 1-tiles. So, the solution of the equation $3x = 12$ is 4.

Check $3(4) = 12$ ✓

PRACTICE Use algebra tiles to model and solve the equation.

1. $5x = 15$ 2. $2x = 4$ 3. $4x = 8$ 4. $4x = 20$

5. $3x = 18$ 6. $7x = 21$ 7. $2x + 3x = 5$ 8. $2x + 4x = 12$

DRAW CONCLUSIONS

9. **WRITING** The example above uses a property called the *division property of equality*, similar to the addition and subtraction properties of equality in the previous lesson. In your own words, explain what this property allows you to do.

7.4 Solving Multiplication and Division Equations

NJ 4.3.D.2.b Using paper-and-pencil, calculators, graphing calculators, spreadsheets, and other technology

Before	You solved addition and subtraction equations.
Now	You'll solve multiplication and division equations.
Why?	So you can find the speed of a blimp, as in Example 4.

KEY VOCABULARY

• **inverse operations,**
  p. 347

Blimps A blimp travels 300 miles in 7.5 hours. The blimp travels at a constant speed. In Example 4, you'll write and solve a multiplication equation to find the speed of the blimp.

Because multiplication and division are inverse operations, you can use division to solve a multiplication equation.

KEY CONCEPT *For Your Notebook*

Division Property of Equality

Words   Dividing each side of an equation by the same nonzero number produces an equivalent equation.

Algebra $ax = b \ (a \ 0) \ \longrightarrow \ \dfrac{ax}{a} = \dfrac{b}{a}$

 EXAMPLE 1 Solving a Multiplication Equation

Solve the equation $-3x = 45$.

$-3x = 45$	**Write original equation.**
$\dfrac{-3x}{-3} = \dfrac{45}{-3}$	**Divide each side by** -3.
$x = -15$	**Simplify.**

WRITE MISSING COEFFICIENTS

In an equation such as $16 = -s$, notice that the coefficient of $-s$ is -1, so you divide each side by -1 to solve.

Check	$-3x = 45$	**Write original equation.**
	$-3(-15) \overset{?}{=} 45$	**Substitute** -15 **for x.**
	$45 = 45 \checkmark$	**Solution checks.**

 GUIDED PRACTICE   for Example 1

Solve the equation. Check your solution.

1. $6a = 54$ **2.** $-13b = 65$ **3.** $16 = -s$

4. $-17 = -b$ **5.** $8g = 88$ **6.** $-12n = 108$

KEY CONCEPT

Multiplication Property of Equality

Words Multiplying each side of an equation by the same nonzero number produces an equivalent equation.

Algebra $\dfrac{x}{a} = b \ (a \neq 0) \longrightarrow a \cdot \dfrac{x}{a} = a \cdot b$

EXAMPLE 2 Solving a Division Equation

 Solve the equation $\dfrac{x}{2} = 0.75$.

$\dfrac{x}{2} = 0.75$	**Write original equation.**
$2 \cdot \dfrac{x}{2} = 2 \cdot 0.75$	**Multiply each side by 2.**
$x = 1.5$	**Simplify.**

✓ **GUIDED PRACTICE** for Example 2

Solve the equation. Check your solution.

7. $\dfrac{c}{2} = 13$ **8.** $-3.4 = \dfrac{d}{5}$ **9.** $\dfrac{s}{-4} = 3$

10. $-11.2 = \dfrac{a}{-10}$ **11.** $\dfrac{z}{7} = -15$ **12.** $5 = \dfrac{r}{6}$

Reciprocals When you are solving an equation containing a fractional coefficient, multiply each side of the equation by the reciprocal, or multiplicative inverse, of the coefficient.

EXAMPLE 3 Solving an Equation Using a Reciprocal

 Solve the equation $-4 = \dfrac{2}{3}x$.

$-4 = \dfrac{2}{3}x$	**Write original equation.**
$\left(\dfrac{3}{2}\right)(-4) = \left(\dfrac{3}{2}\right)\dfrac{2}{3}x$	**Multiply each side by $\dfrac{3}{2}$, the reciprocal of $\dfrac{2}{3}$.**
$-6 = x$	**Simplify.**

✓ **GUIDED PRACTICE** for Example 3

Solve the equation. Check your solution.

13. $\dfrac{4}{5}r = 1$ **14.** $-2 = \dfrac{2}{5}t$ **15.** $-\dfrac{1}{2}p = -10$

EXAMPLE 4 Standardized Test Practice

Blimp What is the speed of the blimp described on page 354?

ⓐ −40 miles per hour Ⓑ 20 miles per hour

Ⓒ 40 miles per hour Ⓓ 200 miles per hour

ELIMINATE CHOICES
You know the speed
of the blimp is not a
negative number, so you
can eliminate choice A.

SOLUTION

Use the formula $d = rt$.

$d = rt$ **Write formula for distance.**

$300 = r(7.5)$ **Substitute 300 for d and 7.5 for t.**

$\dfrac{300}{7.5} = \dfrac{7.5r}{7.5}$ **Divide each side by 7.5.**

$40 = r$ **Simplify.**

▶ **Answer** The speed of the blimp is 40 miles per hour.
The correct answer is C. ⓐ Ⓑ Ⓒ Ⓓ

 GUIDED PRACTICE for Example 4

16. Movie Length A movie is sold as a DVD set that includes 7.5 hours of bonus material. This is 3 times as long as the movie itself. Write and solve an equation to find the length m of the movie.

7.4 **EXERCISES**

HOMEWORK
KEY

★ = **STANDARDIZED TEST PRACTICE**
Exs. 27, 28, 49, 50, 53, 54, 56, and 69

◯ = **HINTS** AND **HOMEWORK HELP**
Exs. 11, 19, 25, 29, 47 at classzone.com

SKILL PRACTICE

VOCABULARY Copy and complete the statement.

1. Multiplication and __?__ are inverse operations.

2. Dividing each side of an equation by __?__ produces an equivalent equation.

SOLVING EQUATIONS Solve the equation. Check your solution.

SEE EXAMPLES
1, 2, AND 3
on pp. 354–355
for Exs. 3–22

3. $14q = 42$

4. $20r = 100$

5. $9s = -27$

6. $-3t = -9$

7. $\dfrac{w}{2} = 8$

8. $-\dfrac{3}{4}y = 12$

9. $-\dfrac{3}{10}z = -6$

10. $30b = 5$

11. $-b = 12.5$

12. $-3.5f = 24.5$

13. $-3 = 1.2y$

14. $-a = -4$

15. $\dfrac{r}{2} = 10$

16. $-36 = \dfrac{r}{5.5}$

17. $-0.7 = \dfrac{z}{3}$

18. $\dfrac{c}{14} = -11$

19. $\dfrac{4}{3}t = 12$

20. $-\dfrac{5}{7}y = 5$

21. $-\dfrac{1}{2}w = -12$

22. $-9 = -\dfrac{3}{4}e$

CHOOSE A STRATEGY Explain how to solve the equation. Then solve.

SEE EXAMPLES 1, 2, AND 3
on pp. 354–355 for Exs. 23–30

23. $3x = 15$

24. $-16x = 4$

(25.) $\dfrac{x}{9} = -2$

26. $\dfrac{x}{15} = -7$

27. ★ **MULTIPLE CHOICE** Which describes how to solve $-8y = 40$ in one step?

    A Divide each side by 40.

    B Multiply each side by -8.

    C Divide each side by -8.

    D Divide each side by 8.

28. ★ **MULTIPLE CHOICE** Which equation has a solution of -2?

    A $4y = 8$ **B** $-4y = 8$ **C** $8y = 4$ **D** $-8y = 4$

ERROR ANALYSIS Describe and correct the error made in solving the equation.

(29.)
$$\frac{4}{5}x = 20$$
$$\frac{4}{5} \cdot \frac{4}{5}x = \frac{4}{5} \cdot 20$$
$$x = 16$$

30.
$$-3.2x = 48$$
$$\frac{-3.2x}{3.2} = \frac{48}{3.2}$$
$$x = 15$$

TRANSLATING SENTENCES Write the verbal sentence as an equation. Then solve.

31. The product of 10 and a number is -22.

32. The quotient of a number and 3 is 6.6.

33. A number divided by -11 is 7.

34. The product of $\dfrac{2}{3}$ and a number is 18.

35. A number multiplied by $-3\dfrac{1}{4}$ is 2.

36. The quotient of a number and -5 is -11.3.

ROUNDING SOLUTIONS Solve the equation. Round to the nearest hundredth.

37. $2x + 3x = 12$

38. $7a - 5a = 15$

39. $10 = b + 8b$

40. $9z + 3z = 6$

41. $3 = m + 3m$

42. $6p - 2p = 9$

CHALLENGE Use mental math to solve the equation.

43. $-\dfrac{48}{x} = 60$

44. $\dfrac{58}{a} = 2.9$

45. $-0.7 = \dfrac{5.6}{y}$

PROBLEM SOLVING

SEE EXAMPLE 4
on p. 356 for Exs. 46–47

46. FLYING DISC You throw a flying disc to your dog. It stays in the air for 2.5 seconds before your dog catches it 30 feet away from you. Write and solve an equation to find the speed of the disc.

(47.) GEOMETRY A rectangle has a length of 7.5 meters and an area of 45 square meters. Write and solve an equation to find the rectangle's width.

48. MIGRATION Use the diagram at the right. Write and solve an equation to find the average speed of the golden plover.

Plover Migration

Canada

United States

2400 miles in 48 hours

South America

49. ★ MULTIPLE CHOICE Your telephone bill lists a call that lasted 18 minutes and cost $1.08. How much were you charged for each minute of the call?

    (A) $0.01   **(B)** $0.06

    (C) $0.08   **(D)** $0.19

50. ★ OPEN-ENDED MATH Opening a door and shutting it can be thought of as inverse operations. Describe two other real-world situations that can be thought of as inverse operations.

JUMP ROPE **In Exercises 51 and 52, use the following information.**

Suppose that in the 3-minute speed event at a jump rope competition, a jumper's right foot strikes the ground 309 times. Assume that the jumper keeps a steady pace.

SEE EXAMPLE 2
on p. 355
for Exs. 51–52

51. Write and solve an equation to find the number of times the jumper's right foot strikes the ground in 1 minute.

52. How many times does the jumper's right foot strike the ground in 1 second? Round your answer to the nearest tenth.

53. ★ WRITING *Describe* a real-world situation that could be solved using the equation $5t = 20$.

54. ★ SHORT RESPONSE In one day, a ski lift can carry 11,200 people. The lift runs from 9:00 A.M. to 4:00 P.M. Write and solve an equation to find the number of people the lift can carry in 1 hour. Estimate the number of people who could ride the lift by noon. *Explain* your reasoning.

55. REASONING Is it possible to solve the equation $5x = 29$ by *multiplying* each side of the equation by the same number? *Explain* your reasoning.

56. ★ EXTENDED RESPONSE The top female runner in the 2001 Boston Marathon completed the 26.2 mile race in about 2 hours 24 minutes. The top female wheelchair racer finished in about 1 hour 54 minutes.

  a. Write the time for each racer as a decimal.

  b. Write and solve equations to find each racer's speed in miles per hour.

  c. About how much faster was the wheelchair racer? *Explain.*

57. BASEBALL In 1932, Ernest Swanson set a record by circling the 4 bases of a baseball diamond in 13.3 seconds. Consecutive bases are 90 feet apart. Assuming that Swanson ran at a constant speed, how fast did he run, in feet per second? Round your answer to the nearest tenth.

58. DISTANCE FORMULA The distance formula $d = rt$ allows you to find distance when given rate and time. Rewrite the formula to find $r = \underline{\ ?\ }$ and $t = \underline{\ ?\ }$. *Justify* each step using the appropriate properties of equality.

59. CHALLENGE A *mil* is used to measure paper thickness. One mil is equal to 0.001 inch. You have a stack of paper that is about 2.5 inches high. Each sheet of paper is 11.8 mils thick. Write and solve an equation to approximate the number of sheets of paper in the stack.

60. CHALLENGE While visiting Mexico, Myles exchanged U.S. dollars for 1338 pesos at an exchange rate of about $11\frac{3}{20}$ pesos for each U.S. dollar. To represent this situation, write an equation that can be solved by multiplying both sides by a reciprocal. *Explain* how you chose your equation. Then solve the equation to find the number of U.S. dollars Myles exchanged.

NEW JERSEY MIXED REVIEW

 TEST PRACTICE at classzone.com

61. The model below represents the equation $x + 4 = 6$. Which step finds the value of x?

(A) Add 4 flowers to each side of the model

(B) Add 6 flowers to each side of the model

(C) Subtract 4 flowers from each side of the model

(D) Subtract 6 flowers from each side of the model

QUIZ *for Lessons 7.1–7.4*

Write the real-world phrase as a variable expression. Be sure to identify what the variable represents. *(p. 337)*

1. Twice the cost of a ticket

2. 4 years younger than Sam

3. MUSEUM ADMISSION The cost of admission to a museum is $32 for 4 adults. Write and solve an equation to find the cost of admission for 1 adult. *(p. 337)*

Identify the coefficients, constant terms, and like terms of the expression. Then simplify the expression. *(p. 342)*

4. $b - 8 - 6b + 10$

5. $10a - 15 + a + 7$

6. $-6 + 6 - 4c$

Solve the equation. Check your solution.

7. $14 + x = 45$ *(p. 347)*

8. $-11 = \frac{a}{8}$ *(p. 354)*

9. $\frac{2}{9}c = -12$ *(p. 354)*

10. $t - 37 = 51$ *(p. 347)*

11. $55 = 2.5p$ *(p. 354)*

12. $0.2 + y + 6.3 = 5$ *(p. 347)*

Lessons 7.1–7.4

1. **GEOMETRY** The length of a rectangle is 3 inches greater than the width. The perimeter of the rectangle is 50 inches. What are the dimensions of the rectangle?

    A. 11 inches by 8 inches

    B. 14 inches by 11 inches

    C. 18.75 inches by 6.25 inches

    D. 26.5 inches by 23.5 inches

2. **WATER TANK** A tank at a water facility is fed by two pipes. One pipe feeds 8 gallons of water per second to the tank. The other feeds 5 gallons per second. The tank has a drain that lets out 3 gallons per second. Let x be the number of seconds after the pipes start filling an empty tank. What does the expression $8x + 5x - 3x$ represent?

    A. The total number of gallons that will pour into the tank

    B. The number of gallons that will drain out of the tank

    C. The total number of gallons that will pour into the tank if the drain is left closed

    D. The number of gallons in the tank if the drain is left open

3. **VIDEO ARCADE** You are using tokens to play arcade games. You use half of your tokens on a racing game, and then 4 tokens on a maze game. You have 2 tokens left after playing the games. Which equation can be used to find t, the total number of tokens you had at the start?

    A. $t - \frac{1}{2}t - 4 = 2$

    B. $\frac{t-4}{2} = 2$

    C. $\frac{1}{2}t + 4 = t$

    D. $\frac{1}{2}t - 4 + 2 = 0$

4. **CHARITY WALK** Each year, you participate in an 8-mile walk for charity. Last year, you completed the walk in 2 hours 40 minutes. This year, you completed the walk in 2 hours 30 minutes. How much faster was your speed this year compared to last year?

    A. 0.2 mile per hour

    B. 0.8 miles per hour

    C. 3.2 mile per hour

    D. 10 miles per hour

5. **SKYSCRAPERS** The Bank of America Tower in Seattle, Washington, is 295 meters tall. The Empire State Building in New York, New York, is 86 meters taller than the Bank of America Tower. How tall is the Empire State Building?

    A. 86 meters

    B. 209 meters

    C. 295 meters

    D. 381 meters

6. **OPEN-ENDED** Deb and Xavier are using tokens to play arcade games. Deb gives $\frac{2}{3}$ of her tokens to Xavier, which is 12 tokens. Deb then spends some of her remaining tokens on a racing game. She then has 2 tokens left.

    - Write and solve an equation to find the number of tokens Deb has at the start.

    - Determine how many tokens Deb has after she gives tokens to Xavier.

    - Write and solve an equation to find the number of tokens Deb spends on the racing game.

7.5 Solving Two-Step Equations

 4.3.D.2.a Multi-step, integer coefficients only (although answers may not be integers)

Before	You solved one-step equations.
Now	You'll solve two-step equations.
Why?	So you can find the time to complete a task, as in Example 3.

KEY VOCABULARY
- inverse operations, *p. 347*

ACTIVITY

Work backward to solve the equation $-3x + 1 = -5$.

STEP 1 **Draw** a box model to represent the equation $-3x + 1 = -5$.

$$\boxed{x} \xrightarrow{\times(-3)} \boxed{?} \xrightarrow{+1} \boxed{-5}$$

STEP 2 **Rewrite** the model using inverse operations. Work from right to left. To undo adding 1, subtract 1. To undo multiplying by -3, divide by -3.

$$\boxed{x} \xleftarrow[\div(-3)]{} \boxed{?} \xleftarrow[-1]{} \boxed{-5}$$

STEP 3 **Solve** the equation. Because $-5 - 1 = -6$ and $-6 \div (-3) = 2$, you know that $x = 2$. So, the solution of the equation $-3x + 1 = -5$ is 2.

$$\boxed{2} \xleftarrow[\div(-3)]{} \boxed{-6} \xleftarrow[-1]{} \boxed{-5}$$

Use a box model to solve the equation.

1. $6x + 1 = 7$ **2.** $2x + 3 = -11$ **3.** $-4x - 5 = 7$

Using Inverse Operations Two-step equations, like $-3x + 1 = -5$ above, require the use of two inverse operations to solve.

EXAMPLE 1 Solving a Two-Step Equation

Solve the equation $5x - 6 = -21$.

$5x - 6 = -21$	Write original equation.
$5x - 6 + 6 = -21 + 6$	Add 6 to each side.
$5x = -15$	Simplify.
$\dfrac{5x}{5} = \dfrac{-15}{5}$	Divide each side by 5.
$x = -3$	Simplify.

EXAMPLE 2 Solving a Two-Step Equation

Solve the equation $\frac{c}{3} + 13 = 0$.

$\frac{c}{3} + 13 = 0$	Write original equation.
$\frac{c}{3} + 13 - 13 = 0 - 13$	Subtract 13 from each side.
$\frac{c}{3} = -13$	Simplify.
$3\left(\frac{c}{3}\right) = 3\,(-13)$	Multiply each side by 3.
$c = -39$	Simplify.

EXAMPLE 3 Writing and Solving a Two-Step Equation

 Bicycle Repair Your bicycle needed to be fixed. A mechanic charged $40 for each hour of labor, and the new parts cost $35. The total cost of fixing the bicycle was $95. How long did it take the mechanic to fix the bicycle?

SOLUTION

STEP 1 **Write** a verbal model. Let n represent the number of hours of labor.

Cost of new parts	$+$	Cost of labor per hour	$\cdot$	Number of hours of labor	$=$	Total cost
35	$+$	40	$\cdot$	n	$=$	95

STEP 2 **Solve** the equation.

$35 + 40n = 95$	Write equation.
$35 - 35 + 40n = 95 - 35$	Subtract 35 from each side.
$40n = 60$	Simplify.
$\frac{40n}{40} = \frac{60}{40}$	Divide each side by 40.
$n = 1.5$	Simplify.

▸ **Answer** The mechanic took 1.5 hours to fix the bicycle.

✓ **GUIDED PRACTICE** for Examples 1, 2, and 3

Solve the equation. Check your solution.

1. $6d - 9 = 15$ 2. $\frac{x}{2} - 10 = -10$ 3. $\frac{m}{4} + 7 = -7$

4. **Landscaping** A landscaper charges $28 per hour for labor and $105 for plants and materials to do a small planting job. If the total cost is $168, how long did the job take?

7.5 EXERCISES

HOMEWORK KEY

★ = STANDARDIZED TEST PRACTICE
Exs. 19, 37, 38, 40, 42, and 53

◯ = HINTS AND HOMEWORK HELP
for Exs. 5, 17, 19, 37 at classzone.com

SKILL PRACTICE

1. **VOCABULARY** Which inverse operation would you use first to solve the equation $7y + 8 = 1$?

2. **VOCABULARY** Describe the operations you would use to solve the equation $5x - 3 = 12$.

SOLVING TWO-STEP EQUATIONS Solve the equation. Check your solution.

SEE EXAMPLES
1 AND 2
on pp. 361–362
for Exs. 3–20

3. $3x - 2 = 4$

4. $-7x + 5 = -9$

5. $\dfrac{x}{9} + 2 = -7$

6. $9y + 4 = -14$

7. $-7b - 7 = -42$

8. $29 - 2x = 13$

9. $\dfrac{e}{9} - 3 = 3$

10. $129 = 12b - 15$

11. $-77 = -t + 55$

12. $0 = 2.5y + 20$

13. $\dfrac{f}{6} + 1.2 = -30$

14. $\dfrac{z}{0.25} - 5 = -12$

15. $\dfrac{3}{8}w - 14 = 10$

16. $\dfrac{5}{13} - 2x = -\dfrac{8}{13}$

17. $-\dfrac{2}{3}s - 1 = \dfrac{5}{6}$

18. **ERROR ANALYSIS** Describe and correct the error made in solving $3x - 9 = 15$.

$$3x - 9 = 15$$
$$\dfrac{3x}{3} - 9 = \dfrac{15}{3}$$
$$x - 9 = 5$$
$$x - 9 + 9 = 5 + 9$$
$$x = 14$$

19. ★ **MULTIPLE CHOICE** Which equation has a solution of -12?

Ⓐ $\dfrac{y}{-2} - 2 = 4$

Ⓑ $2y - 2 = -8$

Ⓒ $-2y + 4 = -20$

Ⓓ $\dfrac{y}{-2} + 4 = -2$

20. **REASONING** Put the steps for solving the equation $7x - 10 = -3$ in order.

A. Add 10 to each side.

B. Check your answer.

C. Write original equation.

D. Divide each side by 7.

SOLVING MULTI-STEP EQUATIONS Solve the equation. Check your solution.

21. $3(x + 1) = 12$

22. $3r + 6 - 9r = 24$

23. $4b - 10b - 9 = -3$

24. $\dfrac{2}{3} + 13y + \dfrac{1}{4} = 2$

25. $2a - 8 + 5a = 20$

26. $6x + 12.3 - 10.2 = -1.5$

TRANSLATING SENTENCES Write the sentence as an equation. Then solve.

27. 7 decreased by twice a number is 11.

28. 8 plus the product of a number and 4 is 4.

29. A number plus twice the number is 15.

30. 6 subtracted from half of a number is 6.

31. **EXAMPLES AND NONEXAMPLES** A test covers only two-step equations, not one-step equations. Give three examples of equations that could be on the test, and three examples of equations that could not.

GEOMETRY **Use the given information to write an equation to find *x*. Then solve the equation.**

32. The rectangle has a perimeter of 26.

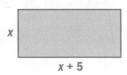

x

x + 5

33. The rectangle has a perimeter of 68.

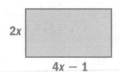

2x

4x − 1

34. CHALLENGE Find two solutions of the equation $-3|x| + 10 = -20$.

PROBLEM SOLVING

SEE EXAMPLE 3
on p. 362
for Exs. 35–37

35. GUIDED PROBLEM SOLVING You and your friend rented a two-person kayak. It costs $15 for the first hour, plus $12.50 for each additional hour. The total cost for renting the kayak was $52.50. For how many total hours did you and your friend rent the kayak?

   a. Write a verbal model that represents the situation.

   b. Use the verbal model to write and solve a two-step equation. Let *x* represent the number of additional hours you and your friend rented the kayak.

   c. Find the *total* hours for which you and your friend rented the kayak.

36. SOUVENIRS You are sightseeing in Chicago and have $20 to spend on souvenirs. You buy a baseball cap for $8. You want to buy key chains to bring home to your friends. Each key chain costs $1.50. Write and solve an equation to find how many key chains you can buy.

37. ★ **MULTIPLE CHOICE** A shoe store is having a sale, and all shoes are half off the original price. You use a coupon for an additional $5 off the sale price, so that you pay $17 for a pair of shoes. What is the original price?

   (A) $11   **(B)** $24   **(C)** $39   **(D)** $44

38. ★ **WRITING** *Explain* how solving the equation $x + 4 = 10$ is different from solving the equation $3x + 4 = 10$.

39. TRIATHLON You travel 15.5 miles while swimming, biking, and running in a triathlon. Use the diagram below to write and solve an equation to find how many minutes you spend running.

Triathlon Stages

swimming — 2 mi/h: 15 min   *biking* — 16 mi/h: 45 min   *running* — 6 mi/h: *t* min

40. ★ **SHORT RESPONSE** You are using a word processor to create a table. The table will be 5 inches wide. The first column of the table will be 3 inches wide, and the remaining 4 columns will have equal widths.

   a. Write and solve an equation to find how wide you should make each of the 4 columns.

   b. You decide to decrease the width of the first column by 1 inch but keep the table 5 inches wide. *Explain* how the widths of the other columns change if these widths stay equal.

41. **BASKETBALL** The length of a basketball court is 34 feet greater than the width. The perimeter of a basketball court is 268 feet. Write and solve an equation to find the width. Then find the length.

42. ★ **OPEN-ENDED MATH** *Describe* a real-world situation that can be modeled by $\frac{1}{2}x - 4 = 5$. Then solve the equation.

43. **CHALLENGE** The formulas below can be used to convert between temperature in degrees Fahrenheit *F* and degrees Celsius *C*. Show that the formulas are different forms of the same expression.

$$F = \frac{9}{5}C + 32 \qquad C = \frac{5}{9}(F - 32)$$

44. **CHALLENGE** On the first three 100-point tests of the grading period, you scored a total of 253 points. What score do you need to get on the fourth 100-point test to have a mean score of 85? *Explain* your reasoning.

NEW JERSEY MIXED REVIEW **TEST PRACTICE** at classzone.com

45. What are the coordinates of point *R*?

   Ⓐ (−4, 2)   Ⓑ (4, −2)

   Ⓒ (−2, 4)   Ⓓ (2, −4)

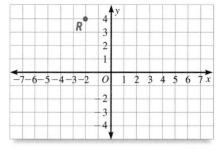

46. Four friends are lining up from oldest to youngest. Paula is older than Michelle and Amanda, but younger than Natalie. What information is needed to determine the order of the girls?

   Ⓐ Who is the oldest?

   Ⓑ Who is the youngest?

   Ⓒ Is Natalie older or younger than Michelle?

   Ⓓ Is Amanda older or younger than Natalie?

7.6 Solving Inequalities

NJ **4.3.D.4.a** Additive inverse

Before You wrote and solved equations.

Now You'll write and solve inequalities.

Why? So you can represent minimum heights, as in Ex. 37.

KEY VOCABULARY
- **inequality,** *p. 366*
- **solution of an inequality,** *p. 366*
- **graph of an inequality,** *p. 366*
- **equivalent inequalities,** *p. 366*

Voting You must be at least 18 years old to vote in the United States. This can be represented by the *inequality* $y \geq 18$.

An **inequality** is a mathematical sentence formed by placing an inequality symbol ($<$, $>$, $\leq$, or $\geq$) between two expressions. The **solution of an inequality** is the set of numbers that you can substitute for the variable to make the inequality true.

The **graph of an inequality** in one variable is the set of points on a number line that represents the solution of the inequality. An open dot on a graph indicates a number that is *not* part of the solution. A closed dot indicates a number that *is* part of the solution.

EXAMPLE 1 Graphing Inequalities

a. $x < 2$ All numbers less than 2   

READING

The inequality symbol $\leq$ is read "is less than or equal to." The inequality symbol $\geq$ is read "is greater than or equal to."

b. $x \leq -1$ All numbers less than or equal to -1 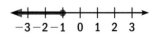

c. $x > 0$ All numbers greater than 0   

d. $x \geq -2$ All numbers greater than or equal to -2 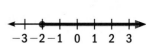

Equivalent inequalities are inequalities that have the same solution. You can produce an equivalent inequality in the following ways.

TAKE NOTES

Compare and contrast solving equations and solving inequalities.

- Add or subtract the same number on each side.

- Multiply or divide each side by the same *positive* number.

$$1 < 3 \quad \boxed{\text{Multiply each side by 2.}} \quad 2 < 6$$

- Multiply or divide each side by the same negative number and reverse the direction of the inequality.

$$1 < 3 \quad \boxed{\text{Multiply each side by } -2.} \quad -2 > -6$$

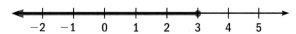

EXAMPLE 2 Solving an Inequality

Solve $d - 2 \leq 1$. Then graph the solution.

$$d - 2 \leq 1 \qquad \text{Write original inequality.}$$
$$d - 2 + 2 \leq 1 + 2 \qquad \text{Add 2 to each side.}$$
$$d \leq 3 \qquad \text{Simplify.}$$

To graph $d \leq 3$, use a closed dot and draw an arrow pointing to the left.

AVOID ERRORS
In Example 2, notice that if you check by using $d = 3$, this does *not* confirm that the graph is pointing in the correct direction.

Check To check the solution $d \leq 3$, choose any number less than or equal to 3 to substitute for d. The check below uses $d = 0$.

$$d - 2 \leq 1 \qquad \text{Write original inequality.}$$
$$0 - 2 \overset{?}{\leq} 1 \qquad \text{Substitute 0 for } d.$$
$$-2 \leq 1 \checkmark \qquad \text{Solution checks.}$$

✓ **GUIDED PRACTICE** for Examples 1 and 2

Solve the inequality. Then graph the solution.

1. $x - 3 \geq -1$ **2.** $6 < t - 5$ **3.** $w + 9 < -4$ **4.** $1 \leq k + 7$

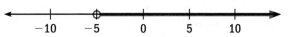

EXAMPLE 3 Solving an Inequality

Solve $-4w < 20$. Then graph the solution.

$$-4w < 20 \qquad \text{Write original inequality.}$$
$$\frac{-4w}{-4} > \frac{20}{-4} \qquad \text{Divide each side by } -4. \text{ Reverse inequality.}$$
$$w > -5 \qquad \text{Simplify.}$$

AVOID ERRORS
Don't forget to reverse the inequality when you multiply or divide each side of an inequality by a *negative* number.

To graph $w > -5$, use an open dot and draw an arrow pointing to the right.

Animated **Math** at classzone.com

✓ **GUIDED PRACTICE** for Example 3

Solve the inequality. Then graph the solution.

5. $-3n \geq -24$ **6.** $6s < -42$ **7.** $-\frac{1}{2}x \leq 5$ **8.** $\frac{3}{4}r > 12$

9. $5z > -10$ **10.** $-6a > -18$ **11.** $\frac{1}{5}k \leq 12$ **12.** $-\frac{2}{3}b \leq 8$

7.6 EXERCISES

HOMEWORK KEY

★ = **STANDARDIZED TEST PRACTICE**
   Exs. 25, 26, 27, 28, 29, 42, 47, 51, 64

◯ = **HINTS AND HOMEWORK HELP**
   for Exs. 3, 17, 19, 37, 41 at classzone.com

SKILL PRACTICE

VOCABULARY Copy and complete the statement.

1. The set of numbers that you can substitute for a variable to make the inequality true is called the __?__ .

2. Inequalities that have the same solution are __?__ .

SEE EXAMPLE 1
on p. 366
for Exs. 3–6

GRAPHING INEQUALITIES Graph the inequality.

3. $a \geq -12$
4. $x \leq -7$
5. $w < 5$
6. $d > 13$

SEE EXAMPLES 2 AND 3
on p. 367
for Exs. 7–24

SOLVING INEQUALITIES Solve the inequality. Then graph the solution.

7. $r - 17 \leq -21$
8. $-b + 17 \geq 8$
9. $-t - 14 \geq -28$
10. $p + 7 < 13$

11. $-w - 21 \leq -32$
12. $19 + e > 41$
13. $-56 + y \geq 113$
14. $z - 8.6 > 16.4$

15. $\frac{x}{3} < -4$
16. $-27n < -108$
17. $\frac{-b}{4} > -5$
18. $\frac{c}{-8} < -17$

19. $-7s \leq 42$
20. $3g > -36$
21. $\frac{x}{9} \geq \frac{1}{3}$
22. $-5y \geq 35$

ERROR ANALYSIS Describe and correct the error.

23. Solve $-5x < 45$.

$$\times \quad \begin{array}{l} -5x < 45 \\ x < -9 \end{array}$$

24. Graph the solution of $-3x \geq 9$.

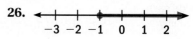

★ **OPEN-ENDED MATH** Write two equivalent inequalities represented by the graph.

25.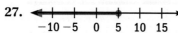

26.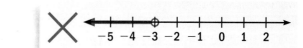

27.

28.

29. ★ **MULTIPLE CHOICE** Which is the solution of the inequality represented by "3 more than double a number is greater than -20"?

Ⓐ $n < 11.5$
Ⓑ $n > -11.5$
Ⓒ $n > -13$
Ⓓ $n < -7$

30. **GRAPHING** The absolute value of a number is its distance from 0 on a number line. Graph: $|x| < 4$ and $|x| \geq 1$.

CHALLENGE *Describe* all of the numbers that are solutions of both inequalities.

31. $4x \geq 2$ and $x + 4 \leq 9$

32. $y - 7 < 21$ and $y + 2 > -23$

In Exercises 33–36, solve the inequality and graph the solution. Then check your answer.

EXTENSION Solving a Two-Step Inequality

$2x + 1 \leq 4$	Original inequality
$2x + 1 - 1 \leq 4 - 1$	Subtract 1 from each side.
$2x \leq 3$	Simplify.
$\dfrac{2x}{2} \leq \dfrac{3}{2}$	Divide each side by 2.
$x \leq \dfrac{3}{2}$	Simplify.

---

33. $3 + 6x \leq 21$ **34.** $2b - 13 > 9$ **35.** $-2y - 5 > 15$ **36.** $-7 - 4x \leq 9$

PROBLEM SOLVING

REAL-WORLD INEQUALITIES Write an inequality to represent the situation. Then graph the inequality.

SEE EXAMPLE 1
on p. 366
for Exs. 37–40

37. You must be at least 42 inches tall to ride the bumper cars.

38. Children under 12 will be admitted to the museum at no charge.

39. In football, you need to gain at least 10 yards for a first down.

40. Adults 65 and over will get a discount at the restaurant.

41. **BOAT LIFT** A boat lift can raise as much as 3600 pounds. An empty boat on the lift weighs 2300 pounds. Write and solve an inequality to find the number of additional pounds allowed in the boat without exceeding the lift's capacity.

42. ★ **WRITING** *Describe* when you use a closed dot and when you use an open dot to graph an inequality.

SHOPPING You have $22 to buy two items *p* and *q* from the list below. Write and use an inequality to tell whether you can buy the given items.

43. Photo album and CD

44. Photo album and magazine

45. Photo album and shirt

46. CD and shirt

Item	Price
Photo album	$10
CD	$15
Magazine	$3
Shirt	$12

47. ★ **MULTIPLE CHOICE** You are buying a rug for a rectangular room. The rug can be at most 16 feet long and 9 feet wide. Which inequality represents the area *A* of the rug in square feet?

    A $A \leq 50$ **B** $A \geq 50$ **C** $A \leq 144$ **D** $A \geq 144$

48. SUBWAY PASS A one-way subway trip costs $1.25. A monthly subway pass costs $41. Write and solve an inequality to find the least number of one-way rides you must take for the subway pass to be a better deal than paying by the ride. If you take an average of 35 one-way trips per month, would you buy the pass? *Justify* your reasoning.

49. REASONING Which values of *m* are solutions of the inequality $m \leq 5$? Write an inequality to represent the values of *m* that are *not* solutions of $m \leq 5$. What is the relationship between the values that are solutions of an inequality and the values that are not?

50. REASONING Are $2x - 12 > 16$ and $16 < 2x - 12$ equivalent inequalities? *Justify* your answer.

51. ★ **SHORT RESPONSE** How is the graph of the solution of an inequality, such as $x + 1 > 2$, different from the graph of a solution of an equation, such as $x + 1 = 2$? *Explain* how each of these compares to the graph of $x + 1 \leq 2$.

ELEVATION The map shows changes in elevation in an area. Use the key to write an inequality for each comparison.

52. How do the elevations of *E* and *F* compare? *Explain* your reasoning.

53. What is the greatest possible difference between *A* and *C*? the least possible difference? *Explain*.

54. Graph the possible elevations for point *B* on a number line.

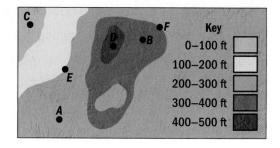

55. CHALLENGE The inequalities $x > a$ and $x < b$ can be written as $a < x < b$. This is called a *compound inequality*. Write a compound inequality for the situation below. What does the variable represent?

> *You had a $10 bill and a $5 bill when you went shopping. After you bought a book, you had a $10 bill and some change.*

 NEW JERSEY MIXED REVIEW

TEST PRACTICE at classzone.com

56. Mr. Woods completed an exercise program. The table shows the length of his workouts in hours for the first few weeks. He continued the pattern for 8 weeks. Which length of time for a workout is NOT included in the 8-week program?

Week	1	2	3
Length of workout	$\frac{4}{5}$	1	$1\frac{1}{5}$

A $1\frac{1}{2}$ hours   **B** $1\frac{2}{5}$ hours

C $1\frac{4}{5}$ hours   **D** 2 hours

7.7 Functions and Equations

 4.3.A.1.a Descriptions using tables, verbal and symbolic rules, graphs, simple equations or expressions

Before	You wrote and evaluated expressions.
Now	You'll write and evaluate function rules.
Why?	So you can analyze relationships, as in Ex. 31.

KEY VOCABULARY
- **function,** *p. 371*
- **input,** *p. 371*
- **output,** *p. 371*
- **domain,** *p. 371*
- **range,** *p. 371*

A **function** is a pairing of each number in a given set with exactly one number in another set. Starting with a number called an **input**, the function associates it with exactly one number called an **output**. A function can be represented by a rule, a table, or a graph.

EXAMPLE 1 Evaluating a Function

 Evaluate the function $y = 5x$ when $x = 7$.

$y = 5x$	**Write rule for function.**
$= 5(7)$	**Substitute 7 for x.**
$= 35$	**Multiply.**

Domain and Range The set of all input values is the **domain** of a function. The set of all output values is the **range** of a function.

EXAMPLE 2 Making an Input-Output Table

 Make an input-output table for the function $y = x - 1.3$ using the domain 0, 1, 2, and 3. Then state the range of the function.

SOLUTION

Input x	0	1	2	3
Substitution	$y = 0 - 1.3$	$y = 1 - 1.3$	$y = 2 - 1.3$	$y = 3 - 1.3$
Output y	-1.3	-0.3	0.7	1.7

The range of the function is the set of outputs -1.3, -0.3, 0.7, and 1.7.

✓ GUIDED PRACTICE for Examples 1 and 2

 1. Make an input-output table for the function $y = 2x + 2$ using the domain -2, -1, 0, 1, and 2. Then state the range of the function.

EXAMPLE 3 Writing a Function Rule

Write a function rule for the input-output table.

Input x	−2	−1	0	1	2	3	4
Output y	0.5	1.5	2.5	3.5	4.5	5.5	6.5

SOLUTION

Compare each output to its corresponding input. You will see that you obtain each output by adding 2.5 to the input.

▸ **Answer** A function rule for the input-output table is $y = x + 2.5$.

Animated **Math** at classzone.com

EXAMPLE 4 Solve a Multi-Step Problem

Making Cuts In the cheese-slicing diagram below, the input c is the number of cuts made across the center of the cheese, and the output p is the resulting total number of pieces of cheese. Write a rule for the function. Then use the rule to find the number of pieces made with 9 cuts.

SOLUTION

STEP 1 **Make** an input-output table.

Input c	1	2	3	4
Output p	2	4	6	8

STEP 2 **Write** a function rule. Notice that each output value is twice the input value. So, a rule for the function is $p = 2c$.

STEP 3 **Evaluate** the function when $c = 9$ to find the number of pieces made with 9 cuts. Because $p = 2(9) = 18$, there are 18 pieces made with 9 cuts.

✓ **GUIDED PRACTICE** for Examples 3 and 4

Write a function rule for the input-output table. Then use the rule to find the output y when $x = 12$.

2.

Input x	−1	0	1	2
Output y	−4	−3	−2	−1

3.

Input x	2	4	6	8
Output y	−1	−2	−3	−4

Sequences A *sequence* is an ordered list of numbers, and each number in the sequence is called a *term*. It is a special type of function whose domain includes only positive integers such as 1, 2, 3, and so on.

 EXAMPLE 5 Standardized Test Practice

Which statement describes the relationship between a term and *n*, its position in the sequence?

Position	1	2	3	4	5	n
Value of term	−1	1	3	5	7	?

ELIMINATE CHOICES Multiplying the position by −1, as in choice A, would result in all negative values. Because only the first value is negative, choice A can be eliminated.

(A) Multiply *n* by −1.

(B) Multiply *n* by 2 and then add −3.

(C) Multiply *n* by −2 and then add 1.

(D) Multiply *n* by 3 and then add −4.

SOLUTION

The terms differ by 2. If you double the position number and subtract 3, you get the value of the term. So, the correct answer is B. **(A) (B) (C) (D)**

✓ **GUIDED PRACTICE** for Example 5

4. Describe the relationship between a term and its position *n*.

Position	1	2	3	4	5	n
Value of term	2	5	8	11	14	?

7.7 EXERCISES

HOMEWORK KEY

★ = **STANDARDIZED TEST PRACTICE**
Exs. 15, 28, 30, 33, and 44

○ = **HINTS AND HOMEWORK HELP**
for Exs. 5, 7, 11, 17, 31 at classzone.com

SKILL PRACTICE

1. **VOCABULARY** Copy and complete: For a given function, the set of all input values is called the   ? ; the set of all output values is called the   ? .

SEE EXAMPLE 1
on p. 371
for Exs. 2–5

FUNCTIONS Evaluate the function $y = 3x - 2$ for the given value of *x*.

2. 4   3. 0   4. 1   **5.** −3

FINDING RANGE Make an input-output table for the function using the domain −2, −1, 0, 1, and 2. Then state the range of the function.

SEE EXAMPLE 2
on p. 371
for Exs. 6–14

6. $y = x + 11$ **7.** $y = -20x$ 8. $y = x - 4.56$ 9. $y = 15 - 2x$

10. $y = 3.7x$ **11.** $y = 0.8x - 1$ 12. $y = -9.1x + 7.22$ 13. $y = -5.4 + 1.6x$

14. **ERROR ANALYSIS** Describe and correct the error in making an input-output table for the function $y = x - 2$.

Input x	−2	−1	0	1
Output y	0	1	2	3

SEE EXAMPLE 3
on p. 372
for Exs. 15–23

15. ★ **MULTIPLE CHOICE** The input x of a function is centimeters. The output y is the equivalent number of millimeters. Which rule represents the function?

    A $y = 0.01x$ **B** $y = 0.1x$ **C** $y = 10x$ **D** $y = 100x$

WRITING FUNCTION RULES Tell whether the table represents a function. If so, write the function rule. If not, *explain* why not.

16.

Input x	1	2	3	4
Output y	5	10	15	20

17.

Input x	−2	−1	0	1
Output y	13	14	15	16

18.

Input x	2	3	4	5
Output y	0.8	1.8	2.8	3.8

19.

Input x	−3	0	3	6
Output y	1	0	−1	−2

20.

Input p	−1	0	1	2
Output q	1	0	1	4

21.

Input s	1	1	4	4
Output t	−1	1	−2	2

22.

Input m	−2	0	2	4
Output n	−3	1	5	9

23.

Input a	−3	−1	1	3
Output b	13	3	−7	−17

SEE EXAMPLE 5
on p. 373
for Ex. 24

24. **SEQUENCES** *Describe* the relationship between a term and its position, n.

Position	0	1	2	3	4	5	n
Value of term	−3	1	5	9	13	17	?

CHALLENGE Write three functions for the given input-output pair.

25. input: −3; output: 15   26. input: 6; output: −18   27. input: −4; output: −11

PROBLEM SOLVING

SEE EXAMPLE 4
on p. 372
for Exs. 28–29

28. ★ **MULTIPLE CHOICE** You can estimate the number of miles m you are from a lightning strike. Use the function $m = 0.2t$, where t is the time in seconds between seeing lightning and hearing thunder. You hear thunder 6 seconds after seeing lightning. About how far away is the lightning?

    A 0.6 mile   **B** 0.83 mile   **C** 1.2 miles   **D** 3 miles

29. ◆ **MULTIPLE REPRESENTATIONS** The cost for renting a cabin for the weekend at a ski resort is $185, plus $36 per person for a weekend lift pass. The cost in dollars is $C = 185 + 36n$, where n is the number of people.

  a. Make an input-output table using the domain 1, 2, 3, 4, 5, and 6.

  b. Write a function rule for the total cost if the cabin rents for $191 and the lift passes are $30 per person. Which situation gives skiers a better deal? *Explain.*

30. ★ **WRITING** *Describe* how to write a function rule to represent the unit conversion of years to months.

SEE EXAMPLE 2
on p. 371
for Ex. 31

31. **SCUBA DIVING** The pressure on a scuba diver is given by the function $p = 64d + 2112$, where p is pressure in pounds per square foot, and d is depth in feet. Make an input-output table for depths of 0, 20, 40, 60, 80, and 100 feet. As the depth increases, what happens to the pressure?

SEE EXAMPLE 4
on p. 372
for Ex. 32

32. **MULTI-STEP PROBLEM** In the diagram of a folded piece of string, the input c is the number of times you cut across the string, and the output p is the total number of pieces of string after you make the cut(s).

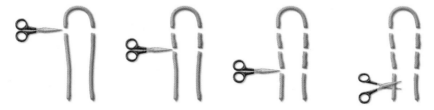

    a. Model Make an input-output table.

    b. Interpret Write a statement in words that shows the relationship between c and p. Then write a rule for the function.

    c. Calculate How many pieces of string do you have if you make 18 cuts?

33. ★ **SHORT RESPONSE** A parking garage charges $5 to park for less than 2 hours, $7 to park for 2 to 4 hours, and $10 to park for the day. Is this an example of a real-life function? If so, identify the domain and range. *Justify* your answers.

34. **REASONING** A store sells used DVDs for $9.99 and new DVDs for $18.99. Is the cost of buying several DVDs a function of the number of DVDs you buy? *Explain* your reasoning.

35. **CHALLENGE** A triangle has side lengths of 8 inches, 8 inches, and x inches. Write a function rule for the perimeter P in terms of x. Do the domain and range have minimum and maximum values? *Explain* why or why not. Then create an input-output table for all possible integer values.

 NEW JERSEY MIXED REVIEW   **TEST PRACTICE** at classzone.com

36. Which of the following coordinates lie within the triangle graphed at the right?

    A $(-2, 0)$

    B $(0, -3)$

    C $(0, 3)$

    D $(2, 0)$

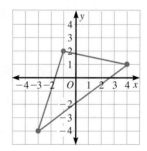

7.8 Graphing Functions

 4.3.B.1.a   Equations involving two variables

Before	You graphed ordered pairs in a coordinate plane.
Now	You'll graph functions in a coordinate plane.
Why?	So you can graph costs, as in Example 2.

KEY VOCABULARY
- linear function, *p. 377*

Fabric You are in a craft shop, choosing fabric for a sewing project. The fabric you choose costs $2.50 for each yard. In Example 2, you will find out how to use a graph to represent this situation.

You can graph a function by creating an input-output table, forming ordered pairs, and plotting the ordered pairs.

EXAMPLE 1 Graphing a Function

 Graph the function $y = 2x + 1$.

STEP 1 **Make** an input-output table by choosing several input values and finding the output values.

STEP 2 **Use** the table to write a list of ordered pairs:

$(-2, -3)$ $(1, 3)$
$(-1, -1)$ $(2, 5)$
$(0, 1)$

x	*Substitution*	y
-2	$y = 2(-2) + 1$	-3
-1	$y = 2(-1) + 1$	-1
0	$y = 2(0) + 1$	1
1	$y = 2(1) + 1$	3
2	$y = 2(2) + 1$	5

CHOOSE A DOMAIN
When the domain of a function is not given, assume that it includes every x-value for which the function can produce a corresponding y-value.

STEP 3 **Plot** the ordered pairs in a coordinate plane.

STEP 4 **Notice** that all of the points lie on a line. Any other ordered pairs satisfying $y = 2x + 1$ would also lie on the line when graphed. The line represents the complete graph of the function $y = 2x + 1$.

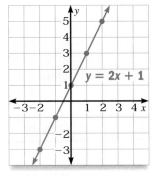

Animated **Math** at classzone.com

 GUIDED PRACTICE   for Example 1

Graph the function.

1. $y = x - 3$ **2.** $y = 2x - 3$ **3.** $y = -3x$ **4.** $y = -x + 4$

EXAMPLE 2 Writing and Graphing a Function

The situation described at the top of page 376 can be represented by the function $y = 2.50x$, where y is the total cost of the fabric and x is the number of yards of fabric. Follow these steps to graph the function.

page 376

AVOID ERRORS
In Example 2, note that you cannot have fewer than 0 yards of fabric, so you cannot use any numbers less than 0 in the domain.

STEP 1 Make an input-output table.

Input x	Output y
0	0
1	2.5
2	5
3	7.5
4	10

STEP 2 Plot the ordered pairs and connect them as shown.

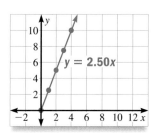

Linear Functions The functions in Examples 1 and 2 are *linear functions*. A **linear function** is a function whose graph is a line or part of a line. Not all graphs are lines, nor do all graphs represent functions.

EXAMPLE 3 Identifying Linear Functions

Tell whether each graph represents a function of x. If it does, tell whether the function is linear.

a.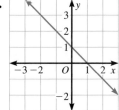

b.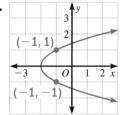

c.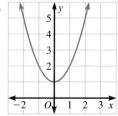

SOLUTION

a. This graph represents a function of x. The function is linear because the graph is a line.

VOCABULARY
Recall that a function pairs each input value with *exactly* one output value.

b. This graph does *not* represent a function of x. For each value of x in the domain, excluding -2, there is more than one value of y.

c. This graph represents a function of x. The function is not linear because the graph is not a line or part of a line.

✓ **GUIDED PRACTICE** for Examples 2 and 3

5. **Cost** Write and graph a function for the cost, y, of x pens that cost $3 each.

6. Is the graph at the right a function? Is it linear? *Explain.*

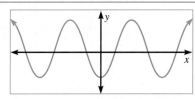

7.8 EXERCISES

SKILL PRACTICE

1. **VOCABULARY** Copy and complete: A function pairs each input value with exactly __?__ output value(s).

2. **VOCABULARY** What is the difference between a linear function and a function that is *not* linear?

GRAPHING FUNCTIONS Graph the function.

SEE EXAMPLE 1
on p. 376
for Exs. 3–12

3. $y = x$

4. $y = 10 - x$

5. $y = \frac{1}{3}x$

6. $y = x + 3$

7. $y = 3x - 5$

8. $y = -4x + 1$

9. $y = -\frac{1}{4}x + 2$

10. $y = 0.5x - 2$

11. $y = -x - 4$

12. **ERROR ANALYSIS** Describe and correct the error made in listing 5 ordered pairs for the function $y = -3x + 2$: $(8, -2)$, $(5, -1)$, $(2, 0)$, $(-1, 1)$, $(-4, 2)$.

IDENTIFYING LINEAR FUNCTIONS Tell whether the graph represents a function of x. If it does, tell whether the function is linear.

SEE EXAMPLE 3
on p. 377
for Exs. 13–15

13.

14.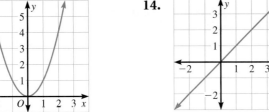

15.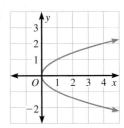

16. ★ **MULTIPLE CHOICE** Which function is graphed at the right?

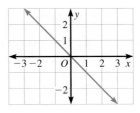

Ⓐ $y = -x$ Ⓑ $y = x$

Ⓒ $y = x - 1$ Ⓓ $y = x - 2$

MAKING TABLES Make an input-output table from the graph. Then write a rule for the function.

17.

18.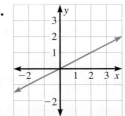

19.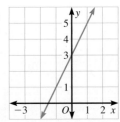

MEASUREMENT Write and graph a function that converts the units.

20. x yards to y feet

21. x days to y weeks

22. x pints to y cups

23. x millimeters to y centimeters

INTERSECTING LINES Graph the functions in the same coordinate plane. Then name the point where they intersect.

24. $y = x$ and $y = 3x - 4$

25. $y = 5 - x$ and $y = \frac{1}{2}x + 2$

26. $y = -x - 3$ and $y = 3x + 1$

27. $y = x + 1$ and $y = 3x - 1$

28. CHALLENGE The graphs of two functions intersect at a point. *Explain* how you could use input-output tables to find the coordinates of the point of intersection without graphing the functions.

In Exercises 29–34, write y as a function of x. Then graph the function.

> **EXTENSION** Writing y as a Function of x
>
> | | |
> |---|---|
> | $8x + 4y = 1200$ | Write original equation. |
> | $8x - 8x + 4y = 1200 - 8x$ | Subtract $8x$ from each side. |
> | $4y = 1200 - 8x$ | Simplify. |
> | $\dfrac{4y}{4} = \dfrac{1200 - 8x}{4}$ | Divide each side by 4. |
> | $y = 300 - 2x$ | Simplify. |
>
> ▶ **Answer** You can write $8x + 4y = 1200$ as $y = 300 - 2x$.

29. $-6x + 2y = 4$

30. $14x + 7y = 56$

31. $15x + 5y = 30$

32. $7x + 2y = -42$

33. $x - \frac{1}{2}y = 6$

34. $\frac{2}{3}x + 2y = 10$

PROBLEM SOLVING

SEE EXAMPLE 2
on p. 377
for Exs. 35–37

35. EXERCISE When you walk slowly, your body burns about 2 calories every minute. This situation can be represented by the function $y = 2x$, where y is the number of calories burned and x is the number of minutes you walk. Graph the function.

36. SHOPPING Papayas cost $1.50 per pound. Write and graph a function that models the cost y of x pounds of papayas.

37. ★ MULTIPLE CHOICE Which function converts gallons x to quarts y?

(A) $y = 4x$ **(B)** $y = 8x$ **(C)** $y = \frac{1}{4}x$ **(D)** $y = \frac{1}{8}x$

SEE EXAMPLE 2
on p. 377
for Exs. 38–40

38. ★ **SHORT RESPONSE** A cable company charges $50 for a one-time installation fee and $30 per month for service. Write and graph a function that models the total cost y after x months of cable service. After how many months will cable costs total $230? *Explain.*

39. ◆ **MULTIPLE REPRESENTATIONS** A unicycle rider travels $6\frac{1}{4}$ feet for every rotation the unicycle wheel makes, as shown below.

1 rotation equals $6\frac{1}{4}$ feet

$6\frac{1}{4}$ ft

Not drawn to scale.

   a. **Write an Equation** Write a function that models the distance y the unicycle rider travels in x rotations.

   b. **Make a Table** Make an input-output table using the domain 0, 4, 8, 12, 16, and 20 rotations.

   c. **Draw a Graph** Graph the function.

40. ★ **WRITING** Write a function for the perimeter P of a rectangle with a length of 4 inches and a width of x inches. *Explain* your reasoning.

41. ★ **OPEN-ENDED MATH** Write a real-world function whose output value is always less than the input value. Make an input-output table and graph the function.

READING IN MATH Read the passage below for Exercises 42–44.

Physics The amount of force needed to move an object depends on its mass and its acceleration. Mass is a measure of the amount of material making up an object. Acceleration is how quickly an object's velocity (speed) is changing over time.

Object	Mass (kg)	Force (N)
Bowling ball	7	70
Large rock	4.5	45
Math book	1	10
Baseball	0.15	1.5

Gravity is a force that causes objects near Earth to fall towards its surface. The acceleration due to gravity of such objects is about 10 meters per second per second. The table shows the masses in kilograms of several everyday objects, and the gravitational force F, in *newtons*, that acts upon them as they fall.

42. Graphing Representing mass on the x-axis and force on the y-axis, plot the ordered pairs and connect them. Does your graph appear to represent a linear function? *Explain.*

43. Write a Rule Write a rule for the function relating force, F, and mass, m. What does your coefficient represent? *Explain.*

44. Newton's Second Law Based on your rule, write a formula relating force, mass, and acceleration.

45. COOLING The table below shows the temperature y of a cup of soup after cooling for x minutes.

Time (min)	0	2	5	10	20	30	40	50	60
Temperature (°C)	90	85	79	68	58	49	43.5	39.5	37

   a. Use the table to write a list of ordered pairs.

   b. Plot the ordered pairs and draw a line or curve through the points.

   c. Tell whether the graph represents a function. If so, is it a linear function? *Explain.*

46. CHALLENGE You make a sketch of a garden you are planning. In your sketch, 3 inches represent 4 feet. Write a function rule that gives a, the actual dimension (in feet), in terms of the sketch's dimension s (in inches). *Explain* the meaning of writing the domain as $0 \le s \le 6$. Then graph the function using this domain.

NEW JERSEY MIXED REVIEW

TEST PRACTICE at classzone.com

47. Which description shows the relationship between the value of a term and n, its position in the sequence?

Position	1	2	3	4	n
Value of Term	3	7	11	15	?

   (A) Add 5 to n

   (B) Multiply n by 3, then add 1

   (C) Multiply n by 3, then subtract 1

   (D) Multiply n by 4, then subtract 1

QUIZ *for Lessons 7.5–7.8*

Solve the equation. Check your solution. *(p. 361)*

   1. $10 + 5u = -25$ **2.** $40 = 6t - 14$ **3.** $\frac{w}{28} + 6.5 = 11$

   4. THEATER Each student ticket to a school musical costs \$5, and each adult ticket costs \$6. The music department collected \$1400 in ticket sales and sold 150 adult tickets. How many student tickets were sold? *(p. 361)*

Solve the inequality. Then graph the solution. *(p. 366)*

   5. $-3w > 51$ **6.** $x - 15 \le -17$ **7.** $34 + y \ge 47$ **8.** $\frac{x}{-4} < 5$

Make an input-output table for the function. Then graph the function. *(pp. 371, 376)*

   9. $y = -x + 2$ **10.** $y = 7 + 2x$ **11.** $y = -\frac{1}{3}x$ **12.** $y = \frac{1}{2}x - 4$

7.8 Graphing Functions

EXAMPLE Graph *y* = 3*x* − 2 and find ordered pairs using the *trace* feature on your graphing calculator.

SOLUTION

STEP 1 Select Y= to enter the function *y* = 3*x* − 2 into the graphing of calculator.

STEP 2 Select WINDOW and set up the window for the graph *y* = 3*x* − 2 as shown.

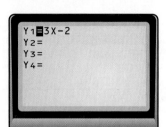

This determines the increment between *x*-values that you see using the trace feature.

STEP 3 Select GRAPH to view the graph of the function. Then select TRACE to see the coordinates of points on the graph. Use the left and right arrows to move the cursor along the graph.

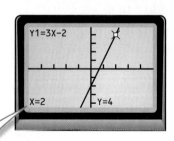

Notice that X = 2 and Y = 4 correspond to the ordered pair (2, 4).

PRACTICE Use a graphing calculator to graph the function and find the unknown value in the given ordered pairs.

1. *y* = 2*x*, (? , 1.6) and (2.1, ?)

2. *y* = −*x*, (−4.3, ?) and (? , 0)

3. *y* = −3*x* + 1, (? , −2) and (−2, ?)

4. *y* = 5*x* − $\frac{1}{2}$, (4.5, ?) and (? , 1.5)

5. *y* = −3*x* − 1, (? , 0.8) and (0.2, ?)

6. *y* = 2*x* + 2.3, (0, ?) and (? , 5.5)

DRAW CONCLUSIONS

7. REASONING Use a graphing calculator to graph *y* = 2*x* + 5 and *y* = −*x* + 2 in the same coordinate plane. Tell where they intersect. Check your answer by substituting the values into each equation.

Direct Variation

Use after Lesson 7.8

GOAL Identify relationships and write equations that represent direct variation.

If you know the cost of one movie ticket, then you can find the cost of 2, 3, or more movie tickets. These two quantities, total cost and number of tickets, are *directly proportional*. In other words, when you divide the total cost by the number of tickets, you will always get the same number, the cost of one ticket.

A relationship in which two quantities have a constant quotient is a *direct variation*.

EXAMPLE 1 Identifying Direct Variation

 Tell whether the relationship represents direct variation.

a.

Input x	Output y
1	2
2	4
3	6
4	8

b.

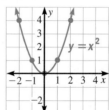

c. $y = 2x - 1$

SOLUTION

a. Use the table to find the quotient of y and x.

Input x	1	2	3	4
Output y	2	4	6	8
$y \div x$	2	2	2	2

▶ **Answer** Notice that the quotient is always 2. This relationship represents direct variation.

b. Make an input-output table and find the quotient of y and x.

Input x	−2	−1	1	2
Output y	4	1	1	4
$y \div x$	−2	−1	1	2

▶ **Answer** Notice that the quotient is not constant. This relationship does not represent direct variation.

c. Make an input-output table. Choose any input values. Then find the quotient of y and x.

Input x	−4	−2	2	4
Output y	−9	−5	3	7
$y \div x$	2.25	2.5	1.5	1.75

▶ **Answer** Notice that the quotient is not constant. This relationship does not represent direct variation.

Model for Direct Variation

Words   The quantity y varies directly with the quantity x.

Algebra $y = kx$ or $\dfrac{y}{x} = k$, where $k \neq 0$ (k is the constant of variation.)

Graph   The graph of a direct variation is a line through the origin.

EXAMPLE 2   Writing a Direct Variation Equation

Movies The total cost of movie tickets varies directly with the number of tickets. The cost of 3 tickets is $27. Write a direct variation equation to represent the situation.

SOLUTION

Use the given values to find the constant of variation, k.

Since $\dfrac{\text{total cost}}{\text{number of tickets}}$ = price of one ticket, $\dfrac{y}{x} = \dfrac{27}{3} = 9$.

▶ **Answer** The direct variation equation is $y = 9x$. To buy x tickets, it costs $9x = y$ dollars.

EXERCISES

In Exercises 1–6, tell whether the relationship represents direct variation. *Justify* your answer.

1.
Input x	2	3	4
Output y	10	15	20

2. $y = 4x + 3$

3. $y = 6x$

4.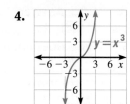

5.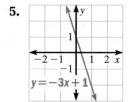

6.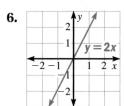

7. **SAVING MONEY** The amount of money you save varies directly with the number of weeks during which you save. In 6 weeks, you save $120. Write a direct variation equation to represent this situation.

8. **MEMBERSHIP FEES** Louise joins a fitness center. After 4 weeks, she has paid a total of $130. After 8 weeks, she has paid a total of $160. Does the total cost vary directly with the number of weeks? *Explain.*

Lessons 7.5–7.8

1. **ADMISSION** An amusement park has a sign showing the admission prices. Children who are 3–12 years of age pay $5, adults pay $10, seniors aged 65 and over pay $8, and children under 3 are free. Which graph represents the ages of people who pay $8 or more for admission to the park?

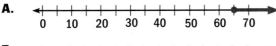

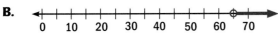

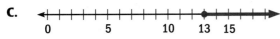

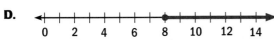

2. **LIFT TICKETS** A daily lift ticket at a ski resort costs $42.50. A season pass costs $510. You want to find the least number of lift tickets you must buy for the season pass to be a better deal than paying by the day. Which inequality can be used to solve this problem?

A. $42.5 \times 12 < n$ C. $510 \div n > 42.5$

B. $42.5n > 510$ D. $510n < 42.5n$

3. **BABY-SITTING** Every time you baby-sit you get a $5 tip. The graph shows the money you earn for various numbers of hours that you baby-sit. Which function models the money y earned after a baby-sitting shift of x hours?

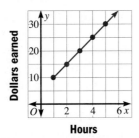

Hours

A. $y = 10x$

B. $y = 10x - 5$

C. $y = x + 5$

D. $y = 5x + 5$

4. **CELLULAR PHONE BILL** The table below shows the cost y of owning a cellular phone after x months. Which statement best describes the data in the table?

Number of months, x	Cost, y ($)
0	60
2	132
4	204
6	276
12	492
20	780

A. The graph represents a linear function.

B. The graph does not represent a function.

C. As the number of months increases, the cost decreases.

D. The graph of the data is not linear.

5. **FROZEN YOGURT** You work in a frozen yogurt shop. You sold 145 frozen juice bars and 150 frozen yogurt cones over the weekend. You took in a total of $399 from these sales. You sold each frozen yogurt cone for $1.50. What was the price, in dollars, of one frozen juice bar?

A. $1.00

B. $1.20

C. $1.30

D. $1.45

6. **OPEN-ENDED** You earn $5 per hour for a baby-sitting job, and you get a $5 tip.

• Write a function that models the money earned y after baby-sitting for x hours.

• Graph the function.

• How many hours would you have to baby-sit to earn $20? How can you tell just by looking at the graph?

REVIEW KEY VOCABULARY

- verbal model, *p. 338*
- terms, *p. 342*
- like terms, *p. 342*
- equivalent variable expressions, *p. 342*
- coefficient, *p. 342*
- constant term, *p. 342*

- inverse operations, *p. 347*
- equivalent equations, *p. 347*
- inequality, *p. 366*
- solution of an inequality, *p. 366*
- graph of an inequality, *p. 366*
- equivalent inequalities, *p. 366*

- function, *p. 371*
- input, *p. 371*
- output, *p. 371*
- domain, *p. 371*
- range, *p. 371*
- linear function, *p. 377*

VOCABULARY EXERCISES

Copy and complete the statement.

1. Two equations that have the same solution(s) are ___?___.

2. ___?___ are operations that "undo" each other.

3. The set of all input values is called the ___?___ of a function.

4. The number 3 in a term such as $3x$ is called the ___?___ of x.

5. The set of all output values is called the ___?___ of a function.

REVIEW EXAMPLES AND EXERCISES

7.1 Writing Expressions and Equations
pp. 337–341

EXAMPLE

Write the phrase or sentence as an expression or equation.

Phrase/Sentence	Expression/Equation
a. A number increased by 7	$n + 7$
b. 6 less than triple a number is 9.	$3n - 6 = 9$

EXERCISES

Write the verbal phrase or sentence as a variable expression or equation. Let w represent the number.

SEE EXAMPLES 1 AND 2 on pp. 337–338 for Exs. 6–10

6. 2 more than a number

7. Twice the sum of a number and 4

8. 8 less than a number is -25.

9. A number divided by 7 is 6.

10. A plane climbs 20,000 feet to reach an elevation of 21,250 feet. Write and solve an equation to find the elevation from which the plane took off.

7.2 Simplifying Expressions

pp. 342–345

EXAMPLE

Simplify the expression $4(2z + 1) - 3z$.

$$
\begin{aligned}
4(2z + 1) - 3z &= 8z + 4 - 3z & &\text{Distributive property} \\
&= 8z + 4 + (-3z) & &\text{Write as a sum.} \\
&= 8z + (-3z) + 4 & &\text{Commutative property of addition} \\
&= 5z + 4 & &\text{Combine like terms.}
\end{aligned}
$$

EXERCISES

SEE EXAMPLES 1 AND 3
on pp. 342–343
for Exs. 11–16

Simplify the expression.

11. $9x + 4 - x - 8$　　　**12.** $14 + 2y + 3 - 6y$　　　**13.** $8 - 3(g + 2)$

14. $-11 + 5b + 6 - 2b$　　　**15.** $10 - 7(d - 4)$　　　**16.** $5x + 9 - 4x - 15$

7.3 Solving Addition and Subtraction Equations

pp. 347–352

EXAMPLE

a. Solve the equation $n + 31 = 50$.

$$
\begin{aligned}
n + 31 &= 50 & &\text{Write original equation.} \\
n + 31 - 31 &= 50 - 31 & &\text{Subtract 31 from each side.} \\
n &= 19 & &\text{Simplify.}
\end{aligned}
$$

b. Solve the equation $-15 = y - 10$.

$$
\begin{aligned}
-15 &= y - 10 & &\text{Write original equation.} \\
-15 + 10 &= y - 10 + 10 & &\text{Add 10 to each side.} \\
-5 &= y & &\text{Simplify.}
\end{aligned}
$$

EXERCISES

SEE EXAMPLES 1, 2, AND 4
on pp. 347–349
for Exs. 17–23

Solve the equation. Check your solution.

17. $x - 3 = 13$　　　**18.** $-5 = z - 19$　　　**19.** $9.6 + g = 11.4$

20. $a + 4 = 9$　　　**21.** $7.4 + y = -19.2$　　　**22.** $-11 = m - 7$

23. Hawaiian Islands The island of Kauai is 55 square miles less in area than the island of Oahu. Kauai has an area of 553 square miles. Write and solve an equation to find the area of Oahu.

7.4 Solving Multiplication and Division Equations

pp. 354–359

EXAMPLE

a. Solve the equation $6m = -78$.

$$6m = -78 \qquad \text{Write equation.}$$

$$\frac{6m}{6} = \frac{-78}{6} \qquad \text{Divide each side by 6.}$$

$$m = -13 \qquad \text{Simplify.}$$

b. Solve the equation $\frac{x}{2} = 3.5$.

$$\frac{x}{2} = 3.5 \qquad \text{Write equation.}$$

$$2 \cdot \frac{x}{2} = 2 \cdot 3.5 \qquad \text{Multiply each side by 2.}$$

$$x = 7 \qquad \text{Simplify.}$$

EXERCISES

SEE EXAMPLES 1, 2, AND 3
on pp. 354–355
for Exs. 24–29

Solve the equation. Check your solution.

24. $-8p = 40$

25. $-36 = -2.25t$

26. $-\frac{2}{5}y = -6$

27. $-k = 12$

28. $-11z = -33$

29. $-90 = 3.75b$

7.5 Solving Two-Step Equations

pp. 361–365

EXAMPLE

a. Solve the equation $4x + 6 = 22$.

$$4x + 6 = 22$$

$$4x + 6 - 6 = 22 - 6$$

$$4x = 16$$

$$\frac{4x}{4} = \frac{16}{4}$$

$$x = 4$$

b. Solve the equation $\frac{c}{5} + 60 = 10$.

$$\frac{c}{5} + 60 = 10$$

$$\frac{c}{5} + 60 - 60 = 10 - 60$$

$$\frac{c}{5} = -50$$

$$5 \cdot \frac{c}{5} = 5(-50)$$

$$c = -250$$

EXERCISES

SEE EXAMPLES 1, 2, AND 3
on pp. 361–362
for Exs. 30–33

Solve the equation. Check your solution.

30. $12r - 8 = -32$

31. $2s + 6 = 64$

32. $-2 = \frac{t}{20} + 8$

33. Computers A computer repair store charges you $28 per hour for labor, and you buy anti-spam software for $36. If your total bill is $85, write and solve an equation to find how long they worked on your computer.

EXAMPLE

Solve the inequality $-3x \le 48$**. Then graph the solution.**

$$-3x \le 48 \qquad \text{Write original inequality.}$$

$$\frac{3x}{-3} \ge \frac{48}{-3} \qquad \text{Divide each side by } -3. \text{ Reverse inequality.}$$

$$x \ge -16 \qquad \text{Simplify.}$$

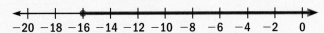

EXERCISES

Solve the inequality. Then graph the solution.

SEE EXAMPLES 1, 2, AND 3
on pp. 366–367
for Exs. 34–37

34. $x - 8 > 3$

35. $\dfrac{y}{5} \le -3$

36. $-7w > -84$

37. Travel Your suitcase weighs 3.6 pounds empty. The luggage weight limit is 40 pounds. Write an inequality to represent how much the contents c of your suitcase can weigh. Give 3 examples of allowable values of c.

EXAMPLE

Write a function rule for the input-output table.

Input x	−4	−3	−2	−1	0	1	2
Output y	2	3	4	5	6	7	8

You get each output by adding 6 to each input. So, the function rule for the table is $y = x + 6$.

EXERCISES

Write a function rule for the input-output table.

SEE EXAMPLE 3
on p. 372
for Exs. 38–41

38.

Input x	0	1	2	3
Output y	4	5	6	7

39.

Input x	−2	0	2	4
Output y	0.5	0	−0.5	−1

40.

Input x	0	2	4	6
Output y	0	4	8	12

41.

Input x	−2	−1	0	1
Output y	−7	−6	−5	−4

Graphing Functions

EXAMPLE 1

Graph the function $y = -2x - 3$.

STEP 1 **Make** an input-output table by choosing several input values and finding the output values.

STEP 2 **Use** the table to make a list of ordered pairs:
$(-2, 1), (-1, -1), (0, -3), (1, -5)$.

x	Substitution	y
−2	$y = -2(-2) - 3$	1
−1	$y = -2(-1) - 3$	−1
0	$y = -2(0) - 3$	−3
1	$y = -2(1) - 3$	−5

STEP 3 **Plot** the ordered pairs in a coordinate plane. Draw a line through the points to make a graph of the function.

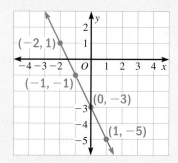

EXAMPLE 2

Tell whether each graph represents a function of x. *Explain*.

a. This graph does not represent a function of x. For each value of x in the domain, excluding $x = -1$, there is more than one y-value.

b. This graph represents a function of x. For each x-value there is exactly one y-value.

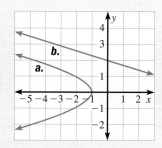

EXERCISES

Graph the function.

SEE EXAMPLES 1 AND 3
on pp. 376–377
for Exs. 42–46

42. $y = x - 5$

43. $y = -3x + 3$

44. $y = \dfrac{2}{3}x$

45. In Example 2, are either of the graphs linear functions? *Explain* why or why not.

46. Tell whether the graph represents a function of x. *Explain*.

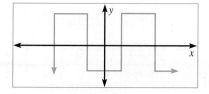

CHAPTER TEST

@HomeTutor
classzone.com
Chapter Test Practice

Write the verbal phrase or sentence as a variable expression or equation. Let x represent the number.

1. 5 more than twice a number
2. 12 less than a number is -19.
3. 18 more than a number is 2.
4. 7 less than triple a number

Simplify the expression.

5. $3b - 2 + 4b$
6. $10h + 9 + h - 10$
7. $7x - 4(3 - x)$
8. $3 - 6s - 5 + 2s$

Solve the equation. Check your solution.

9. $-3 = x + 4$
10. $12 = n + 7$
11. $c - 10.7 = 14.3$
12. $20k = -320$
13. $\dfrac{m}{6} = -13$
14. $\dfrac{2}{7}y = -10$
15. $8 = -5r + 18$
16. $4 - \dfrac{s}{12} = -6$

Solve the inequality. Then graph the solution.

17. $5n \le -10$
18. $z - 3 > 5$
19. $-2p \ge 6$
20. $\dfrac{3}{4}d < -6$
21. $-2x < 22$
22. $-\dfrac{1}{3}a \ge 9$
23. $-5z + 2 > 5$
24. $b - 11 \le -6$

Write a function rule for the input-output table.

25.

Input x	-2	0	2	4
Output y	-20	0	20	40

26.

Input x	-2	-1	0	1
Output y	10	11	12	13

27.

Input x	-3	0	3	6
Output y	-8	-5	-2	1

28.

Input x	-2	-1	0	1
Output y	8	4	0	-4

Graph the function.

29. $y = 5x + 2$
30. $y = x - 7$
31. $y = 2x - 2$
32. $y = \dfrac{1}{3}x + 1$

33. **GEOMETRY** Write and simplify an expression for the perimeter of the rectangle shown.

$x + 1$

$3x$

34. **BASKETBALL** In 1993, Bobby Hurley broke the NCAA all-time assist record for Division I men's basketball. Hurley had 1076 assists, which was 38 more than the previous record. Write and solve an equation to find the previous assist record.

35. **BAKING** It takes you 0.2 hour to decorate 1 dozen cookies. Write a function for the dozens of cookies y you can decorate in x hours. How many dozen cookies can you decorate in 6 hours?

REVIEWING EQUATIONS AND FUNCTIONS

You can use patterns and relationships to write, graph, and solve equations or functions. For instance, in the example below you will write and graph a function used for converting customary measures.

KEY CONCEPT   *For Your Notebook*

Customary Units of Length and Volume

Length   1 yard = 3 feet   **Volume**   1 gallon = 4 quarts
               1 foot = 12 inches   1 cup = 8 fluid ounces

EXAMPLE

Write and graph a function that converts x feet to y yards.

Solution

STEP 1   **Write** an equation that converts feet into yards.

         To convert from a smaller unit, feet, to a larger unit, yards, you divide.

         There are 3 feet in 1 yard, so the number of y yards in x feet is given by the function $y = \dfrac{x}{3}$.

STEP 2   **Make** an input-output table for the function. For convenience, use values of x that are divisible by 3.

Input *x*	0	3	6	9	12
Output *y*	0	1	2	3	4

STEP 3   **Use** the table to make a graph.

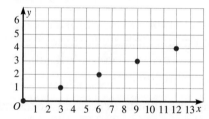

EQUATION AND FUNCTION PROBLEMS

Below are examples of equations and functions in multiple choice format. Try solving the problems before looking at the solutions. (Cover the solutions with a piece of paper.) Then check your solutions against the ones given.

1. The model below represents the equation $x + 2 = -4$.

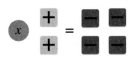

Key

$+ = +1$ $- = -1$

What is the value of x?

A. $x = -6$

B. $x = -2$

C. $x = -1$

D. $x = 2$

Solution

To get the x-tile by itself, you can add the same number of −1 tiles to each side to create zero pairs. So, add two −1 tiles to each side.

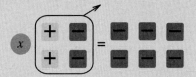

$x + 2 + (-2) = -4 + (-2)$

You can remove the zero pairs from the left side.

$x = -6$

So, the correct answer is A.

2. Which of the following relationships is best represented by the data in the graph?

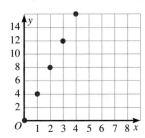

A. Conversion of yards to feet

B. Conversion of feet to inches

C. Conversion of cups to fluid ounces

D. Conversion of gallons to quarts

Solution

Use the graph to make an input-output table.

Input x	0	1	2	3	4
Output y	0	4	8	12	16

From the table, you can see that the outputs are 4 times the inputs, so $y = 4x$. There are 4 quarts in 1 gallon, so the conversion of gallons to quarts is being represented by the data in the graph.

The correct answer is D.

TEST PREPARATION

TEST PREPARATION

1. Spring water costs $1.39 per bottle. Which equation models the cost y of x bottles?

   A. $x = y + 1.39$

   B. $x = 1.39y$

   C. $y = 1.39x$

   D. $y = x + 1.39$

2. Which of the following relationships is best represented by the data in the graph?

   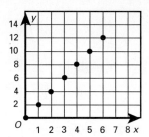

   A. Conversion of pints to cups

   B. Conversion of cups to pints

   C. Conversion of cups to fluid ounces

   D. Conversion of fluid ounces to cups

3. The model below represents the equation $x - 4 = 1$.

   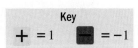

   What is the value of x?

   A. $x = -5$

   B. $x = -3$

   C. $x = 4$

   D. $x = 5$

4. The length of a rectangle is 3 times as long as its width w. Which equation gives the perimeter P of the rectangle?

   A. $P = 2w$

   B. $P = 3w$

   C. $P = 4w$

   D. $P = 8w$

5. Which unknown quantity can be found using the equation $5x = 40$?

   A. The cost of each movie when you buy 5 movies for $40

   B. The distance traveled when driving 40 miles per hour for 5 hours

   C. The total number of students in a grade that is divided into 40 groups containing 5 students each

   D. The amount of money you receive as change when paying a $5 bill with a $40 check

6. The table shows the daily low temperatures for one week. Which statement is supported by this data?

Day	Temperature	Day	Temperature
Sun	−5°C	Thur	−2°C
Mon	0°C	Fri	2°C
Tues	−8°C	Sat	5°C
Wed	1°C		

   A. The lowest temperature occurred on Monday.

   B. All of the temperatures are below −8°C.

   C. All of the temperatures are above −9°C.

   D. The highest temperature occurred on Tuesday.

7. Water boils at 212°F. Use the formula $F = \frac{9}{5}C + 32$ to convert this temperature to degrees Celsius.

   A. 100°C

   B. 135.6°C

   C. 324°C

   D. 439.2°C

8. A pickleball court has a perimeter of 128 feet. The width of the court is 20 feet. Which expression can be used to find the length l of the court?

   A. $128 = l + 20$

   B. $128 = 2l + 20$

   C. $128 = 2l + 40$

   D. $128 = 2l - 40$

9. Which ordered pair is on the line whose graph is shown below?

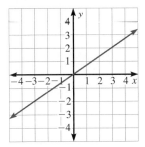

   A. $(2, 3)$

   B. $(3, 2)$

   C. $(-2, 3)$

   D. $(3, -2)$

10. What is the solution of $-5 = \frac{4}{5}x$?

   A. $-\frac{25}{4}$

   B. -4

   C. 4

   D. 6.25

11. Which description shows the relationship between a term and n, its position in the sequence?

Position	−1	0	1	2	n
Value of term	−2	−1	0	1	

   A. Add 1 to n

   B. Subtract 1 from n

   C. Subtract n from 1

   D. Multiply n by 2

12. One half of the difference of 4 and a number is 9. Which equation matches the verbal sentence?

   A. $\frac{1}{2}(4 - x) = 9$

   B. $\frac{1}{2}(x - 4) = 9$

   C. $\frac{1}{2}x - 4 = 9$

   D. $2 - x - 9$

13. **OPEN-ENDED** You are ordering almonds for wedding favors. There are about 110 almonds in 1 pound, and you want the 140 guests to get 11 almonds each.

   Part A Write and solve an equation to find about how many pounds of almonds you must buy.

   Part B The almonds cost $4.95 per pound at a store. On an Internet website, the almonds cost $4.00 per pound, but there is an additional $10.00 shipping charge. Which is the better deal? *Explain* your reasoning.

TEST PREPARATION

8 Ratios and Proportions

Before

In previous chapters you've . . .

- Found equivalent fractions
- Solved multiplication equations

Now

 New Jersey Standards

4.1.A.3	8.1	Ratios
4.1.A.3	8.2	Rates
4.1.A.3	8.3	Slope
4.1.A.3	8.4	Proportions
4.1.A.3	8.5	Cross products
4.2.A.2.b	8.6	Scale drawings

Why?

So you can solve real-world problems about . . .

- roller coasters, p. 400
- volcanoes, p. 410
- in-line skating, p. 418
- penguins, p. 424

 **Math**
at classzone.com

- Rates, p. 404
- Modeling Proportions, p. 420
- Scale Drawings and Models, p. 431

Get-Ready Games

Review Prerequisite Skills by playing *Fraction Action*.

Skill Focus: Finding equivalent fractions

FRACTION ACTION

MATERIALS

- colored chips
- number cubes
- game board

HOW TO PLAY Each player rolls a number cube. The player with the highest roll goes first and chooses one color of chips to use. Players take turns. On your turn, follow the steps on the next page.

 **1** **ROLL** both of the number cubes.

2 **FORM** a fraction from the numbers rolled. One number is the numerator and the other is the denominator.

3 **COVER** the fractions on the board (that are not already covered) that are equivalent to the fraction formed.

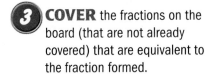

HOW TO WIN Be the first player to cover three spaces in a row (either horizontally, vertically, or diagonally), or be the first player to use all of your chips.

Stop and Think

1. **WRITING** How did you decide which of the numbers you rolled would be the numerator and which would be the denominator?

2. **CRITICAL THINKING** How many spaces can you cover if you roll the same number on both number cubes?

Review Prerequisite Skills

REVIEW WORDS
- **equation,** *p. 25*
- **solution,** *p. 25*
- **fraction,** *p. 176*
- **coordinate plane,** *p. 313*
- **x-axis,** *p. 313*
- **y-axis,** *p. 313*
- **ordered pairs,** *p. 313*

VOCABULARY CHECK

Copy and complete using a review word from the list at the left.

1. A(n) __?__ of an equation is a number that you can substitute for the variable to make the equation true.

2. A(n) __?__ is formed by the intersection of a horizontal number line, called the *x*-axis, and a vertical number line, called the *y*-axis.

3. Points in a coordinate plane are represented by __?__ .

SKILL CHECK

Write the fraction or mixed number as a decimal. *(p. 199)*

4. $\frac{3}{5}$

5. $6\frac{1}{2}$

6. $\frac{19}{20}$

7. $47\frac{1}{4}$

8. $\frac{7}{10}$

9. $\frac{15}{150}$

10. $2\frac{3}{4}$

11. $6\frac{3}{8}$

Plot the point and describe its location in a coordinate plane. *(p. 313)*

12. $(2, 5)$

13. $(0, 6)$

14. $(-1, 1)$

15. $(3, -4)$

Solve the equation. Check your solution. *(p. 354)*

16. $7t = 28$

17. $12p = 72$

18. $\frac{w}{4} = 5$

19. $\frac{x}{3} = 10$

20. $3k = 6$

21. $6.3y = 25.2$

22. $\frac{z}{8} = 36$

23. $\frac{m}{9.9} = 2$

@HomeTutor Prerequisite skills practice at classzone.com

Notetaking Skills   Showing Multiple Methods

In each chapter you will learn a new notetaking skill. In Chapter 8 you will apply the strategy of showing multiple methods to Example 3 on p. 424.

As you learn multiple methods for solving a problem, write the methods in your notebook. Each method should solve the same problem. An example is shown below.

Methods for Finding the GCF

List common factors.	Use prime factorization.
12: **1, 2, 3, 4,** 6, **12**	12: 2 × 2 × 3
18: **1, 2, 3,** 6, **9, 18**	18: 2 × 3 × 3
GCF: 6	GCF: **2 × 3 = 6**

8.1 Ratios

NJ 4.1.A.3 Understand and use ratios, proportions, and percents (including percents greater than 100 and less than 1) in a variety of situations.

Before	You wrote and compared fractions.
Now	You'll write and compare ratios.
Why?	So you can compare sports data, as in Example 1.

KEY VOCABULARY
• ratio, *p. 399*
• equivalent ratios, *p. 399*

Baseball How can you compare a baseball team's wins to its losses during spring training?

A **ratio** uses division to compare two numbers. There are three ways to write a ratio of two numbers.

Spring Training		
Team	**Wins**	**Losses**
San Diego Padres	16	11
L.A. Dodgers	18	13
Chicago Cubs	17	14

KEY CONCEPT   *For Your Notebook*

Writing a Ratio

Words	Numbers	Algebra
wins to losses	18 to 13	a to b, where b is nonzero
$\dfrac{\text{wins}}{\text{losses}}$	$\dfrac{18}{13}$	$\dfrac{a}{b}$, where b is nonzero
wins : losses	18 : 13	$a : b$, where b is nonzero

All three ways of writing the ratio of two numbers are read "the ratio of a to b," so 18 : 13 is read "the ratio of eighteen to thirteen." Two ratios are **equivalent ratios** when they have the same value.

EXAMPLE 1   Writing a Ratio

Use the table above to make comparisons about games played.

a. Cubs' wins to losses

   wins = 17

   losses = 14

   ▶ **Answer** 17 : 14, or $\dfrac{17}{14}$

b. Cubs' wins to games played

   wins = 17

   games = 17 + 14 = 31

   ▶ **Answer** 17 : 31, or $\dfrac{17}{31}$

✓ **GUIDED PRACTICE**   for Example 1

1. Write the ratio of wins to games played for the Padres.

EXAMPLE 2 · Writing Ratios in Simplest Form

Amusement Parks You wait in line for $1\frac{1}{2}$ hours to ride a roller coaster. The ride lasts 2 minutes. What is the ratio of time spent in line to time spent on the ride?

SOLUTION

STEP 1 Write hours as minutes so that the units match.

$1\text{ h} + \frac{1}{2}\text{ h} = 60\text{ min} + 30\text{ min}$ **Write hours as minutes.**

$= 90\text{ min}$ **Add.**

STEP 2 Write the ratio of time spent in line to time spent on the ride.

AVOID ERRORS
Be sure that the first quantity in the ratio goes in the numerator and that the second quantity goes in the denominator.

$\dfrac{\text{Time in line}}{\text{Time on ride}} = \dfrac{90}{2}$ **Write ratio.**

$= \dfrac{45}{1}$ **Simplify fraction.**

▶ **Answer** The ratio of time spent in line to time spent on the ride is 45 : 1.

Animated Math at classzone.com

Comparing Ratios To compare ratios, you can write them as fractions and compare the fractions. You can also compare ratios in their decimal form.

EXAMPLE 3 · Comparing Ratios

Music According to the table, who has the greater ratio of rock CDs to pop CDs, Luis or Ana?

	Rock	Pop	Hip-hop
Luis	9	24	16
Ana	28	70	40

SOLUTION

REWRITE FRACTIONS
Need help with writing fractions as decimals? See p. 199.

STEP 1 Write the ratios as fractions.

Luis   **Ana**

$\dfrac{\text{Rock}}{\text{Pop}} = \dfrac{9}{24}$ $\dfrac{\text{Rock}}{\text{Pop}} = \dfrac{28}{70}$

STEP 2 Write the fractions as decimals. $= 0.375$ $= 0.4$

▶ **Answer** Because $0.4 > 0.375$, Ana has a greater ratio of rock to pop CDs.

✓ **GUIDED PRACTICE** | for Examples 2 and 3

2. **What If?** In Example 2, suppose you wait for $1\frac{1}{3}$ hours. Find the ratio of time in line to time on the ride.

3. In Example 3, who has a greater ratio of pop CDs to hip-hop CDs?

4. In Example 3, who has a greater ratio of hip-hop CDs to rock CDs?

8.1 EXERCISES

HOMEWORK KEY

★ = STANDARDIZED TEST PRACTICE
Exs. 22, 50, 51, 55, 57, 59, and 65

◯ = HINTS AND HOMEWORK HELP
for Exs. 5, 15, 17, 23, 47 at classzone.com

SKILL PRACTICE

1. VOCABULARY What do you call two ratios that have the same value?

SEE EXAMPLE 1
on p. 399 for
Exs. 2–5

WRITING RATIOS Write the ratio of the first number to the second number in three ways.

2. 1, 7   **3.** 1, 1   **4.** 3, 10   **5.** 15, 2

SIMPLIFYING RATIOS Write the ratio as a fraction in simplest form.

SEE EXAMPLE 2
on p. 400 for
Exs. 6–26

6. $\frac{7}{14}$ **7.** $\frac{12}{15}$ **8.** 8 : 14   **9.** 9 : 30

10. 9 to 5   **11.** 20 to 35   **12.** 32 : 48   **13.** 30 : 75

14. 10 to 64   **15.** 65 to 130   **16.** $\frac{54}{72}$ **17.** $\frac{6}{33}$

18. $\frac{26}{91}$ **19.** $\frac{18}{63}$ **20.** 12 to 35   **21.** 56 to 119

22. ★ **MULTIPLE CHOICE** Which ratio is *not* equivalent to 6 to 10?

(A) 6 : 10   **(B)** 3 : 5   **(C)** $\frac{3}{5}$ **(D)** $\frac{5}{3}$

MEASUREMENT Write the ratio of the first measurement to the second measurement. Write both measurements using the same unit.

23. 2 lb, 18 oz   **24.** 600 m, 5 km   **25.** 7 min, 25 sec

26. ERROR ANALYSIS Zach wants to find the ratio of his T-shirts to jeans. He has 14 T-shirts and 9 pairs of jeans. Describe and correct his error.

$$\times \quad \frac{\text{T-shirts}}{\text{Jeans}} = \frac{9}{14}$$

COMPARING RATIOS Copy and complete the statement using <, >, or =.

SEE EXAMPLE 3
on p. 400 for
Exs. 27–35

27. 9 : 15 ? 8 : 20   **28.** 18 : 12 ? 54 : 36   **29.** 72 : 96 ? 56 : 80

30. 10 : 12 ? 48 : 72   **31.** 81 : 63 ? 60 : 35   **32.** 12 : 51 ? 20 : 85

33. 12 : 16 ? 21 : 28   **34.** 18 : 63 ? 20 : 75   **35.** 51 : 39 ? 36 : 27

ORDERING RATIOS Write the ratios in order from least to greatest.

36. 5 : 8, 3 : 6, 15 : 5   **37.** 4 : 3, 6 : 5, 11 : 9   **38.** 3 : 8, 1 : 7, 2 : 9

ALGEBRA Find a value of x that makes the two ratios equivalent.

39. x to 6, 20 to 24   **40.** x to 72, 5 to 8   **41.** x to 12, 6 to 9

42. x to 16, 9 to 12   **43.** x to 5, 2 to 8   **44.** x to 6, 9 to 15

45. CHALLENGE The ratio of a to b is 3 to 8, and the ratio of b to c is 4 to 5. What is the ratio of a to the sum of a, b, and c?

PROBLEM SOLVING

SEE EXAMPLE 1
on p. 399 for
Ex. 46

46. WRITING RATIOS Count the number of ribbons and the number of trophies. Write the ratio of ribbons to trophies.

STUDENT RATIOS The table shows the numbers of boys and girls in the 7th and 8th grades at a school. Use the table to write the specified ratio.

SEE EXAMPLE 2
on p. 400 for
Exs. 47–54

47. 8th grade girls to 8th grade boys

48. 7th grade girls to all 7th graders

49. 8th grade boys to all 8th graders

	Boys	Girls
7th	48	42
8th	36	44

50. ★ MULTIPLE CHOICE You used 3 yards of fleece to make a blanket and 2 feet of fleece to make a vest. What is the ratio of fleece used for the blanket to fleece used for the vest?

(A) $\frac{2}{9}$ (B) $\frac{2}{3}$ (C) $\frac{3}{2}$ (D) $\frac{9}{2}$

51. ★ WRITING For a fundraiser, the ratio of tickets you sold to tickets your friend sold was 11 to 5. Does this mean that you sold 11 raffle tickets and your friend sold 5 raffle tickets? *Explain* your reasoning.

52. SCIENCE There are about 4000 known kinds of lizards and 1600 known kinds of snakes. Write the ratio of known kinds of lizards to known kinds of snakes.

53. TIME RATIOS You spend a total of $1\frac{3}{4}$ hours at a restaurant. You spend 20 minutes eating. What is the ratio of your time spent at the restaurant to your time spent eating?

Jackson's chameleon, Madagascar

54. ART A recipe for papier-mâché paste uses 2 quarts of white glue and 2 pints of water. What is the ratio of pints of glue to pints of water?

SEE EXAMPLE 3
on p. 400 for
Exs. 55, 56

55. ★ SHORT RESPONSE In a basketball game, Albert made 11 out of 15 free throws and Jake made 10 out of 13 free throws. Who had the greater ratio of free throws made to free throws attempted? *Explain* your reasoning.

56. HIGHER EDUCATION The table shows the number of men and women who earned master's degrees in the United States in 1970 and in 1998.

a. For each year, write the ratio of degrees earned by men to all degrees earned. Repeat for women. Express the ratios as decimals rounded to the nearest hundredth.

Master's Degrees Earned		
Year	1970	1998
Men	126,000	184,000
Women	83,000	246,000

b. Which of the two ratios showing the degrees earned by men in part (a) is less? Which ratio is less for the women? *Describe* how the ratios for men and the ratios for women changed over time.

57. ★ OPEN-ENDED MATH Ashley has 10 CDs in her collection and Carrie has 16 CDs. Ashley adds *x* CDs to her collection and Carrie adds *y* CDs. Find two possible values for *x* and *y* so that the ratio of Ashley's CDs to Carrie's CDs remains the same. *Explain* how you found your answer.

58. CHECKING REASONABLENESS Use the diagram to write the ratio of the distance the person ran to the distance the dog ran. Write your answer as a fraction with a numerator of 1. *Describe* how the diagram can help you check that your answer is reasonable.

Distance run in 15 seconds

150 ft   97 yd

59. ★ EXTENDED RESPONSE In this exercise, you'll compare the areas of two squares when one square has sides that are twice as long as the other.

 a. **Use Algebra** One square has side length *s* and another square has side length 2*s*. Find the ratio of the area of the larger square to the area of the smaller square.

 b. **Draw a Diagram** Choose a value for the side length *s* of a square. Draw a square with this side length on graph paper. Then draw a square with side length 2*s* on graph paper. Find the ratio of the area of the larger square to the area of the smaller square.

 c. **Compare** Compare and contrast the two methods.

60. CHALLENGE Is it always possible to find whole numbers *a* and *b* where $\frac{a}{b} > \frac{a}{a+b}$? where $\frac{a}{b} = \frac{a}{a+b}$? where $\frac{a}{b} < \frac{a}{a+b}$? Give examples to support your answers.

 NEW JERSEY MIXED REVIEW  **TEST PRACTICE** at classzone.com

61. Which of the following relationships is best represented by the data in the graph?

 (A) Side length and perimeter of a square

 (B) Side length and area of a square

 (C) Perimeter and area of a square

 (D) Width and length of a rectangle

62. Camilla spent half of her money on a shirt and half of the remaining amount on a CD. After she spent $6.50 on lunch, she had $12.10 left. How much money did Camilla originally have?

 (A) $37.20   **(B)** $74.40   **(C)** $111.60   **(D)** $223.20

8.2 Rates

 4.1.A.3 Understand and use ratios, proportions, and percents (including percents greater than 100 and less than 1) in a variety of situations.

Before You used ratios to compare two quantities.

Now You'll use rates to compare two quantities with different units.

Why? So you can find unit rates of speed, as in Ex. 44.

KEY VOCABULARY

• **rate,** *p. 404*
• **unit rate,** *p. 404*

ACTIVITY

You can rewrite fractions to compare two rates.

STEP 1 **Count** the number of times your heart beats in 10 seconds. Use a watch. Record your result as a fraction.

STEP 2 **Ask** your partner to count his or her pulse for 15 seconds. Record the result as a fraction.

STEP 3 **Decide** whose pulse is faster. Explain how you decided.

A **rate** is a ratio of two quantities measured in different units. A **unit rate** is a rate that has a denominator of 1 unit. The three unit rates below are equivalent.

READING
....
The fraction bar, the slash, and the word "per" mean "for every."

$$\frac{15 \text{ mi}}{1 \text{ h}} \qquad 15 \text{ mi/h} \qquad 15 \text{ miles per hour}$$

EXAMPLE 1 Finding a Unit Rate

Kudzu During peak growing season, the kudzu vine can grow 6 inches in 12 hours. What is the peak growth rate of kudzu in inches per hour?

SOLUTION

First, write a rate comparing the inches grown to the hours it took to grow. Then rewrite the fraction so that the denominator is 1.

$$\frac{6 \text{ in.}}{12 \text{ h}} = \frac{6 \text{ in.} \div 12}{12 \text{ h} \div 12} \qquad \text{Divide numerator and denominator by 12.}$$

$$= \frac{0.5 \text{ in.}}{1 \text{ h}} \qquad \text{Simplify.}$$

▶ **Answer** The peak growth rate of kudzu is about 0.5 inch per hour.

Animated Math at classzone.com

Average Speed If you know the distance traveled and the travel time for a moving object, you can find the average rate, or average speed, by dividing the distance by the time.

$$\text{average rate} = \frac{\text{distance}}{\text{time}}$$

Average rate is usually written as a unit rate.

 EXAMPLE 2 Standardized Test Practice

Speed Skating A skater took 2 minutes 30 seconds to complete a 1500 meter race. What was the skater's average speed?

(A) $\dfrac{1 \text{ sec}}{100 \text{ m}}$ (B) $\dfrac{1 \text{ sec}}{10 \text{ m}}$ (C) $\dfrac{10 \text{ m}}{1 \text{ sec}}$ (D) $\dfrac{100 \text{ m}}{1 \text{ sec}}$

ELIMINATE CHOICES
The units for speed should be distance over time, not time over distance. So choices A and B can be eliminated.

SOLUTION

STEP 1 **Rewrite** the time so that the units are the same.

2 min + 30 sec = 120 sec + 30 sec = 150 sec

STEP 2 **Find** the average speed by dividing the distance by the time.

$$\frac{1500 \text{ m}}{150 \text{ sec}} = \frac{1500 \text{ m} \div 150}{150 \text{ sec} \div 150}$$ **Divide numerator and denominator by 150.**

$$= \frac{10 \text{ m}}{1 \text{ sec}}$$ **Simplify.**

▶ **Answer** The skater's average speed was 10 meters per second. The correct answer is C. (A) (B) (C) (D)

EXAMPLE 3 Comparing Unit Rates

Pasta A store sells the same pasta the following two ways: 10 pounds of bulk pasta for $15.00 and 2 pounds of packaged pasta for $3.98. To determine which is the better buy, find the unit price for both types.

FIND UNIT PRICE
A unit price is a type of unit rate.

Bulk pasta: $\dfrac{\$15.00}{10 \text{ lb}} = \dfrac{\$1.50}{1 \text{ lb}}$ **Write as a unit rate.**

Packaged pasta: $\dfrac{\$3.98}{2 \text{ lb}} = \dfrac{\$1.99}{1 \text{ lb}}$ **Write as a unit rate.**

▶ **Answer** The bulk pasta is the better buy because it costs less per pound.

✓ **GUIDED PRACTICE** | for Examples 1, 2, and 3

1. **Biking** You biked 68 miles in 4 days. Find the unit rate.

2. **Average Speed** It takes you 1 minute 40 seconds to walk 550 feet. What is your average speed?

3. **Compare Costs** Which of the following is the better buy: 2 batteries for $1.50 or 6 batteries for $4.80?

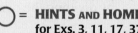
SKILL PRACTICE

VOCABULARY Copy and complete.

1. A(n) __?__ is a ratio of two measures with different units.

2. Dollars per pound and miles per hour are real-world examples of __?__ .

FINDING UNIT RATE Find the unit rate.

SEE EXAMPLE 1
on p. 404
for Exs. 3–18

3. $\dfrac{12 \text{ L}}{2 \text{ days}}$

4. $\dfrac{\$56}{8 \text{ lb}}$

5. $\dfrac{\$16}{5 \text{ persons}}$

6. $\dfrac{\$21}{6 \text{ oz}}$

7. $\dfrac{153 \text{ m}}{5 \text{ sec}}$

8. $\dfrac{48 \text{ students}}{3 \text{ teachers}}$

9. $\dfrac{24 \text{ servings}}{9 \text{ packages}}$

10. $\dfrac{\$124.50}{6 \text{ tickets}}$

11. $\dfrac{468 \text{ visitors}}{4 \text{ days}}$

12. $15 for 2 plants

13. 9 cups in 5 pies

14. 14 cups for 8 servings

15. 7 phone calls in 2 hours

16. 12 inches in 4 years

17. 45 e-mails in 5 days

18. ★ **MULTIPLE CHOICE** You spend $36 for 8 hats. What is the unit rate?

  (A) $\dfrac{\$.22}{1 \text{ hat}}$ **(B)** $\dfrac{\$4.50}{1 \text{ hat}}$ **(C)** $\dfrac{\$9}{1 \text{ hat}}$ **(D)** $\dfrac{\$36}{1 \text{ hat}}$

SEE EXAMPLE 2
on p. 405
for Exs. 19–26

19. ★ **MULTIPLE CHOICE** Which speed is *not* equivalent to 55 mi/h?

  (A) $\dfrac{110 \text{ mi}}{2 \text{ h}}$ **(B)** $\dfrac{265 \text{ mi}}{6 \text{ h}}$ **(C)** $\dfrac{385 \text{ mi}}{7 \text{ h}}$ **(D)** $\dfrac{550 \text{ mi}}{10 \text{ h}}$

FINDING AVERAGE SPEED In Exercises 20–25, find the average speed.

20. 27 meters in 18 seconds

21. 51 meters in 4 minutes 15 seconds

22. 160 feet in 5 minutes 20 seconds

23. 700 feet in 1 minute 10 seconds

24. 240 kilometers in 3 hours 20 minutes

25. 90 miles in 2 hours 40 minutes

26. **FINDING AVERAGE SPEED** Find the average speed of a butterfly that flies 24.4 miles in 4 hours.

27. **FINDING UNIT PRICE** You buy a package of 6 pairs of socks for $8.94. Write this rate as a unit price.

28. **ERROR ANALYSIS** You spend $19.50 for 3 books. Describe and correct the error made in finding the unit rate for the books.

$$\times \quad \dfrac{19.50}{3} = 6.50$$
$$6.50 \text{ books/\$}$$

CHALLENGE Write the average speed in *feet per second*. Round to the nearest whole number.

29. 75 mi in 2 h   **30.** 150 mi in 3 h   **31.** 100 mi in 4 h   **32.** 425 mi in 9 h

SEE EXAMPLE 2
on p. 405
for Exs. 33–34

33. ★ **SHORT RESPONSE** It takes you 2 hours 30 minutes to travel 155 miles by car. *Explain* how to find the car's average speed in miles per hour.

34. **TRAIN SPEEDS** A bullet train in Japan can travel 93 miles in 30 minutes. Find its average speed in miles per hour.

35. **HOVERCRAFT SPEEDS** A hovercraft scooter is traveling at 12 miles per hour. At this rate, how many minutes will it take the hovercraft scooter to travel 1 mile?

SEE EXAMPLE 3
on p. 405
for Exs. 36–38

36. **GUIDED PROBLEM SOLVING** To be considered a "fast talker," you should be able to clearly speak at least 350 words in 60 seconds. Sean can speak 60 words in 15 seconds.

   a. Write the "fast talker" rate as a unit rate. Round your answer to the nearest tenth.

   b. Write Sean's rate of talking as a unit rate.

   c. *Compare* the unit rates. Is Sean a "fast talker"?

BETTER BUY In Exercises 37 and 38, determine which is the better buy.

37.

2 qt
$2.78

1.5 qt
$2.25

38.

17 oz
$3.40

14 oz
$3.08

39. ★ **MULTIPLE CHOICE** A school has 892 students. There are about 10 computers for every 42 students. *Estimate* to find about how many computers the school has.

   (A) 20   **(B)** 90   **(C)** 200   **(D)** 860

40. ★ **WRITING** Is every ratio a rate? Is every rate a ratio? *Explain*.

41. ★ **MULTIPLE CHOICE** There are 275 students going on a field trip. The school wants a student-teacher ratio less than or equal to 15 students to 1 teacher. What is the least number of teachers needed?

   (A) 16   **(B)** 17   **(C)** 18   **(D)** 19

SCIENCE The *density* of a substance is the ratio of its mass to its volume. Write the density of the substance as a unit rate.

42. A 500 cubic centimeter sample of sea water has a mass of 514 grams.

43. A 300 cubic centimeter sample of an iceberg has a mass of 267 grams.

44. ◆ **MULTIPLE REPRESENTATIONS** The diagram shows the maximum distance a NASA Mars rover can travel in the given amount of time.

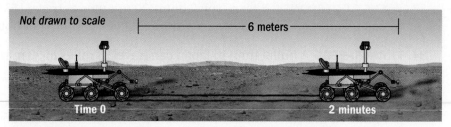

Not drawn to scale 　　　　 6 meters

Time 0 　　　　　　　　　　　　　　 2 minutes

   a. Write a Ratio Write the maximum speed of a rover as a unit rate in kilometers per day.

   b. Make a Table Make a table that shows the number of kilometers a rover can move at maximum speed in 1, 2, 3, 4, and 5 days.

   c. 🆇🆈 **Write an Equation** Write an equation relating the number of kilometers *d* a rover can move at maximum speed in *t* days.

45. ★ **EXTENDED RESPONSE** A recipe for rice pudding uses $\frac{1}{2}$ cup of rice and serves 6 people.

   a. Write the cups of rice per person as a unit rate.

   b. How many cups of rice do you need to serve 75 people?

   c. One cup of rice weighs 6.4 ounces. How many ounces of rice do you need to serve 75 people?

   d. A 1-pound box of rice costs $.99. How much does the rice for 75 servings of rice pudding cost? *Explain* your reasoning.

46. **REASONING** You run the first 2 miles of a 5 mile run at a rate of 300 yards per minute. Then you run the last 3 miles at a rate of 220 yards per minute. Is your average rate for the run 260 yards per minute? *Explain* your reasoning.

47. **CHALLENGE** Emma and Trevor start walking in opposite directions from the same point. Emma walks 0.8 kilometer every 10 minutes, and Trevor walks 2.8 kilometers every 30 minutes. How far apart are Emma and Trevor after 1 hour? after 2 hours?

NEW JERSEY MIXED REVIEW 　　　　 🔍 **TEST PRACTICE** at classzone.com

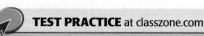

48. Which of the following relationships is best represented by the data in the graph?

   Ⓐ Conversion of feet to inches

   Ⓑ Conversion of kilometers to meters

   Ⓒ Conversion of meters to centimeters

   Ⓓ Conversion of miles to yards

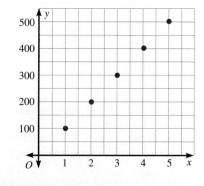

8.3 Slope

 4.1.A.3 Understand and use ratios, proportions, and percents (including percents greater than 100 and less than 1) in a variety of situations.

Before	You used a table to graph a linear function.
Now	You'll find the slope of a line.
Why?	So you can find pay rates, as in Ex. 30.

KEY VOCABULARY
• slope, *p. 409*

ACTIVITY

You can use ratios to describe the slope of a line.

STEP 1 **Draw** an *x*-axis and a *y*-axis on graph paper.

STEP 2 **Start** at the origin. Move 3 units up and 2 units to the right. Plot this point and label it *A*.

STEP 3 **Start** at *A*. Move 6 units up and 4 units to the right. Plot this point and label it *B*.

STEP 4 **Draw** a line through *A*, *B*, and the origin.

STEP 5 **Find** the ratio of rise to run for each of the movements described in Steps 2 and 3. What do you notice?

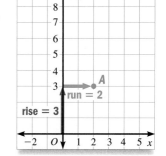

RISE AND RUN

Rise is positive when moving up and negative when moving down.

Run is positive when moving to the right and negative when moving to the left.

The **slope** of a nonvertical line is the ratio of the rise (vertical change) to the run (horizontal change) between any two points on the line, as shown below. A line has a constant slope.

$$\text{slope} = \frac{\text{rise}}{\text{run}} = \frac{-1}{5} = -\frac{1}{5}$$

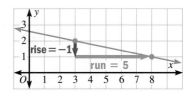

Examples of lines with positive, negative, and zero slopes are shown below. The slope of a vertical line is undefined.

A line that rises from left to right has a **positive** slope.	A line that falls from left to right has a **negative** slope.	A horizontal line has a **slope of 0.**
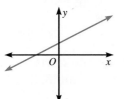	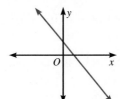	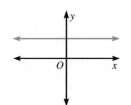

EXAMPLE 1 Finding the Slope of a Line

Find the slope of a line by finding the ratio of the rise to the run between any two points on the line.

a.
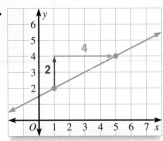

b.
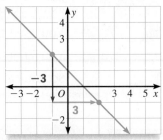

$$\text{slope} = \frac{\text{rise}}{\text{run}} = \frac{2}{4}$$
$$= \frac{1}{2}$$

$$\text{slope} = \frac{\text{rise}}{\text{run}} = \frac{-3}{3}$$
$$= -1$$

Slope as a Rate When the graph of a line represents a real-world situation, the slope of the line can often be interpreted as a rate.

EXAMPLE 2 Interpreting Slope as a Rate

Volcanoes The graph represents the distance traveled by a lava flow over time. To find the speed of the lava flow, find the slope of the line.

SOLUTION

$$\text{slope} = \frac{\text{rise}}{\text{run}} \qquad \text{Definition of slope}$$

$$= \frac{6 \text{ mi}}{4 \text{ h}} \qquad \text{Write rise over run.}$$

$$= \frac{1.5 \text{ mi}}{1 \text{ h}} \qquad \text{Find unit rate.}$$

▶ **Answer** The speed of the lava flow is 1.5 miles per hour.

Animated Math at classzone.com

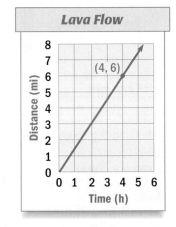

✓ **GUIDED PRACTICE** for Examples 1 and 2

1. Plot the points (3, 4) and (6, 3). Then find the slope of the line that passes through the points.

2. **What If?** In Example 2, suppose the line starts at the origin and passes through the point (3, 6). Find the speed of the lava flow.

EXAMPLE 3 Using Slope to Draw a Line

Draw the line that has a slope of –3 and passes through (2, 5).

STEP 1 Plot (2, 5).

STEP 2 Write the slope as a fraction.

$$\text{slope} = \frac{\text{rise}}{\text{run}} = \frac{-3}{1}$$

STEP 3 Move 3 units down and 1 unit to the right to plot a second point.

STEP 4 Draw a line through the two points.

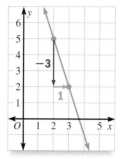

:**ANOTHER WAY**
:You can also write the
:slope as $\frac{3}{-1}$. Move
:3 units up and 1 unit left
:to plot a second point.

✓ **GUIDED PRACTICE** for Example 3

3. Draw the line that has a slope of $\frac{1}{3}$ and passes through (2, 5).

4. Draw the line that has a slope of −4 and passes through (−1, 3).

8.3 EXERCISES

HOMEWORK KEY

★ = **STANDARDIZED TEST PRACTICE**
Exs. 12, 13, 31, 32, 33, 37, 42, and 57

○ = **HINTS AND HOMEWORK HELP**
for Exs. 5, 9, 15, 31 at classzone.com

SKILL PRACTICE

1. VOCABULARY Copy and complete: The slope of a nonvertical line is the ratio of the ? to the ? between any two points on the line.

2. VOCABULARY What is the slope of a vertical line?

FINDING SLOPE Find the slope of the line.

:**SEE EXAMPLE 1**
:on p. 410
:for Exs. 3–11

3.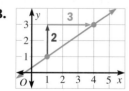

4.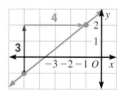

5.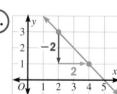

6.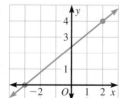

7.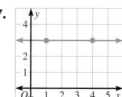

8.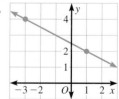

DRAWING LINES Draw the graph of the line that passes through the points. Then find the slope of the line.

9. (3, 4), (5, 6)　　　　**10.** (2, 5), (5, −2)　　　　**11.** (−1, −3), (3, −4)

SEE EXAMPLE 1
on p. 410
for Exs. 12–14

12. ★ **MULTIPLE CHOICE** What is the slope of the blue line?

     Ⓐ $-\dfrac{3}{2}$ Ⓑ $-\dfrac{2}{3}$ Ⓒ $\dfrac{2}{3}$ Ⓓ $\dfrac{3}{2}$

13. ★ **MULTIPLE CHOICE** What is the slope of the red line?

     Ⓐ $-\dfrac{3}{2}$ Ⓑ $-\dfrac{2}{3}$ Ⓒ $\dfrac{2}{3}$ Ⓓ $\dfrac{3}{2}$

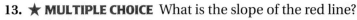

14. **ERROR ANALYSIS** Describe and correct the error made in finding the slope of the line passing through $(0, 0)$ and $(3, 7)$.

$$\times \quad slope = \dfrac{rise}{run} = \dfrac{3}{7}$$

USING SLOPE Draw the line that has the given slope and passes through the given point.

SEE EXAMPLE 3
on p. 411
for Exs. 15–20

⑮ slope = 3, $(3, -1)$ 16. slope = 1, $(0, -1)$ 17. slope = -2, $(4, 0)$

18. slope = $\dfrac{2}{3}$, $(-2, -2)$ 19. slope = $\dfrac{3}{4}$, $(-2, -1)$ 20. slope = $-\dfrac{5}{6}$, $(5, 5)$

COMPARING SLOPES Copy and complete the statement using <, >, or =.

     line a: passes through $(1, -3)$ and $(2, 0)$

     line b: passes through $(1, 1)$ and $(7, 3)$

     line c: slope = $\dfrac{1}{3}$, passes through $(-2, 5)$

21. slope of line a _?_ slope of line b 22. slope of line b _?_ slope of line c

23. slope of line c _?_ slope of line a 24. slope of line b _?_ slope of a horizontal line

ⓧⓨ ALGEBRA Use the points and slope of the line to find the value of a.

25. slope = $\dfrac{a}{2}$, $(-2, -1)$, $(2, 5)$ 26. slope = $\dfrac{-3}{a}$, $(-3, -1)$, $(1, 5)$

27. slope = $-\dfrac{4}{3}$, $(-3, 4)$, $(6, a)$ 28. slope = $\dfrac{9}{4}$, $(a, 7)$, $(2, -11)$

29. **CHALLENGE** Use a rise of $\dfrac{1}{3}$ and a run of $-\dfrac{5}{6}$ to find the slope of a line. Graph the line with this slope that passes through $\left(-\dfrac{1}{3}, 4\dfrac{1}{3}\right)$. Name two points on the line whose coordinates are whole numbers.

PROBLEM SOLVING

SEE EXAMPLE 2
on p. 410
for Ex. 30

30. **GUIDED PROBLEM SOLVING** Use the graph, which shows two pay rates for baby-sitting.

     a. Find two points on each line.

     b. Use the points to find each person's pay rate.

     c. Compare the answers in part (b) to find who has the greater pay rate.

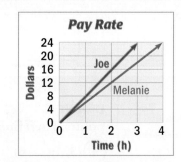

SEE EXAMPLE 2
on p. 410
for Exs. 31–32

31. ★ **OPEN-ENDED MATH** Give an example of a rate describing a relation that can be represented as a line in a coordinate plane. *Explain* your example.

CANOEING In Exercises 32 and 33, use the graph representing the distance that you traveled in a canoe for 2 hours.

32. ★ **MULTIPLE CHOICE** What was your speed?

    (**A**) 1 mile per hour   (**B**) 2 miles per hour

    (**C**) 3 miles per hour   (**D**) 4 miles per hour

33. ★ **SHORT RESPONSE** You went canoeing the following day and traveled 3.5 miles in 1.75 hours. How does this compare to your speed the previous day? *Explain.*

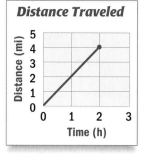

REASONING In Exercises 34–36, use the graph showing the distance you are from home and the time since you left home while you are on a walk.

34. Between which two points were you walking the fastest?

35. What could explain the slope of the line between points B and C?

36. The slope between points O and A is positive and the slope between points C and D is negative. *Interpret* the meaning of positive and negative slopes in the context of this problem.

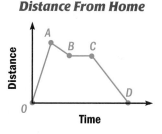

37. ★ **EXTENDED RESPONSE** Use the graph showing the distance traveled by two sea turtles.

  a. Which turtle swam at a greater speed? *Explain.*

  b. About how many more feet per second is the faster sea turtle swimming than the slower sea turtle? *Explain* how you found your answer.

  c. A third turtle swims at a rate of 2.25 feet per second. How does the swimming rate of the third turtle compare with the rates of the other two turtles? *Explain* your reasoning.

38. **REASONING** A line passing through the origin has a negative slope. Through which quadrants does the line pass? *Explain.*

GEOMETRY In Exercises 39–41, use the table that lists the side lengths of four squares.

39. Copy and complete the table.

40. Graph your results as points whose x-coordinates are the side lengths and y-coordinates are the perimeters. Draw a line through the points.

Side length	1	2	3	4
Perimeter	?	?	?	?

41. **INTERPRET** *Explain* what the slope of the line in Exercise 40 tells about the relationship between the side length of a square and its perimeter.

42. ★ **WRITING** You are given a graph of a line that shows the cost of mixed nuts based on the number of pounds. *Describe* how to use the graph to find the cost per pound of the nuts.

43. **CHALLENGE** The points $(x - 4, y)$ and $(x, y + b)$ lie on a line. Find the slope of the line.

44. **CHALLENGE** *Describe* three real-world situations whose graphs would have respectively a positive slope, a negative slope, and zero slope. Choose situations that are not in this lesson.

NEW JERSEY MIXED REVIEW

 TEST PRACTICE at classzone.com

45. A rowing crew took 6 minutes and 40 seconds to finish a 2000-meter race. What was the team's average speed?

   (A) $\dfrac{1 \text{ sec}}{50 \text{ m}}$ (B) $\dfrac{1 \text{ sec}}{5 \text{ m}}$ (C) $\dfrac{5 \text{ m}}{1 \text{ sec}}$ (D) $\dfrac{50 \text{ m}}{1 \text{ sec}}$

46. Which description relates the position n of a term in the sequence and the value of the term?

   (A) Add 4 to n

   (B) Multiply n by 5

   (C) Divide n by 5

   (D) Subtract 4 from n

Position n	1	2	3	4	5
Value of term	5	10	15	20	25

QUIZ *for Lessons 8.1–8.3*

In Exercises 1–4, write the ratio as a fraction in simplest form. *(p. 399)*

1. $\dfrac{12}{16}$ 2. 5 to 6   3. 18 to 4   4. 20 : 5

Copy and complete the statement using <, >, or =. *(p. 399)*

5. 12 : 20 ? 9 : 15   6. 11 : 12 ? 32 : 36   7. 24 : 18 ? 44 : 30

8. **ZOOLOGY** The number of teeth in the upper and lower jaws for each of two animals is shown in the table. Which animal has the greater ratio of teeth in the upper jaw to teeth in the lower jaw? *(p. 399)*

Animal	Upper teeth	Lower teeth
Elk	14	20
Bear	20	22

Find the unit rate. *(p. 404)*

9. $2.25 for 5 pounds   10. $6 for 5 pens   11. 4 laps in 10 minutes

Draw the graph of the line that passes through the points. Then find the slope of the line. *(p. 409)*

12. (3, 4), (0, −2)   13. (1, 1), (−3, −3)   14. (−5, 5), (−1, 3)

8.3 Finding Slope

EXAMPLE Find the slope of the line $y = \frac{2}{3}x$.

SOLUTION

STEP 1 Press (2 ÷ 3) x .

STEP 2 Press 2nd [FORMAT] and make sure that the grid is on.

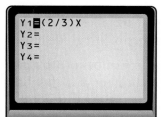

STEP 3 Press ZOOM 4 to graph the line.

STEP 4 Use the grid to find the slope of the line.

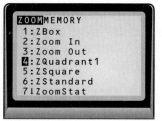

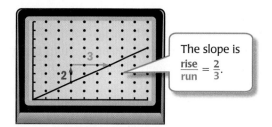

The slope is $\frac{rise}{run} = \frac{2}{3}$.

PRACTICE Graph the line. Then find the slope of the line.

1. $y = 4x$ 2. $y = \frac{3}{4}x$ 3. $y = -3x + 8$ 4. $y = -\frac{1}{3}x + 5$

DRAW CONCLUSIONS

5. **WRITING** What is the relationship between the slope of the line and the coefficient of x in each of Exercises 1–4?

6. **REASONING** What do you think is the slope of the line $y = \frac{2}{5}x$? Graph the line and find its slope to check your answer.

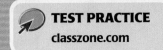
Lessons 8.1–8.3

1. COMPARING PRICES Soup comes in three different sizes. An 8-ounce can costs $1.28, a 12-ounce can costs $1.80, and a 16-ounce can costs $2.48. What can you conclude?

   A. The 8-ounce can is the best buy.

   B. The 12-ounce can is the best buy.

   C. The 16-ounce can is the best buy.

   D. Two 8-ounce cans cost the same as one 16-ounce can.

2. GARDEN You have a garden in the shape of a rectangle. The ratio of the length of the garden to the width of the garden is 8 : 3. Which measurements CANNOT be the dimensions of the garden?

   A. 24 feet by 9 feet

   B. 40 feet by 15 feet

   C. 64 feet by 24 feet

   D. 82 feet by 32 feet

3. CAR SPEED Two battery-operated toy cars were tested to see how fast and consistently they travel. The data are shown in the graph. What is the speed of each car?

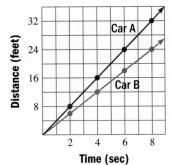

   A. Car A: 4 ft/sec   Car B: 3 ft/sec

   B. Car A: 3 ft/sec   Car B: 4 ft/sec

   C. Car A: 32 ft/sec   Car B: 24 ft/sec

   D. Car A: 24 ft/sec   Car B: 32 ft/sec

4. ENROLLMENT The table shows the number of boys and girls in grades 9–12 at a school. How can you find the ratio of girls in 9th grade to girls in the whole school?

Grade	Boys	Girls
9	110	88
10	75	90
11	70	80
12	84	63

   A. Divide the number of 9th grade girls by the number of 9th grade boys.

   B. Divide the number of 9th grade girls by the total number of high school boys.

   C. Divide the total number of high school girls by the number of 9th grade girls.

   D. Divide the number of 9th grade girls by the total number of high school girls.

5. TORTOISE EGGS The female Angonoka tortoise lays eggs in groups called clutches. One female tortoise lays 5 clutches and a total of 30 eggs. What is her average number of eggs per clutch?

   A. 5

   B. 6

   C. 7

   D. 30

6. OPEN-ENDED During a long trip, the number of gallons of gasoline y in your car's tank after driving x miles is given by the function $y = 15 - \frac{1}{24}x$.

   • Make an input-output table for 0, 60, 120, 180, 240, 300, and 360 miles.

   • Use the table to graph the function.

   • As the number of miles traveled increases, what happens to the number of gallons of gasoline in your car's tank?

INVESTIGATION
Use before Lesson 8.4

GOAL
Use a model to find a missing term in a proportion.

MATERIALS
• chips of two different colors (or pennies and dimes)

8.4 Modeling Proportions

An equation stating that two ratios are equivalent, such as $\frac{2}{4} = \frac{1}{2}$, is called a *proportion*. You can use a chip model to find a missing term in a proportion.

EXPLORE Use a chip model to find the missing term in the proportion $\frac{2}{3} = \frac{n}{6}$.

STEP 1 Model the proportion using red and yellow chips.

> The ratio tells you there should be 2 red chips for every 3 yellow chips.

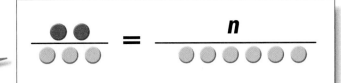

STEP 2 Because the first ratio has a denominator of 3, separate the 6 yellow chips in the second ratio into groups of 3.

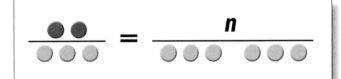

STEP 3 Place 2 red chips in the numerator of the second ratio for every 3 yellow chips in the denominator. Four red chips are placed, so $n = 4$.

PRACTICE Use a chip model to find the missing term.

1. $\frac{1}{3} = \frac{x}{15}$ 2. $\frac{n}{6} = \frac{5}{2}$ 3. $\frac{z}{8} = \frac{3}{2}$ 4. $\frac{3}{4} = \frac{s}{16}$

DRAW CONCLUSIONS

5. **WRITING** In Step 2, how many times more yellow chips are in the second ratio than in the first? How could you use this relationship to find n?

6. **OPEN-ENDED** Find two more ratios that are equivalent to $\frac{2}{3}$. *Explain* how to find ratios that are equivalent to any ratio you are given.

8.4 Writing and Solving Proportions

 4.1.A.3 Understand and use ratios, proportions, and percents (including percents greater than 100 and less than 1) in a variety of situations.

Before You learned how to write ratios.

Now You'll solve proportions using equivalent ratios and algebra.

Why? So you can find calories burned, as in Example 1.

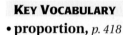

KEY VOCABULARY
• proportion, *p. 418*

Sports A person burned about 210 calories while in-line skating for 30 minutes. About how many calories would the person burn while in-line skating for 60 minutes? In Example 1, you will use a *proportion* to answer this question.

KEY CONCEPT *For Your Notebook*

Proportion

Words A **proportion** is an equation that states that two ratios are equivalent.

Numbers $\dfrac{3}{5} = \dfrac{6}{10}$ The proportion is read "3 is to 5 as 6 is to 10."

Algebra $\dfrac{a}{b} = \dfrac{c}{d}$, where b and d are nonzero numbers.

Using Equivalent Ratios When one of the numbers in a proportion is unknown, you can find the number by *solving the proportion*. One way to solve a proportion is to use mental math to find an equivalent ratio.

EXAMPLE 1 Using Equivalent Ratios

Find the number C of calories the person discussed above would burn while in-line skating for 60 minutes by solving the proportion $\dfrac{210}{30} = \dfrac{C}{60}$.

SOLUTION

STEP 1 Ask yourself: What number can you multiply 30 by to get 60?

$$\frac{210}{30} = \frac{C}{60}$$
$\times\ ?$

STEP 2 Because $30 \times 2 = 60$, multiply the numerator by 2 to find C.

$\times\ 2$
$$\frac{210}{30} = \frac{C}{60}$$
$\times\ 2$

▶ **Answer** Because $210 \times 2 = 420$, $C = 420$. So, the person would burn about 420 calories while in-line skating for 60 minutes.

Using Algebra The same method you used to solve division equations in Lesson 7.4 can be used to solve proportions that have the variable in the numerator.

EXAMPLE 2 Solving Proportions Using Algebra

 Solve the proportion $\frac{6}{10} = \frac{x}{25}$.

$$\frac{6}{10} = \frac{x}{25}$$ **Write original proportion.**

$$25 \cdot \frac{6}{10} = 25 \cdot \frac{x}{25}$$ **Multiply each side by 25.**

$$\frac{150}{10} = x$$ **Simplify.**

$$15 = x$$ **Simplify fraction.**

▶ **Answer** The solution is 15.

✓ **GUIDED PRACTICE**   for Examples 1 and 2

Use equivalent ratios to solve the proportion.

1. $\frac{1}{5} = \frac{z}{20}$ **2.** $\frac{8}{3} = \frac{k}{18}$ **3.** $\frac{27}{c} = \frac{9}{12}$ **4.** $\frac{9}{n} = \frac{99}{22}$

Use algebra to solve the proportion.

5. $\frac{4}{14} = \frac{m}{49}$ **6.** $\frac{25}{30} = \frac{x}{12}$ **7.** $\frac{h}{33} = \frac{2}{6}$ **8.** $\frac{b}{8} = \frac{7}{28}$

Setting Up a Proportion A proportion may be set up several ways. Consider the following problem.

> **Yesterday you bought 8 folders for $4.**
> **Today you need to buy 5 more folders.**
> **How much will 5 folders cost?**

The information is arranged in the two tables below, in which x represents the cost of 5 folders. Either of the proportions that follow from the tables can be used to solve the problem.

	Yesterday	Today
Cost	4	x
Folders	8	5

	Folders	Cost
Today	5	x
Yesterday	8	4

Proportion: $\frac{4}{8} = \frac{x}{5}$ Proportion: $\frac{5}{8} = \frac{x}{4}$

So, you may use either the ratios formed by the columns or the rows of the table to write a proportion.

EXAMPLE 3 Writing and Solving a Proportion

Empire State Building The elevators in the Empire State Building can pass 80 floors in 45 seconds. Follow the steps below to find the number of floors that the elevators can pass in 9 seconds.

STEP 1 **Write** a proportion. Let x represent the number of floors passed in 9 seconds.

$$\frac{80}{45} = \frac{x}{9} \longleftarrow \text{floors} \atop \longleftarrow \text{seconds}$$

STEP 2 **Solve** the proportion.

$$\frac{80}{45} = \frac{x}{9}$$ Write original proportion.

$$9 \cdot \frac{80}{45} = 9 \cdot \frac{x}{9}$$ Multiply each side by 9.

$$\frac{720}{45} = x$$ Simplify.

$$16 = x$$ Simplify fraction.

▸**Answer** The elevators can pass 16 floors in 9 seconds.

AVOID ERRORS
Don't confuse numerators and denominators in a proportion. For example:
$$\frac{80 \text{ floors}}{45 \text{ sec}} \neq \frac{9 \text{ sec}}{x \text{ floors}}$$

Animated Math
at classzone.com

✓ **GUIDED PRACTICE** for Example 3

9. **What If?** Suppose the elevators in Example 3 could pass 70 floors in 63 seconds. How many floors could the elevator pass in 9 seconds?

8.4 **EXERCISES**

HOMEWORK KEY

★ = **STANDARDIZED TEST PRACTICE**
    Exs. 19, 26, 32, 41, and 49

○ = **HINTS AND HOMEWORK HELP**
    for Exs. 5, 11, 17, 31 at classzone.com

SKILL PRACTICE

VOCABULARY Copy and complete.

1. An equation that states that two ratios are equivalent is a(n) _?_.

2. The proportion in Step 1 of Example 3 above is read _?_.

SOLVING PROPORTIONS Use equivalent ratios to solve the proportion.

SEE EXAMPLE 1
on p. 418
for Exs. 3–14

3. $\dfrac{5}{6} = \dfrac{x}{18}$

4. $\dfrac{15}{20} = \dfrac{x}{4}$

5. $\dfrac{x}{6} = \dfrac{4}{2}$

6. $\dfrac{x}{5} = \dfrac{5}{25}$

7. $\dfrac{3}{7} = \dfrac{a}{21}$

8. $\dfrac{4}{36} = \dfrac{w}{9}$

9. $\dfrac{2}{s} = \dfrac{18}{45}$

10. $\dfrac{4}{c} = \dfrac{2}{10}$

11. $\dfrac{14}{8} = \dfrac{42}{m}$

12. $\dfrac{51}{z} = \dfrac{3}{2}$

13. $\dfrac{11}{4} = \dfrac{121}{x}$

14. $\dfrac{65}{s} = \dfrac{13}{6}$

SEE EXAMPLE 2
on p. 419
for Exs. 15–18

Ⓧ **USING ALGEBRA** **Use algebra to solve the proportion.**

15. $\dfrac{h}{8} = \dfrac{3}{12}$ **16.** $\dfrac{k}{27} = \dfrac{4}{6}$ **17.** $\dfrac{6}{14} = \dfrac{m}{21}$ **18.** $\dfrac{20}{16} = \dfrac{n}{12}$

SEE EXAMPLE 3
on p. 420
for Exs. 19–25

19. ★ **MULTIPLE CHOICE** A recipe that makes 12 pints of salsa uses 35 tomatoes. Choose the proportion you can use to determine the number t of tomatoes needed to make 2 pints of salsa.

Ⓐ $\dfrac{12}{35} = \dfrac{t}{2}$ Ⓑ $\dfrac{t}{35} = \dfrac{12}{2}$ Ⓒ $\dfrac{35}{12} = \dfrac{t}{2}$ Ⓓ $\dfrac{t}{12} = \dfrac{2}{35}$

WRITING PROPORTIONS **Write and solve the proportion.**

20. 8 is to 3 as w is to 12.

21. 6 is to 16 as z is to 40.

22. p is to 30 as 10 is to 12.

23. m is to 32 as 3 is to 4.

24. 36 is to 42 as d is to 28.

25. 80 is to 100 as n is to 45.

26. ★ **OPEN-ENDED MATH** Write a proportion with an unknown value using the ratio 2 : 5. *Describe* how to solve the proportion using equivalent fractions.

CHALLENGE **Solve the proportion.**

27. $\dfrac{30}{v} = \dfrac{12}{16}$ **28.** $\dfrac{8}{x} = \dfrac{6}{15}$ **29.** $\dfrac{22}{33} = \dfrac{16}{y}$ **30.** $\dfrac{4}{24} = \dfrac{6}{z}$

PROBLEM SOLVING

SEE EXAMPLE 3
on p. 420
for Exs. 31–34

31. **PAINTING** It takes 4 quarts of paint to cover 560 square feet. How many quarts of the same paint are needed to cover 140 square feet?

32. ★ **SHORT RESPONSE** You can buy 3 CDs for $27 from a music club. How many CDs can you buy for $63? *Explain* your reasoning.

33. **NUTRITION** The average American eats 57 pounds of apples over 3 years. At this rate, how many pounds of apples does a person eat in 15 years?

34. **REASONING** Is it possible to write a proportion using $\dfrac{11}{13}$ and $\dfrac{55}{65}$? *Explain* your reasoning.

35. **ERROR ANALYSIS** To make orange food coloring, 2 drops of red are mixed with 3 drops of yellow. Describe and correct the error in the proportion used to find the number r of drops of red to add to 12 drops of yellow.

$$\cancel{\dfrac{3}{2} = \dfrac{r}{12}}$$

36. **PET CARE** The table lists the flour needed to make dough for a given number of dog biscuits. Copy and complete the table.

Biscuits	32	48	?
Flour (cups)	2	?	5

37. Reasoning How long would a 150-pound person have to ballroom dance to burn as many calories as they would while high-energy dancing for 45 minutes? *Explain* your reasoning.

38. Computation How many calories would a 150-pound person burn after 45 minutes of ballroom dancing?

39. Compare To the nearest minute, how much longer would you have to spend ballroom dancing than doing Latin dance to burn 500 calories?

Dancing and Calories

Dancing is not only fun, it's also healthy, because it's an effective means of burning calories. Recent research shows that during 30 minutes of high-energy dancing, like hip-hop or Latin dance, a 150-pound person burns approximately 212 calories. The same person burns roughly 106 calories while ballroom dancing for 30 minutes. So, whatever style of dance you prefer, dancing is a healthy exercise alternative.

40. HISTORY The length of a Viking ship is given below. What is its width?

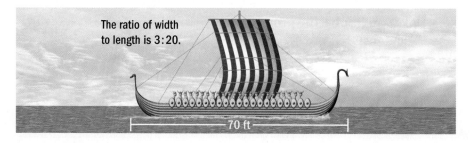

The ratio of width to length is 3 : 20.

70 ft

41. ★ EXTENDED RESPONSE In the United States, 21 out of every 100 people are under the age of 15. In a town of 20,000 people, how many people would you expect to be under the age of 15? 15 and over? Would you expect these ratios to be equivalent in every town in the United States? *Explain* your reasoning.

42. CHALLENGE A ship moves 49 feet 6 inches for every gallon of fuel that it burns. The ship travels 100 miles. How many gallons of fuel does it burn?

 NEW JERSEY MIXED REVIEW   **TEST PRACTICE** at classzone.com

43. The model represents the equation $x + 2 = -5$. What is the value of x?

(**A**) $x = -7$

(**B**) $x = -3$

(**C**) $x = 2$

(**D**) $x = 5$

Key

$+$ = +1 $-$ = −1

8.5 # Solving Proportions Using Cross Products

NJ 4.1.A.3   Understand and use ratios, proportions, and percents (including percents greater than 100 and less than 1) in a variety of situations.

Before	You solved proportions using equivalent ratios and algebra.
Now	You'll solve proportions using cross products.
Why?	So you can use proportions to solve problems, as in Example 3.

KEY VOCABULARY
• **cross products,**
  p. 423

Science A person who weighs 105 pounds on Earth would weigh about 17.5 pounds on the moon. About how much would a 60-pound dog weigh on the moon? You'll use *cross products* to find the answer in Example 2.

In the proportion $\frac{2}{3} = \frac{4}{6}$, the products 2 • 6 and 3 • 4 are called **cross products**. Notice that the cross products are equal. This relationship suggests the following property.

KEY CONCEPT *For Your Notebook*

Cross Products Property

Words The cross products of a proportion are equal.

Numbers $\frac{3}{4} = \frac{15}{20}$ $4 \cdot 15 = 60$
                                          $3 \cdot 20 = 60$

Algebra If $\frac{a}{b} = \frac{c}{d}$ where b and d are nonzero numbers, then $ad = bc$.

EXAMPLE 1 **Solving a Proportion Using Cross Products**

Use the cross products property to solve $\frac{2}{9} = \frac{3}{d}$.

VOCABULARY
The phrase *cross products* comes from the "X" shape formed by the diagonal numbers in a proportion.

$\frac{2}{9} = \frac{3}{d}$ **Write original proportion.**

$2d = 9 \cdot 3$ **Use cross products property.**

$\frac{2d}{2} = \frac{9 \cdot 3}{2}$ **Divide each side by 2.**

$d = 13.5$ **Simplify.**

 GUIDED PRACTICE for Example 1

Use the cross products property to solve the proportion.

1. $\frac{b}{10} = \frac{3}{4}$ **2.** $\frac{a}{15} = \frac{5}{6}$ **3.** $\frac{4}{5} = \frac{28}{c}$

EXAMPLE 2 Writing and Solving a Proportion

Science To find the weight w of a 60-pound dog on the moon, as described on page 423, write and solve a proportion using the weight of the person.

as described on page 423

Person   Dog

$$\frac{105}{17.5} = \frac{60}{w} \quad\longleftarrow \text{weight on Earth}$$
$$\longleftarrow \text{weight on moon}$$

$105w = 17.5 \cdot 60$ **Use cross products property.**

$$\frac{105w}{105} = \frac{17.5 \cdot 60}{105} \quad \textbf{Divide each side by 105.}$$

$w = 10$ **Simplify.**

▶ **Answer** A 60-pound dog would weigh about 10 pounds on the moon.

ANOTHER WAY
You can also find the dog's weight by using the equivalent proportion:

$$\frac{17.5}{105} = \frac{w}{60}$$

EXAMPLE 3 Solve a Multi-Step Problem

Penguins There are 50 penguins at an aquarium. The ratio of rockhopper penguins to African penguins is 3 to 7. How many are rockhoppers?

SOLUTION

STEP 1 **Determine** the ratio of rockhoppers to total penguins.

$$\frac{3}{3 + 7} = \frac{3}{10} \quad \textbf{For every 10 penguins, 3 are rockhoppers.}$$

STEP 2 **Write** and solve a proportion to find the number r of rockhoppers.

$$\frac{3}{10} = \frac{r}{50} \quad\longleftarrow \text{rockhoppers}$$
$$\longleftarrow \text{total penguins}$$

$3 \cdot 50 = 10r$ **Use cross products property.**

$$\frac{3 \cdot 50}{10} = \frac{10r}{10} \quad \textbf{Divide each side by 10.}$$

$15 = r$ **Simplify.**

▶ **Answer** There are 15 rockhoppers at the aquarium.

Rockhopper penguin

TAKE NOTES
In your notes, also show how to solve proportions using the methods of Lesson 8.4, Examples 1 and 2.

(1) $\overset{\times\,5}{\overbrace{\frac{3}{10} = \frac{r}{50}}} \longrightarrow r = 15$
$\underset{\times\,5}{}$

(2) $5\!0 \cdot \dfrac{3}{1\!0} = \dfrac{r}{5\!0} \cdot 5\!0$
$\quad\;\;1 \qquad\quad 1$

$\quad\quad 15 = r$

✓ **GUIDED PRACTICE**   for Examples 2 and 3

4. **What If?** In Example 2, suppose that a 150-pound astronaut stood on the moon. How much would the astronaut weigh?

5. In John's class, the ratio of boys to girls is 5 to 8. There are 39 students in his class. How many are girls?

6. The ratio of tubes of acrylic paint to tubes of oil paint in an art teacher's supply cabinet is 3 to 2. There are 65 tubes of paint in the cabinet. How many are acrylic?

EXAMPLE 4 Standardized Test Practice

Botany A scientist is studying the growth rate of conifer trees. In these trees, the weight of the needles and stems grow at a rate proportional to the root weight. One sample tree has a needle and stem weight of 21.1 pounds and a root weight of 5.3 pounds. The needle and stem weight of a second tree is 35.2 pounds. *Estimate* the weight w of its roots.

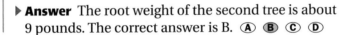

(A) 5 pounds   **(B)** 9 pounds   **(C)** 12 pounds   **(D)** 19 pounds

SOLUTION

Write and solve a proportion to find the weight w. Use the compatible numbers 20 pounds and 5 pounds for the weights of the first tree.

$$\frac{20}{5} = \frac{35.2}{w}$$ ◄── Needle and stem weight
◄── Root weight

$$\frac{4}{1} \approx \frac{36}{w}$$ Simplify the ratio and replace 35.2 with a compatible number.

$$w \approx 9$$ Solve.

▶ **Answer** The root weight of the second tree is about 9 pounds. The correct answer is B. **(A) (B) (C) (D)**

✓ **GUIDED PRACTICE** for Example 4

7. **What If?** Suppose another tree has a needle and stem weight of 78.4 pounds. *Estimate* to find the root weight of the tree.

8.5 EXERCISES

HOMEWORK KEY

★ = **STANDARDIZED TEST PRACTICE**
Exs. 19, 43, 44, 45, 46, and 63

○ = **HINTS AND HOMEWORK HELP**
for Exs. 3, 7, 15, 45 at classzone.com

SKILL PRACTICE

1. **VOCABULARY** What are the cross products of the proportion $\frac{2}{7} = \frac{10}{35}$?

SOLVING PROPORTIONS Use cross products to solve the proportion.

2. $\frac{5}{2} = \frac{y}{10}$

3. $\frac{n}{8} = \frac{3}{12}$

4. $\frac{5}{20} = \frac{3}{d}$

5. $\frac{8}{6} = \frac{12}{s}$

6. $\frac{9}{2} = \frac{36}{n}$

7. $\frac{a}{24} = \frac{7}{8}$

8. $\frac{30}{6} = \frac{b}{7}$

9. $\frac{3}{x} = \frac{4}{28}$

10. $\frac{4}{p} = \frac{14}{28}$

11. $\frac{6.8}{z} = \frac{2}{5}$

12. $\frac{a}{4} = \frac{3.5}{2}$

13. $\frac{7}{10} = \frac{k}{8}$

14. $\frac{20}{m} = \frac{16}{5}$

15. $\frac{6}{9.6} = \frac{9}{d}$

16. $\frac{22}{c} = \frac{5.5}{11}$

17. $\frac{3.6}{3} = \frac{y}{14.4}$

SEE EXAMPLE 1
on p. 423
for Ex. 18

18. ERROR ANALYSIS Describe and correct the error in solving the proportion $\frac{4}{9} = \frac{x}{18}$.

$$\times \quad \begin{array}{c} \frac{4}{9} = \frac{x}{18} \\ 4 \cdot x = 9 \cdot 18 \\ x = 40.5 \end{array}$$

SEE EXAMPLE 2
on p. 424
for Exs. 19–20

19. ★ MULTIPLE CHOICE Hair grows an average of 0.5 inch in 1 month. Choose the proportion that you can use to determine the number of months m it will take for hair to grow 6 inches.

(A) $\frac{0.5}{1} = \frac{6}{m}$ **(B)** $\frac{0.5}{1} = \frac{m}{6}$ **(C)** $\frac{0.5}{m} = \frac{6}{1}$ **(D)** $\frac{m}{0.5} = \frac{1}{6}$

20. MEASUREMENT There are about 16 kilometers in 10 miles. Write a proportion you can use to find the number k of kilometers in 250 miles.

21. ESTIMATION There are about 18.3 meters in 20 yards. *Estimate* the number of meters in one yard.

SEE EXAMPLE 3
on p. 424
for Exs. 22–29

USING PROPORTIONS Use the ratio of boys to girls and the class size to find the number of boys and number of girls in each class.

22. $3 : 5, 80$ **23.** $5 : 4, 45$ **24.** $4 : 3, 35$ **25.** $3 : 4, 84$

26. $7 : 3, 70$ **27.** $5 : 7, 60$ **28.** $2 : 3, 65$ **29.** $6 : 7, 52$

SEE EXAMPLE 4
on p. 425
for Exs. 30–33

ESTIMATION Estimate to solve the proportion.

30. $\frac{0.77}{2.4} = \frac{m}{6}$ **31.** $\frac{4.1}{m} = \frac{4.3}{34.5}$ **32.** $\frac{59.7}{35.8} = \frac{83.9}{m}$ **33.** $\frac{m}{12} = \frac{44.6}{18.7}$

ALGEBRA Solve the proportion.

34. $\frac{15}{4} = \frac{9}{2n}$ **35.** $\frac{b-3}{16} = \frac{5}{8}$ **36.** $\frac{3}{4} = \frac{x}{x+3}$ **37.** $\frac{2}{t} = \frac{5}{t-6}$

38. CHALLENGE If $\frac{a}{b} = \frac{c}{d}$, then is $\frac{d}{b} = \frac{c}{a}$ also true? *Explain* your reasoning.

In Exercises 39–42, tell whether the ratios form a proportion.

EXTENSION Deciding Whether Ratios Form a Proportion

Only ratios that form a proportion are equal.

$\frac{2}{9} \overset{?}{=} \frac{5}{16}$ **Write the possible proportion.**

$2 \cdot 16 \overset{?}{=} 9 \cdot 5$ **Find cross products.**

$32 \neq 45$ **Multiply. The cross products are not equal.**

▶ **Answer** The ratios don't form a proportion.

39. $\frac{24}{104}, \frac{3}{13}$ **40.** $\frac{6}{7}, \frac{21}{18}$ **41.** $\frac{3.4}{4.3}, \frac{5.6}{6.5}$ **42.** $\frac{9}{4.3}, \frac{54}{25.8}$

PROBLEM SOLVING

SEE EXAMPLE 2
on p. 424 for
Exs. 43–44, 46

43. ★ **SHORT RESPONSE** The average person blinks about 360 times in 30 minutes. How many times does the average person blink in 9 minutes? Is a rate of 90 blinks in 9 minutes greater or less than average? *Explain.*

44. ★ **OPEN-ENDED MATH** During the Gold Rush, one pioneer tried to travel west in a wagon with a sail. An advertisement for this *wind wagon* claimed that it could travel 15 miles per hour. How far could the advertisement say the wagon traveled in 30 minutes? Give another equivalent speed that the advertisement could use.

(45.) ★ **WRITING** *Describe* three ways to solve the proportion $\frac{9}{5} = \frac{x}{15}$.

46. ★ **MULTIPLE CHOICE** A digital subscriber line (DSL) Internet connection can transfer 42 megabits of information in 5 minutes. How long would it take to transfer 75.6 megabits of information?

    A 1 min 48 sec   **B** 6 min 35 sec   **C** 9 min   **D** 15 min

47. **MULTI-STEP PROBLEM** Use the dimensions of two ocean waves shown in the table.

Ocean Wave Dimensions		
	Height (meters)	Wavelength (meters)
Wave 1	10.2	71.4
Wave 2	12.7	88.9

Not drawn to scale

  a. Compare Is the ratio of height to wavelength the same for both waves? *Explain* your reasoning.

  b. Interpret The ratio of height to the wavelength of a wave when it breaks is 1 to 7. Were the measures of the waves in the table taken just as the waves broke? *Explain* your reasoning.

48. **MUSIC** The ratio of the number of Taylor's CDs to the number of Dave's CDs is 7 to 8. Taylor has 84 CDs. Together how many CDs do they have?

49. **SPORTS** At a typical National Football League game, the ratio of males to females in attendance is 3 : 2. There are 12,000 female spectators. What is the ratio of the number of male spectators to the total number of spectators?

50. **MEASUREMENT** On a sunny day, go outside and have a classmate measure your height and the length of your shadow. Then measure the length of the shadow of a tall object, such as a tree or flagpole. The height to shadow ratio is the same for both you and the object. Use this fact to find the height of the tall object.

51. ◆ **MULTIPLE REPRESENTATIONS** There are 5 grams of protein in 3 teaspoons of peanut butter.

   a. Write a Proportion Write a proportion that relates grams of protein, *y*, in peanut butter to the number of teaspoons *x*.

   b. Make a Table Let *x* be the input value. Make an input-output table for inputs of 3, 4.5, 6, and 12 teaspoons of peanut butter.

   c. Draw a Graph Plot the ordered pairs. Use the graph to find how many grams of protein are in 9 teaspoons of peanut butter.

52. SURVEYS A survey at a school found that the ratio of students who use a pen to do their math homework to the students who use a pencil is 2 to 7. The number of students surveyed who use a pencil is 35 more than the number of students surveyed who use a pen. How many of the students surveyed use a pen to do their math homework?

53. NATIONAL ZOO The National Zoo in Washington, D.C. had a vertebrate animals to staff ratio of about 7.8 to 1. The number of vertebrate animals outnumbered the staff by 1986 animals. *Estimate* the number of staff.

54. CHALLENGE If *a, b, c,* and *d* are all integers greater than zero and $\frac{a}{b} < \frac{c}{d}$, is it always true that $ad < bc$? In other words, can you use cross products to solve an inequality? If so, *explain* and give an example to support your answer.

 NEW JERSEY MIXED REVIEW  **TEST PRACTICE** at classzone.com

55. Which sequence follows the rule $7n + 5$, where *n* represents the position of a term in the sequence?

   (**A**) 5, 12, 19, 26, 33, . . .   (**B**) 12, 17, 22, 27, 32, . . .

   (**C**) 12, 19, 26, 33, 40, . . .   (**D**) 19, 26, 33, 40, 47, . . .

56. Mr. Pilatos drives between 50 kilometers per hour and 70 kilometers per hour for 3.5 hours. Which is the best estimate of the total number of kilometers he traveled?

   (**A**) From 105 km to 175 km

   (**B**) From 175 km to 245 km

   (**C**) From 245 km to 315 km

   (**D**) From 315 km to 385 km

57. An 18.25-foot board was cut into pieces that measure 36.5 inches each. How many pieces are there?

   (**A**) 5   (**B**) 6   (**C**) 7   (**D**) 8

8.6 Making a Scale Drawing

EXPLORE Make a *scale drawing* of a rectangular bedroom that is 16 feet long and 12 feet wide. In your drawing, let 1 inch represent 8 feet.

STEP 1 Write and solve a proportion to find the length l of the bedroom in the drawing.

$$\frac{1}{8} = \frac{l}{16} \quad \begin{array}{l}\leftarrow\text{inches} \\ \leftarrow\text{feet}\end{array}$$

$$1 \cdot 16 = 8 \cdot l$$

$$2 = l$$

STEP 2 Write and solve a proportion to find the width w of the bedroom in the drawing.

$$\frac{1}{8} = \frac{w}{12} \quad \begin{array}{l}\leftarrow\text{inches} \\ \leftarrow\text{feet}\end{array}$$

$$1 \cdot 12 = 8 \cdot w$$

$$1.5 = w$$

STEP 3 Use a ruler to draw a rectangle with a length of 2 inches and a width of 1.5 inches.

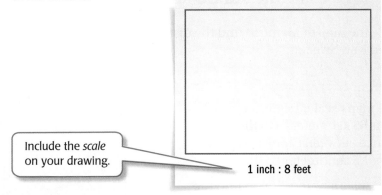

Include the *scale* on your drawing.

1 inch : 8 feet

PRACTICE Make a scale drawing of the rectangular or square top of the object. In your drawing, let 1 inch represent 8 feet.

1. Dresser:
   $l = 4$ ft, $w = 2$ ft

2. Bed:
   $l = 6$ ft, $w = 4$ ft

3. Nightstand:
   $s = 2$ ft

DRAW CONCLUSIONS

4. **WRITING** Cut out the scale drawings from Exercises 1–3. Arrange the pieces on the scale drawing of the bedroom. *Explain* why this method might be used to decide the arrangement of the furniture.

8.6 Scale Drawings and Models

Before	You learned how to solve proportions.
Now	You'll use proportions with models.
Why?	So you can find the scale of a model, as in Example 3.

KEY VOCABULARY
- scale drawing, *p. 430*
- scale, *p. 430*
- scale model, *p. 431*

The floor plan is an example of a *scale drawing*. A **scale drawing** is a diagram of an object in which the dimensions are in proportion to the actual dimensions of the object.

The **scale** on a scale drawing tells how the drawing's dimensions and the actual dimensions are related. The scale "1 in. : 12 ft" means that 1 inch in the floor plan represents an actual distance of 12 feet.

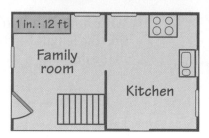

EXAMPLE 1 Using the Scale of a Map

Maps Use the map of Maine to find the distance between the towns of China and New Sweden.

SOLUTION

From the map's scale, 1 centimeter represents 65 kilometers. On the map, the distance between China and New Sweden is 4.5 centimeters.

Write and solve a proportion to find the distance *d* between the towns.

WRITE PROPORTIONS
Need help with writing a proportion? See p. 418.

$$\frac{1}{65} = \frac{4.5}{d} \quad \begin{matrix} \leftarrow \text{ centimeters} \\ \leftarrow \text{ kilometers} \end{matrix}$$

$$1 \cdot d = 65 \cdot 4.5$$

$$d = 292.5$$

▶ **Answer** The actual distance between China and New Sweden is about 293 kilometers.

1 cm : 65 km

 GUIDED PRACTICE for Example 1

1. Use the map to find the distance (in kilometers) between Paris and Marshfield.

READING
When a scale is written as a ratio, it usually takes the form scale model : actual object.

Scale Models A **scale model** is a model of an object in which the dimensions are in proportion to the actual dimensions of the object. The scale of a scale model is often given as a ratio. The two scales listed below are equivalent.

Scale with units	Scale without units
1 in. : 4 ft	1 : 48 ◄— **Express 4 ft as 48 in.**

The second scale can also be written as $\frac{1}{48}$. A scale that is written as a fraction without units is called a *scale factor*.

EXAMPLE 2 **Finding a Dimension on a Scale Model**

White House There is a scale model of the White House in Tobu World Square in Japan. The scale used for the model is 1 : 25. The height of the main building of the White House is 85 feet. Find this height on the model.

SOLUTION

Write and solve a proportion to find the height, h, of the main building of the model of the White House.

$$\frac{1}{25} = \frac{h}{85} \quad \leftarrow \quad \text{scale model} \\ \leftarrow \quad \text{building}$$

$1 \cdot 85 = 25 \cdot h$ **Cross products property**

$3.4 = h$ **Divide each side by 25.**

▸ **Answer** The height of the main building of the model is 3.4 feet.

Check After using the cross product property, you can reason that 85 is greater than 25×3 but less than 25×4. So, h is between 3 and 4. The answer, $h = 3.4$, is reasonable.

Animated **Math** at classzone.com

✓ **GUIDED PRACTICE**   for Example 2

2. **Eiffel Tower** The model of the Eiffel Tower in Tobu World Square is 12 meters high. Use the scale factor of 1 : 25 in Example 2 to estimate the height of the actual Eiffel Tower.

3. **Carpenter Ants** A museum of natural history is making a scale model of a carpenter ant. The scale used is 12.5 cm : 1 mm. If the actual length of the ant is 6.4 mm, what is the length of the model?

EXAMPLE 3 Finding the Scale

Dinosaurs A museum is creating a full-size *Tyrannosaurus rex* from a model. The model is 40 inches in length, from the nose to the tail. The resulting dinosaur will be 40 feet in length. What is the model's scale?

SOLUTION

Write a ratio. Make sure that both measures are in inches. Then simplify.

$$\frac{40 \text{ in.}}{40 \text{ ft}} = \frac{40 \text{ in.}}{480 \text{ in.}} = \frac{1}{12} \begin{array}{l} \longleftarrow \text{ scale model} \\ \longleftarrow \text{ full size} \end{array}$$

▶ **Answer** The model's scale is 1 : 12.

✓ **GUIDED PRACTICE** for Example 3

4. **What If?** Suppose the model of the *Tyrannosaurus rex* in Example 3 were 80 inches in length. What is the model's scale?

8.6 EXERCISES

HOMEWORK KEY

★ = **STANDARDIZED TEST PRACTICE**
Exs. 24, 30, 31, 34, and 52

◯ = **HINTS AND HOMEWORK HELP**
for Exs. 9, 13, 17, 21, 29 at classzone.com

SKILL PRACTICE

VOCABULARY Tell whether the statement is *true* or *false*. *Explain.*

1. The scale on a scale drawing tells how the drawing's dimensions and the actual dimensions are related.

2. An object and its scale model are the same size, but have different shapes.

SEE EXAMPLE 1
on p. 430
for Exs. 3–10

MATCHING DISTANCES The scale on a floor plan is 1 in. : 15 ft. Match the distance on the floor plan with the actual distance.

3. 2 in.   4. 3.5 in.   5. 2.2 in.   6. 1.6 in.

A. 33 ft   B. 30 ft   C. 24 ft   D. 52.5 ft

FINDING DISTANCES The scale on a map is 1 cm : 25 mi. Find the actual distance in miles for the given length on the map.

7. 3 cm   8. 10 cm   9. 5.2 cm   10. 8.7 cm

FINDING LENGTH The scale used to build the scale model of an airplane is 1 : 72. Find the wingspan of the model airplane to the nearest tenth of a centimeter. Check for reasonableness.

SEE EXAMPLE 2
on p. 431
for Exs. 11–14

11. *Wright Flyer* wingspan: 12.3 m   12. *Spirit of St. Louis* wingspan: 14 m

13. Boeing 747 wingspan: 59.6 m   14. Airbus A380 wingspan: 79.8 m

SEE EXAMPLE 2
on p. 431
for Ex. 15

15. ERROR ANALYSIS The scale used in a drawing is 1 in. : 5 ft. The width of the actual object is 15 feet. Describe and correct the error made in finding the drawing width.

$$\frac{1}{5} = \frac{x}{15}$$
$$1 \cdot 15 = 5 \cdot x$$
$$x = 3$$

The drawing width is 3 feet.

FINDING THE SCALE Write the ratio as a scale without units.

SEE EXAMPLE 3
on p. 432
for Exs. 16–23

16. $\frac{5 \text{ in.}}{2 \text{ ft}}$

17. $\frac{7 \text{ cm}}{7 \text{ m}}$

18. $\frac{12 \text{ cm}}{5 \text{ km}}$

19. $\frac{6 \text{ in.}}{14 \text{ yd}}$

20. $\frac{2 \text{ m}}{16 \text{ km}}$

21. $\frac{1 \text{ ft}}{8 \text{ yd}}$

22. $\frac{18 \text{ mm}}{10 \text{ cm}}$

23. $\frac{9 \text{ in.}}{20 \text{ ft}}$

24. ★ MULTIPLE CHOICE A child's picnic table is a scale model of an adult picnic table. The child's picnic table is 22 inches tall, and the adult picnic table is 33 inches tall. What is the model's scale factor?

A $\frac{3}{2}$ **B** $\frac{2}{3}$ **C** $\frac{1}{11}$ **D** $\frac{1}{15}$

25. WHICH ONE DOESN'T BELONG? A 2-foot by 2.5-foot scale drawing is created from an 8-inch by 10-inch photograph. Which scale does *not* belong with the others?

A. 1 ft : 4 in. **B.** 2 : 8 **C.** $\frac{3}{1}$ **D.** $\frac{1}{4}$

26. REASONING A model's scale is 1 : 0.2. Is the scale model larger or smaller than the actual object? *Explain.*

27. CHALLENGE The width of an object is 8 feet. You make a model of the object using a scale factor of $\frac{1}{2}$. Then you make a model of the model using the same scale factor. In total, you make four models by this process. What is the value of x in the scale x inches : 8 feet, where x is the width of the fourth model?

PROBLEM SOLVING

SEE EXAMPLE 2
on p. 431
for Exs. 28

28. SCULPTURE Each bowling pin in the sculpture is a scale model of a normal bowling pin. The model's scale is 1 : 0.05. The height of a normal bowling pin is 38 centimeters. *Estimate* the height of a bowling pin in the model.

SEE EXAMPLE 3
on p. 432
for Ex. 29

29. MINIATURE FURNITURE A carpenter makes miniature replicas of Victorian furniture. The scale model of a table that he made is 3 inches long. The full-size table is 36 inches long. What is the model's scale?

30. ★ WRITING *Explain* what it means if a drawing is "not to scale"?

Flying Pins by Claes Oldenburg and Coosje van Bruggen

31. ★ **MULTIPLE CHOICE** You decide to use a scale of 1 in. : 8 ft to make a scale drawing of your classroom. The actual length of your classroom is 36 feet. What should be the length of the classroom in the drawing?

(**A**) 1 in.   (**B**) 4.5 in.   (**C**) 36 in.   (**D**) 288 in.

PAINTING In Exercises 32 and 33, an artist is making a scale drawing of a 4-foot wide mural. The drawing is 8 inches wide.

32. What is the drawing's scale?

33. The length of the mural is 5 feet. What is the length of the scale drawing? *Explain* your reasoning.

34. ★ **SHORT RESPONSE** A model of a chessboard was made using a scale factor of 3 : 1. The original chessboard was 5 inches by 5 inches. Find the perimeter and area of the original chessboard and its model. Compare your findings to the scale factor. *Describe* what you notice.

35. **MEASUREMENT** Use a ruler to measure the sides of the hexagon shown. Create an approximate scale drawing of the hexagon with a scale of 5 cm : 1 cm.

36. **TIMELINE** The table lists seven recent U.S. Presidents and the year each took office. Make a timeline showing the length of the completed terms of the first six Presidents listed. Use the scale 0.5 centimeters : 2 years.

President	Nixon	Ford	Carter	Reagan	G. Bush	Clinton	G. W. Bush
Year took office	1969	1974	1977	1981	1989	1993	2001

37. ◆ **MULTIPLE REPRESENTATIONS** A scaled picture of a maple leaf is shown at the right. The leaf is on a 5 centimeter by 5 centimeter grid. The scale shown in the picture is of the form scale model : actual object.

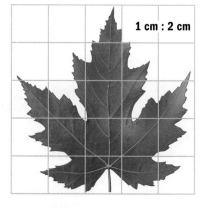

1 cm : 2 cm

  a. Draw at Actual Size Make a drawing of the leaf at its actual size.

  b. Draw a Smaller Model Use the drawing in part (a) to make a model drawing using the scale 5 mm : 2 cm.

  c. Area *Estimate* the area of the maple leaf in the picture and the two drawings in parts (a) and (b).

38. **CHALLENGE** A scale drawing of a rectangular garden has a length of 5 inches and a width of 3.5 inches. The scale is 1 in. : *x* ft. Write a ratio of the area of the scale drawing to the area of the actual garden. Write a ratio of the perimeter of the scale drawing to the perimeter of the actual garden. *Compare* each ratio to the scale.

39. **LOOK FOR A PATTERN** Draw a rectangle, choose a scale, and make a scale drawing of it. Write and compare ratios as done in Exercise 38. Repeat this process for several other rectangles. What do you notice?

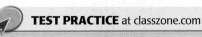
40. Yesterday Mrs. Krause drove 121 miles in 2 hours. Today she drove 3.5 hours at the same rate as yesterday. About how far did she drive today?

    (A) 182 mi   **(B)** 197 mi   **(C)** 212 mi   **(D)** 242 mi

41. Jackie bought 3 shirts for $39. She later bought another shirt for $15. What was the mean cost of all the shirts?

    (A) $13.00   **(B)** $13.50   **(C)** $15.25   **(D)** $18.00

42. Mrs. Taylor bought a dozen roses at $0.75 each and 18 carnations at 6 for $3.15. What is the total amount she spent, not including tax?

    (A) $3.90   **(B)** $10.20   **(C)** $15.30   **(D)** $18.45

QUIZ *for Lessons 8.4–8.6*

In Exercises 1–4, solve the proportion. Tell what method you used. *(p. 418)*

1. $\dfrac{a}{15} = \dfrac{2}{6}$ **2.** $\dfrac{9}{b} = \dfrac{2}{8}$ **3.** $\dfrac{2}{3} = \dfrac{7}{y}$ **4.** $\dfrac{10}{8} = \dfrac{x}{5.6}$

5. **DISCOUNTS** The CDs in the discount bin at a CD store cost $12 for 2 CDs. How much will 5 CDs from the discount bin cost? *(p. 423)*

6. **ADVERTISING** In a magazine, the ratio of pages with advertisements to pages without advertisements is 6 : 5. The magazine has 143 pages. How many pages have advertisements? *(p. 423)*

7. **MAPS** The scale on a map is 1 cm : 65 km. The distance between two cities on the map is 5.5 centimeters. Estimate the actual distance. *(p. 430)*

8. **RECIPES** You need 2.5 pounds of ground beef to make tacos for 16 people. How many pounds of ground beef do you need to make tacos for 24 people? *(p. 423)*

Brain Game

Shape Association

Use the two true statements below to copy and complete the proportions at the right.

$$\frac{\triangle}{\blacksquare} = \frac{\blacksquare}{\bigcirc} \qquad \frac{\bigcirc}{\bigcirc} = \frac{\triangle}{\blacksquare}$$

1. $\dfrac{\triangle}{\blacksquare} = \dfrac{?}{?}$ **2.** $\dfrac{\blacksquare}{\bigcirc} = \dfrac{\triangle}{?}$

3. $\dfrac{\triangle}{\bigcirc} = \dfrac{?}{\blacksquare}$ **4.** $\dfrac{?}{\bigcirc} = \dfrac{\triangle}{?}$

Lessons 8.4–8.6

1. **FUNDRAISER** The seventh grade class sold ice cream cones to raise money for a class trip. The ratio of small to medium cones sold was 3 to 1, and the ratio of medium to large cones sold was 9 to 25. The class sold 81 small cones. Which is the best strategy to find the number of large cones that were sold?

   A. Break into Parts

   B. Draw a Diagram

   C. Act it Out

   D. Use a Venn Diagram

2. **CURRENCY EXCHANGE** One U.S. dollar is equivalent to 1.79 Aruban guilders. You purchase something for 190 Aruban guilders. What is the equivalent price, to the nearest cent, in U.S. dollars?

   A. $.01

   B. $1.06

   C. $106.15

   D. $340.10

3. **BASEMENT PLANS** Mark wants to build a basement playroom for his children. He begins sketching the drawing below. What width in the scale drawing should Mark use to represent a door 2 feet wide?

   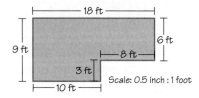
   Scale: 0.5 inch : 1 foot

   A. 0.5 in.

   B. 1 in.

   C. 2 in.

   D. 4 in.

4. **SUMMER CAMP** The ratio of counselors to campers at a camp is 1 : 9. The ratio of campers who can swim to campers who cannot swim is 7 : 2. There are 13 counselors. How many campers can swim?

   A. 10   **C.** 91

   B. 18   **D.** 410

5. **READING** You read a book for Language Arts class. Each day you record the page number of the last page you read that day. The table shows the results. On which of the days did you read 3 pages for every 2 pages that you read on the previous day?

Day	1	2	3	4	5	6	7
Page	15	35	49	70	82	100	112

   A. Days 1 and 4   **C.** Days 4 and 6

   B. Days 2 and 6   **D.** Days 4 and 7

6. **DRIVING TIME** The scale on a map is given as 1 inch : 40 miles. The distance that you plan to drive measures 4.75 inches on the map. You drive at an average speed of 50 miles per hour. About how long will it take you to drive this distance?

   A. 0.1 h   **C.** 5.9 h

   B. 3.8 h   **D.** 10.5 h

7. **OPEN-ENDED** Mark decides to build a shed in his backyard. He makes a scale drawing of the shed using a scale of 0.5 inch : 1 foot.

   • Mark wants a window in the shed to be 2 feet wide. How wide should the window in his scale drawing be? *Explain* your answer.

   • The rectangular floor of the shed in the scale drawing is 12 inches by 18 inches. Find the actual dimensions of the floor. *Explain* how you found your answer.

REVIEW KEY VOCABULARY

- ratio, *p. 399*
- equivalent ratios, *p. 399*
- rate, *p. 404*
- unit rate, *p. 404*

- slope, *p. 409*
- proportion, *p. 418*
- cross products, *p. 423*
- scale drawing, *p. 430*

- scale, *p. 430*
- scale model, *p. 431*

VOCABULARY EXERCISES

Match the definition with the corresponding word.

1. Uses division to compare two numbers

2. A ratio of two quantities measured in different units

3. The ratio of the rise to the run between two points on a line

4. An equation stating that two ratios are equivalent

5. A rate that has a denominator of 1 unit

6. The relationship between a drawing's dimensions and the actual dimensions

A. Proportion

B. Slope

C. Rate

D. Scale

E. Ratio

F. Unit rate

REVIEW EXAMPLES AND EXERCISES

8.1 Ratios

pp. 399–403

EXAMPLE

Animal Kennel On which day did the boarding kennel have a greater ratio of cats to dogs?

	Friday	Saturday
Cats	3	10
Dogs	15	25

SOLUTION

Friday: $\dfrac{\text{cats}}{\text{dogs}} = \dfrac{3}{15}$

$= \dfrac{1}{5}$

$= 0.2$

Saturday: $\dfrac{\text{cats}}{\text{dogs}} = \dfrac{10}{25}$

$= \dfrac{2}{5}$

$= 0.4$

Because $0.4 > 0.2$, there was a greater ratio of cats to dogs on Saturday.

EXERCISES

SEE EXAMPLES
1, 2, AND 3
on pp. 399–400
for Exs. 7–17

Write the ratio as a fraction in simplest form.

7. 9 to 81   **8.** 63 to 7   **9.** $20:35$

Copy and complete the statement using <, >, or =.

10. $5:10 \ \underline{?} \ 1:5$ **11.** $6:14 \ \underline{?} \ 6:10$ **12.** $1:4 \ \underline{?} \ 13:52$

13. $8:12 \ \underline{?} \ 35:42$ **14.** $9:10 \ \underline{?} \ 27:30$ **15.** $8:14 \ \underline{?} \ 4:12$

16. Gardening A dogwood tree has a height of 10 feet and a width of 4 feet. Write the ratio of the height to the width.

17. Bricks A brick has a height of 2 inches and a length of 8 inches. Write the ratio of the height to the length.

8.2   Rates   *pp. 404–408*

EXAMPLE

Pencil Costs A stationery store sells the same mechanical pencils in packages of 2 pencils for $1.98 and packages of 10 pencils for $8.00. To determine which is the better buy, find the unit price for each.

2 pencils: $\dfrac{\$1.98}{2} = \dfrac{\$.99}{1}$ Write as unit rate.

10 pencils: $\dfrac{\$8.00}{10} = \dfrac{\$.80}{1}$ Write as unit rate.

▶ **Answer** The packages of 10 pencils are the better buy.

EXERCISES

SEE EXAMPLES
1, 2, AND 3
on pp. 404–405
for Exs. 18–24

Find the unit rate.

18. $20 for 4 persons   **19.** 22 ounces for 4 servings   **20.** $17.50 for 10 sodas

Better Buy Determine which is the better buy.

21. 6 oz can of tuna for $1.25; 9 oz can of tuna for $1.99

22. 16 oz bottle of salad dressing for $2.29; 20 oz bottle of salad dressing for $2.89

23. 1.4 ounce bag of popcorn for $2.10; 2.2 ounce bag of popcorn for $2.64

24. Sports Salary A football player signs a contract that pays him $28 million over 7 years. What is his average annual salary?

8.3 Slope

EXAMPLE

Find the slope of the line.

To find the slope of a line, find the ratio of the rise to the run between two points on the line.

$$\text{slope} = \frac{\text{rise}}{\text{run}} = \frac{-3}{4} = -\frac{3}{4}$$

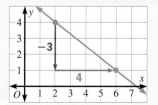

EXERCISES

SEE EXAMPLE 1
on p. 410
for Exs. 25–28

25. Find the slope of the line.

Graph the line that passes through the points. Then find the slope of the line.

26. $(-2, 0), (-1, 4)$ **27.** $(1, -6), (3, 8)$ **28.** $(-3, -2), (5, -5)$

8.4 Writing and Solving Proportions

pp. 418–422

EXAMPLE

Solve the proportion $\frac{5}{4} = \frac{a}{20}$.

$$\frac{5}{4} = \frac{a}{20} \qquad \text{Write original proportion.}$$

$$20 \cdot \frac{5}{4} = 20 \cdot \frac{a}{20} \qquad \text{Multiply each side by 20.}$$

$$\frac{100}{4} = a \qquad \text{Simplify.}$$

$$25 = a \qquad \text{Simplify fraction.}$$

EXERCISES

*SEE EXAMPLES
1 AND 2*
on pp. 418–419
for Exs. 29–32

Solve the proportion.

29. $\frac{8}{10} = \frac{24}{s}$ **30.** $\frac{6}{w} = \frac{12}{18}$ **31.** $\frac{10}{25} = \frac{m}{5}$ **32.** $\frac{7}{21} = \frac{x}{6}$

Chapter Review **439**

Solving Proportions Using Cross Products

EXAMPLE

Car Wash A group of students washes 3 cars in 10 minutes. Write and solve a proportion to find how many cars the students can wash in 30 minutes.

$$\frac{3}{10} = \frac{c}{30}$$ ⟵ cars
⟵ minutes

$3 \cdot 30 = 10 \cdot c$ **Cross products property**

$9 = c$ **Divide each side by 10.**

EXERCISES

Solve the proportion.

SEE EXAMPLES 1, 2, AND 3 on pp. 423–424 for Exs. 33–38

33. $\dfrac{k}{16} = \dfrac{5}{10}$ **34.** $\dfrac{y}{12} = \dfrac{4}{16}$ **35.** $\dfrac{8}{18} = \dfrac{6}{n}$ **36.** $\dfrac{7.5}{b} = \dfrac{9}{24}$

37. Savings You are saving money to buy a new bicycle. You save $100 every 4 months. How long will it take you to save $250?

38. Stationery There are 35 writing utensils in a drawer. The ratio of pens to pencils is 2 : 5. How many pens are in the drawer?

Scale Drawings and Models

EXAMPLE

Submarine The scale used to make a scale model of a submarine is 1 : 35. The length of the actual submarine is 98 meters. Write and solve a proportion to find the length of the model.

$$\frac{1}{35} = \frac{l}{98}$$ ⟵ scale model
⟵ submarine

$1 \cdot 98 = 35 \cdot l$ **Cross products property**

$2.8 = l$ **Divide each side by 35.**

EXERCISES

SEE EXAMPLES 2 AND 3 on pp. 431–432 for Exs. 39–43

39. Use the scale in the example above to find the length of the scale model of a submarine that has an actual length of 308 feet.

Write the ratio as a scale without units.

40. $\dfrac{7 \text{ g}}{2 \text{ kg}}$ **41.** $\dfrac{15 \text{ in.}}{4 \text{ ft}}$ **42.** $\dfrac{6 \text{ mm}}{6 \text{ cm}}$ **43.** $\dfrac{16 \text{ ft}}{1 \text{ mi}}$

Write the ratio as a fraction in simplest form.

1. $\dfrac{168}{28}$

2. 76 to 19

3. $23 : 184$

4. $46 : 1012$

Copy and complete the statement using <, >, or =.

5. $9 : 2 \underline{\ ?\ } 25 : 2$

6. $20 : 8 \underline{\ ?\ } 50 : 20$

7. $11 : 12 \underline{\ ?\ } 96 : 144$

8. $440 : 5 \underline{\ ?\ } 510 : 6$

Graph the line that passes through the points. Then find the slope of the line.

9. $(1, -2), (2, 1)$

10. $(-3, -4), (0, 0)$

11. $(5, 0), (1, 1)$

12. Draw the line that has a slope of $-\dfrac{3}{4}$ and passes through $(6, 3)$.

13. Find the slope of the line.

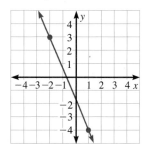

Solve the proportion. Tell what method you used.

14. $\dfrac{5}{8} = \dfrac{75}{a}$

16. $\dfrac{8}{b} = \dfrac{2}{3}$

16. $\dfrac{c}{9} = \dfrac{4}{16}$

17. $\dfrac{12}{5} = \dfrac{d}{8}$

18. $\dfrac{1.25}{5} = \dfrac{x}{18}$

19. $\dfrac{y}{3} = \dfrac{24.8}{8}$

20. $\dfrac{9}{10} = \dfrac{3.6}{z}$

21. $\dfrac{5}{r} = \dfrac{6}{8.4}$

22. **SPEED** A car travels 315 miles in 6 hours. What is the average speed of the car as a unit rate in miles per hour?

23. **FLOWERS** Determine which of the following is the better buy: 6 cut flowers for $5.94 or 9 cut flowers for $8.99.

24. **STAINING** Three gallons of oil-based stain cover about 1050 square feet of a flat surface. How many gallons of stain are needed to cover 3150 square feet?

FLOOR PLANS In Exercises 25–27, use the following information.

The floor plan of the first floor of a house was drawn using the scale 1 cm : 1.5 m. Find the actual length and width of the room given its length and width on the drawing.

25. **Living room**
    length: 5 cm
    width: 4 cm

26. **Kitchen**
    length: 4 cm
    width: 3.5 cm

27. **Family room**
    length: 5.25 cm
    width: 4.5 cm

REVIEWING PROPORTION PROBLEMS

In some real-life situations, you can find an unknown quantity by using a proportion. A proportion is an equation that states that two ratios are equivalent. One type of ratio is a unit rate. These can be used to compare quantities.

EXAMPLE

Prices The prices of four different bottles of lotion are given in the table.

Lotion Prices	
Bottle Size (fluid ounces)	**Price**
2	$1.85
6	$3.15
10	$5.30
24	$6.24

List the bottles from the highest to the lowest price per fluid ounce.

Solution

To compare the prices per fluid ounce, find the unit price for all four bottles.

2-fluid ounce bottle: $\dfrac{\$1.85}{2 \text{ fl oz}} = \dfrac{\$0.925}{1 \text{ fl oz}}$

6-fluid ounce bottle: $\dfrac{\$3.15}{6 \text{ fl oz}} = \dfrac{\$0.525}{1 \text{ fl oz}}$

10-fluid ounce bottle: $\dfrac{\$5.30}{10 \text{ fl oz}} = \dfrac{\$0.53}{1 \text{ fl oz}}$

24-fluid ounce bottle: $\dfrac{\$6.24}{24 \text{ fl oz}} = \dfrac{\$0.26}{1 \text{ fl oz}}$

List the prices per ounce from most expensive to least expensive:

$0.925, $0.53, $0.525, and $0.26

▶ **Answer** From highest to lowest price per ounce, the sizes are 2 fluid ounces, 10 fluid ounces, 6 fluid ounces, and 24 fluid ounces.

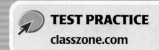

PROPORTION PROBLEMS

Below are examples of proportion problems in multiple choice format. Try solving the problems before looking at the solutions. (Cover the solutions with a piece of paper.) Then check your solutions against the ones given.

1. Tonya drew a floor plan of her house. She used a scale of 1 inch equals 2 feet. The length of her kitchen is 15 feet. What distance on Tonya's floor plan represents the length of her kitchen?

   A. 5.5 in.

   B. 7.5 in.

   C. 10 in.

   D. 30 in.

Solution

Write and solve a proportion to find the length l of her kitchen on the floor plan.

$$\frac{1}{2} = \frac{l}{15} \quad \longleftarrow \text{ inches}$$
$$\qquad\qquad \longleftarrow \text{ feet}$$

$$1 \cdot 15 = 2 \cdot l$$
$$l = 7.5$$

The length of her kitchen on the floor plan is 7.5 inches, so the correct answer is B.

2. An athlete on the school swim team can swim 25 yards in 15.2 seconds. During the last swim meet, he swam the 100-yard event at the same rate of speed. About how long did it take him to swim this race?

   A. 25 sec

   B. 32 sec

   C. 61 sec

   D. 80 sec

Solution

Write and solve a proportion to find the amount of time t in seconds that it took the swimmer to finish the race.

$$\frac{15.2}{25} = \frac{t}{100} \quad \longleftarrow \text{ time}$$
$$\qquad\qquad \longleftarrow \text{ yards}$$

$$15.2 \cdot 100 = 25 \cdot t$$
$$t = 60.8$$

It takes the swimmer about 61 seconds to finish the race, so the correct answer is C.

3. A recipe that makes 30 cookies calls for 1.25 cups of flour. How much flour is needed to make 3 dozen cookies using this recipe?

   A. 1.5 c

   B. 1.75 c

   C. 2.25 c

   D. 7.2 c

Solution

Write and solve a proportion to find the number of cups c of flour needed.

$$\frac{1.25}{30} = \frac{c}{36} \quad \longleftarrow \text{ cups of flour}$$
$$\qquad\qquad \longleftarrow \text{ cookies}$$

$$1.25 \cdot 36 = 30 \cdot c$$
$$c = 1.5$$

The amount of flour needed to make 3 dozen cookies is 1.5 cups, so the correct answer is A.

TEST PREPARATION

1. The graph represents the distance traveled by a car over time. Find the speed of the car.

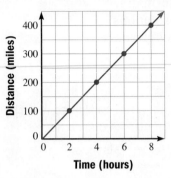

   A. 25 mph

   B. 40 mph

   C. 50 mph

   D. 100 mph

2. The table shows the prices of 4 different boxes of cereal.

Cereal Prices	
Box size (ounces)	Price
16.75	$2.98
18	$3.15
19.25	$3.99
27	$4.89

   Which box has the lowest price per ounce?

   A. 16.75-oz box

   B. 18-oz box

   C. 19.25-oz box

   D. 27-oz box

3. A recipe uses 2 tablespoons of cinnamon to make 20 cookies. How much cinnamon is needed to make 5 dozen cookies?

   A. 0.5 tbsp

   B. 4 tbsp

   C. 6 tbsp

   D. 10 tbsp

4. The scale on a blueprint is 0.5 inch equals 1 foot. What are the actual dimensions of a room that is 4 inches by 5 inches on the blueprint?

   A. 4 feet by 5 feet

   B. 8 feet by 10 feet

   C. 16 feet by 20 feet

   D. 20 feet by 25 feet

5. James read 25 pages yesterday in 35 minutes. Today he read 18 pages at the same rate as yesterday. About how long did he read today?

   A. 20 min

   B. 25 min

   C. 30 min

   D. 31 min

6. What are the coordinates of point R?

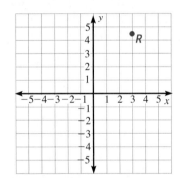

   A. (3, 3.5)

   B. (3, 4.5)

   C. (4.5, 3)

   D. (4.5, 3.5)

7. Which expression is represented by the model below?

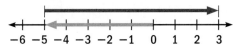

A. $-5 - 2$

B. $-5 + 3$

C. $-5 + 5$

D. $-5 + 8$

8. What is the value of $(-4)^2 - 3 + 10$?

A. -9

B. -3

C. 3

D. 23

9. Which problem situation matches the equation below?

$$\frac{75 + 90 + 85 + x}{4} = 84$$

A. The weights of three children are 75 pounds, 90 pounds, and 85 pounds. Find x, the sum of the weights of the three children.

B. The heights of three people are 75 inches, 90 inches, and 85 inches. Find x, the height of a fourth person so that the average height of the four people is 84 inches.

C. The times it took three students to finish an assignment were 75 minutes, 90 minutes, and 85 minutes. Find x, the average time it took the students to complete the assignment.

D. Derek's first four quiz scores were 75, 90, 85, and 84. Find x, the average of his scores.

10. Each square on the grid represents 6 square feet.

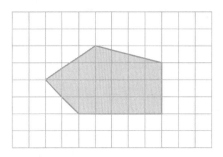

What is the approximate area of the shaded region?

A. 20 ft^2

B. 50 ft^2

C. 96 ft^2

D. 126 ft^2

11. OPEN-ENDED A class sold hoagies to raise money for a trip. The ratio of small to medium hoagies sold was 4 to 1, and the ratio of small to large hoagies sold was 36 to 17. The class sold 18 medium hoagies.

Part A How many small hoagies were sold? *Explain* your reasoning.

Part B How many large hoagies were sold? *Explain* your reasoning.

Part C The class sold small hoagies for $2, medium hoagies for $3.50, and large hoagies for $5. The class needed to raise $350 to go on the trip. Did the class raise enough money by selling hoagies to go on the trip? *Justify* your answer.

TEST PREPARATION

9 Percents

Before

In previous chapters you've . . .

• **Written fractions as decimals and decimals as fractions**
• **Used ratios and proportions**

Now

NJ New Jersey Standards

4.1.A.3	9.1	Percents and fractions
4.1.A.3	9.2	Using proportions
4.1.A.5	9.3	Percents and decimals
4.1.A.3	9.4	The percent equation
4.5.E.1.d	9.5	Circle graphs
4.1.A.3	9.6	Percent of change
4.1.A.3	9.7	Changes in price
4.1.A.3	9.8	Simple interest

Why?

So you can solve real-world problems about . . .

• the Martian atmosphere, p. 452
• surfing, p. 455
• jeans, p. 485

Animated Math

at classzone.com

• Percents and Proportions, p. 457
• Using a Protractor, p. 472
• Simple Interest, p. 490

Get-Ready Games

Review Prerequisite Skills by playing *Sunny Days* and *Lightning Math*.

Sunny Days

Upland: There are 5 sunny days for every 2 cloudy days.

Zellwood: There are 6 sunny days per week.

Arlington: 17 out of 21 days are sunny.

Ashton: There are 11 sunny days every 2 weeks.

Yellowfield: For every 3 days, 2 are sunny.

Milltown: 5 out of 21 days are cloudy.

Skill Focus: Writing ratios

You have asked some friends to report how sunny their towns are. Unfortunately, their reports give data in different ways.

• Write each report as a ratio of sunny days to cloudy days. Write the ratios as fractions. Order the fractions from least to greatest.

• Copy the spaces below. In the spaces, write the first letters of the towns in the order you determined. The answer will spell the name and state of the sunniest city in the United States.

? ? ? ? , ? ?

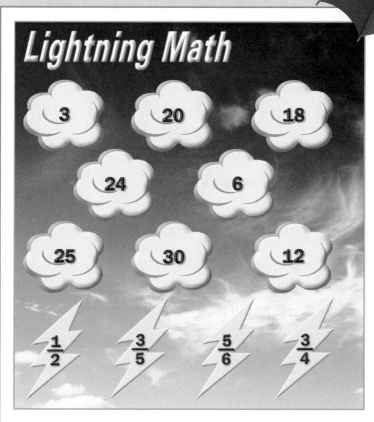

Lightning Math

Clouds: 3, 20, 18, 24, 6, 25, 30, 12

Lightning bolts: $\frac{1}{2}$, $\frac{3}{5}$, $\frac{5}{6}$, $\frac{3}{4}$

Skill Focus: Writing proportions

Use the numbers on the clouds above to form ratios with the same values as the ratios on the lightning bolts. Use each cloud one time.

Stop and Think

1. **WRITING** Explain the procedure you used to order the fractions you wrote in *Sunny Days*.

2. **EXTENSION** Use the cloud numbers in *Lightning Math* to write 4 ratios that are different from the ratios shown above.

Review Prerequisite Skills

VOCABULARY CHECK

REVIEW WORDS
- **decimal,** *p. 56*
- **ratio,** *p. 399*
- **proportion,** *p. 418*

Copy and complete using a review word from the list at the left.

1. A(n) __?__ is an equation that states that two ratios are equivalent.

2. A(n) __?__ uses division to compare two numbers.

SKILL CHECK

Write the fraction as a decimal. *(p. 199)*

3. $\dfrac{1}{2}$ **4.** $\dfrac{3}{4}$ **5.** $\dfrac{4}{5}$ **6.** $\dfrac{7}{10}$

7. $\dfrac{2}{8}$ **8.** $\dfrac{3}{10}$ **9.** $\dfrac{5}{20}$ **10.** $\dfrac{25}{75}$

Write the decimal as a fraction. *(p. 199)*

11. 0.6 **12.** 0.1 **13.** 0.95 **14.** 0.45

15. 0.5 **16.** 0.2 **17.** 0.25 **18.** 0.4

Find the product or quotient. *(pp. 66, 71)*

19. 82×0.64 **20.** 0.78×105 **21.** 0.5×120 **22.** 0.8×76

23. $15 \div 0.12$ **24.** $58 \div 0.29$ **25.** $18 \div 0.2$ **26.** $95 \div 0.05$

Use the cross products property to solve the proportion. *(p. 418)*

27. $\dfrac{11}{4} = \dfrac{33}{n}$ **28.** $\dfrac{a}{28} = \dfrac{6}{7}$ **29.** $\dfrac{25}{5} = \dfrac{b}{6}$ **30.** $\dfrac{3}{x} = \dfrac{5}{45}$

@HomeTutor Prerequisite skills practice at classzone.com

Notetaking Skills   Highlighting the Key Step

In each chapter you will learn a new notetaking skill. In Chapter 9 you will apply the strategy of highlighting the key step to Example 3 on p. 456.

Leave space in your notebook to take notes from your textbook. As you use your textbook to review a lesson covered in class, take additional notes. You may want to highlight the key step in an example.

$\dfrac{3}{x} = \dfrac{5}{15}$ **Write proportion.**

$3 \cdot 15 = x \cdot 5$ **Cross product property**

$\dfrac{3 \cdot 15}{5} = \dfrac{x \cdot 5}{5}$ **Divide each side by 5.**

$9 = x$ **Simplify.**

9.1 Percents and Fractions

4.1.A.3 Understand and use ratios, proportions, and percents (including percents greater than 100 and less than 1) in a variety of situations.

Before You multiplied fractions and whole numbers.

Now You'll use a fraction to find the percent of a number.

Why? So you can calculate percents, as in Example 4.

KEY VOCABULARY
• percent, *p. 449*

The word *percent* means "per hundred." A **percent** is a ratio whose denominator is 100. The symbol for percent is %.

> *VOCABULARY*
> You can remember that percent means "per hundred" by thinking of how many cents are in a dollar.

KEY CONCEPT *For Your Notebook*

Understanding Percent

The model at the right has 16 out of 100 squares shaded. You can say that 16 percent of the squares are shaded.

16 percent

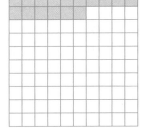

Numbers You can write 16 percent as $\frac{16}{100}$ or as 16%.

Algebra You can write p percent as $\frac{p}{100}$ or as p%.

EXAMPLE 1 **Writing Percents as Fractions**

Write the percent as a fraction.

a. $37\% = \frac{37}{100}$

b. $50\% = \frac{50}{100} = \frac{1}{2}$

EXAMPLE 2 **Writing Fractions as Percents**

To write a fraction as a percent, rewrite the fraction with a denominator of 100.

a. $\frac{4}{5} = \frac{4 \times 20}{5 \times 20} = \frac{80}{100} = 80\%$

b. $\frac{3}{4} = \frac{3 \times 25}{4 \times 25} = \frac{75}{100} = 75\%$

✓ **GUIDED PRACTICE** for Examples 1 and 2

Write the percent as a fraction or the fraction as a percent.

1. 24%

2. 55%

3. $\frac{7}{10}$

4. $\frac{1}{50}$

Common Percents					
$10\% = \dfrac{1}{10}$	$20\% = \dfrac{1}{5}$	$25\% = \dfrac{1}{4}$	$30\% = \dfrac{3}{10}$	$40\% = \dfrac{2}{5}$	$50\% = \dfrac{1}{2}$
$60\% = \dfrac{3}{5}$	$70\% = \dfrac{7}{10}$	$75\% = \dfrac{3}{4}$	$80\% = \dfrac{4}{5}$	$90\% = \dfrac{9}{10}$	$100\% = 1$

TAKE NOTES
Be sure to write these common percents in your notebook.

EXAMPLE 3   Finding a Percent of a Number

Find 60% of 75. Use the fact that $60\% = \dfrac{3}{5}$ and then multiply.

60% of $75 = \dfrac{3}{5} \cdot 75$ Write percent as a fraction.

$= \dfrac{3 \cdot \overset{15}{\cancel{75}}}{\underset{1}{\cancel{5}} \cdot 1}$ Use rule for multiplying fractions.
Divide out common factor.

$= 45$ Multiply.

EXAMPLE 4   Using Percents

Tennis In March of 2005, 14 of the top 100 women's tennis players were from the United States. What percent of players were *not* from the United States?

SOLUTION

You know that $\dfrac{14}{100} = 14\%$ of the players were from the United States. To find the percent of tennis players who were *not* from the United States, use the fact that the entire group of players represents 100%.

$$100\% - 14\% = 86\%$$

▶ **Answer** In March of 2005, 86% of the top 100 women's tennis players were *not* from the United States.

Animated Math at classzone.com

✓ **GUIDED PRACTICE**   for Examples 3 and 4

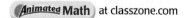

5. Find 70% of 900.   **6.** Find 25% of 200.

7. Tennis In March of 2005, 12 of the top 100 men's tennis players were from the Unites States. What percent of the players were *not* from the United States?

8. Class President During an election 112 out of 200 students in seventh grade voted for Lupe for class president. What percent of students did *not* vote for Lupe?

9.1 EXERCISES

HOMEWORK KEY

★ = **STANDARDIZED TEST PRACTICE**
Exs. 34, 55, 58, 59, 60, and 67

◯ = **HINTS AND HOMEWORK HELP**
for Exs. 3, 9, 13, 25, 57 at classzone.com

SKILL PRACTICE

1. VOCABULARY What does percent mean?

REWRITING PERCENTS Write the percent as a fraction in simplest form.

SEE EXAMPLE 1
on p. 449
for Exs. 2–11, 35

2. 11%   **3.** 23%   **4.** 82%   **5.** 20%   **6.** 8%

7. 67%   **8.** 34%   **9.** 92%   **10.** 14%   **11.** 25%

REWRITING FRACTIONS Write the fraction as a percent.

SEE EXAMPLE 2
on p. 449
for Exs. 12–21

12. $\frac{3}{10}$ **13.** $\frac{13}{25}$ **14.** $\frac{77}{100}$ **15.** $\frac{3}{5}$ **16.** $\frac{3}{20}$

17. $\frac{11}{25}$ **18.** $\frac{13}{50}$ **19.** $\frac{14}{25}$ **20.** $\frac{1}{10}$ **21.** $\frac{7}{20}$

FINDING PERCENTS Find the percent of the number.

SEE EXAMPLE 3
on p. 450
for Exs. 22–34

22. 80% of 55   **23.** 30% of 90   **24.** 50% of 250   **25.** 60% of 85

26. 20% of 75   **27.** 50% of 32   **28.** 45% of 180   **29.** 90% of 20

30. 40% of 95   **31.** 75% of 52   **32.** 25% of 368   **33.** 60% of 200

34. ★ **MULTIPLE CHOICE** What is 40% of 120?

(A) 3   (B) 24   (C) 48   (D) 300

35. ERROR ANALYSIS Describe and correct the error made in writing the percent as a fraction.

$$\times \quad 80\% = \frac{8}{100} = \frac{2}{25}$$

MENTAL MATH Find the percent of the number mentally.

36. 10% of 60   **37.** 25% of 40   **38.** 20% of 80   **39.** 75% of 36

40. 50% of 68   **41.** 30% of 200   **42.** 40% of 20   **43.** 60% of 90

⟨xy⟩ ALGEBRA Write the percent as a fraction. Then solve the proportion.

44. $\frac{13}{20} = x\%$ **45.** $\frac{9}{25} = y\%$ **46.** $\frac{1}{10} = z\%$ **47.** $\frac{3}{50} = w\%$

ORDERING RATIOS Order the given ratios from least to greatest.

48. 6 to 25, 23%, $\frac{1}{4}$ **49.** 81%, $\frac{41}{50}$, 4 to 5   **50.** 73%, $\frac{7}{10}$, 18 to 25

51. $\frac{9}{10}$, 23 to 25, 89%   **52.** $\frac{13}{20}$, 66%, 16 to 25   **53.** 3 to 20, $\frac{7}{50}$, 12%

54. CHALLENGE Is 80% of 80% of 125 the same as 64% of 125? *Justify* your reasoning. What number property do you need to use?

55. ★ **WRITING** What does 100% of a set represent? For example, what part of your class is 100% of it? *Explain.*

SEE EXAMPLE 4
on p. 450
for Exs. 56–59

56. **RECYCLING** In the United States, 10 states refund money for the return of bottles. What percent of states do *not* refund money for recycling of bottles?

57. **GARAGES** On your street, 18 out of 20 houses have attached garages. What percent of houses on your street have attached garages?

58. ★ **MULTIPLE CHOICE** A bake sale raised $300 for a school trip. If 20% of the money covered bake sale expenses, how much went toward the trip?

ⓐ $20   ⓑ $60   ⓒ $240   ⓓ $280

59. ★ **SHORT RESPONSE** Katherine correctly answered 80% of the questions on her Spanish test. The test had 60 questions. How many questions did Katherine answer incorrectly? *Explain* how you found your answer.

60. ★ **EXTENDED RESPONSE** The atmosphere of Mars is made up of about 95% carbon dioxide and about 3% nitrogen.

   a. **Rewrite** Write the percents above as fractions.

   b. **Interpret** About what percent of the atmosphere of Mars consists of gases other than carbon dioxide and nitrogen? What fraction is this?

   c. **Analyze** A probe on Mars took a 500-milliliter sample of the atmosphere. How many milliliters of the sample would you expect to be gases other than carbon dioxide and nitrogen? *Explain* your reasoning.

61. **CHALLENGE** Aaron received 320 points out of a possible 400 in his History class. What percent of the possible points did Aaron receive? How many more points did he need to receive an A, 93%, in History?

 NEW JERSEY MIXED REVIEW   **TEST PRACTICE** at classzone.com

62. Todd can swim 200 meters in 3 minutes 45 seconds. If he competes in the 800-meter race, about how many minutes will it take him to swim the race if he swims at the same rate?

ⓐ 1 min   ⓑ 7.5 min   ⓒ 15 min   ⓓ 900 min

63. Rachel has a map of her hometown. The map uses a scale in which 1 inch equals 2.5 miles. What distance on Rachel's map represents the 10 miles between her school and the museum?

ⓐ 0.25 in.   ⓑ 2 in.   ⓒ 4 in.   ⓓ 25 in.

GOAL
Use a percent bar model to find a percent.

MATERIALS
• paper and pencil

9.2 Using Percent Bar Models

You can find a percent using a percent bar model.

EXPLORE Find what percent 4 is of 9.

STEP 1 **Draw** a percent bar model and label it as shown.

Label the left side of the bar from 0 to the whole amount, 9. Then shade the bar to the part of the whole, 4.

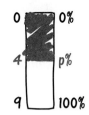

Label the right side of the bar from 0% to 100%. Use $p\%$ to represent the unknown percent.

STEP 2 **Use** the percent bar model to write and solve a proportion.

The arrangement of the numbers in the percent bar model tells you how to set up the proportion.

$$\frac{4}{9} = \frac{p}{100}$$ **Write proportion.**

$$100 \cdot \frac{4}{9} = 100 \cdot \frac{p}{100}$$ **Multiply each side by 100.**

$$\frac{400}{9}, \text{ or } 44\frac{4}{9} = p$$ **Simplify.**

▶ **Answer** The number 4 is $44\frac{4}{9}\%$ of 9.

PRACTICE Use a percent bar model to find the percent.

1. What percent of 48 is 6?

2. What percent of 135 is 90?

DRAW CONCLUSIONS

3. **REASONING** *Describe* how to use a percent bar model to find what number is 72% of 200. Then find the number.

4. **REASONING** *Describe* how to use a percent bar model to find a percent of any number.

9.2 Percents and Proportions

 4.1.A.3 Understand and use ratios, proportions, and percents (including percents greater than 100 and less than 1) in a variety of situations.

Before You used a fraction to find a percent of a number.

Now You will use proportions to solve percent problems.

Why? So you can find a number from a percent, as in Example 2.

KEY VOCABULARY
- **proportion,** p. 418
- **percent,** p. 449

You can use proportions to solve percent problems.

KEY CONCEPT
For Your Notebook

Solving Percent Problems

You can represent "a is p percent of b" with the proportion

$$\frac{a}{b} = \frac{p}{100}$$

where a is part of the base b and $p\%$, or $\frac{p}{100}$, is the percent.

EXAMPLE 1 Finding a Percent

READING
In a percent problem, the word that follows "of" is usually the base b.

 What percent of 3 is 1?

$\dfrac{a}{b} = \dfrac{p}{100}$ **Write proportion.**

$\dfrac{1}{3} = \dfrac{p}{100}$ **Substitute 1 for *a* and 3 for *b*.**

$100 \cdot \dfrac{1}{3} = 100 \cdot \dfrac{p}{100}$ **Multiply each side by 100.**

$33\dfrac{1}{3} = p$ **Simplify.**

▶ **Answer** 1 is $33\dfrac{1}{3}\%$ of 3.

✓ **GUIDED PRACTICE** for Example 1

Use a proportion to answer the question.

1. What percent of 40 is 16?   **2.** What percent of 400 is 52?

3. What percent of 80 is 15?   **4.** What percent of 144 is 12?

5. Sandals In a classroom of 25 students, 16 students are wearing sandals. What percent of the students are wearing sandals?

Writing Fractions as Percents By using a proportion, you can write any fraction as a percent. Example 1 showed that $\frac{1}{3} = 33\frac{1}{3}\%$. Here are some other common percents that you should remember.

Common Percents					
$12\frac{1}{2}\% = \frac{1}{8}$	$33\frac{1}{3}\% = \frac{1}{3}$	$37\frac{1}{2}\% = \frac{3}{8}$	$62\frac{1}{2}\% = \frac{5}{8}$	$66\frac{2}{3}\% = \frac{2}{3}$	$87\frac{1}{2}\% = \frac{7}{8}$

In Lesson 9.1, you found a common percent of a number using a fraction. Now you can use a proportion to find any percent of a number.

EXAMPLE 2 Finding a Part of a Base

Surfing In a survey, 525 teenagers were asked to name the water sport that they would most like to try, and 20% said "surfing." How many teenagers said "surfing"?

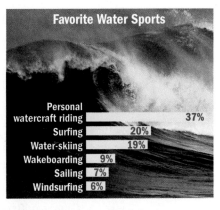
Favorite Water Sports

Personal watercraft riding 37%
Surfing 20%
Water-skiing 19%
Wakeboarding 9%
Sailing 7%
Windsurfing 6%

SOLUTION

To find the number of teenagers who said "surfing," use a proportion.

$$\frac{a}{b} = \frac{p}{100}$$ Write proportion.

$$\frac{a}{525} = \frac{20}{100}$$ Substitute 525 for *b* and 20 for *p*.

$$525 \cdot \frac{a}{525} = 525 \cdot \frac{20}{100}$$ Multiply each side by 525.

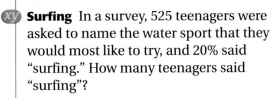 Use rule for multiplying fractions. Divide out common factors.

$$a = 105$$ Multiply.

▶ **Answer** In the survey, 105 of the teenagers said "surfing."

Check 20% of 525 is about $\frac{1}{5}$ of 500, or about 100, so 105 is reasonable.

✓ **GUIDED PRACTICE** for Example 2

Use a proportion to answer the questions.

6. What number is 76% of 25?

7. What number is 5% of 400?

8. What number is 12% of 50?

9. What number is 37% of 200?

Cross Product Property When you are asked to find the base in a percent problem, you solve for b in the proportion $\frac{a}{b} = \frac{p}{100}$. In this case, you should use the cross products property, as shown in Example 3.

EXAMPLE 3 Finding a Base

 42 is 30% of what number?

SOLUTION

$$\frac{a}{b} = \frac{p}{100}$$ Write proportion.

$$\frac{42}{b} = \frac{30}{100}$$ Substitute 42 for a and 30 for p.

$$42 \cdot 100 = b \cdot 30$$ Cross product property

$$\frac{42 \cdot 100}{30} = \frac{b \cdot 30}{30}$$ Divide each side by 30.

$$140 = b$$ Simplify.

▶ **Answer** 42 is 30% of 140.

Check 30% of 140 is about $\frac{1}{3}$ of 150, which is 50. Since 50 is close to 42, the answer is reasonable.

TAKE NOTES
To help you remember the process of solving a percent problem, you may want to highlight the key step in the process.

 GUIDED PRACTICE   for Example 3

10. 14 is 56% of what number?

11. 9 is 45% of what number?

9.2 EXERCISES

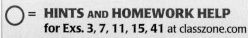

HOMEWORK KEY

★ = **STANDARDIZED TEST PRACTICE**
Exs. 19, 40, 42, 47, and 64

◯ = **HINTS** AND **HOMEWORK HELP**
for Exs. 3, 7, 11, 15, 41 at classzone.com

SKILL PRACTICE

VOCABULARY Copy and complete the proportion for the given question.

1. What percent of 20 is 8?

$$\frac{?}{?} = \frac{p}{100}$$

2. What number is 30% of 50?

$$\frac{a}{?} = \frac{?}{100}$$

MATCHING Match the question with the correct proportion.

SEE EXAMPLES 1, 2, AND 3
on pp. 454–456
for Exs. 3–5

3. 60 is 25% of what number?

A. $\frac{a}{60} = \frac{25}{100}$

4. What percent of 60 is 25?

B. $\frac{25}{60} = \frac{p}{100}$

5. What is 25% of 60?

C. $\frac{60}{b} = \frac{25}{100}$

USING PROPORTIONS Use a proportion to answer the question. Check your answer for reasonableness.

SEE EXAMPLES 1, 2, AND 3
on pp. 454–456
for Exs. 6–19

6. What percent of 30 is 3?

7. What percent of 50 is 47?

8. 51 is 17% of what number?

9. 16 is 80% of what number?

10. What number is 14% of 350?

11. 12 is 8% of what number?

12. What percent of 600 is 180?

13. What number is 75% of 44?

14. 18 is 45% of what number?

15. What percent of 20 is 6?

16. What number is $12\frac{1}{2}$% of 64?

17. What number is $66\frac{2}{3}$% of 81?

Animated Math at classzone.com

18. ERROR ANALYSIS Describe and correct the error made in answering the following question.

What number is 30% of 62?

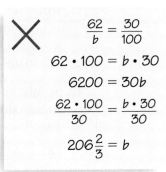

$$\frac{62}{b} = \frac{30}{100}$$
$$62 \cdot 100 = b \cdot 30$$
$$6200 = 30b$$
$$\frac{62 \cdot 100}{30} = \frac{b \cdot 30}{30}$$
$$206\frac{2}{3} = b$$

19. ★ MULTIPLE CHOICE What percent of 155 is 62?

  Ⓐ $2\frac{1}{2}$%   Ⓑ 25%

  Ⓒ 40%   Ⓓ 96%

INTERPRETING MODELS Write the fraction represented by the model as a percent. Round your answer to the nearest whole percent.

20.

21.

22.

23.

ESTIMATION Estimate the answer. Use common percents.

24. What percent of 256 is 52?

25. 88 is what percent of 359?

26. 25 is 64% of what number?

27. What is 35% of 313?

28. What is 73% of 195?

29. What is 39% of 78?

30. MENTAL MATH If 1% of a number is 6, what is the number? *Explain.*

31. REASONING If 5% of a number is y, then what is 100% of the number?

✗ CHALLENGE Use a proportion to answer the question in terms of x.

32. What number is 25% of $8x$?

33. $25x$ is 10% of what number?

34. What percent of $5x$ is $3x$?

35. What percent of $40x$ is $15x$?

36. 5% of what number is x?

37. What number is 80% of $75x$?

SEE EXAMPLES 1, 2, AND 3
on pp. 454–456
for Exs. 38–43

38. THEATER Students are auditioning for a school play. Only 18 out of the 45 students auditioning will get a part in the play. What percent of the students who audition will be in the play?

39. AUTO RACING The first lap of an auto race is 2500 meters. This is 10% of the total race distance. What is the total race distance?

40. ★ WRITING *Describe* how you can identify the base in a percent problem. Include three examples.

41. **HOMEWORK** So far you have completed 80% of your math homework. Your assignment has 45 problems. How many problems do you have left to do?

42. ★ MULTIPLE CHOICE A business made a $5650 profit this month. Last month the business made about 92% of this month's profit. About how much was last month's profit?

  (A) $1628   **(B)** $5198   **(C)** $5558   **(D)** $6141

43. MULTI-STEP PROBLEM Eighty students at Jackson Middle School were asked if they prefer to exercise before school or after school. The results are given in the percent bar model below.

a. **Write a Percent Problem** Use the diagram to copy and complete.

   Before School: 28 is what percent of __?__?

   After School: __?__ is what percent of 80?

b. **Write a Proportion** Identify which value represents *the base, the part of the base,* and *the percent* in each of the percent problems in part (a). Then write a proportion for each problem.

c. **Solve the Proportion** Jackson Middle School enrolls a total of 400 students. Predict how many of these students would prefer to exercise after school. *Explain* your reasoning.

44. ESTIMATION A total of 243 vehicles visited a car wash today. About 62% of these vehicles were cars. Estimate the number of cars washed today.

45. VOLCANOES There are about 65 active volcanoes in the United States. This is about $4\frac{1}{3}\%$ of the total number of volcanoes on Earth. Estimate the number of volcanoes on Earth.

46. ORANGUTANS In 1997, there were about 35,900 orangutans remaining in Borneo and Sumatra. In 1998, the population had fallen by about 43%. About how many orangutans were left in Borneo and Sumatra in 1998? If the population fell by this percent again, what would the population have been the following year?

47. ★ **SHORT RESPONSE** *Explain* how you can mentally find the equivalent percent for $\frac{1}{6}$ using the common percents on page 455.

48. RAKING LEAVES You rake leaves to earn extra money, charging $25 per lawn. On Saturday, you rake 6 lawns. On Sunday you rake 2 lawns. You decide that you want to save 60% of your earnings and spend the rest. How much money do you spend? How much money do you save?

49. WOMEN'S SOCCER A season record for the Boston Breakers, a women's professional soccer team, is shown in the table. What percent of the games did the Breakers lose? What percent did they tie? Round your answers to the nearest whole percent.

Boston Breakers		
Wins	**Losses**	**Ties**
8	10	3

50. REASONING Your friend spends about 35% of each year sleeping, about 10% eating, about 25% on summer vacation, about 15% on weekends, and about 5% on grooming. He claims that leaves about 10% of each year, or about 36 days, to go to school. What is the error in this reasoning?

51. CHALLENGE You took a science test that contained 30 multiple choice questions and 15 true-or-false questions. Each question is worth the same number of points. You answered 12 true-or-false questions correctly, and you answered 90% of the multiple choice questions correctly. What percent of the entire test did you answer correctly? *Explain* your reasoning.

NEW JERSEY MIXED REVIEW

TEST PRACTICE at classzone.com

52. Shundra is saving $\frac{3}{5}$ of her allowance each week. What percent of her allowance is she saving?

(A) 35%   (B) 45%   (C) 60%   (D) 80%

53. Jamal bought 18 boxes of juice and a dozen bottles of water. The juice was priced at 6 boxes for $2.50, and the water was priced at 4 bottles for $2.20. What is the total amount of money he spent, not including tax?

(A) $4.70   (B) $9.10   (C) $9.70   (D) $14.10

9.3 Percents and Decimals

  4.1.A.5   Use whole numbers, fractions, decimals, and percents to represent equivalent forms of the same number.

Before   You wrote percents as fractions and fractions as percents.

Now   You'll write percents as decimals and decimals as percents.

Why?   So you can determine changes in income, as in Ex. 59.

KEY VOCABULARY
- decimal, *p. 56*
- percent, *p. 449*

You can write a percent as a decimal and a decimal as a percent by first writing the percent or decimal as a fraction. Here are two examples:

$$37\% = \frac{37}{100} = 0.37 \qquad\qquad 0.63 = \frac{63}{100} = 63\%$$

Notice that to write a percent as a decimal, you drop the percent sign and move the decimal point two places to the left. To write a decimal as a percent, you move the decimal point two places to the right and add a percent sign.

EXAMPLE 1   Writing Percents as Decimals

a. $48\% = 48\%$
$= 0.48$

b. $9\% = 09\%$
$= 0.09$

c. $75.5\% = 75.5\%$
$= 0.755$

EXAMPLE 2   Writing Decimals as Percents

a. $0.13 = .13$
$= 13\%$

b. $0.04 = .04$
$= 4\%$

c. $0.027 = .027$
$= 2.7\%$

★ EXAMPLE 3   Standardized Test Practice

Joe saves $\frac{5}{6}$ of his allowance. What percent of his allowance does Joe save?

(A) 35%   **(B)** 56.8%   **(C)** 83.3%   **(D)** 90%

SOLUTION

$\frac{5}{6} \approx 0.833$ **Divide 5 by 6. Round to the nearest thousandth.**

$= 83.3\%$ **Write as a percent.**

▶ **Answer** Joe saves about 83.3% of his allowance.
The correct answer is C. (A) (B) **(C)** (D)

READING
The symbol $\approx$ is read "is approximately equal to." It indicates that a result has been rounded and is not exact.

Write the percent as a decimal or the decimal as a percent.

1. 25%   **2.** 5.2%   **3.** 0.06   **4.** 0.578

5. Saving Mary saves $\frac{5}{8}$ of her allowance. What percent of her allowance does Mary save?

Animated Math at classzone.com

Small and Large Percents Percents less than 1% represent numbers less than 0.01, or $\frac{1}{100}$. Percents greater than 100% represent numbers greater than 1. For example, the models below represent **0.5%** and **150%**.

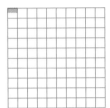   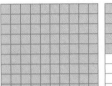

           0.5%   **150%**

EXAMPLE 4   **Rewrite Small and Large Percents**

Geography The surface area of Lake Tarpon is 0.5% of the surface area of Lake Okeechobee. The surface area of Lake Weohyakapka is 300% of the surface area of Lake Tarpon. Write these percents as decimals.

SOLUTION

To write the percents as decimals, follow the same rules as for percents between 1% and 100%.

Lake Tarpon: 0.5% = 00.5%

                  = 0.005

Lake Weohyakapka: 300% = 300%

                              = 3

✓ **GUIDED PRACTICE**   **for Example 4**

Write the percent as a decimal.

6. 0.25%   **7.** 250%   **8.** 375%   **9.** 0.0014%

EXAMPLE 5 Using a Percent Less Than 1%

Water The total amount of water on Earth, including salt water and fresh water, is about 326,000,000 cubic miles. Of this amount, 0.009% is in fresh water lakes. What is the amount of water in fresh water lakes?

SOLUTION

$$0.009\% \text{ of } 326{,}000{,}000 = 0.00009 \times 326{,}000{,}000 \qquad \text{Write percent as a decimal.}$$

$$= 29{,}340 \qquad \text{Multiply.}$$

▶ **Answer** The amount of water in fresh water lakes is 29,340 cubic miles.

Check 0.009% is about 0.01%, or about 0.0001. You move the decimal point in 326,000,000 four places to the left to estimate 0.0001 × 326,000,000 = 32,600. So 29,340 is reasonable. ✓

AVOID ERRORS
When you multiply a number by a percent less than 100%, the result should be less than the original number. Multiplying by a percent greater than 100% results in a number greater than the original.

✓ **GUIDED PRACTICE** for Example 5

10. **Heart Rate** Trang's resting heart rate is 72 beats per minute. During intense exercise, his heart rate is 250% of his resting heart rate. What is Trang's heart rate during intense exercise?

9.3 **EXERCISES**

HOMEWORK KEY

★ = **STANDARDIZED TEST PRACTICE**
Exs. 40, 58, 59, 62, and 73

◯ = **HINTS AND HOMEWORK HELP**
for Exs. 3, 9, 17, 25, 53 at classzone.com

SKILL PRACTICE

1. **VOCABULARY** Write a decimal that is greater than 100%. Write a decimal that is less than 1%.

2. **VOCABULARY** What steps would you take to write 52% as a decimal?

REWRITING PERCENTS Write the percent as a decimal.

SEE EXAMPLES 1 AND 4
on pp. 460–461
for Exs. 3–15

3. 47%
4. 3%
5. 8%
6. 11%
7. 0.15%
8. 0.02%
9. 0.3%
10. 0.7%
11. 42.5%
12. 3.01%
13. 125%
14. 210%

15. **ERROR ANALYSIS** Describe and correct the error made in writing the percent as a decimal.

0.002% = 0.002% = 0.2

REWRITING DECIMALS Write the decimal as a percent.

SEE EXAMPLE 2
on p. 460
for Exs. 16–23

16. 0.26
17. 0.07
18. 0.205
19. 2.03
20. 15.5
21. 1.184
22. 0.0085
23. 0.00105

REWRITING FRACTIONS Write the fraction as a percent. Round to the nearest tenth of a percent.

SEE EXAMPLE 3
on p. 460
for Exs. 24–31

24. $\frac{11}{15}$ **25.** $\frac{13}{21}$ **26.** $\frac{17}{18}$ **27.** $\frac{23}{30}$

28. $\frac{14}{39}$ **29.** $\frac{5}{26}$ **30.** $\frac{5}{1000}$ **31.** $\frac{52}{10,000}$

PERCENTS AND MIXED NUMBERS Write the percent as a decimal and as a mixed number. Write the mixed number as a decimal and as a percent.

32. 450% **33.** 252% **34.** $3\frac{1}{4}$ **35.** $6\frac{4}{5}$

SEE EXAMPLE 5
on p. 462
for Exs. 36–39

USING PERCENTS Find the percent of the number.

36. 0.8% of 200 **37.** 0.003% of 550 **38.** 350% of 12 **39.** 465% of 30

40. ★ **MULTIPLE CHOICE** Which list of values is in order from least to greatest?

(**A**) 1018%, 10.2, 102, 1016   (**B**) 10.2, 1018%, 102, 1016

(**C**) 10.2, 102, 1018%, 1016   (**D**) 10.2, 102, 1016, 1018%

NUMBER SENSE Copy and complete the statement using <, >, or =.

41. 0.14% _?_ 0.014 **42.** 3.4 _?_ 34% **43.** 0.59 _?_ 59% **44.** 44.80% _?_ $\frac{6}{7}$

45. $\frac{4}{9}$ _?_ 51% **46.** 85% _?_ $\frac{21}{25}$ **47.** 0.62 _?_ $\frac{16}{25}$ **48.** 0.52 _?_ $\frac{13}{25}$

CHALLENGE Order the values from least to greatest.

49. 0.33%, 0.00311, $\frac{1}{300}$, 0.0031   **50.** $\frac{461}{50}$, 920%, 9.02, 9.202

PROBLEM SOLVING

51. MENTAL MATH What is 200% of 8? What is 300% of 8? What is 400% of 8? *Describe* how you can find these answers using mental math.

SEE EXAMPLE 5
on p. 462
for Exs. 52–53

52. MENTAL MATH What is 0.1% of 9? What is 0.01% of 9? What is 0.001% of 9? *Describe* how you can find these answers using mental math.

53. TOY CARS The price of a miniature toy car in 1968 was 0.295% of its current price. Today the car is a collector's item and is priced at $200. What was the price of the toy car in 1968?

REASONING Tell whether the statement is reasonable. *Explain.*

54. "Work" was listed as an after school activity by 110% of your classmates.

55. Of the 100 people surveyed, 0.05% said that they drive mopeds.

56. Your math test score is 125% of your last test score.

57. MOVIE SEQUELS A movie made $1,582,000 at the box office. Its sequel made 104% of the original. How much money did the sequel make?

58. ★ MULTIPLE CHOICE LCD TV sales represented about 0.676% of the total sales of electronics in 2003. Which value is *not* equal to 0.676%?

(A) 0.00676   (B) $\frac{676}{1000}$ (C) $\frac{676}{100,000}$ (D) $\frac{169}{25,000}$

59. ★ SHORT RESPONSE The money you earned this summer is 120% of the money you earned last summer. Did you earn more or less money this summer than you did last summer? What information do you need to find how much you made this year? *Explain* your reasoning.

60. HOUSING COSTS The median sale price of a house in San Bernardino, California, in 2002 was $176,000. In 2005, the median sale price rose to $343,000. What percent of $176,000 is $343,000? Using this calculation, did the median price of a house in San Bernardino, California, double? *Explain* your reasoning.

61. POPULATION In 2005, Argentina's population was about 0.613% of the world population of about 6,446,000,000 people. Find a high and a low estimate of the population of Argentina in 2005.

62. ★ OPEN-ENDED MATH *Describe* a real life situation in which a percent greater than 100% makes sense, and one where it does not make sense.

63. APPLES In 2001, 229 million cartons of apples were produced in the U.S. Of these apples, 61% were eaten as fresh fruit. Of the apples used for other apple products, 21% were used for cider and juice. Estimate how many of the total cartons of apples were *not* used for cider and juice. *Justify* your answer.

64. CHALLENGE You enlarge a 4-inch by 4-inch graph on a photo copier to 150%. Then you enlarge the enlargement to 150%. Are the dimensions of your graph now 200%, 225%, or 300% of the original dimensions? *Justify* your answer.

 NEW JERSEY MIXED REVIEW 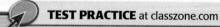 **TEST PRACTICE** at classzone.com

65. In a classroom of 20 students, 70% of the students are wearing jeans. Which proportion can be used to determine how many students are wearing jeans?

(A) $\frac{20}{a} = \frac{70}{100}$ (B) $\frac{a}{100} = \frac{70}{20}$ (C) $\frac{20}{70} = \frac{a}{100}$ (D) $\frac{a}{20} = \frac{70}{100}$

66. Kendra bought 10.5 gallons of gasoline for $25.20. How much did she pay for each gallon of gasoline?

(A) $2.38   (B) $2.40   (C) $2.52   (D) $2.60

9.4 The Percent Equation

 4.1.A.3 Understand and use ratios, proportions, and percents (including percents greater than 100 and less than 1) in a variety of situations.

Before You used proportions to solve percent problems.

Now You'll use equations to solve percent problems.

Why? So you can find a percent of a goal, as in Example 1.

KEY VOCABULARY
• percent, *p. 449*
• percent equation, *p. 465*

In Lesson 9.2, you solved percent problems using the proportion $\frac{a}{b} = \frac{p}{100}$, where a is part of the base b and p is the percent. You can solve this proportion for a. Then you obtain the percent equation described below.

KEY CONCEPT *For Your Notebook*

The Percent Equation

You can represent "a is p percent of b" with the equation

$$a = p\% \cdot b$$

where a is part of the base b and $p\%$ is the percent.

EXAMPLE 1 Finding a Part of a Base

Fundraising Your class has raised 80% of its goal of $8000 for a trip to Washington, D.C. How much money has your class raised for the trip?

SOLUTION

$a = p\% \cdot b$	**Write percent equation.**
$= 80\% \cdot 8000$	**Substitute 80 for p and 8000 for b.**
$= 0.8 \cdot 8000$	**Write percent as a decimal.**
$= 6400$	**Multiply.**

▶ **Answer** Your class has raised $6400 for the trip to Washington, D.C.

✔ **GUIDED PRACTICE** for Example 1

1. What number is 20% of 110?

2. What number is 25% of 88?

3. What number is 40% of 150?

4. What number is 75% of 800?

EXAMPLE 2 Finding a Percent

CHECK REASONABLENESS
You can use common percents to check the reasonableness of the answer. You know that 50%, or $\frac{1}{2}$, of 150 is 75. Because 90 is more than 50% of 150, 60% seems reasonable.

 What percent of 150 is 90?

$$a = p\% \cdot b \qquad \text{Write percent equation.}$$

$$90 = p\% \cdot 150 \qquad \text{Substitute 90 for } a \text{ and 150 for } b.$$

$$\frac{90}{150} = \frac{p\% \cdot 150}{150} \qquad \text{Divide each side by 150.}$$

$$\frac{3}{5} = p\% \qquad \text{Simplify fraction.}$$

$$= 60\% \qquad \text{Write as a percent.}$$

▶ **Answer** The number 90 is 60% of 150.

EXAMPLE 3 Finding a Base

The number 117 is 45% of what number?

$$a = p\% \cdot b \qquad \text{Write percent equation.}$$

$$117 = 45\% \cdot b \qquad \text{Substitute 117 for } a \text{ and 45 for } p.$$

$$\frac{117}{0.45} = \frac{0.45 \cdot b}{0.45} \qquad \begin{array}{l}\text{Write percent as a decimal.}\\\text{Then divide each side by 0.45.}\end{array}$$

$$260 = b \qquad \text{Simplify.}$$

▶ **Answer** The number 117 is 45% of 260.

EXAMPLE 4 Finding a Commission

VOCABULARY
A *commission* is money earned by many sales people. It is usually a percent of each sale.

Shoe Sales A shoe salesperson sells a pair of shoes for $60. The sales person receives a 9% commission on the sale. How much is the commission?

SOLUTION

$$a = p\% \cdot b \qquad \text{Write percent equation.}$$

$$= 9\% \cdot 60 \qquad \text{Substitute 9 for } p \text{ and 60 for } b.$$

$$= 0.09 \cdot 60 \qquad \text{Write percent as a decimal.}$$

$$= 5.4 \qquad \text{Multiply.}$$

▶ **Answer** The commission is $5.40.

✓ **GUIDED PRACTICE** for Examples 2, 3, and 4

5. 50 is what percent of 250? **6.** 130 is 65% of what number?

7. Commission A clothing salesperson sells a suit for $350. The salesperson receives an 8% commission on the sale. How much is the commission?

EXAMPLE 5 Standardized Test Practice

> **Publishing** A company published 132 books last year, and 18 became bestsellers. Which best represents the percent of books the company published last year that did *not* become bestsellers?
>
> **(A)** 14%   **(B)** 18%   **(C)** 86%   **(D)** 114%

ELIMINATE CHOICES
When dealing with percent of books that were not bestsellers, you cannot have a percentage greater than 100. So, you can eliminate choice D.

SOLUTION

You know that $132 - 18 = 114$ books did not become bestsellers.

$$a = p\% \cdot b$$ **Write percent equation.**

$$114 = p\% \cdot 132$$ **Substitute 114 for *a* and 132 for *b*.**

$$\frac{114}{132} = \frac{p\% \cdot 132}{132}$$ **Divide each side by 132.**

$$\frac{19}{22} = p\%$$ **Simplify fraction.**

$$86.36\% \approx p\%$$ **Write as a percent. Round to the nearest hundredth.**

ANOTHER WAY
You could also find the percent of books that became best sellers and then subtract from 100%.

▶ **Answer** Approximately 86% of the books did not become bestsellers. The correct answer is C. **(A) (B) (C) (D)**

✓ **GUIDED PRACTICE** for Example 5

8. **What If?** Suppose the company in Example 5 published 24 bestsellers. What percent of books published were *not* bestsellers?

9.4 EXERCISES

HOMEWORK KEY

★ = **STANDARDIZED TEST PRACTICE**
Exs. 19, 33, 35, 40, and 51

○ = **HINTS AND HOMEWORK HELP**
for Exs. 3, 5, 13, 17, 31 at classzone.com

SKILL PRACTICE

1. **VOCABULARY** State the percent equation in words.

2. **VOCABULARY** Does the answer to the following question represent *part of the base*, the *base*, or the *percent:* Ten is 25% of what number?

USING THE PERCENT EQUATION Find the base or the part of the base.

SEE EXAMPLES 1 AND 3
on pp. 465–466
for Exs. 3–12

3. What number is 20% of 200?
4. What number is 40% of 500?
5. 45 is 25% of what number?
6. 91 is 65% of what number?
7. What number is 35% of 300?
8. What number is 15% of 200?
9. 65 is 65% of what number?
10. 8 is 32% of what number?
11. What number is 32% of 125?
12. 180 is 150% of what number?

FINDING THE PERCENT Use the percent equation to find the percent.
Round to the nearest whole percent if necessary.

SEE EXAMPLE 2
on p. 466
for Exs. 13–19

13. 35 is what percent of 50?

14. 54 is what percent of 60?

15. What percent of 300 is 51?

16. 42 is what percent of 62?

17. What percent of 111 is 80?

18. What percent of 65 is 39?

19. ★ **MULTIPLE CHOICE** What percent of 75 is 33 to the nearest whole percent?

(A) 23%   (B) 44%   (C) 228%   (D) 440%

NUMBER SENSE Copy and complete the statement using <, >, or =.

20. 40% of 120 _?_ 120% of 40

21. 20% of 60 _?_ 30% of 50

22. 160% of 15 _?_ 1% of 240

23. 25% of 100 _?_ 50% of 50

PATTERNS Copy and complete the pattern.

24. 15% of _?_ is 3

15% of _?_ is 6

15% of _?_ is 9

15% of _?_ is 12

15% of _?_ is $3n$

25. _?_ % of 80 = 2

_?_ % of 80 = 4

_?_ % of 80 = 6

_?_ % of 80 = 8

_?_ % of 80 = $2n$

(XV) CHALLENGE Tell if the statement is *true* or *false*. *Justify* your answer.

26. 25% of 25% of x is 50% of x

27. 5% of $(x + 5)$ is $5 + 5\%$ of x

28. 10% more than x is $1.1x$

29. 10% less than x is $0.9x$

PROBLEM SOLVING

30. BASKETBALL The Los Angeles Sparks won 87.5% of 32 regular season games before winning the WNBA championship in 2001. How many games did they win?

SEE EXAMPLE 4
on p. 466
for Ex. 31

31. **ART GALLERY** An art gallery receives a 15% commission on paintings sold. One day the gallery sells $575 worth of art. What commission is given to the art gallery?

SEE EXAMPLE 5
on p. 467
for Exs. 32–33

32. PRECIPITATION In Los Angeles, California, it rains an average of 35 days per year. About what percent of days in a year does it *not* rain in Los Angeles? Round your answer to the nearest percent.

33. ★ **MULTIPLE CHOICE** In Phoenix, Arizona, the average temperature is 85°F or higher during 25% of the year. During about how many *weeks* of the year is the average temperature below 85°F?

(A) 13   (B) 21   (C) 39   (D) 64

★ = **STANDARDIZED TEST PRACTICE**   ◯ = **HINTS AND HOMEWORK HELP** *at classzone.com*

34. COMMISSIONS Which is more money: a 10% commission on $630 or a 15% commission on $480?

35. ★ SHORT RESPONSE The Lions tied one game and won 80% of the 35 games they played this year. How many games did the team lose? *Explain* how you found your answer.

36. MUSIC SALES The table shows the percent of the total recording sales earned by each type of music in 2003. The total sales for the year were about $12 billion. Which type(s) of music earned over $2 billion that year? *Justify* your answer.

2003 Recording Sales	
Type of music	**Percent of total sales**
Rock	25%
Country	10%
Pop	9%
Rap/Hip-Hop	13%
Other	43%

37. WRITE AN EQUATION Kayla's weekly salary is 120% of the weekly salary of her sister Cecily. The total of their salaries is $165. What is Cecily's weekly salary?

38. MULTI-STEP PROBLEM The following results were found in a survey asking 2100 students how they get to school: 1365 take the school bus, 7% get a ride from their parents, 9% walk to school, and 294 ride their bikes. The remainder of the students take public transportation to school.

   a. What percent of students take the school bus to school?

   b. How many students walk to school?

   c. What percent of students and how many students take public transportation to school?

   d. *Explain* how you could check your answers to parts (a) – (c) for reasonableness.

39. GEOMETRY The length of a rectangle is 150% of its width, w. Use the percent equation to find the length of the rectangle in terms of w. Then write a formula for the area of the rectangle using only the variable w.

40. ★ WRITING *Explain* how you could use mental math to find a 15% tip for a $26 restaurant bill.

41. CHALLENGE You have $200, and you would like to rent a sailboat for 4 hours. It costs $45 per hour or $130 per day to rent a sailboat. What percent of your total money will you save by choosing the better rate? *Explain* how you found your answer.

42. CHALLENGE You receive an 87%, an 89%, and a 94% on three science tests. Each test was worth 215 points. How many questions did you correctly answer on each test? The final exam is worth 350 points. How many questions will you need to correctly answer to get a 90% in Science class? Each question, on every test, is worth 1 point.

43. Which problem situation matches the equation $x = 0.04 \cdot 375$?

   Ⓐ A salesperson sells a computer for $375, and receives a 4% commission on the sale. What is x, the commission?

   Ⓑ In a convention room with 375 people, 4 are professors. What is x, the percent of the people who are professors?

   Ⓒ Four percent of a town's population, or 375 people, are moving out of the town. What is x, the town's population?

   Ⓓ Your school has 375 students. Vera's school has 4% more students than your school. What is x, the number of students at Vera's school?

QUIZ *for Lessons 9.1–9.4*

Write the percent as a fraction or the fraction as a percent. *(p. 449)*

1. 18%   **2.** 74%   **3.** $\frac{17}{20}$ **4.** $\frac{12}{25}$

Use a proportion to answer the question. *(p. 454)*

5. What number is 82% of 50?   **6.** 11 is 22% of what number?

Use the percent equation to answer the question. *(p. 465)*

7. 82 is 205% of what number?   **8.** What percent is 28 of 50?

9. **CLASS PRESIDENT** Kathy and Joshua are the only candidates running for class president. Joshua got 45% of the votes. If all 40 students in the class voted, how many votes did Joshua receive? How many votes did Kathy receive? *(p. 465)*

Brain Game

Who should take the kick?

Your soccer team gets to take a penalty kick for a chance to score a goal and win the game. Data from past games are given for the 5 best players on the team. Based on the data, who should take the kick?

Name	Past Kicks
Brad	Has made 5 goals out of 15 attempts
Tommy	Has made 32% of goals attempted
Aaron	Has made $\frac{3}{10}$ of goals attempted
Sean	Has made 9 goals out of 24 attempts
John	Has made 0.35 of goals attempted

Lessons 9.1–9.4

1. **OUTDOOR ACTIVITIES** In a survey asking 1600 people their favorite outdoor activity, the following results were found: 352 chose hiking, 144 chose swimming, 14% chose camping, and 17% chose biking. Which statement below is best supported by this information?

   A. 62% of the people chose an activity other than the four listed.

   B. 0.22% of the people chose hiking.

   C. 48 more people chose biking than camping.

   D. 14.4% of the people chose swimming.

2. **SURVEY QUESTION** Of the 576 people who responded to a survey, 62.5% answered *yes* to a certain question and 25% answered *no*. Which equation can be used to find *x*, the number of people who answered neither *yes* nor *no*?

   A. $x = 0.125 \cdot 576$

   B. $x = 0.25 \cdot 576$

   C. $x = 0.625 \cdot 576$

   D. $x = 0.875 \cdot 576$

3. **MODELING A SITUATION** Which problem situation below could be described by the percent equation $x = 20\% \cdot 150$?

   A. You paid $150 for a desk that was on sale for 20% off the regular price.

   B. You missed 20 points on a 150-point test.

   C. A salad dressing contains 20% olive oil and 150 milliliters of vinegar.

   D. Of the 150 students in your grade, 20% used the computer lab today.

4. **OCEAN WATER** Ocean water is made up of about 86% oxygen, 11% hydrogen, and 2% chlorine by weight. What fraction of ocean water consists of elements other than oxygen, hydrogen, and chlorine?

   A. $\dfrac{1}{100}$

   B. $\dfrac{1}{10}$

   C. $\dfrac{1}{5}$

   D. $\dfrac{99}{100}$

5. **FAVORITE LUNCH** In a survey of seventh graders, 24 students said that their favorite lunch food was pizza. This was 40% of the students surveyed. How many students were surveyed?

   A. 40

   B. 60

   C. 64

   D. 96

6. **OPEN-ENDED** You are organizing a volleyball tournament. The number of players in this year's tournament is 125% of the number of players in last year's tournament. Last year, 28 players signed up.

   • How many players will be in this year's tournament?

   • How many more people are in this year's tournament than last year's?

   • Suppose the increase in the number of players in next year's tournament is 200% of the increase from last year. How many players will be in next year's tournament? *Explain.*

GOAL
Measure and draw angles using a protractor.

MATERIALS
• protractor
• compass
• tracing paper

9.5 Measuring Angles

You can use a protractor to measure and draw angles.

EXPLORE 1 Measure the angle.

An *angle* is formed by connecting two *rays*, as shown at the right. An angle is measured in units called *degrees* (°). The measure of an angle can be found by using a *protractor.*

ray

ray

STEP 1 **Place** the protractor on the angle so the protractor's center point is on the point where the two rays meet called the *vertex* of the angle. Line up one ray with the 0° line.

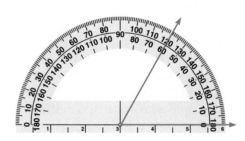

STEP 2 **Read** the angle measure. The measure of the angle is determined by reading where the other ray crosses the curved portion of the protractor. The measure of the angle is 60°.

Animated **Math** at classzone.com

The first ray lines up with the 0° mark on the inside scale, so read the measure from the inside scale.

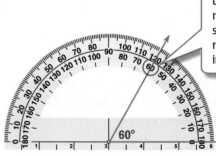

PRACTICE Use tracing paper to copy the angle. Then extend the rays and measure the angle using a protractor.

1.

2.

3.

4.

EXPLORE 2 **Draw an angle that measures 115°.**

STEP 1 **Draw** a ray using the straight edge of the protractor.

STEP 2 **Place** your protractor on the ray so that the endpoint lies on the center point of the protractor and the ray coincides with one of the 0° lines.

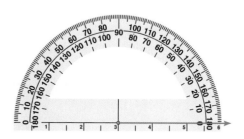

STEP 3 **Mark** your paper where the protractor reads 115°. To draw the angle, use the straight edge of the protractor to draw a ray from the endpoint of the first ray through the mark.

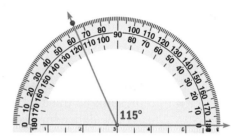

115°

PRACTICE **Draw an angle with the given measure.**

5. 120°   **6.** 80°   **7.** 55°   **8.** 105°

9. Use each of the angles from Exercises 5–8. Place the point of a compass at the vertex of the angle. Draw an *arc* across the two rays so the figure looks like a pie wedge. Use the same compass setting for each angle. Cut out the 4 figures and put them together so that the vertices coincide and there are no gaps or overlaps between the sides. What shape do these arcs form? What is the sum of the angle measures?

DRAW CONCLUSIONS

10. REASONING If an angle measure of 360° represents 100%, what percent does the measure of each angle in Exercises 5–8 represent? Round to the nearest tenth of a percent.

11. REASONING If an angle measure of 360° represents 100%, how many degrees correspond to 25%?

9.5 Circle Graphs

 4.5.E.1.d Graphical representations (e.g., a line graph)

Before	You found the percent of a number.
Now	You'll use percents to interpret and make circle graphs.
Why?	So you can compare means of transportation, as in Ex. 19.

KEY VOCABULARY
- **circle graph,** *p. 474*
- **ray,** *p. 474*
- **angle,** *p. 474*
- **vertex,** *p. 474*
- **degrees** (°), *p. 474*

Class Survey The results of a survey are displayed in the *circle graph* shown. What conclusions can you make about the data?

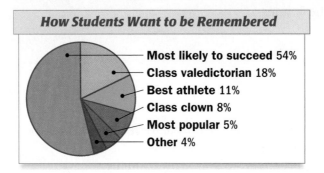

How Students Want to be Remembered

- Most likely to succeed 54%
- Class valedictorian 18%
- Best athlete 11%
- Class clown 8%
- Most popular 5%
- Other 4%

ADD THE DATA
When the data in a circle graph are expressed as fractions, decimals, or percents, the sum of the data must be 1, or 100%.

A **circle graph** displays data as sections of a circle. The entire circle represents all the data. Each section is labeled using the actual data or using the data expressed as fractions, decimals, or percents of the sum of the data.

EXAMPLE 1 Interpreting a Circle Graph

You can make conclusions about the data in the circle graph above.

- The largest section in the circle graph is labeled "most likely to succeed." So, this is how most students want to be remembered.

- More students want to be remembered as "class valedictorian" than as "class clown."

- Together, "class clown" and "best athlete" are more popular than "class valedictorian."

Using Angles The sections of a circle graph can be described mathematically using *angles*. A **ray** is part of a line. It begins at a point and extends in one direction without end. An **angle** consists of two rays that begin at a common point, called the **vertex**. The plural of vertex is *vertices*.

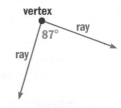

vertex
ray
87°
ray

You can use a protractor to find the measure of an angle, as shown on pages 472–473. Angles are measured in units called **degrees** (°).

Making Circle Graphs To make a circle graph, you need to find the appropriate angle measure for each section. The sum of all the angle measures must equal 360°.

EXAMPLE 2 Making a Circle Graph Using Percents

Siblings The table shows the results of a survey that asked students how many siblings (brothers and sisters) they have. Display the data in a circle graph.

Siblings	Percent
None	10%
One	40%
Two	25%
Three or more	25%

SOLUTION

USE A COMPASS
Need help using a compass? See p. 754.

STEP 1 **Find** the angle measure for each section.

None	**One sibling**
10% of 360° = **0.10** × 360°	40% of 360° = **0.40** × 360°
= 36°	= 144°

Two siblings	**Three or more siblings**
25% of 360° = **0.25** × 360°	25% of 360° = **0.25** × 360°
= 90°	= 90°

STEP 2 **Draw** a circle using a compass.

AVOID ERRORS
Make sure the vertices of the angles are at the center of the circle.

STEP 3 **Use** a protractor to draw an angle measuring 36°. Then label the section "None 10%."

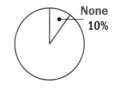

STEP 4 **Draw** and label the remaining sections.

STEP 5 **Write** a title for the graph.

Siblings

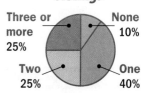

✓ GUIDED PRACTICE   for Examples 1 and 2

1. **Best Athlete** Use the circle graph on page 474. Can you determine, from the graph, the number of people who chose "Best athlete"? *Explain* your reasoning.

2. **Clothing** The table shows the results of a survey that asked students what they wear to school. Display the data in a circle graph.

3. **Conclude** Make a conclusion about the data in the circle graph in Exercise 2.

Clothing	Percent
Jeans	55%
Skirts	15%
Dress pants	30%

EXAMPLE 3 **Making a Circle Graph Using Data**

Exercising The table shows the results of a survey that asked people their favorite type of exercise. Display the data in a circle graph.

Favorite Exercise	People
Aerobics	8
Jogging	22
Cycling	6
Weightlifting	12

STEP 1 **Find** the total number of people surveyed: $8 + 22 + 6 + 12 = 48$.

STEP 2 **Find** the angle measure for each section. Write the data for each group as a fraction of all the people and multiply by 360°.

> **AVOID ERRORS**
> When you round percents or degree measures, they may not add up to 100% or 360°, but they should be close to one of those values.

Aerobics

$$\frac{8}{48} \times 360° = \frac{1}{6} \times 360° = 60°$$

Jogging

$$\frac{22}{48} \times 360° = \frac{11}{24} \times 360° = 165°$$

Cycling

$$\frac{6}{48} \times 360° = \frac{1}{8} \times 360° = 45°$$

Weightlifting

$$\frac{12}{48} \times 360° = \frac{1}{4} \times 360° = 90°$$

STEP 3 **Draw** and label the circle graph.

Animated Math at classzone.com

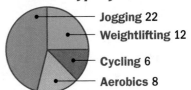

Favorite Type of Exercise

Jogging 22
Weightlifting 12
Cycling 6
Aerobics 8

✓ **GUIDED PRACTICE** **for Example 3**

4. What If? In Example 3, suppose that 12 people favored aerobics and 18 people favored jogging. Make a circle graph of the new data.

9.5 EXERCISES

HOMEWORK KEY

★ = **STANDARDIZED TEST PRACTICE**
Exs. 19, 21, 22, 23, and 32

○ = **HINTS** AND **HOMEWORK HELP**
for Exs. 3, 5, 17, 19 at classzone.com

SKILL PRACTICE

1. **VOCABULARY** Describe the steps for making a circle graph when the data are given in percents.

2. **VOCABULARY** A(n) __?__ consists of two rays that begin at a common point, called the __?__ .

> **SEE EXAMPLE 2**
> on p. 475
> for Exs. 3–6

FINDING ANGLE MEASURES **Find the angle measure that corresponds to the percent of a circle.**

(3.) 5%   **4.** 70%   **(5.)** 45%   **6.** 20%

SEE EXAMPLES 2 AND 3

on pp. 475–476 for Exs. 7–11

7. ERROR ANALYSIS The table shows the results of a survey that asked students where they most often buy their CDs. Ali wants to make a circle graph of the data. Describe and correct the error he made in finding the angle for *Online*.

Buying CDs	Percent
Online	24%
Retail store	56%
CD club	20%

$$\times \quad \frac{1}{24} \times 360° = \frac{360}{24}, \text{ or } 15°$$

MAKING CIRCLE GRAPHS Display the data in a circle graph.

8.

School Involvement	Students
Very involved	30%
Somewhat involved	50%
Not that involved	15%
Not involved at all	5%

9.

Favorite Fruit	Students
Apples	45%
Grapes	25%
Bananas	10%
Oranges	20%

10.

Favorite Movie Type	People
Comedy	15
Horror	5
Science fiction	2
Action	18

11.

Favorite Drink	People
Milk	18
Soda	10
Water	16
Juice	36

CHALLENGE Find the percent of a circle that corresponds to the angle measure.

12. 36° **13.** 153° **14.** 234° **15.** 99°

PROBLEM SOLVING

TRAVELING In Exercises 16–19, use the circle graphs.

SEE EXAMPLES 1 AND 2

on pp. 474–475 for Exs. 16–19

16. What percent of people do *not* travel by car in the United States?

17. What percent of people either bicycle or walk in the Netherlands?

18. Do more people walk or use public transit in the United States?

19. ★ **SHORT RESPONSE** The ratio of the population of the Netherlands to the population of the United States is 1 to 18. What is the ratio of the number of walkers in the two countries? *Justify* your answer.

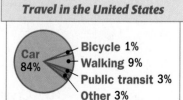

Travel in the Netherlands

Car 45% · Bicycle 30% · Walking 18% · Public transit 5% · Other 2%

Travel in the United States

Car 84% · Bicycle 1% · Walking 9% · Public transit 3% · Other 3%

20. UNITED STATES SYMBOL The table shows the results of a survey that asked people to name the item that most symbolizes the United States. Display the data in a circle graph. Round the angle measures to the nearest degree. Make a conclusion about the data in your graph.

Item	Percent
American flag	67%
Statue of Liberty	17%
Bald eagle	8%
White House	5%
Liberty Bell	2%
Mount Rushmore	1%

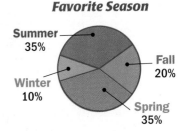

21. ★ WRITING *Describe* the similarities and the differences between a circle graph and a bar graph.

22. ★ EXTENDED RESPONSE Make a bar graph and a circle graph using the data of students' favorite vegetables. Tell which graph more clearly shows that more than half of the students prefer carrots or corn. *Justify* your answer.

Vegetables	Students
Carrots	30
Potatoes	15
Corn	25
Broccoli	5

23. ★ MULTIPLE CHOICE A survey asked 100 people what their favorite season was. The results are shown in the circle graph. Estimate how many people out of 500 would say that fall is their favorite season.

Ⓐ 50   Ⓑ 100
Ⓒ 125   Ⓓ 175

Favorite Season

Summer 35%
Fall 20%
Winter 10%
Spring 35%

24. CHALLENGE The chemical composition of the layers of Earth by mass is shown. Copy and complete the table. Display the data in a circle graph.

Chemical	Iron	Oxygen	Silicon	Magnesium	Other
Fraction	$\frac{173}{500}$	?	$\frac{19}{125}$	$\frac{127}{1000}$	?
Percent	?	?	?	?	8%

NEW JERSEY MIXED REVIEW

TEST PRACTICE at classzone.com

25. The table shows the results of a class election. Which of the following statements is supported by the data in the table?

Ⓐ Sandra received over 50% of the votes.

Ⓑ The mean number of votes received is 108.

Ⓒ T.J. and Jimmie together received about 25% of the votes.

Ⓓ Crystal received fewer than 30% of the votes.

Candidate	Votes received
T.J.	50
Jimmie	22
Sandra	130
Crystal	93

 **ONLINE QUIZ** at classzone.com

9.5 Making Circle Graphs

EXAMPLE The results of a survey in which students were asked their favorite subject in school are shown below. Use spreadsheet software to make a circle graph.

SOLUTION

STEP 1 Enter the data in the first two columns of a spreadsheet as shown.

	A	B
1	Subject	Students
2	Math	42
3	English	30
4	History	24
5	Science	18
6	Art	6

STEP 2 Highlight the data in cells A2 : B6. The expression A2 : B6 refers to the rectangular array of cells that has A2 and B6 at the corners.

STEP 3 Use the Insert menu to insert a chart. Select a pie graph. Then choose the options for your graph, such as the title and labels.

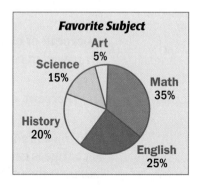

STEP 4 To change other features of your graph after it has been created, double click on the part of the graph that you want to change and adjust the formatting.

PRACTICE Use spreadsheet software to complete the following exercises.

1. **CARS** The table shows the results of a survey that asked people in the United States what type of car they buy. Make a circle graph of the data.

Car Type	People
Luxury	86
Large	35
Midsize	242
Small	142

2. **SPORTS** Ask a group of your classmates to name their favorite sport. Make a circle graph of the data.

9.6 Percent of Increase and Decrease

NJ 4.1.A.3 Understand and use ratios, proportions, and percents (including percents greater than 100 and less than 1) in a variety of situations.

Before You found a percent of a number.

Now You'll find a percent of change in a quantity.

Why? So you can calculate increased sales, as in Ex. 22.

KEY VOCABULARY
- **percent of change,** *p. 480*
- **percent of increase,** *p. 480*
- **percent of decrease,** *p. 480*

ACTIVITY

You can use graph paper to find a percent of change.

The area of the red square below is being added to the area of the blue squares. Each square has an area of one square unit.

Original ⟶ **New**

STEP 1 Find the change in area and write the ratio of the change to the original area.

STEP 2 Express the ratio in Step 1 as a percent, called the *percent of change*.

STEP 3 Suppose 2 red squares instead of just 1 red square are added to the 4 blue squares. What is the percent of change?

A **percent of change** shows how much a quantity has increased or decreased in comparison with the original amount:

$$\text{Percent of change, } p\% = \frac{\text{Amount of increase or decrease}}{\text{Original amount}}$$

If the new amount is greater than the original amount, the percent of change is called a **percent of increase**. If the new amount is less than the original amount, the percent of change is called a **percent of decrease**.

EXAMPLE 1 Finding a Percent of Increase

What is the percent of increase from 8 to 13?

REVIEW COMMON PERCENTS

Need help with common percents? See pp. 450 and 455.

$$p\% = \frac{\text{Amount of increase}}{\text{Original amount}}$$ Write percent of increase formula.

$$= \frac{13 - 8}{8}$$ Substitute amount of increase and original amount.

$$= \frac{5}{8} = 62.5\%$$ Subtract. Then express fraction as a percent.

▶ **Answer** The percent of increase is 62.5%.

EXAMPLE 2 Finding a Percent of Decrease

What is the percent of decrease from 49 to 35?

$$p\% = \frac{\text{Amount of decrease}}{\text{Original amount}}$$ Write percent of decrease formula.

$$= \frac{49 - 35}{49}$$ Substitute amount of decrease and original amount.

$$= \frac{14}{49}$$ Subtract.

$$= \frac{2}{7}$$ Simplify.

$$\approx 0.286 = 28.6\%$$ Express this fraction as a rounded decimal and as a percent.

▶ **Answer** The percent of decrease is 28.6%.

 at classzone.com

CHECK REASONABLENESS
Note that decreasing from 49 to 35 is about the same as decreasing from 50 to 35. Because $\frac{50 - 35}{50} = \frac{3}{10} = 30\%$, the answer is reasonable.

EXAMPLE 3 Using a Percent of Change

Packaging A taco company puts 24 taco shells in every box. Recently the company expanded the box and put 25% more shells in each box. How many shells are in every box now?

SOLUTION

STEP 1 **Find** the amount of increase, 25% of 24.

$$\text{Increase} = 25\% \text{ of } 24$$

$$= 0.25 \times 24$$ Write percent as a decimal.

$$= 6$$ Multiply.

STEP 2 **Add** the increase to the original amount.

$$\text{New amount} = \text{Original amount} + \text{Increase}$$

$$= 24 + 6 = 30$$

▶ **Answer** Every box now has 30 taco shells.

 GUIDED PRACTICE   for Examples 1, 2, and 3

Find the percent of change.

1. Original: 16
   New: 28

2. Original: 35
   New: 91

3. Original: 60
   New: 12

4. **What If?** Suppose the taco company in Example 3 also has boxes that contain 20 taco shells. The company expands this box and puts 25% more shells in each box. How many shells are in every box now?

9.6 EXERCISES

SKILL PRACTICE

1. **VOCABULARY** How can you tell whether a percent of change is a percent of increase or a percent of decrease?

PERCENT OF CHANGE Identify the percent of change as an *increase* or a *decrease.* Then find the percent of change. Use estimation to check.

SEE EXAMPLES 1 AND 2
on pp. 480–481
for Exs. 2–13

2. Original: 30
   New: 51

3. Original: 87
   New: 116

4. Original: 124
   New: 62

5. Original: $1953
   New: $1085

6. Original: 150
   New: 63

7. Original: 10
   New: 12

8. Original: $900
   New: $250

9. Original: 110
   New: 200

10. Original: 20
    New: 26

11. ★ **MULTIPLE CHOICE** What is the percent of decrease from 70 to 42?

    A 33.3%   **B** 40%   **C** 60%   **D** 66.7%

12. **ERROR ANALYSIS** Describe and correct the error made in finding the percent of increase from 94 to 110.

$$\times \quad p\% = \frac{110 - 94}{110}$$
$$= \frac{8}{55} \approx 0.145 = 14.5\%$$

13. **WHICH ONE DOESN'T BELONG?** Which of the following is *not* an example of a percent of decrease?

    A. $\frac{83 - 47}{83}$ **B.** $\frac{73 - 25}{73}$ **C.** $\frac{18 - 7}{18}$ **D.** $\frac{33 - 16}{16}$

FINDING ORIGINAL AMOUNTS Find the original amount.

SEE EXAMPLE 3
on p. 481
for Exs. 14–17

14. Amount of increase: $25
    Percent of increase: 20%

15. Amount of increase: $18
    Percent of increase: 9%

16. Amount of decrease: $30
    Percent of decrease: 24%

17. Amount of decrease: $6
    Percent of decrease: 8%

18. **DOUBLE INCREASES** A $100 purchase increases in value over two years. Each column of the table shows the possible percents of increase for the two years. Find the amount of increase over two years, and find the percent increase over the initial value to copy and complete the table.

Percent of increase in first year	5%	10%	20%	30%	40%
Percent of increase in second year	5%	10%	20%	30%	40%
Total amount of increase	?	?	?	?	?
Percent increase over $100	?	?	?	?	?

19. CHALLENGE A value increases by *a*% and then by *b*% more. *Explain* why the total increase is not (*a* + *b*)%. Write an expression to justify your results.

PROBLEM SOLVING

SEE EXAMPLE 3
on p. 481
for Exs. 20–25

20. ★ SHORT RESPONSE Last year, your class held a fundraiser and donated $850 to a local charity. This year, your donation increased by 24%. *Explain* how to estimate your class's donation for this year.

21. SOAP SHOP During the first week a soap shop was open, it made $2000 in sales. During the second week the soap shop had a 100% increase in sales. Find the soap shop's sales during the second week.

22. HOT DOGS During the last half hour of a baseball game, hot dog sales decreased by about 80% from the previous half hour's sales of 50 hot dogs. How many hot dogs were sold in the last half hour?

23. ★ MULTIPLE CHOICE A school's population increased from 1250 to 2000 students. What was the percent of increase?

Ⓐ 0.375%   Ⓑ 0.6%   Ⓒ 37.5%   Ⓓ 60%

24. HISTORY In 1800, the area of the United States was 891,364 square miles. After the Louisiana Purchase in 1803, the area increased by about 93%. What was the area of the United States after the Louisiana Purchase? Round to the nearest square mile.

United States

Louisiana Purchase (1803)

25. SALARY The average level I engineer's salary is $50,043. A promotion to a level II raises the salary to $59,956. What is the percent of the raise?

26. NUTRITION Two brands of potato chips reduced the fat content of their chips. Brand A had 8 grams of fat per serving, and reduced fat by 30%. Brand B had 10 grams of fat per serving, and reduced fat by 40%. Which brand now has less fat per serving? *Explain.*

27. SOCCER In your first year as the soccer team's goalie, 25 goals were scored against you, followed by only 15 goals in your second year and only 10 goals in your third year. What was the percent of decrease in the amount of goals scored against you from the first to the third year?

28. REASONING The owner of a restaurant increases his prices by 15%. After about a month, the owner notices that business has slowed and decides to decrease the current prices by 15%. Are the menu items back to their original prices? *Explain* your reasoning.

29. ★ WRITING Is the percent of increase from 50 to 70 the same as the percent of decrease from 70 to 50? Why or why not?

Winter Sports Skiing and ice skating were at one time the most popular winter sports. Since the first snowboard was created in 1965, the sport of snowboarding has steadily grown in popularity. In 1998, the sport made its first appearance in the Winter Olympics in Nagano, Japan.

Since the surge of snowboarding into mainstream sports, skiing has dropped in popularity by more than 5 million participants in the United States from its peak of about 12 million in 1988.

Winter Sports Participation in the U.S. (in millions)			
Year	Skiing	Snowboarding	Ice Skating
1998	7.7	3.6	7.8
2003	6.8	6.3	5.1

30. Calculate Use the table to find the percent of increase or decrease for each sport from 1998 to 2003. Round to the nearest tenth.

31. Calculate What is the percent of decrease in skiing from its peak in 1988 to 2003? Round to the nearest tenth.

32. Predict *Predict* the number of people who will participate in these three sports in 2008. Round to the nearest million.

33. CHALLENGE A new car lost 20% of its original value the first year it was owned and lost another 15% the second year. If the car had a value of $10,200 at the end of the second year, how much was the car worth originally? *Explain* how you found your answer.

34. CHALLENGE From 1994 to 1999, the average price of a gallon of gasoline fell 8%. From 1999 to 2004, the average price rose 73% over its 1999 price to $1.61. What was the average price of gasoline in 1994? *Explain* how you found your answer.

 NEW JERSEY MIXED REVIEW **TEST PRACTICE** at classzone.com

35. Which list shows the fractions $\frac{3}{5}$, $\frac{1}{2}$, $\frac{5}{8}$, and $\frac{1}{4}$ written as percents from greatest to least?

Ⓐ 62.5%, 25%, 6%, 5%

Ⓑ 0.625%, 0.6%, 0.5%, 0.25%

Ⓒ 25%, 50%, 60%, 62.5%

Ⓓ 62.5%, 60%, 50%, 25%

 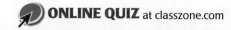

9.7 Discounts, Markups, Sales Tax, and Tips

N♪ 4.1.A.3 Understand and use ratios, proportions, and percents (including percents greater than 100 and less than 1) in a variety of situations.

Before You solved percent problems.

Now You'll find discounts, markups, sales tax, and tips.

Why? So you can find a sale price, as in Example 1.

KEY VOCABULARY
• percent, *p. 449*

Discount A decrease in the price of an item is a *discount*. To find the sale price of an item, do the following:

STEP 1 **Find** the amount of the discount.

STEP 2 **Subtract** the discount from the original price.

EXAMPLE 1 Finding a Sale Price

Clothing You buy a pair of jeans that is 30% off the original price of $29. What is the sale price?

STEP 1 **Find** the amount of the discount.

$$\text{Discount} = \textbf{30\% of \$29}$$

$$= \textbf{0.3} \times 29 \qquad \textbf{Write 30\% as a decimal.}$$

$$= 8.7 \qquad \textbf{Multiply.}$$

STEP 2 **Subtract** the discount from the original price.

$$\text{Sale price} = \text{Original price} - \text{Discount}$$

$$= 29 - 8.7 = 20.30$$

▶ **Answer** The sale price is $20.30.

ANOTHER WAY
Because 30% is the amount of the discount, you are paying 70% of the price. So you could also solve by finding 70% of $29.

✓ **GUIDED PRACTICE** for Example 1

1. **Sale Items** A store is selling flip-flops at 20% off their original price. What is the sale price of a pair of flip-flops originally priced at $20?

Markup A retail store buys items from manufacturers at *wholesale prices*. The store then sells the items to customers at higher *retail prices*. The increase from the wholesale price to the retail price is the *markup*. To find the retail price of an item, do the following:

STEP 1 **Find** the amount of the markup.

STEP 2 **Add** the markup to the wholesale price.

EXAMPLE 2 Finding a Retail Price

Skateboards A store that sells skateboards buys them from a manufacturer at a wholesale price of $57. The store's markup is 150%. What is the retail price?

SOLUTION

AVOID ERRORS
In Example 2, don't stop after multiplying 1.5 × 57. You have to add the result, $85.50, to the wholesale price to get the retail price.

STEP 1   **Find** the amount of the markup.

$$\text{Markup} = \textbf{150\% of \$57}$$
$$= \textbf{1.5} \times \textbf{57} \qquad \textbf{Write 150\% as a decimal.}$$
$$= 85.50 \qquad \textbf{Multiply.}$$

STEP 2   **Add** the markup to the wholesale price.

$$\text{Retail price} = \text{Wholesale price} + \text{Markup}$$
$$= 57.00 + 85.50 = 142.50$$

▶ **Answer** The retail price is $142.50.

Sales Tax and Tips Sales tax and tips are amounts that are added to the price of a purchase. Sales tax and tips are usually calculated using a percent of the purchase price.

EXAMPLE 3 Solve a Multi-Step Problem

Restaurants At a restaurant, you order a meal that costs $12. You leave a 20% tip. The sales tax is 5%. What is the total cost of the meal?

SOLUTION

AVOID ERRORS
The tip at a restaurant is based on the food bill only. Do not include the sales tax when finding a tip.

STEP 1   **Find** the tip.   20% of $12 = **0.20** × 12 = 2.40

STEP 2   **Find** the sales tax.   5% of $12 = **0.05** × 12 = 0.60

STEP 3   **Add** the food bill, tip,   12 + 2.40 + 0.60 = 15.00
             and sales tax.

▶ **Answer** The total cost of the meal is $15.00.

✓ **GUIDED PRACTICE**   for Examples 2 and 3

2. **Guitars** A store buys guitars from a manufacturer at a wholesale price of $38. The store's markup is 85%. What is the retail price?

3. **What If?** Suppose the bill from Example 3 was $15. Find the total cost of the meal if you want to leave a 20% tip and the sales tax is 5%.

EXAMPLE 4 **Standardized Test Practice**

Tipping Scott and Karen's meal costs $16.18. They want to leave a tip of about 20%. Which of the following is the tip they want to leave?

(A) $1.50 **(B)** $2.00 **(C)** $2.40 **(D)** $3.25

ELIMINATE CHOICES
After rounding the cost to $16, a 10% tip would be $1.60. So, you can eliminate choice A.

SOLUTION

To estimate the tip, round the cost of the meal to $16.

$$20\% \text{ of } \$16 = \mathbf{0.20} \times 16$$
$$= 3.2$$

▶ **Answer** The tip is about $3.20. The correct answer is D.

 GUIDED PRACTICE **for Example 4**

4. **What If?** Suppose the bill from Example 4 was $18.78. Approximate the 20% tip they want to leave.

9.7 EXERCISES

HOMEWORK KEY

★ = **STANDARDIZED TEST PRACTICE**
Exs. 16, 24, 26, 30, 31, and 42

○ = **HINTS AND HOMEWORK HELP**
for Exs. 5, 9, 21, 25 at classzone.com

SKILL PRACTICE

VOCABULARY Based on the calculations shown, identify the dollar value or percent that matches the description.

$$0.05 \times 15 = 0.75$$
$$15 + 0.75 = 15.75$$

1. Original price   2. Amount of sales tax   3. Total cost   4. Sales tax percent

FINDING PRICES Use the given information to find the new price.

SEE EXAMPLES 1, 2, AND 3
on pp. 485–486
for Exs. 5–10

 Original price: $36
Discount: 30%

6. Wholesale price: $55
Markup: 50%

7. Food bill before tax: $25
Sales tax: 6%

8. Food bill before tax: $45
Tip: 15%

9. Wholesale price: $70
Markup: 125%

10. Original price: $24
Discount: 20%

ESTIMATION Use the information to estimate the total cost of the meal.

SEE EXAMPLE 4
on p. 487
for Exs. 11–14

11. Cost of meal: $35.27
Tax: 6%; tip: 18%

12. Cost of meal: $23.18
Tax: 4.5%; tip: 17%

13. Cost of meal: $17.49
Tax: 5%; tip: 20%

14. Cost of meal: $42.75
Tax: 6%; tip: 22%

15. ERROR ANALYSIS You hear someone say that the retail price on an item with a wholesale price of $80 is $100 after a markup of 125%. Describe and correct the error in the person's statement.

16. ★ **MULTIPLE CHOICE** Which expression represents the price of an item with an original price p after a discount of 25%?

$\textbf{A}$ $0.25p$ $\qquad$ $\textbf{B}$ $p - 0.25p$ $\qquad$ $\textbf{C}$ $p + 0.25p$ $\qquad$ $\textbf{D}$ $p + 0.75p$

CHALLENGE Let p represent the original price. Match the given discount and markup with the correct expression for the new price.

17. 80% markup, then 20% discount $\qquad$ **A.** New price $= 0.2 \times 2.2p$

18. 120% markup, then 80% discount $\qquad$ **B.** New price $= 0.8 \times 1.8p$

19. 20% markup, then 20% discount $\qquad$ **C.** New price $= 0.8 \times 1.2p$

PROBLEM SOLVING

20. GUIDED PROBLEM SOLVING A bicycle helmet is on sale for 25% off the original price. The original price is $48. What is the sale price?

    a. What is 25% of the original price?

    b. Is the amount from part (a) a discount or a markup? What must you do with this amount?

    c. Find the sale price.

SEE EXAMPLE 4 on p. 487 for Exs. 21–22

21. ESTIMATION A baseball hat with an original price of $19 is on sale for 10% off the original price. Estimate the sale price.

22. BOOKS You have a $20 gift card from a bookstore. You use it to buy two books for a total of $18.49. The sales tax is 5.75%. Will your gift card cover the cost? *Explain* your reasoning.

23. SPORTING GOODS A sporting goods store purchases in-line skates, skateboards, and scooters for the wholesale prices listed in the table. Find the retail price of each item.

Item	Wholesale Price	Markup
In-line skates	$80	105%
Skateboard	$100	125%
Scooter	$60	110%

24. ★ **WRITING** You know the cost of an item and its total cost including sales tax. *Explain* how you can find the sales tax rate.

25. MENTAL MATH You have $50 to spend at a clothing store. You find a sweater that is on sale for 15% off the original price. The original price of the sweater is $60 and there is no sales tax. Do you have enough money to buy the sweater? *Explain* your reasoning.

26. ★ **MULTIPLE CHOICE** A pair of sneakers costs $46.99. You have a coupon for 15% off. What is the total cost of the sneakers after 5% sales tax is included? (*Hint:* You pay tax on the discounted price, not the full price.)

$\textbf{A}$ $37.59 $\qquad$ $\textbf{B}$ $41.94 $\qquad$ $\textbf{C}$ $42.29 $\qquad$ $\textbf{D}$ $56.74

27. COMPARE Your dinner bill for Monday is $22.79. The sales tax is 7% and you leave a 20% tip. Your dinner bill for Tuesday is $23.84. The sales tax is 6% and you leave a 15% tip. For which meal do you pay more?

28. REASONING A $140 car stereo is marked up 50% and then discounted 50%. Will the final price of the car stereo be $140? *Explain.*

29. WATERCOLOR KIT You have a coupon for an additional 25% off any sale item at a craft store. The store has a watercolor kit on sale for 15% off of $40. What is the price of the watercolor kit after both discounts?

30. ★ **MULTIPLE CHOICE** Six friends go to lunch. They plan to split the bill evenly, and they plan to leave a 20% tip. The bill comes to $55.50. The sales tax is 7%. How much will each person pay?

  (A) $18.87   (B) $13.99

  (C) $11.75   (D) $11.66

31. ★ **SHORT RESPONSE** You have a coupon for $10 off a purchase of $50 or more. You also have a coupon for 15% off the purchase price. If you make a $60 purchase, in which order do you want these two coupons processed? Does it make a difference? *Explain* your reasoning.

32. WORK BACKWARD You belong to a CD club run by a local music store. You get 10% off the price of any CD. You pay $18 for a double CD. How much does a person who doesn't belong to the club pay for the same double CD?

33. CHALLENGE A sign says that the price marked on all music equipment is 30% off the original price. You buy a guitar for $315 and guitar strings for $8. What was the original price of each? How much money did you save?

NEW JERSEY MIXED REVIEW

TEST PRACTICE at classzone.com

34. Which of the following represents the greatest percent of change?

  (A) Rita's allowance increased from $10 per week to $13 per week.

  (B) The wholesale price of a camera, $110, is marked up to a retail price of $154.

  (C) A coat that was originally priced at $90 is now on sale for $55.

  (D) The number of stamps in Paul's collection went from 80 to 115.

35. Shirley has a photograph that is 8 inches long. She wants to reduce the length of the photograph so that it is 65% of its original size. Which equation can be used to find x, the length of the reduced photograph?

  (A) $x = 0.65 + 8$ (B) $x = 0.65 - 8$ (C) $x = 0.65 \cdot 8$ (D) $x = 0.65 \div 8$

9.8 Simple Interest

4.1.A.3 Understand and use ratios, proportions, and percents (including percents greater than 100 and less than 1) in a variety of situations.

Before You calculated discounts, markups, sales tax, and tips.

Now You'll calculate simple interest.

Why? So you can find the interest earned in a bank account, as in Ex. 27.

KEY VOCABULARY
- interest, *p. 490*
- principal, *p. 490*
- simple interest, *p. 490*
- annual interest rate, *p. 490*
- balance, *p. 490*

The amount earned or paid for the use of money is called **interest**. The amount of money deposited or borrowed is the **principal**. When interest is earned or paid only on the principal, it is **simple interest**. The **annual interest rate** is the percent of the principal earned or paid per year. The sum of the interest and the principal is called the **balance**.

Simple Interest

Words Simple interest I is the product of the principal P, the annual interest rate r written as a decimal, and the time t in years.

Algebra $I = Prt$

Numbers A $500 deposit earns 6% simple annual interest for 4 years.
$I = (\$500)(0.06)(4) = \$120$

EXAMPLE 1 Finding a Balance

Family Loan Tim's parents lend Tim $100 so he can buy a radio-controlled airplane. They charge Tim 5% simple annual interest. What will be the total amount that Tim will owe his parents in 1 year?

SOLUTION

$I = Prt$ **Write simple interest formula.**

$= (100)(0.05)(1)$ **Substitute 100 for P, 0.05 for r, and 1 for t.**

$= 5$ **Multiply.**

To find the balance, add the interest to the principal.

▶ **Answer** Tim will owe a balance of $100 + $5, or $105.

Animated Math at classzone.com

USE A CALCULATOR
The **%** key on a calculator changes a percent to a decimal. For example, 5 **%** will be displayed as 0.05.

EXAMPLE 2 Finding an Interest Rate

 Investment You deposit $600 into a 6-month certificate of deposit. After 6 months the balance is $618. Find the simple annual interest rate.

STEP 1 **Find** the interest by subtracting the principal from the balance.

$$\$618 - \$600 = \$18$$

AVOID ERRORS
When using the simple interest formula, make sure you write the number of months as a fraction of a year. For example, 7 months should be written as $\frac{7}{12}$.

STEP 2 **Use** the simple interest formula and solve for r.

$I = Prt$	Write simple interest formula.
$18 = (600)(r)\left(\dfrac{6}{12}\right)$	Substitute 18 for I, 600 for P, and $\dfrac{6}{12}$ for t.
$18 = 300r$	Multiply.
$\dfrac{18}{300} = \dfrac{300r}{300}$	Divide each side by 300.
$0.06 = r$	Simplify.
$6\% = r$	Write decimal as a percent.

▶ **Answer** The simple annual interest rate is 6%.

EXAMPLE 3 Finding an Amount of Time

 Investment You put $750 into a certificate of deposit. Your simple annual interest rate is 4%. You receive a check for the interest at the end of each year. How long will it take to earn $150 in interest?

$I = Prt$	Write simple interest formula.
$150 = (750)(0.04)t$	Substitute 150 for I, 750 for P, and 0.04 for r.
$150 = 30t$	Multiply.
$\dfrac{150}{30} = \dfrac{30t}{30}$	Divide each side by 30.
$5 = t$	Simplify.

▶ **Answer** It will take 5 years to earn $150 in simple interest.

✓ **GUIDED PRACTICE** for Examples 1, 2, and 3

1. **Balance** You deposit $500 into an account that earns 6% simple annual interest. What will the account's balance be after 2 years?

2. **Interest Rate** You deposit $1000 into a 3-month certificate of deposit. After 3 months the balance is $1005. Find the simple annual interest rate.

3. **What If?** Suppose the simple interest rate in Example 3 is 5%. How long will it take to earn $150 in interest?

9.8 EXERCISES

HOMEWORK KEY

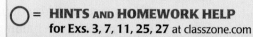

★ = STANDARDIZED TEST PRACTICE
Exs. 13, 26, 31, 32, 35, and 44

◯ = HINTS AND HOMEWORK HELP
for Exs. 3, 7, 11, 25, 27 at classzone.com

SKILL PRACTICE

1. **VOCABULARY** What is the amount of money deposited or borrowed called?

2. **VOCABULARY** What is the amount of money earned or paid called?

CALCULATING SIMPLE INTEREST For an account that earns simple annual interest, find the interest earned, and the balance of the account.

SEE EXAMPLE 1
on p. 490
for Exs. 3–14

3. $30 at 1% for 10 months

4. $100 at 8% for 3 years

5. $50 at 10% for 4 years

6. $200 at 4.5% for 8 months

7. $252 at 8% for 2 months

8. $450 at 4% for 6 months

9. $6240 at 10.4% for 9 months

10. $2000 at 9.6% for 8 months

11. $5000 at 4.5% for 1 year

12. $400 at 3% for 1 month

13. ★ **MULTIPLE CHOICE** What is the balance after 18 months of a savings account that begins with $700 and earns 6% simple annual interest?

    Ⓐ $756   Ⓑ $763   Ⓒ $1456   Ⓓ $1463

14. **ERROR ANALYSIS** Describe and correct the error made in finding the interest earned on a savings account of $200 that earns 4% simple annual interest after 36 months.

    $$I = (200)(0.04)(36)$$
    $$= \$288$$

ⅩⅤ ALGEBRA Find the unknown quantity. Use a calculator or paper and pencil.

SEE EXAMPLES 2 AND 3
on p. 491
for Exs. 15–22

15. $I = $ _?_
    $P = \$2000$
    $r = 9.8\%$
    $t = 5$ years

16. $I = \$84$
    $P = $ _?_
    $r = 7\%$
    $t = 2$ years

17. $I = \$468$
    $P = \$6240$
    $r = $ _?_
    $t = 9$ months

18. $I = \$9$
    $P = \$450$
    $r = 4\%$
    $t = $ _?_

19. Balance = $1530
    $I = \$30$
    $r = 6\%$
    $t = $ _?_

20. Balance = $620
    $I = \$20$
    $r = $ _?_
    $t = 8$ months

21. Balance = _?_
    $I = \$110$
    $r = 5.5\%$
    $t = 1$ year

22. Balance = $960
    $I = $ _?_
    $r = 4\%$
    $t = 5$ years

23. **CHECKING REASONABLENESS** Use estimation and mental math to check the reasonableness of the amount of interest shown at the right. *Explain* your reasoning.

    $P = \$98$
    $r = 5\%$
    $t = 1$
    $I = \$4.90$

24. **CHALLENGE** You put $500 in a savings account that earns 4.5% simple annual interest, and your friend puts $400 in a savings account that earns 6% simple annual interest. Which of you will reach $600 first?

PROBLEM SOLVING

SEE EXAMPLE 2
on p. 491
for Ex. 25

25. **INVESTMENTS** You deposit $250 into an account. At the end of 6 months your balance is $255. What is the simple annual interest rate?

26. ★ **WRITING** If you borrow money, would you want a higher or lower interest rate? If you open a savings account, would you want a higher or a lower interest rate? *Explain* your choice.

SEE EXAMPLE 3
on p. 491
for Ex. 27

27. **SAVINGS** You put $750 into a savings account that earns 2% simple annual interest. How long will it take to have $45 in interest?

28. **CREDIT CARDS** A credit card charges 9.6% annual interest on any unpaid balance each month. During the past month your brother had an unpaid balance of $375. What is the interest charge for that month?

29. **SECURITY DEPOSIT** When signing a lease for an apartment, your sister pays a security deposit that earns 4% simple annual interest. At the end of a year, the interest earned on the security deposit is $54. How much was the security deposit?

30. **INTEREST** Ann has $300 in a savings account that earns 1.75% simple annual interest. In how many years will she have $21 in interest?

31. ★ **MULTIPLE CHOICE** Joe put $350 into a 6-month certificate of deposit. After 6 months, the certificate earned 4.2% simple annual interest. How much interest did the certificate earn?

    A $7.35   **B** $14.70   **C** $29.40   **D** $88.20

32. ★ **OPEN-ENDED MATH** Find two different principals and lengths of time needed to earn $50 interest at 5% simple annual interest.

33. **REASONING** Three months ago you deposited $250 into a savings account, and now your balance is $253. Eight months ago your friend deposited $250 into a different savings account, and her balance is now $257.50. Which account has the greater simple annual interest rate? *Explain* your reasoning.

34. **COMPARE** You put $300 into an account that pays 5% simple interest. Your brother puts $400 into an account that has 2% simple interest. Who has more money in their account after 10 years? Who has earned more interest? *Justify* your answer.

35. ★ **SHORT RESPONSE** Rick wants to borrow $4500 to buy a car. His sister will lend him the money at a simple annual interest rate of 9% for 6 years, and his uncle will lend him the money at a rate of 11.5% for 4 years. From whom should Rick borrow the money? *Explain* your reasoning.

36. CHALLENGE Amanda has $600 in a savings account that earns 4% simple annual interest. At the beginning of each month, she deposits $200 into the savings account. How much is in the account at the beginning of the seventh month before she makes her seventh deposit? *Justify* your answer.

 NEW JERSEY MIXED REVIEW

 TEST PRACTICE at classzone.com

37. Tina's meal costs $8.23. She wants to leave a 20% tip. Which of the following is closest to the tip she wants to leave?

(A) $1.00   (B) $1.65   (C) $1.75   (D) $2.00

38. Philip can walk 1.5 miles in 21 minutes. At this rate, how long will it take him to walk 5 miles?

(A) 6.3 min   (B) 42 min   (C) 70 min   (D) 157.5 min

39. The circle graph shows a breakdown of items sold at an electronics store. Which of the following statements is NOT supported by the data in the graph?

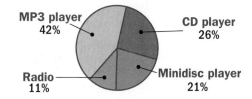

Portable Audio Players

(A) The store sold twice as many MP3 players as Minidisc players.

(B) Over 50% of the items sold were CD players or Minidisc players.

(C) The store sold almost 4 times as many MP3 players as regular radios.

(D) If the store sold a total of 300 portable audio players, 33 of the items sold would be radios.

QUIZ *for Lessons 9.5–9.8*

1. PETS The table shows the results of a survey that asked people to name their favorite pet. Display the data in a circle graph. *(p. 474)*

Pet	Dog	Cat	Bird	Other
People	35%	30%	20%	15%

PERCENT OF CHANGE Identify the percent of change as an *increase* or a *decrease*. Then find the percent of change. *(p. 480)*

2. Original: 240; new: 300   **3.** Original: 150; new: 90

4. CONCERT At a concert, you buy a souvenir T-shirt for $25 and a hat for $16. The sales tax on the items is 5%. Find the total cost. *(p. 485)*

5. SAVINGS Suppose you put $800 into a savings account that earns 2.5% simple annual interest. How long will it take to earn $60 in interest? *(p. 490)*

Lessons 9.5–9.8

1. **ANNUAL GOLF TOURNAMENTS** Last year, 20 people played in an annual golf tournament. This year's tournament saw a 125% increase in players. Next year, the golf club wants to have a 140% increase in players over this year's tournament. How many players does the club want in the tournament next year?

   A. 28

   B. 35

   C. 63

   D. 108

2. **EARNINGS** Michael was earning $120 per week when he had to take a 10% decrease in pay. Six months later he received a 10% increase in pay. Now how much does he earn for a week of work?

   A. $12.00

   B. $118.80

   C. $120.00

   D. $132.00

3. **INTEREST** Marie deposited $125 in a savings account that paid 3.2% simple annual interest. Two years later she took out her principal and the interest it had earned, and deposited the money in another bank, which paid 4% simple annual interest. How much was in the new account, including principal and interest, two and a half years later?

   A. $8.00

   B. $13.30

   C. $133.00

   D. $146.30

4. **BANK ACCOUNT** After 18 months, a bank account that originally contained $80 has grown to $83 at a simple annual interest rate. What is the bank's interest rate?

   A. 0.2%   **C.** 2.5%

   B. 0.25%   **D.** 20.8%

5. **WORKING STUDENTS** The circle graph shows the results of a survey that asked 240 high school students how many hours they work in a typical week. How many of the students work 10 hours or fewer in a typical week?

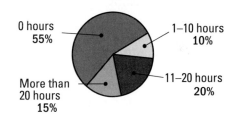

   Hours Students Work

   0 hours 55%
   1–10 hours 10%
   More than 20 hours 15%
   11–20 hours 20%

   A. 24   **C.** 132

   B. 108   **D.** 156

6. **OPEN-ENDED** The layout for your model train is shown below. You are planning to make a new layout whose area is 40% greater than this one.

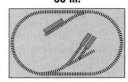

   60 in.

   40 in.

   • What is the area of the current layout? of the new layout?

   • Each dimension must be at least 40 inches. What is one pair of whole number dimensions for the new layout?

   • By what percent has each dimension increased?

REVIEW KEY VOCABULARY

- percent, *p. 449*
- percent equation, *p. 465*
- circle graph, *p. 474*
- ray, *p. 474*
- angle, *p. 474*

- vertex, *p. 474*
- degrees, *p. 474*
- percent of change, *p. 480*
- percent of increase, *p. 480*
- percent of decrease, *p. 480*

- interest, *p. 490*
- principal, *p. 490*
- simple interest, *p. 490*
- annual interest rate, *p. 490*
- balance, *p. 490*

VOCABULARY EXERCISES

Copy and complete the statement.

1. A(n) _?_ shows how much a quantity has increased or decreased relative to the original amount.

2. A(n) _?_ is a ratio whose denominator is 100.

3. A(n) _?_ displays data as sections of a circle.

4. Angles are measured in units called _?_.

5. The amount of money deposited or borrowed is called the _?_.

6. Simple interest is the product of the principal, the _?_, and the time (in years).

7. A(n) _?_ is 2 rays that begin at a common point.

8. The amount earned or paid for the use of money is called _?_.

REVIEW EXAMPLES AND EXERCISES

9.1 Percents and Fractions
pp. 449–452

EXAMPLE

Write the percent as a fraction or the fraction as a percent.

a. $41\% = \dfrac{41}{100}$

b. $\dfrac{13}{25} = \dfrac{52}{100} = 52\%$

EXAMPLE

To find 75% of 120, use the fact that $75\% = \dfrac{3}{4}$ and multiply.

$$75\% \text{ of } 120 = \frac{3}{4} \cdot 120 = \frac{3 \cdot \overset{30}{\cancel{120}}}{\underset{1}{\cancel{4}}} = 90$$

EXERCISES

Write the percent as a fraction.

SEE EXAMPLES
1, 2, 3, AND 4
on pp. 449–450
for Exs. 9–20

9. 19%   **10.** 65%   **11.** 36%   **12.** 98%

Write the fraction as a percent.

13. $\dfrac{23}{50}$ **14.** $\dfrac{2}{25}$ **15.** $\dfrac{7}{10}$ **16.** $\dfrac{3}{5}$

17. Find 30% of 80.   **18.** Find 25% of 130.   **19.** Find 16% of 75.

20. Criminal Justice Nine out of twelve members of a jury are over 35 years old. What percent of the jury is *not* over 35 years old?

9.2   Percents and Proportions   pp. 454–459

EXAMPLE

What percent of 120 is 72?

$$\frac{a}{b} = \frac{p}{100}$$ **Write proportion.**

$$\frac{72}{120} = \frac{p}{100}$$ **Substitute 72 for *a* and 120 for *b*.**

$$100 \cdot \frac{72}{120} = 100 \cdot \frac{p}{100}$$ **Multiply each side by 100.**

$$\frac{\overset{5}{\cancel{100}} \cdot \overset{12}{\cancel{72}}}{\underset{\underset{1}{\cancel{6}}}{\cancel{120}}} = p$$ **Use rule for multiplying fractions.**
Divide out common factors.

$$60 = p$$ **Multiply.**

▶ **Answer** 72 is 60% of 120.

EXERCISES

Use a proportion to answer the question.

SEE EXAMPLES
1, 2, AND 3
on pp. 454–456
for Exs. 21–29

21. What number is 16% of 75?   **22.** 42 is 60% of what number?

23. What number is 80% of 240?   **24.** 51 is 15% of what number?

25. What number is 35% of 200?   **26.** 18 is 90% of what number?

27. 72 is 40% of what number?   **28.** What number is 9% of 200?

29. A vitamin pill provides 14% of an adult's daily magnesium need. If there are 40 mg of magnesium in the vitamin pill, how many mg of magnesium does an adult need per day?

9.3 Percents and Decimals

pp. 460–464

EXAMPLE

Write the percent as a decimal or the decimal as a percent.

a. 14% = 14%
= 0.14

b. 0.25% = 00.25
= 0.0025

c. 0.705 = .705
= 70.5%

EXERCISES

Write the percent as a decimal.

SEE EXAMPLES 1, 2, AND 4 on pp. 460–461 for Exs. 30–37

30. 31% **31.** 210% **32.** 6% **33.** 92.5%

Write the decimal as a percent.

34. 1.39 **35.** 0.0041 **36.** 0.28 **37.** 0.032

9.4 The Percent Equation

pp. 465–470

EXAMPLE

12 is 40% of what number?

$a = p\% \cdot b$ Write percent equation.

$12 = 40\% \cdot b$ Substitute 12 for a and 18 for p.

$12 = 0.40 \cdot b$ Write percent as a decimal.

$\dfrac{12}{0.40} = \dfrac{0.40b}{0.40}$ Divide each side by 0.40.

$30 = b$ Simplify.

▶ **Answer** 12 is 40% of 30.

EXERCISES

Use the percent equation to answer the question.

SEE EXAMPLES 1, 2, 3, AND 4 on pp. 465–467 for Exs. 38–43

38. What number is 125% of 60? **39.** What percent of 500 is 2?

40. What percent of 400 is 252? **41.** 24 is 32% of what number?

42. Test Scores On a recent test, John answered 80% of the questions correctly. There were 30 questions on the test. How many questions did John answer correctly?

43. Car Dealership If 25% of the 64 cars on a lot are white, how many cars are white?

9.5 Circle Graphs

pp. 474–478

EXAMPLE

Colors In a survey that asked 120 teens their favorite color, 40 said red, 55 said green, and 25 said blue. Display the data in a circle graph.

Red $\quad \frac{40}{120} \times 360° = \frac{1}{3} \times 360° = 120°$

Green $\quad \frac{55}{120} \times 360° = \frac{11}{24} \times 360° = 165°$

Blue $\quad \frac{25}{120} \times 360° = \frac{5}{24} \times 360° = 75°$

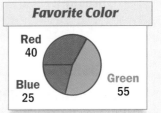

Favorite Color

Red 40
Blue 25
Green 55

EXERCISES

SEE EXAMPLE 2
on p. 475
for Ex. 44

44. Survey In a survey that asked 150 adults their favorite color, 20% said red, 50% said green, and 30% said blue. Display the data in a circle graph.

9.6 Percent of Increase and Decrease

pp. 480–404

EXAMPLE

Trail Mix Yesterday you sold 8 packets of trail mix. Today you sold 15 packets of trail mix. Find the percent of increase in sales.

$p = \dfrac{15 - 8}{8}$

$\quad = \dfrac{7}{8}$

$\quad = 87.5\%$

EXERCISES

**SEE EXAMPLES
1, 2, AND 3**
on pp. 480–481
for Exs. 45–47

45. Talent Show Eighty tickets were sold on the first night of a talent show. On the second night, 150 tickets were sold. What was the percent of increase?

46. Attendance There were 420 fans at a high school basketball game and 399 at the next. Find the percent decrease in attendance.

47. Golf Phil shot 120 for 18 holes of golf the first time he played a new course. The next time he played that course he decreased his score by 15%. What was his score the second time?

9.7 Discounts, Markups, Sales Tax, and Tips
pp. 485–489

EXAMPLE

Furniture A $750 sofa is now 30% off. To find the sale price of the sofa, find the amount of the discount and subtract it from the regular price.

Discount: 30% of $750 = **0.30** × $750 = $225

Sale Price: $750 − $225 = $525

EXERCISES

Use the given information to find the new price.

SEE EXAMPLES
1, 2, AND 3
on pp. 485–486
for Exs. 48–52

48. Regular price: $72
Discount: 75%

49. Wholesale price: $67
Markup: 115%

50. Regular price: $60
Discount: 9%

51. Wholesale price: $124
Markup: 120%

52. Dining You and your family are eating at a restaurant. The food bill is $40. Your family leaves a 20% tip. The sales tax is 6%. What is the total cost of the meal?

9.8 Simple Interest
pp. 490–494

EXAMPLE

Interest You have $180 in an account that earns 5% simple annual interest. How much interest will the account earn in 6 months?

$$I = Prt = (180)(0.05)\left(\frac{6}{12}\right) = \$4.50$$

▶ **Answer** In 6 months, the account will earn $4.50 in interest.

EXERCISES

Use the simple interest formula to find the unknown quantity.

SEE EXAMPLES
1, 2, AND 3
on pp. 490–491
for Exs. 53–57

53. $I = \$590$
$P = \underline{\ ?\ }$
$r = 2.5\%$
$t = 10$ years

54. $I = \underline{\ ?\ }$
$P = \$550$
$r = 14.5\%$
$t = 4$ years

55. $I = \$7$
$P = \$175$
$r = 16\%$
$t = \underline{\ ?\ }$

56. $I = \$1210$
$P = \$15,000$
$r = \underline{\ ?\ }$
$t = 11$ months

57. Banking Maggie had $600 in a savings account. In 3 months she earned $6 in interest. What was the annual interest rate?

Write the percent as a fraction or the fraction as a percent.

1. 65%
2. 40%
3. $\frac{12}{25}$
4. $\frac{4}{5}$

Use a proportion to answer the question.

5. What number is 15% of 30?
6. What number is 30% of 210?
7. 12 is 60% of what number?
8. What percent of 40 is 18?

Write the percent as a decimal or the decimal as a percent.

9. 0.037
10. 208%
11. 0.45%
12. 1.35

Use the percent equation to answer the question.

13. What number is 134% of 20,000?
14. 32 is 40% of what number?
15. What percent of 25 is 24?
16. What percent of 60 is 3?

17. **ADVERTISING** An advertisement says that 4 out of 5 doctors prefer a certain product. What percent of doctors do not prefer the product?

18. **SAVINGS** You have decided to put 12% of your weekly paycheck into a savings account. You made $85.50 last week. How much did you put into the savings account?

19. **BREAKFAST FOOD** The table below shows the results of a survey that asked 200 students what they normally eat for breakfast. Display the data in a circle graph.

Food	Eggs	Cold cereal	Pancakes	French toast	Other
Students	27.5%	45%	15%	7.5%	5%

20. **ENROLLMENT** One fall, 500 students were enrolled in a middle school. The enrollment at the same school in the fall of the following year was 580 students. Find the percent of increase.

21. **BACKPACKS** Which backpack costs less after the discounts are taken? *Justify* your reasoning.

Backpack Sale	
Nylon Original	$40
Sale	20% off
Canvas Original	$50
Sale	40% off

22. **LOAN** You borrow $240 from your friend. One year later you pay back $270 to show your appreciation for the loan. How much interest did you pay your friend? What was the simple annual interest rate?

REVIEWING PERCENT PROBLEMS

You probably noticed in Chapter 9 that there are many different types of percent word problems. Some percent word problems may include (but are not limited to):

- rewriting percents as fractions and decimals
- rewriting fractions and decimals as percents
- finding a percent of change
- finding discounts, markups, sales tax, or tips
- computing simple interest

EXAMPLE 1

Baseball Aiden plays on a summer league baseball team. He gets a hit about 45% of the time. Write the percent as a fraction and as a decimal.

Solution

Fraction

$$45\% = \frac{45}{100} = \frac{9}{20}$$

Decimal

$$45\% = 0.45$$

EXAMPLE 2

Shopping A portable CD player is on sale for 20% off the regular price. The sale price is $125. What is the regular price of the portable CD player?

Solution

Write a verbal model. Let x represent the regular price of the portable CD player.

Regular price − **Percent off** • Regular price = **Sale price**

$x - 0.2x = 125$	**Write an equation using the verbal model. Use 0.2 for 20%.**
$0.8x = 125$	**Combine like terms.**
$\dfrac{0.8x}{0.8} = \dfrac{125}{0.8}$	**Divide each side by 0.8.**
$x = 156.25$	**Simplify.**

▶ **Answer** The regular price of the portable CD player is $156.25.

PERCENT PROBLEMS

Below are examples of percent problems in multiple choice format. Try solving the problems before looking at the solutions. (Cover the solutions with a piece of paper.) Then check your solutions against the ones given.

1. A store is selling all DVDs at 15% off their original price. What is the sale price of a DVD originally priced at $18?

   A. $2.70

   B. $15.30

   C. $18.00

   D. $20.70

Solution

Use the following steps to find the sale price of the DVD.

1) Find the amount of the discount.

   Discount = 15% of $18

   $= 0.15 \times 18 = 2.7$, or $2.70

2) Subtract the discount from the original price.

   Sale price = Original price − Discount

   $= 18 - 2.70 = 15.30$

The sale price is $15.30. So, the correct answer is **B**.

2. Which problem situation matches the equation below?

   $x = 60 + 1.5 \times 60$

   A. A store is selling all jackets at 15% off their original price. What is x, the sale price of a jacket originally priced at $60?

   B. At a restaurant, your dinner party's meal costs $60. You leave a 20% tip. The sales tax is 5%. What is x, the total cost of the meal?

   C. A store that sells scooters buys them from a manufacturer at a wholesale price of $60 per scooter. The store's markup is 150%. What is x, the retail price?

   D. You borrow $60 from a friend so you can buy a skateboard. Your friend charges you 5% simple annual interest. What is x, the total amount that you owe your friend after 1 year?

Solution

Examine each answer choice until you find the correct answer.

Answer choice A

Discounts involve subtraction, not addition. This answer choice can be eliminated.

Answer choice B

The percent being added is about 25%. It is not $1.5 = 150\%$. This answer choice can be eliminated.

Answer choice C

A markup of 150% of $60 is added to $60. So, the correct answer is **C**.

TEST PREPARATION

1. Ethan worked a total of 30 hours this week, 16 of which were on the weekend. Which of the following best represents the percent of hours that he did NOT work on the weekend?

    A. 14%

    B. 47%

    C. 53%

    D. 67%

2. Which problem situation matches the equation below?

    $$x = 500 - 0.15 \times 500$$

    A. A store is selling computer products at 15% off their original prices. What is x, the sale price of a computer system originally priced at $500?

    B. When a company manager takes an entire department out for lunch, the meal costs $500. The manager wants to leave a 15% tip. What is x, the total cost of the meal?

    C. A store that sells tires buys a certain brand of tire from a manufacturer at a wholesale price of $500 per tire. The store's markup is 150%. What is x, the retail price?

    D. You deposit $500 into an account that earns a simple annual interest rate of 5%. What is x, the total amount in your account after 1 year?

3. The cost of Yolanda and Amy's dinner is $24.80. They want to leave a 20% tip. Which of the following is closest to the amount of the tip they want to leave?

    A. $3.50

    B. $4.00

    C. $4.50

    D. $5.00

4. Mrs. Shaffer advises the school yearbook committee. The committee has 6 members who are sixth graders, 9 who are seventh graders, and 10 who are eighth graders. What percent of the committee members are seventh graders?

    A. 9%

    B. 24%

    C. 36%

    D. 40%

5. A landscaper designed a plan for a flower bed in a rectangular front lawn, as shown in the shaded part of the grid below. What percent of the front lawn will be a flower bed?

    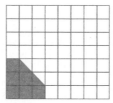

    A. 7%

    B. 8%

    C. 12.5%

    D. 20%

6. Evaluate the expression $(-7x + y)^2$ when $x = -2$ and $y = 6$.

    A. -400

    B. -64

    C. 64

    D. 400

7. Which list shows the fractions $\frac{3}{10}$, $\frac{9}{20}$, $\frac{7}{25}$, and $\frac{21}{50}$ written as percents in order from least to greatest?

A. 0.28%, 0.3%, 0.42%, 0.45%

B. 2.8%, 3%, 4.2%, 4.5%

C. 28%, 30%, 42%, 45%

D. 45%, 42%, 30%, 28%

8. Which sequence follows the rule $3n + 2$, where *n* represents the position of a term in the sequence?

A. 1, 4, 7, 10, 13, . . .

B. 4, 7, 10, 13, 16, . . .

C. 5, 7, 9, 11, 13, . . .

D. 5, 8, 11, 14, 17, . . .

9. The table shows scores on a math test in one of Miss Simon's classes. Which measure of data is represented by a test score of 91?

Name	Score
Tina	84
Wesley	87
Kaleb	93
Madison	95
Emily	87
Rayna	93
Tim	88

Name	Score
Jacob	70
Yi	100
Matt	93
Hailey	85
Chen	100
Colby	96
Sarah	89

A. Mean

B. Median

C. Mode

D. Range

10. Which area model represents the expression $2(5 - 1)$?

A.

B.

C.

D.

11. How many centimeters are in 341.6 millimeters?

A. 3.416 cm

B. 34.16 cm

C. 341.6 cm

D. 3416 cm

12. **OPEN-ENDED** Students at a middle school made 5000 paper roses for a parade float. The color distribution of the roses is shown in the circle graph.

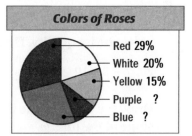

Colors of Roses

Red 29%
White 20%
Yellow 15%
Purple ?
Blue ?

Part A *Explain* how to use the information in the circle graph to find the combined number of blue and purple roses.

Part B The students made three times as many blue roses as purple roses. How many purple roses did they make? How many blue roses did they make?

TEST PREPARATION

9 CUMULATIVE REVIEW *Chapters 1–9*

Use the formula for distance to find the unknown value. *(p. 25)*

1. $d = 180$ miles, $r = 30$ miles per hour, $t = \underline{\ ?\ }$

2. $d = 135$ feet, $r = \underline{\ ?\ }$, $t = 9$ minutes

Copy and complete the statement using <, >, or =. *(pp. 189, 194)*

3. $\frac{8}{17} \underline{\ ?\ } \frac{4}{9}$

4. $\frac{5}{9} \underline{\ ?\ } \frac{15}{27}$

5. $\frac{7}{13} \underline{\ ?\ } \frac{6}{11}$

6. $\frac{11}{12} \underline{\ ?\ } \frac{23}{25}$

7. $\frac{13}{4} \underline{\ ?\ } 3\frac{3}{16}$

8. $\frac{16}{7} \underline{\ ?\ } 2\frac{4}{7}$

9. $\frac{17}{6} \underline{\ ?\ } 2\frac{5}{6}$

10. $\frac{23}{5} \underline{\ ?\ } 4\frac{5}{8}$

Copy and complete the statement. *(p. 250)*

11. $6\frac{1}{2}$ ft $= \underline{\ ?\ }$ in.

12. $3\frac{3}{8}$ lb $= \underline{\ ?\ }$ oz

13. 22 fl oz $= \underline{\ ?\ }$ c

Simplify the expression. *(p. 342)*

14. $6x + 9 - 2x - 14$

15. $5(y + 3) + 2y$

16. $8 - 4(z - 5) - 17$

17. $18a - 4 + 6 - 7a$

18. $33 + 4b - 6(3 - b)$

19. $12(2c - 4) - 8c$

Solve the equation. Check your solution. *(pp. 347, 354, 361)*

20. $n + 8 = -4$

21. $w - 7.6 = -3.1$

22. $\frac{5}{6} + r - 2 = \frac{1}{6}$

23. $-6p = 54$

24. $\frac{b}{8} = -3.5$

25. $\frac{2}{5}t = 8$

26. $7f - 3 = 25$

27. $6 - \frac{d}{4} = -8$

28. $9(g + 2) = 3$

Solve the inequality. Then graph the solution. *(p. 366)*

29. $j + 8 < 10$

30. $\frac{h}{7} > -3$

31. $-8k \le 64$

Draw the graph of the line that passes through the points. Then find the slope of the line. *(p. 409)*

32. $(2, 4), (5, 8)$

33. $(1, 3), (5, -4)$

34. $(-6, -7), (0, 9)$

35. $(3, 2), (-1, -1)$

36. $(-3, -5), (-1, 2)$

37. $(1, 2), (6, -1)$

Solve the proportion. *(p. 423)*

38. $\frac{3}{8} = \frac{x}{40}$

39. $\frac{y}{12} = \frac{22}{8}$

40. $\frac{5}{7.5} = \frac{7}{z}$

41. $\frac{6.3}{w} = \frac{2.7}{9.9}$

Write the fraction or decimal as a percent.

42. $\frac{13}{25}$ *(p. 449)*

43. $\frac{9}{20}$ *(p. 449)*

44. 0.364 *(p. 460)*

45. 0.0497 *(p. 460)*

46. **CAT FOOD** The amount of food a cat needs is proportional to its weight. The label says an 8 pound cat should get 1.25 ounces of food. Your cat weighs 9 pounds 4 ounces. To the nearest tenth, how many ounces should you feed your cat? *(pp. 250, 418)*

47. **SHOPPING** You purchase 5 shirts which are on sale for $17.98 each. Write an expression for the total cost of the shirts. Then use the distributive property to evaluate the expression. *(p. 307)*

48. **GASOLINE** A service station is selling gasoline for $2.11 per gallon. A customer wants to purchase $25 worth of gas. Write and solve an equation to find how many gallons of gasoline the customer will purchase. Round your answer to the nearest hundredth. *(p. 354)*

49. **CAR WASH** A manual car wash station allows customers to use a hose to spray off their cars. For $1, a customer can use the hose for 1.5 minutes. Write a function rule that represents minutes y in terms of dollars spent x. Create an input-output table using the domain 2, 4, 6, and 8. Then graph the function. *(pp. 371, 376)*

50. **AIRPLANE** An airplane traveled at a speed of 150 miles per hour for 2 hours. Then, due to weather problems, the plane traveled at a speed of 75 miles per hour for 3 hours. Find the average speed of the plane in miles per hour. *(pp. 361, 404)*

51. **STATUE OF LIBERTY** The height of the Statue of Liberty from the base to the torch is approximately 151 feet. You have a picture of the Statue of Liberty from the base to the torch that has a height of 8 inches. What is the scale of the photo? *(pp. 250, 430)*

52. **BASEBALL CAPS** A minor league baseball team is giving away a free baseball cap to the first 500 fans who attend the game. The total attendance for the game is 5,250. What percent of the crowd will receive a free cap? Round your answer to the nearest tenth of a percent. *(p. 465)*

53. **CEREAL** A cereal company normally sells 16 ounce boxes of cereal. For a limited time, the company is selling 20 ounce boxes for the same price. Find the percent of increase of the box size. *(p. 480)*

54. **COMPACT DISCS** A store has compact discs marked at $14 each, and is taking off a 15% discount when you check out. You have $25. Do you have enough money to pay for 2 compact discs after 6% sales tax is included in the sale price? *Explain.* *(p. 485)*

55. **CERTIFICATE OF DEPOSIT** You deposit $500 into a 6-month certificate of deposit that has a simple annual interest rate of 4%. What is the value of the certificate after 6 months? *(p. 490)*

10 Geometric Figures

Before

In previous chapters you've . . .

• Multiplied and divided decimals
• Used ratios and proportions

Now

 New Jersey Standards

	10.1 Angles
	10.2 Angle pairs
4.5.E.1.a	10.3 Triangles
4.2.A.1.a	10.4 Polygons
4.2.A.3	10.5 Similar polygons
4.2.A.2.a	10.6 Proportions
4.2.B.1.c	10.7 Symmetry
4.2.C.2	10.8 Transformations

Why?

So you can solve real-world problems about . . .

• hockey, p. 514
• drawbridges, p. 525
• paintings, p. 538

 **Math**

at classzone.com

• Angles, p. 512
• Drawing Quadrilaterals, p. 530
• Lines of Symmetry, p. 549

Get-Ready Games

Review Prerequisite Skills by playing *Rapid Ratios*.

Skill Focus: Finding equivalent ratios

RAPID RATIOS

MATERIALS

• 1 deck of number cards

• 1 deck of ratio cards

HOW TO PLAY Deal three number cards to each player and place the rest face down to form a draw pile. Turn over one number card from the draw pile to form a discard pile. Place five ratio cards face up between you and your partner. Take turns following the directions on the next page.

1 **DRAW** a number card so that you have four cards in your hand. You may take the card from the top of the draw pile or from the top of the discard pile.

2 **DECIDE** whether you can use two of your cards to form a ratio that is equivalent to one of the displayed ratios. If you can, then take the displayed ratio and place it and your pair of cards in front of you.

3 **FINISH** your turn by drawing one card to replenish your hand, or by discarding one card if you were unable to form an equivalent ratio. You should have three cards at the end of your turn.

HOW TO WIN Be the first player to form three equivalent ratios.

Stop and Think

1. **CRITICAL THINKING** Based on the number cards you saw as you played *Rapid Ratios*, which ratio do you think is easier to form, $\frac{8}{9}$ or $\frac{1}{2}$? Explain your reasoning.

2. **WRITING** Explain how you decided which cards to discard in *Rapid Ratios*.

10 *Getting Ready*

Review Prerequisite Skills

REVIEW WORDS

- **coordinate plane,** *p. 313*
- ***x*-axis,** *p. 313*
- ***y*-axis,** *p. 313*
- **origin,** *p. 313*
- **quadrant,** *p. 313*
- **ray,** *p. 474*
- **angle,** *p. 474*
- **vertex,** *p. 474*
- **degrees,** *p. 474*

VOCABULARY CHECK

Copy and complete using a review word from the list at the left.

1. A coordinate plane is formed by the intersection of a horizontal number line, called the __?__, and a vertical number line, called the __?__.

2. A(n) __?__ consists of two rays that begin at a common point, called the __?__.

SKILL CHECK

Plot the point and describe its location in a coordinate plane. *(p. 313)*

3. $A(7, 0)$ 4. $B(-3, -4)$ 5. $C(9, -5)$ 6. $D(-1, 2)$

Use the cross products property to solve the proportion. *(p. 423)*

7. $\dfrac{3}{a} = \dfrac{4}{9}$ 8. $\dfrac{2}{3} = \dfrac{12}{m}$ 9. $\dfrac{2}{5} = \dfrac{p}{40}$ 10. $\dfrac{b}{4} = \dfrac{5}{2}$

Use a protractor to draw an angle with the given measure. *(p. 474)*

11. $45°$ 12. $135°$ 13. $155°$ 14. $75°$

@HomeTutor   Prerequisite skills practice at classzone.com

Notetaking Skills   Connecting

In each chapter you will learn a new notetaking skill. In Chapter 10 you will apply the connecting strategy to Example 1 on p. 529.

Try to connect the new ideas and procedures you learn to concepts you have studied previously. You can include diagrams like the one below in your notebook to show how new concepts are related to those you have already studied.

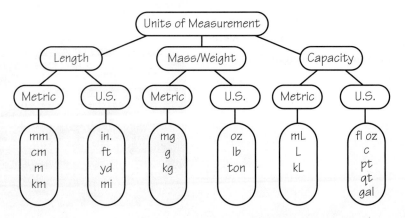

510

10.1 Angles

Before	You used angles to make circle graphs.
Now	You'll classify angles by their measures.
Why?	So you can find angles in everyday objects, as in Ex. 40.

KEY VOCABULARY
- acute angle, *p. 511*
- right angle, *p. 511*
- obtuse angle, *p. 511*
- straight angle, *p. 511*
- complementary, *p. 512*
- supplementary, *p. 512*

Gymnastics The gymnast's arm makes a *right angle* with his body as he performs on the rings. A right angle has a measure of 90°.

Angles are classified by their measures. The notation ∠A is read "angle A," and the notation m∠A is read "the measure of angle A."

KEY CONCEPT   *For Your Notebook*

Classifying Angles

An **acute angle** is an angle whose measure is less than 90°.

A **right angle** is an angle whose measure is exactly 90°.

Indicates a right angle

An **obtuse angle** is an angle whose measure is between 90° and 180°.

A **straight angle** is an angle whose measure is exactly 180°.

EXAMPLE 1   Classifying an Angle

ANOTHER WAY
You can also check the size of an angle by comparing it to the corner of a piece of paper, which has a measure of 90°.

Estimate to classify the angle as *acute, right, obtuse,* or *straight.*

Because *m∠A* is between 90° and 180°, ∠A is obtuse.

A

Animated Math at classzone.com

Angle Pairs Two angles are **complementary** if the sum of their measures is 90°. Two angles are **supplementary** if the sum of their measures is 180°.

EXAMPLE 2 Complementary and Supplementary Angles

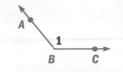
Tell whether the angles are *complementary*, *supplementary*, or *neither*.

a.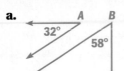

b.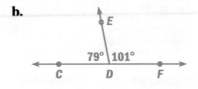

SOLUTION

a. $32° + 58° = 90°$ So, ∠*A* and ∠*B* are complementary.

b. $79° + 101° = 180°$ So, ∠*CDE* and ∠*EDF* are supplementary.

at classzone.com

✓ **GUIDED PRACTICE** for Examples 1 and 2

Classify the angle as *acute*, *right*, *obtuse*, or *straight*.

1. $m\angle A = 90°$ 2. $m\angle B = 118°$ 3. $m\angle C = 180°$ 4. $m\angle D = 55°$

5. Give the measures of two angles that are supplementary.

★ **EXAMPLE 3** Standardized Test Practice

Furniture For the lounge chair at the right, ∠1 and ∠2 are supplementary. If $m\angle 1$ is 130°, what is $m\angle 2$?

Ⓐ 40°   Ⓑ 50°

Ⓒ 130°   Ⓓ 230°

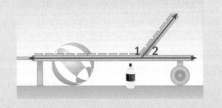

SOLUTION

$m\angle 1 + m\angle 2 = 180°$ **Definition of supplementary angles**

$130° + m\angle 2 = 180°$ **Substitute 130° for $m\angle 1$.**

$m\angle 2 = 50°$ **Subtract 130° from each side.**

▶ **Answer** The measure of ∠2 is 50°. The correct answer is B. Ⓐ **Ⓑ** Ⓒ Ⓓ

✓ **GUIDED PRACTICE** for Example 3

6. ∠*D* and ∠*E* are supplementary, and $m\angle D = 84°$. Find $m\angle E$.

7. ∠*R* and ∠*S* are complementary, and $m\angle S = 9°$. Find $m\angle R$.

10.1 EXERCISES

HOMEWORK KEY

★ = **STANDARDIZED TEST PRACTICE**
Exs. 9, 22, 39, 42, 44, 45, 46, and 61

◯ = **HINTS** AND **HOMEWORK HELP**
for Exs. 1, 7, 11, 17, 41 at classzone.com

SKILL PRACTICE

VOCABULARY Match the angle measure with its classification.

1. 78°　　　　**2.** 90°　　　　**3.** 168°　　　　**4.** 180°

A. Right　　**B.** Straight　　**C.** Obtuse　　**D.** Acute

CLASSIFYING ANGLES Classify the angle as *acute*, *right*, *obtuse*, or *straight*.

SEE EXAMPLE 1
on p. 511
for Exs. 5–9

5. 　　**6.** 　　**7.** 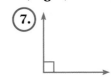　　**8.**

9. ★ **MULTIPLE CHOICE** What type of angle is ∠RST if m∠RST = 56°?

A Right　　**B** Straight　　**C** Obtuse　　**D** Acute

SEE EXAMPLE 2
on p. 512
for Exs. 10–12

COMPLEMENTARY AND SUPPLEMENTARY ANGLES Tell whether the angles
are *complementary*, *supplementary*, or *neither*. *Explain* your reasoning.

10. 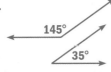　　**11.** 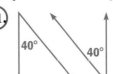　　**12.**

FINDING ANGLE MEASURES For the given angle measure, find the
measure of a supplementary angle and the measure of a complementary
angle, if possible.

SEE EXAMPLE 3
on p. 512
for Exs. 13–22

13. 19°　　**14.** 73°　　**15.** 118°　　**16.** 90°

17. 22°　　**18.** 162°　　**19.** 180°　　**20.** 3°

21. ERROR ANALYSIS ∠A and ∠B are
supplementary angles, and
m∠A = 70°. Describe and correct
the error made in finding m∠B.

$$m\angle A + m\angle B = 90°$$
$$70° + m\angle B = 90°$$
$$m\angle B = 20°$$

22. ★ **MULTIPLE CHOICE** ∠C and ∠D are complementary angles, and
m∠C = 26°. What is m∠D?

A 26°　　**B** 64°　　**C** 90°　　**D** 154°

ALGEBRA Find the measures of all the angles.

23. 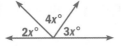　　**24.** 　　**25.**

10.1 Angles　**513**

26. (XY) **ALGEBRA** An angle that measures 16° and an angle that measures $(x + 6)°$ are complementary. What is the value of x?

27. (XY) **ALGEBRA** An angle that measures $(2y - 13)°$ and an angle that measures 29° are supplementary. What is the value of y?

INTERPRETING A DIAGRAM In Exercises 28–31, refer to the diagram at the right.

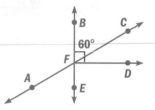

28. Find $m\angle CFD$.   **29.** Find $m\angle AFB$.

30. Find $m\angle AFE$.   **31.** Find $m\angle AFD$.

REASONING Copy and complete the statement using *always*, *sometimes*, or *never*. *Justify* your reasoning.

32. An angle supplementary to an acute angle is __?__ acute.

33. An angle supplementary to a right angle is __?__ a right angle.

(XY) **ALGEBRA** Write an expression for the angle measure.

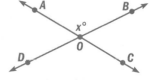

34. $m\angle BOC$ **35.** $m\angle AOD$ **36.** $m\angle DOC$

37. CHALLENGE Suppose the measure of $\angle AOB$ is three times the measure of its complement. What is $m\angle AOB$?

38. CHALLENGE $\angle DCG$ is a straight angle. $\angle ECF$ is a right angle and $m\angle DCE = 40.7°$. What are the possible measures of $\angle FCG$?

PROBLEM SOLVING

39. ★ **MULTIPLE CHOICE** On the roof truss at the right, $\angle 1$ and $\angle 2$ are complementary. The measure of $\angle 1$ is 50°. What is the measure of $\angle 2$?

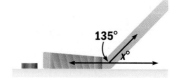

(A) 40°   (B) 50°

(C) 130°   (D) 140°

SEE EXAMPLE 3
on p. 512
for Ex. 40

40. FOLDING FAN A folding fan forms a straight angle when fully opened. If the fan is opened to a 138° angle, how many more degrees does it need to be opened to be fully opened?

41. HOCKEY STICK The *lie* is the angle the blade of a hockey stick makes with the shaft. The diagram shows a stick with a lie of 135°. What is the value of x?

135°

$x°$

42. ★ **SHORT RESPONSE** Which has a greater measure, an angle complementary to an angle measuring 15° or an angle supplementary to an angle measuring 125°? *Explain.*

43. KITES The line of a kite is tied to the ground as shown. Name the two supplementary angles. Then find $m\angle LMK$.

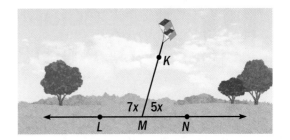

44. ★ **WRITING** Refer to the diagram for Ex. 43. John said that $m\angle M = 75°$. What is wrong with this statement?

45. ★ **OPEN-ENDED MATH** Give an example of an item that can be used to illustrate each of the following types of angles: acute, right, and obtuse.

46. ★ **EXTENDED RESPONSE** Make a table with three columns. Label the headings "$m\angle x$," "Complement of $\angle x$," and "Supplement of $\angle x$." Complete the table for five different acute angles x. What do you notice about the measures of the complement and supplement of the same angle?

47. CHALLENGE Draw five points A, B, C, D, and E such that the following statements are true. What type of angle is $\angle DBA$?

- $\angle DBE$ is a straight angle.
- $\angle DBC$ is a right angle.
- $\angle ABE$ is an obtuse angle.

48. CHALLENGE What must be true about the measure of an angle that has (a) a supplement but no complement, (b) both a supplement and a complement, (c) neither a supplement nor a complement? *Explain* your reasoning.

 NEW JERSEY MIXED REVIEW

TEST PRACTICE at classzone.com

49. Some farmers calculate that 42.8% of their farmland is planted with corn or alfalfa. Which number is NOT equivalent to 42.8%?

Ⓐ $\frac{42.8}{100}$ Ⓑ $\frac{428}{1000}$ Ⓒ 0.0428   Ⓓ 0.428

50. Josephine deposits $200 into a savings account that earns simple annual interest. What other information is necessary to know what the balance will be after 10 months?

Ⓐ The annual interest rate for Josephine's checking account

Ⓑ The annual interest rate for Josephine's savings account

Ⓒ The monthly fee for Josephine's checking account

Ⓓ The wage Josephine is paid at work

51. Of the 140 cars in a parking lot, 35 cars are blue. What percent of cars in the parking lot are NOT blue?

Ⓐ 25%   Ⓑ 35%   Ⓒ 65%   Ⓓ 75%

10.2 Special Pairs of Angles

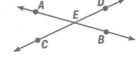

Before	You classified angles according to their measures.
Now	You'll identify special pairs of angles and types of lines.
Why?	So you can find angle measures, as on a map in Example 3.

KEY VOCABULARY
- **adjacent angles**, *p. 516*
- **vertical angles**, *p. 516*
- **congruent angles**, *p. 516*
- **intersecting lines, parallel lines, perpendicular lines,** *p. 517*
- **corresponding angles,** *p. 517*

ACTIVITY

You can find angle relationships when lines meet.

STEP 1 Draw and label $\overleftrightarrow{AB}$, the line containing points A and B. Then draw $\overleftrightarrow{CD}$ so it meets line $\overleftrightarrow{AB}$ as shown.

STEP 2 Measure each angle to the nearest degree and record the results.

STEP 3 Make a conclusion about the angles that are opposite each other.

STEP 4 Draw and label another pair of lines. Then repeat Step 2. Is your conclusion from Step 3 still true?

Two angles that share a common side and a vertex and do not overlap are called **adjacent angles**. When two lines meet at a point, as in the activity, adjacent angles are supplementary.

EXAMPLE 1 Identifying Adjacent Angles

Name all pairs of adjacent, supplementary angles.

∠1 and ∠2   ∠2 and ∠3

∠3 and ∠4   ∠1 and ∠4

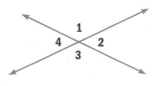

Vertical Angles When two lines meet at a point, as in the activity, the angles that are opposite each other are called **vertical angles**. Vertical angles are **congruent angles**, meaning they have the same measure.

READING
The symbol ≅ indicates congruence and is read "is congruent to."

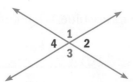

Vertical angles: $\angle 1 \cong \angle 3$

Vertical angles: $\angle 2 \cong \angle 4$

516   Chapter 10   Geometric Figures

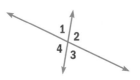

EXAMPLE 2 Using Vertical Angles

ANOTHER WAY
You can also find $m\angle 2$ using supplementary angles. Apply the definition first to $\angle 1$ and $\angle 4$, and then to $\angle 1$ and $\angle 2$.

Given that $m\angle 4 = 105°$, find $m\angle 2$.

SOLUTION

Because $\angle 4$ and $\angle 2$ are vertical angles, they are congruent. So, $m\angle 2 = m\angle 4 = 105°$.

✓ **GUIDED PRACTICE** **for Examples 1 and 2**

Refer to the diagram in Example 2.

1. Name all pairs of adjacent, supplementary angles.

2. Given that $m\angle 4 = 105°$, find $m\angle 1$.

3. Use your answer from Exercise 2 to find $m\angle 3$.

Lines in a Plane You can think of a *plane* as a flat surface that extends without end. In figures, it appears as shown at the right. Two lines that meet at a point, as shown, are called **intersecting lines**.

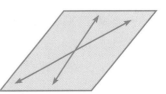

Two lines in the same plane that do not intersect are called **parallel lines**. **Perpendicular lines** intersect to form four right angles. The symbol ∥ is used to indicate parallel lines, and the symbol ⊥ is used to indicate perpendicular lines.

UNDERSTAND SYMBOLS
Arrowheads are used to indicate that lines are parallel.

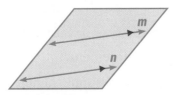

Parallel lines in a plane ($m \parallel n$)

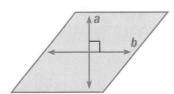

Perpendicular lines in a plane ($a \perp b$)

Angles that occupy corresponding positions when a line intersects two other lines are called **corresponding angles**. When a line intersects two parallel lines, corresponding angles are congruent.

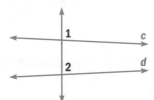

Lines c and d are not parallel, so corresponding angles, such as $\angle 1$ and $\angle 2$, are *not* congruent.

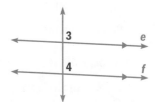

Lines e and f are parallel, so corresponding angles, such as $\angle 3$ and $\angle 4$, are congruent.

EXAMPLE 3 Using Corresponding Angles

Maps The map shows a section of New York City. Streets shown on maps often appear to form parallel or intersecting lines.

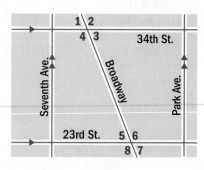

a. Name two streets that are parallel and two streets that intersect.

b. Given that $m\angle 7 = 68°$, find $m\angle 1$.

SOLUTION

a. Several answers are possible. For example, 34th Street is parallel to 23rd Street, and 34th Street intersects Broadway.

b. Because $\angle 7$ and $\angle 5$ are vertical angles, $m\angle 5 = m\angle 7 = 68°$. Because 34th Street and 23rd Street are parallel lines, $\angle 5$ and $\angle 1$ are congruent corresponding angles. So, $m\angle 1 = m\angle 5 = 68°$.

✓ **GUIDED PRACTICE** **for Example 3**

4. Refer to the map above. Find $m\angle 6$ and $m\angle 2$. *Explain* your reasoning.

10.2 EXERCISES

HOMEWORK KEY

★ = **STANDARDIZED TEST PRACTICE**
Exs. 13, 16, 20, 32, 33, and 38

◯ = **HINTS AND HOMEWORK HELP**
for Exs. 3, 5, 7, 11, 21 at classzone.com

SKILL PRACTICE

VOCABULARY Copy and complete the statement.

1. When two lines intersect, __?__ angles are supplementary.

2. When two lines intersect to form four right angles, the lines are __?__.

USING INTERSECTING LINES In Exercises 3–6, refer to the diagram.

SEE EXAMPLES 1 AND 2
on pp. 516–517
for Exs. 3–7, 13

3. Name all pairs of adjacent, supplementary angles.

4. Name all pairs of vertical angles.

5. Given that $m\angle 3 = 147°$, find $m\angle 1$.

6. Given that $m\angle 3 = 147°$, find $m\angle 2$.

USING PARALLEL LINES In Exercises 7–12, refer to the diagram.

7. Name two pairs of vertical angles.

SEE EXAMPLE 3
on p. 518
for Exs. 8–12

8. Name two pairs of corresponding angles.

9. Find $m\angle 3$.

10. Find $m\angle 7$.

11. Find $m\angle 4$.

12. Find $m\angle 6$.

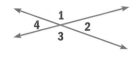

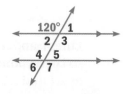

13. ★ **MULTIPLE CHOICE** Which of the following pairs of angles are congruent?

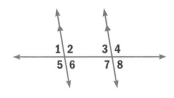

    A ∠1 and ∠4   **B** ∠3 and ∠4

    C ∠4 and ∠8   **D** ∠6 and ∠8

14. **FINDING MEASURES** Use the diagram in Ex. 13. If you know only $m\angle 5$, tell how you can find the measures of all the other angles.

15. **ERROR ANALYSIS** In the diagram at the right, $m\angle 1 = 38°$. Describe and correct the error made in finding $m\angle 3$.

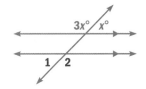

$$m\angle 1 + m\angle 3 = 180°$$
$$38° + m\angle 3 = 180°$$
$$m\angle 3 = 142°$$

16. ★ **OPEN-ENDED MATH** Draw two parallel lines and a third line that crosses them. Label all the angles. Identify all the congruent angles.

17. ⓧⱽ **CHALLENGE** Write and solve an equation to find the values of x and $3x$. Then find $m\angle 1$ and $m\angle 2$.

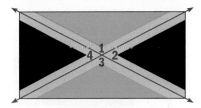

PROBLEM SOLVING

18. **JAMAICAN FLAG** Name two pairs of adjacent angles and two pairs of vertical angles in the flag of Jamaica. Then find $m\angle 2$, given that $m\angle 1 = 127°$.

19. **MULTI-STEP PROBLEM** In the diagram of the cabinet door, $m\angle 3 = 96°$.

  a. Identify Name all pairs of adjacent, supplementary angles. Then name all pairs of vertical angles.

  b. Calculate Find $m\angle 1$, $m\angle 2$, and $m\angle 4$.

  c. Justify *Explain* how you found each of the angle measures in part (b).

20. ★ **WRITING** Your friend says two lines in a plane must either intersect or be parallel. Is your friend correct? *Explain.*

ROAD MAP Refer to the road map.

SEE EXAMPLE 3
on p. 518
for Exs. 21–28

21. Name a street parallel to Elm Street.

22. Name two streets that intersect 1st Ave.

23. Find $m\angle 1$.   24. Find $m\angle 2$.

25. Find $m\angle 3$.   26. Find $m\angle 4$.

27. Find $m\angle 5$.   28. Find $m\angle 6$.

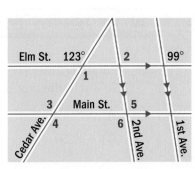

READING IN MATH Read the information below for Exercises 29–31.

The construction of homes and buildings is a major industry. Common building materials are adobe, brick, cement, glass, iron, and wood. Beams, girders, and posts support buildings. Beams and girders run horizontally, and posts are vertical supports.

29. Identify Name the endpoints of a beam. Name the endpoints of a post.

30. Identify Name five angles that have a measure of 53°.

31. Calculate What is $m\angle ADJ$? *Explain* how you found your answer.

32. ★ SHORT RESPONSE Two lines intersect to form an angle that measures 72°. Draw a diagram and find the measures of the three other angles that are not straight. *Explain* your reasoning.

33. ★ MULTIPLE CHOICE In the diagram of the zip line, lines a and b are parallel, and $m\angle 2 = 95°$. Which statement about the zip line is true?

A $\angle 4 \cong \angle 2$ and $\angle 4 \cong \angle 10$

B $\angle 4 \cong \angle 2$ and $m\angle 4 > m\angle 10$

C $m\angle 4 > m\angle 2$ and $\angle 4 \cong \angle 10$

D $m\angle 4 > m\angle 2$ and $m\angle 4 > m\angle 10$

34. CHALLENGE In the diagram at the right, $m\angle 1 = 51°$ and $m\angle 2 = 87°$. What are $m\angle 3$, $m\angle 4$, $m\angle 5$, and $m\angle 6$? *Explain* how you found your answers.

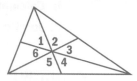

 NEW JERSEY MIXED REVIEW  **TEST PRACTICE** at classzone.com

35. A digital camera costs $336.87 and is subject to a 6% sales tax. Which is closest to the amount of the sales tax?

A $20.00

B $20.20

C $20.50

D $357.00

520 **EXTRA PRACTICE** for Lesson 10.2, p. 785   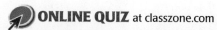 **ONLINE QUIZ** at classzone.com

10.3 Triangles

4.5.E.1.a — Concrete representations (e.g., base-ten blocks or algebra tiles)

Before	You classified angles.
Now	You'll classify triangles.
Why?	So you can analyze triangles, as with tripod angles in Ex. 34.

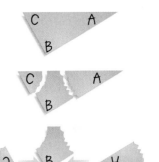

KEY VOCABULARY
- acute, right, obtuse triangle, *p. 522*
- congruent sides, *p. 523*
- equilateral, isosceles, scalene triangle, *p. 523*

ACTIVITY

You can find the sum of the angle measures in a triangle.

STEP 1 **Draw** a triangle and cut it out. Label the angles $\angle A$, $\angle B$, and $\angle C$.

STEP 2 **Tear** the corners off the triangle.

STEP 3 **Rearrange** $\angle A$, $\angle B$, and $\angle C$ so that they are adjacent. Repeat the activity with two more triangles. Then make a conclusion about the angle measures of a triangle.

READING
A triangle is identified by its vertices. In the activity, triangle *ABC* can be written $\triangle ABC$.

In the activity, you found that the sum of the angle measures in $\triangle ABC$ is 180°. The sum of the angle measures in any triangle is 180°.

EXAMPLE 1 Finding an Angle Measure in a Triangle

xy **Find the value of x in the triangle.**

$$x° + 83° + 26° = 180°$$ Sum of angle measures in a triangle is 180°.

$$x + 109 = 180$$ Simplify.

$$x = 71$$ Subtract 109 from each side.

▶ **Answer** The value of x is 71.

Interior and Exterior Angles The three angles of any triangle are called *interior angles*. The sides of a triangle can be extended to form angles outside of the triangle that are adjacent and supplementary to the interior angles. These angles are called *exterior angles*. You can use the measures of interior angles to find the measures of exterior angles.

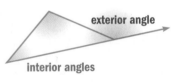

exterior angle

interior angles

EXAMPLE 2 Finding the Measure of an Exterior Angle

Find the value of *y* in the figure.

SOLUTION

To find the value of *y*, use the fact that adjacent interior and exterior angles of a triangle are supplementary.

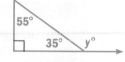

$$y° + 35° = 180°$$ Definition of supplementary angles

$$y = 145$$ Subtract 35 from each side.

▶ **Answer** The value of *y* is 145.

✓ **GUIDED PRACTICE** for Examples 1 and 2

Find the value of *x* or *y*.

1.

2.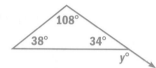

Classifying Triangles When you classify a triangle, be as specific as possible. You can classify a triangle by the measures of its interior angles.

KEY CONCEPT *For Your Notebook*

Classifying Triangles by Angle Measures

Acute Triangle	**Right Triangle**	**Obtuse Triangle**
An **acute triangle** has three acute angles.	A **right triangle** has one right angle.	An **obtuse triangle** has one obtuse angle.

EXAMPLE 3 Classifying a Triangle by Angle Measures

Use the triangle in the plant hanger at the right. Classify the triangle by its angle measures.

The triangle has one right angle, so it is a right triangle.

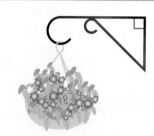

COMPARE ANGLES

The angles opposite congruent sides in a triangle are congruent. The arcs in the triangles show that the angles are congruent.

Congruent Sides Sides of a triangle that have the same length are **congruent sides**. The two marks on the sides of the triangle at the right indicate that sides $\overline{XY}$ and $\overline{XZ}$ are congruent. You can write this as $\overline{XY} \cong \overline{XZ}$.

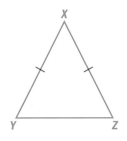

The notation $\overline{XY}$ is read "line segment XY" and represents a *line segment* with endpoints X and Y. The notation XY represents *the length* of XY. You can classify triangles by the lengths of their sides.

KEY CONCEPT — *For Your Notebook*

Classifying Triangles by Side Lengths

An **equilateral triangle** has 3 congruent sides.

An **isosceles triangle** has at least 2 congruent sides.

A **scalene triangle** has no congruent sides.

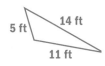

★ **EXAMPLE 4** Standardized Test Practice

Which statement is *not* true about the triangle?

Ⓐ It is isosceles. Ⓑ It is equilateral.

Ⓒ Its 3 angles are congruent. Ⓓ It is scalene.

SOLUTION

All three sides of the triangle are congruent, so the triangle is both isosceles and equilateral. In addition, the angles opposite the three congruent sides are equal in measure. The triangle is not scalene, because it has congruent sides.

▸ **Answer** The correct answer is D. Ⓐ Ⓑ Ⓒ ⬤

 GUIDED PRACTICE for Examples 3 and 4

Classify the triangle by its angle measures.

3. 40°, 60°, 80°   **4.** 45°, 35°, 100°   **5.** 37°, 53°, 90°

6. 59°, 62°, 59°   **7.** 90°, 76°, 14°   **8.** 12°, 114°, 54°

Classify the triangle by its side lengths.

9. 3 ft, 2 ft, 2 ft   **10.** 6 cm, 15 cm, 18 cm   **11.** 17 m, 17 m, 17 m

12. 112 yd, 80 yd, 112 yd   **13.** 19 in., 19 in., 19 in.   **14.** 25 km, 26 km, 27 km

10.3 EXERCISES

SKILL PRACTICE

VOCABULARY In Exercises 1 and 2, tell whether the statement is *true* or *false*. *Explain* your reasoning.

1. A triangle with one angle measure greater than 90° is an acute triangle.

2. An equilateral triangle can also be classified as an isosceles triangle.

XY **ALGEBRA** Find the value of *x*.

SEE EXAMPLE 1
on p. 521
for Exs. 3–6

3.

4.

5.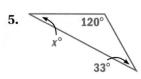

6. **ERROR ANALYSIS** Describe and correct the error made in finding the value of *x*.

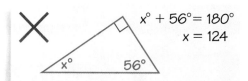

SEE EXAMPLE 2
on p. 522
for Exs. 7–9

XY **ALGEBRA** Find the value of *y*.

7.

8.

9.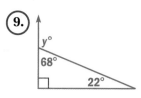

CLASSIFYING BY ANGLE MEASURES Classify the triangle by its angle measures.

SEE EXAMPLE 3
on p. 522
for Exs. 10–15

10. 68°, 22°, 90°

11. 82°, 64°, 34°

12. 135°, 24°, 21°

13. 17°, 60°, 103°

14. 58°, 49°, 73°

15. 54°, 90°, 36°

CLASSIFYING BY SIDE LENGTHS Classify the triangle by its side lengths.

SEE EXAMPLE 4
on p. 523
for Exs. 16–21

16. 12 cm, 6 cm, 11 cm

17. 6 m, 6 m, 6 m

18. 11 ft, 6 ft, 11 ft

19. 15 in., 15 in., 12 in.

20. 2 mm, 2 mm, 2 mm

21. 19 cm, 7 cm, 21 cm

XY **ALGEBRA** Find the values of *x* and *y*.

22.

23.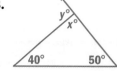

24.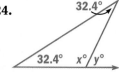

DRAWING TRIANGLES In Exercises 25 and 26, draw each triangle.

25. A right scalene triangle

26. An acute isosceles triangle

27. ★ **MULTIPLE CHOICE** Which of the following describes the triangle at the right?

    Ⓐ right, scalene   Ⓑ obtuse, isosceles

    Ⓒ acute, isosceles   Ⓓ acute, equilateral

28. **FINDING ANGLE MEASURES** Find the unknown angle measures in the triangle shown in Exercise 27.

29. **REASONING** Find the measure of each angle of an equilateral triangle. *Explain* your reasoning.

30. **CHALLENGE** The measure of one angle in a triangle is $x°$. The other two angles are congruent to each other. Write an expression for the measure of each of the other angles. *Explain* your reasoning.

PROBLEM SOLVING

SEE EXAMPLE 2
on p. 522
for Exs. 31, 33

31. **DRAWBRIDGE** A castle has a drawbridge that can be raised or lowered. When the drawbridge is lowered, what is the measure of the angle that the chain forms with the road leading up to the castle?

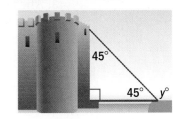

32. ★ **MULTIPLE CHOICE** You are making a triangular piece of glass for a stained glass window. Two of the angles of the triangle measure 65° and 61°. What is the measure of the third angle?

    Ⓐ 54°   Ⓑ 63°   Ⓒ 65°   Ⓓ 126°

33. **RESEARCH TRIANGLE PARK** Duke University, the University of North Carolina, and North Carolina State University make up the three vertices of Research Triangle Park in North Carolina. The distances between the three universities are 9 miles, 21 miles, and 23 miles. Classify Research Triangle Park by its side lengths.

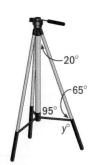

34. **CAMERA TRIPOD** A tripod keeps a camera steady. A tripod has three legs that are each connected to a vertical bar. Find the value of *y*.

REASONING In Exercises 35 and 36, copy and complete the statement using *always, sometimes,* or *never. Justify* your reasoning.

35. An isosceles triangle is __?__ a right triangle.

36. An obtuse triangle __?__ has 3 congruent sides.

37. ★ **WRITING** Is is possible for the exterior angle of a triangle to be acute? obtuse? right? *Explain.*

38. ★ **SHORT RESPONSE** Draw three different isosceles triangles. Mark the congruent sides and congruent angles. How can you tell which angles are congruent when you know which sides are congruent?

39. CONSTRUCTION In some houses, wall posts and ceiling beams are connected by support braces. Find the values of x and y in the diagram.

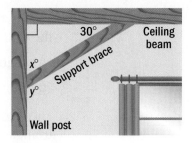

40. REASONING A triangle has angle measures of 40°, 60°, and 80°. One exterior angle is drawn at each vertex of the triangle. What is the sum of the measures of the three exterior angles? *Explain*.

41. ★ SHORT RESPONSE Draw a triangle with an interior angle that is congruent to its corresponding exterior angle. Classify the triangle and find the sum of the other two exterior angles. *Explain* your reasoning.

42. CHALLENGE *Explain* how to make a precise drawing of a triangle with side lengths 10 centimeters, 12 centimeters, and 15 centimeters.

 NEW JERSEY MIXED REVIEW   **TEST PRACTICE** at classzone.com

43. The table at the right represents the relationship between the base x and area y of a rectangle with a height of 2 inches. Which graph best represents the data in the table?

Base x (in.)	1	2	3	4
Area y (in.²)	2	4	6	8

Ⓐ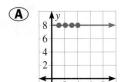

Ⓑ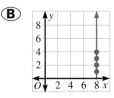

Ⓒ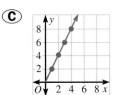

Ⓓ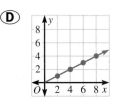

Brain Game   *The Shape of Things*

Draw a square with a side length of 4 inches on a piece of paper. Divide the square into 16 smaller squares with side length 1 inch. Then mark off the lines shown in blue on the diagram. Carefully cut along these lines to produce the seven pieces of a tangram.

Arrange all seven tangram pieces to form each figure.

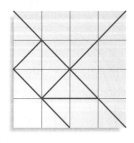

Extension

Use after Lesson 10.3

Constructions

GOAL Construct geometric figures.

KEY VOCABULARY
• **arc,** *p. 527*

You can use a straightedge and a compass to construct geometric figures. To draw an **arc**, or part of a circle, with a given center, first place the point of a compass on the center. Then rotate the compass to draw the arc.

EXAMPLE 1 Copying an Angle

You can use a straightedge and a compass to copy an angle.

STEP 1 **Draw** any ∠*A*. Use a straightedge to draw a ray with endpoint *P*. Use a compass to draw an arc with center *A*. Label *B* and *C* as shown. Then, with the same compass setting, draw an arc with center *P*. Label *Q* as shown.

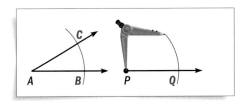

> **REVIEW USING A COMPASS**
> Need help using a compass? See p. 754.

STEP 2 **Put** the compass point at *B* and adjust the compass so you can draw an arc through *C*. Then, with the same compass setting, draw an arc with center *Q*. Label *R* as shown.

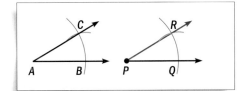

STEP 3 **Use** a straightedge to draw $\overrightarrow{PR}$, the ray from *P* through *R*. ∠*P* is congruent to ∠*A*.

EXAMPLE 2 Bisecting an Angle

You can use a straightedge and a compass to *bisect* an angle, or divide an angle into two congruent parts.

STEP 1 **Draw** any ∠*J*. Then use a compass to draw an arc with center *J* that intersects both sides of ∠*J*. Label *K* and *L* as shown.

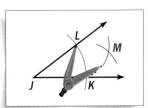

STEP 2 **Use** a compass to draw an arc with center *K*. Then, with the same compass setting, draw an arc with center *L*. Label the intersection *M*.

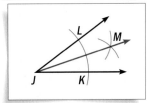

STEP 3 **Use** a straightedge to draw $\overrightarrow{JM}$. This ray bisects ∠*J*.

EXAMPLE 3 Constructing an Isosceles Triangle

You can use a straightedge and a compass to construct an isosceles triangle.

STEP 1 Draw $\overline{AB}$. With the compass opened more than half the length of $\overline{AB}$, draw an arc with center A as shown.

STEP 2 Use the same compass setting to draw an arc with center B. Label the point of intersection C.

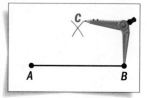

STEP 3 Use a straightedge to draw $\overline{AC}$ and $\overline{BC}$. $\triangle ABC$ is an isosceles triangle with $\overline{AC} \cong \overline{BC}$.

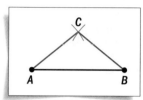

EXERCISES

In Exercises 1 and 2, use a straightedge to draw the specified type of angle. Then copy the angle.

1. An acute angle

2. An obtuse angle

3. Bisect the angle in Exercise 1.

4. Bisect the angle in Exercise 2.

5. Construct perpendicular lines by bisecting a straight angle. *Explain* how you know that the lines are perpendicular.

6. Construct an equilateral triangle using the steps in Example 3. In Step 1, first open your compass to the length of $\overline{AB}$. Then use this setting to draw the two arcs. *Explain* how you know the triangle is equilateral.

7. Follow the steps below to construct parallel lines.

   STEP 1 Draw a line m.

   STEP 2 Choose a point on m and draw a line l perpendicular to m at that point. (*Hint:* See Exercise 5.)

   STEP 3 Choose another point on m and draw a line p perpendicular to m at that point. Lines l and p are parallel.

10.4 Polygons

NJ 4.2.A.1.a Quadrilaterals, including squares, rectangles, parallelograms, trapezoids, rhombi

Before	You classified triangles.
Now	You'll classify quadrilaterals and other polygons.
Why?	So you can classify shapes, as in Ex. 28.

KEY VOCABULARY
- **quadrilateral,** *p. 529*
- **trapezoid,** *p. 529*
- **parallelogram,** *p. 529*
- **rhombus,** *p. 529*
- **polygon,** *p. 530*
- **pentagon,** *p. 530*
- **hexagon,** *p. 530*
- **heptagon,** *p. 530*
- **octagon,** *p. 530*
- **diagonal,** *p. 531*

A **quadrilateral** is a geometric figure that is made up of four line segments, called sides, which intersect only at their endpoints.

Special Quadrilaterals		
Trapezoid		A **trapezoid** is a quadrilateral with exactly 1 pair of parallel sides.
Parallelogram		A **parallelogram** is a quadrilateral with 2 pairs of parallel sides.
Rectangle		A *rectangle* is a parallelogram with 4 right angles.
Rhombus		A **rhombus** is a parallelogram with 4 congruent sides.
Square		A *square* is a parallelogram with 4 right angles and 4 congruent sides.

EXAMPLE 1 Classifying a Quadrilateral

TAKE NOTES
To help you classify quadrilaterals, you could draw a diagram that shows how the special quadrilaterals are related to each other.

Sketch and classify a quadrilateral with opposite sides parallel, one side of length 3 centimeters, and another side of length 1 centimeter.

STEP 1 **Draw** two sides, one of length 3 centimeters and one of length 1 centimeter. The angle between the two sides does not matter.

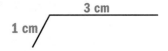

STEP 2 **Draw** sides parallel to the first two sides to complete the figure.

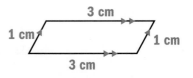

▶ **Answer** The figure is a parallelogram.

1. A quadrilateral has 4 right angles, 4 congruent sides of length 2.5 centimeters, and both pairs of opposite sides parallel. Classify the quadrilateral. Then use a ruler and a protractor to draw it.

Polygons A **polygon** is a geometric figure that is made up of three or more line segments that intersect only at their endpoints. The number of sides determines the name of the polygon.

KEY CONCEPT — *For Your Notebook*

Classifying Polygons

VOCABULARY
The prefix used in the name of a polygon tells you the number of sides the figure has.

Prefix	Meaning
tri-	three
quad-	four
penta-	five
hexa-	six
hepta-	seven
octa-	eight

Triangle
3 sides

Quadrilateral
4 sides

Pentagon
5 sides

Hexagon
6 sides

Heptagon
7 sides

Octagon
8 sides

EXAMPLE 2 Classifying Polygons

Tell whether the figure is a polygon. If it is, classify it. If it is not, explain why not.

a.

b.

SOLUTION

a. This figure is not a polygon because it is not made up entirely of line segments.

b. This figure is a polygon with 5 sides. So, it is a pentagon.

✓ **GUIDED PRACTICE** | **for Example 2**

Tell whether the figure is a polygon. If it is, classify it. If it is not, explain why not.

2.

3.

4.

Animated Math at classzone.com

Regular Polygons A *regular polygon* is a polygon with all sides equal in length and all angles equal in measure. Matching angle marks indicate that the angles are congruent. The figures below are examples of regular polygons.

You can draw *diagonals* to divide polygons into triangles to find the sum of the measures of their angles. A **diagonal** of a polygon is a segment, other than a side, that connects two vertices of the polygon.

EXAMPLE 3 Using a Regular Polygon

The polygon shown is a regular pentagon. Find the perimeter of the pentagon. Then find the sum of the angle measures in the pentagon.

▶ A regular pentagon has 5 sides of equal length, so the perimeter of the pentagon is 5(3) = 15 feet.

▶ A pentagon can be divided into three triangles. The sum of the angle measures in a triangle is 180°, so the sum of the angle measures in any pentagon is 180° + 180° + 180° = 540°.

 GUIDED PRACTICE | **for Example 3**

5. What If? Suppose a polygon is a regular octagon with a side length of 5 feet. What is the perimeter of the octagon? What is the sum of its angle measures?

10.4 EXERCISES

HOMEWORK KEY

★ = **STANDARDIZED TEST PRACTICE**
Exs. 17, 27, 31, 32, and 47

○ = **HINTS AND HOMEWORK HELP**
for Exs. 5, 9, 11, 15, 29 at classzone.com

SKILL PRACTICE

1. VOCABULARY What two types of quadrilaterals have four right angles?

VOCABULARY Match the polygon with its classification.

2.

3.

4.

A. Pentagon

B. Octagon

C. Hexagon

DRAWING QUADRILATERALS **Use the clues to classify the quadrilateral described. Then use a ruler and a protractor to draw it.**

SEE EXAMPLE 1 on p. 529 for Exs. 5–7

5. This figure has four right angles. Not all of the sides are the same length.
6. This figure's opposite sides are parallel. Not all of the angles are congruent.
7. This figure has exactly one pair of opposite sides that are parallel.

IDENTIFYING POLYGONS **Tell whether the figure is a polygon. If it is a polygon, classify it. If it is not, *explain* why not.**

SEE EXAMPLES 2 AND 3 on pp. 530–531 for Exs. 8–17

8. 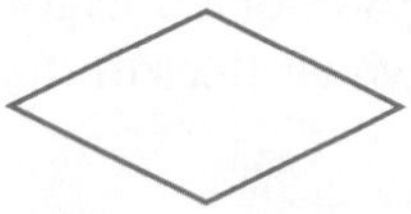

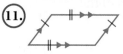

9. 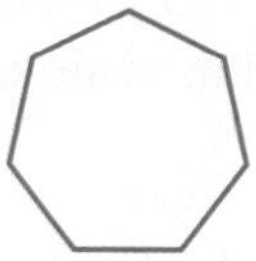

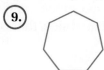

10. 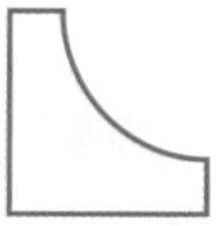

CLASSIFYING POLYGONS **Classify the polygon and tell if it is regular. If it is not regular, *explain* why not.**

11. 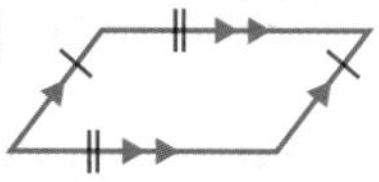

12. 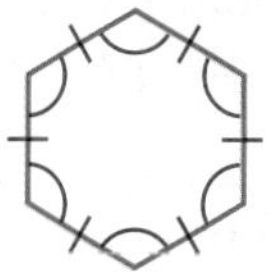

13. 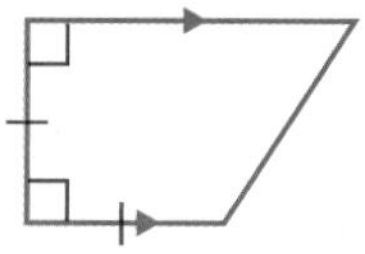

14. 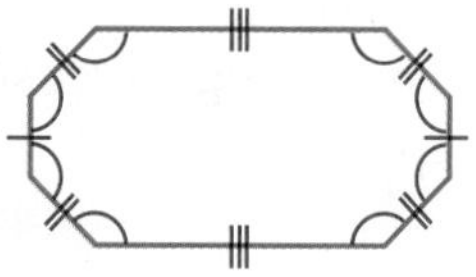

15. 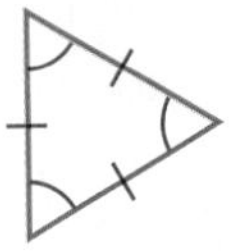

16. 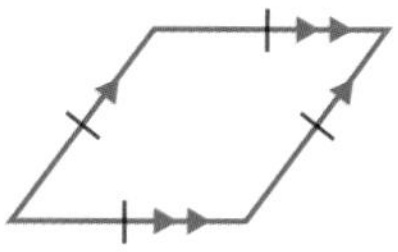

17. ★ **MULTIPLE CHOICE** What is the perimeter of a regular octagon with a side length of 4 centimeters?

(A) 12 cm (B) 16 cm (C) 32 cm (D) 64 cm

18. **ERROR ANALYSIS** Describe and correct the error made in classifying the figure.

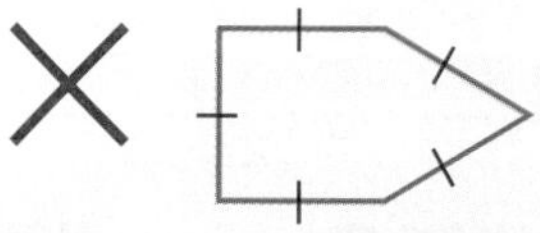

The figure is a regular pentagon because the lengths of all five sides are equal.

REASONING **Tell whether the statement is *true* or *false*. *Explain* your reasoning.**

19. All squares are rectangles.
20. A scalene triangle is regular.
21. A trapezoid is a parallelogram.
22. Every rhombus is a square.

NUMBER SENSE **Find the measures for the polygon described.**

SEE EXAMPLE 3 on p. 531 for Exs. 23–24

23. A side and an angle of a regular octagon with a perimeter of 46 centimeters
24. A side and an angle of a regular heptagon with a perimeter of 52.5 inches
25. **CHALLENGE** What is the sum of the angle measures of any quadrilateral? *Explain* your reasoning.

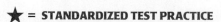

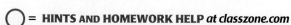

PROBLEM SOLVING

**SEE EXAMPLES
1, 2, AND 3**
on pp. 529–531
for Exs. 26–29

26. GUIDED PROBLEM SOLVING The quilt design shown repeatedly uses regular hexagons and other polygons. What is the sum of the angle measures in a hexagon?

  a. Sketch a hexagon on a piece of paper.

  b. Draw three line segments from one vertex to divide the hexagon into triangles.

  c. Use the triangles to find the sum of the angle measures in a hexagon.

27. ★ MULTIPLE CHOICE The top surface of a picnic table is a regular hexagon with a side length of 2 feet. What is the perimeter of the top surface of the picnic table?

  (A) 8 ft   **(B)** 12 ft   **(C)** 14 ft   **(D)** 16 ft

28. STAINED GLASS WINDOW Sketch and classify four different polygons contained in the stained glass window at the right. Do any of the polygons appear to be regular polygons? *Explain* your reasoning.

29. COORDINATE GEOMETRY Graph and connect the ordered pairs (0, 5), (3, 2), (2, −2), (−2, −1), (−3, 2), and (0, 5) in the order given. Is the resulting figure a polygon? If it is, classify it and tell if it is regular. If it is not a polygon, *explain* why not.

30. FORMULAS Write a formula for the perimeter of (a) a regular pentagon with a side length of s, (b) a regular hexagon with a side length of s, and (c) a regular heptagon with a side length of s. Then write a formula for the perimeter of a regular polygon with r sides with a side length of s.

31. ★ EXTENDED RESPONSE Complete the following parts to examine the angle measures of polygons.

**REVIEW
STRATEGIES**
Need help
with these
problem solving
strategies? See
pp. 766 and 767.

  a. Break into Parts Copy and complete the table below.

Polygons	Triangle	Quadrilateral	Pentagon	Hexagon
Sum of angle measures	?	?	?	?
Measure of each angle in a regular polygon	?	?	?	?

  b. Look for a Pattern What pattern do you notice in the sum of the angle measures in the table?

  c. Predict Use the pattern you identified in part (b) to predict the sum of the angle measures in a heptagon. What do you predict is the measure of each angle in a regular heptagon?

32. ★ WRITING Identify a type of quadrilateral and a type of triangle that are always regular polygons. *Explain* your reasoning.

33. **CHALLENGE** Refer to the results of Exercise 31.

    a. Write an expression for the sum of the angle measures in a regular polygon with *n* sides. *Explain* your reasoning.

    b. Write an expression for the measure of each angle in a regular polygon with *n* sides. *Explain* your reasoning.

---

34. Which of the following best describes the triangle below?

    Ⓐ Right   **Ⓑ** Scalene

    Ⓒ Isosceles   **Ⓓ** Equilateral

35. There were 4 songs that became hit singles from an album that contained 13 songs. Which best represents the percent of songs on the album that did NOT become hit singles?

    Ⓐ 30%   **Ⓑ** 31%   **Ⓒ** 69%   **Ⓓ** 70%

36. What kind of angles are $\angle 1$ and $\angle 2$?

    Ⓐ Congruent   **Ⓑ** Complementary

    Ⓒ Supplementary   **Ⓓ** Vertical

QUIZ *for Lessons 10.1–10.4*

In Exercises 1–4, use the diagram shown below.

  1. Name all pairs of adjacent, supplementary angles. *(p. 511)*

  2. Name all pairs of vertical angles. *(p. 516)*

  3. Given that $m\angle 2 = 125°$, find $m\angle 3$. *(p. 511)*

  4. Given that $m\angle 2 = 125°$, find $m\angle 4$. *(p. 516)*

  5. Find the value of *y*. *(p. 521)*

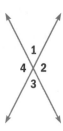

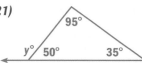

  6. Classify a triangle that has side lengths 7 cm, 12 cm, and 7 cm. *(p. 521)*

  7. STOP SIGN The shape of a stop sign is an octagon. Find the sum of the angle measures in a stop sign. *(p. 529)*

Lessons 10.1–10.4

1. ROAD SIGN A yield sign has the shape of a triangle as shown. Which of the following best describes the triangle?

36 in.

36 in.   36 in.

YIELD

A. right   **C.** scalene

B. equilateral   **D.** obtuse

2. SUM OF ANGLE MEASURES What is the sum of the angle measures of a polygon with ten sides?

A. $18°$ **C.** $1620°$

B. $1440°$ **D.** $1800°$

3. ANGLES In the diagram, $m\angle 4 = 29°$. Which process will NOT tell you the measure of $\angle 1$?

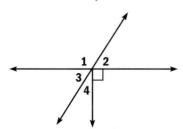

A. Find the complement of $\angle 4$ and subtract its angle measure from $180°$.

B. Subtract $(m\angle 4 + 90°)$ from $180°$ and find the supplement of the resulting angle.

C. Add $m\angle 4$ and $90°$.

D. Find the supplement of $\angle 4$ and subtract $90°$ from its angle measure.

4. QUILT The measures of two angles of a triangular quilt piece are $52°$ and $32°$. What is the measure of the third angle?

A. $6°$ **C.** $84°$

B. $70°$ **D.** $96°$

5. GRAPHING POINTS Graph and connect points A, B, C, and D in alphabetical order: $A(0, 2)$, $B(-1, 0)$, $C(0, -2)$, $D(1, 0)$. Then connect points D and A. Which description best fits the resulting shape?

A. Rhombus   **C.** Trapezoid

B. Rectangle   **D.** Square

6. CORRESPONDING ANGLES In the diagram, m, n, and p are parallel. The measure of $\angle 1$ is $128°$ and the measure of $\angle 2$ is $113°$. Find $m\angle 5$, in degrees.

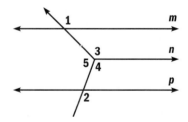

A. $52°$ **C.** $119°$

B. $67°$ **D.** $128°$

7. OPEN-ENDED Use the two sets of ordered pairs to complete the following.

Set A: $(0, 0)$, $(3, 4)$, $(5, 4)$, $(2, 0)$, $(0, 0)$

Set B: $(2, 2)$, $(-2, 2)$, $(-2, -2)$, $(2, -2)$, $(2, 2)$

- Graph and connect the ordered pairs from Set A in the order that they are given.
- Repeat for Set B.
- *Compare* the polygons formed in both sets. How are they alike? How are they different? Is either one regular? *Explain.*

GOAL
Construct and explore similar rectangles.

MATERIALS
• graph paper
• ruler

10.5 Investigating Similar Rectangles

Similar rectangles have the same shape but not necessarily the same size. You can draw rectangles on graph paper to identify properties of similar rectangles.

EXPLORE Find the ratio relating the lengths and widths of two similar rectangles.

STEP 1 **Draw** a rectangle on a piece of graph paper. Use a ruler to draw a diagonal line segment from the lower left corner of the rectangle through the upper right corner.

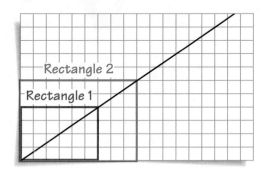

Rectangle 2

Rectangle 1

STEP 2 **Draw** a second rectangle that shares the lower left vertex. The opposite vertex should be on the diagonal line, as shown. The two rectangles are similar.

STEP 3 **Copy** and complete the table by recording the length and width of each rectangle.

	Rectangle 1	Rectangle 2
Length	?	?
Width	?	?

STEP 4 **Find** each of the following ratios from the table. What do you notice?

$$\frac{\text{Length of rectangle 1}}{\text{Length of rectangle 2}} \qquad \frac{\text{Width of rectangle 1}}{\text{Width of rectangle 2}}$$

DRAW CONCLUSIONS

1. **LOOK FOR A PATTERN** Draw rectangle 3 that shares the lower left corner and diagonal line with rectangle 1 that you drew. Then repeat Steps 3 and 4, comparing rectangle 1 and rectangle 3.

2. **REASONING** Rectangle A is similar to rectangle B. Rectangle B is 21 units long and 7 units wide. If rectangle A has a width of 6 units, how long is rectangle A? *Explain* your reasoning.

10.5 Similar and Congruent Polygons

4.2.A.3 Use logic and reasoning to make and support conjectures about geometric objects.

Before You classified polygons.

Now You'll use properties of similar and congruent polygons.

Why? So you can compare side lengths, as with sails in Ex. 20.

KEY VOCABULARY
- **similar polygons,** *p. 537*
- **congruent polygons,** *p. 537*

Two polygons are **similar** if they have the same shape but not necessarily the same size. The symbol ~ is used to indicate that two polygons are similar. **Congruent polygons** are similar polygons that have the same shape *and* the same size.

Similar Polygons	Congruent Polygons
△*LMN* ~ △*PQR*	△*ABC* ≅ △*DEF*
Angles Corresponding angles are congruent:	**Angles** Corresponding angles are congruent:
∠*L* ≅ ∠*P*, ∠*M* ≅ ∠*Q*, and ∠*N* ≅ ∠*R*	∠*A* ≅ ∠*D*, ∠*B* ≅ ∠*E*, and ∠*C* ≅ ∠*F*
Sides Ratios of lengths of corresponding sides are equal:	**Sides** Corresponding sides are congruent:
$\dfrac{LM}{PQ} = \dfrac{MN}{QR} = \dfrac{LN}{PR}$	$\overline{AB} \cong \overline{DE}$, $\overline{AC} \cong \overline{DF}$, and $\overline{BC} \cong \overline{EF}$

EXAMPLE 1 Finding Measures of Congruent Polygons

AVOID ERRORS
When naming congruent or similar polygons, be sure to list the letters for the corresponding vertices in the same order.

△*RST* is congruent to △*XYZ*. Name the corresponding sides and corresponding angles. Then find *XY*.

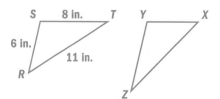

SOLUTION

Corresponding sides: $\overline{RS}$ and $\overline{XY}$, $\overline{RT}$ and $\overline{XZ}$, $\overline{ST}$ and $\overline{YZ}$

Corresponding angles: ∠*R* and ∠*X*, ∠*S* and ∠*Y*, ∠*T* and ∠*Z*

Because $\overline{XY}$ and $\overline{RS}$ are corresponding sides, they are equal in length. So, *XY* = *RS* = 6 inches.

Similarity and Scale Factor If two polygons are similar, the ratio of the lengths of corresponding sides is called the *scale factor*.

EXAMPLE 2 Finding the Ratio of Lengths

AVOID ERRORS
When you write the ratios, be sure you compare the sides of △*ABC* to △*DEF*, not △*DEF* to △*ABC*.

Given that △*ABC* ~ △*DEF*, find the ratio of the lengths of the corresponding sides of △*ABC* to △*DEF*.

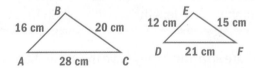

SOLUTION

Write a ratio for each pair of corresponding sides. Then substitute the lengths of the sides and simplify each ratio.

$$\frac{AB}{DE} = \frac{16}{12} = \frac{4}{3} \qquad \frac{BC}{EF} = \frac{20}{15} = \frac{4}{3} \qquad \frac{AC}{DF} = \frac{28}{21} = \frac{4}{3}$$

▸ **Answer** The ratio of the lengths of the corresponding sides, or the scale factor, is $\frac{4}{3}$.

EXAMPLE 3 Checking for Similarity

Drawing An art student is copying a detail of a painting. The copy is 48 inches long and 36 inches wide. The rectangular region she is copying is 16 inches long and 12 inches wide. Are the original and the copy similar figures?

SOLUTION

Because both figures are rectangles, all angles are right angles, so corresponding angles are congruent. To determine whether the figures are similar, see if the ratios of the lengths of the corresponding sides are equal.

$$\frac{\text{Length of original}}{\text{Length of copy}} \overset{?}{=} \frac{\text{Width of original}}{\text{Width of copy}} \qquad \text{Write ratios for lengths of corresponding sides.}$$

$$\frac{16}{48} \overset{?}{=} \frac{12}{36} \qquad \text{Substitute values.}$$

$$\frac{1}{3} = \frac{1}{3} \qquad \text{Simplify.}$$

▸ **Answer** The corresponding angles are congruent and the ratios of the lengths of the corresponding sides are equal, so the figures are similar.

✓ **GUIDED PRACTICE**   for Examples 1, 2, and 3

In Exercises 1 and 2, use the fact that *ABCD* ≅ *EFGH*.

1. Name the corresponding sides and corresponding angles.

2. Find the unknown angle measures.

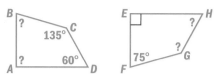

3. **What If?** Suppose the dimensions of the rectangular sketch of the painting described in Example 3 had a length of 44 inches and a width of 27 inches. Would the original and the sketch still be similar figures? *Explain.*

10.5 EXERCISES

HOMEWORK KEY

★ = **STANDARDIZED TEST PRACTICE**
Exs. 10, 21, 22, 25, 26, and 38

◯ = **HINTS AND HOMEWORK HELP**
for Exs. 3, 5, 7, 11, 19 at classzone.com

SKILL PRACTICE

VOCABULARY Copy and complete the statement.

1. Two polygons that have the same shape but not necessarily the same size are __?__ polygons.

2. When two similar polygons have congruent corresponding angles and congruent corresponding sides, the polygons are __?__.

FINDING MEASURES Name the corresponding sides and the corresponding angles of the congruent polygons. Then find the unknown measures.

SEE EXAMPLE 1
on p. 537
for Exs. 3–10

3. *KLMN* ≅ *QRST*

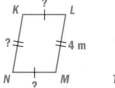

4. △*FGH* ≅ △*JKL*

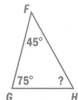

IDENTIFYING CORRESPONDING PARTS Given △*UVW* ≅ △*XYZ*, **name the part in △***UVW* **corresponding to the given part in △***XYZ*.

5. ∠*X*   6. ∠*ZYX*   7. $\overline{XZ}$ 8. $\overline{ZY}$

9. **ERROR ANALYSIS** Describe and correct the error made at the right.

10. ★ **MULTIPLE CHOICE** Suppose that △*LMN* ≅ △*XYZ* and both triangles are scalene. Which of the following is *not* true?

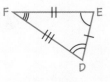

△ABC ≅ △DEF

Ⓐ $\overline{LN}$ ≅ $\overline{XZ}$ Ⓑ $\overline{LM}$ ≅ $\overline{YZ}$ Ⓒ ∠*M* ≅ ∠*Y*   Ⓓ ∠*N* ≅ ∠*Z*

10.5 Similar and Congruent Polygons   **539**

RATIOS Tell whether the two polygons are similar. If they are, find the ratio of the lengths of the corresponding sides of figure A to figure B.

SEE EXAMPLES 2 AND 3
on p. 538
for Exs. 11–14

11.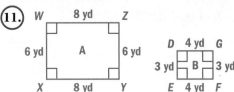

12.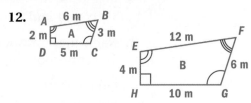

13.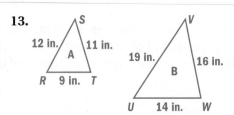

14.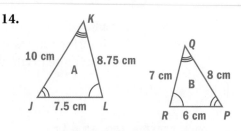

REASONING Tell whether the statement is *true* or *false*. If false, *explain* why.

15. Two rectangles are congruent if they have the same perimeter.

16. Two squares are congruent if they have the same perimeter.

17. **CHALLENGE** Two rectangles are similar. The ratio of the lengths of their corresponding sides is 1 : 2. Find the ratio of the perimeters of the two rectangles. Then find the ratio of the areas. *Explain* your answers.

18. **CHALLENGE** Two rectangles are similar. The area of the first rectangle is 150 square feet. Its width is 10 feet. The area of the second rectangle is 24 square feet. Find the dimensions of the second rectangle.

PROBLEM SOLVING

SAILS In Exercises 19 and 20, use the diagram of the two sailboat sails and the fact that $\triangle ABC \sim \triangle DEF$.

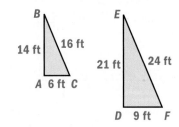

SEE EXAMPLES 1 AND 2
on pp. 537–538
for Exs. 19–20

19. Name the corresponding sides and the corresponding angles.

20. Find the ratio of the lengths of the corresponding sides of $\triangle ABC$ to $\triangle DEF$.

21. ★ **WRITING** Are all squares similar? Are they all congruent? *Explain.*

22. ★ **MULTIPLE CHOICE** Which statement about the triangular scarves is *true*?

Ⓐ The ratio of the lengths of the corresponding sides is 2 : 3.

Ⓑ Both scarves are scalene right triangles.

Ⓒ The scarves are congruent.

Ⓓ $\triangle RST \sim \triangle XYZ$

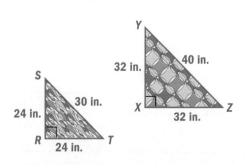

SEE EXAMPLE 3
on p. 538
for Ex. 23

23. **PHOTO STICKERS** A standard photograph is a rectangle that is 6 inches long by 4 inches wide. Rectangular photo stickers are 1.4 inches by 0.9 inch. Are a photograph and a sticker similar figures? *Explain* your reasoning.

24. **REASONING** On a coordinate plane, draw a rectangle *similar* to rectangle *DEFG*, shown. Then draw a rectangle *congruent* to *DEFG*. *Explain* why each rectangle is similar or congruent to *DEFG*.

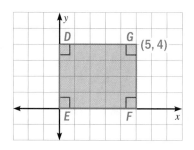

25. ★ **OPEN-ENDED MATH** Sketch two polygons whose corresponding sides are congruent but whose corresponding angles are not congruent. Are the polygons similar? Why or why not?

26. ★ **SHORT RESPONSE** A college football field has a width of 160 feet and a length of 360 feet. A college soccer field can vary from 195 feet to 240 feet in width and from 330 feet to 360 feet in length.

   a. Can college football and soccer fields ever be similar rectangles? *Explain.*

   b. A tennis court for doubles is 78 feet long by 36 feet wide. Is this similar to either of the fields in part (a)? *Explain.*

27. **SCALE FACTORS** Triangle $ABC \sim \triangle XYZ$, and the ratio of the lengths of the corresponding sides of $\triangle ABC$ to $\triangle XYZ$ is $\frac{5}{8}$. What is the ratio of the lengths of the corresponding sides of $\triangle XYZ$ to $\triangle ABC$? *Explain.*

28. **BANNERS** Chloe wants to make three banners similar to the rectangular one she already has. It is 2 ft high and 8 ft wide. Should she change the banner's width and length by multiplying by the same factor or by adding the same amount to each side? *Explain.*

29. **CHALLENGE** A long and narrow rectangular painting is matted with a border 2.5 inches wide all the way around the edges of the painting. Is the inner rectangle of the border similar to the outer rectangle of the border? *Explain.*

 NEW JERSEY MIXED REVIEW **TEST PRACTICE** at classzone.com

30. Cliff is competing in a bicycle race. So far he has completed $\frac{2}{3}$ of the race, or 16 miles. What fraction of the race has he completed after biking 20 miles?

   Ⓐ $\frac{4}{5}$ Ⓑ $\frac{5}{6}$ Ⓒ $\frac{7}{8}$ Ⓓ $\frac{3}{3}$

31. Steve traded $\frac{3}{8}$ of his baseball card collection. What percent of his card collection did he trade?

   Ⓐ 12.5%   Ⓑ 26.7%   Ⓒ 37.5%   Ⓓ 38%

EXTRA PRACTICE for Lesson 10.5, p. 785   🔵 **ONLINE QUIZ** at classzone.com   **541**

10.6 Using Proportions with Similar Polygons

 4.2.A.2.a Using proportions to find missing measures

Before	You identified corresponding parts of polygons.
Now	You'll use similar triangles to find lengths.
Why?	So you can find lengths without measuring, as in Ex. 15.

KEY VOCABULARY
- **proportion,** *p. 418*
- **cross products property,** *p. 423*
- **similar polygons,** *p. 537*

You know that the lengths of corresponding sides of similar polygons are proportional. So when two polygons are similar, you can use proportions to find unknown lengths.

EXAMPLE 1 Finding an Unknown Length

 Quadrilaterals *ABCD* and *EFGH* are similar. Find *FG*.

SOLUTION

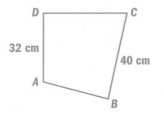

Use the ratios of the lengths of corresponding sides to write a proportion involving the unknown length.

WRITE AND SOLVE A PROPORTION

Need help with writing and solving proportions? See p. 418.

$$\frac{AD}{EH} = \frac{BC}{FG}$$ **Write proportion involving *FG*.**

$$\frac{32}{20} = \frac{40}{x}$$ **Substitute known values.**

$$32x = 20 \cdot 40$$ **Use cross products property.**

$$\frac{32x}{32} = \frac{20 \cdot 40}{32}$$ **Divide each side by 32.**

$$x = 25$$ **Simplify.**

▶ **Answer** The length of $\overline{FG}$ is 25 centimeters.

✓ **GUIDED PRACTICE** for Example 1

Find the unknown length *x*, given that the polygons are similar.

1.
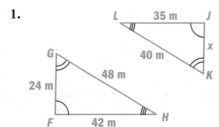

2.
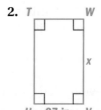
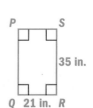

Indirect Measurement The sun's rays hit objects that are perpendicular to the ground at the same angle. These objects and their shadows form similar triangles. You can use these similar triangles to find lengths that are difficult to measure directly.

EXAMPLE 2 Making an Indirect Measurement

 Groundhog Day A 16 inch tall groundhog emerges on Groundhog Day near a tree and sees its shadow. The length of the groundhog's shadow is 5 inches, and the length of the tree's shadow is 35 inches. What is the height of the tree?

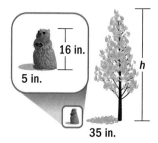

SOLUTION

Use the ratios of the lengths of corresponding parts. Write a proportion involving the unknown height h.

$$\frac{\text{Height of tree}}{\text{Height of groundhog}} = \frac{\text{Length of tree's shadow}}{\text{Length of groundhog's shadow}}$$

$$\frac{h}{16} = \frac{35}{5} \qquad \text{Substitute known values.}$$

$$16 \cdot \frac{h}{16} = 16 \cdot \frac{35}{5} \qquad \text{Multiply each side by 16.}$$

$$h = 16 \cdot 7 \qquad \text{Simplify.}$$

$$h = 112 \qquad \text{Multiply.}$$

▶ **Answer** The tree has a height of 112 inches, or 9 feet 4 inches.

Check You can estimate to check that your answer is reasonable. The groundhog is slightly taller than 3 times its shadow, so the tree should be slightly taller than 3 times its shadow. Because $3 \times 35 = 105$, the height of 112 inches is reasonable.

> *ANOTHER WAY*
> As you saw in Lesson 8.4, you can also write the ratio of the height of the tree to the length of the tree's shadow.

✓ **GUIDED PRACTICE** for Example 2

3. **What If?** Suppose the groundhog in Example 2 emerges and sees its shadow next to a building. The length of the groundhog's shadow is 5 inches, and the length of the building's shadow is 95 inches. Draw a diagram for the situation. Then find the height of the building.

4. **Lighthouse Height** The shadow cast by a lighthouse is 30 feet long. At the same time, the shadow cast by a 4 foot tall sign is 3 feet long. How tall is the lighthouse?

10.6 EXERCISES

HOMEWORK
KEY

★ = **STANDARDIZED TEST PRACTICE**
Exs. 10, 16, 18, 19, and 31

◯ = **HINTS AND HOMEWORK HELP**
for Exs. 3, 5, 9, 11, 17 at classzone.com

SKILL PRACTICE

VOCABULARY Copy and complete the statement.

1. An equation that states that two ratios are equivalent is called a(n) ? .

2. You can use the ? property to rewrite $\frac{a}{b} = \frac{c}{d}$ as $ad = bc$.

FINDING LENGTHS Find length x, given that the polygons are similar.

SEE EXAMPLE 1
on p. 542
for Exs. 3–7

3.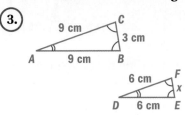

4.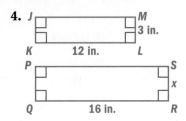

5.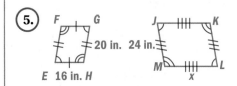

6.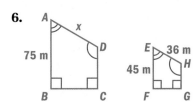

7. **ERROR ANALYSIS** Quadrilaterals *ABCD* and *QRST* are similar. Describe and correct the error made in finding the value of *x*.

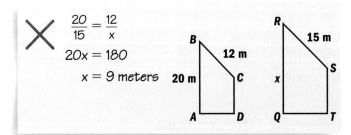

COMPARING AREAS Find the area of the smaller, similar rectangle.

8. [rectangle 12 cm × 8 cm and 6 cm × 6 cm]

9. [rectangle 27 ft × 9 ft and 4 ft × 4 ft]

10. ★ **MULTIPLE CHOICE** Rectangles *RSTU* and *LMNP* are similar and
    RS = 7 cm, *ST* = 4 cm, and *LM* = 21 cm. Which proportion can you use
    to find the width of rectangle *LMNP*?

    (A) $\frac{7}{21} = \frac{MN}{4}$ (B) $\frac{7}{21} = \frac{4}{MN}$ (C) $\frac{21}{7} = \frac{4}{MN}$ (D) $\frac{21}{7} = \frac{7}{MN}$

FINDING PERIMETERS **Find the perimeters of the similar polygons.**

 11.

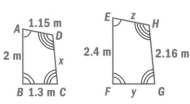

12.

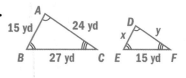

13. FINDING RATIOS Find the ratios of the perimeters in Ex. 11 and in Ex. 12. How do the ratios of the perimeters compare to the ratio of the sides?

14. CHALLENGE In the figure, $\triangle RST \sim \triangle QSP$.

  a. Find RQ, ST, and TP.

  b. Does $\dfrac{ST}{TP} = \dfrac{SR}{PQ}$? Does $\dfrac{ST}{TP} = \dfrac{TR}{PQ}$? *Explain.*

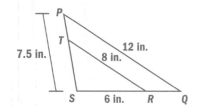

PROBLEM SOLVING

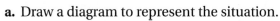

SEE EXAMPLE 2
on p. 543
for Exs. 15–17

15. GUIDED PROBLEM SOLVING A tourist who is 5 feet tall stands next to a cactus. The length of the tourist's shadow is 2 feet, and the length of the cactus's shadow is 13 feet. How tall is the cactus?

  a. Draw a diagram to represent the situation.

  b. Write a proportion involving the unknown height of the cactus.

  c. Solve the proportion.

16. ★ MULTIPLE CHOICE A person who is 6 feet tall stands next to a life-sized model of a dinosaur. The person's shadow is 4 feet long. At the same time, the shadow cast by the dinosaur model is 12 feet long. How tall is the dinosaur model?

  A 6 feet   **B** 12 feet   **C** 18 feet   **D** 48 feet

17. BUILDING HEIGHT A girl places a mirror on the ground and stands so that she can just see the top of a building. If she measures the distance x from the base of the building to the mirror and the distance y from where she is standing to the mirror, how can she use a proportion with her own height h to find the height z of the building?

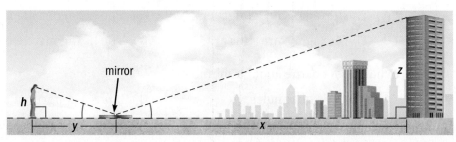

18. ★ **SHORT RESPONSE** *Explain* why you agree or disagree with each of the following statements: (a) All congruent figures are similar; (b) All similar figures are congruent.

19. ★ **OPEN-ENDED MATH** Give an example of a real-life situation in which you would use a proportion to find an indirect measurement.

20. **CHECKING REASONABLENESS** Your friend looks at the diagram at the right. She says that because the building is about 3 times the height of the flagpole, the length of the building's shadow is about 30 feet. Is this reasonable? *Explain.*

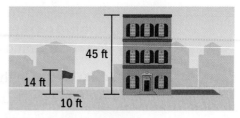

21. ◆ **MULTIPLE REPRESENTATIONS** A flagpole is 24 feet tall and casts a 20 foot shadow. A tree next to the flagpole casts a shadow *x* feet long.

    a. Draw a Diagram Draw and label a diagram to represent the situation.

    b. Write a Proportion Write a proportion you can use to find the height *y* of the tree.

    c. Make a Table Make a table that shows the heights of trees next to the flagpole whose shadow lengths are 10, 15, and 20 feet.

    d. Write a Function Use the table to write a function that models the height *y* of a tree next to the flagpole in terms of the length of the tree's shadow *x*. Then use the function to find the height of a tree that casts a shadow 17.3 feet long.

22. **CHALLENGE** The three overlapping right triangles in the figure are similar. Find the value of *x*. Then find the unknown side lengths.

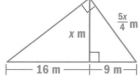

23. **CHALLENGE** Rectangles *ABCD* and *PQRS* are similar.

    a. Suppose you triple the width of each rectangle. Are the rectangles still similar? *Explain.*

    b. Suppose you triple both the length and the width. Are the rectangles still similar? What is the ratio of their perimeters? their areas? *Explain.*

NJ **NEW JERSEY MIXED REVIEW**   **TEST PRACTICE** at classzone.com

24. Two hexagons are drawn so that the ratios of lengths of corresponding sides are equal and corresponding angles are congruent. Which of the following statements is always true?

    (A) The hexagons are congruent.   **(B)** The hexagons are not congruent.

    (C) The hexagons are similar.   **(D)** The hexagons are not similar.

25. What must be true about a rhombus?

    (A) It has 4 right angles.   **(B)** It has 4 congruent angles.

    (C) It has 4 congruent sides.   **(D)** A rhombus is also a square.

 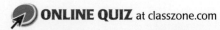

INVESTIGATION
Use before Lesson 10.7

GOAL
Investigate line and
rotational symmetry.

MATERIALS
• tape
• paper

10.7 Investigating Symmetry

A figure has *line symmetry* if you can fold it into two halves that are mirror
images. A figure has *rotational symmetry* if you can turn it 180° or less about
a fixed point so that it matches up with itself again. You can fold and turn
paper to investigate symmetry in a rectangle.

EXPLORE 1 **Determine whether a rectangle has line symmetry.**

STEP 1 **Fold** a rectangular piece of paper horizontally.

STEP 2 **Open** the paper and fold it vertically. Notice
that both the horizontal and vertical folds
produce two mirror images.

STEP 3 **Fold** the paper along its diagonals. Notice that
for each of these folds the two halves are not
mirror images. Experiment with other folds.
You will find that a rectangle has only 2 lines
of symmetry.

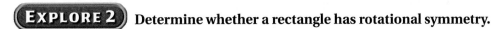

EXPLORE 2 **Determine whether a rectangle has rotational symmetry.**

STEP 1 **Tape** a rectangular piece of paper down on your desk. Place a
second piece of paper over the first so that they match up.

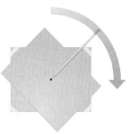

STEP 2 **Place** the tip of your pencil on the center of the top piece of
paper. Slowly turn the top piece of paper clockwise. Notice that
the pieces of paper match up again after a turn of 180°, so the
rectangle has 180° rotational symmetry.

DRAW CONCLUSIONS

1. **REASONING** Determine the line symmetry and rotational symmetry
   of a square. *Explain* your reasoning.

2. **REASONING** Draw a triangle that has three lines of symmetry. Does it
   have rotational symmetry? *Explain* your reasoning.

10.7 Transformations and Symmetry

NJ 4.2.B.1.c   Reflections, rotations, and translations result in images congruent to the pre-image

Before   You identified congruent figures.

Now   You'll identify transformations and symmetry in figures.

Why?   So you can identify a translation, as in Example 1.

KEY VOCABULARY
- **image,** *p. 548*
- **transformations: translation, reflection, rotation,** *p. 548*
- **line of reflection,** *p. 548*
- **center of rotation,** *p. 548*
- **angle of rotation,** *p. 549*
- **line symmetry, rotational symmetry,** *p. 550*

A **transformation** is a movement of a figure in a plane. The new figure formed by a transformation is the **image**. In this book, the original figure will always be blue and the image will always be red.

Each of the three transformations illustrated below results in an image that is congruent to the original figure.

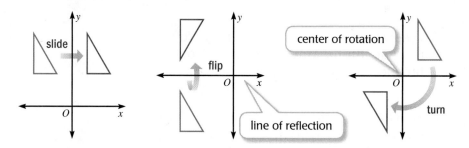

In a **translation**, or *slide*, each point of a figure is moved the same distance in the same direction. In the translation above, the triangle is translated to the right.

In a **reflection**, or *flip*, a figure is reflected in a line called the **line of reflection**, creating a mirror image of the figure. In the reflection above, the triangle is reflected in the *x*-axis.

In a **rotation**, or *turn*, a figure is rotated through a given angle and in a given direction about a fixed point called the **center of rotation**. In the rotation above, the triangle is rotated 180° about the origin.

EXAMPLE 1   Identifying a Translation

Tell whether the red image is a translation of the original blue figure. *Explain* **your reasoning.**

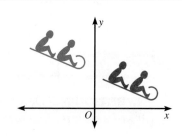

SOLUTION

Each point on the original figure is moved the same number of units in a "downhill" direction. The image is a translation of the original figure.

EXAMPLE 2 Standardized Test Practice

ELIMINATE CHOICES
The orientation of the figure changes, so it is not a translation. You can eliminate choice A.

Which word best describes the transformation shown at the right?

    (A) Translation   **(B)** Reflection in *x*-axis

    (C) Reflection in *y*-axis   **(D)** Rotation

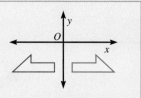

SOLUTION

The two figures are mirror images of each other, so the image is a reflection of the original figure. The line of reflection is the *y*-axis.

▶ **Answer** The correct answer is C.   (A) (B) **(C)** (D)

VOCABULARY
Clockwise means to rotate in the direction of the hands on a clock. *Counterclockwise* means to rotate in the opposite direction.

Rotations The center of rotation for all rotations in this book will be the origin. Rays drawn from the center of rotation through corresponding points on an original figure and its image form an angle called the **angle of rotation**.

Rotations are described by the angle and direction of rotation, either *clockwise* or *counterclockwise*. The figure at the right is rotated 45° clockwise about the origin.

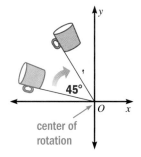

center of rotation

EXAMPLE 3 Identifying a Rotation

Tell whether the image is a rotation of the original figure. If it is, give the angle and direction of rotation.

The image is a rotation of the original figure about the origin. The original figure is rotated 90° counterclockwise.

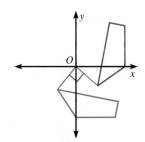

✓ **GUIDED PRACTICE** for Examples 1, 2, and 3

Identify the transformation. If it is a reflection, identify the line of reflection. If it is a rotation, give the angle and direction of rotation.

1. 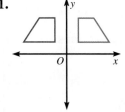   **2.** 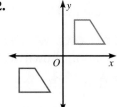   **3.**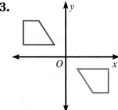

 Animated Math at classzone.com

Symmetry A figure has **line symmetry** if it can be divided by a line, called a *line of symmetry*, into two parts that are mirror images of each other. A figure has **rotational symmetry** if a turn of 180° or less produces an image that fits exactly on the original figure.

EXAMPLE 4 Identifying Symmetry

AVOID ERRORS

Make sure that when you draw a figure that has a line of symmetry, the line divides the figure into mirror images.

Incorrect   Correct

Tell whether the mirror at the right has *line symmetry*, *rotational symmetry*, or *both*. Explain.

The mirror has line symmetry. There are 4 lines of symmetry.

The mirror also has rotational symmetry. A turn of 90° or 180° clockwise (or counterclockwise) produces an image that fits exactly on the original figure.

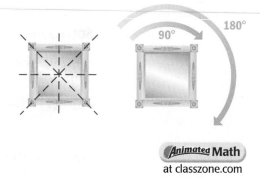

Animated **Math**
at classzone.com

✓ **GUIDED PRACTICE**   for Example 4

Tell whether the figure has *line symmetry*, *rotational symmetry*, *both*, or *neither*. Explain.

4.   5.  6.

10.7 EXERCISES

HOMEWORK KEY

★ = **STANDARDIZED TEST PRACTICE**
   Exs. 3, 28, 29, 30, 32, 34, and 44

◯ = **HINTS AND HOMEWORK HELP**
   for Exs. 5, 9, 11, 13, 29 at classzone.com

SKILL PRACTICE

VOCABULARY Copy and complete the statement.

1. A transformation that moves each point of a figure the same distance and the same direction is called a(n) __?__ .

2. A transformation that forms a mirror image of the original figure is a(n) __?__ .

SEE EXAMPLES 1, 2, AND 3
on pp. 548–549
for Ex. 3

3. ★ **MULTIPLE CHOICE** Which choice best describes the transformation shown at the right?

Ⓐ Translation   Ⓑ Reflection in the *x*-axis

Ⓒ Rotation   Ⓓ Reflection in the *y*-axis

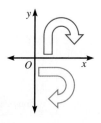

**SEE EXAMPLES
1, 2, AND 3**
on pp. 548–549
for Exs. 4–6

IDENTIFYING TRANSFORMATIONS Identify the transformation. If it is a reflection, identify the line of reflection. If it is a rotation, give the angle and direction of rotation.

4.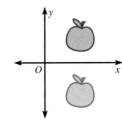

5.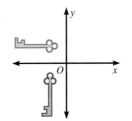

6.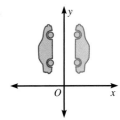

7. ERROR ANALYSIS Describe and correct the error made in identifying the symmetry in the parallelogram.

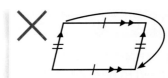

The parallelogram has both line symmetry and rotational symmetry.

SEE EXAMPLE 4
on p. 550
for Exs. 8–10

IDENTIFYING SYMMETRY Sketch the figure and draw any line(s) of symmetry. Then tell whether the figure has rotational symmetry. If it does, give the angle(s) and direction of rotation.

8.

9.

10.

IDENTIFYING SYMMETRY In Exercises 11–14, consider the capital letters of all 26 letters in the English alphabet.

11. Which letters have a vertical line of symmetry?

12. Which letters have a horizontal line of symmetry?

13. Which letters have both a vertical line of symmetry and a horizontal line of symmetry?

14. Which letters have rotational symmetry? Give the angle(s) and direction of rotation.

SYMMETRY IN POLYGONS Tell how many lines of reflection and angles of rotational symmetry the regular polygon has. What is the measure of the smallest angle of rotation?

15. **16.** **17.** **18.**

TYPOGRAPHY The letters below are transformations of one another. *Describe* the line of reflection or angle of rotation used in the transformation.

19. b to **d**

20. d to **p**

21. p to **b**

22. d to **q**

23. CHALLENGE A figure has line symmetry. Does the number of lines of symmetry in the figure change when the figure is translated? rotated? reflected? *Explain* your reasoning.

CHALLENGE **Identify a quadrilateral that meets each condition. Then sketch the quadrilateral and draw all lines of symmetry, if there are any.**

24. No lines of symmetry

25. Exactly one line of symmetry

26. Exactly two lines of symmetry

27. More than two lines of symmetry

PROBLEM SOLVING

28. ★ **WRITING** *Explain* why the words *clockwise* and *counterclockwise* do not need to be used to describe a 180° rotation.

SEE EXAMPLE 4
on p. 550
for Exs. 29–30

29. ★ **SHORT RESPONSE** A person's face appears to have line symmetry, but the two parts are not exact mirror images.

One of the pictures at the right is a normal photograph of a woman. The other is the right side of the woman's face and its exact mirror image.

Which photograph is a normal photograph of the woman? *Explain* your reasoning.

30. ★ **OPEN-ENDED MATH** Draw two polygons that have rotational symmetry but are not regular. Then give the angle(s) and direction of rotation.

31. COMPARE AND CONTRAST *Explain* how the line symmetry and rotational symmetry of a non-square rectangle are like those of a rhombus, and how they are different.

32. ★ **MULTIPLE CHOICE** You are making a collage using geometric figures. You want to use figures that have two or more lines of symmetry. Which figure could *not* be used in your collage?

(A) Circle **(B)** Equilateral triangle

(C) Trapezoid **(D)** Regular pentagon

33. ◆ **MULTIPLE TRANSFORMATIONS** Reflect the shape at the right over the *x*-axis, and then over the *y*-axis. *Compare* the results to the effect of a 180° rotation.

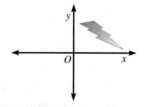

34. ★ **OPEN-ENDED MATH** *Describe* a real-world situation that is a translation. Does it ever involve other transformations? If so, which ones? *Explain*.

★ = **STANDARDIZED TEST PRACTICE** ◯ = **HINTS AND HOMEWORK HELP** *at classzone.com*

35. BIOLOGY The bodies of most animals show some symmetry. Many animals have *bilateral symmetry*, meaning that their bodies can be divided into roughly identical halves along a single plane. Where would a plane divide this stag beetle into two identical halves? How are bilateral symmetry and line symmetry alike? How are they different?

36. MULTI-STEP PROBLEM Use the diagram below to complete the following.

   a. Use a ruler and a protractor to copy the trapezoid and the two lines on a piece of paper.

   b. Sketch the reflection of *ABCD* in line *m*. Name it *EFGH*.

   c. Sketch the reflection of *EFGH* in line *n*. Name it *JKLM*.

   d. Identify the transformation from *ABCD* to *JKLM*. *Explain.*

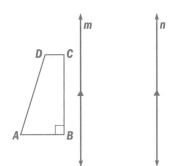

37. CHALLENGE Refer to Exercise 36. How is the distance between the parallel lines related to the distance between *ABCD* and *JKLM*? Why do you think this occurs?

38. REASONING If a regular polygon has *n* sides, how many lines of symmetry does it have? What is the measure of the smallest angle that will rotate the figure onto itself? *Explain.*

 NEW JERSEY MIXED REVIEW   **TEST PRACTICE** at classzone.com

39. Which of the following represents the *least* percent of change?

   A A shirt priced at $20 is now $15.

   B An employee's hourly wage changed from $7 to $9.

   C A plant grew from 10 inches to 30 inches in 1 month.

   D The number of students in a class changed from 33 to 27.

40. Which line contains the ordered pair (2, −3)?

   A Line *q*

   B Line *r*

   C Line *s*

   D Line *t*

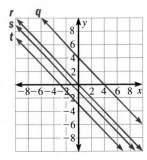

Tessellations

GOAL Recognize and design tessellations.

KEY VOCABULARY
• **tessellation,** *p. 554*
• **regular tessellation,** *p. 554*

A **tessellation** is a covering of a plane with congruent copies of the same pattern so that there are no gaps or overlaps. A **regular tessellation** is made from only one type of regular polygon. The figure below is a regular tessellation made from equilateral triangles.

EXAMPLE 1 Identifying Polygons that Tessellate

Tell whether each type of polygon can form a regular tessellation.

a. Square

b. Regular pentagon

SOLUTION

a. Start with a square. Make copies of the square and fit them together so that they cover the plane without gaps or overlaps. One possible arrangement is shown. So, a square forms a regular tessellation.

b. Start with a regular pentagon. Make copies of the pentagon. When you try to fit them together, you find that three pentagons can share a common vertex, but there is a gap that is too small to fit a fourth pentagon. So, a regular pentagon does not form a regular tessellation.

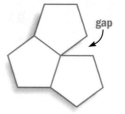

gap

Other Tessellations You can also make tessellations using one or more nonregular polygons. You translate, reflect, or rotate the figures to cover a plane. An isosceles triangle is reflected and translated to form the tessellation below.

EXAMPLE 2 Making a Tessellation

Make a tessellation of the quadrilateral shown. Describe the transformation(s) you use.

STEP 1 **Mark** the point at the middle of one of the sides of the quadrilateral. Then rotate the quadrilateral 180° about that point.

STEP 2 **Translate** the new figure as shown. The pattern that results covers the plane without gaps or overlaps. So, the quadrilateral forms a tessellation.

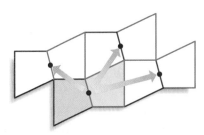

EXERCISES

Tell whether the polygon can form a regular tessellation. If it can, draw the tessellation.

1. Regular hexagon

2. Regular heptagon

In Exercises 3 and 4, make a tessellation of the indicated polygon. *Describe* the transformation(s) you use.

3. Parallelogram

4. Right triangle

5. Can you make a tessellation of the quadrilateral shown in Example 2 using *only* rotations? *only* translations? *only* reflections? *Explain* your reasoning.

In Exercises 6 and 7, tell whether the two polygons can be used to make a tessellation. If they can, draw the tessellation.

6. A regular octagon and a square with all sides from both figures equal in length

7. A regular triangle and a rhombus with all sides from both figures equal in length

8. **Reasoning** In the tessellation at the top of page 554, six triangles fit around a common vertex because each angle at the vertex measures 60°, for a total of 360°. *Explain* how this observation applies to the square and pentagon in Example 1.

9. **Using Polygons** Refer to the photo. Draw the polygon that forms the complete tessellation.

10.8 Transformations in the Coordinate Plane

NJ 4.2.C.2 Use a coordinate grid to model and quantify transformations (e.g., translate right 4 units).

Before You identified translations, reflections, and rotations.

Now You'll graph transformations in a coordinate plane.

Why? So you can describe transformations, as in Example 1.

KEY VOCABULARY
- coordinate plane, *p. 313*
- transformation, *p. 548*
- image, *p. 548*
- translation, *p. 548*
- reflection, *p. 548*
- rotation, *p. 548*

Computer Graphics Computer and video game programmers use transformations to create patterns and animations. How can you use coordinates to describe the transformation shown?

The transformation is a translation. You can use *coordinate notation* to describe a translation. An arrow is used in coordinate notation to signify "goes to."

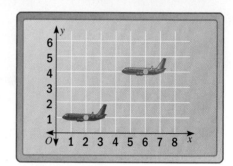

Coordinates of original point → Coordinates of image

$$(x, y) \rightarrow (x + a, y + b)$$

The number *a* tells how many units to shift the figure to the left or right.

The number *b* tells how many units to shift the figure up or down.

EXAMPLE 1 Describing a Translation

Describe the translation shown above using words and using coordinate notation.

Words: Each point on the original figure is moved 4 units to the left and 3 units down.

Coordinate notation: $(x, y) \rightarrow (x + (-4), y + (-3))$ or $(x, y) \rightarrow (x - 4, y - 3)$

 GUIDED PRACTICE for Example 1

1. Describe the translation using words: $(x, y) \rightarrow (x - 7, y + 2)$.

2. Describe the translation using coordinate notation: A figure is moved 5 units to the right and 4 units up.

EXAMPLE 2 **Translating a Figure**

Draw quadrilateral *JKLM* with vertices *J*(−5, 3), *K*(−4, 5), *L*(−3, 3), and *M*(−4, 1). Then find the coordinates of the vertices of the image after the translation $(x, y) \rightarrow (x + 6, y - 2)$ and draw the image.

SOLUTION

For each vertex of the original figure, add 6 to the *x*-coordinate and subtract 2 from the *y*-coordinate.

READING

Each point on an image is labeled with a *prime*. The notation *J*′ is read "*J* prime."

Original		Image
J(−5, 3)	→	*J*′(1, 1)
K(−4, 5)	→	*K*′(2, 3)
L(−3, 3)	→	*L*′(3, 1)
M(−4, 1)	→	*M*′(2, −1)

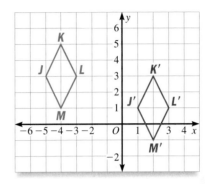

Each point on the original figure is translated 6 units to the right and 2 units down. The graph shows both figures.

Animated Math at classzone.com

✓ **GUIDED PRACTICE** for Example 2

Draw △*ABC* with vertices *A*(−4, 0), *B*(0, −4), and *C*(0, 0).

3. Find the coordinates of the vertices of the image after the translation $(x, y) \rightarrow (x + 4, y + 6)$.

4. Draw the image △*A*′*B*′*C*′.

Reflections You can also use coordinate notation to describe reflections in the *x*- and *y*-axes.

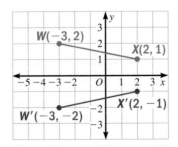 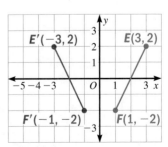

AVOID ERRORS

To keep from confusing the two patterns, remember that a reflection in the *x*-axis keeps the *x*-coordinates the same.

Reflection in the *x*-axis:

Multiply *y*-coordinate by −1.

$$(x, y) \rightarrow (x, -1 \cdot y) \text{ or}$$
$$(x, y) \rightarrow (x, -y)$$

Reflection in the *y*-axis:

Multiply *x*-coordinate by −1.

$$(x, y) \rightarrow (-1 \cdot x, y) \text{ or}$$
$$(x, y) \rightarrow (-x, y)$$

EXAMPLE 3 Reflecting a Figure

Draw parallelogram *ABCD* with vertices $A(-3, 3)$, $B(2, 3)$, $C(4, 1)$, and $D(-1, 1)$. Then find the coordinates of the vertices of the image after a reflection in the *x*-axis and draw the image.

SOLUTION

For each vertex of the original figure, multiply the *y*-coordinate by -1.

Original		Image
$A(-3, 3)$	$\rightarrow$	$A'(-3, -3)$
$B(2, 3)$	$\rightarrow$	$B'(2, -3)$
$C(4, 1)$	$\rightarrow$	$C'(4, -1)$
$D(-1, 1)$	$\rightarrow$	$D'(-1, -1)$

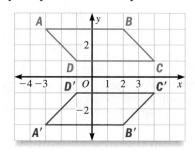

✓ **GUIDED PRACTICE** for Example 3

5. Draw parallelogram *ABCD* with vertices $A(1, 3)$, $B(4, 3)$, $C(6, 1)$, and $D(3, 1)$. Then find the coordinates of the vertices of the image after a reflection in the *y*-axis and draw the image.

10.8 EXERCISES

HOMEWORK KEY

★ = **STANDARDIZED TEST PRACTICE**
Exs. 23, 24, 25, 26, and 36

◯ = **HINTS AND HOMEWORK HELP**
for Exs. 3, 7, 9, 13, 25 at classzone.com

SKILL PRACTICE

VOCABULARY Copy and complete the statement.

1. The figure that results from the transformation of a figure is called the   ? .

2. To reflect a figure in the *y*-axis, multiply the   ?   of each vertex by -1.

SEE EXAMPLE 1
on p. 556
for Exs. 3–4

TRANSFORMATIONS *Describe* the transformation using coordinate notation.

 3.

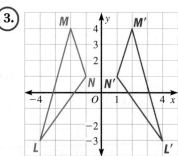

4.

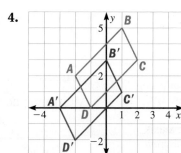

SEE EXAMPLE 1
on p. 556
for Ex. 5

5. ERROR ANALYSIS Describe and correct the error made in using $(x, y) \rightarrow (x + 4, y + 2)$ for the translation shown at the right.

TRANSLATING A FIGURE Draw the given triangle. Then find the coordinates of the vertices of the image after the translation and draw the image.

SEE EXAMPLE 2
on p. 557 for
Exs. 6–10

6. $P(1, 1)$, $Q(3, 5)$, $R(5, 4)$; $(x, y) \rightarrow (x - 2, y - 4)$

7. $F(-2, 3)$, $G(3, 3)$, $H(3, -1)$; $(x, y) \rightarrow (x - 3, y - 6)$

8. $L(-6, 0)$, $M(-6, -4)$, $N(-3, -4)$; $(x, y) \rightarrow (x + 4, y + 5)$

DRAWING TRANSFORMATIONS Draw rectangle *FGHJ* with vertices $F(-2, 3)$, $G(3, 3)$, $H(3, -1)$, and $J(-2, -1)$. Then find the coordinates of the vertices of the image after the given transformation and draw the image.

9. $(x, y) \rightarrow (x + 3, y + 6)$

10. $(x, y) \rightarrow (x - 7, y)$

SEE EXAMPLE 3
on p. 558 for
Exs. 11–12

11. Reflect *FGHJ* in the *x*-axis.

12. Reflect *FGHJ* in the *y*-axis.

ROTATING A FIGURE The vertices of a triangle are given. Find the coordinates of the vertices of the image after a rotation of 90° clockwise about the origin. The coordinate notation $(x, y) \rightarrow (y, -x)$ describes such a rotation.

13. $F(0, 2)$, $G(-3, 1)$, $H(-1, 1)$

14. $L(2, 2)$, $M(4, -1)$, $N(2, -2)$

15. $R(-3, 3)$, $S(-3, 0)$, $T(-1, 0)$

16. $W(0, 0)$, $X(5, -3)$, $Y(3, 4)$

In Exercises 17–19, draw the image of *ABCD* after the dilation.

EXTENSION Drawing a Dilation

Enlarging or reducing a figure by a scale factor to create a similar figure is called a *dilation*. To draw a dilation of square *ABCD* with a scale factor of 3, multiply the *x*- and *y*-coordinates by 3. You can describe this dilation using the coordinate notation $(x, y) \rightarrow (3x, 3y)$.

Original		Image
$A(1, 2)$	$\rightarrow$	$A'(3, 6)$
$B(2, 2)$	$\rightarrow$	$B'(6, 6)$
$C(2, 1)$	$\rightarrow$	$C'(6, 3)$
$D(1, 1)$	$\rightarrow$	$D'(3, 3)$

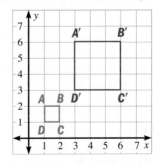

---

17. Scale factor of 5

18. Scale factor of 4

19. Scale factor of 6

20. CHALLENGE What is the effect of a dilation using scale factor *a* on the perimeter and the area of a figure?

21. CHALLENGE Rectangle *ABCD* has vertices *A*(0, 2), *B*(6, 2), *C*(6, 0), and *D*(0, 0).

    a. Draw rectangle *ABCD*. Then draw a dilation of rectangle *ABCD* using a scale factor of 1.5.

    b. Find the ratio in simplest form of the perimeter of the image to the perimeter of the original figure. How does this ratio compare to the scale factor?

    c. Find the ratio in simplest form of the area of the image to the area of the original figure. How does this ratio compare to the scale factor?

PROBLEM SOLVING

22. MOTION Use coordinate notation. *Describe* the transformation of the drummer from one picture to the next picture.

 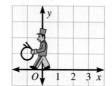 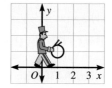 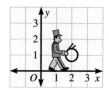

23. ★ MULTIPLE CHOICE Which of the following describes a translation of a game token 8 units to the left and 3 units up?

    (A) $(x, y) \rightarrow (x - 8, y - 3)$ **(B)** $(x, y) \rightarrow (x + 3, y - 8)$

    (C) $(x, y) \rightarrow (x - 8, y + 3)$ **(D)** $(x, y) \rightarrow (x - 3, y + 8)$

24. ★ MULTIPLE CHOICE A computer game reflects quadrilateral *ABCD* in the *x*-axis to produce the image *A′B′C′D′*. The coordinates of point *A* are $(-2, 3)$. What are the coordinates of *A′*?

    (A) $(2, 3)$ **(B)** $(2, -3)$ **(C)** $(-2, 3)$ **(D)** $(-2, -3)$

25. ★ SHORT RESPONSE Draw △*EFG* with vertices (2, 1), (3, 4), and (4, 1) and △*XYZ* with vertices $(-4, 1)$, $(-3, 4)$, and $(-2, 1)$. *Describe* two transformations that could move △*EFG* onto △*XYZ*.

26. ★ WRITING Draw a rectangle with vertices *K*(0, 0), *L*(-3, 0), *M*(-3, 4), and *N*(0, 4). Find the length, width, perimeter, and area of the rectangle. Then translate the rectangle 2 units to the right. Find the length, width, perimeter, and area of the image. *Compare* and explain the results.

27. REASONING The vertices of quadrilateral *ABCD* are *A*(-3, 4), *B*(2, 4), *C*(3, 2), and *D*(-4, -1). After a translation, the coordinates of *A′* are $(-5, 1)$. *Describe* the translation using coordinate notation. *Explain* your method. Then find the coordinates of *B′*, *C′*, and *D′*.

28. REASONING Suppose you reflect a figure in a line and then reflect its image in the same line. What do you notice? *Describe* how you can use coordinate notation to justify this result for this double reflection.

29. ROTATIONS Line segment *EF* has endpoints *E*(4, 3) and *F*(4, −3). Its image after a 180° rotation has endpoints *E′*(−4, −3) and *F′*(−4, 3). *Describe* the 180° rotation using coordinate notation.

30. REASONING △*HJK* has the vertices *H*(−3, 1), *J*(0, 2), and *K*(−2, 7). Reflect △*HJK* in the *x*-axis to produce △*H′J′K′*. Then reflect △*H′J′K′* in the *y*-axis to produce △*H″J″K″*. *Explain* how to use coordinate notation to describe the transformation from △*HJK* to △*H″J″K″*. What are the coordinates of the final image? Is *H″J″K″* a translation of *HJK*? *Explain* your reasoning.

31. CHALLENGE Quadrilateral *WXYZ* has vertices *W*(2, 1), *X*(3, 3), *Y*(6, 4), and *Z*(6, 1). The coordinates of its image after two transformations are *W″*(−6, 4), *X″*(−5, 2), *Y″*(−2, 1), and *Z″*(−2, 4). *Describe* a combination of two transformations that would produce this result.

32. Which word best describes the transformation shown at the right?

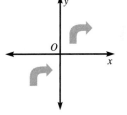

   A Translation

   B Reflection across *x*-axis

   C Reflection across *y*-axis

   D Rotation

33. Which model represents 3^2?

   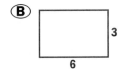   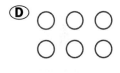

QUIZ *for Lessons 10.5–10.8*

In Exercises 1 and 2, use the diagram and the fact that △*JKL* ∼ △*FGH*.

1. Name the corresponding sides and corresponding angles. *(p. 537)*

2. Find *m*∠*G*. *(p. 537)*

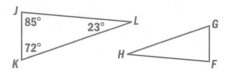

3. GEOMETRY Sketch a regular pentagon and draw any lines of symmetry. Then tell whether the figure has rotational symmetry. If it does, give the angle(s) and direction of rotation. *(p. 548)*

Draw quadrilateral *QRST* with vertices *Q*(3, 2), *R*(4, 5), *S*(−2, 4), and *T*(−1, 1). Then find the coordinates of the vertices of the image after the given transformation and draw the image. *(p. 556)*

   4. (*x*, *y*) → (*x* − 4, *y* − 8)

   5. Reflect *QRST* in the *x*-axis.

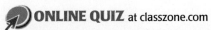

10.8 Translating Points

EXAMPLE Translate the point (3, 4) left 1 unit and up 2 units.

STEP 1 Enter the labels for and the coordinates of the original point in rows 1 and 2.

	A	B
1	Original x	3
2	Original y	4
3	Translate left/right	−1
4	Translate up/down	2
5	Image x	=B1+B3
6	Image y	=B2+B4

STEP 2 Enter the labels and the numbers for the translation in rows 3 and 4.

STEP 3 Enter the labels and the formulas for the coordinates of the image in rows 5 and 6.

STEP 4 Draw the graph by selecting Insert, then Chart. Choose XY (Scatter) as the chart type, and click Next. Under the Series tab, click Add and enter "=Sheet1!$B$1" for X values and "=Sheet1!$B$2" for Y values.

Then click Add, and enter "=Sheet1!$B$5" for X values and "=Sheet1!$B$6" for Y values. Click Next, and make sure that the Major Gridlines boxes are checked under the Gridlines tab. Click Next, then Finish.

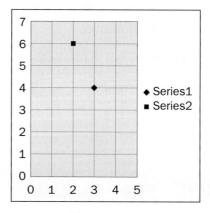

STEP 5 Change the numbers in cells B3 and B4 to produce other translations of the original point.

PRACTICE Use a spreadsheet to translate the point (3, 4) as specified.

1. 3 units to the right and 6 units down

2. 2 units to the left and 7 units up

3. $(x, y) \rightarrow (x - 5, y - 2)$

4. $(x, y) \rightarrow (x + 1, y + 3)$

Lessons 10.5–10.8

1. **TRANSFORMATIONS** In the graph below, which combination of two transformations will move figure A to figure B?

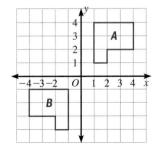

   A. Reflect in x-axis, then reflect in y-axis.

   B. Translate 5 units to the left, then reflect in x-axis.

   C. Reflect in y-axis, then reflect in x-axis.

   D. Reflect in y-axis, then translate 5 units down.

2. **SIMILARITY** Rectangles $PQRS$ and $JKLM$ are similar. Rectangle $PQRS$ has a length of 18 feet and a width of 10 feet. Rectangle $JKLM$ has a width of 25 feet. What is the length of rectangle $JKLM$?

   A. 13.9 feet

   B. 17 feet

   C. 33 feet

   D. 45 feet

3. **SYMMETRY** Which statement is supported by the figures below?

   A. Three figures have line symmetry.

   B. All the figures have line symmetry.

   C. All the figures have rotational symmetry.

   D. Two figures have rotational symmetry.

4. **TILE** A ceramic tile is shaped like a regular pentagon. How many lines of symmetry does the tile have?

   A. 3

   B. 4

   C. 5

   D. 10

5. **LIBERTY BELL** A model of the Liberty Bell is about 0.76 foot wide and 0.6 foot high. The actual bell is 3 feet high. About how wide is the actual bell?

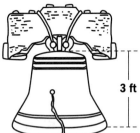

3 ft

   A. 2.28 feet

   B. 2.4 feet

   C. 3.6 feet

   D. 3.8 feet

6. **SHADOWS** A 7 foot tall welcome sign in a city park casts a shadow that is 2 feet long. At the same time, a monument in the park casts a shadow that is 16 feet long. What is the height of the monument, in feet?

   A. 14 feet

   B. 32 feet

   C. 56 feet

   D. 112 feet

7. **OPEN-ENDED** A set of colored tiles has 7 shapes: scalene triangle, isosceles triangle, equilateral triangle, rhombus, parallelogram, rectangle, and square.

   • For each, tell whether it has line or rotational symmetry.

   • Which tile has the most symmetries?

   • What is true about the sides of tiles with both symmetries?

REVIEW KEY VOCABULARY

- angles: acute, right, obtuse, straight, *p. 511*
- complementary, *p. 512*
- supplementary, *p. 512*
- adjacent angles, *p. 516*
- vertical angles, *p. 516*
- congruent angles, *p. 516*
- parallel lines, *p. 517*
- intersecting lines, *p. 517*
- perpendicular lines, *p. 517*

- corresponding angles, *p. 517*
- triangles: acute, right, obtuse, *p. 522*
- congruent sides, *p. 523*
- triangles: equilateral, isosceles, scalene, *p. 523*
- quadrilaterals: trapezoid, parallelogram, rhombus, *p. 529*
- polygons: pentagon, hexagon, heptagon, octagon, *p. 530*
- diagonal, *p. 531*

- similar polygons, *p. 537*
- congruent polygons, *p. 537*
- image, *p. 548*
- transformations: translation, reflection, rotation, *p. 548*
- line of reflection, *p. 548*
- center of rotation, *p. 548*
- angle of rotation, *p. 549*
- line symmetry, *p. 550*
- rotational symmetry, *p. 550*

VOCABULARY EXERCISES

1. What is the measure of a straight angle?

2. How are parallel lines different from perpendicular lines?

3. How many congruent sides does a scalene triangle have?

4. Which type of quadrilateral is not a parallelogram? *Explain* why it is not.

5. In your own words, describe a line of symmetry.

6. Draw a figure that has rotational symmetry.

REVIEW EXAMPLES AND EXERCISES

10.1 Angles
pp. 511–515

EXAMPLE 1

Classify the angle as *acute*, *right*, *obtuse*, or *straight*.

a.

100°

A

b.

55°

B

c.

C

∠A is an obtuse angle. The angle measure is between 90° and 180°.

∠B is an acute angle. The angle measure is less than 90°.

∠C is a right angle. The angle measure is exactly 90°.

EXAMPLE 2

Tell whether the angles are *complementary*, *supplementary*, or *neither*.

Because $80° + 110° = 190°$, $\angle A$ and $\angle B$ are neither complementary nor supplementary.

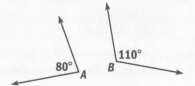

EXERCISES

Classify the angle as *acute*, *right*, *obtuse*, or *straight*.

SEE EXAMPLES
1 AND 2
....
on pp. 511–512
for Exs. 7–16

7. $m\angle A = 65°$ **8.** $m\angle A = 125°$ **9.** $m\angle A = 90°$ **10.** $m\angle A = 180°$

Tell whether $\angle C$ and $\angle D$ are *complementary*, *supplementary*, or *neither*. *Explain* your reasoning.

11. $m\angle C = 42°$, $m\angle D = 48°$ **12.** $m\angle C = 113°$, $m\angle D = 67°$

13. $m\angle C = 76°$, $m\angle D = 114°$ **14.** $m\angle C = 82°$, $m\angle D = 8°$

15. $m\angle C = 37°$, $m\angle D = 43°$ **16.** $m\angle C = 126°$, $m\angle D = 54°$

10.2 Special Pairs of Angles

pp. 516–520

EXAMPLE

Given $m\angle 1 = 115°$, find $m\angle 7$.

Because $\angle 1$ and $\angle 3$ are vertical angles, $m\angle 1 = m\angle 3 = 115°$.

Because lines l and m are parallel lines, $\angle 3$ and $\angle 7$ are congruent corresponding angles. So, $m\angle 3 = m\angle 7 = 115°$.

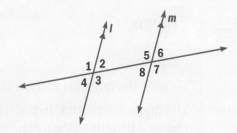

EXERCISES

In Exercises 17–21, find the measure of the given angle in the diagram above. *Explain* your reasoning.

SEE EXAMPLES
1 AND 2
....
on pp. 516–517
for Exs. 17–23

17. $\angle 2$ **18.** $\angle 4$ **19.** $\angle 5$ **20.** $\angle 6$ **21.** $\angle 8$

In Exercises 22–23, refer to the diagram.

22. Name all pairs of adjacent, supplementary angles.

23. Name all pairs of vertical angles.

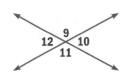

10.3 Triangles

pp. 521–526

EXAMPLE

Find the value of *y*. Then classify the triangle by its angle measures.

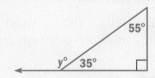

$$35° + y° = 180°$$

$$y = 180 - 35$$

$$y = 145$$

▶ **Answer** The value of *y* is 145. The triangle is a right triangle.

EXERCISES

Find the values of *x* and *y*. Then classify the triangle by its angle measures.

SEE EXAMPLES 1, 2, AND 3 on pp. 521–522 for Exs. 24–26

24.

25.

26.

10.4 Polygons

pp. 529–534

EXAMPLE

Classify the polygon and tell if it is regular.

The figure has 6 sides, so it is a hexagon. The side lengths of the hexagon are not equal, so it is not a regular hexagon.

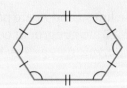

EXERCISES

Classify the polygon and tell if it is regular. If it is not regular, explain why not. If the polygon is quadrilateral, tell which type it is.

SEE EXAMPLE 2 on p. 530 for Exs. 27–29

27.

28.

29.

10.5 Similar and Congruent Polygons

pp. 537–541

EXAMPLE

Given that △BCD ~ △FGH, find the ratio of the lengths of the corresponding sides of △BCD to △FGH.

Write a ratio for each pair of corresponding sides. Then substitute the lengths of the sides and simplify each ratio.

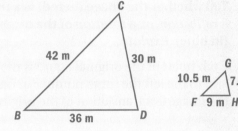

$$\frac{BC}{FG} = \frac{42}{10.5} = \frac{4}{1} \qquad \frac{CD}{GH} = \frac{30}{7.5} = \frac{4}{1} \qquad \frac{BD}{FH} = \frac{36}{9} = \frac{4}{1}$$

EXERCISES

SEE EXAMPLE 2
on p. 538
for Ex. 30

30. Rectangles *QRST* and *CDFG* are similar. *QRST* is 8 inches long and 6 inches wide. *CDFG* is 20 inches long and 15 inches wide. Find the ratio of the lengths of the corresponding sides of *QRST* to *CDFG*.

10.6 Using Proportions with Similar Polygons

pp. 542–546

EXAMPLE

Quadrilaterals *JKLM* and *WXYZ* are similar. Find *YZ*.

Use the ratios of the lengths of corresponding sides to write and solve a proportion involving the unknown length.

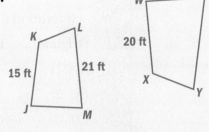

$$\frac{JK}{WX} = \frac{LM}{YZ} \qquad \text{Write proportion involving } \textit{YZ.}$$

$$\frac{15}{20} = \frac{21}{YZ} \qquad \text{Substitute known values.}$$

$$YZ = 28 \text{ ft} \qquad \text{Use cross products property and simplify.}$$

EXERCISES

SEE EXAMPLE 2
on p. 543
for Ex. 31

31. Monument Height A monument casts a 60-foot shadow at the same time that a 5-foot tall person casts a 12-foot shadow. How tall is the monument?

10.7 Transformations and Symmetry
pp. 548–553

EXAMPLE

Tell whether the image (in red) is a *translation*, a *reflection*, or a *rotation* of the original figure (in blue). *Explain*.

Each point of the original figure is moved up and to the left the same number of units. So, the image is a translation of the original figure.

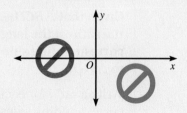

EXERCISES

SEE EXAMPLE 1
on p. 548
for Ex. 32

32. Tell whether the image (in red) is a *translation*, a *reflection*, or a *rotation* of the original figure (in blue). *Explain* your reasoning.

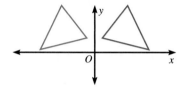

10.8 Transformations in the Coordinate Plane
pp. 556–561

EXAMPLE

Draw △*ABC* with vertices *A*(4, 1), *B*(1, 2), and *C*(5, 2). Then find the coordinates of the vertices of the image after a reflection in the *y*-axis, and draw the image.

For each vertex of the original figure, multiply the *x*-coordinate by −1.

Original		Image
$A(4, 1)$	$\rightarrow$	$A'(-4, 1)$
$B(1, 2)$	$\rightarrow$	$B'(-1, 2)$
$C(5, 2)$	$\rightarrow$	$C'(-5, 2)$

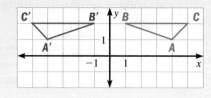

EXERCISES

You are given △*FGH* with vertices *F*(−2, 1), *G*(−3, 3), and *H*(−6, 3).

SEE EXAMPLE 3
on p. 558
for Exs. 33–35

33. Draw △*FGH*.

34. Find the coordinates of the vertices of the image after a reflection in the *x*-axis and draw the image.

35. Find the coordinates of the vertices of the image after a translation 2 units to the right and 3 units down.

Classify the angle as *acute, right, obtuse,* or *straight*.

1.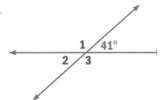

2.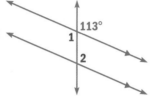

3.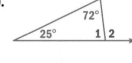

Tell whether ∠A and ∠B are *complementary, supplementary,* or *neither*. *Explain* your reasoning.

4. $m\angle A = 21°, m\angle B = 79°$

5. $m\angle A = 45°, m\angle B = 135°$

6. $m\angle A = 19°, m\angle B = 71°$

Find the angle measures of the numbered angles.

7.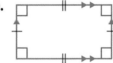

8.

9.

Classify the polygon and tell if it is regular. If not, explain why not.

10.

11.

12.

13. Given that $\triangle QRS \cong \triangle XYZ$, name the corresponding sides and the corresponding angles. Then find XZ and YZ.

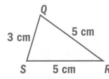 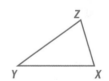

14. Draw a polygon that has exactly 4 lines of symmetry.

15. The measures of two of the angles in a triangle are 63° and 26°. Find the measure of the third angle. Then classify the triangle by its angle measures.

16. **BUILDING HEIGHT** A building casts a 50-foot shadow at the same time that a 5-foot sign casts a 2-foot shadow. What is the height of the building?

17. Draw rectangle *CDEF* with vertices $C(0, 0)$, $D(0, -4)$, $E(-4, -4)$, and $F(-4, 0)$. Then find the coordinates of the vertices of the image after the translation $(x, y) \rightarrow (x - 5, y + 2)$, and draw the image.

18. Draw $\triangle FGH$ with vertices $F(-8, 6)$, $G(-4, 7)$, and $H(-2, 4)$. Then find the coordinates of the vertices of the image after a reflection in the *y*-axis, and draw the image.

OPEN-ENDED QUESTIONS

Scoring Rubric

Full Credit
- solution is complete and correct

Partial Credit
- solution is complete but errors are made, *or*
- solution is without error, but incomplete

No Credit
- no solution is given, *or*
- solution makes no sense

> **PROBLEM**
>
> **GEOMETRY** Quadrilateral *ABCD* is similar to quadrilateral *MNOP*. The length of $\overline{AB}$ is 5 centimeters, the length of $\overline{BC}$ is 2 centimeters, and the opposite sides of quadrilateral *ABCD* are parallel. All four angles are *not* congruent.
>
> **Part A** Sketch and classify quadrilateral *ABCD*.
>
> **Part B** The lengths of $\overline{NO}$ and $\overline{MP}$ are each 6 centimeters. Find the missing dimensions of quadrilateral *MNOP*. *Explain* how you found your answer.

Below are sample solutions to the problem. Read each solution and the comments on the left to see why the sample represents full credit, partial credit, or no credit.

SAMPLE 1: Full Credit Solution

Sketch and classify quadrilateral *ABCD*.

The steps for sketching and classifying a quadrilateral are correct and clearly stated.

Draw sides $\overline{AB}$ and $\overline{BC}$ so that $AB = 5$ cm and $BC = 2$ cm. The angle between the two sides does not matter as long as it does not equal 90°.

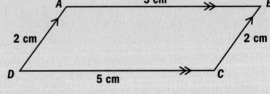

Then draw sides $\overline{CD}$ and $\overline{AD}$ each parallel to the first two sides. Quadrilateral *ABCD* is a parallelogram.

Find the missing dimensions of quadrilateral *MNOP*.

You know the measures of $\overline{NO}$ and $\overline{MP}$. Find the measures of $\overline{MN}$ and $\overline{OP}$. Quadrilaterals *ABCD* and *MNOP* are similar parallelograms.

The proportion is set up correctly and each mathematical calculation is justified.

$$\frac{AB}{MN} = \frac{AD}{MP}$$

$$\frac{5}{MN} = \frac{2}{6}$$

$$2 \cdot MN = 5 \cdot 6$$

$$2 \cdot MN = \frac{5 \cdot 6}{2} = 15$$

The answer is correct and the explanation is clear.

Because the opposite sides of a parallelogram are congruent, the lengths of both $\overline{MN}$ and $\overline{OP}$ are 15 centimeters.

SAMPLE 2: Partial Credit Solution

Quadrilateral *ABCD* is sketched and classified correctly. →

A ——— 5 cm ——— B

2 cm

Parallelogram

2 cm

D ——— 5 cm ——— C

The proportion is written incorrectly. →

You know that quadrilaterals *ABCD* and *MNOP* are similar. Using the ratio of the lengths of the corresponding sides, write a proportion involving *MN*.

$$\frac{AB}{BC} = \frac{NO}{MN}$$

$$\frac{5}{2} = \frac{6}{MN}$$

$$MN = \frac{2 \cdot 6}{5} = \frac{12}{5} \text{ or } 2.4$$

The answer is incorrect, but it reflects correct mathematical reasoning. →

Because quadrilaterals *ABCD* and *MNOP* are similar and *AB* = *CD*, the lengths of $\overline{MN}$ and $\overline{OP}$ are also equal. So, the lengths of both $\overline{MN}$ and $\overline{OP}$ are 2.4 cm.

PRACTICE   Apply the Scoring Rubric

A student's solution to the problem on the previous page is shown below. Score the solution as *full credit, partial credit,* or *no credit*. *Explain* your reasoning. If you choose partial credit or no credit, explain how you would change the solution so that it earns a score of full credit.

1.

A ——— B

D ——— C

Quadrilateral *ABCD* is a rectangle with a length of 5 cm and a width of 2 cm.

You know that quadrilaterals *ABCD* and *MNOP* are similar. Quadrilateral *MNOP* must be a rectangle with a width of 6 cm. Write a proportion to find the length of rectangle *MNOP*.

$$\frac{AB}{MN} = \frac{AD}{MP}$$

$$\frac{5}{MN} = \frac{2}{6}$$

$$MN = \frac{5 \cdot 6}{2} = 15$$

So, the length of rectangle *MNOP* is 15 cm.

TEST PREPARATION

1. Which pair of angles are complementary?

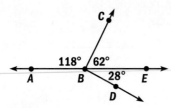

   A. ∠ABC and ∠CBE

   B. ∠CBE and ∠EBD

   C. ∠CBD and ∠EBD

   D. ∠CBD and ∠CBE

2. Which term best describes the triangle shown below?

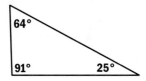

   A. Acute

   B. Equilateral

   C. Obtuse

   D. Right

3. What kind of quadrilateral is shown below?

   A. Rhombus

   B. Rectangle

   C. Square

   D. Trapezoid

4. The transformation of the triangle from which quadrant (Q) to which quadrant (Q) is a rotation?

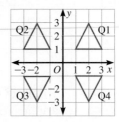

   A. Q3 to Q1

   B. Q2 to Q1

   C. Q2 to Q3

   D. Q4 to Q1

5. A map is 3 feet long and 2 feet wide. A smaller version of the map on the cover of the map booklet is 2.7 inches wide. The maps are similar. What is the perimeter of the smaller map?

   A. 4.05 in.

   B. 9 in.

   C. 13.5 in.

   D. 10 ft

6. ∠A and ∠B are supplementary. ∠B and ∠C are complementary. Which of the following statements must be true?

   A. ∠A is acute.

   B. ∠B is acute.

   C. ∠C is obtuse.

   D. ∠A and ∠C are complementary.

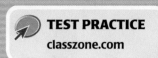

7. The measure of ∠J is 3 times greater than the measure of ∠K. The angles are supplementary. What is the measure of ∠K?

   A. 22.5°

   B. 45°

   C. 67.5°

   D. 135°

8. △DEF and △JKL are similar. The ratio of lengths of corresponding sides is $\frac{1}{4}$. Let P represent the perimeter of △DEF, which is the smaller of the two triangles. Which expression best represents the perimeter of △JKL?

   A. $\frac{P}{4}$

   B. $\frac{P}{12}$

   C. 4P

   D. 12P

9. Lines c and d below are parallel. The measure of ∠1 is 98.7°. What is the measure of ∠2?

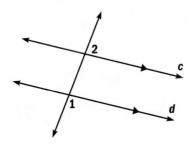

   A. 8.7°

   B. 81.3°

   C. 91.3°

   D. 98.7°

10. Which of the following statements is true about similar and congruent figures?

    A. Two congruent figures must be similar.

    B. Two similar figures must be congruent.

    C. Two similar figures cannot be congruent.

    D. The corresponding side lengths are congruent in both similar and congruent figures.

11. The dimensions of rectangle A are 60% of the dimensions of rectangle B. About how many times greater than the area of rectangle A is the area of rectangle B?

    A. 60%

    B. 167%

    C. 180%

    D. 278%

12. **OPEN-ENDED** Sketch the tile design below and draw any line(s) of symmetry.

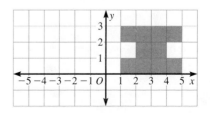

    Part A Does the figure have rotational symmetry? *Explain* why or why not.

    Part B Draw a reflection of the figure in the y-axis. Does the reflected figure have the same number of line(s) of symmetry as the original figure? *Explain* why or why not.

11 Measurement and Area

Before

In previous chapters you've ...

- Evaluated powers
- Classified polygons
- Explored congruent and similar polygons

Now

New Jersey Standards

	11.1 Square roots
	11.2 Approximations
	11.3 Pythagorean Theorem
	11.4 Parallelograms
4.2.E.1.a	11.5 Triangles and trapezoids
4.2.E.1.a	11.6 Circumference
4.2.E.1.b	11.7 Area of a circle

Why?

So you can solve real-world problems about ...

- pole vaulting, p. 578
- television screens, p. 588
- giant sequoias, p. 609

 **Math**
at classzone.com

- The Pythagorean Theorem, p. 589
- Area of a Triangle, p. 601
- Area of a Circle, p. 613

Get-Ready Games

Review Prerequisite Skills by playing *Exponent Suspension* and *Building Bridges*.

Skill Focus: Evaluating powers

- Evaluate the powers. Order the answers from least to greatest. Then write the letters associated with these answers in the same order to spell out the name of the world's longest suspension bridge. The name consists of two six-letter words.

- Now cross off the answers that are divisible by 3. Cross off the answers that are greater than 100 but less than 200. Add the three remaining numbers to find the length, in feet, of the main span of the bridge. The main span lies between the two towers of the bridge.

Skill Focus: Classifying polygons

The bridge above is drawn on graph paper. All line segments that appear to be equal in length are equal in length. All yellow segments intersect at right angles, and yellow segments that have the same slope are parallel.

• Find at least 20 triangles in the bridge.

• Find at least 3 rectangles in the bridge.

• Find at least 9 parallelograms in the bridge.

• Find at least 13 trapezoids in the bridge.

Stop and Think

1. **WRITING** In *Exponent Suspension*, how can you tell by looking at the base of a power whether the power is divisible by 3?

2. **CRITICAL THINKING** In *Building Bridges*, all the triangles are isosceles right triangles. Each triangle has two congruent angles. What is the measure of each of these angles? Explain how you know.

Getting Ready

Review Prerequisite Skills

REVIEW WORDS
- **perimeter,** *p. 32*
- **area,** *p. 32*
- **trapezoid,** *p. 529*
- **parallelogram,** *p. 529*

VOCABULARY CHECK

Copy and complete using a review word from the list at the left.

1. A(n) __?__ is a quadrilateral with exactly one pair of parallel sides.

2. The __?__ of a figure is measured in units such as square inches (in.^{2}) and square meters (m^2).

3. The __?__ is the distance around a polygon.

SKILL CHECK

Evaluate the expression when $p = 3$ and $q = 6$. (pp. 17, 291, 296)

4. p^3 **5.** $p^3 + q$ **6.** $q^2 - 4p$

7. $-6q + q^3$ **8.** $-3p^2 + pq$ **9.** pq^2

10. $\frac{1}{2}q + \frac{2}{3}p^2$ **11.** $\frac{12}{q} \cdot 3p$ **12.** $\frac{4p}{3q}$

Find the perimeter and the area of the rectangle. (pp. 32, 66, 232)

13.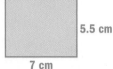
5.5 cm
7 cm

14.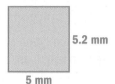
5.2 mm
5 mm

15.
$1\frac{1}{2}$ ft
$\frac{3}{4}$ ft

@HomeTutor   Prerequisite skills practice at classzone.com

Notetaking Skills   Illustrating with Examples

In each chapter you will learn a new notetaking skill. In Chapter 11 you will apply the strategy of illustrating with examples to Example 2 on p. 595.

In your notebook, include examples that illustrate how a math concept is applied or how a formula is used. You may want to divide your notebook page in half lengthwise, with concepts or formulas on the left and examples on the right.

Formula

distance = rate × time

$$d = rt$$

Example

You drive for 3.5 hours at 60 miles per hour. How far do you travel?

$d = rt$

$= \frac{60 \text{ mi}}{1 \text{ h}} \cdot \frac{3.5 \text{ h}}{1}$

$= 210 \text{ miles}$

11.1 Square Roots

Before	You evaluated expressions involving squares.
Now	You'll evaluate expressions involving square roots.
Why?	So you can find the side length of a dance floor, as in Ex. 50.

KEY VOCABULARY
• square root, perfect square, square number, *p. 577*
• radical expression, *p. 578*

A **square root** of a number n is a number m which, when multiplied by itself, equals n.

If $m^2 = n$, then m is a square root of n.

Numbers that are squares of integers, such as $1 = 1^2$ and $4 = 2^2$, are called **perfect squares**, or **square numbers**. You may find it useful to memorize perfect squares up to 225.

EXAMPLE 1 Finding Square Roots

a. You know that $9^2 = 81$ and $(-9)^2 = 81$. Therefore, the square roots of 81 are 9 and -9.

b. You know that $7^2 = 49$ and $(-7)^2 = 49$. Therefore, the square roots of 49 are 7 and -7.

Radical Signs The symbol $\sqrt{}$, called a *radical sign*, represents a nonnegative square root. For example, $\sqrt{4} = 2$ is the positive square root of 4, and $-\sqrt{4} = -2$ is the negative square root of 4.

EXAMPLE 2 Evaluating Square Roots

a. $\sqrt{36} = 6$ because $6^2 = 36$. So, $-\sqrt{36} = -6$.

b. $\sqrt{16} = 4$ because $4^2 = 16$. So, $-\sqrt{16} = -4$.

c. $\sqrt{0} = 0$ because $0^2 = 0$.

✓ **GUIDED PRACTICE**   for Examples 1 and 2

Find the two square roots of the number.

1. 9   **2.** 64   **3.** 100   **4.** 169

Evaluate the square root.

5. $\sqrt{25}$ **6.** $-\sqrt{1}$ **7.** $-\sqrt{144}$ **8.** $\sqrt{121}$

EXAMPLE 3 Solving a Square Root Equation

Pole Vaulting The equation $s = 8\sqrt{h}$ expresses the minimum speed s, in feet per second, needed by a pole vaulter to clear a height of h feet. How fast should a pole vaulter run to vault over a height of 16 feet?

SOLUTION

$s = 8\sqrt{h}$	Write equation for speed of a pole vaulter.
$= 8\sqrt{16}$	Substitute 16 for h.
$= 8(4)$	Evaluate square root.
$= 32$	Multiply.

▶ **Answer** The pole vaulter needs a minimum speed of 32 feet per second.

Radical Expressions An expression involving a radical sign is called a **radical expression**. The radical sign acts as a grouping symbol, so you evaluate the expression under a radical sign before evaluating the square root.

EXAMPLE 4 Evaluating Radical Expressions

Evaluate the expression when $z = 7$ and $m = -2$.

a. $\sqrt{29 + z}$

b. $\sqrt{z^2 + m^2 + 11}$

SOLUTION

a.
$\sqrt{29 + z} = \sqrt{29 + 7}$	Substitute 7 for z.
$= \sqrt{36}$	Add.
$= 6$	Evaluate square root.

b.
$\sqrt{z^2 + m^2 + 11} = \sqrt{7^2 + (-2)^2 + 11}$	Substitute 7 for z and -2 for m.
$= \sqrt{49 + 4 + 11}$	Evaluate powers.
$= \sqrt{64}$	Add.
$= 8$	Evaluate square root.

EVALUATE EXPRESSIONS
Need help with order of operations? See p. 17.

✓ **GUIDED PRACTICE** for Examples 3 and 4

9. Geometry Use the equation $s = \sqrt{A}$ to find the side length s, in inches, of a square that has an area A of 100 square inches.

Evaluate the expression when $x = -3$ and $y = 4$.

10. $\sqrt{5 + y}$ **11.** $\sqrt{78 - x}$ **12.** $\sqrt{y^2 + xy - 4}$ **13.** $\sqrt{y^2 - x^2 - 6}$

EXAMPLE 5 Solving Equations Using Square Roots

Solve the equation.

a. $x^2 = 25$

b. $h^2 + 5 = 54$

SOLUTION

a.
$x^2 = 25$	Write original equation.
$x = \pm\sqrt{25}$	Use definition of square root.
$x = \pm 5$	Evaluate square root.

READING
The symbol $\pm$ is read "plus or minus." The statement $x = \pm 5$ means that 5 and -5 are both solutions of $x^2 = 25$.

b.
$h^2 + 5 = 54$	Write original equation.
$h^2 + 5 - 5 = 54 - 5$	Subtract 5 from each side.
$h^2 = 49$	Simplify.
$h = \pm\sqrt{49}$	Use definition of square root.
$h = \pm 7$	Evaluate square root.

✓ **GUIDED PRACTICE** for Example 5

Solve the equation.

14. $x^2 = 1$ **15.** $x^2 + 7 = 88$ **16.** $12x^2 = 108$ **17.** $x^2 - 5 = -1$

11.1 EXERCISES

HOMEWORK KEY

★ = **STANDARDIZED TEST PRACTICE**
Exs. 39, 50, 52, 53, 55, and 66

○ = **HINTS AND HOMEWORK HELP**
for Exs. 3, 17, 25, 31, 49 at classzone.com

SKILL PRACTICE

VOCABULARY Copy and complete the statement.

1. A(n) _?_ is an expression involving a radical sign.

2. Numbers that are squares of integers are called _?_ , or _?_ .

FINDING SQUARE ROOTS Find the two square roots of the number.

SEE EXAMPLE 1
on p. 577
for Exs. 3–14

3. 625   **4.** 900   **5.** 289   **6.** 729

7. 484   **8.** 10,000   **9.** 441   **10.** 529

11. 0.16   **12.** 2.25   **13.** 0.0256   **14.** 0.0025

EVALUATING SQUARE ROOTS Evaluate the square root.

SEE EXAMPLE 2
on p. 577
for Exs. 15–22

15. $\sqrt{81}$ **16.** $\sqrt{225}$ **17.** $-\sqrt{169}$ **18.** $-\sqrt{324}$

19. $-\sqrt{1225}$ **20.** $-\sqrt{676}$ **21.** $\sqrt{361}$ **22.** $\sqrt{1024}$

SEE EXAMPLE 2
on p. 577
for Ex. 23

23. ERROR ANALYSIS Describe and correct the error made in finding $\sqrt{16}$.

$$\times \quad \begin{array}{l} \sqrt{16} = 8 \\ \text{Check: } 8 \times 2 = 16 \end{array}$$

ⓧⓨ EVALUATING Evaluate the expression when $x = 3$, $y = 4$, and $z = -1$.

**SEE EXAMPLES
3 AND 4**
on p. 578
for Exs. 24–29

24. $-\sqrt{7x + 100}$

25. $\sqrt{-4z}$

26. $\sqrt{60 - xy + 1}$

27. $\sqrt{z^2 - yz + 11}$

28. $\sqrt{3(x + y) + y}$

29. $-\sqrt{x^2 + y^2}$

ⓧⓨ ALGEBRA Solve the equation.

SEE EXAMPLE 5
on p. 579
for Exs. 30–35

30. $3w^2 = 675$

31. $11x^2 = 891$

32. $-w^2 = -576$

33. $d^2 - 12 = 132$

34. $5 + 14c^2 = 229$

35. $13r^2 - 5 = 203$

GEOMETRY Find the side length of a square having the given area.

36. $A = 49 \text{ cm}^2$

37. $A = 64 \text{ yd}^2$

38. $A = 196 \text{ m}^2$

39. ★ MULTIPLE CHOICE The model shown can help you find $\sqrt{25} = 5$. Which arrangement of small squares can be used to find $\sqrt{144}$?

Ⓐ 4 rows of 36 squares

Ⓑ 6 rows of 24 squares

Ⓒ 12 rows of 12 squares

Ⓓ 13 rows of 13 squares

REASONING Evaluate the expression. Assume that $x > 0$.

40. $\sqrt{2^2}$

41. $(\sqrt{4})^2$

42. $(\sqrt{4})^3$

43. $\sqrt{2^4}$

44. $\sqrt{x^2}$

45. $(-\sqrt{x^2})^2$

46. $\sqrt{x^4}$

47. $x^2\sqrt{x^2}$

48. ⓧⓨ CHALLENGE Is the statement $\sqrt{x + y} = \sqrt{x} + \sqrt{y}$ *always* true, *sometimes* true, or *never* true? *Justify* your answer.

PROBLEM SOLVING

SEE EXAMPLE 3
on p. 578
for Ex. 49

49. DISTANCE TO THE HORIZON When you are at a height h, the distance d to the horizon can be approximated using the equation $d = 112.88\sqrt{h}$. Both h and d are measured in kilometers. Approximate the distance to the horizon if you are on top of a mountain that is 4 kilometers high.

50. ★ SHORT RESPONSE The area of a square dance floor is 1600 square feet. What is the side length of the dance floor? How many 2 foot by 2 foot square panels are needed to cover the floor? *Explain.*

51. CRATERS The Barringer Meteor Crater in Winslow, Arizona, is approximately the shape of a square. The crater covers an area of about 1,690,000 square meters. What is the approximate side length of the crater?

52. ★ WRITING *Explain* how to find the perimeter of a square with an area of x square feet.

★ = **STANDARDIZED TEST PRACTICE**   ◯ = **HINTS AND HOMEWORK HELP** *at classzone.com*

53. ★ **EXTENDED RESPONSE** The maximum speed s, in knots or nautical miles per hour, for some boats can be found using the equation $s = \frac{4}{3}\sqrt{x}$ where x is the waterline length of a boat, in feet.

├─16 ft─┤   ├──────64 ft──────┤

   a. Find the maximum speed for each boat shown.

   b. Compare the waterline lengths of the two boats. Does the same relationship hold for the maximum speeds of the boats? *Explain.*

54. **GEOMETRY** The figure is made of squares of the same size. The area of the figure is 324 square meters. Find the side length of the squares.

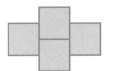

55. ★ **MULTIPLE CHOICE** The area of a square is 242 m². The area of a second square is half that of the first. What is the side length of the second square?

   Ⓐ 7.8 m   Ⓑ 11 m   Ⓒ 60.5 m   Ⓓ 121 m

56. ◆ **MULTIPLE REPRESENTATIONS** Consider the function $y = \sqrt{x}$.

   a. **Make a Table** Make a table of values for the function using the domain 0, 1, 4, 9, and 16.

   b. **Draw a Graph** Graph the ordered pairs from the table. Tell whether the function is linear. *Explain* your reasoning.

57. **CHALLENGE** The figure shown is composed of two squares. The area of the shaded region is 48 square centimeters. What is the side length of the larger square? *Explain* your reasoning.

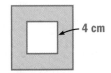
← 4 cm

NEW JERSEY MIXED REVIEW

TEST PRACTICE at classzone.com

58. The figure at the right was transformed from Quadrant I to Quadrant III. Which type of transformation does this represent?

   Ⓐ Translation

   Ⓑ Tessellation

   Ⓒ Rotation

   Ⓓ Reflection

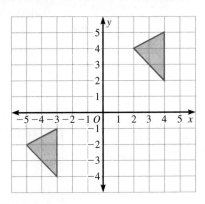

11.2 Approximating Square Roots

Before	You found square roots of perfect squares.
Now	You'll approximate square roots of numbers.
Why?	So you can find flow rates, as in Ex. 45.

KEY VOCABULARY
- **irrational number,** *p. 583*
- **real number,** *p. 583*

You know how to evaluate square roots like $\sqrt{1}$, $\sqrt{4}$, and $\sqrt{9}$ because 1, 4, and 9 are perfect squares. But what about square roots like $\sqrt{2}$, $\sqrt{3}$, and $\sqrt{5}$? The values of these square roots fall between whole numbers, as shown on the number line below.

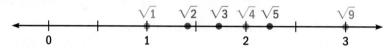

EXAMPLE 1 Approximating to a Whole Number

Approximate $\sqrt{7}$ to the nearest whole number.

STEP 1 **Determine** the two whole numbers closest to $\sqrt{7}$.

$4 < 7 < 9$	**Identify perfect squares closest to 7.**
$\sqrt{4} < \sqrt{7} < \sqrt{9}$	**Take positive square root of each number.**
$2 < \sqrt{7} < 3$	**Evaluate square roots.**

STEP 2 **Square** the decimal halfway between 2 and 3: $2.5^2 = 6.25$.

Because 7 is between 2.5^2 and 3^2, $\sqrt{7}$ is between 2.5 and 3. $\sqrt{7}$ is closer to 3 than 2.

▸ **Answer** To the nearest whole number, $\sqrt{7} \approx 3$.

EXAMPLE 2 Approximating to the Nearest Tenth

Approximate $\sqrt{7}$ to the nearest tenth.

You know from Example 1 that $\sqrt{7}$ is between 2.5 and 3.

$2.5^2 = 6.25$
$2.6^2 = 6.76$
$2.7^2 = 7.29$
$2.8^2 = 7.84$
$2.9^2 = 8.41$

STEP 1 **Make** a list of squares of 2.5, 2.6, . . . , 2.9.

From the list you can see that 7 is between 2.6^2 and 2.7^2, so $\sqrt{7}$ is between 2.6 and 2.7.

STEP 2 **Square** the decimal halfway between 2.6 and 2.7: $2.65^2 = 7.0225$.

Because 7 is between 2.6^2 and 2.65^2, $\sqrt{7}$ is between 2.6 and 2.65. $\sqrt{7}$ is closer to 2.6 than 2.7.

▸ **Answer** To the nearest tenth, $\sqrt{7} \approx 2.6$.

EXAMPLE 3 Using Square Roots

Animals Dr. R. McNeill Alexander studies the motion of animals. He has found that the maximum speed s, in feet per second, that an animal can walk is $s = 5.66\sqrt{l}$ where l is the animal's leg length in feet. What is the maximum walking speed for a giraffe with a leg length of 7 feet?

SOLUTION

You can use the approximation of $\sqrt{7}$ from Example 2.

$s = 5.66\sqrt{l}$	**Write maximum walking speed formula.**
$= 5.66\sqrt{7}$	**Substitute 7 for l.**
$\approx 5.66(2.6)$	**Use approximation of $\sqrt{7}$ to the nearest tenth.**
≈ 15	**Multiply.**

▶ **Answer** The giraffe's maximum walking speed is about 15 feet per second.

✓ **GUIDED PRACTICE** | **for Examples 1, 2, and 3**

Approximate the square root to the nearest whole number and then to the nearest tenth.

1. $\sqrt{10}$ **2.** $\sqrt{22}$ **3.** $\sqrt{45}$ **4.** $\sqrt{115}$

5. What If? In Example 3, suppose the giraffe has a leg length of 10 feet. Estimate the maximum walking speed of the giraffe. Use an estimate of the square root rounded to the nearest tenth. Round your answer to the nearest whole number.

Irrational Numbers The number $\sqrt{7}$ is an example of an *irrational number*. An **irrational number** cannot be written as a quotient of two integers, and the decimal form of an irrational number neither terminates nor repeats. If n is a positive integer which is not a perfect square, then $\sqrt{n}$ is an irrational number.

The set of **real numbers** consists of all rational and irrational numbers. The Venn diagram shows the relationships among the types of real numbers.

DRAW DIAGRAMS
Need help with Venn diagrams? See p. 756.

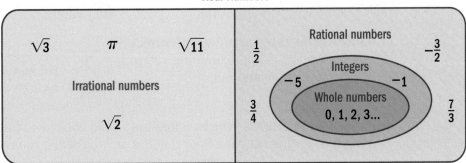

Real Numbers

EXAMPLE 4 **Identifying Rational and Irrational Numbers**

Tell whether the number is *rational* or *irrational*. Explain.

a. $\sqrt{2}$ b. $-\dfrac{1}{9}$ c. $-\sqrt{169}$ d. $1.21121112\ldots$

SOLUTION

a. $\sqrt{2}$ is irrational because 2 is a positive integer but not a perfect square.

b. $-\dfrac{1}{9}$ is rational because $-\dfrac{1}{9} = \dfrac{-1}{9}$, which is a quotient of integers.

c. $-\sqrt{169}$ is rational because $-\sqrt{169} = -13$, which is an integer.

d. $1.21121112\ldots$ is irrational because it neither terminates nor repeats.

✓ **GUIDED PRACTICE** | for Example 4

Tell whether the number is *rational* or *irrational*. Explain.

6. $\sqrt{144}$ 7. $-\dfrac{11}{7}$ 8. $-\sqrt{46}$ 9. $5.151551555\ldots$

11.2 EXERCISES

HOMEWORK KEY

★ = **STANDARDIZED TEST PRACTICE**
Exs. 18, 42, 44, 45, and 56

○ = **HINTS AND HOMEWORK HELP**
for Exs. 5, 7, 13, 15, 43 at classzone.com

SKILL PRACTICE

VOCABULARY Tell whether the statement is *true* or *false*. *Justify* your answer.

1. All integers are irrational.

2. All real numbers are rational.

3. All whole numbers are rational.

4. All repeating decimals are irrational.

APPROXIMATING SQUARE ROOTS Approximate the square root to the nearest whole number and then to the nearest tenth.

5. $\sqrt{15}$ 6. $\sqrt{23}$ 7. $\sqrt{42}$ 8. $\sqrt{131}$

9. $\sqrt{35}$ 10. $\sqrt{89}$ 11. $\sqrt{57}$ 12. $\sqrt{63}$

13. $\sqrt{125}$ 14. $\sqrt{188}$ 15. $\sqrt{200}$ 16. $\sqrt{253}$

17. **ERROR ANALYSIS** Describe and correct the error made in approximating $\sqrt{29}$ to the nearest whole number.

 29 falls between 25 and 36. Because 29 is much closer to 25, $\sqrt{29} \approx 25$.

18. ★ **MULTIPLE CHOICE** Which expression would you use to find the side length of a square kitchen floor that has an area of 260 square feet?

Ⓐ $\sqrt{260}$ Ⓑ $\dfrac{260}{2}$ Ⓒ $260 \cdot 4$ Ⓓ 260^2

SEE EXAMPLE 4
on p. 584
for Exs. 19–26

IDENTIFYING RATIONAL AND IRRATIONAL NUMBERS Tell whether the number is *rational* or *irrational*. Explain your reasoning.

19. -2.6

20. $\sqrt{1600}$

21. $\sqrt{45}$

22. $-\sqrt{115}$

23. $\sqrt{21}$

24. $5\frac{3}{8}$

25. $1.\overline{375}$

26. $30.23233\ldots$

APPROXIMATING SQUARE ROOTS Find the square root to the nearest hundredth.

27. $\sqrt{87}$

28. $\sqrt{91}$

29. $\sqrt{140}$

30. $\sqrt{210}$

NUMBER SENSE Plot the numbers on a number line and order them from least to greatest.

31. $\sqrt{5}, 5, \sqrt{9}, 1.5$

32. $4.3, 4.\overline{3}, \sqrt{17}, \frac{17}{3}$

33. $\sqrt{21}, \sqrt{27}, 5, \frac{27}{5}, 4.8$

(XY) ALGEBRA Solve the equation. Round solutions to the nearest tenth.

34. $5x^2 = 65$

35. $14x^2 = 112$

36. $9x^2 + 3 = 48$

37. $5x^2 + 4 = 10$

38. $2x^2 - 3 = 6$

39. $16x^2 + 7 = 41$

40. (XY) CHALLENGE Is the statement $\sqrt{2a} = 2\sqrt{a}$ *always* true, *sometimes* true, or *never* true? *Explain* your reasoning.

PROBLEM SOLVING

SEE EXAMPLES 1 AND 2
on p. 582
for Exs. 41–42

41. GUIDED PROBLEM SOLVING You buy 14 rolls of sod to cover a square patch of dirt in your yard, as shown. After covering the patch, there are 12 square feet of sod left over. How long is the patch of dirt to the nearest tenth of a foot?

1 roll = 10 ft²

a. How many square feet of sod did you use to cover the lawn?

b. The amount of sod used falls between which two perfect squares?

c. What is the side length of the lawn to the nearest tenth of a foot?

42. ★ SHORT RESPONSE You use one gallon of paint to apply a base coat on a square wall mural. The paint covers 350 square feet per gallon. Find the side length of the mural to the nearest tenth of a foot. If you double the length of each side, how many gallons of paint do you need? *Explain.*

43. CAR SPEED To find how fast a car was going before an accident, investigators can use the equation $s = \sqrt{30df}$ where s is the car's speed in miles per hour, d is the length in feet of the skidmark left by the tires, and f is the coefficient of friction for the road. Find the speed of a car that left an 85 foot skidmark. Use a coefficient of friction of 0.5. Round your answer to the nearest whole number.

44. ★ **MULTIPLE CHOICE** To find the time it takes for a dropped object to hit the ground, you can use the equation $h = 16t^2$, where h is height, in feet, and t is time, in seconds. If an object is dropped from a height of 48 feet, how long (to the nearest tenth of a second) does the object fall?

(**A**) 1.7 sec   (**B**) 1.8 sec   (**C**) 2.4 sec   (**D**) 5.7 sec

45. ★ **SHORT RESPONSE** A firehose's flow rate r in gallons per minute can be approximated by the equation $r = 29.7d^2\sqrt{p}$ where d is the diameter of the nozzle in inches and p is the nozzle pressure in pounds per square inch.

    a. Find the flow rate of a hose with a diameter of 2 inches and a pressure of 60 pounds per square inch. *Explain.*

    b. What nozzle pressure is needed for a hose with a diameter of $1\frac{3}{4}$ inches to have the same flow rate as in part (a)? *Explain.*

46. **REASONING** Find whole number values for a and b such that $\pi < \frac{a}{b} < \sqrt{10}$. Is there a rational number between every pair of irrational numbers? *Explain.*

47. **CHALLENGE** Approximate the two values of x to the nearest tenth that solve the equation $x^2 = \sqrt{24}$. *Explain* how you found your answer.

 NEW JERSEY MIXED REVIEW   **TEST PRACTICE** at classzone.com

48. Angle A and angle B are supplementary. The measure of $\angle A$ is 65°. What is the measure of $\angle B$?

(**A**) 25°   (**B**) 65°   (**C**) 115°   (**D**) 125°

49. The three angles of a triangle measure 40°, 90°, and 50°. Which word describes the triangle?

(**A**) Acute   (**B**) Obtuse   (**C**) Right   (**D**) Straight

---

Brain Game

Who nose?

Evaluate the square roots. Use the code to find the answer to the riddle:
Why can't your nose be 12 inches long?

| 3 | 2 | 10 | 9 | 11 | 12 | 2 | | 8 | 5 |

| 4 | 7 | 11 | 13 | 6 | | 5 | 15 | 2 | 14 |

| 3 | 2 | | 9 | | 16 | 7 | 7 | 5 |

A = $\sqrt{81}$	B = $\sqrt{9}$	C = $\sqrt{100}$
D = $\sqrt{36}$	E = $\sqrt{4}$	F = $\sqrt{256}$
H = $\sqrt{225}$	I = $\sqrt{64}$	L = $\sqrt{169}$
N = $\sqrt{196}$	O = $\sqrt{49}$	S = $\sqrt{144}$
T = $\sqrt{25}$	U = $\sqrt{121}$	W = $\sqrt{16}$

INVESTIGATION
Use before Lesson 11.3

GOAL
Use graph paper to relate the side lengths of a right triangle.

MATERIALS
• graph paper
• scissors

11.3 Modeling the Pythagorean Theorem

You can use graph paper to find the length of a right triangle's *hypotenuse*, which is the side opposite the right angle.

EXPLORE **Find the length of the hypotenuse of a right triangle if the other side lengths are 3 units and 4 units.**

STEP 1 **Draw** the right triangle on graph paper. For each of the triangle's known side lengths, draw a square that has the same side length and shares a side with the triangle.

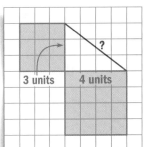

STEP 2 **Find** the sum of the areas of the two squares:

$$3^2 + 4^2 = 9 + 16 = 25 \text{ square units}$$

Use scissors to cut out a third square whose area is equal to the sum of the areas of the two drawn squares.

STEP 3 **Place** the cut-out square against the hypotenuse. You can see that the length of the hypotenuse is 5 units.

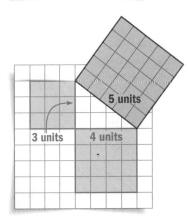

PRACTICE

1. Repeat Steps 1–3 to find the length of the hypotenuse of the right triangle shown.

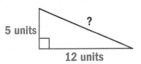

DRAW CONCLUSIONS

2. **REASONING** For the right triangle shown, suppose the lengths *a* and *b* are known. Show how to find the unknown length *c* by relating it to *a* and *b*.

11.3 The Pythagorean Theorem

Before	You classified triangles.
Now	You'll find the length of a side of a right triangle.
Why?	So you can find the length of a ramp, as in Ex. 30.

KEY VOCABULARY
- **right triangle,** *p. 522*
- **hypotenuse,** *p. 588*
- **legs,** *p. 588*
- **Pythagorean Theorem,** *p. 588*

Televisions The size of a television screen is equal to the length of a diagonal. The screen below is 15 inches by 20 inches. What is the length of the diagonal? In Example 1 you'll use right triangle relationships to answer this question.

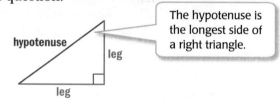

The hypotenuse is the longest side of a right triangle.

In a right triangle, the side opposite the right angle is the **hypotenuse**. The two sides that form the right angle are **legs**. The lengths of the sides of any right triangle are related by the *Pythagorean Theorem*.

KEY CONCEPT *For Your Notebook*

Pythagorean Theorem

Words   For any right triangle, the sum of the squares of the lengths of the legs equals the square of the length of the hypotenuse.

Algebra $a^2 + b^2 = c^2$

EXAMPLE 1 Finding the Length of a Hypotenuse

To find c, the length of the television's diagonal described above, use the Pythagorean Theorem. Let $a = 15$ and $b = 20$.

$$a^2 + b^2 = c^2 \qquad \text{Write Pythagorean Theorem.}$$
$$15^2 + 20^2 = c^2 \qquad \text{Substitute 15 for } a \text{ and 20 for } b.$$
$$625 = c^2 \qquad \text{Simplify.}$$
$$\sqrt{625} = c \qquad \text{Take positive square root of each side.}$$
$$25 = c \qquad \text{Evaluate square root.}$$

AVOID ERRORS
Take the positive square root because length is never negative.

▶ **Answer** The length of the television's diagonal is 25 inches.

EXAMPLE 2 · Approximating the Length of a Hypotenuse

For the right triangle shown, find the length of the hypotenuse to the nearest tenth of a millimeter.

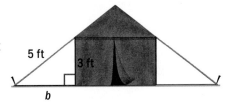

$$a^2 + b^2 = c^2 \qquad \text{Write Pythagorean Theorem.}$$

$$8^2 + 8^2 = c^2 \qquad \text{Substitute 8 for } a \text{ and 8 for } b.$$

$$128 = c^2 \qquad \text{Simplify.}$$

$$\sqrt{128} = c \qquad \text{Take positive square root of each side.}$$

$$11.3 \approx c \qquad \text{Approximate square root.}$$

▶ **Answer** The length of the hypotenuse is about 11.3 millimeters.

APPROXIMATE SQUARE ROOTS

You may find it useful to use the Table of Squares and Square Roots on p. 793 to help with approximation.

EXAMPLE 3 · Finding the Length of a Leg

Camping You are setting up a tent. The ropes that are used to hold the tent down are 5 feet long, and each rope attaches to the tent 3 feet above the ground. How far from the base of the tent should each rope be staked down?

SOLUTION

$$a^2 + b^2 = c^2 \qquad \text{Write Pythagorean Theorem.}$$

$$3^2 + b^2 = 5^2 \qquad \text{Substitute 3 for } a \text{ and 5 for } c.$$

$$9 + b^2 = 25 \qquad \text{Evaluate powers.}$$

$$b^2 = 16 \qquad \text{Subtract 9 from each side.}$$

$$b = \sqrt{16} \qquad \text{Take positive square root of each side.}$$

$$b = 4 \qquad \text{Evaluate square root.}$$

▶ **Answer** Each rope should be staked down 4 feet from the base of the tent.

Animated Math at classzone.com

✓ GUIDED PRACTICE   for Examples 1, 2, and 3

Find the length of the hypotenuse. Round to the nearest tenth, if necessary.

1.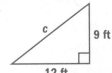

2.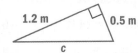

3.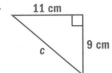

4. **What If?** In Example 3, suppose each rope is 6 feet long. How far from the base should each rope be staked down? Round to the nearest tenth.

11.3 EXERCISES

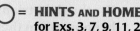

★ = **STANDARDIZED TEST PRACTICE**
Exs. 13, 14, 25, 29, 33, and 41

◯ = **HINTS** AND **HOMEWORK HELP**
for Exs. 3, 7, 9, 11, 25 at classzone.com

SKILL PRACTICE

VOCABULARY Copy and complete the statement.

1. The ___?___ is the side opposite the right angle in a right triangle.

2. The two sides that form the right angle in a right triangle are called ___?___ .

FINDING LENGTHS Find the unknown length. Round to the nearest tenth.

SEE EXAMPLES
1, 2, AND 3
on pp. 588–589
for Exs. 3–14

3.
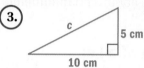

4.
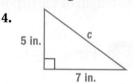

5.
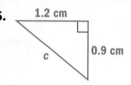

6.
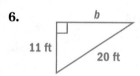

7.
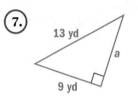

8.
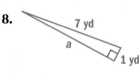

9. legs: 24 in. and 25 in.
hypotenuse: ___?___ in.

10. legs: ___?___ m and 1.6 m
hypotenuse: 3 m

11. legs: ___?___ ft and 9.6 ft
hypotenuse: 11 ft

12. ERROR ANALYSIS Describe and correct the error made in finding the side length.

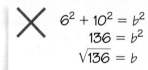

13. ★ **MULTIPLE CHOICE** The length of one leg of a right triangle is 12 meters and the hypotenuse is 20 meters. What is the length of the other leg?

Ⓐ 8 m　　　Ⓑ 12 m　　　Ⓒ 16 m　　　Ⓓ 23.3 m

14. ★ **MULTIPLE CHOICE** A square park has a side length of 100 yards. Which expression represents the yards between opposite corners of the park?

Ⓐ $\sqrt{100}$　　　Ⓑ $\sqrt{200}$　　　Ⓒ 100　　　Ⓓ $\sqrt{100^2 + 100^2}$

GEOMETRY A right triangle has legs of lengths a and b and hypotenuse of length c. Find the perimeter. Round to the nearest tenth, if necessary.

15. $a = 10$ ft, $b = 24$ ft

16. $a = 5$ cm, $c = 13$ cm

17. $b = 1.5$ mm, $c = 2.5$ mm

18. $b = 11$ in., $c = 13$ in.

19. $a = 8$ ft, $b = 6.2$ ft

20. $a = 3$ in., $c = 5.42$ in.

21. $a = 1$ ft, $c = \sqrt{2}$ ft

22. $a = 1$ m, $b = \sqrt{3}$ m

23. $b = \frac{5}{8}$ yd, $c = \frac{3}{4}$ yd

24. CHALLENGE The length of the hypotenuse of an isosceles right triangle is 32 meters. Find the length of the legs. Round to the nearest tenth.

SEE EXAMPLE 3
on p. 589
for Ex. 25

25. ★ **MULTIPLE CHOICE** What is the altitude of the airplane shown?

Ⓐ 47 ft   Ⓑ 95 ft

Ⓒ 105 ft   Ⓓ 1559 ft

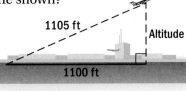

1105 ft

Altitude

1100 ft

Not drawn to scale

26. REASONING Can sticks of lengths 3 inches, 4 inches, and 6 inches be sides of a right triangle? *Justify* your answer.

27. MEASUREMENT Measure the length and width of a book in centimeters. Use the Pythagorean Theorem to calculate the length of a diagonal. Then measure the length of the diagonal to check. What percent of the measured length is your calculated length?

28. MULTI-STEP PROBLEM You are tiling a floor. You cut several 1 foot by 1 foot tiles along a diagonal.

   a. Find the length of a diagonal of a tile to the nearest tenth of a foot.

   b. How many whole diagonal edges will fit along a wall that is 6 feet in length? along a wall that is 10 feet in length? *Explain.*

29. ★ **SHORT RESPONSE** The kite shown has line symmetry. Round your answers to the nearest tenth.

   a. Find the wingspan of the kite.

   b. Find the perimeter of the kite.

   c. *Explain* why you shouldn't use the equation $1^2 + x^2 = (0.7 + 1.2)^2$ to find x.

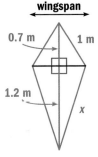

wingspan

0.7 m   1 m

1.2 m

x

READING IN MATH Read the information below for Exercises 30–32.

Handicap Ramps According to federal construction codes, the slope of a handicap exit ramp should be as small as possible. At most, ramps should decrease 1 foot in height for every 12 feet in horizontal length.

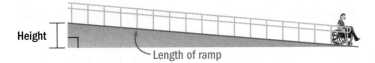

Height

Length of ramp

30. Ramp Length Find the horizontal length required and the minimum acceptable length for a ramp that is 3.5 feet high. Round to the nearest hundredth.

31. Ramp Height You have 18 feet along the ground to put a ramp. Find the maximum height that you could make the ramp and the minimum acceptable ramp length.

32. Code Check A ramp is 2.1 feet high and 25.3 feet in length. Does it meet the construction code? *Explain* why or why not.

33. ★ **WRITING** *Describe* what happens to the length of the hypotenuse when you double the lengths of the legs of a right triangle. Support your answer with an example.

34. **CHALLENGE** In the figure at the right, all of the triangles are right triangles. Find *AB*, *AC*, *AD*, *AE*, *AF*, and *AG*. What pattern do you observe? If the figure is extended to include two more right triangles with hypotenuses $\overline{AH}$ and $\overline{AI}$, what will be the length of $\overline{AI}$? *Justify* your answer.

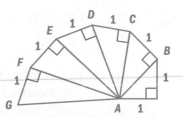

35. The area of a square rug is 24.95 square feet. What is the approximate side length of the rug?

   A Less than 4 ft   **B** Between 4 ft and 5 ft

   C Between 5 ft and 6 ft   **D** More than 6 ft

36. Which of the following can be used to find the area of a rectangle with length *l* and width *w*?

   A $l + w$ **B** lw

   C l^2 **D** $2l + 2w$

QUIZ *for Lessons 11.1–11.3*

Evaluate the expression when $h = -3$ and $x = 2$. *(p. 577)*

  1. $\sqrt{3h + 73}$ **2.** $\sqrt{8x}$ **3.** $\sqrt{24x + 4h}$ **4.** $\sqrt{3h^2 - 2}$

Solve the equation. *(p. 577)*

  5. $3r^2 = 363$ **6.** $t^2 + 33 = 114$ **7.** $\frac{1}{5}s^2 = 45$ **8.** $z^2 - 400 = -391$

Tell whether the number is rational or irrational. *Explain* your reasoning. *(p. 582)*

  9. $-\sqrt{256}$ **10.** -18.45 **11.** $\frac{2}{9}$ **12.** $3.34353\ldots$

13. **RUGS** A square rug has an area of 60 square feet. Find the side length of the rug to the nearest tenth of a foot. *(p. 582)*

Find the unknown length. Round to the nearest tenth, if necessary. *(p. 588)*

14.
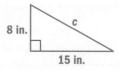

15.

16.
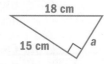

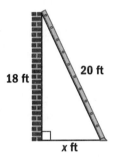
Lessons 11.1–11.3

1. **LADDER PLACEMENT** A 20 foot ladder is placed against a wall, as shown. For safety reasons, the base of the ladder should be at least one foot away from the wall for every three feet of height. Which statement is correct?

18 ft   20 ft   x ft

A. The ladder is placed properly.

B. The base of the ladder is too close to the wall.

C. The base of the ladder is too far away from the wall.

D. There is not enough information to reach a conclusion.

2. **FALLING PENNY** The equation $h = 16t^2$ models how long it will take a dropped object to hit the ground. The height h is measured in feet and the time t is measured in seconds. A penny is dropped from a height of 64 feet. How long will it take for the penny to hit the ground?

A. 2 seconds   C. 8 seconds

B. 4 seconds   D. 16 seconds

3. **WALKING SPEED** The maximum speed s, in feet per second, that an animal can walk is $s = 5.66\sqrt{l}$, where l is the animal's leg length in feet. What is the maximum walking speed for a large bull with a leg length of 5 feet?

A. 5.3 ft/sec   C. 28.3 ft/sec

B. 12.7 ft/sec   D. 141.5 ft/sec

4. **GRAPHING** Points $A(2, 4)$ and $B(7, 16)$ are plotted on a coordinate grid and connected with a line segment. How can you find the distance between the points?

A. Multiply $(16 - 4)$ by $(7 - 2)$.

B. Divide $(16 - 4)$ by $(7 - 2)$.

C. Find the square root of the sum $(16 - 4)^2 + (7 - 2)^2$.

D. Find the square root of the difference $(16 - 4)^2 - (7 - 2)^2$.

5. **SAIL** For the triangular sail shown below, find the length of the hypotenuse in meters. Round your answer to the nearest tenth.

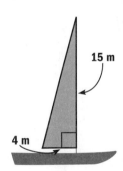

15 m

4 m

A. 15.2 cm   C. 29.0 cm

B. 15.5 cm   D. 241.0 cm

6. **OPEN-ENDED** The area of a square parking lot is 729 square yards.

• What is the side length of the parking lot?

• What is the length of a diagonal, to the nearest tenth?

• Traffic cones are being set up to block off half of the lot for repairs. A cone is placed in one corner of the lot. Then one cone is placed every 2 to $2\frac{1}{2}$ feet along the diagonal until a cone is placed in the opposite corner. What is the minimum number of cones needed to block off the lot?

11.4 Area of a Parallelogram

Before	You found the areas of rectangles and squares.
Now	You'll find the areas of parallelograms.
Why?	So you can find treadmill dimensions, as in Example 2.

KEY VOCABULARY
• base of a parallelogram, p. 594
• height of a parallelogram, p. 594

ACTIVITY

You can find the area of a parallelogram.

STEP 1 **Use** graph paper to draw the parallelogram shown.

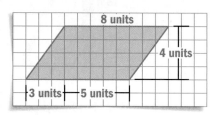

STEP 2 **Cut** a right triangle from one side of the parallelogram and move it to the other side to form a rectangle.

STEP 3 **Find** the area of the rectangle. How does the area of the rectangle compare with the area of the parallelogram?

The **base of a parallelogram** is the length of any one of the sides. The **height of a parallelogram** is the perpendicular distance between the side whose length is the base and the opposite side.

Sometimes the height lies outside the parallelogram.

KEY CONCEPT   *For Your Notebook*

Area of a Parallelogram

Words   The area A of a parallelogram is the product of a base and the corresponding height.

Algebra $A = bh$

Finding the Area of a Parallelogram

Find the area of the parallelogram.

SOLUTION

$A = bh$ **Write formula for area.**

$= 10(6)$ **Substitute 10 for b and 6 for h.**

$= 60$ **Multiply.**

▶ **Answer** The area of the parallelogram is 60 square centimeters.

AVOID ERRORS
Area is measured in square units, not linear units.

 GUIDED PRACTICE   **for Example 1**

Find the area of the parallelogram with the given base b and height h.

  1. $b = 8$ in., $h = 11$ in.   **2.** $b = 9.3$ m, $h = 7$ m   **3.** $b = 3.25$ ft, $h = 12$ ft

EXAMPLE 2 **Finding the Base of a Parallelogram**

Exercising A treadmill's belt is in the shape of a parallelogram before its ends are joined to form a loop. The belt's area is 2052 square inches. The belt's width, which is the height of the parallelogram, is 18 inches. Find the length of the belt, which is the base of the parallelogram.

Not drawn to scale

SOLUTION

$A = bh$ **Write formula for area of a parallelogram.**

$2052 = b(18)$ **Substitute 2052 for A and 18 for h.**

$\dfrac{2052}{18} = \dfrac{b(18)}{18}$ **Divide each side by 18.**

$114 = b$ **Simplify.**

▶ **Answer** The length of the treadmill's belt is 114 inches.

TAKE NOTES
In your notebook, you may want to copy an example of finding the base of a parallelogram next to the formula for the area of a parallelogram.

 GUIDED PRACTICE   **for Example 2**

Use the area A of the parallelogram to find its base b or height h.

  4. $A = 56$ in.^{2} **5.** $A = 36$ mm^2 **6.** $A = 54$ cm^2

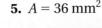

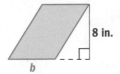

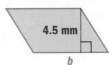

EXAMPLE 3 Comparing Areas of Parallelograms

The base of a parallelogram is 4 feet and its height is 9 feet. It is enlarged to have dimensions 3 times that of the original. Compare the areas of the parallelograms.

SOLUTION

The dimensions of the enlarged parallelogram are 3 times those of the original parallelogram. The larger parallelogram's base is 3(4) = 12 feet and its height is 3(9) = 27 feet. Find the area of each parallelogram.

Original parallelogram	**Enlarged parallelogram**
$A = bh$	$A = bh$
$= 4(9)$	$= 12(27)$
$= 36$	$= 324$

▶ **Answer** Because $\frac{324}{36} = 9$, the area of the enlarged parallelogram is 9 times the area of the original parallelogram.

ANOTHER WAY

You could also compare the areas without evaluating the formulas.

Original area:

$A = bh$

Enlarged area:

$A = 3b \cdot 3h$

$= (3)(3)bh$

$= 9bh$

 GUIDED PRACTICE for Example 3

7. **What If?** Suppose the original parallelogram in Example 3 is reduced so that the dimensions are half the original. Compare the areas.

11.4 EXERCISES

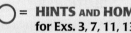

HOMEWORK KEY

★ = **STANDARDIZED TEST PRACTICE**
Exs. 14, 23, 24, 27, and 37

◯ = **HINTS** AND **HOMEWORK HELP**
for Exs. 3, 7, 11, 13, 21 at classzone.com

SKILL PRACTICE

1. **VOCABULARY** Draw a parallelogram. Label a base and the height.

2. **VOCABULARY** Copy your parallelogram from Exercise 1 and label a different base and height.

FINDING PERIMETER AND AREA Find the perimeter and the area.

SEE EXAMPLE 1
on p. 595
for Exs. 3–8

3.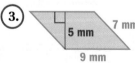

4.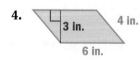

5.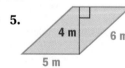

6.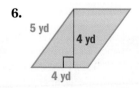

7.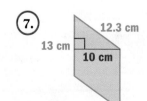

8.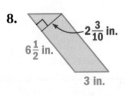

SEE EXAMPLE 1
on p. 595
for Ex. 9

9. ERROR ANALYSIS Describe and correct the error made in finding the area of the parallelogram.

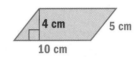

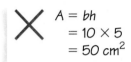

$$A = bh$$
$$= 10 \times 5$$
$$= 50 \text{ cm}^2$$

FINDING THE BASE OR HEIGHT Use the area A of the parallelogram to find its base b or height h.

SEE EXAMPLE 2
on p. 595
for Exs. 10–13

10. $A = 48 \text{ cm}^2$, $b = 12 \text{ cm}$, $h = \underline{\ ?\ }$

11. $A = 117 \text{ ft}^2$, $b = \underline{\ ?\ }$, $h = 9 \text{ ft}$

12. $A = 80 \text{ m}^2$, $b = \underline{\ ?\ }$, $h = 15 \text{ m}$

13. $A = 15 \text{ in.}^2$, $b = \frac{5}{6} \text{ in.}$, $h = \underline{\ ?\ }$

SEE EXAMPLE 3
on p. 596
for Exs. 14–17

14. ★ MULTIPLE CHOICE The area of the large parallelogram is twice the area of the small parallelogram. What is the value of x?

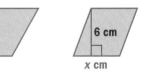

(A) 3   **(B)** 6   **(C)** 12   **(D)** 24

COMPARING AREAS Predict the ratio of the areas of parallelograms P and Q with the given base b and height h. Then find the areas to check.

15. P: $b = 5 \text{ m}$; $h = 3 \text{ m}$
Q: $b = 20 \text{ m}$; $h = 12 \text{ m}$

16. P: $b = 6 \text{ in.}$; $h = 9 \text{ in.}$
Q: $b = 2 \text{ in.}$; $h = 3 \text{ in.}$

17. P: $b = 4 \text{ cm}$; $h = 7 \text{ cm}$
Q: $b = 12 \text{ cm}$; $h = 21 \text{ cm}$

18. FINDING HEIGHT The area of a parallelogram is 216 square feet and the base is 6 times the height. Find the parallelogram's height.

CHALLENGE Identify two possible values for (x, y) that can be connected to the given points to form a parallelogram. Plot and connect the points. Then find the area of both parallelograms. Compare your answers.

19. $R(2, -2)$, $S(-1, -2)$, $T(1, 2)$, $U(x, y)$

20. $A(-3, 3)$, $B(-1, 3)$, $C(2, 0)$, $D(x, y)$

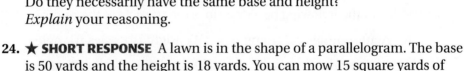

PROBLEM SOLVING

**SEE EXAMPLES
1 AND 2**
on p. 595
for Exs. 21–22

21. STAINED GLASS The area of a parallelogram in a stained glass window is 71.5 square inches, and the height is 6.5 inches. What is the base?

22. MULTI-STEP PROBLEM The state of Missouri has approximately the shape of a parallelogram, as shown.

a. Use a metric ruler to measure the base and height of the parallelogram.

b. Use the scale 1 cm : 120 miles to estimate the area of Missouri.

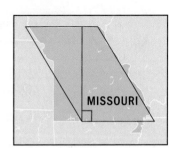

MISSOURI

23. ★ WRITING Two parallelograms have the same area. Do they necessarily have the same base and height? *Explain* your reasoning.

24. ★ SHORT RESPONSE A lawn is in the shape of a parallelogram. The base is 50 yards and the height is 18 yards. You can mow 15 square yards of grass per minute. How long will it take you to mow the lawn? *Explain.*

GEOMETRIC ART The figures are from the sculpture at the right. Approximate the height of the rhombus. Then estimate the area to the nearest square inch.

25.

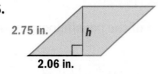

2.75 in.

h

2.06 in.

26.

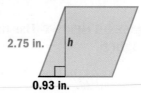

2.75 in.

h

0.93 in.

27. ★ **EXTENDED RESPONSE** On lined paper, sketch any parallelogram $ABCD$ with a base of 4 centimeters. Label the top left vertex A. Then extend $\overline{AB}$ and $\overline{AD}$ to double their initial lengths and complete the enlarged parallelogram. How does the height change? How do the perimeter and area change? Predict the results if you extend $\overline{AB}$ and $\overline{AD}$ to 3 times their original lengths. Check your prediction.

SEE EXAMPLE 3
on p. 596
for Ex. 28

28. **REASONING** The base of a parallelogram is 24.5 feet, and the height is 10 feet. If you divide the base and the height by 4, what happens to the area of the parallelogram? *Explain* your reasoning.

29. **CHALLENGE** Two similar parallelograms are shown below. Find the lengths of the sides x and y and base z. Round decimal answers to the nearest tenth. Then calculate and compare the perimeters and areas of the two parallelograms.

12 cm

x

8 cm

4 cm

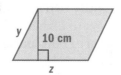

y

10 cm

z

30. **CHALLENGE** A regular hexagon can be divided into 3 congruent parallelograms as shown. The area of the hexagon shown is about 509.2 square inches and the side lengths are 14 inches. Find the distance x between two parallel sides. Round to the nearest tenth. *Explain* how you found your answer.

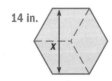

14 in.

x

 NEW JERSEY MIXED REVIEW

TEST PRACTICE at classzone.com

31. All four sides of a quadrilateral have the same length. Which of the following CANNOT describe the quadrilateral?

(A) Trapezoid

(B) Rectangle

(C) Parallelogram

(D) Rhombus

32. Which of the following best describes the triangle at the right?

(A) Acute equilateral triangle

(B) Right isosceles triangle

(C) Right scalene triangle

(D) Acute isosceles triangle

45°   45°

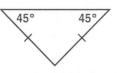 **ONLINE QUIZ** at classzone.com

GOAL

Use graph paper to find the areas of triangles and trapezoids.

MATERIALS

• graph paper
• scissors

11.5 Modeling Areas of Triangles and Trapezoids

You can use a parallelogram to find the area of a triangle and of a trapezoid.

EXPLORE 1 **Find the area of the triangle shown.**

STEP 1 **Use** graph paper to draw two triangles that are congruent to the one shown. Cut out both triangles.

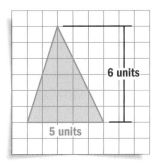

STEP 2 **Fit** the triangles together to form a parallelogram by rotating one of the triangles. Then find the area of the parallelogram.

The area of the parallelogram is 5 • 6 = 30 square units.

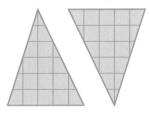

STEP 3 **Use** the area of the parallelogram to find the area of one triangle. Because two congruent triangles make up the parallelogram, the area of the triangle is $\frac{1}{2}$ • 30 = 15 square units.

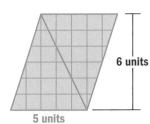

PRACTICE

1. Repeat Steps 1–3 to find the area of the triangle shown.

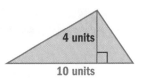

DRAW CONCLUSIONS

2. **REASONING** For the triangle shown, suppose the lengths *b* and *h* are known. *Explain* how to find the area of the triangle in terms of *b* and *h*.

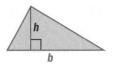

Continued on next page

INVESTIGATION

EXPLORE 2 **Find the area of the trapezoid shown.**

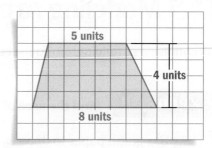

STEP 1 **Use** graph paper to draw two trapezoids that are congruent to the one shown. Cut out both trapezoids.

STEP 2 **Fit** the trapezoids together to form a parallelogram by flipping one of the trapezoids over. Then find the area of the parallelogram.

The area of the parallelogram is
13 • 4 = 52 square units.

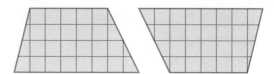

STEP 3 **Use** the area of the parallelogram to find the area of one trapezoid. Because two congruent trapezoids make up the parallelogram, the area of the trapezoid is $\frac{1}{2}$ • 52 = 26 square units.

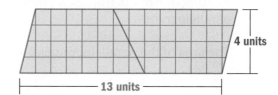

PRACTICE

3. Repeat Steps 1–3 to find the area of the trapezoid shown.

DRAW CONCLUSIONS

4. **REASONING** For the trapezoid shown, suppose the lengths b_1 (read "*b* sub one"), b_2 (read "*b* sub two"), and *h* are known. *Explain* how to find the area of the trapezoid in terms of b_1, b_2, and *h*.

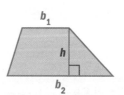

5. **REASONING** *Describe* how you could use the formula for the area of a trapezoid to find the area of a regular hexagon. Draw a diagram to help you solve this problem.

11.5 Areas of Triangles and Trapezoids

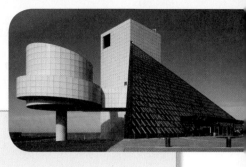

 4.2.E.1.a Develop and apply strategies for finding perimeter and area: Geometric figures made by combining triangles . . .

Before You found the areas of parallelograms.

Now You'll find the areas of triangles and trapezoids.

Why? So you can find the area of a wall, as in Example 1.

KEY VOCABULARY
- base of a triangle, height of a triangle, *p. 601*
- bases of a trapezoid, height of a trapezoid, *p. 602*

You can use the *base* and *height* of a triangle to find the area of the triangle. The **base of a triangle** is the length of any one of the sides. The **height of a triangle** is the perpendicular distance between the side whose length is the base and the vertex opposite that side.

KEY CONCEPT   *For Your Notebook*

Area of a Triangle

Words The area A of a triangle is half the product of a base and the corresponding height.

Algebra $A = \frac{1}{2}bh$

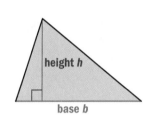

EXAMPLE 1   Finding the Area of a Triangle

Museums The Rock and Roll Hall of Fame and Museum in Cleveland, Ohio, has a triangular shaped wall as shown. What is the area of the wall?

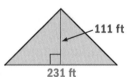

SOLUTION

$A = \frac{1}{2}bh$ **Write formula for area of a triangle.**

$= \frac{1}{2}(231)(111)$ **Substitute 231 for *b* and 111 for *h*.**

$= 12,820.5$ **Multiply.**

▶ **Answer** The area of the wall is 12,820.5 square feet.

Animated **Math** at classzone.com

 GUIDED PRACTICE   for Example 1

Find the area of the triangle with the given base *b* and height *h*.

1. $b = 7$ m, $h = 13$ m   **2.** $b = 6.4$ in., $h = 14$ in.   **3.** $b = 4.5$ ft, $h = 8.6$ ft

EXAMPLE 2 Finding the Base of a Triangle

Flatiron Building From above, the Flatiron Building in New York has a shape that can be approximated by a right triangle with a height of 87 feet. The area of the triangle is 7525.5 square feet. Find its base.

$A = \frac{1}{2}bh$ **Write formula for area of a triangle.**

$7525.5 = \frac{1}{2}b(87)$ **Substitute 7525.5 for A and 87 for h.**

$7525.5 = 43.5b$ **Simplify.**

$173 = b$ **Divide each side by 43.5.**

▶ **Answer** The base of the triangle is about 173 feet.

87 ft

b

Top view

✓ **GUIDED PRACTICE**   for Example 2

Find the unknown base b or height h of the triangle.

4. $A = 61.6 \text{ m}^2$, $b = 11$ m, $h = \underline{\ ?\ }$ **5.** $A = 108.5 \text{ ft}^2$, $b = \underline{\ ?\ }$, $h = 14$ ft

---

Trapezoids You can use the *bases* and the *height* of a trapezoid to find the area of the trapezoid. The lengths of the parallel sides of a trapezoid are the **bases of a trapezoid**. The **height of a trapezoid** is the perpendicular distance between the bases.

KEY CONCEPT   *For Your Notebook*

Area of a Trapezoid

Words   The area A of a trapezoid is half the product of the sum of the bases and the height.

Algebra $A = \frac{1}{2}(b_1 + b_2)h$

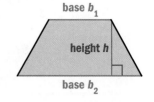

base b_1

height h

base b_2

EXAMPLE 3 Finding the Area of a Trapezoid

READING

Because a trapezoid has two bases, they are usually labeled b_1 and b_2. You read b_1 as "b sub one."

Find the area of the trapezoid shown.

$A = \frac{1}{2}(b_1 + b_2)h$ **Write formula for area of a trapezoid.**

$= \frac{1}{2}(5 + 10)(8)$ **Substitute 5 for b_1, 10 for b_2, and 8 for h.**

$= 60$ **Simplify.**

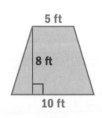

5 ft

8 ft

10 ft

▶ **Answer** The area of the trapezoid is 60 square feet.

EXAMPLE 4 Finding the Height of a Trapezoid

A trapezoid has an area of 66 square meters. The bases are 8 meters and 14 meters. Find the height.

$$A = \frac{1}{2}(b_1 + b_2)h \qquad \text{Write formula for area of a trapezoid.}$$

$$66 = \frac{1}{2}(8 + 14)h \qquad \text{Substitute 66 for } A, \text{ 8 for } b_1, \text{ and 14 for } b_2.$$

$$66 = \frac{1}{2}(22)h \qquad \text{Add.}$$

$$66 = 11h \qquad \text{Multiply.}$$

$$6 = h \qquad \text{Divide each side by 11.}$$

▶ **Answer** The height of the trapezoid is 6 meters.

Animated **Math**
at classzone.com

★ **EXAMPLE 5** Standardized Test Practice

Landscaping Flowers are planted in a public garden in the shape shown. What is the area of the garden covered by flowers?

(A) 22 yd^2 **(B)** 35 yd^2

(C) 47 yd^2 **(D)** 94 yd^2

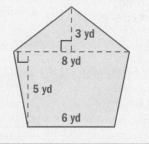

ELIMINATE CHOICES
The area is greater than that of a 5 yd by 6 yd rectangle, which is 30 yd^2. Choice A can be eliminated.

SOLUTION

STEP 1 Find the area of the triangle and the trapezoid.

Area of the triangle	Area of the trapezoid
$A = \frac{1}{2}(8)(3)$	$A = \frac{1}{2}(6 + 8)(5)$
$= 12$	$= 35$

STEP 2 Add the areas to find the total area: $12 + 35 = 47$

▶ **Answer** The area of the garden is 47 square yards. The correct answer is C.   Ⓐ Ⓑ **Ⓒ** Ⓓ

✓ **GUIDED PRACTICE** for Examples 3, 4, and 5

Find the unknown area *A* or height *h* of the trapezoid.

6. $A = \underline{\ ?\ }$, $b_1 = 13$ in., $b_2 = 15$ in., $h = 6$ in.

7. $A = 216 \text{ m}^2$, $b_1 = 11$ m, $b_2 = 13$ m, $h = \underline{\ ?\ }$

8. Find the area of the figure at the right.

11.5 EXERCISES

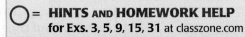
SKILL PRACTICE

1. **VOCABULARY** Draw a triangle and trapezoid. Label the bases and heights.

FINDING AREA Find the area of the triangle.

SEE EXAMPLE 1
on p. 601
for Exs. 2–4

2.
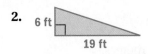

3.
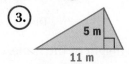

4.
11 in. [triangle] 22 in.

TRIANGLES Find the unknown base or height of the triangle.

SEE EXAMPLE 2
on p. 602
for Exs. 5–8

5. $A = 45 \text{ km}^2$, $b = \underline{\ ?\ }$, $h = 15$ km

6. $A = 71.5 \text{ mm}^2$, $b = 11$ mm, $h = \underline{\ ?\ }$

7. $A = 98 \text{ mi}^2$, $b = 21$ mi, $h = \underline{\ ?\ }$

8. $A = 13 \text{ cm}^2$, $b = \underline{\ ?\ }$, $h = 2.5$ cm

FINDING AREA Find the area of the trapezoid.

SEE EXAMPLE 3
on p. 602
for Exs. 9–12

9.
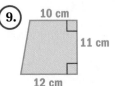

10.
7 in.
6 in.
9 in.

11.
13 m
4 m
9 m

12. **ERROR ANALYSIS** Describe and correct the error made in finding the area of the trapezoid shown.

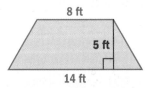

8 ft
5 ft
14 ft

$$\begin{aligned} A &= (b_1 + b_2)h \\ &= (8 + 14)(5) \\ &= 110 \text{ ft}^2 \end{aligned}$$

TRAPEZOIDS Find the unknown base or height of the trapezoid.

SEE EXAMPLE 4
on p. 603
for Exs. 13–17

13. $A = 180 \text{ ft}^2$, $b_1 = \underline{\ ?\ }$, $b_2 = 26$ ft, $h = 9$ ft

14. $A = 114 \text{ cm}^2$, $b_1 = 13$ cm, $b_2 = 6$ cm, $h = \underline{\ ?\ }$

15. $A = 444.5 \text{ m}^2$, $b_1 = 18$ m, $b_2 = 17$ m, $h = \underline{\ ?\ }$

16. $A = 33 \text{ in.}^2$, $b_1 = 3\frac{3}{4}$ in., $b_2 = \underline{\ ?\ }$, $h = 6$ in.

17. **FINDING HEIGHT** A trapezoid has an area of 311.2 square feet. The bases are 25.2 feet and 13.7 feet. Find the height of the trapezoid.

18. ★ **MULTIPLE CHOICE** What is the area of the quadrilateral shown? The length of the diagonal is 25 centimeters.

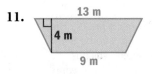

A 200 cm^2 **B** 400 cm^2

C 750 cm^2 **D** 1500 cm^2

6 cm
10 cm

FINDING AREA **Find the area of the figure.**

SEE EXAMPLE 5
on p. 603
for Exs. 19–24

19.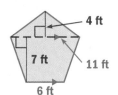

20.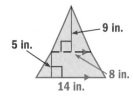

21.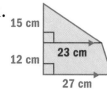

22.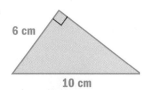

23.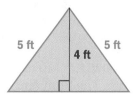

24.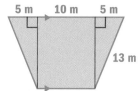

XY ALGEBRA **Use the area of the trapezoid to find the value of x.**

25. Area = 44 in.^{2}

26. Area = 168 cm^2

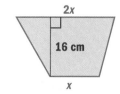

27. Area = 81 m^2

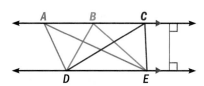

28. **REASONING** *Explain* why triangles ADE, BDE, and CDE have the same area.

29. **CHALLENGE** In a trapezoid, b_2 is three times as great as b_1 and the height h is twice b_1. The area of the trapezoid is 144 square inches. Sketch the trapezoid and find b_1, b_2, and h.

PROBLEM SOLVING

SEE EXAMPLE 4
on p. 603
for Ex. 30

30. ★ **MULTIPLE CHOICE** The top of a table in your classroom is shaped like the trapezoid shown. The area of the trapezoid is 1131 square inches. What is its height?

   (A) 6.5 in.   (B) 15.7 in.   (C) 26 in.   (D) 83.8 in.

31. **BACKPACKS** You are making a reflective patch for your backpack. The patch is a triangle with a base of 12 centimeters and a height of 6 centimeters. What is the area of the patch?

32. ★ **WRITING** The base and height of a triangle are both doubled. How does the area change? Give an example to support your conclusion.

33. **ORIGAMI** A student folds a piece of paper into the shape shown. Find the area by using a triangle, a rectangle, and a trapezoid. Then find the area using two trapezoids. Compare your results.

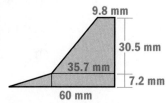

34. CAR WINDOWS On each side of a car, two windows are similar to the shape of a trapezoid and one window is similar to the shape of a triangle, as shown. What is the approximate total area of the windows on both sides of the car?

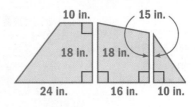

35. ★ **SHORT RESPONSE** A trapezoid's bases are 10 inches and 15 inches, and the height is 5 inches. What happens to the area of the trapezoid if you double only the bases? if you double only the height? if you double the bases and the height? *Explain* your reasoning.

36. ★ **SHORT RESPONSE** A hip roof consists of four polygons. The front and back of the roof are congruent trapezoids. The sides are congruent triangles.

  a. Find the area of the entire roof using the dimensions shown.

  b. Shingles are sold in *bundles*. A bundle of shingles contains three *squares*. Each square covers 100 square feet. How many whole bundles of shingles would you need to cover the roof?

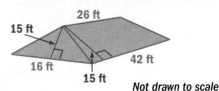

Not drawn to scale

37. ★ **OPEN-ENDED MATH** Sketch two triangles and two trapezoids that each have an area of 24 cm².

38. CHALLENGE The wings of a hang glider are composed of two congruent obtuse triangles as shown. Find the total area of the wings to the nearest square foot.

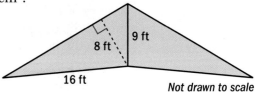

Not drawn to scale

39. CHALLENGE In an isosceles trapezoid, the two *nonparallel* sides are congruent. Find the area of an isosceles trapezoid with bases of 32 meters and 20 meters and congruent sides of 10 meters.

 NEW JERSEY MIXED REVIEW **TEST PRACTICE** at classzone.com

40. Use a metric ruler to measure the height and the base of the parallelogram in centimeters. Which of the following is closest to the area of the parallelogram?

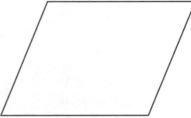

  A 12 cm²

  B 13 cm²

  C 14 cm²

  D 16 cm²

11.6 Circumference of a Circle

 4.2.E.1.a Develop and apply strategies for finding perimeter and area: Geometric figures made by combining . . . circles or parts of circles

Before	You found the perimeters of polygons.
Now	You'll find the circumferences of circles.
Why?	So you can find the circumference of a wheel, as in Ex. 29.

KEY VOCABULARY
- **circle,** *p. 607*
- **center,** *p. 607*
- **radius,** *p. 607*
- **diameter,** *p. 607*
- **circumference,** *p. 607*

ACTIVITY

You can approximate the formula for the *circumference* of a circle.

STEP 1 **Use** a metric ruler to find the distance *d*, in millimeters, across a bottle cap through its center as shown.

STEP 2 **Wrap** a piece of string around the bottle cap until it meets the beginning as shown. Measure this portion of the string, in millimeters, to find the circumference *C*.

STEP 3 **Write** the ratio of *C* to *d* as a decimal.

STEP 4 **Repeat** Steps 1–3 using two other circular objects.

STEP 5 **Compare** the ratios. What do you notice? What does this suggest about the relationship between circumference and the distance *d*?

A **circle** is the set of all points in a plane that are the same distance from a fixed point called the **center**. The distance from the center to any point on the circle is the **radius**. The distance across the circle through the center is the **diameter**.

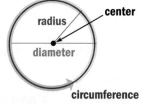

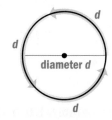

The **circumference** of a circle is the distance around the circle. The ratio of a circle's circumference to its diameter is represented by the Greek letter π (*pi*). As you may have seen in the activity, and in the figure above, π is slightly greater than 3. The values 3.14 and $\frac{22}{7}$ are often used as approximations of the irrational number π. The exact value for π is a non-terminating, non-repeating decimal: 3.14159. . . .

Circumference of a Circle

Words   The circumference C of a circle is the product of π and the diameter, or twice the product of π and the radius.

diameter d

radius r

Algebra $C = \pi d$ $C = 2\pi r$

EXAMPLE 1   Finding the Circumference of a Circle

Find the circumference of the clock. Use 3.14 for π.

SOLUTION

$C = \pi d$ Write formula for circumference.

$\approx 3.14(25)$ Substitute 3.14 for π and 25 for d.

$= 78.5$ Multiply.

▸ **Answer** The circumference of the clock is about 78.5 centimeters.

AVOID ERRORS
Be sure to substitute the diameter into the formula $C = \pi d$, not the radius.

Choosing Approximations When the radius or diameter of a circle is divisible by 7, use $\frac{22}{7}$ as the approximation for π.

EXAMPLE 2   Finding the Circumference of a Circle

Find the circumference of the circle. Use $\frac{22}{7}$ for π.

21 in.

SOLUTION

$C = 2\pi r$ Write formula for circumference.

$\approx 2\left(\frac{22}{7}\right)(21)$ Substitute $\frac{22}{7}$ for π and 21 for r.

$= 132$ Multiply.

▸ **Answer** The circumference of the circle is about 132 inches.

ANOTHER WAY
You may be asked to leave your answers in terms of π. For example, the answer to Example 2 in terms of π is $C = 2\pi(21) = 42\pi$.

✓ **GUIDED PRACTICE**   for Examples 1 and 2

Find the circumference of the circle. Use $\frac{22}{7}$ or 3.14 for π.

1.

9 mm

2.

100 cm

3.

49 in.

EXAMPLE 3 Finding the Diameter of a Circle

Giant Sequoias The largest living tree in the United States is a giant sequoia in Sequoia National Park in California. Its trunk is roughly circular and has a circumference of 1231 inches at ground level. What is the tree's diameter at ground level?

SOLUTION

$C = \pi d$	Write formula for circumference.
$1231 \approx 3.14d$	Substitute 1231 for C and 3.14 for π.
$\dfrac{1231}{3.14} = \dfrac{3.14d}{3.14}$	Divide each side by 3.14.
$392 \approx d$	Simplify.

> **CONVERT UNITS**
> To find the diameter in feet, multiply:
> $392 \text{ in.} \times \dfrac{1 \text{ ft}}{12 \text{ in.}} =$
> $32\frac{2}{3}$ ft

▶ **Answer** The tree's diameter is about 392 inches, or $32\frac{2}{3}$ feet, at ground level.

✓ **GUIDED PRACTICE** for Example 3

4. **Tree Limbs** In Example 3, the circumference of the tree's largest limb at its widest point is about 256 inches. Find its diameter.

11.6 EXERCISES

HOMEWORK KEY

★ = **STANDARDIZED TEST PRACTICE**
Exs. 16, 23, 26, 27, 28, 31, and 38

◯ = **HINTS AND HOMEWORK HELP**
for Exs. 3, 7, 11, 13, 23 at classzone.com

SKILL PRACTICE

1. **VOCABULARY** Sketch a circle. Label its diameter, center, and radius.

2. **VOCABULARY** Copy and complete: __?__ is the distance around a circle.

CIRCUMFERENCE Find the circumference of the circle. Use $\frac{22}{7}$ or 3.14 for π.

> **SEE EXAMPLES 1 AND 2**
> on p. 608
> for Exs. 3–8

 3. $d = 9$ in.

4. $d = 30$ in.

5. $d = 6.5$ cm

6. $r = 3.4$ in.

 7. $r = 14$ cm

8. $d = 1.205$ in.

SEE EXAMPLE 2
on p. 608
for Ex. 9

9. ERROR ANALYSIS A student says that the circumference of a circle with a radius of 5 meters is 15.7 meters. Describe and correct the student's error.

FINDING DIAMETER AND RADIUS Find the diameter and the radius of the circle with the given circumference *C*. Use $\frac{22}{7}$ or 3.14 for π.

SEE EXAMPLE 3
on p. 609
for Exs. 10–15

10. *C* = 28.26 in.　　　　**11.** *C* = 119.32 m　　　　**12.** *C* = 81.64 mm

13. *C* = 42.39 km　　　　**14.** $C = 37\frac{5}{7}$ cm　　　　**15.** $C = 14\frac{1}{7}$ ft

16. ★ MULTIPLE CHOICE A circle has a circumference of 2400π inches. What is its radius in yards?

Ⓐ $\dfrac{33\frac{1}{3}}{\pi}$ yd 　　Ⓑ $33\frac{1}{3}$ yd 　　Ⓒ $66\frac{2}{3}$ yd 　　Ⓓ $33\frac{1}{3}\pi$ yd

FINDING CIRCUMFERENCES Find the circumference of both circles.

17. 　　**18.** 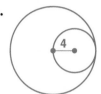　　**19.**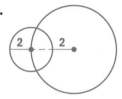

CHALLENGE The figure is a section of a circle graph. Find the value of *x* to the nearest tenth.

20. 　　**21.** 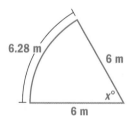　　**22.**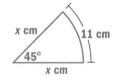

PROBLEM SOLVING

SEE EXAMPLE 1
on p. 608 for
Ex. 23

23. ★ MULTIPLE CHOICE The Astrodome in Houston, Texas, is circular and has a diameter of 710 feet. What is the approximate circumference of the Astrodome?

Ⓐ 1110 ft　　　Ⓑ 2230 ft

Ⓒ 4460 ft　　　Ⓓ 15,600 ft

24. OBSERVATION WHEEL The London Eye, also known as the Millennium Wheel, opened to the public in March, 2000. It rotates at a speed of about 0.26 meters per second and is 135 meters in diameter. What is the circumference of the London Eye? About how many minutes does it take for the wheel to make 1 full rotation?

London Eye

25. REASONING To 9 decimal places, the number π is 3.141592654. To how many decimal places is $\frac{22}{7}$ an accurate approximation of π? Is 3.14 or $\frac{22}{7}$ a more accurate approximation? *Explain.*

26. ★ SHORT RESPONSE The ends of the track shown are approximately semicircles. How much farther would you run in 10 laps in the center of Lane B than if you ran in the center of Lane A? *Explain.*

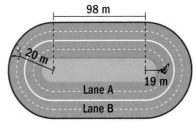

98 m

20 m

19 m

Lane A

Lane B

27. ★ OPEN-ENDED MATH Find a circular object in your house. Measure the diameter and the circumference of the object. Then calculate the circumference. Compare the results.

28. ★ MULTIPLE CHOICE A circular wading pool has a diameter of 4 feet. A circular swimming pool has a radius of 16 feet. How many times greater is the circumference of the swimming pool than the wading pool?

(A) 2 times   **(B)** 4 times   **(C)** 8 times   **(D)** 12 times

29. MULTI-STEP PROBLEM A giant unicycle wheel has a diameter of 7 feet. What is the circumference of the wheel? Use $\frac{22}{7}$ for π. How many rotations does it take for the wheel to travel 176 feet? *Explain.*

30. TIRES A car tire rotates 15 times when it travels 78.5 feet. Find the radius of the tire in inches. Use 3.14 for π.

31. ★ WRITING You triple the diameter of a given circle. What happens to the circle's circumference? Give an example to support your conclusion.

32. CHALLENGE How fast does the tip of a 5-inch minute hand on a clock travel? How fast does the tip of a 6-inch second hand on a clock travel? Express your answers in inches per hour.

NEW JERSEY MIXED REVIEW

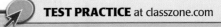

TEST PRACTICE at classzone.com

33. Mr. Clark wants to paint a wall that surrounds a sliding glass door, as shown below.

How many square feet of wall does Mr. Clark need to paint?

(A) 107.5 ft^2

(B) 125 ft^2

(C) 148 ft^2

(D) 188.5 ft^2

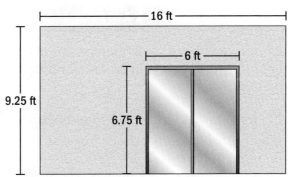

16 ft

6 ft

9.25 ft

6.75 ft

11.7 Area of a Circle

4.2.E.1.b Develop and apply strategies for finding perimeter and area: Estimation of area using grids of various sizes.

Before You found the areas of polygons.

Now You'll find the areas of circles.

Why? So you can estimate areas of circular objects, as in Ex. 33.

The circle shown has a radius of 3 units. To estimate the area of the circle, you can count the number of squares entirely inside the circle, almost entirely inside the circle, and about halfway inside the circle.

- **16** of the squares are *entirely* inside the circle.

- **8** of the squares are *almost entirely* in the circle.

- **8** of the squares are about *halfway* inside the circle.

You can then estimate the area of the circle.

$$\text{Area} \approx 16 + 8 + \frac{1}{2}(8) = 16 + 8 + 4 = 28 \text{ square units}$$

The following formula gives the exact area of a circle.

KEY CONCEPT *For Your Notebook*

Area of a Circle

Words The area A of a circle is the product of π and the square of the radius.

Algebra $A = \pi r^2$

EXAMPLE 1 Finding the Area of a Circle

To find the area of the circle at the top of the page, use 3.14 for π and 3 for r in the area formula.

$A = \pi r^2$ **Write formula for area of a circle.**

$\approx (3.14)(3)^2$ **Substitute 3.14 for π and 3 for r.**

$= 28.26$ **Simplify.**

▶ **Answer** The area of the circle is about 28.26 square units.

EXAMPLE 2 Finding the Area of a Circle

Circus The central performance area at a circus is a circular ring having a diameter of 42 feet. Find the area of the ring.

SOLUTION

STEP 1 **Find** the radius: $r = \dfrac{42}{2} = 21$ ft

STEP 2 **Find** the area.

$A = \pi r^2$ **Write formula for area of a circle.**

$\approx \dfrac{22}{7}(21)^2$ **Substitute $\dfrac{22}{7}$ for π and 21 for r.**

$= 1386$ **Simplify.**

▶ **Answer** The area of the ring is about 1386 square feet.

 Animated Math at classzone.com

★ EXAMPLE 3 Standardized Test Practice

Parks A circular pond in a park has an area of 615.44 square yards. What expression can be evaluated to find the radius of the pond?

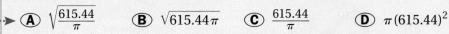

ELIMINATE CHOICES
From the area formula, you can see that the radius will be less than 615.44. Choice D is too great, so it can be eliminated.

  Ⓐ $\sqrt{\dfrac{615.44}{\pi}}$ Ⓑ $\sqrt{615.44\,\pi}$ Ⓒ $\dfrac{615.44}{\pi}$ Ⓓ $\pi(615.44)^2$

SOLUTION

$A = \pi r^2$ **Write formula for area of a circle.**

$615.44 = \pi r^2$ **Substitute 615.44 for A.**

$\dfrac{615.44}{\pi} = r^2$ **Divide each side by π.**

$\sqrt{\dfrac{615.44}{\pi}} = r$ **Take positive square root of each side.**

$14 \approx r$ **Simplify.**

▶ **Answer** The expression that gives the radius of the pond is $\sqrt{\dfrac{615.44}{\pi}}$, which is about 14 yards. The correct answer is A. Ⓐ Ⓑ Ⓒ Ⓓ

✓ GUIDED PRACTICE for Examples 1, 2, and 3

Find the area of the circle. Use $\dfrac{22}{7}$ or 3.14 for π.

  1. radius = 8 mm   **2.** diameter = 14 in.   **3.** radius = 11 ft

  4. What If? In Example 3, suppose the pond has an area of 907.46 square yards. Write and evaluate an expression to find the radius of the pond.

11.7 EXERCISES

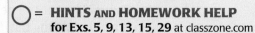
SKILL PRACTICE

VOCABULARY Match the measurement with the value for the circle.

1. radius, in feet   **A.** 28.26
2. area, in square feet   **B.** 18.84
3. diameter, in feet   **C.** 6
4. circumference, in feet   **D.** 3

3 ft

FINDING AREA Find the area of the circle. Use 3.14 for π.

SEE EXAMPLES 1 AND 2
on pp. 612–613
for Exs. 5–11

5. $d = 13$ in.

6. $d = 24.2$ cm

7. $r = 5$ in.

8. $d = 34$ mm

9. $r = 13.25$ mm

10. $r = 1.3$ in.

11. ERROR ANALYSIS Describe and correct the error made in finding the area of a circle with a diameter of 4 inches.

$$\times \quad \begin{aligned} A &= \pi r^2 \\ &\approx (3.14)(4)^2 \\ &= 50.24 \text{ in.}^2 \end{aligned}$$

USING AREA Find the radius and the diameter of the circle with the given area. Use 3.14 for π.

SEE EXAMPLE 3
on p. 613
for Exs. 12–17

12. $A = 200.96$ cm^2
13. $A = 254.34$ ft^2
14. $A = 2122.64$ m^2
15. $A = 706.5$ km^2
16. $A = 1133.54$ mm^2
17. $A = 2640.74$ in.^{2}

USING CIRCUMFERENCE Find the area of the circle with the given circumference. Use 3.14 for π.

18. $C = 15.7$ mm
19. $C = 18.84$ m
20. $C = 62.8$ ft
21. $C = 9.42$ in.
22. $C = 37.68$ cm
23. $C = 21.98$ yd

24. ★ **MULTIPLE CHOICE** The circumference of a circle is 25 centimeters. Which estimate is closest to the area of the circle?

(A) 8 cm^2 **(B)** 16 cm^2 **(C)** 50 cm^2 **(D)** 156 cm^2

COMBINED FIGURES Find the area of the shaded region. Use 3.14 for π.

25.
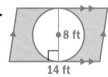
8 ft
14 ft

26.
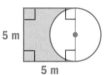
5 m
5 m

27.
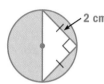
2 cm

28. **CHALLENGE** The figure shows a right triangle with $a < b$. Semicircles are drawn on each side. How does the area of the smallest semicircle compare to the areas of the other two semicircles? *Explain.*

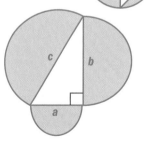
c
b
a

PROBLEM SOLVING

SEE EXAMPLES
1 AND 2

on pp. 612–613
for Exs. 29–31

29. **CALENDARS** The top of an Aztec calendar stone is a circle 12 feet in diameter. What is the area of the top of the stone? Use 3.14 for π.

30. **WORLD MAP** There is a circular world map with a radius of 50 feet at the U.S. Navy Memorial in Washington, D.C. What is the area of the world map?

31. ★ **MULTIPLE CHOICE** A penny has a diameter of 19.05 millimeters. What is the approximate area of one side of the coin?

(A) 19.05π mm^2 (B) 38.1π mm^2 (C) 90.7π mm^2 (D) 362.9π mm^2

32. ★ **WRITING** *Explain* how to find the area of a circle, given its circumference.

33. ★ **SHORT RESPONSE** A circular fountain has a diameter of 8.5 meters. What is the area of the fountain? The outermost meter of the fountain is a pool where water collects and recirculates. What is the area of the pool? Round your answers to the nearest tenth and *explain.*

34. ◆ **MULTIPLE REPRESENTATIONS** Use the table below that relates the radius, circumference, and area of circles.

a. **Making a Table** Copy and complete the table at the right.

b. **Making a Graph** Plot the ordered pairs (r, C) and (r, A) using data from the table. *Describe* how changing the radius affects circumference and area.

Radius, r (m)	Circumference, C (m)	Area, A (m²)
2	$2\pi(2) = 4\pi$	$\pi(2)^2 = 4\pi$
4	?	?
6	?	?
8	?	?

c. **Writing an Equation** Write an equation relating the circumference C of a circle to its area A.

35. NUMBER SENSE Is it possible for a circle to have the same value for its circumference and area? *Explain* your reasoning.

36. CHALLENGE All of the circles on the target have the same center. The distance between circles is 2 inches and the area of the red circle is π square inches. What is the area of the blue portion?

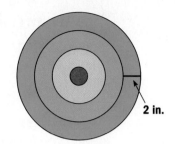

2 in.

 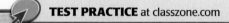
37. The figure at the right was transformed from quadrant II to quadrant III. Which type of transformation does this represent?

    (A) Dilation

    (B) Tessellation

    (C) Rotation

    (D) Reflection

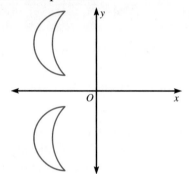

QUIZ *for Lessons 11.4–11.7*

Find the area of the triangle, trapezoid, or circle. Use 3.14 for π.

1. 16 cm *(p. 601)* 6 cm

2. 9 in. *(p. 601)* 7.5 in. 15 in.

3. *(p. 612)* 4 m

4. WRISTWATCH The face of a wristwatch is a parallelogram. The base is 2.75 centimeters, and the height is 2 centimeters. Find the area. *(p. 594)*

Find the unknown height, diameter, or base of the figure. Use 3.14 for π.

5. $A = 11.7 \text{ m}^2$ *(p. 594)*

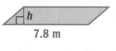

h 7.8 m

6. $C = 396 \text{ cm}$ *(p. 607)*

d

7. $A = 10.72 \text{ mm}^2$ *(p. 601)*

1.9 mm 4 mm b_2

8. A triangle has an area of 14.6 square inches. Its height is 4 inches. Find its base. *(p. 601)*

11.7 Using Square Roots and Pi

You can use the keystrokes 2nd [√] and the π key to evaluate expressions.

EXAMPLE 1 A square field has an area of 4840 square yards, or 1 acre. Between what two whole-number lengths does the length of a side of the field fall? Use a calculator to check your answer.

SOLUTION

Because 4840 falls between the perfect squares $4761 = 69^2$ and $4900 = 70^2$, you know that $\sqrt{4840}$ falls between 69 and 70.

Check your answer by evaluating $\sqrt{4840}$.

Keystrokes	Display
2nd [√] **4840**) =	69.57010852

▶ **Answer** The length falls between 69 yards and 70 yards.

EXAMPLE 2 Evaluate 16π. Round to the nearest hundredth.

SOLUTION

Keystrokes	Display
16 π =	50.26548246

▶ **Answer** $16\pi \approx 50.27$

PRACTICE

Approximate the square root to the nearest whole number. Then use a calculator to check your answer.

1. $\sqrt{467}$ **2.** $\sqrt{1056}$ **3.** $\sqrt{4356}$ **4.** $\sqrt{37{,}888}$

Use a calculator to evaluate the expression. Round to the nearest hundredth.

5. 41π **6.** 36π **7.** π^3 **8.** $14\pi^2$

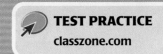
Lessons 11.4–11.7

1. ORIGAMI The figure shown is created when folding a piece of paper. Which equation will NOT give the area of the figure?

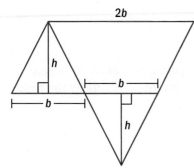

A. $A = \frac{1}{2}(b + 2b)(h) + 2\left(\frac{1}{2}\right)bh$

B. $A = (2b)(h) + \frac{1}{2}bh$

C. $A = \frac{1}{2}bh + \frac{1}{2}(2b)(2h)$

D. $A = (2b)(2h) + 2\left(\frac{1}{2}\right)bh$

2. KITCHEN TILE A square kitchen tile has a circular design on it, as shown. What is the ratio of the circumference of the circle to the perimeter of the square?

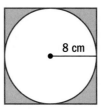
8 cm

A. $\frac{\pi}{4}$ **C.** $\frac{\pi}{2}$

B. $\frac{4}{\pi}$ **D.** $\frac{2}{\pi}$

3. LARGEST CLOCKS One of the largest inclined clocks in the world is being constructed in the United Arab Emirates. The front of the finished circular clock will have an area of about 91.6 square meters. What is the approximate diameter of the clock?

A. 2.7 meters   **C.** 10.8 meters

B. 5.4 meters   **D.** 29.2 meters

4. BASEBALL During a baseball game, a player may stand in the on-deck circle while waiting for a turn at bat. The on-deck circle has a diameter of 5 feet. Find the area of the circle, in square feet. Round your answer to the nearest tenth.

A. 7.9 ft^2

B. 15.7 ft^2

C. 19.6 ft^2

D. 78.5 ft^2

5. OPEN-ENDED A teacher hands out four sheets of $8\frac{1}{2}$ by 11 inch paper to each student. The instructions are to cut out a circle, a triangle, a parallelogram, and a trapezoid that have the same area. The first shape you cut is a circle with a diameter of 7 inches. What are possible dimensions of the remaining shapes? Use $\pi = \frac{22}{7}$.

REVIEW KEY VOCABULARY

- square root, *p. 577*
- perfect square, *p. 577*
- square number, *p. 577*
- radical expression, *p. 578*
- irrational number, *p. 583*
- real number, *p. 583*

- hypotenuse, legs, *p. 588*
- Pythagorean Theorem, *p. 588*
- base of a parallelogram, *p. 594*
- height of a parallelogram, *p. 594*
- base of a triangle, *p. 601*
- height of a triangle, *p. 601*

- bases of a trapezoid, *p. 602*
- height of a trapezoid, *p. 602*
- circle, *p. 607*
- center, *p. 607*
- radius, diameter, *p. 607*
- circumference, *p. 607*

VOCABULARY EXERCISES

Copy and complete the statement.

1. The expression $\sqrt{5(3 + 4)}$ is called a(n) __?__.

2. The side opposite the right angle in a right triangle is the __?__.

3. The lengths of the legs and the hypotenuse of any right triangle are related by the __?__.

4. The distance across a circle through the center is its __?__.

5. The number π is a(n) __?__ number.

6. The distance around a circle is its __?__.

REVIEW EXAMPLES AND EXERCISES

11.1 Square Roots
pp. 577–581

EXAMPLE

Evaluate $\sqrt{36 - x + y}$ when $x = -28$ and $y = 36$.

$$\sqrt{36 - x + y} = \sqrt{36 - (-28) + 36}$$ Substitute −28 for *x* and 36 for *y*.

$$= \sqrt{100}$$ Simplify under the radical.

$$= 10$$ Evaluate square root.

EXERCISES

Find the two square roots of the number.

*SEE EXAMPLES
1 AND 4*
on pp. 577–578
for Exs. 7–14

7. 49   8. 25   9. 441   10. 169

Evaluate the expression when $t = 4$ and $d = 6$.

11. $\sqrt{9t}$ 12. $-\sqrt{3t^3 + 4}$ 13. $\sqrt{d^2 + dt - 11}$ 14. $\sqrt{6dt}$

11.2 Approximating Square Roots

pp. 582–586

EXAMPLE

Approximate $\sqrt{86}$ to the nearest whole number.

STEP 1 **Determine** the whole numbers closest to $\sqrt{86}$.

$$81 < 86 < 100$$ **Identify perfect squares closest to 86.**

$$\sqrt{81} < \sqrt{86} < \sqrt{100}$$ **Take positive square root of each number.**

$$9 < \sqrt{86} < 10$$ **Evaluate square roots.**

STEP 2 **Square** the decimal halfway between 9 and 10: $9.5^2 = 90.25$.

Because 86 is between 9^2 and 9.5^2, $\sqrt{86}$ is between 9 and 9.5. $\sqrt{86}$ is closer to 9.

▶ **Answer** To the nearest whole number, $\sqrt{86} \approx 9$.

EXERCISES

SEE EXAMPLES 1 AND 4 on pp. 582, 584 for Exs. 15–18

Tell whether the number is *rational* or *irrational*. If it is irrational, approximate to the nearest whole number. If it is rational, evaluate.

15. $\sqrt{29}$ **16.** $\sqrt{52}$ **17.** $\sqrt{9}$ **18.** $\sqrt{230}$

11.3 The Pythagorean Theorem

pp. 588–592

EXAMPLE

Find the unknown length in the right triangle shown.

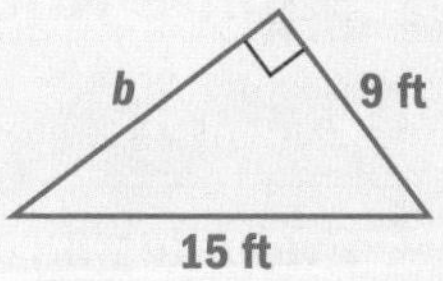

$$a^2 + b^2 = c^2$$ **Write Pythagorean Theorem.**

$$9^2 + b^2 = 15^2$$ **Substitute 9 for *a* and 15 for *c*.**

$$b^2 = 144$$ **Simplify.**

$$b = \sqrt{144}$$ **Take positive square root of each side.**

$$b = 12 \text{ ft}$$ **Evaluate square root.**

EXERCISES

SEE EXAMPLES 1, 2, AND 3 on pp. 588–589 for Exs. 19–24

A right triangle has legs of lengths *a* and *b* and hypotenuse of length *c*. Find the unknown length. Round to the nearest tenth, if necessary.

19. $a = 6$ in., $c = 10$ in. **20.** $a = 2.9$ cm, $b = 1.2$ cm **21.** $b = 45$ mm, $c = 53$ mm

22. $b = 10$ m, $c = 12$ m **23.** $a = 7$ ft, $b = 24$ ft **24.** $a = 0.9$ in., $c = 4.1$ in.

11.4 Area of a Parallelogram

pp. 594–598

EXAMPLE

Find the area of the parallelogram shown.

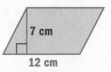

$A = bh$ Write formula for area of a parallelogram.

$= 12(7)$ Substitute 12 for b and 7 for h.

$= 84 \text{ cm}^2$ Multiply.

SEE EXAMPLES
1 AND 2
on p. 595
for Exs. 25–26

EXERCISES

Find the unknown area, base, or height of the parallelogram.

25. $A = \underline{\ ?\ } \text{ in.}^2$, $b = 6$ in., $h = 10.5$ in.   **26.** $A = 61.6 \text{ m}^2$, $b = 11.2$ m, $h = \underline{\ ?\ }$ m

11.5 Areas of Triangles and Trapezoids

pp. 601–606

EXAMPLE

Find the area of the triangle or trapezoid.

a.

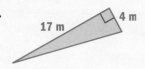

$A = \frac{1}{2}bh$

$= \frac{1}{2}(17)(4)$

$= 34 \text{ m}^2$

b.

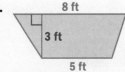

$A = \frac{1}{2}(b_1 + b_2)h$

$= \frac{1}{2}(5 + 8)3$

$= 19.5 \text{ ft}^2$

SEE EXAMPLES
1, 2, 3, AND 4
on pp. 601–603
for Exs. 27–31

EXERCISES

Find the area or the unknown base or height of the triangle or trapezoid.

27. $A = 12 \text{ in.}^2$

28.

29.

30. $A = 35 \text{ yd}^2$

31. Architecture The wall above a garage door is an isosceles triangle with base 24 feet and height 8 feet. What is the area of this wall?

11.6 Circumference of a Circle
pp. 607–611

EXAMPLE

Find the circumference of the circle. Use 3.14 for π.

1.5 ft

$C = 2\pi r$ **Write formula for circumference of a circle.**

$\approx 2(3.14)(1.5)$ **Substitute 3.14 for π and 1.5 for r.**

$= 9.42$ ft   **Multiply.**

▶ **Answer** The circumference of the circle is about 9.42 feet.

EXERCISES

Find the circumference of the circle with the given radius r or diameter d. Use $\frac{22}{7}$ or 3.14 for π.

SEE EXAMPLES 1 AND 2
on p. 608
for Exs. 32–36

32. $d = 19$ mm   **33.** $d = 42$ cm   **34.** $r = 28$ in.   **35.** $r = 17$ m

36. Trim How many inches of trim are needed to put an edging around a circular tablecloth that is 60 inches in diameter?

11.7 Area of a Circle
pp. 612–616

EXAMPLE

Find the area of the circle shown. Use 3.14 for π.

1.5 ft

$C = \pi r^2$ **Write formula for area of a circle.**

$\approx 3.14(1.5)^2$ **Substitute 3.14 for π and 1.5 for r.**

$= 7.065$ ft^2 **Multiply.**

▶ **Answer** The area of the circle is about 7.065 square feet.

EXERCISES

Find the area of the circle with the given radius r or diameter d. Use $\frac{22}{7}$ or 3.14 for π.

SEE EXAMPLES 1 AND 2
on pp. 612–613
for Exs. 37–41

37. $r = 7$ km   **38.** $r = 13$ mm   **39.** $d = 34$ in.   **40.** $d = 9$ mi

41. Gardening Shonda is putting a circular tulip bed in her backyard. The radius is 3.2 feet. How many square feet of her lawn will she lose when she puts in the tulip bed?

Find the two square roots of the number.

1. 225   **2.** 1   **3.** 16   **4.** 324

Evaluate the expression when $a = 25$ and $b = 7$.

5. $\sqrt{a^2 + 104}$ **6.** $\sqrt{10b + 11}$ **7.** $\sqrt{3b + 15}$ **8.** $\sqrt{a^2 + 150b - 75}$

Approximate the square root to the nearest whole number.

9. $\sqrt{18}$ **10.** $\sqrt{43}$ **11.** $\sqrt{105}$ **12.** $\sqrt{135}$

Tell whether the number is *rational* or *irrational*. *Explain* your reasoning.

13. $\sqrt{5}$ **14.** $\sqrt{121}$ **15.** $\sqrt{54}$ **16.** 2.67

Find the unknown length. Round to the nearest tenth if necessary.

17. 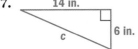   **18.**   **19.**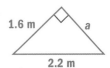

Find the area of the parallelogram, triangle, or trapezoid.

20. 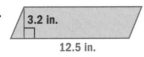   **21.** 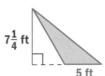   **22.**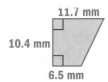

Use the area of A to find the unknown base or height of the parallelogram, triangle, or trapezoid.

23. $A = 289 \text{ m}^2$ **24.** $A = 126.1 \text{ yd}^2$ **25.** $A = 202.5 \text{ in.}^2$

Find the circumference and the area of the circle with the given radius r or diameter d. Use $\frac{22}{7}$ or 3.14 for π.

26. $r = 20 \text{ ft}$ **27.** $r = 0.4 \text{ mm}$ **28.** $d = 28 \text{ in.}$

29. EYEGLASSES The circumference of a circular eyeglass lens is 4 inches. What is the approximate radius? Use 3.14 for π. Round your answer to the nearest tenth of an inch.

MULTIPLE CHOICE QUESTIONS

If you have difficulty solving a multiple choice problem directly, you may be able to use another approach to eliminate incorrect answer choices and obtain the correct answer.

PROBLEM 1

A parallelogram's area is 75 square meters. The base of the parallelogram is three times as long as its height. What are the base and height of the parallelogram?

A. $b = 75$ m   **B.** $b = 21.3$ m   **C.** $b = 15$ m   **D.** $b = 10.5$ m
  $h = 25$ m $h = 7.1$ m $h = 5$ m $h = 3.5$ m

METHOD 1

SOLVE DIRECTLY Use the formula $A = bh$ to find the base and height of the parallelogram.

STEP 1 **Write** an expression for the base. Because the base is three times as long as the height, you can represent the base with the equation $b = 3h$.

STEP 2 **Substitute** the base into the formula for the area of a parallelogram.

$A = bh$	Write formula.
$75 = (3h)(h)$	Substitute for *A* and *b*.
$75 = 3h^2$	Multiply.
$25 = h^2$	Divide each side by 3.
$\sqrt{25} = h$	Take positive square root.
$5 = h$	Evaluate.

The height of the parallelogram is 5 meters.

STEP 3 **Substitute** 5 for *h* to find the base.

$$b = 3h = 15$$

The base of the parallelogram is 15 meters.

The correct answer is C.

METHOD 2

ELIMINATE CHOICES In some multiple choice questions, you can identify answer choices that can be eliminated.

First check that all bases are three times the height. This is true for all choices.

Next use the formula and mental math to try to eliminate choices.

Choice A: $b = 75$ m, $h = 25$ m

Because the base is 75 m, the only height that will give an area of 75 m² is $h = 1$ m. ✗

You can eliminate choice A.

Choice B: $b = 21.3$ m, $h = 7.1$ m

$$A = bh = 21.3(7.1) \approx 20(7) = 140 \text{ ✗}$$

You can eliminate choice B.

Choice C: $b = 15$ m, $h = 5$ m

Substitute 15 for *b* and 5 for *h* in the area formula.

$$A = bh = 15(5) = 75 = 75 \text{ ✓}$$

The correct answer is C.

PROBLEM 2

Eight identical square tiles are used to create a mosaic that covers an area of 98 square centimeters. What is the side length of each tile?

A. 3 cm **B.** 3.5 cm **C.** 4.25 cm **D.** 12.25 cm

METHOD 1

SOLVE DIRECTLY Write and solve an equation for the side length of one tile.

STEP 1 **Find** the area of one of the eight identical tiles.

$98 \div 8 = 12.25$

The area of one tile is 12.25 cm^2.

STEP 2 **Use** the formula for the area of a square to find the side length.

$A = s^2$ **Write formula.**

$12.25 = s^2$ **Substitute for A.**

$\sqrt{12.25} = s$ **Take positive square root.**

$3.5 = s$ **Evaluate.**

The correct answer is B.

METHOD 2

ELIMINATE CHOICES In some multiple choice questions, you can identify answer choices that can be eliminated.

Let x be the side length of a tile. Because the tiles are identical and square, the area of 8 tiles is $8x^2$.

Choice A: 3 cm

Substitute 3 for x in $8x^2$.

$8x^2 = 8(3)^2 = 8(9) = 72 \neq 98$✗

A side length of 3 cm produces too small an area. You can eliminate choice A.

Choice B: 3.5 cm

Substitute 3.5 for x in $8x^2$.

$8x^2 = 8(3.5)^2 = 8(12.25) = 98$✓

The correct answer is B.

PRACTICE

Explain why you can eliminate the highlighted answer choice.

1. The foundation of a square garage has an area of 78 square yards. What is the approximate length of a side of the foundation?

   A. 7.8 yd **B.** 8.8 yd **C.** 8.9 yd ✗ **D.** 19.5 yd

2. A section of a park is designated as an off-leash area for dogs. This fenced-in section is triangular and has an area of 1760 square feet. The base is 80 feet. What is the height of the triangle?

   A. 20 ft ✗ **B.** 22 ft **C.** 44 ft **D.** 88 ft

3. A parallelogram has an area of 168.56 square inches. The base is 17.2 inches. What is the height of the parallelogram?

   A. 9.8 in. **B.** 12.98 in. **C.** 19.6 in. ✗ **D.** 67.18 in.

1. What is the combined area of the two right triangles?

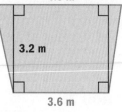

4.8 m

3.2 m

3.6 m

A. 1.92 m²

B. 7.68 m²

C. 11.52 m²

D. 13.44 m²

2. What is the area of the shaded region inside the parallelogram?

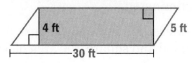

4 ft

5 ft

30 ft

A. 20 ft²

B. 108 ft²

C. 120 ft²

D. 150 ft²

3. A small window is shaped like a quarter circle, as shown. The area of the window is about 28.26 square inches. What is the radius of the circle? Use 3.14 for π.

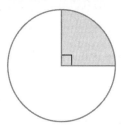

A. 4 in.

B. 5 in.

C. 6 in.

D. 7 in.

4. What method can be used to find the side length of a square, given the area of the square?

A. Divide the area by 2.

B. Find the positive square root of the area.

C. Square the area.

D. Divide the area by 4.

5. The model below represents the equation $2x + 4 = 6$.

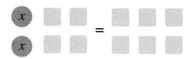

What is the first step in finding the value of x?

A. Add 6 squares to each side of the model.

B. Subtract 4 squares from each side of the model.

C. Subtract 2 squares from each side of the model.

D. Add 2 squares to the left side of the model.

6. A woodworker made 15 dressers and sold 4 of them. Which best represents the percent of dressers the woodworker made that were NOT sold?

A. 5%

B. 11%

C. 27%

D. 73%

TEST PREPARATION

7. A recipe that makes 2 loaves of bread calls for $\frac{3}{4}$ cup of sugar. Which expression could be used to find the amount of sugar needed to make 5 loaves of bread using this recipe?

A. $2 \times \frac{3}{4}$

B. $2.5 \times \frac{3}{4}$

C. $2 + \frac{3}{4}$

D. $5 \div \frac{3}{4}$

8. Which expression represents the perimeter of the figure?

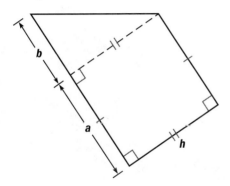

A. $a + b + 2h$

B. $2a + b + h + \sqrt{a^2 + h^2}$

C. $2a + b + h + \sqrt{h^2 + b^2}$

D. $2a + b + h + \sqrt{a^2 + b^2}$

9. A \$215 camera is on sale for 30% off. What is the amount of the discount?

A. \$7.20

B. \$64.50

C. \$150.50

D. \$185.00

10. Triangle *RST* and triangle *LMN* are similar.

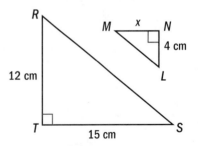

What is the length of $\overline{MN}$?

A. 2 cm

B. 3 cm

C. 3.2 cm

D. 5 cm

11. OPEN-ENDED A rotating sprinkler waters a circular garden with a radius of 24 meters. A second rotating sprinkler waters another circular garden with one-third the radius.

Part A How many times greater is the area of the larger garden than the area of the smaller garden?

Part B Is this relationship true for any pair of circles where the radius of the smaller circle is one-third the radius of the larger circle? *Explain.*

TEST PREPARATION

12 Surface Area and Volume

Before

In previous chapters you've ...

- Evaluated expressions
- Used area formulas

Now

 New Jersey Standards

4.2.A.2.c	12.1	Classifying solids
4.2.A.2.c	12.2	Sketching solids
4.2.A.2.c	12.3	Prism surface area
4.2.A.2.c	12.4	Cylinder surface area
4.2.A.2.c	12.5	Prism volume
4.2.A.2.c	12.6	Cylinder volume

Why?

So you can solve real-world problems about ...

- stadium cushions, p. 643
- balance boards, p. 650
- watermelons, p. 658
- coins, p. 666

 **Math**
at classzone.com

- Classifying Solids, p. 632
- Sketching Solids, p. 637
- Volume of Cylinders and Rectangular Prisms, p. 667

Get-Ready Games

Review Prerequisite Skills
by playing *Basketball Blitz*.

Skill Focus:
Using area formulas

BASKETBALL BLITZ

Did you know that basketball is the most popular indoor sport in the world? In this get-ready game, you'll find the areas of different parts of a basketball court in order to find the year in which basketball was invented.

HOW TO PLAY

1 **FIND** the areas of the different parts of a basketball court, as described on the next page.

2 **USE** the numbers from your answers to evaluate the expression below. The value of the expression is the year in which basketball was invented.

(− + 14) × (+ 43)

6 ft

19 ft

4 ft

12 ft

The blue rectangle and half circle are called the key. Find the area of the key to the nearest square foot.

18 in.

The rim of the basket is a circle. Find the area enclosed by the rim to the nearest square inch. Use 3.14 for π.

2 ft

1.5 ft

3.5 ft

6 ft

The diagram above shows a rectangular backboard. Find the area of the red region.

Stop and Think

1. **CRITICAL THINKING** A player stands on the edge of the key as far from the basket as possible. How far is the player from the basket?

2. **WRITING** In the diagram of the backboard, are the large and small rectangles similar? Explain your reasoning.

Review Prerequisite Skills

VOCABULARY CHECK

Copy and complete using a review word from the list at the left.

1. A(n) __?__ is the set of all points in a plane that are the same distance from a fixed point.

2. The distance around a circle is called its __?__.

3. The __?__ of a rectangle is the sum of the lengths of the sides.

SKILL CHECK

Find the perimeter and the area of the rectangle. *(p. 32)*

4.
4 cm
3 cm

5.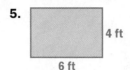
4 ft
6 ft

6.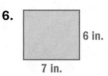
6 in.
7 in.

Evaluate the expression.

7. $4^2 + 3 \times 4 - 10$ *(p. 17)*   **8.** $3.14(5^2)(6)$ *(p. 66)*   **9.** $2(3.14)(7^2)$ *(p. 66)*

Find the radius and the diameter of the circle with the given area. Use 3.14 for π. *(p. 612)*

10. $A = 78.5$ in.^{2} **11.** $A = 530.66$ ft^2 **12.** $A = 314$ cm^2

@HomeTutor   Prerequisite skills practice at classzone.com

Notetaking Skills   Summarizing

In each chapter you will learn a new notetaking skill. In the last lesson of Chapter 12 you can apply the strategy of summarizing.

When you finish a lesson or group of lessons, write a summary of the main ideas in your notebook. Later, when you prepare for a test, you can use your summary as a starting point for checking your knowledge of the material.

Circles

A circle has a radius r and a diameter d.

Area $= \pi r^2$

Circumference $= \pi d = 2\pi r$

$A = \pi r^2$ $C = \pi d$

π is an irrational number approximately equal to 3.14 and to $\frac{22}{7}$.

12.1 Classifying Solids

4.2.A.2.c Models of 3D objects

Before	You classified polygons.
Now	You'll classify solids and identify their parts.
Why?	So you can describe the shapes of real-world objects, as in Example 1.

KEY VOCABULARY
- **solid,** *p. 631*
- **prism,** *p. 631*
- **pyramid,** *p. 631*
- **cylinder,** *p. 631*
- **cone,** *p. 631*
- **sphere,** *p. 631*
- **face, edge, vertex,** *p. 632*

A **solid** is a three-dimensional figure that encloses a part of space.

Classifying Solids

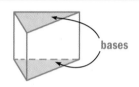

A **prism** is a solid formed by polygons. Prisms have two congruent bases that lie in parallel planes.

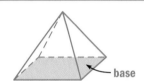

A **pyramid** is a solid formed by polygons. The base can be any polygon, and the other polygons are triangles.

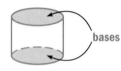

A **cylinder** is a solid with two congruent circular bases that lie in parallel planes.

A **cone** is a solid with one circular base.

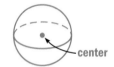

A **sphere** is a solid formed by all points in space that are the same distance from a fixed point called the center.

EXAMPLE 1 Classifying Solids

Classify the solid as a prism, pyramid, cylinder, cone, or sphere.

a.

cone

b.

pyramid

c.

cylinder

 GUIDED PRACTICE for Example 1

1. Classify the glass solid pictured in the photo at the top of the page.

Prisms and Pyramids Prisms and pyramids can be more specifically classified by the shapes of their bases. For example, a prism whose bases are triangles, such as the one at the top of the previous page, is a *triangular prism*.

 EXAMPLE 2 Standardized Test Practice

Geometry Which solid is made up of a pentagon and five triangles?

(A) Pentagonal prism   **(B)** Triangular prism

(C) Pentagonal pyramid   **(D)** Square pyramid

ELIMINATE CHOICES
All but one of the faces in the solid are triangles. This means the solid must be a pyramid. So, choices A and B can be eliminated.

SOLUTION

A pyramid is a solid made up of triangles and a polygonal base. When its base is a pentagon, a pyramid is a *pentagonal pyramid*.

▶ **Answer** A pentagonal pyramid is made up of a pentagon and five triangles. The correct answer is C. **(A) (B) (C) (D)**

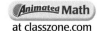
Animated Math
at classzone.com

Faces, Edges, and Vertices When polygons form the sides of a solid, the sides are called **faces**. The line segments where the faces meet are **edges**. Each point where the edges meet is a **vertex**.

EXAMPLE 3 Counting Faces, Edges, and Vertices

A *cube* is a rectangular prism whose faces are all congruent squares. Count the number of faces, edges, and vertices in a cube.

AVOID ERRORS
Don't forget to count the hidden edges of a solid. The dashed lines are used to show the hidden edges.

6 faces   **12 edges**   **8 vertices**

▶ **Answer** A cube has 6 faces, 12 edges, and 8 vertices.

 GUIDED PRACTICE   for Examples 2 and 3

Classify the solid. Be as specific as possible.

2.   **3.**   **4.**

5. Count the number of faces, edges, and vertices in the solid in Exercise 2.

12.1 EXERCISES

HOMEWORK KEY

★ = **STANDARDIZED TEST PRACTICE**
Exs. 12, 24, 25, 27, 28, 29, and 35

◯ = **HINTS AND HOMEWORK HELP**
for Exs. 3, 7, 9, 23 at classzone.com

SKILL PRACTICE

1. **VOCABULARY** Copy and complete: The polygons that form the sides of a prism or pyramid are called ___?___.

2. **VOCABULARY** Name three types of solids that do not have any faces or edges.

CLASSIFYING SOLIDS Classify the solid as a *prism, pyramid, cylinder, cone,* or *sphere.*

on p. 631
for Exs. 3–8

3.

4.

5.

6.

7.

8.

PRISMS AND PYRAMIDS Classify the solid. Be as specific as possible. Then count the number of faces, edges, and vertices in the solid.

SEE EXAMPLES
2 AND 3
on p. 632
for Exs. 9–12

9.

10.

11.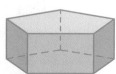

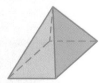

12. ★ **MULTIPLE CHOICE** What is the name of the solid shown?

    (A) Triangular pyramid   (B) Rectangular prism

    (C) Triangular prism   (D) Rectangular pyramid

13. **ERROR ANALYSIS** Describe and correct the error made in classifying the solid.

 The solid has rectangular faces, so it is a rectangular prism.

REASONING In Exercises 14–17, tell whether the statement is *true* or *false*. If it is false, change one word in the statement to make it true.

14. A prism has one base that is a polygon.

15. A cube has 12 congruent edges.

16. A cylinder has two congruent circular bases.

17. Any pair of opposite faces of a rectangular prism can be the bases.

18. ✖ **ALGEBRA** A pyramid has *x* vertices. How many sides does the base have? *Explain* your reasoning.

19. **CHALLENGE** The ice cube tray shown below makes ice cubes whose faces are slanted outward on four sides for easier removal from the tray. Are the ice cubes prisms? *Explain* your reasoning.

Side view

Front view

In Exercises 20–22, use the definition of *skew* in the following example, and use the lines that contain the edges of the triangular prism in the diagram.

IDENTIFY LINES
Need help with parallel and perpendicular lines? See p. 516.

EXTENSION Parallel, Perpendicular, and Skew Lines

Two lines are *skew* if they do *not* intersect and are *not* parallel. Identify a pair of parallel lines, perpendicular lines, and skew lines that contain edges of the rectangular prism shown.

SOLUTION

Lines *e* and *f* are parallel.

Lines *g* and *f* are perpendicular.

Lines *e* and *g* are skew because they do *not* intersect and are *not* parallel.

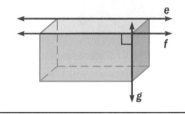

---

20. Name a pair of parallel lines.

21. Name a pair of perpendicular lines.

22. Name a pair of skew lines.

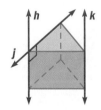

PROBLEM SOLVING

SEE EXAMPLES 2 AND 3
on p. 632 for Ex. 23

23. **ARCHITECTURE** Classify the solid represented by the house shown. Be as specific as possible. Then give the number of faces, edges, and vertices.

24. ★ **WRITING** *Describe* the differences and similarities between a cylinder and a cone. *Describe* the differences and similarities between a pyramid and a prism.

25. ★ MULTIPLE CHOICE The unsharpened end of a wooden pencil is a regular hexagon. You saw off a piece of the pencil along the red line segments shown. Which term best classifies the shape of the piece you sawed off?

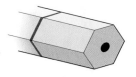

(**A**) Prism   (**B**) Pyramid   (**C**) Cylinder   (**D**) Cone

26. COMPOSITE FIGURE The solid shown at the right is a composite figure formed by joining a pentagonal pyramid and a pentagonal prism. Count the number of faces, edges, and vertices in the solid.

27. ★ OPEN-ENDED MATH Name three types of prisms that are *not* triangular.

28. ★ WRITING The diagram at the right shows a *hemisphere*. What do you think the prefix "hemi" means? *Explain* your reasoning.

29. ★ SHORT RESPONSE What happens to the shape of a pyramid as the number of faces increases? *Explain.*

30. CHALLENGE Copy and complete the table for each solid shown. Then use your results to describe the relationship between the number of edges and the sum of the number of faces and number of vertices.

Solid				
Faces F	?	?	?	?
Vertices V	?	?	?	?
Edges E	?	?	?	?
F + V	?	?	?	?

NEW JERSEY MIXED REVIEW

TEST PRACTICE at classzone.com

31. A circle of crops has an area of 908 square yards. Which expression can be used to find the diameter of the circle?

(**A**) $\sqrt{\dfrac{908}{\pi}}$ (**B**) $2\sqrt{\dfrac{908}{\pi}}$

(**C**) $2\sqrt{908\pi}$ (**D**) $908\pi^2$

32. What is the approximate area of the shaded region?

(**A**) 177 mm^2 (**B**) 353 mm^2

(**C**) 530 mm^2 (**D**) 707 mm^2

15 mm

12.2 **Sketching Solids**

Before	You classified solids.
Now	You'll sketch solids.
Why?	So you can sketch objects, such as buildings in Ex. 20.

KEY VOCABULARY
- **prism,** *p. 631*
- **pyramid,** *p. 631*
- **cylinder,** *p. 631*
- **cone,** *p. 631*
- **sphere,** *p. 631*
- **face, edge, vertex,**
  p. 632

City Buildings The building shown in the photograph is shaped like a rectangular prism. Artists use various methods to draw solids so that they appear to be three-dimensional.

In Example 1, you will learn a method to sketch a rectangular prism. You can use this method to sketch other solids.

EXAMPLE 1 **Sketching a Prism**

Sketch a rectangular prism.

STEP 1
Sketch two congruent rectangles.

STEP 2
Connect corresponding vertices using line segments.

STEP 3
Change any "hidden" lines to dashed lines.

SHOW PERSPECTIVE
Four of the faces of the prism appear to be parallelograms even though they are actually rectangles. The parallelograms give the illusion of depth.

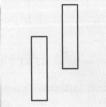

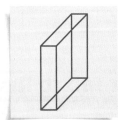

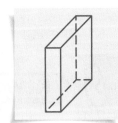

✓ **GUIDED PRACTICE** **for Example 1**

Sketch the solid.

1. Triangular prism
2. Prism with square bases

3. Copy and complete the sketch of an octagonal prism.

EXAMPLE 2 Sketching a Pyramid

Sketch a pentagonal pyramid.

STEP 1
Sketch a pentagon for the base and draw a dot directly above the pentagon.

STEP 2
Connect the vertices of the pentagon to the dot.

STEP 3
Change any "hidden" lines to dashed lines.

Animated Math at classzone.com

Three Views Another way to represent a three-dimensional figure using a two-dimensional drawing is to sketch three different views of the figure: a *top* view, a *side* view, and a *front* view.

EXAMPLE 3 Sketching Three Views of a Solid

Sketch the top, side, and front views of the triangular prism.

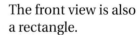

SOLUTION

The top view is a triangle.

The side view is a rectangle.

The front view is also a rectangle.

✓ **GUIDED PRACTICE**   for Examples 2 and 3

4. Sketch a rectangular pyramid.

5. Sketch the top, side, and front views of the rectangular pyramid you sketched in Exercise 4.

6. Sketch the top, side, and front views of the Pentagon Building in the photograph.

12.2 EXERCISES

SKILL PRACTICE

VOCABULARY Name the shape of the base of the solid.

1. Triangular prism
2. Rectangular pyramid
3. Cone

SEE EXAMPLES
1 AND 2
on pp. 636–637
for Exs. 4–11

4. SKETCHING A PYRAMID Copy the partial sketch of a pyramid with a square base. Then complete the drawing.

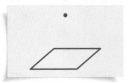

SKETCHING SOLIDS Sketch the solid.

5. Pentagonal prism
6. Hexagonal prism
7. Cone

8. Hexagonal pyramid
9. Octagonal pyramid
10. Cylinder

11. ERROR ANALYSIS Describe and correct the error made in sketching a rectangular prism.

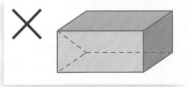

SKETCHING THREE VIEWS Sketch the top, side, and front views of the solid.

SEE EXAMPLE 3
on p. 637
for Exs. 12–16

12.

Front

13.

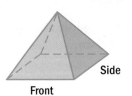

Side

Front

14.

Front

15. ★ MULTIPLE CHOICE Which solid has the three views shown?

Top

Side

Front

Ⓐ Triangular prism
Ⓑ Triangular pyramid

Ⓒ Square prism
Ⓓ Square pyramid

16. GIFT BOX Sketch the top, side, and front views of the gift box shown.

CHALLENGE Sketch a solid with the given numbers of faces, edges, and vertices.

17. 5 faces, 8 edges, 5 vertices

18. 4 faces, 6 edges, 4 vertices

(19.) ★ **MULTIPLE CHOICE** What is the shape of the front view of the cylindrical coliseum in the photo shown at the right?

Ⓐ Circle   Ⓑ Rectangle

Ⓒ Triangle   Ⓓ Oval

SEE EXAMPLE 3
on p. 637
for Ex. 20

20. **BUILDINGS** Sketch the top, side, and front views of the building shown in the photo on page 636.

21. ★ **SHORT RESPONSE** Sketch a triangular pyramid. Then count the number of faces, edges, and vertices in the pyramid. *Explain* how knowing the number of edges in a solid can help you sketch the solid.

22. **REASONING** A student sketches a solid that has five faces. Four of the faces are triangles, and one of the faces is a rectangle. What type of solid did the student sketch? Be as specific as possible. *Justify* your answer.

23. **REASONING** For which solid(s) is at least one of the three views a rectangle? a triangle? a circle?

A.   B.   C.

24. **CHALLENGE** When you slice through a solid, you create a cross section. One cross section of a cube creates a hexagon, as shown. Draw separate sketches of a cube that show cross sections of a triangle, a rectangle, and a pentagon.

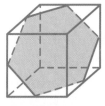

NEW JERSEY MIXED REVIEW
TEST PRACTICE at classzone.com

25. Which of the following solids always has at least one triangular face?

Ⓐ Prism   Ⓑ Pyramid   Ⓒ Cone   Ⓓ Cylinder

26. Mrs. Vasquez wants to paint a 16 foot by 10 foot wall, but not the door on the wall. How many square feet of wall does Mrs. Vasquez need to paint?

Ⓐ 24 ft^2 Ⓑ 136 ft^2

Ⓒ 160 ft^2 Ⓓ 184 ft^2

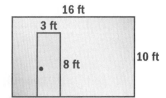

Viewing and Building Solids

GOAL Use top, side, and front views to build or draw a solid.

The solid shown below can be built using unit cubes. There are 9 unit cubes on the bottom layer and 3 unit cubes on the top layer. Modeling with unit cubes can help you identify the top, side, and front views of a solid.

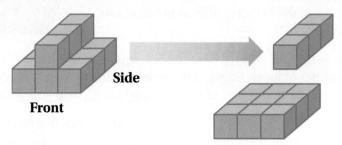

Front   Side

EXAMPLE 1   Drawing Top, Side, and Front Views

VIEWING SOLIDS
For the solids shown here, assume that there are no missing blocks in views that are not shown.

Draw the top, side, and front views of the solid shown above.

SOLUTION

STEP 1 To draw the top view, imagine what you would see if you were looking at the solid from directly above.

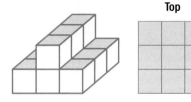

Top

STEP 2 To draw the side view, imagine what you would see if you were looking directly at one of the sides.

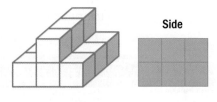

Side

STEP 3 To draw the front view, imagine what you would see if you were looking directly at the front.

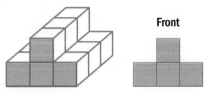

Front

Drawing a Solid Given the top, side, and front views of a solid, you can build or draw the solid. You need to use the information about the solid that each view gives to piece together the shape of the entire solid. You should look at more than one view at the same time to get a complete picture of the solid.

EXAMPLE 2 Using Top, Side, and Front Views

Use the three views of a solid to build and draw the solid.

Top

Side

Front

SOLUTION

STEP 1 The top view gives you information about the bottom layer of the solid.

Top

STEP 2 The side view gives you information about the number of layers and how to form them.

Side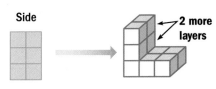

STEP 3 The front view also gives you information about the number of layers and how to form them.

Front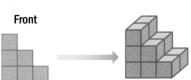

EXERCISES

Use unit cubes to build the solid. Then draw the top, side, and front views.

1.

2.

3.

Use the three views of a solid to build the solid using unit cubes. Then draw the solid.

4.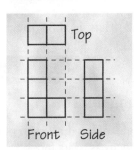

5.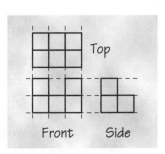

6. **REASONING** It is possible for two different solids to have the same top, side, and front views. Use the three views of a solid in Example 2 to draw a different solid.

12.3 Surface Area of Rectangular Prisms

4.2.A.2.c Models of 3D objects

Before You found the areas of rectangles and squares.

Now You'll find surface areas of rectangular prisms.

Why? So you can analyze sculptures, as in Ex. 32.

KEY VOCABULARY
- surface area, *p. 642*
- net, *p. 642*

The **surface area** of a solid is the sum of the areas of its outside surfaces. A two-dimensional representation of a solid, such as the rectangular prism below, is called a **net**. The surface area of a rectangular prism is equal to the area of its net.

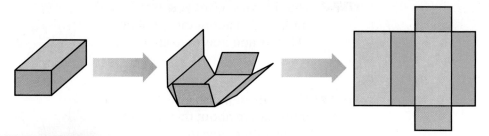

EXAMPLE 1 Finding Surface Area Using a Net

Find the surface area of the rectangular prism.

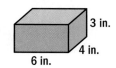

STEP 1 **Draw** a net and find the area of each face.

Area of top or bottom: $6 \times 4 = 24$

Area of front or back: $6 \times 3 = 18$

Area of either side: $4 \times 3 = 12$

STEP 2 **Add** the areas of all six faces.

$24 + 24 + 18 + 18 + 12 + 12 = 108$

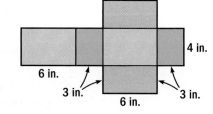

▶ **Answer** The surface area of the prism is 108 square inches.

> **VOCABULARY**
> In this book, every prism is also a *right prism*, which means that the edges connecting the bases are perpendicular to the bases.

KEY CONCEPT   *For Your Notebook*

Surface Area of a Rectangular Prism

Words   The surface area *S* of a rectangular prism is the sum of the areas of its faces.

Algebra $S = 2lw + 2lh + 2wh$

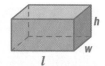

EXAMPLE 2 Finding Surface Area Using a Formula

Find the surface area of the rectangular prism.

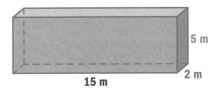
5 m
2 m
15 m

SOLUTION

$S = 2lw + 2lh + 2wh$ **Write formula for surface area.**

$= 2(15)(2) + 2(15)(5) + 2(2)(5)$ **Substitute 15 for *l*, 2 for *w*, and 5 for *h*.**

$= 60 + 150 + 20$ **Multiply.**

$= 230$ **Add.**

▶ **Answer** The surface area of the prism is 230 square meters.

EXAMPLE 3 Solve a Multi-Step Problem

READING
Read the problem carefully so that you can make a plan to solve it. The *surface area* of the cushion will tell you how much *fabric* you need.

Stadium Cushion You are making the stadium cushion shown. The foam for the cushion costs $1.50, and the fabric costs $.50 per square foot. How much does it cost to make the cushion?

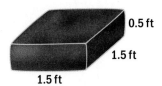
0.5 ft
1.5 ft
1.5 ft

SOLUTION

STEP 1 **Use** a formula to find the surface area of the cushion.

$S = 2lw + 2lh + 2wh$ **Write formula.**

$= 2(1.5)(1.5) + 2(1.5)(0.5) + 2(1.5)(0.5)$ **Substitute values.**

$= 7.5 \text{ ft}^2$ **Simplify.**

STEP 2 **Multiply** to find the fabric cost: $7.5 \text{ ft}^2 \times \$.50/\text{ft}^2 = \$3.75$.

STEP 3 **Add** to find the cost of fabric and foam: $\$3.75 + \$1.50 = \$5.25$.

▶ **Answer** It costs $5.25 to make the stadium cushion.

✓ **GUIDED PRACTICE**   **for Examples 1, 2, and 3**

Find the surface area of the rectangular prism.

1.
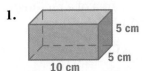
5 cm
5 cm
10 cm

2.
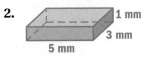
1 mm
3 mm
5 mm

3.
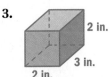
2 in.
3 in.
2 in.

4. What If? Suppose the dimensions of the cushion in Example 3 were 2 feet by 2 feet by 0.75 foot. The foam for a cushion that size costs $1.75. How much would it cost to make the cushion?

12.3 EXERCISES

HOMEWORK
KEY
★ = **STANDARDIZED TEST PRACTICE**
Exs. 14, 27, 29, 32, and 40
◯ = **HINTS** AND **HOMEWORK HELP**
for Exs. 5, 7, 11, 25 at classzone.com

SKILL PRACTICE

VOCABULARY **Copy and complete the statement.**

1. The __?__ of a rectangular prism is the sum of the areas of its faces.

2. A two-dimensional representation of a solid is called a(n) __?__ .

SEE EXAMPLE 1
on p. 642
for Exs. 3–6

3. **USING NETS** Find the surface area of the rectangular prism whose net is shown.

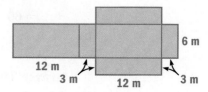

DRAWING NETS **Draw a net for the rectangular prism. Then use the net to find the surface area of the prism.**

4.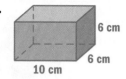

5.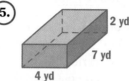

6.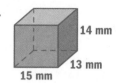

FINDING SURFACE AREA **Find the surface area of the rectangular prism.**

SEE EXAMPLE 2
on p. 643
for Exs. 7–14

7.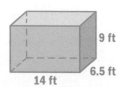

8.

9.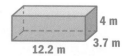

10.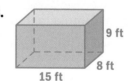

11.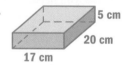

12.

13. **ERROR ANALYSIS** A rectangular prism has dimensions 6 feet by 2 feet by 8 feet. Lana found the surface area of the prism by evaluating the expression $(6 \times 8) + (6 \times 2) + (8 \times 2)$. Describe and correct her error.

14. ★ **MULTIPLE CHOICE** What is the surface area of a rectangular prism that is 8 inches long, 4 inches wide, and 12 inches high?

　Ⓐ 176 in.^{2}　　Ⓑ 332 in.^{2}　　Ⓒ 352 in.^{2}　　Ⓓ 384 in.^{2}

FINDING SURFACE AREA **Find the surface area of a cube with the given side length.**

15. $s = 1.5$ ft　　16. $s = 3$ in.　　17. $s = 4.5$ cm　　18. $s = 0.75$ mm

19. REASONING In Exercises 15–18, what is the relationship between the edge length and surface area of the cube?

20. CHALLENGE The surface area of a cube is 96 square centimeters. Find the length of each edge of the cube. Show your work.

In Exercises 21–23, find the surface area of the prism. Use the steps in the following example. The area of a base B is given.

EXTENSION Finding Surface Areas of Non-Rectangular Prisms

Find the surface area of the triangular prism at the right.

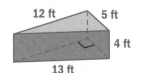

SOLUTION

STEP 1 Find the area of each face.

Area of a base: $B = \frac{1}{2}(5)(12) = 30 \text{ ft}^2$

Area of face 1: $A_1 = 13 \times 4 = 52 \text{ ft}^2$

Area of face 2: $A_2 = 5 \times 4 = 20 \text{ ft}^2$

Area of face 3: $A_3 = 12 \times 4 = 48 \text{ ft}^2$

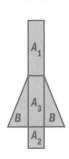

STEP 2 Add the areas of all the faces.

$S = B + B + A_1 + A_2 + A_3$ **Write sum of areas of faces.**

$= 30 + 30 + 52 + 20 + 48$ **Substitute values.**

$= 180$ **Add.**

▶ **Answer** The surface area of the prism is 180 square feet.

---

21. $B = 10.4 \text{ mm}^2$

22. $B = 6 \text{ cm}^2$

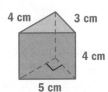

23. $B = 19 \text{ ft}^2$

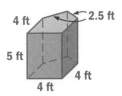

PROBLEM SOLVING

SEE EXAMPLE 3
on p. 643
for Exs. 24–25

24. STORAGE BOX You are building a storage box out of plywood using the dimensions shown. Plywood costs $1.50 per square foot. Find the total cost of the plywood.

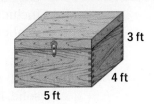

25. WRAPPING PAPER You are wrapping a gift box that is 18 inches by 12 inches by 3 inches. What is the least amount of wrapping paper that you need to wrap the box?

26. PHOTO CUBE The length of each edge of a photo cube is 3 inches. Does the photo cube have *more* or *less* viewing surface than a flat photograph that is 8 inches wide and 10 inches long? *Explain* your reasoning.

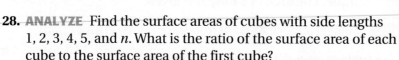

27. ★ WRITING Write a formula for the surface area of a cube with edges of length *s*. *Explain* how you found your answer.

28. ANALYZE Find the surface areas of cubes with side lengths 1, 2, 3, 4, 5, and *n*. What is the ratio of the surface area of each cube to the surface area of the first cube?

29. ★ SHORT RESPONSE A room is 13 feet long, 11 feet wide, and 10 feet high. In the room, 3 windows are each 4 feet wide and 5 feet tall. A gallon of paint covers 350 square feet. How many gallons of paint do you need to paint the 4 walls, not including the windows? *Explain.*

30. ✗✓ ALGEBRA The surface area of a rectangular prism is 1194 square inches. The height is 12 inches. The length is 27 inches. Find the width.

31. BUILDINGS The building below is composed of three rectangular prisms. What is the surface area of the building? Include doors and windows but not the bottom surface.

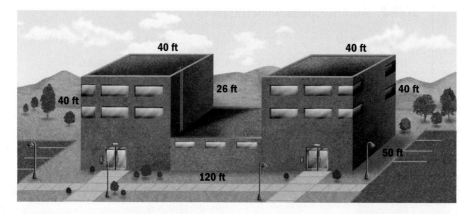

32. ★ EXTENDED RESPONSE The red cube shown in the photo on page 642 has an edge length of about 13.86 feet. Two of the faces have a circular hole of the same size. Estimate the radius of a hole. *Explain* your answer. Then find the total area of the red surfaces. Round to the nearest square foot.

33. DOGHOUSES A small flat-topped doghouse measures 28 inches by 24 inches by 20 inches. For the same style doghouse in a medium size, each dimension is 25% longer. Find the surface area of each doghouse, including the floor. What is the ratio of the surface area of the medium doghouse to the surface area of the small one?

34. CHALLENGE A rectangular hole is cut into the solid, as shown. What is the surface area of the solid, including the faces created by the hole? *Explain* your steps.

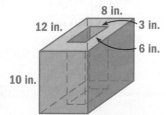

35. CHALLENGE Solids A and B are made up of unit cubes where each edge is 1 unit. Solid A has a surface area of 36 square units. Solid B has a surface area of 40 square units. *Explain* how this is possible. Include a drawing of solid B from a different angle in your explanation.

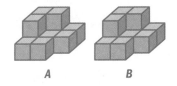

A   B

36. The table shows the time Rory has spent on homework this week. What is the total time Rory has spent on homework?

Day	Mon.	Tues.	Wed.	Thurs.
Time (hours)	1.3	$\frac{7}{10}$	$2\frac{1}{2}$	2.7

(A) 4 h   **(B)** $6\frac{3}{4}$ h   **(C)** 7 h   **(D)** 7.2 h

---

QUIZ *for Lessons 12.1–12.3*

Classify the solid. Be as specific as possible. *(p. 631)*

1.

2.

3.

Sketch the solid. Then count the number of faces, edges, and vertices. *(p. 636)*

4. Triangular prism   **5.** Cube   **6.** Pentagonal pyramid

7. SCHOOL PLAY You are making sets for a school play. One of the set pieces is the rectangular prism shown, which will be used as a raised platform. You paint all of the faces except the bottom surface. What is the total area painted? *(p. 642)*

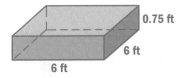

0.75 ft
6 ft
6 ft

Brain Game

Face Painting

You have a cube made out of 27 smaller cubes of the same size. You paint the six faces of the large cube. How many of the 27 smaller cubes have three faces painted? two faces painted? one face painted? no faces painted?

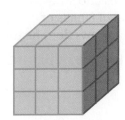

Lessons 12.1–12.3

1. **IDENTIFYING SOLIDS** What kind of solid has 5 vertices?

   A. square prism

   B. square pyramid

   C. triangular prism

   D. triangular pyramid

2. **PYRAMID** A face of a hexagonal pyramid with a regular base is shown.

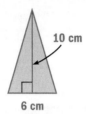

10 cm

6 cm

   A net of the pyramid is shown below. What are the values of *x* and *y*?

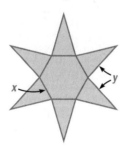

x
y

   A. $x = 3$ cm, $y = 10$ cm

   B. $x = 6$ cm, $y = 10$ cm

   C. $x = 6$ cm, $y = \sqrt{109}$ cm

   D. $x = 6$ cm, $y = \sqrt{136}$ cm

3. **BUILDING MODELS** Zack is building a model of a prism. He uses balls of clay for the vertices and straws for the edges. He uses a total of 8 balls of clay for the model. How many straws does he use?

   A. 8   B. 10   C. 12   D. 16

4. **SHIPPING** The dimensions of two wooden crates are shown. The prices of the crates are based on the amount of wood used to make them. Which crate is cheaper and why?

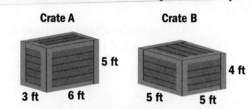

Crate A   Crate B

5 ft   4 ft

3 ft   6 ft   5 ft   5 ft

   A. Crate A because it has a smaller surface area than B.

   B. Crate A because it is not as long as B.

   C. Crate B because it is not as high as A.

   D. Crate B because it has a smaller surface area than A.

5. **CARDBOARD** Below is an unfolded cardboard box. How much cardboard, in square inches, was used to make the box?

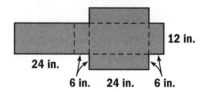

12 in.

24 in.

6 in.   24 in.   6 in.

   A. 792 in^2

   B. 864 in^2

   C. 936 in^2

   D. 1,008 in^2

6. **OPEN-ENDED** *Describe* two ways you can represent a three-dimensional figure using two-dimensional drawings.

   • Represent a triangular prism using each way.

   • Count the number of faces, edges, and vertices in the prism. Which drawing did you use to help you count? *Explain.*

12.4 Surface Area of Cylinders

4.2.A.2.c Models of 3D objects

Before You found the surface areas of rectangular prisms.

Now You'll find surface areas of cylinders.

Why? So you can find dimensions of objects, as in Example 2.

KEY VOCABULARY
- **cylinder,** *p. 631*
- **surface area,** *p. 642*
- **net,** *p. 642*

ACTIVITY

You can make a model to find the surface area of a cylinder.

STEP 1 **Cut** out pieces of paper to cover a cylindrical can. What shape are the pieces of paper that cover the top and bottom of the can? What shape is the piece of paper that covers the side of the can?

STEP 2 **Describe** the relationship between the circumference of the paper used to cover the top of the can and the length of the paper that covers the side of the can.

STEP 3 **Use** the pieces of paper to find the surface area of the can.

In the activity, you saw that the net of a cylinder consists of two circles that form the bases and a rectangle that forms the curved (or lateral) surface of the cylinder. The circumference of a base, $2\pi r$, is equal to the length of the rectangle.

TAKE NOTES

In this book, all cylinders are *right cylinders*, which means that the line connecting the centers of the bases is perpendicular to the bases.

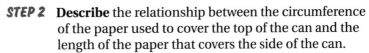

Cylinder   **Unfold.**   **Net**

Top $A = \pi r^2$

Curved surface $A = 2\pi rh$

Bottom $A = \pi r^2$

KEY CONCEPT

For Your Notebook

Surface Area of a Cylinder

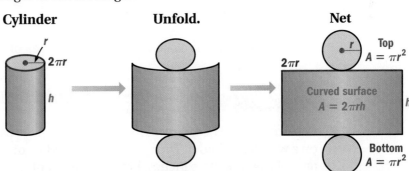

Words The surface area S of a cylinder is the sum of twice the area of a base and the product of the base's circumference and height.

Algebra $S = 2\pi r^2 + 2\pi rh$

♦ **EXAMPLE 1** Finding the Surface Area of a Cylinder

Find the surface area of the cylinder at the right. Use 3.14 for π.

3 cm

8 cm

SOLUTION

METHOD 1 **Use** a net to find the surface area.

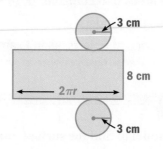

3 cm

8 cm

$2\pi r$

3 cm

Area of base:
$A = \pi r^2$
$\approx 3.14(3)^2 = 28.26 \text{ cm}^2$

Area of curved surface:
$A = 2\pi rh$
$\approx 2(3.14)(3)(8) = 150.72 \text{ cm}^2$

Surface area:
$S = 28.26 + 28.26 + 150.72 = 207.24$

METHOD 2 **Use** the formula for the surface area of a cylinder.

$S = 2\pi r^2 + 2\pi rh$ **Write formula for surface area.**

$\approx 2(3.14)(3)^2 + 2(3.14)(3)(8)$ **Substitute values.**

$= 56.52 + 150.72$ **Multiply.**

$= 207.24$ **Add.**

AVOID ERRORS
....
When finding the surface area of a cylinder, don't forget to add the areas of *both* bases.

▶**Answer** The surface area is about 207 square centimeters.

Check To check that your answer is reasonable, use 3 for π.

$S \approx 2(3)(3)^2 + 2(3)(3)(8)$ **Substitute values into formula.**

$= 54 + 144$ **Multiply.**

$= 198$ **Add.**

Because 198 is close to 207, a surface area of 207 cm^2 is reasonable.

EXAMPLE 2 Finding the Height of a Cylinder

Balance Board The balance board shown on page 649 rocks back and forth on a wooden cylinder. The cylinder has a radius of 3 inches and a surface area of 244.92 square inches. Find the height of the cylinder. Use 3.14 for π.

$S = 2\pi r^2 + 2\pi rh$ **Write formula for surface area.**

$244.92 \approx 2(3.14)(3)^2 + 2(3.14)(3)h$ **Substitute values.**

$244.92 = 56.52 + 18.84h$ **Multiply.**

$244.92 - 56.52 = 56.52 + 18.84h - 56.52$ **Subtract 56.52 from each side.**

$188.4 = 18.84h$ **Simplify.**

$10 = h$ **Divide each side by 18.84.**

▶**Answer** The height of the wooden cylinder is about 10 inches.

Find the surface area of the cylinder. Use 3.14 for π.

1.
5 mm
3 mm

2.
4 ft
12 ft

3.
11 m
11 m

4. Find the height of a cylinder that has a radius of 20 feet and a surface area of 9700 square feet. Use 3.14 for π. Round your answer to the nearest foot.

12.4 EXERCISES

HOMEWORK KEY

★ = **STANDARDIZED TEST PRACTICE**
Exs. 6, 24, 25, 26, and 36

◯ = **HINTS** AND **HOMEWORK HELP**
for Exs. 3, 9, 11, 23 at classzone.com

SKILL PRACTICE

VOCABULARY Copy and complete the statement.

1. The net for a cylinder consists of two __?__ and a(n) __?__.

2. The expression $2\pi r^2 + 2\pi rh$ gives the __?__ of a cylinder.

DRAWING NETS Draw a net for the cylinder and label the dimensions. Then use the net to find the surface area of the cylinder. Use 3.14 for π.

SEE EXAMPLE 1
on p. 650
for Exs. 3–9

3.
9 in.
6 in.

4.
2 cm
7 cm

5.
5 ft
6 ft

6. ★ **MULTIPLE CHOICE** Which of the following is the net for a cylinder?

Ⓐ   Ⓑ   Ⓒ   Ⓓ

SURFACE AREA Find the surface area of the cylindrical object. Use 3.14 for π.

7.
8 cm
19 cm

8.   0.25 in.

lip balm
2 in.

9.
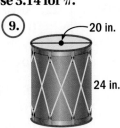
20 in.
24 in.

SEE EXAMPLE 1
on p. 650
for Ex. 10

10. ERROR ANALYSIS The diameter of a cylinder is 5 feet and the height is 10 feet. Describe and correct the error made in finding the surface area of the cylinder.

$$
\begin{aligned}
S &= 2\pi r^2 + 2\pi rh \\
&\approx 2(3.14)(5)^2 + 2(3.14)(5)(10) \\
&= 157 + 314 \\
&= 471
\end{aligned}
$$
The surface area is about 471 ft².

SEE EXAMPLE 2
on p. 650
for Exs. 11–13

ALGEBRA Find the height of a cylinder with the given radius and surface area. Use 3.14 for π.

11. $r = 25$ cm
$S = 4867$ cm²

12. $r = 10$ in.
$S = 1570$ in.²

13. $r = 4.5$ ft
$S = 141.3$ ft²

SURFACE AREA Find the surface area of a cylinder with the given dimensions. Use 3.14 for π. *Compare* the results to the surface area of a cylinder with radius 1 cm and height 2 cm.

14. radius: 3 cm
height: 6 cm

15. radius: 6 cm
height: 12 cm

16. radius: 9 cm
height: 18 cm

17. REASONING Use your answers to Exercises 14–16. How does a change in the dimensions of a cylinder by a factor of x affect the surface area?

18. WHICH ONE DOESN'T BELONG? Which net does *not* belong? *Explain.*

A.   **B.**   **C.**   **D.**

19. ALGEBRA The surface area of a cylinder is 6π square feet. The height is 2 feet. What is the radius of the cylinder? *Justify* your reasoning.

20. CHALLENGE The surface area of a cylinder is 408.2 square feet. The area of one of the bases is 78.5 square feet. Find the height. Use 3.14 for π.

21. CHALLENGE The height and the radius of a cylinder are equal. The cylinder has a surface area of 113.04 square feet. Find the height of the cylinder. Use 3.14 for π.

PROBLEM SOLVING

SEE EXAMPLE 1
on p. 650
for Exs. 22–23

22. FOOD PRESERVATION A cylindrical cheese wheel has a diameter of 8 inches and a height of 5 inches. A wax coating covers the cheese wheel to keep the cheese fresh. How much surface area must the wax coating cover? Use 3.14 for π.

23. ESTIMATION Use a metric ruler to estimate the surface area of the battery to the nearest square centimeter.

24. ★ **SHORT RESPONSE** Cylinder *A* has a radius of 3 meters and a height of 6 meters. Cylinder *B* has a radius of 6 meters and a height of 3 meters. Which cylinder has the greater surface area? *Explain.*

SEE EXAMPLE 2
on p. 650
for Ex. 25

25. ★ **MULTIPLE CHOICE** The surface area of a cylindrical keychain flashlight is about 1608 square millimeters, and its diameter is 8 millimeters. What is the approximate height?

(A) 12 mm   (B) 24 mm   (C) 30 mm   (D) 60 mm

26. ★ **WRITING** Write out a procedure to find the surface area of the figure shown at the right, not including the surface created by the circular hole. Then use your procedure to find the surface area.

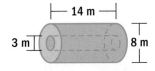

27. **DRAW A DIAGRAM** You are frosting a circular cake that has three layers. Each layer has a 5 inch diameter and is 2 inches tall. You frost the curved surface and the top of each layer. Draw a diagram of the cake. To the nearest square inch, what is the total area that you frost? Use 3.14 for *π*.

28. **CHALLENGE** The figure shown is a cylinder inside a unit cube. The cylinder is the largest possible cylinder that can fit inside the cube. Find the surface area of the cylinder. *Explain* how you found your answer.

29. **CHALLENGE** The figure shown is the net of a cone. Find the radius of the base of the cone. *Explain* your steps. Then find the surface area of the cone.

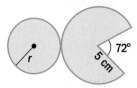

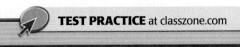

NEW JERSEY MIXED REVIEW

TEST PRACTICE at classzone.com

30. A log has a circumference of 80 inches. Which expression could be used to find the radius of the log?

(A) 80π (B) 160π (C) $\dfrac{80}{2\pi}$ (D) $\dfrac{80}{\pi}$

31. Which of the following CANNOT be used to find the surface area of a cube with side length *s*?

(A) $6s^2$

(B) $6(s \times s)$

(C) $3(s^2 \times s^2)$

(D) $s^2 + s^2 + s^2 + s^2 + s^2 + s^2$

GOAL
Investigate the volumes
of rectangular prisms.

MATERIALS
• unit cubes

12.5 Investigating Volume

The *volume* of a solid is a measure of how much space it occupies. Volume is measured in cubic units. You can use unit cubes to build rectangular prisms and find their volumes.

EXPLORE **Find the volume of a rectangular prism that is 4 units long, 2 units wide, and 1 unit high.**

STEP 1 **Build** a rectangular prism that is 4 units long, 2 units wide, and 1 unit high. Use unit cubes.

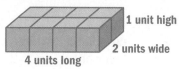

1 unit high
2 units wide
4 units long

STEP 2 **Count** the number of unit cubes used to build the prism. The rectangular prism is made up of 8 unit cubes. This means that the rectangular prism has a volume of 8 cubic units.

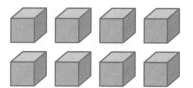

PRACTICE **Complete the following exercises.**

1. Copy the table. Build all of the rectangular prisms whose dimensions are given in the table. Then find the volume of each rectangular prism by counting the number of unit cubes you used to build the prism. Record your results in the table.

Length *l*	Width *w*	Height *h*	Volume *V*
4	2	1	8
2	1	5	?
1	1	7	?
2	2	3	?

2. Use 12 unit cubes to build three different rectangular prisms. What are the length, width, height, and volume of each prism? Include your results in the table.

DRAW CONCLUSIONS

3. **REASONING** Look for a pattern in the table. Then write an equation that relates the volume V of a rectangular prism with its length l, width w, and height h.

4. **REASONING** What does the expression $l \times w$ represent for each prism?

12.5 Volume of Rectangular Prisms

 4.2.A.2.c Models of 3D objects

Before	You found the surface areas of rectangular prisms.
Now	You'll find volumes of rectangular prisms.
Why?	So you can compare volumes, as with sand in Example 3.

KEY VOCABULARY
• **volume,** *p. 655*

The **volume** of a solid is the amount of space that the solid contains. Volume is measured in cubic units, such as cubic feet (ft^3) and cubic meters (m^3).

KEY CONCEPT   *For Your Notebook*

Volume of a Rectangular Prism

Words   The volume *V* of a rectangular prism is the product of the length, width, and height.

Algebra $V = lwh$

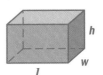

EXAMPLE 1   Volume of a Rectangular Prism

Aquarium An aquarium shaped like a rectangular prism has a length of 120 centimeters, a width of 60 centimeters, and a height of 100 centimeters. How much water is needed to fill the aquarium?

SOLUTION

To find the amount of water needed, find the volume of the aquarium.

$V = lwh$ **Write formula for volume of rectangular prism.**

$= (120)(60)(100)$ **Substitute 120 for *l*, 60 for *w*, and 100 for *h*.**

$= 720,000$ **Multiply.**

▶**Answer** You need 720,000 cubic centimeters of water to fill the aquarium.

> **ANOTHER WAY**
> You can also find the volume *V* of a rectangular prism by multiplying the area *B* of a base by the corresponding height *h* of the prism.
> $V = Bh$

✓ **GUIDED PRACTICE**   **for Example 1**

Find the volume of the rectangular prism.

1. 10 in. 6 in. 16 in.

2. 6 ft 5 ft 4 ft

3. 2 m 3.5 m 1 m

EXAMPLE 2 | Finding the Height of a Rectangular Prism

The rectangular prism shown has a volume of 1440 cubic millimeters. Find the height of the prism.

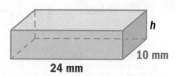

24 mm

10 mm

h

$$V = lwh$$ Write formula for volume of rectangular prism.

$$1440 = (24)(10)h$$ Substitute 1440 for *V*, 24 for *l*, and 10 for *w*.

$$1440 = 240h$$ Multiply.

$$\frac{1440}{240} = \frac{240h}{240}$$ Divide each side by 240.

$$6 = h$$ Simplify.

AVOID ERRORS
Make sure you use the correct units when writing your answer. Linear units should be used to describe the length, width, or height of an object.

▶ **Answer** The height of the prism is 6 millimeters.

EXAMPLE 3 | Solve a Multi-Step Problem

Sand Sculpture The truck at the right is delivering sand for a sand sculpture competition. How many trips must the truck make to deliver 15 cubic yards of sand?

12 ft 5 ft

3 ft

SOLUTION

CHECK WORK
You can use estimation to check that your work in Step 1 is reasonable.
$V \approx (10)(5)(3) = 150 \text{ ft}^3$

STEP 1 **Find** the volume of the bed of the truck.

$$V = lwh = 12(5)(3) = 180 \text{ ft}^3$$

STEP 2 **Convert** 15 cubic yards to cubic feet. Use unit analysis; that is, multiply by forms of 1.

$$15 \text{ yd}^3 \times \frac{3 \text{ ft}}{1 \text{ yd}} \times \frac{3 \text{ ft}}{1 \text{ yd}} \times \frac{3 \text{ ft}}{1 \text{ yd}} = 405 \text{ ft}^3$$

STEP 3 **Divide** 405 ft^3 by 180 ft^3 to find the number of trips that the truck must make.

$$405 \text{ ft}^3 \div 180 \text{ ft}^3 = 2.25$$

▶ **Answer** Because 2.25 trips doesn't make sense, the truck must make 3 trips.

✓ **GUIDED PRACTICE** | for Examples 2 and 3

4. Find the length of the rectangular prism with a volume of 125 cubic meters, a width of 2 meters, and a height of 12.5 meters.

5. **What If?** Suppose the bed of the truck in Example 3 is 10 feet long, 6 feet wide, and 3 feet high. How many trips must the truck make to deliver 12 cubic yards of sand?

12.5 EXERCISES

HOMEWORK KEY
★ = **STANDARDIZED TEST PRACTICE**
Exs. 15, 18, 24, 29, 30, and 39

◯ = **HINTS** AND **HOMEWORK HELP**
for Exs. 3, 7, 13, 23 at classzone.com

SKILL PRACTICE

1. **VOCABULARY** *Explain* the difference between volume and surface area.

2. **VOCABULARY** *Describe* how to find the volume of a rectangular prism.

FINDING VOLUME **Find the volume of the rectangular prism.**

SEE EXAMPLE 1
on p. 655
for Exs. 3–11

3.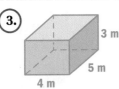
3 m
5 m
4 m

4.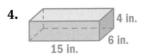
4 in.
6 in.
15 in.

5.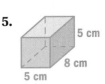
5 cm
8 cm
5 cm

6.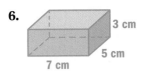
3 cm
5 cm
7 cm

7.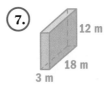
12 m
18 m
3 m

8.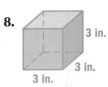
3 in.
3 in.
3 in.

9.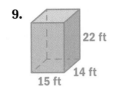
22 ft
14 ft
15 ft

10.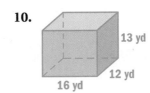
13 yd
12 yd
16 yd

11.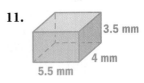
3.5 mm
4 mm
5.5 mm

DIMENSIONS **Find the unknown dimension of the rectangular prism.**

SEE EXAMPLE 2
on p. 656
for Exs. 12–14

12. $V = 400 \text{ ft}^3$, $l = 10$ ft, $w = 5$ ft, $h = \underline{\ ?\ }$

13. $V = 160 \text{ cm}^3$, $l = 10$ cm, $w = \underline{\ ?\ }$, $h = 8$ cm

14. $V = 1200 \text{ mm}^3$, $l = \underline{\ ?\ }$, $w = 12$ mm, $h = 4$ mm

15. ★ **MULTIPLE CHOICE** A rectangular prism has a volume of 432 cubic feet. Its bases are squares with side lengths of 6 feet. What is its height?

Ⓐ 3 ft Ⓑ 6 ft Ⓒ 12 ft Ⓓ 72 ft

REASONING **Find the volume and the total area of all outside surfaces of the solid.** *Explain* **your method. Check your answer using estimation.**

16.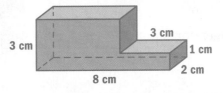
3 cm
3 cm
3 cm
1 cm
2 cm
8 cm

17.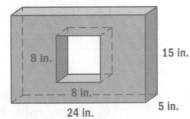
8 in.
15 in.
8 in.
24 in.
5 in.

18. ★ **OPEN-ENDED MATH** A rectangular prism has dimensions 3 inches, 4 inches, and 5 inches. Find another rectangular prism with the same volume but less surface area.

19. ❌ **CHALLENGE** A rectangular prism is built using 40 red cubes and 3 green cubes. The green cubes are twice as wide as the red cubes. Find the total volume of the prism in terms of the width x of a red cube. Write your answer in simplest form.

In Exercises 20–22, find the volume of the prism. Use the example below to help you. Check your answer using estimation.

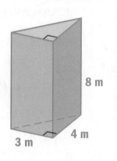

EXTENSION Finding Volumes of Non-Rectangular Prisms

You can find the volume of non-rectangular prisms, such as the triangular prism shown, by multiplying the area B of one base by the corresponding height.

$V = Bh$ **Write formula for volume.**

$= \left(\frac{1}{2}(3)(4)\right)(8)$ **Substitute the area of the triangular base for B and 8 for h.**

$= 48$ **Simplify.**

▶ **Answer** The volume of the triangular prism is 48 cubic meters.

20.

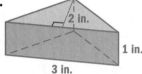

21.

22.

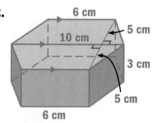

PROBLEM SOLVING

SEE EXAMPLE 1 on p. 655 for Ex. 23

23. **WATERMELONS** In Japan, farmers have developed watermelons that are shaped like cubes and therefore fit better in refrigerators. What is the volume of a cubic watermelon whose edge length is 18 centimeters?

24. ★ **MULTIPLE CHOICE** Which of the following items would likely have a volume of 300 cubic inches?

(A) Sugar cube   (B) Cereal box

(C) Microwave   (D) Refrigerator

SEE EXAMPLE 3 on p. 656 for Ex. 25

25. **ERROR ANALYSIS** Your friend calculates the number of cubic yards of concrete needed for a driveway that is 18 feet by 30 feet by 0.5 feet. Describe and correct your friend's error.

$V = (18 \text{ ft})(30 \text{ ft})(0.5 \text{ ft})$
$= 270 \text{ ft}^3$
$= 90 \text{ yd}^3$

SEE EXAMPLE 3
on p. 656
for Exs. 26–27

26. **MULTI-STEP PROBLEM** A window box shaped like a rectangular prism has a length of 12 feet, a width of 9 inches, and a height of 9 inches.

   a. **Convert** Convert the width and height of the window box to feet. Then find the volume of the window box. Check using estimation.

   b. **Calculate** One bag contains 2 cubic feet of soil. How many bags of soil must you buy to fill the window box? You must buy full bags of soil.

   c. **Estimate** Each bag of soil costs $1.97, including tax. Estimate the cost of filling the window box with soil.

27. **MEASUREMENT** The dimensions of an aquarium are half those of the aquarium on page 655. The aquarium is filled with water. What is the mass of the water, in kilograms? Use this fact for water: $1 \text{ cm}^3 = 1 \text{ g}$.

28. **AIR CONDITIONING** Refer to the Extension on page 658 for help with this exercise. You are buying an air conditioner to cool an attic apartment whose end walls have a vertical line of symmetry and have the dimensions shown in the drawing. The attic is 36 feet long and 28 feet wide. Find the volume of the apartment to be cooled. Check using estimation.

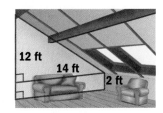

29. ★ **SHORT RESPONSE** What happens to the volume of a prism when its dimensions are doubled? tripled? quadrupled? *Explain* your reasoning and give examples to support your answers.

30. ★ **EXTENDED RESPONSE** Make an input-output table for a cube's edge length *x* and its volume *y* for edge lengths of 1 unit, 2 units, 3 units, and 4 units. Plot the ordered pairs in a coordinate plane. Then use the graph to decide whether the volume of a cube is a linear function of the cube's edge length. *Explain* your reasoning.

31. **CHALLENGE** *Explain* how you can find the volume of the triangular prism shown by first finding the volume of a rectangular prism. Then use your method to find the volume.

4 in.   4 in.   9 in.

32. **CHALLENGE** A woodworker needs to design a cabinet with at most 300 square inches of wood. What whole number dimensions will give the cabinet the greatest volume?

  **NEW JERSEY MIXED REVIEW**   **TEST PRACTICE** at classzone.com

33. Which net can be used to make a cube?

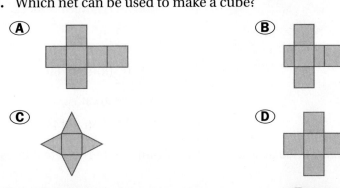

Ⓐ   Ⓑ

Ⓒ   Ⓓ

Surface Area and Volume of Pyramids

GOAL Find the surface areas and volumes of pyramids.

Louvre Museum The entrance to the Louvre Museum in Paris, France, is an example of a regular pyramid. A *regular pyramid* is a pyramid whose base is a regular polygon.

You can find the surface area of a pyramid by finding the area of the base and of each triangular face and then adding the areas. In this book, all pyramids are regular pyramids, so the triangular faces are congruent isosceles triangles.

The volume of a pyramid is related to its height h and the area B of its base. The surface area of a regular pyramid whose base has n sides is related to the height of each triangular face, called the slant height l, and the length s of each side of the base.

$$V = \frac{1}{3}Bh$$

$$S = B + n\left(\frac{1}{2}sl\right)$$

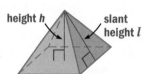

EXAMPLE 1 Finding the Surface Area of a Pyramid

Find the surface area of the square pyramid.

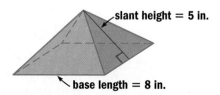

slant height = 5 in.

base length = 8 in.

SOLUTION

You can use a net to find the areas of the faces.

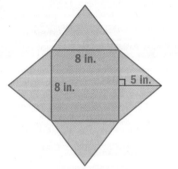

8 in.

8 in.   5 in.

Area of base:

$A = s^2$

$\quad = 8^2 = 64$

Area of triangular faces:

$A = 4\left(\frac{1}{2}sl\right)$

$\quad = 4\left(\frac{1}{2}(8)(5)\right) = 80$

Surface area:

$S = 64 + 80 = 144$

▶ **Answer** The surface area of the pyramid is 144 square inches.

EXAMPLE 2 Finding the Volume of a Pyramid

Find the volume of the pyramid in Example 1.

SOLUTION

STEP 1 **Find** the height h of the pyramid by using the Pythagorean Theorem.

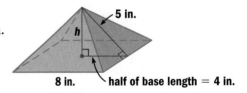
5 in.
h
8 in.   half of base length = 4 in.

$$h^2 + 4^2 = 5^2$$

$$h^2 + 16 = 25$$

$$h^2 = 9$$

$$h = 3$$

STEP 2 **Calculate** the volume using the formula.

Volume $= \frac{1}{3}Bh$	**Write formula for volume of pyramid.**
$= \frac{1}{3}(8^2)(3)$	**Substitute. *B* is the area of square base.**
$= 64$	**Multiply.**

▸ **Answer** The volume of the pyramid is 64 cubic inches.

Comparing Volumes The volume of the square pyramid in Example 2 is equal to $\frac{1}{3}$ the volume of a square prism that has the same dimensions.

Square Pyramid

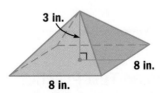
3 in.
8 in.
8 in.

Square Prism

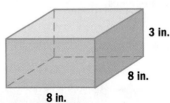
3 in.
8 in.
8 in.

Volume $= \frac{1}{3}Bh = 64$ in.^{3}

Volume $= lwh = 192$ in.^{3}

EXERCISES

Find the surface area and volume of the regular pyramid with the given measurements.

1. Square:
$l = 13$ ft,
$s = 24$ ft,
$h = 5$ ft

2. Triangular:
$l = 13$ m,
$s = 10$ m, $B \approx 43.3$ m^2,
$h = 12$ m

3. Pentagonal:
$l = 30$ yd,
$s = 24$ yd, $B \approx 991$ yd^2,
$h = 25$ yd

4. Louvre The square pyramid entrance to the Louvre shown on page 660 is 35.42 meters wide and 21.64 meters tall. It has a slant height of 27.96 meters. Find the surface area and volume of the solid.

12.6 Volume of Cylinders

NJ 4.2.A.2.c

Models of 3D objects

Before	You found the volumes of rectangular prisms.
Now	You'll find volumes of cylinders.
Why?	So you can find volumes of cylindrical objects, such as haystacks in Ex. 19.

KEY VOCABULARY
- cylinder, *p. 631*
- volume, *p. 655*

In Lesson 12.5, you may have observed that the volume of a rectangular prism is the product of the area of a base (length × width) and the height. The volume of a cylinder can be found the same way.

The area of the base is the number of unit squares that cover the base.

The height is the number of layers of unit cubes that fit in the solid.

TAKE NOTES
You have learned many formulas and properties related to solids. You may want to write a summary of all these formulas and properties in your notebook.

> **KEY CONCEPT** *For Your Notebook*
>
> ### Volume of a Cylinder
>
> **Words**   The volume *V* of a cylinder is the product of the area of a base and the height.
>
> **Algebra** $V = Bh$ or $V = \pi r^2 h$
>
>

★ **EXAMPLE 1** **Standardized Test Practice**

ELIMINATE CHOICES
You can get a low estimate of the volume by using 3 for π:
$$V = \pi r^2 h \approx$$
$$(3)(2)^2(3) = 36.$$
The volume must be greater than 36 m³, so you can eliminate choices A and B.

What is the volume of the cylinder? Use 3.14 for π.

Ⓐ 15.6 m³   Ⓑ 18.8 m³

Ⓒ 37.7 m³   Ⓓ 75.4 m³

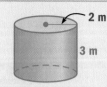

SOLUTION

$$V = \pi r^2 h$$ **Write formula for volume of cylinder.**

$$\approx (3.14)(2)^2(3)$$ **Substitute values.**

$$\approx 37.7$$ **Multiply.**

▶ **Answer** The volume of the cylinder is about 37.7 cubic meters. The correct answer is C. Ⓐ Ⓑ Ⓒ Ⓓ

EXAMPLE 2 Comparing Volumes of Cylinders

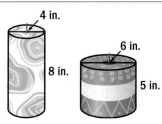

4 in.

6 in.

8 in.

5 in.

Candles You buy the two cylindrical candles shown at the right. Which candle contains more wax?

SOLUTION

To find which candle contains more wax, find their volumes.

STEP 1 **Find** the radius, which is half the diameter, of each candle.

AVOID ERRORS

Be sure to use the radius, *not* the diameter, in the formula for the volume of a cylinder.

Tall candle: $r = \dfrac{4}{2} = 2$ in.　　　Short candle: $r = \dfrac{6}{2} = 3$ in.

STEP 2 **Calculate** the volume of each candle. Use 3.14 for π.

Tall candle: $V = \pi r^2 h$　　　　Short candle: $V = \pi r^2 h$

$\approx (3.14)(2)^2(8)$　　　　　$\approx (3.14)(3)^2(5)$

≈ 100 in.^{3}　　　　　≈ 141 in.^{3}

▶ **Answer** The short candle contains more wax than the tall candle.

EXAMPLE 3 Finding the Radius of a Cylinder

A cylinder has a height of 9 feet and a volume of 706.5 cubic feet. Find the radius of the cylinder. Use 3.14 for π.

$V = \pi r^2 h$	Write formula for volume of cylinder.
$706.5 \approx (3.14)r^2(9)$	Substitute values.
$706.5 = 28.26r^2$	Multiply.
$25 = r^2$	Divide each side by 28.26.
$\sqrt{25} = r$	Take positive square root of each side.
$5 = r$	Evaluate square root.

SOLVE SQUARE ROOT EQUATIONS

Need help with solving equations using square roots? See p. 577.

▶ **Answer** The radius of the cylinder is about 5 feet.

✓ **GUIDED PRACTICE** for Examples 1, 2, and 3

1. Find the volume of each cylinder below. Use 3.14 for π. Which cylinder has the greater volume?

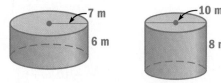

7 m

6 m

10 m

8 m

2. Find the radius of a cylinder that has a height of 5 inches and a volume of 251.2 cubic inches. Use 3.14 for π.

12.6 EXERCISES

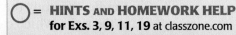
SKILL PRACTICE

SEE EXAMPLE 1
on p. 662
for Exs. 2–8

1. **VOCABULARY** Copy and complete: To find the volume of a cylinder, multiply the area of a(n) __?__ and the __?__.

FINDING VOLUME Find the volume of the cylinder. Use 3.14 for π. Check your answer using estimation.

2.
1 in.
3 in.

3.
5 m
4 m

4.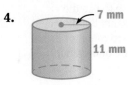
7 mm
11 mm

5. $r = 8$ ft, $h = 8$ ft

6. $d = 6$ in., $h = 4$ in.

7. $d = 8$ cm, $h = 9$ cm

8. **ERROR ANALYSIS** Describe and correct the error made in calculating the volume of the cylinder at the right.

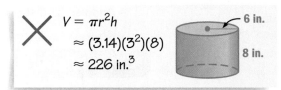

$$V = \pi r^2 h$$
$$\approx (3.14)(3^2)(8)$$
$$\approx 226 \text{ in.}^3$$

6 in.
8 in.

SEE EXAMPLE 2
on p. 663
for Exs. 9–10

COMPARING VOLUMES Tell which cylinder has the greater volume.

9. Cylinder A: $r = 6$ m, $h = 13$ m;
   Cylinder B: $r = 8$ m, $h = 7.5$ m

10. Cylinder C: $r = 3$ yd, $h = 9$ yd;
    Cylinder D: $r = 6$ yd, $h = 4.5$ yd

SEE EXAMPLE 3
on p. 663
for Exs. 11–13

xy ALGEBRA Find the unknown dimension of the cylinder. Use 3.14 for π.

11. $V = 5024$ in.^{3}
    $d = 16$ in.
    $h = $ __?__

12. $V = 25.12$ cm^3
    $r = $ __?__
    $h = 8$ cm

13. $V = 5338$ ft^3
    $d = $ __?__
    $h = 17$ ft

14. ★ **MULTIPLE CHOICE** Which of the following are possible dimensions of a cylinder that has a volume of about 250 cubic units?

    (A) $r = 8, h = 10$ (B) $r = 1, h = 4$ (C) $r = 2, h = 6$ (D) $r = 3, h = 9$

FINDING VOLUMES OF SOLIDS Find the volume of the solid.

15.
4 ft
10 ft
10 ft

16.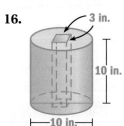
3 in.
10 in.
10 in.

17.
10 yd
2 yd
8 yd
9 yd

18. **CHALLENGE** The volume of the cone at the right is 100π. How is this volume related to the volume of a cylinder with the same base and height? Predict the formula for the volume of a cone.

12 cm
5 cm

PROBLEM SOLVING

SEE EXAMPLE 1
on p. 662
for Ex. 19

19. ★ **MULTIPLE CHOICE** A cylindrical haystack has a diameter of 6 feet and a height of 7 feet. What is the approximate volume of the haystack?

Ⓐ 198 ft^3 Ⓑ 462 ft^3 Ⓒ 791 ft^3 Ⓓ 923 ft^3

20. GUIDED PROBLEM SOLVING A cheese-filled pretzel snack is a cylinder that has a radius of 0.7 centimeter and a height of 2.2 centimeters. The cheese center has a radius of 0.3 centimeter and height of 2.2 centimeters. What percent of the snack is cheese?

  a. Find the volume of the snack. Use 3.14 for π.

  b. Find the volume of the cheese. Use 3.14 for π.

  c. What percent of the snack is cheese? Round to the nearest percent.

21. ★ **WRITING** A cylindrical drinking glass has a diameter of 3 inches and a height of 9 inches. A square pan has a side length of 5 inches and a height of 3 inches. Suppose the glass is full of water and you pour the water into the pan. Will the pan overflow? *Explain.*

22. ★ **SHORT RESPONSE** What is the volume of the chest shown at the right? *Explain* how you found your answer. Check using estimation.

20 in.

26 in.   38 in.

23. REASONING A cylindrical above-ground swimming pool has a diameter of 16 feet and a height of 4 feet. A cylindrical kiddie pool has a diameter of 8 feet and a height of 2 feet. The larger pool can hold 25 tons of water. Write and solve a proportion to find how much water the smaller pool can hold.

READING *IN* MATH Read the information below for Exercises 24–26.

Biosphere The Myriad Gardens Crystal Bridge is a nature conservatory in Oklahoma City. The bridge is composed of two solids. The building is shaped approximately like a cylinder with a diameter of 70 feet and a height of 224 feet. A small cylindrical biosphere room that houses rainforest reptiles is attached to one end of the bridge. This room has a diameter of 10 feet and a height of 20 feet.

24. Calculate Find the surface area of the Myriad Gardens Crystal Bridge, including the biosphere room.

25. Calculate The air in the Crystal Bridge has to be regulated for temperature and humidity. How many cubic feet of air does the bridge contain?

26. Compare *Compare* the volume of the biosphere room with the volume of a greenhouse in the shape of a rectangular prism of length 20 feet, width 10 feet, and height 8 feet. Which has a greater volume, and by how many cubic feet?

27. CHECKING REASONABLENESS The table gives dimensions of different coins. To the nearest hundred cubic millimeters, find the volume of a $1.00 stack of each coin. Use estimation to check the reasonableness of your answers.

Coin	Penny	Nickel	Dime	Quarter
Diameter (mm)	19.05	21.21	17.91	24.26
Thickness (mm)	1.55	1.95	1.35	1.75

28. CHALLENGE Three tennis balls fit tightly in a can. Find the volume of the can. Round to the nearest cubic centimeter.

— 3.25 cm

 NEW JERSEY MIXED REVIEW TEST PRACTICE at classzone.com

29. The top, side, and front views of a solid figure made of cubes are shown below. Which solid figure is best represented by these views?

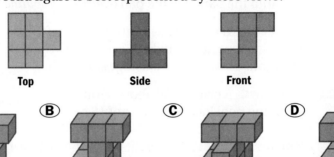

Top   Side   Front

Ⓐ   Ⓑ   Ⓒ   Ⓓ

QUIZ *for Lessons 12.4–12.6*

Find the volume of the rectangular prism. *(p. 655)*

1.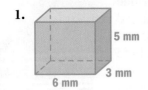
5 mm
6 mm   3 mm

2.
7 cm
4 cm   4 cm

3.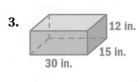
12 in.
15 in.
30 in.

Find the surface area and volume of the cylinder. Use 3.14 for π. *(pp. 649, 662)*

4.
9 yd
13 yd

5.
5 m
2.4 m

6.
32 ft
10 ft

7. BUILDING MATERIALS A brick has a width of 3.75 inches, a height of 2.25 inches, and a volume of 67.5 cubic inches. Find the length of the brick. *(p. 655)*

Technology **ACTIVITY** *Use after Lesson 12.6*

GOAL
Use spreadsheet software to calculate the surface area and volume of a solid.

12.6 Surface Area and Volume

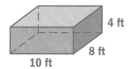

Animated **Math**
at classzone.com

EXAMPLE Find the volume and surface area of the rectangular prism shown. Then double all the dimensions and compare the surface area and volume of the new prism with those of the original prism.

4 ft
8 ft
10 ft

SOLUTION

STEP 1 **Label** five columns for length, width, height, surface area, and volume in the first row. Then enter the dimensions of the original prism and the formulas for surface area and volume as shown. Use * for multiplication.

	A	B	C	D	E
1	Length	Width	Height	Surface area	Volume
2	10	8	4	=2*A2*B2+2*A2*C2+2*B2*C2	=A2*B2*C2

STEP 2 **Enter** the doubled dimensions into row 3. Then use the *Fill down* feature to have the spreadsheet calculate the surface area and volume of the new prism.

	A	B	C	D	E
1	Length	Width	Height	Surface area	Volume
2	10	8	4	304	320
3	20	16	8	1216	2560

▸ **Answer** The surface area of the new prism is 4 times the surface area of the original prism. Its volume is 8 times the volume of the original.

PRACTICE Use the spreadsheet to find the surface area and volume of a rectangular prism with the given dimensions.

1. $l = 4$ in., $w = 3$ in., $h = 2.3$ in.   **2.** $l = 6.5$ cm, $w = 2.5$ cm, $h = 1.5$ cm

3. REASONING Make a conjecture about the effect that tripling all three dimensions of a rectangular prism has on the surface area and volume of the prism. Use the spreadsheet program to check your conjecture.

4. REASONING The dimensions of a prism are increased n times. Write a formula comparing the volume V of the smaller prism to the volume V' of the larger.

5. Create a spreadsheet that calculates the surface area and volume of a cylinder given its radius and height. Use PI() for π and ^2 for squaring.

12.6 Volume of Cylinders **667**

Lessons 12.4–12.6

1. **VOLUME** A mechanical spacer can be wrapped around a hollow cylindrical core, as shown. What is the volume of the mechanical spacer to the nearest cubic inch? Use 3.14 for π.

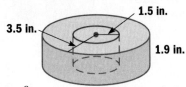

3.5 in.   1.5 in.   1.9 in.

   A.   42 in.^{3}

   B.   60 in.^{3}

   C.   73 in.^{3}

   D.   91 in.^{3}

2. **PACKAGING** A block of cheese in the shape of a rectangular prism has dimensions 7.5 centimeters by 7.5 centimeters by 4 centimeters. The cheese comes encased in a layer of wax. The manufacturer needs to encase the same volume of cheese using less wax without changing the thickness of the wax. The cheese will still be in the shape of a rectangular prism. Which set of dimensions does NOT meet the manufacturer's needs?

   A.   4.5 cm $\times$ 5 cm $\times$ 10 cm

   B.   4.5 cm $\times$ 6.25 cm $\times$ 8 cm

   C.   5 cm $\times$ 5 cm $\times$ 9 cm

   D.   6 cm $\times$ 6 cm $\times$ 6.25 cm

3. **ICE** A block of ice in the shape of a cube has a surface area of 96 square centimeters. What is its volume, in cubic centimeters?

   A.   16

   B.   36

   C.   64

   D.   256

4. **CHANGING DIMENSIONS** How do the volume and surface area of a cylinder change if the radius and height are doubled?

   A.   The volume increases by a factor of 8 and the surface area increases by a factor of 4.

   B.   The volume increases by a factor of 4 and the surface area increases by a factor of 8.

   C.   The volume and surface area both increase by a factor of 4.

   D.   The volume and surface area both increase by a factor of 8.

5. **MEASUREMENT** A chemist uses a glass cylinder to measure volumes of liquid chemicals. The cylinder comes in a box in the shape of a rectangular prism with square ends that are 4 inches wide, and a height of 8 inches. The cylinder fits snugly inside the box. Which expression gives the maximum number of cubic inches that the chemist can measure in the cylinder?

   A. $\pi(2^2)(8)$

   B. $\pi(4^2)(8)$

   C. $2\pi(2)(8) + 2\pi(2^2)$

   D. $2\pi(4)(8) + 2\pi(4^2)$

6. **OPEN-ENDED** The radius of a cylindrical stirring rod is 0.1 inch, and its height is 6 inches.

   • Find the surface area of the stirring rod.

   • Find the volume of the stirring rod.

   • How do the surface area and volume of the stirring rod change if the dimensions are doubled? *Explain* your answer.

REVIEW KEY VOCABULARY

- solid, *p. 631*
- prism, *p. 631*
- pyramid, *p. 631*
- cylinder, *p. 631*

- cone, *p. 631*
- sphere, *p. 631*
- face, *p. 632*
- edge, *p. 632*

- vertex, *p. 632*
- surface area, *p. 642*
- net, *p. 642*
- volume, *p. 655*

VOCABULARY EXERCISES

Copy and complete the statement.

1. The __?__ of a rectangular prism is the sum of the areas of its faces.

2. The __?__ of a solid is the amount of space it contains.

3. Polygons that form the sides of a prism or pyramid are called __?__.

4. The two-dimensional representation of a solid is called a(n) __?__.

5. A(n) __?__ is a solid with two congruent circular bases that lie in parallel planes.

6. A solid that has *n* triangular faces and a polygonal base with *n* sides is a(n) __?__.

7. All points in space that are the same distance from a fixed point form a(n) __?__.

REVIEW EXAMPLES AND EXERCISES

12.1 Classifying Solids

pp. 631–635

EXAMPLE

Classify the solid. Be as specific as possible.

a.

b.

SOLUTION

a. The solid has one circular base. It is a cone.

b. The solid has 2 parallel bases. The bases are triangles, so the solid is a triangular prism.

EXERCISES

Classify the solid. Be as specific as possible.

SEE EXAMPLES
1, 2, AND 3
on pp. 631–632
for Exs. 8–11

8.

9.

10. Count the number of faces, edges, and vertices in the solid in Exercise 9.

11. The base of a prism is an *n*-sided polygon. How many faces does the prism have? How many edges? How many vertices? *Explain.*

12.2 Sketching Solids

pp. 636–639

EXAMPLE

Sketch a hexagonal prism.

SOLUTION

STEP 1
Sketch two congruent hexagons.

STEP 2
Connect corresponding vertices using line segments.

STEP 3
Change any "hidden" lines to dashed lines.

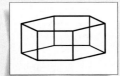
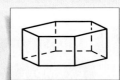

EXERCISES

Sketch the solid.

SEE EXAMPLES
1, 2, AND 3
on pp. 636–637
for Exs. 12–17

12. Pentagonal prism

13. Triangular pyramid

14. Triangular prism

15. Pentagonal pyramid

16. Sketch the top, side, and front views of the square pyramid at the right.

17. Sketch the top, side, and front views of the hexagonal prism in the Example above.

12.3 Surface Area of Rectangular Prisms

pp. 642–647

EXAMPLE

Find the surface area of the rectangular prism.

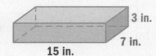

3 in.
7 in.
15 in.

SOLUTION

$$S = 2lw + 2lh + 2wh$$ Write formula for surface area.

$$= 2(15)(7) + 2(15)(3) + 2(7)(3)$$ Substitute values.

$$= 210 + 90 + 42$$ Multiply.

$$= 342 \text{ in.}^2$$ Add.

EXERCISES

SEE EXAMPLE 2
on p. 643
for Ex. 18

18. Find the surface area of the rectangular prism.

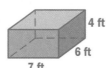

4 ft
6 ft
7 ft

12.4 Surface Area of Cylinders

pp. 649–653

EXAMPLE

Find the surface area of the cylinder. Use 3.14 for π.

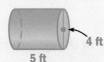

4 ft
5 ft

SOLUTION

Because the diameter is 4 feet, the radius is 2 feet.

$$S = 2\pi r^2 + 2\pi rh$$ Write formula for surface area.

$$\approx 2(3.14)(2)^2 + 2(3.14)(2)(5)$$ Substitute values.

$$= 25.12 + 62.8$$ Multiply.

$$= 87.92 \text{ ft}^2$$ Add.

EXERCISES

SEE EXAMPLE 1
on p. 650
for Ex. 19

19. Find the surface area of the cylinder. Use 3.14 for π.

11 in.
6 in.

12.5 Volume of Rectangular Prisms

pp. 655–659

EXAMPLE

Find the volume of the rectangular prism.

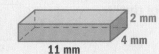

SOLUTION

$V = lwh$ **Write formula for volume.**

$= (11)(4)(2)$ **Substitute values.**

$= 88 \text{ mm}^3$ **Multiply.**

EXERCISES

Find the volume of the rectangular prism.

SEE EXAMPLE 1
on p. 655
for Exs. 20–22

20.
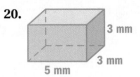

21.
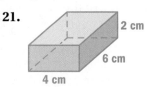

22.
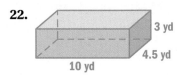

12.6 Volume of Cylinders

pp. 662–666

EXAMPLE

Find the volume of the cylinder. Use 3.14 for π.

SOLUTION

$V = \pi r^2 h$ **Write formula for volume.**

$\approx (3.14)(10)^2(5)$ **Substitute values.**

$= 1570 \text{ cm}^3$ **Simplify.**

EXERCISES

*SEE EXAMPLES
1 AND 3*
on pp. 662–663
for Exs. 23–24

23. Find the volume of a cylinder that has a diameter of 6 inches and a height of 6.5 inches. Use 3.14 for π.

24. Find the radius of a cylinder that has a height of 9 centimeters and a volume of 11,304 cubic centimeters. Use 3.14 for π.

12 CHAPTER TEST

In Exercises 1 and 2, use the diagram of the solid.

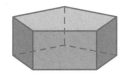

1. Classify the solid. Be as specific as possible.

2. Count the number of faces, edges, and vertices in the solid.

3. Sketch a rectangular pyramid.

4. Order the rectangular prisms from least to greatest surface area.

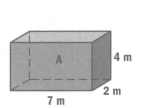 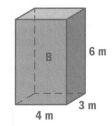 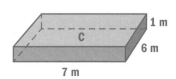

Find the volume of the rectangular prism.

5.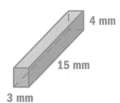

6.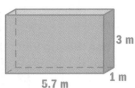

7.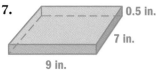

Find the surface area and volume of the cylinder. Use 3.14 for π.

8.

9.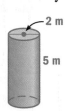

10.

11. Find the height of a cylinder that has a radius of 3 centimeters and a surface area of 108.33 square centimeters. Use 3.14 for π.

12. Find the length of a rectangular prism that has a width of 4.5 inches, a height of 5 inches, and a volume of 135 cubic inches.

13. Find the radius of a cylinder that has a height of 3 centimeters and a volume of 942 cubic centimeters. Use 3.14 for π.

14. **DRUMS** Find the surface area and volume of the drum at the right. Use 3.14 for π.

15. **DVD CASE** A standard DVD case is a rectangular prism that is 19 centimeters long, 13.5 centimeters wide, and 1.4 centimeters high. Find the surface area and volume of the DVD case.

REVIEWING SOLID FIGURE PROBLEMS

You can use what you learned about solids in Chapter 12 to:

- draw a solid given its top, side, and front views
- classify a solid given its net
- find the volumes of prisms ($V = lwh$) and cylinders ($V = \pi r^2 h$)

> **EXAMPLE**
>
> **Use the three views of a solid to build and draw the solid.**
>
>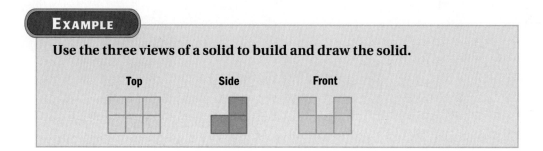
>
> Top   Side   Front

Solution

STEP 1   **Use** the top view. It gives you information about the bottom layer of the solid.

STEP 2   **Use** the side view. It gives you information about the number of layers and how to form them.

STEP 3   **Use** the front view. It also gives you information about the number of layers and how to form them.

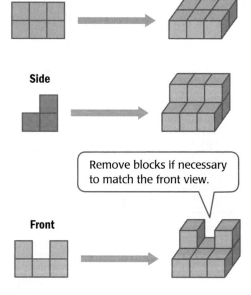

Remove blocks if necessary to match the front view.

TEST PREPARATION

SOLID FIGURE PROBLEMS

Below are examples of solid figure problems in multiple choice format. Try solving the problems before looking at the solutions. (Cover the solutions with a piece of paper.) Then check your solutions against the ones given.

1. The net shown at the right represents which of the following solids?

   A. Triangular prism

   B. Rectangular prism

   C. Rectangular pyramid

   D. Triangular pyramid

   Solution

   The net represents a solid whose base is a triangle. The other polygons in the net are also triangles, so the net represents a triangular pyramid.

   The correct answer is D.

2. Eighteen blocks like the one shown below will fit in a box arranged as shown. Which expression gives the volume of the box in cubic inches?

   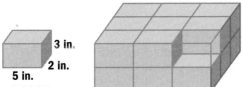

   A. 5(2)(3)

   B. 3[5(2)(3)]

   C. 18[5(2)(3)]

   D. 18[15(6)(6)]

   Solution

   The volume of a rectangular prism is the product of the length, width, and height.

   The volume of each block is 5(2)(3).

   There are 18 blocks that fit in the box, so the volume of the box is given by the expression 18[5(2)(3)].

   The correct answer is C.

3. What is the volume of the triangular prism shown below?

   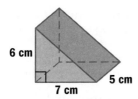

   A. 42 cm^3

   B. 94.5 cm^3

   C. 105 cm^3

   D. 210 cm^3

   Solution

   The volume of a triangular prism is the product of the area of the base and the height.

   $$V = Bh$$
   $$= \left[\frac{1}{2}(6)(7)\right] \cdot 5$$
   $$= 105$$

   The volume of the triangular prism is 105 cubic centimeters, so the correct answer is C.

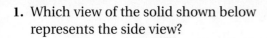
TEST PREPARATION

1. Which view of the solid shown below represents the side view?

A.

B.

C.

D.

2. What is the volume of a rectangular block of cheese that is 4 inches wide, 6 inches long, and 1.5 inches high?

   A. 24 in.^{3}

   B. 36 in.^{3}

   C. 48 in.^{3}

   D. 78 in.^{3}

3. What kind of solid has exactly one circular base?

   A. Circular pyramid

   B. Cylinder

   C. Sphere

   D. Cone

4. The net shown below represents which of the following solids?

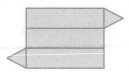

   A. Rectangular prism

   B. Rectangular pyramid

   C. Triangular prism

   D. Triangular pyramid

5. A swimming pool has the dimensions shown. The height of the water in the pool is 3 feet. About how much water needs to be added for the water level to be 4 feet? Use 3.14 for π.

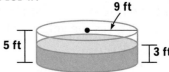

   A. 254 ft^3

   B. 763 ft^3

   C. 1018 ft^3

   D. 1272 ft^3

6. A student's work for Exercise 5 leads to an answer of 550 cubic feet. Why is the answer unreasonable?

   A. It is smaller than the volume of the water already in the pool.

   B. The volume of the pool is less than 550 cubic feet.

   C. The pool can hold significantly more water than 550 cubic feet.

   D. The pool cannot hold that much additional water.

7. Which kind of solid is shown below?

- **A.** Hexagonal prism
- **B.** Pentagonal prism
- **C.** Octagonal pyramid
- **D.** Pentagonal pyramid

8. The graph correctly represents the dimensions mentioned in which of the following statements?

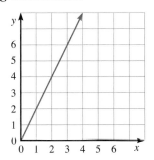

- **A.** The volume y of a cube with side length x
- **B.** The volume y of a rectangular prism with base area 2 and height x
- **C.** The volume y of a cylinder with radius x and height 2
- **D.** The volume y of a cylinder with radius 2 and height x

9. The area of one face of a nickel is about 350 mm². What method would you use to find the number of cubic millimeters in a stack of 8 nickels, each 2 mm thick?

- **A.** Divide the area of one face by 16.
- **B.** Divide the area of one face by 16π.
- **C.** Multiply the area of one face by 16.
- **D.** Multiply the area of one face by 16^2.

10. What is the approximate volume of the glue stick shown below?

3 cm

12 cm

- **A.** 57 cm³
- **B.** 85 cm³
- **C.** 113 cm³
- **D.** 339 cm³

11. Which equation can be used to find the surface area S of the glue stick in Exercise 10?

- **A.** $S = 2\pi(1.5)(12) + 2\pi(1.5)^2$
- **B.** $S = 2\pi(1.5)(12) + 2\pi(1.5)$
- **C.** $S = 2\pi(3)(12) + 2\pi(3)^2$
- **D.** $S = 2\pi(3) + 2\pi(3)^2(12)$

12. OPEN-ENDED The Giant Ocean Tank at the New England Aquarium in Boston is a cylindrical tank that has a radius of 20 feet and a height of 23 feet.

Part A How much water, in gallons, can the tank hold? Use the fact that 1 cubic foot is approximately equal to 7.5 gallons.

Part B If water is pumped into the tank at a rate of 100 gallons per minute, how many hours will it take to fill the tank? *Explain.*

TEST PREPARATION

13 Probability

Before

In previous chapters you've . . .

• Used Venn diagrams
• Worked with fractions, decimals, and percents

Now

 New Jersey Standards

4.4.B.1	13.1	Probability
4.4.C.3	13.2	Tree diagrams
4.4.C.3	13.3	The counting principle
4.4.C.1.a	13.4	Arrangements
4.4.B.3	13.5	Disjoint events
4.4.B.3	13.6	Compound event

Why?

So you can solve real-world problems about . . .

• basketball, p. 686
• lockers, p. 699
• sunglasses, p. 704
• sign language, p. 711

 **Math**
at classzone.com

• Introduction to Probability, p. 683
• Finding Outcomes, p. 691
• Disjoint Events, p. 709

Get-Ready Games

Review Prerequisite Skills by playing *Ocean Discovery* and *Collecting Seashells*.

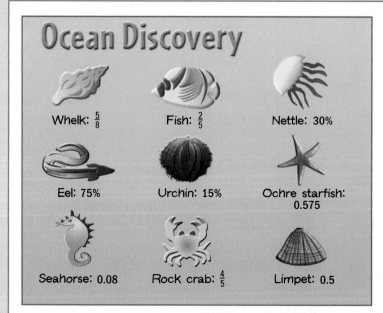

Ocean Discovery

Whelk: $\frac{5}{8}$ Fish: $\frac{2}{5}$ Nettle: 30%

Eel: 75%   Urchin: 15%   Ochre starfish: 0.575

Seahorse: 0.08   Rock crab: $\frac{4}{5}$ Limpet: 0.5

Skill Focus: Working with fractions, decimals, and percents

• Order the numbers from least to greatest. Write the names associated with the numbers in the same order. The first letters of the names will spell out the largest and fastest-moving type of starfish.

• Write all the numbers as decimals. Add the decimals and round to the nearest whole number to find how quickly, in feet per minute, this starfish can move.

Collecting Seashells

Broken Colored

Patterned

Skill Focus:

- Using Venn diagrams

- Using logical reasoning

Suppose you find 76 seashells. You want to sort them into the categories shown in the Venn diagram above. Copy the diagram and use the information below to complete it.

- You have 8 seashells that are broken and are neither colored nor patterned.

- You have 51 unbroken seashells and 25 broken ones.

- You have 17 colored seashells and 16 patterned seashells.

- One of the 3 colored and patterned seashells is broken.

- You have 7 colored seashells that are broken.

Stop and Think

1. **CRITICAL THINKING** In *Ocean Discovery*, you had to add decimals. Suppose you had to find the sum of the repeating decimals $0.\overline{3}$ and $0.\overline{6}$. Use fractions to show that the sum of these numbers is 1.

2. **WRITING** In *Collecting Seashells*, suppose you find 5 additional unbroken seashells. These seashells are colored and patterned. Explain how you would change your Venn diagram.

Review Prerequisite Skills

REVIEW WORDS
- **decimal,** *p. 56*
- **frequency table,** *p. 138*
- **fraction,** *p. 176*
- **percent,** *p. 449*
- **Venn diagram,** *p. 756*
- **data,** *p. 757*

VOCABULARY CHECK

Copy and complete using a review word from the list at the left.

1. A(n) _?_ uses shapes to show how sets are related.

2. A(n) _?_ is a number written in the form $\frac{a}{b}$ $(b \neq 0)$.

3. A(n) _?_ is a ratio whose denominator is 100.

SKILL CHECK

Use the Venn diagram to tell whether the statement is *true* or *false*. (p. 756)

4. Lisa plays basketball.

5. Two students play soccer but not basketball.

6. More students play basketball than play soccer.

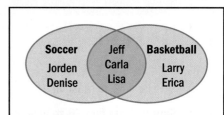

@HomeTutor   Prerequisite skills practice at classzone.com

Notetaking Skills   Concept Grid

In each chapter you will learn a new notetaking skill. In Chapter 13 you will apply the strategy of using a concept grid to Example 1 on p. 709.

You can use a concept grid to take notes on new concepts you learn. A concept grid includes a definition and a list of characteristics, as well as examples and nonexamples.

Definition: A proportion is an equation that states that two ratios are equivalent.	**Characteristics:** The cross-products of a proportion are equal.
Examples: $\frac{8}{10} = \frac{20}{25}$ and $\frac{4}{12} = \frac{20}{x}$	**Nonexamples:** The ratios $\frac{3}{7}$ and $\frac{6}{15}$ do not form a proportion because 3×15 is not equal to 7×6.

proportion

INVESTIGATION
Use before Lesson 13.1

GOAL
Use an experiment to find the probability of an event.

MATERIALS
• two number cubes

13.1 Investigating Probability

The *probability* of an event is a measure of the likelihood that the event will occur. You can conduct an experiment to find the probability of an event.

EXPLORE Two number cubes are rolled. Find the probability that the sum of the resulting numbers is 7.

STEP 1 **Roll** two number cubes 50 times. Record the sums of the resulting numbers and the corresponding frequencies in a frequency table like the one shown below.

Sum	2	3	4	5	6	7	8	9	10	11	12
Tally	?	?	?	?	?	?	?	?	?	?	?
Frequency	?	?	?	?	?	?	?	?	?	?	?

STEP 2 **Find** the probability of a sum of 7 by dividing the number of rolls that have a sum of 7 by the total number of rolls.

$$\text{Probability of a sum of 7} = \frac{\text{Number of rolls that have a sum of 7}}{\text{Total number of rolls}}$$

PRACTICE Complete the following exercises.

1. To find the sums of the numbers that can result when two number cubes are rolled, copy and complete the table at the right.

2. Use your completed table to find the fraction of the outcomes that have a sum of 7. How does your answer compare with the probability that you found in Step 2?

	1	2	3	4	5	6
1	2	3	?	?	?	?
2	3	4	?	?	?	?
3	?	?	?	?	?	?
4	?	?	?	?	?	?
5	?	?	?	?	?	?
6	?	?	?	?	?	?

DRAW CONCLUSIONS

3. **REASONING** Suppose that two number cubes are rolled 90 times. For each roll, the product of the resulting numbers is found. How many rolls would you expect to have a product of 6? *Explain* your reasoning.

13.1 Introduction to Probability

NJ 4.4.B.1 Interpret probabilities as ratios, percents, and decimals.

Before	You wrote ratios.
Now	You'll find probabilities.
Why?	So you can describe animal behavior, as in Example 2.

KEY VOCABULARY
- outcomes, *p. 682*
- event, *p. 682*
- favorable outcomes, *p. 682*
- probability, *p. 682*
- theoretical probability, *p. 683*
- experimental probability, *p. 683*

When you perform an experiment, the possible results are called **outcomes**. An **event** is a collection of outcomes. Once you specify an event, the outcomes for that event are called **favorable outcomes**.

The **probability** of an event is a measure of the likelihood that the event will occur. Use the formula below to find the probability *P* of an event when all of the outcomes are equally likely.

$$P(\text{event}) = \frac{\text{Number of favorable outcomes}}{\text{Total number of outcomes}}$$

EXAMPLE 1 Finding a Probability

Find the probability of randomly choosing a blue marble from the marbles shown at the right.

$P(\text{blue}) = \dfrac{3}{10}$ ← There are 3 blue marbles.
← There are 10 marbles in all.

WRITE PROBABILITIES
You can write probabilities as fractions, decimals, or percents.

▶ **Answer** The probability of choosing a blue marble is $\frac{3}{10}$, 0.3, or 30%.

Probabilities can range from 0 to 1. The closer the probability of an event is to 1, the more likely it is that the event will occur.

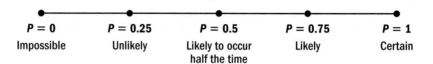

| *P* = 0 | *P* = 0.25 | *P* = 0.5 | *P* = 0.75 | *P* = 1 |
| Impossible | Unlikely | Likely to occur half the time | Likely | Certain |

✓ **GUIDED PRACTICE**   for Example 1

1. **What If?** In Example 1, suppose you randomly choose a green marble. Find the probability of this event.

2. **Coins** Find the probability of getting tails when you flip a coin.

3. **Number Cube** Find the probability of rolling a 5 on a number cube.

Types of Probability The probability found in Example 1 is a **theoretical probability** because it is based on knowing all of the equally likely outcomes.

Probability that is based on repeated *trials* of an experiment is called **experimental probability**. Each trial in which the event occurs is a *success*. You can use the formula below to find the experimental probability of an event.

$$\text{Experimental probability of an event} = \frac{\text{Number of successes}}{\text{Number of trials}}$$

EXAMPLE 2 Finding an Experimental Probability

Animal Training A cat that knows the shake command offers one of its front paws to shake. The table shows the number of times the cat offered each of its paws when asked to shake.

Paw Offered to Shake	
Left paw	38
Right paw	12

What is the experimental probability that the cat will offer its right paw when asked to shake?

SOLUTION

STEP 1 **Determine** the number of successes and the number of trials.

Because a success is offering a right paw, there are **12** successes.

There are $38 + 12 = $ **50** trials.

STEP 2 **Find** the probability.

$$P(\text{right paw}) = \frac{12}{50} \quad \longleftarrow \text{There are 12 successes.}$$
$$\phantom{P(\text{right paw}) = \frac{12}{50}} \quad \longleftarrow \text{There are 50 trials.}$$

$$= \frac{6}{25} \quad \text{Simplify.}$$

▶ **Answer** The probability that the cat will offer its right paw when asked to shake is $\frac{6}{25}$, 0.24, or 24%.

Animated **Math** at classzone.com

✓ **GUIDED PRACTICE** for Example 2

4. **What If?** In Example 2, what is the probability that the cat will offer its left paw when asked to shake?

5. **Election** Of the 20 voters polled after an election for class president, 14 of the voters voted for Sean. What is the probability that a randomly chosen voter voted for Sean?

6. **Survey** Of the 30 students surveyed in the school hallway, 8 of them said their favorite class was science. What is the probability that a randomly chosen student likes science class best?

EXAMPLE 3 Standardized Test Practice

MP3 Players A survey of 200 twelve to seventeen year olds indicated that 54 of them own a portable MP3 player. Which equation could you use to predict the number of twelve to seventeen year olds out of 500 who own a portable MP3 player?

ELIMINATE CHOICES
The value of x must be less than or equal to 500. So, choices B and D can be eliminated.

(A) $\frac{54}{200} = \frac{x}{500}$ **(B)** $\frac{54}{200} = \frac{500}{x}$ **(C)** $\frac{54}{500} = \frac{x}{200}$ **(D)** $\frac{200}{54} = \frac{x}{500}$

SOLUTION

You can solve the problem by using ratios to form a proportion.

$$\frac{\text{Number surveyed with an MP3 player}}{200} = \frac{\text{Number predicted with an MP3 player}}{500}$$

$$\frac{54}{200} = \frac{x}{500}$$

▶ **Answer** You can solve $\frac{54}{200} = \frac{x}{500}$ to predict that 135 of 500 teens own a portable MP3 player. The correct answer is A. **Ⓐ Ⓑ Ⓒ Ⓓ**

✓ **GUIDED PRACTICE**   **for Example 3**

7. **Remote Controls** A survey of 100 households found that 48% had 2 or 3 TV remote controls. Write and solve an equation to predict the number of households out of 2500 who have 2 or 3 TV remote controls.

13.1 **EXERCISES**

HOMEWORK KEY

★ = **STANDARDIZED TEST PRACTICE**
Exs. 14, 30, 35, 36, 37, and 46

◯ = **HINTS AND HOMEWORK HELP**
for Exs. 3, 5, 7, 11, 31 at classzone.com

SKILL PRACTICE

VOCABULARY Copy and complete the statement.

1. The _?_ of an event is a measure of the likelihood that the event will occur.

2. The possible results of an experiment are called _?_.

SEE EXAMPLE 1
on p. 682 for
Exs. 3–6

MATCHING You spin the spinner at right, which is divided into equal parts. Match the event with the letter on the number line that indicates the probability of the event.

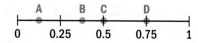

3. Pointer lands on green.

4. Pointer lands on 7.

5. Pointer lands on an even number.

6. Pointer lands on a prime number.

SEE EXAMPLE 1
on p. 682
for Exs. 7–10, 14

THEORETICAL PROBABILITY **You randomly choose a marble from the marbles below. Find the probability of choosing a marble of the given color. Write the probability as a fraction, a decimal, and a percent.**

7. Blue   **8.** Red   **9.** Green   **10.** Yellow

EXPERIMENTAL PROBABILITY **A bag contains red, blue, and green tiles. You randomly choose a tile from the bag, record the result, and then replace it. The table shows the results of several trials. Write the probability of the event as a fraction.**

SEE EXAMPLE 2
on p. 683
for Exs. 11–13

11. You choose a red tile.

12. You choose a blue tile.

13. You choose a green tile.

Tile color	red	blue	green
Times chosen	9	5	6

14. ★ **MULTIPLE CHOICE** What is the probability that you randomly choose a green ticket from a stack of 3 red, 2 green, and 5 blue tickets?

   Ⓐ $\frac{1}{5}$ Ⓑ $\frac{2}{8}$ Ⓒ $\frac{2}{5}$ Ⓓ $\frac{8}{10}$

THEORETICAL PROBABILITY **You roll a number cube. Find the probability of the event. Write the probability as a decimal rounded to the nearest hundredth. Predict the number of times the event will occur in 200 rolls.**

SEE EXAMPLES 1 AND 3
on pp. 682–684
for Exs. 15–21

15. You roll a 3 or a 6.   **16.** You roll a 9.

17. You roll a positive number.   **18.** You roll a prime number.

19. You roll a multiple of 2.   **20.** You roll a number less than 4.

21. ERROR ANALYSIS Describe and correct the error made in finding the probability of randomly choosing a red bean from a bag containing 5 red beans and 9 blue beans.

$P(\text{red}) = \dfrac{\text{Number of red beans}}{\text{Number of blue beans}} = \dfrac{5}{9}$ ✗

So, the probability of choosing a red bean is $\dfrac{5}{9}$.

22. UNDERSTANDING PROBABILITIES Sketch a copy of the spinner shown below. Then color it so that the given probabilities hold true for one spin of the spinner. *Explain* your reasoning.

$P(\text{red}) = \dfrac{1}{6}$ $P(\text{blue}) = \dfrac{1}{2}$

$P(\text{yellow}) = \dfrac{1}{3}$ $P(\text{green}) = 0$

23. REASONING Is it possible to correctly color the spinner in Exercise 22 in several different ways? *Explain* why or why not.

24. REASONING Seven people are drawing straws from a bunch of 6 long straws and 1 short straw. *Describe* how the probability of drawing the short straw changes as each person removes a straw.

25. CHALLENGE You roll two number cubes. What is the probability that the sum of the numbers is less than 5? *Explain* how you can make and use a table to find the answer.

In Exercises 26–28, you are playing a game which uses the spinner shown below. The spinner is divided into equal parts. Find the odds in favor of and the odds against the event.

EXTENSION   Finding Odds

The *odds in favor* and the *odds against* the pointer landing on orange are shown.

▸ Odds in favor $= \dfrac{\text{Favorable outcomes}}{\text{Unfavorable outcomes}} = \dfrac{3}{7}$

   The odds in favor of landing on orange are 3 to 7.

▸ Odds against $= \dfrac{\text{Unfavorable outcomes}}{\text{Favorable outcomes}} = \dfrac{7}{3}$.

   The odds against landing on orange are 7 to 3.

---

26. Landing on blue   **27.** Landing on green   **28.** Landing on yellow

---

PROBLEM SOLVING

29. BLOOD DRIVE At a blood drive held at a school, 2 students out of the 40 students who gave blood have type AB blood. Find the probability that a randomly chosen student has type AB blood. Write the probability as a fraction, a decimal, and a percent.

SEE EXAMPLE 1 on p. 682 for Ex. 30

30. ★ **MULTIPLE CHOICE** Tanya decides to listen to a CD with 12 songs, 3 of which are her favorite songs. If Tanya listens to the songs in random order, what is the probability that the first song played is one of her favorites?

   (A) $\dfrac{1}{4}$ **(B)** $\dfrac{1}{3}$ **(C)** $\dfrac{1}{2}$ **(D)** $\dfrac{3}{4}$

BASKETBALL The table below shows the shots attempted and made by a basketball player during a season. Find the probability that the player makes the given shot. Write the probability as a decimal rounded to the nearest hundredth.

SEE EXAMPLE 2 on p. 683 for Exs. 31–33

31. Free throw

32. Two point

33. Three point

	Free throw	Two point	Three point
Attempted	589	1597	132
Made	488	749	33

34. MULTI-STEP PROBLEM The ability to roll your tongue into a U-shape is inherited from your parents.

  a. You asked 80 students whether they can roll their tongues, and 64 said yes. Find the probability that a randomly selected student can roll his or her tongue. Write the probability as a fraction in simplest form.

  b. There are a total of 2500 students in your school. Predict how many can roll their tongues.

35. ★ WRITING *Compare* theoretical probability to experimental probability. Use examples of each in your comparison.

36. ★ OPEN-ENDED MATH *Describe* a real-world event that has two outcomes that are not equally likely. *Explain* how to use an experiment to find the probability of each outcome.

37. ★ SHORT RESPONSE Flip a coin 20 times and record the outcomes. Find the experimental probability of getting "tails" and compare it with the theoretical probability. Can the theoretical and experimental probabilities be different? *Explain.*

38. MARBLES A bag contains red and blue marbles. The probability of randomly choosing a red marble is 25%, and the probability of randomly choosing a blue marble is 75%. There are 33 blue marbles in the bag. What is the total number of marbles in the bag?

39. GEOMETRY *Geometric probability* is based on areas of geometric regions. You can find geometric probability using the following formula.

$$P(\text{event}) = \frac{\text{Area of favorable outcomes}}{\text{Area of possible outcomes}}$$

What is the probability that a randomly tossed dart that hits the target shown will *not* hit the red circle?

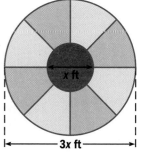

40. CHALLENGE A bus stops at the end of your street every 30 minutes. If you wait for a bus at a randomly chosen time, what is the probability that you wait 10 minutes or less? *Explain.*

 NEW JERSEY MIXED REVIEW  **TEST PRACTICE** at classzone.com

41. What is the volume of the cylinder? Use 3.14 for π.

  A 188.4 in.^{3}

  B 471 in.^{3}

  C 565.2 in.^{3}

  D 2260.8 in.^{3}

Number Sets and Probability

GOAL Apply set theory to numbers and probability.

KEY VOCABULARY

• **set,** *p. 688*
• **element** *p. 688*
• **empty set** *p. 688*
• **universal set** *p. 688*
• **union** *p. 688*
• **intersection** *p. 688*

A **set** is a collection of distinct objects. Each object in a set is an **element** or **member** of the set. You can define a set with set notation. The set A of integers between -3 and 3 can be written as

$$A = \{-2, -1, 0, 1, 2\} \quad \text{or} \quad A = \{x: |x| < 3, \text{ and } x \text{ is an integer}\}.$$

Two special sets are the *empty set* and the *universal set*. The **empty set** is the set with no elements and is written as $\varnothing$. The **universal set** is the set of all elements under consideration and is written as U.

KEY CONCEPT *For Your Notebook*

Union and Intersection of Two Sets

The **union** of two sets A and B is the set of all elements in *either* A or B and is written as $A \cup B$.

The **intersection** of two sets A and B is the set of all elements in *both* A and B and is written as $A \cap B$.

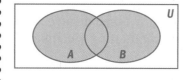

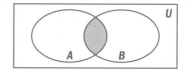

EXAMPLE 1 Find the Union and Intersection of Two Sets

Let U be the set of real numbers. The number line shows that set $A = \{x: |x| < 4\}$ and set $B = \{x: x \geq 0\}$.

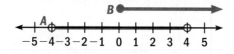

a. Graph $A \cup B$: From the number line you can see that the numbers that are in either set are the numbers greater than -4

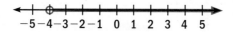

b. Graph $A \cap B$: From the number line you can see that the numbers where sets A and B overlap extend from 0 to 4. The point 0 is included, but the point 4 is not.

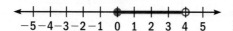

Probability and Sets You can find the probability that an element of set U is in set A as you did for other probabilities.

$$P(\text{event}) = \frac{\text{Number of favorable outcomes}}{\text{Total number of outcomes}} = \frac{\text{Number of elements in set } A}{\text{Number of elements in } U}$$

EXAMPLE 2 Finding Probabilities for Intersection and Union

Universal set U is the odd integers from 10 to 29: $\{11, 13, 15, 17, \ldots, 29\}$. Set A is the set of multiples of five, set B is the set of prime numbers, and set C is the set of multiples of three. Find the probability that a number randomly chosen from Set U is in $A \cup B$ and find the probability that a number chosen randomly is in $(A \cup B) \cap C$.

SOLUTION

STEP 1 List the elements of A, B, and C in the given universal set.

$$A = \{15, 25\} \qquad B = \{11, 13, 17, 19, 23, 29\} \qquad C = \{15, 21, 27\}$$

STEP 2 Find $A \cup B$ and $(A \cup B) \cap C$.

$$A \cup B = \{11, 13, 15, 17, 19, 23, 25, 29\} \qquad \text{The combined sets}$$

$$(A \cup B) \cap C = \{15\} \qquad \text{Elements in both } A \cup B \text{ and } C$$

STEP 3 Calculate the probabilities.

$$P(A \cup B) = \frac{\text{Number of elements in } A \cup B}{\text{Number of elements in } U} = \frac{8}{10} = \frac{4}{5}$$

$$P((A \cup B) \cap C) = \frac{\text{Number of elements in } (A \cup B) \cap C}{\text{Number of elements in } U} = \frac{1}{10}$$

EXERCISES

SEE EXAMPLE 1
on p. 688
for Exs. 1–4

Graph the set of numbers described where $A = \{x: x < 3\}$, $B = \{x: x > 3\}$, $C = \{x: x < 5\}$, and $D = \{x: x > 5\}$.

1. $A \cup D$ **2.** $B \cap C$ **3.** $B \cap D$ **4.** $A \cup C$

Let U be the set of integers whose absolute value is less than or equal to 12. Let A be the set of multiples of four. Let B be the set of even numbers. Let C be the set of multiples of three. Find the probability.

EXAMPLE 2
on p. 689
for Exs. 5–14

5. $P(B \cap C)$ **6.** $P(B \cup C)$

7. $P(A \cup B)$ **8.** $P(A \cap C)$

9. $P(A \cup C)$ **10.** $P(A \cap B)$

11. $P(A \cup (B \cap C))$ **12.** $P(A \cap (B \cup C))$

13. $P((A \cup B) \cap (A \cup C))$ **14.** $P((A \cap B) \cup (A \cap C))$

13.2 Tree Diagrams

NJ 4.4.C.3 Apply techniques of systematic listing, counting, and reasoning in a variety of different contexts.

Before	You used outcomes to find a probability.
Now	You'll use a tree diagram to find all possible outcomes.
Why?	So you can count possibilities, as for groups at science camp in Example 2.

KEY VOCABULARY
- tree diagram, *p. 690*

Fruit Smoothies You are ordering a fruit smoothie. You can choose a small, medium, or large smoothie in one of the following fruit flavors: strawberry, banana, or orange. How many different choices of smoothies do you have?

A **tree diagram** can help you identify and count all the possible outcomes of an event by using branching (as seen on trees) to list choices. The set of all possible outcomes is sometimes called the *sample space*.

 EXAMPLE 1 Making a Tree Diagram

Make a tree diagram to list all of the possible choices of smoothies.

STEP 1 List the sizes. **STEP 2** List the fruit choices for each size. **STEP 3** List the outcomes.

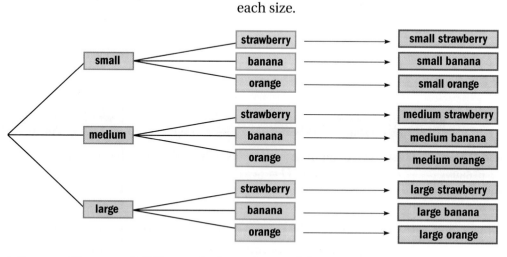

▶ **Answer** There are 9 different choices of smoothies.

✓ **GUIDED PRACTICE** for Example 1

1. **Refreshments** Popcorn at a movie theater comes in regular, large, and jumbo sizes, and it comes either plain or buttered. How many choices of popcorn do you have? Make a tree diagram to solve the problem.

EXAMPLE 2 **Standardized Test Practice**

Science Camp You will be attending two sessions at a science camp. At each session, you will be assigned to one of the following groups: red (R), green (G), blue (B), or yellow (Y). You will not be assigned to the same group for both sessions. Which list gives all possible group assignments?

(A) RG, RB, RY, GB, GY, BY

(B) RG, RB, RY, GR, GB, GY, BR, BG, BY

(C) RG, RB, RY, GR, GB, GY, BR, BG, BY, YR, YG, YB

(D) RR, RG, RB, RY, GG, GR, GB, GY, BB, BR, BG, BY, YY, YR, YG, YB

ELIMINATE CHOICES
You will *not* be assigned to the same group for both sessions, so RR, GG, BB, and YY are not possible. Choice D can be eliminated.

SOLUTION

Because you cannot be in the same group for both sessions, do not include the same group in both sessions in the tree diagram.

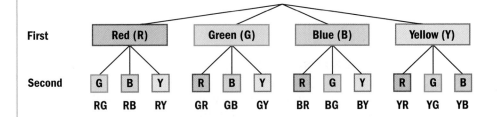

▶ **Answer** The possible group assignments are RG, RB, RY, GR, GB, GY, BR, BG, BY, YR, YG, and YB. The correct answer is C. (A) (B) ● (D)

Animated **Math** at classzone.com

Notice in Example 2 that RG and GR represent two different group assignments. In RG, your first session is with the red group and your second session is with the green group. In GR, your group assignments are in reverse order.

 GUIDED PRACTICE for Example 2

2. **Fruit** You have a plum, a banana, an apple, an orange, and a pear. If you eat one now with lunch and eat one later for a snack, what are all the possible pairs of fruit you can select for lunch and the snack?

3. **Scheduling** You have 6 movies. You want to watch one now, and a different one later. How many ways can you choose two movies to watch?

4. **What If?** In Example 2, how would the diagram of possible outcomes change if you *could* be assigned to the same color group for both sessions? *Explain.*

EXAMPLE 3 Using a Tree Diagram

Find the probability of getting at least 2 heads when tossing a coin 3 times.

Make a tree diagram to list the outcomes, or *sample space*, of the experiment. Circle the successful outcomes.

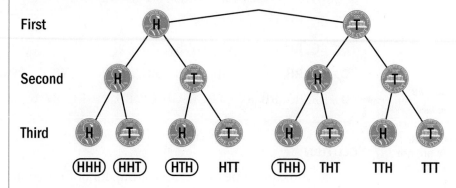

First
Second
Third

(HHH) (HHT) (HTH) HTT (THH) THT TTH TTT

▶ **Answer** Because 4 of the 8 outcomes have at least 2 heads, the probability is $\frac{4}{8}$, or $\frac{1}{2}$.

✓ **GUIDED PRACTICE** **for Example 3**

5. You roll a number cube and flip a coin. Make a list of possible outcomes. What is the probability that you get a 3 and tails?

13.2 EXERCISES

HOMEWORK KEY

★ = **STANDARDIZED TEST PRACTICE**
Exs. 7, 21, 22, 25, and 32

◯ = **HINTS** AND **HOMEWORK HELP**
for Exs. 3, 5, 7, 9, 19 at classzone.com

SKILL PRACTICE

1. **VOCABULARY** Copy and complete: You can use a tree diagram to help you list all the possible __?__ of an event.

2. **VOCABULARY** *Explain* how to draw a tree diagram that shows the possible outcomes of rolling a number cube twice.

MAKING TREE DIAGRAMS **Make a tree diagram to find the number of possible outcomes involving a number cube and a coin.**

SEE EXAMPLE 1
on p. 690
for Exs. 3–7

3. Roll the number cube twice.   4. Roll the number cube and flip the coin.

5. Flip the coin four times.   6. Roll the number cube once and flip the coin twice.

7. ★ **MULTIPLE CHOICE** You randomly choose the answers for 3 multiple choice questions with answer choices A, B, C, and D. How many outcomes are possible?

Ⓐ 3   Ⓑ 4   Ⓒ 12   Ⓓ 64

COUNTING OUTCOMES Make a tree diagram to find the number of possible outcomes for the event. Each spinner is divided into equal parts.

SEE EXAMPLE 1
on p. 690
for Exs. 8–10

8. Spin spinner A two times.

9. Spin spinner B three times.

10. Spin spinner A and spinner B.

Spinner A

2 3
5 4

Spinner B

ELIMINATING CHOICES You have the given colors of pants and shirts. How many shirt-pants pairs are possible with the given restriction?

SEE EXAMPLE 2
on p. 691
for Exs. 11–14

11. Pants: black, white, gray
    Shirts: black, white, gray
    Restriction: no pairs the same color

12. Pants: black, blue, brown, gray
    Shirts: black, red, blue, brown, orange
    Restriction: no pairs the same color

13. Pants: blue, black, gray
    Shirts: blue, green, black
    Restriction: all pairs the same color

14. Pants: white, red, green, pink
    Shirts: white, purple, red, yellow
    Restriction: maximum of 1 pair the same color

FINDING PROBABILITY You roll two number cubes. Use a tree diagram to find the probability of the event.

SEE EXAMPLE 3
on p. 692
for Exs. 15–16

15. The numbers add up to 7.

16. You roll two numbers less than 3.

17. **DRAW A DIAGRAM** The possible outcomes of an event are A1X, A1Y, A2X, A2Y, A3X, A3Y, B1X, B1Y, B2X, B2Y, B3X, and B3Y. Make a tree diagram of the situation.

18. **CHALLENGE** A number cube is rolled x times. What is the probability after x rolls that x results are a number less than 3? *Explain* your reasoning.

PROBLEM SOLVING

SEE EXAMPLE 1
on p. 690
for Ex. 19

19. **SCHOOL LUNCH** A school cafeteria offers students one of three entrées: chicken fajita, turkey sandwich, or yogurt with fresh fruit. Students are also offered one of the following side dishes: broccoli, potato wedges, salad, or pretzels. Make a tree diagram to find all of the possible lunch combinations.

SEE EXAMPLE 3
on p. 692
for Ex. 20

20. **GUIDED PROBLEM SOLVING** A store sells inflatable chairs in two styles: a low-back chair and a high-back chair. The chairs come in five colors: black, clear, orange, lime, and purple. The store receives a shipment of inflatable chairs. Each box contains one of every kind of chair. You randomly choose a chair from a box. What is the probability that the chair is black?

  a. List all the possible outcomes.

  b. Circle the outcomes where the chair is black.

  c. Use parts (a) and (b) to find the probability that the chair is black.

21. ★ **SHORT RESPONSE** Refer to Exercise 19 on page 693. Does adding another entrée result in the same number of additional choices as adding another side dish? *Explain*.

SEE EXAMPLE 2
on p. 691
for Ex. 22

22. ★ **MULTIPLE CHOICE** You randomly choose a mug from the shelf below. Then you randomly choose a second mug without replacing the first mug. Which list gives all of the possible outcomes?

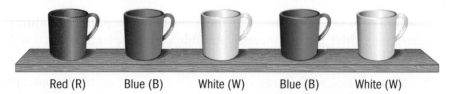

Red (R)   Blue (B)   White (W)   Blue (B)   White (W)

Ⓐ RW, RB, WB

Ⓑ RR, RW, RB, WW, WB, BB

Ⓒ RW, RB, WR, WB, BR, BW

Ⓓ RW, RB, WR, WW, WB, BR, BW, BB

23. **BAKERY** A bakery offers blueberry, cranberry, bran, corn, chocolate, and carrot muffins. A muffin is randomly chosen and eaten from a bag with one of each muffin. Then a second muffin is randomly chosen.

Make a tree diagram showing the ways 2 muffins can be chosen. What is the probability that *at least* one of the two muffins has berries?

SEE EXAMPLE 3
on p. 692
for Ex. 24

24. **CHEERLEADING** Cheerleaders who do stunts are called *flyers*. A coach has to choose the right outside flyer and the left outside flyer for a stunt from the squad's five flyers: Anne, Mandy, Zoe, Laura, and Janie.

Make a tree diagram showing the ways that the 2 flyers can be chosen. What is the probability that Mandy and Laura are *not* the two flyers? *Explain*.

25. ★ **WRITING** You roll two number cubes. Is it more likely for exactly one of the numbers to be 2 or for both of the numbers to be odd? *Explain*.

26. **CHALLENGE** A bag holds 2 green, 1 blue, and 2 red marbles. You randomly choose a marble and do not replace it. *Compare* the probability of randomly choosing a green marble and then a blue marble with the probability of choosing a red marble and then the other red marble. Does the comparison change if you replace the first marble? *Explain*.

NEW JERSEY MIXED REVIEW   **TEST PRACTICE** at classzone.com

27. Kallie is replacing a circular coil on her stove that measures about 25 inches in circumference. Which equation can she use to find d, the diameter of the coil?

Ⓐ $d = \dfrac{25}{\pi}$ Ⓑ $d = \dfrac{50}{\pi}$ Ⓒ $d = \dfrac{25}{2\pi}$ Ⓓ $d = \dfrac{50}{2\pi}$

28. Which of the following solids has exactly one base that is NOT a polygon?

Ⓐ Cone   Ⓑ Prism   Ⓒ Pyramid   Ⓓ Cylinder

INVESTIGATION
Use before Lesson 13.3

GOAL
Determine the number of possible outcomes.

MATERIALS
• paper
• pencil

13.3 Determining Outcomes

EXPLORE Find the number of outcomes of spinning each spinner once. Each spinner is divided into equal parts.

Spinner 1

Spinner 2

Spinner 3

STEP 1 **Make** a tree diagram to determine the number of outcomes of spinning spinner 1, followed by spinner 2, followed by spinner 3.

STEP 2 **Count** the different letters for each spinner in your tree diagram. How many different letters are listed for spinner 1? spinner 2? spinner 3?

STEP 3 **Find** the product of the three numbers from Step 2. What do you notice?

PRACTICE

1. Use the spinner at the right in place of Spinner 3. It is divided into equal parts. Repeat Steps 1–3.

DRAW CONCLUSIONS

2. **WRITING** You know the number of ways that event A can occur and the number of ways that event B can occur. *Explain* how can you find the number of ways that event A followed by event B can occur.

3. **REASONING** Suppose that each of the three spinners is divided into 26 equal parts so that each spinner can include all of the letters of the alphabet. Find the number of outcomes of spinning spinner 1, followed by spinner 2, followed by spinner 3, without using a tree diagram. *Explain* your method.

13.3 The Counting Principle

NJ 4.4.C.3 Apply techniques of systematic listing, counting, and reasoning in a variety of different contexts.

Before You used a tree diagram to find outcomes.

Now You'll use the counting principle to count outcomes.

Why? So you can count choices, as in Example 1.

KEY VOCABULARY
• outcomes, *p. 682*
• event, *p. 682*
• probability, *p. 682*

Track Events A track meet has 6 running events, 3 throwing events, and 2 relay events. You want to compete in one running event, one throwing event, and one relay event. How many different choices do you have for competing in one of each type of event?

In the activity on page 695, you may have noticed a way to use multiplication to count the number of possible outcomes for a series of events. This method, called the *counting principle*, is stated below.

KEY CONCEPT   *For Your Notebook*

The Counting Principle

If one event can occur in m ways, and for each of these a second event can occur in n ways, then the number of ways that the two events can occur together is $m \cdot n$.

The counting principle can be extended to three or more events.

EXAMPLE 1   Using the Counting Principle

To find the number of different choices at the track meet described above, use the counting principle.

Find the product of the number of choices for each track event.

Number of running events	×	Number of throwing events	×	Number of relay events	=	Number of choices
6	×	3	×	2	=	36

▸ **Answer** There are 36 different ways for you to compete in one of each type of track event.

✓ **GUIDED PRACTICE**   for Example 1

1. **What If?** In Example 1, suppose the track meet added 2 more running events and 1 more relay event. How many choices would you have?

EXAMPLE 2 Using the Counting Principle

License Plates The standard New York state license plate has 3 letters followed by 4 digits. How many different license plates are possible if the digits and letters can be repeated?

SOLUTION

Use the counting principle to find the number of different license plates.

> There are 26 choices for each of the 3 letters.

> There are 10 choices for each of the 4 digits.

$$26 \times 26 \times 26 \times 10 \times 10 \times 10 \times 10 = 175{,}760{,}000$$

▶ **Answer** There are 175,760,000 different license plates possible.

AVOID ERRORS
In both Example 2 and Example 3, notice that the digits 0 through 9 represent 10 digits, not 9 digits.

EXAMPLE 3 Solve a Multi-Step Problem

Passwords You are assigned a computer-generated 4-digit password to access your new voice mail account. If the digits can be repeated, what is the probability that your assigned password is 1234?

SOLUTION

STEP 1 **Use** the counting principle to find the total number of different passwords.

$$10 \times 10 \times 10 \times 10 = 10{,}000$$

STEP 2 **Find** the number of favorable outcomes. Only one outcome is 1234.

STEP 3 **Find** the probability that your password is 1234.

$$P(1234) = \frac{1}{10{,}000}$$

▶ **Answer** The probability that your password is 1234 is $\frac{1}{10{,}000}$, or 0.0001.

✓ **GUIDED PRACTICE** for Examples 2 and 3

2. You roll a green number cube, a red number cube, and a blue number cube. How many outcomes are possible?

3. In Exercise 2, what is the probability that the green number cube is a 2, the red number cube is a 6, and the blue number cube is a 3?

4. **What If?** In Example 3, suppose the password had 5 digits. What is the probability that your assigned password is an odd number?

13.3 EXERCISES

HOMEWORK KEY

★ = **STANDARDIZED TEST PRACTICE**
Exs. 14, 21, 22, 25, 29, and 36

○ = **HINTS AND HOMEWORK HELP**
for Exs. 5, 7, 9, 11, 23 at classzone.com

SKILL PRACTICE

1. **VOCABULARY** One event has 5 outcomes and another event has 12 outcomes. What does 5 • 12 represent?

2. **VOCABULARY** Copy and complete: You can use the counting principle to count the number of possible __?__ of a series of events.

COUNTING OUTCOMES Use the number of outcomes of the events to find the number of ways that the events can occur together.

SEE EXAMPLE 1
on p. 696
for Exs. 3–9

3. **Event A:** 6 outcomes
   Event B: 15 outcomes

4. **Event J:** 12 outcomes
   Event K: 13 outcomes

5. **Event C:** 11 outcomes
   Event D: 12 outcomes

6. **Event M:** 18 outcomes
   Event N: 9 outcomes

7. **Event F:** 10 outcomes
   Event G: 26 outcomes
   Event H: 10 outcomes

8. **Event P:** 19 outcomes
   Event Q: 15 outcomes
   Event R: 4 outcomes

9. **ERROR ANALYSIS** Describe and correct the error made in counting the possible outcomes when you roll a number cube three times.

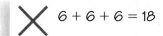
$6 + 6 + 6 = 18$

COUNTING CODES A safe's unlocking code is composed of 6 letters or digits. Find the number of codes that fit the given description.

SEE EXAMPLE 2
on p. 697
for Exs. 10–14

10. 6 digits

11. 1 letter followed by 5 digits

12. 3 letters followed by 3 digits

13. 4 letters followed by 2 digits

14. ★ **MULTIPLE CHOICE** A license plate has 2 letters followed by 4 digits. How many different license plates are possible?

Ⓐ 8   Ⓑ 92   Ⓒ 676,000   Ⓓ 6,760,000

FINDING PROBABILITIES A website randomly generates a 6-letter confirmation code for purchases. Find the probability that a code has the given characteristic. Count the letters A, E, I, O, and U as vowels.

SEE EXAMPLE 3
on p. 697
for Exs. 15–18

15. code is XYNFGO

16. all letters are the same

17. starts with a vowel

18. includes no vowels

19. **EXAMPLES AND NONEXAMPLES** A company wants to offer x flavors of iced tea in y different bottle sizes with z different label styles. The number, n, of possible iced tea bottles must be somewhere from 50 to 60. Find three examples and three nonexamples of possible values for x, y, and z.

20. **CHALLENGE** Jay wants you to guess his password, which has 4 letters followed by 2 digits. He gives you the following clues: The first letter is "P" and the two digits are the same. What is the probability that you guess the password correctly on your first try? *Explain.*

SEE EXAMPLE 1
on p. 696
for Exs. 21, 23

21. ★ **MULTIPLE CHOICE** You have 8 kinds of writing paper and 5 envelope colors. How many pairings of one kind of writing paper and one envelope color are possible?

Ⓐ 8   Ⓑ 13   Ⓒ 40   Ⓓ 80

22. ★ **SHORT RESPONSE** The number of ways that events A and B can occur together is 36. Event B can occur in 3 ways. In how many ways can event A occur? *Explain*.

㉓ **CLASS ELECTION** Your class is having an election. There are 3 candidates for president, 5 for vice president, 2 for secretary, and 6 for treasurer. How many different groups of winning candidates can be chosen?

SEE EXAMPLE 2
on p. 697
for Ex. 24

24. **LOCKERS** The combinations for the lockers at your school consist of 3 numbers. Each number in the combination can be a number from 0 through 49. How many locker combinations are possible?

25. ★ **WRITING** What are the advantages of using the counting principle instead of making a tree diagram when counting possibilities?

SEE EXAMPLE 3
on p. 697
for Ex. 26

26. **MULTI-STEP PROBLEM** A sandwich shop has 5 kinds of bread, 4 kinds of cheese, and 2 kinds of ham to use on a ham-and-cheese sandwich.

   a. You are limited to 1 kind of bread, 1 kind of cheese, and 1 kind of ham. How many different ham-and-cheese sandwiches are possible?

   b. The shop has a pre-made ham-and-cheese sandwich. What is the probability that the sandwich has the kinds of bread, cheese, and ham that you want, if the sandwich was made at random?

27. **BICYCLE LOCKS** A bicycle lock has a 4-digit combination. Each of the digits is a number from 0 through 9. Find the probability that the lock has a combination in which 3 of the 4 digits are 3s.

28. **DIGITAL CLOCKS** On a digital clock, the numbers 1 through 12 are used for the hour display and the numbers 00 through 59 are used for the minute display. How many time displays are possible? If a light for A.M. and P.M. is added, how does this affect the possible number of displays?

29. ★ **EXTENDED RESPONSE** A music shop wants to sell guitar-amplifier-effects pedal packages. The individual costs are shown below.

   a. How many packages are possible?

   b. How many packages can be sold for $395 if the shop wants to make at least $50 profit?

   c. *Describe* two ways to find the answer to part (b).

30. WORK BACKWARD You have many choices of wrapping paper, ribbons, and bows to wrap a gift. There are 385 possible ways to wrap the gift. You have 11 different kinds of ribbons and you have more kinds of wrapping paper than bows. How many kinds of wrapping paper and bows do you have?

31. CHALLENGE You work at an ice cream stand that offers 8 different flavors. On a busy day, you take requests for one-scoop cones from 6 people, but forget the flavors. How many flavors do you have to remember for the probability that you randomly get all the other flavors correct on the first try to be greater than 0.01? *Explain.*

 NEW JERSEY MIXED REVIEW **TEST PRACTICE** at classzone.com

32. You roll a number cube that is numbered from 1 to 6 and spin a spinner that is divided into 3 equal sections labeled A, B, and C. Which choice shows all the possible unique combinations of an even number on the number cube and an A or a B on the spinner?

Ⓐ

Cube	2	2	4	4	6	6
Spinner	A	B	A	B	A	B

Ⓑ

Cube	2	2	4	4	6	6
Spinner	A	A	A	B	B	B

Ⓒ

Cube	1	2	3	4	5	6
Spinner	A	B	A	B	A	B

Ⓓ

Cube	2	2	2	4	4	4
Spinner	A	B	C	A	B	C

QUIZ *for Lessons 13.1–13.3*

1. What is the probability of getting 1, 3, or 5 when rolling a number cube? *(p. 682)*

2. VACATION You are planning a family vacation. You have the choice of 2 modes of transportation: bus or plane. You have the choice of 4 destinations: Las Vegas, San Francisco, Miami, or Denver. Make a tree diagram to find the number of possibilities. *(p. 690)*

3. COINS What is the probability of getting at least 3 tails when flipping a coin 4 times? *(p. 690)*

4. WEB PAGE DESIGN You are designing a Web page. You have a choice of 6 different borders, 12 different fonts, and 40 different background colors. How many possible designs are there for the Web page? *(p. 696)*

5. CLOTHING A T-shirt comes in 2 sleeve lengths, 8 colors, and 3 sizes. Your friend randomly chooses one of these to give to you. What is the probability that the T-shirt is the sleeve length, color, and size that you want? *(p. 696)*

 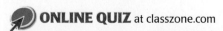

Lessons 13.1–13.3

1. **BUILDING MATERIALS** The circle graph shows the most common materials used for the exterior of new homes in the U.S. Which equation could you use to predict the number of new homes that would NOT be made of brick in a neighborhood that has 50 new homes?

Materials for New Homes

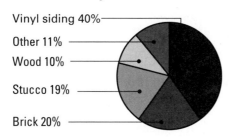

Vinyl siding 40%
Other 11%
Wood 10%
Stucco 19%
Brick 20%

   A. $\dfrac{x}{50} = \dfrac{20}{100}$

   B. $\dfrac{50}{80} = \dfrac{x}{100}$

   C. $\dfrac{x}{50} = \dfrac{80}{100}$

   D. $\dfrac{50}{x} = \dfrac{80}{100}$

2. **LOCKER COMBINATIONS** A locker combination has 3 one-digit numbers. If the digits can repeat, what is the probability that a randomly chosen combination will NOT have all the same digits?

   A. 0.01

   B. 0.09

   C. 0.91

   D. 0.99

3. **NUMBERED DICE** A box contains 5 numbered dice that have 4, 6, 8, 12, and 20 sides, respectively. Each one has sides labeled with consecutive whole numbers starting with 1. Felix selects one of these and rolls it 60 times. The number 3 comes up 13 times. Which numbered die did Felix most likely select?

   A. 4

   B. 6

   C. 8

   D. 12

4. **SECURITY CODES** Joe has a new home security system with a 3 digit entry code. He remembers only that the first digit is a 4. What is the probability that he randomly guesses the last two digits in a single attempt?

   A. $\dfrac{1}{20}$

   B. $\dfrac{1}{10}$

   C. $\dfrac{1}{90}$

   D. $\dfrac{1}{100}$

5. **OPEN-ENDED** You want to redecorate your bedroom with 1 new comforter, 1 pair of curtains, and 1 rug. Your color choices are shown in the table below.

Item	Comforter	Curtains	Rug
Available colors	white, tan, blue, gray	white, blue, gray	white, tan, blue

   • Use a tree diagram to show the number of different ways you can redecorate.

   • Use the counting principle to justify your answer.

   • Suppose you choose one of each item at random. What is the probability that all three items are the same color?

13.4 Permutations and Combinations

 4.4.C.1.a Permutations: ordered situations with replacement . . . vs. ordered situations without replacement . . .

Before	You used tree diagrams and the counting principle.
Now	You'll use permutations and combinations.
Why?	So you can count groupings of people, as in Example 1.

KEY VOCABULARY
- **permutation,** *p. 702*
- **combination,** *p. 703*

ACTIVITY

You can investigate numbers of arrangements.

STEP 1 **Line** up 4 chairs and choose 4 students.

STEP 2 **Determine** how many ways 1 of the 4 students can be chosen to sit in the first chair. Have one of the students sit in the first chair.

STEP 3 **Repeat** Step 2 for the second, third, and fourth chairs.

STEP 4 **Apply** the counting principle to your answers from Steps 2 and 3 to find the number of arrangements of 4 students in 4 chairs.

Permutations In the activity, you found the number of *permutations* of 4 students. A **permutation** is an arrangement of a group of objects in a particular order. For example, the 6 permutations of the 3 letters in the word CAT are shown below.

| CAT | CTA | ACT | ATC | TCA | TAC |

EXAMPLE 1 Counting Permutations

ANOTHER WAY

Draw and count the possibilities:

YBC
YCB
BCY
BYC
CBY
CYB

Amusement Parks Yen, Brianna, and Carlos go to an amusement park. How many ways can they stand in line to buy tickets for the rides?

SOLUTION

Use the counting principle.

Choices for first in line	×	Choices for second in line	×	Choices for third in line	=	Ways to stand in line
3	×	2	×	1	=	6

▶ **Answer** There are 6 ways that the 3 friends can stand in line.

EXAMPLE 2 **Counting Permutations**

Stamp Competition There were 52 finalists in a contest to design a federal duck stamp. In how many ways could the first, second, and third places have been awarded?

SOLUTION

Choices for first place	×	Choices for second place	×	Choices for third place	=	Ways to award first, second, and third
52	×	51	×	50	=	132,600

▶ **Answer** There were 132,600 ways to award first, second, and third places.

✓ **GUIDED PRACTICE** for Examples 1 and 2

1. In how many ways can you arrange the letters in the word COMPUTER?

2. **Volleyball** There are 8 volleyball teams in a tournament. In how many ways can teams place first, second, third, and fourth?

Combinations In a permutation, the order of the objects is important. A grouping of objects in which the order is *not* important is a **combination**.

EXAMPLE 3 **Listing Combinations**

Choosing Classes You can choose 2 different classes from the following 4 classes: Spanish (S), consumer and family studies (C), industrial technology (I), and art (A). How many different pairs can you choose, if the order in which you choose the classes does not matter?

SOLUTION

Start by listing all of the permutations of 2 classes. Because the order in which you choose the classes does not matter, cross out one of any pair of permutations that lists the same two classes.

ANOTHER WAY
You can also use a tree diagram to find the permutations of 2 classes.

SC   SI   SA
CS   CI   CA
IS   IC   IA
AS   AC   AI

> Because IA and AI list the same classes, cross one of them out.

▶ **Answer** You have 6 different choices for choosing 2 classes.

✓ **GUIDED PRACTICE** for Example 3

3. **Music** You want to buy 5 CDs at a music store. You have enough money for only 2 CDs. How many choices do you have?

Relating Permutations and Combinations In Example 3, there is another way to find the number of combinations. Divide the number of permutations when choosing 2 electives from 4 by the number of permutations when arranging 2 electives, as shown below.

$$\frac{\text{Permutations when choosing 2 objects from 4}}{\text{Permutations when arranging 2 objects}} = \frac{4 \times 3}{2 \times 1} = 6 \text{ combinations}$$

This method is useful when there are too many arrangements to list.

(**EXAMPLE 4**)   **Relating Permutations and Combinations**

READING

When objects can be arranged in different orders and still represent the same choice, order is not important. If order is not important in a given problem, you count combinations.

Sunglasses You win a door prize at the grand opening of a department store. For your prize, you can choose 5 different pairs of sunglasses from the 20 styles that the store carries. How many choices do you have?

SOLUTION

Because the order in which you choose the sunglasses does not matter, you need to find the number of combinations.

STEP 1 **Find** the number of permutations when choosing 5 pairs from 20 styles.

$$20 \times 19 \times 18 \times 17 \times 16 = \mathbf{1,860,480}$$

STEP 2 **Find** the number of permutations when arranging 5 objects.

$$5 \times 4 \times 3 \times 2 \times 1 = \mathbf{120}$$

STEP 3 **Divide** the number of permutations when choosing 5 pairs from 20 styles by the number of permutations when arranging 5 objects.

$$\frac{\mathbf{1,860,480}}{\mathbf{120}} = 15,504$$

▸ **Answer** There are 15,504 ways for you to choose the sunglasses.

✓   **GUIDED PRACTICE**   **for Example 4**

4. **What If?** In Example 4, how many choices would you have if you could choose 6 different pairs of sunglasses?

5. **Reading** For a summer reading program, you need to read 4 books. You choose from a list of 15 books. How many different groups of 4 books can you choose if the order in which you choose is not important?

13.4 EXERCISES

★ = **STANDARDIZED TEST PRACTICE**
Exs. 11, 21, 22, 23, 24, and 38

◯ = **HINTS** AND **HOMEWORK HELP**
for Exs. 5, 7, 11, 21, 23 at classzone.com

SKILL PRACTICE

VOCABULARY **Copy and complete the statement.**

1. A __?__ is a grouping of objects in which the order is not important.

2. A __?__ is an arrangement of a group of objects in a particular order.

FINDING PERMUTATIONS **Find the number of permutations.**

SEE EXAMPLES 1 AND 2
on pp. 702–703
for Exs. 3–6

3. Ways to arrange the letters in the word GUITAR

4. Ways to arrange 7 DVDs on a shelf

5. Ways to choose first, second, and third prize from 27 posters in a contest

6. Ways to choose a president, vice-president, treasurer, and secretary from the 18 members of a club

FINDING COMBINATIONS **Find the number of combinations.**

SEE EXAMPLES 3 AND 4
on pp. 703–704
for Exs. 7–10

7. You choose 3 different kinds of apples from the following kinds: Red Delicious, Granny Smith, Empire, McIntosh, and Fuji.

8. You choose 4 different colors from the following colors: red, blue, purple, yellow, green, and orange.

9. From 14 students, you choose 8 students to be extras in a play.

10. You choose 4 different fish from 26 kinds of fish.

SEE EXAMPLE 4
on p. 704
for Exs. 11–16

11. ★ **MULTIPLE CHOICE** Which expression can you use to find how many different groups of 2 students can be chosen from 8 students to hold signs for a car wash?

   Ⓐ $\frac{8 \times 7}{6 \times 5}$ Ⓑ $\frac{2 \times 1}{8 \times 7}$ Ⓒ $\frac{8 \times 7}{2 \times 1}$ Ⓓ 8×7

12. **ERROR ANALYSIS** A disc jockey chooses 3 songs from a list of 10 songs. Describe and correct the error made in finding the number of different groups of 3 songs.

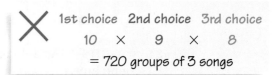

1st choice   2nd choice   3rd choice
   10   ×   9   ×   8
= 720 groups of 3 songs

PERMUTATION OR COMBINATION? **Tell whether the situation describes a permutation or a combination. Then answer the question.**

13. How many ways can you choose 3 different pizza toppings from 15?

14. How many ways can the coach arrange the batting order of the 9 starting players of a baseball team?

15. How many ways can a disc jockey choose 4 different songs from 10?

16. How many ways can a judge award first, second, and third places at a science fair with 23 entries?

FINDING PROBABILITY Use the list of students at the right. Find the probability of the outcome described, if the choices are made randomly.

Al	Di
Gil	Fay
Bea	Kim
Hal	Lee
Otis	Ian

17. Al, Fay, Gil, and Di are chosen to form a 4-person committee.

18. Otis is chosen to go first, Bea is chosen to go 2nd, and Lee is chosen to go 3rd.

19. **CHALLENGE** You are using colored pencils to color a map of three U.S. states. You want each state to be a different color. If there are 504 ways to color the map, how many pencils do you have?

PROBLEM SOLVING

20. **GUIDED PROBLEM SOLVING** You want to choose 3 different colors of balloons to be used as decorations at a school graduation. The balloons are available in 24 colors. How many choices do you have for 3 different balloon colors?

   a. Decide whether the situation describes a permutation or a combination.

   b. Find the number of permutations or combinations.

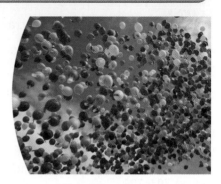

SEE EXAMPLES
1 AND 2
on pp. 702–703
for Ex. 21

21. ★ **SHORT RESPONSE** Does the list below contain all of the permutations of the 3 symbols? *Explain.* If the list is incomplete, sketch any missing permutations of the 3 symbols.

22. ★ **OPEN-ENDED MATH** *Describe* a real-world situation that involves a permutation and a real-world situation that involves a combination.

23. ★ **MULTIPLE CHOICE** A swim team has 12 members. How many different 4-person groups can be chosen to be the relay race team?

   (A) 11,880   **(B)** 2970   **(C)** 495   **(D)** 24

24. ★ **WRITING** A padlock's combination is 7 right, 12 left, 32 right. Your friend buys this padlock and says, "It's not a combination padlock, it's actually a *permutation* padlock." Is your friend right? *Explain.*

SEE EXAMPLES
2 AND 3
on p. 703
for Ex. 25

25. ◆ **MULTIPLE REPRESENTATIONS** At a restaurant, you can have your eggs cooked 4 different ways, and you can choose from 3 kinds of bread for your toast.

   a. Make a List Make an organized list of the possible eggs-toast breakfasts.

   b. Make a Diagram Make a tree diagram showing the possible eggs-toast breakfasts.

   c. Analyze Does this situation represent a permutation or a combination? *Explain.*

26. **Count Outcomes** Find the number of possible outcomes for first, second, and third place in the eighth grade 100 meter dash. Then find the number of possible outcomes for second and third place if Ivan Swanson finishes first.

27. **Analyze** The sixth grade's 100-yard dash has 6 runners and the seventh grade's 100-yard dash has 6 runners. In which race is there a greater number of possible ways ribbons can be awarded? *Explain.*

Henson Ready for First Track Meet

Henson Middle School travels to Elm City today for the first track meet of the season. There are 9 track events and 6 field events for eighth grade competitors, 6 track and 4 field events for seventh grade competitors, and 4 track and 3 field events set for sixth grade competitors.

Two-time champion Ivan Swanson will be running against 7 other competitors in the eighth grade 100 meter dash. Many expect another record-breaking season for the young athlete.

The sixth grade is using a new reward system this year. The top three finishers in each event will receive excellence ribbons. Seventh and eighth grade competitors will still receive the usual first, second, and third place ribbons.

28. **COMPUTERS** A group of 40 computers contains exactly 2 defective computers. Suppose 2 computers are randomly selected from the group. What is the probability that both computers are defective? Write the probability as a decimal rounded to the nearest ten thousandth.

29. **CHALLENGE** The 8 members of the Student Council plan to pose for the yearbook photo by standing in a line, with the president and vice-president standing together in the middle. How many different ways can they line up?

 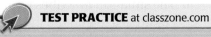

NEW JERSEY MIXED REVIEW TEST PRACTICE at classzone.com

30. Tyler surveyed 10 band students on whether they play the clarinet, the flute, both, or neither. Which of the following displays gives the most detailed information about the results of the survey?

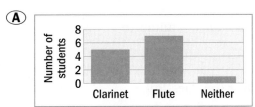

(A)

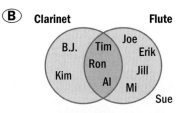

(B) Clarinet   Flute
B.J. Tim Joe
      Ron Erik
Kim   Jill
      Al   Mi
              Sue

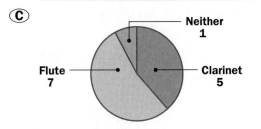

(C) Neither 1 / Flute 7 / Clarinet 5

(D)

Instrument	Number of students
Clarinet	5
Flute	7

13.4 Finding Permutations and Combinations

Many calculators include special functions in their menus that allow you to calculate numbers of permutations and combinations.

EXAMPLE **There are 14 school bands participating in a competition.**

a. In how many ways can first, second, and third places be awarded?

b. After the top 3 places have been awarded, in how many ways can 2 honorable mentions be awarded?

SOLUTION

a. The situation describes a permutation. Use the following keystrokes to find the number of permutations of 3 bands chosen from 14 bands.

> *nPr* represents the number of permutations of *r* objects chosen from *n* objects.

Keystrokes

14 PRB = 3 =

Display

14 nPr 3
                    2184

▶ **Answer** There are 2184 ways for first, second, and third places to be awarded.

b. The situation describes a combination. Use the following keystrokes to find the number of combinations of 2 bands chosen from the remaining 11 bands.

> *nCr* represents the number of combinations of *r* objects chosen from *n* objects.

Keystrokes

11 PRB ▶ = 2 =

Display

11 nCr 2
                    55

▶ **Answer** There are 55 ways for 2 honorable mentions to be awarded.

PRACTICE **Use a calculator to answer the question.**

1. A bowling league has 19 teams. In how many ways can teams place first, second, third, and fourth?

2. How many different groups of 6 people can be chosen from 25 people?

3. How many different 3-person committees can the French Club elect from the 20 members?

13.5 Disjoint Events

4.4.B.3 Estimate probabilities and make predictions based on experimental and theoretical probabilities.

Before You found the probability of a single event.

Now You'll find the probability that either of two events occurs.

Why? So you can analyze games, as in Ex. 38.

KEY VOCABULARY
- disjoint events, *p. 709*
- overlapping events, *p. 709*
- complementary events, *p. 711*

Disjoint events are events that have no outcomes in common. **Overlapping events** are events that have one or more outcomes in common. The Venn diagrams below show how the events that involve rolling a number cube are related.

Disjoint events

Event A: Roll an odd number.

Event B: Roll a 4.

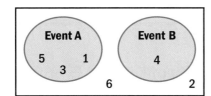

Overlapping events

Event C: Roll a number less than 3.

Event D: Roll an even number.

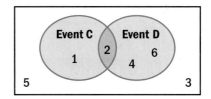

EXAMPLE 1 Disjoint and Overlapping Events

TAKE NOTES
To help you understand the difference between disjoint and overlapping events, you can make a concept grid for each term.

Tell whether the events involving the spinner are *disjoint* or *overlapping*.

    Event P: Spin an odd number.

    Event Q: Spin a prime number.

SOLUTION

Make a list of the outcomes for each event. Then determine whether the events have any outcomes in common.

    Event P: 3, 7, 9, 15   **List the odd numbers.**

    Event Q: 2, 3, 7   **List the prime numbers.**

▶ **Answer** There are outcomes in common, so the events are overlapping.

Animated Math
at classzone.com

 GUIDED PRACTICE for Example 1

1. **What If?** In Example 1, suppose Event P is "spin a number divisible by 4." Are the events *disjoint* or *overlapping*? *Explain.*

Probability of Disjoint Events The Venn diagram at the right shows two disjoint events that involve rolling a number cube.

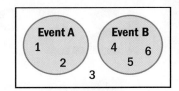

Event A: 1 2

Event B: 4 5 6

3

Event A: Roll a number less than 3.

Event B: Roll a number greater than 3.

The probability of event A *or* event B is $\frac{5}{6}$ because there are 5 favorable outcomes out of 6 possible outcomes. Another way to find the probability of event A *or* event B is to add the probabilities of each event: $\frac{2}{6} + \frac{3}{6} = \frac{5}{6}$.

KEY CONCEPT *For Your Notebook*

Probability of Disjoint Events

Words For two disjoint events, the probability that *either* of the events occurs is the sum of the probabilities of the events.

Algebra If A and B are disjoint events, then
$P(A \ or \ B) = P(A) + P(B)$.

EXAMPLE 2 **Probability of Disjoint Events**

Arena Events The table shows the probability that an arena event is of the given type. What is the probability that a randomly chosen event is an ice hockey game or a basketball game?

Event	Basketball	Ice hockey	Concert	Ice show	Trade show	Other
Percent	24%	23%	16%	11%	8%	18%

AVOID ERRORS
You can't add to find the probability that either of two events occurs unless the events are disjoint events.

SOLUTION

The events are disjoint because two arena events cannot occur at the same time. So, you can add to find the probability.

$P(\text{ice hockey}) + P(\text{basketball}) = 23\% + 24\%$

$= 47\%$

▶ **Answer** The probability that an arena event is either an ice hockey game or a basketball game is 47%.

Complementary Events Two disjoint events in which one or the other must occur are called **complementary events**. If event A and event B are complementary events and you know the probability of one event, you can use the following rule to find the probability of the other event.

$$P(B) = 1 - P(A)$$

> This rule comes from the fact that the sum of the probabilities of two complementary events is 1.

EXAMPLE 3 Probability of Complementary Events

Sign Language At your school, 3% of the students know sign language.

a. What is the probability that a randomly chosen student does *not* know sign language?

b. There are 267 seventh graders at your school. Estimate how many do *not* know sign language.

SOLUTION

a. $P(\text{does not know}) = 1 - P(\text{knows})$ **Use rule for complementary events.**

$= 1 - 0.03$ **Substitute 3%, or 0.03, for P(knows).**

$= 0.97$ **Subtract.**

▶ **Answer** The probability that a randomly chosen student does not know sign language is 0.97, or 97%.

ANOTHER WAY
You can also use a proportion to find the answer in part (b).
$$\frac{97}{100} = \frac{x}{267}$$
$97 \cdot 267 = 100x$
$25{,}899 = 100x$
$259 \approx x$

b. From part (a), you know that 97% of students do not know sign language. So, find 97% of 267.

$a = p\% \cdot b$ **Write percent equation.**

$= 97\% \cdot 267$ **Substitute 97 for *p* and 267 for *b*.**

$= 0.97 \cdot 267$ **Write percent as decimal.**

≈ 259 **Multiply.**

▶ **Answer** About 259 seventh graders do not know sign language.

✓ **GUIDED PRACTICE** **for Examples 2 and 3**

2. Arena Events In Example 2, what is the probability that a randomly chosen event is a concert or a trade show?

3. Subway On a subway, 30% of the passengers have briefcases. What is the probability that a randomly chosen passenger does *not* have a briefcase?

13.5   Disjoint Events   **711**

13.5 EXERCISES

HOMEWORK KEY

★ = **STANDARDIZED TEST PRACTICE**
Exs. 14, 37, 39, 40, 41, 42, and 52

◯ = **HINTS AND HOMEWORK HELP**
for Exs. 5, 7, 13, 19, 35 at classzone.com

SKILL PRACTICE

1. **VOCABULARY** Describe the difference between disjoint events and overlapping events.

2. **VOCABULARY** Copy and complete: The ___?___ of the probabilities of complementary events is 1.

IDENTIFYING EVENTS Use a list or Venn diagram to tell whether the events are *disjoint* or *overlapping*. *Explain* your reasoning.

SEE EXAMPLE 1
on p. 709
for Exs. 3–7

3. **Event A:** Roll a 4 with a number cube.
   Event B: Roll a number less than 4 with a number cube.

4. **Event A:** Roll an odd number with a number cube.
   Event B: Roll a prime number with a number cube.

5. **Event A:** Roll a multiple of 2 with a number cube.
   Event B: Roll a number greater than 3 with a number cube.

6. **Event A:** A student knows how to play a musical instrument.
   Event B: A student doesn't know how to play a musical instrument.

7. **Event A:** A student plays on the football team during fall.
   Event B: A student joins the spring track team.

FINDING PROBABILITY Events A and B are disjoint events. Find P(A or B).

SEE EXAMPLE 2
on p. 710
for Exs. 8–14

8. $P(A) = 0.3$
   $P(B) = 0.2$

9. $P(A) = 0.25$
   $P(B) = 0.35$

10. $P(A) = 0.12$
    $P(B) = 0.3$

11. $P(A) = 0.24$
    $P(B) = 0.37$

12. $P(A) = 33\%$
    $P(B) = 8\%$

13. $P(A) = 16.1\%$
    $P(B) = 28.2\%$

14. ★ **MULTIPLE CHOICE** The spinner at the right is divided into equal parts. What is the probability that the spinner lands on green or an odd number?

    Ⓐ $\frac{1}{6}$

    Ⓑ $\frac{1}{3}$

    Ⓒ $\frac{1}{2}$

    Ⓓ $\frac{5}{6}$

FINDING PROBABILITY Events A and B are complementary events. Find P(A).

SEE EXAMPLE 3
on p. 711
for Exs. 15–20

15. $P(B) = 0.4$

16. $P(B) = 0.75$

17. $P(B) = 0.23$

18. $P(B) = 0.51$

19. $P(B) = \frac{2}{5}$

20. $P(B) = 64\%$

21. **MENTAL MATH** You have made 16 out of 33 basketball shots so far. Use mental math to estimate the probability of missing your next shot.

22. ERROR ANALYSIS You roll a number cube. Your friend says that the events "roll an odd number" and "roll a number less than 4" are complementary, because the sum of their probabilities is 1. Is your friend correct? *Explain.*

COMPARING PROBABILITIES You randomly choose a letter from the word EXAGGERATE. Compare the probability of the events using <, >, and =.

23. $P(T) \underline{\;?\;} P(E)$

24. $P(E) \underline{\;?\;} P(A \text{ or } R)$

25. $P(E \text{ or } R) \underline{\;?\;} P(A \text{ or } T)$

26. $P(E) \underline{\;?\;} P(\textit{not } E)$

27. $P(P) \underline{\;?\;} P(G \text{ or } A)$

28. $P(\textit{not } E) \underline{\;?\;} P(\textit{not } X)$

REASONING Tell whether the statement is *always, sometimes,* or *never* true. *Explain* your reasoning.

29. Two disjoint events are complementary.

30. Two overlapping events are disjoint.

31. Two complementary events are overlapping.

32. CHALLENGE There are red, blue, and green marbles in a bag. The probability of randomly choosing a blue marble is 0.3, and the probability of randomly choosing a blue or red marble is 0.7. There are a total of 20 marbles in the bag. How many marbles of each color are in the bag? *Explain.*

PROBLEM SOLVING

HISTORY Use the survey results in the circle graph. Find the probability that a randomly chosen student who answered the survey responded as indicated.

SEE EXAMPLES
2 AND 3
on p. 711
for Exs. 33–39

33. Chose ancient Egypt or the Aztecs

34. Chose ancient Greece or the Incas

35. Did *not* choose ancient Egypt

36. Did *not* choose the Aztecs

Which ancient civilization would you visit?

Ancient Greece 29%
Aztecs 11%
Incas 8%
Ancient Egypt 52%

37. ★ **SHORT RESPONSE** *Explain* why the sum of two complementary events must be 1. Use an example.

38. CHESS On your first move in chess, you can move one of ten pieces, two of which are knights. You choose a piece at random for your first move. What is the probability that you do *not* choose a knight?

39. ★ **MULTIPLE CHOICE** A weather forecast says there is a 30% probability of rain tomorrow. What is the probability that it will *not* rain tomorrow?

(A) 29%   **(B)** 30%   **(C)** 70%   **(D)** 97%

40. ★ **WRITING** Events A and B are possible outcomes when you roll two number cubes. The probability of event A is 0.75 and the probability of event B is 0.5. Are events A and B disjoint events? *Explain.*

41. ★ **EXTENDED RESPONSE** A group of students volunteer to clean up the grounds at a community center. The table shows the number of volunteers who will be randomly assigned to work in specific areas.

Job and work area	Volunteers
Clean front yard	6
Clean back yard	6
Clean side yard	2
Clean playground	4
Paint playground	2

   a. Calculate Find the probability that a student will be assigned to work in the playground area.

   b. Apply Use your answer to part (a) and your knowledge of complementary events. *Explain* how to find the probability that a student will be assigned to work in the yard area. Then find this probability.

   c. Conjecture For three disjoint events, is it possible to find the probability that any one of the events will occur by adding the probabilities of the events? *Explain* why or why not, based on your answer to part (b).

42. ★ **OPEN-ENDED MATH** Describe three different events involving randomly choosing one or more integers from −10 to 10. Then describe their complementary events, and find the probability of these events.

43. **CHALLENGE** A clearance sale rack holds 84 comedy, drama, and action DVDs. If you choose a DVD randomly, then P(comedy or drama) = P(action or drama). If the probability of *not* choosing a drama DVD is $\frac{5}{21}$, how many comedy DVDs are on the clearance rack?

44. **CHALLENGE** You know that events A and B are disjoint events and events B and C are disjoint events. Does this mean that events A and C are disjoint events? *Explain.*

 NEW JERSEY MIXED REVIEW 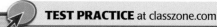 **TEST PRACTICE** at classzone.com

45. Which model best represents the expression $\frac{1}{2} \times \frac{3}{5}$?

 A

B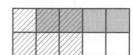

C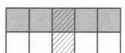

D

ONLINE QUIZ at classzone.com

13.6 Independent and Dependent Events

NJ 4.4.B.3   Estimate probabilities and make predictions based on experimental and theoretical probabilities.

Before   You found the probability of disjoint events.

Now   You'll find the probability of compound events.

Why?   So you can analyze events, as in Exercise 3.

KEY VOCABULARY
- compound events, *p. 715*
- independent events, *p. 715*
- dependent events, *p. 715*

ACTIVITY

You can find the probability of two events occurring under different circumstances.

STEP 1   A bag contains 9 pieces of paper, with 5 pieces having an O and 4 pieces having an X. You randomly choose a piece of paper from the bag, you get an O, and you don't put it back.

You randomly choose a second piece of paper. What is the probability that the second piece of paper has an X?

STEP 2   You repeat Step 1, but this time the first piece of paper has an X. What is the probability that the second piece of paper also has an X? Why is this probability different from the probability in Step 1?

Compound Events When you consider the outcomes of two events, the events are called **compound events**. Two compound events are **independent events** if the occurrence of one event does *not* affect the likelihood that the other event will occur. Two compound events are **dependent events** if the occurrence of one event *does* affect the likelihood that the other will occur.

EXAMPLE 1   Independent and Dependent Events

In Step 1 of the activity, you chose an O first and then an X. Are these events *independent* or *dependent*?

In the activity, whether or not you choose an O first *does* affect the likelihood that you choose an X second. This is because the first piece of paper is chosen and *not put back*. This affects the ratio of X's to O's in the bag when choosing the second letter.

▶ **Answer** The events are dependent.

Independent Events A coin is flipped and a number cube is rolled. The table of outcomes helps you see the relationship between the probability of the compound events and the probabilities of the individual events.

$$P(\text{H and odd}) = \frac{1 \cdot 3}{2 \cdot 6} \longleftarrow \text{ favorable outcomes}$$
$$\qquad\qquad\qquad \longleftarrow \text{ total outcomes}$$

$$= \frac{1}{2} \cdot \frac{3}{6}$$

$$= P(\text{H}) \cdot P(\text{odd})$$

	H	T
1	H, 1	T, 1
2	H, 2	T, 2
3	H, 3	T, 3
4	H, 4	T, 4
5	H, 5	T, 5
6	H, 6	T, 6

KEY CONCEPT · *For Your Notebook*

Probability of Independent Events

Words For two independent events A and B, the probability that *both* events occur is the product of the probabilities of the events.

Algebra If A and B are independent events, then
$P(\text{A } and \text{ B}) = P(\text{A}) \cdot P(\text{B})$.

EXAMPLE 2 Probability of Independent Events

Game Show On a game show, you spin the wheel at the right. It is divided into equal sections. Find the probability that you get $200 on your first spin and go bankrupt on your second spin.

SOLUTION

STEP 1 **Find** the probability of each event.

$P(\$200) = \dfrac{2}{8} = 0.25$ "$200" appears 2 times.

$P(\text{bankrupt}) = \dfrac{1}{8} = 0.125$ "Bankrupt" appears once.

STEP 2 **Multiply** the probabilities, because the events are independent.

$P(\$200 \text{ and bankrupt}) = P(\$200) \times P(\text{bankrupt})$

$\qquad\qquad\qquad\qquad\qquad = 0.25 \times 0.125$

$\qquad\qquad\qquad\qquad\qquad = 0.03125$

▶ **Answer** The probability that you get $200 on your first spin and go bankrupt on your second spin is 0.03125, or about 3%.

Dependent Events If A and B are dependent events, the probability that B occurs given A has occurred is *not* the same as the probability of B. So, you should use $P(\text{B given A})$ instead of $P(\text{B})$ to represent the probability that B will occur given that A has occurred.

Probability of Dependent Events

Words For two dependent events, the probability that *both* events occur is the product of the probability of the first event and the probability of the second event given the first.

Algebra If A and B are dependent events, then
$P(\text{A } and \text{ B}) = P(\text{A}) \cdot P(\text{B given A})$.

EXAMPLE 3 Probability of Dependent Events

Aquarium The 25 fish in your aquarium are 12 loaches, 7 barbs, and 6 tetras. You want to give 2 fish to a friend. You randomly choose 1 fish from the aquarium, then randomly choose another fish without replacing the first. Find the probability that both are loaches.

loaches   barbs   tetras

SOLUTION

The events are dependent. Find the probability of the first event and the probability of the second event given the first. Then multiply the probabilities.

STEP 1 $P(\text{loach}) = \dfrac{12}{25}$ **Of the 25 fish, 12 are loaches.**

STEP 2 $P(\text{loach given loach}) = \dfrac{11}{24}$ **Of the remaining 24 fish, 11 are loaches.**

STEP 3 $P(\text{loach and loach}) = \dfrac{12}{25} \times \dfrac{11}{24}$ **Multiply probabilities.**

$= \dfrac{11}{50}$ **Simplify.**

▶ **Answer** The probability that both fish are loaches is $\dfrac{11}{50}$, or 22%.

AVOID ERRORS

The probability of choosing the second loach is $\dfrac{11}{24}$, not $\dfrac{12}{25}$, because the first fish is not placed back into the tank.

✓ **GUIDED PRACTICE**   for Examples 1, 2, and 3

1. **Marbles** From a jar of 5 red and 7 blue marbles, you randomly choose a marble, replace it, then randomly choose another. Are the events "choose a red marble first" and "choose a blue marble second" *independent* or *dependent*? Find the probability of both events occurring.

2. **Kennel** You work at a kennel walking dogs. The 10 dogs being boarded on a given day include 3 black, 4 brown, 2 white, and 1 spotted dog. You randomly choose 1 dog to walk, return it to its pen, and choose a different dog to walk. What is the probability that both dogs you walk are brown?

13.6 EXERCISES

SKILL PRACTICE

VOCABULARY Copy and complete the statement.

1. Independent events and dependent events are types of __?__ events.

2. If A and B are independent events, then $P(A$ and $B)$ equals __?__ .

CLASSIFYING EVENTS Tell whether the events are *independent* or *dependent*.

SEE EXAMPLE 1
on p. 715
for Exs. 3–4

3. While you are watching a baseball game, the third batter in the lineup hits a home run. Then the fourth batter in the lineup hits a home run.

4. Your CD player randomly plays each song on a CD once. You hear track 3 first and track 1 second.

SEE EXAMPLE 2
on p. 716 for
Exs. 5–7, 13–15

INDEPENDENT EVENTS Events A and B are independent. Find $P(A$ and $B)$.

5. $P(A) = 0.3$
$P(B) = 0.7$

6. $P(A) = 0.5$
$P(B) = 0.5$

7. $P(A) = 0.8$
$P(B) = 0.2$

SEE EXAMPLE 3
on p. 717 for
Exs. 8–11, 16–18

DEPENDENT EVENTS Events A and B are dependent. Find $P(A$ and $B)$.

8. $P(A) = 0.9$
$P(B$ given $A) = 0.5$

9. $P(A) = 0.6$
$P(B$ given $A) = 0.25$

10. $P(A) = 0.25$
$P(B$ given $A) = 0.2$

11. ERROR ANALYSIS Describe and correct the error made in finding the probability that you and your friend are the 2 people randomly chosen from a group of 10.

$$\times \quad \frac{1}{10} \cdot \frac{1}{10} = \frac{1}{100}$$

12. ★ MULTIPLE CHOICE Which expression can you evaluate to find the probability that a pink mint and then a yellow mint are randomly chosen and eaten out of a dish of 7 pink, 8 yellow, and 5 green mints?

A $\frac{7}{20} + \frac{8}{19}$
B $\frac{7}{19} \cdot \frac{8}{19}$
C $\frac{7}{20} \cdot \frac{8}{19}$
D $\frac{7}{20} \cdot \frac{8}{20}$

XIV ALGEBRA Events A and B are independent. Events C and D are dependent. Find the unknown probability.

13. $P(A) = 0.2$
$P(B) = $ __?__
$P(A$ and $B) = 0.08$

14. $P(A) = $ __?__
$P(B) = 0.5$
$P(A$ and $B) = 0.35$

15. $P(A) = 0.75$
$P(B) = $ __?__
$P(A$ and $B) = 0.\overline{3}$

16. $P(C) = 0.9$
$P(D$ given $C) = $ __?__
$P(C$ and $D) = 0.72$

17. $P(C) = 0.4$
$P(D$ given $C) = $ __?__
$P(C$ and $D) = 0.36$

18. $P(C) = $ __?__
$P(D$ given $C) = 0.3$
$P(C$ and $D) = 0.09$

19. CHALLENGE You put 9 paper slips numbered 1 through 9 in a hat. You randomly choose a slip from the hat. Without replacing the first slip, you randomly choose a second slip. What is the probability that the sum of the two chosen numbers is greater than 12? *Explain.*

PROBLEM SOLVING

SEE EXAMPLES 2 AND 3
on pp. 716–717
for Exs. 20–21

Tell whether the situation describes *independent events* or *dependent events*. Then answer the question.

20. VENDING MACHINE You put money in the rubber ball machine at the right and get a rubber ball. You repeat the process to get another rubber ball. What is the probability that both rubber balls are green?

21. SHOPPING There are 12 small, 24 medium, and 14 large T-shirts on display at a clothing store. You randomly choose one T-shirt and put it back. Then you randomly choose a second T-shirt. What is the probability that the first T-shirt is small and the second T-shirt is large?

22. ★ MULTIPLE CHOICE The integers from 1 through 10 are written on separate pieces of paper. You randomly choose two numbers one at a time, but you do not replace them. What is the probability that both numbers are odd?

    A $\frac{2}{9}$ **B** $\frac{1}{4}$ **C** $\frac{1}{2}$ **D** $\frac{17}{18}$

SHOES **The tables give data about the shoes manufactured at a factory during a day. Assume that the events are independent. Find the probability that a randomly chosen pair of shoes has the given description.**

23. Men's athletic shoes

24. Women's casual shoes

25. Men's casual shoes

Gender	Percent
men's	46%
women's	54%

Shoe Style	Percent
athletic	22%
casual	61%
dress	17%

26. ★ WRITING *Describe* a way to randomly choose one of the 6 lettered tiles, and then another, so that the events are independent.

27. ★ SHORT RESPONSE For two compound events A and B, does $P(A)$ have to be greater than $P(A \text{ and } B)$? *Explain.*

28. PERFORM AN EXPERIMENT Roll two number cubes 25 times. For each roll, record the sum of the two cubes. What is the experimental probability that the sum is less than 7? Use your results to predict the probability of getting a sum of less than 7 for (a) both and (b) neither of the next two rolls.

29. REASONING The 11 letters that spell the word PROBABILITY are written on slips of paper and put in a bag. You randomly choose two letters, one at a time, from the bag. Is the probability of getting two B's greater if you replace the first letter chosen or if you don't replace it? *Explain.*

30. **CHALLENGE** A jar of coins includes 15 dimes. The probability of choosing a quarter is 20%. The probability of choosing a dime and then a quarter (after replacing the dime) is 6%. How many quarters are in the jar?

31. **CHALLENGE** The table shows the size and color of paper clips in a box. There are 65 in all. The probability of *not* randomly choosing a yellow paper clip is $\frac{7}{13}$.

	Small	Large
Red	10	10
Blue	10	?
Yellow	?	15

You randomly choose paper clips one at a time without replacing them. What is the probability that the first three paper clips you choose are small and yellow?

In Exercises 32 and 33, use a simulation as shown below.

EXTENSION **Simulating Events**

You and a friend each randomly choose 1 of 6 buses to ride to school. What is the probability that you both ride the same bus?

SOLUTION

You can approximate the probability using a model, or *simulation*. Let the numbers on two number cubes represent buses 1, 2, 3, 4, 5, and 6. Roll two number cubes to represent the buses chosen by you and your friend. A *success* occurs when the same number appears on both cubes.

Your friend rides bus 4.

You ride bus 1.

The table shows the results of 25 rolls of the cubes. You can use the results to find the experimental probability of taking the same bus.

Outcomes	Frequency
Success	4
Total	25

$$P(\text{same bus}) = \frac{\text{successful trials}}{\text{total trials}} = \frac{4}{25} = \frac{16}{100} = 16\%$$

▶ **Answer** About 16% of the time, you and your friend ride the same bus.

---

32. **ROSES** A box contains 6 roses: 3 red, 2 pink, and 1 white. *Explain* how to use simulations to approximate the probability of choosing a red rose, then another red rose when you (a) replace the first rose and (b) do not replace the first rose. Then do the simulations to find these probabilities.

33. **GAMES** You win a prize by choosing 4 white tiles out of a bag of 6 tiles before choosing one of 2 red tiles in the bag. Once a tile is removed, it is not replaced. Use a simulation to find the experimental probability of winning. *Explain* how this compares to the theoretical probability of winning.

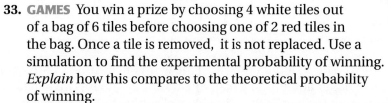 = STANDARDIZED TEST PRACTICE   ◯ = HINTS AND HOMEWORK HELP *at classzone.com*

34. David has 2 red marbles, 2 blue marbles, and 1 white marble in a bag. Which list shows all the possible unique outcomes if David chooses 2 marbles, M1 and M2, at one time from the bag?

Ⓐ

M1	M2
Red	Red
Red	Blue
Red	White
Blue	Blue
Blue	White

Ⓑ

M1	M2
Red	Red
Red	Blue
Red	White
Blue	Red
Blue	Blue
White	White

Ⓒ

M1	M2
Red	Red
Red	Blue
Red	White
Blue	Red
Blue	Blue
Blue	White

Ⓓ

M1	M2
Red	Blue
Red	White
Blue	Red
Blue	White
White	Red
White	Blue

QUIZ *for Lessons 13.4–13.6*

1. COMPUTER PASSWORD A 5-letter computer password is randomly assigned to you. The letters are lower case and may not repeat. How many different passwords are possible? *(p. 702)*

2. FLOWERS You are making floral arrangements. You choose to use only 3 different types of flowers from the 6 types of flowers available. How many ways can you choose 3 different types of flowers? *(p. 702)*

3. AGE DISTRIBUTION The estimated distribution of the U.S. population in 2010 is shown in the table. Find the probability that a randomly chosen person is in the age group 15–19 *or* the age group 60 and over. *(p. 709)*

Age Group	14 and under	15–19	20–24	25–39	40–59	60 and over
Percent	20.0%	6.9%	7.0%	20.0%	27.6%	18.4%

Events A and B are dependent events. Find $P(A \text{ and } B)$. *(p. 715)*

4. $P(A) = 0.6$, $P(B \text{ given } A) = 0.3$ **5.** $P(A) = 0.11$, $P(B \text{ given } A) = 0.45$

Brain Game

What's in the bag?

A bag contains blue, red, orange, and green cubes, and there are 50 cubes in the bag. The probability of randomly choosing each cube is given at the right. How many cubes of each color are in the bag?

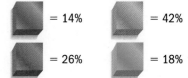

= 14%   = 42%

= 26%   = 18%

Lessons 13.4–13.6

1. **HOMEWORK** The circle graph shows the results of a survey that asked students in your school who usually helps them with their homework. What is the probability that a randomly selected student gets homework help from a friend or teacher?

Who Helps with Homework?

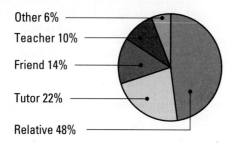

Other 6%
Teacher 10%
Friend 14%
Tutor 22%
Relative 48%

   A. 10%

   B. 12%

   C. 14%

   D. 24%

2. **TENNIS** A bin holds 9 yellow (Y), 12 orange (O), and 5 white (W) tennis balls. You randomly choose a ball from the bin, use it to hit a serve, and then choose another ball. Which series of choices of balls would result in $P(Y) = P(O) = P(W)$ for the next ball chosen?

   A. O, Y, O, Y, O, Y, O, Y

   B. O, Y, O, Y, O, Y, O, Y, O, O, O

   C. O, Y, W, O, Y, W, O, Y, W

   D. O, O, Y, Y, O, O

3. **GUMBALLS** A gumball machine has 400 gumballs. There are 150 red, 75 blue, 50 green, and 125 yellow gumballs in the machine. What is the probability that you choose a yellow gumball and then a red gumball if you don't replace them?

   A. 0.07

   B. 0.12

   C. 0.04

   D. 0.69

4. **SCIENCE FAIRS** There are 22 entries at a science fair. A judge awards a total of 3 ribbons to the first, second, and third place winners. In how many ways can the judge award the ribbons?

   A. 63

   B. 189

   C. 9,240

   D. 10,648

5. **OPEN-ENDED** Explain why you cannot use the expression $4 \times 3 \times 2 \times 1$ to find the number of different arrangements of the letters in the word OHIO. Then find the number of different ways the letters in the word can be arranged. *Justify* your answer.

REVIEW KEY VOCABULARY

- outcomes, *p. 682*
- event, *p. 682*
- favorable outcomes, *p. 682*
- probability, *p. 682*
- theoretical probability, *p. 683*

- experimental probability, *p. 683*
- tree diagram, *p. 690*
- permutation, *p. 702*
- combination, *p. 703*
- disjoint events, *p. 709*

- overlapping events, *p. 709*
- complementary events, *p. 711*
- compound events, *p. 715*
- independent events, *p. 715*
- dependent events, *p. 715*

VOCABULARY EXERCISES

Match the definition with a review word from the list above.

1. The possible results of an experiment

2. A collection of outcomes

3. A measure of the likelihood that an event will occur

4. A probability based on repeated trials of an experiment

5. An arrangement of a group of objects in a particular order

6. A grouping of objects in which order is not important

REVIEW EXAMPLES AND EXERCISES

13.1 Introduction to Probability

pp. 682–687

EXAMPLE

Letters Each letter in PENNSYLVANIA is written on a separate piece of paper and put into a bag. You randomly choose a piece of paper from the bag. Find the probability of choosing an N.

$$P(\text{N}) = \frac{\text{Number of favorable outcomes}}{\text{Total number of outcomes}} = \frac{3}{12} = \frac{1}{4}$$

▶ **Answer** The probability of choosing an N is $\frac{1}{4}$, 0.25, or 25%.

EXAMPLE

Corn You pick up and look at 12 ears of corn at the grocery store. Of these, 8 are bicolor. What is the probability that a randomly chosen ear of corn will be bicolor?

$$P(\text{N}) = \frac{\text{Number of favorable outcomes}}{\text{Total number of outcomes}} = \frac{8}{12} = \frac{2}{3}$$

▶ **Answer** The probability of choosing a bicolor ear is $\frac{2}{3}$, $0.\overline{6}$, or $66\frac{2}{3}$%.

EXERCISES

SEE EXAMPLE 1
on p. 682
for Exs. 7–11

7. In the first Example, what is the probability of randomly choosing an A?

You spin the spinner shown, which is divided into equal parts. Find the probability of the given event. Write the probability as a fraction, a decimal, and a percent.

8. Pointer lands on green.

9. Pointer lands on 5.

10. Pointer lands on an odd number.

11. Pointer lands on yellow.

13.2 Tree Diagrams
pp. 690–694

EXAMPLE

School Newspaper The openings for your school newspaper are for reporters and editors in the areas of sports, student government, or student life. Find the number of options you have.

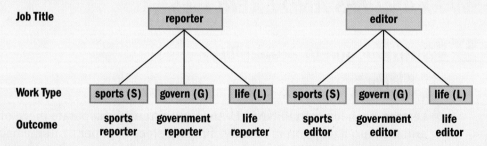

▶ **Answer** You have 6 different options.

EXERCISES

SEE EXAMPLES 1 AND 3
on pp. 690, 692
for Exs. 12–14

12. **Menu** A restaurant offers choices of a chicken, beef, or pork entrée, soup or salad, and baked potato, mashed potatoes, or rice. Make a tree diagram to find the number of meal options.

13. What is the probability of getting at least one head when you toss a coin 3 times?

14. **New Car** You want a new 2-door or 4-door car in blue, black, or red. You may or may not get a CD player. Make a tree diagram to find the number of possible cars you can choose.

The Counting Principle *pp. 696–700*

EXAMPLE

Pizza A pizza comes with a choice of crust (thin or thick), one meat topping (sausage, pepperoni, or ham), and one vegetable topping (peppers, mushrooms, or onions). How many different pizzas are possible?

Number of crust choices	×	Number of meat toppings	×	Number of vegetable toppings	=	Number of pizzas
2	×	3	×	3	=	18

▸ **Answer** There are 18 different possible pizzas.

EXERCISES

SEE EXAMPLE 1
on p. 696
for Ex. 15

15. **What If?** If 2 more meat choices and 3 more vegetable toppings are added to the above example, how many pizzas are possible?

13.4 **Permutations and Combinations** *pp. 702–707*

EXAMPLE

Car Music Your car has a pocket that can hold 8 CDs. You have a set of 10 CDs you would like to take on a trip. How many different groups of 8 CDs can you pick from the total set of 10?

Find the permutations when choosing 8 from 10:
$10 \times 9 \times 8 \times 7 \times 6 \times 5 \times 4 \times 3 = 1{,}814{,}400$

Find the number of permutations of 8 choices:
$8 \times 7 \times 6 \times 5 \times 4 \times 3 \times 2 \times 1 = 40{,}320$

Divide the first number by the second:
$1{,}814{,}400 \div 40{,}320 = 45$

▸ **Answer** There are 45 different sets of CDs you could take.

EXERCISES

**SEE EXAMPLES
1, 2, AND 3**
on pp. 702–703
for Exs. 16–17

16. **Menu Choices** At lunch, you may choose 3 different vegetable side dishes from the 10 available. Is this a permutation or a combination? *Explain.* Then find the number of possibilities.

17. **Prizes** A poetry contest has 12 entries. In how many ways can first and second prizes be awarded? *Justify* your answer.

13.5 Disjoint Events

pp. 709–714

EXAMPLE

Blood Type The table shows the blood types of donors during a week at a hospital. What is the probability that a randomly selected donor has type O+ or type B+ blood?

Type	O	A	B	AB
+	38%	34%	9%	3%
−	7%	6%	2%	1%

The events are disjoint because a person can have only one blood type.

$P(\text{O}+ \text{ or } \text{B}+) = P(\text{O}+) + P(\text{B}+) = 38\% + 9\% = 47\%$

▶ **Answer** The probability that a donor has type O+ or type B+ blood is 47%.

EXERCISES

SEE EXAMPLES
2 AND 3
on pp. 710–711
for Exs. 18–20

In Exercises 18 and 19, use the table above.

18. Find $P(\text{B}- \text{ or } \text{O}-)$.

19. Find $P(\text{A}- \text{ or } \text{B}-)$.

20. **Flowers** At a garden shop, 35% of the chrysanthemums are red. What is the probability that a randomly chosen chrysanthemum is *not* red? There are 140 chrysanthemum plants at the shop. Estimate how many are *not* red.

13.6 Independent and Dependent Events

pp. 715–721

EXAMPLE

Fruit A bowl has 3 plums and 5 pears. A second bowl has 2 plums and 4 pears. You randomly choose 1 piece of fruit from the first bowl and 1 piece of fruit from the second bowl. What is the probability that both are plums?

The choice you make from the first bowl does *not* affect the choice you make from the second bowl. So, the events are independent.

$P(\text{plum from each bowl}) = \dfrac{3}{8} \times \dfrac{2}{6} = \dfrac{\cancel{3}^{1} \times \cancel{2}^{1}}{\cancel{8}_{4} \times \cancel{6}_{2}} = \dfrac{1}{8}$

▶ **Answer** The probability that both pieces of fruit are plums is $\dfrac{1}{8}$, or 12.5%.

EXERCISES

SEE EXAMPLE 3
on p. 717
for Ex. 21

21. You randomly choose a piece of fruit from the first bowl described above, do not replace it, and randomly choose a second piece from the same bowl. What is the probability that both pieces of fruit are pears?

13 CHAPTER TEST

In Exercises 1–3, you randomly choose a marble from the marbles below.
Find the probability of choosing a marble of the given color. Write the
probability as a fraction, a decimal, and a percent.

1. Red   **2.** Blue   **3.** Green

4. Find the number of possible arrangements of the letters in the
word VIDEO.

5. How many groups of 3 forwards can you choose from 7 soccer players?

In Exercises 6–8, events A and B are independent events. Find the
unknown probability.

6. $P(A) = 0.2$
   $P(B) = 0.4$
   $P(A \text{ and } B) = \underline{\ ?\ }$

7. $P(A) = 0.5$
   $P(B) = \underline{\ ?\ }$
   $P(A \text{ and } B) = 0.2$

8. $P(A) = \underline{\ ?\ }$
   $P(B) = 0.7$
   $P(A \text{ and } B) = 0.21$

SURVEY You asked 60 students at your school to name their favorite
type of juice. Of the students surveyed, 42 chose orange juice.

9. Find the probability that orange juice is the favorite juice of a randomly
selected student who participated in the survey. Write the probability as
a fraction, a decimal, and a percent.

10. Predict how many students out of 210 would choose orange juice.

11. **PAINTING** You are painting your dog's house. You can choose red,
green, dark blue, or light blue for the main color, and white or tan for
the trim color. Make a tree diagram to find the number of color pairs
you can choose to paint the dog's house.

RELAXATION The circle graph shows the
results of a survey. Find the probability that
a randomly chosen student who participated
in the survey responded as indicated.

Favorite Way to Relax

- Listen to music 46%
- Watch TV 23%
- Exercise 17%
- Read 14%

12. Chose TV or music

13. Chose music or reading

14. Didn't choose exercise

15. **BED LINENS** There are 18 pillowcases stacked in your linen closet. Four
of the pillowcases are blue. You randomly choose one pillowcase, and
then randomly choose another pillowcase without replacing the first.
Find the probability that both pillowcases chosen are blue.

REVIEWING PROBABILITY PROBLEMS

After completing Chapter 13 you will be able to:

- count the number of outcomes of a real-life event
- find the probability of a real-life event

> ### EXAMPLE
>
> Kevin has a jar containing 2 red marbles, 3 blue marbles, 1 green marble, and 4 yellow marbles.
>
> **Part A** He randomly chooses 1 marble from the jar and then replaces it. Then he chooses another marble. What is the probability that Kevin chooses a blue marble and then a yellow marble?
>
> **Part B** He randomly chooses 1 marble from the jar, but he does not replace it. Then he chooses another marble. What is the probability that Kevin chooses a blue marble and then a yellow marble?

Solution

Because Kevin replaces the first marble, these two events are independent.

$$P(\text{blue and then yellow}) = P(\text{blue}) \cdot P(\text{yellow})$$

$$= \frac{3}{10} \cdot \frac{4}{10} = \frac{3}{25}$$

▶ **Answer** So, the probability that he chooses a blue marble and then a
▶ yellow marble with replacement is $\frac{3}{25}$.

Because Kevin does not replace the first marble, these two events are dependent.

$$P(\text{blue and then yellow}) = P(\text{blue}) \cdot P(\text{yellow given blue})$$

$$= \frac{3}{10} \cdot \frac{4}{9} = \frac{2}{15}$$

▶ **Answer** So, the probability that he chooses a blue marble and then a
▶ yellow marble without replacement is $\frac{2}{15}$.

PROBABILITY PROBLEMS

Below are examples of probability problems in multiple choice format. Try solving the problems before looking at the solutions. (Cover the solutions with a piece of paper.) Then check your solutions against the ones given.

1. You randomly choose a letter from the word TOMATO. What is the probability of choosing either an M or an O?

   A. $\frac{1}{6}$

   B. $\frac{1}{3}$

   C. $\frac{1}{2}$

   D. $\frac{3}{4}$

Solution

The events are disjoint because two letters cannot be chosen at the same time.

$$P(M) + P(O) = \frac{1}{6} + \frac{2}{6} = \frac{3}{6} = \frac{1}{2}$$

The probability of choosing either an M or an O is $\frac{1}{2}$, so the correct answer is C.

2. A café offers ham, turkey, and chicken for meat choices in a sandwich, and American and Swiss for cheese choices. If you choose one meat and one cheese at random for your sandwich, what is the probability that you choose a turkey and Swiss sandwich?

   A. $\frac{1}{3}$

   B. $\frac{1}{5}$

   C. $\frac{1}{6}$

   D. $\frac{1}{9}$

Solution

Find the number of possible outcomes using the counting principle.

Number of meat choices		Number of cheese choices		Number of possible outcomes
3	×	2	=	6

There are 6 possible sandwich combinations and only 1 is turkey and Swiss, so the probability of choosing turkey and Swiss is $\frac{1}{6}$. The correct answer is C.

3. In your class, 45% of the students play an instrument. What is the probability that a randomly chosen student in your class does NOT play an instrument?

   A. 25%

   B. 45%

   C. 55%

   D. 65%

Solution

Playing an instrument and not playing an instrument are complementary events.

$$P(\text{does not play}) = 1 - P(\text{plays})$$
$$= 1 - 0.45$$
$$= 0.55$$

The probability that a randomly chosen student does not play an instrument is 0.55, or 55%, so the correct answer is C.

TEST PREPARATION

TEST PREPARATION

1. Eugene collected data on the number of students in each homeroom that are trying out for the lead role in a school play. The table below shows the results.

School Play	
Homeroom Teacher	**Number of Students**
Mrs. Smith	0
Mrs. Carson	2
Mr. Williams	1
Mr. Kendall	3
Miss Stoltz	1
Mrs. Davis	5

What is the probability that the student chosen for the lead role is in Mr. Kendall's homeroom if each student is equally likely to be chosen?

A. 0.2

B. 0.25

C. 0.3

D. 0.4

2. The line plot shows the results of a questionnaire asking students how many pets they own.

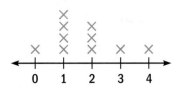

A student is chosen at random. What is the probability that the student has 2 or fewer pets?

A. 0.1

B. 0.2

C. 0.3

D. 0.8

3. The spinner below is divided into equal parts. You spin the spinner twice. What is the probability of spinning a 2 and then an odd number?

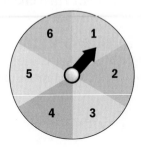

A. $\frac{1}{12}$

B. $\frac{1}{6}$

C. $\frac{1}{4}$

D. $\frac{2}{3}$

4. A sporting goods store is having a sale. The table shows the regular price r and the sale price s of three items.

Sale		
Item	**Regular Price r**	**Sale Price s**
A	$7.40	$3.70
B	$12.50	$6.25
C	$15.90	$7.95

Which formula can be used to calculate the sale price?

A. $s = r - 3.70$

B. $s = r \times 2$

C. $s = r \times 0.5$

D. $s = r - 0.5$

5. The cost of Simon and Alexa's dinner was $15.72. They want to leave a 15% tip. Which of the following is closest to the amount of the tip they want to leave?

   A. $2.00

   B. $2.50

   C. $3.00

   D. $3.50

6. The radius of a circle is 13 inches. Which of the following is closest to the circumference of the circle?

   A. 26 in.

   B. 41 in.

   C. 52 in.

   D. 82 in.

7. The fraction $\frac{3}{7}$ is found between which pair of fractions on a number line?

   A. $\frac{4}{14}$ and $\frac{8}{21}$

   B. $\frac{5}{14}$ and $\frac{10}{21}$

   C. $\frac{7}{14}$ and $\frac{11}{21}$

   D. $\frac{8}{14}$ and $\frac{12}{21}$

8. Angle X and angle Y are supplementary. The measure of angle Y is 30°. What is the measure of angle X?

   A. 30°

   B. 60°

   C. 150°

   D. 160°

9. Mr. Schein asked 27 students how many times they used a calculator today in his class. The responses are shown in the table.

Calculator Use	
Number of Times Used	Number of Students
2	5
3	12
4	4
5	6

   Which measure of the data represents the most common number of times the students used the calculator?

   A. Mean

   B. Median

   C. Mode

   D. Range

10. **OPEN-ENDED** You want to remodel your kitchen by painting the walls, replacing the countertop, and replacing the floor tiles. Your color choices for each item are given in the table below.

Item	Paint	Countertop	Floor tiles
Available colors	white, tan, blue	white, green, blue, gray, tan	white, tan

   Part A Use a tree diagram to show the number of different ways you can remodel your kitchen by choosing 1 color of each item.

   Part B Use the counting principle to justify your answer.

   Part C Suppose you choose the color of each item at random. What is the probability that all three items are the same color? *Explain.*

Find the mean, median, mode(s), and range of the data. *(p. 109)*

1. 0, 1, 2, 4, 4, 5, 7, 8, 10, 12, 13

2. 5.5, 6.3, 4.7, 4.6, 4.6, 7.1, 6.3, 7.4, 6, 7.5

Write the decimal as a fraction or mixed number in simplest form. *(p. 199)*

3. 0.75   **4.** 0.06   **5.** 5.125   **6.** 3.3125

Make an input-output table for the function. Then graph the function. *(p. 376)*

7. $y = -x - 8$ **8.** $y = 4x + 5$ **9.** $y = \frac{1}{3}x - 2$ **10.** $y = -2.5x + 4$

Use the percent equation or a proportion to solve. *(p. 465)*

11. 2 is 8% of what number?   **12.** What number is 1% of 44?

Classify the angle as *acute*, *right*, *obtuse*, or *straight*. Then find the measure of a supplementary angle and the measure of a complementary angle, if possible. *(p. 511)*

13. $m\angle A = 25°$ **14.** $m\angle B = 140°$ **15.** $m\angle C = 5°$ **16.** $m\angle D = 90°$

Find the unknown length. Round to the nearest tenth, if necessary. *(p. 588)*

17.
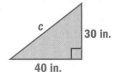

18.
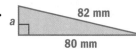

19.
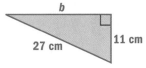

Find the unknown dimension or volume of the rectangular prism. *(p. 655)*

20. $V =$ __?__ , $l = 20$ in., $w = 4$ in., $h = 5$ in.   **21.** $V = 81$ cm³, $l = 9$ cm, $w = 4.5$ cm, $h =$ __?__

In Exercises 22 and 23, use the cylinders below.

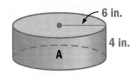
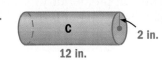
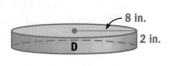

22. Order the cylinders from greatest to least surface area. *(p. 649)*

23. Order the cylinders from greatest to least volume. *(p. 662)*

Events A and B are disjoint events. Find *P*(A or B). *(p. 709)*

24. $P(A) = 0.2; P(B) = 0.7$ **25.** $P(A) = 0.13; P(B) = 0.27$

Events A and B are independent events. Find *P*(A and B). *(p. 715)*

26. $P(A) = 0.4; P(B) = 0.6$ **27.** $P(A) = 0.5; P(B) = 0.3$

28. SKATING The surface of the Olympic Oval's ice skating rink in Salt Lake City, Utah, was created by repeatedly spraying water to make 24 layers of ice for a total thickness of $\frac{3}{4}$ inch. How thick is each layer of ice? *(p. 237)*

29. FREEZE-DRIED ICE CREAM During the freeze-drying process, all of the water content is removed from the food item. To freeze-dry ice cream, regular ice cream is frozen at a temperature of $-40°F$ and then dried in a vacuum. Convert this temperature to degrees Celsius. *(p. 296)*

30. BREAKFAST 200 students were asked what they eat for breakfast. Display the results, shown below, in a circle graph. *(p. 474)*

Food	Eggs	Cold cereal	Pancakes	French toast	Other
Students	27.5%	45%	15%	7.5%	5%

31. DINING You and your family are eating at a restaurant. The food bill is $40. Your family chooses to leave a 20% tip before tax. The sales tax is 6%. What is the total cost of the meal? *(p. 485)*

32. MOVIE POSTERS A rectangular movie poster has a length of 28 inches and a width of 22 inches. A print of the poster is similar to the original and has a length of 14 inches. What is the width of the print? *(p. 542)*

33. BASKETBALL The circumference of the rim of a basketball hoop is about 56.52 inches. What is the diameter of the rim? Use 3.14 for π. *(p. 607)*

34. PENCILS An unsharpened wooden pencil is a cylinder that has a radius of 3.5 millimeters and a height of 175 millimeters. The pencil's lead is a cylinder that has a radius of 2 millimeters. Find the volume of the wood in the pencil. Use 3.14 for π. *(p. 662)*

CAR COLORS As you wait for the bus, you keep track of the color of each passing car, as shown. Find the probability a car that passes is the given color. *(p. 682)*

35. White
36. Black
37. Silver
38. Blue
39. Green
40. Red

White	5	Silver	8
Blue	14	Red	7
Green	6	Black	10

41. DIARY LOCK A diary lock has a 3 digit unlocking code. Each of the digits is a whole number from 1 through 5. Find the probability that the lock has an unlocking code in which all of the digits are the same number. *(p. 696)*

42. SHOES You have 8 pairs of shoes (16 individual shoes) in the back of your closet. Because your closet is dark, you randomly choose one shoe, and without replacing it, you randomly choose another shoe. What is the probability that you choose a matching pair? *(p. 715)*

ADDITIONAL LESSONS

MATH COURSE 2

The additional lessons have been written to ensure complete state standard coverage. These lessons provide content addressing material to encompass individual state needs. They are offered to help teach all of the standards or to provide enrichment and challenge opportunities.

A   Estimation and Accuracy of Measurement A2

B   Metric/Customary Conversions A4

C   Rules of Exponents A6

D   Introduction to Recursive Functions for Sequences A8

E   Vertex-Edge Graphs, Circuits, Networks, and Routing A10

F   Coordinate Geometry and Geometric Figures A12

G   Angles and Polygons A14

H   Volumes of Pyramids and Cones A16

I   Circles and Sectors A18

J   Similarity and Dilations A20

K   Stem-and-Leaf Plots A22

L   Misleading Data Displays A24

M   Designing and Conducting an Investigation A26

N   Experimental vs. Observational Study A28

O   Inductive and Deductive Reasoning A30

P   Triangle Inequalities A32

ADDITIONAL LESSONS

Estimation and Accuracy of Measurement

Use after Chapter 1

GOAL Use estimation strategies reasonably and fluently.

Key Vocabulary

• **estimation**
• **amount of error**

When solving problems in mathematics, we don't always have a calculator or the appropriate measuring tools available to us. When this happens, we can use estimation as a means of approximating a value. **Estimation** is the process of forming an approximation without actual calculation or measurement. When estimating, there is an **amount of error** that depends on the measuring tool. That is, the determined value will err on either side of the value by the smallest increment on the measuring tool.

EXAMPLE 1 **Estimate a reasonable solution**

Estimate: $\sqrt{78}$

Find the perfect squares just less than 78 and just greater than 78.

The perfect squares on either side of 78 are 64 and 81. So $\sqrt{78}$ is between $\sqrt{64}$ and $\sqrt{81}$, which means $\sqrt{78}$ is between 8 and 9.

The difference between 64 and 78 is 14, the difference between 64 and 81 is 17, the difference between 8 and $\sqrt{78}$ is "x" and the difference between 8 and 9 is 1. Solve the following proportion.

$$\frac{14}{17} = \frac{x}{1}$$

$$17x = 14$$

$$x = \frac{14}{17}$$

$$x \approx 0.824$$

Therefore $\sqrt{78} = 8 + 0.8$, or 8.8 with accuracy to the tenths place.

EXAMPLE 2 **Estimate and determine an amount of error**

Estimate the measure of $\angle ABC$ and $\angle DBC$ in the drawing.

Compare $\angle ABC$ with an angle of known measure such as a right or straight angle.

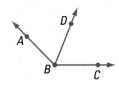

Draw $\angle EBC$ as a straight angle and $\angle FBC$ as a right angle. $\angle ABC$ appears to be approximately $\frac{1}{2}$ of the way between $\angle EBC$ and $\angle FBC$, so $\angle ABC$ is approximately $\frac{(90 + 180)}{2}$, or 135°. $\angle DBC$ is approximately $\frac{1}{2}$ of $\angle ABC$, or approximately 68°, when rounded to the nearest degree.

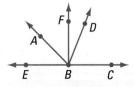

EXAMPLE 3 **Using tools to measure line segments and angles**

What is the measure of line segment $\overline{XY}$?

If the ruler being used has increments of tenths of an inch, the measure is approximately $1\frac{9}{10}$ inch, with an error of $\frac{1}{10}$ inch in either direction. That is, the measure is from $1\frac{8}{10}$ inch to 2 inches.

If the ruler is incremented in eighths of an inch, the measure is $1\frac{7}{8}$ inch with an error of $\frac{1}{8}$ of an inch in either direction. That is, the measure is from $1\frac{6}{8}$ inch to 2 inches.

What is the measure of $\angle ABC$?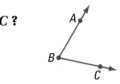

If the protractor being used is incremented every 1°, the angle is about 70°, with an error range of 1° greater or less than 70°. That is, the angle measures from 69° to 71°.

If the protractor being used is incremented every 5°, the angle is about 70°, with an error range of 5° greater or less than 70°. That is, the angle measures from 65° to 75°.

PRACTICE

Complete the following exercises.

EXAMPLE 1
for Exs. 1–3

Estimate the following square roots.

1. $\sqrt{21}$ 2. $\sqrt{110}$ 3. $\sqrt{52}$

Use the figure below to answer exercises 4 and 5.

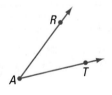

EXAMPLE 2
for Exs. 4–5

4. Estimate the measure of $\angle RAT$.

5. Measure $\angle RAT$.

EXAMPLE 3
for Ex. 6

6. Measure line segment $\overline{PG}$.

Additional Lesson B — Metric/Customary Conversions

Use after Chapter 1

GOAL Use the metric to customary conversion tables to understand how one unit of measure relates to the other.

Key Vocabulary

- **metric system**
- **customary system**

History

The **metric system** was developed in France in the late 18th century to replace the various systems that were being used throughout the world at that time. Today, the metric system is referred to as the International System of Units, abbreviated SI. **Customary Systems** grew out of the customs of the area. The system presently used in the United States is the English System and the United States is the only industrial nation using it.

Abbreviations

Customary	Metric
inch = in.	centimeter = cm
foot = ft.	meter = m
mile = mi.	kilometer = km
quart = qt.	liter = l or L
gallon = gal.	Celsius = C
Fahrenheit = F	

CONVERSION TABLES

| | Into Metric | | | | Into Customary | |

Length						
From	**multiply by**	**To**		**From**	**multiply by**	**To**
in.	2.54	cm		m	39.36	in.
ft.	30.48	cm		cm	0.39	in.
mi.	1.61	km		km	0.62	mi.

Volume						
From	**multiply by**	**To**		**From**	**multiply by**	**To**
qt.	.95	L		L	1.06	qt.
gal.	3.79	L		L	0.26	gal.

Temperature						
From		**To**		**From**		**To**
F	subtract 32 then multiply by $\frac{5}{9}$	C		C	multiply by $\frac{9}{5}$ then add 32	F

EXAMPLE 1 • Convert from Customary into Metric Units

Convert 9.8 in. to centimeters.

Multiply by 2.54 to change from inches to centimeters.

$$9.8 \times 2.54 = 24.89 \text{ cm}$$

Convert 12 miles to kilometers.

Multiply by 1.61 to change from miles to kilometers.

$$12 \times 1.61 = 19.32 \text{ km}$$

EXAMPLE 2 • Convert from Metric into Customary Units

The Granger family is driving a rental car in Canada. They stop and put 45 liters of gas into the car. Determine the number of gallons they put in the car.

To change from liters to gallons, multiply by 0.26.

$$45 \times 0.26 = 11.7 \text{ gallons}$$

The Granger family put 11.7 gallons of gas in the car.

EXAMPLE 3 • Convert from Celsius (C) to Fahrenheit (F)

During their drive, the thermometer in the car said that the temperature was 15°. Knowing that Celsius is the unit used in Canada for temperature, what is the Fahrenheit equivalent?

To change from degrees Celsius to degrees Fahrenheit, multiply by $\frac{9}{5}$ and then add 32.

$$15 \times \frac{9}{5} = 27.0$$

$$27.0 + 32 = 59.0°F$$

The temperature was 59°F.

PRACTICE

Complete the following exercises.

EXAMPLE 1
for Exs. 1, 7

1. Convert 16 gal. to liters.

2. Convert 7.5 m to inches.

EXAMPLE 2
for Exs. 2, 3, 6

3. A pediatrician measured a baby's length at 62 cm. What is the baby's length in inches?

4. A friend from Spain tells you that the current temperature is 35°C. Determine the temperature in Fahrenheit.

EXAMPLE 3
for Exs. 4–5

5. You tell your Spanish friend that the current temperature in your hometown in 77°F. Convert that temperature to °C for your friend.

6. Your friend will be traveling with her family to Barcelona by car next week. The distance is about 300 km from her hometown. What is this distance in miles?

7. You do some research and find that the distance between your hometown in the U.S. and your friend's hometown in Spain is 3,591 miles. How many kilometers is this distance?

Rules of Exponents

GOAL Use laws of exponents to simplify.

Key Vocabulary

- power
- base
- exponent
- Product of Powers Property
- Quotient of Powers Property

Recall that a **power** is a way of writing repeated multiplication. The **base** of a power is the factor, and the **exponent** of a power is the number of times the factor is used.

Exponents follow certain patterns. Two of those patterns are known as the **Product of Powers Property** and the **Quotient of Powers Property.** The properties are defined below.

Product of Powers Property

Words To multiply powers with the same base, add their exponents.

Algebra $a^m \cdot a^n = a^{m+n}$

Numbers $5^2 \cdot 5^7 = 5^{2+7} = 5^9$

Quotient of Powers Property

Words To divide two powers with the same nonzero base, subtract the exponent of the denominator from the exponent of the numerator.

Algebra $\dfrac{a^m}{a^n} = a^{m-n}$ **Numbers** $\dfrac{2^5}{2^3} = 2^{5-3} = 2^2$

EXAMPLE 1 **Using the Product of Powers Property**

Simplify the expression. Write your answer as a power.

a. $x^3 \cdot x^2 = x^{3+2}$ Product of powers property

$= x^5$ Add exponents.

b. $4^3 y^4 \cdot 4^6 y = (4^3 \cdot 4^6) \cdot (y^4 \cdot y)$ Use properties of multiplication.

$= 4^{3+6} \cdot y^{4+1}$ Product of powers property

$= 4^9 y^5$ Add exponents.

EXAMPLE 2 **Using the Quotient of Powers Property**

Simplify the expression. Write your answer as a power.

a. $\dfrac{m^4}{m^3} = m^{4-3}$ Quotient of powers property

$= m^1$ Subtract exponents.

b. $\dfrac{9^{10}}{9^6} = 9^{10-6}$ Quotient of powers property

$= 9^4$ Subtract exponents.

EXAMPLE 3 Simplifying Fractions with Powers

Simplify the expression. Write your answer as a power.

a. $\dfrac{t^3 t^t}{t^2} = \dfrac{t^4}{t^2}$ Simplify numerator-using product of powers property.

$\qquad\quad = t^{4-2}$ Quotient of powers property

$\qquad\quad = t^2$ Subtract exponents.

b. $\dfrac{x^4 y^2}{y} = x^4 y^{2-1}$ Quotient of powers property

$\qquad\quad = x^4 y$ Subtract exponents.

PRACTICE

Simplify the expression. Write your answer as a power.

EXAMPLE 1
for Exs. 1–4

1. $g^6 \cdot g^2$

2. $5^3 \cdot 5^8$

3. $x^5 \cdot 2x^2$

4. $3^5 h^3 \cdot 3h$

EXAMPLE 2
for Exs. 5–7

5. $\dfrac{t^{13}}{t^8}$

6. $\dfrac{8^{10}}{8^2}$

7. $\dfrac{3^3 m^5}{3m^4}$

EXAMPLE 3
for Exs. 8–10

8. $\dfrac{n^3 \cdot n^6}{n^2}$

9. $\dfrac{k^2 \cdot l^5}{l^4}$

10. $\dfrac{2^5 d^2 \cdot 2^2 f^9}{2^6 f^3}$

Introduction to Recursive Functions for Sequences

Use after Chapter 7

GOAL Evaluate problems using basic recursive formulas.

Key Vocabulary

- **sequence**
- **term notation**
- **recursive**
- **recursive formula**

A **sequence** is a set of numbers in a particular order (pattern), such as 2, 4, 6, 8 ....

Sequences can be referred to by using **term notation,** t_1, t_2, t_3, t_4, ..., t_n where t_1 is the first term, t^2 is the second term, ... and t_n is the number nth term. We can also refer to the term after t_n as t_{n+1}, and the previous term, or term before t_n as t_{n-1}.

The word **recursive** means applying the same rule again and again. So a **recursive formula,** given with the first term or several terms of a sequence, is a rule that can be used to determine additional terms.

EXAMPLE 1   Write terms of sequences

a. Write the first 6 terms of the sequence 1, 5, 9... where $t_n = t_{n-1} + 4$, that is, any term is determined by adding 4 to the previous term.

$$t_4 = t_3 + 4 \qquad\qquad t_4 = 9 + 4 = 13$$

$$t_5 = t_4 + 4 \qquad\qquad t_5 = 13 + 4 = 17$$

$$t_6 = t_4 + 4 \qquad\qquad t_6 = 17 + 4 = 21$$

Thus the first 6 terms of this sequence are 1, 5, 9, 13, 17, 21.

b. Write the first 5 terms of the sequence 2, 3, 8... where $t_n = (t_{n-1})^2 - 1$, that is, 1 is subtracted from the square of the previous term.

$$t_4 = (t_3)^2 - 1 \qquad\qquad t_4 = 8^2 - 1 = 64 - 1 = 63$$

$$t_5 = (t_4) - 1 \qquad\qquad t_5 = 63^2 - 1 = 3969 - 1 = 3968$$

Thus the first 5 terms of this sequence are 2, 3, 8, 63, 3968.

EXAMPLE 2 Write a rule for the *n*th term of a sequence

a. Find the *n*th term, that is, the formula or rule that is used to determine the next term in the sequence 1, 4, 13, 40, 121…

Examine each term. How do you get the second term from the first? How do you get the third term from the second? And so on.

$$1 \times 3 + 1 = 4$$
$$4 \times 3 + 1 = 13$$
$$13 \times 3 + 1 = 40$$
$$40 \times 3 + 1 = 121$$

The previous term is multiplied by 3 and 1 is added to it.
So, the formula for the *n*th term is $t_n = 3(t_{n-1}) + 1$.

b. Find the *n*th term, that is, the formula or rule that is used to determine the next term in the sequence 4096, 2048, 1024, 512, 256, 128…

Examine each term. How do you get the second term from the first? How do you get the third term from the second? And so on.

$$4096 \div 2 = 2048$$
$$2048 \div 2 = 1024$$
$$1024 \div 2 = 512$$
$$512 \div 2 = 256$$
$$256 \div 2 = 128$$

The previous term is divided by 2.
So, the formula for the *n*th term is $t_n = \dfrac{t_{n-1}}{2}$.

PRACTICE

Complete the following exercises.

EXAMPLE 1
for Exs. 1–3

1. Write the first 6 terms of the sequence 1, 6… where $t_n = t_{n-1} + 5$.

2. Write the first 5 terms of the sequence 1, 4… where $t_n = (t_{n-1} + 5)^2$.

3. Write the first 7 terms of the sequence 3, 8… where $t_n = 2t_{n-1} + 2$.

Find the *n*th term, that is, the formula for determining the next term for the sequence.

EXAMPLE 2
for Exs. 4–6

4. 1, 4, 7, 10, 13, 16…

5. 1, 5, 25, 125, 525, 2625…

6. 1, 2, 5, 26, 677, 458330…

Vertex-Edge Graphs, Circuits, Networks, and Routing

Use after Chapter 10

Key Vocabulary

- vertex-edge graph
- network
- vertex
- edge
- path
- adjacent
- circuit
- route
- degree of a vertex

GOAL Use vertex-edge graphs to represent and find solutions to practical problems.

A **vertex-edge graph** or **network** has a finite number of dots (**vertices**) and lines (**edges**) connecting them. A **path** through the graph describes a sequence of vertices, all of which are **adjacent,** or next to one another. A path that starts and ends at the same vertex and travels over each edge only once is called a **circuit.** A **route** is a path through the graph that yields a particular result, such as shortest, cheapest, fastest, etc.

One way to determine if a particular graph is a circuit is to analyze the degree of the vertices. The **degree of a vertex** is the number of edges that connect to that vertex.

- If a graph has any vertices whose degree is odd-numbered, then it cannot be a circuit.

- Further, if a graph has more than two odd vertices, then it cannot have a path.

EXAMPLE 1 **Analyzing a network**

Determine whether the graph is a circuit.

a.

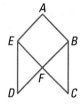

Solution
Analyze the degree of the vertices.
$A = 2$
$B = 3$
$C = 2$
$D = 2$
$E = 3$
$F = 4$

Since the graph has two odd vertices, it is not a circuit, but it does have a path.

b.

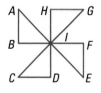

Solution
Analyze the degree of the vertices.

$A = 2$	$F = 2$
$B = 2$	$G = 2$
$C = 2$	$H = 2$
$D = 2$	$I = 8$
$E = 2$	

Since the graph has no odd vertices, it is a circuit. Use your finger to trace this path and see that it is a circuit, beginning and ending at the same point, going over each edge only one time:
$A, B, I, C, D, I, E, F, I, G, H, I, A.$

EXAMPLE 2 Solving a routing problem

The following network shows several cities and the paths connecting them. The vertices represent cities and the edges indicate nonstop airline routes between them.

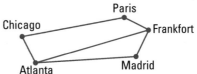

a. List all the paths that describe a trip from Chicago to Frankfort.

Solution
Using the first letter of each city, the paths are CPF, CAF, CAMF.

b. If the cheapest cost is Javier's greatest concern, which path would you suggest for him to take from Chicago to Frankfort?

Chicago to Paris	$865.00	8 hr. 45 min
Paris to Frankfort	$152.00	1 hr. 20 min.
Layover		3 hr. 10 min.
Chicago to Atlanta	$229.00	3 hr. 05 min.
Atlanta to Frankfort	$1053.00	7 hr. 50 min.
Layover		2 hr. 15 min.
Chicago to Atlanta	$229.00	3 hr. 05 min.
Atlanta to Madrid	$658.00	7 hr. 20 min.
Madrid to Frankfort	$89.00	1 hr. 35 min.
2 Layovers		1 hr. 55 min.

Solution
Using the chart, add to find the total cost of each route. The cheapest path is CAMF: Chicago to Atlanta to Madrid to Frankfort.

PRACTICE

Complete the following exercises.

Determine whether the graph is a circuit. If it is, list the path.

EXAMPLE 1
for Exs. 1–2

1.

2.

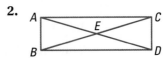

EXAMPLE 2
for Ex. 3

3. From Example 2, if shortest time is Javier's greatest concern, which path would you suggest from Chicago to Frankfort?

Coordinate Geometry and Geometric Figures

Use after Chapter 10

GOAL Given ordered pairs, identify geometric shapes in the coordinate plane using their properties.

Key Vocabulary

- **geometric shapes**
- **coordinate plane**
- **axes**
- **ordered pair**
- **coordinates**
- ***x*-coordinate**
- ***y*-coordinate**
- **origin**
- **quadrant**

Geometric figures are defined by their **geometric shapes.** Geometric shapes are recognizably named areas based on straight lines, angles, and curves such as square, circle, triangle, rectangle, etc.

We can graph geometric figures in the **coordinate plane,** which is formed by two real number lines called **axes.** To graph the figure, we use **ordered pairs,** which are pairs of numbers or **coordinates** used to locate a point in the coordinate plane. The ***x*-coordinate** is the first number of the ordered pair and gives the position relative to the horizontal axis. The ***y*-coordinate** is the second number of the ordered pair and gives the position relative to the vertical axis. The point where the axes intersect is called the **origin.** The coordinates for the origin are (0, 0). The coordinate plane is divided by the axes into four **quadrants.**

EXAMPLE 1 Use coordinate geometry to construct geometric shapes

Plot the given ordered pairs on graph paper. Then, connect them to form a geometric figure. Finally, identify what type of figure is formed.

a. Graph the points.
A (1, 4), B (−2, 0), C (2, −1)

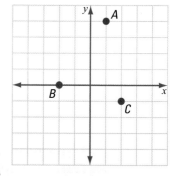

Point A From the origin, move 1 unit to the right. Then move 4 units up.

Point B Because the *x*-coordinate is negative; move 2 units to the left from the origin. The *y*-coordinate is 0, so there is no movement along the vertical axis.

Point C From the origin, move 2 units to the right. Then move 1 unit down.

b. Connect the points to form the geometric figure.

The figure formed is a triangle.

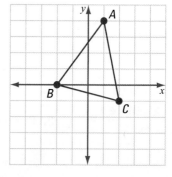

EXAMPLE 2 State the missing coordinate of a given geometric figure based on its properties

Determine the remaining coordinates of the rectangle formed by the three points given in the figure. Each of the squares in the grid represents one unit. Explain how you determined the final ordered pair.

Solution

We know that a rectangle has four sides. Each pair of opposite sides is congruent in length. Locate the fourth point that would form a rectangle and find its coordinates.

The coordinates of the last point are $(4, -2)$.

PRACTICE

For Exercises 1 and 2, graph each point given. Identify the figure formed.

EXAMPLE 1
for Exs. 1–2

1. $(1, 1)$, $(3, 2)$, $(-1, -2)$, $(1, -1)$

2. $(1, 0)$, $(1, 2)$, $(-1, 0)$, $(-1, 2)$

EXAMPLE 2
for Ex. 3

3. The points shown are the endpoints of the base of an isosceles triangle with a height of 4 units. What are the coordinates of the third vertex of the triangle, given that the third point is located above the points shown?

Additional Lesson G Angles and Polygons

Use after Chapter 10

GOAL Find measures of interior and exterior angles.

Key Vocabulary

- polygon
- interior angle
- exterior angle
- convex polygon
- *n*-gon
- regular polygon

A **polygon** is a closed plane figure whose sides are segments that intersect only at their endpoints. An **interior angle** is the angle formed by the sides of the polygon. When you extend a side of a polygon, the angle that is adjacent to the interior angle is an **exterior angle.**

A polygon is a **convex polygon** if no line that contains a side of the polygon contains a point in the interior of the polygon.

The term ***n*-gon** is used to name the polygon where n represents the number of the polygon's sides.

The sum of the measures of the interior angles of a convex *n*-gon is given by the formula $(n - 2) \cdot 180°$.

A polygon is a **regular polygon** if it is equilateral and equiangular.

The measure of an interior angle of a regular *n*-gon is given by the formula $\frac{(n - 2) \cdot 180°}{n}$.

EXAMPLE 1 Finding the Sum of a Polygon's Interior Angles

Find the sum of the measures of the interior angles of the polygon.

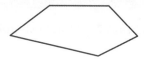

Solution

The polygon has 5 sides. It is a pentagon.

For a convex pentagon, $n = 5$.

$$(n - 2) \cdot 180° = (5 - 2) \cdot 180°$$
$$= 3 \cdot 180°$$
$$= 720°$$

EXAMPLE 2 Finding the Measure of an Interior Angle

Find the measure of an interior angle of a regular hexagon.

Solution

For a regular hexagon, $n = 6$.

Measure of an interior angle $= \frac{(n - 2) \cdot 180°}{n}$ Write formula.

$= (6 - 2) \cdot 180°$ Substitute for *n*.

$= 120°$ Simplify.

EXAMPLE 3 Finding the Measure of an Exterior Angle

An interior angle and an exterior angle at the
same vertex form a straight angle.

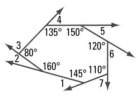

Find $m\angle 1$ **in the diagram.**

Solution

The angle that measures 145° forms a straight angle
with $\angle 1$, which is the exterior angle at the same vertex.

$m\angle 1 + 145° = 180°$ Angles are supplementary.

$m\angle 1 = 35°$ Subtract 145° from each side.

EXAMPLE 4 Using the Sum of Measures of Exterior Angles

Each vertex of a convex polygon has two exterior angles. If you draw one
exterior angle at each vertex, then the sum of the measures of these angles
is 360°.

**Find the unknown angle measure
in the diagram.**

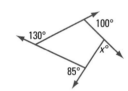

Solution

$x° + 130° + 100° + 85° = 360°$

$x° + 315° = 360°$ Add.

$x° = 45°$ Subtract 315°.

Answer: The angle measure is 45°.

PRACTICE

Complete the following exercises.

*EXAMPLE 1
for Ex. 1*

1. Find the sum of the measures of the interior angles of a convex decagon.

*EXAMPLE 2
for Ex. 2*

2. Find the measure of an interior angle of a regular octagon.

*EXAMPLE 3
for Ex. 3*

3. Find the measures of angles 2, 3, 4, 5, 6, and 7 for the figure in Example 3.

*EXAMPLE 4
for Ex. 4*

4. Find the unknown angle in the diagram to the right.

Volumes of Pyramids and Cones

GOAL Find the volumes of pyramids and cones.

Key Vocabulary

• volume
• cone
• base
• vertex
• pyramid
• lateral faces

The **volume** of a solid is the number of cubic units contained in the interior of a solid.

In this lesson, you will learn the formulas for finding the volume of **cones,** which are solids with a circular **base,** and a **vertex** that is not in the same plane as the base, and **pyramids,** which are polyhedrons in which the base is a polygon and the **lateral faces** are triangles with a common vertex.

Volume of a Pyramid

Words The volume of a pyramid is one third the product of the area of the base and the height.

Algebra $V = \frac{1}{3}Bh$ where B is the area of the base

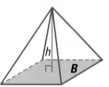

Volume of a Cone

Words The volume of a cone is one third the product of the area of the base and the height.

Algebra $V = \frac{1}{3}Bh$ where B is the area of the base

EXAMPLE 1 **Finding the Volume of a Pyramid**

What is the volume of each of the pyramids shown?

a.

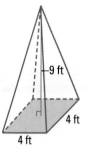

Solution

$V = \frac{1}{3}Bh$ Write the formula for volume of a pyramid.

$= \frac{1}{3}(4^2)(9)$ The base is square, so $B = s^2$.

$= 48$ Evaluate.

Answer: The pyramid has a volume of 48 cubic feet.

b.

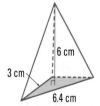

Solution

$V = \frac{1}{3}Bh$ Write the formula for volume of a pyramid.

$= \frac{1}{3}\left(\frac{1}{2}(6.4 \cdot 3)\right)(6)$ The base is a triangle, so $B = \frac{1}{2}bh$.

$= 19.2$ Evaluate.

Answer: The pyramid has a volume of 19.2 cubic centimeters.

EXAMPLE 2 Finding the Volume of a Cone

A paper cup has the shape of a cone. The cup has
a height of 5 inches and a base radius of 2 inches.
What is the capacity of the cup?

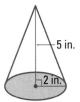

Solution

$V = \frac{1}{3}\pi r^2 h$ Write the formula for volume of a cone.

$\quad = \frac{1}{3}\pi(2^2)(5)$ Substitute 2 for r and 5 for h.

$\quad = \frac{20}{3}\pi$ Simplify.

$\quad \approx 20.94$ Evaluate using a calculator.

Answer: The capacity of the cone is approximately 20.94 cubic inches.

PRACTICE

Complete the following exercises.

Find the volume of the pyramids. Round to the nearest tenth.

EXAMPLE 1
for Exs. 1–2

1.

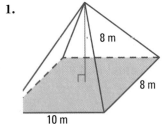

2.

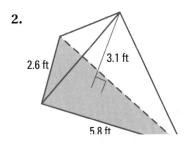

Find the volume of the cone with radius r and height h. Round to the nearest tenth.

EXAMPLE 2
for Exs. 3–5

3. $r = 4$ in., $h = 8$ in.

4. $r = 10$ cm, $h = 12$ cm

5. $r = 15$ ft, $h = 2$ ft

Circles and Sectors

Use after Chapter 11

GOAL Identify parts of a circle and calculate the area of a sector of a circle.

Key Vocabulary
- circle
- center
- chord
- central angle of a circle
- sector
- area of a sector

A **circle** is the set of all points in a plane that are equidistant from a given point, called the **center** of the circle. A **chord** is a segment whose endpoints are on the circle. A **central angle of a circle** is an angle whose vertex is the center of the circle. A **sector** of a circle is the region bounded by a central angle of the circle and the arc of the circle intercepted by the central angle. The **area of a sector** can be found using the formula:

$$\frac{\text{Area of sector}}{\text{Area of entire circle}} = \frac{\text{Measure of central angle}}{\text{Measure of entire circle}}$$

EXAMPLE 1 **Identify Parts of a Circle**

Tell whether the indicated segment is best described as a *radius*, *diameter*, or *chord* of the circle.

   a. $\overline{DA}$ **b.** $\overline{DB}$ **c.** $\overline{CA}$

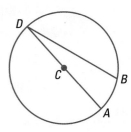

Solution

   a. $\overline{DA}$ is a diameter because it is a chord with the center C as one of its points.

   b. $\overline{DB}$ is a chord because it is a segment whose endpoints are on the circle.

   c. $\overline{CA}$ is a radius because C is the center and A is a point on the circle.

EXAMPLE 2 **Find the Area of a Sector**

Find the area of the sector formed by $\angle RST$.

Write and solve a proportion to find the area of the sector.

Solution

$$\frac{\text{Area of sector}}{\text{Area of entire circle}} = \frac{\text{Measure of central angle}}{\text{Measure of entire circle}}$$

$\dfrac{a}{16\pi} = \dfrac{45°}{360°}$ Substitute.

$a \cdot 360 = 16\pi \cdot 45$ Find cross products.

$360a \approx 2260.8$ Simplify. Use 3.14 for π.

$a \approx 6.28$ Divide both sides by 360.

Answer: Rounded to tenths, the area is 6.3 square feet.

Complete the following exercises.

Tell whether the indicated segment or angle is best described as a radius, diameter, chord, angle, or central angle.

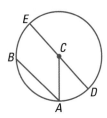
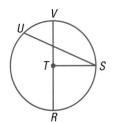

EXAMPLE 1
for Exs. 1–10

1. ∠*BAC*

2. $\overline{AB}$

3. $\overline{EC}$

4. ∠*ACD*

5. $\overline{ED}$

6. $\overline{TS}$

7. ∠*UST*

8. ∠*STR*

9. $\overline{RV}$

10. $\overline{US}$

Find the area of the sector formed by to the nearest tenth. Use 3.14 for π.

EXAMPLE 2
for Exs. 11–14

11.

12.

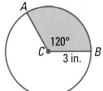

13.

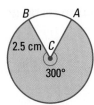

14.

Additional Lesson **J**

Similarity and Dilations

Use after Chapter 10

GOAL Use similar polygons to find missing measures.

Polygons that have the same shape but not necessarily the same size are called **similar polygons.** If two polygons are similar, their corresponding angles are congruent and the lengths of the corresponding sides are proportional. The symbol for "similar to" is ~.

Key Vocabulary

• **similar polygons**
• **scale factor**
• **dilation**

Similar Polygons

△*ABC*: △*XYZ*

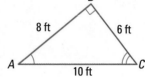

Corresponding angles are congruent.

$$\angle A \cong \angle X \qquad \angle B \cong \angle Y \qquad \angle C \cong \angle Z$$

Corresponding side lengths are proportional.

$$\frac{AB}{XY} = \frac{BC}{YX} \qquad \frac{BC}{YZ} = \frac{AC}{XZ} \qquad \frac{AC}{XZ} = \frac{AB}{XY}$$

The ratio of the lengths of two corresponding sides of two similar polygons is the **scale factor.**

A transformation that stretches or shrinks a figure is called a **dilation.**

Words	To dilate a polygon, multiply the coordinates of each vertex by the scale factor k and connect the vertices.
Numbers	$P(3, 2)$ $P'(6, 4)$
Algebra	$P(x, y)$ $P'(kx, ky)$

EXAMPLE 1 Identifying Similar Polygons

In the diagram, rectangle *ABCD* is similar to rectangle *PQRS*. Find the value of *x*.

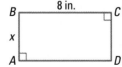 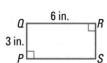

Solution

Corresponding side lengths are proportional.

$$\frac{AB}{PQ} = \frac{BC}{QR} \qquad \text{Write a proportion.}$$

$$\frac{x}{3} = \frac{8}{6} \qquad \text{Substitute given values.}$$

$$x = 4 \qquad \text{Solve the proportion.}$$

Answer: The value of x is 4 inches.

EXAMPLE 2   Dilating a Polygon

Pentagon *ABCDE* has vertices $A(-1, 2)$, $B(-1, -2)$, $C(2, -6)$, $D(10, 0)$, and $E(2, 6)$. Dilate using a scale factor of 0.5. Then graph its image.

Solution

Original	→	Image
(x, y)	→	$(0.5x, 0.5y)$
$A(-1, 2)$	→	$A'(-0.5, 1)$
$B(-1, -2)$	→	$B'(-0.5, -1)$
$C(2, -6)$	→	$C'(1, -3)$
$D(10, 0)$	→	$D'(5, 0)$
$E(2, 6)$	→	$E'(1, 3)$

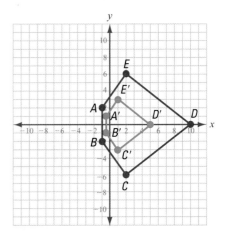

PRACTICE

Complete the following exercises.

Each pair of figures below represents similar polygons. Find the length of *x*.

EXAMPLE 1
for Exs. 1–2

1.

2.

EXAMPLE 2
for Exs. 3–4

Graph the polygon with the given vertices. Then graph its image after dilation by the scale factor *k*.

3. $F(2, 3)$, $G(-2, 4)$, $H(0, 5)$;

$k = 1.5$

4. $A(1, -1)$, $B(-2, 2)$, $C(2, 5)$, $D(3, 1)$;

$k = 3$

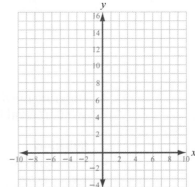

Stem-and-Leaf Plots

Use after Chapter 3

GOAL Make and interpret stem-and-leaf plots.

Key Vocabulary

• stem-and-leaf plot

A **stem-and-leaf plot** is a data display that organizes data based on their digits. Each value is separated into a *stem* (the leading digit(s)) and a *leaf* (the last digit). A stem-and-leaf plot has a key that tells you how to read the data. A stem-and-leaf plot shows how the data are distributed.

EXAMPLE 1 Making a Stem-and-Leaf Plot

Skateboarding The scores for the top 10 finishers of a street skateboarding competition are shown below.

a. How can the data be displayed to show the distribution of the scores?

92.5	91.5	92.0	90.5	88.6
88.7	86.0	86.5	90.6	88.4

Solution

You can display the scores in a stem-and-leaf plot.

1. Identify the stems and leaves. The scores range from 86.0 through 92.5. Let the stems be the digits in the tens' and ones' places. Let the leaves be the tenths' digits.

2. Write the stems first. Then record each score by writing its tenths' digit on the same line as its corresponding stem. Include a key that shows what the stems and leaves represent.

3. Make an ordered stem-and-leaf plot. The leaves for each stem are listed in order from least to greatest.

Unordered Plot		**Ordered Plot**	
86 | 5 0		86 | 0 5	
87 |		87 |	
88 | 6 7 4		88 | 4 6 7	
89 |		89 |	
90 | 6 5		90 | 5 6	
91 | 5		91 | 5	
92 | 5 0		92 | 0 5	

Key: 86 | 5 = 86.5   Key: 86 | 5 = 86. 5

b. Describe the data using the stem-and-leaf plot from part **a.** What interval includes the most data?

Solution

The highest score was 92.5 and the lowest score was 86.0. The range of scores is 6.5. Most of the scores are in the 88.0 to 88.9 interval.

EXAMPLE 2 **Making a Double Stem-and-Leaf Plot**

Test Scores The data below show the test scores for the students in two math classes. Overall, which class had the highest test scores?

Class A: 82, 88, 71, 73, 75, 93, 98, 99, 94, 80, 88, 84, 89, 90, 75

Class B: 74, 93, 95, 96, 98, 82, 86, 88, 90, 93, 72, 94, 94, 86, 87

Solution

You can use a double stem-and-leaf plot to compare the test scores of the two classes.

					4	2	7	1	3	5	5	
		8	7	6	6	2	8	0	2	4	8	8	9
8	6	5	4	4	3	3	0	9	0	3	4	4	8	9

Key: 2 | 8 | 0 represents 82 and 80

Answer: The students from Class B had higher test scores than Class A because Class B had more students score in the 90's.

PRACTICE

Complete the following exercises.

EXAMPLE 1
for Ex. 1

1. The prices for a small, eight slice pizza (in dollars) for 10 different restaurants are found below. Make a stem-and-leaf plot of the data, and then describe the data, giving the minimum value, the maximum value, the range of the data, and the interval which includes the most data.

   7.50, 7.85, 7.60, 7.75, 7.95, 7.90, 7.80, 7.65, 7.70, 7.95

EXAMPLE 2
for Ex. 2

2. The players in two football teams were asked how much time they spent weightlifting (in minutes), on average, in a given day. The results are shown below. Make a double stem-and-leaf plot of the data. Overall, which team spends more time working out in a given day?

   Team A: 35, 45, 48, 50, 52, 54, 55, 30, 38, 40, 42, 45

   Team B: 30, 35, 38, 40, 51, 40, 38, 35, 38, 30, 38, 30

Misleading Data Displays

Use after Chapter 3

GOAL Determine if and how the data displayed is giving a misleading impression.

Key Vocabulary

- **data**
- **display**
- **range**
- **scale**
- **interval**
- **misleading display**

Information that is presented in the form of a graph can be misleading. That is, when looking at a graph, one might get the wrong idea, or not see all the information in a clear and accurate way. This can happen for various reasons. Let's first look at some of the components of a graph that can come into play.

Data is a collection of numerical facts. A **display** is a visual representation of data, including bar graphs, circle graphs, line graphs, scatter plots, and other picture displays. The **range** of the data is the difference between the lowest and highest values. The range of the data is used to determine the **scale,** or unit of measure on the horizontal and vertical axes. The difference between every consecutive unit on an axis is called the **interval.** The choices for such things as the scale and interval can create a **misleading display,** in which the design of the display may lead to incorrect conclusions. Some reasons for misleading displays include broken scales, intervals that are too large or too small, or unequal intervals.

EXAMPLE 1 Analyze a graph to determine how an incorrect conclusion may be drawn

The line graph shows the change in Grace's annual salary over time. What incorrect conclusion might be drawn from this graph? Explain why it is a misleading display.

Answer: Someone might conclude that Grace has had drastic increases in her annual salary over time. The y-axis scale goes from $33,000 to $38,000, which are the lowest and highest data values. This has the effect of spreading the data points out from the very bottom to the very top of the display, making the changes look more dramatic than if the scale started at 0. The reality is that Grace's salary has only increased a total of $5,000 over the course of 20 years.

Grace's Annual Salary

Complete the following exercises.

EXAMPLE 1
for Exs. 1–3

1. The bar graph shows the number of students that were able to complete a given amount of sit-ups in a one-minute physical fitness test. What incorrect conclusion might be drawn from this graph? Explain why it is a misleading display.

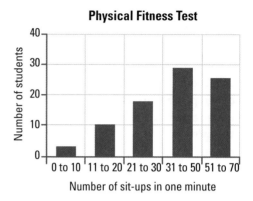

2. The bar graph shows the results of a survey in which teenagers were asked about their favorite leisure time activities. It appears as if twice as many teenagers prefer watching television as playing sports, when asked about their favorite leisure activity. But this is not true. Explain why this graph is misleading.

3. The line graph here shows the change in monetary donations given to a charitable organization over the 5 days of a fundraising campaign. What might someone be led to believe from this graph? Explain why it is a misleading display.

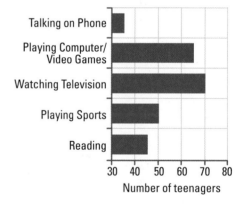

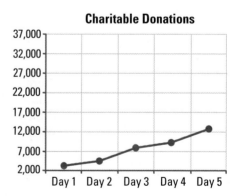

Use after Chapter 3

GOAL Use statistical methods to analyze and communicate data.

Key Vocabulary

- statistics
- descriptive statistics
- inferential statistics
- sample
- mean
- median
- mode
- standard deviation

Statistics is the branch of mathematics that deals with the collection, organization, and interpretation of data. **Descriptive statistics** involves collecting data and tabulating results using tables, charts, or graphs to make the data meaningful and more understandable. **Inferential statistics** involves collecting data from a sample population that is large enough to be accurate for the needs of the statistical study. Conclusions are drawn about the entire group based on the sample group. A **sample** is a small group of people or objects selected to represent the entire group called the population.

Once data is collected, it is interpreted using different measures. One of these measures is called the **mean.** The mean of a data set is the average of a set of numbers determined by adding the numbers and dividing by the number of numbers, denoted by m. A second measurement in statistics is called the **median.** The median is the number that is in the middle of a set of numbers when the numbers are arranged in order from smallest to largest. If there is an odd number of numbers, then the median is the middle number. If there is an even number of numbers, then the median is the average of the two middle numbers. The **mode** of the data is the number that occurs the most number of times in a set of numbers. If no number appears more than once, then there is no mode. If several numbers appear the same number of times, then the set has multiple modes.

The **standard deviation** describes the spread of scores, a deviation of each data value from the mean, denoted s. The formula for standard deviation is:

$$S = \sqrt{\sum_{i=1}^{n} \frac{(x_i - \overline{m})^2}{n-1}}$$

where x_i = each number in the set (1 to n); m is the mean and n is the number of numbers; the divisor, $n-1$, is used for a sample population, while n is used for the whole population. The graphing calculator is very helpful in determining the standard deviation.

EXAMPLE 1

Analyze data to determine how an incorrect conclusion may be drawn

Two students did a science project testing the battery life of AA batteries from two different brands. Each student tested the batteries in the same DVD player. The length of the life of the batteries (in hours) is recorded below.

Battery Test	Brand A	Brand B
1	6.02	7.05
2	6.50	7.20
3	7.05	7.36
4	7.09	7.38
5	7.20	7.40
6	7.80	7.46
7	8.02	7.53
8	8.08	8.02
9	8.19	8.04
10	8.20	8.05
11	8.30	8.19
12	8.50	9.00
13	8.50	9.00
14	8.59	9.32
15	9.60	9.66
Mean	7.842667	8.044
Median	8.08	8.02
Mode	8.50	9.00
Standard Deviation	0.91771	0.833176

The means are similar, but Brand A has a slightly lower mean than Brand B. The median of Brand B is lower than the median for Brand A. The mode is higher for Brand B than for Brand A. However, the standard deviation of Brand A (0.91771) is greater than the standard deviation of Brand B (0.833176). Brand B has less variability and will have a longer battery life than Brand A.

PRACTICE

Complete the following exercises.

EXAMPLE 1
for Ex. 1

1. Design your own survey of interest or use the following data.

John was conducting an experiment to determine if the growth of a certain plant was greater depending on the type of soil where it was planted. The growth (in inches) for each of the two plants was recorded daily and the results are displayed at the right. Determine the mean, median, mode, and standard deviation to determine the soil that had the greatest growth.

Growth (in inches)

	M	T	W	Th	F
Plant A	0.3	1.4	0.7	1.6	1.2
Plant B	0.4	0.5	0.8	1.2	0.8

Experimental vs. Observational Study

Use after Chapter 3

GOAL Differentiate between an experiment and an observational study.

Key Vocabulary

- **descriptive statistics**
- **inferential statistics**
- **population**
- **sample**
- **simple random**
- **systematic**
- **stratified**
- **convenience**
- **self-selected**
- **biased**
- **parameter**
- **statistic**

Descriptive statistics involves collecting data and tabulating results using tables, charts, or graphs to make the data meaningful and more understandable. **Inferential statistics** involves collecting data from a sample **population** that is large enough to be accurate for the needs of the statistical study. Conclusions are drawn about the entire group based on the sample group. A **sample** is a small group of people or objects selected to represent the entire group called the population.

In a **simple random** sample, each person or object has an equally likely chance of being selected. In a **systematic** sample, members are chosen using a pattern, such as selecting every other person. In a **stratified** sample, a population is first divided into groups, and then members are randomly chosen from each group. For a **convenience** sample, members are chosen because they are easily accessible. In a **self-selected** sample, members volunteer to participate.

A sample is considered to be **biased** if it is not representative of the population. A biased sample can be underrepresented if one or more parts of the population are not included. It is overrepresented if a greater emphasis is placed on one or more of the population when choosing the sample.

The **parameter** is a numerical measurement describing a characteristic of a population. The **statistic** is the numerical measurement describing a characteristic of a sample.

EXAMPLE 1 **Classifying samples and determining if the sample is biased**

1. The principal at a certain school has decided to change the colors of the school. There are approximately 1500 students in the school. The principal wants to know which colors students prefer and decides to ask a sample of about 100 students. Classify each sample.

   a. The principal randomly chooses 3 students from each of the 32 clubs in the school. *Stratified*

   b. The principal chooses the first 100 students that volunteer their opinions. *Self-selected*

   c. The principal has a computer generate a list of 100 students from a database that includes all the students in the school. *Simple Random*

2. The directors of a theater company want to know which play to produce next season and want the opinion of the members of the company. Decide whether the sampling method could result in a biased sample. Explain your reasoning.

   a. Survey every member older than 30 years old.
   This method could result in a biased sample because it underrepresents the members who are younger than 30 years old.

   b. Survey every 10th person coming in the door of the performance hall for rehearsal.
   This method is not likely to result in a biased sample because a wide range of members will be surveyed.

Complete the following exercises.

EXAMPLE 1
for Exs. 1–5

Identify the population and the sample.

1. The manager of a store wants to know how many of the 140 employees would order lunch if they were offered a discounted price for the luncheon. She asks 20 randomly chosen employees.

2. The owners of a cafeteria want to know if they should add a new salad to their menu. They ask 30 randomly selected customers out of an average of 350 customers they have each week.

In Exercises 3–4, classify the sample related to the following situation.

A local TV station wants to know if they should add high school sports results to their morning news broadcast.

3. Survey the first 50 people they see on the street in front of the news station building.

4. Survey every 15th person who crosses the street in front of the station.

Decide whether the sampling method could result in a biased sample. Explain your reasoning.

5. The owner of an ice cream parlor wants to know which flavor out of 30 new flavors of ice cream should be added to the flavors sold in that particular store. He asks the first ten customers who come in the door on a Monday morning.

Additional Lesson O — Inductive and Deductive Reasoning

Use after Chapter 3

GOAL Solve simple logic problems using inductive and deductive reasoning.

Key Vocabulary

- inductive reasoning
- deductive reasoning
- Law of Detachment
- Law of Syllogism

Inductive reasoning is reasoning from detailed facts to general principles. **Deductive reasoning** uses facts, definition, accepted properties, and the laws of logic to form a logical argument. Deductive reasoning goes from the general to the particular or from cause to effect.

Law of Detachment
If the hypothesis of a true conditional statement is true, then the conclusion is also true.

Law of Syllogism
If these statements are true,
   If hypothesis p, then conclusion q.
   If hypothesis q, then conclusion r.
Then the following statement is true.
   If hypothesis p, then conclusion r.

EXAMPLE 1   Use the Law of Detachment

Use the Law of Detachment to make a valid conclusion in the true situation.

If two sides of a polygon have the same measure, then they are congruent. You know that $m\overline{AB} = m\overline{CD}$.

Solution

First, identify the hypothesis and the conclusion of the first statement. The hypothesis is "If two sides of a polygon have the same measure." The conclusion is "then they are congruent."

Because $m\overline{AB} = m\overline{CD}$ satisfies the hypothesis of a true conditional statement, the conclusion is also true. So, $m\overline{AB} = m\overline{CD}$.

EXAMPLE 2   Use the Law of Syllogism

If possible, use the Law of Syllogism to write the conditional statement that follows from the pair of true statements.

  a. If it is Sunday, then George goes to the ball park.
     If George goes to the ball park, then he plays baseball.
  b. If $4x > 40$, then $4x > 30$.
     If $x > 10$, then $4x > 40$.

Solution

  a. The conclusion of the first statement is the hypothesis of the second statement, so you can write the following statement.
     If it is Sunday, then George plays baseball.
  b. Notice that the conclusion of the second statement is the hypotheses of the first statement.
     If $x > 10$, then $4x > 30$.

EXAMPLE 3   Use inductive and deductive reasoning

What conclusion can you make about the sum of two odd integers?

Solution

Step 1   Look for a pattern in several examples. Use inductive reasoning to make a conjecture.

$$-3 + 7 = 4, \; 1 + 3 = 4, \; 3 + 9 = 12, \; -7 + 1 = -6$$

Conjecture: Odd integer + Odd integer = Even integer

Step 2   Let n and m be any integer. Use deductive reasoning to show the conjecture is true.

$2n + 1$ and $2m + 1$ are odd integers because any integer multiplied by 2 is even, so when 1 is added, the number is odd.

$(2n + 1) + (2m + 1)$ represents the sum of two odd integers.

$2n + 2m + 2$ can be written as $2(n + m + 1)$

The sum of two integers and 1 is an integer and any integer multiplied by 2 is even.

The sum of two odd integers is an even integer.

PRACTICE

Complete the following exercises.

EXAMPLES 1, 2
for Exs. 1–3

1. If A is complementary to B and B is complementary to C, what conclusion can you make using the Law of Syllogism?

2. If M is the midpoint of AB, what conclusion can you make about AM and MB using the Law of Detachment?

3. If $y < x$, then $y < m$. If $y < m$, then $x < p$. What conclusion can you make using the Law of Syllogism?

EXAMPLE 3
for Ex. 4

4. Use inductive and deductive reasoning to make a conclusion given the following: If two angles are supplementary to a third angle, then the two angles are congruent.

Additional Lesson P Triangle Inequalities

Use after Chapter 10

GOAL Use triangle measurements to decide which side is longest and which angle is largest. Determine possible and impossible side lengths of a triangle.

Key Vocabulary

• **Triangle Inequality Theorem**
• **opposite side**

An important relationship exists between the angles of a triangle and their opposite sides. In addition, there is a relationship among the sides of all triangles called the **Triangle Inequality Theorem.** These relationships are summarized below using the triangle shown. Arrows point from each angle to its **opposite side.**

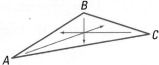

Words If one side of a triangle is longer than another side, then the angle opposite the longer side is larger than the angle opposite the shorter side.

Symbols If $AC > BC$, then $m\angle B > m\angle A$.

Words If one angle of a triangle is larger than another angle, then the side opposite the larger angle is longer than the side opposite the smaller angle.

Symbols If $m\angle B > m\angle C$, then $AC > AB$.

Words The **Triangle Inequality Theorem** states that the sum of the lengths of any two sides of a triangle is greater than the length of the third side.

Symbols $AB + BC > CA$
$BC + CA > AB$
$CA + AB > BC$

EXAMPLE 1 Order Angle Measures

Name the angles from largest to smallest.

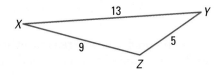

Solution

$XY > XZ$, so $m\angle Z > m\angle Y$.

$XZ > YZ$, so $m\angle Y > m\angle X$.

The order of the angles from largest to smallest is $\angle Z$, $\angle Y$, $\angle X$.

EXAMPLE 2 **Order Side Lengths**

Name the sides from longest to shortest.

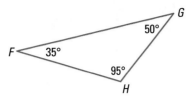

Solution

$m\angle H > m\angle G$, so $FG > FH$.

$m\angle G > m\angle F$, so $FH > GH$.

The order of the sides from longest to shortest is FG, FH, GH.

EXAMPLE 3 **Use the Triangle Inequality Theorem**

Can the side lengths form a triangle? Explain.

    a. 2, 7, 10   **b.** 2, 7, 9   **c.** 2, 7, 8

Solution

    a. These lengths *do not* form a triangle because $2 + 7 < 10$.

    b. These lengths *do not* form a triangle because $2 + 7 = 9$.

    c. These lengths *do* form a triangle because $2 + 7 > 8$, $2 + 8 > 7$, and $7 + 8 > 2$.

PRACTICE

Complete the following exercises.

EXAMPLE 1
for Ex. 1

    1. Name the angles from largest to smallest.

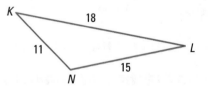

EXAMPLE 2
for Ex. 2

    2. Name the sides from longest to shortest.

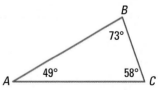

Can the side lengths given form a triangle? Explain.

EXAMPLE 3
for Exs. 3–5

    3. 8, 9, 6

    4. 12, 8, 21

    5. 3, 7, 4

Contents of Student Resources

Skills Review Handbook
pp. 735–760

Whole Number Place Value	735	Solving Problems Using Addition and Subtraction	749
Comparing and Ordering Whole Numbers	736	Solving Problems Using Multiplication and Division	750
Rounding Whole Numbers	737	Units of Time	751
Number Fact Families	738	Solving Problems Involving Time	752
Divisibility Tests	739	Using a Ruler	753
Modeling Fractions	740	Using a Compass	754
Using a Number Line to Add and Subtract	741	Basic Geometric Figures	755
Addition and Subtraction of Whole Numbers	742	Venn Diagrams and Logical Reasoning	756
Multiplication of Whole Numbers	743	Reading Bar Graphs and Line Graphs	757
Division of Whole Numbers	744	Reading and Making Line Plots	758
Estimating Sums	745	Commutative and Associative Properties of Addition	759
Estimating Differences	746	Commutative and Associative Properties of Multiplication	760
Estimating Products	747		
Estimating Quotients	748		

Problem Solving Handbook: Strategy Review
pp. 761–770

Make a Model	761	Look for a Pattern	766
Draw a Diagram	762	Break into Parts	767
Guess, Check, and Revise	763	Solve a Simpler Problem	768
Work Backward	764	Use a Venn Diagram	769
Make a List or Table	765	Act It Out	770

Problem Solving Handbook: Strategy Practice
pp. 771–775

Extra Practice for Chapters 1–13
pp. 776–788

Tables
pp. 789–794

Symbols	789	Properties	792
Measures	790	Finding Squares and Square Roots	793
Formulas	791	Squares and Square Roots	794

English-Spanish Glossary
pp. 795–830

Index
pp. 831–845

Credits
pp. 847–848

Selected Answers
pp. SA1–SA24

Skills Review Handbook

Whole Number Place Value

The **whole numbers** are the numbers 0, 1, 2, 3, ... A **digit** is any of the numbers 0, 1, 2, 3, 4, 5, 6, 7, 8, or 9. For example, the whole number 16 has the digits 1 and 6. The value of each digit in a whole number depends on its position within the number. For example, in the number 146,783 the 8 has a value of $8 \times 10 = 80$ because it is in the tens' place.

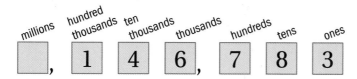

EXAMPLE 1

Write the number 65,309 in expanded form.

$65,309 = 60,000 + 5000 + 300 + 9$ **The zero in the tens' place is a placeholder.**

$\qquad = 6 \times 10,000 + 5 \times 1000 + 3 \times 100 + 9 \times 1$

EXAMPLE 2

Write the number in standard form.

a. $8 \times 10,000 + 2 \times 1000 + 4 \times 100 + 1 \times 1$

b. Three million, six hundred ten thousand, fifty

SOLUTION

a. $8 \times 10,000 + 2 \times 1000 + 4 \times 100 + 1 \times 1 = 80,000 + 2000 + 400 + 1$

$\qquad\qquad\qquad\qquad\qquad\qquad\qquad\qquad = 82,401$

b. Write 3 in the millions' place, 6 in the hundred thousands' place, 1 in the ten thousands' place, and 5 in the tens' place. Use zeros as placeholders for the other places. The answer is 3,610,050.

PRACTICE

Write the number in expanded form.

1. 3802   **2.** 10,649   **3.** 901,003   **4.** 4,003,506

Write the number in standard form.

5. $4 \times 10,000 + 5 \times 1000 + 9 \times 10 + 7 \times 1$ **6.** $7 \times 100,000 + 6 \times 1000 + 4 \times 100 + 5 \times 10$

7. Two thousand, three hundred sixty-one   **8.** Eight million, forty-five thousand, ten

Comparing and Ordering Whole Numbers

A **number line** is a line whose points are associated with numbers. You can use a number line to compare and order whole numbers. First graph the numbers on a number line. The numbers from left to right are in order from least to greatest. Remember that the symbol < means *is less than* and the symbol > means *is greater than*.

EXAMPLE 1

Use a number line to order 11, 3, 5, 10, 8, and 15 from least to greatest.

Graph all six numbers on the same number line.

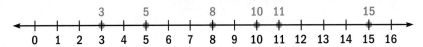

▶ **Answer** From the positions of the graphed numbers, you can see that the order from least to greatest is 3, 5, 8, 10, 11, 15.

EXAMPLE 2

Use a number line to compare the numbers.

  a. 14 and 2   **b.** 25 and 42

SOLUTION

a.
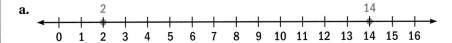

    ▶ **Answer** 14 is to the right of 2, so 14 is greater than 2. Write 14 > 2.

b.
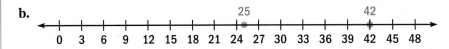

    ▶ **Answer** 25 is to the left of 42, so 25 is less than 42. Write 25 < 42.

PRACTICE

Use a number line to order the numbers from least to greatest.

  1. 4, 10, 0, 2, 1, 8   **2.** 12, 5, 6, 7, 2, 16   **3.** 29, 9, 0, 19, 11, 6   **4.** 26, 20, 18, 13, 31, 15

Use a number line to compare the numbers.

  5. 5 and 12   **6.** 6 and 16   **7.** 15 and 11   **8.** 43 and 34

Rounding Whole Numbers

To **round** a whole number means to approximate the number to a given place value. When rounding, look at the digit to the right of the given place value. If the digit to the right is less than 5 (0, 1, 2, 3, or 4), round down. If the digit to the right is 5 or greater (5, 6, 7, 8, or 9), round up.

EXAMPLE 1

Round the number to the place value of the red digit.

a. 7839.

b. 19,712

SOLUTION

a. Because the 8 is in the hundreds' place, round 7839 to the nearest hundred. Notice that 7839 is between 7800 and 7900, so it will round to one of these two numbers.

7839 is closer to 7800 than to 7900.

The digit to the right of the 8 in the hundreds' place is the 3 in the tens' place. Because 3 is less than 5, round down.

▶ **Answer** 7839 rounded to the nearest hundred is 7800.

b. Because the 9 is in the thousands' place, round 19,712 to the nearest thousand. Notice that 19,712 is between 19,000 and 20,000, so it will round to one of these two numbers.

19,712 is closer to 20,000 than to 19,000.

The digit to the right of the 9 in the thousands' place is the 7 in the hundreds' place. Because 7 is 5 or greater, round up.

▶ **Answer** 19,712 rounded to the nearest thousand is 20,000.

PRACTICE

Round the number to the place value of the red digit.

1. 342

2. 8351

3. 27,945

4. 184,920

5. 9395

6. 652

7. 298,725

8. 644,087

9. 58,920

10. 349,657

11. 5205

12. 24,618

13. 27,830,643

14. 156,970

15. 1,463,562

Number Fact Families

Inverse operations are operations that "undo" each other, such as addition and subtraction or multiplication and division. A **number fact family** consists of three whole numbers related by inverse operations. For example, the facts $8 + 2 = 10$, $2 + 8 = 10$, $10 - 2 = 8$, and $10 - 8 = 2$ are in the same number fact family.

EXAMPLE 1

Copy and complete the number fact family.

$6 + 3 = 9$ $\qquad$ $3 + \underline{\ ?\ } = 9$ $\qquad$ $9 - \underline{\ ?\ } = 3$ $\qquad$ $9 - \underline{\ ?\ } = 6$

SOLUTION

The numbers in this fact family are 6, 3, and 9. Identify which of the three numbers is missing in each of the last three equations.

The 6 is missing in $3 + \underline{\ ?\ } = 9$ and in $9 - \underline{\ ?\ } = 3$.

The 3 is missing in $9 - \underline{\ ?\ } = 6$.

▶ **Answer** $6 + 3 = 9$ $\qquad$ $3 + 6 = 9$ $\qquad$ $9 - 6 = 3$ $\qquad$ $9 - 3 = 6$

EXAMPLE 2

Copy and complete the equation $\underline{\ ?\ } \div 3 = 4$.

Use the multiplication and division number fact family that contains 3 and 4 to find the missing number. The equation $4 \times 3 = 12$ is in this family. This means that 12 is missing in the equation $\underline{\ ?\ } \div 3 = 4$.

▶ **Answer** $12 \div 3 = 4$

PRACTICE

Copy and complete the number fact family.

1. $7 + 9 = 16$ $\qquad$ $\underline{\ ?\ } + 7 = 16$ $\qquad$ $16 - \underline{\ ?\ } = 7$ $\qquad$ $\underline{\ ?\ } - 7 = 9$

2. $9 \times 3 = 27$ $\qquad$ $\underline{\ ?\ } \times 9 = 27$ $\qquad$ $\underline{\ ?\ } \div 3 = 9$ $\qquad$ $27 \div \underline{\ ?\ } = 3$

3. $7 - 4 = 3$ $\qquad$ $7 - \underline{\ ?\ } = 4$ $\qquad$ $\underline{\ ?\ } + 3 = 7$ $\qquad$ $3 + \underline{\ ?\ } = 7$

4. $8 \div 2 = 4$ $\qquad$ $8 \div \underline{\ ?\ } = 2$ $\qquad$ $2 \times \underline{\ ?\ } = 8$ $\qquad$ $4 \times \underline{\ ?\ } = 8$

Copy and complete the equation.

5. $\underline{\ ?\ } \div 8 = 7$ $\qquad$ 6. $6 + \underline{\ ?\ } = 14$ $\qquad$ 7. $\underline{\ ?\ } - 3 = 8$ $\qquad$ 8. $72 \div \underline{\ ?\ } = 9$

9. $\underline{\ ?\ } \times 5 = 35$ $\qquad$ 10. $8 + \underline{\ ?\ } = 16$ $\qquad$ 11. $\underline{\ ?\ } - 6 = 4$ $\qquad$ 12. $9 \times \underline{\ ?\ } = 63$

Divisibility Tests

When two nonzero whole numbers are multiplied together, each number is a **factor** of the product. A number is **divisible** by another number if the second number is a factor of the first. For example, $3 \times 6 = 18$, so 3 and 6 are factors of 18, and 18 is divisible by both 3 and 6.

You can use the following tests to test a number for divisibility by 2, 3, 5, 6, 9, and 10.

Divisible by 2:	The last digit of the number is 0, 2, 4, 6, or 8.
Divisible by 3:	The sum of the digits of the number is divisible by 3.
Divisible by 5:	The last digit of the number is 0 or 5.
Divisible by 6:	The number is divisible by both 2 and 3.
Divisible by 9:	The sum of the digits of the number is divisible by 9.
Divisible by 10:	The last digit of the number is 0.

EXAMPLE 1

Test the number for divisibility by 2, 3, 5, 6, 9, and 10.

a. 3564   **b.** 20,415

SOLUTION

a. The last digit of 3564 is 4, so it is divisible by 2 but not by 5 or 10. The sum of the digits is $3 + 5 + 6 + 4 = 18$, so it is divisible by 3 and 9. Because 3564 is divisible by both 2 and 3, it is divisible by 6.

▸ **Answer** 3564 is divisible by 2, 3, 6, and 9.

b. The last digit of 20,415 is 5, so it is divisible by 5 but not by 2 or 10. The sum of the digits is $2 + 0 + 4 + 1 + 5 = 12$, so it is divisible by 3 but not by 9. Because 20,415 is divisible by 3, but not by 2, it is not divisible by 6.

▸ **Answer** 20,415 is divisible by 3 and 5.

PRACTICE

Test the number for divisibility by 2, 3, 5, 6, 9, and 10.

1. 26	**2.** 99	**3.** 183
4. 348	**5.** 990	**6.** 1300
7. 1785	**8.** 2340	**9.** 3125
10. 4455	**11.** 17,820	**12.** 25,002
13. 47,320	**14.** 79,191	**15.** 93,295

Modeling Fractions

A **fraction** is used to describe one or more parts of a set or a whole. Each part must have the same size. A **mixed number** is a sum of a whole number and a fraction.

EXAMPLE 1

Write a fraction to represent the shaded part of the set.

There are 9 objects in this set, and 5 of the objects are shaded.

▶ **Answer** The fraction that represents the shaded part of the set is $\frac{5}{9}$.

EXAMPLE 2

Write a mixed number to represent the shaded region.

Each region is divided into 4 equal parts. The whole first region is shaded along with 3 parts of the second region.

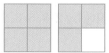

▶ **Answer** The mixed number that represents the shaded region is $1\frac{3}{4}$.

PRACTICE

Write a fraction to represent the shaded part of the set or region.

1.

2.

3.

4.

5.

6.

Write a mixed number to represent the shaded region.

7.

8.

9.

10.

11.

12.

Using a Number Line to Add and Subtract

To **add** two whole numbers on a number line:

STEP 1   Start at 0. Move to the right to locate the first number.

STEP 2   To add the second number, start at the location of the first number and move to the *right* the amount indicated by the second number. The final location is the **sum** of the two numbers.

To **subtract** two whole numbers on a number line:

STEP 1   Start at 0. Move to the right to locate the first number.

STEP 2   To subtract the second number, start at the location of the first number and move to the *left* the amount indicated by the second number. The final location is the **difference** of the two numbers.

EXAMPLE 1

Use a number line to find the sum 8 + 6.

Start at 0. Move 8 units to the right. Then move 6 more units to the right.

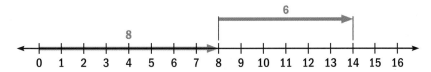

▶ **Answer** $8 + 6 = 14$

EXAMPLE 2

Use a number line to find the difference 18 − 11.

Start at 0. Move 18 units to the right. Then move 11 units to the left.

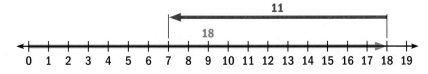

▶ **Answer** $18 - 11 = 7$

PRACTICE

Use a number line to find the sum or difference.

1. $5 + 8$	**2.** $11 - 4$	**3.** $10 + 5$	**4.** $13 + 7$	**5.** $15 - 7$
6. $25 - 10$	**7.** $16 + 9$	**8.** $12 - 8$	**9.** $20 - 16$	**10.** $14 + 8$

Addition and Subtraction of Whole Numbers

To add and subtract whole numbers, start with the digits in the ones' place. Moving to the left, add or subtract the digits one place value at a time, regrouping as needed.

EXAMPLE 1

Find the sum 329 + 75.

STEP 1 Add the ones. Regroup 14 ones as 1 ten and 4 ones.

$$
\begin{array}{r}
1 \\
329 \\
+\ 75 \\
\hline
4
\end{array}
$$

STEP 2 Add the tens. Regroup 10 tens as 1 hundred and 0 tens.

$$
\begin{array}{r}
1\,1 \\
329 \\
+\ 75 \\
\hline
04
\end{array}
$$

STEP 3 Add the hundreds.

$$
\begin{array}{r}
1\,1 \\
329 \\
+\ 75 \\
\hline
404
\end{array}
$$

EXAMPLE 2

Find the difference 402 − 235.

STEP 1 Start with the ones. There are not enough ones in 402 to subtract 5.

$$
\begin{array}{r}
402 \\
-\ 235 \\
\hline
\end{array}
$$

STEP 2 Move to the tens. There are no tens in 402, so regroup 1 hundred as 9 tens and 10 ones.

$$
\begin{array}{r}
9 \\
3\ \,10\,12 \\
4\ 0\ 2 \\
+2\ 3\ 5 \\
\hline
\end{array}
$$

STEP 3 Subtract.

$$
\begin{array}{r}
9 \\
3\ \,10\,12 \\
4\ 0\ 2 \\
-2\ 3\ 5 \\
\hline
1\ 6\ 7
\end{array}
$$

Check Because addition and subtraction are inverse operations, you can check your answer by adding: 167 + 235 = 402.

PRACTICE

Find the sum or difference.

1. 79 + 23

2. 53 + 38

3. 206 + 84

4. 515 + 196

5. 62 − 28

6. 97 − 59

7. 312 − 27

8. 283 − 195

9. 4259 + 57

10. 1207 − 78

11. 2725 − 807

12. 3052 + 958

13. 12,235 + 876

14. 10,782 − 927

15. 23,008 + 6913

16. 27,091 − 3493

Multiplication of Whole Numbers

To **multiply** two whole numbers, multiply the entire first number by the digit in each place value of the second number to obtain partial products. To find the **product** of the original numbers, add the partial products.

EXAMPLE 1

Find the product 935 × 306.

STEP 1 Multiply 935 by the ones' digit in 306.

```
   23
   935
×  306
  5610
```

STEP 2 Skip the 0 in the tens' place, and multiply by the hundreds' digit. Start the partial product in the hundreds' place.

```
    11
   935
×  306
  5610
  2805
```

STEP 3 Add the partial products.

```
    935
×   306
   5 610
   280 5
  286,110
```

To multiply a whole number by a *power of 10*, such as 10, 100, or 1000, write the number followed by the number of zeros in the power. Because multiplying by such powers of 10 shifts each digit of the number to a higher place value, the zeros are needed as placeholders.

EXAMPLE 2

Find the product.

a. 823×100

b. 4200×1000

SOLUTION

a. 100 is a power of 10 with 2 zeros, so write 2 zeros after 823.

$823 \times 100 = 82,300$

b. 1000 is a power of 10 with 3 zeros, so write 3 zeros after 4200.

$4200 \times 1000 = 4,200,000$

PRACTICE

Find the product.

1. 89×54

2. 326×12

3. 452×708

4. 6290×2050

5. 167×100

6. $52 \times 10,000$

7. 970×1000

8. 2000×100

Division of Whole Numbers

In a division problem, the number being divided is called the **dividend** and the number it is being divided by is called the **divisor**. The result of the division is called the **quotient**. To **divide** two whole numbers, you start with the leftmost digits of the dividend and move to the right. If the divisor does not divide the dividend evenly, then there is a **remainder**.

EXAMPLE 1

Find the quotient 252 ÷ 7.

STEP 1
Because 7 is between 2 and 25, place the first digit above the 5. Because $7 \times 3 = 21$, estimate that 7 divides 25 about 3 times.

$$\begin{array}{r} 3 \\ \text{divisor} \longrightarrow 7\overline{)252} \longleftarrow \text{dividend} \end{array}$$

STEP 2
Multiply 3 and 7. Then subtract 21 from 25. Be sure the difference is less than the divisor: 4 < 7.

$$\begin{array}{r} 3 \\ 7\overline{)252} \\ \underline{21} \\ 4 \end{array}$$

STEP 3
Bring down the next digit, 2. Divide 42 by 7 to get 6. Multiply 6 and 7. Subtract 42 from 42. There are no more digits to bring down.

$$\begin{array}{r} 36 \longleftarrow \text{quotient} \\ 7\overline{)252} \\ \underline{21} \\ 42 \\ \underline{42} \\ 0 \end{array}$$

EXAMPLE 2

Find the quotient 2533 ÷ 63.

STEP 1
Because 63 is between 25 and 253, place the first digit above the first 3. Because $60 \times 4 = 240$, estimate that 63 divides 253 about 4 times.

$$\begin{array}{r} 4 \\ 63\overline{)2533} \end{array}$$

STEP 2
Multiply 4 and 63. Then subtract 252 from 253. Be sure the difference is less than the divisor: 1 < 63.

$$\begin{array}{r} 4 \\ 63\overline{)2533} \\ \underline{252} \\ 1 \end{array}$$

STEP 3
Bring down the last digit, 3. Because 13 < 63, write a 0 in the quotient. Then write the remainder next to the quotient.

$$\begin{array}{r} 40 \text{ R}13 \\ 63\overline{)2533} \\ \underline{252} \\ 13 \longleftarrow \text{remainder} \end{array}$$

PRACTICE

Find the quotient.

1. 225 ÷ 5   **2.** 413 ÷ 8   **3.** 276 ÷ 12   **4.** 430 ÷ 61

5. 5286 ÷ 48   **6.** 5776 ÷ 361   **7.** 1048 ÷ 131   **8.** 13,327 ÷ 665

Estimating Sums

To **estimate** the solution of a problem means to find an approximate answer. One way to estimate a sum is to use *front-end estimation*: First add the front-end digits. Then estimate the sum of the remaining digits. Finally, add the two sums together.

EXAMPLE 1

Estimate the sum 575 + 220 + 365.

STEP 1 **Add** the digits in the hundreds' place.

$$
\begin{array}{r} 575 \\ 220 \\ + \ 365 \end{array} \quad\longrightarrow\quad \begin{array}{r} 500 \\ 200 \\ + \ 300 \\ \hline 1000 \end{array}
$$

STEP 2 **Round** the remaining digits to the nearest ten and add.

$$
\begin{array}{r} 80 \\ 20 \\ + \ 70 \\ \hline 170 \end{array}
$$

STEP 3 **Add** the two sums.

$$1000 + 170 = 1170$$

▶ **Answer** The sum 575 + 220 + 365 is *about* 1170.

When numbers being added have about the same value, you can use *clustering* to estimate their sum.

EXAMPLE 2

Estimate the sum 482 + 529 + 498.

$$
\begin{array}{r} 482 \\ 529 \\ + \ 498 \end{array} \quad\longrightarrow\quad \begin{array}{r} 500 \\ 500 \\ + \ 500 \\ \hline 1500 \end{array}
$$

The numbers all cluster around the value 500.

▶ **Answer** The sum 482 + 529 + 498 is *about* 1500.

PRACTICE

Estimate the sum.

1. 221 + 389 + 105

2. 524 + 168 + 912

3. 729 + 376 + 857

4. 4568 + 2157 + 1982

5. 5649 + 6125 + 2914

6. 9270 + 7632 + 5718

7. 659 + 719 + 684

8. 734 + 658 + 709

9. 931 + 863 + 874 + 917

SKILLS REVIEW HANDBOOK

Estimating Differences

One way to estimate a difference is to first subtract the digits in the greatest place. Then round the remaining parts of the numbers and subtract the lesser number from the greater number. Finally, combine the two differences using addition or subtraction as shown below.

EXAMPLE 1

Estimate the difference.

a.   46,398
   − 21,759

b.   7276
   − 3814

SOLUTION

a. First subtract the digits in the
   ten thousands' place.

$$\begin{array}{r} 46{,}398 \\ -\ 21{,}759 \end{array} \Longrightarrow \begin{array}{r} 40{,}000 \\ -\ 20{,}000 \\ \hline 20{,}000 \end{array}$$

   Then round the remaining parts to
   the nearest thousand. Subtract the lesser
   number from the greater number.

$$\begin{array}{r} 6{,}000 \\ -\ 2{,}000 \\ \hline 4{,}000 \end{array}$$

   Because the greater remaining number was
   originally on the *top*, you *add* the differences.

$$20{,}000 + 4{,}000 = 24{,}000$$

   ▶ **Answer** The difference 46,398 − 21,759 is *about* 24,000.

b. First subtract the digits in the
   thousands' place.

$$\begin{array}{r} 7276 \\ -\ 3814 \end{array} \Longrightarrow \begin{array}{r} 7000 \\ -\ 3000 \\ \hline 4000 \end{array}$$

   Then round the remaining parts to
   the nearest hundred. Subtract the lesser
   number from the greater number.

$$\begin{array}{r} 800 \\ -\ 300 \\ \hline 500 \end{array}$$

   Because the greater remaining number was originally
   on the *bottom*, you *subtract* the differences.

$$4000 - 500 = 3500$$

   ▶ **Answer** The difference 7276 − 3814 is *about* 3500.

PRACTICE

Estimate the difference.

1. 891 − 252

2. 921 − 542

3. 587 − 175

4. 674 − 328

5. 3245 − 1097

6. 7658 − 3109

7. 9123 − 2345

8. 55,903 − 14,872

Estimating Products

One way to estimate a product is to find a range for the product by finding a low estimate and a high estimate.

EXAMPLE 1

Find a low and high estimate for the product 47 × 34.

For the low estimate, round both factors *down*.

$$\begin{array}{r} 40 \\ \times\ 30 \\ \hline 1200 \end{array}$$

For the high estimate, round both factors *up*.

$$\begin{array}{r} 50 \\ \times\ 40 \\ \hline 2000 \end{array}$$

▶ **Answer** The product 47 × 34 is between 1200 and 2000.

Another way to estimate a product is to use *compatible numbers,* which are numbers that make a calculation easier.

EXAMPLE 2

Use compatible numbers to estimate the product 345 × 18.

$$\begin{array}{r} 345 \\ \times\ 18 \\ \end{array}$$ ⟹ **Round 345 to 350.** ⟹ **Round 18 to 20.** ⟹ $$\begin{array}{r} 350 \\ \times\ 20 \\ \hline 7000 \end{array}$$

▶ **Answer** The product 345 × 18 is *about* 7000.

PRACTICE

Find a low and high estimate for the product.

1. $\begin{array}{r} 28 \\ \times\ 12 \\ \hline \end{array}$
2. $\begin{array}{r} 46 \\ \times\ 81 \\ \hline \end{array}$
3. $\begin{array}{r} 56 \\ \times\ 29 \\ \hline \end{array}$
4. $\begin{array}{r} 74 \\ \times\ 32 \\ \hline \end{array}$

5. $\begin{array}{r} 387 \\ \times\ 21 \\ \hline \end{array}$
6. $\begin{array}{r} 640 \\ \times\ 74 \\ \hline \end{array}$
7. $\begin{array}{r} 183 \\ \times\ 27 \\ \hline \end{array}$
8. $\begin{array}{r} 819 \\ \times\ 55 \\ \hline \end{array}$

Use compatible numbers to estimate the product.

9. 452 × 153

10. 389 × 173

11. 628 × 921

12. 476 × 293

13. 807 × 504

14. 127 × 836

15. 6509 × 23

16. 7091 × 98

Estimating Quotients

One way to estimate a quotient is to find a low estimate and a high estimate by using numbers that divide with no remainder.

EXAMPLE 1

Find a low and high estimate for the quotient 14,682 ÷ 63.

When the divisor has more than one digit, round it as described below.

For a *low* estimate, round the divisor *up* and replace 14,682 with a number that is divisible by 70 and is *less* than 14,682.

$$\overset{200}{70\overline{)14,000}}$$

For a *high* estimate, round the divisor *down* and replace 14,682 with a number that is divisible by 60 and is *greater* than 14,682.

$$\overset{300}{60\overline{)18,000}}$$

▶ **Answer** The quotient 14,682 ÷ 63 is between 200 and 300.

Another way to estimate a quotient is to use compatible numbers.

EXAMPLE 2

Use compatible numbers to estimate the quotient 147 ÷ 22.

Look for numbers close to 147 and 22 that divide evenly.

$$22\overline{)147} \quad \longrightarrow \quad \overset{7}{20\overline{)140}}$$

▶ **Answer** The quotient 147 ÷ 22 is *about* 7.

PRACTICE

Find a low and high estimate for the quotient.

1. 133 ÷ 4 **2.** 2397 ÷ 6 **3.** 1580 ÷ 6 **4.** 1957 ÷ 8

5. 528 ÷ 28 **6.** 8091 ÷ 92 **7.** 1735 ÷ 34 **8.** 3196 ÷ 42

9. 14,453 ÷ 6 **10.** 21,895 ÷ 9 **11.** 55,912 ÷ 59 **12.** 29,021 ÷ 74

Use compatible numbers to estimate the quotient.

13. 238 ÷ 5 **14.** 8319 ÷ 9 **15.** 4175 ÷ 7 **16.** 3214 ÷ 4

17. 633 ÷ 32 **18.** 4332 ÷ 78 **19.** 1462 ÷ 53 **20.** 2581 ÷ 83

21. 36,012 ÷ 8 **22.** 13,906 ÷ 3 **23.** 32,164 ÷ 62 **24.** 67,428 ÷ 76

Solving Problems Using Addition and Subtraction

You can use the following guidelines to tell whether to use addition or subtraction to solve a word problem.

- Use addition when you need to combine, join, or find a total.

- Use subtraction when you need to separate, compare, take away, find how many are left, or find how many more are needed.

SKILLS REVIEW HANDBOOK

EXAMPLE 1

You paid $14 for a CD and $30 for a DVD. How much did you pay in all?

You need to find a total, so you need to add.

$14 + $30 = $44

▶ **Answer** You paid $44 in all.

EXAMPLE 2

You have 25 invitations to your birthday party. You hand out 16 invitations. How many invitations do you have left?

You need to find how many are left, so you need to subtract.

$25 - 16 = 9$

▶ **Answer** You have 9 invitations left.

PRACTICE

1. You have $18 to spend. You buy a book for $6. How much money do you have left?

2. You spend $25 for a shirt and $35 for a pair of jeans. How much more did you spend for the jeans?

3. You invited 18 boys and 26 girls to your party. How many people did you invite in all?

4. You need to study 6 hours for your tests. You have studied for 4 hours. How many more hours do you need to study?

5. You have $35. Your sister gives you $9 more. How much money do you have now?

6. You have 200 sheets of notebook paper. You give your friend 65 sheets. How many sheets do you have left?

Solving Problems Using Multiplication and Division

You can use the following guidelines to tell whether to use multiplication or division to solve a word problem.

- Use multiplication when you need to find the total number of objects that are in groups of equal size.

- Use division when you need to find the number of equal groups or find the number in each equal group.

EXAMPLE 1

You bought 3 packages of socks. Each package contains 6 pairs of socks. How many pairs of socks did you buy?

You need to find the total number of objects, so you need to multiply.

$$3 \times 6 = 18$$

▸ **Answer** You bought 18 pairs of socks.

EXAMPLE 2

You bake 36 cookies. You put the same number of cookies in 9 bags. How many cookies do you put in each bag?

You need to find the number in each equal group, so you need to divide.

$$36 \div 9 = 4$$

▸ **Answer** You put 4 cookies in each bag.

PRACTICE

1. You order 3 packages of pencils for the school store. Each package contains 12 pencils. How many pencils do you get?

2. You bought 4 bags of apples. Each bag contains 6 apples. How many apples did you buy?

3. You bought 6 packages of muffins and have a total of 24 muffins. How many muffins are in a package?

4. You have 5 boxes of dog biscuits. Each box contains 10 dog biscuits. How many dog biscuits do you have?

5. You split a deck of 52 playing cards evenly among 4 people. How many cards does each person get?

Units of Time

Use the equivalent units of time given below to convert one unit of time to another. Multiply to convert from a larger unit to a smaller unit. Divide to convert from a smaller unit to a larger unit.

$$1 \text{ week (wk)} = 7 \text{ days (d)}$$
$$1 \text{ day (d)} = 24 \text{ hours (h)}$$
$$1 \text{ hour (h)} = 60 \text{ minutes (min)}$$
$$1 \text{ minute (min)} = 60 \text{ seconds (sec)}$$

EXAMPLE 1

Copy and complete.

a. 21 d = __?__ wk

b. 3 h = __?__ min

SOLUTION

a. You are converting days to weeks, a smaller unit to a larger unit. There are 7 days in one week, so divide by 7.

21 d = (21 ÷ 7) wk
= 3 wk

b. You are converting hours to minutes, a larger unit to a smaller unit. There are 60 minutes in one hour, so multiply by 60.

3 h = (3 × 60) min
= 180 min

EXAMPLE 2

Compare 1 h 20 min and 120 min.

To compare times you must express them in the same units, so convert 1 hour 20 minutes to minutes.

1 h 20 min = 1 h + 20 min
= 60 min + 20 min
= 80 min

▶ **Answer** Because 80 min < 120 min, 1 h 20 min < 120 min.

PRACTICE

Copy and complete.

1. 5 h = __?__ min

2. 120 sec = __?__ min

3. 3 d = __?__ h

4. 4 wk = __?__ d

5. 48 h = __?__ d

6. 4 min = __?__ sec

Copy and complete the statement using <, >, or =.

7. 1 min 15 sec __?__ 65 sec

8. 2 d 12 h __?__ 62 h

9. 190 min __?__ 3 h 10 min

10. 75 h __?__ 5 d 5 h

11. 14 wk 2 d __?__ 100 d

12. 425 sec __?__ 7 min 5 sec

Solving Problems Involving Time

When given a start time and an end time, you can find the *elapsed time* by subtracting the end time from the start time.

EXAMPLE 1

A study session began at 9:40 A.M. and ended at 10:10 A.M. How long did the study session last?

Subtract to find the elapsed time.
Subtract the minutes first, then the hours.

$$\begin{array}{r} 10{:}10 \\ -9{:}40 \end{array}$$

You cannot subtract 40 from 10. Rename 1 hour as 60 minutes. Then subtract.

$$\begin{array}{r} {}^{9}\ \ {}^{70} \\ \cancel{10}{:}\cancel{10} \\ -9{:}40 \\ \hline 30 \end{array}$$

▶ **Answer** The study session lasted 30 minutes.

When you need to estimate solutions of problems involving minutes, round times to the nearest 10 minutes or 15 minutes.

EXAMPLE 2

Solve the following problem.

You spent 22 minutes doing your math homework, 1 hour 27 minutes writing a book report, and 44 minutes working on your science project. Estimate how much time you spent doing your homework.

$$\begin{array}{r} 22 \text{ min} \\ 1 \text{ h } 27 \text{ min} \\ + \ \ \ 44 \text{ min} \end{array} \longrightarrow \begin{array}{r} 20 \text{ min} \\ 1 \text{ h } 30 \text{ min} \\ + \ \ \ 40 \text{ min} \\ \hline 2 \text{ h } 30 \text{ min} \end{array}$$

These rounded times add up to 1 hour.

▶ **Answer** You spent about 2 hours 30 minutes doing your homework.

PRACTICE

1. How long was a soccer game that started at 1:15 P.M. and ended at 3:30 P.M.?

2. A movie started at 8:40 P.M. and ended at 10:05 P.M. How long did it last?

3. You talked with your grandfather for 18 min, your friend for 25 min, and your lab partner for 22 min. Estimate how long you were on the phone.

4. Some friends are working at a car wash. If it takes them 14 minutes to wash a car, about how many cars can they wash in 3 hours?

Using a Ruler

An **inch ruler** has markings for inches, halves of an inch, fourths of an inch, eighths of an inch, and sixteenths of an inch. As the lengths get shorter, so do the markings.

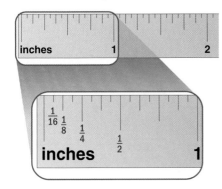 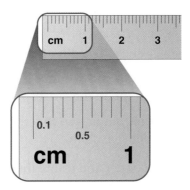

A **centimeter ruler** has markings for centimeters, halves of a centimeter, and tenths of a centimeter (also called *millimeters*). Like an inch ruler, as the lengths get shorter, so do the markings.

EXAMPLE 1

Use a ruler to draw a segment with the given length.

a. $1\frac{3}{4}$ inches

b. 2.9 centimeters

SOLUTION

a. Start at the leftmost mark on the ruler.

Draw a segment so that the other end is at the $1\frac{3}{4}$ in. mark.

b. Start at the leftmost mark on the ruler.

Draw a segment so that the other end is at the 2.9 cm mark.

PRACTICE

Use a ruler to draw a segment with the given length.

1. $\frac{9}{16}$ inch

2. $4\frac{1}{4}$ inches

3. 1.8 centimeters

4. 6.2 centimeters

5. $3\frac{7}{8}$ inches

6. 2.3 centimeters

7. 5.5 centimeters

8. $1\frac{1}{2}$ inches

Using a Compass

A **compass** is an instrument used to draw circles. A **straightedge** is any object that can be used to draw a segment.

EXAMPLE 1

Use a compass to draw a circle with radius 1 cm.

Recall that the *radius* of a circle is the distance between the center of the circle and any point on the circle.

Use a metric ruler to open the compass so that the distance between the point and the pencil is 1 cm.

Place the point on a piece of paper and rotate the pencil around the point to draw the circle.

EXAMPLE 2

Use a straightedge and a compass to draw a segment whose length is the sum of the lengths of $\overline{AB}$ and $\overline{CD}$.

A ———————— B C ———————————— D

SOLUTION

Use a straightedge to draw a segment longer than both given segments.

Open your compass to measure segment *AB*. Using this compass setting, place the point at the left end of your segment and make a mark that crosses your segment.

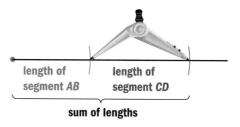

Then open your compass to measure segment *CD*. Using this compass setting, place the point at the first mark you made on your segment and make another mark that crosses your segment.

PRACTICE

1. Use a compass to draw a circle with radius 5 centimeters.

2. Use a compass to draw a circle with radius 1 inch.

3. Use a straightedge and a compass to draw a segment whose length is the *sum* of the lengths of the two given segments.

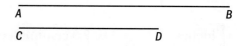

4. Use a straightedge and a compass to draw a segment whose length is the *difference* of the lengths of the two given segments in Exercise 3.

Basic Geometric Figures

A **triangle** is a geometric figure having 3 sides and 3 angles.

A **rectangle** has 4 sides and 4 right angles. Opposite sides have the same length.

A **square** is a rectangle with all four sides the same length.

The distance around a figure is called its **perimeter**. If a figure has straight sides, you can find its perimeter by adding the lengths of the sides.

EXAMPLE 1

Find the perimeter.

The perimeter is 5 in. + 4 in. + 4 in. = 13 in.

EXAMPLE 2

Draw and label a rectangle with a length of 3 cm and a width of 2 cm. Then find its perimeter.

Draw a horizontal side 3 cm long. Then draw the two vertical sides 2 cm long. Finally, draw the second horizontal side 3 cm long.

The perimeter is 3 cm + 2 cm + 3 cm + 2 cm = 10 cm.

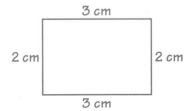

PRACTICE

Find the perimeter.

1.
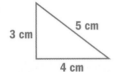

2.

3.
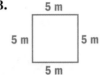

4.

Draw and label the figure described. Then find its perimeter.

5. A square with sides 1 in. long

6. A square with sides 4 cm long

7. A rectangle with a length of 4 cm and a width of 3 cm

8. A rectangle with a length of 2 in. and a width of 1 in.

Venn Diagrams and Logical Reasoning

A **Venn diagram** uses shapes to show how sets are related.

EXAMPLE 1

Draw and use a Venn diagram.

a. Draw a Venn diagram of the whole numbers between 10 and 20 where set A consists of odd numbers and set B consists of multiples of 3.

b. Is the following statement *true* or *false*? Explain.
No odd whole number between 10 and 20 is a multiple of 3.

c. Is the following statement *always*, *sometimes*, or *never* true? Explain.
A multiple of 3 between 10 and 20 is even.

SOLUTION

a.

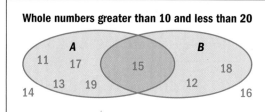

b. False. 15 is an odd whole number that is a multiple of 3.

c. Sometimes. It is true that 12 and 18 are multiples of 3 that are even, but 15 is a multiple of 3 that is odd.

PRACTICE

Draw a Venn diagram of the sets described.

1. Of the whole numbers less than 10, set A consists of numbers that are greater than 7 and set B consists of even numbers.

2. Of the whole numbers less than 15, set C consists of multiples of 4 and set D consists of odd numbers.

Use the Venn diagrams from Exercises 1 and 2 to answer the question.
***Explain* your reasoning.**

3. Is the following statement *true* or *false*? *There is only one even number greater than 7 and less than 10.*

4. Is the following statement *always*, *sometimes*, or *never* true? *A whole number less than 15 is both a multiple of 4 and odd.*

Reading Bar Graphs and Line Graphs

Data are numbers or facts. Two ways to display data are **bar graphs**, which use bars to show how quantities compare, and **line graphs**, which use line segments to show how a quantity changes over time.

EXAMPLE 1

The bar graph shows the results of a survey on favorite pizza toppings. Which topping is favored the most? Which is favored the least?

SOLUTION

The longest bar on the graph represents the 7 students who favor pepperoni, and the shortest bar represents the 2 students who favor mushrooms. So, pepperoni is most favored, and mushrooms are least favored.

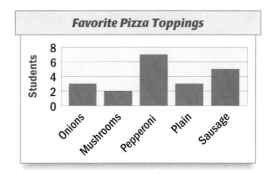

EXAMPLE 2

The line graph shows temperature data collected hourly for 5 times on Monday. Between which two consecutive times was the greatest increase in temperature? What was the increase?

SOLUTION

The steepest segment in the line graph is from 11 A.M. to 12 P.M. The students recorded a temperature of 55°F at 11 A.M. and a temperature of 62°F at 12 P.M., which is an increase of 7°F.

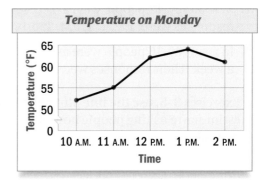

PRACTICE

Use the graphs shown above.

1. How many students chose sausage as a favorite pizza topping?

2. Which two pizza toppings were chosen by the same number of students?

3. At what time was the temperature 52°F?

4. Between which two consecutive times did the temperature decrease?

Reading and Making Line Plots

A **line plot** uses a number line to show how often data values occur.

EXAMPLE 1

You surveyed 15 of your neighbors and asked them how many brothers and sisters they have. Their responses were:
5, 3, 2, 1, 6, 3, 4, 3, 1, 2, 3, 2, 5, 3, 4.

   a. Make a line plot of the data.

   b. What was the least frequent response?

SOLUTION

   a.

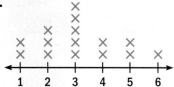

   b. There is only one × above 6, so 6 was the least frequent response.

PRACTICE

Make a line plot of the data.

   1. In a survey, 12 people were asked how many pets they own. Their responses were: 1, 2, 1, 1, 0, 4, 1, 0, 0, 2, 1, 3.

   2. In a survey, 16 people were asked how many times they exercise during a week. Their responses were: 1, 3, 4, 2, 3, 3, 3, 5, 3, 4, 5, 2, 3, 3, 5, 6.

In Exercises 3–5, use the line plot below, which shows the results of a questionnaire asking people how many hours of television they watch each week.

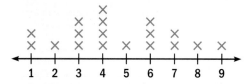

   3. How many people completed the questionnaire?

   4. How many more people watch 3 hours of television each week than watch 5 hours of television?

   5. How many people watch less than 4 hours of television each week?

Commutative and Associative Properties of Addition

The properties below can help you add numbers.

Commutative Property of Addition		Associative Property of Addition	
Words	In a sum, you can add numbers in any order.	**Words**	Changing the grouping of the numbers in a sum does not change the sum.
Numbers	$2 + 4 = 4 + 2$	**Numbers**	$(3 + 8) + 6 = 3 + (8 + 6)$
Algebra	$a + b = b + a$	**Algebra**	$(a + b) + c = a + (b + c)$

EXAMPLE 1   Identifying Properties of Addition

Identify the property that the statement illustrates.

a. $(43 + 9) + 7 = (9 + 43) + 7$ **b.** $13 + (7 + 15) = (13 + 7) + 15$

SOLUTION

a. The order of two of the numbers in the sum has changed. This illustrates the commutative property of addition.

b. The grouping of the numbers in the sum has changed. This illustrates the associative property of addition.

EXAMPLE 2   Using Properties of Addition

Evaluate the expression $8 + 16 + 42$. Justify each step.

$8 + 16 + 42 = (8 + 16) + 42$	**Use order of operations.**
$= (16 + 8) + 42$	**Commutative property of addition**
$= 16 + (8 + 42)$	**Associative property of addition**
$= 16 + 50$	**Add 8 and 42.**
$= 66$	**Add 16 and 50.**

PRACTICE

Identify the property that the statement illustrates.

1. $(77 + 20) + 50 = 77 + (20 + 50)$ **2.** $(8 + 15 + 2) + 1 = (15 + 8 + 2) + 1$

Evaluate the expression. *Justify* **each step.**

3. $5 + (15 + 21)$ **4.** $44 + (16 + 12)$ **5.** $(7 + 61) + 13$

6. $(98 + 36) + 12$ **7.** $16 + 19 + 4$ **8.** $3 + 11 + 97$

Commutative and Associative Properties of Multiplication

The properties below can help you multiply numbers.

Commutative Property of Multiplication	Associative Property of Multiplication
Words In a product, you can multiply the factors in any order.	**Words** Changing the grouping of the factors in a product does not change the product.
Numbers $9 \cdot 3 = 3 \cdot 9$	**Numbers** $(7 \cdot 2) \cdot 4 = 7 \cdot (2 \cdot 4)$
Algebra $ab = ba$	**Algebra** $(ab)c = a(bc)$

EXAMPLE 1   Identifying Properties of Multiplication

Identify the property that the statement illustrates.

   a. $(2 \cdot 11) \cdot 13 = 2 \cdot (11 \cdot 13)$ **b.** $(8 \cdot 21) \cdot 9 = (21 \cdot 8) \cdot 9$

SOLUTION

   a. The grouping of the factors in the product has changed. This illustrates the associative property of multiplication.

   b. The order of two of the factors in the product has changed. This illustrates the commutative property of multiplication.

EXAMPLE 2   Using Properties of Multiplication

Evaluate the expression $5 \cdot 34 \cdot 4$. Justify each step.

$$5 \cdot 34 \cdot 4 = (5 \cdot 34) \cdot 4 \qquad \textbf{Use order of operations.}$$
$$= (34 \cdot 5) \cdot 4 \qquad \textbf{Commutative property of multiplication}$$
$$= 34 \cdot (5 \cdot 4) \qquad \textbf{Associative property of multiplication}$$
$$= 34 \cdot 20 \qquad \textbf{Multiply 5 and 4.}$$
$$= 680 \qquad \textbf{Multiply 34 and 20.}$$

PRACTICE

Identify the property that the statement illustrates.

   1. $2(3)(8)(12) = 3(2)(8)(12)$ **2.** $(3 \cdot 25) \cdot 4 = 3 \cdot (25 \cdot 4)$

Evaluate the expression. *Justify* each step.

   3. $(9 \cdot 15) \cdot 2$ **4.** $(32 \cdot 6) \cdot 5$ **5.** $2 \cdot 41 \cdot 5$

   6. $25 \cdot 26 \cdot 4$ **7.** $5 \cdot 33 \cdot 4$ **8.** $25 \cdot 16 \cdot 8$

Problem Solving Strategy Review

Make a Model

Problem Tommy is creating a program for the school play. He plans to use two pieces of paper placed on top of each other and fold them in half. He wants the title on the cover, the inside cover blank, the list of acts and scenes on the first page, the list of cast and crew members on pages 2 and 3, a thank-you list on page 4, and ads on the last page. The back cover will be blank. When Tommy goes to type this program on his computer, in what order should he type everything?

Make a Model
Draw a Diagram
Guess, Check, and Revise
Work Backward
Make a List or Table
Look for a Pattern
Break into Parts
Solve a Simpler Problem
Use a Venn Diagram
Act It Out

1 Read and Understand
You need to figure out what needs to be printed on each piece of paper.

2 Make a Plan
Since it is difficult to visualize this, you can make a model.

3 Solve the Problem

Make a model of the program. Stack two pieces of paper and fold them in half.

Write what needs to go on each page.

Separate the pages.

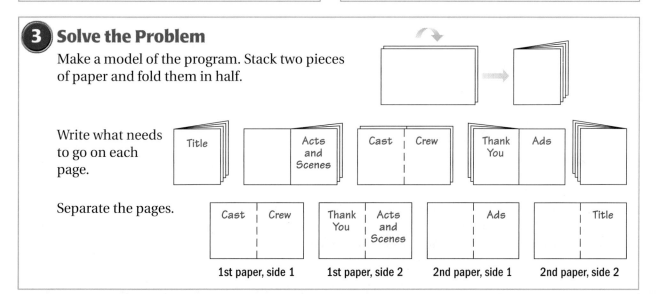

4 Look Back
Get two blank sheets of paper and write the titles on them as shown above. Then create the program with them and check that it looks as you planned.

Practice the Strategy

Maggie, Jack, Brianne, Noah, Zachary, and Sarah are sitting in a row at a movie. Noah and Sarah are not next to each other. Brianne is between Maggie and Jack. There is more than one person between Zachary and Brianne. Give 3 possible seating arrangements.
(See p. 771 for more practice.)

Draw a Diagram

Problem Alan is planting 5 types of flowers in a rectangular flower bed that is 23 feet by 4 feet. He divides the flower bed lengthwise into 5 rectangular sections of equal size, with a 2-foot path between each section. What are the dimensions of each section?

Make a Model
Draw a Diagram
Guess, Check, and Revise
Work Backward
Make a List or Table
Look for a Pattern
Break into Parts
Solve a Simpler Problem
Use a Venn Diagram
Act It Out

① Read and Understand

You need to find the dimensions of each of the 5 rectangular sections in the flower bed.

② Make a Plan

It is hard to figure out what calculations need to be made without seeing how the flower bed is laid out. Drawing a diagram can help.

③ Solve the Problem

Draw a large rectangle for the flower bed and label the length as 23 feet and the width as 4 feet. Draw one of the flower sections in the flower bed. Then draw a path and label the width of the path as 2 feet. Continue drawing sections and paths until you draw the fifth section.

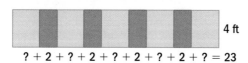

4 ft

? + 2 + ? + 2 + ? + 2 + ? + 2 + ? = 23

From the diagram you can see that there are 4 paths. The combined width of the paths is 4(2) = 8 feet. This leaves 23 − 8 = 15 feet for the combined width of the flower sections. There are 5 flower sections, so the width of each flower section is 15 ÷ 5 = 3 feet. Each flower section is 4 feet by 3 feet.

④ Look Back

Check that your answer is correct by making sure that the sum of the widths of the flower sections and the paths equals 23 feet.

3 + 2 + 3 + 2 + 3 + 2 + 3 + 2 + 3 = 23 ft

Practice the Strategy

You want to use exactly 20 feet of fence to enclose an area for a garden in your backyard. The garden must be rectangular, and each side length of the garden must be a whole number of feet. How many different rectangles can be formed?

(See p. 771 for more practice.)

Guess, Check, and Revise

Make a Model
Draw a Diagram
Guess, Check, and Revise
Work Backward
Make a List or Table
Look for a Pattern
Break into Parts
Solve a Simpler Problem
Use a Venn Diagram
Act It Out

Problem Timory's bedroom is 10 feet by 12 feet. The furniture in her room is arranged as shown in the diagram. Timory wants to buy a bookcase that is 4 feet long. Where in her room can Timory fit the bookcase against a wall?

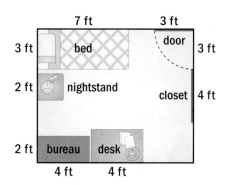

1 Read and Understand

You need to determine where in Timory's room a 4 foot long bookcase can fit against a wall.

2 Make a Plan

There are only four possible walls against which the bookcase can be placed. For this reason, it makes sense to guess, check, and revise a placement of the bookcase until you find the answer.

3 Solve the Problem

Guess that the bookcase will fit against the wall between the nightstand and the bureau. The bed, nightstand, bookcase, and bureau would then take up $3 + 2 + 4 + 2 = 11$ feet of wall space. Since the room is only 10 feet wide, the bookcase cannot fit against that wall.

Now guess that the bookcase will fit against the wall next to the desk. The bureau, desk, and bookcase would then take up $4 + 4 + 4 = 12$ feet of wall space. Since the room is 12 feet long, the bookcase would fit against this wall.

4 Look Back

Check to make sure that the bookcase does not fit against the two remaining walls.

Practice the Strategy

You buy a tube of toothpaste and 3 toothbrushes for a total of $6.25. If a tube of toothpaste costs twice as much as a toothbrush, how much does 1 toothbrush cost?

(See p. 772 for more practice.)

PROBLEM SOLVING HANDBOOK

Work Backward

Problem Your family leaves your house at 6:00 A.M. to drive to New York City. At 11:00 A.M., you reach the halfway mark and decide to stop for a break. After the break, you drive 100 miles and then stop for lunch at 1:00 P.M. After lunch, your mother tells you that there are 200 more miles until you get to New York City. How far is the total drive?

Make a Model
Draw a Diagram
Guess, Check, and Revise
Work Backward
Make a List or Table
Look for a Pattern
Break into Parts
Solve a Simpler Problem
Use a Venn Diagram
Act It Out

1 Read and Understand

The problem asks for total distance. Notice that the times given in the problem are irrelevant.

2 Make a Plan

One way to solve the problem is to work backward. Start with the final 200 miles and work backward.

3 Solve the Problem

Reread the problem. Then work backward starting at 200 miles.

You drove half the total distance before the first break. So you must drive the second half after the first break. If you must drive $200 + 100 = 300$ miles *after* the first break, then you drove 300 miles *before* the first break.

You can use a verbal model to help analyze the situation.

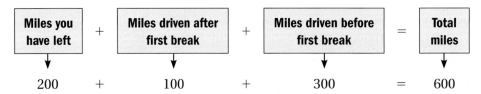

Miles you have left	+	Miles driven after first break	+	Miles driven before first break	=	Total miles
200	+	100	+	300	=	600

So, the total drive is 600 miles.

4 Look Back

Work forward to check that your answer is correct. You drove 300 miles before the first break. Then you drove another 100 miles. After lunch you drove the final 200 miles.

$300 + 100 + 200 = 600$ miles

Practice the Strategy

Jarrod spends 1 hour 15 minutes raking leaves in his yard and 45 minutes mowing his lawn. He then washes his car, which takes 30 minutes. Jarrod finishes working at 1:30 P.M. At what time did he start raking?
(See p. 772 for more practice.)

Make a List or Table

Problem Lena is shopping in the clearance section at her favorite store. The table at the right shows the prices of the clothing in the clearance section. How many ways can Lena spend exactly $30?

Clothing	Price
T-shirt	$6
sweatshirt	$9
jeans	$12
sweater	$15

Make a Model
Draw a Diagram
Guess, Check, and Revise
Work Backward
Make a List or Table
Look for a Pattern
Break into Parts
Solve a Simpler Problem
Use a Venn Diagram
Act It Out

1 Read and Understand

You need to find all the different ways Lena can spend $30 on clothes in the clearance section.

2 Make a Plan

You need to make a list of the different ways Lena can spend $30.

3 Solve the Problem

Make a list of the different combinations of clothes Lena can buy. Start with the greatest number of each item that can be bought with $30. Then see if there is a way to spend exactly $30. Gradually reduce the number of the item to find all possible combinations.

5 T-shirts	$6 \cdot 5 = \$30$
3 T-shirts & 1 pair of jeans	$6 \cdot 3 + \$12 = \$30$
2 T-shirts & 2 sweatshirts	$6 \cdot 2 + \$9 \cdot 2 = \$30$
1 T-shirt & 2 pairs of jeans	$6 + \$12 \cdot 2 = \$30$
1 T-shirt, 1 sweatshirt, & 1 sweater	$6 + \$9 + \$15 = \$30$
2 sweatshirts & 1 pair of jeans	$9 \cdot 2 + \$12 = \$30$
2 sweaters	$15 \cdot 2 = \$30$

You can see from the list that there are 7 different ways Lena can spend $30.

4 Look Back

Make sure that there are no other combinations that add up to $30. For example, if she bought 4 T-shirts, is there anything else she can buy for $6?

Practice the Strategy

In basketball, you can score a 2-point field goal, a 3-point field goal, and a 1-point free throw. If Abby scored at least one of each type of basket and scored 12 points, in how many different ways could she have scored the points?
(See p. 773 for more practice.)

Look for a Pattern

Problem You fold a rectangular piece of paper in half and create 2 rectangles when you open it up again. How many rectangles will you create if you fold the paper in half 8 times?

Make a Model
Draw a Diagram
Guess, Check, and Revise
Work Backward
Make a List or Table
Look for a Pattern
Break into Parts
Solve a Simpler Problem
Use a Venn Diagram
Act It Out

① Read and Understand

You need to predict the number of rectangles created when you fold a piece of paper in half 8 times.

② Make a Plan

Since it is difficult to fold a piece of paper in half 8 times, look for a pattern in the number of rectangles created each time the paper is folded in half.

③ Solve the Problem

Use a piece of paper to find the number of rectangles created by the first 4 folds. Record your results in a table.

Notice that each time the paper is folded in half, the number of rectangles increases. Find the amount by which the number of rectangles increases.

For each additional fold, the number of rectangles is doubled. So, you can expect that 256 rectangles will be created when a piece of paper is folded in half 8 times.

Fold	Rectangles
1	2
2	4
3	8
4	16
5	32
6	64
7	128
8	256

$\cdot 2$

$\cdot 2$

$\cdot 2$

④ Look Back

Make sure that you multiplied correctly. Divide each number of rectangles by the previous number of rectangles and make sure the quotient is 2.

Practice the Strategy

Josh's first class starts at 8:16 A.M. and ends at 9:04 A.M. The next class starts at 9:08 A.M. and ends at 9:56 A.M. Assuming the rest of the day follows this pattern, at what time will Josh's fourth class of the day end?

(See p. 773 for more practice.)

Break into Parts

Problem Rachel is buying cards and envelopes for her party invitations. The costs associated with the invitations are given at the right. How much will it cost for Rachel to buy and decorate 100 invitations?

Cards	$22 for 25
Envelopes	$15 for 25
Stickers	$.50 per invitation

- Make a Model
- Draw a Diagram
- Guess, Check, and Revise
- Work Backward
- Make a List or Table
- Look for a Pattern
- **Break into Parts**
- Solve a Simpler Problem
- Use a Venn Diagram
- Act It Out

1 Read and Understand

You need to find the total cost of buying and decorating 100 invitations.

2 Make a Plan

Since the costs are given in terms of different numbers of items, break the problem into parts by finding the total cost for each type of item.

3 Solve the Problem

First find the cost of 100 cards. The given price is for 25 cards, so multiply this by 4.

$$\$22 \times 4 = \$88$$

Then find the cost of 100 envelopes. The given price is for 25 envelopes, so multiply this by 4.

$$\$15 \times 4 = \$60$$

Now find the cost of decorating 100 invitations.

$$\$.50 \times 100 = \$50$$

Add all the costs.

$$\$88 + \$60 + \$50 = \$198$$

It will cost Rachel $198 for the invitations.

4 Look Back

Estimate to check the reasonableness of your answer. The total cost of 25 cards and envelopes is about $40, so this would be about $40 × 4 = $160 for 100 cards and envelopes. The decorating cost is $1 for 2 invitations, so it is $50 for 100 invitations. The total cost is about $160 + $50 = $210. So, an answer of $198 is reasonable.

Practice the Strategy

Arthur pays $39 a month to have cable TV. Through his cable service, Arthur can also watch recently released movies for $2.50 a movie. If Arthur's bill for the month is $51.50 before tax, how many movies did he watch?

(See pp. 773–774 for more practice.)

Solve a Simpler Problem

Problem A caterpillar is making its way up a telephone pole that is 28 feet tall. Each day the caterpillar manages to climb up 4 feet. Each night because of rain, the caterpillar slips down 3 feet. How many days will it take the caterpillar to reach the top of the pole?

Make a Model
Draw a Diagram
Guess, Check, and Revise
Work Backward
Make a List or Table
Look for a Pattern
Break into Parts
Solve a Simpler Problem
Use a Venn Diagram
Act It Out

① Read and Understand

You need to find how many days it will take the caterpillar to climb to a height of 28 feet.

② Make a Plan

You could list the heights the caterpillar reaches at the end of each day, but this would take a long time. Instead, look for a simpler problem to solve.

③ Solve the Problem

Solve the simpler problem of finding the number of days it will take the caterpillar to reach a height of 7 feet. Record the caterpillar's progress in a table.

Number of days	Height reached by the end of the day (feet)	Height reached by the end of the night (feet)
1	0 + 4 = 4	4 − 3 = 1
2	1 + 4 = 5	5 − 3 = 2
3	2 + 4 = 6	6 − 3 = 3
4	3 + 4 = 7	

It will take 4 days for the caterpillar to reach a height of 7 feet. You can see that the number of days the caterpillar has been climbing is always 3 less than the number of feet reached by the caterpillar at the end of the day. So, it will take the caterpillar 28 − 3 = 25 days to reach the top of the telephone pole.

④ Look Back

You may have thought that because the caterpillar's climbing height increases by 1 foot each day, the caterpillar would reach the top of the pole in 28 days. This is not the case, because if the pole were only 4 feet tall, the caterpillar would reach the top in 1 day, not 4 days.

Practice the Strategy

Jeff is cutting out numbers to sew onto hockey jerseys. All of the numbers are to be double digits, so 01 represents 1. If Jeff needs to sew the numbers 00 through 99 onto jerseys, how many of each digit should be cut out?
(See p. 774 for more practice.)

Use a Venn Diagram

Problem In a survey of people at a health club, 65 people said that they have an aerobics membership only, 67 people said that they have a gym membership only, and 47 people said that they have a pool membership only. 50 people said that they have an aerobics and a pool membership but not a gym membership, and 28 people said that they have an aerobics and a gym membership but not a pool membership. If 300 people were surveyed, how many people said that they have both a pool and a gym membership?

Make a Model
Draw a Diagram
Guess, Check, and Revise
Work Backward
Make a List or Table
Look for a Pattern
Break into Parts
Solve a Simpler Problem
Use a Venn Diagram
Act It Out

① Read and Understand

You need to find out how many people have either all three memberships or a pool and a gym membership but not an aerobics membership.

② Make a Plan

Since some people have three types of membership, some people have two types, and some people have just one type, the answer is not obvious. Draw a Venn diagram to make sense of the given information.

③ Solve the Problem

Draw a Venn diagram to represent the given information.

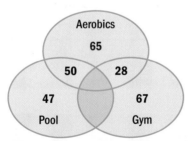

You can see from the Venn diagram that $300 - (65 + 67 + 47 + 50 + 28) = 43$ people who have both a pool and a gym membership.

④ Look Back

Make sure that you placed the numbers in the correct places in the Venn diagram.

Practice the Strategy

There are 60 students in Jason's class, of which 17 have an MP3 player only, 30 have a CD player only, and 5 have neither. How many students have both an MP3 player and a CD player?
(See p. 775 for more practice.)

Act It Out

Problem A kite has five vertical stripes of different colors. The red, yellow, and blue stripes are not next to each other. The red stripe is at one end. Two stripes separate the blue and orange stripes. Between which two stripes is the green stripe?

Make a Model
Draw a Diagram
Guess, Check, and Revise
Work Backward
Make a List or Table
Look for a Pattern
Break into Parts
Solve a Simpler Problem
Use a Venn Diagram
Act It Out

1 Read and Understand

Read the problem carefully. You need to place five colors in order. Red is either first or last. Red, blue, and yellow are not next to each other.

2 Make a Plan

Decide on a strategy to use. You can use colored strips of paper to represent the vertical stripes. Then write down arrangements that work.

3 Solve the Problem

Reread the problem and act it out. Use five colored pieces of paper to represent the five strips on the kite. Make sure that the red, yellow, and blue pieces are not next to each other. List the arrangements.

A list of all possible arrangements is shown, with red first or last. Of these arrangements, only two meet the condition of having two stripes between the blue and orange stripes.

red, orange, yellow, green, blue
red, orange, blue, green, yellow
red, green, yellow, orange, blue
red, green, blue, orange, yellow

blue, green, yellow, orange, red
yellow, green, blue, orange, red
blue, orange, yellow, green, red
yellow, orange, blue, green, red

Whether red is first or last, green is between blue and yellow in all the arrangements.

4 Look Back

You can solve the problem a different way using logical reasoning. If blue is two stripes away from orange, it can be at an end, and green must be next to it, with yellow in the middle.

Practice the Strategy

You are picking the five starting players from a basketball team of 8 players. Both Rasheed and Tim will be part of the starting team. How many ways can you choose all the starting players?
(See p. 775 for more practice.)

Solve the problem and show your work.

Make a Model

1. Two wheels are the same size. Wheel A rolls around the outside of Wheel B, then returns to its original position. How many revolutions does Wheel A make during its trip around Wheel B? *(Problem Solving Strategy Review, p. 761)*

2. You have 24 6-foot sections of fence to enclose a rectangular garden. If you use all the sections, what is the greatest area that you can enclose? What is the least area you can enclose? *(Problem Solving Strategy Review, p. 761)*

3. You have 9 square tiles that measure 1 inch on a side. You arrange the tiles to form polygons. How many different perimeters can you make? Draw a polygon for each perimeter. *(Problem Solving Strategy Review, p. 761)*

4. You fold a rectangular piece of paper in half from left to right, then in half again from top to bottom, and in half again from left to right. Then you cut a rectangle through all the layers of paper like the one shown below. How many holes will there be when you unfold the paper? *(Problem Solving Strategy Review, p. 761)*

5. You have 3 pieces of plastic tubing that you want to connect to form the triangular frame for a kite. Two pieces of the tubing are 14 inches long. What would be the minimum and maximum lengths, in whole inches, of the third piece of tubing? Assume that you do not make any cuts to the third piece of tubing. *(Problem Solving Strategy Review, p. 761)*

Draw a Diagram

6. John has 10 coins in his pocket which are pennies, nickels, dimes, or quarters. Of these coins, 7 are silver in color. The edges of 7 coins are smooth, while the edges of the other 3 coins have ridges. Only one coin is a dime. What is the value of the 10 coins? *(Problem Solving Strategy Review, p. 762)*

7. You live 24 miles from Bensonville. You pass through Attleton when you are two thirds of the way to Bensonville. Spedfield is three fourths of the way from your home to Attleton. How far is Spedfield from your home? *(Problem Solving Strategy Review, p. 762)*

8. On a straight street, a vegetable stand is between a hardware store and a pet store. The hardware store is 2 miles from the vegetable stand. The pet store is 5 miles from the hardware store. How far is the vegetable stand from the pet store? *(Problem Solving Strategy Review, p. 762)*

9. You are thinking about buying a table for your computer. The table is 4 feet long and 2 feet 6 inches wide. You need to fit a 16 inch by 10 inch monitor, an 18 inch by 6 inch printer, a 14 inch by 12 inch scanner, and an 18 inch by 6 inch keyboard on the table. Can you fit everything on the table? *(Problem Solving Strategy Review, p. 762)*

10. Use the following statements about points *A*, *B*, *C*, and *D* on a number line to find the distance from point *B* to point *D*.
    - Point *B* is 6 units right of point *A*.
    - Point *C* is 12 units left of point *A*.
    - Point *D* is halfway between points *A* and *C*. *(Problem Solving Strategy Review, p. 762)*

Guess, Check, and Revise

11. A farm raises cows and ostriches. Rosa can see above and below the horizontal boards of a fence. She sees 78 legs in the lower opening of the fence, and 35 heads above the fence. How many of each kind of animal are there? *(Problem Solving Strategy Review, p. 763)*

12. You are making a scrapbook with pages that are 15 inches by 15 inches. On one page, you want to put two 4 inch by 6 inch photographs, each with blue borders of equal width, as shown. What is the widest border you can use if you want at least 1 inch of space on all sides of the photos? *(Problem Solving Strategy Review, p. 763)*

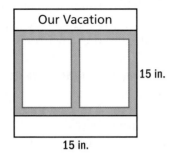

13. At a store that sells school supplies, a package of 2 pens costs $3, a package of 2 pencils costs $1, and notebooks cost $5 each. Kevin bought 14 items (counting each of the multiple items in a package as separate items) and paid $20. How many of each item did he buy if he bought at least one of each item? *(Problem Solving Strategy Review, p. 763)*

14. In the diagram below, the symbols "*" and "#" each represent a digit from 1 to 9, and are different from the other digits in the diagram. They do not represent the same number. The sum of each row and each column is given. Find the value of each symbol. *(Problem Solving Strategy Review, p. 763)*

*	8	#	5	23
2	*	2	#	14
#	#	*	*	20
#	8	5	*	23
19	26	17	18	

Work Backward

15. Derek brought raisins for lunch and shared them with some of his classmates. He gave half of his raisins to Molly, then ate one himself. After that he gave half of the remaining raisins to Tricia and ate another one himself. Finally, he gave half of the remaining raisins to Clark, and had 7 raisins left. How many raisins did Derek start with? *(Problem Solving Strategy Review, p. 764)*

16. Three students played a game in which there were always two winners and one loser. Each player started with a certain number of pebbles. When a player lost a game, the losing player gave each of the winning players the number of pebbles that winning player already had. After 3 games, each player had lost once, and each player ended up with 8 pebbles. How many pebbles did each of the three players start with? *(Problem Solving Strategy Review, p. 764)*

17. A school chess tournament works by elimination. The winners advance to the next round. If Veronica wins the tournament by winning 4 games, how many people played in the competition? *(Problem Solving Strategy Review, p. 764)*

18. Rafael is going grocery shopping. The drive between Rafael's house and the grocery store takes 15 minutes. The grocery shopping takes 35 minutes. If Rafael needs to be home by noon, what is the latest time that he can leave home to go grocery shopping? *(Problem Solving Strategy Review, p. 764)*

19. Ellen takes $\frac{1}{4}$ of the oranges in a bowl. Geoff takes $\frac{1}{3}$ of the oranges that remain in the bowl. Ellen and Geoff later decide that they don't need all their oranges, so they each put one orange back in the bowl. The next day, Carlos takes $\frac{1}{2}$ of the oranges that remain in the bowl. There are 4 oranges left in the bowl. How many oranges were in the bowl originally? *(Problem Solving Strategy Review, p. 764)*

Make a List or Table

20. A bus company charges a $1 fare on one route, which normally has 80 riders. The company is thinking of raising the fare, but they estimate that each increase of $.10 will lose 4 riders. What fare will give them the most revenue (number of riders times fare per rider)? *(Problem Solving Strategy Review, p. 765)*

21. A marching band is 120 meters long when lined up to march. It marches along a street at 30 meters per minute. A drum major marches at 45 meters per minute, starting from the back of the band. How long does it take the drum major to reach the front of the band? *(Problem Solving Strategy Review, p. 765)*

22. Margot has a choice of joining a music club in which she gets 3 CDs for $1 and pays $7 per CD after that, or joining a club in which the price of each CD is $4.50. How many CDs would Margot have to buy in order to pay the same amount to each club? *(Problem Solving Strategy Review, p. 765)*

23. A video game awards 300 points, 400 points, and 900 points for doing each of 3 different activities. If you complete 3 activities, how many different point totals are possible? *(Problem Solving Strategy Review, p. 765)*

24. You are organizing the schedule for a youth hockey season. If there are 6 teams and each team plays each of the other teams twice, how many games must you schedule? *(Problem Solving Strategy Review, p. 765)*

Look for a Pattern

25. Gavin works at a restaurant where each table is rectangular and seats 6 people: 2 places on each long side and 1 place at each end. Gavin makes 3 long tables of 6 tables each, with the tables in each row placed end to end. How many seats are there? *(Problem Solving Strategy Review, p. 766)*

26. If you slice a pie with one cut, there will be 2 pieces. If you slice the pie again so that the second cut intersects the first, there will be 4 pieces. You keep slicing the pie so that no cut goes through the intersection of any two cuts and each new cut intersects all the previous cuts. How many pieces will there be if you make 10 cuts? *(Problem Solving Strategy Review, p. 766)*

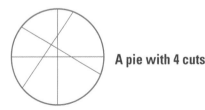

A pie with 4 cuts

27. Rory is making a quilt by sewing together small squares of the same size. The quilt will have 24 rows of 24 small squares on each side. How many points where 4 small squares meet will the quilt contain? *(Problem Solving Strategy Review, p. 766)*

28. You fold a square piece of paper in thirds, which makes 3 rectangles when you unfold it. How many rectangles will you make if you fold the paper in thirds 4 times? *(Problem Solving Strategy Review, p. 766)*

29. Describe the pattern shown below. Then draw the next figure in the pattern. *(Problem Solving Strategy Review, p. 766)*

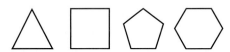

Break Into Parts

30. You are making a birthday card for your friend. You want to frame the picture on the front of the card with construction paper. The front of the card is 10 inches long and 8 inches wide. You want the frame to be 2 inches wide. What is the area of the frame? *(Problem Solving Strategy Review, p. 767)*

31. Jack wants to buy molding to put around the bottom and top of the walls of his bedroom. How much molding does he need to buy? *(Problem Solving Strategy Review, p. 767)*

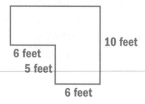

32. Some of your family is going to an amusement park for the day. Your group includes 3 adults, 1 senior citizen, 2 teenagers, 4 children between 5 and 12 years old, and one 3 year old. Use the table below to find the total cost to enter the park for your family. *(Problem Solving Strategy Review, p. 767)*

Amusement Park Admission Prices	
Seniors	$6
Adults	$20
Teenagers	$15
Children ages 5–12	$12
Children under 5	Free

33. Paula began painting a mural at 7:45 A.M. and finished working on it at 2:20 P.M. She took a break from 12:30 P.M. to 1:00 P.M. How long did she spend painting? *(Problem Solving Strategy Review, p. 767)*

34. The table below lists the percent discounts off the original prices at a clothing store sale. You buy 4 shirts, 1 pair of jeans, and a coat. You also buy a $10 hat that is *not* on sale. How much, in dollars and cents, do you spend at the store, assuming there is no sales tax? *(Problem Solving Strategy Review, p. 767)*

Item	Original Price	Discount
shirt	$18	one half off
jeans	$30	one tenth off
coat	$50	one fifth off

Solve a Simpler Problem

35. To connect 3 cities by airline routes so that each city is connected to every other city by exactly one route, you need 3 routes. How many routes are needed to connect 4 cities, with one route directly connecting each pair? How many routes are needed to connect 15 cities? *(Problem Solving Strategy Review, p. 768)*

36. Richard makes souvenir medallions of metal. One day he made 27 medallions but realized that he had mixed the metals incorrectly for one medallion, so it was slightly heavier than the others. His co-worker Edward told Richard that he could determine which of 3 medallions was overweight by comparing any 2 of the 3 medallions using a balance scale. How can Richard identify the one overweight medallion of the 27 medallions using the balance scale only 3 times? *(Problem Solving Strategy Review, p. 768)*

37. A bag contains tags numbered from 1 to 10. Eight of the tags are red, and two are blue. You draw a tag without looking in the bag. You look at the tag, put it back, and draw another tag without looking in the bag. How many different ordered pairs of tags can you draw with at least one red tag? *(Problem Solving Strategy Review, p. 768)*

38. A chapter that begins on page 1 and ends on page 20 is 20 pages long. How long is a chapter that begins on page 470 and ends on page 527? *(Problem Solving Strategy Review, p. 768)*

39. You are going to a geography bee where all contestants shake hands before beginning the contest. How many handshakes happen if there are 5 contestants? How many handshakes happen if there are 12 contestants? *(Problem Solving Strategy Review, p. 768)*

40. You are collecting pennies for a food bank. You collect 2 pennies per day for each of the first 3 days. After every 3 day period, the number of pennies you collect each day doubles. How many pennies will you collect on day 29? *(Problem Solving Strategy Review, p. 768)*

Use a Venn Diagram

41. A deli offers soup and salad as side dishes. One afternoon, 25 people order only soup, 18 people order only salad, and 9 people order both soup and salad. How many more people have soup than have only salad? *(Problem Solving Strategy Review, p. 769)*

42. In your gym class there are 12 students who know how to inline skate, but not ice skate. There are 6 students who know how to ice skate, but not inline skate. There are 8 students who know how to inline skate and ice skate. How many students know how to ice skate in your class? *(Problem Solving Strategy Review, p. 769)*

43. There are 26 families that live on Countryside Drive. Twelve families own a dog only. Eight families own a cat only. Three families own both a cat and a dog. How many families do not own a cat or a dog? *(Problem Solving Strategy Review, p. 769)*

44. You are selling chocolate for a fundraiser. Thirty-four people buy a plain chocolate bar but not a crispy chocolate bar. Fifteen people buy a crispy chocolate bar but not a plain chocolate bar. Twenty-three people buy both a plain chocolate bar and a crispy chocolate bar. How many people buy a plain chocolate bar? *(Problem Solving Strategy Review, p. 769)*

45. In a class of 25 students, 10 students play after-school street hockey on Mondays, and 19 students play after-school softball on Thursdays. If 2 students do not play either softball or street hockey, how many students play both sports? *(Problem Solving Strategy Review, p. 769)*

46. In a survey, 100 people were asked what else they do while online. Of these, 52 people listened to music on the radio, and 62 people watched TV. If 18 people didn't watch TV or listen to music on the radio, how many people surveyed watch TV and listen to music on the radio while online? *(Problem Solving Strategy Review, p. 769)*

Act It Out

47. The number of people who get on and off a city bus at each stop are listed below. How many passengers are on the bus after the fourth stop? *(Problem Solving Strategy Review, p. 770)*

Stop	People who get on the bus	People who get off the bus
1	25	0
2	7	12
3	3	3
4	13	9

48. You are having a holiday party. Twelve people arrive, then one quarter of them leave an hour later to go to another party. Twice the number of people who left to go to the other party show up during that hour. If 9 people leave the party later on that night, how many people remain at your party? *(Problem Solving Strategy Review, p. 770)*

49. You and a friend are about to eat some pistachios. You have 3 times as many pistachios as your friend. You give your friend 4 of your pistachios, but still have 4 more than your friend. How many pistachios did you have at the beginning? *(Problem Solving Strategy Review, p. 770)*

50. Six pennies are arranged on the left. Describe how to get the arrangement on the right by moving only two pennies. *(Problem Solving Strategy Review, p. 770)*

51. A photo album has 1 black-and-white photo for every 4 color photos. If there are 40 photos in the album, how many are color photos? *(Problem Solving Strategy Review, p. 770)*

Extra Practice

Chapter 1

1.1 **Describe the pattern. Then write the next three numbers.**

1. 57, 49, 41, 33, . . .   **2.** 5, 15, 45, 135, . . .   **3.** 1600, 800, 400, 200, . . .

4. Describe the pattern.
Then draw the next figure.

1.2 **Evaluate the expression for the given value of the variable.**

5. $75 \div m$ when $m = 5$ **6.** $k - 26$ when $k = 43$ **7.** $4x$ when $x = 9$

8. The expression $60h$ can be used to find the number of minutes in h
hours. Find the number of minutes in 24 hours.

1.3 **Write the product as a power.**

9. $11 \cdot 11 \cdot 11$ **10.** $8 \cdot 8 \cdot 8 \cdot 8 \cdot 8$ **11.** $y \cdot y \cdot y \cdot y$ **12.** $a \cdot a \cdot a \cdot a \cdot a \cdot a$

Evaluate the power.

13. 10^2 **14.** 7^4 **15.** 0^6 **16.** 2^8

1.4 **Evaluate the expression.**

17. $1 + (7 - 3)^3$ **18.** $\dfrac{36 - 8}{2 + 5}$ **19.** $72 \div 4 \div 3$ **20.** $(3^3 - 2)(1 + 2)$

1.5 **Solve the equation using mental math.**

21. $x + 6 = 13$ **22.** $\dfrac{z}{8} = 2$ **23.** $1 = 10 - p$ **24.** $280 = 20t$

1.6 **Find the perimeter and the area of the rectangle or square with the given dimensions.**

25. $l = 11$ feet, $w = 7$ feet   **26.** $l = 8$ yards, $w = 7$ yards   **27.** $s = 16$ centimeters

1.7 **28.** You are ordering pitchers of lemonade for you and 6 of your friends.
One pitcher of lemonade can fill 5 glasses. How many pitchers should
you order if each person wants 3 glasses of lemonade?

29. There are 5 tennis players in a tournament. If each tennis player plays
every other player once, how many games will be played?

30. The items that Frank needs to buy for his cookout are given in the table.
If Frank spends $7, how much does each ear of corn cost?

Item	Total Cost
1 package of ground beef	$3
1 bag of rolls	$2
4 ears of corn	?

Chapter 2

2.1 **Order the numbers from least to greatest.**

1. 0.25, 0.5, 0.05, 5.2   **2.** 7.9, 9.7, 0.97, 0.79   **3.** 6.2, 6.08, 6.28, 6.82

4. Round 8.4746 to the nearest thousandth.

2.2 **Find the sum or difference. Use estimation to check your answer.**

5. $8.33 - 7.41$ **6.** $16.7 + 129.413$ **7.** $702.85 + 35.2$ **8.** $42.9 - 26.74$

Evaluate the expression when $a = 13.2$ and $b = 7.49$.

9. $6.4 + a$ **10.** $a + b$ **11.** $8.613 - b$ **12.** $8 + a - b$

2.3 **Find the product. Then check that your answer is reasonable.**

13. 2.7×0.8 **14.** 3.05×0.26 **15.** 1.48×0.037 **16.** 46×2.718

17. 0.89×8.76 **18.** 3.5×6.3 **19.** 6.4×9.05 **20.** 0.006×1.2

2.4 **Find the quotient. Then check that your answer is reasonable.**

21. $84.14 \div 7$ **22.** $19.98 \div 2.7$ **23.** $6.4 \div 0.08$ **24.** $0.115 \div 5.75$

25. $0.126 \div 2.8$ **26.** $0.884 \div 0.26$ **27.** $23.24 \div 1.12$ **28.** $3.91 \div 3.4$

29. Find the quotient $18 \div 3.21$. Round your answer to the nearest hundredth.

2.5 **Write the number in scientific notation.**

30. 5210   **31.** 8,200,000,000   **32.** 900,000   **33.** 431.6

Write the number in standard form.

34. 1.4×10^4 **35.** 4.221×10^8 **36.** 6×10^1 **37.** 5.3761×10^6

2.6 **Copy and complete using the appropriate metric unit.**

38. The mass of a pencil is 6 __?__ .   **39.** A bottle of mouthwash holds 710 __?__ .

40. A pair of scissors is 14 __?__ long.   **41.** The mass of a pair of sneakers is 1 __?__ .

2.7 **Copy and complete the statement.**

42. 24 cm = __?__ mm   **43.** 0.4 g = __?__ mg

44. 795 g = __?__ kg   **45.** 120 L = __?__ kL

46. 0.07 kL = __?__ mL   **47.** 36,100 mm = __?__ km

Copy and complete the statement using <, >, or =.

48. 3 km __?__ 3200 m   **49.** 9450 g __?__ 9.45 kg   **50.** 5.4 L __?__ 540 mL

Chapter 3

3.1 **Find the mean, median, mode(s), and range of the data.**

1. 18, 22, 57, 29, 22, 41   **2.** 7, 7.5, 7.1, 7.9, 7.5, 7, 7.3, 7.5

3. 8, 7, 2, 9, 11, 7, 10, 3, 12, 2, 6   **4.** 94, 108, 145, 171, 162, 197, 186, 76, 88, 143

5. The record low temperatures in July in 8 cities are 43°F, 69°F, 35°F, 51°F, 40°F, 35°F, 44°F, and 35°F. Which average best represents the data? *Explain* your reasoning.

3.2 **6.** The table below shows the life spans of various U.S. currency bills. Make a bar graph of the data. Make a conclusion about the data.

Denomination (dollars)	1	5	10	20	50
Life Span (years)	1.5	2	3	4	9

7. *Describe* a real-life data set that could be displayed in a line graph.

3.3 **8.** Make an ordered stem-and-leaf plot of the data in Exercise 5. Then make a conclusion about the data.

3.4 **In Exercises 9–12, use the prices, in dollars, of several DVD players and VCRs listed below.**

DVD PLAYERS 250, 200, 160, 180, 160, 300, 185, 190, 130, 115, 250, 160, 200, 180

VCRs 130, 100, 80, 200, 100, 100, 100, 90, 90, 120, 200, 230

9. Using the same number line, make a box-and-whisker plot for each data set.

10. Use the box-and-whisker plots from Exercise 9 to make a conclusion about the price of a DVD player as compared with the price of a VCR.

3.5 **11.** Make a frequency table of each data set using the intervals 70–109, 110–149, 150–189, 190–229, 230–269, and 270–309.

12. Use the frequency tables from Exercise 11 to make a histogram for each data set.

3.6 **13.** *Explain* why the data display below could be misleading.

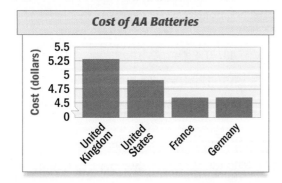

14. You want to display the winning long jump distances for men and women in various years of the summer Olympics. What type of data display should you use? *Explain* your choice.

Chapter 4

4.1 Tell whether the number is *prime* or *composite*. Then write all the factors of the number.

   1. 75   **2.** 71   **3.** 83   **4.** 91

Use a factor tree to write the prime factorization of the number.

   5. 84   **6.** 117   **7.** 125   **8.** 225

4.2 Find the greatest common factor of the numbers using prime factorization. Then tell whether the numbers are relatively prime.

   9. 72, 96   **10.** 35, 105   **11.** 32, 76   **12.** 51, 175

4.3 Write the fractions in simplest form. Tell whether they are equivalent.

   13. $\dfrac{20}{24}, \dfrac{30}{36}$ **14.** $\dfrac{21}{56}, \dfrac{28}{84}$ **15.** $\dfrac{12}{16}, \dfrac{14}{18}$ **16.** $\dfrac{14}{35}, \dfrac{22}{55}$

4.4 Find the least common multiple of the numbers by listing multiples.

   17. 12, 16   **18.** 20, 25   **19.** 9, 14   **20.** 32, 160

4.5 Copy and complete the statement using <, >, or =.

   21. $\dfrac{5}{6}$? $\dfrac{3}{4}$ **22.** $\dfrac{2}{5}$? $\dfrac{1}{4}$

   23. $\dfrac{35}{42}$? $\dfrac{30}{36}$ **24.** $\dfrac{3}{10}$? $\dfrac{1}{3}$

   25. $\dfrac{23}{45}$? $\dfrac{4}{9}$ **26.** $\dfrac{14}{56}$? $\dfrac{18}{72}$

   27. $\dfrac{7}{18}$? $\dfrac{7}{10}$ **28.** $\dfrac{22}{25}$? $\dfrac{9}{10}$

4.6 Write the mixed number as an improper fraction.

   29. $7\dfrac{1}{3}$ **30.** $2\dfrac{3}{10}$ **31.** $5\dfrac{4}{9}$ **32.** $10\dfrac{1}{4}$

Write the improper fraction as a mixed number.

   33. $\dfrac{25}{7}$ **34.** $\dfrac{52}{11}$ **35.** $\dfrac{33}{8}$ **36.** $\dfrac{47}{6}$

4.7 Write the fraction or mixed number as a decimal.

   37. $\dfrac{7}{9}$ **38.** $\dfrac{26}{125}$ **39.** $8\dfrac{9}{10}$ **40.** $3\dfrac{7}{12}$

Write the decimal as a fraction or mixed number.

   41. 0.68   **42.** 0.5   **43.** 5.625   **44.** 1.925

Chapter 5

5.1 **Find the sum or difference.**

1. $\frac{5}{8} + \frac{1}{8}$

2. $\frac{1}{6} + \frac{5}{12}$

3. $\frac{8}{11} - \frac{3}{11}$

4. $\frac{8}{9} - \frac{5}{6}$

5. $\frac{7}{18} + \frac{1}{3}$

6. $\frac{3}{7} + \frac{5}{7}$

7. $\frac{13}{15} - \frac{1}{5}$

8. $\frac{11}{12} - \frac{7}{12}$

5.2 **Find the sum or difference.**

9. $3\frac{1}{4} + 3\frac{3}{4}$

10. $8\frac{7}{9} + 1\frac{8}{9}$

11. $2\frac{2}{5} + 4\frac{3}{10}$

12. $7\frac{3}{4} + 1\frac{5}{6}$

13. $11\frac{3}{5} - 8\frac{4}{5}$

14. $5\frac{1}{2} - 3\frac{3}{8}$

15. $6 - 5\frac{4}{7}$

16. $8\frac{3}{8} - 3\frac{2}{3}$

5.3 **Find the product.**

17. $\frac{7}{9} \cdot \frac{3}{4}$

18. $\frac{7}{10} \cdot 24$

19. $3\frac{1}{5} \cdot 1\frac{1}{4}$

20. $\frac{5}{8} \cdot 4\frac{4}{9}$

21. $12 \times \frac{1}{6}$

22. $\frac{7}{24} \times \frac{8}{14}$

23. $4\frac{2}{5} \times \frac{2}{11}$

24. $10\frac{1}{2} \times 5\frac{1}{3}$

5.4 **Write the reciprocal of the number.**

25. $\frac{2}{9}$

26. $\frac{1}{5}$

27. $3\frac{1}{6}$

28. $1\frac{9}{10}$

Find the quotient.

29. $\frac{3}{4} \div \frac{7}{8}$

30. $\frac{6}{25} \div 4$

31. $7\frac{4}{5} \div \frac{13}{15}$

32. $2\frac{1}{6} \div 1\frac{1}{3}$

5.5 **Copy and complete using the appropriate customary unit.**

33. A hockey rink is 200 __?__ long.

34. A hockey puck weighs 6 __?__ .

35. A washing machine holds 24 __?__ .

36. A bottle of lotion holds $8\frac{1}{2}$ __?__ .

37. A watermelon weighs 11 __?__ .

38. A computer keyboard is $18\frac{1}{2}$ __?__ long.

5.6 **Copy and complete the statement.**

39. 3 yd = __?__ in.

40. 5 pt = __?__ c

41. 4 lb = __?__ oz

42. 8000 lb = __?__ T

43. 19 qt = __?__ gal __?__ qt

44. 13,200 ft = __?__ mi __?__ ft

Find the sum or difference.

45.   7 qt 1 pt
   + 2 qt 1 pt

46.   3 ft 7 in.
   + 1 ft 9 in.

47.   3 T 100 lb
   − 1 T 400 lb

48.   5 c 2 fl oz
   − 4 c 7 fl oz

Chapter 6

6.1 **Order the integers from least to greatest.**

    1. $-3, 0, 6, -10, 3$ **2.** $63, -48, -9, 32, -106$ **3.** $71, -70, 15, 99, -10, -84$

    4. Write the integer that represents a depth of 128 feet below sea level. Then write the opposite of that integer.

6.2 **Find the sum.**

    5. $-18 + 14$ **6.** $75 + (-38)$ **7.** $12 + 27 + (-12)$ **8.** $-8 + (-5) + 6$

6.3 **Find the difference.**

    9. $7 - 11$ **10.** $-25 - 10$ **11.** $64 - (-15)$ **12.** $-8 - (-7)$

6.4 **Find the product.**

    13. $-9(-8)$ **14.** $20(-7)$ **15.** $-3(-4)(-1)$ **16.** $6(0)(-100)$

6.5 **Find the quotient.**

    17. $65 \div (-5)$ **18.** $0 \div (-3)$ **19.** $-42 \div (-14)$ **20.** $-60 \div 12$

6.6 **Show that the number is rational by writing it in $\frac{a}{b}$ form. Then give the multiplicative inverse and the additive inverse of the number.**

    21. -0.9 **22.** $8\frac{1}{6}$ **23.** -1 **24.** $-\frac{7}{9}$

    Evaluate the expression. Justify each step you take.

    25. $-6 \cdot 10 \cdot \left(-\frac{1}{6}\right)$ **26.** $-\frac{3}{5} + \frac{7}{11} + \frac{3}{5}$ **27.** $50 \cdot 13 \cdot 2$ **28.** $0.5 + (-9 + 2.5)$

6.7 **Use the distributive property to evaluate the expression.**

    29. $8(9.1) + 8(0.9)$ **30.** $11\left(\frac{5}{9}\right) + 11\left(\frac{4}{9}\right)$ **31.** $12\left(\frac{5}{8}\right) - 12\left(\frac{1}{8}\right)$ **32.** $6(4.8)$

    33. You buy 4 teddy bears for $24.95 each. Write an expression that will allow you to use the distributive property to find the total cost of the teddy bears. Then evaluate the expression.

6.8 **Plot the point and describe its location in a coordinate plane.**

    34. $W(-3, -4)$ **35.** $Z(0, 2)$ **36.** $N(6, -1)$ **37.** $L(-1, 6)$

    38. Plot and connect the points $P(-4, 5)$, $Q(-4, 1)$, $R(2, 1)$, and $S(2, 5)$ to form a rectangle. Find the length, width, and area of the rectangle.

    39. The table shows the pressures at various depths underwater. Make a scatter plot of the data. Then make a conclusion about the data.

Depth (ft)	5	10	15	20	25	30	35
Pressure (lb/in.²)	17	19	21	23.5	26	28	30

Chapter 7

7.1 **Write the verbal phrase as a variable expression. Let x represent the number.**

    1. 17 fewer than a number

    2. The quotient of a number and 7

Write the verbal sentence as an equation. Let y represent the number.

    3. Half of a number is equal to -5.

    4. 1 more than 6 times a number is 19.

7.2 **Simplify the expression.**

    5. $-r + 4 - 2 + r$

    6. $6 + z + 3z - 4$

    7. $6y + 12 - 4y$

    8. $8a - 2(3 + 4a)$

    9. $2(3 - x) - 12 - 3x$

    10. $3(2t - 5) + 4t$

7.3 **Solve the equation. Check your solution.**

    11. $n + 6 = -4$
    12. $15 = d - 3$
    13. $1.4 = 3.8 + w$
    14. $z - (-7) = 3$

7.4 **Solve the equation. Check your solution.**

    15. $-7y = -49$
    16. $1.2 = \dfrac{k}{4}$
    17. $18 = -\dfrac{2}{3}m$
    18. $10c = -110$

7.5 **Solve the equation. Check your solution.**

    19. $2x - 7 = 6$
    20. $\dfrac{p}{4} + 1 = -1$
    21. $8.1 = 5j - 7.4$
    22. $6 = 6(-x + 1)$

7.6 **Write an inequality represented by the graph.**

    23.

    24.

Solve the inequality. Then graph the solution.

    25. $-24 + b > -30$
    26. $\dfrac{t}{-3} \le 1$
    27. $s - 3.5 \le 1.5$
    28. $9r < -45$

7.7 **Make an input-output table for the function using the domain $-4, -2, 0, 2,$ and 4. Then state the range of the function.**

    29. $y = x - 1.5$
    30. $y = -9x$
    31. $y = 8 - x$
    32. $y = \dfrac{3}{2}x + 1$

Write a function rule for the input-output table.

33.

Input x	−2	−1	0	1
Output y	−8	−7	−6	−5

34.

Input x	−4	0	4	8
Output y	1	0	−1	−2

7.8 **Graph the function.**

    35. $y = -0.5x$
    36. $y = 6 - x$
    37. $y = 2x + 3$
    38. $y = -2 + \dfrac{1}{2}x$

Chapter 8

8.1 In the 2001–2002 season, the Michigan State men's hockey team had 18 wins, 6 losses, and 4 ties in their conference. Use this information to write the specified ratio.

1. Wins to losses **2.** Wins to games played **3.** Losses to games played

Write the ratio as a fraction in simplest form.

4. 30 : 36 **5.** 12 to 48 **6.** 28 to 70

8.2 Find the unit rate.

7. $11.89 for 8.2 gallons **8.** $370 for 40 hours **9.** 432 words in 12 minutes

10. Find the average speed of a runner who completes a 1500 meter race in 4 minutes 10 seconds.

11. Determine which bottle of shampoo is the better buy: 15 fluid ounces for $2.59 or 20 fluid ounces for $3.59.

8.3 Draw the graph of the line that passes through the points. Then find the slope of the line.

12. $(7, 2), (-5, 4)$ **13.** $(-6, 0), (-5, 1)$

14. $(3, 4), (5, 9)$ **15.** $(-2, -3), (1, -3)$

16. Draw a line that has a slope of -2 and passes through $(0, -5)$.

8.4 Use equivalent ratios or algebra to solve the proportion.

17. $\dfrac{x}{30} = \dfrac{5}{6}$ **18.** $\dfrac{28}{24} = \dfrac{r}{6}$ **19.** $\dfrac{t}{36} = \dfrac{3}{4}$ **20.** $\dfrac{12}{15} = \dfrac{c}{10}$

8.5 Use the cross products property to solve the proportion.

21. $\dfrac{a}{39} = \dfrac{6.5}{13}$ **22.** $\dfrac{30}{12} = \dfrac{6}{z}$ **23.** $\dfrac{9}{x} = \dfrac{5}{14}$ **24.** $\dfrac{2.4}{9} = \dfrac{n}{1.5}$

25. There are 180 calories in a 30 gram serving of walnuts. How many calories are there in a 100 gram serving of walnuts?

8.6 In Exercises 26–28, use the fact that a floor plan of a house is drawn using a scale of 1 in. : 8 ft.

26. Find the actual dimensions of a rectangular basement that is 2.5 inches long and 2.25 inches wide on the floor plan.

27. Find the actual dimensions of a rectangular deck that is 3.75 inches long and 1.875 inches wide on the floor plan.

28. Find the actual dimensions of a rectangular bedroom that is 2.75 inches long and 1.75 inches wide on the floor plan.

Chapter 9

9.1   **Write the percent as a fraction.**

1. 60%   **2.** 49%   **3.** 84%   **4.** 56%

Write the fraction as a percent.

5. $\frac{2}{5}$ **6.** $\frac{9}{10}$ **7.** $\frac{1}{4}$ **8.** $\frac{17}{25}$

9.2   **Use a proportion to answer the question.**

9. What percent of 25 is 16?   **10.** 54 is 75% of what number?

11. What number is 27% of 250?   **12.** What percent of 32 is 12?

9.3   **Write the percent as a decimal or the decimal as a percent.**

13. 2%   **14.** 20.4%   **15.** 106%   **16.** 0.94%

17. 0.575   **18.** 0.082   **19.** 0.0012   **20.** 4.2

9.4   **Use the percent equation to answer the question.**

21. 57 is 125% of what number?   **22.** What number is 3% of 18?

23. What percent of 64 is 20?   **24.** 60 is 40% of what number?

9.5   **25.** The table shows Jake's work schedule at a video store during the week. Display the data in a circle graph.

Day	Monday	Tuesday	Wednesday	Thursday	Friday
Hours	3.5	5	6	3	2.5

9.6   **Identify the percent of change as an *increase* or a *decrease*. Then find the percent of change.**

26. Original: 32
New: 28   **27.** Original: 48
New: 45   **28.** Original: $375
New: $400   **29.** Original: $32
New: $35

9.7   **Use the given information to find the new price.**

30. Original price: $58
Discount: 25%   **31.** Wholesale price: $96
Markup: 120%   **32.** Food bill before tax: $62
Sales tax: 7%

9.8   **For an account that earns simple annual interest, find the interest and the balance of the account.**

33. $250 at 2.5% for 2 years

34. $1000 at 3% for 8 months

35. $600 at 4.4% for 1 month

36. Suppose you deposit $500 into an account that earns 4% simple annual interest. How long will it take to earn $10 in interest?

Chapter 10

10.1 **For the given angle measure, find the measure of a supplementary angle and the measure of a complementary angle, if possible.**

1. $86°$ **2.** $151°$ **3.** $90°$ **4.** $7°$

10.2 **Find the unknown angle measures.**

5.    **6.** 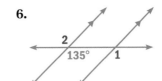   **7.**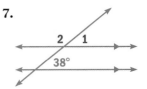

10.3 **8.** The measures of two of the angles in a triangle are $52°$ and $38°$. Find the measure of the third angle. Then classify the triangle by its angle measures.

     9. The side lengths of a triangle are 11 feet, 8 feet, and 11 feet. Classify the triangle by the lengths of its sides.

10.4 **10.** Sketch a parallelogram that is both a rectangle and a rhombus. Then classify the parallelogram.

     11. Find the sum of the angle measures in an octagon.

10.5 **12.** Given that $\triangle ABC \cong \triangle DEF$, name the corresponding sides and the corresponding angles.

     13. One square has a side length of 8 meters, and another square has a side length of 10 meters. Are the squares similar? Explain.

10.6 **14.** Find the unknown lengths given that the triangles are similar.

     15. The shadow cast by a tree is 18 feet long. At the same time, a girl who is 5 feet tall casts a 3 foot long shadow. How tall is the tree?

10.7 **16.** Sketch an equilateral triangle and draw any line(s) of symmetry. Then tell whether the triangle has rotational symmetry. If it does, give the angle(s) and direction of rotation.

10.8 **Draw triangle *ABC* with vertices $A(-2, 1)$, $B(-5, 2)$, and $C(-1, 4)$. Then find the coordinates of the vertices of the image after the specified transformation, and draw the image.**

     17. $(x, y) \rightarrow (x + 7, y - 4)$ **18.** $(x, y) \rightarrow (x - 3, y + 2)$

     19. Reflect $\triangle ABC$ in the *y*-axis.   **20.** Reflect $\triangle ABC$ in the *x*-axis.

Chapter 11

11.1 **Evaluate the expression when $x = 5$ and $y = 12$.**

1. $\sqrt{3y}$ **2.** $-\sqrt{61 - xy}$ **3.** $\sqrt{x^2 + y^2}$ **4.** $\sqrt{y - x + 2}$

Solve the equation.

5. $a^2 - 4 = 140$ **6.** $5b^2 = 500$ **7.** $2c^2 + 9 = 81$ **8.** $2 + 3d^2 = 194$

11.2 **Approximate the square root to the nearest whole number and then to the nearest tenth.**

9. $\sqrt{19}$ **10.** $\sqrt{94}$ **11.** $\sqrt{135}$ **12.** $\sqrt{229}$

Tell whether the number is *rational* or *irrational*. Explain your reasoning.

13. $1.23456789\ldots$ **14.** $2.\overline{62}$ **15.** $-\sqrt{49}$ **16.** $\sqrt{11}$

11.3 **Find the unknown length. Round to the nearest tenth if necessary.**

17. 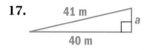   **18.** 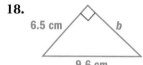   **19.**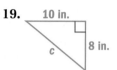

11.4 **Find the unknown area, base, or height of the parallelogram.**

20. $b = 14$ cm, $h = 9$ cm, $A = \underline{\ ?\ }$

21. $A = 96$ ft^2, $b = 12$ ft, $h = \underline{\ ?\ }$

22. $A = 20$ in.^{2}, $b = \underline{\ ?\ }$, $h = 1.6$ in.

23. $b = 8$ m, $h = 4$ m, $A = \underline{\ ?\ }$

11.5 **Find the area of the triangle or trapezoid.**

24. 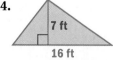   **25.** 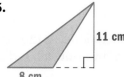   **26.**

11.6 **Find the circumference of the circle with the given radius or diameter. Use $\frac{22}{7}$ or 3.14 for π. Check using estimation.**

27. $r = 42$ mi   **28.** $r = 12$ in.   **29.** $d = 50$ cm   **30.** $d = 35$ mm

11.7 **Find the area of the circle with the given radius or diameter. Use $\frac{22}{7}$ or 3.14 for π. Check using estimation.**

31. $r = 40$ yd   **32.** $r = 84$ m   **33.** $d = 14$ ft   **34.** $d = 0.2$ km

Chapter 12

12.1 Classify the solid. Be as specific as possible.

1.

2.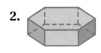

3.

4.

Count the number of faces, edges, and vertices in the solid.

5. Triangular pyramid

6. Rectangular prism

7. Hexagonal pyramid

12.2 Sketch the solid.

8. Cube

9. Triangular prism

10. Pentagonal prism

11. Sketch the top, side, and front views of the cylinder shown at the right.

12.3 Find the surface area of the rectangular prism.

12.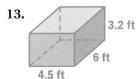
3 in.
2 in.
10 in.

13.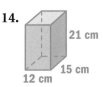
3.2 ft
6 ft
4.5 ft

14.
21 cm
15 cm
12 cm

12.4 Find the surface area of the cylinder. Use 3.14 for π.

15.
2 m
1 m

16.
7 in.
2 in.

17.
3 ft
10 ft

12.5 Find the volume of the rectangular prism with the given dimensions.

18. 3 m by 4 m by 0.5 m

19. 14 in. by 10 in. by 2 in.

20. 7 ft by 7 ft by 3.5 ft

21. 5 cm by 2.5 cm by 11 cm

22. 9 yd by 20 yd by 15 yd

23. 8 mm by 6 mm by 5.25 mm

24. Find the width of a rectangular prism that has a length of 15 meters, a height of 9 meters, and a volume of 1080 cubic meters.

12.6 Find the unknown volume, radius, or height of the cylinder. Use 3.14 for π.

25. $V = $ _?_

$r = 6$ in.

$h = 10$ in.

26. $V = 25.12$ cm^3

$r = 2$ cm

$h = $ _?_

27. $V = 39.25$ ft^3

$r = $ _?_

$h = 0.5$ ft

Chapter 13

13.1 **Each number from 1 to 20 is written on a separate piece of paper and put in a bag. You randomly choose a piece of paper from the bag. Find the probability of the event. Write the probability as a fraction, a decimal, and a percent.**

1. You choose a multiple of 6.

2. You choose a factor of 12.

3. When a bottle cap is tossed, it lands top side down 36 times and top side up 14 times. Find the probability that the next time the bottle cap is tossed, it will land top side down.

13.2 4. A store sells sweatshirts in blue, black, and white. The sizes available are small, medium, large, and extra large. Make a tree diagram to find all the possible sweatshirt choices you have to choose from.

5. Suppose a pitcher can throw a fastball, a curve ball, or a slider. If the pitcher chooses any two pitches at random, what is the probability that one pitch is a fastball and one is a slider?

13.3 **A monogram consists of the first letters of a person's first, middle, and last names.**

6. How many different monograms are possible?

7. If a monogram is chosen at random, what is the probability that the monogram is ABC? Assume that all monograms are equally likely.

13.4 8. How many 4 digit numbers can be formed from the digits 1, 2, 3, 4, 5, and 6 if each digit is used only once?

9. A teacher chooses 3 students from a class of 30 students to present their projects during today's class. If the order in which the students are chosen does not matter, how many different ways are there for the students to be chosen?

13.5 **Two number cubes are rolled. Find the probability of the event(s).**

10. Either both numbers are odd or both are even.

11. The sum of the numbers is *not* 11.

13.6 **A bag contains 10 red beads and 6 white beads. You randomly choose one bead, and then randomly choose another bead.**

12. Find the probability that both beads are red if you replace the first bead before choosing the second bead.

13. Find the probability that both beads are red if you do not replace the first bead before choosing the second bead.

Tables

Table of Symbols

Symbol	Meaning	Page
. . .	continues on	3
=	equals, is equal to	8, 25
$\frac{14}{2}$	14 divided 2	9
$3 \cdot x$ $3(x)$ $3x$	3 times x	9
<	is less than	10, 736
>	is greater than	10, 736
4^3	4 to the third power	13
( )	parentheses—a grouping symbol	18
[ ]	brackets—a grouping symbol	18
$\stackrel{?}{=}$	is equal to?	25
$\neq$	is not equal to	25
28.6	decimal point	56
$1.1\overline{6}$	repeating decimal 1.16666 . . .	199
−3	negative 3	269
−3	the opposite of 3	269
$|a|$	the absolute value of a number a	278
(x, y)	ordered pair	313
$\leq$	is less than or equal to	366
$\geq$	is greater than or equal to	366
$a : b, \frac{a}{b}$	ratio of a to b	399

Symbol	Meaning	Page
$\approx$	is approximately equal to	425, 460
%	Percent	449
°	degree(s)	472
$\angle PQR$	angle PQR	511
$m\angle B$	measure of angle B	511
⌐	right angle	511
$\cong$	is congruent to	516
$\overleftrightarrow{AB}$	line AB	516
⇉	parallel lines	517
‖	is parallel to	517
$\perp$	is perpendicular to	517
$\triangle ABC$	triangle with vertices A, B, and C	521
$\overline{AB}$	line segment AB	523
AB	the length of line segment AB	523
$\overrightarrow{AB}$	ray AB	527
$\sim$	is similar to	537
A'	the image of point A	557
$\sqrt{a}$	the positive square root of a number a where $a > 0$	577
$\pm$	plus or minus	579
π	pi—a number approximately equal to 3.14	607

Table of Measures

Time

60 seconds (sec) = 1 minute (min)	$\left.\begin{array}{l}\text{365 days} \\ \text{52 weeks (approx.)} \\ \text{12 months}\end{array}\right\}$ = 1 year
60 minutes = 1 hour (h)	
24 hours = 1 day (d)	
7 days = 1 week (wk)	10 years = 1 decade
4 weeks (approx.) = 1 month	100 years = 1 century

Metric

Length

10 millimeters (mm) = 1 centimeter (cm)

$\left.\begin{array}{l}\text{100 cm} \\ \text{1000 mm}\end{array}\right\}$ = 1 meter (m)

1000 m = 1 kilometer (km)

Area

100 square millimeters = 1 square centimeter
(mm^2)   (cm^2)

10,000 cm^2 = 1 square meter (m^2)

10,000 m^2 = 1 hectare (ha)

Volume

1000 cubic millimeters = 1 cubic centimeter
(mm^3)   (cm^3)

1,000,000 cm^3 = 1 cubic meter (m^3)

Liquid Capacity

$\left.\begin{array}{l}\text{1000 millimeters (mL)} \\ \text{1000 cubic centimeters (cm}^3\text{)}\end{array}\right\}$ = 1 liter (L)

1000 L = 1 kiloliter (kL)

Mass

1000 milligrams = 1 gram (g)

1000 g = 1 kilogram (kg)

1000 kg = 1 metric ton (t)

Temperature Degrees Celcius (°C)

0°C = freezing point of water

37°C = normal body temperature

100°C = boiling point of water

United States Customary

Length

12 inches (in.) = 1 foot (ft)

$\left.\begin{array}{l}\text{36 in.} \\ \text{3 ft}\end{array}\right\}$ = 1 yard (yd)

$\left.\begin{array}{l}\text{5280 ft} \\ \text{1760 yd}\end{array}\right\}$ = 1 mile (mi)

Area

144 square inches (in.^{2}) = 1 square foot (ft^2)

9 ft^2 = 1 square yard (yd^2)

$\left.\begin{array}{l}\text{43, 560 ft}^2 \\ \text{4840 yd}^2\end{array}\right\}$ = 1 acre (A)

Volume

1728 cubic inches (in.^{3}) = 1 cubic foot (ft^3)

27 ft^3 = 1 cubic foot (yd^3)

Liquid Capacity

8 fluid ounces (fl oz) = 1 cup (c)

2 c = 1 pint (pt)

2 pt = 1 quart (qt)

4 qt = 1 gallon (gal)

Weight

16 ounces (oz) = 1 pound (lb)

2000 lb = 1 ton

Temperature Degrees Fahrenheit (°F)

32°F = freezing point of water

98.6°F = normal body temperature

212°F = boiling point of water

Table of Formulas

Geometric Formulas

Rectangle (p. 32)

Area   **Perimeter**
$A = lw$ $P = 2l + 2w$

Square (p. 32)

Area   **Perimeter**
$A = s^2$ $P = 4s$

Parallelogram (p. 552)

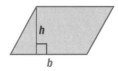

Area
$A = bh$

Triangle (p. 558)

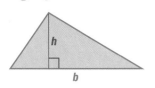

Area
$A = \frac{1}{2}bh$

Trapezoid (p. 559)

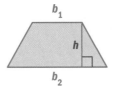

Area
$A = \frac{1}{2}(b_1 + b_2)h$

Circle (pp. 563, 567)

Area   **Circumference**
$A = \pi r^2$ $A = \pi d$ or
               $C = 2\pi r$

Rectangular Prism (pp. 594, 607)

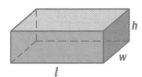

Surface Area   **Volume**
$S = 2lw + 2lh + 2wh$ $V = lwh$

Cylinder (pp. 602, 611)

Surface Area   **Volume**
$S = 2\pi r^2 + 2\pi rh$ $V = \pi r^2 h$

Other Formulas

Distance traveled (p. 27)	$d = rt$ where d = distance, r = rate, and t = time
Temperature (p. 279)	$F = \frac{9}{5}C + 32$ and $C = \frac{5}{9}(F - 32)$ where F = degrees Fahrenheit and C = degrees Celsius
Simple interest (p. 454)	$I = Prt$ where I = simple interest, P = principal, r = annual interest rate, and t = time in years
Pythagorean theorem (p. 546)	In a right triangle, $a^2 + b^2 = c^2$ where a and b are the length of the legs, and c is the length of the hypotenuse.

Table of Properties

Number Properties		
Commutative Property of Addition *(p. 284)* In a sum, you can add terms in any order.	**Numbers** **Algebra**	$-2 + 5 = 5 + (-2)$ $a + b = b + a$
Associative Property of Addition *(p. 284)* Changing the grouping of terms in a sum will not change the sum.	**Numbers** **Algebra**	$(2 + 4) + 6 = 2 + (4 + 6)$ $(a + b) + c = a + (b + c)$
Commutative Property of Multiplication *(p. 284)* In a product, you can multiply factors in any order.	**Numbers** **Algebra**	$3(-6) = -6(3)$ $ab = ba$
Associative Property of Multiplication *(p. 284)* Changing the grouping of factors in a product will not change the product.	**Numbers** **Algebra**	$(6 \times 2.5) \times 4 = 6 \times (2.5 \times 4)$ $(ab)c = a(bc)$
Inverse Property of Addition *(p. 285)* The sum of a number and its additive inverse, or opposite, is 0.	**Numbers** **Algebra**	$4 + (-4) = 0$ $a + (-a) = 0$
Identity Property of Addition *(p. 285)* The sum of a number and the additive identity, 0, is the number.	**Numbers** **Algebra**	$7 + 0 = 7$ $a + 0 = a$
Inverse Property of Multiplication *(p. 285)* The product of a nonzero number and its multiplicative inverse, or reciprocal, is 1.	**Numbers** **Algebra**	$\frac{2}{3} \cdot \frac{3}{2} = 1$ For any nonzero integers a and b, $\frac{a}{b} \cdot \frac{b}{a} = 1$.
Identity Property of Multiplication *(p. 285)* The product of a number and the multiplicative identity, 1, is the number.	**Numbers** **Algebra**	$3 \cdot 1 = 3$ $a \cdot 1 = a$
Distributive Property *(p. 307)* You can multiply a number and a sum by multiplying each term of the sum by the number and then adding these products. The same property applies to subtraction.	**Numbers** **Algebra**	$3(4 + 6) = 3(4) + 3(6)$ $2(8 - 5) = 2(8) - 2(5)$ $a(b + c) = a(b) + a(c)$ $a(b - c) = a(b) - a(c)$
Cross Products Property *(p. 394)* The cross products of a proportion are equal.	**Numbers** **Algebra**	If $\frac{3}{4} = \frac{6}{8}$, then $3 \cdot 8 = 4 \cdot 6$. If $\frac{a}{b} = \frac{c}{d}$ and b and d do not equal 0, then $ad = bc$.

Finding Squares and Square Roots

EXAMPLE 1 Finding a Square

Find 54^2.

Find 54 in the column labeled *No.* (an abbreviation for *Number*). Read across to the column labeled *Square*.

No.	Square	Sq. Root
51	2601	7.141
52	2704	7.211
53	2809	7.280
54	2916	7.348
55	3025	7.416

▶ **Answer** So, $54^2 = 2916$.

EXAMPLE 2 Finding a Square Root

Find a decimal approximation of $\sqrt{54}$.

Find 54 in the column labeled *No.* Read across to the column labeled *Sq. Root.*

No.	Square	Sq. Root
51	2601	7.141
52	2704	7.211
53	2809	7.280
54	2916	7.348
55	3025	7.416

▶ **Answer** So, to the nearest thousandth, $\sqrt{54} \approx 7.348$.

EXAMPLE 3 Finding a Square Root

Find a decimal approximation of $\sqrt{3000}$.

Find the two numbers in the *Square* column that 3000 is between. Read across to the column labeled *No.*; $\sqrt{3000}$ is between 54 and 55, but closer to 55.

No.	Square	Sq. Root
51	2601	7.141
52	2704	7.211
53	2809	7.280
54	2916	7.348
55	3025	7.416

▶ **Answer** So, $\sqrt{3000} \approx 55$. A more accurate approximation can be found using a calculator: 54.772256.

TABLES

Table of Squares and Square Roots

No.	Square	Sq. Root	No.	Square	Sq. Root	No.	Square	Sq. Root
1	1	1.000	51	2601	7.141	101	10,201	10.050
2	4	1.414	52	2704	7.211	102	10,404	10.100
3	9	1.732	53	2809	7.280	103	10,609	10.149
4	16	2.000	54	2916	7.348	104	10,816	10.198
5	25	2.236	55	3025	7.416	105	11,025	10.247
6	36	2.449	56	3136	7.483	106	11,236	10.296
7	49	2.646	57	3249	7.550	107	11,449	10.344
8	64	2.828	58	3364	7.616	108	11,664	10.392
9	81	3.000	59	3481	7.681	109	11,881	10.440
10	100	3.162	60	3600	7.746	110	12,100	10.488
11	121	3.317	61	3721	7.810	111	12,321	10.536
12	144	3.464	62	3844	7.874	112	12,544	10.583
13	169	3.606	63	3969	7.937	113	12,769	10.630
14	196	3.742	64	4096	8.000	114	12,996	10.677
15	225	3.873	65	4225	8.062	115	13,225	10.724
16	256	4.000	66	4356	8.124	116	13,456	10.770
17	289	4.123	67	4489	8.185	117	13,689	10.817
18	324	4.243	68	4624	8.246	118	13,924	10.863
19	361	4.359	69	4761	8.307	119	14,161	10.909
20	400	4.472	70	4900	8.367	120	14,400	10.954
21	441	4.583	71	5041	8.426	121	14,641	11.000
22	484	4.690	72	5184	8.485	122	14,884	11.045
23	529	4.796	73	5329	8.544	123	15,129	11.091
24	576	4.899	74	5476	8.602	124	15,376	11.136
25	625	5.000	75	5625	8.660	125	15,625	11.180
26	676	5.099	76	5776	8.718	126	15,876	11.225
27	729	5.196	77	5929	8.775	127	16,129	11.269
28	784	5.292	78	6084	8.832	128	16,384	11.314
29	841	5.385	79	6241	8.888	129	16,641	11.358
30	900	5.477	80	6400	8.944	130	16,900	11.402
31	961	5.568	81	6561	9.000	131	17,161	11.446
32	1024	5.657	82	6724	9.055	132	17,424	11.489
33	1089	5.745	83	6889	9.110	133	17,689	11.533
34	1156	5.831	84	7056	9.165	134	17,956	11.576
35	1225	5.916	85	7225	9.220	135	18,225	11.619
36	1296	6.000	86	7396	9.274	136	18,496	11.662
37	1369	6.083	87	7569	9.327	137	18,769	11.705
38	1444	6.164	88	7744	9.381	138	19,044	11.747
39	1521	6.245	89	7921	9.434	139	19,321	11.790
40	1600	6.325	90	8100	9.487	140	19,600	11.832
41	1681	6.403	91	8281	9.539	141	19,881	11.874
42	1764	6.481	92	8464	9.592	142	20,164	11.916
43	1849	6.557	93	8649	9.644	143	20,449	11.958
44	1936	6.633	94	8836	9.695	144	20,736	12.000
45	2025	6.708	95	9025	9.747	145	21,025	12.042
46	2116	6.782	96	9216	9.798	146	21,316	12.083
47	2209	6.856	97	9409	9.849	147	21,609	12.124
48	2304	6.928	98	9604	9.899	148	21,904	12.166
49	2401	7.000	99	9801	9.950	149	22,201	12.207
50	2500	7.071	100	10,000	10.000	150	22,500	12.247

English-Spanish Glossary

absolute value (p. 278) The absolute value of a number a is the distance between a and 0 on a number line. The absolute value of a is written $|a|$.

valor absoluto (pág. 278) El valor absoluto de un número a es la distancia entre a y 0 en una recta numérica. El valor absoluto de a se escribe $|a|$.

$$|4| = 4 \qquad |-7| = 7 \qquad |0| = 0$$

---

acute angle (p. 511) An angle whose measure is less than 90°.

ángulo agudo (pág. 511) Un ángulo que mide menos de 90°.

---

acute triangle (p. 522) A triangle with three acute angles.

triángulo acutángulo (pág. 522) Un triángulo que tiene tres ángulos agudos.

---

addition property of equality (p. 348) Adding the same number to each side of an equation produces an equivalent equation.

propiedad de igualdad en la suma (pág. 348) Al sumar el mismo número a cada lado de una ecuación se produce una ecuación equivalente.

If $x - 5 = 2$, then $x - 5 + 5 = 2 + 5$, so $x = 7$.
If $x - a = b$, then $x - a + a = b + a$.

Si $x - 5 = 2$, entonces $x - 5 + 5 = 2 + 5$, por lo tanto $x = 7$.
Si $x - a = b$, entonces $x - a + a = b + a$.

---

additive identity (p. 302) The number 0 is the additive identity because the sum of any number and 0 is the original number.

identidad de la suma (pág. 302) El número 0 es la identidad de la suma porque la suma de cualquier número y 0 es el número original.

$$-7 + 0 = -7$$
$$a + 0 = a$$

---

additive inverse (p. 302) The additive inverse of a number a is the opposite of the number, or $-a$. The sum of a number and its additive inverse is 0.

inverso aditivo (pág. 302) El inverso aditivo de un número a es el opuesto del número, o $-a$. La suma de un número y su inverso aditivo es 0.

The *additive inverse* of 6 is -6, so $6 + (-6) = 0$.

El *inverso aditivo* de 6 es -6, por lo tanto $6 + (-6) = 0$.

---

adjacent angles (p. 516) Two angles that share a common side and a vertex and do not overlap.

ángulos adyacentes (pág. 516) Dos ángulos que comparten un lado común y un vértice y no se superponen.

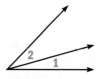

$\angle 1$ and $\angle 2$ are *adjacent angles*.

$\angle 1$ y $\angle 2$ son *ángulos adyacentes*.

angle (p. 474) A figure formed by two rays that begin at a common point, called a vertex.

ángulo (pág. 474) Figura formada por dos semirrectas que comienzan en un punto común, llamado vértice.

vertex/vértice
ray/semirrecta
ray/semirrecta

angle of rotation (p. 549) In a rotation, the angle formed by two rays drawn from the center of rotation through corresponding points on the original figure and its image.

ángulo de rotación (pág. 549) En una rotación, el ángulo formado por dos semirrectas trazadas desde el centro de rotación a través de puntos correspondientes en la figura original y su imagen.

See **rotation.**

Véase **rotación.**

annual interest rate (p. 490) The percentage of the principal earned or paid per year.

tasa de interés anual (pág. 490) El porcentaje sobre el capital ganado o pagado por año.

See **simple interest.**

Véase **interés simple.**

arc (p. 527) Part of a circle.

arco (pág. 527) Parte de un círculo.

The *arc* intersects $\angle A$ at points B and C.

El *arco* interseca $\angle A$ en los puntos B y C.

area (p. 32) The number of square units needed to cover a figure.

área (pág. 32) La cantidad de unidades cuadradas que se necesitan para cubrir una figura.

3 units
3 unidades
7 units
7 unidades

Area = 21 square units

Área = 21 unidades cuadradas

associative property of addition (p. 302) Changing the grouping of terms in a sum does not change the sum.

propiedad asociativa de la suma (pág. 302) Cambiar la manera en que se agrupan los términos en una suma no cambia la suma.

$$(9 + 4) + 6 = 9 + (4 + 6)$$
$$(a + b) + c = a + (b + c)$$

associative property of multiplication (p. 302) Changing the grouping of factors in a product does not change the product.

propiedad asociativa de la multiplicación (pág. 302) Cambiar la manera en que se agrupan los factores en un producto no cambia el producto.

$$(2 \cdot 5) \cdot 3 = 2 \cdot (5 \cdot 3)$$
$$(ab)c = a(bc)$$

balance (p. 490) The sum of the interest and the principal.

balance (pág. 490) La suma del interés y el capital.

See simple interest.

Véase interés simple.

---

bar graph (p. 117) A type of graph in which the lengths of bars are used to represent and compare data.

gráfica de barras (pág. 117) Un tipo de gráfica en el que las longitudes de las barras se usan para representar y comparar datos.

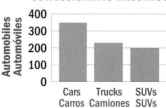

---

base of a parallelogram (p. 594) The length of any side of the parallelogram can be used as the base.

base de un paralelogramo (pág. 594) La longitud de cualquier lado del paralelogramo puede usarse como la base.

---

base of a power (p. 13) The number or expression that is used as a factor in a repeated multiplication.

base de una potencia (pág. 13) El número o la expresión que se usa como factor en una multiplicación repetida.

In the power 5^3, the base is 5.

La base de la potencia 5^3 es 5.

---

base of a triangle (p. 601) The length of any side of the triangle can be used as the base.

base de un triángulo (pág. 601) La longitud de cualquier lado de un triángulo puede usarse como base.

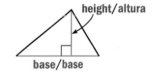

---

bases of a trapezoid (p. 602) The lengths of the parallel sides of the trapezoid.

bases de un trapecio (pág. 602) Las longitudes de los lados paralelos del trapecio.

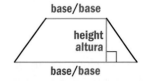

---

biased sample (p. 115) A sample that is not representative of the population from which it is selected.

muestra parcial (pág. 115) Una muestra que no es representativa de la población de la cual fue seleccionada.

The members of a football team are a *biased sample* if you want to determine the average amount of time students spend playing sports each week.

Los miembros de un equipo de fútbol son una *muestra parcial* para determinar la cantidad promedio de tiempo a la semana que los estudiantes practican deportes.

ENGLISH-SPANISH GLOSSARY

box-and-whisker plot (p. 133) A data display that divides a data set into four parts using the lower extreme, lower quartile, median, upper quartile, and upper extreme.

diagrama de líneas y bloques (pág. 133) Diagrama que divide un conjunto de datos en cuatro partes usando el extremo inferior, el cuartil inferior, la mediana, el cuartil superior y el extremo superior.

0 10 20 30 40 50

8 19 26 37 45

C

center of a circle (p. 607) The point inside the circle that is the same distance from all points on the circle.

centro de un círculo (pág. 607) El punto en el interior del círculo que está a la misma distancia de todos los puntos del círculo.

See circle.

Véase círculo.

---

center of rotation (p. 548) The point about which a figure is turned when the figure undergoes a rotation.

centro de rotación (pág. 548) El punto alrededor del cual gira una figura cuando la figura sufre una rotación.

See rotation.

Véase rotación.

---

circle (p. 607) The set of all points in a plane that are the same distance, called the radius, from a fixed point, called the center.

círculo (pág. 607) El conjunto de todos los puntos en un plano que están a la misma distancia, llamada radio, de un punto fijo, llamado centro.

radius
radio

center
centro

diameter
diámetro

circumference
circunferencia

---

circle graph (p. 474) A circle graph displays data as sections of a circle. The entire circle represents all the data. Each section is labeled using the actual data or using data expressed as fractions, decimals, or percents of the sum of the data.

gráfica circular (pág. 474) Una gráfica circular representa los datos como secciones de un círculo. El círculo completo representa todos los datos. Cada sección está rotulada con los datos reales o usando datos expresados como fracciones, decimales o porcentajes de la suma de los datos.

Siblings
Hermanos

Three or more
Tres o más
25%

None/Ninguno
10%

Two/Dos
25%

One/Uno
40%

---

circumference (p. 607) The distance around a circle.

circunferencia (pág. 607) La distancia alrededor de un círculo.

See circle.

Véase círculo.

---

coefficient (p. 342) The number in a term that is the product of a number and a variable.

coeficiente (pág. 342) La parte de un término que es el producto de un número y una variable.

The *coefficient* of $7x$ is 7.

El *coeficiente* de $7x$ es 7.

---

combination (p. 703) A grouping of objects in which the order is not important.	There are 6 *combinations* of 2 letters chosen from the 4 letters in the word VASE: VA VS VE AS AE SE
combinación (pág. 703) Agrupación de objetos en la cual el orden no es importante.	Existen 6 *combinaciones* de 2 letras tomadas de la palabra VASO: VA VS VO AS AO SO
common factor (p. 170) A whole number that is a factor of two or more nonzero whole numbers.	The *common factors* of 8 and 12 are 1, 2, and 4.
factor común (pág. 170) Un número natural que es factor de dos o más números naturales distintos de cero.	Los *factores comunes* de 8 y 12 son 1, 2 y 4.
common multiple (p. 182) A multiple that is shared by two or more numbers.	The *common multiples* of 4 and 6 are 12, 24, 36, ...
múltiplo común (pág. 182) Un múltiplo compartido por dos o más números.	Los *múltiplos comunes* de 4 y 6 son 12, 24, 36,...
commutative property of addition (p. 302) In a sum, you can add terms in any order. **propiedad conmutativa de la suma** (pág. 302) En una suma, puedes sumar los términos en cualquier orden.	$$4 + 7 = 7 + 4$$ $$a + b = b + a$$
commutative property of multiplication (p. 302) In a product, you can multiply factors in any order. **propiedad conmutativa de la multiplicación** (pág. 302) En un producto, puedes multiplicar los factores en cualquier orden.	$$5(-8) = -8(5)$$ $$ab = ba$$
compatible numbers (p. 71) Numbers that make a calculation easier.	To estimate the quotient $377.25 \div 21$, use *compatible numbers*: $377.25 \div 21 \approx 380 \div 20 = 19$
números compatibles (pág. 71) Números que hacen más fácil un cálculo.	Para estimar el cociente de $377.25 \div 21$, usa *números compatibles*: $377.25 \div 21 \approx 380 \div 20 = 19$
complementary angles (p. 512) Two angles whose measures have a sum of 90°. **ángulos complementarios** (pág. 512) Dos ángulos cuyas medidas suman 90°.	32° 58°
complementary events (p. 711) Two disjoint events such that one or the other of the events must occur. **eventos complementarios** (pág. 711) Dos eventos disjuntos, de modo que uno u otro de los eventos debe ocurrir.	When rolling a number cube, the events "getting an odd number" and "getting an even number" are *complementary events*. Al lanzar un cubo numerado, obtener un número par y obtener un número impar son *eventos complementarios* o *complementos*.

composite number (p. 165) A whole number greater than 1 that is not prime.	6 is a *composite number* because its factors are 1, 2, 3, and 6.
número compuesto (pág. 165) Un número natural mayor que 1 que no es primo.	6 es un *número compuesto* porque sus factores son 1, 2, 3 y 6.
compound events (p. 715) Two or more events that can happen either at the same time or one after the other.	*See* independent events *and* dependent events.
eventos compuestos (pág. 715) Dos o más eventos que pueden ocurrir al mismo tiempo o uno después del otro.	*Véase* eventos independientes y eventos dependientes.
cone (p. 631) A solid with one circular base.	
cono (pág. 631) Un cuerpo geométrico que tiene una base circular.	base/base
congruent angles (p. 516) Angles that have the same measure.	*See* congruent polygons.
ángulos congruentes (pág. 516) Ángulos que tienen medidas iguales.	*Véase* polígonos congruentes.
congruent polygons (p. 537) Similar polygons that have the same shape and the same size. For congruent polygons, corresponding angles are congruent and corresponding sides are congruent. The symbol ≅ indicates congruence and is read "is congruent to."	$\triangle ABC \cong \triangle DEF$
polígonos congruentes (pág. 537) Polígonos similares que tienen la misma forma y el mismo tamaño. Para polígonos congruentes, los ángulos correspondientes son congruentes y los lados correspondientes son congruentes. El signo ≅ indica congruencia y se lee "es congruente con".	
congruent sides (p. 523) Sides that have the same length.	*See* congruent polygons.
lados congruentes (pág. 523) Lados que tienen igual longitud.	*Véase* polígonos congruentes.
constant term (p. 342) A term that has a number but no variable.	In the expression $5y + 9$, the term 9 is a *constant term.*
término constante (pág. 342) Un término que tiene un número pero no una variable.	En la expresión $5y + 9$, el término 9 es un *término constante.*

coordinate plane (p. 313) A coordinate system formed by the intersection of a horizontal number line, called the *x*-axis, and a vertical number line, called the *y*-axis.

plano de coordenadas (pág. 313) Un sistema de coordenadas formado por la intersección de una recta numérica horizontal, llamada eje *x*, y una recta numérica vertical, llamada eje *y*.

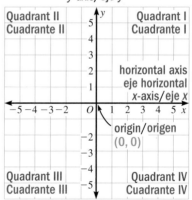

corresponding angles (p. 517) Angles that occupy corresponding positions when a line intersects two other lines.

ángulos correspondientes (pág. 517) Ángulos que ocupan posiciones correspondientes cuando una recta interseca otras dos rectas.

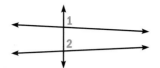

$\angle 1$ and $\angle 2$ are *corresponding angles*.

$\angle 1$ y $\angle 2$ son *ángulos correspondientes*.

counting principle (p. 696) If one event can occur in *m* ways, and for each of these a second event can occur in *n* ways, then the number of ways that the two events can occur together is $m \cdot n$. The counting principle can be extended to three or more events.

If a T-shirt is made in 5 sizes and in 7 colors, then the number of different T-shirts that are possible is $5 \cdot 7 = 35$.

principio de conteo (pág. 696) Si un evento puede ocurrir de *m* maneras, y para cada una de éstas un segundo evento puede ocurrir de *n* maneras, entonces el número de maneras en las que pueden ocurrir ambos eventos juntos es $m \cdot n$. El principio de conteo puede extenderse a tres o más eventos.

Si una camiseta se hace en 5 tallas y 7 colores, entonces el número de camisetas diferentes posibles es $5 \cdot 7 = 35$.

cross products (p. 423) For the proportion $\frac{a}{b} = \frac{c}{d}$, where $b \neq 0$ and $d \neq 0$, the cross product are *ad* and *bc*.

The *cross products* of the proportion $\frac{2}{3} = \frac{4}{6}$ are $2 \cdot 6$ and $3 \cdot 4$.

productos cruzados (pág. 423) Para la proporción $\frac{a}{b} = \frac{c}{d}$, donde $b \neq 0$ y $d \neq 0$, los productos cruzados son *ad* y *bc*.

Los *productos cruzados* de la proporción $\frac{2}{3} = \frac{4}{6}$ son $2 \cdot 6$ y $3 \cdot 4$.

cross products property (p. 423) The cross products of a proportion are equal.

If $\frac{4}{9} = \frac{x}{27}$, then $4 \cdot 27 = 9x$.
If $\frac{a}{b} = \frac{c}{d}$ where $b \neq 0$ and $d \neq 0$, then $ad = bc$.

propiedad de los productos cruzados (pág. 423) Los productos cruzados de una proporción son iguales.

Si $\frac{4}{9} = \frac{x}{27}$, entonces $4 \cdot 27 = 9x$.
Si $\frac{a}{b} = \frac{c}{d}$ donde $b \neq 0$ y $d \neq 0$, entonces $ad = bc$.

cylinder (p. 631) A solid with two congruent circular bases that lie in parallel planes.

cilindro (pág. 631) Un cuerpo geométrico que tiene dos bases circulares congruentes que se ubican en planos paralelos.

bases/bases

D

data (p. 757) Information, facts, or numbers that describe something.

datos (pág.757) Información, hechos o números que decriben algo.

Numbers of cars sold annually at a dealership:
340, 350, 345, 347, 352, 360, 365

Cantidades de carros vendidos anualmente en un concesionario:
340, 350, 345, 347, 352, 360, 365

---

decimal (p. 56) A number written using the base-ten place value system where a decimal point separates the ones' and tenths' digits.

decimal (pág. 56) Un número que se escribe usando el sistema de valor posicional de base diez en el que un punto decimal separa el dígito en la posición de las unidades del dígito en la posición de las décimas.

2.6 and 7.053 are *decimals*.

2.6 y 7.053 son *decimales*.

---

degrees (p. 474) Unit of measure for angles. The symbol for degrees is °. There are 360° in a circle.

grados (pág. 474) Unidad de medida para ángulos. El símbolo para los grados es °. Hay 360° en un círculo.

---

denominator (p. 176) The number b in the fraction $\frac{a}{b}$ where $b \neq 0$.

denominador (pág. 176) El número b en la fracción $\frac{a}{b}$ donde $b \neq 0$.

The *denominator* of $\frac{7}{13}$ is 13.

El *denominador* de $\frac{7}{13}$ es 13.

---

dependent events (p. 715) Two events such that the occurrence of one affects the likelihood that the other will occur.

eventos dependientes (pág. 715) Dos eventos tales que la ocurrencia de uno afecta la probabilidad de que ocurra el otro.

A bag contains 5 red and 8 blue marbles. You randomly choose a marble, do not replace it, then randomly choose another marble. The events "first marble is red" and "second marble is red" are *dependent events*.

Una bolsa contiene 5 canicas rojas y 8 azules. Tomas una canica al azar y no la reemplazas, luego tomas otra canica al azar. Los eventos "primera canica es roja" y "segunda canica es roja" son *eventos dependientes*.

---

diagonal (p. 531) A segment, other than a side, that connects two vertices of a polygon.

diagonal (pág. 531) Un segmento, distinto de un lado, que conecta dos vértices de un polígono.

diagonals/ diagonales

diameter of a circle (p. 607) The distance across the circle through its center.	*See* circle.
diámetro de un círculo (pág. 607) La distancia que atraviesa el círculo por el centro.	*Véase* círculo.
difference (p. 742) The result when one number is subtracted from another.	The *difference* of 7 and 3 is 7 − 3, or 4.
diferencia (pág. 742) El resultado cuando un número se resta de otro número.	La *diferencia* de 7 y 3 es 7 − 3, ó 4.
disjoint events (p. 709) Events that have no outcomes in common.	When rolling a number cube, the events "getting an odd number" and "getting a 4" are *disjoint events.*
eventos disjuntos (pág. 709) Eventos que no tienen resultados en común.	Al lanzar un cubo numerado, los eventos "obtener un número impar" y "obtener 4" son *eventos disjuntos.*
distributive property (p. 307) For all numbers a, b, and c, $a(b + c) = ab + ac$ and $a(b − c) = ab − ac$.	$$8(10 + 4) = 8(10) + 8(4)$$ $$3(4 − 2) = 3(4) − 3(2)$$
propiedad distributiva (pág. 307) Para todos los números a, b y c, $a(b + c) = ab + ac$ y $a(b − c) = ab − ac$.	
dividend (p. 744) A number that is divided by another number.	In $18 \div 6 = 3$, the *dividend* is 18.
dividendo (pág. 744) Un número que es dividido por otro número.	En $18 \div 6 = 3$, el *dividendo* es 18.
division property of equality (p. 354) Dividing each side of an equation by the same nonzero number produces an equivalent equation.	If $6x = 54$, then $\frac{6x}{6} = \frac{54}{6}$, so $x = 9$. If $ax = b$ and $a \neq 0$, then $\frac{ax}{a} = \frac{b}{a}$.
propiedad de igualdad en la división (pág. 354) Al dividir cada lado de una ecuación por el mismo número distinto de cero se obtiene una ecuación equivalente.	Si $6x = 54$, entonces $\frac{6x}{6} = \frac{54}{6}$, por lo tanto $x = 9$. Si $ax = b$ y $a \neq 0$, entonces $\frac{ax}{a} = \frac{b}{a}$.
divisor (p. 744) The number by which another number is divided.	In $18 \div 6 = 3$, the *divisor* is 6.
divisor (pág. 744) El número por el que otro número es dividido.	En $18 \div 6 = 3$, el *divisor* es 6.
domain of a function (p. 371) The set of all input values for the function.	*See* function.
dominio de una función (pág. 371) El conjunto de todos los valores de entrada para la función.	*Véase* función.

edge of a solid (p. 632) A line segment where two faces of the solid meet.

arista de un cuerpo geométrico (pág. 632) Un segmento de recta donde se encuentran dos caras del cuerpo geométrico.

element (p. 688) An object in a set.

elemento (pág. 688) Un objeto en un conjunto.

5 is an *element* of the set of whole numbers, $W = \{0, 1, 2, 3, 4, 5, \ldots\}$.

5 es un *elemento* en el conjunto de los números naturales $N = \{0, 1, 2, 3, 4, 5, \ldots\}$.

empty set (p. 690) The set with no elements, written as $\varnothing$.

conjunto vacío (pág. 690) El conjunto que no tiene elementos, que se expresa como $\varnothing$.

The set of fraction whole numbers $= \varnothing$.

El conjunto de números naturales que son fracciones $= \varnothing$.

equation (p. 25) A mathematical sentence formed by setting two expressions equal.

ecuación (pág. 25) Un enunciado matemático que se forma al establecer como iguales dos expresiones.

$3 \cdot 6 = 18$ and $x + 7 = 12$ are *equations*.

$3 \cdot 6 = 18$ y $x + 7 = 12$ son *ecuaciones*.

equilateral triangle (p. 523) A triangle with three congruent sides.

triángulo equilátero (pág. 523) Un triángulo que tiene tres lados congruentes.

equivalent equations (p. 347) Equations that have the same solution(s).

ecuaciones equivalentes (pág. 347) Ecuaciones que tienen la misma solución o soluciones.

$2x - 6 = 0$ and $2x = 6$ are *equivalent equations* because the solution of both equations is 3.

$2x - 6 = 0$ y $2x = 6$ son *ecuaciones equivalentes* porque la solución de ambas ecuaciones es 3.

equivalent expressions (p. 307) Expressions that have the same value when simplified.

expresiones equivalentes (pág. 307) Expresiones que tienen el mismo valor cuando se las simplifica.

$4(3 + 5)$ and $4(3) + 4(5)$ are *equivalent expressions* because $4(3 + 5) = 4(8) = 32$ and $4(3) + 4(5) = 12 + 20 = 32$.

$4(3 + 5)$ y $4(3) + 4(5)$ son *expresiones equivalentes* porque $4(3 + 5) = 4(8) = 32$ y $4(3) + 4(5) = 12 + 20 = 32$.

equivalent fractions (p. 176) Fractions that represent the same part-to-whole relationship. Equivalent fractions have the same simplest form.

fracciones equivalentes (pág. 176) Fracciones que representan la misma relación entre la parte y el todo. Las fracciones equivalentes tienen la misma mínima expresión.

$\frac{6}{8}$ and $\frac{9}{12}$ are *equivalent fractions* that both represent $\frac{3}{4}$.

$\frac{6}{8}$ y $\frac{9}{12}$ son *fracciones equivalentes* porque ambas representan $\frac{3}{4}$.

equivalent inequalities (p. 366) Inequalities that have the same solution.	$3x \le 12$ and $x \le 4$ are *equivalent inequalities* because the solution of both inequalities is all numbers less than or equal to 4.
desigualdades equivalentes (pág. 366) Desigualdades que tienen la misma solución.	$3x \le 12$ y $x \le 4$ son *desigualdades equivalentes* porque la solución de ambas desigualdades es todos los números menores que o iguales a 4.
equivalent ratios (p. 399) Ratios that have the same value.	$\frac{15}{12}$ and $\frac{25}{20}$ are *equivalent ratios* because $\frac{15}{12} = 1.25$ and $\frac{25}{20} = 1.25$.
razones equivalentes (pág. 399) Razones que tienen el mismo valor.	$\frac{15}{12}$ y $\frac{25}{20}$ son *razones equivalentes* porque $\frac{15}{12} = 1.25$ y $\frac{25}{20} = 1.25$.
equivalent variable expressions (p. 342) Expressions that are equal for every value of each variable they contain.	$5(x - 3)$ and $5x - 15$ are *equivalent variable expressions*.
expresiones variables equivalentes (pág. 342) Expresiones que son iguales para cada valor de cada variable que contienen.	$5(x - 3)$ y $5x - 15$ son *expresiones variables equivalentes*.
evaluating a variable expression (p. 8) Substituting a value for each variable in the expression and simplifying the resulting numerical expression.	Evaluating $2x + 3y$ when $x = 1$ and $y = 4$ gives $2(1) + 3(4) = 2 + 12 = 14$.
hallar el valor de una expresión variable (pág. 8) Sustituir con un valor cada variable de la expresión y simplificar la expresión numérica resultante.	Al hallar el valor de $2x + 3y$ cuando $x = 1$ e $y = 4$ se obtiene $2(1) + 3(4) = 2 + 12 = 14$.
event (p. 682) A collection of outcomes of an experiment.	An *event* that involves tossing a coin is "getting heads."
evento (pág. 682) Un conjunto de resultados de un experimento.	Al lanzar una moneda, "obtener cara" es un *evento*.
experimental probability (p. 683) A probability based on repeated trials of an experiment. The experimental probability of an event is given by: $$P(\text{event}) = \frac{\text{Number of successes}}{\text{Number of trials}}$$	During one month, your school bus is on time 17 out of 22 school days. The *experimental probability* that the bus is on time is: $$P(\text{bus is on time}) = \frac{17}{22} \approx 0.773$$
probabilidad experimental (pág. 683) Una probabilidad basada en el número de ensayos de un experimento. La probabilidad experimental de un evento se expresa: $$P(\text{evento}) = \frac{\text{Número de éxitos}}{\text{Número de ensayos}}$$	Durante un mes, tu autobús llega a tiempo 17 de 22 días escolares. La *probabilidad experimental* de que el autobús llegue a tiempo es: $$P(\text{autobús a tiempo}) = \frac{17}{22} \approx 0.773$$
exponent (p. 13) A number that represents how many times a base is used as a factor in a repeated multiplication.	In the power 5^3, the *exponent* is 3.
exponente (pág. 13) Un número que representa cuántas veces una base se usa como factor en una multiplicación repetida.	El *exponente* de la potencia 5^3 es 3.

ENGLISH-SPANISH GLOSSARY

F

face of a solid (p. 632) A polygon that is a side of the solid.

cara de un cuerpo geométrico (pág. 632) Un polígono que forma un lado del cuerpo geométrico.

See edge of a solid.

Véase arista de un cuerpo geométrico.

factor (p. 165) When whole numbers other than zero are multiplied together, each number is a factor of the product.

factor (pág. 165) Cuando los números naturales distintos de cero se multiplican entre sí, cada número es un factor del producto.

Because $2 \times 3 \times 7 = 42$, 2, 3, and 7 are *factors* of 42.

Como $2 \times 3 \times 7 = 42$, 2, 3 y 7 son *factores* de 42.

factor tree (p. 166) A diagram that can be used to write the prime factorization of a number.

árbol de factores (pág. 166) Un diagrama que puede usarse para escribir la descomposición de un número en factores primos.

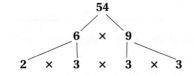

favorable outcomes (p. 682) Outcomes corresponding to a specified event.

resultados favorables (pág. 682) Los resultados correspondientes a un evento determinado.

When rolling a number cube, the *favorable outcomes* for the event "getting a number greater than 4" are 5 and 6.

Al lanzar un cubo numerado, los *resultados favorables* para el evento "obtener un número mayor que 4" son 5 y 6.

fraction (p. 176) A number of the form $\frac{a}{b}$ where $b \neq 0$.

fracción (pág. 176) Un número de la forma $\frac{a}{b}$ donde $b \neq 0$.

$\frac{5}{7}$ and $\frac{18}{10}$ are *fractions*.

$\frac{5}{7}$ y $\frac{18}{10}$ son *fracciones*.

frequency (p. 138) The number of data values that lie in an interval of a frequency table or histogram.

frecuencia (pág. 138) El número de valores en un conjunto de datos que se ubican en un intervalo de una tabla de frecuencias o histograma.

See frequency table *and* histogram.

Véase tabla de frecuencias e histograma.

frequency table (p. 138) A table used to group data values into intervals.

tabla de frecuencias (pág. 138) Una tabla que se usa para agrupar valores de un conjunto de datos en intervalos.

Interval Intervalo	Tally Marca	Frequency Frecuencia
0–9	II	2
10–19	IIII	4
20–29	JHT	5
30–39	III	3
40–49	IIII	4

front-end estimation (p. 61) A method for estimating the sum of two or more numbers. In this method, you add the front-end digits, estimate the sum of the remaining digits, and then add the results.

estimación por la izquierda (pág. 61) Un método para estimar la suma de dos o más números. En este método, se suman los dígitos de la izquierda, se estima la suma de los dígitos restantes y luego se suman los resultados.

To estimate $3.81 + 1.32 + 5.74$, first add the front-end digits: $3 + 1 + 5 = 9$. Then estimate the sum of the remaining digits: $0.81 + (0.32 + 0.74) \approx 1 + 1 = 2$. The sum is about $9 + 2 = 11$.

Para estimar la suma de $3.81 + 1.32 + 5.74$, suma primero los dígitos de la izquierda: $3 + 1 + 5 = 9$. Luego estima la suma de los dígitos restantes: $0.81 + (0.32 + 0.74) \approx 1 + 1 = 2$. La suma es aproximadamente $9 + 2 = 11$.

function (p. 371) A pairing of each number in a given set with exactly one number in another set. Starting with a number called an input, the function associates with it exactly one number called an output.

función (pág. 371) La asociación de cada número en un conjunto dado con exactamente un número de otro conjunto. Comenzando con un número llamado de entrada, la función asocia con él exactamente un número llamado de salida.

Input/Entrada, x	1	2	3	4
Output/Salida, y	2	4	6	8

The input-output table above represents a *function*.

La tabla anterior de entrada y salida representa una *función*.

graph of an inequality (p. 366) A set of points on a number line that represents the solution of the inequality. An open dot on a graph indicates a number that is not part of the solution. A closed dot indicates a number that is part of the solution.

gráfica de una desigualdad (pág. 366) Conjunto de puntos en una recta numérica que representa la solución de la desigualdad. Un punto hueco en una gráfica indica un número que no es parte de la solución. Un punto sólido indica un número que es parte de la solución.

The *graph of the inequality* $x < 2$ is shown below. The open dot at 2 shows that 2 is not part of the solution of the inequality.

A continuación se muestra la *gráfica de la desigualdad* $x < 2$. El punto hueco muestra que 2 no es parte de la solución de la desigualdad.

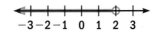

greatest common factor (GCF) (p. 170) The greatest whole number that is a factor of two or more nonzero whole numbers.

máximo común divisor (MCD) (pág. 170) El mayor número natural que es un factor de dos o mas números naturales distintos de cero.

The *GCF* of 18 and 27 is 9.
The *GCF* of 48, 24, and 36 is 12.

El *MCD* de 18 y 27 es 9.
El *MCD* de 48, 24 y 36 es 12.

height of a parallelogram (p. 594) The perpendicular distance between the side whose length is the base and the opposite side.

altura de un paralelogramo (pág. 594) La distancia perpendicular entre el lado cuya longitud es la base y el lado opuesto.

See base of a parallelogram.

Véase base de un paralelogramo.

height of a trapezoid (p. 602) The perpendicular distance between the bases of the trapezoid.

altura de un trapecio (pág. 602) La distancia perpendicular entre las bases de un trapecio.

See bases of a trapezoid.

Véase bases de un trapecio.

---

height of a triangle (p. 601) The perpendicular distance between the side whose length is the base and the vertex opposite that side.

altura de un triángulo (pág. 601) La distancia perpendicular entre el lado cuya longitud es la base y el vértice opuesto a ese lado.

See base of a triangle.

Véase base de un triángulo.

---

heptagon (p. 530) A polygon with seven sides.

heptágono (pág. 530) Polígono que tiene siete lados.

---

hexagon (p. 530) A polygon with six sides.

hexágono (pág. 530) Polígono que tiene seis lados.

---

histogram (p. 139) A graph that displays data from a frequency table. A histogram has one bar for each interval of the table that contains data values. The length of the bar indicates the frequency for the interval.

histograma (pág. 139) Una gráfica que muestra datos de una tabla de frecuencias. Un histograma tiene una barra para cada intervalo de la tabla que contiene valores de datos. La longitud de la barra indica la frecuencia para el intervalo.

---

horizontal axis (p. 118) The horizontal number line of a graph.

eje horizontal (pág. 118) La recta numérica horizontal de una gráfica.

See coordinate plane.

Véase plano de coordenadas.

---

hypotenuse (p. 588) The side of a right triangle that is opposite the right angle.

hipotenusa (pág. 588) El lado de un triángulo rectángulo que está opuesto al ángulo recto.

I

identity property of addition (p. 302) The sum of a number and the additive identity, 0, is the number. **propiedad de identidad de la suma** (pág. 302) La suma de un número y la identidad de la suma, 0, es el mismo número.	$8 + 0 = 8$ $a + 0 = a$
identity property of multiplication (p. 302) The product of a number and the multiplicative identity, 1, is the number. **propiedad de identidad de la multiplicación** (pág. 302) El producto de un número y la identidad de la multiplicación, 1, es el mismo número.	$4 \cdot 1 = 4$ $a \cdot 1 = a$
image (p. 548) The new figure formed by a transformation. **imagen** (pág. 548) La figura nueva formada por una transformación.	*See* reflection, rotation, *and* translation. *Véase* reflexión, rotación *y* traslación.
improper fraction (p. 194) A fraction whose numerator is greater than or equal to its denominator. **fracción impropia** (pág. 194) Una fracción en la cual el numerador es mayor que el denominador o igual a él.	$\frac{8}{7}$ is an *improper fraction*. $\frac{8}{7}$ es una *fracción impropia*.
independent events (p. 715) Two events such that the occurrence of one event does not affect the likelihood that the other will occur. **eventos independientes** (pág. 715) Dos eventos tales que la ocurrencia de uno no afecta la probabilidad de que ocurra el otro.	You toss a coin and roll a number cube. The events "getting heads" and "getting a 6" are *independent events*. Lanzas una moneda y después lanzas un cubo numerado. Los eventos "obtener cara" y "obtener 6" son *eventos independientes*.
inequality (p. 366) A mathematical sentence formed by placing an inequality symbol between two expressions. **desigualdad** (pág. 366) Un enunciado matemático formado colocando un símbolo de desigualdad entre dos expresiones.	$3 < 5$ and $x + 2 \geq -4$ are *inequalities*. $3 < 5$ y $x + 2 \geq -4$ son *desigualdades*.
input (p. 371) A number on which a function operates. An input value is in the domain of the function. **entrada** (pág. 371) Número sobre el que opera una función. Un valor de entrada está en el dominio de la función.	*See* function. *Véase* función.
integers (p. 269) The numbers . . . , $-4, -3, -2, -1, 0, 1, 2,$ $3, 4, \ldots$ consisting of the negative integers, zero, and the positive integers. **números enteros** (pág. 269) Los números ..., $-4, -3, -2,$ $-1, 0, 1, 2, 3, 4, \ldots$ que constan de los números enteros negativos, cero y los números enteros positivos.	-8 and 14 are *integers*. $-8\frac{1}{3}$ and 14.5 are not *integers*. -8 y 14 son *números enteros*. $-8\frac{1}{3}$ y 14.5 no son *números enteros*.

interest (p. 490) The amount earned or paid for the use of money. **interés** (pág. 490) La cantidad ganada o pagada por el uso de dinero.	*See* **simple interest.** *Véase* **interés simple.**
interquartile range (p. 133) The difference between the upper and lower quartiles in a box-and-whisker plot. **rango entre cuartiles** (pág. 133) La diferencia entre los cuartiles superior e inferior en un diagrama de líneas y bloques.	 The *interquartile range* is 37 − 19, or 18. El *rango entre cuartiles* es 37 − 19, ó 18.
intersecting lines (p. 517) Two lines that meet at a point. **rectas secantes** (pág. 517) Dos rectas que se encuentran en un punto.	
intersection of a set (p. 688) The set of all elements in both set A and set B, written as $A \cap B$. **intersección de conjuntos** (pág. 688) El conjunto de todos los elementos que están tanto en el conjunto A como en el conjunto B, que se expresa como $A \cap B$.	
inverse operations (p. 347) Operations that "undo" each other. **operaciones inversas** (pág. 347) Operaciones que se "deshacen" mutuamente.	Addition and subtraction are *inverse operations.* Multiplication and division are also *inverse operations.* La suma y la resta son *operaciones inversas.* La multiplicación y la división también son *operaciones inversas.*
inverse property of addition (p. 302) The sum of a number and its additive inverse, or opposite, is 0. **propiedad inversa de la suma** (pág. 302) La suma de un número y su inverso aditivo u opuesto, es cero.	$5 + (-5) = 0$ $a + (-a) = 0$
inverse property of multiplication (p. 302) The product of a nonzero number and its multiplicative inverse, or reciprocal, is 1. **propiedad inversa de la multiplicación** (pág. 302) El producto de un número distinto de cero y su inverso multiplicativo, o recíproco, es 1.	$\dfrac{3}{4} \cdot \dfrac{4}{3} = 1$ $\dfrac{a}{b} \cdot \dfrac{b}{a} = 1 \quad (a, b \neq 0)$

irrational number (p. 583) A real number that cannot be written as a quotient of two integers. The decimal form of an irrational number neither terminates nor repeats.

$\sqrt{2}$ and 0.313113111... are *irrational numbers*.

número irracional (pág. 583) Un número real que no puede escribirse como un cociente de dos números enteros. La forma decimal de un número irracional no termina ni se repite.

$\sqrt{2}$ y 0.313113111... son *números irracionales*.

---

isosceles triangle (p. 523) A triangle with at least two congruent sides.

triángulo isósceles (pág. 523) Un triángulo que tiene al menos dos lados congruentes.

L

leading digit (p. 66) The first nonzero digit in a number.

The *leading digit* of 725 is 7.
The *leading digit* of 0.002638 is 2.

dígito dominante (pág. 66) El primer dígito distinto de cero en un número.

El *dígito dominante* de 725 es 7.
El *dígito dominante* de 0.002638 es 2.

---

least common denominator (LCD) (p. 189) The least common multiple of the denominators of two or more fractions.

The *LCD* of $\frac{7}{10}$ and $\frac{3}{4}$ is 20, the least common multiple of 10 and 4.

mínimo común denominador (m.c.d.) (pág. 189) El mínimo común múltiplo de los denominadores de dos o más fracciones.

El *m.c.d.* de $\frac{7}{10}$ y $\frac{3}{4}$ es 20, que es el mínimo común múltiplo de 10 y 4.

---

least common multiple (LCM) (p. 182) The least number that is a common multiple of two or more numbers.

The *LCM* of 4 and 6 is 12.
The *LCM* of 3, 5, and 10 is 30.

mínimo común múltiplo (m.c.m.) (pág. 182) El menor de los múltiplos comunes de dos o más números.

El *m.c.m.* de 4 y 6 es 12.
El *m.c.m.* de 3, 5 y 10 es 30.

---

legs of a right triangle (p. 588) The two sides of a right triangle that form the right angle.

See hypotenuse.

catetos de un triángulo rectángulo (pág. 588) Los dos lados de un triángulo rectángulo que forman el ángulo recto.

Véase hipotenusa.

---

like terms (p. 342) Terms that have identical variable parts. (Two or more constant terms are considered like terms.)

In the expression $x + 4 - 2x + 1$, x and $-2x$ are *like terms*, and 4 and 1 are *like terms*.

términos semejantes (pág. 342) Términos que tienen partes variables idénticas. (Dos o más términos constantes se consideran términos semejantes.)

En la expresión $x + 4 - 2x + 1$, x y $-2x$ son *términos semejantes*, y 4 y 1 son *términos semejantes*.

line graph (p. 118) A type of graph in which points representing data pairs are connected by line segments.

gráfica lineal (pág. 118) Un tipo de gráfica en la que los puntos que representan pares de datos se conectan por segmentos de recta.

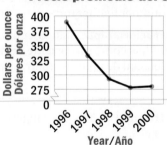

line of reflection (p. 548) The line in which a figure is flipped when the figure undergoes a reflection.

línea de reflexión (pág. 548) La recta sobre la que se invierte una figura cuando dicha figura se refleja.

See reflection.

Véase reflexión.

line of symmetry (p. 550) A line that divides a figure into two parts that are mirror images of each other.

línea de simetría (pág. 550) Una recta que divide una figura en dos partes que son imágenes reflejas entre sí.

See line symmetry.

Véase simetría lineal.

line plot (p. 758) A number line diagram that uses X marks to show the frequencies of items or categories being tallied.

diagrama lineal (pág. 758) Un diagrama de recta numérica que usa marcas X para mostrar las frecuencias con las que se marcan artículos o categorías.

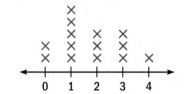

line symmetry (p. 550) A figure has line symmetry if it can be divided by a line, called a line of symmetry, into two parts that are mirror images of each other.

simetría lineal (pág. 550) Una figura tiene simetría lineal si puede dividirse por una recta, llamada línea de simetría, en dos partes que son imágenes reflejas entre sí.

A square has 4 *lines of symmetry*.

Un cuadrado tiene 4 *líneas de simetría*.

linear function (p. 377) A function whose graph is a line or part of a line.

función lineal (pág. 377) Una función cuya gráfica es una recta o parte de una recta.

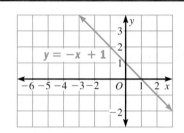

lower extreme (p. 133) The least value in a data set.	*See* **box-and-whisker plot.**
extremo inferior (pág. 133) El menor valor en un conjunto de datos.	*Véase* **diagrama de líneas y bloques.**
lower quartile (p. 133) The median of the lower half of a data set.	*See* **box-and-whisker plot.**
cuartil inferior (pág. 133) La mediana de la mitad inferior de un conjunto de datos.	*Véase* **diagrama de líneas y bloques.**

M

mean (p. 109) The sum of the values in a data set divided by the number of values.	The *mean* of the data set $$85, 59, 97, 71$$ is $\frac{85 + 59 + 97 + 71}{4} = \frac{312}{4} = 78.$
media (pág. 109) La suma de los valores en un conjunto de datos dividida por el número de valores.	La *media* del conjunto de datos $$85, 59, 97, 71$$ es $\frac{85 + 59 + 97 + 71}{4} = \frac{312}{4} = 78.$
median (p. 109) The middle value in a data set when the values are written in numerical order. If the data set has an even number of values, the median is the mean of the two middle values.	The *median* of the data set $$8, 17, 21, 23, 26, 29, 34, 40, 45$$ is the middle value, 26.
mediana (pág. 109) El valor que está en el medio de un conjunto de datos cuando los valores están escritos en orden numérico. Si el conjunto de datos tiene un número par de valores, la mediana es la media de los dos valores que están en el medio.	La *mediana* del conjunto de datos $$8, 17, 21, 23, 26, 29, 34, 40, 45$$ es 26, el valor que está en el medio.
mixed number (p. 194) A number that has a whole number part and a fraction part.	$3\frac{2}{5}$ is a *mixed number.*
número mixto (pág. 194) Un número que tiene una parte que es un número natural y una parte que es una fracción.	$3\frac{2}{5}$ es un *número mixto.*
mode (p. 109) The value in a data set that occurs most often. A data set can have no mode, one mode, or more than one mode.	The *mode* of the data set $$73, 42, 55, 77, 61, 55, 68$$ is 55 because it occurs most often.
moda (pág. 109) En un conjunto de datos, el valor que ocurre con mayor frecuencia. Un conjunto de datos puede no tener moda, o puede tener una moda o más de una moda.	La *moda* del conjunto de datos $$73, 42, 55, 77, 61, 55, 68$$ es 55 porque es el valor que aparece más veces.
multiple (p. 182) The product of a number and any nonzero whole number.	The *multiples* of 3 are 3, 6, 9, ...
múltiplo (pág. 182) El producto de un número y cualquier número natural distinto de cero.	Los *múltiplos* de 3 son 3, 6, 9, ...

ENGLISH-SPANISH GLOSSARY

multiplication property of equality (p. 355) Multiplying each side of an equation by the same nonzero number produces an equivalent equation. **propiedad de igualdad en la multiplicación** (pág. 355) Al multiplicar cada lado de una ecuación por el mismo número distinto de cero se obtiene una ecuación equivalente.	If $\frac{x}{3} = 7$, then $3 \cdot \frac{x}{3} = 3 \cdot 7$, so x = 21. If $\frac{x}{a} = b$ and $a \neq 0$, then $a \cdot \frac{x}{a} = a \cdot b$. Si $\frac{x}{3} = 7$, entonces $3 \cdot \frac{x}{3} = 3 \cdot 7$, por lo tanto x = 21. Si $\frac{x}{a} = b$ y $a \neq 0$, entonces $a \cdot \frac{x}{a} = a \cdot b$.
multiplicative identity (p. 302) The number 1 is the multiplicative identity because the product of any number and 1 is the original number. **identidad de la multiplicación** (pág. 302) El número 1 es la identidad de la multiplicación porque el producto de cualquier número y 1 es el número original.	$$9 \cdot 1 = 9$$ $$a \cdot 1 = a$$
multiplicative inverse (p. 302) The multiplicative inverse of a number $\frac{a}{b}$ ($a, b \neq 0$) is the reciprocal of the number, or $\frac{b}{a}$. The product of a number and its multiplicative inverse is 1. **inverso multiplicativo** (pág. 302) El inverso multiplicativo de un número $\frac{a}{b}$ ($a, b \neq 0$) es el recíproco de dicho número, es decir, $\frac{b}{a}$. El producto de un número y su inverso multiplicativo es 1.	The *multiplicative inverse* of $\frac{3}{2}$ is $\frac{2}{3}$, so $\frac{3}{2} \cdot \frac{2}{3} = 1$. El *inverso multiplicativo* de $\frac{3}{2}$ es $\frac{2}{3}$, por lo tanto $\frac{3}{2} \cdot \frac{2}{3} = 1$.

N

negative integers (p. 269) The integers that are less than zero. **números enteros negativos** (pág. 269) Números enteros menores que cero.	The *negative integers* are $-1, -2, -3, -4, \ldots$. Los *números enteros negativos* son $-1, -2, -3, -4, \ldots$
net (p. 642) A two-dimensional representation of a solid. **red** (pág. 642) Representación bidimensional de un cuerpo geométrico.	
numerator (p. 176) The number a in the fraction $\frac{a}{b}$. **numerador** (pág. 176) El número a en la fracción $\frac{a}{b}$.	The *numerator* of $\frac{7}{13}$ is 7. El *numerador* de $\frac{7}{13}$ es 7.

O

obtuse angle (p. 511) An angle whose measure is between 90° and 180°. **ángulo obtuso** (pág. 511) Ángulo cuya medida es mayor que 90° y menor que 180°.	

obtuse triangle (p. 522) A triangle with one obtuse angle. **triángulo obtusángulo** (pág. 522) Triángulo que tiene un ángulo obtuso.	 120° 35° 25°
octagon (p. 530) A polygon with eight sides. **octágono** (pág. 530) Polígono que tiene ocho lados.	
opposites (p. 269) Two numbers that are the same distance from 0 on a number line but are on opposite sides of 0. **opuestos** (pág. 269) Dos números que están a la misma distancia de 0 en una recta numérica pero en lados opuestos de 0.	−3 and 3 are *opposites*. −3 y 3 son *opuestos*.
order of operations (p. 17) A set of rules for evaluating an expression involving more than one operation. **orden de las operaciones** (pág. 17) Conjunto de reglas para hallar el valor de una expresión que tiene más de una operación.	To evaluate $3 + 2 \cdot 4$, you perform the multiplication before the addition: $$3 + 2 \cdot 4 = 3 + 8 = 11$$ Para hallar el valor de $3 + 2 \cdot 4$, haz la multiplicación antes que la suma: $$3 + 2 \cdot 4 = 3 + 8 = 11$$
ordered pair (p. 313) A pair of numbers (x, y) that can be used to represent a point in a coordinate plane. The first number is the x-coordinate, and the second number is the y-coordinate. **par ordenado** (pág. 313) Par de números (x, y) que se puede usar para representar un punto en un plano de coordenadas. El primer número es la coordenada x y el segundo número es la coordenada y.	$(-2, 1)$
origin (p. 313) The point $(0, 0)$ where the x-axis and the y-axis meet in a coordinate plane. **origen** (pág. 313) El punto $(0, 0)$ donde se encuentran el eje x y el eje y en un plano de coordenadas.	*See* coordinate plane. *Véase* plano de coordenadas.
outcomes (p. 682) The possible results when an experiment is performed. **resultados** (pág. 682) Resultados posibles cuando se realiza un experimento.	When tossing a coin, the *outcomes* are heads and tails. Al lanzar una moneda, los *resultados* son cara y cruz.
output (p. 371) A number produced by evaluating a function using a given input. An output value is in the range of the function. **salida** (pág. 371) Número producido al hallar el valor de una función usando una entrada dada. Un valor de salida está dentro del rango de la función.	*See* function. *Véase* función.

ENGLISH-SPANISH GLOSSARY

overlapping events (p. 709) Events that have one or more outcomes in common.

eventos superpuestos (pág. 709) Eventos que tienen uno o más resultados en común.

When rolling a number cube, the events "getting a number less than 3" and "getting an even number" are *overlapping events* because they have the outcome 2 in common.

Al lanzar un cubo numerado, los eventos "obtener un número menor que 3" y "obtener un número par" son *eventos superpuestos*, ya que tienen el resultado 2 en común.

P

parallel lines (p. 517) Two lines in the same plane that do not intersect. The symbol ∥ is used to indicate parallel lines.

rectas paralelas (pág. 517) Dos rectas en el mismo plano que no se intersecan. Se usa el símbolo ∥ para indicar rectas paralelas.

parallelogram (p. 529) A quadrilateral with two pairs of parallel sides.

paralelogramo (pág. 529) Cuadrilátero que tiene dos pares de lados paralelos.

pentagon (p. 530) A polygon with five sides.

pentágono (pág. 530) Polígono que tiene cinco lados.

percent (p. 449) A ratio whose denominator is 100. The symbol for percent is %.

porcentaje (pág. 449) Razón cuyo denominador es 100. El símbolo de porcentaje es %.

$$\frac{17}{20} = \frac{17 \cdot 5}{20 \cdot 5} = \frac{85}{100} = 85\%$$

percent equation (p. 465) You can represent "*a* is *p* percent of *b*" with the equation $a = p\% \cdot b$ where *a* is the part of base *b* and *p*% is the percent.

ecuación de porcentaje (pág. 465) Puedes representar "*a* es *p* por ciento de *b*" con la ecuación $a = p\% \cdot b$, donde *a* es parte de la base *b* y *p*% es el porcentaje.

4.5 is 10 percent of 45 can be written as the equation $4.5 = 10\% \cdot 45$.

4.5 es el 10 por ciento de 45 se puede escribir como la ecuación $4.5 = 10\% \cdot 45$.

percent of change (p. 480) A percent that shows how much a quantity has increased or decreased in comparison with the original amount:

Percent of change $p = \dfrac{\text{Amount of increase or decrease}}{\text{Original amount}}$

porcentaje de cambio (pág. 480) Porcentaje que muestra cuánto ha aumentado o disminuido una cantidad en comparación con la cantidad original:

Porcentaje de cambio $p = \dfrac{\text{Cantidad de aumento o disminución}}{\text{Cantidad original}}$

The *percent of change p* from 15 to 19 is:
$$p = \frac{19 - 15}{15} = \frac{4}{15} \approx 0.267 = 26.7\%$$

El *porcentaje de cambio p* de 15 a 19 es:
$$p = \frac{19 - 15}{15} = \frac{4}{15} \approx 0.267 = 26.7\%$$

percent of decrease (p. 480) The percent of change in a quantity when the new amount of the quantity is less than the original amount.

See **percent of change.**

porcentaje de disminución (pág. 480) Porcentaje de cambio en una cantidad cuando el valor nuevo de una cantidad es menor que la cantidad original.

Véase **porcentaje de cambio.**

percent of increase (p. 480) The percent of change in a quantity when the new amount of the quantity is greater than the original amount.

See **percent of change.**

porcentaje de aumento (pág. 480) Porcentaje de cambio en una cantidad cuando el valor nuevo de una cantidad es mayor que la cantidad original.

Véase **porcentaje de cambio.**

perfect square (p. 577) A number that is the square of an integer.

49 is a *perfect square* because $49 = 7^2$.

cuadrado perfecto (pág. 577) Un número que es el cuadrado de un número entero.

49 es un *cuadrado perfecto* porque $49 = 7^2$.

perimeter (p. 32) The distance around a figure. For a figure with straight sides, the perimeter is the sum of the lengths of the sides.

perímetro (pág. 32) La distancia alrededor de una figura. Para una figura de lados rectos, el perímetro es la suma de las longitudes de los lados.

Perimeter = 22 ft

Perímetro = 22 pies

permutation (p. 702) An arrangement of a group of objects in a particular order.

There are 6 *permutations* of the 3 letters in the word CAT:

CAT ACT TCA CTA ATC TAC

permutación (pág. 702) Disposición de un grupo de objetos en un orden particular.

Hay 6 *permutaciones* de las 3 letras de la palabra MAR:

MAR AMR RMA MRA ARM RAM

perpendicular lines (p. 517) Two lines that intersect to form four right angles. The symbol $\perp$ is used to indicate perpendicular lines.

rectas perpendiculares (pág. 517) Dos rectas que se intersecan formando cuatro ángulos rectos. El símbolo $\perp$ se usa para indicar rectas perpendiculares.

$a \perp b$

plane (p. 517) A plane can be thought of as a flat surface that extends without end.

plano (pág. 517) Se puede pensar en un plano como una superficie plana que se extiende infinitamente.

polygon (p. 530) A geometric figure made up of three or more line segments that intersect only at their endpoints.

polígono (pág. 530) Figura geométrica compuesta de tres o más segmentos de recta que se intersecan sólo en sus extremos.

Polygon
Polígono

Not a polygon
No polígono

---

population (p. 115) In statistics, the entire group of people or objects about which you want information.

población (pág. 115) En estadística, todo el grupo de personas u objetos sobre los que se busca información.

If a biologist wants to determine the average age of the elephants in a wildlife refuge, the *population* consists of every elephant in the refuge.

Si un biólogo quiere determinar la edad promedio de los elefantes de un santuario animal, la *población* consiste en cada elefante del santuario.

---

positive integers (p. 269) The integers that are greater than zero.

números enteros positivos (pág. 269) Números enteros mayores que cero.

The *positive integers* are 1, 2, 3, 4, ...

Los *números enteros positivos* son 1, 2, 3, 4, ...

---

power (p. 13) A product formed from repeated multiplication by the same number or expression. A power consists of a base and an exponent.

potencia (pág. 13) Producto que se obtiene de la multiplicación repetida por el mismo número o expresión. Una potencia está compuesta de una base y un exponente.

2^4 is a *power* with base 2 and exponent 4.

2^4 es una *potencia* con base 2 y exponente 4.

---

prime factorization (p. 166) Expressing a whole number as a product of prime numbers.

descomposición en factores primos (pág. 166) Expresar un número natural como producto de números primos.

The *prime factorization* of 54 is $54 = 2 \times 3 \times 3 \times 3 = 2 \times 3^3$.

La *descomposición en factores primos* de 54 es $54 = 2 \times 3 \times 3 \times 3 = 2 \times 3^3$.

---

prime number (p. 165) A whole number greater than 1 whose only whole number factors are 1 and itself.

número primo (pág. 165) Número natural mayor que 1 cuyos únicos factores que son números naturales son 1 y él mismo.

5 is a *prime number* because its only whole number factors are 1 and 5.

5 es un *número primo*, porque sus únicos factores que son números naturales son 1 y 5.

---

principal (p. 490) An amount of money that is deposited or borrowed.

capital (pág. 490) Una cantidad de dinero que se deposita o se solicita en préstamo.

See simple interest.

Véase interés simple.

---

prism (p. 631) A solid, formed by polygons, that has two congruent bases lying in parallel planes.

prisma (pág. 631) Cuerpo geométrico formado por polígonos, que tiene dos bases congruentes ubicadas en planos paralelos.

bases/bases

Rectangular prism   **Triangular prism**
Prisma rectangular   **Prisma triangular**

---

probability of an event (p. 682) A number from 0 to 1 that measures the likelihood that the event will occur.

probabilidad de un evento (pág. 682) Número de 0 a 1 que mide la posibilidad de que ocurra un evento.

See **experimental probability** *and* **theoretical probability**.

Véase **probabilidad experimental** *y* **probabilidad teórica**.

---

product (p. 743) The result when two or more numbers are multiplied.

producto (pág. 743) Resultado cuando se multiplican dos o más números.

The *product* of 3 and 4 is 3×4, or 12.

El *producto* de 3 y 4 es 3×4, ó 12.

---

proper fraction (p. 194) A fraction whose numerator is less than its denominator.

fracción propia (pág. 194) Una fracción cuyo numerador es menor que su denominador.

$\frac{7}{8}$ is a *proper fraction*.

$\frac{7}{8}$ es una *fracción propia*.

---

proportion (p. 418) An equation stating that two ratios are equivalent.

proporción (pág. 418) Una ecuación que establece que dos razones son equivalentes.

$\frac{3}{5} = \frac{6}{10}$ and $\frac{x}{12} = \frac{25}{30}$ are *proportions*.

$\frac{3}{5} = \frac{6}{10}$ y $\frac{x}{12} = \frac{25}{30}$ son *proporciones*.

---

pyramid (p. 631) A solid, formed by polygons, that has one base. The base can be any polygon, and the other polygons are triangles.

pirámide (pág. 631) Cuerpo geométrico, formado por polígonos, que tiene una base. La base puede ser cualquier polígono, y los otros polígonos son triángulos.

base/base

Pythagorean theorem (p. 588) For any right triangle, the sum of the squares of the lengths a and b of the legs equals the square of the length c of the hypotenuse: $a^2 + b^2 = c^2$.

teorema de Pitágoras (pág. 588) Para cualquier triángulo rectángulo, la suma de los cuadrados de las longitudes a y b de los catetos es igual al cuadrado de la longitud c de la hipotenusa: $a^2 + b^2 = c^2$.

15   c

20

$15^2 + 20^2 = c^2$

Q

quadrant (p. 313) One of the four regions that a coordinate plane is divided into by the x-axis and the y-axis.

cuadrante (pág. 313) Una de las cuatro regiones en las que el eje x y el eje y dividen un plano de coordenadas.

See **coordinate plane**.

Véase **plano de coordenadas**.

quadrilateral (p. 529) A geometric figure made up of four line segments, called sides, that intersect only at their endpoints; a polygon with four sides. **cuadrilátero** (pág. 529) Figura geométrica formada por cuatro segmentos de recta, llamados lados, que se intersecan sólo en sus extremos; polígono de cuatro lados.	
quotient (p. 744) The result of a division. **cociente** (pág. 744) Resultado de una división.	The *quotient* of 18 and 6 is $18 \div 6$, or 3. El *cociente* de 18 y 6 es $18 \div 6$, ó 3.

R

radical expression (p. 578) An expression involving a radical sign, √. **expresión radical** (pág. 578) Expresión que tiene un signo radical, √.	$\sqrt{3(22 + 5)}$ is a *radical expression*. $\sqrt{3(22 + 5)}$ es una *expresión radical*.
radius of a circle (p. 607) The distance between the center and any point on the circle. **radio de un círculo** (pág. 607) Distancia entre cualquier punto del círculo y su centro.	*See* circle. *Véase* círculo.
random sample (p. 115) A sample selected in such a way that each member of the population has an equally likely chance to be part of the sample. **muestra aleatoria** (pág. 115) Muestra seleccionada de tal manera que cada miembro de la población tiene la misma probabilidad de formar parte de la muestra.	A *random sample* of 5 seventh graders can be selected by putting the names of all seventh graders in a hat and drawing 5 names without looking. Una *muestra aleatoria* de 5 estudiantes de séptimo grado puede seleccionarse colocando los nombres de todos los alumnos de séptimo grado en un sombrero y sacando 5 nombres sin mirar.
range of a data set (p. 110) The difference of the greatest and least values in the data set. **rango de un conjunto de datos** (pág. 110) La diferencia entre el valor mayor y el valor menor en un conjunto de datos.	The *range of the data set* $\qquad$ 60, 35, 22, 46, 81, 39 is $81 - 22 = 59$. El *rango del conjunto* de datos $\qquad$ 60, 35, 22, 46, 81, 39 es $81 - 22 = 59$.
range of a function (p. 371) The set of all output values for the function. **rango de una función** (pág. 371) Conjunto de todos los valores de salida posibles para la función.	*See* function. *Véase* función.

rate (p. 404) A ratio of two quantities measured in different units.	An airplane climbs 18,000 feet in 12 minutes. The airplane's *rate* of climb is $\frac{18{,}000 \text{ ft}}{12 \text{ min}} =$ 1,500 ft/min.
tasa (pág. 404) Razón entre dos cantidades medidas en unidades diferentes.	Un avión asciende 18,000 pies en 12 minutos. La *tasa* de ascenso del avión es $\frac{18{,}000 \text{ pies}}{12 \text{ min}} =$ 1,500 pies/min.
ratio (p. 399) A comparison of two numbers using division. The ratio of a to b (where $b \neq 0$) can be written as a to b, as $\frac{a}{b}$, or as $a : b$.	The *ratio* of 17 to 12 can be written as 17 to 12, as $\frac{17}{12}$, or as $17 : 12$.
razón (pág. 399) Comparación entre dos números usando la división. La razón de a a b (donde $b \neq 0$) puede escribirse como a a b, como $\frac{a}{b}$ o como $a : b$.	La *razón* de 17 a 12 puede escribirse como 17 a 12, como $\frac{17}{12}$ o como $17 : 12$.
rational number (p. 301) A number that can be written as $\frac{a}{b}$ where a and b are integers and $b \neq 0$.	$6 = \frac{6}{1}$, $-\frac{3}{5} = \frac{-3}{5}$, $0.75 = \frac{3}{4}$, and $2\frac{1}{3} = \frac{7}{3}$ are all *rational numbers*.
número racional (pág. 301) Un número que se puede escribir como $\frac{a}{b}$ donde a y b son números enteros y $b \neq 0$.	$6 = \frac{6}{1}$, $-\frac{3}{5} = \frac{-3}{5}$, $0.75 = \frac{3}{4}$ y $2\frac{1}{3} = \frac{7}{3}$ son todos *números racionales*.
ray (p. 474) A part of a line that begins at a point and extends in one direction without end.	
semirrecta (pág. 474) Una parte de una recta que comienza en un punto y se extiende infinitamente en una dirección.	
real numbers (p. 583) The set of all rational numbers and irrational numbers.	0, $-\frac{5}{9}$, 2.75, and $\sqrt{3}$ are all *real numbers*.
números reales (pág. 583) Conjunto de todos los números racionales e irracionales.	0, $-\frac{5}{9}$, 2.75 y $\sqrt{3}$ son todos *números reales*.
reciprocals (p. 237) Two nonzero numbers whose product is 1.	$\frac{2}{3}$ and $\frac{3}{2}$ are *reciprocals*.
recíprocos (pág. 237) Dos números distintos de cero cuyo producto es 1.	$\frac{2}{3}$ y $\frac{3}{2}$ son *recíprocos*.
reflection (p. 548) A transformation that reflects a figure in a line, called the reflection line, creating a mirror image of the figure; also known as a *flip*.	
reflexión (pág. 548) Transformación que refleja una figura en una recta, llamada línea de reflexión, creando una imagen espejo de la figura; también llamada *inversión*.	

regular polygon (p. 531) A polygon with all sides equal in length and all angles equal in measure.

polígono regular (pág. 531) Un polígono cuyos lados tienen igual longitud y cuyos ángulos tienen la misma medida.

Regular pentagon
Pentágono regular

regular pyramid (p. 660) A pyramid whose base is a regular polygon.

pirámide regular (pág. 660) Una pirámide cuya base es un polígono regular.

height/altura   slant height / altura inclinada

regular tessellation (p. 554) A tessellation made from only one type of regular polygon.

teselado regular (pág. 554) Teselado hecho con un solo tipo de polígono regular.

relatively prime numbers (p. 171) Two or more nonzero whole numbers whose greatest common factor is 1.

números relativamente primos (pág. 171) Dos o más números naturales distintos de cero cuyo máximo común divisor es 1.

9 and 16 are *relatively prime* because their GCF is 1.

9 y 16 son *relativamente primos* porque su MCD es un 1.

repeating decimal (p. 199) A decimal that has one or more digits that repeat without end.

decimal periódico (pág. 199) Decimal que tiene uno o más dígitos que se repiten infinitamente.

$0.7777\ldots$ and $1.\overline{29}$ are *repeating decimals*.

$0.7777\ldots$ y $1.\overline{29}$ son *decimales periódicos*.

rhombus (p. 529) A parallelogram with four congruent sides.

rombo (pág. 529) Paralelogramo que tiene cuatro lados congruentes.

right angle (p. 511) An angle whose measure is exactly 90°.

ángulo recto (pág. 511) Un ángulo que mide exactamente 90°.

right triangle (p. 522) A triangle with one right angle.

triángulo rectángulo (pág. 522) Un triángulo que tiene un ángulo recto.

50°   40°

rotation (p. 548) A transformation that rotates a figure through a given angle, called the angle of rotation, and in a given direction about a fixed point, called the center of rotation; also known as a *turn*.

rotación (pág. 548) Transformación que rota un figura por un ángulo dado, llamado ángulo de rotación, en una dirección dada alrededor de un punto fijo, llamado centro de rotación; también se conoce como *giro*.

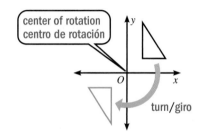

rotational symmetry (p. 550) A figure has a rotational symmetry if a turn of 180° or less produces an image that fits exactly on the original figure.

simetría de rotación (pág. 550) Una figura tiene simetría de rotación si un giro de 180° o menor produce una imagen que es igual a la figura original.

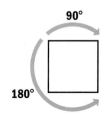

A square has *rotational symmetry*.

Un cuadrado tiene *simetría de rotación*.

 S

sample (p. 115) A part of a population.

muestra (pág. 115) Una parte de una población.

To predict the results of an election, a survey is given to a *sample* of voters.

Para predecir los resultados de unas elecciones, se encuesta a una *muestra* de votantes.

sample space (p. 690) The set of all possible outcomes.

espacio muestral (pág. 690) El conjunto de todos los resultados posibles.

The *sample space* for rolling a number cube is {1, 2, 3, 4, 5, 6}.

El *espacio muestral* de un cubo numérico que se ha lanzado es {1, 2, 3, 4, 5, 6}.

scale (p. 430) In a scale drawing, the scale gives the relationship between the drawing's dimensions and the actual dimensions.

escala (pág. 430) En un dibujo a escala, la escala muestra la relación entre las dimensiones del dibujo y las dimensiones reales.

The *scale* "1 in. : 10 ft" means that 1 inch in the scale drawing represents an actual distance of 10 feet.

La *escala* "1 pulg. : 10 pies" significa que una pulgada en el dibujo a escala representa una distancia real de 10 pies.

scale drawing (p. 430) A diagram of an object in which the dimensions are in proportion to the actual dimensions of the object.

dibujo a escala (pág. 430) Un diagrama de un objeto cuyas dimensiones están en proporción con las dimensiones reales del objeto.

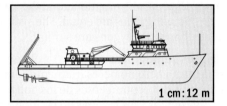

1 cm : 12 m

scale model (p. 431) A model of an object in which the dimensions are in proportion to the actual dimensions of the object.

modelo a escala (pág. 431) Un modelo de un objeto cuyas dimensiones están en proporción con las dimensiones reales del objeto.

A *scale model* of the White House appears in Tobu World Square in Japan. The scale used is 1 : 25.

En Tobu World Square, en Japón, hay un *modelo a escala* de la Casa Blanca. La escala utilizada es de 1 : 25.

---

scalene triangle (p. 523) A triangle with no congruent sides.

triángulo escaleno (pág. 523) Un triángulo cuyos lados no son congruentes.

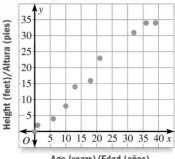

5 ft/5 pies   14 ft/14 pies   11 ft/11 pies

---

scatter plot (p. 315) The graph of a set of a data pairs (x, y), which is a collection of points in a coordinate plane.

diagrama de dispersión (pág. 315) La gráfica de un conjunto de pares de datos (x, y), que es un grupo de puntos en un plano de coordenadas.

Pine Tree Growth
Crecimiento del pino

(graph: Height (feet)/Altura (pies) on y-axis, Age (years)/Edad (años) on x-axis)

---

scientific notation (p. 78) A number is written in scientific notation if it has the form $c \times 10^n$ where c is greater than or equal to 1 and less than 10, and n is an integer.

notación científica (pág. 78) Un número está escrito en notación científica si tiene la forma $c \times 10^n$ donde c es mayor que o igual a 1 y menor que 10, y n es un número entero.

In *scientific notation*, 328,000 is written as 3.28×10^5, and 0.00061 is written as 6.1×10^{-4}.

En *notación científica*, 328,000 se escribe como 3.28×10^5 y 0.00061 se escribe como 6.1×10^{-4}.

---

set (p. 688) A collection of distinct objects.

conjunto (pág. 688) Una agrupación de objetos distintos.

The *set* of whole numbers is
$$W = \{0, 1, 2, 3, 4, 5, \ldots\}.$$

El *conjunto* de los números naturales es
$$N = \{0, 1, 2, 3, 4, 5, \ldots\}.$$

---

similar polygons (p. 537) Polygons that have the same shape but not necessarily the same size. Corresponding angles of similar polygons are congruent, and the ratios of the lengths of corresponding sides are equal. The symbol ~ is used to indicate that two polygons are similar.

polígonos semejantes (pág. 537) Polígonos que tienen la misma forma pero no necesariamente el mismo tamaño. Los ángulos correspondientes de los polígonos semejantes son congruentes y las razones de las longitudes de los lados correspondientes son iguales. Se utiliza el símbolo ~ para indicar que dos polígonos son semejantes.

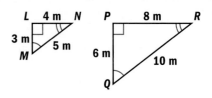

$\triangle LMN \sim \triangle PQR$

simple interest (p. 490) Interest that is earned or paid only on the principal. The simple interest I is the product of the principal P, the annual interest rate r written as a decimal, and the time t in years: $I = Prt$.

interés simple (pág. 490) El interés ganado o pagado sólo sobre el capital. El interés simple I es el producto del capital P, la tasa de interés anual r escrita en forma decimal y el tiempo t en años: $I = Prt$.

Suppose you deposit $700 into a savings account. The account earns 3% *simple annual interest*. After 5 years, the interest is $I = Prt = (700)(0.03)(5) = \$105$, and your account balance is $700 + $105 = $805.

Imagina que depositas $700 en una cuenta de ahorros. La cuenta genera un *interés anual simple* del 3%. Después de 5 años, el interés es $I = Prt = (700)(0.03)(5) = \$105$, y el saldo de tu cuenta es $700 + $105 = $805.

---

simplest form of a fraction (p. 177) A fraction is in simplest form if its numerator and denominator have a greatest common factor of 1.

mínima expresión de una fracción (pág. 177) Una fracción está en su mínima expresión si el máximo común divisor del numerador y del denominador es 1.

The *simplest form of the fraction* $\frac{6}{8}$ is $\frac{3}{4}$.

La *mínima expresión de la fracción* $\frac{6}{8}$ es $\frac{3}{4}$.

---

slant height (p. 660) The height of any face that is not the base of a regular pyramid.

altura inclinada (pág. 660) En una pirámide regular, la altura de cualquier cara que no sea la base.

See regular pyramid.

Véase pirámide regular.

---

slope (p. 409) The slope of a nonvertical line is the ratio of the rise (vertical change) to the run (horizontal change) between any two points on the line.

pendiente (pág. 409) La pendiente de una recta no vertical es la razón entre la distancia vertical (cambio vertical) y la distancia horizontal (cambio horizontal) entre dos puntos cualesquiera de la recta.

The *slope* of the line above is:
$$\text{slope} = \frac{\text{rise}}{\text{run}} = \frac{2}{7}$$

La *pendiente* de la recta anterior es:
$$\text{pendiente} = \frac{\text{distancia vertical}}{\text{distancia horizontal}} = \frac{2}{7}$$

---

solid (p. 631) A three-dimensional figure that encloses a part of space.

cuerpo geométrico (pág. 631) Figura tridimensional que encierra una parte del espacio.

See cone, cylinder, prism, pyramid, *and* sphere.

Véase cono, cilindro, prisma, pirámide y esfera.

---

solution of an equation (p. 25) A number that, when substituted for the variable in the equation, makes the equation true.

solución de una ecuación (pág. 25) Número que, cuando sustituye la variable en la ecuación, hace verdadera la ecuación.

The *solution of the equation* $n - 3 = 4$ is 7.

La *solución de la ecuación* $n - 3 = 4$ es 7.

solution of an inequality (p. 366) The set of all numbers that, when substituted for the variable in the inequality, make the inequality true.	The *solution of the inequality* $y + 2 > 5$ is $y > 3$.
solución de una desigualdad (pág. 366) Conjunto de todos los números que, cuando sustituyen la variable en la desigualdad, hacen verdadera la desigualdad.	La *solución de la desigualdad* $y + 2 > 5$ es $y > 3$.
solving an equation (p. 26) Finding all solutions of the equation by using mental math or the properties of equality.	To *solve the equation* $4x = 20$, find the number that can be multiplied by 4 to equal 20; $4(5) = 20$, so the solution is 5.
resolver una ecuación (pág. 26) Hallar todas las soluciones de la ecuación usando el cálculo mental o las propiedades de igualdad.	Para *resolver la ecuación* $4x = 20$, halla el número que multiplicado por 4 sea igual a 20; $4(5) = 20$, por lo tanto la solución es 5.
sphere (p. 631) A solid formed by all points in space that are the same distance from a fixed point called the center.	center centro
esfera (pág. 631) Cuerpo geométrico formado por todos los puntos en el espacio que se encuentran a la misma distancia de un punto fijo llamado centro.	
square numbers (p. 577) Numbers that are squares of integers.	Because 3×3 is 9, 9 is a *square number*.
números cuadrados (pág. 577) Números que son el cuadrado de número enteros.	Como 3×3 es 9, 9 es un *número cuadrado*.
square root (p. 577) A square root of a number n is a number m which, when multiplied by itself, equals n.	The *square roots* of 81 are 9 and -9 because $9^2 = 81$ and $(-9)^2 = 81$.
raíz cuadrada (pág. 577) La raíz cuadrada de un número n es un número m, el cual, cuando se multiplica por sí mismo, es igual a n.	Las *raíces cuadradas* de 81 son 9 y -9 porque $9^2 = 81$ y $(-9)^2 = 81$.
stem-and-leaf plot (p. 126) A data display that helps you see how data values are distributed. Each data value is separated into a leaf (the last digit) and a stem (the remaining digits). In an ordered stem-and-leaf plot, the leaves for each stem are listed in order from least to greatest.	stems/tallos leaves/hojas 10 | 8 11 | 2 2 5 12 | 1 3 4 7 13 | 0 6 Key/Clave: 10 | 8 = 108
diagrama de tallo y hojas (pág. 126) Diagrama que muestra cómo se distribuyen los valores en un conjunto de datos. Cada valor está separado en una hoja (el último dígito) y un tallo (los dígitos restantes). En un diagrama de tallo y hojas ordenado, las hojas para cada tallo están en orden de menor a mayor.	
straight angle (p. 511) An angle whose measure is exactly $180°$.	
ángulo llano (pág. 511) Ángulo que mide exactamente $180°$.	

subtraction property of equality (p. 347) Subtracting the same number from each side of an equation produces an equivalent equation.

propiedad de igualdad en la resta (pág. 347) Al restar el mismo número de cada lado de una ecuación se obtiene una ecuación equivalente.

If $x + 7 = 9$, then $x + 7 - 7 = 9 - 7$, so $x = 2$.
If $x + a = b$, then $x + a - a = b - a$.

Si $x + 7 = 9$, entonces $x + 7 - 7 = 9 - 7$, por lo tanto $x = 2$.
Si $x + a = b$, entonces $x + a - a = b - a$.

---

sum (p. 742) The result when two or more numbers are added.

suma (pág. 742) El resultado cuando se suman dos o más números.

The *sum* of 2 and 5 is $2 + 5$, or 7.

La *suma* de 2 y 5 es $2 + 5$, ó 7.

---

supplementary angles (p. 512) Two angles whose measures have a sum of 180°.

ángulos suplementarios (pág. 512) Dos ángulos cuyas medidas suman 180°.

$79°$ \ $101°$

---

surface area of a solid (p. 642) The sum of the areas of the outside surfaces of the solid.

área de la superficie de un cuerpo geométrico (pág. 642) La suma de las áreas de las superficies exteriores del cuerpo geométrico.

3 in./3 pulg.
4 in./4 pulg.
6 in./6 pulg.

Surface area $= 2(6)(4) + 2(6)(3) + 2(4)(3) = 108$ in.^{2}

Área de la superficie $= 2(6)(4) + 2(6)(3) + 2(4)(3) = 108$ pulg.^{2}

T

terminating decimal (p. 199) A decimal that has a final digit.
decimal exacto (pág. 199) Decimal que tiene un dígito final.

0.4 and 3.6125 are *terminating decimals*.
0.4 y 3.6125 son *decimales exactos*.

---

terms of an expression (p. 342) The parts of an expression that are added together.

términos de una expresión (pág. 342) Las partes de una expresión que se suman entre sí.

The *terms* of $2x + 3$ are $2x$ and 3.

Los *términos* de $2x + 3$ son $2x$ y 3.

---

tessellation (p. 554) A covering of a plane with congruent copies of the same pattern so that there are no gaps or overlaps.

teselado (pág. 554) La cobertura de un plano con copias congruentes del mismo patrón de modo que no haya huecos o superposiciones.

theoretical probability (p. 683) A probability based on all of the equally likely outcomes of an experiment. The theoretical probability of an event is given by:

$$P(\text{event}) = \frac{\text{Number of favorable outcomes}}{\text{Total number of outcomes}}$$

probabilidad teórica (pág. 683) Probabilidad basada en que todos los resultados de un experimento son igualmente probables; la probabilidad de un evento se expresa como:

$$P(\text{evento}) = \frac{\text{Número de resultados favorables}}{\text{Número total de resultados}}$$

A bag of 20 marbles contains 7 red marbles. The *theoretical probability* of randomly choosing a red marble is:

$$P(\text{red}) = \frac{7}{20} = 0.35$$

Una bolsa de 20 canicas contiene 7 canicas rojas. La *probabilidad teórica* de tomar al azar una canica roja es:

$$P(\text{roja}) = \frac{7}{20} = 0.35$$

---

transformation (p. 548) A movement of a figure in a plane.

transformación (pág. 548) Movimiento de una figura en un plano.

See translation, reflection, *and* rotation.

Véase traslación, reflexión y rotación.

---

translation (p. 548) A transformation that moves each point of a figure the same distance in the same direction; also known as a *slide*.

traslación (pág. 548) Transformación que mueve cada punto de una figura la misma distancia en la misma dirección.

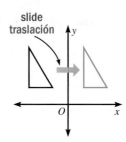

---

trapezoid (p. 529) A quadrilateral with exactly one pair of parallel sides.

trapecio (pág. 529) Cuadrilátero que tiene exactamente un par de lados paralelos.

---

tree diagram (p. 690) A branching diagram that shows all the possible outcomes of a process carried out in several stages.

diagrama de árbol (pág. 690) Diagrama ramificado que muestra todos los resultados posibles de un proceso llevado a cabo en varias etapas.

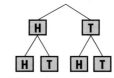

---

union (p. 688) The set of all elements in either set *A* or set *B*, written as $A \cup B$.

unión de conjuntos (pág. 688) El conjunto que incluye todos los elementos del conjunto *A* y el conjunto *B*, que se expresa como $A \cup B$.

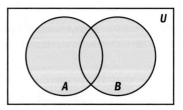

---

unit rate (p. 404) A rate that has a denominator of 1 unit.

tasa unitaria (pág. 404) Una tasa cuyo denominador es 1 unidad.

$9 per hour is a *unit rate*.

$9 por hora es una *tasa unitaria*.

universal set (p. 688) A set of all elements under consideration and written as U. **conjunto universal** (p. 688) Un conjunto de todos los elementos bajo consideración que se expresa como U.	If the *universal set* is the set of positive integers, then $U = \{1, 2, 3, \ldots\}$. Si el *conjunto universal* es el conjunto de los números enteros positivos, entonces $U = \{1, 2, 3, \ldots\}$.
upper extreme (p. 133) The greatest value in a data set. **extremo superior** (pág. 133) El mayor valor en un conjunto de datos.	*See* box-and-whisker plot. *Véase* diagrama de líneas y bloques.
upper quartile (p. 133) The median of the upper half of a data set. **cuartil superior** (pág. 133) La mediana de la mitad superior de un conjunto de datos.	*See* box-and-whisker plot. *Véase* diagrama de líneas y bloques.

V

variable (p. 8) A letter that is used to represent one or more numbers. **variable** (pág. 8) Letra que se usa para representar uno o más números.	In the expression $m + 5$, the letter m is the *variable*. En la expresión $m + 5$, la letra m es la *variable*.
variable expression (p. 9) An expression that consists of numbers, variables, and operations. **expresión variable** (pág. 9) Expresión compuesta por números, variables y operaciones.	$n - 3$, $\frac{2s}{t}$, and $x + 4yz + 1$ are *variable expressions*. $n - 3$, $\frac{2s}{t}$ y $x + 4yz + 1$ son *expresiones variables*.
Venn diagram (p. 756) A diagram that uses shapes to show how sets are related. **diagrama de Venn** (pág. 756) Un diagrama que usa formas para mostrar cómo se relacionan los conjuntos.	Whole numbers from 1 to 10 Números naturales de 1 a 10 3 10 Prime numbers Números primos 2 4 Even numbers Números pares 7 5 8 6 1 9
verbal model (p. 338) A word equation that represents a real-world situation. **modelo verbal** (pág. 338) Ecuación expresada en palabras que representa una situación de la vida real.	Distance traveled $=$ Speed of car $\cdot$ Time traveled Distancia recorrida $=$ Velocidad del carro $\cdot$ Tiempo de viaje
vertex of an angle (p. 474) The common endpoint of the two rays that form the angle. **vértice de un ángulo** (pág. 474) El extremo común de las dos semirrectas que forman el ángulo.	*See* angle. *Véase* ángulo.

vertex of a solid (p. 632) A point where the edges of the solid meet.	*See* edge of a solid.
vértice de un cuerpo geométrico (pág. 632) Punto donde se encuentran las aristas de un cuerpo geométrico.	*Véase* arista de un cuerpo geométrico.
vertical angles (p. 516) A pair of opposite angles formed when two lines meet at a point. **ángulos opuestos por el vértice** (pág. 516) Par de ángulos opuestos entre sí formados por dos rectas que se intersecan.	 ∠1 and ∠3 are *vertical angles*. ∠2 and ∠4 are also *vertical angles*. ∠1 y ∠3 son *ángulos opuestos por el vértice*. ∠2 y ∠4 también son *ángulos opuestos por el vértice*.
vertical axis (p. 118) The vertical number line of a graph.	*See* coordinate plane.
eje vertical (pág. 118) La recta numérica vertical de una gráfica.	*Véase* plano de coordenadas.
volume of a solid (p. 655) The amount of space the solid contains. **volumen de un cuerpo geométrico** (pág. 655) Cantidad de espacio que contiene el cuerpo geométrico.	 $Volume = \pi r^2 h \approx (3.14)(2)^2(3) \approx 37.7 \text{ m}^3$ $Volumen = \pi r^2 h \approx (3.14)(2)^2(3) \approx 37.7 \text{ m}^3$

X

***x*-axis** (p. 313) The horizontal axis in a coordinate plane.	*See* coordinate plane.
eje *x* (pág. 313) Eje horizontal de un plano de coordenadas.	*Véase* plano de coordenadas.
x*-coordinate** (p. 313) The first number in an ordered pair representing a point in a coordinate plane. **coordenada *x (pág. 313) El primer número en un par ordenado que representa un punto en un plano de coordenadas.	The *x-coordinate* of the ordered pair $(-2, 1)$ is -2. La *coordenada x* del par ordenado $(-2, 1)$ es -2.

Y

***y*-axis** (p. 313) The vertical axis in a coordinate plane.	*See* coordinate plane.
eje *y* (pág. 313) Eje vertical en un plano de coordenadas.	*Véase* plano de coordenadas.
y*-coordinate** (p. 313) The second number in an ordered pair representing a point in a coordinate plane. **coordenada *y (pág. 313) El segundo número de un par ordenado que representa un punto en un plano de coordenadas.	The *y-coordinate* of the ordered pair $(-2, 1)$ is 1. La *coordenada y* del par ordenado $(-2, 1)$ es 1.

Index

A

Absolute value
  adding integers with, 278–282
  definition of, 278
  finding, 278–280, 352
Act it out, problem solving strategy, 12, 404, 427, 702, 770, 775
Activity, *See also* Games; Investigations; Technology activities
  algebra
    evaluating expressions, 8
    solving addition equations, 25
    solving division equations, 296
    working backward to solve equations, 361
  geometry and measurement
    angle relationships, 516
    area of parallelograms, 594
    circumference of a circle, 607
    sum of angle measures, 521
    surface area of cylinder, 649
  number operations
    adding and subtracting decimals, 60
    adding and subtracting fractions, 219
    multiplication rules for integers, 291
    percent of change, 480
    writing prime numbers, 165
  probability and statistics
    data collection and display, 144
    number arrangements, 702
    probability of two events, 715
  ratios and proportions
    rewriting fractions to compare rates, 404
    using ratios to describe slope, 409
Acute angle, 511
Acute triangle, 522
Addition
  of angles, A14–A15
  of decimals, 60–65, 70, 76, 80, 95, 98, 101, 143
  equations,
    modeling, 25, 346
    solving, 25, 347–353, 388
    writing, 372–380, 384, 388–389
  expressions, 25, 337–341, 343
  of fractions
    with common denominators, 219, 221
    with different denominators, 220–225, 230, 257

    using a calculator, 243
  of integers
    modeling, 276, 277
    using absolute value, 278–282, 323, 345, 370
  of like terms, 342–346
  of mixed customary units, 252, 253
  of mixed numbers
    with common denominators, 226
    with different denominators, 227–230, 242, 258, 273
    modeling, 225
    using a calculator, 243
  of numbers in scientific notation, 80
  order of operations, 17–22
  place value and, 56
  properties of,
    associative, 302–306, 325, 759–760
    commutative, 302–306, 325, 759–760
    identity, 302
    inverse, 302
  property of equality, 348
  rounding and, 57, 58, 73
Additive identity, 302
Additive inverse, 302
Algebra
  describing patterns, 3–7, 11, 12, 16, 22, 43, 47, 58, 62, 69, 160, 204, 312–315, 370, 372–380, 389
  equation, 25–30, 347–352, 353–359, 361–365
    absolute value, 364
    addition, 25–30, 197, 338, 346–352, 389
    direct variation, 383–384
    division, 26–30, 65, 353–359
    multiplication, 26–30, 353–359
    percent, 465–470, 498
    solving, 25–30, 36, 41, 45, 65, 70, 178, 338, 353–359
    square root, 578
    subtraction, 26–30, 197, 348–352
    two-step, 361–365, 370
    writing, 338–341, 448–352, 357–359, 362–365
  expression(s)
    equivalent, 307–309, 342–345, 359
    evaluating, 8–11, 14–16, 17–18, 20, 22,
    numeric, 13–16, 17–20, 22–23, 36, 44, 54, 62, 74, 82, 160
    order of operations, 17–21

    simplifying, 342–345, 359
    variable, 8–11, 14–16, 17–18, 20, 22, 44–45, 61–62, 160
    writing, 16, 337–341
  formula. *See* Formulas
  function
    direct variation, 383–384
    evaluating, 371–375, 389
    graphing, 376–384, 390
    linear, 377–381, 383–384
    nonlinear, 377–381, 383–384
    writing rules for, 373–375, 378–381, 384
  inequality
    graphing, 366–370
    solving, 366–370
  number properties
    associative, 302–306, 325, 759–760
    commutative, 302–306, 325, 759–760
    distributive, 307–311, 341
    identity, 302–306
    inverse, 302–306
  properties of equality
    addition, 348
    division, 354
    multiplication, 355
    subtraction, 347
  rational numbers, 301–306, 325
  real numbers, 583–586
  slope of a line, 409–414
Algorithm
  adding and subtracting, 219–220, 226, 278, 285
  comparing and ordering, 56–57, 189, 269–270
  finding mean, median, mode, 109–110
  graphing functions, 376
  making frequency tables, 138
  making graphs, 313–315
  measuring length, 83
  multiplying and dividing, 66, 72, 232, 237, 291, 296
  order of operations, 17
  rewriting fractions
    and decimals, 199
    and percents, 449, 455
  rounding decimals, 57
  solving equations, 347, 354, 361
  solving problems, 26, 38
  surface area, 642, 649
  write function rules, 372
Alternative method. *See* Another Way
Analyze exercises, 192
Angle(s), 472–473, 474, A14–A15

acute, 511–515, 564–565

adjacent, 516–518, 534

bisecting, 527

in a circle graph, 474

classifying, 511–515, 564–565

complementary, 512–515, 565

congruent, 516–520, 523, 537–540, 565

copying, 527–528

corresponding, 517–518

estimating measures of, A2–A3

exterior, 521–522, A14–A15

finding in triangles, 521–522, 524–526, 534, 539, 566

interior, 521–522, A14–A15

obtuse, 511–515, 564–565

pairs, 512–515, 516–520, 565

rays of, 472, 474

right, 511–515

of rotation, 549

straight, 511–515

supplementary, 512–515, 565

vertex of, 474

vertical, 516–520, 565

Animated Math, 4, 18, 26, 33, 38, 57, 60, 66, 71, 87, 117, 126, 133, 171, 178, 185, 196, 201, 221, 227, 233, 237, 239, 247, 251, 270, 292, 301, 308, 310, 317, 337, 348, 367, 372, 376, 400, 404, 410, 431, 450, 457, 461, 476, 481, 490, 511, 512, 530, 549, 550, 557, 589, 601, 613, 632, 637, 683, 691, 709

Annual interest rate, 490

Another Way, *Throughout. See for example* 61, 71, 79, 183, 226, 279, 285, 343, 347, 411, 424, 467, 485, 511, 517, 543, 596, 608, 655, 702

Applications

advertising, 145, 186, 435, 501

agriculture, 11, 68

animals, 27, 29, 94, 112, 126, 203, 223, 235, 251, 294, 299, 583, 678

aquarium, 655, 717

architecture, 46, 78, 420, 431, 441, 543, 545, 567, 569, 574–575, 591, 621, 634, 636, 639, 660, 661, 665

art, 35, 36, 47, 275, 402, 421, 433, 434, 538, 598

attendance, 499

automobiles, 145, 153, 479, 498, 585, 606, 611

baseball, 39, 98, 106–107, 155, 226, 246, 358, 399

basketball, 6, 35, 149, 177, 365, 468, 628–629, 686

biking, 28, 127, 148, 362, 404, 476, 699

books and print media, 116, 122, 152, 242, 488, 551

botany, 136, 141, 315, 404, 425, 609, 720

boxes and packaging, 253, 259, 481, 638, 645

business, 145, 306, 319, 467, 491

calendars, 185, 615

caves, 337, 338

code counting, 698

construction, 35, 81, 221, 438, 452, 464, 526, 533, 666

consumer economics, 21, 36, 101, 173, 230, 241, 279, 286, 289, 311, 322, 341, 377, 384, 404, 405, 435, 438, 440, 461, 490, 491, 493, 494, 500, 501, 507, 749–750

crafts, 6, 40, 47, 180, 230, 235, 258, 597, 605

decorating, 47, 99, 308, 349, 500, 512, 541, 592, 646

directions, 64

employment, 149, 438, 483

entertainment, 22, 36, 64, 71, 95, 110, 173, 216–217, 307, 310, 351, 356, 359, 381, 384, 428, 458, 464, 468, 477, 499, 601, 656, 752, 758

environment, 93, 148, 154, 452

eyeglasses, 623

family life, 129, 152, 229, 327, 475, 752, 758

fashion, 113, 134, 211, 249, 454, 475, 507, 616, 700

fitness, 47, 90, 185, 223, 229, 379, 462, 476

flag, 519

folding fan, 514

food, 23, 76, 88, 94, 101, 147, 177, 185, 192, 232, 236, 240, 255, 260, 310, 405, 435, 464, 477, 483, 499, 501, 507, 658, 690, 691, 693, 694, 750, 757

football, 135, 179, 272

games, 16, 19, 44, 52–53, 69, 266–267, 281, 294, 396–397, 508–509, 687, 717, 720

geography, 4, 152, 201, 286, 288, 292, 295, 323, 327, 370, 387, 430, 435, 461, 518, 519, 615

government, 129, 179, 233, 366, 431, 478, 497, 683

history, 75, 129, 179, 185, 254, 272, 317, 334–335, 434, 483

hobbies, 35, 73, 88, 154, 182, 223, 243, 310, 433, 463, 525, 682, 700

holidays, 168, 543

home improvement, 30, 34, 64, 88, 192, 311, 326, 362, 441, 459, 603

membership, 113, 384

motion, 560

movies, 752

music, 17, 37, 38, 116, 130, 139, 170, 224, 258, 400, 427, 486, 494, 673

Olympic games, xxii–1, 56

parks, 28, 63, 67, 111, 133, 192, 202, 288, 400, 507, 610, 613, 702

pets, 15, 155, 421, 437, 494, 507, 646, 655, 717

photo sticker, 541

population, 324, 464

prices, 141, 154, 485, 489

recreation, 11, 41, 117, 142, 189, 197, 238, 242, 252, 272, 338, 341, 357, 358, 369, 381, 389, 413, 438, 455, 477, 484, 515, 540, 589, 622, 691, 700

restaurants, 155, 486, 487, 500

retail sales, 46, 65, 145, 466, 469, 483, 485, 488, 499

schedules, 3, 143, 183, 691

school, 749, 750

science, 11, 13, 69, 79, 82, 94, 109, 138, 288, 292, 298, 300, 326, 349, 358, 402, 407, 408, 410, 423, 424, 432, 462, 553, 580

shopping, 76, 369, 379, 407, 438, 507

souvenirs, 168, 364

sports, xxii–1, 6, 9, 21, 22, 33, 35, 47, 56, 108, 113, 118, 125, 129, 144, 148, 152, 193, 198, 203, 281, 299, 364, 375, 405, 418, 427, 438, 450, 458, 459, 475, 483, 484, 499, 507, 511, 514, 578, 696, 703, 752

structures, 525, 574–575

student life, 40, 46, 54, 101, 115, 119, 127, 139, 141, 165, 168, 173, 197, 208, 327, 351, 402, 450, 458, 470, 474, 477, 498, 501, 605, 647, 693, 694, 699, 703

surveys, 114, 428, 498, 683

technology, 119, 136, 143, 155, 203, 318, 324, 388, 507, 525, 534, 556, 588, 659, 673, 684, 696, 699, 700

television, 758

time, 752

transportation, 28, 41, 46, 70, 81, 118, 137, 294, 317, 327, 354, 356, 370, 407, 507, 525 volunteering, 74, 155, 319, 465, 507, 686

weather, 122, 125, 204, 270, 286, 288, 289, 297, 305, 327, 341, 380, 446–447, 468, 757

wildlife, 108, 176, 140, 251, 424, 431, 459

Area

of a circle, 612–616, 622

of a composite figure, 35, 36, 581, 603–606, 615

in a coordinate plane, 314

definition, 32

estimating, 75, 597, 612

model for decimals, 66

model for fractions, 75, 187

of a parallelogram, 596–598, 621

of a rectangle, 31–36, 41, 46–47, 67, 69, 75, 93, 173

of a square, 31–36, 46–47, 94, 611

of a trapezoid, 600–606, 616, 621

of a triangle, 599, 601–606, 616, 621

Arithmetic sequence, 373–375, 389

Assessment, *See also* Internet; Online Quiz; Review; State Test Practice

Chapter Test, 47, 101, 155, 211, 261, 327, 391, 441, 501, 569, 623, 673, 727

Guided Practice, *Throughout. See for example* 4, 8, 9, 14, 18, 19, 26, 33, 34, 37, 38, 57, 61, 67, 68, 71, 72, 73, 78, 79, 86, 91, 92, 109, 111, 117, 119, 127, 134, 135, 139, 140, 145

Pre-Course Problem Solving Practice, 771–775

Pre-Course Problem Solving Review, 761–770

Quiz, 22, 41, 76, 95, 130, 149, 180, 204, 242, 255, 289, 319, 359, 381, 414, 435, 470, 494, 534, 561, 592, 616, 647, 666, 700, 721

Skill Check, 2, 54, 108, 164, 218, 268, 336, 398, 448, 510, 576, 630, 680

Skill Practice, *Throughout. See for example* 5, 10, 15, 19–20, 27–28, 34–35, 39, 58, 62–63, 68–69, 73–74, 80, 87–88, 92–93, 111–112, 120–121, 128–129, 135–136, 141–142, 146

Standardized Test Practice, 50–51, 104–105, 158–159, 214–215, 264–265, 330–331, 394–395, 444–445, 504–505, 572–573, 626–627, 676–677, 730–731

Associative property

of addition, 302–305, 325, 759

of multiplication, 302–305, 325, 759

@HomeTutor, *Throughout. See for example* 2, 43, 47, 54, 97, 101, 108, 151, 155, 164, 207, 211, 218, 257, 261, 268, 322, 327, 336, 386, 391, 398, 441, 448, 496, 501, 510, 564, 569, 576, 619, 623, 630, 669, 673, 680, 723, 727

Average rate formula, 405

Averages, 109–110, *See also* Mean; Median; Mode

choosing the best, 110

Avoid Errors, *See* Error Analysis

Axis (axes)

in coordinate plane, 313

for line graphs, 118–119

Bar graph

double, 118–120

interpreting, 124, 144–148, 152, 155, 757

making, 117–120, 124, 152

Bar notation, 199–202, 204, 210–211

Base(s)

of a cone, 631, 638, 653

of a cylinder, 631, 634, 649–653, 662–666

of a parallelogram, 594–598, 616, 621

of a percent, 455–456, 466–467

of a prism, 631, 634, 638, 658

of a pyramid, 631–632, 637, 638, 660–661

of a trapezoid, 602–606, 616, 621

of a triangle, 601–606, 616, 621

Base-ten pieces, *See* Manipulatives

Benchmarks

for customary units, 245–247

for metric units, 84–86

Biased questions, 116

Biased sample, 115–116, A28–A29

Box-and-whisker plots

comparing, 135–136

definition of, 133

interpreting, 134–137

making, 133–137, 153, 295, 345

Brain Games, *See* Games

Break a problem into parts, problem-solving strategy, 533, 635, 767, 773

Capacity, 86, 247

customary units, 247–249, 251–255, 259–260

benchmarks, 247

converting between, 251–255, 260, A4–A5

cup, 247

fluid ounce, 247

gallon, 247

measuring, 248–249, 252–255

pint, 247

quart, 247

metric units, 86–89, 100

benchmarks, 86

converting between, 91–95, 100

kiloliter, 86

liter, 86

measuring, 86, 88

milliliter, 86

Center

of a circle, 607

of rotation, 548

of a sphere, 631

Centimeter, 84, 87–89

ruler, measuring with, 87–89, 753

Challenge exercises, *Throughout. See for example* 6, 7, 10, 11, 15, 16, 20, 22, 28, 29, 30, 35, 36, 39, 41, 58, 59, 63, 65, 69, 70, 74, 76, 81, 89, 93, 95, 112, 114, 121, 123, 129, 130, 136, 137, 142, 143, 146, 148

Changing dimensions

effect on area, 540, 596–598, 605–606, 615

effect on circumference, 611, 615

effect on perimeter, 540, 545, 546

effect on surface area, 646

effect on volume, 659, 665

Chapter Review, 43–46, 97–100, 151–154, 207–210, 257–260, 322–326, 386–390, 437–440, 496–500, 564–568, 619–622, 669–672, 723–726

Chapter Test, *See* Assessment

Check reasonableness, *See* Reasonableness

Check solutions, *Throughout. See for example* 71, 79, 189, 238, 251, 347, 348, 354, 361, 367

Choose a method exercise, 192, 222, 228

Choosing problem-solving strategies, *Throughout. See for example* 41, 65, 149, 169, 185, 318, 341, 403, 494, 526, 611, 635

Circle

arc of, 527–528, 622

area of, 612–616, 622

center, 607

chord of, A18–A19

circumference of, 607–612, 622

diameter, 607–611, 614–615, 622
drawing with a compass, 546, 754
radius of, 607–611, 612–616, 622
sectors of, A18–A19
Circle graph, 474–479
interpreting, 474–475, 477–478, 727
making, 475–479, 484, 499
using a spreadsheet, 479
Circuits, A10–A11
Circumference, 607–611
formula for, 607, 791
Clockwise rotation, 549, 551, 552
Clustering, to estimate, 745
Coefficient(s), 342–344, 354, 359
Combinations, 703–707, 725
finding on calculator, 708
Combining like terms, 342–345, 348, 350
Common denominators
adding with
fractions, 219–224
mixed numbers, 225–230
subtracting with
fractions, 219–224
mixed numbers, 225–230
Common factor, 170, 176
Common multiple, 182, 184
Communication, *See also* Error Analysis
describing in words, 6, 76, 89, 94, 116, 160, 191, 232, 237, 278, 285, 291, 296, 297, 347, 348, 354, 384, 399
reading, *See* Reading in Math; Reading math
writing, *See* Writing
Commutative property
of addition, 302–305, 325, 759
of multiplication, 302–305, 325, 759
Comparing
areas of parallelograms, 596
data displays, 135–136, 142, 143, 148
decimals, 54, 56–59, 76, 89, 97, 101, 160
fractions, 187–193, 195–197, 209, 211
integers, 270–273, 280–281, 322
measurements, 91, 93, 160, 253
mixed numbers and fractions, 195–197, 204, 210–211
numbers in scientific notation, 79–81, 161
percents, 463, 468
rates, 404
rational numbers, 305, 365
ratios, 400
unit rates, 405
Compass, 754

drawing geometric construction, 527–528
using, 473, 754
Compatible numbers, 71, 73–74, 306
estimating with, 747, 748
Complementary events, 711–714
Composite numbers, 165–168, 207
Compound events, 715–721, 725
Computer
making circle graphs on, 479
Concept grid, 680
Conclusions, *See* Draw conclusions
Cone, 631, 633, 653, 664
volume of, A16–A17
Congruent figures, 516–520, 523–525, 537, 539, 540, 548
Conjecture, *See* Draw conclusions
Connections, *See* Applications
Constant term, 342–345
definition of, 342
Constructions (geometric), 527–528
Conversion
between customary and metric units, 297–300, 606, 790, 791, A4–A5
between customary units, 75, 250–255, 359, 379
between metric units, 90–95, 100, 101, 110, 379
between units of time, 95, 149, 180, 379
Coordinate plane
definition of, 313
finding segment lengths and area, 314
graphing in, 313–319, 320, 326, 376–381, 382, 383–384, 390, 556–561, 568, A12–A13
ordered pairs, 313, A12–A13
origin, 313
quadrant, 313
transformations, 556–561
x-coordinate, 313, A12–A13
y-coordinate, 313, A12–A13
Copy and complete the statement, *Throughout. See for example* 2, 10, 19, 20, 27, 34, 55, 57, 76, 79, 85, 91, 92, 93, 95, 97, 100, 101, 108, 114, 123, 151
Corresponding angles, 517
Counterclockwise rotation, 549
Counting principle, 696–697, 725
Critical thinking, *See* Reasoning
Cross product, 423
property, 456
using to solve proportions, 423–424, 440, 542
Cumulative Review, 160–161, 332–333, 506–507, 732–733

Cup (c), 247, 250
Customary units, 245–255
adding mixed units, 252
benchmarks, 245–247
of capacity, *See* Capacity
of length, 245, 250, 753
converting units of, 250, 260, A4–A5
measuring with a ruler, 753, A2–A3
subtracting mixed units, 252
table of, 790
units of measure, 250
of weight, 246
converting units of, 251
Cylinders, 631
identifying, 631, 633
surface area, 649–653, 671
volumes
comparing, 663
finding, 662–666, 672
formula for, 662

Data
analyzing
choosing a display, 144–149, 154, 161
comparing data displays, 135–136, 142–144, 148, 154
descriptive statistics, A26–A27
extremes, 133–137, 153
inferential statistics, A26–A27
interpreting data displays, 38, 118–123, 127–130, 132, 134, 137–140, 201, 474
interquartile range, 134–135
measures of central tendency, 109–114, 130, 151, 160, 297
measures of dispersion, 110–114, 130, 151–152, 155, 160
misleading, 115–116, 145–148, A24–A25
quartiles, 133, 153
samples, A26–A27
collecting, 12, 132, 133, 165, 681, 703
displaying
in a bar graph, 114, 117–124, 144–149, 152, 155, 161, 757
in a box-and-whiskers plot, 133–137, 144–149, 153
in a circle graph, 475–479, 499
in a line graph, 115–124, 144–149, 152, 155, 757
in a scatter plot, 312, 315–317
misleading displays, A24–A25
organizing
in a frequency table, 138, 142, 160, 681

in a histogram, 139–143, 144–
149, 154, 155
in an input-output table, 371–
372, 376–377, 383
in a line plot, 108, 113, 123
in a stem-and-leaf plot, 126,
144–149, 153, 155, 160,
A22–A23
in a tree diagram, 690–692, 695
in a Venn diagram, 365, 688,
710, 769
Decimal
addition, 60, 76, 95, 98, 101
bar notation for, 199–204, 210–211
common, 200
comparisons, 54, 56–59, 76, 89, 97,
101, 123
division, 71–76, 92, 99, 101
by a decimal, 72, 81, 130, 174
modeling on a number line, 74
placing decimal point in, 71–72
rounding quotient in, 73
by a whole number, 71, 109,
130
expanded form of, 62
fractions, mixed numbers, and,
198–204, 210–211, 268
modeling
using an area model, 66
using base-ten pieces, 55, 60
using a number line, 57, 58, 62
multiplication, 66–70, 76, 89, 98,
101, 143, 289, 582–583, 608–
611, 650–653
using area model, 66
by a whole number, 67, 69
ordering, 54, 57, 65, 89, 108, 186
percent and, 460–464, 498
place value and, 56
reading, 56
repeating, 199–203, 380, 459
rounding, 54, 57, 68, 71, 97, 160
subtraction, 60, 76, 98, 101
terminating, 199–203, 380, 459
Deductive Reasoning, A30–A31
Degrees, 474
of angle, 472
Denominator(s), 176
common
adding fractions with, 219–224
subtracting fractions with,
220–224
different
adding fractions with, 220–224
subtracting fractions with,
220–224
least common (LCD)
comparing fractions, 189–190
Dependent events, 715–721, 726
probability of, 717

Diagonal, of polygon, 531
Diagram(s)
drawing, 403, 546, 693
interpreting, 514
in notebook, 2
Venn, 756
Diameter, 607–611, 614–615, 622
Difference, *See* Subtraction
definition of, 741
Digit, 735
Dilation, A20–A21
scale factor in, 559
Dimensions
effect of change
on area, 540, 596–598, 605–606,
615
on circumference, 611, 615
on perimeter, 540, 545, 546
on surface area, 646
on volume, 659, 665
Direct variation, 383–384
identifying, 383
model for, 384
writing, 384
Discounts, 485–489, 500
Discrete mathematics
combinations, 702–707, 725
using a calculator, 707
composite number, 165–168, 174,
180, 207, 211
counting methods, 690–694,
695–700, 702–707, 709–714,
724–725
Goldbach's conjecture, 169
greatest common factor, 170–174,
177, 180, 186, 208, 211
least common denominator, 189–
193, 204, 208
least common multiple, 182–186,
189, 193, 198, 204, 209, 211
permutations, 702–707, 725
using a calculator, 707
prime factorization, 165–169, 207
prime number, 165–168, 180, 207,
211
relatively prime numbers, 165–
169, 171–174, 180, 183–185,
204, 207, 211, 375
set theory, 679, 688–689, 769
tree diagram, 690–694, 695, 700,
724
Disjoint events, 709–714, 726
Distance
in a coordinate plane, 314, 316
formula, 26–29, 359
Distributive property, 307–311,
325–326
definition of, 307
using, 308, 325
Dividend, 744

Divisibility, 11, 149, 169, 739
tests, 739
Division
in converting units, 90–95, 250–254
of decimals, 71–76, 81, 92, 99, 101,
130, 174
rounding quotient, 73
using a model, 55, 60, 74
dividend, 744
divisor, 744
equation, 26–29, 45, 356–359
estimating quotients, 71, 239, 748
with exponents, A6–A7
expression, 9, 44, 337–341
of fractions, 239–242, 259
using a calculator, 243
of integers, 296–300, 324, 351
of mixed numbers, 239–242
using a calculator, 243
order of operations, 17
ways of writing, 9
of whole numbers, 744
Divisor, 744
Domain
definition of, 371
of function, 376
Draw a diagram, problem solving
strategy, 41, 238, 241, 340,
341, 546, 693, 762, 771, 772
Draw conclusions
from data, 475
exercises, 12, 31, 55, 83, 132, 175,
188, 225, 231, 276, 284, 312,
346, 353, 382, 415, 417, 429,
453, 473, 536, 547, 587, 599,
600, 654, 681, 695
Drawing
a circle with a compass, 754
line segments of given measures,
753
segments with a compass, 754

E

Edges, 632
Elapsed time, 752
Element, 688
Eliminate choices, *Throughout.*
See for example 19, 34
Empty set, 690
Equation(s)
addition, 25–30, 197, 346–352
division, 26–30, 65, 354–359
functions and, 371–375
modeling, 25, 346, 353, 361
multiplication, 26–30, 353–359
percent, 465–470, 498
proportions, 417–428
solving, 25
with mental math, 25–30

square root, 578
subtraction, 26–30, 347–352
two-step, 361–365
writing, 338–341, 465–470
Equilateral triangles, 523
Equivalent equations, 347
Equivalent expressions, 307–309,
342–345, 359
Equivalent fractions, 175–180
identifying, 176, 208
modeling, 175
writing, 176
Equivalent inequalities, 366
Equivalent ratios, 399
proportions, 418
writing, 399
Error Analysis
Avoid Errors, *Throughout. See for
example* 9, 17, 61, 72, 84, 91,
92, 110, 133, 139, 145
exercises, *Throughout. See for
example* 5, 10, 15, 19, 28, 34,
39, 58, 62, 68, 74, 80, 88, 93,
120, 128, 141, 146
Estimation
in addition, 54, 61, 745
of area, 75, 597, 612
benchmarks, 84–86, 245–247
checking answers, 66, 67, 220
with fractions, 190, 191, 192
of geometric figures, A2–A3
in multiplication, 66, 747
square root, 582–586, 589–592,
A2–A3
techniques
compatible numbers, 71, 73–74
front-end, 61
with leading digits, 66, 69
using rounding, 607–616
using scale, 430, 431, 432
Evaluating
algebraic expressions, 8–11, 16–21,
30, 44, 59, 61, 62, 67, 69, 81,
222, 228, 234, 268, 292–295,
306
functions, 371
numeric expressions, 13–16, 17–
18, 20, 22, 44–45, 47, 62, 74
on a calculator, 23, 82
square roots, 577
Events
complementary, 711
compound, 715–720
dependent, 717
disjoint, 709, 726
independent, 716
Examples and nonexamples, 80,
168, 249, 363, 698
Expanded form
of decimals, 55

of whole numbers, 7, 41, 735
Experiment, A28–A29
Experimental probability, 682–684
Exponent(s), 13, 15–16, 44, 108
evaluating, 76
negative, 274
notation, 13–16, 44, 108, 149, 180
rules, A6–A7
zero, 274–275
Exponential form, 14
Expressions, 8–11. *See also* Variable
expressions
addition, 8–11
algebraic, 8–11, 337–345
numeric, 13–16, 17–20, 22, 36, 44,
54, 62, 74
using a calculator, 23, 82
radical, 534–537
simplifying, 342–345
variable
evaluating, 8–11, 14–16, 17–18,
20, 22, 44–45, 61, 62, 160
evaluating with two variables,
10, 11, 18, 20, 22, 30, 59,
67–69, 74, 81
Extended response practice,
Throughout. See for example 7, 21,
41, 64, 123, 130, 143
Extensions
activities, 115, 274, 383, 527, 554,
640, 660, 688
examples, 379, 426, 559, 686, 720
Exterior angles, 521–526
Extra Practice, 776–788

F

Faces of a solid, 632
Factor(s), 165, 739
common, dividing out, 233
divisibility tests and, 739
tree, 165, 166, 273
Favorable outcomes, 682
Find the error, *See* Error Analysis
Fluid ounce (fl oz), 247, 250, 251, 252
Foot (ft), 245, 250
Formula(s)
for area
circle, 612–616, 622
parallelogram, 594–598, 621
rectangle, 32–36, 46, 75
square, 31–36, 46–47, 94
trapezoid, 602–606, 616, 621
triangle, 599, 601–606, 616, 621
for circumference, 607–611, 791
for distance, 26, 356
for Fahrenheit/Celsius
temperature, 297–300, 606,
790, 791
for percent of change, 480

for perimeter, 32–36, 75
for probability, 682
complementary events, 711
dependent events, 717
disjoint events, 710
independent events, 716
for simple interest, 490–494, 500
for surface area
cylinder, 649–653, 671
prism, 643–647, 667, 671
pyramid, 660
table of, 791
for volume, 655, 660, 662
cylinder, 662–666, 672
prism, 654–659, 667, 672
pyramid, 661
Four-step problem solving plan,
See Problem solving plan
Fraction(s)
adding, 219–230
with common denominators,
219–224
with different denominators,
220–224
using models, 219
comparing, 187–193
using approximations, 190, 191,
192
using cross products, 188
using least common
denominator, 189–192
using models, 187–188
dividing, 237–243
using models, 237
using reciprocals, 237–243
equivalent, 175–180
with exponents, A6–A7
improper, 194–198
mixed numbers, 194–198, 232–241
multiplying, 231–236
using models, 231
ordering, 187–193
proper, 194
reciprocals and, 237–241
repeating decimals and, 199–200
simplifying, 177–178
subtracting, 219–230
with common denominators,
219–224
with different denominators,
220–224
using models, 219
Frequency table, 138
making, 138, 142, 160
Front-end estimation, 61, 745
Function(s), 371
domain of, 376
evaluating, 371–375, 389
graphing, 376–382, 390
linear, 376, 377, 380, 381

making input-output tables for,
371–377
nonlinear, 378
recursive, A8–A9
writing rules for, 372, 380, 389

G

Gallon (gal), 247, 250
Games
   Brain Games, 30, 65, 114, 169, 242,
      319, 352, 435, 470, 526, 586,
      647, 721
   Get-Ready games, xxii–1, 52–53,
      106–107, 162–163, 216–217,
      266–267, 334–335, 396–397,
      446–447, 508–509, 574–575,
      628–629, 678–679
GCF, *See* Greatest common factor
Geometry, *See also,* Area; Perimeter;
      Surface area; Volume
   angles, 511–520
   circles, 474, 607–616
   congruent figures, 523, 525,
      537–541
   constructions, 527–528
   coordinate, A12–A13
   figures, A12–A13
   line symmetry, 547, 550–553
   net, 642, 649, 660
   plane, 517
   polygons, 529–534, 537–541,
      542–546
      hexagon, 530–531, 533
      octagon, 530–532
      parallelogram, 529, 594–598
      quadrilateral, 529–534
      rectangle, 31–36, 529, 532, 536
      rhombus, 529
      square, 755
      triangle, 521–526, 587–592, 755
   Pythagorean theorem, 588–592
   ray, 472–473, 474
   rotational symmetry, 547, 548–
      553
   segment, 314, 316
   similar figures, 542–546
   solids, 631–641
      cone, 631, 633–635
      cylinder, 631, 633–635, 638–639,
         649–653, 662–667, 671–672
      prism, 631–635, 642–647, 654–
         659, 661, 667
      pyramid, 631–635, 637–639,
         660–661
      sphere, 631, 633
   tessellation, 554–555
   transformation, 548–553, 556–561
      reflection, 548–553
      rotation, 548–553

translation, 548–553
Goldbach's conjecture, 169
Gram(s), 85
   benchmarks, 85
Graph(s), *See also* Box-and-whisker
      plot; Histogram; Line plot;
      Scatter plot
   bar, 117–120, 124, 144–148, 152,
      155, 757
   circle, 474–479, 727
   in a coordinate plane, 313–319,
      320, 326, 376–384, 390, 556–
      561, 568
   of an inequality, 366–370
   line, 115–124, 144–149, 152, 155,
      757
   misleading, 115–116, 145–148
   networks, A10–A11
   vertex-edge, A10–A11
Greatest common factor (GCF),
      170–174, 180, 186, 208
Grouping symbols, 18–23
Guess, check, and revise, problem
      solving strategy, 341, 635, 763,
      771
Guided Practice, *See* Assessment
Guided Problem Solving,
      Throughout. See for example
      6, 20, 63, 93, 121

H

Height
   of cylinder, 650–651
   of parallelogram, 594
   of rectangular prism, 656
   slant, 660
   of trapezoid, 602–603
   of triangle, 601
Heptagon, 530
Hexagon, 530
Histogram, 139
   making, 139–143, 154
Homework Help, *Throughout. See*
      for example 5, 10, 15, 19, 27,
      34, 39, 58, 62, 68, 73, 80, 87,
      92, 111, 120, 128, 136, 141,
      146
Horizontal axis, 118
Hypotenuse, 588–589

I

Identity property
   of addition, 302–305
   of multiplication, 302–305
Image, 548
Improper fractions, 194
   writing, 196, 204, 218
Inch (in.), 245, 250, 753

Increments
   large, compressing into vertical
      graph, 145
Independent events, 715–716, 726
   probability of, 716
Inductive Reasoning, A30–A31
Inequalities, 366
   graphing, 366–370
   reading, 366
   solution of, 366
   solving, 366–370
      of triangles, A32–A33
Inferences, *See* Draw conclusions
Input, 371
Integer(s), 269
   adding, 276–282
      multiple addends, 279–282
      using absolute value, 278–282
      using models, 276
   comparing, 269–273
   dividing, 296–300
   expressions, 292, 293–295
   multiplying, 291–295
   negative, 269, 274, 275
   ordering using a number line,
      270–273, 289
   positive, 269
   subtracting, 285–289
      using models, 283–284
   zero, 269, 274, 275
Interest
   simple, 490, 492, 500
Internet, *See* Animated Math;
      @HomeTutor; Homework
      Help; Online Quiz
Interquartile range, 134
Intersecting lines, 516, 518–520
Intersection
   of two sets, 688, 689
Intervals, 138, 145
   in data displays, A24–A25
Inverse operations, 738
   solving equations with, 347–348,
      361–362
Inverse property
   of addition, 302–305
   of multiplication, 302–305
Investigation(s)
   compare fractions, 187–188
   designing and conducting, A26–
      A27
   geometry
      area of rectangles and squares, 31
      area of triangles and trapezoids,
         599–600
      measuring length, 83
      Pythagorean theorem, 587
      similar rectangles, 536
      symmetry, 547
      volume, 654

making scale drawings, 429
modeling
    addition equations, 346
    addition of mixed numbers, 225
    decimals, 55
    equivalent fractions, 175
    integer addition, 276
    integer subtraction, 283
    multiplication equations, 353
    proportions, 417
multiplying fractions, 231
repeated multiplication, 12
statistics and probability
    determining outcomes, 695
    organizing data using median, 132
    probability, 681
using a percent bar model, 453
Irrational numbers, 583–586
Isosceles triangle, 523
constructing, 528

Journal, *See* Notetaking skills

Key Concepts, *Throughout. See for example* 9, 13, 17, 26, 32, 38, 56, 57, 66, 72, 78, 109, 144, 189, 194, 195, 219, 220, 226, 232, 237, 250, 269, 274, 278, 285, 291, 296, 297, 302, 307, 347, 348, 354, 355, 384, 399, 418, 423, 449, 454, 465, 490
Kilogram (kg), 85, 87–89
benchmarks, 85
Kiloliter (kL), 86, 87–89
benchmarks, 86
Kilometer (km), 84, 87–89

Lateral surface, of a cylinder, 649
Law of Detachment, A30–A31
Law of Syllogism, A30–A31
LCD, *See* Least common denominator
LCM, *See* Least common multiple
Leading digit, 66
Least common denominator (LCD), 189–190, 204, 222
comparing fractions, 189–190
Least common multiple (LCM), 182
finding, 182–184, 193, 204, 209
    using prime factorization, 183
using, 183
Left-to-right rule, 18

Legs, of right triangle, 588
Length, 81, 84–86, 241, 245, 248–249, 252–255, 273, 424
benchmarks, 84–86, 245
converting
    customary units, 250–255
    metric units, 90–95
finding, on coordinate plane, 314, 316
of a hypotenuse
    approximating, 589
    finding, 588
units of measure, 84, 250, 790
    customary system of, 245, 248–249, 753
    metric units, 84, 87–89, 753
Like terms, 342
combining, 342, 344–345, 348
Line(s), 411–414
drawing, using slope, 411–414
identifying, 634
intersecting, 516
parallel, 516, 634
perpendicular, 516, 517, 634
skew, 634
of symmetry, 547, 550
Line segments, measurement of, A2–A3
Linear functions, 377–381
Linear relationships
non-proportional, 297–300, 790, 791
proportional, 176, 178–180, 186, 208, 218, 305, 316, 377, 378–381, 435
Line graph, 118, 757
interpreting, 118, 121
making, 119, 121, 152
reading and interpreting, 757
Line of reflection, 548
Line plot, 108, 113, 123, 757, 758
Line segment
drawing with a compass, 754
Line slope, *See* Slope
Liquid amount, *See* Capacity
Liter (L), 86
benchmarks, 86
Look for a pattern, problem solving strategy, 403, 533, 536, 766, 773
Lower extreme, 133
Lower quartile, 133

Make a list, problem solving strategy, 341, 765, 772
Make a model, problem solving strategy, 761, 771
Make a table, problem solving strategy, 403, 408, 428, 546, 581, 615, 635, 765, 772

Manipulatives, *See also* Calculator
algebra tiles, 346, 353
base-ten pieces, 55, 60
chips, 25, 417
coins, 417
colored pencils, 175, 187, 231
compass, 472
graph paper, 31, 312, 409, 536, 587, 594, 599
integer chips, 25
measuring tools, 83, 144, 312, 404, 429, 472, 516, 536
number cube, 681
paper, 8, 12, 521, 547, 649
real-world objects, 429, 547, 587, 599, 607, 649, 702
tracing paper, 472
unit cube, 654
Markups, 500
Mass, 85, 87, 790, *See also* Weight
benchmarks, 85
gram, 85
kilogram, 85
measuring, 85
metric units, 85
    converting, 91
milligram, 85
Mean, 109, 151, A26–A27
finding, 109–114, 123, 130, 152, 299, 659
Measurement(s), *See also* Area; Measurement tools; Perimeter; Surface area; Volume; *See also specific measures*
accuracy of measurement, 83–86, A2–A3
adding, 252–255
angles, 472–473, 474–478, 510–515, 521–526
capacity
    customary units, 247–249
    metric units, 86–89
choosing appropriate units, 85, 86, 87, 246–247
comparing, 253
congruent figures and, 537–540
converting
    customary units, 250–255, A4–A5
    metric units, 90–95, A4–A5
estimation of, A2–A3
exercises, 63, 70, 93, 241, 252–255, 259, 379, 401, 515, 591
indirect, 543–546
    to find unknown length of polygon, 543
length
    customary units, 245, 248–249, 753
    metric units, 84, 87–89, 753

mass, 85, 87–89
ordering, 253
perimeter, 32–36, 755
precision, 83, A2–A3
similar figures and, 536–541
subtracting, 252–255
temperature, 297–300, 606, 790, 791
time, 751–752
units of measure, 84, 250, 790
customary system of, 245, 248–249, 753
metric units, 84, 87–89, 753
weight, 246, 248, 249
Measurement tools
compass, 472–483, 474–478, 527–528, 754
measuring cup, 86, 88, 247, 248
protractor, 472–473, 474–478, 527–528
ruler, 83, 84, 88, 245, 753
scale, 85, 87, 246, 248
Median, 109
examples, 110, 152
finding, 110, 111–114, 123, 130, 152
organizing data using, 132, A26–A27
Mental math
prices, 488
to solve percents, 457, 463
using to solve equations, 20, 26, 27, 36, 41, 45, 281, 287, 294, 304, 318, 336
Meter (m), 84
converting to kilometers, 90
Metric units, 83–89, 90–95
of capacity, 86
converting, 91, A4–A5
comparing measurements, 91
converting, 90–95, A4–A5
of length, 81, 84
converting, A4–A5
of mass, 84, 85
measuring with a ruler, 753
table of, 790
Mile (mi), 245, 250
Milligram (mg), 85
benchmarks, 85
Milliliter (mL), 86
benchmarks, 86
Millimeter (mm), 84
Mixed numbers
adding, 224, 226, 229, 242, 258
with calculator, 243
with common denominator, 226
modeling of, 225
comparing with fractions, 195, 197, 210
conversion to decimal, 205
definition of, 194

dividing, 239, 242, 259
with calculator, 243
and fractions
ordering, 196
modeling, 740
multiplying, 233, 234–236, 242, 258
with calculator, 243
rounding to estimate, 227
subtracting, 224, 226, 229, 242
with calculator, 243
with common denominator, 227
renaming for, 227
writing, 197, 218, 268
Mixed Review, 24, 42, 77, 96, 131, 150, 181, 206, 244, 256, 290, 321, 360, 385, 416, 436, 471, 495, 535, 563, 593, 618, 648, 668, 701, 722
Mixed Review by lesson, 7, 11, 16, 22, 30, 36, 41, 59, 65, 70, 76, 81, 89, 95, 114, 123, 130, 137, 143, 149, 169, 174, 180, 186, 193, 198, 204, 224, 230, 236, 241, 249, 255, 273, 282, 289, 295, 300, 306, 311, 318, 341, 345, 352, 359, 365, 370, 375, 381, 403, 408, 414, 422, 428, 435, 452, 459, 464, 470, 478, 484, 489, 494, 515, 520, 526, 534, 541, 546, 553, 561, 581, 586, 592, 598, 606, 611, 639, 647, 653, 666, 700
Mode, 109, 110, 152, A26–A27
finding, 110, 111–112, 113–114, 123, 130, 152, 659
Model, interpret, calculate, 375
Modeling, 16, 74, 179, 300, 457
addition
of mixed numbers, 225
of whole numbers, 741
addition equations, 346
areas of triangles and trapezoids, 599–600
decimals, 55
for direct variation, 384
fractions, 740
integer addition, 276
mixed numbers, 740
multiplication equations, 353
products, 66
proportions, 417
Pythagorean theorem, 587
subtraction
of integers, 283–284
of whole numbers, 736
Models
algebraic, 13, 26, 219, 232, 285, 297, 302, 307, 347, 348, 354, 355, 361, 384, 399, 418, 423, 449, 490, 588, 594, 601, 602,

608, 612, 642, 649, 655, 662, 710, 716, 717
area, 31, 35, 175, 178, 187, 197, 219, 225, 231, 237, 307, 461, 480, 587, 596, 599–600
graphical, 133–137, 269–273, 276, 277–282, 283–284, 285–289, 293, 315, 317–318, 336, 366, 367, 389, 453, 536, 582, 682, 688
numeric, 13, 26, 66, 72, 194, 195, 219, 232, 237, 278, 285, 291, 296, 297, 302, 307, 399, 418, 423, 449, 490
physical, 12, 25, 55, 60, 346, 353, 417, *See also* Manipulatives
verbal, 338, 349, 362
Money
commissions, 466, 469
discounts, 485–486
discounts, markups, tax, tips, 487–489
interest, 490–493
sales tax, 485–486
tips, 486
wages, 149, 438, 483
Multiple, 182, 184
least common, *See* Least common multiple
Multiple choice practice
Throughout. See for example 5, 6, 7, 10, 11, 16, 20, 28, 29, 35, 36, 39, 40, 41, 58, 59, 62, 64, 65, 69, 70, 74, 76, 80, 81, 88, 89, 93, 94, 112, 113, 121, 122, 123, 128, 130, 136, 141, 142, 146, 147, 149
Multiple representations,
Throughout. See for example 6, 16, 29, 94, 142, 179, 223, 241, 293, 374, 380, 408, 428, 434, 546, 581, 615
Multiplication
in conversions, 7, 11, 14, 65, 67, 76, 89
between customary units, 250
of metric units, 90
of decimals, 66–70, 98, 101, 143, 289
estimating products, 747
with exponents, A6–A7
expressions, 9
fact families, 738
factors and, 739
of fractions, 234
dividing out common factors, 233
modeling of, 231
using a calculator, 243
and whole numbers, 233
of integers, 292, 300, 324
with different sign, 291

with same sign, 291
uses for, 292
with zero, 291
of mixed numbers, 233, 242
using a calculator, 243
patterns, to find rules for
multiplying numbers, 291
by powers of ten, 743
problem solving and, 750
properties of
associative property of, 302, 304
communicative property of,
302, 304, 760
identity property of, 302
inverse property of, 302
product of powers property of,
A7–A8
repeated, 12
translating verbal phrases and
sentences, 337–338
whole number, 743
Multiplication equations
modeling, 353
solving, 354, 356–359
Multiplication property of equality,
355
Multiplicative identity, 302
Multiplicative inverse, 302
Multi-step problems
exercises, *Throughout. See for*
example 29, 94, 113, 148, 174,
186, 204, 223, 254, 318, 352,
375
solving, 372, 643, 656
using cross products, 424

N

Negative exponent, 274
Negative integers, 269
Net(s), 642, 651
Networks, A10–A11
Notation
coordinate, 556
scientific, *See* Scientific notation
Notetaking skills, *Throughout. See*
for example 18, 32, 66, 134,
165, 167, 200, 233, 355, 366,
424, 450, 456, 529, 595, 649,
662, 703, 709
comparing and contrasting, 336
concept grid, 680
connecting, 510
highlighting the key step, 448
including vocabulary notes, 108
items in, 2
keeping a notebook, 2
previewing the chapter, 54
recording the process, 268
showing multiple methods, 398

summarizing, 630
using your homework, 164
using your notes, 218
Number(s)
absolute value of, 278–279, 280–282
comparing in scientific notation, 79
irrational, 583–585
mixed, 194–198
ordering, 186, 197, 202
powers and exponents, 13
prime, 165–169
rational, 301, 583–585
real, 583
reciprocal, 237
scientific notation, 78, 79
square, 577
Number line, 736
for adding
integers, 277
whole numbers, 741
for comparing
whole numbers, 736
for ordering
integers, 270–273
whole numbers, 736
for subtracting
whole numbers, 741
Number sense, 16, 28, 40, 62, 80, 88,
172, 240, 294, 463, 468, 532,
585, 616, *See also* Comparing;
Equation(s); Estimation;
Ordering; Pattern(s);
Properties
comparing whole numbers, 736
divisibility tests, 739
expanded form, whole numbers,
735
operations
addition, 741, 742
divisibility tests, 739
division, 744
fact families, 738
multiplication, 743
subtraction, 741, 742
ordering whole numbers, 736, 737
place value
decimal, 56
whole number, 54, 735
Number sets
intersection of, 688–689
probability and, 688–689
union of, 688–689
Numerator, 176

O

Observational Study, A28–A29
Obtuse triangle, 522
Octagon, 530
Odds, finding, 686

Online Quiz, *Throughout. See for*
example 7, 11, 16, 22, 30, 36,
41, 59, 65, 76, 81, 89, 95, 114,
123, 130, 137, 149
Open-ended exercises, *Throughout.*
See for example 6, 11, 22, 29,
58, 59, 89, 94, 114, 122, 125,
130, 137, 142, 148, 168, 174,
178
Opposite(s), 269, 271, 282
comparing and contrasting with
integers, 336
Ordered pairs, 313, 315–318, 326
Ordering
decimals, 54, 57, 97, 108
fractions, 191, 209
integers using a number line, 270,
271–273, 311
measurements, 253
mixed numbers and fractions, 196
numbers, 65, 123, 197, 202, 268, 300
numbers in scientific notation, 80
rational numbers, 311
ratios, 451
stem-and-leaf plots, 126
whole numbers, 736
Order of operations, 17, 19–22, 45
on a calculator, 23
following, 17
grouping symbols, 18
left-to-right rule, 18
Origin, 313
Ounce (oz), 246, 250
Outcomes
counting, 693, 698
determining, 695
favorable, 682
Outliers, 129
Output, 371
Overlapping events, 709

P

Parallel lines, 516, 517, 518–520, 634
Parallelogram, 529, 596–598, 621
area of, 621
comparing, 596
finding, 594–595
base of, 594, 595
height of, 594
Pattern(s), 4, 5–7, 11, 16, 22, 40, 43,
58, 69, 222, 370, 468
describing, 3–7, 43
drawing, 6
extending, 3–4
letter, 5
looking for, problem-solving
strategy, 3–7, 38, 40, 58, 274,
291, 403, 434, 766, 773
number, 3–5

in problem solving, 38, 766, 773

recognizing, 3

using to find multiplication rules, 291

visual, 4, 5

extending, 4

Pentagon, 530

Percent(s), 449, 450, 470, 496

of change, 480, 481, 482–484, 494

circle graphs and, 474–476, 477–478

common, 455

decimals and, 460–464, 498

of decrease, 480–484, 499

equation, 465–470

estimating, 450, 470, 496

finding, 450, 454

a base, 456, 466

part of a base, 455

fractions and, 449, 451–452, 459, 496

of increase, 480–484, 499

interest, 492, 494

large and small, rewriting, 461

proportions and, 454, 456–459, 497

using percent bar model, 453

Perfect squares, 577

Perimeter, 30, 32, 34–36, 41, 93, 98, 310, 531–534, 545, 596

finding, 32, 46

formulas, 32, 755, 791

using, 33

Permutations, 702–707, 725

Perpendicular lines, 516, 517, 634

Perspective, 636

Pi (π), 607

finding

using a calculator, 617

Pie chart, See Circle graphs

Pint (pt), 247, 250

Place values

decimals and, 56

rounding and, 737

whole numbers, 735

Plane

lines in, 517

Points, locating on a number line, 736

Polygon(s), 529, 531–534, 544–546, 567, A14–A15

classifying, 530–532, 566–567

congruent, finding measures of, 537–538, 566–567

dilation, A20–A21

finding perimeters of, 531–534

finding the ratio of lengths, 538

finding an unknown length, 542–543

regular, 531

similar, 537, 539–541, 544–546, 566–567, A20–A21

checking for similarity, 538

scale factor, 538, A20–A21

using proportions with, 542–543, 567

tessellations, 554–555

Population, 115, A28–A29

Positive integers, 269

Pound (lb), 246, 250

Power(s), 13, 89, 149

evaluating, 14, 15–16, 44, 76, 274, 275

with variables, 14

of ten, multiplication by, 743

rules of multiplication and division, A7–A8

writing, 13, 15–16

Prerequisite skills, review of, 2, 54, 108, 164, 218, 268, 336, 398, 448, 510, 576, 630, 680

Prices

discounts, markups, tax, tips, 487–489

markup, 485

retail, 485–486

sales tax, 486

tips, 486

Prime

notation in transformation, 557

Prime factorization, 166–169, 207, 273

in finding GCF, 171, 172, 180

in finding LCM, 183, 204

using a factor tree, 165

Prime number, 165

identifying, 165–169, 174, 180

relatively prime, 171

Principal, 490

Prism

non-rectangular

surface area, 645, 671

volume, 658

properties of, 631, 632

rectangular, 657–659

finding surface area of, 644–647

height of, 656

volume of, 655

right, 642

sketching, 636, 638–639

surface area, 642, 644–647

Probability, 685, 698–700, 703, 712–714, 723, 724

combinations, 725

counting permutations, 702–703

counting principle, 696–697, 725

of events

complementary 711

compound, 715–720

dependent, 717

disjoint, 710

independent, 716

experimental, 682

finding, 681

listing combinations, 703

number sets and, 688–689

outcomes

counting, 693, 698

determining, 695

favorable, 682

permutations, 725

relating permutations and combinations, 703

sample space, 681–687, 690–694, 695–700, 702–706, 709–714

success, 720

theoretical, 682

Problem solving, See also Choosing problem-solving strategies; Eliminate choices; Guided problem solving; *Throughout. See for example* 6–7, 11, 15–16, 20–22, 28–30, 35–36, 40–41, 59, 63–65, 69–70, 74–76, 81, 88–89, 93–95, 112–114, 121–123, 129–130, 136–137, 142–143, 147–148

Problem Solving Handbook

Strategy Practice, 771–775

Strategy Review, 761–770

Problem-solving plan, 39–41, 46–47

solving and looking back, 38

understanding and planning, 37

Problem-solving strategies, See also Choosing problem-solving strategies

act it out, 12, 404, 427, 702, 770, 775

break into parts, 635, 767, 773

draw a diagram, 41, 238, 241, 340, 341, 546, 653, 693, 762, 771, 772

find a pattern, 38, 40, 274, 291, 403, 434, 533, 766

guess, check and revise, 25, 30, 341, 635, 763, 771

look for a pattern, 403, 766, 773

make a list, 341, 765, 772

make a model, 761, 771

make a table, 29, 372, 375, 403, 408, 419, 428, 546, 581, 615, 635, 765, 772

solve a simpler problem, 768, 774

use a Venn diagram, 769, 774

use a verbal model, 338, 349, 362

work backwards, 30, 361, 403, 700, 764, 772

Product, 743

cross, 432

find the product, 319

modeling, 66

placing decimal in, 66–67
writing powers as, 13–15
Product form
writing numbers in, 78, 275
Proper fraction, 194
Properties
of addition, 302–305, 325, 759–760
distributive, 307–308
identifying, 302
of exponents, A7–A8
of multiplication, 302–305, 325, 759–760
table of, 792
using, 303
Proportion(s), 418
cross products, 423
modeling, 417
percents and, 454, 456–459, 497
solving, 418–422, 423–428, 439, 440
multiple-step problems, 424
using algebra, 419
using equivalent ratios, 418
using with similar polygons, 542–543, 544–546, 567
writing, 424, 439
Proportional reasoning, 417–422, 423–428
percents, 454–459
rates, 404–408
ratios, 399–403
scale drawings, 429–435
Protractor
using to measure angles, 472–473, 474–478
Pyramid(s), 631, 632, 660
regular, 660
sketching, 637, 638–639
surface area, finding, 660
volume, finding, 661, A16–A17
Pythagorean theorem
finding the length of a hypotenuse, 588, 620
formula for, 791
modeling, 587

Q

Quadrant, 313
Quadrilateral(s), 529–530
Quantitative reasoning, *Throughout.*
See for example 10, 15, 28, 30, 56–59, 75, 79, 93, 97, 113, 136, 137
Quart (qt), 247, 250
Quotient, 744, *See also* Division
estimating, 236, 352
finding, 7, 70, 71, 72, 73, 76, 81, 130, 239, 295, 318
rounding, 73

R

Radical expression, 577, 578
Radius, 607
Random sample, 115
Range
of a data set, 110, 111–114, 130, 659, A24–A25
of a function, 371
interquartile, 134
of a product, 747
of a quotient, 748
Rate(s), 404
average rate formula, 405
finding unit, 404
interpreting slope as, 410
unit comparisons, 405
unit price, 405, 406
Ratio(s), *See also* Proportion; Rate(s); Scale
comparing, 400
definition of, 399
equivalent, 399, 418
ordering, 451
in simplest form, 400
unit rate and, 399–403, 404–408
using to describe slope, 409
using to form proportions, 426
writing, 399–400, 437
Rational numbers, 301
associative property of, 325
commutative property of, 325
identifying, 301
ordering, 301
Ray, 474
Readiness
Get-Ready exercises, 7, 11, 16, 22, 30, 36, 41, 59, 65, 70, 76, 81, 89, 95, 114, 123, 130, 137, 143, 149, 169, 174, 180, 186, 193, 198, 204, 224, 230, 236, 241, 249, 255, 273, 282, 289, 295, 300, 306, 311, 318, 341, 345, 352, 359, 365, 370, 375, 381, 403, 408, 414, 422, 428, 435, 452, 459, 464, 470, 478, 484, 489, 494, 515, 520, 526, 534, 541, 546, 553, 561, 581, 586, 592, 598, 606, 611, 616, 635, 639, 653, 659, 666, 687, 694, 700, 707, 714
Get-Ready games, xxiv–1, 52–53, 106–107, 162–163, 216–217, 266–267, 334–335, 396–397, 446–447, 508–509, 574–575, 628–629, 678–679
prerequisite skills, 2, 54, 108, 164, 218, 268, 336, 398, 448, 510, 576, 630, 680

Skills Review Handbook, 735–760
Reading in Math
biosphere, 665
bowling, 21
construction, 520
dancing, 422
marsupials, 203
music, 224
physics, 380
pyramids, 254
ramps, 591
stock trading, 306
tour de France, 148
track meet, 707
westward expansion, 75
winter sports, 484
Reading math, 3, 14, 25, 79, 118, 166, 176, 194, 232, 246, 269, 308, 338, 342, 366, 404, 431, 454, 460, 512, 516, 521, 557, 579, 602, 643
Real numbers, 583–586
Reasonableness
checking, *Throughout. See for example* 66, 76, 191, 403, 492, 546, 666
Reasoning, *See also* Error analysis; Games; Proportional reasoning; Spatial reasoning
exercises, 1, 7, 12, 20, 21, 31, 53, 74, 75, 122, 124, 128, 132, 142, 163, 167, 172, 174, 180, 185, 198, 203, 217, 222, 225, 229, 230, 235, 249, 253, 254, 267, 276, 284, 300, 304, 306, 316, 335, 346, 350, 358, 363, 370, 375, 382, 397, 408, 413, 415, 421, 422, 433, 447, 453, 457, 459, 463, 483, 489, 493, 509, 514, 525, 526, 532, 536, 540, 541, 547, 553, 555, 560, 561, 575, 580, 586, 587, 589, 591, 600, 611, 629, 634, 639, 645, 654, 665, 667, 679, 681, 686, 695
inductive and deductive, A30–A31
Reciprocals, 237
to divide fractions, 237–241
to divide mixed numbers, 238–241
to solve division equations, 355–359
Recursive functions, sequences, A8–A9
Rectangle(s), 529, 755
area of, 31, 32, 41
congruent, 540
perimeter of, 32, 755
properties of, 2
similar, 536, 540
Reflection, 548

in the coordinate plane, 557–561
line of, 548
Regular polygon, 531
Relatively prime numbers, 171, 180
Remainder, 744
Renaming
to subtract mixed numbers, 227
units of measure, 252
Repeating decimals, 199, 202, 381
writing fractions as, 200
Representations, *See* Multiple
representations
Review, *See* Chapter Review;
Cumulative Review; Extra
Practice; Mixed Review;
Mixed Review by lesson;
Prerequisite skills; Skills
Review Handbook
Rhombus, 529
Right trangle, 522
Rotation, 548–553
angle of, 549
center of, 548
identifying, 549
Rotational symmetry, 547, 550
Rounding, 7, 54, 57, 73, 97, 357, 737
decimals, 56–59, 71–76
degree measures, 476
to estimate
whole number differences, 746
whole number products, 747
whole number sums, 745
quotients, 73
whole numbers, 737
Routing, A10–A11

S

Sales tax, 486, 500
Sample(s), 115–116, A26–A27
biased, 115, A28–A29
random, 115, A28–A29
Sample space, 681–687, 690–694,
695–700, 702–706, 709–714
use combinations to find, 703
use a tree diagram to find, 690–694
Scale, 430
in data displays, A24–A29
drawing, 440
finding, 432
making, 429
on a map, 430
model, 431, 440
using, 432–435, 440
Scale drawing, 429–435
making, 429
Scale factor
in dilations, 559, A20–A21
of similar polygons, 538, 541,
A20–A21

Scale model, 431–435
Scalene triangle, 523
Scatter plot, 312–319
making, 312
Science, *See* Applications
Scientific notation
comparing numbers in, 79–81
writing numbers in, 78–81, 89, 99,
275, 359
Sectors, A18–A19
Segment, drawing with a compass,
754
Sequences, 373, 374
recursive functions for, A8–A9
Set(s)
element of, 688
empty, 688
intersection of, 688
union of, 688
universal, 688
Venn diagrams and, 688, 756
Short response practice
Throughout. See for example 6, 11,
16, 21, 29, 35, 40, 59, 63, 70,
75, 81, 89, 95, 113, 114, 129,
136, 142, 143, 147
Similarity, A20–A21
Simple interest, 490
formula for, 791
Simplest form, 177
Simplifying expressions, 343–345,
359, 387
Skew lines, 634
Skill Check, *See* Assessment
Skill Practice, *See* Assessment
Skills Review Handbook, 735–760
data displays
bar graph, 757
line graph, 757
line plot, 758
estimation
differences, 746
products, 747
quotients, 748
sums, 745
fractions, 740
logical reasoning, Venn diagrams,
756
measurement
perimeter, 755
time, 751, 752
using a compass, 754
using a ruler, 753
number sense
comparing whole numbers, 736
ordering whole numbers, 736,
737
rounding whole numbers, 737
whole number place value, 735
operations

addition, 741, 742
divisibility tests, 739
division, 744
fact families, 738
multiplication, 743
subtraction, 741, 742
problem solving, 749, 750, 752
properties
of addition, 759
of multiplication, 760
Slant height, 660
Slide, *See* Translation(s)
Slope, 409–414
to draw a line, 411
negative, 409
positive, 409
as a rate, 410
zero, 409
Solids
building, 640–641
classifying, 631, 669
drawing, 636–639, 670
edges of, 632
faces of, 632
vertices of, 632
viewing, 640–641
views of, 637
volume of, 654
Solution, 25
of an equation, 26
of an inequality, 366
Solve a simpler problem, problem
solving strategy, 768, 774
Solving equations, *See* Equations
Spatial reasoning
nets, 642, 649
sketching solids, 636
surface area, 642–647, 649–653,
660–661
Venn diagram, 756
views of a solid, 637, 640–641
visualizing volume, 655–656, 662–666
Sphere, 631
Spreadsheet, 562
Square, 529, 755
area of, 31, 32, 41
perimeter of, 32, 755
properties of, 2
Square numbers, 577
Square roots, 577–581
approximating, 582, 620, 793, A2–A3
evaluating, 577
using a calculator, 617
finding, 793
radical expressions, 577, 578
table of, 794
Standard deviation, A26–A27
Standard form
of a whole number, 735
writing numbers in, 14, 16, 78, 79,

80, 99, 186, 204, 275

Standardized Test Practice, 50–51, 104–105, 158–159, 214–215, 264–265, 330–331, 394–395, 444–445, 504–505, 572–573, 626–627, 676–677, 730–731

Standardized Test Preparation, 48–49, 102–103, 156–157, 212–213, 262–263, 328–329, 392–393, 442–443, 502–503, 570–571, 624–625, 674–675, 728–729

examples, 19, 34, 68, 92, 111, 140, 201, 221, 238, 247, 277, 297, 314, 356, 405, 425, 460, 512, 549, 603, 613, 632, 662, 684

State Test Practice, *Throughout. See for example* 24, 42, 50–51, 77, 96, 104–105, 131, 150, 158–159, 181, 206, 214–215

Statistics, *See also* Data; Data display; Graphs
descriptive, A41, A26–A29
extremes, 133
inferential, A41, A43, A26–A29
interquartile range, 134
mean, 109, A26–A27
median, 109, A26–A27
mode, 109, A26–A27
outlier, 129
population, 115, A28–A29
quartile, 133–134
range, 110

Stem-and-leaf plots, 126–130
interpreting, 127–130, A22–A23
making, 126–130, A22–A23
order in, 126

Stop and Think questions, 1, 53, 107, 163, 217, 267, 335, 397, 447, 509, 575, 629, 679

Straight angle, 511
Straightedge, 754
Substitution, 8
Subtraction
checking, 742
of decimals, 60, 98, 101, 143
elapsed time and, 752
estimating differences, whole number, 746
fact families, 738
of fractions, 219–224, 230, 257
using a calculator, 243
with common denominators, 219
with different denominators, 220
of integers, 285–289, 295, 323, 370
modeling, 283–284
order of, 286
measurements, 252, 253
of mixed numbers, 226–231
with common denominators,

226, 227
renaming for, 227
using a calculator, 243
problem solving and, 749
solving equations, 348–352, 387
whole number, 741, 742

Subtraction property of equality, 347
Sum, *See* Addition
Supplementary angles, 512
Surface area, 642
of cylinders, 649–654
nets, 642, 649
of prisms, 642–647, 671
of pyramids, 660
Surveys
circle graphs and, 474–478
questions, 115–116
biased, 115–116
Symbols, 516
grouping, 18
meaning of, 25, 579
table of, 789
Symmetry, 547
identifying, 550
line, 550
rotational, 547, 550

T

Table(s)
of formulas, 791
frequency, 138
input-output, 371, 378, 381
of measures, 790
of properties, 792
of squares and square roots, 794
of symbols, 789
Tangrams, 526
Technology activities
calculator
evaluating square roots, 617
finding permutations and combinations, 708
fraction and decimal conversion, 205
fraction operations, 243
graphing functions, 382
using order of operations, 23
using pi, 617
using scientific notation, 82
computer
finding surface area and volume, 667
making circle graphs, 479
making data displays, 124–125
translating points, 562
finding slope, 415
graphing in a coordinate plane, 320

spreadsheet, 562
Technology support, *See* Animated Math; @HomeTutor; Online Quiz; State Test Practice
Temperature
Celsius, 297, 790, 791
conversions, 297–300, 790, 791, A4–A5
Fahrenheit, 297, 790, 791
Terminating decimal, 199
Term(s), 342
constant, 342
like, 342
of a sequence, 373, A8–A9
Tessellation, 554–555
Test-taking strategies
choose a strategy exercise, *Throughout. See for example* 41, 65, 149, 169, 185, 236, 282, 318, 341, 357, 403, 494, 526, 561, 611, 635, 700
eliminate choices, *Throughout. See for example* 19, 34, 68, 92, 111, 190, 201, 221, 238, 247, 277, 297, 314, 373, 405, 425, 467, 487, 512, 549, 613, 662, 693
Theoretical probability, 682
Three-dimensional figures, *See* Solids
Time, 26, 149, 402
comparing, 751
converting among units of, 751
elapsed, 752
estimation and, 752
units of, 751, 790
Tips, 486–489, 500
Ton, 246, 250
Transformation(s), 548–553
in coordinate plane, 556–561
notation in, 556, 557
reflection, 548–553
rotation, 548–553
symmetry, 548
tessellation, 554–555
translation, 548–553
Translation(s), 548–553
in the coordinate plane, 556
identifying, 548
Trapezoid, 529–534
area of, 600, 601–606
modeling, 600
Tree diagram, 690–695
Triangle(s), 755
acute, 522
angle measures of, 521–526
area of, 599, 601–606
modeling, 599
base of, 601
classifying

by angle measures, 522
by side lengths, 523
equilateral, 523
height of, 601
hypotenuse, 588–589
inequalities, A32–A33
isosceles, 523, 528
obtuse, 522
perimeter of, 755
properties of, 523, 530
right, 522
scalene, 523
Two-dimensional figures, *See*
Polygons

Union of two sets, 688–689
Unit conversion
between customary and metric,
297–300, 791
within customary, 250–255
within metric, 90–95
Unit price, 405, 406
Unit rate, 404–408
average speed, 405, 406
comparing, 406
density, 407
unit price, 405, 406
Universal set, 688
Upper extreme, 133
Upper quartile, 133
U.S. customary system, *See*
Customary units
Use a Venn diagram, problem-
solving strategy, 769, 774

Validate conclusions, *See* Draw
conclusions; Reasoning
Variable expressions, 8–11
evaluating, 17–22, 292–295, 309,
319, 336
simplifying, 342–345
writing, 337–341
Variables, 8–11
assigning, 338
equations and, 25–30
expressions and, 8–11
powers and, 14–16
Venn diagram, 40, 365, 680, 756
of disjoint events, 709
logical reasoning and, 756
of overlapping events, 709
as a problem-solving strategy, 769,
774
Verbal model, 337
in problem solving, 176, 177, 286,
314, 338, 349, 362, 399, 400,

480–481, 485–486, 538, 543,
684, 696, 702, 703, 710, 711
Vertex
of an angle, 474
of a solid, 632
Vertex-Edge graphs, A10–A11
Vertical angles, 516–517
Vertical axis, 118
Vocabulary
exercises, *Throughout. See for*
example 5, 10, 15, 19, 27, 34,
39, 43, 58, 62, 68, 73, 78, 80,
87, 88, 92, 97, 111, 120, 128,
135, 141, 146, 151
learning, 78, 182, 199, 237, 278,
377, 410, 423, 466
prerequisite, 2, 54, 108, 164, 218,
268, 336, 398, 448, 510, 576,
680
review, 43, 97, 151, 207, 257
Volume
converting units of, A4–A5
of a cone, A16–A17
of a cylinder, 662–666
of a pyramid, 661, A16–A17
of a rectangular prism, 654–659,
667

Weight, 246, 790, *See also* Mass
benchmarks for, 246
converting units of, 251–255
measuring, 246, 250, 259
What If? questions, 9, 19, 33, 34, 38,
68, 73, 85, 86, 92, 111, 134,
145, 170, 177, 183, 221, 239,
252, 269, 279, 292, 307, 308,
315, 400, 410, 420, 424, 425,
432, 467, 476, 481, 486, 487,
491, 531, 539, 543, 583, 589,
596, 613, 656, 682, 683, 691,
696, 697
Which One Doesn't Belong?
questions, *Throughout. See*
for example 74, 87, 136, 184,
309, 433
Whole numbers, 197
adding, 741, 742
approximating, 582
comparing, 736
dividing, 70, 164, 193, 198, 744
estimation
differences, 746
products, 747
quotients, 748
sums, 745
fact families, 22, 738
in expanded form, 735
in standard form, 735

multiplying, 65, 164
with decimals, 67
with fractions, 233
by powers of ten, 743
ordering, 123, 736
place value, 735
rounding, 737
in standard form, 735
subtracting, 741, 742
word form of, 76, 186, 735
Work backwards, problem solving
strategy, 764, 772
Writing exercises, *Throughout. See*
for example 1, 6, 7, 10, 11, 12,
15, 16, 19, 20, 21, 22, 29, 30,
31, 34, 35, 36, 39, 40, 41, 53,
55, 59, 63, 64, 69, 70, 74, 75,
76, 80, 81, 83, 88, 89, 95, 101,
107, 112, 113, 114, 116, 120,
121, 122, 123, 125, 129, 130,
134, 136, 137, 140, 141, 142,
143, 146, 147, 148, 149, 155

***x*-axis,** 313
***x*-coordinate,** 313

Yard (yd), 245, 250
***y*-axis,** 313
***y*-coordinate,** 313

Zero
dividing by, 296
as an exponent, 274
as an integer, 269
as a place holder
decimal addition, 60
decimal multiplication, 67
decimal subtraction, 60
slope of a horizontal line, 409
Zero exponent, 274

Credits

Cover *center* Royalty-Free/Getty Images; **ML9** Gail Burton/AP Images; **ML10** Walter Bibikow/Getty Images; **ML11** Ezra Shaw/Getty Images; **ML12** Photograph by Jonathan Wiggs. Republished with permission of Globe Newspaper Company, Inc., from the 7/25/01 issue of The Boston Globe, 2001; **ML13** Terry Husebye/Getty Images; **ML14** age fotostock/SuperStock; **ML15** Stephen Frink/Corbis; **ML16** Jim Sugar/Corbis; **ML17** Patrik Giardino/Corbis; **ML18** Amanda Clement/Getty Images; **ML19** Neil Emmerson/Robert Harding World Imagery/Getty Images; **ML20** Imagemore/SuperStock; **ML21** i2Stock/Getty Images; **ML 24** Image Source/Alamy; **xxiv** *center, from top,* Royalty-Free/Corbis, Anatoly Malstev/AFP/Getty Images, Wally McNamee/Corbis, *background* Royalty-Free/Corbis, *gold medal* George Frey/AFP/Getty Images; **1** *top row, from left,* Royalty-Free/Corbis, Free Agents Limited/Corbis, *center row, from left,* Alan Schein Photography/Corbis, Royalty-Free/Corbis, Royalty-Free/Corbis, *bottom row, from left,* Sandy Felsenthal/Corbis, Royalty-Free/Corbis, AFP/Getty Images; Chris Trotman/Duomo/Corbis; **3** GDT/Getty Images; Monica Stevenson/FoodPix; **6** Michelle D. Bridwell/PhotoEdit; **7** Andy Williams/Getty Images; **8** Dawn Villella/AP Images; **9** School Division/Houghton Mifflin Co.; **11** Keren Su/Corbis; **13** Getty Images; **15** Alison Barnes Martin/Masterfile; **16** Frank Siteman/McDougal Littell/Houghton Mifflin Co.; **17** *top* Myrleen Ferguson Cate/PhotoEdit; *bottom* School Division/Houghton Mifflin Co.; **19** Naki Rocker Pad 2002 Naki International/Photograph by Ken O'Donoghue/McDougal Littell/Houghton Mifflin Co.; **20** Daniell Bonanno/Bruce Coleman Inc.; **21** Pedro Ugarte/AFP/Getty Images; **24** Tony Freeman/PhotoEdit; **25** Gail Mooney/Masterfile; **27** Bembaron Jeremy/Corbis Sygma; **28** Erwin Bud Nielsen/Index Stock Imagery; **32** Karl DeBlaker/AP Images; **35** Tony Freeman/PhotoEdit; **36** Donald Cooper/Shakespeare's Globe; **37** Paul A. Souders/Corbis; **38** Myrleen Ferguson Cate/PhotoEdit; **40** Digital Vision/Getty Images; **42** Jim Cummins/Corbis; **53** Ken O'Donoghue/McDougal Littell/Houghton Mifflin Co.; **56** Ben Curtis/AP Images; **59** Phil Long/AP Images; **60** David Young-Wolff/Getty Images; **63** Courtesy of the MAiZE, www.cornfieldmaze.com; **66** Walter Bibikow/Getty Images; **67** Setboun/Corbis; **69** Aura/Kitt Peak/Photo Researchers, Inc.; **71** Dennis MacDonald/PhotoEdit; **73** PhotoDisc Blue/Getty Images; **74** Paul Barton/Corbis; **77** Kimimasa Mayama/Landov/Reuters; **78** 2001 Ripley Entertainment, Inc. "Believe It or Not!" is a registered trademark of Ripley Entertainment, Inc.; **79** NASA/Roger Ressmeyer/Corbis; **81** William Sallaz/Duomo/Corbis; **83** Ken O'Donoghue/McDougal Littell/Houghton Mifflin Co.; **84** Richard Hamilton Smith/Corbis; **89** David Young-Wolff/PhotoEdit; **90** Tim Davis/Photo Researchers, Inc.; **92** Rusty Hill/Foodpix; **95** Ken O'Donoghue/McDougal Littell/Houghton Mifflin Co.; **96** Bob Krist/Corbis; **101** Ken O'Donoghue/McDougal Littell/Houghton Mifflin Co.; **106** Joseph Sohm/ChromoSohm Inc./Corbis; **107** PhotoDisc; **109** Donald Miralle/Getty Images; **110** Chuck Savage/Corbis; **112** Flip Nicklin/Minden Pictures; **113** School Division/Houghton Mifflin Co.; **114** Mary Kate Denny/PhotoEdit; **115** PhotoDisc; **117** Keren Su/Corbis; **118** Michael T. Sedam/Corbis; **120** Royalty-free/Corbis; **121** PhotoDisc; **122** Vicky Kasala/Getty Images; **126** Stefano Rellandini/Reuters; **127** Todd Gipstein/Corbis; **129** Myrleen Ferguson Cate/PhotoEdit; **132** Frank Siteman/McDougal Littell/Houghton Mifflin Co.; **133** Pierre Ducharme/Reuters

NewMedia Inc./Corbis; **134** CSA Plastock/Getty Images; **136** Royalty-Free/Corbis; **138** *top* Jim Sugar/Corbis; *bottom* Spencer Jones/Getty Images; **140** PhotoSpin; **143** Douglas Peebles/Corbis; **144** Tim De Weale/Corbis; **147** Jose Carillo/PhotoEdit; **150** Stephen Frink; **162-163** Lester Lefkowitz/Corbis; **163** *bottom left* Mansfield News Journal/Jason Molyct/AP Images; *top* Craig T. Mathew/AP Images; *right* Rick Norton/AP Images; **165** Buddy Mays/Corbis; **168** *top* School Division/Houghton Mifflin Co.; *bottom* China Photo/Reuters; **170** *top* Photograph by Jonathan Wiggs. Republished with permission of Globe Newspaper Company, Inc., from the 7/25/01 issue of The Boston Globe, 2001.; *bottom* Artville; **173** Vince Bucci/AFP/Getty Images; **174** Larry Kolvoord/The Image Works; **176** plainpicture/Alamy; **179** Maxine Hall/Corbis; **181** David Young-Wolff/PhotoEdit; **182** Tony Freeman/PhotoEdit; **183** Trevor Smithers ARPS/Alamy; **185** Michael T. Sedam/Corbis; **186** Johann Schumacher/Peter Arnold, Inc.; **189** Mike Brinson/Getty Images; **192** Peter Gridley/Getty Images; **193** Barbara Stitzer/PhotoEdit; **194** From *The Unbelievable Bubble Book* by John Cassidy. Photography by Peter Fox, Used with permission. 1987 Klutz; **196** Jeff Greenberg/PhotoEdit; **198** Dennis MacDonald/PhotoEdit; **199** Al Franklin/Corbis; **202** Ric Ergenbright/Corbis; **206** Tony Freeman/PhotoEdit; **217** David Madison/Getty Images; John Slater/Corbis; **219** Scott Manchester/©The Press Democrat, Santa Rosa, CA; **221** Mike Yoder/Lawrence Journal-World/AP Images; **223** Jeffrey L. Rotman/Corbis; **226** Jed Jacobsohn/Getty Images; **229** Michal Heron/Corbis; **230** Frank Siteman/McDougal Littell/Houghton Mifflin Co.; **232** *top badges:* Ken O'Donoghue/McDougal Littell/Houghton Mifflin Co.; *girl:* PhotoDisc; *bottom* Frank Siteman/McDougal Littell/Houghton Mifflin Co.; **233** *badges:* Ken O'Donoghue/McDougal Littell/Houghton Mifflin Co.; *boy:* PhotoDisc; **235** A. Ramey/PhotoEdit; **236** Ken O'Donoghue/McDougal Littell/Houghton Mifflin Co.; **237** Dana White/PhotoEdit; **238** Gregg Adams/Getty Images; **241** Terry Husebye/Getty Images; **244** John Warden/SuperStock; **245** Wolfgang Kaehler/Corbis; **247** Frank Siteman/McDougal Littell/Houghton Mifflin Co.; **249** David R. Frazier/The Image Works; **250** Tim Page/Corbis; **251** Yukimasa Hirota/Getty Images; **252** Martin Bydalek/Corbis; **254** Epix Photography/Getty Images; **256** Tim O'Hara/Corbis; **267** Ken O'Donoghue/McDougal Littell/Houghton Mifflin Co.; **269** Dennis MacDonald/PhotoEdit; **270** Bruno Morandi/Getty Images; **272** Chuck Savage/Corbis; **275** Satoshi Kawata; **277** Peter Mason/Getty Images; **282** Ken O'Donoghue/McDougal Littell/Houghton Mifflin Co.; **285** Kevin R. Morris/Corbis; **286** Alan Puzey/Getty Images; **288** Cydney Conger/Corbis; **290** Michael Freeman; **291** Age Fotostock/SuperStock; **292** Lonely Planet Images; **294** Mitsuaki Iwago/Minden Pictures; **295** Danny Lehman/Corbis; **296** Fritz Polking/Peter Arnold, Inc.; **299** Michael Freeman/Corbis; **301** Ricardo Mazalan/AP Images; **305** E. Schlegel/Dallas Morning News/Corbis Sygma; **306** Chris Hondros/Getty Images; **307** Brigid Davis; **308** Comstock/Jupiter Images; **310** Norm Dettlaff/Las Cruces Sun-News/AP Images; **313** Nancy Sheehan/PhotoEdit; **315** Dale Sanders/Masterfile; **317** *top* Jonathan Blair/Corbis; *bottom* Jeffrey L. Rotman/Corbis; **321** Patrick Ward/Corbis; **334** Staffan Widstrand/Corbis; **335** *top* Christie's Images/Corbis; *bottom* Archivo Iconographico/Corbis; **337** Michael Nichols/National Geographic Image Collection; **341** Jeff Christensen/Reuters; **342** David Young-Wolff/PhotoEdit; **345**

Royalty-Free/Corbis; **347** NASA; **349** NASA; **351** R. Holz/zefa/ Corbis; **354** Getty Images; **357** Lawrence Manning/Corbis; **358** Michael Geissinger/The Image Works; **360** Photofusion Picture Library/Alamy; **361** Walter Hodges/Getty Images; **362** Dimitri Iundt/Corbis; **365** Royalty-Free/Corbis; **366** Pictor International, Ltd./Jupiter Images; **370** Johner/Getty Images; **371** Stephen Frink/Corbis; **374** Tony Freeman/PhotoEdit; **376** Ken O'Donoghue/McDougal Littell/Houghton Mifflin Co.; **379** David Young-Wolff/PhotoEdit; **385** Randy Lincks/ Masterfile; **397** Ken O'Donoghue/McDougal Littell/ Houghton Mifflin Co.; **399** Brian Kersey/AP Images; **400** Joe McBride/Getty Images; **402** Duncan Smith/Getty Images; **404** *top* NASA/AP Images; *center, bottom* Jack Anthony, Dahlonega, Georgia; **405** Jerry Lampen/Reuters; **407** Royalty-Free/Corbis; **409** Mary Kate Denny/PhotoEdit; **410** G. Brad Lewis/Getty Images; **413** Frans Lanting/Minden Pictures; **416** Mike King/Corbis; **418** Scott Markewitz/Getty Images; **420** Johner/Photonica/Getty Images; **421** Brand X Pictures/ Alamy; **423** Mitsuaki Iwago/Minden Pictures; **424** Frans Lanting/Minden Pictures; **425** Steve Terrill/Corbis; **428** National Zoo/AP Images; **429** Ken O'Donoghue/McDougal Littell/Houghton Mifflin Co.; **430** Royalty-Free/Corbis; **431** Michael S. Yamashita/Corbis; **433** *Flying Pins*, 2000, Claes Oldenburg and Coosje van Bruggen. Steel, fiber-reinforced plastic, foam, epoxy; painted with polyester gelcoat and polyurethane enamel. Ten pins, including partially buried pins, combined pins, and individual pins; each 24' 7" (7.5 m) high x 7' 7" (2.3 m) widest diameter; and ball, 9' 2" (2.8 m) high x 21' 12" (6.7 m) diameter, in an area approximately 123' (37.5 m) long x 65' 7" (20 m) wide. Intersection of John F. Kennedylaan and Fellenoord Avenues, Eindhoven, the Netherlands.; **436** Tony Gutierrez/AP Images; **446** StockTreck/Corbis; **447** *top* Martin Barraud/Getty Images; *bottom* Frank Siteman/McDougal Littell/Houghton Mifflin Co.; **449** Bob Child/AP Images; **450** PhotoDisc; **452** Mary A. Dale-Bannister, Washington University in St. Louis. http:// nssdc.gsfc.nasa.gov/photo_gallery/photogallery-mars.html.; **454** Peter Wilson/AP Images; **455** Corbis; **458** Michael Newman/PhotoEdit; **459** Frans Lanting/Minden Pictures; **460** Joe Carini/Index Stock Imagery; **463** HOT WHEELS ® trademark owned by and used with permission from Mattel, Inc. © 2002 Mattel, Inc. All Rights Reserved. Cougar trademark used under license to Mattel, Inc. from Ford Motor Company. Photograph courtesy of David Williamson, ToyCarCollector.com; **465** *top* Annie Griffiths Belt/Corbis; *bottom* Robert Giroux/Reuters; **466** SW Productions/ PhotoDisc Green/Getty Images; **468** Mike Blake/Reuters/ Corbis; **469** Bob Krist/Corbis; **471** Royalty-Free/Corbis; **474** Chris Mellor/Lonely Planet Images; **478** Reza Estakhrian/ Getty Images; **480** Jeff Greenberg/PhotoEdit; **481** Tim Hawley/Foodpix; **483** Ken O'Donoghue/McDougal Littell/ Houghton Mifflin Co.; **484** J L Lloyd/Alamy; **485** *top* Ellen Senisi/The Image Works; *bottom* Ken O'Donoghue/McDougal Littell/Houghton Mifflin Co.; **486** Bob Daemmrich/ PhotoEdit; **489** Ken O'Donoghue/McDougal Littell/ Houghton Mifflin Co.; **490** *top* Thomas Florian/Index Stock Imagery; *bottom* Esa Hiltula/Alamy; **493** *top* Ryan McVay/ Getty Images; *bottom* Sandy Felsenthal/Corbis; **495** David Young-Wolff/PhotoEdit; **511** *top* Imagemore/SuperStock; *bottom* Timothy A. Clary/AFP/Getty Images; **516** Digital Vision/age fotostock; **520** Harris ("Butterfly") House, 1997, designed by Samuel Mockbee and students, Rural Studio,

Auburn University, AL. Photograph by Timothy Hursley; **521** Jeanne Moutoussamy-Ashe/Fifi Oscard Agency, Inc.; **529** Jeff Greenberg/PhotoEdit; **533** *top* Ken Burris/New England Quilt Museum; *bottom* Farrell Grehan/Corbis; **535** David Pollack/ Corbis; **536** Ken O'Donoghue/McDougal Littell/Houghton Mifflin Co.; **537** LMR Group/Alamy; **538** Dave Bartruff/Index Stock Imagery; **541** Lloyd Sutton/Masterfile; **542** B.A.E. Inc./ Alamy; **545** Dave G. Houser/Corbis; **548** LWA/Getty Images; **552** Frank Siteman/McDougal Littell/Houghton Mifflin Co.; **553** Merton Gauster/Getty Images; **555** Neil McAllister/ Alamy; **556** Brand X Pictures/Alamy; **563** Laura Ciapponi/ Getty Images; **574** Oliver Strewe/Lonely Planet Images; **575** Eric O'Connell/Getty Images; **577** David Turnley/Corbis; **578** Kevin R. Morris/Duomo/Corbis; **580** Charles O'Rear/Corbis; **582** Flying Colours LTD/Getty Images; **588** Toby Talbot/AP Images; **593** Alan G. Nelson/Animals Animals; **594** Roberto Candia/AP Images; **598** © 2002 George W. Hart; **601** Bill Ross/ Corbis; **602** Henry Westheim Photography/Alamy; **606** Linda Whitwam/Dorling Kindersley; **607** Eric Sandler; **608** Steve Shott/Dorling Kindersley; **609** *top right, bottom right* School Division/Houghton Mifflin Co.; *all others* PhotoDisc; **610** Allan Baxter/Getty Images; **612** Geri Engberg/The Image Works; **613** Dean Conger/Corbis; **614** *top center* School Division/Houghton Mifflin Co.; *all others* McDougal Littell/ Houghton Mifflin Co.; **615** McDougal Littell/Houghton Mifflin Co.; **618** Raymond Gehman/Corbis; **628** Mike Powell/ Allsport/Getty Images; **629** Mike Powell/Allsport/Getty Images; **631** *top* Elizabeth Simpson/Getty Images; *bottom left, bottom right* Ken O'Donoghue/McDougal Littell/Houghton Mifflin Co.; *bottom center* Dennis MacDonald/PhotoEdit; **633** *top left* PhotoDisc; *top center* Michael S. Yamashita/Corbis; *top right, bottom left* Ken O'Donoghue/McDougal Littell/ Houghton Mifflin Co.; *bottom center* Siede Preis/Getty Images; *bottom right* Comstock/Jupiter Images; **634** Lee Snider/Corbis; **636** *top* Ezra Stoller/Esto; *bottom* Ken O'Donoghue/McDougal Littell/Houghton Mifflin Co.; **637** Digital Vision/Getty Images; **638** Ken O'Donoghue/McDougal Littell/Houghton Mifflin Co.; **639** John Elk III/Lonely Planet Images; **642** Luc Novovitch/Alamy; **646** Ken O'Donoghue/ McDougal Littell/Houghton Mifflin Co.; **648** Bruce Coleman Inc.; **649** Courtesy of IndoBoard.com Rider: Serena Brooke. Photograph by Tom Servais; **653** David Young-Wolff/ PhotoEdit; **655** Rich Pedroncelli/AP Images; **658** Koichi Kamoshida/Getty Images; **660** Stephen Johnson/Getty Images; **662** Superstock; **665** Tom Dietrich/Getty Images; **666** Randall Fung/Corbis; **679** *top* Eric Curry; **679** *bottom* Ken O'Donoghue/McDougal Littell/Houghton Mifflin Co.; **682** *top* FLPA/Alamy; *bottom* Corbis; **685** Corbis; **687** Frank Siteman/McDougal Littell/Houghton Mifflin Co.; **690** *top* Richard T. Nowitz/National Geographic Image Collection; *bottom* Ken O'Donoghue/McDougal Littell/Houghton Mifflin Co.; **693** Monica Lau/Getty Images; **696** David Madison/ Allsport/Getty Images; **701** Gabe Palmer/Corbis; **702** Ryuichi Sato/Getty Images; **703** Hillery Smith Garrison/AP Images; **704** Jose Luis Pelaez, Inc./Corbis; **706** Jey Inoue/Getty Images; **707** Corbis; **709** Jonathan Nourok/PhotoEdit; **710** *both* Ben Garvin/1999 The Christian Science Monitor; **711** Myrleen Ferguson Cate/PhotoEdit; **714** Jeff Greenberg/ PhotoEdit; **715** Bob Daemmrich/The Image Works; **719** Ken O'Donoghue/McDougal Littell/Houghton Mifflin Co.; **720** Botanica/Jupiter Images; **722** Tony Freeman/PhotoEdit; **727** Corbis.

Selected Answers

Chapter 1

1.1 Skill Practice (pp. 5 – 6) **1.** C **3.** D **5.** Multiply the previous number by 5: 625; 3125; 15,625. **7.** Divide the previous number by 2: 40; 20; 10. **9.** Add 11 to the previous number: 44; 55; 66. **11.** Subtract 8 from the previous number: 48; 40; 32. **13.** Multiply the previous number by 6: 1296; 7776; 46,656. **15.** Add 1, then add 3, then add 5, then add 7, and so on: 27; 38; 51. **17.** no; *Sample answer:* The pattern is "Multiply the previous number by 2" so the next number is 8×2 or 16. **19.** Alternate triangle, square, triangle, square, etc.

21. Draw a square of dots where each side has one more dot than the previous square. • • • • •

25. Alternate, going forward from A and backwards from Z: C, X, D. **27.** Alternate, starting backwards from Z and backwards from M: X, K, W. **29.** Go backwards from Z, skipping 9 letters: L, B, R.

1.1 Problem Solving (pp. 6 – 7) **33.** 2nd round: 32 teams; 3rd round: 16 teams; 4th round: 8 teams

37.

39. a. The pattern is the odd numbers, or add 2 to the previous number.
b. *Sample answer:* • •• •• •• •• Each diagram has 2 more dots than the previous diagram.

1.2 Skill Practice (p. 10) **1.** variable **3.** 22 **5.** 28 **7.** 6 **9.** 18 **11.** 9 **13.** 24 **15.** The student misinterpreted the *a* as representing the ones digit. $2a$ means "$2 \times a$." So when $a = 3$, $2a = 2(3) = 6$. **17.** 34 **19.** 4 **21.** 39 **23.** 3 **27.** = **29.** < **31.** >

1.2 Problem Solving (p. 11) **39.** 84 in.

1.3 Skill Practice (p. 15) **1.** base 9, exponent 4 **3.** 10^2 **5.** k^4 **7.** five to the power of two; 25 **9.** zero to the power of eight; 0 **11.** six to the power of two; 36 **13.** five to the power of one; 5 **15.** 18 **17.** 625 **19.** 7776 **23.** 10^2 **25.** 2^5 **27.** 4^4 or 16^2 or 2^8 **29.** 3^5 **31.** < **33.** > **35.** = **37.** <

1.3 Problem Solving (pp. 15 – 16) **43.** 8^2, 64 **47.** $2^2 - 1$, $3^2 - 1$, $4^2 - 1$, or $n^2 - 1$ where $n =$ the number of dots in the first column of each set of dots **49. a.** *Sample answer:* Cut a piece of paper into 3 equal strips. Cut each strip into 3 pieces, and cut each piece into 3 parts. The result is 27 parts. **b.** $3^3 = 27$

1.4 Skill Practice (pp. 19 – 20) **1.** before **3.** 34 **5.** 96 **7.** 81 **9.** 7 **11.** 9 **13.** 2 **15.** The student added $4 + 3$ first instead of subtracting $8 - 4$ first. Use the left-to-right rule; $8 - 4 + 3 = 4 + 3 = 7$. **17.** 20 **19.** 10 **21.** 4 **23.** 44 **25.** × **27.** − **29.** − **31.** ÷ **33.** ÷ **35.** $(20 - 3^2) \times 2 + 8 = 30$

1.4 Problem Solving (pp. 20 – 22) **45.** $1 \times 15 + 4 \times 25 + 2 \times 20 = 155$ kg **47.** You get 6 discounts of $11: $66 \times 4 - 6 \times 11 = 264 - 66 = 198$. **49.** bowling + cake + soft drinks $= 10 \times 5 + 10 \times 2 + 10 \times 1 = \$80$ **51.** At the per person rate, a party for 15 people costs $15 \times 5 + 15 \times 2 + 15 \times 1 = \$120$, and a party of 16 people costs $16 \times 5 + 16 \times 2 + 16 \times 1 = \$128$. So the least number of people is 16 for the group rate of $125 to be less than the per person rate.

1.4 Technology Activity (p. 23) **1.** 23 **3.** 4 **5.** 5 **7.** 13 **9.** about 1080

1.5 Skill Practice (pp. 27 – 28) **1.** solution **3.** yes **5.** no **7.** no **9.** 6 **11.** 9 **13.** 17 **15.** 48 **17.** 6 **19.** 3 **21.** 4 h **23.** 3 sec **25.** $9 \frac{\text{mi}}{\text{h}}$ **27.** The variable and the number 7 are written in the wrong order; $x \div 7 = 28$. **31.** no **33.** no **35.** no solutions **37.** one solution

1.5 Problem Solving (pp. 28 – 30) **43.** 3 min **45.** $\frac{600 \text{ ft}}{\text{min}}$; I used the equation $d = rt$ with $d = 3000$ ft and $t = 5$ min.

49. a.

		d		g		

(diagram showing 1600 m total length)

b.

d	0	50	100	150	200
g	1600	1550	1500	1450	1400

c. When d increases by 50, g decreases by 50. In general, as d increases by an amount, g decreases by the same amount.

1.6 Skill Practice (pp. 34 – 35) **1.** perimeter **3.** $P = 36$ m, $A = 45$ m^2 **5.** The student found the area, not the perimeter. The equation should be for perimeter; $P = 4s = 12$ in. **7.** $P = 32$ m, $A = 63$ m^2 **9.** $P = 44$ ft, $A = 40$ ft^2 **11.** $P = 34$ in., $A = 66$ in.^{2} **13.** $P = 48$ cm, $A = 144$ cm^2 **17.** 2 ft **19.** 8 m **21.** $P = 32$ m, $A = 36$ m^2; *Sample answer:* Think of the figure as a 2 by 3 rectangle taken from a 7 by 6 rectangle.

1.6 Problem Solving (pp. 35 – 36) **27.** $P = 22$ ft, $A = 28$ ft^2 **33.** $A = 1100$ ft^2, $P = 138$ ft **35.** *Sample answer:* The painted area on each side of a door is $3 \times 7 - 3$ or 18 ft^2. So for both sides of 2 doors, the total painted area is $2 \times 2 \times 18$ or 72 ft^2. You will need a minimum of 3 cans $(72 \div 30 = 2 \text{ R}12)$ and no more than 4 cans $(72 \div 22 = 3 \text{ R}6)$. Therefore you should buy 4 cans.

1.7 Skill Practice (pp. 39 – 40) **1.** *Answers may vary. Sample answer:* Step 1: Read the problem and identify the important information. Step 2: Pick a strategy to solve the problem. Step 3: Use the strategy to answer the problem. Step 4: Check your answer.   **3.** You know the individual costs and how much the customer paid. You need to find out the customer's change.   **5.** The value 22 represents the total cost of the tickets and snacks. You have to subtract the cost of the snacks before you divide by 2; $(22 - 6) \div 2 = 8$; the tickets cost \$8 each.

1.7 Problem Solving (pp. 40 – 41)   13. on day 7   **15.** 64 members   **17.** The friend is correct about the number of lanterns needed on each side. But because you only need one lantern on each corner, adding the number needed for each side gives you a number 4 greater than what you need. Only 24 lanterns are needed.**19.** Cindy is first in line, followed by Ty, Mark, and Karen, in that order. I used the strategy Draw a Diagram to model the information in the problem.

Chapter Review (pp. 43 – 46)   1. solution   **3.** an equal sign   **5.** Add 10 to the previous number: 41; 51; 61.
7. Double the previous number: 400; 800; 1600.
9. Subtract 3 from the previous number: 88; 85, 82.
11. Going in a clockwise direction, skip one section and then shade;

13. 63   **15.** 5   **17.** 32   **19.** 7   **21.** 9   **23.** 100   **25.** 32   **27.** 243   **29.** 729   **31.** 15   **33.** 1   **35.** 34   **37.** 75   **39.** 3   **41.** 3   **43.** 64   **45.** 5   **47.** 4   **49.** 21   **51.** 5   **53.** 28   **55.** 30   **57.** 3   **59.** 4   **61.** 120   **63.** $P = 38$ ft, $A = 48$ ft^2 **65.** $P = 140$ in., $A = 1225$ in.^{2} **67.** $P = 60$ yd, $A = 225$ yd^2 **69.** 1 quarter, 1 dime; 1 quarter, 2 nickels; 3 dimes, 1 nickel; 2 dimes, 3 nickels; 1 dime, 5 nickels; 7 nickels

Chapter 2

2.1 Skill Practice (p. 58)   1. tenths   **3.** hundreds   **5.** >   **7.** =   **9.** <   **11.** =   **13.** >   **15.** no; Compare the single digits in the same place values. For the ones' digits, 8 = 8. For the tenths' digits, 4 > 2. So 8.4 > 8.29.   **17.** 7.635, 7.65, 8.56, 8.65   **19.** 7.266, 7.276, 7.3057, 7.34   **21.** 8.999, 9.594, 9.6, 9.701   **23.** 32.1   **25.** 1   **27.** 9.10   **29.** 7.2607   **35.** Divide the previous number by 10; 0.001, 0.0001.

2.1 Problem Solving (p. 59)   39. the 12.2 ft sculpture

2.2 Skill Practice (pp. 62 – 63)   1. Add the whole number parts. Then estimate the sum of the decimal parts, and add that to the previous sum.   *3–13. Checking will vary.*   **3.** 23.4; 16 + 8 = 24   **5.** 67.263; 50 + 15 = 65   **7.** 82.5; 90 − 8 = 82   **9.** 483.83; 467 + 5 + 11 = 483   **11.** 13.95; 9 + 20 − 15 = 14   **13.** 19.068; 26 − 9 + 2 = 19   **15.** The 13 is lined up incorrectly under the 48 in 3.48. Write 13 as 13.00 and line up the decimal points; The sum is 16.48.   **17.** 14.02   **19.** 123.627   **21.** 138.746   **23.** 35.3   *25–33. Estimates may vary. Samples are given.*   **25.** 15   **27.** 18   **29.** 3   **31.** 3   **33.** 13   **35.** 6 + 0.9 + 0.01 + 0.002   **37.** 40 + 3 + 0.07   **39.** >   **41.** >   **43.** <   **45.** Add; you want to find the total cost.   **47.** Subtract; you want to find the difference in the costs.

2.2 Problem Solving (pp. 63 – 65)   *53–55. Checking will vary.*   **53. 9.3 acres; 13 − 3 = 10, reasonable   **55.** 1.35 L;

1 + 0.2 + 0.02 = 1.22, reasonable   **57.** yes; The total time for your team is 22.34 + 25.8 + 30.15, or 78.29 min, which is faster than the total time of 80.63 min for your friend's team.

2.3 Skill Practice (pp. 68 – 79)   1. 4   **3.** 18   **5.** 0.012   **7.** 2.4   **9.** 22.1   **11.** 3.549   **13.** 343.64   **15.** 0.0126   **17.** 13.188   **19.** 1.3   **21.** The decimal point was brought straight down instead of adding the total number of decimal places in both factors. The product should have 2 + 2 = 4 decimal places; 0.2484.   **23.** 13.5 mm^2 **25.** 52.9104 yd^2 **27.** 0.9   **29.** 100   **31.** 420   **33.** 120   **35.** 0.14994   **37.** 0.0872032   **39.** 866.640042   **41.** 223.266   **43.** 32.768   **45.** Divide the previous number by 2: 0.0625; 0.03125; 0.015625.

2.3 Problem Solving (pp. 69 – 70)   49. 26.048 ft^2 **55. a.** pollen: 0.0364 mm; algae: 0.0888 mm; blood cell: 0.0114 mm   **b.** blood cell, pollen, algae

2.4 Skill Practice (pp. 73 – 74)   1. 56 and 7   **3.** 1.25   **5.** 0.053   **7.** 53.64   **9.** 5   **11.** 100   **13.** 7.3   **15.** 1.88   **17.** 5.05   **19.** 5.49   **21.** 35.61   **23.** A; for B, C, and D, the quotient is 12.5, but for A the quotient is 1.25.   *25–33. Estimates may vary. Samples are given.*   **25.** 21   **27.** 1   **29.** 36   **31.** 8   **33.** 7   **35.** 4.37   **37.** 82.2   **39.** 34   **41.** To represent 0.8 ÷ 0.2 on a number line, show how many lengths of 0.2 are needed to show a length of 0.8;

0.8 ÷ 0.2 = 4

2.4 Problem Solving (pp. 74 – 76)   43. *Estimates may vary. Sample answer:* 750 ÷ 5 = 150 cars. (The actual number is 158 cars.)   **49.** 5.05 cm   **51.** about 360,000,000 acres   **53.** Louisiana Territory; about \$18.12 per mi^2; Alaska: about \$12.80 per mi^2; the Louisiana purchase cost about \$5 less per acre than the Alaska purchase.   **55. a.** 4 times   **b.** The area of the second rectangle, 1102.08 ft^2, is 16 times as much as the area of the first rectangle, 68.88 ft^2.

2.5 Skill Practice (p. 80)   1. scientific notation   **3.** standard form   **5.** 4.12×10^4 **7.** 2.92×10^7 **9.** 1.54×10^5 **11.** 1.024×10^2 **13.** 5.35×10^2 **15.** No, the first factor should be ≥ 1 and < 10; It should be 2.95×10^7.   **17.** 2000   **19.** 150   **21.** 5,884,000,000   **23.** 60.7   **25.** <   **27.** =   **29.** *Sample answers:* 1×10^3, 2.3×10^4, and 5.67×10^8 are in scientific notation; 10×10^2, 23×10^3, and 56.7×10^7 are not in scientific notation.   **31.** 7.98×10^4, 3.25×10^5, 3.5×10^5, 2.61×10^6 **33.** 1.10×10^7, 1.1×10^8, 1.101×10^8, 1.11×10^8 **35.** 1.502×10^{10} **37.** 6.7924×10^9

2.5 Problem Solving (p. 81)   39. 2400 lb   **41.** Galileo   **43.** 25,284,000,000,000 mi; 2.5284×10^{13} mi

2.5 Technology Activity (p. 82)   1. 7.3×10^9 **3.** about 3.88 times greater

2.6 Skill Practice (pp. 87–88)   1. mass   *3–7. Estimates may vary. Sample answers are given.*   **3.** 25 cm   **5.** 26.5 cm   **7.** 6 cm   **9.** 0.6 kg   **11.** 5.1 g   **13.** meters   **15.** kilograms   **17.** milliliters   **19.** meters

21. centimeters **23.** kilograms **25.** milliliters **27.** B
29. 350 mL **31.** 1.9 L **35.** No, a mass of 400 g is about
the mass of a box of 400 paper clips, which is too light for
a desk. **37.** D **39.** A

2.6 Problem Solving (pp. 88 – 89) 41. 30 **43.** 3

2.7 Skill Practice (pp. 92 – 93) 1. milliliters **3.** kilogram
5. 4900 **7.** 0.47 **9.** 3750 **11.** 750 **13.** 352.8 **15.** 840
17. 1,280,000 **19.** The student multiplied by 1000
instead of dividing. To convert from milligrams to grams,
divide by 1000. So 50 mg = 0.05 g. **21.** = **23.** > **25.** <
27. > **31.** 3965 mL **33.** 107,025 mg **35.** 1550 mL
37. $P = 6.6$ cm, $A = 2$ cm² **39.** 9.5 mg, 69 mg, 0.04 kg,
45 g, 60 g

2.7 Problem Solving (pp. 93 – 95) 45. 60 paper
clips **47.** 4 kg **53. a.** 6,380,000 m **b.** 6380 km
c. 12,760 km; Double the radius to find the diameter;
1.276×10^4 km

Chapter Review (pp. 97 – 100) 1. *Answers may vary.*
Sample answer: 0.5, 1.6, 100.001 **3.** A number in
scientific notation, such as 5.2×10^3, is written in the
form $c \times 10^n$, where $1 \le c < 10$ and n is an integer. A
number in standard form, such as 5200, is written out in
digits. **5.** meter **7.** < **9.** > **11.** If the thousandths'
digit is greater than 5, round up by adding 1 to the digit in
the hundredths' place. If it is less than 5, round down by
keeping the digit in the hundredths' place the same.
13. 25.895 **15.** 25.102 *17–19. Estimates may vary.*
Sample estimates are given. **17.** 13 **19.** 4 **21.** 23.95
23. 8.57 **25.** 993.6 **27.** 68.8154 **29.** 82.3346
31. 1346.115 **33.** 3001 games **35.** 3.4 **37.** 9.4 **39.** 75.4
41. 0.09 **43.** $.94 **45.** $2.83 **47.** 3.356×10^6
49. 7.0×10^5 **51.** 406,000,000 **53.** 125 **55.** meters
57. D **59.** C **61.** 0.07 **63.** 0.0000094 **65.** >
67. < **69.** =

Chapter 3

3.1 Skill Practice (pp. 111 – 112) 1. true **3.** 33; 38; 38;
25 **5.** 437; 502; 502; 410 **7.** 51; 46; 23 and 46; 58 **9.** 2.3;
2.8; no mode; 4.6 **11.** 5.2; 5.2; 5.2; 0.2 **15.** the median,
24 **17.** the mean and the median, 12 **19.** 3 **21.** 7

3.1 Problem Solving (pp. 112 – 114) 27. 18.75; 15; 32; 32
29. 226.630; 225.608. *Sample answer:* The median is the
better measure because the two larger values make the
mean too large to represent the data well; 1999 to 2001
33. *Sample answer:* All three averages are very close
together. The mean best represents the data; the median
and the mode are both near the higher end of the data.
The range tells little about this data set.
35. a. 83; 85; 95; 27 **b.** *Sample answer:* The mean and
the median are both reasonable averages. The mode,
95, is not. **c.** The mean increases from 83 to 84.7. The
median increases from 85 to 85.5, while the mode stays
at 95.

3.1 Extension (p. 116) 1. biased; Asking people who are
active users of the library could bias the sample in favor
of increased spending. This sample may not reflect the
opinions of voters or taxpayers on the whole. **3.** This is
a good sampling method. The sample is random and not

likely to be biased. **5.** biased; The adjectives "exciting"
and "crying" seem to ask for a response in favor of the
movie. **7.** biased; The information provided by the
statement seems to ask respondents to say yes.

3.2 Skill Practice (pp. 120 – 121) 1. horizontal axis;
vertical axis **3.** 27 **5.** canned drinks **7.** Only 30
seventh graders bought canned drinks, and because
there were eighth graders that bought canned drinks, the
difference has to be less than 30; 6 more seventh graders
bought canned drinks than eighth graders.

9.

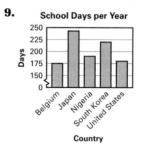

11.

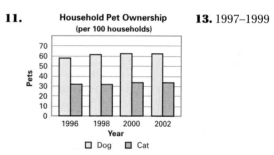

13. 1997–1999

3.2 Problem Solving (pp. 121 – 123)

18. a.

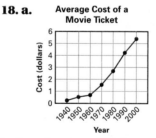

b. *Sample answer:* The line segments vary from nearly
flat (1950–1960) to quite steep, the steepest being 1980 to
1990. Over time, the cost of a ticket has always gone up,
but it increased much more dramatically since 1960.
19. 1992–1993. *Sample answer:* For 1992–1993, the
number of tornadoes decreased by more than one
hundred, while for 1995–1996, the decrease was less
than one hundred. **23.** no; The data are not entirely
numerical and do not show a change in data over time.
Type of pet is a category, and only the frequency for
each type of pet is numerical. **25.** *Sample answer:*
Each year from 1999 to 2003, the circulation of evening
newspapers has decreased, while that of morning papers
has increased, but not enough to make up for the entire
decrease, resulting in an overall decrease in newspaper
circulation.

3.2 Technology Activity (pp. 124 – 125)

1.

Shopping Centers

3. *Sample answer:* In each of the 5 states shown, the number of shopping centers increased from 1999 to 2000.

3.3 Skill Practice (pp. 128 – 129)   **1.** 10; 5

3.
```
0 | 9
1 | 0 2 2 3 5 9
2 | 2 6 7 7 9
```
Key: 1 | 0 = 10

5.
```
0 | 5
1 | 1
2 | 0 2 4 5
3 | 0
4 | 1
5 | 8
6 | 6
```
Key: 4 | 1 = 4.1

7. There is no 6 in the stem;
```
4 | 3 3 5 6
5 | 0 1 2
6 |
7 | 4 4 8 9 9
```
Key: 7 | 4 = 74

3.3 Problem Solving (pp. 129 – 130)   **17.** 61
19. *Sample answer:* The great grandfather's age is an outlier because there is a large difference (37 years) between his age and the age of the next oldest person.

3.4 Skill Practice (pp. 135 – 136)   **1.** false; The upper extreme is 117.   **3.** true   **5.** true

7.

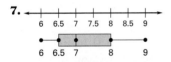

9.

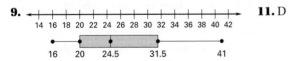

11. D

3.4 Problem Solving (pp. 136 – 137)   **21.** $\frac{1}{4}$

23.

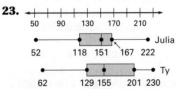

25. *Sample answer:* Ty is, in general, able to drive the ball farther than Julia. His upper extreme is 8 yards greater than Julia's, and his upper quartile is 34 yards greater than Julia's.

3.5 Skill Practice (pp. 141 – 142)   **1.** frequency   **3.** 25-27; 4; 5; 4; 5   **5.** Two of the intervals overlap, so they are not well defined. Change them to 100–149, 150–199, 200–249, and 250–299;

Interval	Frequency
100-149	4
150-199	6
200-249	2
250-299	4

7.

Interval	Frequency
61-70	4
71-80	4
81-90	11
91-100	5

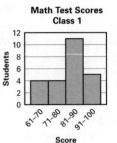

Math Test Scores Class 1

9.

Interval	Frequency
51-100	9
101-150	8
151-200	4
201-250	0
251-300	2
301-350	1

Prices of Wicker Furniture

3.6 Skill Practice (p. 146)   **1.** bar graph, stem-and-leaf plot, histogram, line graph, and box-and-whisker plot   **3.** histogram; A histogram uses numerical intervals of equal width.   **5.** bar graph; The categories here are not numerical. They are the names of basketball teams.
9. a bar graph;

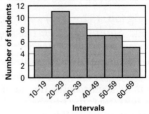

Ages of Students in a CPR Class

3.6 Problem Solving (pp. 147 – 149)   **15.** false; Pasta was selected by about 62 students, while about 48 students chose fish. 48 is more than half of 62.   **17.** false; Twice the other is 80, which is more than the 60 students who chose beef.   **19.** false; Beef was chosen by 60 students, which is less than the 62 students that chose pasta.   **21.** The box-and-whisker plot compares the lengths of the stages without using space for all of the data that has a large range; the stem-and-leaf plot groups the data; and the line plot shows the individual data values.   **23. a.** about twice as much   **b.** about 4 times;

no **c.** *Sample answer:* The graph could be misleading because the artist increased both the height and width of each recycle bin drawn. When making a bar graph, you are supposed to keep the bars of equal width to avoid this type of misleading graph.

Chapter Review (pp. 151 – 154) 1. bar graph **3.** lower extreme, lower quartile, median, upper quartile, and upper extreme **5.** mean **7.** stem-and-leaf plot **9.** 6; 5; 4; 13 **11.** 6; 6.15; 4.6 and 6.3; 2.9 **13.** *Sample answer:* The mean of the data set is 7, while the median is 6.5. The mode is 5. The mode is near the beginning of the data set, so it may not be a good representation of the entire data set. The median and mean are very close in value, so either one would make a good choice. 7 would represent the data well, as it is near the middle of the data.
15. March and April;

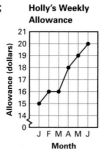

Holly's Weekly Allowance

17.
```
1 | 2 7 8 9
2 | 0 2 3 5 7
3 | 0 5 6 6 7 8 8 9
4 | 1
```
Key: 3 | 7 = 37

19.

Interval	Frequency
20–29	3
30–39	5
40–49	5
50–59	4
60–69	2
70–79	1

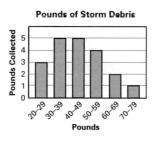

Pounds of Storm Debris

Chapter 4

4.1 Skill Practice (pp. 167 – 168) 1. prime factorization **3.** 1, 2, 4, 5, 10, 20 **5.** 1, 13 **7.** 1, 2, 4, 5, 10, 20, 25, 50, 100 **9.** prime; the only factors are 1 and 23. **11.** composite; $51 = 3 \cdot 17$ **13.** prime; the only factors are 1 and 67. **15.** composite; $99 = 3 \cdot 33$ **17.** composite; $87 = 3 \cdot 29$ **19.** $2^2 \cdot 17$ **21.** 2^6 **23.** $2^4 \cdot 3^2$ **25.** $2^2 \cdot 3 \cdot 7^2$ **27.** $2^5 \cdot 3^3$ **29.** Nine needs to be factored so $9 = 3^2$; $2^2 \cdot 3^2$ **31.** false; 2 is a prime. **33.** false; 2 and 3 are primes, and $2 \cdot 3$ is not odd. **35.** 53, 59, 61, 67, 71, 73, 79 **37.** 181, 191, 193, 197 **39.** 271, 277, 281, 283, 293 **41.** 1, 2, 3, 5, 6, 8, 9 **43.** 1, 2, 4, 5, 7, 10

4.1 Problem Solving (pp. 168 – 169) 47. composite; The total number of stones is the product of the number of stones in a pouch times the number of pouches. It is divisible by at least 2, the minimum number of stones in

each pouch. **49.** factors: 1, 2, 4, 7, 14, 28, possible group sizes: 2, 4, 7, 14 **53.** *Sample answer:* $4 = 2 + 2$; $6 = 3 + 3$; $8 = 3 + 5$; $10 = 3 + 7$

4.2 Skill Practice (pp. 172 – 173) 1. common factor **3.** 7 **5.** 11 **7.** 1 **9.** 5 **11.** 15 **13.** 6 **15.** 4 is a factor of 32; The GCF is 4. **17.** 14; not relatively prime **19.** 2; not relatively prime **21.** 18; not relatively prime **23.** 17; not relatively prime **25.** 24; not relatively prime **27.** 21; not relatively prime **29.** sometimes; The GCF of 2 and 4 is 2, but the GCF of 4 and 8 is 4. **31.** always; The only factors of each number are itself and 1. **33.** *Answers may vary. Sample answer:* 210 and 217; I know that $7 \cdot 30 = 210$, so I used $7 \cdot 30$ and $7 \cdot 31$. **35.** *Answers may vary. Sample answer:* 240 and 248; I know that $8 \cdot 30 = 240$, so I used $8 \cdot 16$ and $8 \cdot 17$. **37.** $A = 35$, $P = 24$. 35 and 24 are relatively prime because their GCF is 1. **39.** $A = 72$, $P = 34$. 72 and 34 are not relatively prime because their GCF is 2.

4.2 Problem Solving (pp. 173 – 174) 43. 3 groups; 5 girls and 4 boys **46.** 12 bunches; 9 red, 12 white, 4 yellow, 6 purple **48.** the cost of 1 apple, 1 orange, 1 banana, and 1 basket **49.** The GCF is the lesser number because it is a factor of both numbers and no number greater than the lesser number is a factor of it. **50.** *Sample answer:* Multiply each common factor the smallest number of times it occurs. **52.** Yes; *Sample answer:* The GCF must be a factor of all the numbers, and a factor cannot be greater than the number. **53. a.** 9 **b.** 9 rows of trombonists, 4 rows of flutists, 6 rows of saxophonists, 3 rows of drummers **c.** *Sample answer:* The GCF of 81, 36, 54, 27, and 8 is not 9, but the GCF of 81, 36, 54, 27, and 45 is 9.

4.3 Skill Practice (pp. 178 – 179) 1. The GCF of the numerator and denominator is 1. *Sample answers for 3–5.* **3.** $\frac{1}{4}, \frac{2}{8}$ **5.** $\frac{2}{3}, \frac{16}{24}$ **11.** $\frac{4}{9}$ **13.** $\frac{5}{7}$ **15.** $\frac{7}{12}$ **17.** $\frac{3}{4}$ **19.** $\frac{7}{15}$ **21.** The GCF is 6, not 3; $\frac{8}{14}$ can be reduced further; $\frac{24}{42} = \frac{4}{7}$ **23.** yes **25.** no **27.** 9 **29.** 42 **31.** 2 **33.** 10

4.3 Problem Solving (pp. 179 – 180) 45. *Answers may vary. Sample answer:* 5, 7 or 8, 10; I used the fact that $\frac{7}{11}$ is a little more than $\frac{1}{2}$ to estimate the numbers of correct answers.

4.4 Skill Practice (p. 184) 1. *Sample answer:* The LCM is the smallest number that both numbers divide evenly, and the GCF is the greatest number that divides both numbers. **3.** 72, 144, 216 **5.** 80, 160, 240 **7.** 120, 240, 360 **9.** 126, 252, 378 **11.** C **15.** 2028 **17.** 10,800 **19.** 2; 1122; the LCM is the product, 2244, divided by the GCF. **21.** 24; 504; the LCM is the product, 12,096, divided by the GCF. **23.** 6; 34 **25.** 36; 24 **27.** $9d$ **29.** $48x^2$

4.4 Problem Solving (pp. 185 – 186) 31. 12 min **35.** *Answers may vary. Sample answer:* I would use prime factorization because 32 and 49 are fairly large numbers,

and it would be quicker to find the prime factorization for them than list out their multiples. **37.** 18,980
41. a. 221 years **b.** 221 is $13 \cdot 17$ **c.** 2219, 2440, 2661, 2882; *Sample answer:* I started with 1998 and kept adding 221.

4.5 Skill Practice (pp. 191 – 192) **1.** least common denominator **3.** < **5.** > **7.** > **9.** $\frac{3}{10}, \frac{1}{3}, \frac{11}{30}, \frac{2}{5}$ **11.** $\frac{1}{3}$, $\frac{3}{7}, \frac{1}{2}, \frac{9}{14}$ **13.** $\frac{2}{3}, \frac{32}{45}, \frac{20}{27}, \frac{7}{9}$ **17.** $\frac{27}{50}$ **19.** $\frac{9}{17}$ **23.** >; paper and pencil; $\frac{1}{4} = \frac{14}{56}$ **25.** <; pencil and paper; $\frac{13}{24} = \frac{52}{96}$ and $\frac{19}{32} = \frac{57}{96}$.

4.5 Problem Solving (pp. 192 – 193) **31.** Broadway Flying Horses **33.** $\frac{3}{8}, \frac{7}{16}, \frac{1}{2}, \frac{5}{8}, \frac{11}{16}, \frac{3}{4}$ **39.** *Sample answer:* Think of cutting a pie into a slices or into b slices. If you cut it into a greater number of slices, then each slice is smaller. So if $a > b$, then $\frac{1}{a} < \frac{1}{b}$.

4.6 Skill Practice (pp. 196 – 197) **1.** improper fraction **3.** mixed number **5.** $\frac{16}{3}$ **7.** $\frac{22}{9}$ **9.** $\frac{33}{8}$ **11.** $\frac{91}{8}$ **13.** $\frac{69}{16}$ **15.** $5\frac{2}{5}$ **17.** $8\frac{3}{8}$ **19.** $2\frac{2}{11}$ **21.** 9 **23.** $9\frac{15}{16}$ **25.** < **27.** > **31.** $\frac{40}{40}, \frac{22}{20}, 1\frac{1}{9}, \frac{49}{42}$
33. 3;

35. 7;

4.6 Problem Solving (pp. 197 – 198) **39.** $\frac{10}{8}$; $1\frac{1}{4}$
41. $18\frac{1}{3}, 18\frac{7}{12}, 18\frac{2}{3}, 18\frac{3}{4}; 18\frac{3}{4}$ ft

4.7 Skill Practice (pp. 201 – 202) **1.** repeating decimal
3. 0.5 **5.** $1.\overline{3}$ **7.** $0.2\overline{7}$ **9.** 2.4 **11.** $3.\overline{4}$ **15.** $5.\overline{21}$
17. $2.\overline{358}$ **19.** $\frac{4}{5}$ **21.** $\frac{19}{40}$ **23.** $6\frac{6}{25}$ **25.** $2\frac{49}{200}$ **27.** 0.2, $0.\overline{2}, 0.25, \frac{2}{7}, \frac{5}{2}$ **29.** $1\frac{4}{9}, 1.9, 1.94, \frac{9}{4}, \frac{8}{3}$ **31.** C **33.** A

4.7 Problem Solving (pp. 202 – 204) **39.** $88\frac{2}{5}$
43. kangaroo: 72.8 in. to 84.3125 in.; koala: 23.625 in. to 29.5625 in.; numbat: 16.3125 in. to 13.8 in.; wombat: 31.5 in. to 51.2 in. **45.** koala **47.** $\frac{1}{8}$; 0.125; 0.125 > 0.12 because 0.12 = 0.120 and 125 > 120. **49. a.** $\frac{1}{9} = 0.\overline{1}; \frac{2}{9} = 0.\overline{2}; \frac{3}{9} = 0.\overline{3}; \frac{4}{9} = 0.\overline{4}$ **b.** *Sample answer:* Each is a repeating decimal, with the repeating digit the same as the numerator.

c.

Fraction	Decimal
$\frac{1}{9}$	$0.\overline{1}$
$\frac{2}{9}$	$0.\overline{2}$
$\frac{3}{9}$	$0.\overline{3}$
$\frac{4}{9}$	$0.\overline{4}$
$\frac{5}{9}$	$0.\overline{5}$
$\frac{6}{9}$	$0.\overline{6}$
$\frac{7}{9}$	$0.\overline{7}$
$\frac{8}{9}$	$0.\overline{8}$

4.7 Technology Activity (p. 205) **1.** $\frac{3}{8}$ **3.** $1\frac{14}{25}$ **5.** $15.8\overline{3}$
7. $6.\overline{6}$

Chapter Review (pp. 207 – 210) **1.** prime number
3. least common multiple **5.** greatest common factor
7. 1, 2, 4, 17, 34, 68; composite **9.** 1, 2, 3, 4, 6, 8, 9, 18, 24, 36, 72; composite **11.** 1, 7, 13, 91; composite **13.** 1, 31; prime **15.** 6; not relatively prime **17.** 8; not relatively prime **19.** 17 **21.** 1 **23.** *Sample answer:* $\frac{6}{10}, \frac{9}{15}$ **25.** $\frac{1}{2}$; *Sample answer:* $\frac{2}{4}$ **27.** $\frac{23}{25}; \frac{9}{10}$; no, $\frac{46}{50} \neq \frac{45}{50}$ **29.** 42 **31.** 1872 **33.** 72 **35.** 770 **37.** $\frac{1}{2}, \frac{8}{15}, \frac{2}{3}, \frac{7}{10}$ **39.** $\frac{6}{13}, \frac{25}{39}, \frac{17}{26}, \frac{5}{6}$ **41.** $\frac{5}{12}, \frac{9}{20}, \frac{4}{7}, \frac{11}{18}$ **43.** $\frac{6}{7}, \frac{7}{8}, \frac{9}{10}, \frac{11}{12}$ **45.** > **47.** = **49.** 5.875 **51.** $4.\overline{7}$ **53.** $1.41\overline{6}$ **55.** 11.6 **57.** $\frac{3}{50}$ **59.** $3\frac{5}{16}$ **61.** $2\frac{1}{4}$ **63.** $\frac{9}{20}$

Chapter 5

5.1 Skill Practice (pp. 221 – 222) **1.** least common denominator **3.** $1\frac{2}{7}$ **5.** $\frac{4}{5}$ **7.** $\frac{1}{6}$ **9.** $\frac{1}{3}$ **11.** $\frac{7}{12}$ **13.** $\frac{1}{3}$
15. $1\frac{3}{8}$ **17.** $1\frac{1}{21}$ **19.** $\frac{17}{18}$ **21.** $\frac{1}{2}$ **23.** $\frac{17}{40}$ **25.** $\frac{11}{36}$ **27.** $\frac{11}{12}$
29. $\frac{1}{5}$ **33.** $\frac{1}{8}$ **35.** $\frac{5}{14}$ **37.** $\frac{12}{45}$ or $\frac{4}{15}$ **39.** $1\frac{1}{12}$ **41.** $\frac{2}{5}$
43. $\frac{47}{120}$ **45–49.** *Methods will vary.* **45.** > **47.** <
49. < **51.** *Sample answer:* After you find the sum, it already is written in simplest form.

5.1 Problem Solving (pp. 223 – 224) **53.** $1\frac{1}{6}$ ft **55.** $\frac{3}{8}$ mi
59. a.

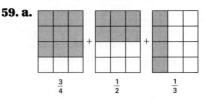

$$\frac{3}{4} \qquad\qquad \frac{1}{2} \qquad\qquad \frac{1}{3}$$

b. $\frac{3}{4} + \frac{1}{2} + \frac{1}{3} = \frac{9}{12} + \frac{6}{12} + \frac{4}{12} = \frac{19}{12} = 1\frac{7}{12}$

61. $\frac{1}{6}$; 124 cards **63.** yes; The sum is $\frac{1}{4} + 2 + \frac{3}{8} + 1 +$ $\frac{3}{8} = 4$. **65.** In $\frac{4}{4}$ time, the note represents $\frac{1}{16}$ of 4 beats.

5.2 Skill Practice (pp. 228 – 229)

1. *Sample answer:* In a proper fraction, the numerator is less than the denominator; In an improper fraction, the numerator is equal to or greater than the denominator.

3. $17\frac{4}{5}$; 13 + 5 = 18 **5.** 13; 9 + 4 = 13 **7.** $1\frac{1}{3}$; 4 − 2 = 2
9. $3\frac{2}{9}$; 8 − 5 = 3 **11.** $7\frac{5}{8}$; 4 + 4 = 8 **13.** $11\frac{5}{12}$; 5 + 7 = 12
15. $17\frac{17}{30}$; 6 + 11 = 17 **17.** $6\frac{1}{2}$; 8 − 2 = 6 **19.** $3\frac{3}{8}$;
6 − 2 = 4 **21.** $3\frac{7}{10}$; 7 − 3 = 4 **25.** $12\frac{11}{15}$ **27.** $5\frac{52}{105}$
29. $3\frac{1}{6}$ **31.** $4\frac{16}{21}$ **33.** =; *Sample answer:* mental math
35. <; *Sample answer:* estimation **37.** =; *Sample answer:* paper and pencil **39.** 5.625 or $5\frac{5}{8}$ **41.** $2\frac{11}{24}$
43. 3.8 or $3\frac{4}{5}$ **45.** $\frac{3}{4}$ **47.** $10\frac{5}{8}$ **49.** $2\frac{1}{4}$

5.2 Problem Solving (pp. 229 – 230) **53.** $4\frac{1}{4}$ in.; $27\frac{3}{4}$
59. $7\frac{1}{2}$ g **63.** *Sample answer:* A half-dollar is twice a quarter's mass and value. A quarter is $2\frac{1}{2}$ times a dime's mass and value.

5.3 Skill Practice (pp. 234 – 235) **1.** simplest form
3. $\frac{5}{14}$ **5.** $\frac{2}{45}$ **7.** 10 **9.** 2 **11.** $6\frac{1}{3}$ **13.** $\frac{3}{4}$ **15.** 6 **17.** 48
19. Write each mixed number as an improper fraction, then multiply; $2\frac{1}{3} \times 3\frac{1}{2} = \frac{7}{3} \times \frac{7}{2} = \frac{49}{6} = 8\frac{1}{6}$. **21.** $\frac{3}{4}$
23. $2\frac{11}{12}$ **25.** $1\frac{17}{32}$ **27.** $\frac{27}{32}$ **29.** $2\frac{1}{4}$ **31.** $\frac{1}{5}$ **33.** <; $1\frac{3}{5}$
35. >; $4\frac{1}{2}$ **37.** <; $34\frac{10}{27}$ **39.** sometimes; *Sample answer:*
$3\frac{1}{4} \times \frac{1}{2}$ is greater than 1; $1\frac{1}{8} \times \frac{1}{2}$ is less than 1. **41.** always;
Sample answer: Each factor is greater than 1, so the product is greater than the larger of the two factors.

5.3 Problem Solving (pp. 235 – 236) **43.** about $5\frac{1}{6}$ ft
47. $1089\frac{3}{8}$ in²

5.4 Skill Practice (pp. 239 – 240) **1.** $\frac{6}{5}$ **3.** 1 **5.** $1\frac{1}{2}$
7. $\frac{3}{20}$ **9.** $\frac{40}{51}$ **11.** $2\frac{2}{5}$ **13.** $\frac{17}{42}$ **15.** $9\frac{1}{10}$ **17.** $3\frac{1}{3}$ **19.** $2\frac{5}{14}$
21. 3 **23.** $1\frac{4}{5}$ **25.** Multiply by the reciprocal of the divisor; $\frac{7}{9} \div \frac{2}{3} = \frac{7}{9} \cdot \frac{3}{2} = \frac{21}{18} = 1\frac{1}{6}$. **29.** $4\frac{4}{5}$ **31.** $\frac{1}{16}$
33. $\frac{6}{7}$ **35.** $1\frac{3}{10}$ **37.** $x = \frac{1}{2}$ **39.** all whole numbers greater than 0

5.4 Problem Solving (pp. 240 – 241)
41. $\frac{1}{2}$ ft

45. a.

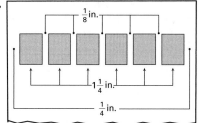

b. $2 \cdot \frac{1}{4} + p \cdot 1\frac{1}{4} + (p − 1) \cdot \frac{1}{8}$; 6; the value of the expression when $p = 6$ is $8\frac{5}{8}$. **47.** $\frac{3}{10}$ h/mi; reciprocal
49. $1\frac{3}{5}$ boxes/oz; reciprocal

5.4 Technology Activity (p. 243) **1.** $1\frac{23}{99}$ **3.** $\frac{1}{5}$ **5.** $2\frac{11}{14}$
7. $23\frac{2}{3}$ **9.** $1\frac{11}{80}$ **11.** $42\frac{13}{16}$ **13.** 6 posters; $77.70

5.5 Skill Practice (pp. 248 – 249) **1.** cup *3–5. Estimates may vary. Sample estimates are given.* **3.** 14 in. **5.** 12 in.
7. $4\frac{1}{2}$ lb **9.** pounds **11.** fluid ounces **13.** The question asked for the weight, not the capacity; 16 oz **15.** $1\frac{1}{2}$ c
17. *Sample answer:* ruler **19.** *Sample answer:* yardstick
21. estimate **23.** exact answer

5.5 Problem Solving (p. 249) **29.** Dave is right; *Sample answer:* 2 lb would be heavy on your head.

5.6 Skill Practice (pp. 252 – 253) **1.** yd **3.** ft **5.** qt
7. $1\frac{1}{2}$ **9.** $2\frac{11}{12}$ **11.** $3\frac{1}{11}$ **13.** 2500 **15.** $12\frac{1}{2}$ **17.** 3; 4
19. 1; 200 **21.** 2; 1 **25.** 15 lb **27.** 3 ft 3 in.
29. 40 mi 470 ft **31.** < **33.** < **35.** <
37. $\frac{37}{5}$ in., $7\frac{3}{4}$ in., 8.7 in., 0.75 ft, $\frac{5}{6}$ ft **39.** $\frac{y}{3600}$

5.6 Problem Solving (pp. 253 – 255) **43.** 2 c 4 fl oz
45. a. 160 c **b.** 27 c **c.** 187 c **47.** Khafre: 157 yd or 471 ft; Menkaure: $71\frac{2}{3}$ yd or 215 ft; Khufu: $160\frac{1}{3}$ yd or 481 ft
49. $88\frac{2}{3}$ yd; 266 ft **51.** yes; *Sample answer:* In inches, the 3 heights are 5652 in., 2580 in., and 5772 in., while the bases, in the same order, are 8448 in., 4128 in., and 9036 in.

Chapter Review (pp. 257 – 260) **1.** reciprocal **3.** yd
5. 36 in. **7.** ounce, pound, ton **9.** $\frac{1}{5}$ **11.** $\frac{4}{5}$ **13.** $\frac{3}{11}$
15. $\frac{19}{28}$ **17.** $\frac{1}{8}$ **19.** $\frac{19}{24}$ **21.** $1\frac{3}{4}$ **23.** $22\frac{5}{14}$ **25.** $\frac{3}{16}$ **27.** $1\frac{2}{3}$
29. $\frac{1}{14}$ **31.** $\frac{1}{10}$ **33.** $7\frac{1}{2}$ **35.** ounces **37.** fluid ounces
41. $4\frac{1}{4}$ **43.** 3 gal 6 pt **45.** 3 lb 2 oz **47.** 8 pt
49. 1 T 1113 lb **51.** 3 mi 1049 yd

Chapter 6

6.1 Skill Practice (pp. 271 – 272) **1.** 2675, 0, −56, 75
3. 1333; −1333 **5.** −9,000,000; 9,000,000 **7.** > **9.** >
11. < **13.** > **17.** −49, −42, −2, 11, 13, 99 **19.** −66,

$-22, -10, 9, 21, 44$ **21.** $-93, -84, -11, -3, 0, 9$
31–45. Answers may vary. **31.** $4, 22$ **33.** $-13, -20$
35. $-3, -1$ **37.** $-4, -9$ **39.** $1, 2$ **41.** $5, 6$ **43.** $0, 2$
45. $-3, 2$ **47.** *Sample answer:* $0, -1, -2$

6.1 Problem Solving (pp. 272 – 273) **49.** $-5, -4, 0, 3$;
Andrew **51.** Syracuse, Carthage, Alexandria, Jerusalem,
Byzantium

6.1 Extension (pp. 274 – 275) **1.** $\frac{1}{36}$ **3.** $\frac{1}{32}$ **5.** 0.021

7. 0.00892 **9.** the diameter of the cell **11.** $1 \cdot 10^{-4}$
13. $9.32 \cdot 10^{-5}$

6.2 Skill Practice (pp. 280 – 281)

1. false; An absolute value is always positive or 0
regardless of the sign of the integer. **3.** $6 + (-1) = 5$
5. 12 **7.** 54 **9.** 37 **11.** 47 **13.** positive; 29
15. negative; -14 **17.** negative; -145 **19.** zero; 0
21. negative; -25 **23.** negative; -10 **25.** The absolute
values of the integers were added instead of subtracted;
$10 + (-15) = -5$. **27.** $<$ **29.** $<$ **31.** $=$ **33.** 4 **35.** 2
37. -2 **39.** -3 **43.** $>$ **45.** $=$ **47.** -17 **49.** 16
51. -10 **53.** $7, -7$ **55.** $23, -23$ **57.** $52, -52$

6.2 Problem Solving (pp. 281 – 282) **59.** 2 spaces
forward **61.** $-60 + 25 + (-10) + 25; -20$

6.3 Skill Practice (p. 287) **1.** opposite **3.** D;
5. B;

7. -12 **9.** -26 **11.** -11 **13.** 14 **15.** -47 **17.** 60
21. 20 **23.** -2 **25.** $<$ **27.** $=$ **29.** $>$ **31.** $>$ **33.** $=$
35. $a = b$ **37.** when $a = b = 0$ and when a and b have
the same sign **39.** $a = 0$ and $b = 0$

6.3 Problem Solving (pp. 288 – 289) **41.** $22{,}965$ ft
43. $11{,}331$ ft **45.** $179°C, 8°C, -153°C, -185°C, -236°C$

6.4 Skill Practice (pp. 293 – 294) **1.** positive **3.** negative
5. -33 **7.** 24 **9.** 0 **11.** -40 **13.** -30 **15.** 28
17. -32 **19.** -45 **23.** -49 **25.** 25 **27.** 24 **29.** -10
31. 525 **33.** -40 **35.** -15;

37. -4;

39. 4 **41.** 10 **43.** -8 **45.** 12 **47.** -2 **49.** $112, -448$

6.4 Problem Solving (pp. 294 – 295) **53.** -60
55. $-4(10) = -40$ **57.** -5 **59.** $-3(9) = -27$ ft; 45 ft

6.5 Skill Practice (pp. 298 – 299) **1.** negative **3.** -4
5. -7 **7.** 4 **9.** -7 **11.** -3 **13.** 0 **15.** -3 **17.** -2
19. The quotient of two negative integers is not negative;
$-20 \div (-5) = 4$ **21.** -1 **23.** -17 **25.** 7 **27.** $-58°F$
29. $-25°C$ **31.** 4 **33.** 10 **35.** -5 **37.** -21 **39.** $<$
41. $=$ **43.** $>$ **45.** $>$ **47.** $<$

6.5 Problem Solving (pp. 299 – 300) **51.** $\frac{4}{9}$ **53.** $212°F$

6.6 Skill Practice (pp. 304 – 305) **1.** 0 **3.** $-\frac{3}{2}, \frac{2}{3}$

5. $\frac{10}{7}, -0.7$ **7.** $\frac{2}{5}$ **9.** $\frac{3}{1}$ **11.** $\frac{11}{5}$ **13.** $-\frac{29}{5}$ **15.** $-4, -3\frac{3}{4},$
$-3.7, -\frac{10}{3}, -3.1$ **17.** $-1\frac{1}{3}, -0.5, 0.02, \frac{3}{10}, 1$ **19.** inverse

prop. of add. **21.** associative prop. of multi.
23. inverse prop. of multi. **25.** associative prop. of add.

29. $4 + 17 + (-4)$ [original expression]
  $= 4 + (-4) + 17$ [commutative property of addition]
  $= [4 + (-4)] + 17$ [associative property of addition]
  $= 0 + 17$ [inverse property of addition]
  $= 17$ [identity property of addition]

31. $43 + 68 + 57$ [original expression]
  $= 43 + 57 + 68$ [commutative property of addition]
  $= (43 + 57) + 68$ [associative property of addition]
  $= 100 + 68 = 168$ [add 43 and 57, then 100 and 68]

33. $-2.4 + [7 + (-0.6)]$ [original expression]
  $= -2.4 + [(-0.6 + 7]$ [commutative property of addition]
  $= [-2.4 + (-0.6)] + 7$ [associative property of addition]
  $= -3 + 7 = 4$ [add -2.4 and -0.6, then -3 and 7]

35. $14 \cdot \frac{2}{3} \cdot \frac{1}{14}$ [original expression]
  $= 14 \cdot \frac{1}{14} \cdot \frac{2}{3}$ [commutative property of multiplication]
  $= (14 \cdot \frac{1}{14}) \cdot \frac{2}{3}$ [associative property of multiplication]
  $= 1 \cdot \frac{2}{3}$ [inverse property of multiplication]
  $= \frac{2}{3}$ [identity property of multiplication]

37. 1 and -1 because $1(1) = 1$ and $-1(-1) = 1$; 0 because
$0 + 0 = 0$ **39.** $\frac{15}{15}$ **41.** $<$ **43.** $>$ **45.** $>$ **47.** 0 **49.** 0

6.6 Problem Solving (pp. 305 – 306) **53.** $-8\frac{4}{25}, -\frac{631}{100},$
$-5.87, 1.97$; Southeast; Southwest **59.** 8 **61.** $-\$100$

6.7 Skill Practice (pp. 309 – 310) **1.** equivalent **3.** $4(4) +$
$4(5)$ **5.** $8(100) - 8(4)$ **7.** $4\left(\frac{3}{5} + \frac{2}{5}\right)$ **11.** 101.1 **13.** 30

15. 180 **17.** 13 **19.** The student multiplied 4 by 8
instead of -8; $-8(5 + 4) = -8(5) + (-8)(4) = -40 +$
$(-32) = -72$. **21.** $8(3) + 14 + 8(-4) = 24 + 14 + (-32) =$
6 or $8(3) + 14 + 8(-4) = 8[3 + (-4)] + 14 = 8(-1) + 14 =$
6 **23.** $17(2) + 16 + 17(8) = 34 + 16 + 136 = 186$ or
$17(2) + 16 + 17(8) = 17(2 + 8) + 16 = 17(10) + 16 =$
$170 + 16 = 186$ **25.** $7(9 - 5) - 13 + 7(2 + 4) = 7(4) -$
$13 + 7(6) = 28 - 13 + 42 = 57$ or $7(9 - 5) - 13 + 7(2 + 4) =$
$7(9 - 5 + 2 + 4) - 13 = 7(10) - 13 = 57$ **27.** inverse
prop. of addition **29.** associative prop. of
multiplication **31.** distributive prop. **33.** identity prop.
of multiplication **35.** B **37.** $mp - mn - mp = -mn$

6.7 Problem Solving (pp. 310 – 311) **43.** $2(l + w)$;
$2(14) + 2(12) = 28 + 24 = 52$ cm; $2(14 + 12) = 2(26) =$
52 cm **47.** 200 min **49.** $20(1 - 0.05); 20 - 1 = \$19$
51. $x(3 + 1 + 1 + 3 + 1 + 3 + 1 + 1) = x(14) = 14x$;
5600 cm; 3959.2 cm

6.8 Skill Practice (pp. 315 – 316) **1.** x-axis **3.** $(2, 2)$
5. $(3, 3)$ **7.** $(4, -3)$ **9.** $(0, 2)$

11–22.

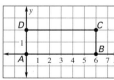

11. Quadrant II
13. Quadrant III
15. Quadrant II
17. Quadrant III
19. Quadrant IV
21. on the y-axis

25. 6 units, 2 units, 12 square units;

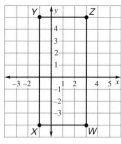

27. 9 units, 4 units, 36 square units;

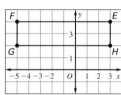

29. 8 units, 2 units, 16 square units;

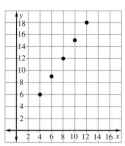

31. Distance is never negative; distance $= |-14 - (-6)| = |-14 + 6| = |-8| = 8$ **33.** Both are positive. **35.** The y-coordinate is zero. **37.** x is negative; y is positive.

39. *Answers may vary. Sample answer:* $\frac{4}{6}, \frac{6}{9}, \frac{8}{12}, \frac{10}{15}, \frac{12}{18}$.

The data is linear;

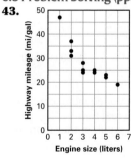

6.8 Problem Solving (pp. 317 – 318) **41.** $(-15, -8)$

43.

45. *Sample answer:* about 21 mi/gal **49.** *C*

6.8 Technology Activity (p. 320) **1.** Quadrant I **3.** Quadrant IV **5.** on the negative x-axis **7.** on the negative y-axis

Chapter Review (pp. 322 – 326) **1.** $-4, 5, -2, 4; 2.3, -2.3; -4, 4$ **3.** The multiplicative inverse of a number is its reciprocal, and the additive inverse of a number is its opposite. **5.** $>$ **7.** $<$ **9.** $-10, -8, 7, 8, 9, 11$ **11.** 15 **13.** -60 **15.** 41 **17.** -55 **19.** -25 **21.** -2 **23.** $-28 + 16; -12$ m **25.** 13 **27.** 75 **29.** 47 **31.** -9 **33.** 26 **35.** -4 **37.** 0 **39.** -54 **41.** -114 **43.** 0 **45.** 105 **47.** -175 **49.** -4 **51.** 0 **53.** 2 **55.** -4 **57.** $-40°$C

59. $2.4 = \frac{12}{5}, -2.1 = -\frac{21}{10}, -2\frac{4}{5} = -\frac{14}{5}, 2 = \frac{2}{1}, 2\frac{1}{9} = \frac{19}{9}$; $-2\frac{4}{5}, -2.1, 2, 2\frac{1}{9}, 2.4$

61. $-\frac{2}{3} + (-\frac{2}{3}) + \frac{2}{3}$ [original expression]
$= -\frac{2}{3} + [(-\frac{2}{3}) + \frac{2}{3}]$ [associative property of addition]
$= -\frac{2}{3} + 0$ [inverse property of addition]
$= -\frac{2}{3}$ [identity property of addition]

63. $\frac{3}{7} \cdot (-1) \cdot \frac{7}{3}$ [original expression]
$= \frac{3}{7} \cdot \frac{7}{3} \cdot (-1)$ [commutative property of multiplication]
$= (\frac{3}{7} \cdot \frac{7}{3}) \cdot (-1)$ [associative property of multiplication]
$= 1 \cdot (-1)$ [inverse property of multiplication]
$= -1$ [identity property of multiplication]

65. $4(1 - 0.02); 3.92$ **67.** $9(2.6 + 5.4); 72$ **69.** $(-2, -2)$ **71.** $(2, 1)$ **73.** $(-3, 2)$ **75–78.**

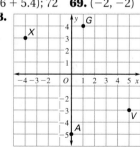

75. on the y-axis **77.** Quadrant II

79. 9 units;

Chapter 7

7.1 Skill Practice (pp. 339 – 340)   **1.** verbal model   **3.** B

5. A   **7.** $-7 + n$ **9.** $\frac{1}{3}n$ **11.** $-50 - n$ **13.** $\frac{n+6}{3}$

15. $n + -9 = 24$ **17.** $3n = 2 \cdot 23$ **19.** $2 + \frac{1}{3}n = -8$

Sample answers for 23–33.   **23.** 13 times b **25.** the quotient of 10 and d **27.** The sum of q and 8 is 34.   **29.** 90 divided by s is equal to 1.   **31.** 11 less than a is equal to 2.   **33.** The sum of k and 9 is 52.   *Sample answers for 35–37.*   **35.** the quotient of the cube of a number and the difference of another number and 8   **37.** the quotient of the sum of a number and 12 and the square of another number

7.1 Problem Solving (pp. 340 – 341)   **41.** $2s$; s = a team's score   **43.** $a - 5$; a = Ann's height in inches.   **49.** 19

7.2 Skill Practice (p. 344)   **1.** coefficients: 5, 2; constant terms: -7, 1; like terms: $5z$, $2z$ and -7, 1   **3.** $2a + 9$ **5.** $-8c - 1$ **7.** $-3k - 3$ **9.** $11x - 4.5$ **11.** $-0.6p + 3$ **13.** coefficients: -4, 5; constant terms: 10, -8; like terms: $-4y$, $5y$ and 10, -8 **15.** no; You need to rewrite the expression as a sum; The coefficients are 6 and -3.   **17.** $5z + 2$ **19.** $5m - 13$ **21.** $8t + \frac{4}{7}$ **23.** $4n - 2p + 1$ **27.** $2x + 2(x + 10)$; $4x + 20$ **29.** no   **31.** yes

7.2 Problem Solving (p. 345)   **35.** $2(3w) + 2w$; $8w$

7.3 Skill Practice (pp. 349 – 350)   **1.** addition and subtraction   **3.** 3   **5.** -17 **7.** $-\frac{5}{7}$ **9.** 9   **11.** 4

13. -20.2 **15.** 37.3   **17.** -14 **21.** 7   **23.** 11   **25.** 27.8   **27.** -4 **29.** -14.6 **31.** $6 + x = 3$; -3 **33.** $t - 1 = -3$; -2 **35.** $-4 + r = 8$; 12   **37.** $z - 7.2 = -12.9$; -5.7 **39.** commutative property of addition; combine like terms; subtraction property of equality; combine like terms   **41.** $4.2 + 5 + 3.9 + x = 21.5$; 8.4 in.   **43.** *Sample answers:* $x + 2 = -3$; $x + (-3) = -8$; $x + 10 = 5$

7.3 Problem Solving (pp. 351 – 352)
47. a. 1 mile plus 2 miles plus a number of miles equals 5 miles.   **b.** $1 + 2 + x = 5$ **c.** 2 mi   **49.** $p - 1.50 = 5.75$; $7.25   **51.** $c + 112 = 127$; 15 lb   **53.** $25 = x + 2.5 \cdot 3.5 + 5.39 + 2 \cdot 1.99 + 4.25$; $2.63   **55. a.** $m = 25 - 4.75$; $20.25   **b.** $c = 20.25 - 12.50$; $7.75   **c.** $7.75 remains, enough for 1 CD, 2 CDs or another package of CD holders, but not enough for a DVD or another game.

7.4 Skill Practice (pp. 356 – 357)   **1.** division   **3.** 3   **5.** -3 **7.** 16   **9.** 20   **11.** -12.5 **13.** -2.5 **15.** 20   **17.** -2.1 **19.** 9   **21.** 24   **23.** Divide both sides by 3; 5   **25.** Multiply both sides by 9; -18 **29.** Multiply both sides by $\frac{5}{4}$ instead of $\frac{4}{5}$; 25   **31.** $10x = -22$; -2.2

33. $\frac{n}{-11} = 7$; -77 **35.** $\frac{-13}{4}n = 2$; $-\frac{8}{13}$ **37.** 2.4   **39.** 1.11

41. 0.75

7.4 Problem Solving (pp. 357 – 359)   **47.** $7.5w = 45$; 6 m

51. $3s = 309$; 103 strikes/min   **55.** yes; $\frac{1}{5}$; Multiplying by

$\frac{1}{5}$ gives the same result as dividing by 5.   **57.** 27.1 ft/sec

7.5 Skill Practice (pp. 363 – 364)   **1.** subtraction   **3.** 2   **5.** -81 **7.** 5   **9.** 54   **11.** 132   **13.** -187.2 **15.** 64

17. $-2\frac{3}{4}$ **21.** 3   **23.** -1 **25.** 4   **27.** $7 - 2n = 11$; -2

29. $n + 2n = 15$; 5   **31.** *Sample answers:* $2x + 3 = 9$,

$3x - 4 = 10$, $\frac{x}{5} + 1 = 6$; $x + 1 = 8$, $7x = 42$, $x - 10 = 11$

33. $2(2x) + 2(4x - 1) = 68$; $5\frac{5}{6}$

7.5 Problem Solving (pp. 364 – 365)   **35. a.** Cost for first hour + cost per additional hour $\times$ number of additional hours = 52.50   **b.** $15 + 12.5x = 52.5$; 3   **c.** 4 h

39. $2(\frac{1}{4}) + 16(\frac{3}{4}) + 6(\frac{t}{60}) = 15.5$; 30 min

41. $2w + 2(w + 34) = 268$; 50 ft; 84 ft

7.6 Skill Practice (pp. 368 – 369)   **1.** solution set

3.

5.

7. $r \le -4$;

9. $t \le 14$;

11. $w \ge 11$;

13. $y \ge 169$;

15. $x < -12$;

17. $b < 20$;

19. $s \ge -6$;

21. $x \ge 3$;

23. The direction of the inequality was not changed when the inequality was divided by a negative; $x > -9$ *Sample answers for 25–27.*   **25.** $x > 2$; $x + 1 > 3$ **27.** $x < 5$;

$-x \ge -5$ **33.** $x \le 3$;

35. $y < -10$;

7.6 Problem Solving (pp. 369 – 370)
37. $h \ge 42$;   **39.** $f \ge 10$;

  41. $h + 2300 \le 3600$;

$h \le 1300$ **43.** $P + q > 22$; no   **45.** $P + q \le 22$; yes
47. C   **49.** All real numbers less than or equal to 5; $m > 5$; The solutions together make up the real number line but have no points in common.   **51.** A graph of the solution

of an inequality has infinitely many numbers on it, while the graph of the solution of an equation has only one solution. The graphs of $x + 1 > 2$ and $x + 1 \le 2$ will have no points in common but will take up the entire number line. The graphs of $x + 1 = 2$ and $x + 1 \le 2$ have one point in common at $x = 1$.   **53.** 300 ft; 100 ft; Greatest possible difference between A and C is the highest possible elevation for A (300 ft) minus the lowest possible elevation for C (0 ft). Least possible difference between A and C is the lowest possible elevation for A (200 ft) minus the lowest possible elevation for C (100 ft).   **55.** $0 < x < 5$; x represents the cost of the book.   **57.** Add 12; 56, 68, 80   **59.** Subtract 4; 7, 3, -1 **61.** -35 **63.** 1

7.7 Skill Practice (pp. 373 – 374)
1. domain; range   **3.** -2 **5.** -11
7. range: $-40, -20, 0, 20, 40$;

Input x	-2	-1	0	1	2
Output y	40	20	0	-20	-40

9. range: 11, 13, 15, 17, 19;

Input x	-2	-1	0	1	2
Output y	19	17	15	13	11

11. range: $-2.6, -1.8, -1, -0.2, 0.6$;

Input x	-2	-1	0	1	2
Output y	-2.6	-1.8	-1	-0.2	0.6

13. range: $-8.6, -7, -5.4, -3.8, -2.2$;

Input x	-2	-1	0	1	2
Output y	-8.6	-7	-5.4	-3.8	-2.2

17. yes; $y = 15 + x$; Each input value has exactly one output.   **19.** yes; $y = \frac{x}{-3}$; Each input value has exactly one output.   **21.** no; Input values 1 and 4 have two different outputs.   **23.** yes; $y = -5x - 2$; Each input value has exactly one output.

7.7 Problem Solving (pp. 374 – 375)
29. a.

Input n	1	2	3	4	5	6
Output C	221	257	293	329	365	401

b. $C = 191 + 30n$; This group will pay less.
31. As the depth increases, the pressure increases;

Input d	0	20	40	60	80	100
Output p	2112	3992	4672	5952	7232	8512

7.8 Skill Practice (pp. 378 – 379)
1. one
3. 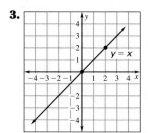   **5.**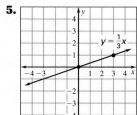

7. 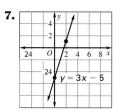   **9.**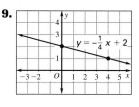

11.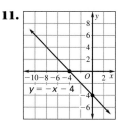

13. function; nonlinear   **15.** not a function
17. $y = 3x$;

Input x	-1	0	1
Output y	-3	0	3

19. $y = 2x + 3$;

Input x	-1	0	1
Output y	1	3	5

21. $y = \frac{x}{7}$;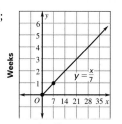

23. $y = \frac{x}{10}$;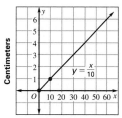

25. $(2, 3)$;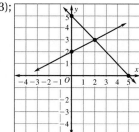

27. $(1, 2)$;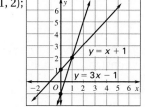

29. $y = 3x + 2$;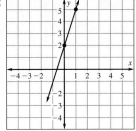

31. $y = -3x + 6$;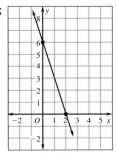

33. $y = 2x - 12$;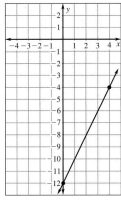

7.8 Problem Solving (pp. 379 – 381)

35.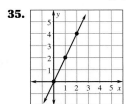

39. a. $y = 6.25x$

b.

Input x	0	4	8	12	16	20
Output y	0	25	50	75	100	125

c.

43. $F = 10m$; the acceleration due to gravity; When on Earth, this force is relatively constant.   **45. a.** (0, 90), (2, 85), (5, 79), (10, 68), (20, 58), (30, 49), (40, 43.5), (50, 39.5), (60, 37)

b.

c. The graph is a function but is not linear because the graph is not a line.

7.8 Technology Activity (p. 382)   **1.** 0.8, 4.2   **3.** 1; 7
5. −0.6; −1.6   **7.** (−1, 3)

7.8 Extension (p. 384)   **1.** yes; $y = 5x$, so $k = 5$ **3.** yes;
$k = 6$ **5.** no; $\dfrac{y}{x}$ is not constant.   **7.** $y = 20x$

Chapter Review (pp. 386 – 390)   **1.** equivalent

3. domain   **5.** range   **7.** $2(w + 4)$ **9.** $\dfrac{w}{7} = 6$ **11.** $8x - 4$

13. $-3g + 2$ **15.** $-7d + 38$ **17.** 16   **19.** 1.8   **21.** -26.6
23. $O = 553 + 55$; $O = 608$ mi^2 **25.** 16   **27.** -12
29. -24 **31.** 29   **33.** $85 = 36 + 28x$; $x = 1.75$ h
35. $y \le -15$;

37. $c + 3.6 \le 40$; $c \le 36.4$ lb; 10 lb, 20 lb, 30 lb   **39.** $y = \dfrac{x}{-4}$
41. $y = x - 5$

43.   **45.** b; The graph is a line.

Chapter 8

8.1 Skill Practice (pp. 401)   **1.** equivalent ratios   **3.** 1 to

1, 1 : 1, $\dfrac{1}{1}$ **5.** 15 to 2, 15 : 2, $\dfrac{15}{2}$ **7.** $\dfrac{4}{5}$ **9.** $\dfrac{3}{10}$ **11.** $\dfrac{4}{7}$

13. $\dfrac{2}{5}$ **15.** $\dfrac{1}{2}$ **17.** $\dfrac{2}{11}$ **19.** $\dfrac{2}{7}$ **21.** $\dfrac{8}{17}$ **23.** 32 : 18 or 2 : $1\dfrac{1}{8}$

or 16 : 9   **25.** 420 : 25 or 7 : $\dfrac{5}{12}$ or 84 : 5   **27.** >   **29.** >

31. <   **33.** =   **35.** <   **37.** 6 : 5, 11 : 9, 4 : 3   **39.** 5   **41.** 8

43. $\dfrac{5}{4}$ or 1.25

8.1 Problem Solving (pp. 402 – 403)   **47.** 44 : 36 or 11 : 9
49. 36 : 80 or 9 : 20   **53.** 105 : 20 or 21 : 4

8.2 Skill Practice (p. 406)   **1.** rate   **3.** 6 L/day

5. \$3.20/person   **7.** 30.6 m/sec   **9.** $2\dfrac{2}{3}$ servings/package

11. 117 visitors/day   **13.** 1.8 c/pie   **15.** 3.5 phone
calls/h   **17.** 9 e-mails/day   **21.** 12 m/min or 0.2 m/sec

23. 600 ft/min or 10 ft/sec   **25.** 33.75 mi/h or 0.5625 mi/min   **27.** $1.49/pair

8.2 Problem Solving (pp. 407 – 408)   **35.** 5 min
37. 2 qt for $2.78   **43.** 0.89 g/cm³

8.3 Skill Practice (pp. 411 – 412)   **1.** rise; run   **3.** $\frac{2}{3}$

5. −1   **7.** 0   **9.** The slope is 1;

11. The slope is $-\frac{1}{4}$;

15.   **17.**

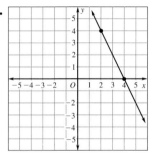

19.   **21.** >   **23.** <   **25.** 3   **27.** −8

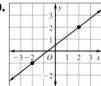

8.3 Problem Solving (pp. 412 – 414)   **35.** You stopped and rested.   **39.** Perimeter: 4; 8; 12; 16   **41.** *Sample answer:* The slope of 4 tells that the perimeter of a square is four times the length of a side.

8.3 Technology Activity (p. 415)

1. 4;

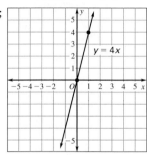

3. −3;   **5.** They are the same.

8.4 Skill Practice (pp. 420 – 421)   **1.** proportion   **3.** 15

5. 12   **7.** 9   **9.** 5   **11.** 24   **13.** 44   **15.** 2   **17.** 9

21. $\frac{6}{16} = \frac{z}{40}$; 15   **23.** $\frac{m}{32} = \frac{3}{4}$; 24   **25.** $\frac{80}{100} = \frac{n}{45}$; 36

8.4 Problem Solving (pp. 421 – 422)   **31.** 1 qt
33. 285 lb   **35.** Corresponding units were not placed in corresponding places in the proportion. The proportion should be red/yellow = $\frac{2}{3} = \frac{r}{12}$; 8 drops of red

37. 90 min; The ratio of the calories burned is 1 to 2, so it will take twice as long to burn the same number of calories.
39. 71 min

8.5 Skill Practice (pp. 425 – 426)   **1.** 70; 70   **3.** 2   **5.** 9
7. 21   **9.** 21   **11.** 17   **13.** 5.6   **15.** 14.4   **17.** 17.28
21. *Sample answer:* about 1 m   **23.** 25 boys, 20 girls
25. 36 boys, 48 girls   **27.** 25 boys, 35 girls   **29.** 24 boys, 28 girls   **31–33.** *Answers may vary. Estimates are given.*
31. 30   **33.** 30   **35.** 13   **37.** −4   **39.** yes   **41.** no

8.5 Problem Solving (pp. 427 – 428)   **43.** 108 blinks;
less than average because $\frac{90 \text{ blinks}}{9 \text{ min}} < \frac{108 \text{ blinks}}{9 \text{ min}}$

45. *Sample answer:* **(1)** Find the cross products, $135 = 5x$, and then divide both sides by 5 to get $x = 27$; **(2)** Multiply both sides by 15 to get $9 \cdot 3 = x$, or $x = 27$. **(3)** In the denominators, 5 is multiplied by 3 to get 15, so multiply 9 by 3 to get x, or $x = 27$.
47. a. yes; *Sample answer:* The cross products are $(10.2)(88.9) = 906.78$ and $(12.7)(71.4) = 906.78$. The cross products are equal; so the ratios are equal.

b. yes; *Sample answer:* The ratios are $\frac{10.2}{71.4} = \frac{12.7}{88.9} = \frac{1}{7}$, so the measures may have been taken just as the waves broke.   **49.** $\frac{3}{5}$

51. a. $\frac{5}{3} = \frac{y}{x}$ **b.**

x	3	4.5	6	12
y	5	7.5	10	20

c. 15 g;

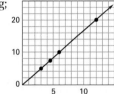

53. *Answers may vary. Sample answer:* about 250 staff members

8.6 Skill Practice (pp. 432 – 433) **1.** true **3.** B
5. A **7.** 75 mi **9.** 130 mi **11.** 17.1 cm **13.** 82.8 cm
15. The wrong unit of measurement is used. The scale is

1 in. : 5 ft, so the unit for x is in.; 3 in. **17.** $\frac{1}{100}$ **19.** $\frac{1}{84}$

21. $\frac{1}{24}$ **23.** $\frac{3}{80}$ **25.** C

8.6 Problem Solving (pp. 433 – 435) **29.** 1 : 12

33. 10 in.; $\frac{1}{6} = \frac{l}{60}$, $l = 10$ in. **39.** *Sample answer:* The

ratio of the areas is the square of the scale, and the ratio
of the perimeters is the same as the scale.

Chapter Review (pp. 437 – 440) **1.** e **3.** b **5.** f **7.** $\frac{1}{9}$

9. $\frac{4}{7}$ **11.** < **13.** < **15.** > **17.** 1 : 4 **19.** 5.5 oz/serving

21. 6 oz for $1.25 **23.** 2.2 oz for $2.64 **25.** $\frac{3}{5}$

27. The slope is 7;

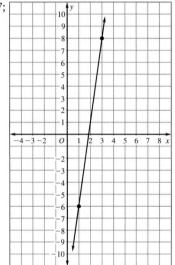

29. 30 **31.** 2 **33.** 8 **35.** 13.5 **37.** 10 months
39. 8.8 m **41.** 15 : 48 or 5 : 16 **43.** 16 : 5280 or 1 : 330

Chapter 9

9.1 Skill Practice (p. 451) **1.** per hundred **3.** $\frac{23}{100}$

5. $\frac{1}{5}$ **7.** $\frac{67}{100}$ **9.** $\frac{23}{25}$ **11.** $\frac{1}{4}$ **13.** 52% **15.** 60%
17. 44% **19.** 56% **21.** 35% **23.** 27 **25.** 51
27. 16 **29.** 18 **31.** 39 **33.** 120 **35.** 80% is $\frac{80}{100}$,

not $\frac{8}{100}$; 80% $= \frac{80}{100} = \frac{4}{5}$ **37.** 10 **39.** 27 **41.** 60

43. 54 **45.** $\frac{y}{100}$; 36 **47.** $\frac{w}{100}$; 6 **49.** 4 to 5, 81%, $\frac{41}{50}$

51. 89%, $\frac{9}{10}$, 23 to 25 **53.** 12%, $\frac{7}{50}$, 3 to 20

9.1 Problem Solving (p. 452) **57.** 90%

9.2 Skill Practice (pp. 456 – 457) **1.** $\frac{8}{20}$ **3.** C **5.** A

7. 94% **9.** 20 **11.** 150 **13.** 33 **15.** 30% **17.** 54
21. 63% **23.** 44% *25-29. Estimates may vary.*
25. 25% **27.** 100 **29.** 0.32 **31.** 20y

9.2 Problem Solving (pp. 458 – 459) **39.** 25,000 m, or
25 km **41.** 9 **43. a.** 80, 52 **b.** 80 is the base, 28 is the
part of the base, x is the percent; 80 is the base, 52 is the

part of the base, y is the percent; $\frac{28}{80} = \frac{x}{100}$, $\frac{52}{80} = \frac{y}{100}$

c. 260 students; When you solve the second proportion
from part (b), you find that 65% of the students prefer to
exercise after school, and 0.65(400) = 260.
45. about 1500 volcanoes **49.** 48%; 14%

9.3 Skill Practice (pp. 462 – 463) **1.** *Sample answer:*
1.25, 0.0045 **3.** 0.47 **5.** 0.08 **7.** 0.0015 **9.** 0.003
11. 0.425 **13.** 1.25 **15.** The decimal point was moved
in the wrong direction; 0.002% = 0.00002 **17.** 7%
19. 203% **21.** 118.4% **23.** 0.105% **25.** 61.9%

27. 76.7% **29.** 19.2% **31.** 0.5% **33.** 2.52, $2\frac{13}{25}$

35. 6.8, 680% **37.** 0.0165 **39.** 139.5 **41.** < **43.** =
45. < **47.** <

9.3 Problem Solving (pp. 463 – 464) **51.** 16; 24; 32;
Convert the percents to decimals, 200% = 2, 300% = 3,
and 400% = 4, and then multiply by 8. **53.** $.59
55. no; You can only get integer percents in a group
of 100 people. **57.** $1,645,280 **61.** *Sample answer:*
39,481,750; 39,546,210 **63.** about 210 million cartons;
Find the number of cartons used for cider and juice and
subtract it from 229 million; 0.39(0.21)(229) = about 19,
and 229 − 19 = 210.

9.4 Skill Practice (pp. 467 – 468) **1.** The part of the base
is equal to the percent times the base. **3.** 40 **5.** 180
7. 105 **9.** 100 **11.** 40 **13.** 70% **15.** 17% **17.** 72%
21. < **23.** = **25.** 2.5, 5, 7.5, 10, 2.5n

9.4 Problem Solving (pp. 468 – 470) **31.** $86.25
37. $75 **39.** $l = 1.5w$; $A = 1.5w^2$

9.5 Skill Practice (pp. 476 – 477) **1.** Change each
percent to a decimal and multiply by 360° to find the
measure of each angle. Draw a circle, and then use a
protractor to mark each angle. Label the sections. **3.** 18°

5. 162° **7.** 24% is not equal to $\frac{1}{24}$; 0.24 · 360° = 86.4°

9. Favorite Fruit

Oranges 20%
Apples 45%
Bananas 10%
Grapes 25%

11. Favorite Drink

Milk 18
Juice 36
Soda 10
Water 16

9.5 Problem Solving (pp. 477 – 478) **17.** 48%

9.5 Technology Activity (p. 479)

1. Car Purchases

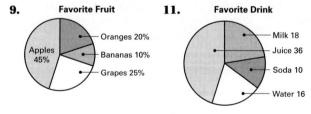

Large 35
Luxury 86
Small 142
Midsize 242

9.6 Skill Practice (pp. 482 – 483) **1.** If the new value is greater than the original value, there was a percent of increase; if the new value is less than the original value, there was a percent of decrease. **3.** increase; about 33.3% **5.** decrease; about 44.4% **7.** increase; 20% **9.** increase; about 81.8% **13.** D **15.** $200 **17.** $75

9.6 Problem Solving (pp. 483 – 484) **21.** $4000 **25.** about 19.8% **27.** 60% decrease **31.** 43.3% decrease

9.7 Skill Practice (pp. 487 – 488) **1.** $15 **3.** $15.75 **5.** $25.20 **7.** $26.50 **9.** $157.50 *11–13. Estimates may vary.* **11.** $45 **13.** $22 **15.** To find the retail price, you must add the markup and the wholesale price; The markup is $100, so the retail price is 80 + 100 = $180.

9.7 Problem Solving (pp. 488 – 489) **21.** $17 **23.** in-line skates: $164; skateboard: $225; scooter: $126 **25.** no; The sale price of the jacket is $51. **27.** Monday's meal **29.** $25.50

9.8 Skill Practice (p. 492) **1.** principal **3.** $.25; $30.25 **5.** $20; $70 **7.** $3.36; $255.36 **9.** $486.72; $6726.72 **11.** $225; $5225 **15.** $980 **17.** 10% **19.** 4 months **21.** $2110 **23.** *Sample answer:* It is reasonable. 5% of $100 is $5, so I should be around $5.

9.8 Problem Solving (pp. 493 – 494) **25.** 4% **27.** 3 years **29.** $1350 **33.** Yours; Your interest rate is 4.8%, and your friend's is 4.5%.

Chapter Review (pp. 496 – 500) **1.** percent of change

3. circle graph **5.** principal **7.** angle **9.** $\frac{19}{100}$ **11.** $\frac{9}{25}$

13. 46% **15.** 70% **17.** 24 **19.** 12 **21.** 12 **23.** 192 **25.** 70 **27.** 180 **29.** about 285.7 mg **31.** 2.1 **33.** 0.925 **35.** 0.41% **37.** 3.2% **39.** 0.4% **41.** 75 **43.** 16 white cars **45.** 87.5% increase **47.** 102 **49.** $144.05 **51.** $272.80 **53.** $2360 **55.** 3 months **57.** 4%

Chapter 10

10.1 Skill Practice (pp. 513 – 514) **1.** D **3.** C **5.** straight **7.** right **11.** neither; The sum of the angles is neither 90° nor 180°; 40° + 40° = 80° **13.** 161°; 71° **15.** 62°; none **17.** 158°; 68° **19.** none; none **21.** The sum of the angles should be 180°; 110° **23.** 40°; 80°; 60° **25.** 72°; 90°; 18° **27.** 82 **29.** 120° **31.** 150° **33.** always; A right angle has measure 90°, so the supplement will also be 90°. **35.** 180° − x

10.1 Problem Solving (pp. 514 – 515) **41.** 45° **43.** ∠LMK and ∠NMK; 105°

10.2 Skill Practice (pp. 518 – 519) **1.** adjacent **3.** ∠1 and ∠2; ∠2 and ∠3; ∠3 and ∠4; ∠4 and ∠1 **5.** 147° **7.** ∠1 and ∠2; ∠5 and ∠6 **9.** 120º **11.** 120° **15.** ∠1 and ∠3 are vertical angles and are congruent, not supplementary; 38°

10.2 Problem Solving (pp. 519 – 520) **19. a.** ∠1 and ∠2, ∠2 and ∠3, ∠3 and ∠4, ∠4 and ∠1; ∠3 and ∠1; ∠4 and ∠2 **b.** 96°; 84°; 84° **c.** *Sample answer:* ∠2 and ∠4 are supplements of ∠3. ∠1 is the supplement of ∠4. **21.** Main St. **23.** 123° **25.** 123° **27.** 99° **29.** *Sample*

answer: J and E; G and C **31.** 37; ∠ADJ and ∠LDF are complementary.

10.3 Skill Practice (pp. 524 – 525) **1.** false; The triangle is obtuse. **3.** 96° **5.** 27° **7.** 70° **9.** 112° **11.** acute **13.** obtuse **15.** right **17.** equilateral **19.** isosceles **21.** scalene **23.** 90°; 90° **29.** 60°; All angles are congruent and must add up to 180°.

10.3 Problem Solving (pp. 525 – 526) **31.** 135° **33.** scalene **35.** sometimes; If two sides are congruent, one of the angles of the triangle may or may not measure 90°. **39.** 60°; 120°

10.3 Extension (p. 528) *1–3. Sample constructions are shown.*

1.  **3.**

5. The bisector forms congruent angles on both sides and $\frac{180°}{2}$ = 90°;

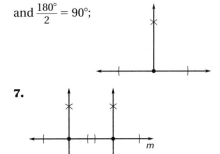

7.

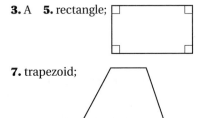

10.4 Skill Practice (pp. 531 – 532) **1.** square, rectangle

3. A **5.** rectangle;

7. trapezoid;

9. yes; heptagon **11.** quadrilateral, parallelogram; no; Not all sides or angles are congruent. **13.** quadrilateral, trapezoid; no; Not all angles are congruent, nor are all sides congruent. **15.** triangle; yes **19.** true; A square has 4 right angles. **21.** false; A trapezoid has only one pair of parallel sides. **23.** 5.75 cm; 135°

10.4 Problem Solving (pp. 533 – 534) **29.** yes; pentagon; no; Not all of the sides and angles are congruent;

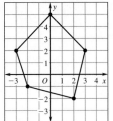

10.5 Skill Practice (pp. 539 – 540) **1.** similar

3. $\overline{KL}$ and $\overline{QR}$, $\overline{LM}$ and $\overline{RS}$, $\overline{MN}$ and $\overline{ST}$, $\overline{NK}$ and $\overline{TQ}$; $\angle K$ and $\angle Q$, $\angle L$ and $\angle R$, $\angle M$ and $\angle S$, $\angle N$ and $\angle T$; $KL = QR = NM = 3$ m; $KN = QT = RS = 4$ m **5.** $\angle U$

7. $\overline{UW}$ **9.** The triangle that corresponds with $\triangle ABC$ is $\triangle EDF$. **11.** yes; $2:1$ **13.** no **15.** false; If one rectangle has dimensions 2 by 3 and another has dimensions 1 by 4, the perimeters would be the same, but the rectangles would not be similar.

10.5 Problem Solving (pp. 540 – 541) **19.** $\overline{AB}$ and $\overline{DE}$, $\overline{BC}$ and $\overline{EF}$, $\overline{AC}$ and $\overline{DF}$; $\angle A$ and $\angle D$, $\angle B$ and $\angle E$, $\angle C$ and $\angle F$ **20.** $2:3$ **23.** no; $\frac{6}{1.4} \neq \frac{4}{0.9}$ **27.** $8:5$; The order of the corresponding sides changes.

10.6 Skill Practice (pp. 544 – 545) **1.** proportion
3. 2 cm **5.** 30 in. **7.** The proportion was not made with corresponding parts; 25 m; $\frac{20}{x} = \frac{12}{15}$, $12x = 300$, $x = 25$. **9.** 48 ft² **11.** 6.25 m, 7.5 m **13.** The ratio of the perimeters in Ex. 11 is 5 to 6; The ratio of the perimeters in Ex. 12 is 9 to 5; The ratios of the perimeters are the same as the ratios of the corresponding sides.

10.6 Problem Solving (pp. 545 – 546)

15. a. 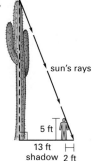 **b.** $\frac{5}{2} = \frac{b}{13}$ **c.** 32.5 ft

sun's rays

5 ft
13 ft
shadow 2 ft

17. Write the proportion $\frac{h}{y} = \frac{z}{x}$. This can be solved for z. $z = \frac{hx}{y}$

21. a.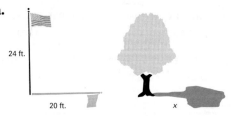

24 ft.

20 ft. x

b. $\frac{24}{y} = \frac{20}{x}$ **c.**

x	10	15	20
y	12	18	24

d. $y = \frac{6}{5}x$; 20.76 ft

10.7 Skill Practice (pp. 550 – 552) **1.** translation
5. rotation 90° counterclockwise **7.** There is no line symmetry. **9.** 120°;

11. A, H, I, M, O T, V, W, X, Y **13.** H, I, O, X **15.** 3; 1; 120°
17. 6; 3; 180° **19.** reflection; y-axis **21.** reflection; x-axis

10.7 Problem Solving (pp. 552 – 553) **31.** A rhombus and rectangle both have two lines of symmetry. The lines of symmetry for the rectangle run through the midpoints of the parallel sides, but the lines of symmetry for the rhombus are the diagonals. Both polygons have 180° rotational symmetry. **33.** The results are the same. **35.** vertically through its body and head; The two symmetries cut the image into mirror images. Bilateral symmetry occurs in space, while line symmetry occurs in a plane.

10.7 Extension (p. 555)

1. yes;

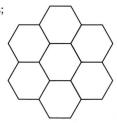

3. translation; Parallelograms: stack and extend the rows. Right triangles: alternate right angle from lower right to upper left;

5. yes; See Example 2; no; There are no sides that are the same length; no. A reflection will create gaps.

7. yes; 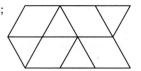 **9.**

10.8 Skill Practice (pp. 558 – 560) **1.** image
3. $(x, y) \rightarrow (-x, y)$ **5.** The translation is 2 units down instead of 2 units up; $K'(2, 3)$, $L'(1, 4)$, $M'(2,6)$, $N'(4, 4)$

7. $F'(-5, -3)$, $G'(0, -3)$ $H'(0, -7)$;

9. $F'(1, 9)$, $G'(6, 9)$, $H'(6, 5)$, $J'(1, 5)$;

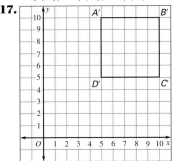

11. $F'(-2, -3)$, $G'(3, -3)$, $H'(3, 1)$, $J'(-2, 1)$;

13. $F'(2, 0)$, $G'(1, 3)$, $H'(1, 1)$ **15.** $R'(3, 3)$, $S'(0, 3)$, $T'(0, 1)$

17.

19.

10.8 Problem Solving (pp. 560 – 561)
27. $(x, y) \rightarrow (x - 2, y - 3)$; Compare the x- and y-coordinates of the original and the image. $B'(0, 1)$, $C'(1, -1)$, $D'(-6, -4)$ **29.** $(x, y) \rightarrow (-x, -y)$

10.8 Technology Activity (p. 562) **1.** $(6, -2)$ **3.** $(-2, 2)$

Chapter Review (pp. 564 – 568) **1.** $180°$ **3.** none
5. A line that divides the figure in half so one side is the image of the other. **7.** acute **9.** right
11. complementary; The sum is $90°$. **13.** neither; The sum is neither $90°$ or $180°$. **15.** neither; The sum is neither $90°$ or $180°$. **17.** $65°$; $\angle 2$ forms a straight angle with $\angle 1$. **19.** $115°$; $\angle 5$ is corresponding with $\angle 1$. **21.** $65°$; $\angle 8$ forms a straight angle with $\angle 5$. **23.** $\angle 12$ and $\angle 10$; $\angle 9$ and $\angle 11$ **25.** $x = 48$; $y = 132$ **27.** heptagon; yes **29.** triangle; no; The sides are not all congruent.

31. 25 ft **33.**

35. $F'(0, -2)$, $G'(-1, 0)$, $H'(-4, 0)$

Chapter 11

11.1 Skill Practice (pp. 579 – 580) **1.** radical expression
3. $25, -25$ **5.** $17, -17$ **7.** $22, -22$ **9.** $21, -21$ **11.** $0.4, -0.4$ **13.** $0.16, -0.16$ **15.** 9 **17.** -13 **19.** -35
21. 19 **23.** The student divided by 2 instead of finding
the square root; $\sqrt{16} = 4$; Check: $4 \cdot 4 = 16$. **25.** 2 **27.** 4
29. -5 **31.** ± 9 **33.** ± 12 **35.** ± 4 **37.** 8 yd **41.** 4
43. 4 **45.** x^2 **47.** x^3

11.1 Problem Solving (pp. 580 – 581) **49.** 225.76 km
51. 1300 m

11.2 Skill Practice (pp. 584 – 585) **1.** false; All integers can be written as rational numbers. **3.** true; All whole numbers can be written as rational numbers. **5.** 4; 3.9
7. 6; 6.5 **9.** 6; 5.9 **11.** 8; 7.5 **13.** 11; 11.2 **15.** 14; 14.1
17. The error is not taking the square root of 25;

$\sqrt{29} \approx \sqrt{25} = 5$ **19.** rational; $-2.6 = -\frac{2.6}{1}$ **21.** irrational;

45 is not a perfect square. **23.** irrational; 21 is not a
perfect square. **25.** rational; A repeating decimal is a

rational number. **27.** 9.33 **29.** 11.83 **31.** $1.5, \sqrt{5}, \sqrt{9}, 5$

33. $\sqrt{21}, 4.8, 5, \sqrt{27}, \frac{27}{5}$ **35.** ± 2.8 **37.** ± 1.1 **39.** ± 1.5

11.2 Problem Solving (pp. 585 – 586) **41. a.** 128 ft^2
b. 121 and 144 **c.** 11.3 ft **43.** 36 mi/h

11.3 Skill Practice (p. 590) **1.** hypotenuse **3.** 11.2 cm
5. 1.5 cm **7.** 9.4 yd **9.** 34.7 in. **11.** 5.4 ft **15.** 60 ft
17. 6 mm **19.** 24.3 ft **21.** 3.4 ft **23.** 1.8 yd

11.3 Problem Solving (pp. 591 – 592) **27.** *Sample answer:*
26.8 cm by 22.2 cm; 34.8 cm; measure 35 cm; 99.4%
31. height: 1.5 ft; ramp length: 18.06 ft

11.4 Skill Practice (pp. 596 – 597) **3.** $P = 32$ mm;
$A = 45$ mm^2 **5.** $P = 22$ m; $A = 20$ m^2 **7.** $P = 50.6$ cm;
$A = 130$ cm^2 **9.** Use the height rather than the side
length; $A = bh = 10 \times 4 = 40$ cm^2 **11.** 13 ft
13. 18 in. **15.** 1 : 16; 15 m^2; 240 m^2 **17.** 1 : 9; 28 cm^2;
252 cm^2

11.4 Problem Solving (pp. 597 – 598) **21.** 11 in.
25. $h = 1.82$ in.; $A = 5$ in.^{2}

11.5 Skill Practice (pp. 604 – 605) **3.** 27.5 m^2 **5.** 6 km

7. $9\frac{1}{3}$ mi **9.** 121 cm^2 **11.** 44 m^2 **13.** 14 ft **15.** 25.4 m

17. 16 ft **19.** 81.5 ft^2 **21.** 472.5 cm^2 **23.** 12 ft^2 **25.** 4 in.

27. $3\frac{3}{8}$ cm **29.** $b_1 = 6$ in., $b_2 = 18$ in., $h = 12$ in.

11.5 Problem Solving (pp. 605 – 606) **31.** 36 cm²
33. 1038.395 mm²; 1038.395 mm²; They are the same.

11.6 Skill Practice (pp. 609 – 611) **3.** 28.26 in.
5. 20.41 cm **7.** 88 cm **9.** The student calculated πr
rather than $2\pi r$; $C = 2\pi r = 2 \cdot 3.14 \cdot 5 = 31.4$ m
11. $d = 38$ m; $r = 19$ m **13.** $d = 13.5$ km; $r = 6.75$ km
15. $d = 4.5$ ft; $r = 2.25$ ft **17.** 31.4; 50.24
19. 12.56; 25.12

11.6 Problem Solving (pp. 609 – 611) **25.** *Sample*
answer: $\frac{22}{7} = 3.1428...$, so $\frac{22}{7}$ is accurate to 2 decimal
places. The difference between π and 3.14 is 0.00159...,
and the difference between π and $\frac{22}{7}$ is 0.00126..., so $\frac{22}{7}$ is
a more accurate approximation. **29.** 22 ft; 8 revolutions;
Sample answer: Use $C = \pi d$ with $d = 7$ ft, and then
$C = \frac{22}{7} \cdot 7 = 22$ ft. The number of revolutions needed to
travel 176 ft is $176 \div 22 = 8$ revolutions.

11.7 Skill Practice (pp. 614 – 615) **1.** D **3.** C
5. 132.665 in.² **7.** 78.5 in.² **9.** 551.27 mm² **11.** The
solution used the diameter, not the radius; $A = \pi r^2 =$
$(3.14)(2)^2 = 12.56$ in.² **13.** $r = 9$ ft, $d = 18$ ft
15. $r = 15$ km, $d = 30$ km **17.** $r = 29$ in., $d = 58$ in.
19. 28.26 m² **21.** 7.065 in.² **23.** 38.465 yd² **25.** 61.76 ft²
27. 4.28 cm²

11.7 Problem Solving (pp. 615 – 616) **29.** 113.04 ft²
35. yes; If $r = 2$ then $C = 2\pi r = 4\pi$ and $A = \pi r^2 = 4\pi$.

11.7 Technology Activity (p. 617) **1.** 21 **3.** 66 **5.** 128.81
7. 31.01

Chapter Review (pp. 619 – 622) **1.** radical expression
3. Pythagorean Theorem **5.** irrational **7.** ± 7 **9.** ± 21
11. 6 **13.** 7 **15.** irrational; 5 **17.** rational; 3 **19.** 8 in.
21. 28 mm **23.** 25 ft **25.** 63 **27.** 3 in. **29.** 120 ft²
31. 96 ft² **33.** 132 cm **35.** 106.76 m **37.** 154 km²
39. 907.46 in.² **41.** 32.15 ft²

Chapter 12

12.1 Skill Practice (pp. 633 – 634) **1.** faces **3.** sphere
5. cone **7.** cylinder **9.** hexagonal pyramid; 7 faces,
12 edges, 7 vertices **11.** pentagonal prism; 7 faces,
15 edges, 10 vertices **13.** Even though the solid has 3
rectangular faces, it is not a rectangular prism. The bases
are triangles, so it is a triangular prism. **15.** true
17. true **21.** lines h and j

12.1 Problem Solving (pp. 634 – 635) **23.** pentagonal
prism; 7 faces, 15 edges, 10 vertices

12.2 Skill Practice (p. 638) **1.** triangle **3.** circle

5. **7.** **9.**

11. The dashed line connecting the bottom back left
corner to the top front left corner is wrong. It should
connect the bottom back left corner to the top back left
corner; **13.**

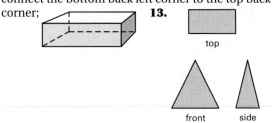

12.2 Problem Solving (p. 639) **23.** B and C; A; A and C

12.2 Extension (p. 641)

1.

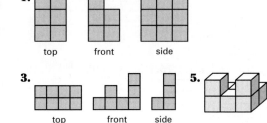

3.

5.

12.3 Skill Practice (pp. 644 – 645) **1.** surface area
3. 252 m² **5.** 100 yd² **7.** 180 in.² **9.** 1050 cm²
11. 10 in.² **13.** She forgot to multiply the area of each
face by 2; $2(6)(8) + 2(6)(2) + 2(8)(2) = 152$ ft² **15.** 13.5 ft²
17. 121.5 cm² **19.** The surface area is 6 times the square
of the edge length. **21.** 68.8 mm² **23.** 123 ft²

12.3 Problem Solving (pp. 645 – 647) **25.** 612 in.²
31. 20,120 ft² **33.** surface area of small doghouse =
3424 in.²; surface area of medium doghouse = 5350 in.²;
25 : 16

12.4 Skill Practice (pp. 651 – 652) **1.** circles; rectangle
3. 848 in.² **5.** 133 ft² **7.** 1360 cm² **9.** 2140 in.²
11. 6 cm **13.** 0.5 ft **15.** 678 cm²; 36 times as large
17. When you multiply the dimensions of a cylinder by x,
the surface area is increased by a factor of x^2.
19. 1 ft; $6\pi = 2\pi r(2) + 2\pi r^2$, so you can use the strategy
Guess, Check, and Revise to find that $r = 1$.

12.4 Problem Solving (pp. 652 – 653) **23.** 25 cm²
27. 153 in.²

12.5 Skill Practice (pp. 657 – 658)

1. The volume is the space an object fills up. The surface
area is the total area of all of its surfaces. **3.** 60 m³
5. 200 cm³ **7.** 648 m³ **9.** 4620 ft³ **11.** 77 mm³
13. 2 cm **17.** 1480 in.³; 1142 in.²; *Sample answer:* To find
the volume, draw vertical lines passing through the figure
along the inner edges of the cutout square. Two pairs of
congruent rectangular prisms are formed. The first pair
have dimensions 8 in. by 5 in. by 15 in., and the second
pair have dimensions 8 in. by 5 in. by 3.5 in. To find the
surface area, find the areas of each face and add them.
21. 4410 ft³

12.5 Problem Solving (pp. 658 – 659) **23.** 5832 cm³
25. Even though 1 yd = 3 ft, 1 yd³ ≠ 3 ft³. There are 27 ft³
in 1 yd³; V = (18 ft)(30 ft)(0.5 ft) = 270 ft³ = 10 yd³
27. 90 kg

12.6 Skill Practice (pp. 664 – 665) **1.** base; height
3. 314 m³ **5.** 1610 ft³ **7.** 452 cm³ **9.** cylinder B
11. 25 in. **13.** 20 ft **15.** 659 ft³ **17.** 689 yd³

12.6 Problem Solving (pp. 665 – 666) **23.** $\frac{804}{25}$ =

$\frac{100}{x}$, 804x = 2500, $x \approx$ 3.11 tons **25.** about 863,000 ft³

27. penny: 44,200 mm³; nickel: 13,800 mm³; dime:
3400 mm³; quarter: 3200 mm³

12.6 Technology Activity (p. 667) **1.** 56.2 in.²; 27.6 in.³
3. The surface area will be 9 times as great as the original
surface area, and the volume will be 27 times as great as
the original volume.

Chapter Review (pp. 669 – 672) **1.** surface area
3. faces **5.** cylinder **7.** sphere **9.** hexagonal pyramid
11. n + 2 faces, 3n edges, 2n vertices; The prism has the
top and bottom plus n other faces. The prism has n edges
in each of the two bases plus n edges connecting the two
bases, and the prism has n vertices in each of the two
bases. **13.** **15.**

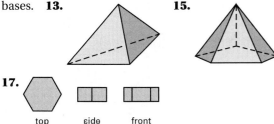

17.

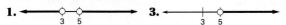

top   side   front

19. 1170 in.² **21.** 48 cm³ **23.** 184 in.³

Chapter 13

13.1 Skill Practice (pp. 684 – 686) **1.** probability

3. C **5.** D **7.** $\frac{3}{10}$, 0.3, 30% **9.** $\frac{1}{5}$, 0.2, 20% **11.** $\frac{9}{20}$

13. $\frac{3}{10}$ **15.** 0.33; 67 **17.** 1.0; 200 **19.** 0.5; 100

21. The number of possible outcomes is 14, not 9;

P(red) = $\frac{\text{Number of red beans}}{\text{Number of beans}} = \frac{5}{14}$ so the probability of

choosing a red bean is $\frac{5}{14}$. **23.** Yes; the colors do not

have to be in any particular order. **27.** 3 to 7; 7 to 3

13.1 Problem Solving (pp. 686 - 687) **29.** $\frac{1}{20}$; 0.05; 5%

31. 0.83 **33.** 0.25 **39.** $\frac{8}{9}$ or 89%

13.1 Extension (p. 689)

1. <--○--○--> **3.** <--|--○-->
     3 5   3 5

5. $\frac{1}{5}$ **7.** $\frac{13}{25}$ **9.** $\frac{13}{25}$ **11.** $\frac{9}{25}$ **13.** $\frac{9}{25}$

13.2 Skill Practice (pp. 692 - 693) **1.** outcomes
3. 36;

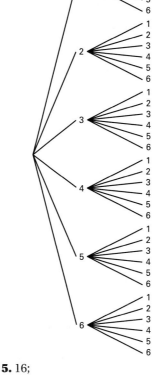

5. 16;

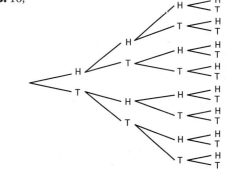

9. 27 outcomes;

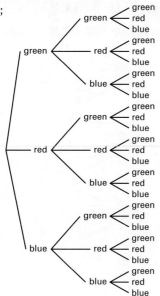

11. 6 pairs   **13.** 2 pairs

15. $\frac{1}{6}$;

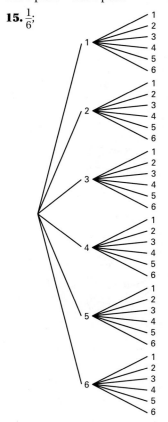

17.

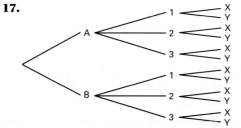

19.

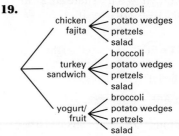

23. a. $\frac{1}{15}$;

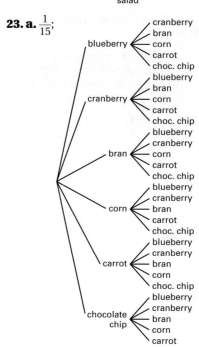

13.3 Skill Practice (pp. 698 – 698)

1. the number of ways that the two events can occur together   **3.** 90   **5.** 132   **7.** 2600   **9.** The outcomes from each roll should not be added, they should be multiplied;

$6 \times 6 \times 6 = 216$ **11.** 2,600,000   **13.** 45,697,600   **15.** $\frac{1}{26^6}$

17. $\frac{5}{26}$ **19.** *Sample answer:* examples: 2, 3, and 9; 2, 4, and 7; 2, 5, and 6; non-examples: 4, 5, and 6; 2, 3, and 8; 3, 5, and 6

13.3 Problem Solving (pp. 699 – 700)   **23.** 180 groups
25. *Sample answer:* The counting principle is faster and is much easier to use if there are a lot of possibilities, like finding the number of locker combinations above.

27. $\frac{9}{2500}$

13.4 Skill Practice (pp. 705 – 706)   **1.** combination
3. 720 ways   **5.** 17,550 ways   **7.** 10 choices   **9.** 3003 choices   **13.** combination; 455 ways   **15.** combination;

210 ways   **17.** $\frac{1}{210}$

13.4 Problem Solving (pp. 706–707) **25. a.** E1B1, E1B2, E1B3, E2B1, E2B2, E2B3, E3B1, E3B2, E3B3, E4B1, E4B2, and E4B3

b.

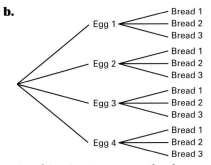

c. Combination; Because order does not matter, it is a combination. **27.** The seventh grade's 100-yard dash has more possible ways ribbons can be awarded because the order matters.

13.4 Technology Activity (p. 708) **1.** 93,024 ways **3.** 1140 committees

13.5 Skill Practice (pp. 712–713)

1. Disjoint events have no outcomes in common, while overlapping events have one or more outcomes in common. **3.** Disjoint; Event B does not say less than or equal to 4. **5.** Overlapping; Both events have 4 and 6 in common. **7.** Overlapping; A student could play a sport in the fall and another one in the spring. **9.** 0.60

11. 0.61 **13.** 44.3% **15.** 0.6 **17.** 0.77 **19.** $\frac{3}{5}$ **21.** $\frac{1}{2}$

23. < **25.** > **27.** < **29.** sometimes; Two disjoint events are complementary only if one or the other must occur. **31.** never; Complementary events must be disjoint events.

13.5 Problem Solving (pp. 713–714) **33.** 63% **35.** 48%

13.6 Skill Practice (pp. 718–719) **1.** compound **3.** independent **5.** 0.21 **7.** 0.16 **9.** 0.15 **11.** The second choice is dependent on the first choice, so the number of possible outcomes is 9; $\frac{1}{10} \cdot \frac{1}{9} = \frac{1}{90}$ **13.** 0.4

15. $0.\overline{4}$ **17.** 0.9

13.6 Problem Solving (pp. 719–721) **21.** independent events; $\frac{42}{625}$ **23.** 0.1012 **25.** 0.2806 **29.** If you choose a B first, then the probability is greater if you replace it, so there are still two B's to choose for the second pick. **33.** *Sample answer:* The experimental probability is close to the theoretical probability, $\frac{1}{15}$.

Chapter Review (pp. 723–726) **1.** outcomes

3. probability **5.** permutation **7.** $\frac{1}{6}$ **9.** $\frac{1}{8}$, 0.125, 12.5%

11. $\frac{5}{8}$, 0.625, 62.5% **13.** $\frac{7}{8}$ **15.** 60 pizzas **17.** 132; There are 12 choices for first place, leaving 11 choices for second place; $12 \cdot 11 = 132$. **19.** 8% **21.** $\frac{5}{14}$

Skills Review Handbook

Whole Number Place Value (p. 735) **1.** $3 \times 1000 + 8 \times 100 + 2 \times 1$ **3.** $9 \times 100,000 + 1 \times 1000 + 3 \times 1$ **5.** 45,097 **7.** 2,361

Comparing and Ordering Whole Numbers (p. 736) **1.** 0, 1, 2, 4, 8, 10 **3.** 0, 6, 9, 11, 19, 29 **5.** 5 < 12 **7.** 15 > 11

Rounding Whole Numbers (p. 737) **1.** 340 **3.** 28,000 **5.** 9000 **7.** 300,000 **9.** 58,900 **11.** 5210 **13.** 28,000,000 **15.** 1,500,000

Number Fact Families (p. 738) **1.** 9; 9; 16 **3.** 3; 4; 4 **5.** 56 **7.** 11 **9.** 7 **11.** 10

Divisibility Tests (p. 739) **1.** 2 **3.** 3 **5.** 2, 3, 5, 6, 9, 10 **7.** 3, 5 **9.** 5 **11.** 2, 3, 5, 6, 9, 10 **13.** 2, 5, 10 **15.** 5

Modeling Fractions (p. 740) **1.** $\frac{7}{8}$ **3.** $\frac{2}{7}$ **5.** $\frac{5}{8}$ **7.** $1\frac{1}{8}$ **9.** $1\frac{2}{3}$ **11.** $1\frac{5}{6}$

Using a Number Line to Add and Subtract (p. 741) **1.** 13 **3.** 15 **5.** 8 **7.** 25 **9.** 4

Addition and Subtraction of Whole Numbers (p. 742) **1.** 102 **3.** 290 **5.** 34 **7.** 285 **9.** 4316 **11.** 1918 **13.** 13,111 **15.** 29,921

Multiplication of Whole Numbers (p. 743) **1.** 4806 **3.** 320,016 **5.** 16,700 **7.** 970,000

Division of Whole Numbers (p. 744) **1.** 45 **3.** 23 **5.** 110 R6 **7.** 8

Estimating Sums (p. 745) *1–9. Estimates may vary.* **1.** 720 **3.** 1970 **5.** 14,600 **7.** 2100 **9.** 3600

Estimating Differences (p. 746) *1–7. Estimates may vary.* **1.** 640 **3.** 410 **5.** 2100 **7.** 6800

Estimating Products (p. 747) *1–7. Estimates may vary.* **1.** 200; 600 **3.** 1000; 1800 **5.** 6000; 12,000 **7.** 2000; 6000 *9–15. Estimates may vary.* **9.** 50,000 **11.** 540,000 **13.** 400,000 **15.** 130,000

Estimating Quotients (p. 748) *1–11. Estimates may vary.* **1.** 30; 35 **3.** 250; 300 **5.** 17; 18 **7.** 50; 60 **9.** 2000; 2500 **11.** 900; 950 *13–23. Estimates may vary.* **13.** 48 **15.** 600 **17.** 21 **19.** 30 **21.** 4500 **23.** 550

Solving Problems Using Addition and Subtraction (p. 749) **1.** $12 **3.** 44 people **5.** $44

Solving Problems Using Multiplication and Division (p. 750) **1.** 36 pencils **3.** 4 muffins **5.** 13 cards

Units of Time (p. 751) **1.** 300 **3.** 72 **5.** 2 **7.** > **9.** = **11.** =

Solving Problems Involving Time (p. 752) **1.** 2 h 15 min **3.** about 1 h

Using a Compass (p. 754) **3.** The length of the segment should be about $3\frac{3}{4}$ in. long.

Geometric Figures (p. 755) **1.** 12 cm **3.** 20 m
5. 4 in.; **7.** 14 cm;

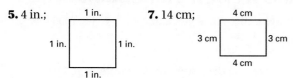

Venn Diagrams and Logical Reasoning (p. 756)

1.

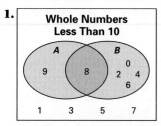

3. true; 8 is the only number in both set *A* and set *B*.

Reading Bar Graphs and Line Graphs (p. 757)
1. 5 students **3.** 10 A.M.

Reading and Making Line Plots (p. 758)
1.

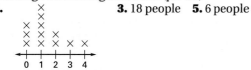

3. 18 people **5.** 6 people

Commutative and Associative Properties for Addition (p. 759) **1.** Associative property of addition **3.** 5 + (15 + 21) = (5 + 15) + 21 [Associative property of addition] = 20 + 21 [Add 5 and 15] = 41 [Add 20 and 21] **5.** (7 + 61) + 13 = (61 + 7) + 13 [Commutative property of addition] = 61 + (7 + 13) [Associative property of addition] = 61 + 20 [Add 7 and 13] = 81 [Add 61 and 20] **7.** 16 + 19 + 4 = (16 + 19) + 4 (Use order of operations] = (19 + 16) + 4 [Commutative property of addition] = 19 + (16 + 4) [Associative property of addition] = 19 + 20 [Add 16 and 4] = 39 [Add 19 and 20]

Commutative and Associative Properties of Multiplication (p. 760) **1.** Commutative property of multiplication **3.** (9 × 15) × 2 = 9 × (15 × 2) [Associative property of multiplication] = 9 × 30 [Multiply 15 and 2] = 270 [Multiply 9 and 30] **5.** 2 × 41 × 5 = (2 × 41) × 5 [Order of operations] = (41 × 2) × 5 [Commutative property of multiplication] = 41 × (2 × 5) [Associative property of multiplication] = 41 × 10 [Multiply 2 and 5] = 410 [Multiply 41 and 10] **7.** 5 × 33 × 4 = (5 × 33) × 4 [Order of operations] = (33 × 5) × 4 [Commutative property of multiplication] = 33 × (5 × 4) [Associative property of multiplication] = 33 × 20 [Multiply 5 and 4] = 660 [Multiply 33 and 20]

Problem Solving Practice

Make a Model (p. 771) **1.** 2 **3.** 5 perimeters **5.** 1 inch minimum; 27 inch maximum

Draw a Diagram (p. 771) **7.** 12 miles **9.** Yes

Guess, Check, and Revise (p. 772) **11.** 31 ostriches and 4 cows **13.** 2 notebooks, 4 pens, and 8 pencils

Work Backward (p. 772) **15.** 62 raisins **17.** 16 people **19.** 12 oranges

Make a List or a Table (p. 773) **21.** 8 minutes **23.** 10 different scores

Look for a Pattern (p. 773) **25.** 78 seats **27.** 529 points **29.** The next figure will be a regular heptagon (7-sided figure).

Break into Parts (pp. 773 – 774) **31.** 88 feet **33.** 6 hours and 5 minutes

Solve a Simpler Problem (pp. 774) **35.** 6 routes; 105 routes **37.** 96 pairs **39.** 10 handshakes; 66 handshakes

Use a Venn Diagram (p. 775) **41.** 16 people **43.** 3 families **45.** 6 students

Act It Out (p. 775) **47.** 24 passengers **49.** 18 pistachios **51.** 32 color photos

Extra Practice

Chapter 1 (p. 776) **1.** Each number is 8 less than the previous number; 25, 17, 9 **3.** Each number is the previous number divided by 2; 100, 50, 25 **5.** 15 **7.** 36 **9.** 11^3 **11.** y^4 **13.** 100 **15.** 0 **17.** 65 **19.** 6 **21.** 7 **23.** 9 **25.** 36 ft; 77 ft^2 **27.** 64 cm; 256 cm^2 **29.** 10 games

Chapter 2 (p. 777) **1.** 0.05, 0.25, 0.5, 5.2 **3.** 6.08, 6.2, 6.28, 6.82 **5.** 0.92 **7.** 738.05 **9.** 19.6 **11.** 1.123 **13.** 2.16 **15.** 0.05476 **17.** 7.7964 **19.** 57.92 **21.** 12.02 **23.** 80 **25.** 0.045 **27.** 20.75 **29.** 5.61 **31.** 8.2×10^9 **33.** 4.316×10^2 **35.** 422,100,000 **37.** 5,376,100 **39.** milliliters **41.** kilogram **43.** 400 **45.** 0.12 **47.** 0.0361 **49.** =

Chapter 3 (p. 778) **1.** 31.5; 25.5; 22; 39 **3.** 7; 7; 2 and 7; 10 **5.** median; *Sample answer:* The mode is 35, which is also the smallest data value. It is not very representative of the data set as a whole. The mean is 44, while the median is 41.5. The median is the best representative of the data, since it is close to most of the values. The mean is a little high because of the one reading of 69, which is a little bit larger than the other data values. **7.** *Sample answer:* the amount of money you earn each week with your paper route

9.

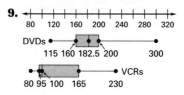

11.

DVD Players	Interval	VCRs
0	70–109	7
2	110–149	2
6	150–189	0
3	190–229	2
2	230–269	1
1	270–309	0

13. *Sample answer:* Since there is a break in the vertical scale, the bar heights appear to differ a lot more than the data would indicate.

Chapter 4 (p. 779) **1.** composite; 1, 3, 5, 15, 25, 75 **3.** prime; 1, 83 **5.** $2^2 \times 3 \times 7$ **7.** 5^3 **9.** 24; not relatively prime **11.** 4; not relatively prime **13.** $\frac{5}{6}, \frac{5}{6}$; equivalent **15.** $\frac{3}{4}, \frac{7}{9}$; not equivalent **17.** 48 **19.** 126 **21.** > **23.** = **25.** > **27.** < **29.** $\frac{22}{3}$ **31.** $\frac{49}{9}$ **33.** $3\frac{4}{7}$ **35.** $4\frac{1}{8}$ **37.** $0.\overline{7}$ **39.** 8.9 **41.** $\frac{17}{25}$ **43.** $5\frac{5}{8}$

Chapter 5 (p. 780) **1.** $\frac{3}{4}$ **3.** $\frac{5}{11}$ **5.** $\frac{13}{18}$ **7.** $\frac{2}{3}$ **9.** 7 **11.** $6\frac{7}{10}$ **13.** $2\frac{4}{5}$ **15.** $\frac{3}{7}$ **17.** $\frac{7}{12}$ **19.** 4 **21.** 2 **23.** $\frac{4}{5}$ **25.** $\frac{9}{2}$ **27.** $\frac{6}{19}$ **29.** $\frac{6}{7}$ **31.** 9 **33.** feet **35.** gallons **37.** pounds **39.** 108 **41.** 64 **43.** 4; 3 **45.** 10 qt **47.** 1 T 1700 lb

Chapter 6 (p. 781) **1.** $-10, -3, 0, 3, 6$ **3.** $-84, -70, -10, 15, 71, 99$ **5.** -4 **7.** 27 **9.** -4 **11.** 79 **13.** 72 **15.** -12 **17.** -13 **19.** 3 **21.** $\frac{-9}{10}; -\frac{10}{9}; \frac{9}{10}$ **23.** $\frac{-1}{1}; -1; 1$ **25.** $-6 \cdot 10 \cdot (-\frac{1}{6})$ [original expression] = $-6 \cdot (-\frac{1}{6}) \cdot 10$ [commutative property of multiplication] = $[-6 \cdot (-\frac{1}{6})] \cdot 10$ [associative property of multiplication = $1 \cdot 10$ [multiplicative inverses] = 10 [multiplicative identity] **27.** $50 \cdot 13 \cdot 2$ [original expression] = $50 \cdot 2 \cdot 13$ [commutative property of multiplication] = $(50 \cdot 2) \cdot 13$ [commutative property of multiplication] = $100 \cdot 13$ [multiplication fact] = 1300 [multiplication fact] **29.** 80 **31.** 6 **33.** $4(\$25 - \$.05) = \$100 - \$.20 = \$99.80$

34–37.

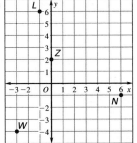

35. y-axis **37.** Quadrant II **39.** Pressure increases as the depth increases;

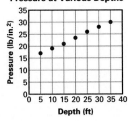

Pressure at Various Depths

Chapter 7 (p. 782) **1.** $x - 17$ **3.** $\frac{y}{2} = -5$ **5.** 2 **7.** $2y + 12$ **9.** $-6 - 5x$ **11.** -10 **13.** -2.4 **15.** 7 **17.** -27 **19.** 6.5 **21.** 3.1 **23.** $x > -7$ **25.** $b > -6$;

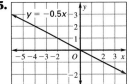

27. $s \leq 5$;

29. range: $-5.5, -3.5, -1.5, 0.5, 2.5$;

Input x	Output y
-4	-5.5
-2	-3.5
0	-1.5
2	0.5
4	2.5

31. range: 4, 6, 8, 10, 12;

Input x	Output y
-4	12
-2	10
0	8
2	6
4	4

33. $y = x - 6$ **35.**

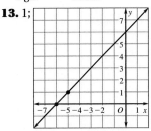

37.

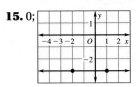

Chapter 8 (p. 783) **1.** 3 to 1 **3.** 3 to 14 **5.** $\frac{1}{4}$ **7.** $\frac{\$1.45}{1 \text{ gal}}$ **9.** $\frac{36 \text{ words}}{1 \text{ min}}$ **11.** 15 fl oz **13.** 1;

15. 0;

17. 25   **19.** 27   **21.** 19.5   **23.** 25.2   **25.** 600 calories
27. 30 ft by 15 ft

Chapter 9 (p. 784)   **1.** $\frac{3}{5}$ **3.** $\frac{21}{25}$ **5.** 40%   **7.** 25%

9. 64%   **11.** 67.5   **13.** 0.02   **15.** 1.06   **17.** 57.5%

19. 0.12%   **21.** 45.6   **23.** 31.25%

25.

Work Schedule
at Video Store
— Tuesday: 5 h
— Monday: 3.5 h
— Friday: 2.5 h
— Thursday: 3 h
— Wednesday: 6 h

27. decrease; 6.25%   **29.** increase; 9.375%   **31.** $211.20
33. $12.50; $262.50   **35.** $2.20; $602.20

Chapter 10 (p. 785)   **1.** 94°; 4°   **3.** 90°; no complementary
angle   **5.** 123°; 57°   **7.** 38°; 142°   **9.** isosceles   **11.** 1080°
13. yes; Any two squares are similar, since all of their
angles are congruent, each with a measure of 90°, and
each pair of corresponding sides has the same ratio. Here,
the ratio is 4 to 5.   **15.** 30 ft   **17.** $A'(5, -3)$, $B'(2, -2)$,
$C'(6, 0)$;

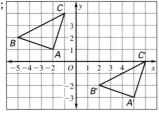

19. $A'(2, 1)$, $B'(5, 2)$, $C'(1, 4)$;

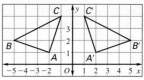

Chapter 11 (p. 786)   **1.** 6   **3.** 13   **5.** 12, −12   **7.** 6, −6
9. 4; 4.4   **11.** 12; 11.6   **13.** Irrational; It is not a finite or
repeating decimal.   **15.** Rational; 49 is a perfect square.
17. 9 m   **19.** 12.8 in.   **21.** 8 ft   **23.** 32 m²   **25.** 44 cm²
27. 264 mi   **29.** 157 cm   **31.** 5024 yd²   **33.** 154 ft²

Chapter 12 (p. 787)   **1.** sphere   **3.** rectangular pyramid
5. 4; 6; 4   **7.** 7; 12; 7
9.   **11.**

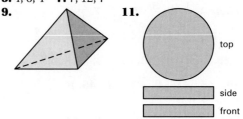

top

side

front

13. 121.2 ft²   **15.** 37.7 m²   **17.** 245 ft²   **19.** 280 in.³
21. 137.5 cm³   **23.** 252 mm³   **25.** 1130 in.³   **27.** 5 ft

Chapter 13 (p. 788)   **1.** $\frac{3}{20}$; 0.15; 15%   **3.** 72%   **5.** $\frac{2}{9}$

7. $\frac{1}{17,576}$ **9.** 4060 ways   **11.** $\frac{17}{18}$ **13.** $\frac{3}{8} = 0.375$

NEW JERSEY MATHEMATICS CORE CURRICULUM CONTENT STANDARDS

Standard 4.1: Number and Numerical Operations

All students will develop number sense and will perform standard numerical operations and estimations on all types of numbers in a varietly of ways.

4.1.A Number Sense

4.1.A.1 Extend understanding of the number system by constructing meanings for the following (unless otherwise noted, all indicators for grade 7 pertain to these sets of numbers as well):

    4.1.A.1.a Rational numbers

    4.1.A.1.b Percents

    4.1.A.1.c Whole numbers with exponents

4.1.A.2 Demonstrate a sense of the relative magnitudes of numbers.

4.1.A.3 Understand and use ratios, proportions, and percents (including percents greater than 100 and less than 1) in a variety of situations.

4.1.A.4 Compare and order numbers of all named types.

4.1.A.5 Use whole numbers, fractions, decimals, and percents to represent equivalent forms of the same number.

4.1.A.6 Understand that all fractions can be represented as repeating or terminating decimals.

4.1.B Numerical Operations

4.1.B.1 Use and explain procedures for performing calculations with integers and all number types named above with:

    4.1.B.1.a Pencil-and-paper

    4.1.B.1.b Mental math

    4.1.B.1.c Calculator

4.1.B.2 Use exponentiation to find whole number powers of numbers.

4.1.B.3 Understand and apply the standard algebraic order of operations, including appropriate use of parentheses.

4.1.C Estimation

4.1.C.1 Use equivalent representations of numbers such as fractions, decimals, and percents to facilitate estimation.

STANDARDS

Standard 4.2:
Geometry and Measurement

All students will develop spatial sense and the ability to use geometric properties, relationships, and measurement to model, describe and analyze phenomena.

4.2.A Geometric Properties

4.2.A.1   Understand and apply properties of polygons.

    4.2.A.1.a Quadrilaterals, including squares, rectangles, parallelograms, trapezoids, rhombi

    4.2.A.1.b Regular polygons

4.2.A.2   Understand and apply the concept of similarity.

    4.2.A.2.a Using proportions to find missing measures

    4.2.A.2.b Scale drawings

    4.2.A.2.c Models of 3D objects

4.2.A.3   Use logic and reasoning to make and support conjectures about geometric objects.

4.2.B Transforming Shapes

4.2.B.1   Understand and apply transformations.

    4.2.B.1.a Finding the image, given the pre-image, and vice-versa

    4.2.B.1.b Sequence of transformations needed to map one figure onto another

    4.2.B.1.c Reflections, rotations, and translations result in images congruent to the pre-image

    4.2.B.1.d Dilations (stretching/shrinking) result in images similar to the pre-image

4.2.C Coordinate Geometry

4.2.C.1   Use coordinates in four quadrants to represent geometric concepts.

4.2.C.2   Use a coordinate grid to model and quantify transformations (e.g., translate right 4 units).

4.2.D Units of Measurement

4.2.D.1 Solve problems requiring calculations that involve different units of measurement within a measurement system (e.g., 4'3" plus 7'10" equals 12'1").

4.2.D.2 Select and use appropriate units and tools to measure quantities to the degree of precision needed in a particular problem-solving situation.

4.2.D.3 Recognize that all measurements of continuous quantities are approximations.

4.2.E Measuring Geometric Objects

4.2.E.1 Develop and apply strategies for finding perimeter and area.

4.2.E.1.a Geometric figures made by combining triangles, rectangles and circles or parts of circles

4.2.E.1.b Estimation of area using grids of various sizes

4.2.E.2 Recognize that the volume of a pyramid or cone is one-third of the volume of the prism or cylinder with the same base and height (e.g., use rice to compare volumes of figures with same base and height).

Standard 4.3:
Patterns and Algebra

All students will represent and analyze relationships among variable quantities and solve problems involving patterns, functions, and algebraic concepts and processes.

4.3.A Patterns

4.3.A.1 Recognize, describe, extend, and create patterns involving whole numbers, rational numbers, and integers.

> **4.3.A.1.a** Descriptions using tables, verbal and symbolic rules, graphs, simple equations or expressions
>
> **4.3.A.1.b** Finite and infinite sequences
>
> **4.3.A.1.c** Generating sequences by using calculators to repeatedly apply a formula

4.3.B Functions and Relationships

4.3.B.1 Graph functions, and understand and describe their general behavior.

> **4.3.B.1.a** Equations involving two variables

4.3.C Modeling

4.3.C.1 Analyze functional relationships to explain how a change in one quantity can result in a change in another, using pictures, graphs, charts, and equations

4.3.C.2 Use patterns, relations, symbolic algebra, and linear functions to model situations.

> **4.3.C.2.a** Using manipulatives, tables, graphs, verbal rules, algebraic expressions/equations/inequalities
>
> **4.3.C.2.b** Growth situations, such as population growth and compound interest, using recursive (e.g., NOW-NEXT) formulas (cf. science standard 5.5 and social studies standard 6.6)

4.3.D Procedures

4.3.D.1 Use graphing techniques on a number line.

    4.3.D.1.a Absolute value

    4.3.D.1.b Arithmetic operations represented by vectors (arrows) (e.g., "$-3 + 6$" is "left 3, right 6")

4.3.D.2 Solve simple linear equations informally and graphically.

    4.3.D.2.a Multi-step, integer coefficients only (although answers may not be integers)

    4.3.D.2.b Using paper-and-pencil, calculators, graphing calculators, spreadsheets, and other technology

4.3.D.3 Create, evaluate, and simplify algebraic expressions involving variables.

    4.3.D.3.a Order of operations, including appropriate use of parentheses

    4.3.D.3.b Substitution of a number for a variable

4.3.D.4 Understand and apply the properties of operations, numbers, equations, and inequalities.

    4.3.D.4.a Additive inverse

    4.3.D.4.b Multiplicative inverse

STANDARDS

Standard 4.4:
Data Analysis, Probability, and Discrete Mathematics

All students will develop an understanding of the concepts and techniques of data analysis, probability, and discrete mathematics, and will use them to model situations, solve problems, and analyze and draw appropriate inferences from data.

4.4.A Data Analysis

4.4.A.1 Select and use appropriate representations for sets of data, and measures of central tendency (mean, median, and mode).

    4.4.A.1.a Type of display most appropriate for given data

    4.4.A.1.b Box-and-whisker plot, upper quartile, lower quartile

    4.4.A.1.c Scatter plot

    4.4.A.1.d Calculators and computer used to record and process information

4.4.A.2 Make inferences and formulate and evaluate arguments based on displays and analysis of data.

4.4.B Probability

4.4.B.1 Interpret probabilities as ratios, percents, and decimals.

4.4.B.2 Model situations involving probability with simulations (using spinners, dice, calculators and computers) and theoretical models.

    4.4.B.2.a Frequency, relative frequency

4.4.B.3 Estimate probabilities and make predictions based on experimental and theoretical probabilities.

4.4.B.4 Play and analyze probability-based games, and discuss the concepts of fairness and expected value.

4.4.C Discrete Mathematics—Systematic Listing and Counting

4.4.C.1 Apply the multiplication principle of counting.

    4.4.C.1.a Permutations: ordered situations with replacement (e.g., number of possible license plates) vs. ordered situations without replacement (e.g., number of possible slates of 3 class officers from a 23 student class)

4.4.C.2 Explore counting problems involving Venn diagrams with three attributes (e.g., there are 15, 20, and 25 students respectively in the chess club, the debating team, and the engineering society; how many different students belong to the three clubs if there are 6 students in chess and debating, 7 students in chess and engineering, 8 students in debating and engineering, and 2 students in all three?).

4.4.C.3 Apply techniques of systematic listing, counting, and reasoning in a variety of different contexts.

4.4.D Discrete Mathematics—Vertex-Edge Graphs and Algorithms

4.4.D.1 Use vertex-edge graphs to represent and find solutions to practical problems.

    4.4.D.1.a Finding the shortest network connecting specified sites

    4.4.D.1.b Finding the shortest route on a map from one site to another

    4.4.D.1.c Finding the shortest circuit on a map that makes a tour of specified sites

STANDARDS

Standard 4.5:
Mathematical Processes

All students will use mathematical processes of problem solving, communication, connections, reasoning, representations, and technology to solve problems and communicate mathematical ideas.

4.5.A Problem Solving

4.5.A.1 Learn mathematics through problem solving, inquiry, and discovery.

4.5.A.2 Solve problems that arise in mathematics and in other contexts (cf. workplace readiness standard 8.3).

    4.5.A.2.a Open-ended problems

    4.5.A.2.b Non-routine problems

    4.5.A.2.c Problems with multiple solutions

    4.5.A.2.d Problems that can be solved in several ways

4.5.A.3 Select and apply a variety of appropriate problem-solving strategies (e.g., "try a simpler problem" or "make a diagram") to solve problems.

4.5.A.4 Pose problems of various types and levels of difficulty.

4.5.A.5 Monitor their progress and reflect on the process of their problem solving activity.

4.5.B Communication

4.5.B.1 Use communication to organize and clarify their mathematical thinking.

    4.5.B.1.a Reading and writing

    4.5.B.1.b Discussion, listening, and questioning

4.5.B.2 Communicate their mathematical thinking coherently and clearly to peers, teachers, and others, both orally and in writing.

4.5.B.3 Analyze and evaluate the mathematical thinking and strategies of others.

4.5.B.4 Use the language of mathematics to express mathematical ideas precisely

4.5.C Connections

4.5.C.1 Recognize recurring themes across mathematical domains (e.g., patterns in number, algebra, and geometry).

4.5.C.2 Use connections among mathematical ideas to explain concepts (e.g., two linear equations have a unique solution because the lines they represent intersect at a single point).

4.5.C.3 Recognize that mathematics is used in a variety of contexts outside of mathematics.

4.5.C.4 Apply mathematics in practical situations and in other disciplines.

4.5.C.5 Trace the development of mathematical concepts over time and across cultures (cf. world languages and social studies standards).

4.5.C.6 Understand how mathematical ideas interconnect and build on one another to produce a coherent whole.

4.5.D Reasoning

4.5.D.1 Recognize that mathematical facts, procedures, and claims must be justified.

4.5.D.2 Use reasoning to support their mathematical conclusions and problem solutions.

4.5.D.3 Select and use various types of reasoning and methods of proof.

4.5.D.4 Rely on reasoning, rather than answer keys, teachers, or peers, to check the correctness of their problem solutions.

4.5.D.5 Make and investigate mathematical conjectures.

    4.5.D.5.a Counterexamples as a means of disproving conjectures

    4.5.D.5.b Verifying conjectures using informal reasoning or proofs.

4.5.D.6 Evaluate examples of mathematical reasoning and determine whether they are valid.

4.5.E Representations

4.5.E.1 Create and use representations to organize, record, and communicate mathematical ideas.

> **4.5.E.1.a** Concrete representations (e.g., base-ten blocks or algebra tiles)
>
> **4.5.E.1.b** Pictorial representations (e.g., diagrams, charts, or tables)
>
> **4.5.E.1.c** Symbolic representations (e.g., a formula)
>
> **4.5.E.1.d** Graphical representations (e.g., a line graph)

4.5.E.2 Select, apply, and translate among mathematical representations to solve problems.

4.5.E.3 Use representations to model and interpret physical, social, and mathematical phenomena.

4.5.F Technology

4.5.F.1 Use technology to gather, analyze, and communicate mathematical information.

4.5.F.2 Use computer spreadsheets, software, and graphing utilities to organize and display quantitative information.

4.5.F.3 Use graphing calculators and computer software to investigate properties of functions and their graphs.

4.5.F.4 Use calculators as problem-solving tools (e.g., to explore patterns, to validate solutions).

4.5.F.5 Use computer software to make and verify conjectures about geometric objects.

4.5.F.6 Use computer-based laboratory technology for mathematical applications in the sciences.